CW00665875

# 125 YEARS ON THE BORDERLINE

## The Complete History of Chester City F.C. 1885 ~ 2010

Published by:
Yore Publications
12 The Furrows, Harefield,
Middx. UB9 6AT.



British Library Cataloguing-in-Publication Data.
A catalogue record for this book is available from the British Library.

ISBN 978 0 9569848 2 1

Managed and Manufactured by
Jellyfish Solutions Ltd.

# INTRODUCTION

When I completed the original version of On The Borderline in 1997 the last line of the book read: "Having survived a traumatic 10 years some stability has finally returned to the club and Chester are now in a position to look forward to the future." Sadly this proved to be a wildly inaccurate statement but I don't think anyone could possibly have predicted quite what was in store for the next 13 years as the club stumbled from crisis to crisis.

This updated edition of the book completes the story of Chester City which ended on March 10th 2010 when the club was wound up in the High Court. While it was a sad way for the club to end there is no doubt in my mind that Chester City was well beyond salvage at that point and needed to be put out of its misery. In the meantime, the emergence of Chester FC has been like a breath of fresh air and the new supporter's run team has placed a club back in the hands of local people for the first time since Reg Rowlands stepped down in 1982. In many ways it harks back to the 19th century when Cestrians like Lockwood, Tatler and Walley were instrumental in forming the original club.

It's an understatement to say that a lot has happened since 1997 and the years under Terry Smith and the Vaughan family could easily fill two volumes in their own right. The formation of Chester FC is also worthy of more extensive coverage but I made a conscious decision to only briefly cover the new club and thus bring the history to a natural conclusion.

I hope that the book brings back some happy memories and that they override the less enjoyable events which overshadowed the club in its later years. I know that the original book resolved many queries and arguments and I hope that this will also be the case with this new edition.

I am always interested to hear from anyone with photographs and memorabilia associated with the club and I can be contacted either through the club itself or the publisher. As secretary of the Chester City Former Players Association I am also interested to hear from former players and more details can be found on our website at www.formerchesterplayers.com

Chas Sumner
September 2011

# ACKNOWLEDGMENTS

In addition to all the people who helped out with the original edition of On The Borderline I would like to express my thanks to the following who assisted with this updated version. Sue Choularton and Richard Prince checked through the text for me and pointed out my errors. Rick Matthews of the Leader provided invaluable assistance with the photographs and Dave Triggs of the Chester Chronicle helped fill in the gaps. Martin Huxley of Martin Huxley Graphic Design performed an excellent job in designing the cover while Steve Mansley's unofficial Chester website www.chester-city.co.uk proved to be a vital source in piecing together the tangled web of the last few seasons. Also thanks to Dave Twydell, Michael Joyce and programme editor Rob Ashcroft as well as everyone else who has contacted me since the original book was published and who have helped either directly or indirectly. Sincere apologies to anyone I have unintentionally omitted.

I would also like to thank everyone at City Fans United who worked so hard to establish the new Chester FC and who made watching football fun again.

Last but not least thanks to my wife Diane who once again offered encouragement while I buried myself in this latest project.

# CONTENTS:

# EARLY FOOTBALL IN CHESTER
# CHAPTER 1

Football in the modern era appears to have commenced in Chester in the early 1870s. There is evidence however, that a version of the game was being played in the city in the late 15th and 16th century. On Shrove Tuesday it was traditional for the corporation of shoemakers in the city to meet the company of drapers at the Cross on the Roodee. It was here that the drapers were presented with a ball of leather, called a foote-ball, to the value of 3s-4d. The young people in the city would then, '*by force and stronge hande*', bring the ball to the Mayor's house or one of the two Sheriff's houses. It appeared to be a dangerous game with many people getting maimed or suffering from broken limbs, this caused considerable damage to the participants and resulted in the Mayor and Common Council abolishing the game in 1539 and replacing it with a foot race. However this failed to quash the interest of the citizens of Chester and by 1564 it was recorded that *'there was a great frost, and the Dee was frozen over, so that the people played at football thereon'*.

Three hundred years later, the game as we know it was beginning to take shape, with early games being played in the educational establishments of the city. In October 1874 the King's School lost a game 4-0 at Chester College, a defeat that was put down to the fact that the school team did not have proper knowledge of the Association rules. Early the following year a game was recorded on the Roodee (site of Chester Racecourse) between Arnold House School and the Garrison, where a tape was used as a crossbar. The Roodee proved to be the focus for many of the early teams including Chester Ramblers, the GPO, Trinity Lever and Chester Rangers. Over the next few years a number of other clubs were formed including Chester Wanderers (based in Sealand Road), Hoole Rovers (Hoole Road) and Chester St.Oswalds, who started off on the Roodee but later moved to Cheyney Road opposite Bouverie Street.

In the 1870s and 1880s the principal games played by male citizens were quoits, skittles, rowing and rugby. Another popular sport was cricket and one of the chief protagonists was a club called Chester Rovers who played on the Roodee. Their team included Jack Hack, Fred Maddocks and Joe Tomkinson who had also been playing football for Chester Wanderers and St. Oswalds. By 1880 the Rovers had formed a football team to occupy the winter months and matches that season were recorded against Northwich Victoria Reserves and Wrexham Civil Service. The following season the fixture list was expanded and included a match with Everton in which they achieved a creditable 1-1 draw. Chester Rovers emerged as one of the principal clubs in the city, alongside St.Oswalds and Chester College, and this was reflected in attendances with 300 turning up for a Reserve match against Trinity Ramblers in March 1883.

In parallel to this the members of the King's School, who had helped in the growth of football in the city, had formed an Old King's Scholars team. Although only playing occasional games they reached the Semi-Final of the Cheshire Senior Cup in 1882/83 when they were beaten by all-conquering Northwich Victoria who had retained the cup every year since its inception in 1879/80. Among the Scholars team were A.Carden Lockwood, Alf Tatler and W.V.J.Walley, all of whom had also played for other clubs in the city.

Towards the end of the 1883/84 season an attempt was made to form a more representative team which could challenge the supremacy of Northwich Victoria and Crewe Alexandra in Cheshire. With this in mind two trial matches were held between picked members of all the Chester clubs. After the second of these trials a team was selected which became known as the Chester Football Association. The committee formed to choose this team created a great deal of controversy with its selection policy. A high proportion of players came from Chester Rovers and it looked like other clubs were being ignored so that the committee, with a heavy Rovers bias, could get members of their own club represented. One of the players excluded from the team was Corey of Chester St. Johns who scored 4 out of 5 goals in the second trial match and could therefore consider himself unlucky not to be selected.

Despite this, on April 5th 1884, Chester Association played a scratch team with the proceeds of the game going to an injured player. The Association, comprising mainly of players from Chester Rovers, Old King's Scholars and Chester Novices, won the match 1-0 in front of between 400 and 500 spectators. The following players represented the Association :- Tatler, Walley, Wright, Lloyd, Thomas, Lythgoe, Wycherley, Banks, Tomkinson, Thrash, Lockwood.

However the efforts to establish a united team appear to have floundered with no mention of the Chester Football Association appearing again. It seems the most likely reason for the failure of this venture was the antagonism created by the selection policy and the fact that the committee seemed to have no particular aim in mind.

By holding the Trial matches in March, so close to the end of the season, it was difficult to arrange matches against other clubs of note and so all momentum was lost.

The start of the 1884/85 season saw Chester Rovers move from their base on the Roodee to a new ground at Faulkner Street in the Hoole area of Chester. This ground was rented from the Earl of Kilmorey by the Weaver Brothers, coach and cab proprietors in Flookersbrook, and was initially known as Weaver's Field. The club continued to play friendly matches throughout the season, against clubs from the Chester, North Wales and Liverpool areas, but despite success on the field they struggled financially.

***CHESTER ROVERS 1884/85***
*Players include: Hack, James, Lythgoe, Thrash, Southworth. McMillan, Lockwood, Tomkinson, Banks, Jones.*

Meanwhile Old King's Scholars were still playing the occasional friendly match, including games against Market Drayton and Tranmere, but were finding difficulty in raising a team each week. Because of the irregular nature of their matches the three key players, Lockwood, Tatler and Walley, all appeared at various times in the season for Chester Rovers. It therefore seems logical that, at the end of the season, the three Old King's Scholars would try to make this relationship more permanent bearing in mind the problems the two teams were experiencing.

Although the formation of Chester has been previously presented as an amalgamation of Chester Rovers and Old King's Scholars, in terms of playing staff there were virtually no changes in the Chester Rovers team that finished 1884/85 and the new Chester team that started the following season. The last team to represent Chester Rovers at Faulkner Street on April 6th 1885, against Liverpool St. Benedicts, was :-
James, Southworth, Higginson, Hack, Tomkinson, Roberts, Lockwood, McMillan, Thrash, Jones, Banks. Eight of these players were in the first recorded Chester team in September 1885 and Tomkinson and Jones, who missed that game, both featured in one of the next two matches.

Most of the changes made were at the committee level and many of the people behind the new club had also been involved in the Chester Assoc-iation project. Al-though presented as a new club, in reality Chester were just Chester Rovers by another name with the same ground and same players. The in-flux of new committee men, including the Old King's Scholars, all-owed them to consider them-selves as the premier club in the city thus stealing a march over other clubs like Chester St.Johns and Chester St.Oswalds. The adoption of the name Chester did cause some resentment, especially with St.Oswalds, and goes some way to explaining the bitter rivalry that existed between the two for the remainder of the decade.

Trying to pinpoint the actual date of the formation of Chester Football Club has not proved possible, but the first meeting would probably have taken place in July or August 1885. On June 23rd 1885, at the AGM of the Cheshire Football Association, it had been noted that the number of member clubs had expanded from 8 to 16 teams. At this point Chester Rovers were still one of the committee members although Old King's Scholars had been replaced by Chester St.Johns. It therefore seems likely that Lockwood, Tatler and Walley now realised that the Scholars could not continue in their current form although they had yet to formally join up with the Rovers. In the 1930s, A.Carden Lockwood, by now a solicitor in Newgate Street, reflected on the formation of the club. He recalled that the first negotiations were held at the Crown Vaults in Lower Bridge Street. At the time these premises were owned by Mrs Tomkinson the mother of the Chester Rovers captain. It seems that the meeting did not go quite as smoothly as planned with some dispute occurring over the name for the new club. One section of the committee who had belonged to the Rovers were reluctant to expunge the Rovers name. A compromise was reached on this matter and for some time the actual title of the club was 'Chester Football Club (later Chester Rovers)'.

# FRIENDLIES AND NOT SO FRIENDLIES 1885 - 1890
# CHAPTER 2

At the inaugural meeting in the Crown Vaults, the first officials and committee of Chester Football Club were appointed, and comprised the following:-

*President* - Captain Fluitt; *Vice Presidents* - Mr J.B.McMillan and Mr W.Marsh; *Captain* - Mr J.Hack; *Vice-Captain* - Mr J.Tomkinson; *Treasurer* - Mr W.Wilks; *Hon. Secretary* - Mr A.C.Lockwood Jnr, "Hop Pole" Hotel, Chester; *Assistant Secretary* - Mr J.James; *Committee* - Mr Bryan, Mr S.Pickering, Mr H.J.Moss, Mr G.James, Mr E.Hughes, Mr A.A.Tatler and Mr J.Short.

Initially the team used the Ermine Hotel on Hoole Road as a dressing room. At the time it was owned by George Barnes who also used to transport the team to away matches.

The first game of the new club was a friendly played at Earlestown on September 5th 1885. Unfortunately the result of this game has been lost over time, although it is known that Chester were defeated. A week later the following team lined up for Chester at Oswestry's Victoria Road ground:-

Goal: G James; Backs: Southworth, Higginson; Half backs: Hack, Roberts, A.Evans; Right wing: J.B.McMillan, A.C.Lockwood; Left wing: Banks, Groves; Centre: H.Clare.

Although Evans and Groves were late substitutes it proved to be a disastrous start with Chester a goal down after only 5 minutes and 4-0 behind at half-time. In the second half they were totally overwhelmed and eventually defeated 10-0.

Chester made their first appearance at Faulkner Street on September 26th 1885 against Northwich Victoria. In front of between 700 and 800 spectators the following teams lined up:-

Chester - James, Southworth, Walley, Hack, Turner, Roberts, McMillan, Lockwood, Tomkinson, Maddocks, Clare

Northwich Victoria - Harper, Anderson, Molyneux, Rose, Hughes, Butterworth, Turnbull, Lever, Rhodes-Denton, Hankey, Malam.

After 10 minutes the first goal was scored for Northwich from a corner by Turnbull, headed in by Malam. The second goal came in a similar way with Lever sending in a splendid shot from a corner by Malam.

After half-time play was fast and furious and Northwich had a goal disallowed but near the end Turnbull scored with another header to make the final score 3-0 to Northwich.

Victory was finally achieved in the fourth game, although this was gained under questionable circumstances. In an evenly matched game against Chester College Lockwood scored for Chester with just under 10 minutes to go. However the College disputed the goal with some players claiming it was offside and others that the ball had gone out of play. In either case the College refused to accept the referee's decision and in a very unsporting manner left the pitch.

There were no organised leagues at this stage (the Football League was not founded until 1888) and Chester's first season comprised almost entirely of friendly matches. The club entered the Welsh Cup but were eliminated by a moderate Crewe Brittania team. There was a similar story in the Cheshire Senior Cup where they were defeated by a *'third rate'* Middlewich team in a brutal game in which several players were badly injured. The Middlewich captain stating after the game that he deeply regretted the incident in which Mercer of Chester was kicked in the forehead!

On October 24th 1885 Chester played their first game against rivals Chester St.Oswalds, in a game arranged at one hour's notice, after the cancellation of a county game between Cheshire and Liverpool District. Chester were surprisingly defeated 2-1 but gained their revenge with three victories over St.Oswalds later in the season. The second of these, a Benefit match for Chester Infirmary, drew the largest home gate so far with 1500 present. After expenses had been deducted £10-8s-8d was handed over to the Infirmary in what proved to be an annual fund-raising event in the formative years.

Matches in this first season were very hit and miss affairs as opponents often arrived late or failed to turn up for games. Chester particularly seemed to have trouble with teams from the Liverpool area with both Liverpool Ramblers and Liverpool St.Marys failing to appear as scheduled, and Bootle arriving so late that the match concluded in darkness in a match described as, *'more like blind mans buff'*. However Chester themselves were by no means perfect and a game at Hartford St.Johns had to be terminated early because Chester had only caught a 4pm train for a 3.30pm kick off.

Overall Chester could be happy with their first season despite early elimination from two cup competitions. They had proved their superiority over St.Oswalds and after a shaky start had achieved some fine victories. They also had two players capped for the County, Alf Tatler and Arthur Turner, and the funds raised allowed them to employ Turner as their first professional when they bought him out of the Army for £25 in 1886.

The 1886/87 season saw Chester enter the FA Cup for the first time, where they were drawn against Potteries side Goldenhill. The only goal of the game came from Arthur Turner who dodged through the entire Goldenhill defence to score. As was the tendency in those days, Goldenhill raised a protest after the game, and Chester were disqualified for playing four unregistered players. Interestingly enough none of the Goldenhill players were not bona-fide, but the FA were prepared to accept that a letter had been posted registering them.

Another aspect of 19th Century football that often caused controversy was the fairness (or otherwise) of the referee and umpires. Chester were at the receiving end of a supposedly unfair official when they visited Chirk at the start of the season. After trailing 3-0 they pulled back 2 goals but the referee (an ex-Chirk player) became determined not to let Chirk lose and refused to take notice of his umpires. The Chester umpire and players remonstrated with the referee, who proceeded to call the umpire a rogue, whereupon the Chester group walked off, the game ending abruptly with Chirk winning 3-2. In both the Welsh Cup and Cheshire Senior Cup, Chester were eliminated by Davenham. The county competition attracted a new record crowd of 3000 to Faulkner Street of which 500 came supporting the visiting team. Unfortunately Alf Tatler had a poor game in goal as Davenham, the holders of the trophy, triumphed 6-1.

The playing personnel remained roughly the same as the first season and the Chester Chronicle gave a concise (and sometimes harsh) appraisal of the players after a game against Holywell:
*John Southworth* - Late of Blackburn Olympic, one of the best in the country.
*James Southworth* - Captain, dashing and safe back.
*T.Jones* - Not brilliant, but safe and cool.
*Hack* - Fast but needs more judgement in tackling.
*Higginson* - Good strong steady worker.
*Mercer* - Heads well.
*Geo. Hughes* - Serves partner well and centres beautifully.
*Clare* - Works hard, unselfish.
*McMillan* - Strong and fast, should pass more and learn to shoot as his left foot shots go too high.
*W.Hughes* - Should use more judgement and jump less. A good worker.
*Rogers* - Rather light. Fairly fast and centres well.

The Southworths were two of the most interesting characters to play for Chester in the early years. Both were musicians at the Royalty Theatre, with John playing the violin and James conducting the orchestra. Appearances were governed by musical commitments, they had to return to the city in time for 7.30pm performances, and James missed games over Christmas 1885 because of the pantomime season. After leaving Chester both brothers won FA Cup winners medals for Blackburn, and John proved to be one of football's first, truly great goalscorers with 122 goals in 133 appearances for Rovers. Strangely enough John spent his short career at Chester as a goalkeeper and only turned to outfield after a career-threatening injury. He earned three England caps, and when Everton paid £400 for his services in 1893 reputedly received £2000 for a five year contract.

Once again Chester were able to prove their superiority over St.Oswalds with three victories, and antagonism between the two clubs grew when Chester arranged a match on the same day as St.Oswalds played an important Cheshire Cup match. Relations between the club were such that both sets of spectators (and sometimes players) used to turn up at each others ground to cheer the opposition.

At the AGM, held in the Hop Pole Hotel, the club were able to report a creditable balance of £32. Changes were made on the committee, where Billy Wray was elected as secretary and Hugh Roberts - who often acted as umpire and later became a respected referee - was elected as President. It was Roberts' wife who had the distinction of choosing the original club colours of red and white halves.

The club continued to play friendlies over the next two seasons, including attractive fixtures against Blackburn Olympic, Stoke, Mitchell St.Georges (Birmingham) and a team from Preston North End, all of which attracted large attendances. A record score of 17-0 was achieved against Haydock Central, although the game was played in a severe hail and snow storm with a bitterly cold wind. Haydock were clearly unprepared for these conditions as they appeared minus caps, bare-legged, bare-necked and bare-armed, although this raises interesting questions over what kit Chester were wearing.

The early years saw Chester gain a reputation as a rough side. The Staffordshire Sentinel reported that Crewe Steam Shed were ill-treated when they visited Chester with one of the home team half-backs using language which required the severest censure. They also suggested that Oswestry and Birmingham cancelled fixtures with Chester because of their reputation. One of the main culprits appears to have been Ted Carty (also known as McCarthy); "*a name inseparably associated or a synonym for roughness*" according to the Cheshire Observer.

Against Stoke he fouled in such a barefaced manner that it was suggested that Chester look for a less violent centre half. Carty was not the only offender as Chester had their first player sent off in the final friendly of the 1887/88 season when Cecil Lowe was dismissed for striking a Stafford Rangers player.

The 1887/88 season also saw Chester achieve another first when they reached the Final of the Cheshire Senior Cup, but they were soon brought down to earth with a crushing 9-0 defeat from FA Cup Semi-Finalists Crewe Alexandra. The game was played in front of 4000 at the Alexandra Cricket Ground, Crewe, on March 24th 1888 where the following teams faced each other:-

> Chester - W.Blake, T.Walker, S.Jones, F.Lee, E.Carty, J.Higginson, T.Fleming, A.Turner, J.B.McMillan, W.J.V.Walley, R.Brierley.
> Crewe Alex. - E.Hickton, C.Conde, Bayman, Bell, Halfpenny, Osborne, Pearson, E.Payne, Price, A.Payne, Ellis.

Although the Chester fans were not overly optimistic before the game the scale of the defeat surprised many people and it was only a spirited defence that prevented even more goals from being scored. Jack Higginson, Ted Carty, and Sam Jones, were the only players to do themselves justice while goalkeeper Bill Blake was a bag of nerves throughout the game as Crewe took full advantage. The Chester Chronicle pulled no punches describing the Chester team as '*eleven men croaking with fear, inspired by a feeling of terror, trampled on and outplayed*'.

A few days after the Cheshire Cup Final a concert was held at the Royalty Theatre in aid of the football club. The proprietor of the theatre, Mr J.W.Carter, had been struck by the unsatisfactory state of the Faulkner Street enclosure on a previous visit and the concert was held specifically for ground improvements. The concert, featuring the Bars Orchestral Band conducted by Frank Tasker, raised more than £15 which was used to build a stand 66 yards (c.60 metres) in length.

At the AGM, held in July 1888 at the Boot Inn in Eastgate Street, Higginson was elected captain to replace the retiring Walley, while Tommy Fleming became vice-captain. Prices were also decided for the coming season with the entrance fee set at 6d and 3d. Alternatively, season tickets for the new reserved stand could be obtained for 6s (30p) - a 250% increase - while members could pay 2s-6d (12½p) for the three unreserved sides of the ground. The huge increase in prices caused outrage amongst the supporters who felt that it could not be justified as the stand had already been paid for through the benefit concert. Meanwhile, across the town, St.Oswalds only charged 2s-6d for members in their reserved area.

Chester also became embroiled in a dispute with Boughton Hall Cricket Club over club colours. The secretary of the cricket club had written to Chester requesting that they give up their red and white colours which were the same as Boughton Halls but with a different design. Chester, not wanting to throw away the £5 they had spent on the kit said they would only do so if they received compensation, and when Boughton Hall refused the committee voted to continue in red and white.

Highlight of the 1888/89 season was the club's first appearance in the 4th Qualifying Round of the FA Cup. The run had started with a home match against Macclesfield, a game Chester were expected to win easily. However the home forwards squandered chance after chance as Macclesfield achieved a 2-2 draw after 90 minutes; a creditable score for the visitors who had displayed a strong susceptibility to the hospitality of the Ermine Hotel during the break. At full-time, with extra time scheduled, Macclesfield left the pitch on the pretext that they had to catch a train. Chester, with no opposition, kicked off the extra period of 30 minutes, and simply walked the ball through the goal to win the tie 3-2. The next 2 rounds saw 5-1 victories against Over Wanderers and Vale of Llangollen. In the Llangollen game, Cecil Lowe was badly injured by nails sticking out of an opponents boot, and the spectators were amused to see the referee make both teams sit on the grass facing each other so that he could inspect their boots and identify the culprit. The run finally came to an end with a 3-2 defeat against Wrexham in the first competitive game between the two sides.

Chester had another good run in the Cheshire Senior Cup where they took Northwich to a Semi-Final replay before being narrowly defeated 1-0. The replay of this game was held at Macclesfield for which there was a respectable attendance of 1500, '*despite the intricate and perilous journey lying between Chester and Macclesfield*'. Relationships between the two teams deteriorated quite badly after Northwich scored a controversial goal, with the ensuing 'discussion' almost halting the game. At the end of both games Chester raised a protest on the grounds of rough and foul play, and when Northwich appeared at Faulkner Street for a Welsh Cup Semi-Final the week after the replay they got a very hostile reception. The Northwich players were threatened, mud was thrown at the captain, and a number of players had to be escorted off the pitch at the end of the game. Predictably the Northwich contingent were quite indignant about this behaviour but they received little sympathy from the Chester press who claimed that the behaviour was justified, not only because Northwich were '*masters in the art of fouling*', but also on the dubious grounds that their supporters had treated Crewe players the same way.

The bad blood between the teams carried through to a 'friendly' at the end of the season when it was a miracle that all 22 men got off the pitch alive as many players took the opportunity to settle old scores in a vicious game.

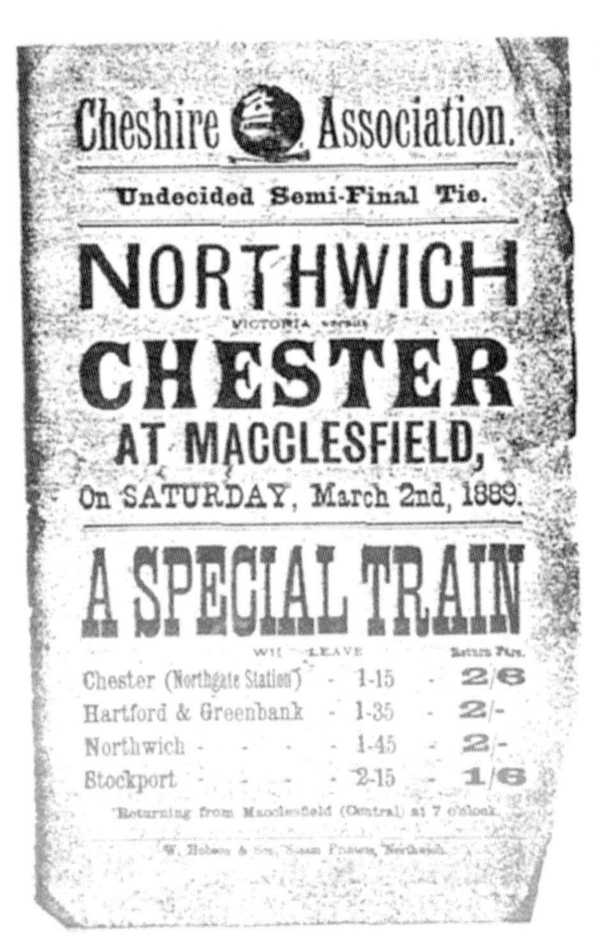


In those days the game was still developing and many actions were permitted which would not be allowed under current rules. This can be seen in a typical incident from Chester's game against Notts Jardines when, with the ball in his hands, the Notts goalkeeper was brought to the ground. A rugby struggle ensued in which nearly all the players on the pitch took part. The goalkeeper managed to keep hold of the ball as the Chester forwards tried to wrest it from his grasp and haul him through the posts before he finally managed to throw the ball among the spectators.

The AGM was once again held at the Boot Inn, and Arthur Turner was appointed captain with Tommy Fleming as his deputy. Despite a good run in the FA Cup, retiring president Hugh Roberts had to report that finances were not in such a good state as in previous years with the club reporting a deficit of £50. This was mainly put down to increased expenses and guarantees paid out to other clubs over cup-ties. Fortunately the debt was wiped out by donations from members but it led to the club looking to alternative sources of finance, and in August 1889 the players took part in an athletics event. The meeting, which attracted 6000 spectators to Faulkner Street, proved a success and became a regular source of income for a number of years.

The 1889/90 season proved to be the most successful season so far for Chester as they won 19, lost 10 and drew 6 games in all competitions. Included in these results were four 7-0 victories, one of which - over Wrexham - prompted the Cheshire Observer to suggest that, '*Wrexham, erstwhile such doughty opponents, were now not worthy to unloosen your shin-pads*'. The team did not compete in the Cheshire Senior Cup but they surpassed the previous season's performance in the FA Cup by reaching the 1st Round proper. In the 1st Qualifying round Chester had a straightforward win against Over Wanderers, which was followed by a narrow win over a Burslem Port Vale side that had beaten Chester only two weeks previously. After the cup game Port Vale put in a *'childish'* protest on the basis that:

a) The grass on the Faulkner Street pitch was so long that it rendered correct football impossible.

b) Chester meted out such rough treatment that it was impossible for Port Vale to do themselves justice. After one of their players had to leave the pitch to get medical attention Port Vale felt that they would rather lose the game than run further risk.

Needless to say this protest was dismissed.

The 3rd Qualifying Round saw the game that the whole footballing fraternity in the city wanted to witness, as Chester and St.Oswalds were paired together with the latter having choice of ground. Having not played each other for two years, the opportunity arose for all the old disagreements to re-surface as St.Oswalds once again disputed the right of Chester to adopt the name of the city. In the weeks leading up to the game relations between the teams deteriorated as Chester expressed their displeasure and disappointment at the game being played at St.Oswalds. An unsuccessful protest was made by Chester on the basis that Exton Park, where St.Oswalds had moved the previous year, lacked convenient accommodation. Meanwhile the Saints carefully measured their pitch to eliminate any protest after the game.

In an attempt to recoup some of the considerable expense that was required to improve their ground, the St.Oswalds committee doubled the entrance fee to 6d (2½p), a price seen as exorbitant by many people. There was a feeling that this amount would exclude the working class spectators and that the increase had really been made to preclude the rowdy element from attending.

In the end the match proved to be a dull anti-climax as Chester won easily 3-0, with spectators losing interest after the third goal was scored, as the Saints lost heart. The only excitement came towards the end when two players (including Bobby Davies of Chester) were sent off for fighting. A crowd of 3500 paid receipts of £60 and effective police arrangements prevented serious disturbances in the crowd.

In the next round Chester achieved a notable victory over Crewe and were rewarded with a tie against Lincoln City of the Midland League, a team who had only been beaten once all season. Four hundred Cestrians travelled to Lincoln and saw their side hold out until the 50th minute when an error of judgement by Dickson, the Chester goalkeeper, result in a goal which was quickly followed by another as Chester legs tired.

In the end Chester were well beaten but it had been a tremendous achievement to reach the last 32. There was outrage a few days after the game when it was revealed in the press that letters (see next column) had been sent to an official of Lincoln prior to the game. It appears as though P.K. was either an official or supporter of St. Oswalds and there was astonishment that any Cestrian, however spiteful, should sink to such depths in betraying the club of his own city.

On May 3rd 1890, Chester won their first trophy when they defeated Northwich in the Chester Charity Cup, for which they won the Yerburgh Cup, named after the local MP who was also a vice-president of the club. This season also saw the first two Chester players to win international honours. Anglesey born Bob Roberts was the first to be honoured when he played for Wales in their 5-2 victory over Ireland, at Shrewsbury, on February 8th 1890 in his only international match. Meanwhile, full-back Sam Jones was selected to play for Wales against Scotland in Glasgow on March 22nd 1890 where he was unfortunately on the end of a 5-0 defeat.

Although the season was a success on a footballing front there were distinct problems behind the scenes. A reserve team had been started but few games were played due to a lack of organisation and when players were missing from the first team Chester had to borrow from other clubs in the district. This was clearly of some concern to a team looking to compete at a higher level. There were also occurrences of drunkenness amongst the players and committee at away games (which could explain why Chester failed to win a game outside the city.). It was felt that the new committee should look to recruit new players who would not use drink as an excuse for defeat.

For the first, but not the last time, the club reported financial problems with a deficit of £107-12s-1d announced at the AGM in May. The reasons behind such a large loss are not entirely clear, but the treasurer, Mr Jarvis, was removed in April because the club had been unable to get a balance sheet from him. There had been a great deal of unpleasantness as the auditors went through the accounts and there was talk of Chester taking legal action against Jarvis in an attempt to recover some of the money. In the event no action was taken because the club recognised his previous service to them and the matter was laid to rest.

Despite all these internal problems, after a meeting in Manchester in May 1890, Chester were invited to participate in the new Combination League along with Blackpool South Shore, Witton (from Blackburn), Halliwell, Burslem Port Vale and Northwich. Other clubs expected to join were Ardwick, Kidderminster, Bury, Heywood Central, Gorton and Leek. In the event the structure of the Combination proved to be somewhat different, but Chester started the 1890/91 season optimistic about their chances in their first organised league.

Chester, 13/1/90.
Dear Sir, - In your match with Chester I must tell you to be prepared for a few knocks, for Chester is a long way off being lambs, but if you play them the same game they will be finished. Their play is a big kick and a rush. Their extreme left, B. Davies, is perhaps the best man to watch, as he is a good one to put the ball in the centre while the others do the rushing. Turner, who generally plays centre, will, I think, play inside right. He is a terror to goalkeepers about here, but if he gets upset a time or two he will soon funk. Please watch the extreme right, T. Fleming, who will stand almost off side all through the game waiting for big kicks, and if the backs keep any where up the field - I mean the opposing backs - he is off like a shot with the ball. It was in this way that they managed to beat Crewe, who were five or six goals better than Chester in point of play. Two solitary breaks away, and then Fleming scores both times. The Crewe backs being well up the field, the ball was sent with a big kick to Fleming, and off he goes, and the Crewe back could not catch him. The extreme left is, I daresay, their strongest point, and if you stop his centres his play is finished. If you give Dixon, their goalkeeper, swift low shots he will not stop one in twelve. He is pretty good at high shots, although very clumsy at catching the ball. I may say that Chester supporters are confident of winning and giving you 4 to 0. Chester have not won a match out of town this season, and when they are at home they won't be beat if the referee can help it. Don't hold them too cheap, the same as Crewe did. I must conclude, hoping you will give them a good dressing. Chester are taking an excursion from here, and you will hear a few who can yell a bit. If Chester win they will have a band to meet them.
P.K.

Dear Sir, - Turner, one of the Chester F.B.C., has I believe gone to Lincoln to see your club at practice so as to see the weak points in your team if any. He is a chap about 24 or 25, light complexion and bare face. He is about 5 feet 5 or 6, and very quick step and a queer swing with his hands. They are confident of beating you. Turner went yesterday (Wednesday) so you might see him if you keep a sharp look out. The Chester right back is rough and a wild kicker, and does a lot of charging, but as a good footballer is not much. Look after the extreme left and this Turner, also Fleming extreme right for his speed. I conclude, hoping you will give them a good dressing. Their umpire is a demon at claiming, and always has a red handkerchief. Watch it flying about. - I remain.
P.K.

# 'THE FLOOKERSBROOK CLUB' 1890 - 1899

# CHAPTER 3

Chester got off to an ideal start in the Combination by achieving their first ever win at Wrexham with the winner coming only 30 seconds from the end. The next game proved even more impressive with a staggering 14-1 win over Stafford, unfortunately this game did not count in the final analysis as Stafford, along with Witton and Derby St.Lukes, failed to complete their fixtures. By the end of November Chester were top of the League and supporters were confidently talking of the championship. Unfortunately they were unable to maintain the momentum and a poor run in February and March saw them finish 3rd, behind Gorton Villa and Macclesfield. In the end it was the points deducted from victories gained against the teams who resigned from the League that cost Chester the title. Although Chester could consider themselves satisfied with their first experience of league football the Combination itself was not regarded as a success because of the many resignations.

In the FA Cup Chester surpassed their performance of the previous season by reaching the 2nd Round proper, where they were defeated by the eventual winners Blackburn Rovers. The run had started with a 6-0 hammering over St.Oswalds who had 'strengthened' their team for the occasion by gaining assistance from players outside the area. A 2-0 victory over Northwich was followed by an exciting encounter at Nantwich in which Chester eventually came out on top by the odd goal in nine. The score was 4-4 at half-time and when Chester scored in the second-half the referee was under the impression that this was the equaliser. Consequently, at the end of 90 minutes, the referee ordered the teams to turn round and play extra time. There was uproar amongst the Chester contingent and a debate ensued between the players which spread to the crowd.

A small number of Nantwich supporters made a rush for the Chester players, who were rescued by the Nantwich committee, and the referee was made to consult the press. At this point the referee admitted that he had made a mistake and apologised for an error which had almost caused a riot.

The 4th Qualifying Round saw an unusual fixture with Chester being drawn against Irish club Cliftonville. This was one of the last seasons in which Irish clubs competed in the FA Cup, but in the end the match was not played as Cliftonville scratched from the competition. The game had been originally scheduled for December 6th, but Cliftonville had a league match arranged on the same day against Linfield Athletic. Bad feeling between the two Irish clubs meant that Linfield refused to re-arrange the game, and when Chester turned down an alternative date Cliftonville were given no alternative but to withdraw.

In the 1st Round Proper Chester gained their revenge over the conquerors of the previous season Lincoln, but in the 2nd Round Chester were drawn at Blackburn Rovers where, without the injured Sam Jones, they were comprehensively beaten 7-0. Three of the goals were scored by Jack Southworth (the ex-Chester goalkeeper) but Blackburn were sufficiently impressed by Chester to agree to play a friendly the following season. The attendance for the game had only been 2000, mainly because of the counter-attraction of Darwen v Sunderland, and the Chester share of the gate was a mere £11.

The biggest shock of the season was Chester's 2-0 defeat at St.Oswalds in the Hospital Charity Cup. This was only the second such victory for St.Oswalds and it came about partly because of the over-confidence of Chester, and partly due to a splendid display by Saints goalkeeper Jack Pay.

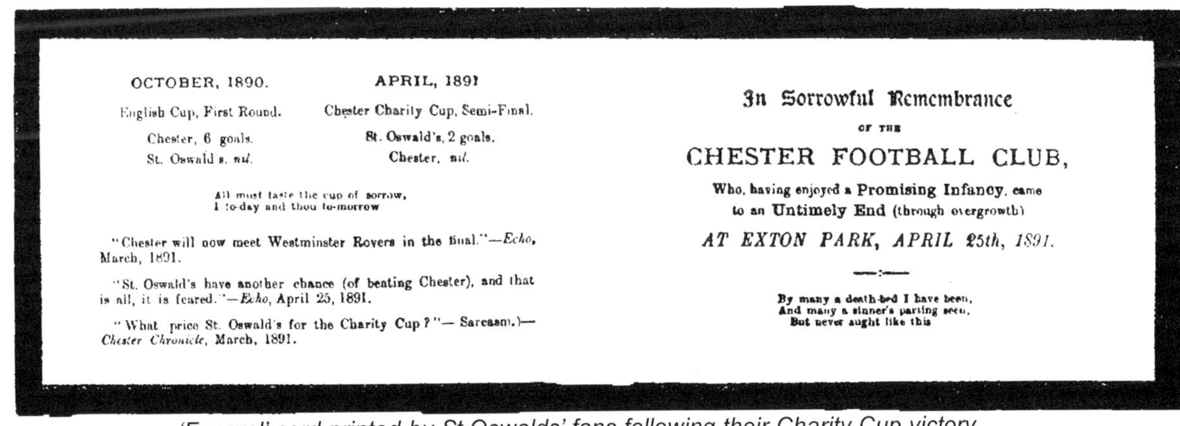

OCTOBER, 1890.
English Cup, First Round.
Chester, 6 goals.
St. Oswald's, *nil.*

APRIL, 1891
Chester Charity Cup, Semi-Final.
St. Oswald's, 2 goals.
Chester, *nil.*

All must taste the cup of sorrow,
I to-day and thou to-morrow

"Chester will now meet Westminster Rovers in the final."—*Echo*, March, 1891.

"St. Oswald's have another chance (of beating Chester), and that is nil, it is feared."—*Echo*, April 25, 1891.

"What price St. Oswald's for the Charity Cup?"— Sarcasm.)—*Chester Chronicle*, March, 1891.

In Sorrowful Remembrance
OF THE
CHESTER FOOTBALL CLUB,
Who, having enjoyed a **Promising Infancy**, came to an **Untimely End** (through overgrowth)
*AT EXTON PARK, APRIL 25th, 1891.*

By many a death-bed I have been,
And many a sinner's parting seen,
But never aught like this

*'Funeral' card printed by St.Oswalds' fans following their Charity Cup victory.*

Chester had another player capped for Wales in Ben Lewis who scored both goals in a 7-2 defeat against Ireland. Also in the Welsh side were J.Davies and W.Owen of Chirk who had helped out Chester earlier in the season. There was also success for the Reserves, after the problems of the previous season, with victory over Nantwich in the Chester Junior Cup Final.

**MATCH TO REMEMBER**
**CHESTER 1 LINCOLN CITY 0**
**FA CUP 1ST ROUND - JANUARY 17TH 1891**

*Chester faced Lincoln looking for revenge over the club who had defeated them 2-0 at the same stage the previous season. Lincoln had a good record in the Midland League and they were accompanied by a large number of supporters who were attracted by the added inducement of an evening visit to the pantomime. The ground was in poor condition, resembling a 'nutmeg-grater', as a severe frost overnight made worse a pitch which had been slushy and rough after a thaw. Chester were led by Bob Roberts who had started the season as Captain, until work commitments had forced a move to London where he had played for London Welsh. He returned to the city especially for the game and on winning the toss elected to play uphill.*

*Chester had the best chances in the early exchanges, with Taylor hitting the crossbar and Bobby Davies shooting inches over. The only goal of the game was scored by Bob Roberts in a scrimmage as he followed in his own shot. The goal was met with great enthusiasm by the Chester fans who saw the first-half end with Lincoln pressing forward. In the second period the game was evenly contested with Chester coming close through Charlie Jones and Roberts, while Dickson pulled off some smart saves from the Lincoln forwards. The game ended with Chester on the attack, and the final whistle was greeted by tremendous cheering as supporters celebrated the club's first appearance in the last 16 of the FA Cup.*

*Chester - Dickson, Roberts, S. Jones, Maddocks, Williams, Taylor, Fleming, Townsend, C. Jones, Lewis, Davies.*
*Lincoln City - Robinson, Jeffrey, Neil, Duckworth, Mollineaux, Rawlinson, Burton, Irving, Smallman, Shaw, Moore.*

The AGM was held at the Boot Inn on May 21st 1891 where once again the club reported a loss on the season.

The committee took great pains to point out that gate receipts no longer covered expenses and a full breakown of payments in connection with the first team was provided:-

In May 1891 the suggestion was put forward by the former president of Chester, Hugh Roberts, that the differences between Chester and St.Oswalds should be settled, and one good club formed from the two. Although Hugh Roberts had resigned as president in 1889 he still took great interest in local football and his views were much respected; it was thanks to his foresight that Chester had been able to establish themselves as the prominent club in the city. While St.Oswalds had always relied on local players, Roberts, by advocating a better standard of fixture for Chester, had recognised that higher class players were required in order to compete. Since this talent was not always available locally Chester had been forced to look outside the area and in order to retain the services of these players had started to pay wages. Roberts himself preferred amateur status but recognised that payments were needed to succeed, unlike St.Oswalds who resolutely held out as amateurs. It had always been Hugh Roberts' ambition to make Chester football a success and he realised that there was only room for one club in the city. He felt that an amalgamation would mean a lower cost of operation and improvements on the playing front as more money became available for players.

Although Chester were in favour of the proposal, St.Oswalds were very much against it, even though they were suffering financial difficulties at the time. Sam Laing, the chairman of St.Oswalds, suggested that this was all a plan by Chester to destroy them. He did not see it as an amalgamation and thought that Chester would just take their best players and leave the rest, an understandable concern as Chester had already taken Harry Lee and were trying to obtain three others.

| | |
|---|---|
| Players wages - | £141 6s 4d |
| Amateurs expenses - | £65 4s 11d |
| Railway fares and travelling expenses - | £59 5s 5d |
| Refreshment allowance - | £18 12s 2d |
| Guarantees, referees and umpires - | £104 1s 10d |
| Police, checkers - | £17 5s 6d |
| Rent, printing and posting | £22 1s 0d |
| Footballs, clothing, improvements on field, boots, repairs and washing | - £33 3s 0d |
| Secretary's expenses re finding players, loss of time, injuries and sundries | -£81 18s 0d |
| Total | - £542 18s 2d |

Gate receipts and subscriptions amounted to £407-3s-1d, with the largest amount coming from the Lincoln City cup-tie which fetched £59-8s-10d. The club did benefit from the Annual Sports which raised £63-19s-11d, together with a number of donations including a substantial sum from local MP Mr Yerburgh. Despite this there was an overall deficiency of £145-2s-4d and there was talk of increasing admission prices for the new season.

For the start of the 1891/92 campaign Chester had to do without Ben Lewis who had joined Wrexham, but there were new arrivals in Bentley (Gainsborough Trinity) and Morris (Bootle). For the first game of the season Ashton and Dawes were promoted from the Reserves, but Chester got off to a bad start with a 4-1 defeat at home to a far superior Northwich team. The following week Chester introduced Billy Lewis from Crewe, a player who had already won 12 caps for Wales and who was to become Chester's most capped player until Angus Eve in 2001.

He created a good impression in his first game against Denton with some good runs and passes, and later in the season he added to his total of caps with games against England, Scotland and Ireland. The Denton match proved to be the last game for centre-half Ted Williams, who joined Crewe. Born near Saltney he was known as one of the fastest players in football and once defeated the England amateur 100 yards champion. He went on to play in the Second Division with Crewe and won 2 Welsh caps in 1893, before ligament trouble forced him to retire from football at the early age of 26.

The first away game of the season was played against Stoke Swifts (the reserve team of Stoke) where, despite a valiant performance, a totally reorganised team was hammered 9-1. The new goalkeeper, Mercer, was not a success, and more changes were made for the Wrexham game with the introduction of Owen (St.Oswalds), Meredith (Saltney) and Stoneley (Over). After another defeat the rumblings of discontent over the selection policy of the committee began to increase. Although Chester beat Rhosllanerchrugog in the FA Cup it was a wretched performance and the team that represented Chester was of very poor quality. The committee was criticised for putting out a team that was a disgrace to the city and it was felt that, after the financial loss of the previous season, they could not have found such a good way of decreasing attendances further. There were even suggestions that the team should be disbanded as the prestige of the club waned.

As a result of this criticism an emergency meeting was held in October to discuss the future of the club with the main outcome being a decision to change the selection policy. Previously it had been the decision of up to 15 people to pick the side, and it was decided that, in future, the selection committee should be reduced to three, namely Mr Wooliscroft, Mr Weston and Mr Clare. It was Weston who had led the Reserves to the Chester Junior Cup the previous season, while Clare, a schoolmaster at Grosvenor St.Johns, had played for Chester in their first season.

The new committee reacted by bringing in Billy Carter from St.Oswalds and two of the players from the previous season, Taylor and Ted Carty (who had just returned from a long suspension by the Cheshire Association). The changes did not bear fruit straight away and defeats against Everton Reserves, Gorton Villa and Macclesfield left Chester firmly anchored at the bottom of the table. They were also eliminated from the FA Cup by Wrexham, although they did show an improvement in form.

A League victory was finally achieved, against Wrexham, and this was followed by an excellent 6-1 win over Gorton Villa on Boxing Day. The latter performance helped rekindle enthusiasm in what was one of the best performances for a long time.

On the other side of town however things were not going so well and by mid-January St.Oswalds were in a critical financial position. Mr Yerburgh MP, who was president of both clubs, put his weight behind an amalgamation but some members of the St.Oswalds committee were still against it, even at this stage. Feelings in the northern part of town had always been strongly against Chester and the Saints fans always referred to them disparagingly as the *'Flookersbrook club'*. With so much hostility between the clubs a merger was always unlikely, and with the Saints on the brink of closure Chester became even more reluctant since they did not want to take on the debts of their rivals.

On January 23rd 1892, St.Oswalds played their last ever game, ironically against Chester, and were outclassed in a 7-0 defeat. Two days later the Saints were dissolved with debts of £100 and Chester lost their only challengers within the city. Goalkeeper Jack Pay and half-back Thompson, two of St.Oswalds better players, immediately joined Chester, and they were soon followed by McNiel. With the demise of St.Oswalds, crowds began to show a small increase as the previously reluctant Saints fans were left with no viable alternative but to switch their allegiance.

In the second-half of the season Chester's performances improved considerably and they achieved some good results, notably 4-1 against Stoke Swifts and 6-2 against Everton Reserves. The Everton result was particularly outstanding because they had lost only one game all season having scored 99 and conceded just 18 goals. This late run helped pull Chester up to a final position of 9th.

The AGM was once again held at the Boot Inn on May 30th 1892, and the club were able to report a reduction in the debt by £21-4s-10d, leaving an outstanding balance of £123-17s-6d. Travel expenses were still high and there was concern about the distances being travelled, but the decision was made to continue in the Combination. Gate receipts rose which was pleasing considering the poor start to the season; this was partly due to an increase in the number of friendlies played. Amongst these friendlies was a game against a touring Canadian team from Toronto which resulted in a 3-3 draw.

For the 1892/93 season the team was augmented by the arrival of Seth Powell, a sturdy full back from West Bromwich Albion, and Fred Porter a hard tackling centre-half from local football. Tommy Fleming, who had been at the club since 1886, was made captain.

Once again Chester got off to a poor start and after four games were bottom of the table having lost all their games. However a win against Nantwich, who were also without a point, marked a change of fortune.

A week later Chester crushed Stanley from Liverpool 11-0 in the FA Cup with an outstanding performance. This game had been scheduled for Liverpool but switched to Chester on the payment of a £10 guarantee. Unfortunately the attendance was dismal and Chester ended up making a loss. In the Second Qualifying Round Chester beat Prescot but were unlucky to be eliminated in the next round by Liverpool Caledonians, despite a good display from Jack Pay and the forwards. A week prior to this tie Chester had signed full-back Wilson from Caledonian to replace Taylor who had gone to work abroad. Caledonians disbanded later in the season due to poor attendances and Chester were again able to take advantage with the signing of Deighton.

Back in the Combination Chester had recovered well and after a comfortable 5-1 win over Wrexham reached fifth position. Lol Heyes was signed from Northwich and he went on to form a good partnership with Billy Lewis. His debut came against Everton Reserves who were running away with the Combination having only dropped one point in 12 games. Chester rose to the occasion and shocked the leaders with a 3-2 win, one of the goals coming from debutant Heyes.

In February Chester turned up an hour and a quarter late for a fixture at Macclesfield which necessitated a second-half of only 15 minutes, surprisingly the result was allowed to stand. The following month the fixture at Gorton was moved to Chester because of a clash with the Cup Final at Fallowfield.

As 50,000 watched Wolves beat Everton a much smaller attendance saw Chester take full advantage by thrashing the Manchester club 6-0. Chester finished the season in 3rd place behind the Reserves of Everton and Stoke, a big improvement on the previous season.

For the first time Chester entered the Liverpool Senior Cup but were well beaten 4-0 by a Liverpool team that had only been formed 12 months previously. In the Cheshire Senior Cup Chester reached the Final for the second time having defeated Marple and Northwich on the way. The victory over Northwich in the Semi-Final attracted 6500 to Crewe and Chester impressed with a 4-2 victory over a team who were then in the Second Division of the Football League.

In the Final, Chester faced Crewe, a club eager for revenge over a team that had embarrassed them in the Final of 1888. Crewe, like Northwich, were then in the Second Division and had already beaten Chester in a friendly, but a close contest was anticipated. The game was played at Macclesfield and a crowd of 6500 saw a goalless draw which Chester deserved to win. In the second half Chester exerted considerable pressure, penning Crewe in their own half, but were unable to break down a solid defence. The replay was held at Northwich two weeks later and attracted a record crowd of 8000 (gate receipts of £150), including 2500 from Chester. The same eleven players turned out for Chester, with some positional changes, and at half-time they were leading 1-0 thanks to a goal from Lol Heyes. However in the second half they faded badly and were well beaten 3-1. Crewe deserved to win and the blame was laid at the feet of the Chester forwards who had played so well in the first game but put no effort into the second 45 minutes of the replay. The team that played for Chester in the deciding game was:- Pay, Wilson, Powell, Carter, Porter, Astbury, Lewis, Heyes, Ashton, Fleming, Deighton.

The AGM was held at the Oddfellows Hall in July 1893 where, despite higher gate receipts, season ticket prices were set at 7s-6d (37½p) and 5s (25p).

For the 1893/94 season the Combination was down to 10 clubs with Chirk and Gorton Villa dropping out. To make up the fixtures, more friendlies were played, but like many clubs Chester were finding that these games no longer attracted the crowds. There was plenty of experience in the Chester side that started the season especially in the forward line where Fleming, Heyes and Lewis were joined by Arthur Turner who had re-joined the club after spells with Stoke and Ardwick. Other new signings included Grewcock from Stockport County and Bob Bull a Tarvin based player who had been playing for Nantwich. Despite this experience Chester found goals hard to come by and the committee came in for a lot of criticism for their re-arranging and experimenting.

In October Chester played a friendly at Crewe which was grandly, and inappropriately, billed as the *'fight for the Cheshire Championship'*. Only £16 was taken at the gate as Chester were beaten 3-1. At the end of the month centre half Fred Porter quit as a professional to become a policeman and joined a new team in the city, Chester Police Athletic. This club, based at Brook Lane in Newton, became a haven for a number of ex-Chester players including Jack Pay who joined a few days after Porter. The Police team joined the Wirral & District League and for a couple of years they were seen as a serious threat to Chester, as attendances at Faulkner Street fell. They met with some success in their short existence finishing 3rd in the Wirral League and reaching the Cheshire Senior Cup Semi-Final in 1894/95.

Chester had a disastrous 6-1 defeat in the FA Cup against Macclesfield, a surprising result because matches between the sides were normally close affairs. Chester clearly missed Porter and Arthur Turner was moved to centre-half with 'old man' Fleming returning to the forwards. At half-time the tactics were changed and Turner moved back up front but it was already too late and Chester were well beaten.

Once again the Combination was dominated by Everton Reserves and when they visited Chester in December the prices were raised to increase funds. Lining up for Everton was a familiar face in Fred Porter who had only left Chester 6 weeks previously. It turned out to be a very rough game, largely instigated by Chester, and it disintegrated into a kicking match as the players were urged to go for the man and not the ball. Porter's decision to leave Chester and join the Police was clearly the catalyst behind the trouble and rumours that there would be a concerted attack on him at the end of the game proved true as he was kicked and pushed by thugs as he left the pitch. Fortunately he was assisted by some friends although the Chester committee were conspicuous by their absence.

It was February before Chester were beaten away from home (at Dresden) and although the defence was strong, the attack was struggling despite a return to form of Billy Lewis which earned him three more Welsh caps. The inability to score goals meant that Chester finished a disappointing 6th out of 10, but once again they reached the Cheshire Senior Cup Final. In the Semi-Final Chester had easily defeated Second Division Northwich 3-0 with goals from Heyes, Grewcock and Bull, and met Combination rivals Macclesfield in the Final, which was held at Northwich in front of 5000 spectators. The following team represented Chester:-

Moore, Thompson, Wilson, Turner, Farrell, Astbury, Bull, Fleming, Lewis, Grewcock, Heyes.

For the second successive season the Final went to a replay with the game finishing 1-1, Macclesfield equalising after Chester had taken a first half lead through Heyes. For the replay, at Crewe, Chester replaced Fleming with Pickering but to no avail as they were beaten 2-1. The game followed the pattern of the 1893 replay with Chester taking a first-half lead, through Lewis, but fading badly after the break. The equaliser came from a penalty after Turner had collided with a Macclesfield forward; this affected the rhythm of Chester who went to pieces and Macclesfield ended up easy winners. Chester had trained for the Final by running round the Roodee at night, but it was felt that it would have been more profitable for them to practice their shooting as their lack of fire power let them down.

There were a number of changes in the Combination for the 1894/95 season, most notably the departure of the reserve teams of Stoke and Everton and a closer contest was expected. There were no major changes on the playing front as an attempt was made to rely more on local players in order to increase support. Lol Heyes left the club and Billy Carter returned after a long term injury, while Bob Bull was elected captain and was joined in the team by his brother Harry from Nantwich. Chester found goalscoring a lot easier this season thanks to the introduction of young Rimmer Brown, and by Christmas they were challenging at the top of the table. However, there was to be no success in the FA Cup as Chester were once again eliminated by Macclesfield at the first hurdle.

The policy of playing local players seemed to pay dividends and the team was strengthened by the introduction of goalkeeper Billy Coventry from Chester Institute and Charles Spencer from Chester Rovers, a team who had reformed in October 1891 and were now playing in local football. Spencer went on to have a long association with Chester, although in the early 1900s he went to work abroad and represented Italy in an International game against Switzerland. He later returned to Chester as trainer, a position he held until the late 1920s. The challenge for the Championship suffered a blow in February with 2 heavy defeats in the Potteries against Dresden and Hanley, however the team recovered well to win the next four games. The crunch came at Easter when leaders Ashton North End brought 1000 fans from Manchester to Faulkner Street. A hard fought game finished goalless and Ashton went on to finish champions with Chester trailing by five points in 3rd place.

For the third season in succession Chester reached the Cheshire Senior Cup Final. In the Semi-Final they had beaten Northwich in a game which did not attract the same interest as in previous years, possibly because Northwich had now dropped out of the Football League and had reverted to amateur status. Chester won the game convincingly 3-1 with goals from Brown, Harry Bull and Farrell. In the Final Chester met Macclesfield at Northwich and in front of a crowd of 3000 won the cup for the first time with a 2-1 victory. On returning to the city the players received an enthusiastic welcome at Northgate Station where a crowd of 1000 and a band awaited their arrival. The team were then driven in a wagonette around the city parading the cup as hundreds of people lined the street. Particular pride was felt in this achievement because the team was made up of so many local players. Coventry, Astbury, Thompson, Spencer and Brown were all from Chester, while the Bull Brothers came from Tarvin. One of the non-Cestrians, Billy Lewis, achieved more international success playing against England, Scotland plus Ireland, and scoring 2 goals in the process.

The local rivalry with Wrexham was not so keen although three friendlies were played during the season. In the first of these it was noted that Chester were playing in their traditional red while Wrexham played in dark blue and white vertical stripes!

Despite success in the Cheshire Cup, gate receipts were falling as Chester continued to face clubs from outside the locality in the Combination. A proposal was put forward for a new League to cover Cheshire, Shropshire and North Wales including the likes of Chester, Wrexham and Oswestry.

Unfortunately this failed to get off the ground and Chester started the 1895/96 season in a Combination League which had now been reduced to 8 teams.

The Chester team was strengthened for the new season with the arrival of Worgan from the Liverpool District and half-back Harry Jones. Chester also welcomed back Ben Lewis from Wrexham who was looking for a better standard of football than the Welsh League, where Wrexham were currently playing. During his time away from Chester, at Middlesbrough and Wrexham, Lewis had added another 9 Welsh caps to his total. The arrival of Lewis and Worgan gave Chester what was reckoned to be one of their best ever forward lines, but despite playing well the results were not forthcoming in a League dominated by Macclesfield and the returned Everton Reserves. The lack of competitiveness in the League led to a further fall in gates, and in December it was announced that soldiers in uniform and women would be allowed in free in an attempt to increase crowds. By the end of February Chester had played all their games although some teams still had more than half their fixtures to complete. At the time Chester were 4th, but by the time the other teams had completed their matches, they had fallen to 5th.

**MATCH TO REMEMBER**
**CHESTER 2 MACCLESFIELD 1**
**CHESHIRE SENIOR CUP FINAL - MARCH 30TH 1895**

*The 1894/95 Cheshire Cup Final saw Chester face the team that had not only beaten them in the previous year's final, but also knocked them out of the FA Cup two seasons in succession. The final was held at the Drill Field, Northwich, and Chester were backed by more than 1,000 supporters.*

*In gloomy weather Chester, playing in all red, kicked off with a strong wind behind them. After 10 minutes Bullock was fouled by Turner and Heapey scored for Macclesfield with a low shot which Coventry could not reach as he slipped in the mud. Two minutes later, at the other end of the pitch, Lewis was fouled, and when Astbury placed the resultant free kick into the goalmouth, Rimmer Brown scored the equaliser in a scrimmage. Up until half-time Chester had the better of the play but Macclesfield held out. The start of the second-half was even but Macclesfield gradually got on top and Coventry had to save six shots in quick succession. As the game progressed Chester started to turn the game around and with seven minutes to go Rimmer Brown scored his second with a beautiful shot after a good run down the left. For the final few minutes Macclesfield pressed hard, but the Chester defence held out to win 2-1. Chester's best players were Coventry, Astbury and Farrell, but the forwards were disappointing and Lewis was not up to his usual form.*

*Chester - Coventry, Thompson, Wilson, Astbury, Farrell, Turner, R. Bull, Spencer, Lewis, H. Bull, Brown.*
*Macclesfield - Kent, Hindley, Gaskell, Hall, Heapey, Bolton, Bullock, Wheeldon, Hall, Burton, Oldham.*

In the cup competitions Chester got past the First Qualifying Round of the FA Cup for the first time in three seasons, thanks to an easy victory over Port Sunlight. However in the Second Qualifying Round they were disappointingly beaten at home by Middleton 3-0. For half the game Chester played with only 10 men and despite strong second-half pressure they were unable to break down the Middleton defence. In the Cheshire Senior Cup Chester were beaten in a Second Round replay by a Macclesfield team who had already defeated them 3 times during the season. Chester did reach the Liverpool Senior Cup Final but this was not much of an achievement as they attained this stage without playing a game, Semi-Final opponents Liverpool having scratched from the competition. In the Final at Goodison Park, Chester lost 4-0 to Everton Reserves in front of only 500 people.

Harry Jones and Billy Lewis both played in the trial games for Wales in February but only Lewis was selected to play and he added another three caps to his growing total. The 1895/96 season also saw the debut of Bert Lipsham who went on to win an FA Cup Winners medal with Sheffield United and an England cap in 1902.

At the end of the season the first attempts were made to convert the club into a Limited Liability Company, and many leading men in the district were approached with a view to taking up shares. An ambitious scheme was proposed to procure a field and build a ground with an athletics and cycling track. It was hoped that the ground would eventually rival Stanley Park in Liverpool which was hired out for pigeon shooting, rabbit coursing, rat catching and sparrow shooting, but the scheme failed to get off the ground at this stage. One of the reasons behind the proposal was the concern over the future of the ground in Faulkner Street. The area was becoming more and more built up as Hoole become a prime area for housing, and it was becoming clear that a move to a new ground would soon be needed.

There were more changes in the structure of the Combination for the 1896/97 season, most notably the arrival of local teams Barnton Rovers, Wrexham and Crewe. Barnton did not prove to be a great addition to the League and there were reputedly only 20 people present for their home game with Chester in January.

The defence remained the same as the previous season and Harry Jones was made captain. Jones, a burly defender, was noted for his peculiar way of spread-eagling himself when tackling. Up front Billy Lewis had left the club for Manchester City although he returned to Faulkner Street later in the season and Chester relied on two youngsters, Blakeman and Speakman for the goals.

In November Worgan and Wilson left the club but the defence was strengthened by the surprising re-appearance of Fred Porter at centre-half.

The following month Tommy Gordon, a young forward from Buckley, made his debut and he went on to become one of the most well-respected players to represent the club.

At the turn of the year Chester were 3rd in the table and a good run at the end of the season, coinciding with the return of Billy Lewis, allowed them to retain this position behind Everton Reserves and Rockferry. In the middle of this run Chester played at Wrexham and took the unusual step of playing Billy Lewis in goal and Billy Coventry at centre-forward. The move paid off, with Lewis keeping a clean sheet in an excellent display, and Coventry scoring one of the goals in a 2-0 victory.
Because of the few Combination games, Chester also joined the Central League along with Macclesfield, Walsall, Dresden and Crewe. Unfortunately the League proved to be a failure with Macclesfield turning up 90 minutes late, with only 9 men, for their game at Faulkner Street, and Chester visiting Walsall to find that their opponents had forfeited the game.

In the FA Cup Chester were again defeated by Middleton, but this setback was compensated with more success in the Cheshire Senior Cup. Victories over Saltney Borderers, Port Sunlight and Congleton Hornets put Chester in the Final where they faced old rivals Northwich with the following team:-
Coventry, Astbury, Jones, Catherall, Porter, Barker, Gordon, Lewis, Spencer, Lipsham, Speakman

A 1-1 draw at Macclesfield meant another game at the same venue the following week, and at half-time in the replay Chester were trailing 1-0. Despite constant pressure in the second-half it was 15 minutes from the end before Chester were able to equalise when Hargreaves sliced the ball into his own net from a corner by Gordon. A few minutes later Speakman netted the winner and Chester captured the cup for the second time in 3 years.

Despite success on the pitch there were serious problems in financial and organisational terms. Total receipts had been falling constantly since 1892, mainly because of declining attendances, however no attempt had been made to cut down on expenditure. The loss on the season was £53-8s-11d which increased total liabilities to £288-9s, including £30 owed to the players who were not paid for the last seven games. Behind the scenes the club had started 1896/97 with a new committee but, as the season progressed, it became more difficult to get them to attend meetings. In the last six weeks of the season no meetings at all were held and the club was being run by the players and Mr Shepherd the secretary. Matters came to a head in July 1897 when the players refused to start the new season with any of the previous seasons committee in control, as relations between the players, the secretary and the committee deteriorated.

The secretary was asked to call a general meeting but he refused and it was discovered that a proper balance sheet could not be submitted because no accounts had been submitted for the last seven weeks of the season.

With the club in total disarray a heated meeting was held at the start of August at which a new committee was appointed, including 3 members of the old committee, 4 ex-members and 5 newcomers, a surprising balance considering the players demands. The committee comprised of J.Crowder (chairman), R.Atherton (secretary), E.Dutton (treasurer), J.Jones, H.Clare, Dr.Butt, W.Coventry (father of the Chester goalkeeper), E.Hallmark, G.Hull, W.Fletcher and W.Shepherd. Controversially they proposed not to take on the liabilities of the old committee so that they could have a completely new beginning. Although legally correct this was not considered very fair and it was believed that the new committee should meet its creditors and clear the name of the old club so that a fresh start could be made with clean hands. The alternative was for the committee to face the criticism, let the old club die, take a new name and possibly sacrifice a season in order to get the finances in order. In the end the club got the best of both worlds as they continued under the old name and avoided paying off their debts.

At the August meeting the players and many of the guarantors agreed to forego their claims if the club was to be run properly, and it appears as though the appointment of the new committee satisfied these demands. Certainly Chester started the following season with a zero balance, and although at the start of the season they were known as the 'new club', it seems that technically they were still the same team. Although some players boycotted the new organisation the backbone of the team remained the same as the previous season.

As if these problems were not enough the ground issue was beginning to cause a major headache as building work moved closer to the playing area. The landlord wanted to increase the rent and there was also a requirement to move the hoardings closer to the pitch at a cost of £50. With the probability that they would have to move in 12 months, there were doubts as to whether it was worthwhile spending money which could not be recouped. The only alternative was to find a new ground, and although there were two or three possible sites available, they required even more money to develop them. In the time available, and with the club still recovering from a traumatic close season, the only real option was to continue at Faulkner Street, although it was clear that a move was now imminent.

Chester started the 1897/98 season without Bert Lipsham, Harry Jones and Astbury, who all joined Rockferry, but Wilson returned from Liverpool.

Lipsham, the second of four brothers to play for Chester, later joined Sheffield United and appeared in the 1901 and 1902 FA Cup Finals; he also won an England cap and later became Millwall's player-manager. The first game of the season, against Northwich, resulted in a goalless draw, but the match attracted a great deal of interest because of the reconstitution of the club. It was the sixth game before Chester achieved a victory, when they beat Dresden 5-0, but the Potteries team resigned from the Combination later in the season due to financial difficulties and their record was deleted. After beating Druids, Chester lost goalkeeper Billy Coventry, who was in dispute with the club, and with Griffiths in goal for the next game they suffered an embarrassing 7-4 defeat at Garston Copper Works who had only been a junior club the year before. The team made up for this in the next game with a 6-0 hammering of fellow strugglers Tranmere, in which Billy Lewis scored 4 goals, but an unpredictable season continued with a 5-2 defeat at Northwich followed by a 3-1 victory over Wrexham.

On February 5th Chester gained their revenge over Garston Copper Works with a 5-0 victory in which debutant Len Hales scored two goals. Hales joined the club from Chester PSA, along with Fred Halliday, and made an immediate impression with his direct and purposeful approach. He was considered a gentleman both on and off the field and in many ways his temperament was not suited to the 'rough and tumble' of football. Unfortunately he was susceptible to injury and few games passed without him limping at some point in the game. Despite this he soon attracted the attention of Crewe where he partnered Bert Lipsham and won Cheshire Cup honours. From there he moved to Stoke where a knee injury terminated a promising career, but he later returned to Chester and became a director of the Football Club.

Chester finished the season third from bottom above Northwich and Tranmere, but bearing in mind the problems at the start of the season it was considered a satisfactory performance. The team had rarely been hammered and had been unlucky not to pick up a few more victories. In the cup competitions Chester were eliminated from the FA Cup at the first stage by Stockport County. In the Cheshire Senior Cup Chester beat Birkenhead Locos and Tranmere before being knocked out by a revitalised Nantwich in the Semi-Final.

At the AGM the club showed a balance in hand of £25 as the club reaped the benefits of better management. The committee worked hard throughout the year and managed to turn round the fortunes of the club with a lot of good work being done by the secretary, Reuben Atherton Although wages had increased, additional income came from subscribers and ticket-holders as well as a new football draw.

Meanwhile the proposal to build an Athletics ground for the city took a step forward following the abortive attempts by members of the football club in 1896. Early in 1898 a prospectus was issued by the Chester Athletics Ground Company with the intention of building a ground capable of holding 20,000 spectators, suitable for football, cycling, cricket, athletics and other pastimes. The proposed site of the ground was the Lead Works Field bounded on one side by the Lead Works and on the other by the railway. A right of way to City Road was acquired making it an ideal site because of its proximity to both the city and the General railway station. The men behind the proposal had met the members of Chester Football Club and it was agreed in principal to hand over the club to the company who would then appoint a committee to run the football.

Shares were issued at £10 each in an attempt to raise the necessary £7,000, but the price proved to be prohibitive and the flotation failed. Although the scheme was instigated by people outside the football club they were heavily reliant on the backing of football followers in the city. However football was very much the sport of the working classes and £10 proved to be well out of the reach of the average supporter.

For the 1898/99 season Chester were forced to leave Faulkner Street where building work had absorbed a large proportion of land. Ironically, for a short period of time, the Faulkner Street ground was occupied by Chester St.Oswalds who had been formed after the demise of Chester PSA. It proved to be a difficult task for Chester to find a new ground, but eventually a field was found in Hoole, close to the old base, on land that had been used for the Royal Agricultural Show in 1893.

New arrivals on the playing front were Salmon (Liverpool), Marshall (Everton) and Donoghue (Blackburn) with Billy Lewis, now playing in defence, as captain. Chester Rovers - who had been playing in local football - became Chester Reserves, and it was the Reserves who played the first game at the new ground against Chester Garrison. The first Combination game at home resulted in a 3-1 defeat against the champions of the previous season, Everton Reserves, although there was some consolation in gate receipts of £23 -12s-4d. Three successive home victories followed thanks to the developing partnership between Gordon and Donoghue. One of these victories was against Wrexham who defeated Chester in the FA Cup the following week largely due to two own goals by Eardley and Halliday in the first 15 minutes.

In November Harry Jones returned to Chester from Crewe at the same time as Len Hales made the move in the opposite direction.

Other players to return to the club during the season were McHugh (Reading) and Charles Spencer (Rockferry). For the game at Everton in November the Chester players were offered a substantial bonus of 10s (50p) per man to beat a team who had only dropped 2 points all season. Despite this incentive Chester were well beaten 4-0 after missing a number of easy chances, and failing to take the advice of their fans to *'shoot bloomin' hard and bloomin' often'*.

Chester returned to form against Buxton, even though trainer Billy Carter was required to make up the eleven, and good results at the turn of the year took Chester up to 5th place. However the Chester committee, who were working hard to clear the debts incurred by the preparation of the new ground, suffered a setback after a storm on January 2nd did £30 of damage. The day after the storm, hoardings were found littered throughout the area along with the remains of the stand and all the work carried out at the start of the season had to be repeated. No sooner had the repairs been finished than the hoardings blew down again, and for the game against Liverpool Reserves the players gave their services for free to help out the committee.

The team was strengthened by the arrival of Bill Poutney from Rossett at centre-forward, and he went on to score nine goals in the last 13 games, as Chester finished in a satisfactory 5th position. In fact the club were lucky to finish the season at all as they were on the point of disbanding after incidents against Crewe in the Cheshire Senior Cup. Chester were drawn against the Alexandra team in the Second Round after a 2-0 victory against Wirral Railway Athletic, and faced ex-players Billy Coventry, Bert Lipsham and Len Hales. Just before half time Donoghue (Chester) and Batho (Crewe) were sent off after getting involved in a fight. In the second half Chester had 3 goals disallowed, while the referee controversially allowed 3 dubious Crewe goals, and they went on to win 4-1. Although the Chester spectators accepted the decisions quietly during the game a huge crowd surrounded the referee after the match.

Thanks to the actions of the police, together with Coventry and a number of Chester players, the referee was safely escorted to the Bee Hive Hotel where he was able to take refuge until the excitement subsided. As a result of these disgraceful scenes a number of spectators were charged with causing a disturbance and the Football Association launched an enquiry. The incident received national coverage and the St.James Gazette alleged that the rowdyism was caused by people who had bet on the match, a charge that Chester vigorously denied. The Star was quite vehement in its condemnation of the club saying that *'The football authorities should mercilessly stamp out the brutal scoundrelism which threatens to engulf the English tradition of fair play on the football field.*

*The Chester rioters whose conduct the county magistrates investigated on Saturday should be punished in some more effectual way than by a fine. . . . It would perhaps be unfair to disqualify a club for the sins of its sympathisers but if the Chester roughs knew that rioting would entail deprivation for the rest of the season of their favourite sport they might be induced to take their beating like Englishman and not like - well, the worst kind of beasts.* '

Chester were clearly concerned about the widespread coverage the incident had received and threatened to disband the club if the ground was suspended. The committee sent a letter to the Cheshire Association expressing regret at the unfortunate incident and said that the demonstration could not be laid against the club as they had done all they could to protect the referee. In addition they arranged for large posters to be put on the hoardings at their ground warning of rowdyism. On March 3rd Mr Atherton represented Chester, in front of the commission appointed by the Football Association, at the Queen Hotel in the city. In a strong defence Mr Atherton and members of the committee picked holes in the referees report and condemned the reporting of the incident which they felt had been grossly exaggerated. Letters from representatives of Liverpool, Everton and other prominent clubs were read out in which the orderliness of the spectators and the work of the committee were praised. Mr Atherton concluded by pointing out to the commission the heavy expenditure incurred in re-erecting the hoarding and stands after recent gales, stressing the real danger of the club being forced to disband.

After deliberation the commissioners issued the following report:- *'The Chester club did not provide proper police protection; that the referee was mobbed on the field at the close of the match, and on the way to the dressing room; that the referee was protected by several policemen in plain clothes and some members of the Chester and Crewe clubs who prevented his being assaulted. The statements laid before the Football Association were much exaggerated and we are satisfied by the evidence that there was no justification for the assertion that betting was the cause of the disturbance. The commission recommend that dressing accommodation for the visiting club and referee be provided on the ground before next season. A disturbance having taken place, the Chester Club is ordered to take measures to prevent a repetition, and to pay the costs of the commission. Donoghue, of Chester, and Batho, of Crewe, must be suspended for one month from this date for fighting on the field.'* As a postscript to this incident Donoghue and Batho made their first appearances after suspension in a friendly match between Chester and Crewe on April 1st at Chester.

No sooner had Chester overcome these difficulties than the stand blew down for the third time, at the beginning of April. Only one home match was left and that was a friendly against the Chester Junior League which had ironically been arranged to help the club with its financial commitments. For this final game only the press box was left standing and the local reporter refused to use it in case it collapsed! A decision was made not to re-erect the stand because the season was coming to an end and the tenure of the ground was due to expire with no possibility of continuing.

In parallel with the 1896/97 season the team had performed well on the field, just as the club were having problems behind the scenes. The home record had been excellent with only four points dropped in Hoole, but the away performances had been disappointing with the only victories coming against bottom clubs Rhyl and Garston Copper Works. However there were quality players in the side including Tommy Gordon, Bill Poutney and Tommy Delaney and the whole team, with the exception of Donoghue, agreed to sign up for the new season.

The AGM was held on June 1st where it was reported that gate receipts had risen to just over £329 as the Combination expanded and became more competitive. Despite the ground problems and the cost of the Football Association hearing a positive balance of £20-13s-2d was recorded. The club was helped in this by the owners of the ground who agreed to waive the rent of £10 when they heard of the difficulties the club had experienced with the gales. Nevertheless, these positive aspects could not disguise the fact that the club were effectively homeless. At the end of the season the committee had disposed of the timber and galvanised sheeting which comprised the stand and hoardings. The sale by auction raised £58 as the committee sought to find a new ground. The favourite site was the Roodee and an application was made to the corporation to enclose some land and build a grandstand.

However it soon became clear that this was not a viable move as the corporation refused to sanction the enclosure of the area. This was decided on the basis that the Roodee belonged to the people of Chester and if land was enclosed for football purposes other people would want to do likewise. Legal opinion was therefore entirely against the enclosing of portions of land on the Roodee. By July Chester were no nearer finding a solution to the ground problem and the Combination were considering whether to include them in the forthcoming fixture list as their membership of the League came close to lapsing. A meeting was held at the Town Hall on July 18th 1899 presided over by the mayor at which the position and future of the club was considered.

A large attendance, including Messrs Hallmark, Fletcher and Atherton, discussed the options, but it was becoming clear that Chester would be unable to start the 1899/1900 season. A site at Brook Lane in Newton was rejected and once again the club looked to the Lead Works Field as the best solution. Despite the failure of the Athletics Ground Company Mr Fletcher thought that a scheme could succeed if the shares were priced at £1 rather than £10 and he proposed the formation of a Limited Liability Company. However, with the Combination deadline fast approaching, the practicalities of getting such an ambitious scheme off the ground in such a short period of time proved insurmountable.

By August the club was finally excluded from the Combination and several players severed their connections with the club. Amongst the departures were Gordon, Delaney and Poutney to Wrexham, Spencer to Druids, Halliday to Crewe and Donoghue to Reading. The core of the committee remained intact with the intention of finding a new ground but Chester Football Club ended the century by temporarily disbanding.

# MUD AND CUPS 1900 - 1910
# CHAPTER 4

As the new century dawned Chester were a club in limbo but all efforts were being made by Messrs. Hallmark, Coventry and Atherton to secure a new ground. In April 1900 attempts were made to revive the club and Chester were entered for the Combination with the possibility of playing at Hoole Park. Although the club were hopeful the deal fell through at the last minute as residents objected to having football played near their houses. Another appeal to use the racecourse was also rejected by the town council.

In June the following year it was revealed that a new ground had been found for the club in Whipcord Lane close to where St.Oswalds used to play. Although Cestrians were cautious about the re-formation of the club the committee was confident that the field would be ready by September and that Chester would have a team for the start of the season.

A new committee was formed comprising E.Hallmark (Chairman), W.Coventry (Treasurer), W.Fletcher, J.Williamson, D.Hewitt, G.Hull and R.Atherton. Ben Eardley, who had been goalkeeper in 1898/99, was made trainer and stalwart player Billy Carter became his assistant. The new Whipcord Lane ground was fully enclosed by August and the local press were very enthusiastic about the new set-up, believing it to be the best ground the club had played on and finding it hard to say how it could be improved upon. Future events proved this evaluation to be somewhat premature.

The playing staff was largely built up of youngsters augmented by players who had played for the club in its previous incarnation. Moore, Barker, Farrell and Delaney all returned to the club, Moore having played for Stockport and Farrell for Gravesend. Newcomers included Morris (Liverpool Reserves), Dawson and Coppack (Newton Rangers), Griffiths and Davies (Rowton), Prescott (Sealand Road), Gibbs (New Brighton) and Wakefield (Chester Locos).

The ground was opened with a friendly against Everton, a club with whom they had always had a good relationship, and over 1000 people were present to see senior football return to the city. A young Chester side did not disgrace themselves, with Glyn Griffiths scoring the first goal at the new ground, but Chester tired in the second half and Everton won 4-1. The club's first competitive game was played against White Star Wanderers at Bootle and Chester, playing in their new green and white shirts, got off to an inauspicious start by losing 6-3. The team was handicapped in this game as two players did not turn up and trainer Eardley had to play at half-back. The following week a determined Chester side opened their Combination account with a 3-1 win over Nantwich. This proved to be the only victory in the first 12 games as Chester struggled to make an impact against some well-established sides. Perhaps the best result in this period was a 2-2 draw with the previous season champions Wrexham who included Bill Poutney and Tommy Gordon in their side.

Chester returned to the FA Cup with a game against Birkenhead, a team who were to become keen rivals over the next few years. After a 1-1 draw at the Birkenhead ground in Chester Road, the replay at Whipcord Lane proved to be a thriller. Chester opened the scoring with an early goal from Spencer but this was soon equalised by an own goal from Morris. Dodd scored for Birkenhead but Spencer netted his second after a pass from Hallmark. Coppack was having a shaky game in goal for Chester, contrasting with Viner who withstood a lot of pressure after Lloyd had put Birkenhead 3-2 in front. In the last minute Griffiths grabbed an equaliser and the game went into extra time. There were no goals in the first period, and it was Prescott who put Chester in the lead shortly after the break with Davies adding a fifth a few minutes later. Right on time Birkenhead added a fourth but it was not enough as Chester won 5-4.

Immediately after the game Birkenhead raised a protest on the basis that the Chester ground was too short, an action that Chester did not defend. This protest exposed the major failing of the new site which effectively prevented Chester from competing in cup competitions while they remained at Whipcord Lane. This was not the only problem with the ground, bad weather meant the postponement of some games and many others were played under dreadful conditions as the pitch often resembled a swamp. Back in the League, Chester were bottom of the table at the turn of the year with only three points having had two deducted for playing an ineligible player. On January 11th Chester hammered a feeble Newton Le Willows team 5-1 in which only 30 minutes each way was played. Two weeks later they came down to earth with an embarrassing 8-1 home defeat to Oswestry. There was a mini-revival in March, which started with a 6-1 victory over Liverpool Police Athletic in the Liverpool Senior Cup. Three successive Combination victories followed against White Star, Rhyl and Chirk, but on Easter Monday Chester were defeated twice in one day.

In the morning they fell 4-2 at home to Skelmersdale in the Liverpool Senior Cup, and in the afternoon a tired Chester lost 2-0 to Birkenhead. Despite the better results after Christmas, Chester finished bottom of the Combination, although the club were able to report a satisfactory season in other respects, for the club had cleared its debts and were in a better financial position.

In addition the attitude of a predominantly young team had also been good. The players had always tried their hardest and never raised objections which gave the committee optimism for the 1902/03 season. Particularly pleasing was the form of full-backs Wakefield and Morris who formed a good partnership. Wakefield, who had been made captain, was a stubborn reliable defender whose form brought him to the attention of Sheffield Wednesday who signed him at the end of the season.

A number of changes were made in the team for the 1902/03 season, headed by full-back Harry Astbury who returned to the club from Rhyl. To partner him Chester signed Stewart of Stockport along with centre-half Turner from Liverpool Reserves. There were major changes up front with the arrival of Bromfield and Hodnett (Oswestry), Copeland (Birkenhead) and Kelly (White Star). A new goalkeeper was tried for the first home game of the season, Ledsham from Melrose, but he had a poor game and was replaced by trainer Eardley for the next game who then kept his place for the rest of the season.

After defeats in the first 2 games Chester put together a good run of eight games without defeat and attendances picked up with this improvement in form. The forward line was strengthened further with the arrival of Sherman from Hudson's, Liverpool, and he formed a promising partnership with Kelly on the left. Another newcomer was Riley, a small but tricky centre-forward who was promoted from the Reserves. An excellent 2-0 victory over second placed Witton showed how much Chester had progressed since the start of the season, but the run ended with a 5-2 defeat at Oswestry where a ten man Chester were forced to re-organise when Barker fell ill shortly before the beginning of the match.

Much to the surprise of many people the committee entered Chester for the Welsh Cup, but they were forced to switch the home match to Wrexham, where they were beaten 2-0. On Christmas Day Chester returned to Wrexham in the League but despite taking a lead through Tommy Delaney early in the second-half they were beaten by the top of the table team; leading goalscorer Delaney was a popular player although it was sometimes felt that he spoilt his play through '*over-excitement*'. Good wins followed against Newton Le Willows, Bangor and Burslem Port Vale, but these results were interspersed by a 9-1 hammering at Nantwich. The heavy defeat can be explained by the fact that Chester were due to play a Cheshire Cup-tie against Sale Holmfield on the same day and decided to play the Reserve team at Nantwich. Unfortunately the game against Sale was subsequently called off because of the state of the Whipcord Lane pitch.

Chester had a good run in the Cheshire Cup where the rules on the size of the pitch were less stringent. Victory over Birkenhead, after a replay in the first round, was followed by a defeat against Tranmere, but Chester went through after successfully appealing that Rovers played an ineligible player. An intriguing third round match saw Chester win at Helsby 3-1 in front of a crowd of 1000. This game saw the re-appearance of Glyn Griffiths at centre-forward, but it was reported that his speed had fallen off deplorably and he was wholly unreliable. Chester were finally defeated in the Semi-Final by Sale Holmfield after a replay, the same team who had knocked them out the previous season.

In the Combination a new centre-forward had been tried, in Lewis from Wrexham Victoria, and in April Chester benefited from the demise of White Star Wanderers with the signing McGuffie and Hardacre. Despite the new players Chester had a disappointing end to the season and finished 7th after winning only one of their last eight games. Overall the team had shown a vast improvement on the previous campaign, and in the autumn they had been one of the best teams in the Combination, it was only the poor run-in at the end that spoiled their record.

For the start of the 1903/04 season the committee aimed for a more local side having been criticised a year earlier for taking on too many players from outside the area. In the new team only 2 players were not local residents, with the home based players including two more members of the Lipsham family, Jacky and Tommy, who had both been regulars in the Reserves. A number of players returned to Chester including Coventry (Crewe), Wakefield (Sheffield Wednesday), Harry Jones (Rhyl) and Poutney (Wrexham). Other newcomers were Billy Matthews (Rhyl) and Smith (Skelmersdale). The local bias gave the committee more control and for the first time it became possible to introduce regular training on a Tuesday and Friday.

The season started in fine style with a 5-0 win over Witton with four of the five forwards scoring, but in the next game serious injuries to Astbury and Poutney resulted in a 2-1 defeat to Birkenhead. Chester soon bounced back with seven successive wins and by the start of November they were top of the table thanks to some outstanding performances by the forwards who scored 28 goals in the seven games. Tommy Lipsham and Matthews had formed a good partnership on the right, while on the left Jacky Lipsham was becoming a firm favourite with the fans thanks to his shooting ability. However there was disappointment in the performances of Wakefield at full-back, who had lost a lot of the form from his earlier stint at Chester.

Challenging at the top of the table were newly formed Broughton United, unbeaten at home when Chester visited their ground in November. Chester returned with a point after a 1-1 draw but it was clear that one of the reasons for Broughton's success was their pitch which was situated on the side of a steep hill. The ground was described as having an enormous slope from one side of the ground to the other with a sharp dip in the middle.

Surprisingly Chester entered the Welsh Cup again but were defeated at the first hurdle by Druids. This loss coincided with two successive Combination defeats but Chester recovered well with two excellent victories over Broughton (3rd) and Wrexham (4th) at Christmas which put them three points clear of Oswestry at the top. Another seven goals against Chirk further boosted hopes but there was surprising criticism that Chester were not scoring enough goals. Billy Matthews in particular was singled out against Chirk for '*playing to the gallery*' instead of concentrating on scoring goals.

A defeat at Tranmere saw Birkenhead go top of the table and Chester's failure to win the following four games saw them slip further behind. There was a return to winning ways at Bangor where Chester had to do without Tommy Lipsham who missed the train, his place being taken by Breen's brother who happened to be at the station to see the team off. In March, Chester lost assistant trainer Billy Carter who died at the early age of 37 from consumption. His valuable experience and sound judgement had proved beneficial to the club after the re-formation and his death was a sad loss.

Chester ended the season with four straight wins to finish runners-up four points behind Birkenhead. Crowds had improved still further and the club benefitted from having a more settled side. It was clear that Chester had the makings of a very good team and the committee were urged to retain as many of the players as possible. Although Chester had to content themselves with second place in the League they won silverware in the Cheshire Senior Cup. They had reached the Final after victories over Wirral Railway (7-0) and Witton Albion (1-0). In the Semi-Final they had beaten Tranmere 3-2 after a replay and had shown great character by pulling back a 2-0 deficit to draw 2-2 in the first game. The 1904 Cheshire Senior Cup Final was played against Nantwich at Northwich on April 16th. Nantwich had done the double over Chester in the Combination and had been particularly impressive in a 4-1 win at Whipcord Lane where they were considered to be the best team seen at the ground all season. The following team represented Chester in front of a crowd of 2,866:-

Coventry, Bather, Poutney, J.Breen, Hall, Barker,
T.Lipsham, Matthews, T.Delaney, Bell, J.Lipsham.

Two evenly matched teams fought out a splendid game with Nantwich taking the lead after five minutes through Lowrie. Tommy Lipsham then missed an open goal before Nantwich were awarded a penalty after Poutney charged down an approaching forward. Astles put the ball in the net for Nantwich but the penalty was ordered to be retaken and Coventry magnificently punched out the second attempt. In the second-half Chester had the bulk of the play with Jacky Lipsham, Matthews and Delaney all coming close, and Hall was a tower of strength in defence. With less than 10 minutes to go Chester won a corner and Delaney was able to score the equaliser.

Chester were unchanged for the replay at Crewe and a crowd of 5000 saw a fast, exciting game. A fairly even first-half remained goalless but Chester took control after the break and when Tommy Lipsham placed a corner into the goalmouth Barnes turned the ball into his own net. Nantwich responded well and Lowrie equalised after a beautiful pass from White. There were no further goals in normal time so an extra 30 minutes was played and as players tired the match became rough with several players getting injured. Amongst these was Nantwich goalkeeper Barnes, who got a nasty kick on the leg, and Delaney scored shortly afterwards when the keeper's injury prevented him from getting to the ball. News of the 2-1 victory reached Chester by telegram and a large crowd awaited the players when they returned to the General Station. As the train steamed into the station there were wild scenes of enthusiasm and Coventry was lifted shoulder high as a procession made its way to the Holborn restaurant to celebrate the victory.

The successful season resulted in a surplus of £40 which helped reduce the debt that had accumulated following improvements to the ground. Surprisingly Chester did not make any money out of the Cheshire Cup because they paid a guarantee to Witton in order to switch the game to Whipcord Lane. A small loss was also made on the Reserve team and the committee decided not to run a second team for the new season. Once again Chester were prevented from entering the FA Cup, but an arrangement had been in place for them to use the YMCA ground in Sealand Road if there was a home draw in the Welsh Cup.

For the 1904/05 season Chester welcomed forwards Case and White from Nantwich who had both played against them in the Cheshire Cup Final. Other new players were Jack Dawson who returned to the club from Shotton, Lewis from Winsford and Hughes, a full-back from Wrexham. Among the departures were captain David Hall and Bell, but there was good news when Coventry committed himself to Chester rather than Crewe who had tried to re-sign him. Tommy Delaney, who had been made captain, also elected to stay at Chester despite a bid of £50 from Doncaster Rovers.

Chester got off to a disastrous start with a 3-0 defeat at Tranmere but made amends in the next game thanks to an unexpectedly easy 6-0 victory over Welsh Cup winners Druids. Chester, by now playing in green and blue, were then defeated at home by Combination champions Birkenhead, who included ex-Chester players Bather and Hardacre in their team. The introduction of Hughes and Dawson against Chirk saw Chester win the next seven games as the forwards hit form and results paralleled those of the previous season. By the time Chester faced old protagonists Nantwich they were top of the table with a narrow lead over Wrexham, but there was a setback when Poutney suffered a twisted knee which put him out for the rest of the season.

There were disgraceful scenes when Chester went to Plas Power to play their next game at the mountainous ground of Broughton. Not only was the game played in thick snow, but after the game the Chester players were bombarded by snow, gravel and cinders as they made their way back to the dressing rooms which were located a mile away from the pitch.

A change had to be made in the side for the top of the table clash against Wrexham as White had been injured at Broughton. The lack of a reserve side meant that Secretary Fletcher had to look elsewhere to fill the gap in the team and the man chosen was Bob Evans, a tall winger from local junior side Saltney. Evans only appeared in one Combination and one Welsh Cup match for Chester (both against Wrexham) but went on to win 10 Welsh caps and four England caps. After finishing the season with Saltney he went on to join Wrexham, where he won his first Welsh cap, before entering the Football League, first with Aston Villa and then Sheffield United. It was in 1910, while Evans was at United, that the FA discovered that he had been born in Chester and not over the border in Wales as had initially been thought. As a result the English FA objected to his qualification and he went on to be selected for England on four occasions. After the war he returned to the area and played for Crichtons Athletic in the Cheshire County League.

By the middle of January, Wrexham had opened a five point lead over Chester at the top of the table but Chester closed the gap in the next four games with victories over Bangor, Port Sunlight, Middlewich and Nantwich. On April 1st Chester faced Wrexham in what was classed as the title decider. A packed Whipcord Lane saw a 1-1 draw, a fair reflection of the game, with Wrexham the better team in the first-half and Chester in the second. Two wins in the last four games were not enough and Chester again finished runners-up, trailing Wrexham by six points.

In cup competitions Chester were defeated at the first stage of the Welsh Cup by Wrexham but once again there was a good run in the Cheshire Cup. Victories over Sale Holmfield, Tranmere and Congleton put Chester in the Final and they defended their title against Altrincham at Northwich.

A crowd of 4000 saw Chester enter the game as favourites but they were beaten 2-1 with Jacky Lipsham scoring the Chester goal. Chester were unfortunate to lose Billy Matthews for the Final as he was selected to play for Wales against Ireland where he won his first cap.

Once again it had proved to be another satisfactory season for the club, although they had no cups to show for some fine performances. With some of the luck they had experienced the previous season it was felt they could have given Wrexham a closer run for the title. Although there was talk of Chester entering the Birmingham League they vowed to continue in the Combination until they had won the Championship.

Away from the League Chester played an interesting friendly against the 1st Battalion of the 22nd Cheshire Regiment who had built up a good reputation as a regimental team. The game attracted a large crowd with Chester winning 3-2, although the regiment was handicapped by the mud of Whipcord Lane which compared unfavourably with the parched fields of India to which they were more familiar. A friendly was also played in March against Chester Wednesday as a benefit match for Harry Astbury who had received an eye injury the previous season and was now in a poor state of health. Astbury, who had played his first game for the club in 1892 sadly died the following month at the early age of 30. Several material improvements, including a new exit gate, were made to the Whipcord Lane ground over the summer, but requests to Lord Crewe, the owner of the field, to enlarge the ground proved to be unsuccessful.

New arrivals for the 1905/06 season included Rainford (West Kirby), Galley (Crewe) and Marshall who returned to the club from Portsmouth. Meanwhile the impressive full-back Dawson had been transferred to Stoke and Billy Barker retired having played for the club since 1894. After a draw in the first game, Chester achieved the highest League victory in their history to that date, with a 9-0 win over Chirk. In a one sided game Chester could have easily reached double figures as both Marshall and Delaney hit hat-tricks. Delaney missed the next game at Crewe and his place at centre-forward was taken by Case who played so badly that his papers were handed to him straight after the game. The following week Case returned to Whipcord Lane as leader of the Nantwich attack but was on the losing side as Chester won 3-1.

A defeat at Tranmere led to more changes in the team as Chester sought some consistency, and for the game against Rhyl, Rainford and Marshall were dropped to be replaced by Cooper (Middlewich) and William Jackson (Flint). Jackson was a former Welsh International who had played in the Football League for Burnley and Newton Heath (later Manchester United).

He made an immediate impression in his first game, linking up well with Jacky Lipsham, as Chester put on their best display of the season to win 8-0. This victory sparked Chester into an eight match unbeaten run which placed them at the top of the table by the end of the year, two points clear of Whitchurch and Druids. Included in this run was another 8-0 win, this time over Middlewich, with Harry Jones from Chester Albion scoring four goals on his debut. Not only was the attack hitting form but the defence only conceded 10 goals up to the end of January.

Unfortunately, this form did not continue into 1906 and Chester had gone off the boil by the time they faced Whitchurch in the top of the table clash in March. Four hundred fans followed the club to Whitchurch and in a blinding snowstorm Chester played a miserable game and were beaten 2-0. Despite the defeat it was clear that Whitchurch were not an outstanding side and hopes of the Championship were raised again after victories over Oswestry and Port Sunlight closed the gap at the top. For the Port Sunlight game Chester had introduced Wallace Jones to the forward line, a reserve Welsh International from Druids, and he was an immediate success. Unfortunately this game also proved to be the last of the season for Matthews who had been suffering from a knee injury for some time.

On Good Friday Chester faced Whitchurch in a crucial top of the table clash and a large crowd of 4000 gathered to see Chester defend their 100% home record. At half-time it appeared as though the record would be maintained as they took a 2-0 lead thanks to goals from Jacky Lipsham and Harry Jones. However, in the second half, Chester struggled against the wind and Whitchurch, showing a vast improvement, snatched 2 goals, and in the end the home team was lucky to escape with a draw. Easter Monday saw Chester achieve a convincing 6-0 victory over Druids and they followed this up two days later with a narrow 1-0 win over Broughton. With only three games to go Chester were in the driving seat with a single point lead over Whitchurch, and although the remaining games were away from home they were all against teams in the bottom half of the table.

Unfortunately, a spectacular collapse saw Chester contrive to lose all these games and once again they had to settle for a runners-up spot as Whitchurch clinched the title by five points. A number of factors were put forward for the disappointing end to the season, including injuries to Matthews and Williams. However A lot of the blame fell on 'Snowy' Jones whose '*clever work and straightforward tactics*' at the start of the season had helped put Chester at the top of the table. Jones had failed to turn up for the game against Chirk, despite telling the committee that he would play, and Chester were subsequently beaten 3-1. It was later discovered that Jones had not appeared for Chester because he was playing in a Flintshire League Charity cup-tie for Hawarden Bridge. The committee reacted to this by stating that he would never play for the club again and Chester missed his trickery in the last few games.

As a postscript to the season a meeting of the Combination was held at which Chester refuted various allegations made against them by the Whitchurch secretary. It was claimed that Chester had come to a financial arrangement with Broughton to throw the match. In addition it was alleged that Chester had bribed Druids by paying for the transfer of a suspended player. At the meeting Mr Roberts, the Whitchurch secretary, admitted that he could not substantiate these claims and Chester let the matter drop.

Chester made a surprise return to the FA Cup when they were given permission to use the Whipcord Lane ground against Northern Nomads, a strong amateur side with a good reputation. In their new kit of green and white halves Chester won convincingly 2-0 but they were surprisingly defeated in the next round by Chirk only a month after beating them 9-0. There was also no extended run in the Cheshire Cup as Chester were defeated 3-2 by Crewe, having overcome Congleton after 3 games in the previous round.

There were a number of significant departures at the end of the season, most notably Jacky Lipsham, the speedy winger, who was transferred to Liverpool. Chester also lost Billy Matthews who returned to Rhyl and Billy Coventry who rejoined Crewe. Coventry had long been considered one of the best goalkeepers in the Combination, having joined Chester from Chester Lane Institute in 1894. He stayed at Chester until the end of 1897 when he joined Crewe but returned to the club in 1903. By 1906 he had played in seven Cheshire Cup Finals (four with Chester), winning on six occasions, and had also represented the county.

At the AGM chairman Edward Hallmark was able to announce a small profit thanks to an increase in attendances. More importantly he was able to reveal plans for a new ground in Sealand Road, a short walk from Whipcord Lane. Attempts the previous season to widen the ground and erect larger stands at Whipcord Lane had proved unsuccessful and so the club turned to Alfred Mond, local MP and supporter, for assistance in finding a new base. He had successfully negotiated with Lord Crewe for the lease of land on Sealand Road with the intention of letting it to the Football Club for a period of 10 years. Initial proposals had been for a ground accommodating 5000 comprising of a stand holding 2500 on the 4d side, a reserved stand for 1500 in the middle and two smaller stands at either end. In fact the plans went through a number of changes over the next few months but significantly it appeared as though Chester had found a spacious ground with opportunities for development.

Because of the scale of the new ground it was clear that a large sum would be required to pay for the development. Once again it was proposed that a Limited Company should be formed to raise the necessary funds. The new company sought to raise £1000 with shares priced at £1, a more reasonable price than the £10 suggested in 1897. When the share list closed on September 30th the number taken up was not as large as anticipated, however the 580 shares that were allotted went some way to paying for the ground as the club at last became a Limited Company.

*The team that started the 1906/07 season with seven wins*

Having finished runners-up for 3 successive seasons, and with an excellent new ground on the way, it was clear that the fortunes of the club were on an upward curve. Interest in the club had expanded considerably as the club had maintained a high standard of performance and Chester were now seen as the best supported team in the Combination. For the start of the 1906/07 season a number of new players were introduced as the committee strived to meet the expectations of their increasing support. In came Jack Jones (Rhyl), Freddy Grainger (Broughton), and Dick Jones (Ruabon) to strengthen the defence, along with Lees (Northwich), Walker (Hoole) and Schofield (Mouldsworth). The committee also had high hopes for Harry Williams, a neat and speedy winger, who was brought in to replace Billy Matthews.

The first game of the new season was played in a heatwave as Chester crushed Nantwich 7-1 with both teams losing players through sunstroke. For the next game Chester introduced two players from Birkenhead, goalkeeper Bill Keeley and Jimmy Russell a promising young full-back. The encouraging start was maintained with a 4-0 win at Tranmere. By the end of October Chester were clear at the top of the table with a 100% record having scored 30 goals and only conceded three in seven games. The perfect record was broken at Wigan Town where Bill Keeley was chaired off the field by Chester fans after his outstanding performance helped them to a 1-1 draw.

On November 10th, Chester beat Birkenhead 4-0 in what was to be the last game at Whipcord Lane. Arr-angements for the provision of the new ground had only been finalised a week before but it was hoped that the Sealand Road enclosure would be completed in time for the next home game. On December 15th 1906, a far from complete Sealand Road enclosure was opened by Mr C.J.Hughes, vice-chairman of the English Association, with Chester entertaining Bangor.

For the first game none of the proposed stands had been completed, although it was hoped they would be ready by the time Chester played Bangor in the Welsh Cup the following month. Although Chester won the inaugural game 4-0 they failed to reach their normal high standards as they struggled to adapt to the larger dimensions of the new pitch. The first goal at Sealand Road was scored by Jenkins who was making his debut having recently joined Chester from Northern Nomads.

For the next home game against Druids, on Christmas Day, 5,000 people saw another fine performance with Chester winning 7-0. The attendance was larger than any at Whipcord Lane where the 4,000 who saw the Good Friday top of the table clash against Whitchurch the previous season was believed to be the highest.

By the end of the year Chester had only dropped one point but incredibly they were only top on goal average from Whitchurch with the clubs having the following records:

| | | | | | | | |
|---|---|---|---|---|---|---|---|
| Chester | P13 | W12 | D1 | L0 | F49 | A5 | P25 |
| Whitchurch | P14 | W12 | D1 | L1 | F52 | A15 | P25 |

A draw at Bangor, with the Bangor equaliser coming in the last five minutes, was followed by a thrilling 3-2 victory over Tranmere. Early in the second-half Chester had found themselves 2-0 down but when Harry Williams pulled one back the crowd had livened up and with their enthusiasm infecting the players Tranmere were forced on the defensive.

As Chester mounted attack after attack, Walker forced an equaliser and Wallace Jones netted the winner in stoppage time. Two weeks later Chester finally lost their unbeaten record with a 4-1 defeat at Nantwich, the team Chester had beaten 7-1 on the opening day of the season. In the same month the ability within the Chester team was recognised by the Welsh selectors who called up Jack Jones, Wallace Jones and Harry Williams for a trial match in Wrexham. Although they all acquitted themselves well they were not selected.

On Good Friday Chester faced Whitchurch at Sealand Road in front of a record crowd of 6,670. Chester included Harry Hughes from Wolves in the team but despite constant pressure they only came away with a 1-1 draw thanks to a last minute equaliser. The result left the picture at the top no clearer and Chester completed the Easter programme with victories over Druids and Wigan. On April 13th the two title challengers met again at Whitchurch, with the Shropshire club holding a one point lead over Chester with a game in hand. Chester had hoped to include Billy Matthews in the team, having re-signed him from Rhyl, but the paperwork had not been completed in time and Chester entered the game knowing they needed to win. On the day the forwards had a poor game and Chester failed to hit the form of earlier in the season as they were comprehensively beaten 4-0. A week later, without Grainger, Jack Jones, Walker and Williams, all chances of the championship disappeared with a 5-1 defeat against Crewe Reserves. A third successive defeat against Wrexham Reserves finally handed the title to Whitchurch, and despite victories in the last two games Chester finished runners-up four points behind Whitchurch.

Overall it had been another successful season marred only by the defeats in mid-April, with Chester also reaching the Semi-Final of the Welsh Cup for the first time. In the end the championship was lost to a Whitchurch team who had an impressive record with only one defeat all season. For the second successive season Whitchurch had also become the only club to take a home point from Chester.

Before the start of the 1907/08 season there were two significant arrivals at Sealand Road, with the re-signing of Jacky Lipsham and Tommy Gordon. Lipsham returned after a season at Liverpool while Gordon had spent eight seasons at Wrexham where he had won 2 Welsh Cup winners medals. Other newcomers were Joe Freeman, also from Wrexham, and goalkeeper Robertson from Tranmere.

The new arrivals made an immediate impression by scoring four of Chester's five goals as they beat Wrexham Reserves in the first game of the season. Once again the goals were flowing freely with the early highlights being an 8-0 win against a declining Birkenhead side, and a 6-0 victory over Rhyl.

However, the goalkeeping position proved to be a problem with both Robertson and Dodd (Chester Kaleyards) proving unreliable. It was Robertson who was in goal when Chester suffered an early exit from the FA Cup with a 4-0 defeat at home to Tranmere. This was Chester's first ever defeat at Sealand Road, and 3 weeks later they suffered their first Combination defeat at home since September 1904, when they were beaten 3-2 by Oswestry.

Bert Goode, a skilful inside-right from Saltney, was brought into the side after defeat at Connah's Quay. He had originally played one match on trial from Hoole at the end of the 1905/06 season but had not been signed on. The re-appearance of Keeley in goal against Welshpool also helped inspire the team and the addition of these 2 players marked a significant change in fortune as Chester began to string together a sequence of excellent results.

On Boxing Day Chester faced leaders Tranmere Rovers at Sealand Road and, in a game worthy of the occasion, defeated them 2-0 with goals from Freeman and Goode. A defeat at Oswestry left Chester trailing Tranmere by four points but three consecutive victories closed the gap as they faced Rovers in the crucial return match at Prenton Park. Bert Goode opened the scoring for Chester after three minutes, only for Tranmere to hit back with a McGuigan equaliser. Rovers were then awarded a penalty after Matthews handled, but Keeley made a magnificent save. In stopping the penalty Keeley fell to the ground and was severely kicked on the arm by the Tranmere forwards trying to force the ball out of his grasp. For a short period of time he was replaced in goal by Gordon and this allowed Tranmere to take a half-time lead through Fishwick. Early in the second half Freeman grabbed an equaliser for Chester who held on for a 2-2 draw thanks to a splendid display from the injured Keeley.

Chester reached the Welsh Cup Final for the first time, where they faced local rivals Connah's Quay, and an appearance in the Cheshire Cup Final meant that they faced two Finals and two vital League games in a period of nine days. The first of these games was the Cheshire Cup encounter, against Altrincham at Crewe, where a crowd of 3500 saw Chester win the trophy for the fourth time. Freeman, Jones and Lees (2) scored the goals for Chester in a 4-2 victory with the following team appearing for Chester:-

Keeley, Wightman, Grundy, Matthews, Grainger,
Gordon, Williams, Lees, Freeman, Jones, Lipsham

On Good Friday Chester beat Whitchurch at Sealand Road for the first time, although they lost full-back Grundy with a serious leg injury which put him out for the remainder of the season.

**MATCH TO REMEMBER**
**CHESTER 3 CONNAH'S QUAY UNITED 1**
**WELSH CUP FINAL - APRIL 2OTH 1908**

*A crowd of 8,000 gathered at the Racecourse Ground, Wrexham, to see Chester's first appearance in the Welsh Cup Final. Former Chester player 'Bloomer' Jones won the toss for Connah's Quay and elected for them to play with the strong wind at their backs. The game got off to a sensational start with Chester taking the lead in the first minute. Harry Williams broke down the right and shot across to Bert Goode who volleyed in a hard drive past Lloyd. Chester continued to press and Freeman almost increased the lead but his shot was charged down by Hewitt. Quay, taking advantage of the strong wind, began to exert some pressure but Chester had the best opportunity when Lipsham hit the upright with a magnificent shot. Quay's best chance was a great shot from O'Neill which appeared to be going in until Keeley threw himself across the goal to save the ball on the line. Just as it looked as though Chester would hold out until half-time, Bloomer Jones lifted the ball to James Roberts who hooked the ball into the net from close range for the equaliser.*

*In the second-half Connah's Quay continued to attack as Chester appeared to suffer from the exertions of a heavy programme leading up to the Final. Gradually Chester came into the game as the half progressed and after a goalmouth scramble the ball came to Arthur 'Coffin' Lees who hit a hard low shot which easily beat Lloyd. The goal greatly encouraged Chester and the forwards began to show improved form. Harry Williams and Bert Goode both had great shots, and with a few minutes to go Lipsham passed to an unmarked Goode who scored Chester's 3rd goal with a terrific drive. A thrilling and memorable game ended with Chester deservedly winning 3-1, although it had not been until the last 20 minutes that they had played to the best of their abilities.*

*Chester - Keeley, Wightman, Russell, Matthews, Grainger, Gordon, Williams, Lees, Freeman, Goode, Lipsham.*
*Connah's Quay United - Lloyd, Penn, Hewitt, Griffiths, Evans, Lumberg, Bates, O'Neill, Jones, J. Roberts, H. Roberts.*

The following day Chester easily overcame Crewe Reserves 4-0, their 6th successive League victory, which left them 2nd behind Tranmere on goal average. On Easter Monday there were memorable scenes as thousands of Cestrians made the short journey to Wrexham for the Welsh Cup Final against Connah's Quay. More than 2,500 fans travelled on five special excursion trains from the General and Northgate stations with many others travelling on scheduled trains. There was also a constant stream of fans making their way along the Wrexham Road which swarmed with cyclists, motorists and pedestrians, all decked out in the club colours of light green and white.

IN LOVING MEMORY OF

CONNAHS QUAY.

O no. we never mention them,
Football must not be heard;
At the very name of goalposts
Their stomachs are bestired.

They are gone but not forgotten,
Never will their memory fade,
Football thoughts will ever linger
Around the spot where they were laid.

Ah ! if they only had not fancied
That football they could play,
We should never had a reason
For a funeral to-day.

Chester won the trophy at the first attempt by 3-1 and Tommy Gordon was presented with the cup by Mr Davies, President of the Welsh Association. There were enthusiastic scenes when Chester returned to the city on the last train with the crowds even greater than those of the previous week when they had won the Cheshire Cup. The team made their way to the city centre along City Road and Foregate Street with both trophies on display. The procession was led by the St Werburgh's band and the win was celebrated with dinner at the Holborn restaurant.

While Chester were winning the Welsh Cup Tranmere beat Bangor 2-0 to open a two point gap at the top of the Combination, and the following Saturday Chester beat Whitchurch as Tranmere completed their season with victory over Connah's Quay. Although Chester still had one game to go and could pull level on points Tranmere's goal average was far superior and a 2-1 victory over Birkenhead was not good enough. For the fifth season in succession Chester had finished runners-up and it was only the goals that had been conceded in the early part of the campaign that cost them the Championship. The defence improved considerably after the return of Keeley in December and Chester lost only one of their last 26 League and cup games, of which the final 12 were all victories.

The 1907/08 season had without doubt been the most successful in the clubs history and they were also now in a strong financial position. Income had reached £1,000 for the first time and the club were able to declare the maximum dividend of 5% on a profit of nearly £200. Money was also spent on ground improvements with the construction of more stand accommodation and improved changing facilities for the players.

On the playing front there had been excellent performances from Russell and Grundy, a pair of reliable and consistent full-backs, and the latter had been unlucky to miss the Welsh Cup Final through injury. Billy Matthews had moved to half-back early in the season and a subsequent improvement in form had resulted in his second Welsh cap against England.

In attack the outstanding performances had come from Bert Goode and Arthur Lees. Goode in particular had been a revelation and his skilful dribbling brought him to the attention of Liverpool who signed him at the end of the season. He found it hard to settle at Anfield and joined Wrexham in 1910 scoring a hat-trick in the 1911 Welsh Cup Final against Connah's Quay. After short spells with Aston Villa and Hull he returned to Wrexham in 1913 where he was a prolific goalscorer until his retirement in 1926.

During the close season Chester also lost Lees and Grundy to Haslingden and Appleton to Grimsby. They were replaced by Ben Roberts of Saltney, Tom Jones (Wrexham) and Harold Lappin (Rhyl). Chester began the 1908/09 season as they had ended the previous one with victory over Birkenhead and after eight games they were top of the Combination. Despite easy victories over Bangor and Rhyl there was a general feeling that the team had not performed to its full potential and a hard working Connah's Quay side almost beat a complacent Chester at Sealand Road. In the FA Cup Chester were beaten by Wrexham in the 3rd Qualifying Round after comfortable wins over Druids and Wellington.

The FA Cup defeat was the only blemish on the record as Chester proved themselves to be a class above the other teams in the Combination. Unlike previous seasons there were no other serious challengers for the title and Chester set a furious pace at the top of the table. At the start of December new signings Stockton (Ellesmere Port) and Bentley (Knutsford) were introduced into the side as Welshpool, one of the nearest challengers to the title, were beaten by 5 goals to 1. Chester ended the year with a draw against Tranmere in front of the largest crowd of the season.

This result meant that Chester had completed 1908 unbeaten in the League with only a defeat in the FA Cup to spoil their record. By mid-January they were seven points clear of Welshpool with a game in hand and it was becoming more a question of whether they would go through the whole season unbeaten as the Championship was already a virtual certainty.

At the start of February Chester faced Saltney for the first time in the League in what was a true local derby. The game was keenly anticipated as Saltney had risen to 2nd in the table and, with the stands full 30 minutes before kick off, a crowd of 6,000 gathered to see the game. Saltney gave Chester a fright and at one point in the game were leading by 3-1 but a penalty from Billy Matthews and a goal from ex-Saltney player Roberts saved Chester's unbeaten record. This proved to be only a temporary respite and Chester surprisingly lost their next game 3-2 at Bangor, a team who had previously given them few problems.

The game was not without controversy as Chester left the field towards the end of the game, having had what they believed to be a perfectly good goal disallowed. This came about due to the referee not turning up, and the selected referee was a nominee from Bangor. Chester appealed to the Combination on the grounds that the match was refereed by a Bangor official but the protest was upheld. This defeat was Chester's first in 31 games, a run that stretched back to December 28th 1907, and proved to be only a temporary setback on the march to the Championship.

Away from the Combination victories over Helsby, Crewe (after a replay) and Macclesfield had put Chester in the Cheshire Cup Final where they faced Northwich Victoria. There was also a second successive appearance in the Welsh Cup Final after easy wins over Nantwich and Aberystwyth and a Semi-Final victory over Wellington St.Georges, whose strong-arm tactics failed to unsettle Chester. Success in cup competitions left Chester with a heavy programme to finish the season and once again they faced the prospect of playing two finals in three days.

On Good Friday Chester beat Oswestry in a Combination fixture and journeyed to Crewe the following day for the Cheshire Cup Final. A crowd of 5,963 saw Chester and Northwich fight out a 1-1 draw, but unfortunately Chester suffered a number of injuries in this game and changes had to be made for the Welsh Cup Final, against Wrexham, on Easter Monday. Freeman, Bentley and Lipsham were all missing from the forward line and were replaced by Tom Jones, Roberts and Cotton from Middlewich who had agreed to help Chester out. In addition Tommy Gordon and Jimmy Russell were not in a fit state to play and with so many changes the odds were against Chester retaining the trophy.

In the first-half, with a strong gale behind them, Chester kept Wrexham pinned in their own half but a predictable lack of understanding amongst the forwards prevented them from taking advantage. In the second half all the pressure came from Wrexham and after 77 minutes Huffadine headed the winner. Although Chester had played well the necessary reshuffling of the side cost them dearly and with a full strength team the result could well have been different.

The following Wednesday Chester made the short journey to Saltney knowing that a victory would give them their first Championship. The ropes were thickly lined with people as Saltney took a half time lead with Hewitt scoring a penalty after Gordon had handled. A determined Chester came out for the second-half and within five minutes Tom Jones hit the equaliser. With time running out a shot by Ben Roberts was deflected into his own net by Hewitt and the full time whistle sounded shortly afterwards leaving Chester 2-1 winners. Chester ended the season with three more victories to finish a comfortable eight points ahead of Saltney.

On April 24th, 3 days after the Saltney game, Chester returned to Crewe to play the Cheshire Cup Final replay against Northwich. In front of a crowd of 4,500 the following team was played:-

Keeley, Russell, Davies, Matthews, Grainger, Gordon, Jones, Roberts, Freeman, Stockton, Lappin

A far superior Chester team outplayed Northwich and were comfortable 3-0 winners. After going three up they were content to show off their skills rather than go for more goals and the cup returned to Chester for the fifth time. The season ended with Chester playing the rest of the Combination in a traditional challenge match for the champions. Chester showed their superiority with a 4-1 victory and after the game they were presented with the Combination cup.

Once again it had been an excellent season for the club and they had shown that they were ready for a higher standard of football. For the second successive season an application to join the Birmingham League was turned down and Chester had to content themselves with another season in the Combination. Attendances had continued to be high with Chester the best supported team in the League, and the club were able to report another substantial profit and pay out another 5% dividend.

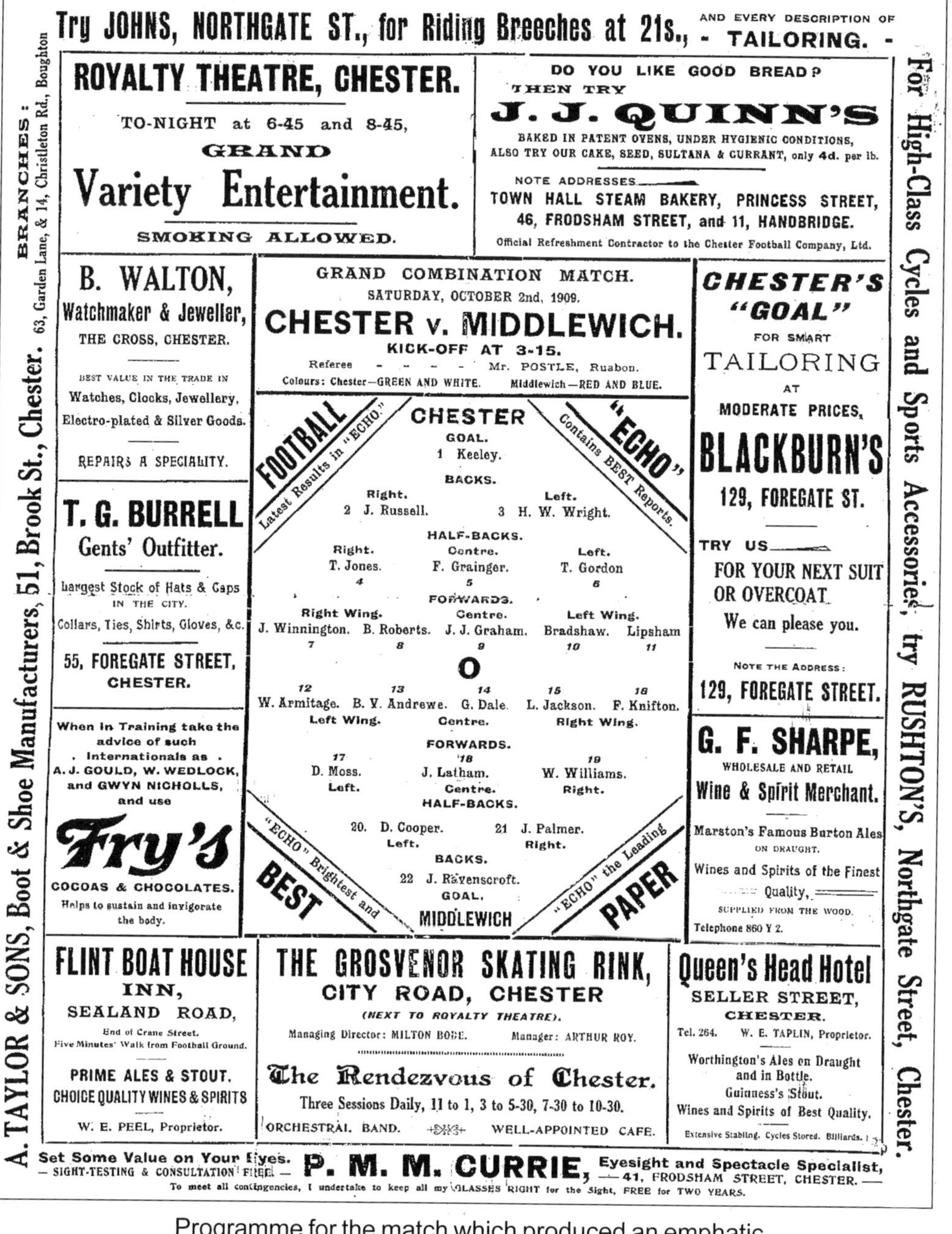

Try JOHNS, NORTHGATE ST., for Riding Breeches at 21s., AND EVERY DESCRIPTION OF TAILORING.

ROYALTY THEATRE, CHESTER.
TO-NIGHT at 6-45 and 8-45,
GRAND
Variety Entertainment.
SMOKING ALLOWED.

DO YOU LIKE GOOD BREAD? THEN TRY
J. J. QUINN'S
BAKED IN PATENT OVENS, UNDER HYGIENIC CONDITIONS,
ALSO TRY OUR CAKE, SEED, SULTANA & CURRANT, only 4d. per lb.
NOTE ADDRESSES
TOWN HALL STEAM BAKERY, PRINCESS STREET, 46, FRODSHAM STREET, and 11, HANDBRIDGE.
Official Refreshment Contractor to the Chester Football Company, Ltd.

B. WALTON,
Watchmaker & Jeweller,
THE CROSS, CHESTER.
BEST VALUE IN THE TRADE IN
Watches, Clocks, Jewellery, Electro-plated & Silver Goods.
REPAIRS A SPECIALITY.

T. G. BURRELL
Gents' Outfitter.
Largest Stock of Hats & Caps IN THE CITY.
Collars, Ties, Shirts, Gloves, &c.
55, FOREGATE STREET, CHESTER.

When in Training take the advice of such Internationals as A. J. GOULD, W. WEDLOCK, and GWYN NICHOLLS, and use
Fry's
COCOAS & CHOCOLATES.
Helps to sustain and invigorate the body.

GRAND COMBINATION MATCH.
SATURDAY, OCTOBER 2nd, 1909.
CHESTER v. MIDDLEWICH.
KICK-OFF AT 3-15.
Referee - - - - Mr. POSTLE, Ruabon.
Colours: Chester—GREEN AND WHITE. Middlewich—RED AND BLUE.

FOOTBALL Latest Results in "ECHO."
"ECHO" Contains BEST Reports.

CHESTER
GOAL.
1 Keeley.
BACKS.
Right. 2 J. Russell. Left. 3 H. W. Wright.
HALF-BACKS.
Right. T. Jones. 4 — Centre. F. Grainger. 5 — Left. T. Gordon. 6
FORWARDS.
Right Wing. J. Winnington. 7, B. Roberts. 8 — Centre. J. J. Graham. 9 — Left Wing. Bradshaw. 10, Lipsham 11

O

12 W. Armitage. 13 B. V. Andrewe. Left Wing. — 14 G. Dale. Centre. — 15 L. Jackson. 16 F. Knifton. Right Wing.
FORWARDS.
17 D. Moss. Left. — 18 J. Latham. Centre. — 19 W. Williams. Right.
HALF-BACKS.
20. D. Cooper. Left. — 21 J. Palmer. Right.
BACKS.
22 J. Ravenscroft.
GOAL.
MIDDLEWICH

"ECHO" Brightest and BEST
"ECHO" the Leading PAPER

CHESTER'S "GOAL"
FOR SMART TAILORING AT MODERATE PRICES,
BLACKBURN'S
129, FOREGATE ST.
TRY US FOR YOUR NEXT SUIT OR OVERCOAT
We can please you.
NOTE THE ADDRESS: 129, FOREGATE STREET.

G. F. SHARPE,
WHOLESALE AND RETAIL
Wine & Spirit Merchant.
Marston's Famous Burton Ales ON DRAUGHT.
Wines and Spirits of the Finest Quality,
SUPPLIED FROM THE WOOD.
Telephone 860 Y 2.

FLINT BOAT HOUSE INN,
SEALAND ROAD,
End of Crane Street. Five Minutes' Walk from Football Ground.
PRIME ALES & STOUT.
CHOICE QUALITY WINES & SPIRITS
W. E. PEEL, Proprietor.

THE GROSVENOR SKATING RINK,
CITY ROAD, CHESTER
(NEXT TO ROYALTY THEATRE).
Managing Director: MILTON BODE. Manager: ARTHUR ROY.
The Rendezvous of Chester.
Three Sessions Daily, 11 to 1, 3 to 5-30, 7-30 to 10-30.
ORCHESTRAL BAND. WELL-APPOINTED CAFE.

Queen's Head Hotel
SELLER STREET, CHESTER.
Tel. 264. W. E. TAPLIN, Proprietor.
Worthington's Ales on Draught and in Bottle.
Guinness's Stout.
Wines and Spirits of Best Quality.
Extensive Stabling. Cycles Stored. Billiards.

Set Some Value on Your Eyes. — SIGHT-TESTING & CONSULTATION FREE —
P. M. M. CURRIE, Eyesight and Spectacle Specialist, — 41, FRODSHAM STREET, CHESTER. —
To meet all contingencies, I undertake to keep all my GLASSES RIGHT for the Sight, FREE for TWO YEARS.

BRANCHES: 63, Garden Lane, & 14, Christleton Rd., Boughton
A. TAYLOR & SONS, Boot & Shoe Manufacturers, 51, Brook St., Chester.

For High-Class Cycles and Sports Accessories, try RUSHTON'S, Northgate Street, Chester.

Programme for the match which produced an emphatic 4-1 home victory in the 1909/10 season.

Before the start of the 1909/10 season Chester lost centre forward Joe Freeman to Scottish club Hamilton, but welcomed Graham, Winnington (Middlewich) and full-back Hubert Wright. There was a major surprise in the first game of the season with defeat at Oswestry.

As a result the committee dropped three players for the return game the following week replacing them with Winnington, Roberts and Tommy Jones, and Chester responded with an easy 3-0 win. Chester suffered a heavy defeat at Tranmere in the FA Cup but there followed five successive Combination victories which returned them to familiar ground at the top of the table.

Having found some consistency in the side Chester faced the reserves of Crewe in a top of the table clash but were beaten 3-1.

This reverse heralded an unprecedented run of four successive defeats including a 5-3 defeat at Bangor, a team they had hammered 7-3 a month earlier. This was the worst run that Chester had endured since the re-formation of the club in 1901 and was a painful experience for Chester fans used to success. Once again the committee rang the changes and the forward line was re-arranged with the appearance of Rainford (Southport), Jack Yuill (Northern Nomads), and Oswald Jones, an 18-year-old from Mold Town. The latter was an immediate success and he scored a gem of a goal on his debut in the derby game against Saltney.

At the start of December Chester secured a convincing 6-1 win over Birkenhead. This proved to be the last game for Birkenhead as they disbanded immediately afterwards and their fixtures were taken over by Brymbo Victoria. There was another heavy defeat at Tranmere at the end of the year, although Chester were handicapped by an injury to Keeley who was replaced in goal by Tommy Gordon. Chester gained their revenge over Tranmere with a 2-1 win in the Cheshire Cup and, more importantly, a 5-1 win in the Combination which came in the middle of a run of eight successive victories.

By the time Chester beat Denbigh they had a one point lead over Crewe at the top of the table, but had played four games more. Crewe took advantage of these extra games and by the end of the season were nine points ahead of Chester who finished 3rd (the lowest position for seven seasons) behind the 'Chain Boys' of Saltney.

Despite their relative failure in the Combination, Chester reached the Welsh Cup Final for the 3rd season in succession. In the early rounds they had secured easy victories over Rhyl and Druids and were drawn against Milford Haven United in the Semi-Final. Chester made the long journey to South Wales the day before the game but despite numerous chances they were unable to score and came away with a goalless draw. The FA of Wales instructed the replay to be played at Aberystwyth but Milford refused to accept the decision and Chester were awarded the tie.

The Final was played at Wrexham on Easter Monday in front of a crowd of 10,000, but the forwards had a poor day as Chester were defeated 2-1. Chester's goal came from Oswald Jones just before half-time equalising an Allman effort after 19 minutes.

In the second half Wrexham were on top but it was the 80th minute before Mason was able to hit the winner. Only a brilliant display by Bancroft prevented a heavier defeat and a promising future was predicted for the amateur goalkeeper who had been playing for Manchester University.

For the first time since the re-formation of the club the directors had to report a heavy financial loss, for attendances had fallen. Despite the poorer financial situation Chester were finally successful in joining a League that offered a better standard of football, as a late application to join the Second Division of the Lancashire Combination was accepted. The directors had been concerned that the calibre of the Combination had been showing no sign of improvement, but they now had an opportunity to show their skills in a League whose First Division contained the reserve sides of many Football League clubs.

A.J.Smith - soon to sign for Chester.

# NEW HORIZONS IN LANCASHIRE 1910 - 1915
# CHAPTER 5

With the prospect of starting in a new League all efforts were made by the Directors to acquire new players. It was evident that a larger squad would be required as a decision was made to continue with a reserve team, who were to replace the first eleven in the Combination. In order to support these requirements the prices in the stand were increased from 6d (2½p) to 9d (4p).

For the first game in the Lancashire Combination, played at Atherton, there were a number of new faces in the team. Dick Bancroft had now established himself in goal but Hubert Wright was joined at full-back by Frank Simpson from Saltney. At centre-half Chester signed Edwin Tremlett, also from Saltney, to support the experienced Tommy Gordon and Billy Matthews. There was also another ex-Saltney player, Blackburn, at centre-forward. On the right-wing Jack Yuill, an amateur who had made a few appearances the previous season, was joined by Wally Smith from Bradford City. Smith, a classy player and fine passer of the ball, elected to join Chester, despite competition from Huddersfield and Southend. On the left the consistent Jacky Lipsham was supported by Chetwood who cost Chester £25 from Everton.

Chester won their first match in the Lancashire Combination 3-0 but were defeated two days later at Hyde, one of the strongest teams in the League. Chester only lost two more games up to the turn of the year at which point they lay 2nd, four points behind Hyde but with two games in hand. The most impressive performances however were saved for the FA Cup where they had the best run since re-forming. In the Preliminary Round Chester beat Druids at Ruabon in a rough game and were drawn against Wrexham in the next round.

For a number of years Wrexham had been the stronger of the two teams, indeed Chester had been facing their reserves in the Combination while the Welsh club's first team played in the Birmingham League. When they had met in the Welsh Cup Final Wrexham had won on both occasions and they had also knocked Chester out of the FA Cup. On this occasion Chester proved themselves to be the superior side thanks to a single goal from Jacky Lipsham. This, despite playing two thirds of the game with only 10 men following an injury to Wright.

In the 2nd Qualifying Round the amateurs from New Brighton Tower were induced to switch the tie to Sealand Road, and Chester took full advantage by easily winning

The next opponents were Witton Albion, top of the Manchester League, and Chester produced their best football of the season to win 7-1. Three of the goals came from Arnold Dargie of Bangor who had agreed to help Chester out when the Welsh club were without a Combination match.

Chester finally met their match in the final qualifying round where they were defeated by Crewe in a thrilling game. Crewe took the lead after five minutes but Chester were level within four minutes thanks to a solo effort from Yuill. At half-time Chester were ahead 3-1 after goals from Dargie and Lipsham, but Bancroft was kept busy at the other end as Crewe forced a succession of corners. Crewe were dominant after the break and pulled a goal back early in the half with an equaliser coming soon after from a 30 yard free kick. Crewe hit the winner with 15 minutes to go and they could afford the luxury of a missed penalty near the end as they triumphed 4-3. It had been a spirited and determined performance by Chester but in the end they had been beaten by the superior stamina of Crewe.

Chester continued to raid Northern Nomads for players to support their Lancashire Combination team. Bancroft, Yuill and Dargie had all represented the Manchester club and they were joined by Tyson and more significantly centre-half A.J.Smith. The latter was an Irishman who served in the Army as a Staff Sergeant at Hulme Barracks in Manchester, and was reputedly *'as hard as nails'*. The high standard of amateurs playing for Chester was recognised with Dargie playing for the Welsh amateur team and Bancroft, who had been performing brilliantly, representing England against Belgium.

In the League Chester continued to perform well and high-scoring victories were achieved over Walkden (7-0) and Padiham (6-0). Despite a run of seven successive away games, which saw them without a League game at Sealand Road for two months, Chester were able to close the gap on Hyde to one point by the start of April. On April 5th Chester faced Hyde at Sealand Road in a crucial top of the table clash. With the score goalless at half-time, Chester came out kicking against a strong wind and scored four times to move to the top of the table. Three wins in the next four games put Chester on the verge of promotion to the First Division which was finally achieved when Hyde failed to win at Heywood.

With promotion now assured Chester required to win their last two games to secure the Championship. The first of these games, against Great Harwood, resulted in a 4-0 victory with George Jordan scoring all the goals. Chester played the last game at Bacup with a weakened team and went behind after half-an-hour play. Despite constant second half pressure Chester were unable to score and eventually had to settle for promotion in 3rd place as Haslingden snatched the Championship with a win at Darwen.

Once again Chester reached the Final of the Cheshire Cup where they faced Macclesfield after victories over Tranmere, Crewe and Altrincham. The game was played at Crewe in front of a crowd of 6000 with the following team representing Chester:-

Morgan, Jones, Rose, Matthews, Tremlett, Gordon, Yuill, Smith, Dargie, Chetwood, Lipsham.

Chester entered the Final as firm favourites but received a shock when Macclesfield scored in the first minute. Playing stylish football Chester were the better side but were unable to break down a dogged Macclesfield defence who held out to win 1-0. It was only a brilliant display by Allen, the Macclesfield goalkeeper, that prevented Chester scoring a hatful of goals and it was a mystery to many observers how Chester failed to score.

The first season in the Lancashire Combination had proved to be a great success, but financially Chester made a loss on the season, as the Reserve team failed to pay its way in the Combination. Although Chester had gained promotion there was a major disappointment with the League going through a major restructuring. Chester had joined the Lancashire Combination because of the attraction of playing the Reserve sides of teams like Manchester United and Liverpool.

Lol Cook

Unfortunately, as Chester reached the First Division, the Reserve teams promptly left to join the Central League and the competition lost a lot of its glamour. As a result 11 teams were promoted to the First Division which started the 1911/12 season with 17 clubs.

The most significant signing for the new season was forward Lol Cook who joined Chester from Bacup. Cook, an all-round sportsman, was also a well known bowler with Lancashire C.C., and he soon proved himself to be an outstanding centre-forward. Also new to the team was Mold Town captain Tommy Matthias who had set a remarkable record by scoring 51 penalties in three seasons. He only spent one season with Chester before joining Wrexham where he won four Welsh Cup winners medals and 12 Welsh caps in 16 seasons.

The season started on a very hot day at Colne with Chester losing 3-2 after being 3-0 down at one stage. A win over Eccles was followed by three indifferent results, but Chester recovered with five successive wins. The first two months of the season were notable for an impressive display of goalscoring by Lol Cook. For many seasons Chester had been fortunate to have some exceptional forwards without finding a consistent goalscorer. Cook changed all this and in his first 14 matches he was on the mark in every game scoring 22 goals in the process. A clever, bustling striker he had a deadly shot and his goals soon brought him to the attention of several League clubs although no move materialised. Also playing well at the start of the season was Billy Matthews who had regained his best form but was unfortunate to suffer a serious knee injury against Northern Nomads which put him out of contention for several months.

Chester had another good run in the FA Cup where they once again reached the 4th Qualifying Round. In the First Qualifying Round they had given Shrewsbury Town of the Birmingham League a 6-1 drubbing with Cook hitting a hat trick. Victories over Birmingham League opposition had always gone down well after the League had rejected Chester's application a few years earlier. There followed a 4-1 victory over Northern Nomads which gave Chester an away tie at Wrexham in the next round. Cook's reputation had gone before him and both he and Wally Smith were closely watched by the Wrexham defenders. This left more space for Jack Yuill who had an outstanding game and scored twice as 'the boys in green' deservedly won 4-1. Chester were finally eliminated 4-1 by Second Division Stockport County in a game in which only Simpson, Matthias and Lipsham did themselves justice.

In December a number of 1st Division scouts were present to watch Wally Smith play in Chester's game against Hyde. Smith, a wizard with the ball, had been one of the club's best captures and two brilliant goals that day prompted Bury to sign him shortly afterwards. A good win against Rochdale in which Cook scored another hat-trick left Chester in 5th place at the end of the year, five points behind leaders Hyde but with three games in hand.

Cook's run of goalscoring continued into 1912 and in February he scored seven goals in two games, including four against his old club Bacup. There were two disappointing draws against Barrow and Accrington over Easter, and after victory over Chorley on Easter Monday full-back Williams was transferred to Aston Villa for £120. The following week Chester clearly missed Williams as they suffered their heaviest defeat of the season, 5-1 at Rossendale. In a disappointing end to the season Chester finished in 6th position as they failed to win any of their last five games.

Chester continued their good form in the Welsh Cup by reaching the Semi-Final where they were drawn against Cardiff City. With Cardiff having the choice of ground Chester made the long journey to South Wales where an evenly contested game resulted in a 1-1 draw. Much to the indignation of Chester the Welsh FA Council proclaimed that the replay should be held at neutral Wrexham rather than Sealand Road and the club rightly objected to this decision. The directors sent a strong letter to the Welsh FA protesting about their decision, claiming it was a gross injustice, but it was all to no avail.

When the game took place Chester took a first-half lead through a Tommy Matthias penalty and despite Cardiff pressure it was seven minutes from the end before Tracey netted their equaliser. An extra 30 minutes was played during which time Burton scored a deserved winner for Cardiff. The match was played in front of an estimated crowd of 5000 although it was swollen by hundreds of striking miners who broke into the ground on the cheap side.

The financial accounts showed a profit of £146-18s-10d, compared with losses on the two previous seasons, and the directors elected to pay a 5% dividend. The profit was largely due to transfer fees received which amounted to £352-10s, while attendances had fallen off considerably despite a fairly good performance from the team.

In the close season Chester lost several key players with Yuill, Bancroft and A.J.Smith all returning to Northern Nomads, leading scorer Lol Cook joining Stockport and Matthias going to Wrexham. Perhaps the most significant departure however was that of Edward Hallmark who resigned as Chairman due to ill health and pressure of business. Hallmark had been with Chester since the days at Hoole and as Chairman had been instrumental in finding the Whipcord Lane ground.
He had also guided Chester through their formation as a Limited Company and devoted a lot of his time and money to the club. His replacement as Chairman was George Hull, who resigned himself after only a few weeks allowing Will Fletcher, another long-standing committee member, to take his place.

The question of which League to compete in was still causing a major problem for the directors and an unsuccessful application was made to join the Central League. The Lancashire Combination had failed to provide the attractive opposition that had initially been hoped for and an unofficial ballot was held amongst the supporters requesting their opinion. A coupon was included in the programmes over Easter asking the spectators if they would prefer Chester to compete in the Lancashire Combination or Birmingham League. Only a quarter of spectators bothered to vote but it showed a 6 to 1 majority in favour of the Birmingham League. Despite the result of the poll the Directors elected to continue in the Lancashire Combination because that League required a definite decision before the Birmingham League met. Understandably there was a reluctance to resign from one League with no guarantee of a place in another.

Amongst the new signings for Chester's 3rd season in the Lancashire Combination were goalkeeper Fletcher (Hyde), Ralphs (Aston Villa), Wynne (Stirling FC, Liverpool) and Andrew Sheargold, a cool, clever centre-half from Wolves who took over as captain from Smith. The first game of the season produced a 3-1 win at Chorley achieved under remarkable circumstances. The basket containing Chester's kit went astray at Warrington railway station and as a result they had to play the game in ordinary boots and an assortment of jerseys and trousers. A few days later Chester secured a convincing 8-1 win over St Helens Town, no doubt buoyed by the incentive offered by a local men's outfitters, of an overcoat for any player who scored tw goals in a match. Ralphs and Wynne both benefitted from this incentive, which was frowned on by the Chester directors, although similar offers were repeated through the season until the practice was eventually wiped out.

For the game against Barrow, Chester included 35 year-old full-back Walter Balmer from Everton. Balmer was an ex-England international who had played in two Cup Finals, but the trial was not a success as he was deemed too slow and past his best.

After beating Eccles, Chester went to the top of the table, but a series of indifferent results followed and the club responded by signing Gordon Best from Hyde. Best arrived with a good reputation having already scored 15 goals that season and there was an all round improvement in the team, with the newcomer scoring a hat-trick in his second game. He was also on target four times in a 9-2 hammering of Nelson on Boxing Day, although Nelson were unfortunate to lose a pair of players early on when the score was only 1-0. For the same game Chester had to re-arrange their team as both full-backs, Gordon Jones and Tommy Hughes, failed to appear and were subsequently suspended by the club. Hughes, a Welsh amateur international had been building a good reputation for himself and like his colleague worked as a collier near Wrexham.

With both regular full-backs out of the team results slumped and by February Chester were mid-table. For the return game against Nelson, secretary Jack Jones - who had last played for the club five years previously - was forced to include himself in the team after a late injury to Jordan. At the beginning of March the League fixture against Hyde was played as a benefit for Jacky Lipsham and Billy Matthews with £82-10s being handed over to the two long-serving players. There were some improved performances at the end of the season including victories over Walkden (7-0) and Denton (8-1), but the final position of 7th was a disappointment.

Performances in cup competitions did not meet the standards of previous seasons and Chester were eliminated at the first stage of the FA Cup and Cheshire Cup by Wrexham and Crewe respectively. They did better in the Welsh Cup however, reaching the Semi-Final, thanks to a last minute goal in the 4th Round against village side Troedyrhiw. The Semi-Final was played at Cardiff where Chester failed to take advantage of a number of good opportunities and were beaten 3-0 by an experienced Pontypridd side. Chester made a protest after the game claiming that one of the Pontypridd players had already played in the competition for Llandudno but the appeal was quickly dismissed and the South Wales team progressed to the Final.

With fewer cup games, and no major outgoing transfers, the club reported a loss on the season of £180, and the decision to declare a dividend the previous year appeared unwise. As attendances continued to fall the annual dilemma of which league to enter came to the fore. Another application to join the Central League was withdrawn at the last minute as the timing of the meetings meant Chester again ran the risk of being left high and dry.

There was a surprise departure in the close season as long-serving Jacky Lipsham joined Wrexham. The move did not please the directors who had put a fee on Lipsham after he had refused to re-sign and they felt let down after staging a benefit for him only two months earlier. He was replaced in the team by young Ernie Lloyd who was promoted from the Reserves. Other departures included Sheargold to Connah's Quay, Jordan to Eccles, Ritchie to Norwich, and Best to Heywood.

To replace them Chester introduced Llewellyn Morris (Gwersyllt), Thomas Flannery (Brighton) and Pat McCarthy (Tranmere), the latter having played for Chester as an amateur four years previously. Also returning was Lol Cook, whose appearances at Stockport had been limited by a severe illness. Perhaps the most impressive capture was Sam Wolstenholme a good tackler who had been captain of Norwich City. Wolstenholme had made his Football League debut with Everton in 1897 and went on to make 160 appearances for the club, winning an England cap in 1904. After transferring to Blackburn he won two further caps against Ireland and Wales before joining Croydon Common and then Norwich. His stay at Chester lasted one season during which time he proved himself to be a great leader and '*responsible for a great part of the brains of the team*'. After leaving Chester he became a coach in Germany and was interred in that country when war was declared.

Although Chester started the season reasonably well with two convincing home wins against St.Helens Town and Accrington, attendances were continuing to show a downward trend. By December Chester were in the bottom half of the table, and when they played struggling Heywood United receipts were down to £15. On the playing front all efforts were being made to improve the side with the notable arrival of Herbert Hughes from Connah's Quay and J.C.Bardsley, an amateur player of distinction from Everton, who was also a dentist in Warrington. Hughes was rated as one of the fastest wingers in the League and his stay proved to be brief but profitable as Chester transferred him to Sheffield Wednesday in April for £150. Results showed no improvement in the second-half of the season and there were only three victories for Chester in the new year. A 6-0 victory over Walkden secured Chester safe from relegation, and for the next game against Hurst a very small attendance saw an apathetic display from the players as the season petered out.

There was some interest in the FA Cup with Chester having three home ties. In the Preliminary Qualifying Round Chester paid a guarantee to Nantwich for them to switch the game to Sealand Road. The decision was vindicated with a victory and a profit of £13. The game itself provided plenty of excitement for the spectators with Flannery opening the score for Chester after 10 minutes. At that point Chester were well on top but the game was turned on its head with three goals in six minutes from Nantwich. Not to be outdone Chester replied with goals from Pat McCarthy and an equaliser from Flannery, leaving the score 3-3 at half-time. Nantwich opened the second-half full of enthusiasm, but it was Cook who put Chester ahead from a well-judged pass by Hornby. With 10 minutes to go Flannery completed his hat-trick as Chester won 5-3. In the next round Chester were the better side in beating Tranmere but they left it late with Cook scoring from the rebound after his penalty was saved by Ashcroft. Chester met their match against Port Vale where they were convincingly beaten 5-2 with three of Vale's goals coming from Billings who was to join Chester at the end of the season.

There was an early exit from the Cheshire Cup at Stalybridge and in the Welsh Cup, Chester lost to holders Swansea Town although they were unlucky not to come away with at least a draw.

All in all the 1913/14 season proved to be a great disappointment and only Matthews and Ankers were left on the retained list. Because of the expense of running two teams the committee decided to concentrate entirely on the Lancashire Combination side for the forthcoming season. Therefore, instead of running a Reserve side, they took on Sealand United as a junior team.

Sealand were allowed to use the ground when Chester were away and all their players signed Lancashire Combination forms so that Chester had players to fall back on. At the AGM held at the Holborn Restaurant in July the club announced a profit of £55-7s-4d, although this was largely due to transfer fees received rather than gate receipts.

Having released virtually the whole team, the committee, led by secretary Jack Jones, put a great deal of effort into re-constructing the side for the 1914/15 season. In came the right-wing pairing of Sidney Billings and Jack Smith from Port Vale that had done so much damage to Chester in the FA Cup. From Merseyside came Peter Malone, a regular goalkeeper with Liverpool Reserves, and Fred Kirby a half-back with Everton Reserves. At full-back Chester welcomed James Rothwell who had played for four seasons with West Ham in the Southern League. The forwards were complemented by Hughes of Llandudno and Horace Brindley of Lincoln City. The re-assembling of the team paid dividends with Chester winning their first seven games, playing high-class football that was good to watch.

The outbreak of war brought into question the whole future of the club and although attendances had initially risen they soon began to fall dramatically as so many men in the area contributed to the war effort.

Unlike many clubs Chester continued to pay the same wages as had been paid prior to war breaking out, and they soon found themselves with severe financial problems. Chester were still top of the table when they played Hurst in December, but gate receipts only amounted to £15 and the directors approached the players to see if they would accept a reduction in wages which they were reluctant to do.

On January 7th a meeting was held at the Holborn Restaurant to discuss the club's future. Receipts over Christmas had been minimal with the club now facing an overall debt of £349, and with the prospect of it continuing to grow. The players were approached again and were more amenable to a wage reduction, but the club were aware that they would have to pay them until the end of the season regardless of whether the club continued or not. Chester were also in a dilemma with regard to the Lancashire Combination, because if they withdrew their membership they would still have to pay guarantees to all the other clubs for unplayed matches. It was finally agreed at the meeting that the club would continue for the time being but would vote for disbandment of the Lancashire Combination at its next meeting.

At the end of January the member clubs of the Lancashire Combination voted almost unanimously to continue; Chester were one of only two clubs to vote for disbanding. As a result Chester declared their intentions to continue on a purely amateur basis, and for the next game against Llandudno, in the Welsh Cup, the professionals were told that they would only be paid a small amount above expenses. This created a great deal of dissatisfaction and after the game five players were put up for transfer, leaving only Matthews, Griffiths, and Ankers as professionals with the club. Applications were received from 66 amateurs as Chester struggled to continue, but the club lost heavily at Tranmere as they had difficulty in putting together a team of adequate standard.

On March 7th Chester lost 6-0 against Eccles with a team made up almost entirely of local amateurs and the gate receipts amounted to a paltry £4. A week later the decision was finally made to discontinue the club and they withdrew their membership of the Lancashire Combination lying in mid-table. With no senior football club in the city the people of Chester were left to contemplate more important matters.

# 'ARSENAL OF THE NORTH' 1919-1931
# CHAPTER 6

At the end of the war the directors were faced with the prospect of building the club from scratch as Chester were left with no ground, no players and virtually no money. They were able to secure the old ground at Sealand Road on a yearly tenancy, with a three year option, and the £300 that the club had in the bank was put towards its refurbishment. Preparation of the ground eventually cost £654 and the club also had to find £65 to pay a fine levied by the Lancashire Combination for their previous withdrawal.

The Lancashire Combination had resumed in 1918/19 with an eight team Manchester Section, and it was these clubs that were behind the formation of the Cheshire County League in 1919/20. Chester were invited to join along with 12 other clubs (although Tranmere resigned early in the season), and all efforts were made to prepare the club for this new venture.

A practice game was held at Sealand Road on August 16th as the committee tried to build a new team without the help of Jack Jones, club secretary before the war, who was killed in the hostilities. The team that started the first Cheshire County League game, against Altrincham, contained a mixture of both new players and those who had represented the club before the war. In goal was Farrell from Queensferry with Hubert Wright and Jimmy Settle, both ex-Chester players, starting at full-back. The half-backs included Evans from Buckley and Lockett, a pre-war regular in the Reserves. At centre-half and captain was the popular figure of Edwin Tremlett, a well known figure in local football, who had previously represented both Chester and Saltney. The forwards included Winnington (Northwich), Petrie (Connah's Quay), Gordon Jones (Gresford) and the welcome return of veteran Jacky Lipsham at outside-left.

The first game resulted in a 4-2 defeat against an Altrincham team that had played throughout the war. Their better football won out and although Chester showed a great deal of enthusiasm they predictably lacked understanding. The following week Chester, playing in colours of dark green, travelled to Witton and were narrowly beaten 4-3, but victory was achieved in the third match against Mossley. The new colours prompted Chester to be nicknamed the 'Ivies' by their supporters although they were also popularly known as the 'Linnets'.

In the FA Cup Chester were easily beaten 5-0 by Nantwich but gained their revenge the following week by beating the same team in the League.

This lack of consistency proved to be the main feature of the season as Chester struggled to find a settled side. Few players made more than 10 appearances and only Lipsham and Settle were guaranteed a regular place, although the arrival of Joe Jenkins and Lewis gave more shape to the forward line. Jimmy Settle was a mainstay in the defence and later in the season he was ably supported by Alf Jones, a half-back who Chester believed had a promising future. The real star of the season was Jacky Lipsham, appearing almost 20 years after he had first played for the club. Although he had lost much of his pace his boundless enthusiasm set a fine example to his colleagues.

The composition of the Cheshire County League meant that Chester now had more local games and they were given a true derby by the presence of Crichton's Athletic who played at Mount Pleasant in Saltney. The club, formed in 1918, were based around Crichton's Shipyard and included in their ranks ex-Chester player and dual international Bob Evans. The first League game between the two sides was played in front of an impressive crowd of 3000 and resulted in a 1-1 draw. The return game, which took place over Christmas, saw the 'Shipbuilders' beaten 3-1 thanks to a hat-trick from Lewis. It was Crichton's who eliminated Chester from the Cheshire Senior Cup at the Semi-Final stage with a goal five minutes from the end in a 3-2 victory. Crichton's went on to win the cup beating Crewe 1-0 in the Final.

Chester continued to gain good results at home, but it was January before they obtained their first away victory, at Northwich. Wins in the next two games took Chester to 4th but failure to win the last four games meant that Chester had to settle for a respectable mid-table position. The second-half of the season was confused by the presence of a subsidiary competition in which two groups of six teams played in a mini-league. Chester tended to use this League for experimentation and they finished equal bottom of their group with Nantwich.

The penultimate game of the season, against champions elect Runcorn, produced disgraceful scenes as Chester slumped to a 4-2 defeat. The ground was in a bad state and good football was impossible, but Runcorn's questionable tactics upset the crowd who reacted in a very unsportsmanlike manner. At the end of the game the officials struggled to reach the dressing room as a few hundred hooligans attempted to blockade it.

When the players left the ground they were bombarded with missiles and their taxis covered in mud. As a result Chester were fined £10 and the ground was closed for the first two Saturdays of the 1920/21 season. These unfortunate incidents took some of the gloss off a season that had otherwise proved satisfactory.

During the close season a number of measures were taken in an attempt to raise money for ground improvements. Finances had been stretched to the limits by the costs involved in starting the club again and the directors sought an extra injection of cash. More shares were made available by the club and an independent supporters committee was formed with the intention of raising £1,000. A sportsday was held at the ground, an event that had proved successful when the club played at Faulkner Street, and although the crowds were not as large as they had been in the 1890s, £62 was raised from spectators who enjoyed a cycle race among other activities. The 1920/21 season also saw the re-introduction of a matchday programme for which the club charged 2d (Chester programmes had first been produced in the 1907/08 season).

There was a major expansion of the Cheshire County League from 12 to 18 clubs for the start of the 1920/21 season. Included in the League were near neighbours Connah's Quay and the reserve teams of Crewe, Tranmere and Stalybridge.

The inconsistencies of the previous year meant that few players were retained for the 1920/21 season with only Settle, Jenkins, Lipsham, Lloyd and Alf Jones remaining. Among the arrivals were defenders Emery and Dawson from Crewe and an excellent goalkeeper, Casey from Birmingham, whose displays earned him the captaincy later in the season. For the first game of the season, however, Chester were without a recognised keeper as reserve Butterworth failed to turn up at Mossley. Popular forward 'Our Joe' Jenkins took over in goal and despite a good performance could not prevent a 4-2 defeat. This proved to be one of only two defeats in the first seven games as Chester benefitted from playing a more settled side. There was an outstanding goalscoring performance when Jimmy Settle scored five penalties in two successive games against Mossley and Tranmere Reserves.

Chester supporters were treated to a new kit during the season having seen their favourites appear in various combinations of green and white since 1901. The new black and white stripes earned them a new nickname of the 'Magpies'. Fans were also given the opportunity of regular organised transport as the club started to run charabancs to away games for the first time.

The early run, which took Chester to a challenging position near the top of the table, was not maintained and a series of ups and downs continued well into 1921. There were numerous alterations in the team with the centre-forward position proving particularly problematical as 16 different players were tried.

The local derbies against Connah's Quay and Crichton's attracted a considerable amount of interest and Crichton's agreed to switch the game from Mount Pleasant in exchange for a larger share of the gate. However the highest attendance of the season gathered for a friendly match in aid of the Local Soldiers and Sailors Association, a game in which Chester did not play. Seven thousand spectators turned up for a match between the famous Dick Kerr International Ladies AFC from Preston and St.Helens Ladies AFC.

In March, Chester suffered a humiliating defeat at the hands of Nantwich in what was described as *'one of the greatest debacles the club had suffered'*. Chester lost the game 9-1 with most of the damage being done by outside-left Mellor who was transferred to Bolton shortly afterwards. This was the worst defeat the club had suffered since 1903 when, in a remarkable coincidence, they were beaten 9-1 by the same team. The defeat prompted a change of fortune as Chester finished the season with six wins out of eight, including a 6-2 revenge victory over Nantwich, which left them in 10th place.

There was disappointment in the Welsh Cup with defeat at the first stage by Chirk, after a prolonged encounter, and an early exit in the Cheshire Senior Cup at Congleton. The first team also played in the Cheshire League Knock-Out Cup, where they were beaten at home by Crichton's in front of 6500, and the Flintshire Charity Cup where they were beaten by Buckley.

Once again there was a big clear out of players at the end of the season with the most notable departure being the retirement of Jacky Lipsham. Chester started the 1921/22 season with an entirely new team, the most exciting signing being that of Joe Donnachie an ex-Scottish International with three caps from Blackpool. In his heyday, at Everton and Oldham, he had been recognised as one of the finest crossers of the ball in the English game and at Sealand Road his mazy dribbling made him in instant crowd favourite, prompting frequent shouts of 'give it to Joe'. Donnachie was immediately made captain and effectively took the role of player-manager as he used his influence to bring new players to the club. Into the club came Sam Ashcroft a goalkeeper from New Brighton and Trevor Jones a full-back and penalty expert from Wrexham. A solid half-back line was built with Robinson and Charlie Jones from Everton alongside Jimmy Pryde, a centre-half who had always been a thorn in Chester's side when playing for Crichton's. In the forward line Donnachie was joined by Frank Timmis (Congleton) and Tommy Cooper (Ellesmere Port Cement).

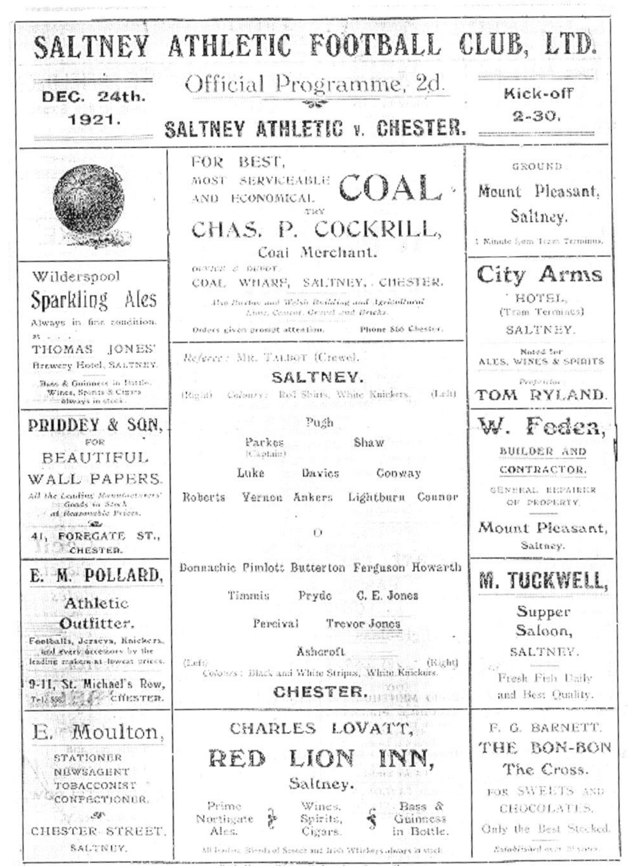

SALTNEY ATHLETIC FOOTBALL CLUB, LTD.

DEC. 24th. 1921.

Official Programme, 2d.

SALTNEY ATHLETIC v. CHESTER.

Kick-off 2-30.

FOR BEST, MOST SERVICEABLE AND ECONOMICAL COAL TRY CHAS. P. COCKRILL, Coal Merchant. OFFICE & DEPOT: COAL WHARF, SALTNEY, CHESTER. Also Buckley and Welsh Building and Agricultural Lime, Cement, Gravel and Bricks. Orders given prompt attention. Phone 556 Chester.

GROUND Mount Pleasant, Saltney. 1 Minute from Tram Terminus.

Wilderspool Sparkling Ales Always in fine condition. at THOMAS JONES' Brewery Hotel, SALTNEY. Bass & Guinness in Bottle. Wines, Spirits & Cigars always in stock.

City Arms HOTEL, (Tram Terminus) SALTNEY. Noted for ALES, WINES & SPIRITS. Proprietor TOM RYLAND.

Referee: MR. TALBOT (Crewe).

SALTNEY.

(Right) Colours: Red Shirts, White Knickers. (Left)

Pugh

Parkes (Captain) Shaw

Luke Davies Conway

Roberts Vernon Ankers Lightburn Connor

O

Donnachie Pimlott Butterton Ferguson Howarth

Timmis Pryde C. E. Jones

Percival Trevor Jones

Ashcroft

(Left) (Right)

Colours: Black and White Stripes, White Knickers.

CHESTER.

PRIDDEY & SON, FOR BEAUTIFUL WALL PAPERS. All the Leading Manufacturers' Goods in Stock at Reasonable Prices. 41, FOREGATE ST., CHESTER.

W. Foden, BUILDER AND CONTRACTOR. GENERAL REPAIRER OF PROPERTY. Mount Pleasant, Saltney.

E. M. POLLARD, Athletic Outfitter. Footballs, Jerseys, Knickers, and every accessory by the leading makers at lowest prices. 9-11, St. Michael's Row, CHESTER.

M. TUCKWELL, Supper Saloon, SALTNEY. Fresh Fish Daily and Best Quality.

E. Moulton, STATIONER NEWSAGENT TOBACCONIST CONFECTIONER. CHESTER STREET, SALTNEY.

CHARLES LOVATT, RED LION INN, Saltney. Prime Northgate Ales. Wines, Spirits, Cigars. Bass & Guinness in Bottle. All leading Blends of Scotch and Irish Whiskeys always in stock.

F. G. BARNETT. THE BON-BON The Cross. FOR SWEETS AND CHOCOLATES. Only the Best Stocked.

*Four goals were shared in this 1921 local derby.*

The season started with a 1-1 draw against Saltney Athletic (the renamed Crichton's), but Chester went on to win the next 10 games outright as they progressed in both the FA Cup and Cheshire Challenge Cup. The FA Cup provided Chester with a record number of games as they played eight ties in reaching the 4th Qualifying Round. After beating Machynlleth of the Welsh National League 7-0 with three goals in the first six minutes, they easily overcame Ellesmere Port, Lostock Gralam and Harrowby. Against Northwich they recovered from 3-1 down with 10 minutes remaining to snatch a draw and won the replay thanks to a penalty from Trevor Jones. Chester eventually met their match in Crewe, of the 3rd Division North, although it took a goal in extra time of the replay to put them out. Chester did not deserve to be beaten and they put in an unsuccessful protest after the game, claiming that the referee had curtailed the first-half of extra time when Chester were pressurising the Crewe goal.

The exertions of the cup game cost Chester dearly when they lost their next home game against Stalybridge and there were more problems the week after when leading scorer Tommy Cooper broke his ankle against Runcorn. Cooper was replaced by Thomas Pimlott, a forward with a powerful shot, from Stalybridge, and Chester went on to complete December unbeaten. At the end of the year Chester were lying 6th, 10 points behind leaders Congleton, but the extended cup run meant that they had seven games in hand.

At the start of February Chester beat Congleton in a top of the table clash played in heavy snow. After the game they were brought before a commission because a complaint was made by Congleton that their linesman had been snowballed by small boys. As a result Chester had to pay the expenses of three witnesses. Defeat in the next two games at Northwich and Sandbach left Chester in 7th place, but the dual signing of Albert Virr on loan from Everton and Robert Taylor, Goole's leading scorer, considerably strengthened the forward line. Virr, an up and coming amateur who went on to become a vital member of Everton's Championship winning side of 1928, made an impressive debut with two goals against Winsford.

A week later he surpassed that with four brilliant strikes against Ashton National, all the goals being scored with first time shots.

Despite the new arrivals Chester lost four of the next five games, including a 4-0 defeat at Congleton, which left the gap at nine points with only four games in hand. In a nail-biting finale to the season Chester hit form and won the next seven games to close the gap to one point. By this time Congleton had completed their fixtures and Chester knew that they only required one win from their last two home games to overhaul them.

In the first of these games, against Cheshire Cup winners Witton Albion, there was an early shock for Chester when Charlie Jones scored an own goal. Chester were quick to reply and the hero of the season, captain Joe Donnachie, hit the equaliser. In the second-half Chester overran Witton with Virr putting them ahead and Pimlott putting the issue beyond doubt after brilliant play by Pryde. The 3-1 victory gave Chester the Championship as they moved to the top of the table for the first time that season. The fixtures ended with a 3-2 win over Sandbach, Chester's 9th successive victory, and the Cheshire County League trophy was presented after the game.

Unfortunately the financial cost of the season was high as Chester made a loss of just over £460. This was mainly due to a doubling in wages as more professionals were introduced to the side. The loss helped sway Chester away from making an application to join the 3rd Division North as they feared a large increase in travel expenses. The club also claimed, rather arrogantly, that the Cheshire County League was of equal standing and the supporters would not see an improvement in the standard of football. There was some good news when a 10 year lease was arranged on the Sealand Road ground. Originally the landlord was only prepared to offer a 12 month tenancy at an increased rent but the lease was extended when Chester agreed to buy some adjoining land for £800 as part of the deal. The intention was to use this land for a new ground but the directors had to sell the plot only two years later for £625.

Chester were able to retain most players for the 1922/23 season but there was one notable absentee in Joe Donnachie who was unable to come to a financial agreement with the directors. One new arrival was left-winger Frank Mellor from Bolton who had terrorised Chester two years earlier in Nantwich's 9-1 victory.

Defending Champions Chester got off to a disastrous start, and after eight games they were 2nd from bottom with only three points; the failure was largely due to the absence of Joe Donnachie. Matters reached a head after two defeats against Saltney and in mid-October negotiations were concluded, and Donnachie re-signed for the rest of the season. Such was his popularity in the city that the news was announced in the middle of a performance at the Music Hall cinema and was greeted by tremendous applause.

*The return of Joe Donnachie.*

There was an immediate improvement in results as Chester won three successive games, but it proved to be a false dawn and at the start of December there was an embarrassing 9-0 defeat against Stockport Reserves. Chester were at a disadvantage in this game as Simpson missed the train and to rub salt in the wounds the club were fined 10s (50p) by the Cheshire Association for failing to play a full team.

By the end of the year the Magpies were 2nd from bottom, above Middlewich, and to make matters worse the financial position had deteriorated with rumours abounding that the club were more than £1000 in debt and in danger of folding. The grave financial position was confirmed at a public meeting in January 1923 and a number of events, including a boxing tournament and a whist drive, were arranged to raise money.

Results showed an improvement in the New Year, largely due to the arrival of McGivney, another loan signing from Everton. McGivney galvanised the team in much the same manner as Virr had done the previous season and he led the attack well, scoring some vital goals in the process.

The best result of the season was saved for the last game when Chester gained revenge over 2nd placed Stockport Reserves with a 6-0 victory, to allow the team to finish 15th. There was no joy in cup competitions with a 4-2 defeat at New Brighton in the FA Cup and elimination in the 3rd Round of the Cheshire Cup by Altrincham. Meanwhile Joe Donnachie retired at the end of the season to become a publican at the Mariner's Arms in New Crane Street.

At the AGM the club reported that the debt was now just under £1000, although the supporters committee had helped by handing over £325. Matters did not improve at the start of the 1923/24 season as once again poor results produced a further drop in attendances. A number of new players were introduced at the start of the season including Westby Heath (Stockport) and Frank Payne (Lancaster Town) but they soon dropped out of the ranks. The forward line in particular proved a problem and the biggest disappointment was McGivney who had played so well at the end of the previous campaign.

At the start of November Chester were narrowly beaten 3-2 at Stockport, after taking a 2-0 lead. Stockport's winning goal came from a disputed penalty taken by Joe Kearslake who joined Chester after the game. His arrival, along with wingers Lydiate and Ingham from Manchester United, helped improve matters, although Chester continued to struggle in the bottom six.

The season continued to follow a similar pattern as the previous year with results showing a slight improvement in the New Year. Much of this was due to the performance of the defence where goalkeeper Pugh, a policeman who had previously been with Ellesmere Port, was outstanding. Perhaps the most unusual signing during the season was Mokhtar, an Egyptian student from Liverpool University, who had also played for Tranmere and Northern Nomads. His eight goals in the final 15 games helped pull Chester up the table but a final position of 16th was again unsatisfactory.

In the FA Cup Chester reached the 2nd Qualifying Round after victories over Ellesmere Port Cement and Lostock Gralam. Their opponents were Ellesmere Port Town and Chester looked to be well on their way as they held a 1-0 lead with 15 minutes to go but two late goals put paid to their chances. In the Cheshire Senior Cup there was defeat by bogey team Nantwich in the 3rd Round following victories over Northwich and Runcorn.

For the 1924/25 season only Syd Hughes, Cecil Williams and Mokhtar were initially re-signed as the directors looked to introduce younger players. The club also attempted to foster their own talent by inviting applications from local players for a trial prior to the start of the season.

Among the professionals signed were Jack Barton, ex Rochdale captain, who had been playing for Colwyn Bay, and Walter Taylor an outside-right of New Mills and Manchester United. Once again Chester looked to an ex-Everton player for experience by signing 35-year-old Tommy Fleetwood from Oldham and he was immediately made Captain.

Fleetwood had made more than 200 appearances for Everton in a 12 year span winning a Championship medal in 1914/15 and playing twice for England in Victory internationals. Early on in the campaign Chester fans also saw the brief re-appearance of Jimmy 'Met' Settle one of the heroes of the 1921/22 season.

At the AGM in September the club reported another deficit of £479, despite large savings on players wages, as gate receipts continued to fall. This was partly due to damage done to the ground by trespassers who persisted in breaking down the fencing in order to enter the ground without paying.

Chester got off to an indifferent start and, in much the same way as the previous season, struggled to find a settled side especially up front. In September Mokhtar returned to Northern Nomads and after playing Bolton 'A' in a friendly, Chester signed three of their opponents forward line, Shaw, Russell and McMaster. Only Shaw made any impression, and in December the forward line was changed again with Ankers and Lightburn arriving from Ellesmere Port Cement. Both players made debuts against their old club with Lightburn scoring Chester's only goal in a 1-1 draw as the Magpies pulled themselves up to 10th at the start of 1925.

There was a surprise for fans in the home game against Witton when Tommy Fleetwood appeared in goal. Chester won the game 1-0 and Fleetwood made some fine saves. In February Chester suffered a humiliating 7-1 home defeat against Port Vale Reserves in a game described as a mud scramble. Chester Fire Brigade had spent the morning pumping water off the pitch and although good football was impossible Vale adapted better to the conditions. The introduction of Ellis, a speedy winger from Holywell, helped Chester achieve an excellent win over League leaders Hurst, and this was followed by a 4-0 hammering of Ellesmere Port Town. However the season finished badly with some high scoring defeats notably at Altrincham, Port Vale and Northwich.

Although the first team had suffered another poor season there was success for the Reserves who finished as runners-up in the West Cheshire League and won the Cheshire Amateur Cup and Wirral Senior Cup. The contrasting fortunes were highlighted when the Reserves beat the first team 2-0 at the end of the season with many observers feeling that the result would have been more comprehensive had the Reserves reproduced their cup form. Several of the Reserves were kept on for the 1925/26 season in the hope that they would form the basis of the first team from which only Bert Ankers and Jack Barton were retained.

The directors also brought in several new players in an attempt to pull the club out of the doldrums and revive support in the city. First to arrive was 22-year-old Harry Bingham, a winger with a good goalscoring record from Cardiff. He immediately hit it off with Harold Peters from Southport and together they formed a formidable left-wing partnership. The defence was bolstered by signing Archie Jackson from Third Lanark and Tweedle Rigg from Rochdale, the latter arriving on the recommendation of captain Jack Barton. Jackson, a tall centre-half with a good turn of speed, had begun his career with Rutherglen in Scotland and then signed for Sunderland. He returned to Scotland with Third Lanark but joined Chester when Thirds were relegated, and his performances soon attracted the attention of scouts from First Division clubs.

Chester got off to a good start with a sparkling 4-0 win over Macclesfield as the change in the offside rule brought a glut of goals in the Cheshire County League. The Chester forwards adapted well to the new rule which gave the opportunity for players to play much further forward. The first away win of the season came at bottom of the table Congleton thanks to another good display from Jack Pugh in goal. Pugh, who joined the club from Saltney, had been a member of the successful Reserve team, and had replaced his namesake in goal at the start of the season.

At the end of October Chester were 7th from bottom but had played several games less than their rivals due to a cup run which had seen them play seven games and reach the 3rd Qualifying Round. The run had started with a victory over Llandudno after a replay. The winning goal had come a minute from time when Peters ran from the halfway line, beat two players, and unleashed a shot from 30 yards which completely deceived the goalkeeper. In the next round Chester beat Sandbach 2-0 but should have scored more as the forwards spurned chance after chance. In the 2nd Qualifying Round against Witton Albion Chester included Caulfield from Crewe, a player with one of the strongest shots in the 3rd Division. Caulfield lived up to his reputation by scoring 2 excellent goals in a 2-2 draw and Chester won the replay despite losing Harry Bingham who was sent off near the end.

Chester were hot favourites to beat Mold in the next round who included ex Chester players Billy Robinson and Syd Hughes. The crowd of 6500 brought back memories of pre-war days and coal carts were used on the reserved side to accommodate the spectators. The game finished 2-2 but Caulfield missed two penalties and Chester were routed 5-0 in the replay at Mold. Curiously enough Chester had an aversion to penalties throughout the season and up until the end of February only four out of 13 awards were converted.

Back in the League a number of changes were made at the start of November which saw Chester embark on a run of 13 successive victories. Tweedle Rigg was moved to left-back with his place at left-half being taken by Jimmy Duckworth from the Reserves. The forward line was changed with the signing of centre-forward Parkin from Southport and the re-signing of Peter Rothwell who had been playing for Northwich and Tranmere.

At the start of December, Chester were involved in an 11 goal thriller at Winsford in a game played on a pitch covered in ice. Harry Bingham gave a brilliant display as Chester recovered from 5-3 down to win 6-5. The following week Chester again pulled back a 2 goal deficit to beat Manchester North End 5-2. On Boxing Day 3000 spectators turned up to see the League game against Ellesmere Port but the game was called off just before kick-off because of a waterlogged pitch. Surprisingly the teams made the decision to play the game as a friendly with 35 minutes each way and no interval.

In mid-January, Chester gave a splendid performance in beating top of the table Port Vale Reserves 3-1. Chester took the lead through Ankers after 30 minutes and added two more before half-time, thanks to Peters and a brilliant solo goal by Bingham. This put them in a strong position as the gap at the top was closed to four points with Chester having five games in hand. The match also marked an upturn in attendances as the Championship came into sight.

Chester finally reached the top of the table over Easter with two wins and a draw, and on April 17th they faced Congleton in a potential title decider. Congleton had put together some good results after a poor start but they were no match for Chester who outplayed them throughout. Owens, a centre-forward from Hull, opened the scoring after 35 minutes and a second was added with a few minutes to go, when Rothwell sent in a high dropping centre for Parkin to head in. The Championship was clinched with a draw against Ashton National and the Cheshire County League points total was broken with victory over Stalybridge.

The hero of the fans had been Archie Jackson who was regarded as the best centre-half in the League, although the skilful Harold Peters had attracted a lot of attention as leading goalscorer. Success on the field also brought success off it and for the first time for many seasons the club were able to post a profit of just under £500 which helped reduce the overall debt.

There were few alterations to the team for the 1926/27 season, although Chester lost Owens to Rochdale and Barton to Manchester North End. Their replacements were Dick Critchlow of New Brighton and George Burley of Ellesmere Port. Critchlow was unfortunate to be carried off in his first game and was immediately replaced by the experienced full-back Jimmy Tootle who was on Derby's transfer list for £2000. Although Tootle remained on Derby's books he proved to be Chester's best player during the season with some outstanding displays.

Chester started the season in much the same way as they had finished the previous one thanks to the sensational goalscoring exploits of George Burley who scored 25 goals in 11 games. Burley had played wartime football for Liverpool Reserves and joined Ellesmere Port in 1920 where he had frequently been watched by Football League clubs. The 11 games brought two hat-tricks, one four goal haul (including a trio of penalties) and five in a 8-3 hammering of Middlewich. The scouts came flooding to Sealand Road, and in October he was inevitably transferred, to Burnley for £750, although Ellesmere Port received half this fee.

By this time Chester were lying 2nd in the table and Burley was replaced by Joe Yearsley, a prolific goalscorer from Northwich. Yearsley carried on the good work by scoring a hat trick in his first game and following up with five in Chester's best League win of the season, 9-1 against Runcorn. There was a lucky escape for Chester in November, when they travelled to Altrincham in thick fog for a Cheshire County League game. Many players arrived late for the game and the referee controversially abandoned the game with only 3 minutes remaining and Altrincham winning 4-1.

Chester continued to find goalscoring easy but they suffered a setback when they were heavily defeated 4-0 at 3rd placed Congleton and had Jackson sent off for striking a player. Jackson was subsequently suspended for a month and Chester badly missed him on New Years Day when they were hammered 5-1 at Runcorn.

It was proving to be tight at the top and Chester welcomed back Jackson for the head of the table game with Crewe Reserves. Chester triumphed 2-1 but had Harry Bingham sent off in a game which also saw a linesman sent off for *'interfering with the players'*. The linesman for the game was in fact Parkin, one of the Chester Reserves, and in a report after the game it was clarified that *'the offending linesman repeatedly pushed Clarke (Crewe) when he was about to throw the ball in from the touch line'*. There was more controversy in the Cheshire Senior Cup-tie, when a Macclesfield player was knocked unconscious by a spectator after the ball had been kicked into the crowd and struck the spectator's wife. The ensuing pitch invasion held the game up for several minutes and the commission appointed to investigate the incident closed the ground for 14 days from March 1st.

Despite the disciplinary problems Chester maintained their good form and although defeats against Stalybridge and Altrincham briefly took them off the top of the table they still had games in hand over their rivals. In April, Chester had to play seven games in 15 days but only dropped two points in the process. A point against Port Vale Reserves in an unimpressive display brought the Championship to Sealand Road for the 2nd successive season and the trophy was presented to captain Rigg before the final home game of the season against Northwich. Chester celebrated by coming back from 1-0 down at half-time to win 7-1 with Yearsley making up for his first half indifference and scoring five goals.

Unfortunately gates had once again been disappointing and it was only the transfer of Burley to Burnley and Reg Jenkins to Lincoln that prevented a loss and the overall debt now stood at £1250.

Before the start of the 1927/28 season Chester made the decision to run a team of '*equal strength*' in the Welsh National League and the club were faced with the problem of building 2 sides. This decision proved to be a financial disaster and after two seasons they withdrew from the League although considerable damage had already been done. Among the new signings for the Cheshire League side were Bimson and King of Southport and Tom Brittleton son of the ex-Sheffield Wednesday and England full-back. Chester also welcomed back Reg Jenkins from Lincoln who was released because he did not want to move over to Lincolnshire.

Unfortunately he was unable to reproduce the form which attracted him to Lincoln in the first place and was soon dropped. Another player who struggled early on was Yearsley who was criticised for being '*slow and cumbersome*', although he returned to form with four successes against Sandbach which sparked off another impressive run of goals. The Sandbach game proved to be the final game for Brittleton who was transferred to Aston Villa after only 10 League games. Two weeks later Chester also lost the popular winger Harry Bingham who joined Wrexham. An impetuous but hard working and enthusiastic player he '*caused much merriment among his comrades at Sealand Road with his racy humour*'.

There was one notable result in the Preliminary Qualifying Round of the FA Cup when Chester beat '*plucky*' Lostock Gralam 10-1 which almost overhauled their record 11-0 FA Cup victory over Stanley in 1892.

At the turn of the year Chester were 7th but the average gate of 1169 was beginning to cause concern to the directors who were seriously considering an application to join the Third Division, if the club could pay off its £1500 overdraft. In February Chester were rocked by the death of Josiah Taplen who had been chairman since 1921. He was succeeded by Harry Mansley, a board member since the war, who became the prime instigator in pushing Chester towards League status.

Back in the Cheshire County League, Chester had started 1928 with a bang scoring 34 goals in six games, but after March results began to tail off although there were high scoring wins over Ashton National (7-3) and struggling Whitchurch (8-0). Much of the excitement was saved for the Cheshire Senior Cup where they reached the Semi-Final after victories over Hyde, Sandbach and Ashton Brothers. A thousand Chester fans went to Crewe to see Chester go down tamely with a 1-0 defeat against Witton. This defeat effectively ended the season as Yearsley again lost form despite the support of Jack Keedwell from Llandudno. Chester finished the season in 5th place, although it was felt that they were only a couple of signings away from having a very good side.

The application for League status proved to be a non-starter as, despite £255 being raised as the result of a public appeal, there was little sign of the overdraft being reduced. When the voting took place Chester came bottom of the poll and it was Carlisle who were elected into the League, in place of Durham City:

| | |
|---|---|
| Nelson | 37 |
| Carlisle United | 33 |
| Durham City | 11 |
| York City | 7 |
| Chester | 2 |

During the close season Chester lost one of their most consistent performers when Archie Jackson joined Tranmere. He was replaced at centre-half by Nevin, captain of Queen of the South. There was also a new full-back in Jackson from New Brighton, and the forward line was bolstered by Freddy Birtles from Crewe plus the return of George Burley from Burnley.

Early season form proved to be very in and out and there was a surprise early exit from the FA Cup at the hands of Northwich. Meanwhile the financial position was getting steadily worse and with gate receipt often falling below £50, rumours began to circulate that the club would disband. Chairman Harry Mansley confirmed the stories and in a drastic attempt to reduce the wage bill several professionals were transferred in mid-November. Burley went to Stalybridge, Duckworth to Sandbach, Pollock and Ecclestone to Winsford and Bimson to Ashton National. Ankers and McConnachie were promoted from the Welsh League side as replacements and centre-forward Schofield arrived from Middlewich.

Surprisingly the departures did not unduly affect the team but the financial position went from bad to worse as receipts continued to fall especially for Welsh League games which frequently failed to reach £10. Travel expenses were also high for the Welsh League team and when the team journeyed to Holyhead they were prevented from crossing the Menai Bridge because the char-a-banc was too heavy. Even when the players dismounted it was still too heavy and the journey had to be completed by two taxis.

The first team continued to hold a mid-table position, but suffered an inglorious exit from the Welsh Cup when they were defeated 5-2 at home by Buckley. There was a much more effective exhibition in the Cheshire Cup where Chester reached the Final for the first time since 1911, beating Runcorn, Sandbach and Tranmere on the way. In the Final they played Northwich at Crewe, a team they had hammered 4-0 a month earlier. A disappointing game in front of 9000 spectators saw Chester hustled off the ball by Northwich's spoiling tactics and they were beaten 2-0 despite hitting the woodwork three times in the 2nd half.

Four wins in the last five games left Chester in 8th position but the club was still in serious financial difficulty. Once again a surprising application was made for admission to the Football League, although the directors acknowledged that the poor support would not enhance their chances. At the time inclusion in the Football League was seen as the club's salvation bringing, as it would, better football and derby matches against teams like Wrexham, Crewe and Tranmere. Unfortunately the club were in a 'Catch 22' situation as they needed better support from the public before they could get in the League.

There was no doubt that a successful team would bring in the crowds as the club had been one of the best supported in the area before the war and even post war crowds had been impressive on occasions. When the voting took place Chester failed to receive a single vote:

| | | | |
|---|---|---|---|
| Hartlepools United | 33 | Prescot Cables | 1 |
| York City | 24 | Chester | 0 |
| Mansfield Town | 16 | Rhyl | 0 |
| Ashington | 14 | Workington | 0 |
| Manchester Central | 2 | | |

As Chester entered the 1929/30 season they suffered a double setback when they were not only excluded from the FA Cup because of a clerical error but also the Cheshire Senior Medals, a competition for the county's league clubs. Chester had originally been invited to play in the competition in 1926 as replacements for New Brighton and their exclusion was a blow as it had given them a chance to test their mettle against Football League clubs.

There were plenty of new faces for the new season including Hicks (ex Nottingham Forest and Preston), Morgan (Torquay), Broome (Mossley), Parry (Preston) and Downey (Buckley). However Chester lost two of their more long-standing members when Tweedle Rigg and Bert Ankers left the club. After an opening day defeat against Stalybridge, Chester obtained the services of the experienced George Parkin, ex-Captain of Burnley, who had been at Turf Moor for more than five years.

Early results were poor, although the defence performed well and Tom Hicks formed a good partnership with the well-respected Jimmy Tootle. Also impressive was Stan Starling, a young goalkeeper from Chester YMCA, who soon signed professional. Most of the problems were in attack where Chester played attractive but ineffective football. The main culprit was Harold Peters, described as one of the best inside forwards in the Cheshire League, but whose '*appetite for pattern weaving nullified good work*'. Everything fell into place for Peters and Chester in a 13-2 mauling of Altrincham in November. Unfortunately just as the forwards hit form they were hampered by a serious injury to Peters who needed eight stitches in his knee after falling on a piece of glass when playing at Northwich.

By the end of the year Chester were 8th, 10 points behind Port Vale Reserves, who they beat 3-2 in one of the best games of the season. The following week Vale turned the tables and outplayed Chester in winning 7-0. In February a new centre-forward, King from Wolves, scored a hat-trick in his first game, but Chester slumped badly the following month as the defence shipped goals. They eventually finished 9th and there was no success in the Welsh Cup where they were eliminated by Colwyn Bay after a replay.

The result was particularly frustrating as Chester were well on top when Colwyn Bay equalised five minutes from time to take the game into extra time.

A week after the end of the season a decision was taken which affected the whole future of Chester Football Club. The directors made the bold decision to 'go for broke' in an attempt to gain League status. The man they chose to spearhead the campaign was Charlie Hewitt, manager of Connah's Quay, who had a wide knowledge of the game and a proven record as manager with Mold, Flint and Wrexham. In 1928/29 he had won the Welsh Cup and Welsh National League, with Connah's Quay, and in 1929/30 had taken the same team to 2nd in the Cheshire County League with a well-balanced team playing attractive football. Chester themselves had twice lost to Quay over Easter and it was hoped that with Hewitt in charge a serious challenge would be made for the title. Chairman Harry Mansley gave Charlie Hewitt a freehand to build a successful team, a task he embarked on with gusto. In order to support these ambitious plans, prices were raised to 1s (5p) for all parts of the ground, with an extra 1s for the grandstand; season tickets were priced at 15s-9d (79p) and £1 11s 6d (£1-58).

**MATCH TO REMEMBER**
**CHESTER 13 ALTRINCHAM 2**
**CHESHIRE COUNTY LEAGUE - NOVEMBER 30TH 1929**

*A remarkable game saw Chester achieve their record score for a competitive fixture in front of a moderate gate at Sealand Road. Incessant rain in the morning considerably affected the surface, and after a few minutes play the pitch became a quagmire with mud inches deep in front of one goal.*

*Chester's form leading up to the game gave no indication of what was to come, but the team ran riot in a game that was a personal triumph for Harry Peters who scored six goals. The game opened with the Chester forwards raining in shots and the first goal was scored by Broome in the 9th minute from a centre by Bromage. Broome also scored the second and Peters opened his account with a goal from close range. A brilliant piece of opportunism by Bromage for the 4th goal was followed by another from Peters as the goalkeeper failed to hold a greasy ball. These five goals had come in a 14 minute spell and Chester added three more before half-time with Birtles pulling one back for Altrincham.*

*In the second-half Chester defended the muddier end, but Altrincham showed no signs of recovery as the Chester forwards revelled in the conditions. Parkin scored goals nine and ten from the penalty spot and missed the chance of a hat-trick when a 3rd penalty was saved by Whitehead the ex-Chester goalkeeper. Peters added goals 11 and 12 and Bromage rounded off the scoring for Chester among enthusiastic scenes. In the last few minutes Fidler added a second for Altrincham who also missed a penalty right on full-time as Edwards shot was saved by Starling.*

*Chester - Starling, Tootle, Hicks, Walsh, Parkin, Parry, Hopkin, Jenkins, Broome, Peters, Bromage.*
*Altrincham - Whitehead, Harrison, Fletcher, Haydock, Edwards, Turner, Rowson, Fidler, Seed, Birtles, Wolstenholme.*

Hewitt brought with him the Connah's Quay trainer 'Jock' Simpson, an ex-Scottish International from Hearts, and his first signing was Joshua Atkinson a 26-year-old centre-half from Barnsley who was made captain. The side was largely built using players who were on the 'available for transfer' list of their respective clubs. Many of these players would have cost Chester upwards of £1000 but as a non-League club they were able to take advantage of this 'loan' system to recruit several experienced and well-known players. In came 'Paddy' Clifford, a little outside-right from Bournemouth, Tom Neale and Walter Webster from Sheffield Wednesday, and crucially, Arthur Gale a school master from Bury. Hewitt also went up to Scotland and returned with Gilroy (Falkirk) and Wilson (Third Lanark).

Another Scottish recruit was James Dickie, on Bristol City's transfer list for £1000, and from the same city came Fred Bennett of Bristol Rovers. Frank Cresswell, brother of England international Warney, joined from West Bromwich Albion although he had recently been playing for Hewitt at Connah's Quay.

It was clear that Chester meant business, and a crowd of 2802 turned up to see the first practice game where prospective first-teamers beat the Reserves 10-1 in the best trial match for years. Before the season got under way Hewitt made one final plea to the public to support the team and back up the propaganda that was being prepared to take Chester into the League. Cestrians responded to this new go-ahead approach and there were unprecedented scenes for the first game of the season against Northwich as crowds flocked to the ground. The reward was a 5-1 victory as Chester's exciting new forward line slipped into gear. This was followed by a narrow win over Witton but there was a massive disappointment the following week when Chester were beaten by Rhyl in the extra-preliminary round of the FA Cup and Port Vale Reserves in the League.

The Rhyl game was a major setback as Hewitt and the directors had been desperate for a good cup run to bring in money and raise the club's profile. Hewitt's response to the defeats was to release Gilroy, Webster and Wilson and replace them with Dave Morris of Preston and George Biswell of Chelsea. If the supporters had any doubts about the directors intentions then they were scotched by the sensational signing of Morris, one of the most talked about players of the day, who had won 6 Scottish caps in the mid-1920s while playing for Raith.

For the next game against Manchester Central, Gale was moved to centre-forward as Chester won 4-0, but the next three games resulted in draws, although a point was only dropped against Altrincham following a late equaliser in a 5-5 thriller.

After this game the problematical left-back spot was solved with the signing of Phil McCloy from Manchester City and he joined the all star Chester team who were now becoming known as the 'Arsenal of the North'. McCloy was another ex-Scottish international who had won 2 caps while playing for Ayr United. At the start of October Gale, already the idol of the crowd with his unselfish play and good ball control, was in irresistible form as Chester beat Whitchurch 10-2. Gale hit eight goals as Whitchurch were totally outplayed to such an extent that Chester were reputedly given instructions at half-time to stop scoring. A few days later Chester annihilated top of the table Congleton 9-1 as Gale grabbed another hat-trick. The next appearance at Sealand Road produced an unfortunate 5-1 defeat against Runcorn, although Chester were hampered by the loss of goalkeeper Jim Jarvie with a badly broken leg.

This proved to be the last reverse for two months as the team hit top form and the forward line produced some dazzling football. The next 11 games were all won with the team hitting an incredible 65 goals and Arthur Gale netting five on four separate occasions. The deluge of goals took Chester to the top of the table and there was no resting on laurels as another ex-international, Bobby Irvine of Portsmouth and Ireland, was recruited to the cause.

Increased attendances helped considerably reduce the bank overdraft and improvements were made to the main stand and the Sealand Road end with the supporters committee contributing £400. At the start of 1931 Chester submitted their application to join the League and also made the decision to increase share capital by £1000 to help fund ground improvements. Plans were submitted to extend the main stand to increase the seating capacity to 1700 and building work started with a target of Easter completion. Hewitt, recognising the value of marketing, took the progressive step of speaking to Chester rotary club on the commercial value of the club to the city as invitations were issued to Football League clubs to visit the ground.

Even when Gale was rested for the Welsh Cup game against Cross Street, the goals kept coming and replacement centre-forward Neale netted a double hat-trick. Gale returned for the next round and helped himself to seven as Chester crushed the amateurs of Llanfairfechan 11-2. In the 5th Round Chester were drawn at New Brighton but paid the Wirral side £100 to switch the game to Sealand Road. A robust game ended in a draw, with Chester not at their best, and the replay was abandoned in extra time as light faded. Chester finally triumphed 4-2 and the enthusiastic crowds and splendid performances proved to many people that Chester would be able to compete at a higher level. They were finally beaten in the Semi-Final by 2nd Division Cardiff, but the attendance was a new Sealand Road record. Just over a week later the crowd record was broken again when the new stand extension was opened for the title clash with Port Vale Reserves.

Chester were now in the middle of an eight match winning sequence and with three games to go were level on points but with an inferior goal average to Vale. On April 25th Chester lost at Manchester North End, as Vale were beating Winsford at home, and the title was effectively secured for the Potteries side when they beat Altrincham 5-1 a few days later. Vale also beat Chester in the Cheshire Challenge Cup Final but a magnificent season did not pass without silverware as the Cheshire Senior Cup was captured for the first time since 1909. Once again Arthur Gale had been among the goals with hat-tricks in earlier rounds against Winsford and Nantwich and six in an 8-1 Semi-Final victory over Congleton. In the Final, Chester played Crewe at Northwich with the following side:

Jarvie, Bennett, McCloy, Atkinson, Morris,
Neale, Clifford, Irvine, Gale, Cresswell, Dickie

Despite being handicapped by the loss of 'Smiler' Neale after three minutes with a double frature of the leg, ten man Chester proved their superiority thanks to a brilliant display by the forwards. The first goal was scored by Gale who beat the Crewe goalkeeper with a dropping shot despite the close attention of two defenders. Dickie scored the second with a nicely placed cross shot after Gale had flicked on an Irvine cross. On 36 minutes Gale pounced on a rebound from the crossbar to score number three, and completed his hat-trick a minute later after another good run by Clifford. Chester went in at the break leading by 5-0 as Irvine scored when the Crewe keeper failed to hold a Gale shot. In the second-half Gale headed in brilliantly from an Atkinson free kick, and a late consolation for Crewe left Chester 6-1 victors. Gale's goals in the Cheshire Senior Cup took his tally to 102 for the season in an overall total of 239.

With the season over, attention switched to the fight for League status and the directors completed the task of canvassing support by personally visiting all 1st and 2nd Division clubs. They had a good story to tell with much improved facilities and a deficit of £1500 being turned into a profit of £1600 as attendances soared. It was anticipated that voting would be close at the League's AGM but many people felt that the odds were against Chester achieving their goal.

The ballot was held In London on June 1st 1931 with the following result:

| | | | |
|---|---|---|---|
| Rochdale | 40 | Nelson | 27 |
| Chester | 27 | Manchester Central | 4 |

The tie between Chester and Nelson necessitated a second ballot and this time 28 votes were cast for Chester against 20 for Nelson.

Eighteen months after nearly going out of business Chester were in the Football League, and Charlie Hewitt started the task of building a team for the new venture.

**MATCH TO REMEMBER**
**CHESTER 2 PORT VALE RESERVES 0**
**CHESHIRE COUNTY LEAGUE - APRIL 3RD 1931**

*When Chester faced Port Vale Reserves at Sealand Road in April 1931, the game held extra significance because of Chester's fight for Football League status. The two teams were neck and neck at the top of the table, and a (then) record home crowd of more than 13,000 gathered to see the match which was played in a cup-tie atmosphere. Before the game the new extension to the main stand was opened by Charles Sutcliffe, vice-president of the Football League, who visited the ground along with Alderman Cropper, chairman of the management committee for Division 3 North.*

*Straight from the kick-off Dickie had the ball in the net for Chester, but the goal was disallowed for a foul on the full-back by Gale. Chester continued to exert pressure and Gale shot straight at the keeper when clean through, then hit the crossbar from only two yards out. The constant pressure was rewarded when Gale put in a brilliant run to the goal line and passed to Paddy Clifford to turn the ball into the net. Shortly afterwards Chester increased their lead when Gale pounced on a poor clearance to score with a first time shot from long range. These two first-half goals took some of the pressure off Chester and as the match progressed they gradually sat back on their lead allowing Port Vale to ease their way back into the game. Although Vale worked well in the middle their finishing left much to be desired and Chester held out for a comfortable 2-0 victory. The win closed the gap at the top of the table, although Chester eventually had to settle for 2nd place. More importantly the sense of occasion created a favourable impression on the visiting dignitaries and went a long way to securing Chester's place in the Football League.*

*Chester - Jarvie, Bennett, McCloy, Atkinson, Morris, Neale, Clifford, Burgess, Gale, Cresswell, Dickie.*
*Port Vale Reserves - Slater, Maddocks, Wooton, Sherlock, Izon, Birke, Anstiss, Rowbottom, Watkin, O'Grady, Baxter.*

Arthur Gale:
Scorer of 102 goals in the 1930/31 season.

Chester players prepare for life in the Football League in summer 1931 as workmen complete the extension to the main stand.

# 'ARISTOCRATS OF THE NORTHERN SECTION' 1931-1939
# CHAPTER 7

Chester had naturally wanted to retain as many players as possible for their first step into the unknown but they were no longer able to exploit the system which allowed them to sign League players without paying a transfe fee. Although Atkinson's signature was secured, ma of the other players left the club. Perhaps the biggest loss was Arthur Gale who was transferred to West Bromwich Albion, with Bury (Gale's original club) receiving £400, and Chester obtaining Frank Cresswell in part exchange. Charlie Hewitt took advantage of his contacts with London clubs by recruiting Skitt, Herod and Thompson from Tottenham and Millsom from Charlton. They were joined by Foster Hedley from Manchester City and two signings from Leeds United, goalkeeper Bill Johnson and Tommy Jennings. Powerful centre-forward Jennings, a wonderful header of the ball, had scored 120 goals in 140 appearances for Leeds after joining them from Raith and he was made captain of the team. Other new players included Burke (Shelbourne), Ranson (Swansea) and Reilly (Gateshead).

Throughout the summer workmen carried out ground improvements and by the start of the season football fever had gripped the city.

Hewitt meanwhile tried to play down expectations by refusing to make rash promises looking to mid-table as a satisfactory position.

More than 12,000 turned up for the first game against Wigan Borough, with an influx of fans from North Wales and the Wirral and a constant stream of buses taking supporters to the ground from the city centre. Four second-half goals won the game for Chester but the result was deleted from the records in October when Wigan resigned from the League. Chester picked up their first 'legitimate' point with a draw at Wrexham, and the following week they were able to include Fred Bennett in the side after his transfer from Bristol Rovers. Chester were beaten 4-1 but this proved to be their only away defeat until December.

At the end of September Chester earned a brave draw against Gateshead after playing part of the game with only nine men after injuries to keeper Johnson and Atkinson. Baden Herod took over in goal and Johnson played on the right-wing with a broken wrist, an injury that was to keep him out for two months. These injuries necessitated changes to the defence for the next game against Wrexham with Johnny Burke making his debut in goal and Harry Skitt moving to right-half to accommodate Alex Lambie from Partick at centre-half.

The changes were instrumental in Chester losing 5-2, but the team began to find their feet and embarked on a nine match unbeaten run which saw them slowly climb the table.

In November, Chester appeared in the FA Cup 1st Round for the first time since the 1890/91 season. Their opponents were Hartlepools who were confident of victory after inflicting defeat on Chester at Sealand Road in the League. Foster Hedley was in fine form as Chester won 4-1, but there was a giant-killing act in the next round when Lancashire Combination side Darwen showed a greater desire to succeed after overcoming a first-half deficit to win 2-1. The defeat cost Chester a money-spinning tie against Arsenal in the 3rd Round.

By the end of the year Chester held a respectable mid-table position and Hewitt strengthened the team by signing Arthur Mercer and Cud Robson from Bristol City for £500. Both players settled quickly but it was 20-year-old Ernie Keeley, a gangling half-back, who was attracting attention with some outstanding performances. Keeley, son of former Chester keeper Billy, had come to Sealand Road from Ellesmere Port and Chester received a record fee of £1,000 when he joined Leicester in February. Also impressive was Tommy Jennings who became the first Chester player to score a hat-trick in the Football League, adding two more for good measure, as Chester overcame Walsall 5-1. He produced another fine goalscoring performance at the end of the season by scoring four when Chester ran riot against Rochdale 7-2.

A final placing of 3rd was the best position for a club in its first League season, and Chester had every reason to be proud of this achievement.

The Semi-Final of the Welsh Cup was reached with defeat, but not disgrace, at home to Swansea and the Reserves retained the Cheshire Senior Cup by defeating Crewe at Gresty Road.

Improvement off the field was maintained and a profit of £903 allowed the club to pay out a dividend for the first time since 1909. Significantly Chester were also in a position to purchase the Sealand Road ground (now known as the Stadium) along with some of the adjoining land. In the weeks leading up to the purchase Chester had seriously investigated the possibility of building a new ground elsewhere in the city. They had been offered land at Boughton Hall, Hough Green, and another site at Sealand Road, but the directors opted to stay at the developing Stadium.

The nucleus of the side remained the same for 1932/33, but Chester welcomed Stevenson, a Scot from Falkirk, Gray (Rotherham) and Armes (Carlisle) the latter a right-winger who performed brilliantly in the trials. Chester also re-signed James Dickie on a free transfer from Bristol City although he only made one appearance before returning to his first love, New Brighton.

After eight games Chester were top of the table but there was still a perceived weakness in the forwards and Tommy Jennings was dropped for the next game against Wrexham. He was replaced as captain by Baden Herod and at centre-forward by new signing Joe Mantle from Plymouth, who was regarded as one of the fastest forwards in the game. Mantle got his Chester career off to an explosive start with a first minute goal against Wrexham described by the Cheshire Observer as a 'sensational goal of luck *opportunism, originality and speed'*.

*Hedley scores the third goal against Fulham.*

He controlled a difficult ball with his chest and then his head, beat the defence with a turn of speed and had the ball in the net before the defence could recover. Chester won the game 2-1 and retained the leadership the following week with an easy win over Carlisle.

**MATCH TO REMEMBER**
**CHESTER 5 FULHAM 0**
**FA CUP 3RD ROUND - JANUARY 14TH 1933**

*The 5-0 win over Fulham was regarded as one of Chester's best ever team performances. In a brilliant collective display of skill and speed an inspired Chester earned themselves a 4th Round tie with Halifax.*

*Chester entered the game on the crest of a wave having just beaten Rotherham 5-0, but it was a cagey opening as both sides weighed each other up. Gradually the game opened out as Sammy Armes created early chances for Mantle and Cresswell. It was Armes who set up the first goal for Chester after 22 minutes when his short pass was picked up by Mercer who shot past Toothill. Seven minutes later Armes put in another cross that appeared to be too close to the keeper, but Hedley slipped in to head the ball into the net. At 2-0 the game was going well for the home club, although Wrightson (who was later to join Chester) had an effort cleared off the line for Fulham. Hedley added a third just before half-time, and he completed his hat-trick in the 55th minute when he headed in after Toothill failed to hold the ball. For the rest of the game Chester toyed with Fulham as Cresswell and Mercer ran rings round the hapless defence. A fifth goal was added when Toothill failed to gather Mantle's shot, and Hedley appeared from nowhere to lift the ball over the keeper and complete a memorable victory.*

*Chester - Johnson, Bennett, Herod, Pitcairn, Skitt, Bell,Armes, Mercer, Mantle, Cresswell, Hedley.*
*Fulham - Toothill, Birch, Barrett, Oliver, Gibbons, Webb, Richards, Hammond, Wrightson, Price, Finch.*

In November Chester faced 2nd placed Hull who snatched an unmerited draw with a late penalty and some baffling offside tactics. Mantle however was in the middle of a rich vein of form, scoring in nine successive League games, and by the end of the year Chester were two points clear of Hull who had two games in hand.

It proved to be an eventful season in the FA Cup with Chester reaching the 4th Round. In the 1st Round Chester had beaten Rotherham in a one-sided game to give themselves a tie against Yeovil and Petters United, a team with a good cup reputation. Chester went 2-0 up in a thrilling game but a Wyper penalty miss saw Yeovil rally and reduce the arrears, although Chester held on to win 2-1.

The 5-0 win over Fulham in the 3rd Round was regarded as one of the best ever performances by a Chester team and when they were drawn at home to struggling Halifax in the next round there was even talk of Wembley in the air. On a frost-bound pitch the Halifax goal led a charmed life and the Yorkshire side held on for a shock 0-0 draw. In the replay Halifax took a 2-0 lead but Chester fought back with goals from Mantle in the 52nd and 75th minutes to take the game into extra time. Chester were extremely unlucky not to win the game in normal time as they were denied a penalty when Flack of Halifax scooped away a Billy Bell header with his hand when the goalkeeper was stranded.

Chester F.C. Bringing Home the "Welsh Cup" May 1933 Park Cook City Walls Chester

Halifax grabbed a winner in the first minute of extra time, and a few days later Chester also lost the leadership of the 3rd Division when they were beaten by Wrexham.

At the start of April Chester journeyed to Humberside for a key game against Hull with some of the directors and supporters flying to the game from Hooton aerodrome. Chester lost the game 2-0, and their title hopes effectively ended (and hence promotion) when they dropped vital points against Rochdale and Darlington over Easter. Chester ended the season in 4th position after an 8-5 defeat at Stockport, but they reached the Welsh Cup Final where they faced Wrexham at Sealand Road.

A torrential downpour before the game restricted the attendance to 15,000, although this was still a new ground record. An exciting game saw Chester take the lead after seven minutes when Gerry Kelly left defenders floundering and cut in from the wing to score with a cross shot which gave the keeper no chance. Early in the 2nd half Kelly, Wrexham's tormentor, weaved past three defenders and shot for goal, the attempt was partially blocked by a defender, but Cresswell followed up to make it 2-0 for Chester. The cup was presented by the Duke of Westminster who had been elected the club's first president the previous year. Earlier in the season Chester had also won the inaugural Cheshire Bowl competition when they beat Crewe 3-1 in the Final with goals from Mantle, Stevenson and Cresswell.

During the close season further improvements were made to the banking at the Saughall Road end and the club also mistakenly started preparing for their Silver Jubilee before realising, later in the season, that they were two years too early!

After two impressive years there was speculation that Chester were in a position to seriously challenge for promotion. Tommy Jennings had left the club to become player/manager of Bangor City, and he later took over at Third Lanark who he took to the 1936 Scottish Cup Final. The promise shown by John Burke allowed Chester to release Bill Johnson on a free transfer and his form was such that the Irish selectors watched him in an early season game against Halifax. Into the club came Thomas Freeman, a full-back from Middlesbrough and George McLachlan who had played in the 1927 Cup Final for Cardiff. Chester had relied heavily on the goals of Joe Mantle the previous season, and Ernie Whittam (Huddersfield) came in to assist at inside-forward.

The season started well with a 5-1 win over Rotherham but this proved to be one of only two victories up to the start of November. Arthur Mercer left to join Halifax but the replacement signing, Upton from Blackpool, was not a success and when little Foster Hedley joined Tottenham it necessitated a shuffling of the pack, with McLachlan moving to the forward line. The brilliant form of McLachlan and Armes on the wing brought Chester 28 goals in four home games, with Mantle and Armes scoring 23 of them. Armes had been reinstated to right-wing having lost his place to Gerry Kelly the previous season, and his new found form alerted Blackpool who signed him for a four figure fee early in 1934.

At the same time Chester also transferred popular Frank Cresswell to Notts County for £2,750 with Hughes (Bolton) and Roberts (Crystal Palace) arriving as replacements. Hughes, a former Wrexham winger, scored five penalties in as many games shortly after his arrival, but this could not disguise the fact that the team were now struggling. Over the season Chester lost too many players without finding adequate replacements and when Chester suffered their heaviest defeat in the League, 9-0 at Barrow, they were 5th from bottom and in danger of having to apply for re-election.

Hewitt responded by signing goalkeeper Bob Middleton from Sunderland, a player who had represented Scotland while playing for Cowdenbeath.

A few weeks later, on March 15th, the forward line was rebuilt with the triple signing of Arthur Wilson, a 23-year-old inside-left from West Ham, Charlie Sargeant, outside-left from Hull, and John Wallbanks of Portsmouth. The 3 players cost a total of £400 and Chester got their moneysworth as they recovered to win eight of their last 10 games and finish 10th.

Away from the League there had been another surprise defeat in the FA Cup as Chester lost to Southend, who were struggling in Division 3 South, in the 2nd Round. In April Chester played a benefit for Alf Jones of Wrexham who had made more than 400 appearances for the Welsh club having started his career as a promising youngster with Chester in 1919/20. At the end of the season an FA Committee investigated a pitch invasion by Chester fans in the home win over League leaders Chesterfield. As a result the club decided to erect a concrete wall behind the two goals and along the popular side to make it harder for people to get on the pitch.

There was a surprise return to Chester for Frank Cresswell at the start of the 1934/35 season. He had found it difficult to settle at Notts County and needed little persuasion to return to Sealand Road. His return at inside-left gave Charlie Hewitt the chance to experiment in the trial games by playing Arthur 'Tug' Wilson at centre-half. Hewitt had been inspired by the ideas of Herbert Chapman who had introduced the defensive centre-half with great success at Arsenal and he saw Wilson as an ideal candidate for this role at Chester. The fans were initially sceptical but Wilson was an immediate success and over the next three seasons he was almost ever-present in this position. Other newcomers over the close season were Ernie Hall (QPR) at full-back and Jack Fantham (Rotherham).

The season started with seven wins in the first eight games, including a 6-2 blitz of Wrexham where Wallbanks scored four goals. But that game was over-shadowed by the local colliery disaster at Gresford where 265 miners had lost their lives on September 22nd. Three successive defeats followed, but Chester then commenced an 18 match unbeaten run which took them well into February. At the same time they also reached the 3rd Round of the FA Cup. In the 1st Round they faced Sheffield District League side Dinnington Athletic who refused to be overawed even after Chester had taken a 2-0 lead in the first 15 minutes. It was a poor display by Chester despite a 3-1 win, but in the next round they produced an improved performance in beating Clapton Orient 3-1 on their first ever visit to London.

The reward was a home draw against 2nd Division Nottingham Forest, and Chester prepared for the game with a relaxing break in Blackpool. Talk of football was banned as the players concentrated on playing golf and snooker and were *'fed like fighting cocks'*.

The change of routine clearly did the players little good as they produced a disappointing display in going down 4-0 on a sea of mud.

In January 1935 Sealand Road staged an England amateur trial between the North and South in which two referees were deployed for the first time, one in each half. The experiment was not a great success with both referees staying in the corner near the touchline making the linesmen superfluous. There was also confusion as to which referee should blow the whistle when an incident occurred on the centre line. Playing in the trial were Hedley Simms, a College Schoolteacher, who made one appearance for Chester and Saltney born Bobby Sanders who made a name for himself four years later in the FA Cup-ties against Sheffield Wednesday.

By now Chester had a number of promising youngsters coming through the ranks including Fred Smallwood who later moved to Southampton, and Guy Wharton a half-back who made his debut in the Division 3 North Cup against Wrexham. Wharton came from the Barnsley area and joined Chester after Charlie Hewitt's wife spotted him playing in local football. He later went on to play for Wolves and won a Cup winners medal with Portsmouth in 1939.

Chester's unbeaten run ended with defeat against fellow title challengers Doncaster as they failed to take advantage of the majority of the play in going down 3-1. After the game leading goalscorer Wallbanks was transferred to Bradford P.A., but this did not prevent Chester winning five of the next six games to go top of the table at the start of April. Unfortunately, despite the re-introduction of Joe Mantle, a poor return of three points over Easter saw Chester finally finish in 3rd place, three points behind Doncaster.

In the Welsh Cup Chester reached the Final where they faced Tranmere. A lively and robust game ultimately proved to be a disappointment with Chester hampered by an early injury to Gerry Kelly. Bert Gray, Tranmere's Welsh International goalkeeper, excelled with a couple of great saves from Sargeant and eight minutes from time Woodward scored what proved to be the winner for Tranmere. Chester did win one trophy when they secured the Cheshire Bowl after defeating Stockport 4-2 with goals from Sargeant (2), Cresswell and Wallbanks.

The disappointing end to the season led to rumours circulating that Chester did not want promotion, a rumour that was to periodically re-surface whenever Chester missed out on promotion in future years. The directors vehemently denied these accusations and brought in a number of new players for the 1935/36 season. First to arrive was Ronnie Williams a Welsh International from Newcastle who cost Chester a record fee of £750.

Williams a strong, bustling forward was known as a player who could *'dish it out'* and was seen as a *'sensational transfer star'*. The right hand side of the forward line was enhanced by the signing of winger Bill Horsman (Birmingham) and inside-forward Frank Wrightson (Exeter). Also new to the team was Ted Common from Preston, a fearless tackler with great positional ability, and Ted Anderson, a long throw expert from West Ham. Anderson came into the side at half-back where he joined Harold Howarth who had signed from Bolton in February. Howarth's wonderful ball control earned him a reputation as one of the Division's best half-backs, and he formed a good partnership with Ernie Hall on the right.

Once again Chester started the season with an emphatic victory, 5-1 over Southport, which included a hat trick in six minutes from debutant Williams. There was a similar burst of goalscoring in the 2nd match where three goals in eight minutes defeated Accrington as Chester's good football earned them the tag of *'aristocrats of the Northern section'*. By October Williams had established himself as the Division's leading goalscorer with 13 goals in 12 games but there was still a lack of cohesion in the forward line. Cresswell and Sargeant were both briefly dropped, and after goalless games against Rotherham and Mansfield, Wrightson lost his place at inside-right.

After a poor October, Chester regained their form in November and there was an unusual incident at Carlisle when Chester won 3-1. A cannonball shot from Cresswell entered the goal and apparently broke the net; as the players lined up for the kick-off the referee surprised everyone by awarding a goal kick much to the displeasure of the Chester players.

The dismissal of Howarth in a League game against Tranmere led to his suspension and the re-appearance of Harry Skitt at centre-half in the 2nd Round FA Cup-tie against Reading. Skitt had not played in the first team for more than a season and the defence was reshuffled as Chester threw away a 3-1 lead to draw 3-3. Chester were comprehensively beaten 3-0 in the replay and completed the month without a victory, although they remained in contact with the League leaders.

At the start of January, Williams, who had been struggling with his form, was injured at Wrexham. Utility man Gerry Kelly took his place at centre-forward and scored a hat-trick against Gateshead. After failing to score in his next game Kelly was unlucky to be dropped and was replaced by 'Paddy' Wrightson who had been in fine form for the Reserves. Hewitt had converted the initially reluctant Wrightson to centre-forward, and the move paid immediate dividends as Paddy scored four in the record 12-0 victory over York, plus hat-tricks in the next pair of League games, as Chester struck form with a vengeance.

Wrightson was in unstoppable form scoring 26 goals in Chester's next 13 games to put pressure on Chesterfield at the top.

Wolf (Carlisle) saves from Joe Mantle in April 1953.

Unfortunately, in mid-March, there was a major setback when arch-schemer Cresswell broke his knee-cap against Walsall as Chester lost 1-0. Chester failed to win the next two games and despite finishing the season with 11 points out of 12 they had to settle for runners-up spot five points behind Chesterfield. The last League game of the season against Halifax was a thriller and when Wilson ran through the defence to score with nine minutes remaining it was Chester's 100th goal of the season. Many people felt that the injury to Cresswell cost Chester the Championship but realistically it was the winless months of October and December that had ruined their chances.

Chester were able to celebrate one cup win when they won the 3rd Division North Cup at Darlington. In a game of high quality football, 'Tug' Wilson was outstanding against Best, Darlington's lively centre-forward. The opening goal for Chester was a gift as Walker fumbled a centre from the left and Horsman scored. Alderson scored an equaliser midway through the second-half but Wrightson scored the winner for Chester with 90 seconds to go.

Three days later Chester appeared in the Welsh Cup Final against Crewe but it was a leg weary team that turned out having played five games in eight days. Crewe were 1-0 up after only three minutes when Swindells scored, and they were much too strong for a tired Chester. Early in the second-half Horsman missed a simple chance when he contrived to head the ball across the goal when standing almost on the goal line, and Crewe made certain of victory when Rigby scored a penalty after a foul by Hall on Swindells.

Both these finals were played without secretary-manager Charlie Hewitt who had resigned on April 1st to take up a similar position at Millwall. The Millwall directors had persuaded Hewitt to take over during an International between England and Wales, and he took the Lions to the FA Cup Semi-Final in 1937 and the 3rd Division Championship the following year.

**MATCH TO REMEMBER**
**CHESTER 12 YORK CITY 0**
**FOOTBALL LEAGUE DIVISION 3 NORTH - FEBRUARY 1ST 1936**

*An irresistible performance from the forwards helped Chester to their biggest League victory, as they overwhelmed a shell-shocked York 12-0. The game was a personal triumph for Frank Wrightson who scored four goals in his first appearance at centre-forward. However, the main architects of the win were inside-forwards Jackie Hughes and Frank Cresswell who exploited the gaps in the York defence and were instrumental in virtually every goal.*

*The game was in doubt right up until midday as melting snow had caused the River Dee to overflow creating severe flooding problems on the Sealand Road pitch, and when the game went ahead it was played on a ground ankle deep in mud.*

*The first goal came after three minutes when Cresswell drove a Horsman centre towards goal. Wilson only made a partial clearance and Sargeant came tearing in to score with ease. Almost immediately afterwards York had a splendid chance to equalise, but Speed missed the target with only Middleton to beat. Chester never looked back and Horsman headed the 2nd after five minutes, with Wrightson pouncing on a through pass by Cresswell to score the 3rd with a tremendous first time shot. Cresswell scored his first with a header from a cross by Horsman and Charlie Sergeant netted the 5th after Wilson had parried a shot from Hughes. By now Chester were goal hungry, and after 36 minutes Wrightson headed home another Horsman cross and three minutes later Horsman himself benefitted from a goalkeeping error to score the 7th. Just before the end of the first period, Sergeant completed his hat-trick with a fine individual goal, and at the break, Chester led by 8-0 - a Football League record half-time score.*

*As soon as the second-half resumed Frank Wrightson completed his hat-trick from a cross by Sergeant, but the fans had to wait more than 20 minutes for Chester to reach double figures, although Wrightson twice hit the woodwork in this period. The 10th goal was scored by Cresswell after a goalmouth scramble, and number 11 arrived in the 85th minute as Sargeant shot into an empty net. The scoring was rounded off two minutes later when Wrightson scored with a magnificent header from Sergeant's centre. In fact Chester could have scored more than 12 had the team not been so intent in getting Hughes's name on the score sheet in the second-half.*

*Surprisingly the game was not always one-sided and it was the confidence of the forward line rather than the weakness of York which resulted in the record score.*

*Chester - Middleton, Common, Hall, Wharton, Wilson, Howarth,*
*Horsman, Hughes, Wrightson, Cresswell, Sargeant.*
*York City - Wilson, Fox, Legge, Lawrie, Wass, Hathway,*
*Green, Routledge, Speed, Lindsay, Spooner.*

He had always wanted to manage a London club and he left Chester saying '*a manager must make for London to be any good*', but Chester had every reason to be very grateful for the work he had done in his six seasons in charge. However during the year gates had fallen, despite success on the field, and Hewitt probably realised he had taken the club as far as he could, as Chester made a loss of £470 on the season.

Chairman Harry Mansley took over for the last few games of the season, but on June 1st Alex Raisbeck became manager under competition from Frank Cresswell's brother Warney. Raisbeck had been one of the finest centre-halves of his day at Liverpool where he won two League Championships and eight caps for Scotland. During the War he had been secretary-manager with Hamilton Academicals and in December 1921 taken over at Bristol City who he took to a pair of 3rd Division Championships. After being sacked by Bristol City in 1929 he became manager of Halifax and had been in charge when they beat Chester in the 4th Round of the FA Cup in 1933. There were also changes in the backroom staff as Hugh Ross left to become trainer-coach at Wrexham, and he was replaced by assistant Jimmy Collins. Meanwhile Raisbeck was left to concentrate on football matters as Billy Peters took over as secretary.

During the close season there were a large number of comings and goings. Johnny Burke followed Charlie Hewitt to Millwall and he was replaced by Bert Gray the Welsh International who had always performed well when playing for Tranmere against Chester. Although now almost 37 he was still a very capable goalkeeper and at 6ft-3ins had a great height advantage. Raisbeck returned to Halifax to sign well-travelled forward Bill Chambers. Other forwards to sign were Jack Gurry (Southampton), Peter Percival (Sheffield Wednesday), Tommy Alderson (Darlington) and Stan Prout (Bristol Rovers). The half-backs were strengthened by the signing of the impressively named Arthur Staveley Griffith Sackville Redvers Trevor Boscawen Trevis or 'Bos' as he was known to his colleagues. His father had been a staunch Conservative and Bos had been given the names of the Conservative candidate for Dudley.

The 1936/37 season got off to an excellent start with eight wins in the first nine games which put Chester firmly on top of the table. They were fortunate to be able to field the same side for all these games but when they played Hartlepools, Trevis broke his ankle in the first few minutes, although Chester went on to win 1-0. The enforced change in defence for the next game saw Chester suffer their only home defeat of the season, 3-2 against Southport. On October 17th Bert Gray became the first Chester player to be capped since Billy Matthews when he played for Wales against England in Cardiff. This proved to be the first of six caps with Chester, taking his total to 24 in an international career spanning 14 years. In November Jack Gurry took the place of Chambers at inside-right and scored a hat-trick in a 7-3 win over Lincoln, but his appearance in the first team was brief, in what proved to be a problem position. At Christmas Arthur Gale, the idol of the 1930/31 season, was re-signed from West Bromwich Albion. More than 11,000 spectators turned up to see his first game back, a 1-1 draw with Halifax on Christmas Day.

Chester entered 1937 on top of the table and after a defeat by struggling Tranmere on New Years Day they were unbeaten in the next nine games. On March 20th, Chester faced title rivals Lincoln at Sincil Bank where they were well beaten 3-0. Worse was to follow on Good Friday when they were heavily defeated at Mansfield, a result that took them off the top. Although they gained revenge over Mansfield on Easter Monday with a 5-1 win, the damage had been done, and Chester once again eventually finished 3rd, seven points behind Champions Stockport. On this occasion it had been the 10 defeats away from home that cost Chester dearly and, despite the goals of Paddy Wrightson, the forward line had not been as potent as the previous season. In six seasons in the League Chester had only finished out of the top four on one occasion, but it was proving frustrating for the fans who were now getting used to seeing their team heading the table and then fading after Easter.

In the FA Cup Chester were exempt until the 3rd Round for the first time. A one week training by the sea at Colwyn Bay did the players no harm on this occasion as they beat Doncaster, bottom of the 2nd Division, by 4-0. In the 4th Round Chester were beaten 2-0 by Coventry City on a pitch resembling a skating rink. Chester once again reached the Final of the 3rd Division North Cup where they faced Southport at Haig Avenue. Southport were the more industrious of the two sides but it was Chester who scored first when Frame steered the ball past his own goalkeeper under pressure from Wrightson. Two minutes later Jackie Davies collected the ball in his own half, dashed upfield and slotted the ball past a bemused goalkeeper. In the second half Southport pulled a goal back from the penalty spot but Chester made sure of retaining the trophy with a close range header from Horsman. Chester also won the Cheshire Bowl for the 3rd time with a Wrightson goal against Tranmere.

One of the success stories of the season had been 20-year-old half-back Jackie Davies. An ex-Welsh schoolboy international who had joined Chester straight from school he was transferred to Everton during the close season for £2,000. Raisbeck started his team building for the new season by returning to his old club Halifax to sign Thomas Feeney and Clem Smith, a player he had discovered playing in Yorkshire League football.

Other newcomers were Beynon (Watford), Walters (Aberaman) and Reg Butcher a 21-year-old half-back who had been playing for the Liverpool 'A' team.

Charlie Sargeant (left) and Arthur 'Tug' Wilson (right)

Unusually the team that faced Halifax for the first game of the 1937/38 season was identical to the one that started the previous one, with the exception of Smith who replaced Chambers. The game finished 1-1, and for the next match Trevor Walters made his debut in place of Arthur Wilson. After losing his place Wilson asked to be put on the transfer list and many supporters were sorry to see him go when he signed for Wolves. Walters however proved to be a fine replacement and showed great promise as a stopper. Chester were only defeated once in the first 13 games but the results were unconvincing and it was proving difficult to find a settled side. By November results were beginning to reflect this and the team suffered a blow when Wrightson dislocated a shoulder against Oldham. At the end of the month Chester played a successful friendly against Charlie Hewitt's Millwall which earned them £200.

By January, Chester were 8th, but the team was not playing the attractive football which had been its hallmark since joining the League. In an effort to bring in new blood to the team they tried to sign three members of a touring South African team but negotiations fell through. Much of the excitement in January was reserved for the FA Cup where Chester faced 1st Division opposition for the first time. Their preparation for Leeds United included a game against Tranmere Rovers - at golf. The cup-tie attendance of more than 37,000 was the largest to watch a Chester game so far and the team went down with honour as only fine goalkeeping by Savage prevented a draw. Leeds had gone ahead in 24 minutes with a goal from ex-Chester winger Sammy Armes, and just before half-time a poor punch by Gray let in Buckley for a 2nd. Chester responded immediately as Gale headed in a Howarth lob. Ainsley scored a 3rd for Leeds but Savage made brilliant saves from Chambers and Smith, with Horsman also having a good opportunity as Leeds won 3-1.

Before the game at Rochdale in February the Chester directors 'treated' the players to turtle soup in a Manchester Hotel. The soup was noted for *'putting pep into football teams'* but it failed dismally for Chester as they went down 4-0. Over the next couple of months there were a number of outgoings as Feeney and Alderson joined Darlington and Clem Smith went to Stoke for a substantial fee.

A bigger loss in March was the transfer of Charlie Sargeant to Stockport for a fee in the region of £2,000. Sargeant had been having a poor run by his standards, but 12 goals in 4 games saw a return to form and as leading scorer he was badly missed.

On April 12th Raisbeck resigned as manager due to the *'non-success of the team in recent weeks'* and disagreement with the board on policy and team selection. The resignation did not come as a total surprise as there had been rumours circulating for some weeks that all was not well behind the scenes. Raisbeck agreed to help the club by continuing until the end of the season as Chester finished 9th. However the club was plunged into crisis when chairman Harry Mansley also resigned saying that he was dissatisfied with the current board of directors. The board themselves, under fire from the shareholders, then resigned en-bloc and in July, at the AGM, the shareholders voted in a new board with Sir Thomas Brocklebank as chairman. Harry Mansley was immediately invited back on the board as the directors tried to regain the confidence of supporters. Their first task was to appoint a manager and the man chosen was Frank Brown who had helped establish Torquay United as a Football League side, having played for Blackpool and Exeter as a centre-half. Brown had a reputation as a manager who could develop young talent and he expressed a desire to give amateurs a chance at Chester.

Before Brown's arrival Chester had already signed Rogers (Manchester City), Owen (Halifax) and Robertson - a constructive centre-half - from Grimsby. Brown then added Arthur Keeley (brother of Ernest) from Bournemouth, Joe McGough (Reading), and Bill Pendergast, ex-Bristol Rovers, who had been playing for non-League Colchester.

Chester started the season with poor displays against Hull and New Brighton and there were six changes in the side for the next game against Lincoln. Albert Robertson and Bill Pendergast made their Chester debuts and Pendergast, adding punch to the attack, marked his first game with a goal. A week later he scored a hat-trick in his first home appearance and went on to create a Football League record by scoring 15 goals in 12 consecutive games. Chester had one of their largest League crowds of the season against Gateshead, when the visitors included veteran Hughie Gallacher in their side. Goalkeeper Cliff Owen was injured in the 2-2 draw, and was replaced by Eric Mansley for the next game against Wrexham, where Chester conceded two goals in the last 10 minutes and lost 3-2. The defeat prompted the immediate signing of goalkeeper Alf Hobson from Liverpool for over £700.

However defensive frailties continued to be exposed as Hobson got off to a less than confident start and full-back Dai Beynon was dropped to make way for new signing Willis Gregg from Manchester City. Chester saved their best scoring performance of the season for the Christmas games against Hartlepools when they scored 13 in two days. In the home game, Chester had trailed 2-0 after four minutes, but recovered to win 8-2.

It was in the FA Cup that Chester made an impression with some excellent performances. A comfortable 3-1 win over Bradford City was followed by a 2-2 draw at home to Hull. It looked like Chester had lost their chance of progressing further but Gregg was immaculate in a brilliant defensive display and Horsman snapped up one of Chester's few chances as Chester won the replay 1-0. In the 3rd Round Chester gained revenge over Coventry for their defeat two years earlier by winning 1-0 on a muddy pitch. The 4th Round encounter with Sheffield Wednesday proved to be a classic as Chester took their illustrious opponents to 3 games. Four thousand Chester fans at Hillsborough saw their favourites weather intense Wednesday pressure in the first 20 minutes and it was only superb goalkeeping by Cliff Owen that kept them at bay.

The deadlock was broken when Millership put Wednesday ahead and it looked like Chester would be swamped. In the second-half Chester came back into the game and equalised when Sanders poked the ball into the net after a Pendergast header had been pushed onto the underside of the crossbar.

In the replay a record crowd saw Chester take the initiative but despite having most of the play they were unable to score in the first-half. Ten minutes into the second-half a Sanders shot was blocked by the Wednesday defence, but then turned into his own net by Hanford. Now it was Wednesday's turn to take control and it was Robinson who got the equaliser to take the game into extra time. Chester had more of the ball in the final period, with Horsman causing plenty of problems, and they almost snatched a winner with a Pendergast shot being well saved by Smith. The third game was held at Manchester City and Chester did everything but score in a valiant display but eventually succumbed 2-0.

In the League it continued to be a very up and down season. Pendergast found goals harder to come by after Christmas and Chester clearly missed Frank Wrightson who continued to suffer with injury problems. In March, Chester introduced a new outside-left, Jack Coulter from Chelmsford, who had won 11 caps for Ireland while playing for Belfast Celtic, Everton and Grimsby. In his day he had been a skilful and adventurous winger but his stay with Chester was brief. In the end it was the left-wing partnership of Worswick and Warburton that helped spark a revival as Chester won 6 of their last 7 games to finish 6th.

Perhaps the biggest disappointment of the season was the huge decline in gate receipts as attendances slumped after Chester had been knocked out of the FA Cup. There was also a fall in income from transfers, which had brought in £5000 the previous season, and at his first AGM chairman Sir Thomas Brocklebank had to report a loss of £3,092.

The declining financial situation meant Chester had to rely more on local players and at the start of the 1939/40 season there was evidence of some exciting new talent coming through the ranks. Reg Butcher had already established himself at half-back and was being watched by Arsenal and Birmingham while two promising youngsters, who had played in the Cheshire County League side, signed as professionals. Both Tommy Astbury (17) from Buckley, and Dick Yates (18) from Queensferry were already on the verge of the first team and Chester had high hopes for both of them. In addition Dave McNeil, a speedy full-back in local football, signed as an amateur. He had played in the same Hoole team as goalkeeper Billy Shortt who Chester had loaned to Wellington to gain experience and was now pressing for a first team place.

When the 1939/40 season started Chester relied on the 'old brigade' from the previous season with Vic Brown, a full back from Coventry, the only newcomer. After a 1-1 draw with York, two more close season signings were introduced against Doncaster. In came Frank Marsh from Bolton and Alec Law from Brighton who had been signed to replace Arthur Keeley. Chester beat Doncaster 1-0 and followed this up a few days later with victory over Tranmere which put them in 4th place. However this game marked the end of normal League football for seven years as the competition was suspended following Britain's declaration of war with Germany on September 3rd 1939.

# THE WAR YEARS 1939-1945
# CHAPTER 8

With the curtailment of the League programme, Chester, like many clubs, played friendly games until a new regionalised League was developed. Chester's first friendly against Liverpool marked the debuts of Tommy Astbury and Dick Yates. Astbury showed great promise with a clever display at inside-left, and it was clear that Chester had a real find on their hands. In October a Northern League of 12 clubs gave Chester the opportunity to play distinguished teams like Everton and Manchester United. Throughout the war a system of guests was operational which allowed clubs like Chester to include some well known names in their team. One of these guest players was Doug McMahon, a Canadian from Wolves, who scored six goals in an 8-1 thrashing of Stockport in December 1939. It was a brilliant personal perf-ormance but there were less than 1000 present to see it.

In 1940/41 Chester played 35 games in a 36 team League and were placed 18th overall. Many of these games counted in two comp-etitions as was the case when Chester played Manchester United in the Semi-Final of the Lancashire Cup. The game was a thriller with Chester pulling back from 4-2 down to draw 4-4 after 90 minutes. Although the result stood as 4-4 for the League game an extra 30 minutes had to be played to settle the cup-tie and two Rowley goals gave United a 6-4 win.

On Christmas Day 1940 Chester played two games against Wrexham, one in the morning and one in the afternoon, and were defeated both times. In the FA Cup Chester were drawn against Tranmere and after a 2-0 win in the first leg they looked favourites to progress into the next round. With 30 minutes to go Chester were well on top, winning 2-1 on the day and 4-1 overall, but in an amazing turnaround Tranmere scored eight times to win 9-4 on aggregate.

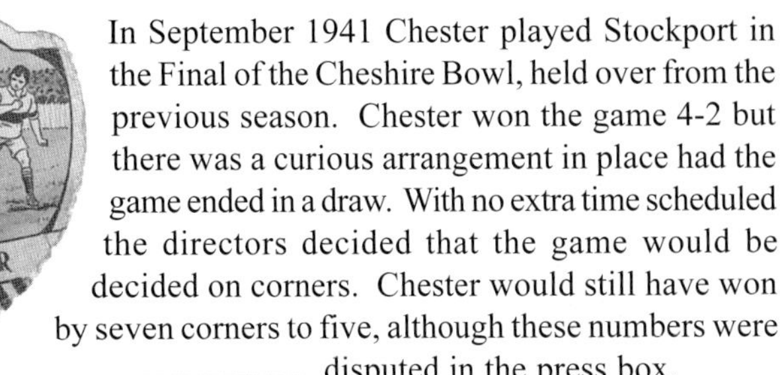


In September 1941 Chester played Stockport in the Final of the Cheshire Bowl, held over from the previous season. Chester won the game 4-2 but there was a curious arrangement in place had the game ended in a draw. With no extra time scheduled the directors decided that the game would be decided on corners. Chester would still have won by seven corners to five, although these numbers were disputed in the press box.

Tommy Astbury

Chester qualified for the final stages of the League War Cup but were beaten by Wolves in the 1st Round and there was also defeat at the first stage of the Lancashire Cup by Liverpool. The 1941/42 season had been split into two League Championships running either side of Christmas, and Chester finished 24th out of 38 in the first half season and 21st out of 22 in the second.

When Chester took on Halifax in September 1942 Ellesmere Port born Joe Mercer played at right-half in a 4-1 win. Mercer had played 158 times for Everton before the war, winning five England caps and was now a regular wartime international. After the war he played for Arsenal and later famously managed Aston Villa, Manchester City and England.

Another famous name to represent the club was Leslie Compton the Arsenal full-back. He made his first appearance, against Manchester City, and scored an 81st minute equaliser from a corner. A few weeks later he played at centre-forward against Everton where his commanding stature brought him a second-half hat-trick in a 5-4 victory. After the war Compton became the oldest player to make his England debut when he played against Wales in 1950 at the age of 38. Chester were also fortunate to have probably one of the best centre-forwards in the country to appear for them when Tommy Lawton of Everton and England played in a friendly against the RAF and scored 5 goals in an 11-4 victory.

Many of the wartime games were high scoring and there could often be a huge turnaround in results over a few days. On November 6th 1943 Chester beat Liverpool 3-1 at Sealand Road but a week later a weakened team travelled to Anfield and were overturned 9-0, with Cyril Done scoring seven times. Chester themselves hit nine in a 9-5 Cheshire Bowl Semi-Final win at Crewe. One of the Chester stars was Billy Hughes the Birmingham full-back who made 10 peace-time and 14 war-time appearances for Wales. Hughes had played in a variety of positions for Chester but had recently been successfully converted to centre-forward. He was also on target in the 2nd Leg against Crewe when a 4-1 win put Chester in the Final by an aggregate score of 13-6. Chester outplayed Stockport in the Final and won 6-1 in front of a meagre attendance.

One of the stars of the 1944/45 season was Scottish International forward Andy Black from Hearts. Black became a popular figure at Sealand Road and Chester tried to sign him after the war but he joined Manchester City for £6,000. It had been against Manchester City in December 1944 that Black had produced one of his best performances for the club as Chester won 7-1. The forward line that day also included fellow Scotsmen Armstrong (Aberdeen) and Hamilton (Hearts) but Black was absent the following week when Chester went to Maine Road for the return match, and were soundly beaten 6-0.

In April 1945 Charlie Sargeant appeared in a Chester shirt for the first time since 1938. He had been a prisoner of war for three and a half years and played against Wrexham only a week after his release. A week later he made his first appearance at Sealand Road and scored one of the goals in a 2-1 win over Wrexham.

The 1945/46 season acted as an interim season with Chester once again lining up against familiar opponents from the 3rd Division North. By now the team had a heavy local bias and in the first-half season they finished 4th out of 10 in the 3rd Division North (West Region). In the FA Cup Chester were drawn against Liverpool in the 3rd Round with the tie being played over two legs. An exuberant Chester, including seven local players, gave a meritorious display and put Liverpool under constant pressure but went down 2-0 to their more experienced opponents. In the 2nd Leg Chester put up another brave display but were 2-0 down by half time. It was four minutes before the end when Chester finally scored a consolation through Astbury and, although of no real value, it gave some evidence of Chester's fighting qualities.

Chester finished the season with an appearance in the 3rd Division North Cup Final after wins over Bradford City, York and Southport. In the Final they met Rotherham and drew the 1st Leg away 2-2 but went down 3-2 at Sealand Road to a team who were faster to the ball and quicker in the tackle.

The war years had given Chester the chance to develop their own talent and Dick Yates had proved himself to be a prolific scorer, while Tommy Astbury's ability had been recognised by Wales who awarded him 2 caps against England in 1945. Astbury also guested for Manchester United against Bolton in the League North Cup Final of 1945 where he finished on the losing side. The other success had been goalkeeper Bill Shortt, who joined Plymouth Argyle for £1,000 in 1946 and went on to win 12 caps for Wales.

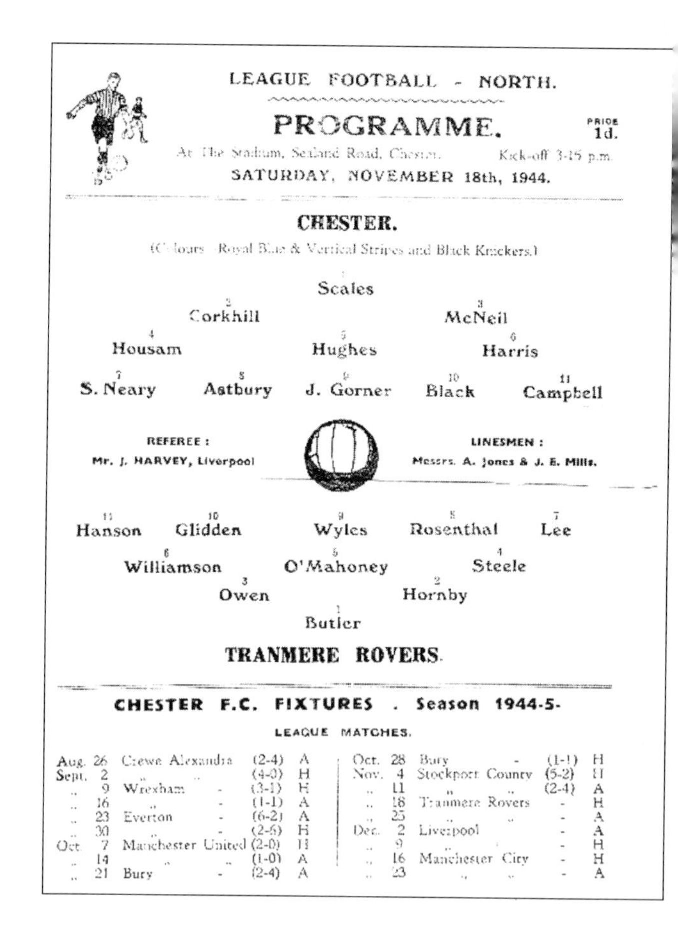

LEAGUE FOOTBALL - NORTH.

PROGRAMME.

PRICE 1d.

At The Stadium, Sealand Road, Chester. Kick-off 3-15 p.m.

SATURDAY, NOVEMBER 18th, 1944.

CHESTER.

(Colours Royal Blue & Vertical Stripes and Black Knickers.)

1 Scales

2 Corkhill    3 McNeil

4 Housam    5 Hughes    6 Harris

7 S. Neary    8 Astbury    9 J. Gorner    10 Black    11 Campbell

REFEREE: Mr. J. HARVEY, Liverpool

LINESMEN: Messrs. A. Jones & J. E. Mills.

11 Hanson    10 Glidden    9 Wyles    8 Rosenthal    7 Lee

6 Williamson    5 O'Mahoney    4 Steele

3 Owen    2 Hornby

1 Butler

TRANMERE ROVERS.

CHESTER F.C. FIXTURES . Season 1944-5.

LEAGUE MATCHES.

| Date | | Opponents | Result | H/A | Date | | Opponents | Result | H/A |
|---|---|---|---|---|---|---|---|---|---|
| Aug. | 26 | Crewe Alexandra | (2-4) | A | Oct. | 28 | Bury - | (1-1) | H |
| Sept. | 2 | " " | (4-0) | H | Nov. | 4 | Stockport County | (5-2) | H |
| " | 9 | Wrexham - | (3-1) | H | " | 11 | " " | (2-4) | A |
| " | 16 | " - | (1-1) | A | " | 18 | Tranmere Rovers | - | H |
| " | 23 | Everton - | (6-2) | A | " | 25 | " " | - | A |
| " | 30 | " - | (2-6) | H | Dec. | 2 | Liverpool | - | A |
| Oct. | 7 | Manchester United | (2-0) | H | " | 9 | " | - | H |
| " | 14 | " " | (1-0) | A | " | 16 | Manchester City | - | H |
| " | 21 | Bury - | (2-4) | A | " | 23 | " " | - | A |

# SEASONS OF STRUGGLE 1946-1958
# CHAPTER 9

The resumption of peace-time football saw Frank Brown place his faith in the players who had helped the club through the war. There were only two new signings, right back George Summerbee (Preston) and Jackie Arthur (Everton), the latter being one of only four full-time professionals, along with Walters, Marsh and Yates. Captain of the team was Tommy Burden, a sergeant instructor in the Army, who had first played for Chester as a guest from Wolves while stationed at Blacon Camp. He had suffered a career threatening injury to his back in the Normandy landings and Chester had been able to acquire him for a reduced fee. However the emphasis was very much on local part-timers, a policy promoted by chairman Sir Thomas Brocklebank who believed that players were better for treating football as a second calling.

After waiting seven years for a League game the spectators had to wait a further 15 minutes as Chester were held up in traffic on the way to York, but they were rewarded with a thrilling match. Chester were 4-2 down with 10 minutes to go, but first Gledhill put through his own goal, then Hamilton hit an equaliser. In the dying moments Chester almost snatched a winner but Burden's effort was disallowed.

George Scales made his debut in goal in the first home game and the rein-troduction of Trevor Walters to centre-half and the move of Eric Lee to left-half further strengthened the defence as Chester embarked on a 16 match unbeaten run which took them to within a point of Doncaster at the top. Eric Lee's performances earned him international recognition when he played for England amateurs against Wales.

The forward line were also gaining plaudits with Burden, Astbury and Yates particularly attracting the scouts. Sheffield Wednesday came in with an offer for all three players, but it was suggested that a fee of £14,000 would be needed to prise them away from Sealand Road. Burden was selected as a Reserve for the FA XI to play the Army and Astbury's performances put him on the verge of the Welsh team.

At the turn of the year all attention switched to the 3rd Round of the FA Cup where Chester were paired with Plymouth Argyle and ex-keeper Bill Shortt. They prepared for the game at Abergele on a diet of sherry, milk and eggs, and a capacity crowd gathered at Sealand Road to see if Chester could prevent Plymouth from scoring for the first time that season. Tommy Astbury opened the account for Chester after five minutes, a lead they held until half-time, but after the break Chester had a lucky escape when Straus hit the bar and Thomas failed to score from the rebound. Burden added a well taken second, after beating the Plymouth defence to a long ball by Selby, and cooly drawing the ball round Shortt. It was Walters who was Chester's hero with a masterly performance at centre-half and it earned Chester a money spinning tie with Stoke City and Stanley Matthews in the 4th Round.

Chester returned to Abergele to prepare for the game and after a goalless draw at Sealand Road they faced a replay at Stoke under Arctic cond-itions. Goals from Steele (2) and Ormston put Stoke 3-0 ahead midway through the second-half, but Burden and Walters inspired Chester to a splendid recovery and two goals in five minutes from Hamilton and Yates put Chester back in the game.

**MATCH TO REMEMBER**
**CHESTER 0 STOKE CITY 0**
**FA CUP 3RD ROUND - JANUARY 25TH 1947**

*The demand for tickets for this FA cup-tie was enormous as Cestrians clamoured to see how Chester would cope with the wizardry of Stanley Matthews. All tickets at the ground were sold within 90 minutes, and shops in the city centre were able to dispose of their allocation in 15 minutes. It was estimated that the club could have sold up to 40,000 tickets for the match.*

*Dave McNeil and Eric Lee were given the difficult task of marking Matthews and they went about their task quietly and confidently. McNeil in particular rose to the occasion in marvellous style as Matthews was frustrated by the constant presence of at least one Chester defender.*

*In the first-half the best opportunities fell to Stoke, and Steele had a shot cleared by McNeil who appeared from nowhere to kick the ball off the line. Baker also hit the bar for Stoke, but it wasn't all one way traffic as Hamilton was pulled down just outside the area when clean through. The Chester strike force was generally kept quiet and Yates had little chance against England centre-half Neil Franklin.*

*After the break McNeil managed two long range shots on goal, but the best chance came near the end when an interchange of passes between Jackie Arthur and Dick Yates, left the former through with only the keeper to beat. His shot looked a winner but Jepson made the save of the match and the game finished goalless. It had been a magnificent performance, especially in defence, and Chester fully deserved the replay at the Victoria Ground.*

*Chester - Scales, Butcher, McNeil, Marsh, Walters, Lee, Arthur, Burden, Yates, Astbury, Hamilton.*
*Stoke City - Jepson, Mould, McCue, Mountford, Franklin, Kirton, Matthews, Peppitt, Steele, Barker, Ormston.*

In the last five minutes Chester bombarded the Stoke goal and it seemed certain that they would grab an equaliser. Both Mould and Franklin made goal-line clearances and Mould appeared to head one attempt away from behind the line as Chester had to settle for a narrow 3-2 defeat.

The cup-ties had been a distraction from the League, where Chester had slumped badly after their excellent start, and a run of only 6 points from 11 games left them trailing Doncaster by 18 points at the end of March. However, a strong finish saw Chester finish 3rd with 56 points, beating their previous best of 55 points in 1935/36. Joe Mantle's record of 34 goals in the 1932/33 season was also broken by Dick Yates who managed an impressive 36 in 40 games.

A long season ended with a Welsh Cup Final appearance against Merthyr Tydfil at Cardiff. Chester were firm favourites to win the cup for the 3rd time but, in a disappointing game their poor finishing failed to match some fine approach work and the match finished goalless. A week later the two sides met in the replay at Wrexham, and after some early scares Chester took the lead when Burden scooped the ball into the net after a Yates header had been turned against the post. After 41 minutes Astbury crashed a shot into the net from Burden's centre but just on the interval Thomas pulled one back for Merthyr. In the second-half Chester took control and goals from Yates, Turner and Burden gave them a convincing 5-1 victory. The goal from Phil Turner was his first in senior football and came after he had flown back from a holiday in the Isle of Man a few hours before the game. The cup was presented to captain Trevor Walters and the players and officials celebrated their win with dinner at the Bars Hotel on their return to Chester

The post-war boom in attendances coupled with a successful season on the playing front allowed the club to show a profit of £530 and they were also able to put aside £1,000 for ground improvements.

In preparation for the 1947/48 season Chester brought in Tommy Best (Milford Haven), Fred Wilcox (Everton), George Williamson (Middlesbrough) and Harry Colville (East Fife). Best, an inside-forward with a devastating shot, became the first coloured footballer to play League football for Chester, and made himself an instant crowd favourite after heading the 2nd goal in an opening day victory over Oldham. Williamson showed outstanding form when he was brought into the side in October capping it with two long range goals in Chester's best display of the season, a 4-1 win over Wrexham.

Chester were unable to maintain the form of the previous season, especially up front where Astbury struggled with a knee injury and Dick Yates failed to reproduce his goalscoring exploits. At the start of October Yates was replaced by local youngster Geoff Coffin who scored on his debut against Carlisle. Coffin had been playing for Heath Rangers in the Chester & District League and went on to give the club eight seasons sterling service. In December, Yates was surprisingly transferred to Wrexham for a four figure fee and promptly made his mark for the Reds with a hat-trick against Halifax.

On Boxing Day Chester pulled off a major coup with the signing of 35-year-old ex-England international Ray Westwood from Bolton for £2,400. Westwood had joined Bolton in 1930, helping them to promotion to the 1st Division in 1934/35, and making six England appearances at inside-left between 1935 and 1937. Although he had lost some of his pace Westwood still showed a mark of class and acted as a steadying influence on the team. Although he scored within 10 minutes of his debut he could not prevent a 3-2 defeat at home to York.

Chester reached the 4th Round of the FA Cup for the second season in succession after a narrow 1-0 win at Crystal Palace. The victory was entirely due to a superlative goalkeeping display from George Scales who had the game of his life, in spite of having to receive attention for injuries on five separate occasions. Scales had been understudy to Frank Swift at Manchester City during the war and his fearless displays had quickly earned him the admiration of Chester fans. In the 4th Round Chester once again faced Stanley Matthews, who by now had joined Blackpool. Unfortunately a tragic mistake by Scales, who allowed a Shimwell clearance to bounce over his head into the net, affected his display and two goals from Mortenson helped Blackpool to a 4-0 win.

Despite some improved results after Christmas Chester finished 3rd from bottom, their worst League position thus far, and their worst finish in any League since they finished bottom of the Combination in 1902. The club also reported a loss on the season of £113, largely as a result of an increase in wages.

At the end of the season long serving Trevor Walters was granted a well-deserved benefit game against Manchester City. A strong, commanding centre-half, he had joined Chester in 1937 but like many players of the era had seen his best footballing years lost to the war. Whilst stationed in the Army as a Sergeant-Instructor he had captained the famous Wanderers team in the Middle East where he had played alongside players of the calibre of Tom Finney and Bob Paisley.

During the close season Chester lost the services of one of their most consistent players when Tommy Burden joined Leeds United.

At Elland Road he linked up with the manager who had discovered him for Wolves at the age of 15, Major Frank Buckley. Burden went on to make more than 200 appearances for both Leeds and his subsequent club Bristol City where he retired in 1961. With Chester also releasing Phil Turner to Carlisle, Bobby Hamilton to Yeovil, and Frank Marsh to Macclesfield, new faces were required for the 1948/49 season. In came Peter Greenwood, the Lancashire cricketer, from Burnley, Mackie and Forsyth from New Brighton, Albert Foulds (Altrincham), Billy Foulkes (Cardiff) and Cliff Mansley (Barnsley). Westwood was made captain and the club were also able to call upon Eric Lee whose appearances the previous season had been limited through his teacher training at Loughborough College.

*Eric Lee (1946 - 1957)*

There were also changes behind the scenes where Trevor Walters briefly took on the role as trainer after the departure of Vic Brown to Haarlem in Holland. Future chairman Reg Rowlands also joined the board of directors for the first time.

In October Tommy Best, who had been successfully converted to centre-forward, was transferred to Cardiff City as Chester struggled at the wrong end of the table. He was replaced by Duncan Harrigan (Aston Villa) and Albert Burgess a strong, brave player from Bolton who became known locally as the 'goal thief' for his opportunism near goal. Both players were on target in their first home game against Accrington where keeper Ted Elliott also made his debut.

Elliott replaced Jimmy McLaren whose performances had been affected by an over-critical crowd, but who went on to make more than 250 appearances for Carlisle.

In the FA Cup Chester were too good for Hartlepools in the 1st Round but a failure to take their chances cost them dearly at Aldershot in Round 2. There was major embarrassment in the Welsh Cup where a poor defensive display resulted in a 6-0 home defeat by Wrexham, although Chester could point to the loss of Ted Elliott with a broken wrist as an excuse.

Another disappointing season ended with some spiritless performances as Chester finished in 18th place. Most of their problems were away from home where they only picked up one victory and suffered 14 defeats. The signings of Foulds, Forsyth and Mackie had not been a success and all three were made available for transfer. Also given a free transfer was Trevor Walters who joined Caernarvon as player-manager.

On the eve of the 1949/50 season there was a surprise in store when Ray Westwood refused to accept terms and left the club. Injuries had limited his appearances and at the time it was calculated that every game he played cost the club £70. This was a large sum to Chester who announced a loss of just under £900 on the previous season, and Chairman Brocklebank announced that the club needed gates of 8,000 to survive.

Among the new players were Frank Hindle and Harry Jackson, regulars in Blackburn's Central League team, along with Eric Sibley and Bill Pearson from Grimsby. A lot was expected of Sibley, who had pre-war experience with Bournemouth and Blackpool, and he was made team captain. Unfortunately he had a poor debut as Chester went down 4-0 at home to Stockport, and Sibley joined Lytham as player-manager after only seven games. His replacement at full-back was John Molyneux, a promising youngster, who had been carefully nurtured in the Reserves by Frank Brown for two seasons.

Goal-scoring proved to be a problem in the early part of the season and Dick Yates, by now playing for New Brighton, showed what they were missing when he scored two beautifully headed goals in the 3-3 draw at the Tower Ground. Albert Burgess clearly took note and scored four goals in the next game against Halifax, on his way to become leading scorer with 24 in 34 games.

In the FA Cup Chester made the long trip to Exeter after a comfortable win over Midland League Goole in the 1st Round. Within the first 12 minutes Chester had conceded one goal and lost Ted Elliott with concussion. Bill Pearson took over in goal but could not prevent a 2-0 defeat against the team bottom of Division 3 South.

During the winter of 1949 former chairman Harry Mansley died and in the Christmas game against Bradford City young Joe Davies badly fractured his leg. Davies had run into form after moving to inside-right, and although he attempted a comeback at the start of the 1951/52 season the injury effectively ended his League career.

In January, Chester threw away a four goal lead against Darlington with pre-war Chester star Guy Wharton getting two of the goals for the Quakers in a 4-4 draw. A month later Chester almost repeated the feat against Rotherham who managed to pull back from 4-0 down to 4-2. One of the highlights of the Rotherham win was the performance of right-winger Billy Foulkes, and it was his brilliant form that led to improved results in 1950 as Chester recovered to finish 12th. The season ended with a Testimonial game for Reg Butcher against Blackpool. Liverpool born Butcher had spent the whole of his professional career with Chester having been signed by Alex Raisbeck in 1937 and former colleagues Tommy Best and Billy Shortt returned for his Benefit game

Financially matters went from bad to worse as gates continued to dwindle and Sir Thomas Brocklebank announced a massive loss of £3,527 in August 1950. It was clear that the club had to change their transfer policy and new signings Devonshire (Brentford), Hankinson (Preston) and Morement (Sheffield United) had only made two League appearances between them when they played in Chester's first game of the season against Lincoln. In September 1950 20-year-old wing-half Ronnie Hughes completed his army service and signed professional terms. Although he had to wait until 1952 for his debut he went on to become one of Chester's greatest servants making nearly 400 League appearances.

The 1950/51 season followed much the same pattern as the previous year as Chester maintained a mid-table position. Foulkes and Molyneux continued to enhance their reputations and Burgess remained the main source of goals. Tattenhall born Harry Threadgold took over from Ted Elliott in goal and also started to attract the attention of the larger clubs with some outstanding performances.

In the FA Cup, Chester were knocked out at the first stage by Bradford Park Avenue, 3 weeks after beating them in the League, and despite taking the lead after only four minutes. Frank Hindle missed a first-half penalty as Chester went out 2-1. In the Welsh Cup Chester were lucky to get past Rhyl, with 2 goals in the last six minutes, from Burgess. In goal for Rhyl was George Scales, on long term loan from Chester, and he proved that he had lost none of his agility by saving a Burgess penalty. In the 6th Round Chester were easily beaten by Southern League leaders Merthyr Tydfil, despite twice taking the lead, and only an inspired performance by Threadgold prevented further embarrassment.

At Christmas Chester played their first ever League match against Shrewsbury Town, winning 3-1 in a game with plenty of thrills but little good football. Later in the season the other northern League babes, Scunthorpe United, paid their first visit to Sealand Road, and after taking a first-half lead were eventually beaten 4-1 thanks to a hat-trick by the dynamic Burgess. The 1950/51 season also marked the end of New Brighton's career in the Football League. Chester were the opponents for the last game at the Tower Ground but were defeated 1-0 in a thrilling game full of goalmouth action.

The season ended with Chester in 13th position, but the financial haemorrhage had been stemmed as the club reported a small profit of £43 thanks to a net gain of more than £3,000 in the transfer market. This was the first AGM for new chairman Sam Argyle who had taken over after the resignation of Sir Thomas Brocklebank midway through the season.

One of the players to leave at the end of the season was Tommy Tilston who had been associated with the club since 1944. His appearances had been limited and he had frequently been the butt of criticism from Chester fans, but he went on to average more than a goal every three games with Tranmere, Wrexham and Crystal Palace. Also departing was stalwart defender Dave McNeil who was awarded a Testimonial against Everton in recognition of his 12 year association with the club.

Frank Brown had a busy summer as he began his 14th season as manager. The most significant signing was that of full-back Ray Gill from Manchester City, who went on to break the appearance record in his 11 seasons at the club. He was joined by Bill Jones, also from Manchester City, along with Fletcher (Birmingham), Port (Hull), Wright (Leeds), Yates (Sheffield United) and Smyth (Cardiff). The influx of players brought a good start to the season and Chester were top after six games. However, by mid-October, Chester had lost their most influential strikers with the transfer of Burgess to Crystal Palace and Billy Foulkes to Newcastle for a record fee of £12,000 plus £500 if and when capped. Within a week Chester had received this bonus as Foulkes played for Wales against England and scored with his first kick in international football. Although left-winger 'Wee Willie' Windle was a sound performer, following his arrival from Lincoln, Chester struggled to find any real consistency in the forward line and they slowly slipped down the table.

In the FA Cup Chester recovered from 1-0 down with 10 minutes to go to beat Accrington 2-1, the winner coming from Kirkpatrick in the dying seconds. In the 2nd Round the amateurs from Leyton were out of their depth as Chester triumphed 5-2, and the club earned themselves a visit to Chelsea in Round 3.

Geoff Coffin looks on as Peter Greenwood (white shirt on ground), just fails to make contact in the F.A.Cup replay. Chelsea players (standing) is future Chester manager John Harris.

**MATCH TO REMEMBER**
**CHESTER 2 CHELSEA 3**
**FA CUP 3RD ROUND REPLAY - JANUARY 16TH 1952**

*After a 2-2 draw at Stamford Bridge the largest home crowd in the club's history gathered at Sealand Road to see if Chester could spring a major surprise in the replay.*

*Although play in the first half was end to end the best chances fell to Chelsea. After 17 minutes Roy Bentley had a goal disallowed for offside, but eight minutes later the same player rocketed a header into the net to give Chelsea the lead. Chester continued to attack but trailed by the only goal at half-time. There was plenty for the crowd to shout about in the second-half. First of all a shot from Greenwood went through Robertson's legs and appeared to cross the line. The Chester players dashed in to make sure but Chelsea cleared the ball for a corner as the home players appealed for a goal. After 55 minutes Chester grabbed an amazing equaliser. Coffin was charged down by Harris as he raced for goal, and as the ball ran loose he appealed for a penalty. With all eyes focused on the referee Willemse, the Chelsea defender, tapped the ball back to his keeper only to see the ball trickle over the line for a Chester goal.*

*With no further scoring the game went into extra time and the turning point came when Harris pulled back the lively Coffin as he had a clear run on goal. The resultant free kick came to nothing and Chelsea took advantage of this lucky break with two quick goals. Firstly the outstanding Lee was unlucky to deflect a Bentley shot into his own net, and then Smith scored from close range after Armstrong's penalty had been saved. Chester responded immediately with Coffin heading in from a corner but there was no further scoring and Chelsea went through to the 4th Round after 210 minutes of battling resistance from Chester.*

*Chester - Threadgold, Molyneux, Morement, Morris, Lee, Astbury, Fletcher, Whitlock, Coffin, Greenwood, Windle.*
*Chelsea - Robertson, Bathgate, Willemse, Armstrong, Harris, Dickson, Gray,D'Arcy, Smith, Bentley, Capbell*

**MATCH TO REMEMBER**
**OLDHAM ATHLETIC 11 CHESTER 2**
**FOOTBALL LEAGUE DIVISION 3 NORTH - JANUARY 19TH 1952**

*Only 3 days after their epic FA cup-tie with Chelsea, a weary Chester travelled to Boundary Park and experienced their heaviest ever League defeat. In a game played in snowy, Arctic, conditions, Chester twice took the lead but were ultimately overwhelmed by a stronger Oldham side.*

*Chester went in front after 16 minutes when 16-year-old goalkeeper Eddie Hopkinson failed to reach a Billy Windle centre, and defender Goodfellow was forced to handle on the line. Ralph Morement scored from the ensuing penalty, but Oldham levelled 5 minutes later with a goal from Eric Gemmell. After 26 minutes Hopkinson, who later went on to play for England, missed another cross and Bill Jones put Chester 2-1 ahead. From then on it was all downhill and five goals in 15 minutes from Goodfellow, Munro, Warner, Smith and Gemmell put Oldham in a commanding position with a 6-2 half-time lead.*

*The second-half was a personal success for Oldham centre-forward Eric Gemmell who scored all five goals to take his own tally to seven in the 11-2 win. It was a display where Chester's form hit rock bottom and it was hard to believe that the same team had only been narrowly beaten by Chelsea. In the end it was only a brilliant goalkeeping performance from Harry Threadgold that kept the score down to 11.*

*Chester - Threadgold, Molyneux, Morement, Morris, Lee, Astbury, Jones, Whitlock, Coffin, Greenwood, Windle.*
*Oldham Athletic - Hopkinson, Bell, Hardwick, Warner, Whyte, Goodfellow, Munro, Smith, Gemmell, McKennan, Ormond.*

They travelled to London without Ray Gill and with promising half-back Sam Morris making only his second appearance for the club. Chester, playing with fervour and spirit, took the lead after 12 minutes when Coffin chested down a Windle cross and hooked the ball past the keeper. Although Chelsea had opportunities to equalise, Chester extended their lead early in the second half when Greenwood calmly placed a Fletcher cross into the net. A cup sensation was now on the cards but Chelsea recovered to draw level with goals from Gray and a controversial penalty from Armstrong after Lee had allegedly handled. Chelsea won the replay 3-2, but the honours had gone to Chester with Lee and Coffin particularly impressive.

By February Chester were 3rd from bottom in the League, although the signing of the strong, bustling centre-forward Don Travis from Oldham and inside-forward Fred Richardson from West Bromwich Albion caused a small improvement in fortunes and they finished the season in 19th position. The sale of Burgess and Foulkes allowed the club to make a record profit of £4,321 and there was another significant departure in the close season when Harry Threadgold joined Sunderland for a four figure fee. After only a season at Roker Park Threadgold moved to Southend where he was first choice keeper for just under 10 years, making more than 300 appearances.

Ralph Morement was appointed captain for the 1952/53 season and Frank Brown increased competition in the forward line with the signing of seven strikers. Unfortunately none of the new signings were able to find the net consistently and the main goalscoring threat continued to come from Don Travis.

After two games the weaknesses in the team were already evident and there were nine positional changes for the game against Bradford City with four players making their debut in a 2-0 win. John Molyneux played full-back in this game but his appearances were limited by National Service and Chester missed his authority in defence.

In October, four successive defeats started alarm bells ringing and a special meeting of the board was held to discuss the poor results. A decision was made to look for a reputable player/coach who could perform a task similar to that of Raich Carter at Hull, or Peter Doherty at Doncaster. As usual money proved to be a major obstacle and after an unsuccessful search a decision was deferred until the end of the season. However it was clear that Frank Brown's position was now under threat and the season continued with reports of the Directors influencing team selection. Inevitably results suffered as the team was chopped and changed, and both Kirkpatrick and Morement asked for transfers after being dropped.

The year ended with a thrilling 4-3 victory over Wrexham in the Welsh Cup, the winner coming from Windle with a superlative shot two minutes from time. Chester continued to find the net regularly in the Welsh Cup and reached the Final for the 8th occasion where they faced non-League Rhyl at Bangor. In the Final all the action came in the first six minutes as Rhyl took a 2-1 lead. Although Chester were the more polished team and attacked for most of the game they could not break down the Rhyl defence and the Welsh club were able to retain the trophy. This proved to be the first of three Finals in just over a week, as Chester also reached the Final of the Cheshire Bowl and the Lancashire Cup. In the Cheshire Bowl they were beaten 3-1 by Stockport with the consolation goal coming from Travis. The same player was on the mark four days later, but he could not prevent a hat-trick of defeats as an experienced Manchester City side outclassed Chester in a 5-1 Lancashire Cup victory.

Results in the League continued to be disappointing and a single win in the last 11 games left Chester in 20th place. The penultimate game of the season proved to be a game to forget as Chester suffered a 7-0 defeat at the hands of Wrexham. The team were dogged by misfortune as keeper Wright was carried off early in the game after a collision with Heggie. Morement took over in goal and was partly responsible for four of the goals, but more seriously the injury to Wright cut short a promising career.

The inevitable parting of the ways with Frank Brown came at the end of the season when his contract was cancelled by mutual consent. Brown, a likeable character, had been a popular manager with the players and had always shown great integrity. He had developed some good young talent but in latter years his hands had been tied in the transfer market. After leaving Chester he went on to manage Stafford Rangers in the Cheshire County League and as scout for Liverpool.

Favourite to replace Brown was Tommy Jones the ex-Everton and Wales centre-half who was player-manager at Pwllheli. However he turned the job down and the eventual appointment of 54-year-old Louis Page came as something of a surprise. The experienced Page, a well-known football personality, had been secretary-manager at Swindon for 8 years having also previously been manager at Yeovil, Newport and Glentoran. During his playing days with Stoke, Northampton, Burnley, Manchester United and Port Vale he had earned six England caps and had once scored six goals in a game for Burnley, a record for a winger.

Another loss of £5,130 gave Page little option but to concentrate on local players although he did bring in ex-Swindon winger John Thomas who had been playing with Headington United in non-League football.

His two other signings, Jimmy Rolfe (Liverpool) and Ken Fletcher (Everton), both arrived on free transfers. Page arranged a series of private trials for local players and 52 amateurs were signed as the club entered teams in the Cheshire County, West Cheshire and Chester and District Leagues.

For the 1953/54 season Chester reverted to blue and white stripes after a season playing in white shirts and black shorts. Although the club played good football at times, they struggled to score goals and soon found themselves at the wrong end of the table. Off the field enthusiasm in the club had also reached a low ebb and membership of the supporters club had dwindled from 1300 to less than 100. Chairman Argyle made an appeal to local businesses for monetary assistance but met with little response as the financial situation worsened.

Just before Christmas Bernard Morrey was signed from Newport and he had an inspired game when Chester faced 2nd placed Gateshead in January. With supporters expecting the worst the team finally clicked and achieved a magnificent 5-0 victory. This result proved to be a flash in the pan and at the end of January Chester were bottom of the 3rd Division North for the first time in their history.

Another two ex-Swindon players arrived before the end of the season, Mike Betteridge and Ken Brandon. Page was able to use his contacts in Swindon to persuade them to waive the fee for Betteridge who had been captain and ever-present for the Robins in 1952/53. Neither player was able to prevent Chester from finishing in last place as the club were forced to make their first ever application for re-election to the League. In the weeks leading up to the end of the season rumours circulated that Chester would not apply for re-election if they finished bottom because of the financial difficulties being experienced. The club vigorously denied these rumours and when the re-election vote took place they came top of the poll and were comfortably re-admitted.

There was another appearance in the Welsh Cup Final where the opposition were Flint Town United of the Welsh League North. The Flint team, including ex-Chester player Ernie Bryan, were captained by Billy Hughes a favourite at Sealand Road during the war. Before the game the Cheshire Observer declared that '*defeat in such a game, by a neighbouring non-League side, would be the last straw*', and Chester plumbed new depths in losing 2-0. Much of the blame fell on the lame attacking display and only Ron Hughes came out of the game with any credit. In the end a dismal season was only rescued by victory in the Cheshire Bowl Final against Tranmere after a replay. The winning goal came from Ray Gill in the 1st minute of extra time, a reward for perhaps the seasons most consistent performer.

Despite stringent economies the club made another huge loss of £5,475 leaving them more than £11,000 in debt. The club decided to make available another 8000 shares at £1 each but the offer met with a lukewarm response.
The only new players that Page could sign were Roy Halstead, an inside-forward from Burnley, and Herbert 'Monty' Wright from Stockport, the latter signed in exchange for John Thomas. Significantly Don Travis, leading goalscorer in the previous two seasons, was transferred to Oldham and with no replacement signed the outlook was not encouraging. The pre-season trial matches did not augur well and for the first few games of the season Ray Gill was surprisingly given the job of leading the attack. The move met with little success despite 5 points from the first 3 games, and Ronnie Hughes was handed the number 9 shirt against Grimsby. With four wins in the next six games, including seven goals from Hughes, it looked like the young 'Pageboys' were in for a better season. Page himself declared that '*the brand of football played is more important than actual playing results. Good football will bring victories in plenty and the present team will win matches*'. However his optimism proved unfounded and after beating Crewe at the start of October Chester only managed another six wins and a mere 28 goals during the remainder of the season.

In the FA Cup a shambling performance against Gateshead resulted in a 6-0 defeat but once again Chester reached the Welsh Cup Final. In the Semi-Final they had unexpectedly beaten 1st Division Cardiff, and for the 3rd season in succession they faced non-League opposition in the Final. It was only brilliant goalkeeping by Bob Jones that allowed Chester to escape with a draw as Barry Town of the Southern League dominated the game. Chester took the lead against the run of play when Brandon scored a soft goal just before the break, and they almost extended the lead in the second-half when Molyneux hit the bar with a 40 yard free kick. Barry equalised shortly afterwards but could not manage a winner despite their overall superiority. Such was Chester's standing that Barry were favourites for the replay, and although they put up a better performance it was the non-League side who snatched a narrow 4-3 win. On the same day another Final was lost when the Reserves were beaten 3-2 by Tranmere in the Cheshire Bowl.

Although the standard of football was often encouraging it was poor finishing that let the team down and three goalless draws in April sealed a second successive re-election appeal. Meanwhile, with rumours circulating in the city about the future of the club, a public meeting was arranged in March to consider the escalating debt. An encouraging turnout of 1,000 debated the issues and a shilling fund was started to meet the £5,000 that was urgently needed to keep the club going.

The Supporters Club and Supporters Committee also agreed to disband their organisations and join a new association in a joint effort to help the club. The new Supporters Association was to make a considerable contribution to the Football Club over the next few years with some sizeable financial donations.

THE CHESTER FOOTBALL CLUB, LTD.
President: T.Sarl-Williams,Esq.

Chairman of Directors:-
S.Argyle, Esq.
Manager:- L.A.Page.
Secretary:- W.P.Peters.

The Stadium,
Sealand Road,
Chester.

16th.February, 1955.

Dear Sir/Madam,

Decreasing support and the ever increasing costs connected with the Company, have caused your Chairman and the Directors much concern for some considerable time.

Expected improvements having to date failed to materialise, you are invited to attend a Meeting of Shareholders, to be held at the Town Hall, Chester, on Tuesday, 1st.March,1955, at 7p.m., to further their efforts to ensure continuity of League Football in the City of Chester.

In addition, a Public Meeting has been called to follow the Shareholders' Meeting, at 7.45p.m. in the Town Hall, at which His Worship the Mayor will preside.

By Order of the Directors,

W.P.Peters,
Secretary.

Admission to the Shareholders' Meeting will be by production of this Notice.

*Letter sent to Shareholders.*

During the close season John Molyneux was transferred to Liverpool for £4,000 with another £1,500 after 12 appearances. Molyneux's development had been impaired by National Service but his speed and stamina proved a great asset to Liverpool and he went on to make 228 appearances at full-back for the Anfield club. The close season also marked the retirement of loyal servant Tommy Astbury, one of the best players to wear a Chester shirt, after 16 years with the club. Every effort was made to strengthen the side for the 1955/56 season and experience was added in the shape of Jack Haines from Rochdale. Haines, an inside-forward, had made nearly 300 appearances for Swansea, Leicester, West Bromwich and Bradford PA and scored two goals in his single international appearance for England against Switzerland.

Other signings included Jimmy Collins, Barrow's captain and leading scorer, Charlie Jolley, an ex-England Youth international from Tranmere, George Allman (Stockport), Bernard Hackett (Aston Villa), Fred Tomley (Liverpool) and John Devine and Keith Griffiths (Rhyl). The restructuring was completed by Frank Wayman a skilful inside-left from Preston.

After crashing to a 6-1 defeat at Grimsby, Chester started to play improved football with Jack Haines a particular influence on the side. Increased interest drew a crowd of more than 15,000 for the visit of Wrexham where Haines was the hero with two second-half goals in a 2-1 win. By the end of October Chester were 6th but the cracks began to show against Oldham and Workington and November heralded a run of seven successive defeats; this included a 5-2 home defeat by 'glamour' side Derby who raced into a 5-0 lead within the first 38 minutes. Chester opened 1956 with their first double of the season, against Darlington, but the following week they were well beaten in atrocious conditions at Accrington.

On a pitch covered in 6 inches of snow and with driving wet snow falling throughout the game Chester lost Ray Griffiths before the end suffering from the extreme cold.

The forward line continued to lack cohesion and Jolley was unlucky not to be given a longer run in the team having scored 21 goals in 24 games for the Reserves. However there were encouraging displays by the whole-hearted Whitlock and the ever-dependable Gill. Five points out of six over Easter helped save Chester from re-election, despite a failure to win their last seven games. By this time a decision had already been made not to renew Louis Page's contract and the search was on for a big name player-manager. Page was unlucky to take over at Chester with the club at its lowest ebb and with little opportunity to move into the transfer market. After leaving Chester he scouted for Leicester City and died in Birkenhead in 1959.

The replacement for Page was John Harris of Chelsea, the man who had been given such a hard time by Geoff Coffin in the 1952 cup-tie. Chelsea were honouring a promise made after this game to do all they could to help Chester, and they offered Harris without a fee and with the strongest recommendation. Harris, a full-back or centre-half, had started his playing career with Swansea in 1934, and went on to play for Tottenham and Wolves. After the war Chelsea paid £8,000 for his services and he made 326 appearances for the Blues, winning a Championship medal in his final season at Stamford Bridge. Harris signed a four year contract, two years as player-manager and two as manager.

For the first time in a number of years prospects appeared favourable for the 1956/57 season. In the previous season total attendances had increased by more than 30,000 and a small profit of £734 was announced, as a wave of enthusiasm gripped the club after the appointment of Harris. The manager's first move was to make Mickey Fields and Ray Griffiths part-time professionals, and his first signing was Ron Hansell an inside-forward from Norwich City. Another cause for optimism was the news that Billy Foulkes was returning to Sealand Road. Foulkes had suffered a slipped disc playing for Southampton and had been regaining his fitness playing for Winsford United.

On his return Foulkes announced that: *'I would not have signed for any other Football League club'*. Harris also signed two half-backs, John Mulholland from Southampton and George Davies a tough tackler with six years experience at Sheffield Wednesday.

Chester showed fine form in drawing the first two games against Wrexham and Derby, but the pre-season optimism soon disintegrated as 10 of the next 11 games were lost. By the end of September they were bottom of the table and Harris was experiencing the same problems as his predecessors in trying to run the club on shoestring finances. Once again the forward line was proving to be a problem as promising approach work was not capitalised on. In November another former player returned to the club when inside-forward Phil Turner signed from Accrington after also playing for Carlisle, Bradford PA and Scunthorpe. His first home game, against Barrow, was Chester's first home FA Cup-tie since 1952. A failure to take chances cost them dearly and Barrow took them back to Holker Street after a goalless draw. In the replay Chester took an early lead when Turner was presented with a gift goal but Barrow equalised just after the break and went on to win comfortably 3-1.

In January, Harris signed centre-forward Barry Jepson from Mansfield. Jepson, a part-time player who worked for the coal board, faced Mansfield in his second game with something to prove to his detractors at Field Mill. He made his point in fine style with a hat-trick in a 6-2 win. This result proved the exception in another disappointing season, and once again it was five points out of six over Easter that pulled them out of the mire.

For the 2nd time in three years Chester surprised First Division Cardiff City in the Welsh Cup as goals from George Davies and Jepson eliminated a side containing seven internationals. In the Semi-Final Chester faced Wrexham but neither side were happy with the Welsh FA's choice of Rhyl as the venue for the game. Both teams preferred to play the game at the Racecourse Ground where a large crowd would have been expected, and there were less than 3,000 present to see a Wrexham victory.

There was a more positive result in the Lancashire Senior Cup Semi-Final where Chester beat Liverpool's Central League championship winning side having eliminated Rochdale and Accrington in earlier rounds. The Final, against Burnley, had to be held over until the 1957/58 season because the Lancashire side were on a continental tour. When the match was held in October 1957 Chester became the first club to take the trophy out of Lancashire, a Mickey Fields goal giving them a 1-0 win. Harris prepared for the 1957/58 season knowing that an improvement in form was vital if Chester wanted to take their place in the new Third Division. A re-structuring of the League meant that the top 12 from the Third Division North and South would form a new Division 3 while the bottom 12 would form the new 4th Division. Sam Argyle and the Chester board had their reservations about the new setup, being concerned about the financial burden involved in the extra travelling.

The remission of entertainment tax and the considerable efforts of the Supporters Association, who had contributed £5,000, helped balance the books and the club made a small profit of £77. John Harris made widespread changes for the new season and among the outgoings were Hansell, Mulholland, Haines, Collins, Turner, Allman and Hackett. Into the squad came left-winger Jimmy Mason, one of Accrington's Scottish contingent, along with another Scot, Jimmy Anderson of Bristol Rovers, for a substantial fee.

Full-back Bill Souter was signed from Burnley as was utility player Aled Williams. The loss of Sam Morris through injury saw the signing of 31-year-old Jack Saunders from Crystal Palace, a player who had played alongside Harris at Chelsea. Billy Foulkes took over as captain replacing Ray Gill who had elected to go part-time. Despite all the changes the faults of the previous year were still evident in the trial games and there were doubts as to whether the side had been strengthened in the right areas.

Early results substantiated these beliefs as the attack continued to lack imagination, but good away wins at York and Accrington kept them in with a chance of making the top 12. At the end of October the search for an inside-forward came to an end with the signing of 38-year-old Stan Pearson from Bury. Pearson, a fine opportunist with excellent distribution, had made his name with Manchester United scoring 128 goals in 315 appearances. He was a scorer in the 1948 Cup Final win over Blackpool and had won eight England caps between 1948 and 1952. Pearson had joined Bury in 1954 and Harris felt that he was the man to bring some steadiness to the attack.

Pearson could not make his debut immediately because of flu, but his signing inspired the forwards to the most convincing performance of the season in beating Stockport 3-0. His long-awaited debut came in the FA Cup 1st Round against Gateshead and Pearson showed a stamp of class with a series of intelligent passes in a real thriller. Chester went into a 2-0 lead with a Jepson header and a goal from Mason, but the Tynesiders pulled back with goals from Baldridge and Callender. Early in the second-half Pearson celebrated his debut with a goal after Bullock had slipped a free kick into his path, but Gateshead scored again to make it 3-3. With time slipping away Foulkes capitalised on a defensive mistake to put Chester into the 2nd Round for the first time since 1952.

*Team talk on the annexe - in the background, the rear of the old stand.*

In the next tie, a first half hat-trick by Jepson put Chester in a commanding position against Bradford City, but a fighting recovery by the Yorkshire side resulted in a 3-3 draw. In the replay at Valley Parade the tables were turned and Bradford City raced into a 3-0 lead but, unlike Chester, they were able to hold on to their lead and go through to the next round.

On Christmas Day Chester beat Bury 2-1 but failed to complete the double the following day when Jepson missed a sitter in a goalless draw. This proved to be the first of five games in which only two goals were scored, both by centre-half Saunders, and Harris signed outside-left Gordon Richards for £750 from Wrexham. Richards had frequently been the bogey man when playing against Chester and he marked his debut with a goal in an encouraging 4-2 win at Southport. A week later York made the journey to Sealand Road and were trounced 9-2 with Barry Jepson becoming the first Chester player to score five in a game since Tommy Jennings in 1932. York were hampered by the loss of their goalkeeper after 30 minutes but Chester could have easily repeated their 12-0 win but for some good saves by replacement Brown.

Despite 16 goals in three games, Chester had left themselves too much to do and a series of drawn games consigned them to the new 4th Division. They saved their best performance of the season for the last game when they hammered runners-up Accrington 5-1 with Pearson in his element.

The 1957/58 season ended with another appearance in the Welsh Cup Final where they played Wrexham at Sealand Road. Wrexham, who had qualified for the new 3rd Division, were the dominant side as Chester failed to make an impression. It was the Reds who took the lead midway through the first-half when a mistake by Gill let in Murray who put the ball into an empty net. Just before half-time Chester surprisingly pulled themselves back into the game when Hughes scored from the spot after a foul on Foulkes. In the second-half 17-year-old goalkeeper Brian Biggins was the hero for Chester with a series of excellent saves as Chester held on for a draw. Prior to the Final Biggins had only made 2 League appearances and, in the replay at the Racecourse, he again stood between Chester and a heavy defeat. Wrexham took the lead after only two minutes through Murray and went further ahead with a header from Bannan. Royson Evans pulled one back for Chester but it was merely a consolation, and Wrexham were comfortably able to retain the cup.

In terms of football played it had been one of the best seasons for many years and a final position of 20th did not reflect the advances that had been made. Pearson had added a new dimension to the attack, but they still needed a strong inside-forward who could score goals. Meanwhile the revival under Harris had not gone unnoticed and in April, Cardiff offered him the position of assistant manager. Harris showed commendable loyalty in turning the job down but it was clear that Chester would have difficulty holding on to their talented young manager as they embarked on a new era in Division 4.

*Assembling goal-posts at the Sealand Road end, under the watchful eye of Stan Pearson (leaning against wall).*

# PROMOTION - AT LAST 1958 - 1975
# CHAPTER 10

In their last season in Division 3 North, Chester had made a surprising profit of £2,600, largely due to the sale of keeper Bob Jones to Blackburn Rovers for £3,000. However this was a long way short of the estimated £16,000 required for floodlights which were now deemed essential for progress. The early kick-offs were costing the club money, for instance only 3,220 turned up for a 3pm mid-week game against Hartlepools compared with 6,655 the following Saturday against Aldershot. A Floodlight Fund was started to raise the money with the Supporters Association leading the way, and by the end of the 1958/59 season £5000 had been raised.

In preparation for the new season Harris brought in Bobby Hunt and Brian Griffiths from Wrexham along with Harry Webster, an inside-forward with 10 years experience at Bolton. Also new to the club, but not to the city, was Chester born George Spruce, a 35-year-old centre-half from Barnsley. Spruce had slipped through Chester's fingers in 1948 when Wrexham had spotted him playing in the Chester and District League for Heath Rangers.

Chester kicked off their first 4th Division campaign with a home game against Torquay. They certainly looked the part in a new 'continental' style kit which featured the City's coat of arms in the centre of the shirt.

Unfortunately a dismal display saw them lose 2-0, but they won plaudits a few days later in their first League game in London when they drew 3-3 at Crystal Palace.

In September Harris signed goalkeeper Ronnie Howells from Worcester City.

*Norman Bullock just fails to get his head to the ball in the Christmas 1958 match v. Millwall.*

Howells had been Cardiff's first team goalkeeper for six seasons, winning two caps for Wales in 1954, but had dropped into non-League football in 1957. The move to Chester gave him a chance to resurrect his League career at the age of 31. In the same month George Spruce made his Chester debut against York, but had the misfortune to head into his own goal with 30 seconds remaining to give York an equaliser. The much maligned forwards hit form in October when Chester won five successive games, their best sequence since 1946. The last of these, a scintillating 4-2 win over 2nd placed Exeter, took Chester to 8th position. The following week it was a case of 'after the Lord Mayor's show' as they were well beaten by another title challenging side, Coventry City.

In the FA Cup Chester were given a hard struggle by Southern League Boston United in the 1st Round. Bobby Williams was surprisingly chosen at centre-forward, but the decision appeared justified as Chester went into an early 2-0 lead. Just before half-time Boston pulled back a goal, and then Howells brilliantly saved a penalty, only for the Lincolnshire side to equalise from the resulting corner.

After 73 minutes Pearson hooked the ball into the net for what proved to be the winner, although Boston still had time to hit the bar near the end. In the 2nd round, 3rd Division Bury came to Sealand Road and went away with a draw after an astonishing refereeing decision.

Chester were leading 1-0 with less than 10 minutes to go when Bullock was brought down in the penalty area and play stopped with all the players expecting a penalty.

The referee ran over to where Bullock was lying and appeared to point to the spot as the linesman flagged to confirm the offence. Meanwhile Bury goalkeeper Adams gathered the ball, punted it up field and to the amazement of everyone the referee waved play on. Before Chester could react Parker had the ball in the net for a Bury equaliser, and pandemonium broke out as the Chester players vigorously protested the goal, but to no avail. The following Tuesday, two snap goals gave Bury a 2-1 victory and Chester missed out on a visit from Arsenal in the 3rd Round.

Chester maintained their League position into 1959 but poor defensive performances against Gillingham and Shrewsbury cost them valuable points. Against Shrewsbury, Chester threw away a two goal lead by conceding five in 14 minutes to go down 5-3. February saw the signing of full-back George Ashfield from Aston Villa and Eric Davis from Scunthorpe. Davis arrived for his debut only 10 minutes before kick-off, but scored Chester's 2nd goal against Bradford PA with a perfect header in the last minute.

In March Chester lost the man who had done so much to turn round the club's fortunes when John Harris accepted the position as manager of Sheffield United. Harris had improved the standard of football at Sealand Road and his departure was a huge blow to the club. There were more than 60 applications to be his successor but the job went to the fan's choice, Stan Pearson, who made the step up from skipper on merit. Pearson marked his appointment with a point-winning goal at Exeter, but had to wait for the last game of the season for his first victory, against Darlington. A final position of 13th proved a disappointment after such a promising first-half to the season .

Pearson retired from playing at the end of the season to concentrate on the management role. When he played his final match, against Crewe on April 22nd, he became Chester's oldest League player at the age of 40 years and 101 days. Jack Saunders, Jimmy Mason and Phil Whitlock were among a number of players released, but few players were signed as Pearson expressed his commitment to develop the youngsters at the club. The new players were Frank Clempson (Stockport), Jack Capper (Lincoln) and John Walton, an England amateur international from Kettering, who had previously played League football with Manchester United, Bury, Burnley and Coventry. Clempson, a wing-half who had made more than 250 appearances at Edgeley Park, was made captain but there was concern that Pearson had not brought in enough new blood to an aging side.

Chester started the season in new club colours of green shirts with gold facings and white shorts. For the first game of the 1959/60 season, a defeat at Notts County, Chester had only one player under 25, in John Pimlott, and defeats in the next three games gave Chester their worst ever start to a League season. After a drab goalless draw against Oldham, Pearson moved to solve the lack of penetration in attack by signing Walter Kelly from Stockport for just under £2,000. The bustling Kelly made a memorable debut by scoring two goals as Chester produced an assured display to recover from a 3-1 deficit and beat Crystal Palace 4-3. Results continued to improve and by the end of the year Chester held a mid-table position.

As the season progressed Pearson gradually gave opportunities for the youngsters to establish themselves in the team. Alex Croft and Jerry Ireland, who had made their debuts the previous season, were both given runs in the side and there were debuts for Jimmy Cooper, Ron Davies, Gerry Citron, Colin Jones, Les Stopford and Derek Owen. Cooper showed great early promise but the jewel in the crown was 17-year-old Ron Davies who, after 11 goals in 19 games for the Reserves, made his debut at Workington. It proved to be an ignominious debut as Chester slumped to a 5-0 defeat, but Davies led the attack well and showed good distribution. Against Torquay, on Easter Saturday, Chester fielded one of their youngest ever forward lines comprising Cooper (18), Stopford (18), Davies (17), Pimlott (20) and Croft (22). Despite the presence of the youngsters Chester slowly slipped down the table in 1960, and there were only three wins in the last 15 games. A final position of 20th left Chester just clear of the re-election zone.

The clear out at the end of the season included Jimmy Anderson, George Ashfield, Eric Davis, Bill Souter and Harry Webster. Also surprisingly released was the virtual ever-present Ron Howells, but Chester could ill-afford to pay his expenses as he continued to live in South Wales. Howells was replaced by Bill Brown the ex-St Mirren goalkeeper from Accrington, while other signings included Tommy Barrett (Plymouth), John Anderson (Rochdale) and John Watson (Everton). Another loss of more than £3,000 put the total liability at £19,000 but, thanks to the Supporters Association, the club were able to commence the erection of floodlights.

The lights were completed in time for Chester's first game in the new League Cup competition, against 2nd Division Leyton Orient. In a dramatic game Orient held a comfortable 2-0 lead at half-time, a lead they maintained until the final four minutes. With time running out 17-year-old debutant Alan Pritchard stroked a pass to Davies who crashed a shot past George in the Orient goal. Two minutes later Cooper let fly with the equaliser to complete a stirring comeback. Orient narrowly won the replay 1-0 and Chester returned to League action where they had got off to a poor start.

Away form had been particularly bad and it was the end of October before the first point was picked up on their travels, at Stockport. Pearson struggled to find the right blend of experience and youth as supporters grew more dissatisfied and patience was stretched to the limit when Chester were defeated at home by Hartlepools. This was 'Pools first away win in 32 games against one of the poorest Chester sides seen at Sealand Road. However, less than a month later, there was an amazing 3-0 win over League leaders Crystal Palace as Chester rolled up their sleeves against the slick Londoners. Palace gained their revenge at the end of January with a classy 5-1 win, and after a dismal 0-0 draw with Crewe, Pearson finally entered the transfer market. In came wing-half Derek Hennin and 21-year-old Malcolm Edwards for a joint fee of £4,000. Hennin, an England youth international, had joined Bolton in 1949 and was the proud possessor of an FA Cup winners medal, while Edwards had won two caps for the Welsh Under-23s.

Both players made their debuts at Wrexham and helped Chester to a 2-1 win, the first points away from home in four months. Despite another win in the next game, against Rochdale, the rot was now well established, and Chester were firmly entrenched in the re-election zone. A first ever visit to champions-elect Peterborough resulted in a 6-0 defeat with the League's leading scorer, Terry Bly, scoring four including a hat-trick in seven minutes. Chester's fate was sealed with dreary defeats against Darlington and Doncaster and they needed a win in the last game against fellow strugglers Hartlepools to avoid the wooden spoon. Chester held a 4-3 lead with three minutes to go, but a late penalty robbed them of a valuable point and they finished one adrift of 'Pools.

Although the youngsters showed promise Pearson had placed too much reliance on their abilities. By the time he entered the transfer market confidence was at a low ebb and, despite some impressive performances by Hennin, the team were faced with an impossible task.

The introduction of floodlights gave Chester a good case when they went cap in hand to the League and they finished comfortably top in the re-election vote. The floodlights had also helped boost finances as the club arranged attractive friendlies against Manchester United and Third Lanark.

*1962: Ron Davies (no.9) in action against Workington.*

Pearson was determined not to repeat the mistakes of the previous year and there was a large turnover in playing staff in preparation for the 1961/62 season. Among the departures was that of Frank Clempson, who was appointed player-manager of Hyde United taking Billy Foulkes with him. The first signing was 35-year-old Joe Kennedy, a solid defender, on a free transfer from West Bromwich Albion. Kennedy had made nearly 400 appearances for Albion in his 12 years and appeared at right back in their 1954 FA Cup winning side. He was followed by five free transfer signings in five days as Billy White (Wrexham), Fred Donaldson (Exeter), Wally Bellett (Leyton Orient), Fred Morris (Gillingham) and John Hardie (Oldham) all arrived at Sealand Road.

The surprise signing however was Republic of Ireland international Peter Fitzgerald from Leeds United for £3,000. Fitzgerald had started his career with his home town club Waterford United joining Dutch champions Sparta Rotterdam for £5,000 in 1959. He returned from Holland in 1960 and played for Leeds United where he gained the first three of his five senior Irish caps. During his first season at Chester Fitzgerald earned another two caps when he played in both World Cup qualifying games against Czechoslovakia. This earned him the distinction of being the first Chester player to be capped at senior level for a country other than Wales. The pre-season signings were completed with the arrival of left-winger Mervyn Jones from Crewe for £1,000. The industrious Hennin was made captain and there was a significant change behind the scenes where Reg Rowlands took over as chairman after the death of Sam Argyle.

The season opened with a narrow win over Oldham and after eight games Chester were 4th, but this was a prelude to the most disastrous series of results in the club's history.

Defeat at Doncaster on September 19th heralded a run of 26 League games without a win, broken only by an FA Cup win over Midland League Ashington. By the time Chester faced Morecambe in the 2nd Round, the club were in the middle of another crisis. With the fans having lost faith in the team the game became important both psychologically and financially with Pearson describing it as '*the most important match of the season*'. Chester, without the masterly Kennedy, had 37-year-old part-timer Ray Gill back in the side and a shaky defence gifted Morecambe a goal after only two minutes. Davies and Cartlidge both missed excellent opportunities but as the game wore on it became clear that Chester did not have the marksmen with the ability to take advantage of the few chances that were being carved out. Sheer desperation in the last few minutes saw Morecambe twice clear the ball off the line, but they held on to their lead and after the game a noisy crowd assembled outside demanding Pearson's resignation.

*Bill Lambton*

The fans got their wish and three days later a disappointed Pearson parted with the club. During his reign limited resources had forced Pearson to rely on youngsters, and although they created an initial impact many of them failed to live up to their early potential. At the start of the season Pearson had gambled on a number of new signings to support the youngsters but the team had failed to gell. A decision on the appointment of a new manager was held over until 1962 and a committee took over team selection. With uncertainty surrounding the club results showed no improvement and it was the end of January before an appointment was finally made.

The man given the task of pulling the club out of the doldrums was Bill Lambton, a former Sergeant Major in the army who had worked with the Army Physical Training Corps. His footballing career had only spanned three games in goal for Doncaster in 1946/47, and he had first made his name as a coach in Denmark with KB Copenhagen in the early 1950s. On returning to England he coached at Scunthorpe, Leeds - where he also spent six months as manager, and Grimsby Town who earned a reputation for their 'super-fitness'. In April 1959 he had set the record for the shortest time spent as a manager with three days in charge at Scunthorpe.

'Iron Man Bill' arrived at the club like a whirlwind and immediately set about re-organising the training schedule. Ominously, for the players, he believed in hard work and had revolutionary ideas on training based on physical fitness and speed. Strenuous workouts were introduced, including trampoline exercises, and he enhanced his reputation as a hard man by hanging a notice above the dressing room door with his motto 'Keep fighting' and a pair of boxing gloves underneath. Lambton's first match in charge, against Rochdale, resulted in another defeat and days later there was a dreadful Welsh Cup defeat at home to Holyhead Town. Results in February showed no improvement and at the beginning of March Lambton made his first signings in inside-forwards Ron Hewitt and Bill Myerscough from Coventry. Flint-born Hewitt had been a great favourite at Wrexham in the 1950s averaging almost a goal every other game. In 1957 he had moved to Cardiff and earned five Welsh caps, including three in the 1958 World Cup Finals in Sweden, but he was now coming to the end of his career.

The first home appearance of the new signings came against fellow strugglers Chesterfield, and a 4-1 win gave Chester their first win in 27 League games. Unfortunately March also saw the resignation of Accrington Stanley from the Football League and Chester lost three valuable points leaving them entrenched at the bottom of the 4th Division. Six defeats in the next seven games proved that fitness was not enough, and the defence continued to leak goals. Despite three wins over Easter Chester finished bottom for the 2nd season in succession and the club were fortunate that the demise of Accrington made re-election a formality as Oxford United took the Lancashire club's place. Surprisingly attendances had shown an increase over the season, but a loss of £4,169 was recorded as more than £8,000 was spent on transfer fees.

Lambton acted quickly to sign new players in preparation for his first full season in charge and showed that he was not afraid to make changes, by releasing long serving Ron Hughes and Ray Gill. Another departure was Jimmy Cooper to Southport, a player of whom Chester had expected so much. The defence, who had conceded 96 goals, came in for particular attention with the signings of Wilson (Accrington), Fleming (Workington), Molyneux (Liverpool), Corbishley (Port Vale) and Butler (Notts County). Burly John Butler, a hard tackling right-back at County, was installed at centre-half as Lambton built a defence of giants, but it was the re-signing of John Molyneux, returning to Sealand Road from Liverpool, that grabbed the attention. A change was also made to the kit as Chester reverted to blue and white after the green and gold shirts had brought the club little luck. When Chester took to the field against Gillingham for the first game of the 1962/63 season there were only two players, Peter Fitzgerald and young goalkeeper Reg Barton, who had not been signed by Lambton.

Unfortunately the new look team failed to blend and there was only one win in the first nine games, although the defence had tightened up significantly.

Ron Davies was put on the transfer list in September after failing to gain a regular first team place, but after a good display in the Reserves against Bangor he earned a recall against Workington. He found form with a vengeance and 10 goals in eight games, including a scintillating four against Southport, attracted the scouts. In mid-October Luton stepped in with a bid of £12,200 for Davies and the young Welshman made the move South. Davies went on to play for Norwich, Southampton, Portsmouth, Manchester United and Millwall, and scored nine goals for his Country in 29 games. His last game for Chester had been a 2-2 draw with Newport where Dave 'Slipper' Read, a promising 21-year-old from Wolves, had scored in the first minute of his debut.

*Peter Hauser*

Chester's first game without Davies resulted in their largest ever cup defeat as they were blitzed 9-2 by Leyton Orient in the League Cup 3rd Round. Lambton immediately signed half-back Jimmy McGill from Crewe who made his debut against Bradford City alongside Dennis Keating, a young winger from the Reserves. This proved to be Keatings only first team appearance as he moved to Wellington shortly afterwards and then, unusually, gave up football to become a monk.

A series of good results moved Chester up to mid-table, but the Big Freeze of 1962/63 left them without a League game for two months and some of the momentum was lost. When they returned to action in February goal-scoring again proved to be a problem, despite the signing of George McGowan from Preston. As Chester started to falter their fellow strugglers began to show improved form and the club entered the last game of the season, at home to Chesterfield, requiring one point to avoid re-election. A tame performance saw Chester go down 2-0 and a Newport win against Oxford consigned them to their 3rd successive re-election. Fortunately the standard of applicant was lower than in recent seasons and Chester were comfortably re-elected.

In spite of the inconsistent form attendances held up well and financially the club were in a better position. The sale of Davies resulted in a profit of £9,142 and with the floodlights paid for the overdraft was reduced by £5,000. The financial contribution of the Supporters Association could not be underestimated and 1963 saw their total donation reach £56,000.

Mervyn Jones, Ron Hewitt and David Cartlidge were among the close season departures along with Bill Myerscough who joined Wrexham in exchange for Stan Bennion and George Evans. Other newcomers included John Currie (Workington), Gil Wheaton (Grimsby), Jimmy Humes (Bristol Rovers), and goalkeeper Frank Adams from Bury who had been at the centre of the controversial goal that knocked Chester out of the 1958/59 FA Cup. As the 1963/64 season approached rumours began to circulate that Lambton was about to leave the club and the stories were confirmed at the end of July when his contract was cancelled by mutual consent.

Lambton's final task was to address the players as they reported back for training, and the directors faced the responsibility of finding a new manager before the season started. Although Lambton had brought more discipline to the side his training methods had not been popular with the players and his constant team changes had often been difficult for the supporters to comprehend. A huge turnover at the start of the season had failed to revitalise the team, but Lambton left the foundations of a sound defence in the shape of Corbishley and the excellent Butler.

Once again the directors surprised everyone by choosing 29-year-old Peter Hauser as player-manager. Hauser, a qualified surveyor, had worked in the gold mines of South Africa and was spotted by a Charlton scout while playing for Johannesburg Ramblers in 1955. At the last minute, Blackpool had stepped in to sign him and after breaking into the first team in 1958 he went on to make 83 appearances for the Lancashire club. In 1961 he was transfer-listed by Blackpool at £15,000, but chose to drop into non-League football as a part-timer with Cheltenham Town, which gave him the opportunity to pursue his surveying career.

Hauser's style of management was a total contrast to that of Lambton, and on his arrival he prophetically announced that he *'would not worry if the opposition scored six as long as his side got seven'*.

There was little time for Hauser to prepare for the new season and his first side, utilising the players brought in by Lambton, lost 2-0 at home to Oxford. His first signing was Brian Bades from Stockport, and when Peter Fitzgerald returned to his native Ireland Hauser brought in part-timer Gary Talbot, a press photographer spotted playing in a celebrity charity match. Both players scored on their debuts, a 3-0 win over Newport, and Talbot added two more in the next game against Barrow. The early results showed that Hauser was beginning to get the best out of his players and on the playing field he put in some inspired performances until injury cut short his season. Gary Talbot also missed out through injury, but on his return he hit all four in a marvellous attacking display against Carlisle. Although the forwards were playing well the team was still lacking a creative inside-forward and in December Mike Metcalf was signed from Wrexham for £5,000. Metcalf, a clever ball player, had an impressive goal-scoring record in his six years at the Race-course and smoothly slotted into the team as a flurry of goals took Chester to within touching distance of the leaders.

Between October and March Chester won 10 successive home games, their best run in the Football League, but this was unfort-unately matched by a wretched away record which ultimately cost them a better place in the table. A win in the last game against Aldershot left them in 12th position, amaz-ingly their first top half finish since 1946/47. The season ended with a testimonial game for Billy Peters who left the club in January after 33 years loyal service as secretary.

Although the club was being turned round on the pitch the club made their biggest ever loss of £14,837, largely due to transfer fees paid out.

It had been a satisfactory first season for Hauser and the team were beginning to build a good reputation with their style of play. They had been unlucky to lose Hauser, George McGowan, John Molyneux and John Evans through long term injury, but there was some compensation in the successful conversion of Malcolm Starkey to full-back and the emergence of young Ray Jones, a tough tackling defender.

It was not surprising that Hauser chose to rely on the same players for the 1964/65 season with only Fleming, Bades and Wheaton re-leased. The squad was supplemented by the addition of Dave Berry, a young centre-half from Blackpool, and Hugh Ryden on a free transfer from Stockport. Ryden had attracted Hauser's attention when he scored the only goal against Chester in September and he became the final piece of the jigsaw in what was to become the club's most prolific forward line. Ryden made his debut in the season opener against Aldershot, but Chester were made to look ordinary as they conceded three goals in the first 8 minutes in a 3-1 defeat. Moly-neux, Corbishley and Lee were all dropped for the next game and Chester faced Brad-ford City with the classic 'Famous Five' forward line of Humes, Metcalf, Talbot, Ryden and Morris. Talbot and Morris were both on target in a 3-1 win, but the first home appearance resulted in a disappointing 1-0 setback against Torquay.

In September the forwards began to show their potential and a 3-0 drubbing of Wrexham in the League Cup was followed by a nine goal thriller at Stockport. Chester had raced into a comfortable 4-1 lead after 53 minutes but with less than 15 minutes to go County were back on level terms. The winner came from Talbot who showed real class in beating a defender and swerving round the goalkeeper to place the ball into an empty net. Less than a month later the epic League Cup-tie against Derby County produced another nine goals, and Hauser signed Dave Durie, an ex-colleague from his Blackpool days. Durie had made more than 300 appearances for Blackpool since 1953, mainly at inside-forward, but had retired at the end of the 1963/64 season to concentrate on his business.

**MATCH TO REMEMBER**
**CHESTER 5 DERBY COUNTY 4**
**LEAGUE CUP 2ND ROUND - SEPTEMBER 23RD 1964**

*Chester's 5-4 League Cup victory over 2nd Division Derby County must go down as one of the most thrilling games ever seen at Sealand Road. Despite trailing three times, Chester could not be subdued and there was never a dull moment as both sides produced some scintillating football.*

*Mike Metcalf was the key player in the Chester side as he covered every blade of grass and helped himself to two goals. He opened the scoring with a penalty after 23 minutes but by the 36th minute Derby were 2-1 in front thanks to two headed goals from Eddie Thomas. The lead lasted only two minutes as Metcalf played a one-two with Talbot and slipped the return ball past Matthews. In the next few minutes Matthews pulled off saves from Corbishley, Humes and Metcalf, before John Butler had the misfortune to turn the ball into his own net to put Derby back in front. Once again Derby's joy was short-lived as Elfed Morris picked up the ball straight from the kick-off and waltzed through the Rams defence before slipping the ball over Matthews to make it 3-3. The second half started at the same frantic pace and after Thomas had missed a sitter for Derby, Chester went behind for the 3rd and final time when Durban slotted home a Buxton pass on 65 minutes. At this point Gary Talbot came into his own firing in a brilliant left foot shot on the turn, followed 10 minutes later by what proved to be the winner. Once again Metcalf caused the Derby defence problems and when his shot was blocked by Matthews it fell to Talbot who forced the ball over the line with his chest.*

*It had been a thrilling nights football that lived long in the memory, as the men in blue and white showed they never knew when they were beaten.*

*Chester - Reeves, Jones, Starkey, Hauser, Butler, Corbishley, Humes, Metcalf, Talbot, Ryden, Morris.*
*Derby County - Matthews, Richardson, Ferguson, Webster, Young, Parry, Hughes, Thomas, Buxton, Durban, Cleevely*

Hauser brought Durie back to League football when the business was sold and utilised him at half-back where he forged an excellent partnership alongside Butler and the player-manager himself.

**MATCH TO REMEMBER**
**MANCHESTER UNITED 2 CHESTER 1**
**FA CUP 3RD ROUND - JANUARY 9TH 1965**

*For 45 glorious minutes Chester stood on the verge of a major cup shock as they held a 1-0 lead over 13-2 Cup favourites Manchester United at Old Trafford. Two goals in five second-half minutes eventually gave United a narrow victory, but Chester put up a titanic struggle and the result remained in doubt until the final minute.*

*Cheered on by thousands of Cestrians, Chester took the game to their illustrious opponents straight from the kick-off, and after only five minutes Ryden hit the crossbar with a speculative shot from fully 30 yards. United hit back strongly and debutant Albert Kinsey had a shot cleared off the line by Dave Durie. In the 9th minute Chester took a shock lead with a brilliant goal from Jimmy Humes who dived to head in Ryden's right wing corner. The goal stunned United who pressed forward but found the Chester defence, superbly marshalled by Hauser, in outstanding form. Much of the danger came from midfield master Bobby Charlton, who lived up to his world class reputation, but in general the Reds were restricted to long range efforts.*

*After the interval United had more and more shots on goal, but keeper Dennis Reeves continued to perform heroics, and when Chester broke out of defence they continued to look dangerous with Ryden forcing Dunne into a good save at the foot of the post. On 56 minutes United finally made a breakthrough, when Charlton threaded a beautiful pass through to Best who escaped the close attention of Ray Jones and slotted the ball past Reeves. Every man in Chester's well-drilled defence appealed for offside, but the goal was allowed to stand and three minutes later Kinsey, a late replacement for Denis Law, side-footed the ball past Reeves from close range after Connelly had hooked the ball back from the by-line. With a 2-1 lead United began to play with more confidence and Herd had a goal ruled out for offside. As the minutes ticked away Chester had one last opportunity when a quick breakaway by Metcalf ended with Talbot putting the ball over the bar. Although United finished well on top Chester belied their lowly status and United knew they had been in a match.*

*Chester - Reeves, Jones, Starkey, Hauser, Butler, Durie, Humes, Metcalf, Talbot, Ryden, Morris.*
*Manchester United - P Dunne, Brennan, A Dunne, Crerand, Foulkes, Stiles, Connelly, Charlton, Herd, Kinsey, Best.*

The win over Derby gave Chester a home tie against another 2nd Division side, Norwich City, although they missed the chance of facing ex-leader Ron Davies who was injured. Norwich were given a fright by a diligent Chester side who pulled back a deficit three times before finally going down 5-3 to the pacey Norfolk team. The thrills in the League Cup games were equalled by an exhilarating FA Cup run which saw their first appearance in the 3rd Round since 1952.

In the 1st Round Chester faced Crewe, a week after the two sides had fought out a 2-2 draw at Sealand Road. At 2-0 a scrappy cup-tie was drawing to a conclusion when Talbot showed how deadly he was with a half chance. Goals in the 86th, 88th and 89th minutes gave Talbot what was believed to be the fastest FA Cup hat trick on record as Chester won 5-0. In the 2nd Round it was Metcalf's turn to make the headlines as his hat-trick helped Chester recover from 2-1 down to beat Barnsley 5-2. A classic encounter with Manchester United in the 3rd Round saw Chester finally eliminated, but they gained many new friends for their enterprising football.

*Gary Talbot scores the final goal in the 6-1 hammering of Wrexham in February 1965.*

Back in the League an unpredictable Chester were conceding goals almost as fast as they could score them. February began with another action packed game, a 4-4 draw with Brighton, and the month ended with the much anticipated derby game against Wrexham. Another exhilarating display by the forwards produced a 6-1 win including a hat-trick for the hard working Jimmy Humes. Unfortunately any chance of promotion was effectively ended by three successive defeats at the start of March as reserve goalkeeper Reg Barton conceded five apiece against Darlington and Crewe. Dennis Reeves was back in the side when Chester faced Wrexham in the Welsh Cup Semi-Final, but Hauser made a misjudgment in resting Ryden, Talbot and Durie, and they were easily beaten 3-0.

The season ended with a flourish of goalscoring. Jimmy Humes notched Chester's 100th League goal of the season at Halifax in a 4-3 win, and this was followed by four goal perform-ances against

Doncaster, Notts County and Barrow. There was nothing at stake for the last game of the season against Doncaster, but for the knowledge that Hugh Ryden needed two goals to join his fellow forwards in scoring more than 20 goals in all English competitions. Every attack focused on Ryden as the whole team tried to assist him in reaching his target. The first of his goals came in the first-half, and just after the hour Talbot had an opportunity to score with only the goalkeeper to beat. Instead of going for goal he passed to Ryden and every heart stood still as the inside-forward failed to make contact and ended up flat on the turf. However the ball was still within reach and the Stadium erupted as Ryden put the ball into the net from a prone position to cap a wonderful season.

Hauser's attacking policy had paid dividends but, in pushing the wing-halves forward, he had sacrificed defensive cover and the 81 goals conceded had cost Chester a higher position. Despite this the supporters had been treated to great entertainment with the 'Famous Five' dominating the goals. In 52 games in the League, League Cup and FA Cup, Chester had scored 141 goals with 138 of them coming from Humes, Metcalf, Talbot, Ryden and Morris. Even in the Welsh Cup it was only an own goal by a Borough defender that prevented a clean sweep for the front five. Hauser had also been fortunate that a lack of serious injuries had allowed him to field a settled side, although John Evans had been forced to retire from the game after a serious back injury against Gillingham in 1963/64. Chester did win some silverware during the season when a mainly Reserve side won the Cheshire Bowl against Tranmere thanks to two goals from captain Stan Bennion.

Financial matters had taken a turn for the better with a profit of £7,860, and the completion of the new social club at the end of the season had opened another source of revenue. Predictably the same squad was retained for the 1965/66 season with the only new arrivals being Graham Chadwick from Walsall and Tommy Singleton from Peterborough, another player who had played alongside Hauser at Blackpool. Singleton had the distinction of being the first substitute used by Chester when he came on for the injured Starkey in the first game of the season against Stockport. The team carried on where they had left off as a Jimmy Humes goal gave them a 1-0 victory, and by the end of September they were top of the League.

However the defence was still causing concern and there were heavy defeats in the League Cup against Wrexham, and at the start of October against Port Vale. Injuries among the forward line meant that Chester were only able to field their classic forward line on two occasions, and diminutive Les Jones, who had been signed from Tranmere in April, took the opportunity to stake his claim.

The major loss was Talbot who struggled with injury throughout the season, although 'Elky' Morris continued to improve amid rumours that he was about to leave for a bigger club.

In the FA Cup, Chester comfortably beat Chesterfield in the 1st Round but were given a hard game by an aggressive Wigan Athletic in the 2nd. The reward was a home draw against Newcastle which attracted more than 18,000 fans, despite a controversial increase in prices. Although Morris gave Chester an early lead, goals from McGarry, Robson and Craig gave Newcastle a convincing 3-1 victory. Meanwhile, back in the League, Chester entered 1966 in 2nd place, a point behind Torquay and four points clear of Darlington in 5th place.

On New Years Day struggling Aldershot visited Sealand Road and disaster struck as both full-backs, Bryn and Ray Jones, suffered broken legs. Determined team spirit carried Chester through to a narrow 3-2 victory but there was further bad news when it was discovered that reserve winger Garth Lee had also fractured his leg playing for the Reserves. Surprisingly no move was made by Hauser to seek replacements, although his confidence in the Reserves appeared justified as Chester were only beaten once in the next eight games. One of these games, a 4-0 win over Bradford City, was televised with Chester receiving a nominal payment of £10. At the start of March, a 2-1 win over Bradford City at Valley Parade put Chester in 2nd place, a point behind new leaders Tranmere but with games in hand over all their nearest rivals. Unfortunately a spectacular end of season collapse saw Chester win only two of their last 15 games and a desperately disappointing season ended with Chester in 7th position.

Much of the blame for missing out on promotion was heaped on Hauser for not taking more positive action after the New Year Day injuries to the full-backs.

The forward line had also struggled to find their form after a promising start. Talbot missed much of the season with injury and was not adequately replaced, while Humes could not reproduce his 1964/65 form and both Morris and Ryden burned themselves out as the season progressed. At the end of the season there was great interest in the Welsh Cup, where Chester had reached the Final after victories over Wrexham, Newport and Bangor. The interest centred on the issue of whether Chester should represent Wales in the European Cup Winners Cup if they won the competition.

The matter came to a head at the start of April when the FA of Wales declared that no English club could represent the Principality, and if Chester won, the place would fall to the runners-up.

Reg Rowlands broadly accepted the viewpoint of the Welsh FA and declared: *'If we win the Welsh Cup the ball will be at the feet of the Welsh FA, but if we are refused entry into the European competition it would be wrong for us to create a disturbance. We will abide by the decision of the Welsh FA but we shall, as diplomatically as possible, endeavour to enter the European Cup Winners Cup. At the same time we do not want to embarrass the Welsh FA, Chester can make as much as £3000 a season in the Welsh Cup so we do not want to jeopardise our chances of entering the competition next year.'* Chester's opponents in the Final were 3rd Division Swansea Town, with the game decided over two matches. A more enterprising Swansea were comfortable 3-0 winners in the first game at the Vetch Field with goals from McLaughlin (2) and Jones. However, the nature of the Final meant that Chester only had to win the second game at Sealand Road to force a play-off.

They got off to a fine start when Morris headed home a Ryden cross after only 13 minutes but, despite heavy pressure, they could not force a second. Just before half-time Dennis Reeves became the hero of the hour when he saved a Swansea penalty after Starkey had brought down Todd. There were no further goals and Chester won the toss for choice of venue for the play-off. There was little to choose between the teams in the decider and Chester took the lead early in the second-half when Les Jones headed Harley's accurate centre over Hayes and into the net. The lead lasted less than 10 minutes when Todd equalised for Swansea. In the end the game was settled by a touch of class from Welsh international Ivor Allchurch, who beat two defenders and placed the ball past Reeves to take Swansea into Europe.

The close season brought the World Cup Finals to England and Chester played host to the Bulgarians in an unusual practice game. With the players not having reported back for training Hauser had to assemble a scratch team. The game lasted 100 minutes, but after seventy-five Chester gave way to a team of amateurs from Manchester. At that point Chester were losing 8-5 with their goals being scored by Talbot (4) and Metcalf. Despite a poor end to the 1965/66 season Hauser continued to place his faith in the same squad and only fringe players Corbishley, Willder, Lee and Howard were released. Although the club made a healthy profit of £10,710, no money was spent on players and the only arrivals were John Bennett, Alan Hignett and John Sealey, all on free transfers from Liverpool.

A poor start to the season, including a 5-2 home defeat by Tranmere in the League Cup, showed up the weaknesses in the team, although Hauser was convinced that there was nothing seriously wrong that a good win would not solve.

The home record was particularly poor throughout the season and an aging eleven struggled to find the net regularly. In November, six players, including Durie and Read, were placed on the transfer list as an attempt was made to lighten the wage bill. A home defeat against Exeter precipitated significant changes in the side including new signings Terry Carling from Walsall and Gordon Seaton from Rhyl. The immediate response was a 3-2 win at Bradford City, and three weeks later Chester returned to Bradford to beat Park Avenue by the same score. Unfortunately Chester continued to struggle just above the re-election zone, although they were unlucky to suffer a number of injuries, including Talbot, Morris and Ray Jones. They also lost the services of Malcolm Starkey who was forced into retirement after a serious illness. In the end six wins in the last 10 games saved them from the bottom four, and Hauser accepted responsibility for the poor campaign by admitting he had retained too many players at the end of the previous season. Chairman Reg Rowlands was even more critical claiming *'the mistake was made in putting loyalty to players before loyalty to the club. Last June we retained far too many players of mediocre ability. Consequently when we had injuries, or when players fell off form, those called upon were just not good enough'.*

The Chester fans were promised new signings for the 1967/68 season, but surprisingly 16 players were still retained, when a much bigger clear-out was expected. Among the departures were forwards Jimmy Humes, who joined Barnsley on a free transfer, and Gary Talbot whose contract was cancelled.

The club made a massive loss of £14,026 on the season but the transfer record was broken with the signing of Ian Moir from Blackpool for £10,000. Moir, a flying winger with brilliant ball skills, had cost Blackpool £27,500 from Manchester United in 1965 having made 46 appearances at Old Trafford in the aftermath of the Munich disaster. Hauser also managed to persuade 22-year-old Mike Sutton to reverse his decision to leave football. Sutton had become disillusioned with the game after failing to gain a regular place at Norwich City, but at Sealand Road his consistency made him one of the first names on the team sheet. The signings were completed with the arrival of young forwards David Hancox from Sheffield United and Eddie Loyden on a free transfer from Carlisle. There was almost a surprise return to the club for Charlie Hewitt, the man who had taken Chester into the League in 1931. Hewitt had returned to the city after being in charge at Millwall and Leyton Orient, but his attempt to join the board of directors failed by some distance.

Such were the state of the finances that Chester's 2nd strip for the season was orange shirts purchased second hand from Blackpool by Peter Hauser on a visit to his former club. There were encouraging performances in pre-season friendlies against Shrewsbury and Sheffield United and an impressive win at Notts County in the season opener. However a 3-0 League Cup defeat at Port Vale proved a real dampener, and when Crewe left Sealand Road with a 4-0 victory it was clear that the team would be in for a long hard season. The defeat by Crewe was made worse by the influential performance of Gary Talbot who went on to score 20 goals for the Alex during the season. In the next home game, against Exeter, there was a surprise return to the side for John Butler after many people had thought his career at Sealand Road had ended. Butler, who had given the club such excellent service, was rewarded with a testimonial against First Division Sheffield United at the end of the season.

In October, Dennis Reeves left Sealand Road in exchange for Tony McLaughlin, who had scored twice for Wrexham against Chester in the previous seasons Welsh Cup Semi-Final. McLaughlin failed to make an impression and after goalless draws against Doncaster and Bradford PA he was dropped along with centre-forward Loyden. David Hancox took over in the middle and promptly scored two goals in his first two games, but could not maintain the momentum and he in turn was replaced by on-loan signing Alan Hughes from Liverpool.

By December the club were struggling in the bottom four but with no money available Hauser had to make do with the players at his disposal. On Boxing Day Chester went down 3-0 at fellow strugglers Lincoln City but, four days later they astonishingly beat the same side 6-0 in what was easily their best performance of the season. All six goals were shared by Moir and the re-instated Loyden, but it proved to be Moir's final League game for the club as he was transferred to Wrexham in exchange for Graham Turner and £8,000. In his short spell at the club Moir had been the shining light in the team but the lack of support up front had reduced his effectiveness.

Despite the Lincoln victory the club were once again in turmoil on the pitch and home performances were matching those of the early 60s. Without Moir, Chester gained only two points from the next eight games and after a home defeat by Workington there was the inevitable parting of the ways with Hauser. The big South African had initially won the admiration and respect of the supporters with his attacking ways, but ironically it was injuries to defenders Ray and Bryn Jones that saw the side slowly disintegrate as the spark was lost. After his sacking Hauser returned to South Africa where he resumed his former career as a surveyor.

The man chosen to replace Hauser was 32-year-old Ken Roberts, recently released by Bradford PA where he had been assistant manager.

Roberts had been the youngest player to make his League debut when he had played for Wrexham at the age of 15 years and 158 days. A fast, elusive winger his career had been cut short by a knee injury in 1958 and he had taken coaching positions at Oswestry and Wrexham before joining Bradford PA. It proved to be an unhappy first game in charge for Roberts as Chester went down 5-1 at Southend in what was the final appearance for Elfed Morris. who joined ex-colleague Hugh Ryden at Halifax. A week later Roberts had the satisfaction of gaining his first points in charge, at his former club Bradford PA. This win started a seven match unbeaten run which included an impressive 3-0 win over promotion chasing Chesterfield, the club who had knocked them out of the FA Cup three months earlier. Unfortunately the Chester were already too far adrift in the bottom four and five defeats in the last six games consigned them to another re-election plea.

By now Roberts had started rebuilding for the new season with the signing of Cliff Sear from Manchester City at the end of April. Sear, a cultured left back, had made nearly 250 appearances at Maine Road and won a Welsh cap against England in 1962.

Re-building continued during the close season with the signing of forceful half-back Eric Brodie from Shrewsbury for £5,000 in a deal which took Eddie Loyden to Gay Meadow for a new record fee of £13,000. Loyden's replacement in the forward line proved to be the familiar figure of Gary Talbot from Crewe, while nippy right-winger Billy Dearden came from the same club. The forward line was completed by the £4,000 signing of Andy Provan, a left-winger from York with an impressive goalscoring record.

Good performances in pre-season friendlies, including a thrilling 4-4 draw with League Champions Manchester City, chased away the spectre of re-election and the club looked forward to the 1968/69 season in their new sky blue kit. The season opened with a 2-0 win over York, in which Sear scored his first and only goal for the club, but the result was reversed a week later at Bradford City. Much of August was taken with an absorbing and gruelling League Cup-tie against 3rd Division Tranmere Rovers. The tie went to four games and Chester were unlucky to lose out on a trip to Everton, as Tranmere eventually came out on top after 420 minutes.

Chester played some flamboyant football at the start of the season and the goals flowed freely as Talbot and Metcalf renewed their partnership, aided by the exciting wing play of Provan and Dearden. A 2-0 win over the massed defence of Port Vale allowed Chester to take an early lead at the top of the table, and after 11 games they had only suffered one League defeat. At the start of October Chester entertained the England Under-23 side in a private practice game but were beaten 3-1.

November proved to be a poor month as only one point was picked up, in a tense derby against Wrexham, although the team put in a ruthless performance in defeating Bradford City in the 1st Round of the FA Cup. This victory gave them a home tie against Lincoln City but an out of sorts display resulted in a 1-1 draw, and in the replay at Sincil Bank Chester failed to take advantage of an injury to the Lincoln goalkeeper and were beaten 2-1.

The change in fortune in League form had seen Chester slip down the table and Roberts moved to strengthen the side with the free transfer signing of Roy Cheetham from Charlton. Cheetham, a former Manchester City half-back, had only been with Charlton for four weeks having spent 10 months playing in the USA with the New York Generals. The year ended with an impressive 5-0 win at Swansea, and after a home defeat against 2nd placed Darlington, Chester embarked on another extended unbeaten run of 11 games which included seven draws. This was enough to take them into 2nd place, four points behind League leaders Doncaster, although their nearest challengers all had games in hand.

One player to emerge during this run was inside-forward Derek Draper who had been signed by Ken Roberts for £5,000 from his old club Bradford PA. Draper, who joined Bradford from Derby County, had earned a Welsh Under-23 cap in 1965 while playing with his first club Swansea Town. Over the next 10 years Draper was to become an influential general for Roberts on the field. Shortly after Draper's arrival Mike Metcalf, one of Chester's most creative players, was transferred to Altrincham.

After another five goal away performance at Newport, Chester were beaten by two John Toshack goals for Cardiff in the Welsh Cup Semi-Final at Sealand Road. This defeat heralded another spectacular end of season collapse as three successive home defeats took Chester out of the top four. Victory over Rochdale briefly raised hopes but five defeats in the last six games left Chester in a disappointing 14th position. An inconsistent season disguised the work that Roberts had done in bringing respectability back to the club but, after 38 years in the lowest division, it was a bitter pill for the supporters to swallow and they were even more convinced that the club did not actively want promotion.

The last home game of the season, against Lincoln, marked the final appearance of Gary Talbot who retired to concentrate on photography. His 22 goals left him the division's leading scorer and he proved to be a difficult man to replace.

The Lincoln game also saw the debuts of two players who were to become great favourites throughout the 1970s, goalkeeper Grenville Millington and full back Nigel Edwards. Millington only made one appearance before joining Rhyl, but returned to Chester in 1973 while Edwards had shown great promise in the Reserves and represented the Welsh youth team in 1968.

During the close season Ray Jones and George Evans were among the players given free transfers as Roberts retained 11 professionals. The forward line was strengthened with the signing of Keith Webber, a well built centre-forward from Doncaster, and Roy Chapman on a free transfer from Port Vale. The experienced Chapman had made his League debut with Aston Villa in 1953, scoring 198 League goals in a prolific career with Lincoln, Mansfield and Port Vale. Roberts also added to an already strong half-back line with the signing of Chester born Albert Harley from Stockport and Terry Bradbury, a former England Schoolboy international, from Wrexham. Roberts later utilised the experience of Bradbury by making him player-coach while Cliff Sear was made captain.

Chester ended their long association with the Cheshire County League at the end of the 1968/69 season when the Reserves withdrew to enter the Northern Floodlit League. Average attendances had fallen to 295 in the final season and the team had struggled despite the withdrawal of the stronger teams to the Northern Premier League.

Once again Chester performed well in pre-season friendlies with the tall Chapman showing he had lost none of his striking instincts by scoring five goals in four games.

*Gary Talbot (centre) prepares for his final game, as Nigel Edwards (left) and Grenville Millington await their debuts.*

He continued this form into the first game of the 1969/70 season when Chester recovered from 2-1 down to beat Scunthorpe 3-2, with Chapman scoring two to take his career total to 200. Unfortunately he could not maintain the scoring rate and by October had dropped out of the team and into non-League football as player-manager with Stafford Rangers. Meanwhile wingers Billy Dearden and Andy Provan continued to enhance their reputation with much of Chester's play being built around their skill and speed. Provan had been particularly impressive in the League Cup 1st Round tie against 2nd Division Aston Villa where Chester had been narrowly beaten 2-1.

A series of disappointing results followed the Villa defeat but, more significantly, the club were once again on the verge of a financial crisis as a loss of £11,860 on the previous season took the overall debt to nearly £30,000. The burden was eased in the short term by the transfer of Eric Brodie to Tranmere for £5,000 but some of this money was immediately spent on full-back Graham Birks from Southend. Two weeks later another £4,000 was spent on Alan Tarbuck a young, highly thought of, inside-forward from Crewe. Tarbuck quickly became the idol of the fans with two goals on his home debut against Exeter, and he inspired Chester to five wins in his first six games. In mid-December Chester visited Notts County and were dealt a cruel blow when Tarbuck tragically broke his leg in a 3-0 defeat. Roberts moved quickly to replace Tarbuck by signing Sammy McMillan from Wrexham for £2,000 and Alan Spence on a free transfer from Oldham. Two Billy Dearden goals against Wrexham on Boxing Day took Chester to 9th in the table, but by now most of the attention was on the FA Cup where Chester had their best run for more than 20 years.

In the 1st Round Chester had deservedly beaten 3rd Division Halifax after a replay and faced another 3rd Division team, Doncaster Rovers, in the next round. The Yorkshire side came to Sealand Road with the intention of taking Chester back to Doncaster, and although they succeeded in their aim they were given a shock three days later in a stirring replay. At Belle Vue Chester took the lead after 23 minutes when Webber got his boot to a cross shot by Provan to score his first goal for the club against his former team-mates. The tie was sealed, with eight minutes to go, when Dearden scored Chester's second with a well-judged lob which earned them a 3rd Round tie against 2nd Division Bristol City. Chester entered this match without tenacious half-back Barry Ashworth who was serving a six week suspension after being sent off against Aldershot. In a hard tackling game Chester took the lead after 90 seconds through Webber, only for Skirton to equalise for the Bristol club midway through the second half. In the dying seconds Dearden latched on to a Provan free kick to put Chester in the 4th Round for the first time since 1948.

When Chester played Swindon in the 4th Round they were not only missing Tarbuck, but also Dearden and Birks, and 19-year-old Gavin Lang was given his debut on the wing. Lang, whose father had played for Chester in the 1950s, made a name for himself by scoring one of Chester's goals in a 4-2 defeat but it was a courageous performance from an injury hit side.

After elimination from the FA Cup Chester were unbeaten in February, and a 2-1 victory over Oldham took them to 7th position. However, despite the return of Tarbuck against York, the season stuttered to a conclusion and six defeats in the last 10 games left them in 11th place.

Chester ended the season with what proved to be their last ever appearance in the Welsh Cup Final where they faced Cardiff City. They had reached the two-legged Final after victories over Llandudno, Llanelli and a gallant Hereford United who had the legendary John Charles at centre-forward. The first leg of the Final was played at Sealand Road and Chester almost took an early lead when a Draper shot was deflected onto the underside of the bar by Carver. Despite this early pressure Cardiff took the lead through Bird after seven minutes and although the home side had more of the play they could not force an equaliser. In the second-half both Turner and McMillan hit the woodwork but Chester went to Cardiff for the second leg trailing by the only goal. The second leg was all over by half-time as goals from Woodruff, Bird, Lea and Clarke gave Cardiff a comfortable 4-0 lead, and although they failed to add to the score the Welshmen retained the trophy for a record 4th successive time.

In April, off the field events came to the fore as the club revealed that they were in dire financial straits. Despite a good cup run and some promising performances the club never captured the imagination of the fans and attendances had failed to reach 5,000 after Christmas. With the club losing £300 a week and an overdraft of £30,000 the whole team was put up for sale. and inevitably the best players swiftly became transfer targets. First to go was Billy Dearden, to Sheffield United, for £11,000 and he was quickly followed by Andy Provan who joined Wrexham for £7,500. The sale was completed when the masterful Sutton went to Carlisle for £10,000. The loss of the popular trio helped disperse the cloud of uncertainty over the club, but left Roberts with the task of rebuilding a team that had shown great potential.

The close season also saw the departure of popular, but volatile, full-back Barry Ashworth. After completing a six week suspension in January he had returned to the side only to be sent off against Oldham in March. He was due to start another six week suspension but was put on the transfer list and joined non-League Altrincham.

The first signing for the 1970/71 season was wing-half Dave Pountney from Shrewsbury, a player who had made more than 100 1st Division appearances with Aston Villa in the mid 1960s. Dearden and Provan were replaced by Chester-born Brian Woodall from Sheffield Wednesday and Alan Groves, a forceful winger from Southport. Both players were under 23, as were fellow signings Dave Kennedy (Tranmere) and goalkeeper John Taylor (Pwllheli).

Pountney made his home debut in a League Cup-tie against his old club Shrewsbury and scored one of the best goals ever seen at Sealand Road when his 40 yard shot flew into the net before the goalkeeper could move, to give Chester a late winner. In the 2nd Round Turner superbly marshalled the defence to give the team an unexpected draw at 2nd Division Norwich City. In the replay a Woodall goal gave Chester a great start but goals by Silvester and Foggo before half-time provided Norwich with a lead which they retained despite constant Chester pressure.

Early League form was encouraging and a 5-0 win over Grimsby put Chester top of the table. Three days later a 4-1 win at struggling Barrow helped strengthen the position, but when Chester were beaten in the next two games by Brentford and Northampton, Roberts reacted quickly by signing Kevin McHale from Crewe for £5,000. The experienced McHale had started his career with Huddersfield where a great future had been predicted after he had won schoolboy international honours, and played for the England youth team. Unfortunately he had failed to live up to his early promise although he made more than 300 appearances for Huddersfield.

McHale made his debut in a 4-2 win over promotion chasing Bournemouth, and another addition was made to the forward line in time for the next home game, against Oldham. The return of Eddie Loyden from Barnsley for £7,000 showed the club was determined to make a serious bid for promotion, but paradoxically the signing disrupted the team who lost four of the next five games and slipped down the table. By the end of the year Chester had dropped to 8th, but there was another appearance in the FA Cup 3rd Round to look forward to.

In the 1st Round Chester had beaten a Preston side making their first ever appearance at that stage of the competition. After a 1-1 draw at Deepdale, Chester won the replay 1-0 despite an unexpected penalty miss by Cheetham which broke his 100% record from the spot. In the next round Chester avenged an earlier heavy 6-3 defeat at Crewe when a Turner header gave them a 1-0 win, although it was not a good performance. The reward was a home game against a Derby side managed by Brian Clough, and although the game did not match the thrills of the 1964 encounter Derby were made to fight all the way for their 2-1 win.

Back in the League the Tarbuck/Loyden combination moved into gear and a 2-1 win over League leaders Notts County heralded a run which put Chester back among the promotion challengers. By the end of March Chester were 5th, on goal average from York, and facing a relatively easy programme to finish the season. The crucial game proved to be the Easter Monday encounter with York watched by the largest home crowd of the season. Nearly 8,000 saw Tarbuck pulled down in the area after only two minutes, but Loyden failed to capitalise and his missed penalty seemed to unsettle the team. After soaking up Chester pressure Aimson hammered home from close range to give York the lead on the hour. As the game moved into stoppage time Hillyard, the York goalkeeper, dropped a high cross from McHale on to Turner's head and the ball rebounded into the net to salvage a late point for Chester. Victory over bottom of the table Barrow kept Chester in the hunt, but defeats at Exeter and struggling Lincoln, consigned Chester to yet another season of football in the basement. A final position of 5th left them ruing the dropped point against York who were promoted a point ahead of Chester.

Perhaps the most encouraging feature of the season was the continuing development of full-back Nigel Edwards, who was by now the subject of constant transfer speculation. At the end of the season he was invited on a tour of New Zealand and the Far East with the Wales team and played in eight of their nine games.

Terry Carling was awarded a Testimonial against Wrexham and left the club during the close season, as did Keith Webber and player-coach Terry Bradbury. Carling was replaced by Gordon Livsey from Wrexham for £2,500 with Bernard Purdie, a young striker, also making the move from the Racecourse. Other signings were Bobby Smith (Brighton) and Tony Moore (Chesterfield), but neither player was to make an impression although they both appeared in the season opener against Cambridge.

Purdie got off to a good start with a goal on his full debut against Tranmere in the League Cup, although there was disappointment when Chester collapsed in the replay at Sealand Road. August ended with a 5-1 win over Gillingham, a surprising result given early season performances, with Purdie claiming four of the goals. This proved to be the best result of a campaign in which Chester once again struggled in front of goal. Purdie failed to match his goal blitz against Gillingham and only Loyden reached double figures.

The leading scorer from the previous season, and the fans favourite, Alan Tarbuck, struggled in the early games but his transfer to Preston for £5,500 did little to please the supporters, after successive goalless draws against Aldershot, Workington and Barrow.

Once again Chester turned to Crewe for a goalscoring replacement, but Pat Morrissey at £4,000 managed only one goal before moving to Watford for £7,000.

Although the forwards were struggling the defence was in excellent form and captain Pountney had formed a fine partnership with the promising Graham Turner. The combination of a strong defence and weak attack gave the fans little to enthuse over and no fewer than 10 games finished goalless during the season.

The development of Nigel Edwards suffered a setback when a sending off against Aldershot was followed by an ankle injury, but Cliff Sear's youth policy started to pay dividends with debuts for Ray Carter and Graham Futcher. Both players had moved up from the Lancashire League team, a competition that Chester entered for the first time.

Ken Roberts was awarded a new contract in December as the club struggled in mid-table, but poor attendances meant that he could not spend money on the team. Joe Ashworth, Rochdale defender and captain, was signed on a free transfer, but Roberts mainly had to rely on loan signings like Tinnion (Wrexham), Sinclair (Watford), Clapham (Shrewsbury) and Bingham (Mansfield). Clapham scored on his debut against Southport and was signed at the end of his loan period.

On New Years Day Chester suffered their first home defeat in more than 12 months when Exeter won 2-1, but the away record was dismal and they failed to win away from Sealand Road all season. There was no improvement in the second-half of the season, and the club slipped dangerously close to the re-election zone. In the end it was only last day defeats for Northampton and Barrow that saved Chester from re-election as they finished 5th from bottom, a complete turnaround from the previous season. The last five games encapsulated the season as Chester failed to score and supporters had to endure four successive goalless draws in 11 days.

Cup competitions brought little relief with Chester being knocked out in the 1st Round of the League Cup and FA Cup. Elimination in the FA Cup was particularly disappointing as a 4-3 defeat gave 3rd Division Mansfield their first home win of the season. In the Welsh Cup, Chester netted seven in a replay against Holyhead after a farcical goalless draw in atrocious conditions on Anglesey drew receipts of only £39. In the 6th Round they were embarrassingly beaten by non-League Rhyl who had Grenville Millington playing in goal.

A poor season had seen attendances continue to fall, and when Barrow failed in their re-election attempt the club received a much needed jolt as they realised they could be next.

In order to raise money the directors decided to realise some assets and two acres of land on the city side of the Stadium was sold to Chester Corporation along with the Social Club which was purchased by Greenalls. Some of the money was spent on Terry Owen from Bradford City (£1,000), Mick Hollis, Barrow's leading scorer (£2,000), Geoff Davies from Wigan (£4,000) and Bob Wallace an industrious midfield player and penalty expert from Halifax (£4,000). Among the departures were the consistent Roy Cheetham, Kevin McHale and Joe Ashworth.

Injuries to regular keepers Livsey and Taylor on the eve of the 1972/73 season forced Roberts to take Jim Eadie on loan from Cardiff City, but Chester got off to a bright start with a 2-0 win over Bury. This was followed by a thrilling encounter against 3rd Division Shrewsbury in the League Cup as Chester recovered from 2-0 down to win 4-3 thanks to a magnificent late header from man of the match Draper.

After the scarcity of goals the previous season, early form proved a welcome surprise to Chester fans and they were given a real treat in the next home game, an astonishing 8-2 win over Peterborough. At half-time Chester were leading 2-1, and had given no indication of what was to happen in the second-half, when Peterborough were hit by a deluge of goals including a hat-trick from Hollis. The momentum was maintained in the next match with a convincing 4-0 win over Colchester, and Chester entered the League Cup-tie at 1st Division Southampton full of confidence. Southampton, with Ron Davies leading their attack, were never allowed to dominate and as the game wore on Chester grew in stature with Bob Wallace directing operations superbly in midfield. The game finished goalless but, in the last five minutes, Chester almost snatched a winner through Purdie who first powered a header against the bar and then, two minutes later, raced clear of a static defence only to hit the ball wide of the post.

In the replay, at Sealand Road, Chester again rose to the occasion and recovered from a Francis Burns goal to equalise through a Mick Hollis volley which took the game into extra time. After a tame 1st period Channon slotted home for the Saints in the 109th minute, but with time running out Draper cleverly headed a Kennedy cross over Martin for a 2nd equaliser. The 2nd replay at West Bromwich Albion, saw Chester go down 2-0, but they came out of the tie with a great deal of credit.

Although Chester were unable to maintain their goalscoring form they were on the fringe of the promotion group by the start of December and had put up another good performance in the FA Cup, where they took 3rd Division leaders Bolton to a replay, before going down 1-0. Unfortunately the goals dried up completely after victory over Stockport, and Chester slowly lost touch with the leaders as they went eight games without a win.

In January the influential Graham Turner was sold to Shrewsbury for a new record fee of £30,000. Turner went on to make more than 300 appearances at Gay Meadow where he later became player-manager, and took them into the 2nd Division in 1979, before managing Aston Villa, Wolves and Hereford. His replacement at centre-half was the experienced Reg Matthewson, who initially arrived on loan from Fulham but signed the following month.

Matthewson made his home debut against Darlington as did John James who was signed from Port Vale for £5,000. Without the suspended Wallace and Clapham, an efficient Chester produced their best performance for some weeks and debutant James was on target in a 5-0 win. This victory proved to be a flash in the pan and the fall down the table continued with three successive home defeats. When Chester finally won at home, 2-0 against Reading, there were only 1264 present. As another season turned sour after a promising start there was one ray of hope when 16-year-old Paul Futcher made an encouraging debut against Cambridge. Paul had joined the club straight from school alongside his twin brother Ron, and followed in the footsteps of brother Graham who had made 10 appearances for the club. Under the tutelage of Cliff Sear a great future was predicted for the twins.

A final position of 15th was by no means satisfactory and the promotion of Aldershot left Chester as the only club in the Football League never to be promoted. With attendances now regularly below the 2,000 mark, chairman Rowlands promised another all out effort for promotion and, after years of speculation, the decision was finally made to sell the Annexe in order to take the club forward. In a 'make or break' attempt to bring success to the club Rowlands stated that '*it is better to use our assets in a bid to get success rather than drift on until we have to use that money just to pay our debts*'. The sale of the Annexe, covering the area between the ground and the Greyhound Stadium, raised £290,000 and secured the future of the club.

With money to spare Chester embarked on a series of ground improvements as Roberts brought in a number of new signings. Having already bought Stuart Mason (Wrexham), Stan Horne (Fulham) and Jim Grummett, the ex-Lincoln captain from Aldershot, Ken Roberts was able to break the club transfer record in signing winger Jimmy Redfern from Bolton for £11,000. On the verge of the new season another winger, Norman Whitehead from Rotherham, was signed for £8,000.

It was a new look Chester side, with five players making their debuts, that took the field for the season opener against Swansea where injuries to new skipper Matthewson and Pountney forced James to play at centre-half. After missing only three games in three seasons, Pountney's injury effectively ended his career at Sealand Road and he moved into non-League football with Oswestry. The 2-0 defeat against Swansea was Chester's first opening day defeat since 1964, and it also marked the end of Dave Kennedy's career at Chester as he moved on to Torquay for £5,000. Local youngster Gary Potter was given his chance at centre-half for the first home game against Hartlepool as Chester won three games in succession, but defeats against Exeter and Mansfield forced Roberts back into the transfer market. For the second time in just over a month the transfer record was broken with the signing of centre-half Chris Dunleavy from Southport for £12,000. A few days later he was joined by talented midfielder Ian Seddon from Bolton.

In October Chester visited Workington and in front of a paltry attendance of 862 Ron Futcher made his debut alongside twin brother Paul. Ron was unlucky not to score as Chester almost ended Workington's run of 25 home games without defeat, but the inconsistent form was causing unrest among the supporters. Having spent nearly £50,000 on new players a great deal was expected of the 'big spenders', and heavy defeats against Colchester and Brentford called for serious action as the expected push for promotion failed to materialise.

After the defeat by Colchester, Ken Roberts offered his resignation, but the club responded by appointing Brian Green as coach to assist the manager, and the club's fortunes took a turn for the better. Although Green had only played his football in the lower leagues he was a qualified FA coach and had coached in Kuwait as well as helping Southport to promotion in 1973. The first League game in December saw a number of changes in the side including the return of Reg Matthewson from injury and the re-appearance of Grenville Millington in goal, four years after his Chester debut. Nigel Edwards was also given the chance to regain his place at full-back. During the previous season Edwards had played for Wales Under-23s against England and Scotland but had lost his place in the side to Stuart Mason, and had spent a short time on loan at Rotherham. Edwards came back into the side after the Colchester debacle and gained a 3rd Welsh Under-23 cap early in 1974. Griffiths meanwhile joined Port Vale in December in an exchange deal with full back Tony Loska.

The 1-1 draw with Torquay marked the final game for Stan Horne who, like Jim Grummett, had failed to impress. Both players moved to Rochdale while the re-vitalised Chester started a slow climb up the table. Grummett had marked his final appearance for Chester with his only goal for the club which helped overcome non-League Telford in the FA Cup.

In the 2nd Round Chester faced Huddersfield Town and a blistering first half display saw them take a 3-1 lead thanks to goals

from Owen, James and Draper. Despite a 2nd half reply from Gowling, the Yorkshiremen could not force a replay and Chester deservedly went through to the 3rd Round where they faced Aston Villa at Villa Park. John James scored Chesters' goal in a 3-1 defeat, but until Morgan netted Villa's 3rd, the game was always in the balance.

In the League Chester were beginning to reap the benefits of Green's coaching and were only beaten in five of the last 28 games. At the end of January Chester played their first ever Sunday game, a 1-1 draw at Barnsley, and two weeks later a Terry Owen goal gave Chester a 1-0 win in the first Sunday match at Sealand Road. The poor start to the season had left Chester too much to do as far as promotion was concerned, but three points out of four against champions-elect Peterborough showed how far Chester had come and augured well for the 1974/75 season.

*Paul Futcher departs from Sealand Road, with Ken Roberts looking on.*

During the close season Chester received another windfall when twins Paul and Ron Futcher were transferred to Luton Town for a joint fee of £125,000. Both players went on to have long and distinguished careers with Paul making nearly 700 appearances for Manchester City, Oldham, Derby, Barnsley, Halifax and Grimsby, as well as winning 11 England Under 21 caps. Ron meanwhile played nearly 400 games for Manchester City, Barnsley, Oldham, Bradford City, Port Vale, Burnley and Crewe, as well as playing in the USA and Holland.

In preparation for the 1974/75 season Ken Roberts once again broke the transfer record in signing Trevor Storton from Liverpool for £20,000. The only other additions to the squad were Dave Coxon, a midfielder from Sheffield United, and Gary Moore, a £10,000 signing from Southend.

In the event Trevor Storton was the only new face for the season opener at Lincoln, and after taking an early lead through Terry Owen the Imps came back into the game to win 2-1.

Chester started at Sealand Road with a fluent 3-0 victory over Hartlepool, and a week later achieved their first away win at Barnsley. The only goal of that game came from Nigel Edwards, but the win was largely due to a heroic performance from keeper Millington who foiled the Barnsley strikers on numerous occasions.

Despite the Barnsley win, the away form in the early games was poor in comparison with home results, where Chester turned Sealand Road into a veritable fortress. James and Draper formed a lethal partnership as Chester rolled over opponent after opponent. It was October 23rd before Chester conceded their first goal and point at home, when Cambridge earned a 1-1 draw but normal service was resumed against Rochdale with a 2nd half hat-trick from Draper in a 4-0 win. Inexplicably Chester struggled to find the net away from home, although a fine point was earned at erstwhile champions Mansfield. It was the start of December before Chester earned their 2nd away win, when they beat 3rd placed Rotherham 1-0 only two weeks after the same side had eliminated them from the FA Cup. It was Rotherham who also ended Chester's proud unbeaten home record, which stretched back more than 12 months, when they won at Sealand Road in January.

The only blot on the landscape was the unfortunate injury to 1973/74 Player of the Year Chris Dunleavy who broke his leg against Torquay in September. In the same month Roberts added skill to the midfield with the signing of Dave Lennard on loan from Cambridge, a move that became permanent the following month.

Chester opened 1975 in fine fettle, standing 3rd in Division 4 and with a League Cup Semi-Final against Aston Villa to look forward to. The first game of the year saw the battle between the Division's best home and best away record as Shrewsbury visited Chester. Inevitably the game finished 1-1, but Chester, without the injured Matthewson, could have snatched both points in an impressive second-half display. Chester completed January without a win as they suffered a 3-0 reverse at the hands of promotion rivals Newport.

This defeat left Chester in 4th place but they now only had a two point advantage over Rotherham and Newport who both had three games in hand.

**MATCH TO REMEMBER**
**CREWE ALEXANDRA 0 CHESTER 1**
**LEAGUE DIVISION 4 - APRIL 26TH 1975**

*Stuart Mason sent 3000 travelling fans ecstatic when his headed goal gave Chester a 1-0 victory in a game they could not afford to lose. News of Lincoln's victory at Workington dampened the celebrations, but the true significance of the goal became apparent a few days later when a Lincoln defeat at Southport sent Chester into Division 3.*

*Although the match was always in the balance, Chester had the extra touch of skill and Dave Lennard, Jimmy Redfern and Terry Owen proved a constant handful to the Crewe defence. Both sides had some near misses in the first-half and John James headed just wide after six minutes while Crewe's best chance fell to former Chester striker Bernard Purdie. In the second half a Purdie header hit the bar, but with 15 minutes to go Mason struck with a classic goal. Lennard was the instigator when his glorious cross-field pass found the hard-working Redfern. The winger took on three Crewe defenders and his final cross was perfectly placed for Mason to send a brave header past Crudgington. There was no way back for Crewe as Chester held out for their first win at Gresty Road in 17 years.*

*Chester - Millington, Edwards, Loska, Storton, Matthewson, Pugh, Redfern, Mason (Seddon), Owen, James, Lennard.*
*Crewe Alexandra - Crudgington, Lowry, Kelley (Melledew), Rimmer, Bowles, Lugg, Snookes, Carter, Purdie, Davies, Nelson.*

With Chester out of the League Cup they were able to concentrate on promotion, and Ken Roberts introduced new blood into the team by signing Chester born midfielder Graham Pugh from Huddersfield for £20,000. Pugh had appeared in the 1966 FA Cup Final for Sheffield Wednesday when only 18, and added a wealth of experience to the midfield. He made an impressive debut against Northampton but it was substitute Terry Owen who stole the show with two spectacular goals in a 2-1 win.

This proved to be the first of five successive wins as Chester completed doubles over Rochdale, Swansea and Barnsley and, more importantly, crushed promotion seeking rivals Newport 4-1. Once again Owen was the hero with a first half hat-trick as he exploited mistakes in the Newport defence.

In mid-March Chester faced their most crucial League match of the season when they played Lincoln at Sealand Road, four days after gaining a hard earned point against League leaders Mansfield. The two teams entered the game level on points but with Lincoln ahead on goal average. In a memorable attacking display Chester tore the Lincoln defence to shreds with Pugh inspirational in midfield. Chester put pressure on the Lincoln defence straight from the kick-off and Grotier made magnificent saves from Mason and Edwards. They took the lead with a majestic header from Storton, his first League goal for the club, but were rocked when Lincoln equalised with a well worked goal from Graham. Chester responded quickly and Moore crashed them into the lead after Cooper had hooked the ball onto the underside of his own bar.

In the 65th minute Redfern threw the Lincoln defence into disarray and from his cross Moore's attempted overhead kick fell to Edwards who beat Grotier from close range. With four minutes left Moore completed the rout with a 25 yard shot to give Chester a boost to their goal average in the 4-1 victory.

The season moved to a thrilling climax, and after Chester had beaten Southport 3-0 in the final home game of the season a narrow defeat at Hartlepool the following Monday left Lincoln in the driving seat for the final promotion place:

| | | | | | | | |
|---|---|---|---|---|---|---|---|
| Chester | P45 | W22 | D11 | L12 | F63 | A38 | P55 |
| Lincoln | P43 | W20 | D14 | L9 | F75 | A45 | P54 |

On the Wednesday a 0-0 draw with Crewe took Lincoln above Chester, and victories on the final Saturday, for Lincoln at Workington and Chester at Crewe, left the Imps needing one point from their last game at Southport to clinch promotion.

Many Chester fans travelled to Haig Avenue for the vital game, while others made the trip to Sealand Road to watch the players turn out in a charity match.

Brian Green's old side did Chester proud in winning a tense match 3-2, and Chester went up by the narrow goal average margin of 0.039. Had goal difference rather than goal average been used, then Lincoln would have taken 4th place. After 44 years in the basement Chester could finally celebrate their first promotion.

A magnificent season was recognised with both Trevor Storton and Derek Draper appearing in the PFA's representative team for the 4th Division while Ken Roberts became Football League Manager of the Month for December. Brian Green's achievements earned him the accolade of Coach of the Year by his fellow professionals. Off the field the club were able to report a record profit of £48,008, and the balance sheet showed assets of £385,000, allowing the club to enter Division Three financially secure after years of struggle.

## 'SIMPLY MAGNIFICENT' - THE LEAGUE CUP RUN OF 1974/75

Although promotion gave Chester supporters plenty to cheer about for most people the enduring memory of the 1974/75 season was the tremendous League Cup run which took the club to within a hairsbreadth of Wembley.

The journey started with an innocuous looking tie against 3rd Division Walsall, 11 days after the Saddlers had beaten Chester in a pre-season friendly. At half-time Chester were heading for early elimination as Walsall lead through an Alan Buckley goal. However the break revitalised Chester and within two minutes they were level as James put Draper in possession and he beat Kearns with a coolly-judged shot. After 75 minutes the James/Draper combination struck again when James back headed a Dunleavy free kick to Draper who beat Kearns from close range.

> Chester - Millington, Edwards, Loska, Storton, Matthewson, Mason (Dunleavy), Whitehead, Seddon, Draper, James, Owen
> Walsall - Kearns, Saunders, Fry, Robinson, Bennett, Atthey, Harrison, Andrews (Sloan), Wright, Buckley, Taylor.

In the 2nd Round Blackpool came to Sealand Road and were swamped in the first 45 minutes as Chester raced into a 3-1 half-time lead. Whitehead was inspirational on the wing and Ian Seddon in brilliant form as Chester produced some of their best football for many years in an all-out attacking display. Nigel Edwards put Chester ahead after only four minutes with a vicious 20 yarder, only for Walsh to equalise following a defence splitting pass from Bentley. Chester now showed their true mettle and two goals in five minutes put the tie beyond Blackpool. First, Terry Owen sent a glancing header past Burridge from a Whitehead cross and then, before Blackpool could recover, Burridge failed to hold a ferocious Owen shot which bounced off his chest and was cooly turned home by Whitehead. Chester almost extended their lead in the second half with Whitehead hitting the bar and James scooping the ball over from close range. Blackpool's best chance came with a Glyn James header which was cleared off the line by Edwards.

> Chester - Millington, Edwards, Loska, Storton, Dunleavy, Matthewson, Whitehead, Seddon, Draper, James (Moore), Owen
> Blackpool - Burridge, Curtis, Bentley, Hart, Hatton, Suddaby, James, Evanson, Walsh, Ainscow (Tong), Harrison

By the time Preston paid a visit in the 3rd Round Chester boasted a proud home record of eight wins out of eight with no League goals conceded. Preston rarely looked like denting this record as the Chester defence, with Storton impeccable, chased and challenged for every ball, while player-manager Bobby Charlton was ineffective as Stuart Mason marked him out of the game. The only goal came after 32 minutes when Dave Lennard superbly volleyed in after Draper had flicked on an Edwards' cross. Reg Matthewson had two efforts cleared off the line and Draper had a 'goal' disallowed as Chester marched into round four.

> Chester - Millington, Edwards, Loska, Storton, Matthewson, Mason, Redfern, Seddon, Draper, James, Lennard
> Preston - Brown, Spark, Burns, Charlton, Bird, Sadler, Lamb, Morley, Elwiss, Holden, Williams

LEAGUE CUP Fourth Round
At SEALAND ROAD STADIUM, CHESTER
Wednesday, 13th Nov., 1974 Kick-off 7-30

CONDITIONS OF SALE
This Ticket is issued subject to the rules & regulations of the FOOTBALL ASSOC. on the distinct condition that no holder thereof shall sell or transfer same for a larger price than appears on the face thereof. In the event of any breach of this condition the Chester Football Club Ltd., reserves the right to cancel this ticket and to retain the money paid therefor on allotment. Price of ticket will NOT be returned in any circumstances if the match has to be abandoned.

CHESTER v. LEEDS

Seat No.
№ 0026

CENTRE STAND S.T.
60p
ENTRANCE F

Secretary Chester F.C.

This portion to be retained

When the draw paired Chester with League Champions Leeds United at Sealand Road few people gave them a chance against a team brimming with internat-ionals, but, on a never to be for-gotten night, Chester pulled off one of the greatest giant-killing acts of all time. There was only one team in it as Chester not only beat but outclassed and outplayed Leeds in a 3-0 victory. John 'Jesse' James was the goalscoring hero as Leeds failed to handle the elusive Draper, who was a constant thorn in their side, while Storton and Matthewson hardly gave Clarke and Jordan a look in.

A packed Stadium erupted after only 16 minutes as Chester took the lead. Mason sent over a fine cross to the near post where Draper's flicked header deceived the Leeds defence to give James a vital opening. His shot was blocked by Harvey, but the keeper could do nothing as James hammered in the rebound. In the first-half the best chance for Leeds fell to Cooper but his 25 yard shot was turned over the bar by Millington. The crucial moment in the game came early in the second-half when Storton made his only mistake, but when Cooper put the ball into the net the 'goal' was disallowed for offside. Hearts were still pounding a minute later, when a long free kick by Whitehead was turned across the area by Draper for Storton to put Chester two up with a fierce shot.

The killer blow for Leeds came in the 58th minute when the unfortunate Cooper brought down Seddon in the penalty area. James made no mistake from the spot to complete the club's finest victory and send the fans into raptures.

The 3-0 win was no more than Chester deserved and Leeds captain Billy Bremner praised Chester by admitting *'The better team won on the night. They were a different class from us.'* Ken Roberts, who had always been confident, said '*we were simply magnificent. We played Leeds off the park and beat them on merit.*'

> Chester - Millington, Edwards, Loska, Storton, Matthewson, Mason, Whitehead, Seddon, Draper, James, Lennard
> Leeds United - Harvey, Reaney, Cooper, Yorath, McQueen, Cherry, Lorimer, Clarke, Jordan, Bremner (Bates), Madeley

After victory over Leeds, Chester had no need to fear anyone at Sealand Road, but the 5th Round gave them their first away tie at Newcastle United. In a spirited performance Chester put their poor away form behind them and came away with a fully deserved goalless draw.
It was Newcastle who exerted the early pressure but the defence held firm and Storton was outstanding in subduing Tyneside hero Malcolm MacDonald. When MacDonald did break through Millington was equal to everything thrown at him. As the game wore on Chester began to show their best form and once again proved that they could match 1st Division opposition for skill. Although they created few clear cut chances Draper almost scored after an excellent seven man move, and James shot inches wide after McFaul had failed to hold a Seddon shot.

> Newcastle - McFaul, Kelly, Clark, Cassidy (Laughton), Keeley, Howard, Barrowclough, Kennedy, MacDonald, Cannell, Nattrass
> Chester - Millington, Edwards, Loska, Storton, Matthewson, Mason, Whitehead, Seddon, Draper, James, Lennard

Having taken Newcastle back to the Stadium, Chester were understandably confident of further progress and Roberts predicted *'We are not dreaming of Wembley, we are planning for it.'*

A week before Christmas the Stadium was again full to the rafters to see if Chester could pull off another cup shock. In a tense, hard-fought encounter both teams found it difficult to create openings. Newcastle's best opportunity fell to MacDonald but his fierce shot, early in the second-half was superbly tipped over by Millington. With only 14 minutes to go a Whitehead corner was headed down by Storton to the lethal James who scored from only two yards out. Newcastle threw everything into a last-ditch attempt to equalise but the 11 man defence held out and Chester were incredibly in the Semi-Finals.

Newcastle manager Joe Harvey was less than charitable in defeat declaring *'I don't rate them at all, not one bit. They are a kick and rush side with no outstanding players.'* Although Chester failed to produce the fluent football of earlier rounds it had been a gutsy, courageous performance and the tone of the encounter had been set by Newcastle with a series of aggressive tackles early in the game.

> Chester - Millington, Edwards, Loska, Storton, Matthewson, Mason, Whitehead, Seddon (Owen), Draper, James, Lennard
> Newcastle - McFaul, Nattrass, Clark, Gibb, Keeley, Howard, Barrowclough, Kennedy, MacDonald, Cannell, Smith.

There were no 1st Division teams left in the competition by the Semi-Final stage, and Chester were drawn against Aston Villa while the other match paired Norwich City with Manchester United. The whole city was now preparing for Wembley and local businesses got behind the team with promises of freezers and a Hillman Imp for each player if they won the cup.

Chester started the 1st leg match at Sealand Road without Stuart Mason who lacked match fitness after a Boxing Day injury. His place was taken by Terry Owen, with Gary Moore as substitute, and it was these players who were the heroes of the evening as Chester played their least convincing football of the run.

The early running came from Chester with a Draper header causing Cumbes problems and Edwards blasting a shot over the bar. Millington also had to save from Graydon, McDonald and Hamilton, and it was McDonald who headed Villa in front after 15 minutes from a Graydon free kick. The goal rattled Chester who struggled to gain a grip on midfield, although Seddon brought a fine save from Cumbes after half-an-hour. A minute before half-time Chester grabbed an equaliser when Owen stabbed the ball home after a mix-up between Nicholl and Cumbes.

The goal came at the right time but Villa quickly recovered and regained the lead in the 50th minute when Graydon, who caused Chester problems all night, latched on to a Brian Little pass and unleashed a fierce shot which left Millington helpless. At this point it looked like Villa would cruise to victory, and Edwards cleared a Leonard effort off the line. With 20 minutes to go Moore replaced James and Chester finally gained the upper hand. There were only 10 minutes to go when Draper broke down the right, took the ball to the by-line and crossed low for Moore to score his first goal for the club. Edwards and Lennard both went close in the last few minutes but Chester had to settle for a 2-2 draw, leaving everything to play for in the second leg at Villa Park.

Chester - Millington, Edwards, Loska, Storton, Matthewson, Owen, Whitehead, Seddon, Draper, James (Moore), Lennard
Aston Villa - Cumbes, Robson, Aitken, Ross, Nicholl, McDonald, Graydon, Little, Leonard, Hamilton, Pimblett

*Ian Seddon (in the net) celebrates Gary Moore's equaliser v. Villa.*

Injuries to Seddon and Draper forced Roberts to reshuffle the side for the 2nd Leg, and 7000 Cestrians made the journey down the M6 to see if the Wembley dream could come true. After 28 minutes it looked all over for Chester as two defensive mistakes were exploited by Keith Leonard. First of all Millington and Storton got in a tangle covering a cross from Graydon and the ball struck Leonard to rebound into an empty net. Nine minutes later the unmarked Leonard powered home a Carrodus cross and Chester trailed 2-0. The response was swift and Stuart Mason hit a stunning 20 yard volley into the top corner for his first goal of the season after 33 minutes.

The task still looked beyond Chester as Villa continued to sweep forward and Millington's goal had a number of narrow escapes. However, after 62 minutes, Chester incredibly put themselves back on level terms when Cumbes failed to gather a Whitehead corner and dropped it at the feet of James who swivelled and hit a left foot shot into the net. For the third time in the tie Chester had courageously fought back to equalise and extra time looked a certainty as both sides struggled for a breakthrough. There were only 10 minutes to go when Villa struck the killer blow as Graydon's corner was headed on by Leonard for Little to dramatically shoot home. It was heartbreaking for Chester who almost snatched another equaliser when Whitehead's angled shot skimmed wide with only four minutes left. It was a cruel way to be eliminated, but Chester had been glorious in defeat and they were given a tremendous ovation by 47000 fans at the end of the game.

Aston Villa - Cumbes, Robson, Aitken, Ross, Nicholl, McDonald, Graydon, Little, Leonard, Hamilton, Carrodus
Chester - Millington, Edwards, Loska, Storton, Matthewson, Mason, Whitehead, Lennard, Moore, James, Owen

**Derek Draper races Ian Ross (Villa) for the ball.**

# SUCCESS AND EMBARRASSMENT 1975 - 1986
# CHAPTER 11

After the euphoria of promotion Ken Roberts and Brian Green settled down to preparing the club for a new era in Division 3. Although both men believed that Chester's style of football would suit a higher League they recognised that the squad would also need to be strengthened. However for the first game, at Crystal Palace, Roberts placed his faith in the players who had won promotion, but Chester went down 2-0. The only summer signing, Barney Daniels from Manchester City for £20,000, made his debut in the opening home game against Southend and scored with a ferocious 25 yard shot to give Chester their first point. A few days later Daniels was the subject of controversy as Chester crashed out of the League Cup to Wrexham. Trailing 3-0 from the 1st leg Daniels was substituted and reacted by tearing off his shirt and throwing it at the trainer's bench. It proved to be an unhappy move for the record signing who made only eight appearances before joining Stockport.

Many of the players found it difficult to adapt to 3rd Division football and it was mid-September before the first win was achieved, 1-0 over Colchester. John James was the first of the promotion heroes to depart when he moved to Tranmere in part-exchange for Paul Crossley. Unfortunately Crossley injured his ankle after scoring on his home debut against Peterborough and missed the next two months action. The early season problems were exacerbated by the loss of Brian Green who left the club to become coach of an Australian national side preparing for the 1978 World Cup. By mid-October Chester were bottom of the table, but the signing of Bob Delgado from Rotherham for £6,000 helped add stability to the defence. When Delgado returned to Millmoor he helped Chester to their first away win of the season, the first game of a nine match unbeaten run.

The New Year commenced with a thumping 8-1 win over Kidderminster in the Welsh Cup, and a home draw with Mansfield which included a spectacular 35 yard goal from Delgado. Revenge was gained over promotion chasing Brighton for a 6-0 defeat in September and the 3-0 win was one of a number of impressive home results which re-established the Stadium as a graveyard for visitors. Unfortunately Chester's away record in 1976 proved to be poor in the extreme, and it was mid-March before the first goal and point was picked up, at Aldershot, and only two more goals and one point were secured on their travels.

The poor away record pulled Chester back towards the relegation zone, although Division 3 safety was secured before they faced Crystal Palace in the last game. Palace, managed by Malcolm Allison and coached by Terry Venables, needed to win this game to gain promotion, and an early penalty by Peter Taylor put them in a strong position but two goals from the recalled Crossley ended their dream.

There was some disappointment at the final position of 17th, but lessons had been learnt and there was encouragement in the form of Player of the Season Grenville Millington and centre-backs Storton and Delgado. Cliff Sear, who had taken the role of Youth Team manager, led the youngsters to the Northern Floodlit League title and two members of that team, Paul Raynor and Mark Nickeas, made their full debuts. In February prodigal son Billy Dearden made a brief but welcome return on loan from Sheffield United and the move was made permanent in July.

The major signing for the 1976/77 season was Alan Oakes, the stalwart Manchester City midfielder, with 565 appearances under his belt. Oakes, who started his career at Maine Road in 1959, had won medals in all three domestic competitions as well as the European Cup Winners cup and had been included in the 40 man England squad for the 1970 Mexico World Cup. The £15,000 transfer was a coup for Ken Roberts and Chester, as Oakes was under no pressure to leave City and he was immediately given the captaincy.

The season opened with an away win at Tranmere courtesy of a remarkable long range own goal by Dave Philpotts. Amazingly Philpotts had performed the same feat 10 days earlier when Chester had beaten Tranmere in the Cheshire Premier Cup. Later in the season Chester completed the League double over the Wirral side thanks to another own goal, this time from Clive Griffiths.

Chester also benefitted from an own goal, in the League Cup, against 2nd Division Hereford. They had travelled to Edgar Street with a two goal first leg lead and at 2-2 in the 2nd leg the tie was put beyond Hereford when Terry Paine scored with a 30 yard attempted back pass. Chester went through with an aggregate score of 5-4 but were beaten 3-2 in the next round by Swansea, who included Gary Moore in their team, thanks to an injury time goal by 16-year-old Jeremy Charles. This setback, the third home defeat in a week, proved to be the final straw for Ken Roberts who tendered his resignation two days later after eight years in charge. Alan Oakes was immediately appointed as his successor although Roberts remained at the club in an advisory capacity.

It was a difficult first match for Oakes, away at promotion favourites Crystal Palace, but Chester recovered a half-time deficit to win 2-1 and give the new player-manager a flying start. When Oakes took over, the team was fundamentally the same as that which had won promotion, but it was clear new blood was needed and gradually he embarked on a rebuilding process.

Oakes's first signing was creative midfielder Paul Richardson from Nottingham Forest for £13,000. A former England Youth international Richardson proved a quality signing and at the end of the season he moved back into the 2nd Division with Stoke for £50,000. Chris Dunleavy and Tony Loska moved on to Halifax in October, while solid full-back Jim Walker came in from Peterborough. Although Paul Crossley was playing well up front Chester lacked a target man and this was remedied with the £18,000 signing of 21-year-old Ian Edwards from West Bromwich Albion. Edwards made his debut against Northampton alongside Ian Howat who was also playing his first full game. It proved a dream debut for Edwards who scored a glorious goal in a 2-1 win.

The signing of Edwards proved a turning point and coincided with Chester's first ever appearance in the FA Cup 5th Round. The cup run started with an ugly battle against Hartlepool which saw Trevor Storton suffer a broken nose in an off the ball incident as 'Pool finished with 10 men. The 1-0 win earned Chester a trip to Grimsby, bottom of the 3rd Division, and they had few problems in disposing of the Mariners more easily than the 1-0 score suggested. In the 3rd Round Chester were given a tough looking tie at 4th Division Southend, a team with an excellent defensive record, who had only been beaten twice all season.

In one of the most clinical FA Cup performances for many years Chester crushed the Essex side 4-0, with Edwards enhancing his growing reputation by scoring an explosive hat-trick. Luton Town were the 4th Round opponents in what was a nostalgic return for the Futcher twins. It took Chester a long time to find their composure but gradually they took control with Oakes masterminding the game in midfield. The tie remained goalless until injury time, when a Dearden cross found Edwards in acres of space allowing the big striker to pick his spot out of keeper Aleksic's reach.

As Edwards celebrated the goal an 8 foot section of perimeter wall at the Kop end collapsed and the crowd spilled on to the pitch. Fortunately there were no serious injuries in what was a potentially dangerous situation. In the 5th Round Chester visited 2nd Division promotion challengers Wolves and were desperately unlucky not to make further progress as they easily matched their illustrious opponents. The only goal of the game came from Hibbitt, nine minutes from time, and was the first goal Chester had conceded in the competition.

With two minutes remaining Edwards crashed a powerful header against the inside angle of the post and bar to deprive Chester of a deserved replay.

Results proved to be equally good in the League and Alan Oakes won his first Manager of the Month award in January 1977. Five wins out of six in February, including an impressive 4-3 win at Preston, took Chester into the top half of the table, but they suffered a setback at the start of March against Rotherham. Ian Edwards had put Chester in line for their fifth successive win, but collided with goalkeeper McAllister in the process of scoring. By continuing he further aggravated the injury and at the end of the game Chester were not only beaten but effectively without the services of their centre-forward for the remainder of the season. It was unfortunate for Edwards who a month earlier had earned a Welsh Under-21 cap against Scotland.

Oakes signed Mick Kearney on loan from Shrewsbury as a replacement and made the move permanent in April at a fee of £8,000. Towards the end of the season two more of Cliff Sear's youngsters, David Burns and Brynley Jones, made their debuts. Burns replaced Paul Crossley who left Chester to spend the summer playing in America.

The 1976/77 season marked the end of Derek Draper's first team career at Chester after more than 300 appearances, while Billy Dearden moved on to Chesterfield. A long season ended with Chester competing in the Debenhams Cup Final, a competition for clubs outside the 1st and 2nd Divisions who advanced furthest in the FA Cup. Their opponents were Port Vale and at half-time in the 2nd Leg at Sealand Road Chester were trailing 2-0 on aggregate, but a tenacious 2nd half display brought them back into the game. Goals from Mason and Burns put Chester level but Beamish responded quickly with an important away goal.

With 20 minutes to go former Chester defender Neil Griffiths put through his own goal and with victory in sight substitute Howat crashed the ball into the net to crown a remarkable aggregate win. There was more silverware before the start of the 1977/78 season when Chester won the Cheshire Premier Cup for the first time. Victories over Stockport (2-1), Tranmere (2-1) and Crewe (2-0) helped Chester to a trophy which had superseded the Cheshire Bowl and was now being played on a League basis.

The only new signing was Derek Jeffries from Crystal Palace, an ex-colleague of Oakes at Manchester City, although the manager failed in an attempt to bring Graham Turner back to the club. After a narrow defeat by 2nd Division Burnley in the League Cup the bread and butter of the League commenced with a crushing 4-1 win over Hereford. Paul Crossley returned from America in September and helped Chester recover a 2-0 deficit against Bradford City in a game which also marked the debut of midfielder Ronnie Phillips, an £8,000 signing from Bury. The 2-2 draw at Valley Parade was one of 22 draws during the season which equalled the Football League record held jointly by Tranmere and Aldershot.

Grenville Millington was dropped after heavy defeats at Oxford and Tranmere in favour of new signing Brian Lloyd from Wrexham. Lloyd, who cost £6,000, had won three caps for Wales but had recently lost his place at the Racecourse Ground. He proved that Wrexham's decision was premature with some outstanding displays, including a penalty save on his debut against Portsmouth, and was deservedly voted Player of the Year. In October a struggling midfield was strengthened with the signing of Doug Livermore, the ex-Liverpool and Norwich player, from Cardiff, for £12,500.

**MATCH TO REMEMBER**
**WREXHAM 1 CHESTER 2**
**LEAGUE DIVISION 3 - APRIL 3RD 1978**

*When Chester made the short trip to Wrexham for this Monday evening encounter,the game was watched by the largest derby day crowd in 30 years. Nearly 20,000 spectators were present to see if top of the table Wrexham could extend their unbeaten home record,while Chester entered the game without an away win in 14 months.*

*On the night, Wrexham's front runners failed to find their rhythm against a composed Chester side, well organised by Oakes. They survived an early Wrexham onslaught, during which Dwyer volleyed against the crossbar, and took the lead after 30 minutes when a neat through pass from Man of the Match Ronnie Phillips fell to Ian Howat who beat Dai Davies on the turn. It was a great moment for Wrexham born Howat who had been unfortunate to miss most of the season through injury. Just before half-time Chester extended their lead when a Phillips corner was headed on by Delgado to Mellor, who had time to control the ball, turn, and shoot high into the net. In the second-half Chester defended their lead well, but Wrexham came back into the game with 15 minutes remaining when Paul Raynor headed into his own goal while trying to clear a corner. In a frantic finale ex-Wrexham keeper Lloyd made magnificent saves from Thomas and Cegielski, while Ian Howat had a chance to extend the lead in the closing minutes but his shot was saved by Dai Davies. The 2-1 victory gave Chester their first win at the Racecourse Ground since 1961.*

*Chester - Lloyd, Nickeas, Raynor, Storton, Jeffries, Oakes, Howat, Livermore, Delgado, Mellor Phillips.*
*Wrexham - D Davies, Hill, Dwyer, G Davies, Roberts (Cegielski), Thomas, Shinton, Sutton, Lyons, Whittle, Cartwright.*

For the second time in three seasons Chester beat Darlington in the FA Cup 1st Round but defeat in the 2nd Round, at Carlisle, cost them a money spinning tie against Manchester United in Round 3. At the turn of the year Chester were in mid-table but the front two of Edwards and Kearney were finding goals hard to come by.

Kearney was dropped in January and moved to Reading for £11,000 shortly after-wards. Edwards meanwhile was still suffering the after affects of his knee injury against Rotherham the previous year, although in September he had won his first full Welsh cap, coming on as substitute for John Tosh-ack against Kuwait.

In February he won a second Under-21 cap against Scotland in a match played at Sealand Road in front of 2,454 with Wales winning 1-0.

In February Oakes signed another ex-colleague, Ian 'Spider' Mellor from Brighton for £25,000. Injuries to Edwards and Howat saw Mellor line up alongside Nigel 'Goller' Clutton in his second game against Carlisle. Clutton, a 23-year-old Sunday League player, interrupted his job as a milkman to play his only game for the club in a 2-2 draw. When Chester played Walsall in March leading scorer Paul Crossley played his last game for the club before joining Seattle Sounders for £10,000. He departed the club, as he joined it, in dramatic style, by scoring a penalty equaliser and dislocating his right arm. The draw left Chester 11th but April provided a fine sequence of results and seven wins out of eight matches pulled Chester up to a final position of 5th, and earned Alan Oakes another Manager of the Month award. The final game provided a dramatic end to the season as Chester beat Peterborough 4-3. All Peterborough's goals were scored by Alan Slough from the penalty spot, and at the end of the game hundreds of angry Chester fans invaded the pitch as the referee was escorted off the field.

Having missed out on promotion by two points the club had every reason to look forward to the 1978/79 season. The building of the new main stand left Alan Oakes with no money to spend, but Cliff Sear had a number of promising youngsters coming through the ranks. The Youth team had achieved their best performance in the Youth Cup by reaching the last 32 thanks to the goal-scoring exploits of 15-year-old Flintshire schoolboy Ian Rush.

*Paul Crossley shoots for the Carlisle goal, watched by Clutton and Mellor.*

The 1978/79 season started with Chester retaining the Cheshire Premier Cup after victories over Stockport (2-0), Tranmere (2-1) and Crewe (2-0), while three straight League wins put them top of Division 3 for the first time. The early weeks of August brought back memories of the 1974/75 season, when Chester faced 1st Division Coventry in the League Cup after easily disposing of Port Vale in the 1st Round. Coventry came to Sealand Road in 4th place but were no match for hard-running Chester who put the Sky Blues defence under constant pressure. Chester took the lead when Edwards soared above the Coventry defence to head in a Livermore free kick and Mellor extended the lead after a mistake by keeper Sealey. A late consolation by Thompson gave a flattering slant on the scoreline in a game dominated by Chester. Another 1st Division side, Norwich City, won 2-0 in the next round but the result could have been different had Mellor not mis-kicked after rounding keeper Keelan.

*Chairman Reg Rowlands presents Ian Edwards with a Welsh under-21 Cap.*

The win over Coventry earned Oakes the Manager of the Month award for August, but September started badly with a first defeat in 17 League and Cup games, 3-0 against Hull. Chester returned to winning ways against League leaders Swansea in a game notable for the sending off of ex-Liverpool defender Tommy Smith, and two weeks later 2nd placed Watford also came to grief at Sealand Road. Just when everything appeared to be going well Chester came down to earth with a disastrous 6-2 defeat at relegation threatened Tranmere, a result that hinged on the first-half dismissal of Derek Jeffries.

Despite the Tranmere result Chester continued to challenge the leaders with a lot of the credit due to Ian Edwards who was back to full fitness after his February injury. Edwards was rewarded with his second Welsh cap in a European Championship game against Malta. Wales won 7-0 and Ed-wards was the hero with four, a feat which equalled the Welsh record for most goals in an International.

The follow-ing Saturday Edwards was again in lethal form with an 18 minute hat-trick against Brentford.

Unfortunately fate stepped in and the big striker had to return to hospital for another operation on his troublesome knee after scoring twice against Hull.

Although Edwards returned to the side in January he was unable to recapture his early form, and Chester's promotion bid started to falter. After hammering Runcorn 5-0 in an FA Cup 1st Round replay Chester played 12 League and cup games without a win. In December winger Peter Sutcliffe arrived from Port Vale with popular Bob Delgado making the move in the opposite direction, and two more forwards, Gary Felix (Leeds) and Peter Henderson (Witton) joined in January. Henderson, a 26-year-old PE teacher in Northwich, had an impressive goalscoring record at Witton with 34 goals in 28 games and had been tracked by many League clubs.

The poor run ended with a 4-1 win over Oxford and this was followed by a 5-1 victory over bottom of the table Lincoln, with Henderson netting his first hat-trick. An unpredictable season continued with a 6-0 defeat at Brentford in the next game, and a final position of 16th was a disappointment after such a promising start.

The Youth team once again reached the last 32 of the FA Youth Cup, when they were narrowly beaten 1-0 by Bristol Rovers. Ian Rush meanwhile made his full debut in a reshuffled side against Sheffield Wednesday wearing the number 4 shirt.

There were two departures during the close season, Doug Livermore and Ian Mellor, while midfielder John Ruggiero joined on a free transfer from Brighton, along with Chesterfield centre-half John Cottam for £12,500. Both players appeared in the League Cup 1st Round tie against Walsall, a game that also marked the opening of the new £630,000 main stand. Once again Chester were top of the table after three games, which included a win at Wimbledon in their first match against the London club.

Injury to Brian Lloyd gave Grenville Millington a chance to re-establish himself in the team against Carlisle at the end of September.

Millington, who had recently turned part-time, was unable to prevent Carlisle snatching a draw with a late Peter Beardsley goal. In the next game however he saved a penalty from Plymouth's Fred Binney as Chester achieved their first win in eight games. October ended with an Ian Edwards goal against Barnsley, but fans were dismayed when the popular striker was sold to arch-rivals Wrexham for what appeared a bargain £125,000 a few days later. In retrospect it proved to be a good deal as the unlucky Edwards continued to be troubled by injury and was forced into an early retirement in 1983.

The Edwards transfer gave Ian Rush the opportunity to stake his claim, and in his first match at centre-forward the youngster scored from 25 yards in a 3-1 win over Wimbledon. Rush never looked back and 10 goals in 15 games took Chester up the table and brought the scouts flocking to Sealand Road. A spectacular winner against Blackpool at the end of 1979 enhanced his reputation still further and he also played a major part in helping Chester to their second appearance in the FA Cup 5th Round in only 4 seasons.

In the 1st Round Chester had little problem in disposing of non-League Workington 5-1, but were given a much harder game against Barnsley in Round 2 where a late Paul Raynor penalty separated the teams. Round 3 provided a tie at Newcastle United, riding high at the top of Division 2 and unbeaten at home.

The Chester defence however were in sterling form with Trevor Storton outstanding in stifling the threat of highly rated number 9 Peter Withe.

Peter Henderson surprised the Geordies with a goal after only three minutes when the Newcastle defence failed to clear a Phillips cross. More than 400 Chester fans, stuck on a football special train near Castleford, missed the goal but they arrived in time to see Ian Rush slam home the second goal with 15 minutes to go, and add another zero to his value. The 4th Round draw proved a disappointment, but Chester were well in command in beating 3rd Division rivals Millwall 2-0, a week after the same team had beaten them 3-1 in London. Ipswich Town, 5th in Division 1, provided a formidable obstacle in Round 5 but the Suffolk side were given a shock after only nine minutes when an apparently harmless header by Jones caught Cooper off his line to give Chester the lead. Gradually the Dutch pair of Thijssen and Muhren took control of midfield and two goals by Burley and Wark, just before half-time, sent Ipswich through.

By now Manchester City and Liverpool had emerged as firm favourites to sign Ian Rush, and in April the Anfield club won the race by signing the Welshman for £300,000. It had been a short but spectacular Sealand Road career for Rush that owed a lot to Cliff Sear and Alan Oakes, and he continued to score goals in an illustrious career with Liverpool, Juventus and Leeds amongst others.

*Watched by Trevor Phillips, Ian Rush scores against Oxford in 1980.*

*Watched by Trevor Phillips, Ian Rush scores against Oxford in 1980.*

In March Chester had broken their own transfer record with the £35,000 signing of striker Trevor Phillips from Hull. The ex-England Youth international had an outstanding goalscoring record with his first club, Rotherham United, but was unable to match this rate at Chester as goals dried up towards the end of the season. However a tight defence, the Oakes trademark, helped Chester to 9th position despite a poor away record which saw no wins after mid-November.

The 1979/80 season marked the end of Chester's long association with the Welsh Cup, a competition they had won three times. During the 1970s interest had faded and matches against Welsh non-League clubs were frequently used for experimentation. It was only the games against Cardiff and particularly Wrexham that attracted much interest, although Chester did reach the Semi-Finals on four occasions during the 1970s. The final Welsh Cup game was played at Merthyr Tydfil, and Chester suffered an ignominious 1-0 defeat without creating any worthwhile chances.

In July Peter Henderson was transferred to Gillingham for £28,000, the third striker to leave in less than 12 months, and it was inevitable that goals would be at a premium in the 1980/81 season. Oakes moved to bolster the attack by signing John Anderson, a triallist from Everton, Trevor Birch (Shrewsbury) and Mike Kearney (Reading), but all three failed to find the net in the League. The signing of Kearney for £25,000 proved a major surprise, but the big striker had finished leading scorer for Reading in 1979/80 with three of his total coming against Chester.

Kearney's second spell at Sealand Road proved to be an unhappy episode, and after only nine games he returned to Elm Park. Inevitably when Chester played Reading early in 1981 Kearney was one of the scorers in a 3-0 win.

Chester's other pre-season signing was 24-year-old midfielder Steve Ludlam from Carlisle for a record £45,000, and he was on target in a 1-0 win over Tranmere in the pre-season Cheshire Premier Cup. The cup was won for the 3rd time in four seasons after additional victories over Stockport (4-1) and Crewe (1-0). Fourth Division Stockport were quick to gain revenge when they defeated Chester by an aggregate 2-1 in the League Cup despite finishing the match at Sealand Road with only 10 men. This disappointing defeat was matched by a poor start in the League and when youngster Terry Cooke marked his debut by scoring a late goal against Exeter, it was one of only two goals in the first seven games. The first away point was picked up at Colchester courtesy of a fluke goal by Brynley Jones when an attempted clearance by Leslie thundered against Jones' shins and into the net.

With the team struggling to find goals, and results disappointing, unrest among the fans started to gain momentum as attendances slumped. Early in 1981 a pessimistic Reg Rowlands warned Chester fans of impending financial problems despite the club reporting a record profit of £370,060 thanks to the sale of Edwards and Rush. Most of the profit had since been used to reduce the bank loan on the new stand with the club being badly hit by a huge increase in interest rates. In addition more than £100,000 had been spent on new players and wages had risen correspondingly as Rowlands announced that the club were currently losing £3,500 a week and expected to lose £200,000 during the season. Hopes of another windfall from the FA Cup were dashed in the 1st Round when Barnsley won 2-1 at Sealand Road, thanks to a late penalty, and Oakes was told that there was no more money available for new players.

*Alan Oakes makes his 750th appearance at Exeter*

In the League four successive wins in October, including a 4-1 victory over Hull, was followed by failure to score in five of the next seven games. The lack of goals was countered by a strong defence in which Cottam and the evergreen Storton were outstanding. In addition the form of Millington, who was elected Player of the Year, and the emergence of Phil Harrington in the Reserves, allowed Oakes to release Brian Lloyd on loan to Port Vale.

Chester reserved their best performance of the season for a 4-0 crushing of League leaders Charlton Athletic, but that result was an exception in a season of few thrills, which had been marked by a series of narrow wins and defeats. In March, Chester received television exposure when they appeared on 'Match of the Day' against Huddersfield, but there was little to entertain the viewers in a goalless draw. Third Division survival was assured with a point at Exeter City where Alan Oakes made his 750th Football League appearance.

Among seven players given free transfers at the end of the season were Brian Lloyd, Derek Jeffries, Trevor Birch and Keith Fear, while Ronnie Phillips had left the club in January. In addition popular full-back Jim Walker was forced into premature retirement after a nine month battle against injury. This left Oakes with only 14 professionals for the 1981/82 season, including the inexperienced Peter Zelem, Terry Cooke and Paul Needham, as the wage bill was cutback. Oakes failed in his attempt to bring in George Telfer (Everton) and Ernie Moss (Chesterfield), but did succeed in signing another Chesterfield striker, 22-year-old Gary Simpson for £6,000. The manager himself was linked with Rotherham and short-listed for the job at Plymouth, but Reg Rowlands made it clear that he did not want Oakes to leave.

The 1981/82 season marked Chester's 50th year as members of the Football League and they looked set for an opening day victory when Zelem and Oakes put them 2-0 up after 22 minutes on their first visit to Bristol Rovers. However Rovers recovered in the second-half to snatch a 2-2 draw. The first three League games at Sealand Road, against Swindon, Millwall, and Walsall were all goalless, and 16-year-old forward John Allen made his full debut against Fulham as Alan Oakes tried to find an answer to the lack of goals. With no money available for signings a number of Cliff Sear's youngsters were given first team opportunities and besides Allen, Paul Blackwell, Phil Harrington, Mark Dean and Mike Williams, were all given debuts during the season. Gary Simpson scored his first League goal at Gillingham to give Chester not only their first success in 16 visits to the Priestfield Stadium but also their first ever three point win.

In the League Cup Chester were paired against Plymouth in what was supposedly a regional draw. The first leg at Sealand Road had a bizarre ending when, with the match evenly balanced at 2-2, Grenville Millington crashed into the goalpost while saving a David Kemp header. Millington was stunned as the bar collapsed on top of him and with no replacement goalposts available the referee was forced to abandon the game.

The re-match, a week later, also finished in a draw, but Plymouth went through with a 1-0 win in the 2nd Leg. At the end of October Plymouth, by then bottom of Division 3, inflicted a humiliating 5-1 defeat, and the following week Mike Kearney was again on target for Reading as Chester threw away another two goal lead to lose 3-2.

By mid-November Chester were 2nd from bottom, without a home win, and facing a tricky FA Cup-tie at Northern League Penrith. Four hundred Chester fans made the trip to the Lake District to experience one of the worst days in the club's history. A Geoff Fell goal midway through the second-half gave the Cumbrians a 1-0 victory, but the manner of defeat brought the dissent among the fans to a new height. Oakes himself said *'It is unbelievable. I am very depressed and disappointed about the result and I can only apologise to the supporters. I feel they were badly let down.'* The following Monday supporter pressure and disagreement with his fellow directors on the club's transfer policy forced Reg Rowlands to quit as chairman.

Once again the club was thrown into turmoil, although Rowlands resumed control in February after settling his differences with the other directors. A massive loss of £137,227 was announced at the AGM and the only 'new' signing was Peter Henderson who returned on trial after an injury hit career at Gillingham.

The return of Henderson coincided with victory at Newport and the first home success, against Portsmouth in January, broke a sequence of 10 home matches without a win. There were brief hopes of a revival in February when Henderson and Simpson hit five goals apiece in as many games. The last of these, against 2nd placed Chesterfield, produced a major shock as Gary Simpson led Chester to a 5-3 win in monsoon conditions. However this proved to be the last win of the season, and defeat at home to fellow strugglers Preston cost Alan Oakes his job after six years in charge. With Chester firmly entrenched at the bottom of the table, Cliff Sear took over as caretaker/manager for the remainder of the season.

Oakes had guided Chester through their most successful seasons since the 1930s. Unfortunately the cash crisis, brought on by the construction of the new stand, had severely limited his options after 1980, and some of his later signings had failed to live up to expectations. After leaving Sealand Road, Oakes moved on to Port Vale but returned to the coaching staff during Graham Barrow's managerial reign.

The size of the task facing Cliff Sear became apparent when Chester faced second from bottom Wimbledon in his first game in charge. Wimbledon had two players sent off in a stormy relegation battle, but still went away with a point in a 1-1 draw. Only one more point and two goals were recorded in the last 12 games as Chester finished 21 points adrift of safety, and returned to Division 4 after seven seasons. The only cause for optimism in a disastrous season were the Welsh Youth caps awarded to Phil Harrington and John Allen.

Sear was confirmed as manager for the 1982/83 season with former full-back Jim Walker appointed as his right hand man. Predictably there was a big turnover of players with John Cottam leaving to become player-manager of Scarborough and taking Brynley Jones and David Burns with him. Other departures included Trevor Phillips (Stockport), Paul Raynor (Oswestry) and Peter Henderson (Telford). Nigel Edwards returned to Sealand Road, with the money being raised by SPAF (Seals Player Appeal Fund) while other signings, on free transfers, were striker John Thomas (Bolton), long throw expert Noel Bradley (Bury), Paul Johnson (Stoke), Tom Sloan and Martin Lane (Manchester United). Sloan arrived with an impressive pedigree having won three caps for Northern Ireland in 1978.

Perhaps the most significant departure was that of chairman Reg Rowlands, a Chester man through and through, who resigned after 34 years of devoted service on the board, 21 of which were as chairman. On this occasion it was an harmonious parting, and the position of chairman went to Manchester businessman Eric Barnes, a former director at Stockport and Wigan. Barnes breezed into the club with fresh ideas but made it clear that there would be no money for players in the immediate future. By now the club was £400,000 in debt and a 39,000 share allocation was agreed to help the cash flow at the club. This took the total share issue up to 49,000, of which 25,000 were owned by Eric Barnes.

*Trevor Phillips in action against Reading.*

The 1982/83 League season opened with a narrow win over Crewe, Nigel Edwards celebrating his return with the only goal of the game. The following week John Thomas opened his League account at Rochdale although he had already impressed with two goals in a 5-0 Football League Trophy win over Shrewsbury. An undisciplined defensive display sent Chester crashing out of the Milk Cup against Blackpool, and Sear responded with the loan signings of promising Manchester City youngsters Steve Kinsey and Clive Wilson. Kinsey, rated at £250,000, scored one goal in his three appearances, but the real revelation was 20-year-old midfielder Wilson who showed maturity beyond his years with some immaculate displays as Chester achieved solid victories over Hereford (5-0) and Darlington (2-0). Without Kinsey, Wilson, and the injured Thomas, Chester suffered a 3-1 home defeat against Mansfield and also lost 1981/82 Player of the Season Millington with a badly bruised arm.
Sear brought in Mike Salmon on loan from Blackburn for the next game against Peterborough, but it was the opposing keeper, 19-year-old David Seaman, who made a name for himself with a last minute penalty save in a 1-1 draw.

In November Chester were beaten 1-0 by Bury, their fourth home defeat in five games, and were thrown into a fresh crisis when Cliff Sear resigned after only eight months in charge. Sear, who had felt increasingly uncomfortable in the role as manager, gratefully stepped down to his former job in charge of the Youth team, while 36-year-old John Sainty took over as 'caretaker coach'. A former player with Reading, Bournemouth, Mansfield and Aldershot, Sainty was initially given six weeks to convince the board he was the man for the job. One of Sainty's first jobs was to return to Manchester City, where he had previously been coach, to bring back Clive Wilson on loan.

Sainty's reign began with another FA Cup defeat at the hands of non-League opposition, when near neighbours Northwich won after a replay. Only an injury time equaliser by Martin Lane had saved Chester from defeat at Sealand Road, but Vics made no mistake in the replay as two goals from Mark Ward secured a 3-1 win in extra time. On a brighter note, Lane was also on target on Boxing Day when he played up-front and scored twice in a 4-2 win over Tranmere, in a game which saw Paul Blackwell and Tranmere's John Williams dismissed.

Sainty's trial period, which brought a mixed bag of results, was extended to Easter but after a goalless draw with Tranmere he was confirmed as manager. Finances had restricted his signings to non-contract players Ian Workman and Paul Manns. Workman was released after only three games and joined the police force, while the skilful Manns signed full-time at the end of the season.

The serious financial situation also affected the backroom staff and in February trainer Jim Walker and physio Vince Pritchard were released as an economy measure. Pritchard's association with the club went back to 1959 and he was awarded a testimonial in 1984.

Chester continued to maintain a mid-table position, despite the inexperience of the team. Two of the youngsters, John Allen and Mike Williams, were offered a trial at Chelsea with a view to a permanent transfer. Unfortunately Williams was stretchered off in the game against Hartlepool while Allen's move was delayed by an injury crisis at Sealand Road and the deal fell through

For the last two home games of the season, Chester fans had to watch while Hull City and Scunthorpe celebrated promotion. The Scunthorpe game saw a recall for Grenville Millington who had been released in December but re-signed on non-contract terms in March.

He had been coaching the Lancashire League team and was called on as emergency cover after Phil Harrington was injured in the win at Torquay.

Under the circumstances a final position of 13th was satisfactory, but the future did not look bright as Sainty was told to halve the wage bill, and Sloan, Bradley, Simpson, Dean, Needham, Johnson, Moffatt and Edwards were all released. The only new signings for 1983/84 were the aggressive Andy Elliott who had been playing in Ireland for Sligo Rovers and Andy Holden, a 19 year old hot property with Rhyl who had been attracting the attention of a number of clubs.

Chester started 1983/84 with a new image as the club officially adopted the name Chester City. For many years the 'City' tag had been popular with the fans and on more than one occasion the name change had been proposed, most notably after the war and at the start of the 1960s. The Seals nickname, introduced in 1973/74 as the result of a competition, was dropped and removed from the club crest.

On the verge of the new season, leading scorer John Thomas was sold to Lincoln for £22,500 to ease the financial burden. Player of the Season Thomas had been one of the successes during 1982/83 as he ploughed a lone furrow up front.

In order to flesh out a squad, pared to the bone, Sainty had to rely on non-contract players. Paul Raynor and Trevor Phillips, who had both been released after relegation in 1982, appeared in the opening day draw against Northampton. Also in the side was David Brett, a Youth team player at Chester in the late 1970s, who had latterly played for Colwyn Bay and Chester Sunday League side Liver Hotel. As the season progressed other non-contract players, John Burke, John Ryan, Stuart Parker and Dennis Wann, all made brief appearances and although Parker scored five goals in nine games, Chester could not afford to meet his wages.

Deficiencies in the team soon became apparent as Chester won only one of the first 12 League games. However, there were two impressive performances in the Milk Cup to savour, against Bolton and Leeds. In the 1st Round, against 2nd Division Bolton, Chester trailed 3-0 from the 1st Leg and were given little hope of progressing against a team who had just thrashed Walsall 8-1. In the second Leg Sainty experimented by pushing Andy Holden up front and the move paid off in remarkable fashion. Holden scored his first goal for the club as Chester pulled back the three goal deficit to send the game into extra time and penalties.

The penalty shoot out saw skipper Peter Zelem and John Allen score for Chester but the hero was keeper Harrington who saved the first 3 Bolton penalties. In Round 2 it was a seriously understrength Chester team that visited 2nd Division Leeds United for the 1st Leg.

Trevor Storton, the only survivor from the 1974 clash, was missing through injury as were Paul Manns and Paul Blackwell. A heroic performance saw Chester triumph 1-0, with the only goal coming from a spectacular Andy Elliott header after 27 minutes. Unfortunately there was no fairy tale ending as Leeds overran City in the 2nd Leg to go through 4-2 on aggregate.

The Milk Cup results could not disguise what was turning into one of Chester's worst ever seasons. In November John Sainty parted company with Chester after only 12 difficult months in charge. Long serving defender Trevor Storton was given the unenviable task of pulling the team around as he was appointed caretaker/coach for two months. Results under Storton showed no improvement, and when Chester lost at home to Aldershot they were watched by only 975 people, their lowest ever League attendance. Storton's chances of getting the managers job permanently effectively disappeared after a 4-0 home defeat by Mansfield and an ill-disciplined performance at Bristol City where Zelem and Sutcliffe were sent off in a 4-2 defeat.

At the start of 1984 Storton quit as player-coach after Ronnie Hildersley and Paul Sanderson were signed on loan from Manchester City without his knowledge. With Cliff Sear once again in temporary charge the club looked for a successor and the short list included Gordon Lee, John King, Doug Livermore and, surprisingly, Alan Oakes. In mid-January ex-Port Vale manager John McGrath, an uncompromising centre-half with Bury, Newcastle and Southampton, took over in the hot seat. He had led Port Vale to promotion the previous season but was sacked in December with the club at the bottom of the table.

McGrath's first game in charge resulted in a 1-1 draw with Crewe but a new low was reached with heavy home defeats against Colchester and Swindon, the latter watched by only 880 spectators. The new manager immediately started to build for the future with the double free transfer signing of Lee Dixon and Andy 'The Rat' Wharton from Burnley. Nineteen year old Dixon had only made a handful of appearances at Turf Moor, but had impressed McGrath in the Central League team. Paul Sanderson also signed after 2 months on loan, while Bobby Coy and David Wintersgill were introduced on loan from Wolves. To make way for the new signings, Storton, Phillips and Sutcliffe were all released.

The injection of new blood into the team saw a slight improvement in form with five wins in the last 17 games, but it was not enough to prevent a bottom place finish and the first application for re-election since 1968.

One glimmer of hope was the form of captain and Player of the Season Andy Holden who was tipped to be Chester's next big money transfer.

A player who always gave 100%, Holden had been an unused substitute for Wales Under-21s against Bulgaria in November, and came off the bench against Yugoslavia the following month to gain his first Under-21 cap. At the end of the season he earned a full Welsh cap, as a substitute against Israel, a tremendous achievement for a player with the League's basement club.

McGrath had the makings of a strong defence in Holden, Dixon, Lane, Zelem and Coy and he concentrated his efforts in bringing some flair players to the club. The financial cutbacks during the previous season gave the manager some leeway and nine players, including Coy, were signed for the start of the season while Andy Elliott, John Allen and Mike Williams were all released. Into the squad came Nigel Walker (Sunderland), Steve Fox (Port Vale), Andy Higgins (Rochdale), Alan Morris (Bangor), Peter Sayer (Preston) and Ronnie Hildersley (Manchester City). Sayer, an ex-Welsh International, had won 7 caps while with Cardiff while Hildersley signed after a successful loan period. Experience was added in the form of goalkeeper John Butcher (Oxford) and Mick Speight, ex Sheffield United, Blackburn and Grimsby, a hard-working midfielder who was appointed player-coach.

McGrath's signings helped generate a new wave of optimism among the fans and the manager's enthusiasm helped put some pride back in the club. Eight of the new signings played in the season opener, a 1-1 draw with Scunthorpe, and there was another new face in the first away game at Aldershot. Owen Brown made a goalscoring debut as Chester achieved their first away win in 16 months, but he was released in November despite three goals in five games. The inspirational Holden, injured in a pre-season friendly against Manchester City, returned to the defence in the Milk Cup against Blackpool but picked up another injury as Chester crashed out to the Seasiders for the 2nd time in three seasons. Bobby Coy and Martin Lane also suffered serious early season injuries as McGrath struggled to field a settled defence, but the real problems existed up-front where the failure to sign a recognised goalscorer proved costly.

A bid to sign former Scottish international Asa Hartford was unsuccessful in September as were Bolton and Lincoln's attempts to sign skipper Holden. Meanwhile the form of young Lee Dixon attracted 1st Division scouts and prompted McGrath to put forward his name to Bobby Robson for the England Under-21s.

After beating bottom of the table Northampton, results took a turn for the worse with only one win in 14 League games and an FA Cup exit at Darlington. A series of dismal performances was summed up in a home defeat by injury hit Torquay where 38-year-old David Webb, playing his first game in 3 years as a makeshift striker, scored the only goal of the game. Another home defeat, against a poor Rochdale side, put the manager's position under threat and when Chester conceded four goals in the first 19 minutes at Stockport in a 5-1 defeat the writing was on the wall, and McGrath was sacked.

McGrath left on amicable terms boldly declaring that *'I was only half an inch away from having a great side.....once they get a centre forward they will cruise away.'* Player coach Mick Speight took over as caretaker/manager, and under his leadership the team showed renewed commitment. His first home game in charge saw a morale boosting 2-1 win over bottom of the table Wrexham, but postponements during a January freeze left Chester bottom of the table. Speight made it his priority to strengthen the forward line and signed 25 year old Ricky Greenhough from Alfreton Town, while two more strikers, Paul O'Berg and Stuart Rimmer, were introduced on loan from Wimbledon and Everton respectively. Twenty-year-old Rimmer, a member of Everton's Youth Cup winning team the previous year, was a consistent scorer in the Central League and came recommended by Howard Kendall, Mick Speight's boss at Blackburn.

Rimmer made a dream debut with a quality hat-trick against Southend and a few days later Greenhough and O'Berg were on target in a 2-0 win over Swindon with the latter scoring a spectacular 40 yard lob after a poor clearance by the goalkeeper. The improved form continued with another five goal onslaught, against promotion chasing Darlington, which briefly hauled Chester out of the bottom four. This proved to be O'Berg's final game and coincided with a run of five matches without a win, in what was an inconsistent end to the season. Part-timers Peter Kitchen and Rory Blease were given brief opportunities in the team while Speight failed in attempts to sign Mark Leonard (Crewe), Alan Taylor (Burnley) and Paul Bannon (Bristol Rovers). There was good news when Stuart Rimmer signed on as a full-time Chester player, after an impressive loan spell, with the money coming from the sale of Peter Zelem to Wolves for £12,500.

After victories at Northampton and Halifax, Speight was confirmed as player-manager and celebrated with a 2-0 victory over Aldershot, the 3rd 'double' of the season. The season ended in fine style with five wins in the last seven games, including a Nigel Walker hat-trick in a 4-4 draw at Swindon. Speight had done a fine job in steering Chester clear of re-election and creating a positive atmosphere with the players, but his outspoken comments did little to endear him to the directors. Shortly after his appointment the blunt Yorkshireman had expressed some forthright views on the running of the club claiming: *'There is no ambition within the club. It is run on an amateur level right through the place.'* With a promised two year contract still unsigned Speight entered the close season still uncertain over his future, and in July he was replaced by Harry McNally the former Wigan Athletic manager.

McNally, who never played in the Football League, spent most of his career at Skelmersdale before managing non-League Altrincham and Southport. The controversial sacking sparked a wave of criticism, but McNally quickly settled to the job in hand by signing Milton Graham (Bournemouth), David Glenn (Blackburn) and John Kelly (Preston). They joined Peter Houghton, who had been signed by Speight from Preston, and Northampton's giant central defender, 6ft-5ins Wakeley Gage.

*Stuart Rimmer scores against Tranmere in the 1985 Milk Cup match.*

Among the players who left the club during the close season was the promising Lee Dixon who disappointingly refused a new contract and joined Bury for £3,500. He went on to play for Stoke and Arsenal and won 22 England caps, justifying John McGrath's earlier confidence in him.

Illness and suspension caused the club problems at the start of the 1985/86 season, and when Chester called off a Milk Cup-tie against Tranmere they were fined £2,500 by the Football League.

**MATCH TO REMEMBER**
**PRESTON NORTH END 3 CHESTER CITY 6**
**CANON LEAGUE DIVISION 4 - OCTOBER 12TH 1985**

*Stuart Rimmer celebrated his 21st birthday by helping himself to four goals in an astonishing 6-3 victory at Deepdale. His 17 goals in 15 games helped extend Chester's unbeaten run to nine games as they challenged for promotion.*

*After a quiet start the game came to life after 31 minutes when five goals were scored in a dramatic 14 minute spell. Milton Graham, who had a magnificent game, set up the first goal when his low cross was met by Rimmer and the skilful midfielder repeated the trick six minutes later, for John Kelly to score against his former club. Preston pulled one back through Wayne Foster after 40 minutes, but by half-time Chester were 4-1 ahead as Stuart Rimmer completed his hat-trick. Graham was the creator of Rimmer's 2nd with a superb pass, and straight from the kick-off Rimmer sprinted through the Preston defence before cooly slipping the ball past Platt.*

*In the second half Ricky Greenhough came on for David Murray and joined the scoring spree when he chested down Brett's corner before firing in City's fifth. Slack defensive play allowed Preston to pull two goals back through Welsh and a Gary Brazil penalty, but four minutes from time Rimmer rounded off the scoring with a twice taken penalty after Atkins had brought down Greenhough. In the last minute Rimmer had an excellent opportunity to add a 7th for Chester but he shot wide when it looked easier to score.*

*After the match the players were typically brought down to earth by Harry McNally who gave them a verbal roasting for the sloppy defending that almost let Preston back into the game.*

*Chester - Butcher, Glenn, Lane, Speight, Gage, Coy, Kelly, Graham, Rimmer, Brett, Murray (Greenhough).*
*Preston North End - Platt, Twentyman, Jones, Atkins, Gibson, Martin, Keen (Welsh), Foster, Thomas, Chippendale, Brazil.*

When the game was eventually played a Stuart Rimmer hat-trick at Prenton Park gave Chester a comfortable 3-1, 1st leg lead, and with the tie effectively settled a goalless draw took Chester through to play Coventry City.

In the 1st leg at Sealand Road it was only the Coventry goalkeeper Steve Ogrizovic who prevented a shock result with a string of fine saves, although he was beaten by a Rimmer penalty. At 1-1, with four minutes to go, a 30 yard Dave Bowman shot completely deceived John Butcher to give Chester an uphill struggle in the 2nd leg. The task was made more difficult by the absence of central defenders Gage and Holden, so Ricky Greenhough was given the unenviable task of marking Cyrille Regis who had missed the first game through injury. Greenhough was given a torrid time as Regis rampaged through the makeshift defence and helped himself to five goals in Coventry's 7-2 victory.

The Milk Cup defeat proved a minor blemish as City produced some exhilarating early season performances. After an opening day draw against Halifax McNally returned to Wigan to sign 22-year-old aggressive striker Gary Bennett, who made his debut in a 3-0 defeat at Peterborough. Bennett was quick to form an effective partnership with Rimmer as Chester won seven of the next nine games, including 4-0 destructions of Crewe and Burnley. The most astonishing performance came in a 6-3 away win at Preston, where Rimmer celebrated his 21st birthday by scoring four goals.

A week later the chance to go top of the League was missed after a home defeat by up and coming Swindon, but this proved to be the last defeat until Boxing Day. A rare Bobby Coy goal gave Chester a 1-1 draw at Wrexham, although it was only the woodwork that prevented City claiming all three points, and successive victories over Aldershot,

Colchester and Exeter saw Chester finally reach the 4th Division summit. Wakeley Gage moved to Peterborough in November while Mick Speight took up a position of player-coach in Norway, and NcNally raided non-League football to sign centre-half Graham Abel from Northwich.

A comprehensive 3-0 win over Orient proved costly when the League's leading scorer, Stuart Rimmer, collided with keeper Peter Wells while scoring. It was Rimmer's 21st goal in 23 games and this phenomenal strike rate put him in the £200,000 class with several big clubs watching his progress. X-Rays revealed badly torn knee ligaments, and McNally quickly signed Ian Richardson, a player in the same mould as Rimmer, from Watford for £15,000. The injury kept Rimmer out for the rest of the season and the 1984/85 Player of the Year, Andy Holden, suffered similar problems as a troublesome knee injury required a series of operations which restricted his appearances.

Four wins and a draw in November earned McNally a deserved Bell's Manager of the Month award although top spot was surrendered at the end of the year to Swindon Town. A resounding 4-1 New Year's Day win over Port Vale was marred by the sending off of the skilful Milton Graham who had formed such an effective midfield partnership with John Kelly. A week later Graham repeated the feat against Hartlepool and was relegated to substitute for the next game, against Tranmere. His place was taken by Barry Butler, a recent signing from non-League Atherton LR, but Graham came off the bench to score the only goal of the game. Two more wins in January, against Halifax and Torquay, earned McNally a second Manager of the Month award. Injuries began to take their toll on a small squad in February and March as the promotion bid began to falter. Billy Wright arrived on loan from Birmingham, and scored a thunderous goal on his final appearance as Chester returned to winning ways against Preston. McNally also recruited full-back Earl Barrett and forward Steve Johnson on loan from Manchester City and Bristol City respectively. Barrett, who later earned three England caps when playing for Oldham, remained until the end of the season while Johnson's aerial power added a new dimension to the attack and he contributed some vital goals as the season gathered pace.

Johnson made his debut in the 2-1 win over Wrexham, although the hero was substitute Gary Bennett who scored a late goal to end his personal lean scoring spell. Injury to Graham Abel forced McNally to play Johnson at centre-half as Chester earned draws against Port Vale and Cambridge, but Johnson returned to the attack against Colchester. In a dramatic game Colchester recovered from 2-0 down to equalise, but a Ricky Greenhough goal, eight minutes from time, gave City a thrilling 3-2 win.

Runaway leaders Swindon clinched promotion with a 4-2 win over Chester where Milton Graham received his third dismissal of the season. Eleven days later it was Chester's turn to celebrate as a goalless draw at Orient secured a return to Division 3. The runners-up spot was assured after victories over Southend and Rochdale.

It had been a remarkable turnaround in fortune for the club and a tribute to the fighting qualities instilled in the side by Harry McNally. Despite a disastrous catalogue of injuries, which saw them lose key players Holden and Rimmer, a tremendous team spirit had pulled them through giving Chester fans something to celebrate after the pain of the preceding few seasons.

*Steve Johnson scores from the spot against Exeter in 1986.*

# INTO EXILE 1986 - 1992

# CHAPTER 12

Harry McNally had produced a minor miracle in taking Chester to Division 3, achieving promotion two years ahead of schedule. Having made the step up McNally now began the task of building for the future and his first move proved controversial when he released Bobby Coy on a free transfer, days after the player had been voted Player of the Year. Meanwhile the manager returned to his former club Wigan to sign midfield player Graham Barrow for £6,000 and keeper Billy Stewart on a free transfer. McNally rated Barrow highly but it took a long time for the hard tackling midfielder to win over the fans. Five bookings in his first seven games did little to help his cause and in November Barrow considered a move to Blackpool. However he gradually imposed his authority on midfield where his ball-winning abilities balanced the skills of John Kelly and Milton Graham.

In preparation for the new season Chester embarked on their first ever foreign tour when they made an unusual visit to the Faroe Islands, despite pressure from Greenpeace who objected to the Islanders annual whale slaughter. However the controversy surrounding this tour was nothing compared to the furore that greeted the announcement of a proposed ground move over the border into Wales. In February 1986, with debts mounting, Eric Barnes announced the intentions of the club to move to a multi-million pound stadium with a 15,000 capacity and facilities for other sports. The move was to be funded by the sale and re-development of Sealand Road together with a grant from the Sports Council. During the summer the new site was revealed to be 50 acres of land on Mill Farm, just over the Welsh border, between Bumpers Lane and the River Dee. The announcement caused an uproar among fans who made their views known before a pre-season friendly with Oldham, and the objections caused Barnes to reconsider his decision.

In September the re-location issue took a backseat when a tax demand for £78,000 coupled with unpaid bills of £70,000 placed the club's whole future in doubt. With the club facing a winding-up order over the unpaid tax bill, two Cheshire businessmen, Dyson Barker and David Cross, injected £132,000 into the club to pay off the outstanding debt which secured the club's short term future. The new owners, trading as BCH, also purchased 26,000 shares from Eric Barnes for £260, thus taking a controlling interest in the club although Barnes remained as chairman.

Out on the field City returned to Division 3 with a bruising encounter against Carlisle. Graham Abel, who had turned full-time during the summer, was sent off along with Carlisle's Scott Endersby in a 2-2 draw. The first goal had come from an Andy Holden penalty, and in October, with the financial crisis worsening, Chester were forced to accept an offer of £50,000 from Wigan for the popular defender. Unfortunately Holden's promising career continued to be injury plagued and over the next 10 years he only managed another 71 appearances with Wigan and later Oldham. Holden's final goal for Chester came in a 1-0 win over Doncaster, the only victory in the first 16 games, where Stuart Rimmer also made a welcome re-appearance as substitute after nearly 12 months out injured. The return of Rimmer saw Ian Richardson move to Scunthorpe for £15,000, but with Rimmer struggling for fitness the goalscoring focus fell on no-nonsense striker Gary Bennett who hit a rich vein of form after being handed the number 9 shirt for the FA Cup-tie against Rotherham.

It proved an excellent season for Chester in cup competitions with the club just missing out on a trip to Wembley. In the Littlewoods Cup there was an impressive away performance at Derby County with Chester winning 1-0, courtesy of a composed defence and a stunning Peter Houghton goal. City were beaten in the second leg, but the form of 17-year-old Colin Woodthorpe over the two games earned him a full-time contract.

In the FA Cup it was perhaps inevitable, after 11 draws in the first 16 League games, that it should take three games to dispose of 3rd Division rivals Rotherham. The deciding match, at Sealand Road, was settled by a fine goal from Brian Croft, but the result would have been more decisive had Bennett not missed a penalty. This victory put Chester in the 2nd Round for the first time since 1979 and they had few problems in brushing aside Doncaster Rovers. Chester entered the 3rd Round match at Wrexham without Graham Barrow, who was serving his second suspension of the season, while new signing Derek Fazackerley from Blackburn missed the game due to an administrative error over his transfer. Fazackerley, a fully qualified coach, had made nearly 600 appearances at Ewood Park and was lined up by Harry McNally to be his successor. The game itself, played on a snow-covered pitch, was dominated by Wrexham in the first-half with Jim Steel putting the Reds ahead, but Chester turned the tie around in the second-half, thanks to the midfield prompting of Graham and Kelly. It was Graham who was brought down in the 75th minute and although Gary Bennett's penalty was saved by Pearce the rebound fell invitingly for him to equalise.

Chester were now looking the most likely team to score and with four minutes remaining 'Psycho' struck again from another perfect Graham pass to put City in the 4th Round. The Wrexham game marked the final appearance for Martin Lane who was transferred to Coventry City for £25,000.

Chester were rewarded with a 4th Round draw at home to Sheffield Wednesday, and they made all the early running in taking the game to their 1st Division opponents. After only seven minutes John Kelly put Chester ahead, but Wednesday survived the onslaught and Lee Chapman equalised just after the break. In the replay at Hillsborough all the headlines were made for the wrong reasons when a clumsy Bennett tackle on Ian Knight, after only three minutes, led to the Wednesday man being stretchered off with a compound fracture of the leg. Bennett later equalised a Chapman strike but the tie went Wednesday's way when Abel headed spectacularly into his own net as Chester eventually lost 3-1.

In the Freight Rover Trophy Chester moved past Crewe and Preston in the Group stage before beating Lincoln on penalties in the 1st round. Billy Stewart was the hero, saving Kevin Kilmore's penalty, after Chester had scored through Bennett, Rimmer, Fazackerley, Croft and Greenhough. Stewart also saved a late penalty in the next round against Bolton to give them a second cup-tie at Wrexham in less than three months. Once again Chester left it late as they trailed Wrexham to a Paul Comstive goal. With only three minutes remaining a teasing cross from substitute Croft was headed home by Barrow, and goals from Fazackerley and Rimmer in extra time put Chester through to the regional final against Mansfield, with the first leg at Field Mill. Chester were confident of reaching Wembley, having come away from Mansfield a month earlier with an impressive 3-2 win, but on the night many of the players froze, and a jittery Chester hardly mounted a threat in going down to goals from Stringfellow and Cassells. In the second leg, Chester got off to a flying start when Woodthorpe blasted home a free kick after only 12 minutes to rekindle the Wembley dream. However a massed Mansfield defence, in which centre-half George Foster was outstanding, continued to hold out and in the second-half City gradually lost their way as the players tired. Despite a gallant effort, Chester went down 2-1 on aggregate and it was Mansfield who met Bristol City in the Final at Wembley.

In the League, Chester gradually acclimatised to life in Division 3 and achieved some impressive victories, including a 2-1 win at promotion favourites Middlesbrough on their first visit to Ayresome Park. There were also high scoring victories over Fulham (5-0) and Darlington (6-0) as Chester achieved a satisfactory final position of 15th. The season ended, as it had started, with a double sending off as Gary Bennett and Port Vale's Bob Hazell were given their marching orders in Chester's 2-1 defeat.

Milton Graham was rewarded for some creative performances by being elected Player of the Season but he lost his midfield partner in the summer when John Kelly joined Swindon for £20,000. Kelly was replaced by Paul Maddy, a former Welsh Under 21 International, from Brentford for £15,000. McNally also signed one of the lower divisions most consistent defenders, Steve Hetzke from Sunderland, while keeper Mick Astbury replaced the released John Butcher. McNally himself signed a new four year contract, despite rumours linking him with Sunderland and Blackpool. Sadly the 1986/87 season saw Cliff Sear end his long association with the club after an acrimonious behind the scenes dispute.

Chester opened the 1987/88 season without Barrow and Bennett, both suspended following dismissals the previous season, and suffered a horrendous 5-0 home defeat by Northampton, followed by another Littlewoods Cup defeat at the hands of Blackpool. Seventeen-year-old Mark Parry made a goalscoring debut at Southend, but in the next away game, at Rotherham, City conceded another five goals and had Steve Hetzke sent off as Carl Airey scored four for the Yorkshire side. Keeper Billy Stewart joined Butler, Houghton, Maddy and long term casualty David Glenn on a lengthening injury list, and with reserve keeper Astbury also injured, Harry McNally turned to fourth choice Everton goalkeeper Mike Stowell as a temporary replacement. The introduction of Stowell prompted an immediate improvement in results as he only conceded one goal in his first five games, and was on the winning side on each occasion. Stowell was particularly impressive at Gillingham and Sunderland, where Chester put in typical hard-working performances to pull off unlikely victories. Stuart Rimmer scored in both these games to prove that he was back to his goalscoring best, and the scouts returned to Sealand Road as he went on to score 19 goals in the first 22 games.

Young central defender Chris Lightfoot made an accomplished debut in a 1-0 win over Grimsby, before being carried off injured, while Milton Graham became the next injury victim after damaging knee ligaments in a training accident. The improvement in form saw Chester shoot up to 2nd in the table, and McNally was awarded the Divisional Manager of the Month for September. Unfortunately the extensive injury list began to take its toll and one win in the next 18 League games saw Chester slide back down the table. There was also early elimination in the FA Cup at home to non-League opposition, when GM Vauxhall Conference side Runcorn won 1-0. The game was marred by a serious injury to Runcorn's Don Page who suffered a broken leg after a reckless challenge by Barrow.

Loan signings Gary Howlett (Bournemouth), Tony Caldwell (Bristol City) and the highly rated Kevin Langley (Manchester City) were brought in to bolster the injury hit squad.

Former Republic of Ireland international Howlett scored his only goal for the club in a thrilling 4-4 draw with Bury, as Chester twice threw away a two goal lead. On Boxing Day Chester were beaten at home by table-topping Sunderland, but full-back David Glenn returned to first team action after 16 months absence. Another player troubled by injury, Steve Hetzke, returned to the side against Wigan but asked to be put on the transfer list after the next game with Northampton, when McNally was critical of a defence which conceded two late goals. Hetzke moved to Colchester for £10,000, while Paul Maddy, another close-season signing, moved to Hereford on a free transfer.

At the start of March, Chester beat Gillingham 3-1 thanks to a Stuart Rimmer hat-trick in the last 10 minutes. This was Rimmer's fourth hat-trick for the club and came after he had missed a penalty early in the second-half. It proved to be Rimmer's last goal action for Chester as he moved to struggling 1st Division Watford the following week for £210,000. Half the fee went to Everton due to a sell-on clause introduced when Rimmer had joined Chester in 1985. McNally refused to be rushed into buying a replacement for Rimmer and the only new signing before the transfer deadline was John Lowey from Preston. Lowey replaced Kevin Langley who ended his loan spell early, and was transferred to Birmingham by Manchester City. It proved a short stay for Lowey who emigrated to Australia at the end of the season.

Gary Bennett took over from Rimmer at centre-forward and scored five goals in five games as fears of relegation were banished before the final game against Bury. A difficult season ended with Chester in 15th position, but there were encouraging signs in the emergence of Chris Lightfoot and the continuing development of Colin Woodthorpe, while Player of the Year Graham Abel excelled at the heart of the defence. The last game of the season, at Bury, had seen a debut for 15-year-old Aidan Newhouse who became the youngest player to represent Chester in a League game. The following season Newhouse was called up to the England Under-17 squad and inevitably earned the tag of the 'new Ian Rush' as he was tracked by Manchester United, Liverpool and Everton.

Departures at the end of the season included Ricky Greenhough, who joined Scarborough for £5,000, Astbury, Houghton and Lowey. Derek Fazackerley also left the club for York City having grown unhappy with progress at Chester, and Graham Barrow took over as assistant manager. Experience was added to the squad in the shape of competitive midfielder Joe Jakub from Dutch side AZ Alkmaar while Joe Hinnigan (Wrexham) took Fazackerley's place in defence. A new look forward line included Ian Benjamin (Cambridge) and Steve Johnson (Scunthorpe), while McNally brought in 22-year-old Carl Dale from Bangor City for £12,000.

Dale had proved to be a natural goalscorer in non-League football with Rhyl, Conwy and Bangor, and after adjusting to full-time training became a prolific scorer in the Football League.

Chester started the 1988/89 season without the influential Milton Graham, who was struggling with a troublesome knee injury, but early results proved encouraging despite a heavy defeat 6-1 at Sheffield United. In the Littlewoods Cup, Chester again overhauled a 1st Leg deficit at Bolton to go through 3-2 on aggregate, and line-up a money-spinning tie with Brian Clough's Nottingham Forest. Unfortunately a 6-0 defeat at the City Ground made the second leg a formality as Chester crashed out 10-0 on aggregate.

Carl Dale marked his first full game with two goals on the plastic pitch at Preston, but the new forward line left little opportunity for Gary Bennett who asked for a transfer in October. Bennett had never fully regained his touch after the Ian Knight incident against Sheffield Wednesday, and his aggressive style made him a marked man. When Knight returned to League football Bennett again became the focus of press attention and he felt it was in everyone's best interests to look for a new club. Bennett joined Southend for £25,000 and signed off with a typically enthusiastic performance as Chester beat Swansea 3-1. Inevitably when Bennett returned to Chester with his new club at the end of November he scored one of the goals, as the Shrimpers won 4-2 to consign City to their first home defeat of the season.

The return of Barry Butler saw the tightening up of a defence which leaked goals alarmingly at the start of the season. Four successive League victories in December earned Harry McNally another Manager of the Month award, although Chester were eliminated from two cup competitions in the same month. Wrexham ended Chester's interest in the Sherpa Van Trophy at the group stage thanks to a 2-1 win at Sealand Road, with the deciding goal coming from Roger Preece. In the FA Cup Chester put up little resistance to Huddersfield in the 2nd round, after a thoroughly professional performance had seen them dispose of Burnley in the preceding tie. The 2-0 win at Turf Moor was rated by McNally as one of Chester's best performances, and Ian Benjamin capped an outstanding personal display with the second goal. This proved to be one of Benjamin's final acts for Chester as he moved on to Exeter after failing to settle in the City.

Chester entered 1989 in 8th place, and made their first League visit to Wolves on the New Year Holiday. In a match packed with goalmouth incident Chester were beaten 3-1, but it could have been different had Steve Johnson not missed a first-half penalty.

In the return game at Sealand Road, Graham Abel was the hero as he not only silenced the free-scoring Steve Bull but also netted the equaliser with a tremendous 30 yard drive.

David Glenn, who had struggled to match his pre-injury form, asked for a transfer in January while Martin Lane became one of a number of players to re-join Chester under McNally, when he returned from Coventry for £25,000. Lane's arrival saw Chester win four successive games without conceding a goal, including a 1-0 win at Littlewoods Cup Semi-Finalists Bristol City.

Chester continued to hover on the verge of the play-offs and reserved their best performance of the season for another team fighting for promotion. An astonishing 7-0 hammering of 5th placed Fulham was the biggest winning margin since the 9-2 defeat of York in 1958, and included Carl Dale's first hat-trick in League football to take him past his personal target of 20 goals. Former Republic of Ireland International, 35 year old Eamon O'Keefe, was also on target from the penalty spot as he returned to English football after a serious knee injury had forced him to quit two years earlier. O'Keefe had been playing in Ireland for St. Patricks Athletic and Cork City, and signed after lengthy negotiations with the Football League over his insurance pay-out.

A final position of 8th was Chester's best since 1977/78, but attendances were disappointing and only 2,106 were present for the final home game against Gillingham when there was still a chance of reaching the play-offs. The style of play had not always been appreciated by Chester fans, but there was no doubt that McNally had achieved a tremendous job in competing with big-spending opponents on limited resources.

The much-improved Billy Stewart became the first player since Grenville Millington in 1980/81 to play in all 46 League games, while leading scorer Carl Dale was elected Player of the Year and earned a call-up for the Wales squad against West Germany.

During the summer Milton Graham rejected a new contract and joined Peterborough for £70,000, while Steve Johnson moved to Scandinavian football, and Joe Jakub returned to former club Burnley for a five figure fee. The success of Carl Dale prompted Harry McNally to look into non-League football for a goal-scoring partner for the ex-Bangor striker, but attempts to sign Mark Carter (Runcorn) and Phil Power (Chorley) were unsuccessful. Left-sided midfielder David Pugh was snapped up from Runcorn for £35000, while defender Alan Reeves, who had started his career with West Cheshire League side Heswall, joined from Norwich.

Other arrivals were utility player David Hamilton, another ex-Wigan man, from Blackburn, while Brian Croft made a swift return from Cambridge.

The 1989/90 season started badly with a home defeat to Mansfield, followed by a comprehensive 6-0 Littlewoods Cup hammering at the hands of Crewe. Chester gained revenge over the Alex. with a gutsy 2-1 League victory, but it took a late Graham Abel header and a last minute penalty save from Billy Stewart. This proved to be the only win in the first 10 games as the midfield, without the injured Barrow and the departed Graham and Jakub, struggled to stamp its authority on games.

Meanwhile, behind the scenes, the financial situation went from bad to worse. The outstanding debt had now reached £1 million and hopes of attracting large attendances against the 'glamour' clubs of Division 3 disappeared when the Kop end of the ground and the covered visitors section were refused safety certificates. Consequently, when Birmingham City visited the Stadium, it was a meagre attendance of 1,882 that saw Chester pull off an excellent 4-0 win. Architect of the victory was Brian Croft who showed his true potential as Chester ran in four goals in 15 minutes. The most popular goalscorer was Barry Butler, who scored his first goal for the club after four years and 119 appearances.

Injuries to Newhouse and Dale left Chester without a recognised goalscorer, and loan signings Kevin Hulme (Bury) and Australian triallist Ross Greer failed to make an impression, with the latter unfortunate to score an own goal against Shrewsbury. After conceding five goals at Rotherham, Graham Barrow returned to the side and although goals remained at a premium, Chester became a much harder team to beat.

In the FA Cup Chester visited Macclesfield, where they conceded an injury time equaliser to Steve Burr, an earlier transfer target for McNally. An incident packed replay saw Macclesfield miss a penalty as Chester narrowly won 3-2 after taking a 2-0 lead in the first six minutes. In the 2nd round, defensive lapses proved costly for Chester as they went down 3-0 at Blackpool.

Harry McNally's search for a striker continued into the New Year as Graham Abel temporarily filled the vacancy at centre-forward. Manchester City reserve striker Andy Milner rejected a possible £20,000 move to Sealand Road as did Nicky Morgan of Stoke. In February, teenage striker Aidan Newhouse, by now a regular member of the England Youth squad, was transferred to Wimbledon for £100,000, with the possibility of another £150,000 depending on appearances.

Away from home Chester were without a goal from October until the end of March, when Barry Butler scored in a 1-1 draw at Walsall. Ironically the Walsall equaliser came from Stuart Rimmer who had moved to Fellows Park after spells at Watford and Notts County. At the end of March, McNally finally got his man when Gary Bennett rejoined City from Southend for £25,000. The pairing of Bennett with Carl Dale, now recovered from injury, inspired Chester to a 2-0 win over Bolton, but three successive defeats over Easter left Chester sixth from bottom with their 3rd Division future in the balance.

**MATCH TO REMEMBER**
**CHESTER CITY 2 ROTHERHAM UNITED 0**
**BARCLAYS LEAGUE DIVISION 3 - APRIL 28TH 1990**

*Chester entered the final home game of the 1989/90 season knowing that a win would secure 3rd Division safety. More significantly the game marked Chester's final game at Sealand Road after 84 years. In a highly charged atmosphere Chester swept to a 2-0 victory on a tide of emotion, and supporters spilled on to the pitch at the end of the game to acknowledge Harry McNally and the players.*

*Despite the sadness of the occasion the players refused to let the pressure get the better of them and the supporters, in defiant mood, gave the team their full backing.*

*In the early stages Rotherham were overwhelmed by a wave of Chester attacks, and after 16 minutes Brian Croft's free kick was headed in by Bennett, his first goal since rejoining the club from Southend. Less than 10 minutes later Graham Abel added a second, the final League goal at Sealand Road, from Croft's pinpoint corner. Rotherham now produced their best spell of the game, but Billy Stewart prevented a comeback with fine saves from Mendonca and Buckley.*

*Chester started the second-half as they had the first, and Dale shot wide from a Bennett pass. Rotherham forced two more saves from Stewart, and late in the game Croft almost added a 3rd for Chester after a thrilling run. However, on the day, nobody could deny Chester a deserved victory, and fans left the ground for the last time still unsure of where they would be watching home games in 1990/91.*

Chester - Stewart, Butler, Woodthorpe, Hamilton, Abel, Lightfoot, Pugh, Barrow, Dale, Bennett (Painter), Croft.
Rotherham United - O'Hanlon, Barnsley, Cash, Goodwin, Johnson,Robinson, Pepper (Hazel), Dempsey, Williamson, (Evans), Mendonca, Buckley

The relegation battle continued to be fought against the backdrop of the sale of Sealand Road (see Chapter 13), and City faced Tranmere for what was the penultimate game at the Stadium. In an absorbing game goals from Dale and Pugh gave Chester a half-time lead, and although Malkin pulled one back it appeared as though City had weathered the storm as the game approached the final minute. However a weak Billy Stewart clearance left Malkin with a clear run on goal, and Woodthorpe brought down the winger as he raced through. For the third successive game points were lost to a penalty, as Ian Muir scored from the resultant spot kick.

**Dale, Stewart, Lane, Painter and Butler take a final look at Sealand Road after the Rotherham game.**

The game at fellow strugglers Blackpool now took on added significance, and Chester got off to a magnificent start with first-half goals from Dale (2) and a Gore own goal.

In the second-half Blackpool pulled a goal back before Chester conceded another penalty, but a tense finale was avoided as Eyres missed from the spot, and City entered the last two games requiring three points to avoid the drop.

On April 28th supporters gathered at Sealand Road for the last time to see Chester take on Rotherham United in a vital game. This time there were no slip-ups as Chester drew the curtain on 84 years of football at the Stadium with an emotional 2-0 victory.

With 3rd Division safety secured Harry McNally started to make plans for the 1990/91 season, hampered by the uncertain future facing the club. A traumatic close season saw Morrisons, the club's new owners, play Russian roulette with the League over a possible ground share, and it was mid-July before Macclesfield was confirmed as the club's new home.

McNally's own future was secured with a four year contract and similar deals were handed to assistant manager Graham Barrow and physio Joe Hinnigan. Darren Wynne and Michael Hayde were released during the summer as was David Hamilton who refused a new contract. Into the club came 19-year-old former Liverpool apprentice Spencer Whelan while Neil Ellis became the latest non-League signing at £7,500 from Bangor City. McNally also snapped up 21-year-old Roger Preece who had made more than 100 appearances for Wrexham before being released.

Preece had a poor disciplinary record at Wrexham, having been sent off five times, but he relished the opportunity of a fresh start at Chester. McNally saw him as the man to fill the role of attacking full-back in his sweeper system, but it was as a midfield player that Preece eventually made his mark.

On the verge of the 1990/91 season, promising full-back Colin Woodthorpe joined Norwich City for £225,000. Woodthorpe was to be the last big money transfer for many years as the move to Macclesfield brought an end to the club's youth development scheme. As a result of the ground share the Reserves had to pull out of the Midland League and join the lower standard Lancashire League Division 1, with their home games played at Moss Farm, home of the Cheshire FA, in Northwich.

*Brian Croft in action versus Exeter, the first League game at Moss Rose.*

After a pre-season tour of Scotland, Chester made their debut at the Moss Rose with a behind closed doors friendly against Manchester United, which they lost 1-0. The season proper started with a tricky away fixture at big spending Bury, who had invested £430,000 on new players during the summer.

Within six minutes Chester were trailing 2-0 and the large away following, still celebrating the club's survival, feared the worst for the season ahead.

A David Pugh goal put City back in the game, but there was no further scoring as Chester went down 2-1, and this was followed days later by a Rumbelows Cup defeat at Preston.

On September 1st, a crowd of just over 1,300 made the long journey to Macclesfield to see the club play the first game in exile against 4th Division Champions, Exeter City. Scott Hiley became the first player to score a League goal at Moss Rose as the Devon side won 2-1, with Chester's late reply coming from Graham Abel.

After three successive defeats there was little interest in the 2nd Leg Rumbelows Cup-tie against Preston, but just over 1,000 saw Chester march into Round two in impressive style as McNally abandoned his favoured sweeper system in favour of all out attack. Brian Croft made amends for his sending off in the first leg with two goals, and the reward was a plum tie against 1st Division Arsenal, who included Chester old boy Lee Dixon. The 1st leg was held at Macclefield, and City were unlucky not to take an 8th minute lead when David Pugh thumped a free-kick against the base of the post. Although Chester harried and chased all evening, they eventually succumbed to a Paul Merson goal, and in the 2nd leg, at Highbury, Arsenal won comfortably 5-0. The game at Arsenal marked the debut of new record £55,000 signing Neil Morton, a 21-year-old striker from Northwich Victoria.

*An aggrieved Carl Dale watches the booking of Tony Adams, and Dave Seaman looks on.*

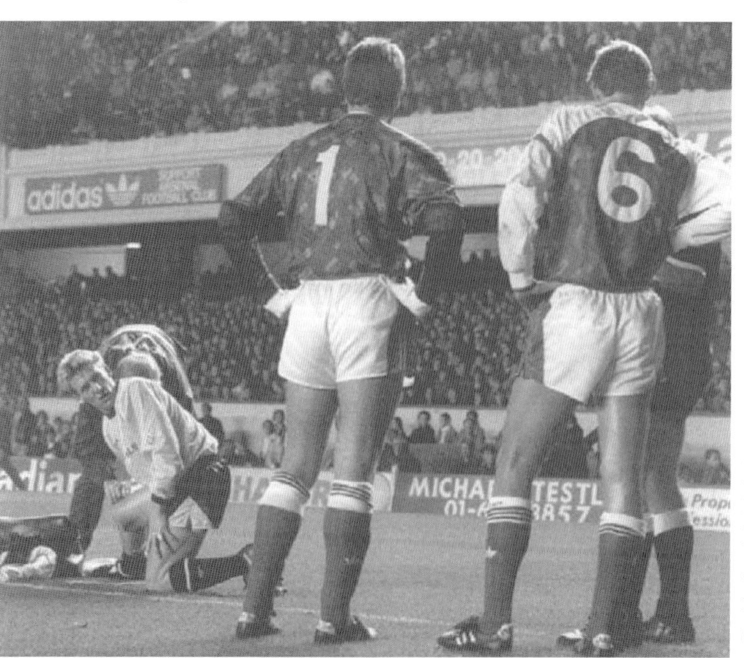


In the League, Chester showed little consistency in their early season form although there were good away wins at Brentford and Tranmere. At the start of October Chester had two players, Billy Stewart and David Pugh, sent off by Preston referee Jim Parker in the first 25 minutes of a 2-1 defeat at Bradford City.

The sending off cost Stewart the chance of breaking the record for most consecutive appearances as he fell three short of Mike Metcalf's 127 games. Fred Barber arrived on loan from Walsall, as Stewart's replacement, and had a second spell on loan towards the end of the season when Stewart suffered a crisis of confidence after three home defeats.

October ended with Neil Morton grabbing two goals against Crewe in a 3-1 away win, but Chester then played nearly two months without a League goal, as form dipped and confidence began to evaporate. Harry McNally, who had been desperate to sign a big striker since the start of the season, had an offer of £75,000 for Andy Garner turned down by Blackpool, but succeeded in signing Keith Bertschin the experienced Walsall striker. Bertschin, a former England Under-21 international, had made more than 400 appearances for Ipswich, Birmingham, Norwich, Stoke and Sunderland, and McNally had great expectations of the Bertschin, Morton, Dale strike-force.

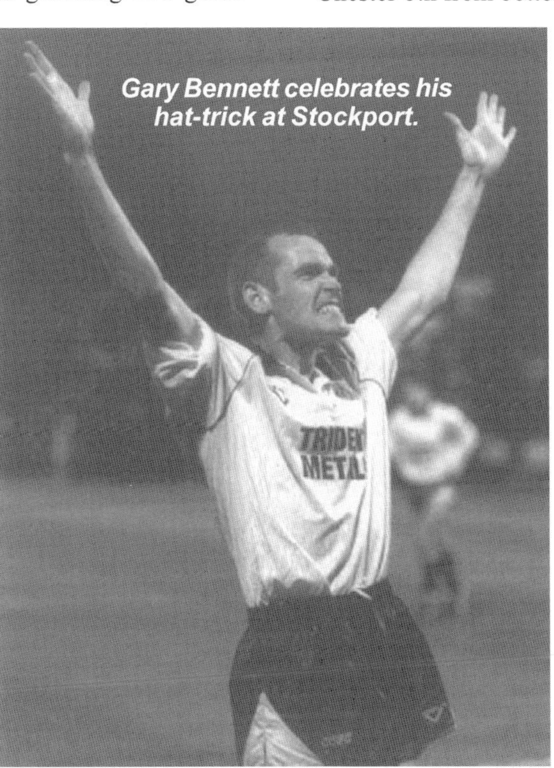
Gary Bennett celebrates his hat-trick at Stockport.

In the Leyland Daf Cup, Chester failed to compete against Wigan in their first group match and were comprehensively beaten 4-0 with future City player Don Page scoring a hat-trick. Three weeks later the ultimate test of supporters loyalty came when City faced Bury at the Moss Rose in the same competition. On a cold, wintry November night 409 spectators, including 100 from Bury, saw Chester win 2-0 with goals from Dale and Morton.

In the FA Cup Doncaster visited Moss Rose and after trailing 2-0 pulled back to 2-2 with a last minute equaliser. In the replay at Doncaster transfer-listed Robbie Painter scored an extra-time winner to give City a 2nd round tie against 'local' rivals Leek Town. Once again Chester failed to exploit the early advantage given to them by Carl Dale's 4th minute goal, and after dominating the game they allowed Leek to equalise in injury time. There was no mistake in the replay as Chester won 4-0 with Keith Bertschin scoring his only goal for the club. The 3rd Round draw proved a massive disappointment as Chester faced 3rd Division rivals Bournemouth.

In a howling gale, Spencer Whelan made his full debut for Chester, but was powerless to prevent Bournemouth take advantage of the wind with two first-half goals. The tables were turned in the second-half, as Brian Croft scored twice in a minute, but when a replay seemed likely a disastrous mistake by Billy Stewart allowed Efan Ekoku to score the winner for Bournemouth.

The year ended with a 4-1 defeat at Fulham, which left Chester 6th from bottom, but for the second time in three months the transfer record was broken with the £80,000 signing of Eddie Bishop from Tranmere. Bishop, who had a wealth of non-League experience with Winsford, Altrincham, Runcorn and Northwich, had been a great favourite at Tranmere, and was seen by McNally as a natural successor to Graham Barrow in midfield. He soon made a name for himself when his two goals helped Chester race into a 3-0 lead at Stoke. Although the Potteries side pulled back to 3-2, Chester rode the storm to pull off their best victory of the season.

A wintry January and February led to a series of postponements, and when the Moss Rose was covered under six inches of snow, prior to the Swansea game, Ray Crofts entered negotiations with Manchester City in an attempt to re-schedule the game at Maine Road. Although Manchester City agreed to the request it was turned down by the Football League and the backlog led to Chester playing six games at Macclesfield in March. Inevitably support suffered, and an attendance of 631, for a midweek game against Reading, set a new record low for the club. A Barry Butler goal gave City the first of three wins in a week but six points from the next 10 games put them back in trouble. Third Division safety was secured before the final home game of the season against Crewe, and with the pressure off, Chester were able to produce some of their best football of the season as a 3-1 win sent the Railwaymen back to Division 4.

Under the circumstances 19th was a remarkable achievement for a club watched by the lowest average crowd in the Football League. Attendances rarely passed the 1500 mark, and the home form suffered as Chester were defeated on 10 occasions. On a brighter note Chris Lightfoot was voted Player of the Year while Spencer Whelan won the Young Player award.

During the close season Pugh, Preece and Whelan all signed new contracts, but terms were rejected by Stewart, Dale and Painter. In anticipation of Stewart's departure, McNally brought in 36-year-old veteran Barry Siddall from Carlisle who made Chester his 13th different club. More experience was added in the form of ex-Manchester United defender Arthur Albiston who solved the problematical left-back role. Albiston had played nearly 400 games at Old Trafford, winning three FA Cup Winners medals and 14 Scottish caps. Meanwhile Chester became embroiled in a tangle with Maidstone United over the triple transfer of Neil Ellis, Robbie Painter and Carl Dale. Ellis moved to Kent for £10,000 while Painter's fee was set at an initial £30,000 by a League tribunal. Dale, valued at more than £100,000 by McNally, also had his fee set by tribunal after protracted negotiations failed to produce an agreement. However when the tribunal valued the Welshman at £65,000 plus bonuses, Maidstone pulled out of the deal and Dale eventually joined Cardiff for a bargain £82,000.

Other players to leave the club during the summer were the reliable Martin Lane (Walsall), Alan Reeves (Rochdale) and Keith Bertschin (Aldershot). Reeves had been on the transfer list all season after experiencing an unhappy time at Chester, but the move to Rochdale revitalised his career, and outstanding performances at his natural position of centre-half resulted in a move to Wimbledon for £300,000 in 1994.

On the verge of the new season McNally made a sensational swoop for the prolific Stuart Rimmer who rejoined his old club from Barnsley for a record £94,000. The signing gave Rimmer the chance to rekindle his love affair with the club where he had played the best football of his career. His return also helped stimulate interest among fans, weary over the lack of progress in building a new ground, and he was given a rapturous welcome before the 2-0 victory over Fulham. Following a 1-0 1st leg Rumbelows Cup victory over Lincoln, Rimmer got off the mark against Wigan, and began to repay his transfer fee with two goals in a pulsating 2nd leg tie at Sincil Bank. Although Chester lost the game 4-3, to a battling Lincoln side, they went through to the 2nd Round, on away goals, where they faced Manchester City. At Maine Road Chester played above themselves and caused problems with some stylish counter attacks. After David White had scored for Manchester City, Chester responded quickly with a Gary Bennett header, and in the end they were unlucky to lose 3-1 following two late Niall Quinn goals. The 2nd leg was played at Stockport because of safety concerns, and the 3-0 defeat did not reflect the chances created in the first-half by an injury hit Chester.

After beating Swansea in the League, only two points were won from the next eight games, including a 3-2 defeat at Birmingham, where goals from Bishop and Rimmer had given Chester a 2-0 lead.

In October Chester returned to Stockport to play a League game and destroyed County's 100% home record with a comprehensive 4-0 victory. Hero of the hour was the tireless Gary Bennett who scored a hat-trick and earned Chester the Barclay's Performance of the Week. Victory over Preston was marred by injury to sweeper David Pugh, prompting a disastrous run of 12 games without a win as Chester slumped to the bottom of the table. The introduction of Paul Comstive from Bolton for £10,000 failed to halt the slump, and there was no relief in the FA Cup where Chester were beaten by Crewe, after a narrow win over Guiseley in the 1st round.

Confidence reached rock bottom when 23rd placed Darlington arrived at the Moss Rose and went away with a 5-2 win after Comstive's first goal for the club had given Chester the lead. Four days later Darlington returned to Macclesfield for an Autoglass trophy game, with David Nolan from Bromborough Pool making his debut. Fifteen members of Nolan's family helped swell the crowd to 416, and the team showed the right attitude in winning 2-1. In the next round they were defeated 3-0 by Rotherham after a first game had been abandoned because of fog.

Defeat at Hartlepool left Chester five points adrift at the bottom of the table, but a draw in the next game, against table topping Brentford, sparked an incredible revival as Chester only lost four of the final 22 games. The revival coincided with the news that work was finally going to commence on the new stadium, and the announcement seemed to inspire the players to ensure that Chester would start the 1992/93 season in the same division. The air of resignation marking recent performances was swept away as the team once again revealed the battling qualities instilled by McNally.

When Chester faced Exeter at Moss Rose, the hard-working Barry Butler took over at centre-forward. Like many players Butler had suffered a dip in form, but he marked the switch with two goals in an inspiring 5-2 victory. A visit to Shrewsbury saw Chester score their first League goal at Gay Meadow, on their 10th appearance. Indeed they scored two in the first 10 minutes, but still had to settle for a 2-2 draw. Two more Butler goals against Hartlepool lifted Chester off the bottom, and a floodlight failure at Bury failed to prevent a 3-1 win as City ended February out of the bottom four. An ugly clash with Darlington saw McNally banished from the dugout, while Mick Tait and Graham Barrow were also sent off. Chester also had a player sent off in the next game against Brentford, when Billy Stewart was dismissed in a 2-0 defeat. Stewart, who had been on a week-to-week contract, had returned to the side after injury to Siddall, and was in excellent form as the season came to a climax.

Unfortunately he missed the game against Birmingham where a partially fit Siddall was at fault for Nigel Gleghorn's late winner as he let a 30 yard free kick squirm under his body. The attendance of 4,895 for this game proved to be the best for a Chester game at Macclesfield.

An Easter Monday victory over Torquay left Chester requiring one win from the last two games to secure safety, and City went to promotion chasing Stoke for a game described by McNally as *'not so much a Cup Final more a World Cup Final'*. On the day Chester packed the midfield and stifled a Stoke team who knew that a win could take them to Division 2. Gary Bennett produced a typical aggressive performance and was rewarded in the 78th minute when he picked up a through ball from Comstive, shrugged off Blake's challenge, and beat keeper Ronnie Sinclair. The goal stunned Stoke and Chester could have extended the lead when Comstive hesitated after beating the keeper allowing the defence to recover. The shock victory earned City another Barclay's Performance of the Week, but surprisingly other results meant relegation still remained a mathematical possibility .

At the beginning of May, Chester fans made the long trek to Macclesfield for the last time to see their favourites take on Leyton Orient.

Out-of-favour Eddie Bishop returned to the side in place of Gary Bennett, who had been bailed earlier in the week on burglary charges, an offence for which he was later cleared. In a nerve-jangling game Billy Stewart kept Orient at bay with some outstanding saves, and five minutes from time a Graham Barrow goal confirmed Chester's place in Division 3 at the expense of Bury.

It had been a remarkable escape with much of the credit going to McNally, whose achievements were recognised by The Sun newspaper who acknowledged him as their Manager of the Year. On the field elder-statesmen Barrow and Albiston had been steadying influences during the latter half of the season, but Player of the Year was Chris Lightfoot for whom McNally had turned down an offer of £80,000 from Motherwell.

Barry Siddall and Paul McGuinness were released at the end of the season while Gary Bennett saw his career blossom when he moved to Wrexham on a free transfer, after turning down a one year contract.

Despite the lowest average attendance in the Football League, Chester had survived their two years in exile, a tribute to everyone associated with the club, especially the supporters, who regularly travelled 40 miles across the county just to see a home game.

*The sorry state of The Sealand Road Stadium, just before 'the end', in 1992.*

# THE SAGA OF SEALAND ROAD

# CHAPTER 13

Chester had always been in the fortunate position of owning their ground, along with a significant amount of the surrounding land. In the 1970s money had been raised by selling some of this land and as debts began to soar in the 1980s, chairman Eric Barnes made it clear that he believed the only realistic future for the club lay in realising their most valuable asset, paying off the debt and relocating.

In 1986 the first attempt to re-develop the Stadium failed when a planning application was rejected by the City Council, and the proposed relocation to land over the Welsh border, along Bumpers Lane, met with a public outcry. A scaled down plan to build a supermarket on the training pitch behind the Kop was put forward in February 1987, but, like the earlier scheme, it was turned down, in November. With the re-development of prime importance to the club, an appeal was planned but before the case was heard the council withdrew their objections in September 1988 and recommended that the scheme be approved. However it proved a mixed blessing as the decision was conditional on the club contributing an index-linked £2.8 million to an access road which immediately rendered the scheme financially impractical.

During these discussions preliminary talks had taken place on a possible location for the new ground, and in November 1988 ambitious plans for a new multi-million pound stadium were announced. The 15,000-20,000 capacity ground was to be part of a sports complex with a restaurant, separate leisure centre, and international athletics track. Once again the site was on Bumpers Lane, but this time it lay on the English side of the border. By April these latest plans were in tatters as the council dealt another blow to the club by rejecting the scheme declaring that the proposal was *'ill-conceived, premature and mischievous'* and not needed because the club did not attract enough supporters.

In November 1989, on the eve of the FA Cup 1st round tie with Macclesfield, financial director David Cross dropped a bombshell when he announced, on television and in the press, that the ground was for sale with vacant possession at the end of the season. Attempts to sell the ground in the past had floundered because prospective buyers had been put off by the club's failure to find an alternative site, and the board hoped that the offer of vacant possession would act as an incentive. Unfortunately this offer was made with the club no nearer to finding a site for a new ground, and with no arrangements in place for a ground for the 1990/91 season. I n March, hours before Chester's vital 1-0 win over Cardiff, months of speculation ended when it was announced that the Stadium and a majority share-holding had been sold to Scottish based property developers Morrisons Developments. The deal allowed for the outstanding debt to be cleared and £2 million was put into trust for the proposed new ground. Morrisons themselves stated that they had no intention of getting involved in the day-to-day running of the club but it soon became clear to them that all was not quite as it first seemed. They entered the deal with Chester in the belief that a ground share agreement had been made and that a supermarket operator had been lined up to acquire the Stadium site, neither of which were in place

The takeover by Morrisons was swiftly followed by the resignation of Eric Barnes, citing *'constant criticism from fans, members of the club and the city council'* as the reason behind his decision. Although Barnes had achieved his goal of clearing all debts he left the club facing a bleak immediate future.

Ray Crofts, the supporters choice, took over as Chairman, with Norman MacLennan and Dan McDonald of Morrisons also joining the board, and their first task was to find a ground for the 1990/91 season. Following the ground for sale announcement in November, the club had embarked on a fruitless search of the North-West for somewhere to play, and as the season drew to a close a solution was no nearer. Among the grounds suggested were Crewe, Stoke, Port Vale, Tranmere, Stockport, Oldham, Blackpool and Manchester City, while deals with non-League clubs Northwich, Runcorn, Altrincham, Witton Albion and Rugby League giants Widnes also proved non-starters. By the start of May the Football League were becoming increasingly concerned about the lack of progress and issued an ultimatum to the club. They insisted on a £500,000 bond to ensure that a new ground be built in the City within two years and gave the troubled club until May 25th to come up with a ground-sharing plan.

As the deadline approached Wrexham emerged as the best option, but opposition from the North Wales police proved an insurmountable obstacle and the alternative of Warrington Rugby League club was rejected by the Football League. By noon on May 25th, there were still no firm plans in front of the League bosses, although Morrisons insisted that a deal was imminent. Finally, a few minutes after the 5pm deadline had passed, details of a ground-share agreement with GM Vauxhall Conference side Macclesfield were faxed to League Headquarters. The late deal left Chester fans facing an 80 mile round trip, but Ray Crofts admitted that *'It's Macclesfield or nowhere'*, and the club agreed to lay on subsidised transport for the 80 mile journey.

The following week the two season deal was approved by the League Management committee, although they insisted on payments of two additional bonds totalling £160,000, one for £115,000 for safety work, and one for £45,000 to increase ground capacity at the Moss Rose to 6,000.

On June 22nd the club's future was again put in the balance when it was revealed that they had failed to come up with one of the promised security bonds for £500,000. Morrisons explained that they were unhappy with the wording of the bonds, while the Football League stated that *'The bonds were not received by the stated deadline and a move to Macclesfield is no longer an option for the club.'* The argument centred on a clause which guaranteed that the club would be relocated within the City of Chester, while Morrisons wanted to ensure that they were covered if the ground straddled the border. The passing of the deadline saw both sides in deadlock as the Football League were adamant that Chester must stay at Sealand Road, while Morrisons insisted that the ground would be developed as a supermarket.

On June 29th, Chester pulled back from the very edge of extinction when both sides re-entered talks, and the League finally gave Macclesfield a written go-ahead as a mutually acceptable version of the wording was agreed. On the same day the bonds were delivered to Football League Headquarters, but Chester were left to wait two weeks until the Management Committee met to discuss the club's future. At 7pm on July 12th, the League finally gave the deal the go-ahead . With the ground-share now settled attention could turn to finding a new ground. Bumpers Lane remained the favourite site and outline plans were again submitted to the Council for a 12,000 stadium behind the local tip. However, initial reports on the land revealed a high level of methane gas below the surface, and in mid-October the site was ruled out because of the potential cost of clearing the problem. In November the council, who became more supportive when Chester were forced into exile, offered the club an alternative site on Bumpers Lane at a rent of £20,000 per year. The new location straddled the border and required applications to both Chester and Alyn and Deeside Councils, but the exact site was no longer an issue for supporters desperate for a return to the city. By the end of January 1991 planning applications for both sides of the border were accepted in principle for a 10,600 capacity stadium. However an agreement had yet to be reached on the development of Sealand Road, and Morrisons needed to raise money for the new ground by building a superstore on the old site.

Although Morrisons were optimistic about the sale of the ground they suffered a setback when Asda, favourites to build the superstore, revealed they were no longer in a position to develop the land. The following month legal charges, held by former owners BCH, preventing the club from developing the ground were lifted when a court ruling allowed the ground to be sold while the BCH claim was discussed. However, as Chester entered their second season in exile, a return by the start of the 1992/93 season still remained a distant dream.

Published accounts at the end of the season revealed losses of more than £800,000, with nearly half this figure made up of charges incurred by the old regime in their efforts to sell the Stadium. The spectre of the former owners continued to haunt the club, but in October a winding-up order, sought by former directors Fred Summers and Eric Barnes, was resolved when Chester paid off the outstanding debt. In November the club faced a vital court hearing with BCH who were suing the club for £3 million, based on an agreement struck with Eric Barnes when they took over the club in 1986. By this agreement any money from the sale of the Stadium would be split so that the first £1 million would go to the club with the rest split 50-50 between the club and BCH. The loss of the case would have threatened the whole future of the club, but a settlement, in the region of £400,000, lifted a huge burden.

By August 1991, even the optimistic chairman had become worried about the new ground, as Morrisons entered another dispute with the Council over the planning application. Morrisons wanted a reduction in the size of the car park to allow for the inclusion of two training pitches, a request which introduced another delay into the planning hearing. In November, Morrisons were forced to back down and the application to build the stadium was finally rubber-stamped by Alyn and Deeside Council in December, although the tight deadline meant that the intended capacity had to be reduced to 6,000.

Although the old ground still remained unsold, Morrisons pledged that the new ground would start regardless of its sale, and on January 28th 1992 a turf-cutting ceremony was held in Bumpers Lane. There was still time for another dispute with the council, as Morrisons started work on the site immediately after the ceremony. The council responded by issuing an injunction preventing any further development as they pointed out that the rental agreement had still not been signed. Days later the injunction was lifted as the paperwork was completed, and work started for a second time on February 3rd.

The builders entered a race against time in an effort to get the ground ready for the 1992/93 season, and amazingly the ground was completed in time for the Coca Cola Cup encounter with Stockport on August 25th. As supporters arrived at the new Deva Stadium for the first time, they passed the sorry sight of their derelict former home which was finally razed to the ground in January 1993. The following month the council gave authority for Morrisons to develop the site as a retail park (the original proposal had been for a supermarket only), and an extraordinary general meeting of the club cleared the way for the land to be sold. Morrisons were then able to sell the site to Chester City Council, in return for a long term lease, and then lease it back for development of the £10 million retail park. The deal enabled Morrisons to clear the club's debts - now having climbed to £2 million following the exile - and with the new ground paid for they could put the club up for sale with a clean slate. The long saga of Sealand Road had finally ended.

# HOME AGAIN 1992 - 1999
# CHAPTER 14

The introduction of the Premier League meant that Chester would start their new era at the Deva Stadium in Division 2, and while build-ers completed work on the ground Harry McNally took the players on a pre-season tour of Scotland.

Trialists Craig Goodwin (Aston Villa) and Darren Ryan (Shrewsbury) created a good impression and were offered 12 month contracts, but the manager returned with a broken leg after playing himself in a game against village side Vale of Atholl. The only other arrivals were free transfer signings Dave Thompson (Preston) and John Kelly (Huddersfield), with the latter starting his second spell at the club. Meanwhile Brian Croft made a surprise move to Premier League QPR for £60,000, although none of this money could be made available to McNally as the club reported a massive, record loss of £1,646,787. The loss was not unexpected, because of the costs involved in playing at Macclesfield, and it was hoped that the debts would be cleared when Sealand Road was finally sold.

*Harry McNally, Chairman Ray Crofts (with scarf) and supporter Les Parry at the turf-cutting ceremony - January 1992.*

Chester started the 1992/93 season with four successive away games, but only returned with one point after a draw at Hull. There was also an early exit from the Coca Cola Cup after a 3-2 aggregate defeat by Stockport. The 2nd leg of this tie marked Chester's first appearance at the Deva Stadium, but Stockport spoiled the party with a deserved 2-1 win. The first goal at the new ground was scored by County's Chris Beaumont, with Eddie Bishop, sent off in the 1st leg, earning the distinction as City's first goalscorer. A disappointing evening ended with Billy Stewart being stretchered off after a brave save at the feet of Kevin Francis.

Stewart's injury forced McNally into the loan market to bring in replacement keeper John Keeley from Oldham.

The first League game at the new ground resulted in victory over Burnley, but this marked the only success until the end of October. Against Mansfield, Stuart Rimmer's goal after 75 seconds was his 84th League goal for Chester and broke Gary Talbot's long standing record. On the night it proved academic, as City succumbed to a late Mansfield winner. The poor start to the season put pressure on Harry McNally, for a season that began with so much optimism turned sour and a disastrous display at Plymouth increased speculation over his future. The following week City threw away a two goal lead against Bolton, and the resultant 2-2 draw left them bottom of the table. A few days later McNally, the League's fourth longest serving manager, was axed after seven years in charge. It was a sad end for McNally whose achievement in keeping Chester in Division 3 while playing at Macclesfield cannot be under-estimated. No stranger to controversy, his outspoken views had often led to conflict, but he was passionate about football and a great motivator of players. After leaving Chester he went on to scout for Preston, Tranmere and Blackpool.

Assistant manager Graham Barrow emerged from McNally's shadow to take temporary charge with the promise to impose his own ideas on the team. He received an immediate boost when David Pugh and Neil Morton asked to come off the transfer list, and the former, restored to his natural position of left mid-field, responded with four goals against Swansea and Rotherham as Chester won two of the next four games.

The short term improve-ment in form and confidence led to the con-firmation of Barrow as manager before the FA Cup-tie against his former club Altrincham. However, it proved to be an inauspicious start as Altrincham won 2-0, after forcing a draw at the Deva. The second goal, a screaming drive from Clive Freeman, won the BBC's Goal of the Month competition.

*Neil Morton (left) scores the first League goal at the Deva Stadium, Rimmer and Kelly look on.*

In the League, new found confidence soon dissipated as Chester lost nine of Barrow's first 10 games as manager, and there was no respite in the Autoglass Trophy where City were defeated by Chesterfield and Stockport. Even the return of Arthur Albiston from Norway, and the £5,000 signing of centre-half Mark Came from Bolton failed to halt the slide as the defence leaked goals at an alarming rate, which culminated in total collapse against Bradford City and Burnley, where elementary mistakes saw five goals conceded on both occasions. Came missed both these matches with a broken collar bone, the result of a collision with Kevin Francis in the first 10 seconds of the season's fifth encounter with Stockport.

Meanwhile the for-wards were struggling to score goals, and in January Barrow exchanged Dar-ren Ryan for Stockport's Paul Wheeler.

The signing had an im-mediate effect on Stuart Rimmer, who scored seven goals in the next six games and was the subject of a £109,000 bid from Preston on tran-sfer deadline day.

By now it was evident that an ageing Chester side was simply not good enough, and by March rele-gation was inevitable. Commendably chairman Ray Crofts stood by Graham Barrow, recog-nising that there was little that the manager could do under the circumstances.

The move to Macclesfield had stemmed the flow of young talent coming into the club, and Barrow could only re-shuffle the players at his disposal, in addition the clubs ownership was once again in question. In December Morrisons had put the club up for sale for £1 million, and were understandably reluctant to invest further money in the club which was once again being run on a tight budget. On the bright side the clubs debts were wiped out in February when the old Stadium site was finally sold for retail development.

Relegation was confirmed with five games remaining, and a dismal season ended with seven straight losses. Chester's final total of 33 defeats equalled the all-time Football League record. The final game was played at Brighton, where Chester went two goals in

**MATCH TO REMEMBER**
**CHESTER CITY 3 BURNLEY 0**
**BARCLAYS LEAGUE DIVISION 2 - SEPTEMBER 5TH 1992**

*After a poor start to the season Chester were desperate to impress in the first ever League game at the Deva Stadium and Burnley were brushed aside as Chester celebrated their first win of the campaign.*

*Despite being without the suspended Bishop and the injured Butler and Stewart, a tightly-organised Chester took a firm grip of the game in the first half-hour as they raced into a 2-0 lead. The lively Neil Morton opened the scoring after 11 minutes when he slotted home a loose ball after Rimmer's effort had been palmed away by Beresford. Eleven minutes later Lightfoot increased the lead when he deflected a Barrow header into the net. Burnley posed little threat and loan keeper John Keeley had little to do as Paul Comstive and John Kelly dominated the midfield. Comstive rounded off a purposeful performance with Chester's 3rd goal in the 65th minute with a shot from the edge of the box. The only blemish on the performance was a missed penalty from Graham Abel which ended the big defender's 100% record from the spot.*

*Unfortunately the 3-0 victory failed to provide a launching pad for success and instead proved to be one of the few highlights in a disastrous season.*

*Chester - Keeley, Preece, Comstive, Whelan, Abel, Lightfoot, Thompson, Barrow, Rimmer, Morton, Kelly.*
*Burnley - Beresford, Measham, Jakub, Randall, Pender, Monington, Painter, Deary, Lancashire, Heath, Harper.*

front in the first two minutes, but still lost 3-2. The second of Chester's goals marked Stuart Rimmer's 100th for the club, while Brighton's first goal, scored by Kurt Nogan, was the 100th League goal conceded, with the final total of 102 falling just short of the 104 conceded in 1960/61. Despite this defensive record keeper Billy Stewart remained relatively immune from criticism and won the Player of the Year award.

In a massive clear out at the end of the season, Albiston, Comstive, Abel, Goodwin, Kelly, Butler and Morton were all released while Thompson and Limbert were re-signed after initially having their contracts cancelled.

The departure of Graham Abel to Crewe ended an eight year association covering nearly 300 League games. The exodus gave Barrow the opportunity to build his own squad, but financial constraints restricted his options to free transfer signings. Into the squad came Iain Jenkins, a 20-year-old defender from Everton, while veteran Joe Jakub re-joined the club from Burnley. Jakub was brought in as Youth Development Officer, and only registered as a player for cover, but went on to make 36 appearances. Two other players to sign were Mark Leonard and centre-half Colin Greenall, both from Preston.

The experienced Leonard, a bustling striker with the ability to hold the ball up, was the sort of player Chester had lacked since the departure of Steve Johnson, while the accomplished Greenall, still only 29, had played more than 400 League games for Blackpool, Gillingham, Oxford, Bury and Preston. Barrow later acknowledged Greenall as his best ever signing and it gave him the option of moving Chris Lightfoot into midfield where Chester had lacked a commanding presence the previous season. Barrow also signed three youngsters from Blackburn, Ian Berry, Lee Moss and Darren Donnelly, but only the latter appeared in the first team.

Most of the talk during the break had centred on the prospective takeover of the club, but a series of offers came to nothing, and Chester remained under Morrisons control at the start of the season. Chester started 1993/94 with a home game against Doncaster and returned to the favoured blue and white stripes for the first time since 1982/83. The season opened with an 8th successive reversal, but the 1-0 defeat did not reflect Chester's control of a game which hinged on the sending off of Eddie Bishop. A week later Chester were the first League visitors to Wycombe Wanderers, but could not spoil the party as they went down 1-0 to the Buckinghamshire club. Sandwiched in between these games was a 3-1 Coca Cola Cup defeat at Sunderland, as City conceded three goals in seven minutes, after Rimmer had given them an early lead.

Despite the poor results Chester were playing a style of football unrecognisable from the previous season, and after halting the run of defeats with a goalless draw, against Sunderland in the second leg, they achieved their first win since March 24th by beating Chesterfield 3-1. Three days later Lincoln were swept aside 3-0 as Barrow kept his promise to play football with style. The revival suffered a temporary setback with defeats against Rochdale and Scunthorpe, but there was a return to winning ways at Scarborough thanks to a late Mark Leonard goal. The win proved costly as Billy Stewart was injured in the pre-match kickabout and had to go off after only three minutes. Without a substitute goalkeeper, Mark Came took over between the sticks and paved the way for victory with a stunning save from Scarborough's Calvert.

With Stewart out for the rest of the season Barrow had to look for an experienced replacement, and after playing Blackpool's Steve McIlhargey in a goalless draw with Carlisle, settled on 33 year old David Felgate who had been on a monthly contract with Wolves. Felgate, capped once for Wales, soon struck up a tremendous rapport with the fans, but had a difficult debut at Wigan where Chester were beaten 6-3, despite pulling back from 3-0 down to 3-3. Chief tormentor for Wigan was Keith Gillespie, on loan from Manchester United.

Once again Chester bounced back quickly with three successive wins, including a 4-0 victory at Mansfield, as they embarked on a run which saw them lose just three of the next 31 games. Paul Wheeler continued his good run with a hat-trick at Mansfield, and in the next away game City went one better with a 5-0 win at Hereford, the best away win since the same score hammering of Fulham in 1987. Man of the Match was the transformed David Thompson who gave Hereford player-manager Greg Downs a torrid time. Thompson had been a peripheral figure during the relegation season but came into his own as Barrow moved Chester away from the physical approach of previous seasons, and he benefitted immensely from the service provided by the new look midfield where Lightfoot and Preece were outstanding. Lightfoot's form prompted Barrow to value him at a somewhat inflated £750,000, while Preece, who had struggled at full-back the previous year, had lost weight and was playing like a man possessed. Preece's non-stop running and tigerish tackling were rewarded when he scored his first goal for the club, a magnificent strike in the FA Cup against Hull.

However, behind the scenes there were still problems as the on-off sale of the club dragged on and prevented Barrow from building up his painfully thin squad. A bid for Winsford's full-back John Whitney failed when it proved impossible to raise the necessary £10,000, and Barrow was also unsuccessful in trying to sign Crewe's Jimmy Harvey on playing terms, although Harvey was later put in charge of Chester's School of Excellence. Also of concern to Barrow was the fact that every prof-essional on the clubs books had his contract up for renewal at the end of the season, and in November he prophetically announced that *'we should be starting to talk to players now with a view to next season, otherwise we could be in trouble'.*

November proved to be a sad month as former chairman Reg Rowlands died, and Ray Crofts was forced to step down as current chairman due to ill health which also prevented him from attending further games.

In December, Wycombe suffered their first away defeat in the Football League when they visited the Deva, and Chester's move up the table continued with a 4-3 win at Doncaster, courtesy of a Mark Leonard hat-trick, as City pulled back a 3-1 deficit with three goals in the last 20 minutes. The largest 3rd Division crowd of the season gathered at Deepdale for the Christmas top of the table clash with Preston, and the 1-1 draw left Chester 3rd, seven points behind Crewe and one behind their hosts, as they entered 1994.

Not only were Chester challenging for promotion but they also entered the New Year in two Cup competitions. In the FA Cup Chester had beaten Bradford City (after a replay) and Hull without conceding a goal, and in the 3rd Round they faced another 2nd Division side, in-form Plymouth. Nearly 1000 Chester fans made the long journey to Devon, but it proved a miserable afternoon as a battling City fell to a late Kevin Nugent header in torrential rain. Chester were still suffering an FA Cup hangover a few days later when they were eliminated from the Autoglass Trophy by Lincoln, where only David Felgate stood between Chester and a massacre.

In the League, Chester started 1994 in sluggish fashion and after scraping a point at Colchester suffered defeat at up and coming Shrewsbury, where Mark Leonard missed a penalty.

David Flitcroft, the third Preston player to join Chester in six months, made his full debut at Torquay and scored as a 3-1 victory ended a barren goal-less spell. With Stuart Rimmer struggling to find the net Graham Barrow boosted the strike force with the loan signing of Graham Lancashire from Burnley. Lancashire proved an immediate hit with a goal against Lincoln, after coming on as a substitute, and continued the good work with goals against Mansfield and Chesterfield, before returning to Burnley.

The win at Chesterfield came through a controversial Mark Leonard goal, and coincided with the shock announcement that Stuart Rimmer and Chris Lightfoot had been put on the transfer list in an attempt to raise money to develop the squad. The announcement came from Graham Wilkes who had been appointed Chief Executive by Morrisons on the departure of Ray Crofts, and was now in charge of the day to day running of the club. A diplomatic Barrow remained silent but the decision caused an outcry among supporters who feared a break-up of the promotion chasing team. In the event the team remained intact with the only offer coming from Carlisle, a £40,000 bid for Rimmer, which was rejected out of hand.

After two months without a home win, City finally slipped into gear and victories over Rochdale and Gillingham closed the gap on Crewe at the top. Dave Thompson became the first Chester player to score a hat-trick at the Deva in a 4-1 win over Scarborough, a game also remembered for keeper Felgate's attempts to dribble the ball round the advancing Scarborough forwards. Three days later Chester went to the top of the table after a hard fought victory over Walsall, with Thompson again on target with a classy strike.

Just before transfer deadline day Barrow secured Graham Lancashire for a second loan spell, consolation for the fact that City were unable to meet Burnley's asking price of £20,000 for a permanent move.

Once again Lancashire proved a hit by scoring two goals in a thrill-ing top of the table encounter with Preston, watched by the Deva

**MATCH TO REMEMBER**
**CHESTER CITY 3 HEREFORD UNITED 1**
**ENDSLEIGH LEAGUE DIVISION 3 - APRIL 23RD 1994**

*Chester clinched promotion to Division 2 in front of their joyous home fans, after a 3-1 victory over Hereford coupled with defeat for Crewe at Rochdale. Champagne flowed after the game, as hundreds of celebrating fans invaded the pitch to acknowledge Graham Barrow and his transformed team who had upset all the odds in securing a promotion that had looked so unlikely at the start of the season.*

*In a blustery wind, Chester got off to a shaky start and Derek Hall missed a simple opportunity to give Hereford an early lead. Chester made the best of their good fortune and after 18 minutes took the lead when Pugh sent a bullet header past Thomas after a pinpoint cross from Whelan. With the wind behind them City had a hatful of chances and Pugh (twice), Leonard, Greenall and Thompson all came close. In the 2nd half Chester stepped up another gear and their superiority was rewarded with a 2nd goal, when Graham Lancashire scored with a spectacular bicycle kick. Hereford briefly came back into the game when Clark pulled the score back to 2-1, but the two goal cushion was restored by Man of the Match Preece who gleefully slotted home a loose ball when Hereford failed to clear a Leonard cross.*

*For the remaining 20 minutes Chester turned on the style, with Lancashire and Lightfoot both coming close to extending the lead, and as news of Crewe's defeat at Rochdale filtered through the promotion celebrations went into overdrive.*

*Chester - Felgate, Whelan, Jakub, Preece, Came, Greenall, Thompson, Lightfoot, Leonard, Lancashire, Pugh.*
*Hereford United - Thomas, Clark (Clements), Downs, Davies, Morris, Reece, Hall, Steele, Pike, Pickard (Eversham), Anderson.*

Stadium's largest attendance to date. City struggled in the first-half against a strong wind, and went in 2-1 down, but after the break they turned on the style and Lancashire's 88th minute strike secured a deserved 3-2 victory. The Preston game marked the end of Graham Barrow's playing career at the age of nearly 40.

*Mark Came, Colin Greenall and Dave Thompson celebrate promotion.*

Last minute goals at Gillingham, and by Lightfoot at home to Colchester, put Chester on the verge of promotion, although top spot was surrendered to Shrewsbury who took advantage of their games in hand.

Failure to cash in on an early Lancashire goal cost Chester the chance of a record-breaking ninth away win at Bury, but promotion was secured after a 3-1 victory over Hereford, the eighth successive home win. The season ended anti-climatically with defeats at bottom-placed Northampton and at home to Crewe, but Chester still finished runners-up, five points behind Shrewsbury.

After relegation the previous season, Chester had started the next as 66-1 title outsiders, but some inspired free transfer signings and Barrow's ability to get the best out of existing players helped turn the tide. Barrow himself received a boost when he was acknowledged by Leeds boss Howard Wilkinson, chairman of the Football Managers Association, as one of the top bosses outside the Premiership, after coming 3rd in the merit awards conducted by the Association.

With promotion under a promising young manager and the sale of the club nearing completion the future looked bright for Chester, but all was to change as another close season upheaval saw the promotion squad disintegrate.

Graham Barrow returned from hol-iday to find that the prospective buyout had collapsed over the guarantee on the 120 year lease for the ground. The threat-ened exo-dus of out-of-contract players became a reality as David Pugh accepted an offer from Bury, and Player of the Year Greenall also expressed a wish to move on. Within days Barrow dropped his own bomb-shell when he tendered his resignation, frustrated by the lack of financial backing from the board, as he sought to build on the previous season's success. It came as a severe blow to the club and was closely followed by the departure of assistant Joe Hinnigan and Youth Officer Joe Jakub.

Within a week Chief Executive Wilkes had unveiled a new management team of Mike Pejic and Kevin Ratcliffe, who were faced with the unenviable task of returning some stability to the club and win over supporters incensed by the departure of Barrow. They arrived at the club with only three players, including Ratcliffe, on the books and one of these, Chris Lightfoot, on the transfer list.

Pejic, the new man in charge had been capped four times by England during a long career as full-back with Stoke, Everton and Aston Villa, but had recently been coaching in Kuwait. Player-coach Ratcliffe, an inspirational centre-back and captain for Everton and Wales, was coming to the end of a distinguished career which had seen him capped 59 times for his country. During his time at Goodison Park, Ratcliffe had led Everton to two League Championships, an FA Cup win and success in the European Cup Winners Cup.

Pejic found his hands tied by the same financial restrictions as Barrow, and had to look to the free transfer market to build up his squad, although a number of the out-of-contract players, including Whelan and Jenkins, eventually re-signed. Into the squad came Jason Burnham (Northampton), Don Page (Doncaster), Andy Milner (Rochdale), Leroy Chambers (Sheffield Wednesday), Gary Shelton (Bristol City), Ray Newland (Plymouth) and Julian

Alsford (Watford), and when the first Division 2 game was played against Bradford City, there were six players making their Chester debuts. Supporters worst fears were con-firmed when City went down to a demoralising 4-1 defeat, and matters went from bad to worse as the opening seven League games were all lost, by a team clearly out of their depth. Elimination from the Coca Cola Cup, by a Lincoln side that included Colin Greenall, meant that by mid-September Chester had suffered a record 11 consecutive defeats stretching back into the previous season. The first point was finally won at Bournemouth, where Gary Shelton made his long-awaited debut after recovering from an injury picked up in the pre-season Isle of Man tournament.

*A worried bench! Shelton, Pejic, Ratcliffe and Felgate.*

Skipper Spencer Whelan broke his leg in the defeat at Plymouth, and Pejic signed 33-year-old Peter Jackson on loan from Huddersfield as a replacement. Jackson, veteran of over 500 League appearances with Newcastle, Bradford City and Huddersfield made his debut in Chester's first win of the season, a surprise 2-0 triumph over top of the table Oxford. Scorers for Chester were Gary Hackett, a recent signing from Shrewsbury, and Chris Priest, a talented midfielder on loan from Everton.

Jackson and Priest were later signed on a permanent basis and there was more good news when Roger Preece, one of the few successes of the season, signed a new deal after spending five months on a week to week contract. Preece had been a target for Graham Barrow, now manager at Wigan, and his signing proved a welcome settlement. In an effort to halt the club's slide Pejic also brought in Nick Richardson (Cardiff) and Neil Tolson (Bradford City) on loan, while Canadian international Geoff Aunger was given a short trial before being released. In October the on-off sale of the club finally came to a conclusion when Morrisons accepted an offer from Manchester businessmen Mark Guter-man and Ian Morris.

The deal was finally completed in February when Mor-risons ended their five year association with the club. Having pro-vided a new stadium and cleared the club's debts they left the club on a much firmer footing than when they had taken over in 1990.

However the tightening of the purse strings, as the club was put up for sale, had made the job more difficult for both Barrow and Pejic. Although a series of consortiums came in with offers, Morrisons made it clear that they would only sell when they were satisfied that the new owners could safeguard the club's future, and none of the prospective buyers met Morrisons criteria. As the sale of the club dragged on it was Morrisons appointee Graham Wilkes who became the focus of supporters dissent, and he resigned late in 1994.

On the footballing side Chester had little trouble in disposing of Witton Albion in the FA Cup but were eliminated in the 2nd Round by Burnley, in a game televised on Sky TV, City's first live appearance in front of the cameras. Despite home wins over Stockport and Blackpool, Pejic came under fire as Chester experienced a series of dreadful home results in December and January.

A 4-0 defeat by a moderate York side proved the final straw and Pejic was dismissed after only six months in charge, with the club bottom of the table. The hard-working Pejic had faced an impossible task in taking over from Barrow, but as results had deteriorated so the patience of the supporters had run out. He had done little to help his cause by publicly condemning the players while refusing to accept the blame for some poor performances. After leaving Chester Pejic went on to become coach at Stoke under Lou Macari.

Youth coach and physio, Derek Mann, was handed the job as caretaker manager, with Kevin Ratcliffe remaining as player-coach. Mann, an apprentice at Shrewsbury before injury ended his career, was a fully qualified coach and had served on the coaching staff at Shrewsbury, Watford, Huddersfield and West Bromwich Albion, as well as managing Telford United. The appointment of Mann led to a recall for Stuart Rimmer, after loan spells with Rochdale and Preston, while Nick Richardson returned to Cardiff after being expected to sign on a permanent basis.

Poor results were being matched by a poor disciplinary record which saw Chester end the season with 12 sendings off and 80 bookings. During February, five players were sent off in eight days, starting with Lightfoot and Bishop in the dramatic local derby with Wrexham. Lightfoot was also dismissed against Shrewsbury and, in an ill-disciplined display at Blackpool, Jackson and Jenkins received their marching orders.

**MATCH TO REMEMBER**
**WREXHAM 2 CHESTER CITY 2**
**ENDSLEIGH LEAGUE DIVISION 2 - FEBRUARY 14TH 1995**

*In one of the most thrilling derbies in recent memory, nine-man Chester earned a well deserved point with a stunning late Andy Milner goal. At half-time, a St.Valentine's Day massacre appeared on the cards. Bottom-placed Chester trailed 2-1, having been outplayed for much of the half, and in a minute of madness just before the break had Lightfoot and Bishop sent off. However, Wrexham were unable to make their numerical advantage count and 45 minutes of grit and determination saw City achieve their best result under Derek Mann.*

*The game started in explosive fashion with former City favourite Gary Bennett having a header disallowed for pushing after only two minutes. A minute later the Wrexham striker won a penalty after being brought down by Flitcroft. However, Felgate went the right way to make a tremendous save. Ten minutes later it was Chester's turn to claim a penalty when Hunter pulled down Milner. Eddie Bishop made no mistake from the spot and the Chester fans went wild. The lead only lasted a minute as Karl Connolly -Wrexham's best player on the night - scored with a cracking shot, and three minutes later set up Gary Bennett for his 35th goal of the season to put the Reds ahead. As half-time approached Wrexham took command as Chester's frustration got the better of them.*

*Lightfoot was the first to go, for a second bookable offence, after a foul on Watkin, and almost immediately Bishop was dismissed following an off-the-ball incident involving Bennett.*

*Chester came out for the second-half with Priest at full-back and Jenkins at the centre of defence. Although Watkin forced Felgate into a fine save and Alsford cleared off the line, the defence was impregnable and as the game wore on Chester grew in confidence. With five minutes to go Milner broke towards goal from the halfway line, but appeared to have missed his chance when he checked back with defenders hot on his trail. However, he wrong-footed Pejic, before curling the ball over Marriott into the net for a magnificent equaliser.*

*There was still time for Bennett to have another 'goal' disallowed for an infringement, but it would have been cruel on City who thoroughly deserved the point.*

*Chester - Felgate, Preece, Jenkins, Shelton, Alsford, Lightfoot, Flitcroft (Burnham), Priest, Milner, Rimmer (Page), Bishop.*
*Wrexham - Marriott, Jones, Hardy, Hughes, Hunter, Pejic, Bennett, Owen, Connolly, Watkin, Durkan (Cross).*

After defeat at Wycombe, an Eddie Bishop goal against relegated Leyton Orient, without an away win in 18 months, gave City only their second win in 28 League games. This result was enough to take Chester off the basement, and the season ended with victory at Swansea, the first away win of the season. However the overall total of six victories was the lowest since entering the League, and the points total of 29 equalled that of the 1992/93 season.

Despite these results, Ratcliffe, who still had to win over many supporters, remained unsure as to whether he wanted to become Chester's fourth manager in less than 12 months. However, at the end of May, he was appointed manager by Mark Guterman who had been impressed by the qualities shown by Ratcliffe in his short period in the caretaker role.

After victory over Plymouth, the first in 18 games, the likeable Mann was given the job on a permanent basis, but it proved a short-lived appointment as City only picked up three points from the next nine games. A goalless draw with Bristol Rovers brought inevitable relegation, and following a home defeat by Crewe Derek Mann sensationally quit to return to his former role with the Youth Development Scheme. Although performances had improved under Mann results had remained poor and Chester won only one of the 19 games in which he was in charge. Kevin Ratcliffe took control for the last three games while the new owners sifted through more than 50 applications for the job. Names in the frame included Ray Matthias, John Beck, Danny Bergera and Graham Barrow - still awaiting a contract at Wigan - but there was no official application from Ratcliffe.

Gary Shelton was appointed as Assistant, and within a week the first signing had been made when 24-year-old utility man Neil Fisher was snapped up on a free transfer from Bolton. Billy Stewart also rejoined the club from Northampton, a move that prompted the release of Felgate to Wigan, while Dave Rogers signed from Tranmere.

Other players released were Gary Hackett and Don Page, while Chris Lightfoot got his wish for a move when he joined Graham Barrow at Wigan for a tribunal decided £87,500. This move after Barrow had put in an initial offer of £30,000, a far cry from the £750,000 valuation of 1993. The biggest coup for the club however was the signing of experienced former England international Cyrille Regis on a free transfer from Wycombe.

Cyrille Regis in action versus Hereford.

Regis had made more than 500 appearances for WBA, Coventry, Aston Villa, Wolves and Wycombe, scoring 152 goals and winning five England caps in the process. Although he had lost some of his pace he read the game well and his strength, ability in the air, and refusal to be shaken off the ball made him an instant cult hero with Chester fans.

The 1995/96 season opened with Roger Preece collecting the previous season's Player of the Year award against Hartlepool. Less than 45 minutes later Preece's season lay in ruins after a clattering tackle from Mick Tait left him with a serious leg injury. Despite the loss of Preece the ecclesiastical duo of Bishop and Priest gave Chester an opening day victory. The win put Chester in an ideal frame of mind for their Coca Cola cup encounter with Wigan, and a head-to-head encounter between Ratcliffe and former favourite Graham Barrow. Although Ratcliffe played down the importance of the tie, it was a crucial personal test for him, and the players did him proud with a superb 4-1 victory. It got worse for Barrow in the second leg when Milner gave City a two minute lead on the way to a crushing 7-2 aggregate victory, as Chris Lightfoot and Roberto Martinez were sent off for the Latics.

In the League, Chester were in magnificent early season form with some flowing football prompted by the masterful Regis. A 3-1 win over promotion favourites Plymouth saw Regis score his first goal for the club with a typical header, while Eddie Bishop, now playing part-time, scored for the fifth consecutive game. At the start of September, winger Kevin Noteman signed on a one month trial, a move later made permanent, and was on target on his debut against Hereford. Club comedian Eddie Bishop missed the game through injury, and was lucky to escape censure when he grabbed hold of the public address microphone during the game and gave the referee his opinion of a penalty incident.

Nick Richardson, a £40,000 signing from Bury, became the next player to join the bandwagon as wins at Colchester and Scunthorpe, the most impressive performance so far, took Chester to the top of the table.

The position was consolidated with an exciting 5-1 win over Lincoln, where Jason Burnham scored his only goal for the club, a cracking 25 yard free kick, and Neil Fisher capped another outstanding performances with his first Chester goal.

Progress in the Coca Cola Cup was halted by Premiership side Spurs, but Chester always tried to play football and the aggregate score of 7-1 was cruel on them. Iain Jenkins received an ankle injury in the 1st leg which put him out of action for six weeks, and defeat at Preston cost Chester top spot. There was a return to form at Orient where the home fans showed their appreciation of Regis with a tremendous ovation after his late substitution.

Four successive wins, in which 15 goals were scored, saw Chester return to the top, although a 4-1 win over an impressive Darlington was flattering. Understandably confidence was sky high when Chester travelled to Blackpool for an FA Cup-tie in November. It looked as though Chester were through, when Andy Milner's bullet header gave them a 77th minute lead, but, after defending so well, two late goals were conceded and City went out. A serious car crash after this game left Iain Jenkins with broken ribs and a punctured lung, but tremendous powers of recovery saw him return to the side in April.

The year ended with victory at a waterlogged St James's Park, Exeter, leaving Chester two points clear of Gillingham at the top, and in much better shape than at the end of 1994. In January, Ratcliffe and Shelton were rewarded for their enterprising management with extended rolling contracts as Mark Guterman pronounced them '*the brightest, most creative young management team in the country*'.

Unfortunately Chester were unable to carry their form through into the second half of the season and they gradually slipped out of the promotion places.

During January and February only one game was won as long term injuries to Flitcroft, Bishop, Preece and Jenkins began to take their toll, while Regis struggled with a thigh injury.

The home game against Scunthorpe in February marked a milestone for Billy Stewart who made his 300th League appearance for the club. This followed on from Peter Jackson who had played his 600th League game at home to Darlington, and Cyrille Regis who reached a similar total at Cambridge.

The defence, leaking too many goals for Ratcliffe's liking, was bolstered by the arrival of hard-tackling Ross Davidson from Sheffield United. Davidson scored his first goal for the club in a 4-0 win over Cardiff as Chester showed some of their early season form. There followed four draws in successive home games, including a goalless match against Wigan where Darren Ryan made a surprise return to the Chester team after joining on non-contract terms from Rochdale. A hot and cold season was summed up over the Easter weekend when a 5-0 demolition of Scarborough was followed by a poor display at Fulham, where two goals were conceded in the first 10 minutes. Defeat at home to Rochdale was marred by a touchline brawl when Ratcliffe's frustration finally got the better of him after team captain and Player of the Year Peter Jackson was sent off. Home wins against Northampton and Mansfield left Chester just outside the play-off zone, as a season that had started so well finished disappointingly.

Jason Burnham, Eddie Bishop, Leroy Chambers and reserve goalkeeper John Bagnall were all released at the end of the season, while Billy Stewart turned down a new contract and joined Southport. With the goalkeeping position as a top priority, Ratcliffe signed Scotsman Ronnie Sinclair from Stoke and teenager Chris Knowles (Peterborough) as reserve. Young Everton defender, Mattie Woods, was the only other signing as Julian Alsford, who had lost his place after a promising start to the previous season, remained on a week to week contract. There was a change in the back room staff where youth team coach and former manager Derek Mann left the club and was replaced by ex-Wrexham player David Fogg.

John Murphy led the attack for the first game of the season at troubled Brighton, having impressed with two goals in a pre-season friendly against Burnley. Although Murphy put City ahead, defensive lapses cost Chester their first ever win at the Goldstone Ground. Four days later, at the other end of the country, they received a battering in the Coca Cola Cup at Carlisle where only a virtuoso performance from Sinclair kept the score down to 1-0. Sinclair broke his jaw in the next game against Cambridge, and Chris Knowles made his debut in the 2-0 victory over Swansea.

Chester's first goal was scored by 38-year-old Gary Shelton who belied his age with some outstanding early season performances. Neil Cutler, on loan from Crewe, took over in goal against Wigan. For Cutler it was his second spell at Chester, having played one game on loan from West Brom. the previous season. Ratcliffe had tried to sign Cutler during the summer but the £25,000 fee had proved prohibitive.

After defeats against Wigan and Carlisle in the Coca Cola Cup, Fisher, Murphy and Rogers were all dropped and replaced by Flitcroft, Davidson and Noteman. A 4-1 win over Lincoln justified the changes but Cutler was sent off for handling outside the area. Peter Jackson took over in goal, a role he had performed the previous season against Orient. On that occasion he let in a soft goal and afterwards had vowed never to appear in goal again. Jackson was also in the news against Scunthorpe, where he was sent off as Chester grabbed an improbable victory with a lucky goal from Fisher.

Nick Richardson shattered his knee in the 2-0 defeat at Hartlepool, an injury that put him out for the season, and Dave Flitcroft was lucky not to break his back after celebrating a sensational goal against Northampton. Ratcliffe finally acquired a target man in October, when 6ft-4ins Ian Helliwell joined the club on loan from Burnley but after one goal in nine games he was allowed to return to Turf Moor.

In October Mark Guterman announced he was heading a consortium to take control of Manchester City with the intention of making Chester a feeder club. Although the offer came to nothing it stirred a hornet's nest and the whole issue of feeder clubs became the subject of national footballing debate.

There was sad news in October when Roger Preece was allowed to leave the club having struggled to regain fitness after injury. He joined Billy Stewart at Southport, and they were later followed by Dave Rogers. Cyrille Regis announced his retirement from football in the same month, having struggled with a series of niggling injuries.

In November, Ratcliffe added some bite to midfield with the loan signing of hard man Shaun Reid from Bury, while striker Rod McDonald was given the chance to resurrect his League career after signing from Southport. Both players made their debuts against Cardiff, where Wayne Brown from Weston Super Mare became the fourth keeper of the season. At the end of January, Reid's move became permanent when Chester paid out £30,000. By the end of December Chester were ninth, with games in hand, and facing an attractive FA Cup 3rd Round tie at Premiership Middlesbrough.

They had reached this stage after defeating two non-League clubs, Stalybridge Celtic and Boston United . The 3-0 win over Stalybridge included two goals from Stuart Rimmer, amazingly his first FA Cup goals for the club. Boston, including old boy Leroy Chambers, put up a hard fight but were beaten by an early Andy Milner goal as Jackson was sent-off and Sinclair saved a penalty.

It was a makeshift Chester side that travelled to Middlesbrough with Davidson, Jackson and Flitcroft all suspended and two players, Reid and McDonald, ineligible. Over 2,500 supporters made the journey - more than most home League attendances - but Middlesbrough won 6-0 with Ravanelli having a hand in five of the goals. Kevin Noteman missed the chance to put Chester on the score-sheet when he ballooned a penalty into the stand.

*Julian Alsford and Ravenelli (Middlesbrough)*

In the League, 1997 started badly with three goalless draws and a 5-1 hammering at promotion rivals North-ampton. However, in February, Chester began a sequence of 12 games without defeat that put them back in the promotion frame. Highlight of this run was a 6-0 hammering of a poor Doncaster side where Andy Milner became the first player, since Stuart Rimmer in 1985, to score four goals in a game. City could even afford the luxury of a missed penalty when Iain Jenkins spurned the opportunity of scoring his first goal for the club.

Jenkins had by now attracted the attention of Northern Ireland manager Bryan Hamilton and after a Man of the Match performance for the 'B' team against Portugal earned a full cap in the World Cup qualifier against Armenia. At the end of the season Jenkins travelled with the Ireland team to the Far East and won a second cap against Thailand.

Chester's march towards the play-offs was partly due to the form of flying winger Sam Aiston, on loan from Sunderland. Aiston became an instant hit as he showed some dazzling skills and remained at the Deva until the end of the season.

A narrow l-0 victory over Scarborough, in a tense encounter, left Chester seventh and a play-off position was confirmed with an extraordinary victory at Exeter. Even psychic Uri Geller, who had placed an energy-infused crystal behind each goal, could not help Exeter as Chester tore the Grecians apart with five second-half goals in a torrential downpour. Defeat at home to Leyton Orient in the final game left Swansea lying between Chester and a first Wembley appearance. The first leg, at the Deva Stadium, proved to be a scrappy encounter with few clear-cut chances and a goalless draw was a fair result. Chester's best chance fell to Andy Milner although David Flitcroft had a goal disallowed for offside.

The return game was a different matter as Swansea over-powered Chester following the 25th minute dismissal of Chris Priest. Two goals in first-half injury-time, from Thomas and Torpey, put Swansea in the driving seat and future loan player, Carl Heggs made it 3-0 in the second period.

Both Peter Jackson and Kevin Noteman were released in summer 1997 while there were two new signings in the form of Gary Bennett and Rod Thomas. Bennett joined Chester for a third time, in a £50,000 deal with local rivals Wrexham, while Thomas, a free transfer signing from Carlisle, was a former England Youth and Under-21 international whose lightning pace had always caused City problems when in opposition. Meanwhile Kevin Ratcliffe announced his own decision to retire from playing and, along with Gary Shelton, signed a new three year management deal which kept him at the club until the year 2000.

Chester started the 1997/98 season with Gary Bennett and Stuart Rimmer leading the attack, the same striking partnership that had taken the Blues to promotion in 1985/86. Typically Bennett was on target in the opening game, a 2-0 home victory against Lincoln City. Bennett scored 11 goals in the first 16 League games of the season including his 200th League goal at Scunthorpe and City's record of scoring in each of the first 16 games was their best run from the start of a season since joining the League. With goals flowing freely, Ratcliffe could afford to let Andy Milner go on loan to Hereford United and later in the year Milner made a permanent move to Morecambe.

The first half of the season proved to be very inconsistent with some excellent home victories, which at one point gave them the best home record in the Football League, balanced by some poor away results. After an excellent 2-0 win at Cardiff they conceded 15 goals in the next four away games at Mansfield, Rotherham, Torquay (where Ronnie Sinclair and Gary Shelton were sent-off) and Scarborough. Perhaps the most impressive performance before Christmas was a backs to the wall display at top of the table Notts County where youngsters Martin Giles and Ryan Dobson made their first and second appearances respectively as the Blues sneaked an unlikely 2-1 victory.

The appearance of Dobson and Giles highlighted the injury problems City were suffering, especially in defence, where Ross Davidson, Matt Woods, Iain Jenkins and Spencer Whelan all missed a number of games. Financial constraints meant that Chester were unable to sign players either permanently or on loan and as gates fell short of the break-even figure, chairman Mark Guterman revealed a revolutionary scheme to attract more fans to the Deva Stadium. Starting with the home game against Rochdale supporters from clubs outside Division Three were allowed free entrance on production of a season ticket. The scheme received widespread media coverage but received a mixed, but mainly negative, reaction from home supporters.

In Cup competitions, City were eliminated from the Coca-Cola Cup at the first stage by Carlisle United for the second successive season although, on this occasion, Chester put up more of a fight. In the FA Cup Chester recovered a one goal half-time deficit to defeat a Winsford United side containing former City stars Paul Wheeler and Mark Came. In the Second Round Chester were drawn to play Wrexham at the Deva Stadium. The game was televised live on Sky television but, after a big build-up, the game proved to be an anti-climax as Wrexham survived early City pressure to comfortably progress to the Third Round. Of more importance to the club was the £75,000 received from Sky which helped relieve the growing financial problems. On December 3rd Chester had faced a winding-up order brought by the Inland Revenue although Mark Guterman explained that the bill had already been settled.

Back in the League there was an eleventh hour postponement at Swansea in November when the Vetch Field was declared unsafe. The home game against Swansea was brought forward at short notice and played at the Deva Stadium the following week in front of only 1,500, although Chester were rewarded with a hard earned three points. At the start of 1998 Chester stood fourth in the table and the good form continued with a 3-1 win at Lincoln where Iain Jenkins scored his first goal for the club after more than 150 appearances. The full-back's form had been attracting interest from other clubs with Ipswich, Sunderland, Birmingham and Stockport all reputed to have shown an interest and in March he made his third appearance for Northern Ireland, against Slovakia. Jenkins was not the only person attracting outside interest as managerless Cardiff put Kevin Ratcliffe at the top of their wanted list, but to no avail.

Rod McDonald's late winner at Cambridge gave City their first victory at the Abbey Stadium after 10 games and a 28-year wait, however this game marked a turning point as the Blues gradually slipped out of play-off contention. Deva Stadium lost its reputation as a fortress as Barnet and Mansfield both left with three points, and it was February 21st before the home fans saw the first goal of 1998, although it was worth waiting for as Rotherham were overwhelmed with four second-half goals and had two players dismissed.

In March the financial problems came to a head as Guterman revealed that he had personally put £1 million into the club and that City were still losing £350,000 a year. Despite these figures he denied that the club was up for sale following speculation that ownership was about to change hands. However, a few days before transfer deadline day it became clear that the financial difficulties were far worse than anyone had anticipated when it was revealed that the players had not been paid and the club were facing a second winding-up order brought by the Inland Revenue for £100,000. With the club in turmoil and facing extinction, Guterman announced a six-point restructuring plan which would inject £600,000 into the club.

Key to the plan was the sale of Iain Jenkins and Julian Alsford to Dundee United for £200,000 and the shock sale of 17-year-old Matt McKay to Everton for an initial £250,000 in a deal which could eventually net £750,000. It was a dream move for McKay who had only made three full appearances for Chester following his first start at Rochdale three weeks earlier.

By now the club were in mid-table and the low point of the season was reached when a clearly demoralised team lost 5-0 at Exeter and had John Murphy sent-off. The in-form Murphy had been one of the bright spots in the second half of the season having finally been given a run in the team after a series of injuries.

Chester gained their first win in nine games when they had the dubious distinction of sending Doncaster Rovers into the Conference, and victory over promotion chasing Colchester was notable for a Spencer Whelan goal from the halfway line. April ended with a nostalgic return to the Moss Rose for a League encounter with Macclesfield. In front of a capacity crowd, with hundreds locked out, Macclesfield clinched promotion at the first attempt with a 3-2 win but City fans will remember it for a remarkable long-range goal from Rod Thomas. The season ended with a 1-1 draw against Scarborough with Chester's goal coming from a Stuart Rimmer header. Fittingly this marked Rimmer's final appearance for the club as Chester's greatest ever goalscorer was given a free transfer along with Ronnie Sinclair, Neil Fisher, Rod McDonald, Ryan Dobson and Martin Giles.

In preparation for the 1998/99 season Kevin Ratcliffe brought in striker Luke Beckett, leading scorer with Barnsley Reserves, left-sided midfielder Alex Smith (Huddersfield), Jonathan Cross (Wrexham), Darlington skipper Andy Crosby and goalkeeper Neil Cutler, who had already spent two periods on loan at the Deva Stadium.

Nevertheless it was the off-the field problems that dominated the close-season and, after Kevin Ratcliffe temporarily paid an outstanding water bill, the friendly game against Everton came under threat when it was revealed that some of the players had not been paid. The game only went ahead when the money was handed over hours before the kick off. The crisis affecting the club prompted action from two quarters. Firstly a small group of Chester supporters, concerned about recent developments, formed the Chester City Independent Supporters Association (ISA) while a consortium, of local businessmen outlined a rescue package, entitled "Phoenix – Fans and Plans", to step in if the club had to call in the receiver. By the end of July Guterman, who had failed in a bid to be elected to the Football League board, had had enough and put the club up for sale blaming disruption to family life and the drain on his own personal resources for his decision.

On the playing field the pre-season friendly, against a strong Everton side, saw the father-son combination of Gary and Andy Shelton feature for the final ten minutes of the game although they never appeared in a League game together. The 1-1 draw with Everton capped an impressive pre-season in which new-signing Beckett and Gary Bennett grabbed 14 goals between them as the goals flowed freely. However this form was not translated to the League and the season opened with a 2-0 defeat to 10-man Leyton Orient.

The first League win of the season came at Southend, at the end of August, where Gary Bennett scored his first League goal since the previous November. This marked Bennett's final League goal as a knee injury forced him out of action in September and he retired the following August. In fact, Chester reserved their best performances for their travels where they won seven games compared with only six at the Deva Stadium. At home, the failure to kill off teams cost Chester dearly and supporters were left increasingly frustrated throughout the season by the habit of opening the scoring and then conceding a late equaliser.

In the Worthington Cup, Chester overcame League Two side Port Vale in the First Round to earn an attractive tie against Sunderland and a first visit to the Stadium of Light. The tie was of particular interest to Shaun Reid, who faced the side managed by his brother Peter, days after he had made his first appearance in 15 months following a cruciate ligament injury. Without the defensive spine of Wayne Brown and Andy Crosby, both suspended after being sent-off in the 3-0 home defeat to Cambridge, the Blues were no match for Sunderland who won 3-0 to make the second leg a formality. A disappointingly small crowd of only 2,738 watched the 1-0 second leg defeat to the Wearsiders.

Away from the action, the club survived a winding-up order on August 10th but the case was adjourned until October 19th as the players continued to suffer from delayed payment of wages and expenses. Meanwhile the increasingly high-profile ISA arranged bucket collections to help meet players' expenses as the PFA assisted in paying wages. Although Guterman had been in negotiation with potential buyers, he conceded defeat in his attempts to sell the club days before the winding-up order and investigated the possibility of placing the club into administration by appointing corporate rescue and recovery specialists Begbies Traynor.

Two days before the winding-up order Chester faced Swansea at the Deva Stadium in what was potentially the last game for the club. Almost 4,000 fans attended the game thanks to a big publicity campaign by the ISA. On an emotional day the game finished 1-1, with John Murphy scoring for the Blues. The following Monday a further adjournment was obtained and on October 27th the club finally went into administration giving David Acland, the Begbies Traynor representative, until December 18th to find a buyer and satisfy the creditors.

With outstanding debts of £500,000, a reduction in costs was the main priority and all the players were put on the transfer list. First to go had been popular winger Rod Thomas who scored two goals in his final game, a 4-2 win at Scarborough, in what was one of the best performances of the season. The sale of Thomas, to Brighton, raised £25,000 and his exit was followed by that of the club's longest serving player, Spencer Whelan, to Shrewsbury for £35,000.

Although there was plenty of interest in buying the club, no bids materialised. The strongest enquiries had come from Oswestry based tele-communications company Total Network Solutions, who had invested heavily in League of Wales side TNS Llansantffraid. However, their interest waned in December as they expressed their intention to change the name of the club to promote their own company.

At the start of December Acland met with the creditors, who gave him an extension until the end of January to find a buyer, while the courts gave the club another stay of execution in the same month as the administrator remained confident that a sale was imminent. Acland had been helped in these negotiations with the news that a financial boost was on the cards as Sky intended to do a live screening of the January meeting between Chester and Brighton. The ISA designated the game as "Fans United 3", a concept invented by Brighton fans to highlight the problems of lower division clubs, and supporters from all over the country were invited to attend the Friday night game.

As activity increased off the field, Ratcliffe continued to manage the players under difficult conditions. Any hopes of a money-spinning run in the FA Cup were abruptly ended in the First Round with an abject performance at Cardiff where the Welshman clinically tore apart Chester to the tune of six unanswered goals. However, despite the financial problems, Ratcliffe was able to bring in two loan players. Winger Sam Aiston returned from Sunderland for a second time, in a deal partially financed by the ISA, while experienced striker Mike Conroy arrived from Blackpool the following month. The new arrivals helped Chester to an unbeaten League run in December earning Ratcliffe his first Manager of the Month award. This came despite Chester's first taste of the Golden Goal when they were defeated in the First Round of the Auto Windscreens Shield by a Hartlepool goal in the 103rd minute.

The televised match against Brighton proved a great success with over 4,000 attending but, for the second successive game, City conceded a 90th minute equaliser after Mike Conroy had given them the lead. Nevertheless the £35,000 earned from Sky helped the club through to the end of February. The sale of Alex Smith, to Port Vale, raised another £75,000 while Julian Alsford briefly returned to the club in February on a week-to-week contract after an unsuccessful spell with Dundee United. Another ex-player, Neil Fisher, also signed on non-contract terms after a spell with Bangor City and Connah's Quay Nomads.

Under the circumstances a final position of 14th was impressive and the final game, against Rotherham, neatly encapsulated the season as Chester took a first-half lead through Luke Beckett, dominated the game and then conceded an equaliser in the 88th minute. However, not for the first time, the game was overshadowed by activities off the field as there had still been no firm offer to buy the club. The administrators had revealed the extent of the problems in April when they stated that the club would be wound up in May unless a buyer was found. Prior to the Rotherham game the ISA organised a march from the Town Hall to the Deva Stadium to highlight the problem as well as celebrate the fact that the club had survived the season against all odds.

During May another potential buyer emerged in the form of a consortium of businessmen fronted by Reg Brearley, major shareholder at Grantham Town and a former chairman of Darlington and Sheffield United. Meanwhile, the ISA had launched their own bid to take over the club alongside a group of local businessmen. With this in mind a Trust Fund was launched and £73,000 was pledged at a Town Hall meeting at the end of May.

With the Football League looking for assurances that Chester would be able to start the 1999/2000 season another candidate emerged as favourite to buy the club in June. Terry Smith, an American based in Manchester, had attended the ISA launch and enthusiastically talked about his revolutionary plans to bring in foreign players and involve the supporters in the running of the club. Backed by his father Gerald, a Florida businessman, Smith had a background in coaching American Football having coached the Manchester Spartans as well as the Great Britain team. In his first interview with the Chester Chronicle he explained how he and his fellow investors had been looking to invest in a British club for some time and ominously stated how he would *"enjoy being involved with the players and the competition."*

The Smith bid quickly gathered pace and on July 19th a deal was finally completed when the creditors approved the Voluntary Arrangement Proposal whereby £251,000 would be paid to the major creditors over 24 months as Mark Guterman accepted an offer for his majority shareholding. On completing the deal an optimistic Smith gave details of his plans for the club which included First Division football in three years, an influx of international signings, sell-outs at every home game as well as full supporter and community involvement with the opportunity to buy shares in the club. Having experienced a traumatic 12 months, supporters were just relieved that a deal had finally been completed. Little did they realise that the problems were just beginning.

# DOWN AND OUT 1999 - 2010
# CHAPTER 15

A buoyant, capacity crowd gathered at the Deva Stadium for the first game of the Terry Smith era as Chester faced a strong Everton side and were narrowly beaten 3-2. Nevertheless, despite the takeover, there were major issues on the playing front as the problems of the last 12 months took the toll on Kevin Ratcliffe's small squad. Prior to takeover there had been eleven players out of contract and during the summer David Flitcroft joined Rochdale while Chris Priest signed for Macclesfield. In addition, Andy Crosby signed for Brighton for £10,000 claiming that the club was *"falling apart"*. Meanwhile the promising John Murphy moved to Blackpool on a Bosman free transfer on the verge of the opening game, leaving the squad desperately short of experience.

Ratcliffe, who had been on the short list for the Wales manager's job following the resignation of Bobby Gould, was given the full backing of Smith who claimed: *"Kevin and I have a good relationship and there are no plans to make any changes"*. However Ratcliffe's plans to bring in experienced professionals to strengthen the squad were clearly at odds with Smith, who was already looking to bring in overseas players on trial. In fact, the only pre-season arrival was the Smith sanctioned signing of Paul Berry from Warrington Town who had impressed the new owner in a pre-season friendly.

The 1999/2000 season opened with a 2-0 home defeat to Barnet, but there was a boost three days later when goals from Nick Richardson and Luke Beckett gave Chester a 2-1 victory over Port Vale in the Worthington Cup despite having Martyn Lancaster sent-off. However, any hope that the club could build from this victory was firmly scotched when Chester suffered a humiliating 4-0 defeat at Rotherham in which two penalties were conceded and Lancaster was dismissed for the second successive game. The inadequacies of the team were already evident and, after a 2-0 home defeat to Northampton, the club was again thrown into turmoil when Kevin Ratcliffe resigned.

Ratcliffe had gradually earned the respect of City fans after his unpopular arrival with Mike Pejic in 1994 and had performed miracles in keeping the team together through the period of administration. Therefore Smith did himself few favours by issuing a statement accusing the former Everton and Wales captain of showing a lack of commitment as well as a *"negative and pessimistic attitude"* that would *"in all likelihood have led to relegation"*. News that there was a clause in Ratcliffe's contract entitling him to walk away with payment for the remainder of his contract if the club changed hands did little to help the financial situation.

Rather than appoint a replacement manager, Smith responded by controversially naming himself as part of a five-man coaching team alongside youth team coach Dave Fogg, Gary Shelton, Shaun Reid and Scott Cooper, a Smith associate who had coached indoor soccer in the USA. He also invited ridicule by taking the novel approach of appointing zonal captains with Ross Davidson captain of defence, Nick Richardson captain of midfield and Luke Beckett captain up front. Shaun Reid remained club captain.

Despite his background in American Football and lack of experience coaching football, Smith justified his hands-on role by stating that *"80% or 90% of coaching is the same in every sport. It is to do with organisation, the disciplinary side and motivation and everything on those lines. I imagine I've had more years of coaching than everybody, including Kevin."*

The first match under the new system saw Smith issue all the players with a seven-page game plan for the second leg Worthington Cup tie against Port Vale. The team responded with a thrilling performance to secure a 4-4 draw as Chester eliminated Vale for the second successive season. Luke Beckett scored twice bringing his total to five in the four games between the sides.

In the second round City were drawn against Aston Villa and produced a fighting display in the first leg. With the game heading for a goalless draw Serbian debutant, Goran Milosavijevic, inexplicably handled the ball in the penalty area with 12 minutes remaining. Although Wayne Brown brilliantly saved Lee Hendrie's penalty he couldn't prevent the midfielder netting the rebound. In the second leg Chester were swept aside 5-0 in a one-sided game.

Milosavijevic was one of a number of foreign players introduced into the team by Smith with Joe Carver, Kamu Laird and Manchester-born Nicky Spooner arriving from America alongside Canadian international Martin Nash and Angus Eve from Trinidad. Laird and Eve both scored on their debuts, a 2-1 win over Halifax in December, but none of the signings were appropriate for a side struggling at the bottom of the table.

Eve proved to be an enigma as he spent much of his time at Chester playing international football for Trinidad. Although he was contracted for two years, Eve spent the second season back in the Caribbean on loan with former club Joe Public. He therefore earned the distinction of becoming the club's most capped player with 35 caps even though he only ever featured in 13 League games.

A more successful loan signing was that of Junior Agogo from Sheffield Wednesday. The Ghanaian scored six goals in his 10 appearances including one of the best goals scored at the Deva Stadium, a brilliant solo effort against Cheltenham. Agogo also scored a 94th minute winner at the Withdean Stadium to secure Chester's first ever win at Brighton, despite the dismissal of Ross Davidson. There was also a first ever win at fellow strugglers Shrewsbury with Nick Richardson scoring the only goal in a poor game.

In the FA Cup, Chester reached the Third Round where the 4-1 scoreline flattered Manchester City who scored two goals in the dying minutes. Nevertheless City had been lucky to reach that stage having survived a scare in the First Round where an awful performance at non-League Whyteleafe saw them come away with a goalless draw after Wayne Brown had saved a late penalty. The replay was won 3-1 but Chester had to recover from a goal down in a game where another Smith signing, Scotsman Steve Malone, was substituted after only half an hour in his one and only game.

Despite these sporadic victories, dissent was growing with the management style and tactical awareness of Smith and this came to a head in December. The defiant American rejected a plea by the ISA for him to stand down as manager and relations with the Supporters Group continued to deteriorate amid claims that an offer to buy shares in the club had been withdrawn.

In the last game of the twentieth century, at home to bottom of the table Leyton Orient, Chester produced a wretched performance in slumping to a 5-1 defeat. The Londoners, who had failed to score for more than nine hours, swapped places with the Blues at the bottom and the embarrassment was compounded by the presence of a documentary crew filming the debacle. A week later Chester started the new century with a humiliating 4-1defeat at fellow strugglers Carlisle United in what proved to be Smith's last game in charge as the owner finally recognised that an experienced manager was required.

Former Northampton manager, Ian Atkins was present at the Carlisle game and he was given the onerous task of turning around what already looked like a hopeless situation in the role as Director of Football, although Smith retained the job title Team Manager. Smith gave Atkins the go-ahead to recruit players and, over the next two months a total of 10 new faces arrived at the Deva Stadium as the team was gradually reshaped. Amongst the newcomers were Paul Carden (Rochdale), Gary Hobson (Brighton), John Keister (Walsall), Tony Hemmings (Ilkeston), Jamie Robinson (Exeter) and Ally Pickering (Altrincham) as well as experienced midfielder Andy Porter (on loan from Port Vale) and commanding central defender Stuart Hicks from Leyton Orient.

It took time for the changes to take effect and after only one victory in Atkins' first six games, Chester were unlucky to lose to a goal deep into injury-time against promotion-chasing Swansea as performances improved. However February ended in disastrous style as City suffered their heaviest home defeat in the Football League with teenager Bobby Zamora scoring a hat-trick for Brighton in a 7-1 thrashing.

That defeat left Chester staring the Conference in the face as they lay three points adrift of Carlisle at the bottom having also played two extra games. However, with Atkins' job already under threat, March saw a gradual change in fortunes amid a growing belief that relegation could be avoided. A trip to the West Country saw the Blues return with three points from Exeter, thanks to goals from Siggi Eyjolfsson , a loan signing from Walsall, and Luke Beckett. This was followed, three days later, by a point in a goalless draw at Plymouth. March ended in spectacular style as City crushed Mansfield 5-0 with Angus Eve scoring a brace. By now the supporters had rallied around Atkins' fighters and the possibility of a "Great Escape" captured the imagination of everyone.

April opened with a tremendous 1-0 win at Halifax as Chester secured back-to-back wins for the first time. A Beckett penalty secured the points but hero of the day was Stuart Hicks who had quickly become a cult hero at the club with some towering defensive performances as City kept six clean sheets in seven games. More than 5,500 fans attended the next game at the Deva, a crucial bottom-of-the-table game against Carlisle. However, in a dramatic finale, substitute Scott Dobie netted a 91st minute injury-time winner made worse by the fact that the visitors only had nine men on the field following the dismissals of Whitehead and Halliday. It was a cruel setback that left Chester two points behind Shrewsbury (now managed by Kevin Ratcliffe) and five behind Carlisle, with five games remaining, as relegation developed into a three-way battle.

The following week the Great Escape was back on track as goals from loanee Carl Heggs (Rushden) and Neil Fisher gave Chester a 2-1 win at Leyton Orient after they had trailed to an early goal. Backed by amazing vocal support from over 500 fans the three points hauled the Blues off the basement as Shrewsbury lost at home to Rochdale.

Over Easter, a point at former home Macclesfield, with Beckett again on target, and a 2-0 win over York at the Deva put Chester in the driving seat. They entered the last two games, away at Cheltenham and at home to Peterborough, needing just one point to secure safety. Chester's first League visit to Whaddon Road saw an unconvincing performance with the Blues falling to a 77th minute header from John Brough. The following week Chester were consigned to the Conference, after 69 years in the Football League, as Richie Hanlon's 64th minute goal settled the game in Peterborough's favour at the same time as Shrewsbury won at Exeter and Carlisle lost narrowly at Brighton.

Recriminations quickly followed with many supporters blaming Smith's ill-advised attempts at management for relegation. Meanwhile, Smith's press statements immediately after the game merely served to widen the gap between himself and the fans as he claimed that *"I have no regrets about my time in charge, in fact I have achieved 10 of the 11 targets I set for the club when I took over."* He also refused to guarantee the future of the popular Atkins, stating that twenty three points from his time in charge was *"a poor return after doubling the wage bill"*. There was further bad news, two days after relegation, when Kevin Ratcliffe won his compensation claim as the club was ordered to pay £200,000 after a League tribunal ruled in his favour.

**MATCH TO REMEMBER**
**CHESTER CITY 0 PETERBOROUGH UNITED 1**
**NATIONWIDE LEAGUE DIVISION 3 – MAY 6TH 2000**

***Chester's 69 years in the Football League ended with a 1-0 home defeat to Peterborough United. Needing only one point for safety, the Great Escape failed at the final hurdle as Ian Atkins' team failed to rise to the occasion amidst emotional scenes.***

***On a sunny afternoon the game kicked off with a party atmosphere and, after a goalless first-half, Chester still had one foot in the League. However the Blues had created few chances and it was the visitors who had come closest to scoring when Gareth Jelleyman struck Wayne Brown's post from outside the area on the half hour. For Chester the best chances had fallen to Steve Finney who had his shot well blocked by Mark Tyler in the 12th minute, while winger Tony Hemmings screwed his shot wide on the brink of half- time after good work by Carl Heggs and Luke Beckett.***

***The game was turned on its head on 64 minutes when Peterborough substitute Ritchie Hanlon struck a firm 20 yard shot past Brown into the bottom corner with virtually his first touch of the ball. News that Shrewsbury had taken a 2-0 lead at Exeter did little to settle nerves as an increasingly desperate Chester struggled to make any headway against the visitors' defence. In the closing stages Hemmings had a vicious free kick well saved by Tyler while Beckett just failed to connect with a Darren Wright cross.***

***In injury-time, hopes were briefly raised by an erroneous rumour of an Exeter equaliser against Shrewsbury, and this was accompanied by a long-range Paul Carden strike that brushed the top of the crossbar. In the end Peterborough deserved the victory and Chester supporters were left to reflect on Terry Smith's managerial reign as well as Carlisle's injury-time winner and the seven goals conceded against Brighton.***

***Chester – Brown, Fisher (Wright), Carden, Hobson, Hicks, Woods, Porter, Hemmings (Lancaster), Heggs, Beckett, Finney (Moss)***
***Peterborough United – Tyler, Drury, Farrell, Knight (Hanlon),Cullen, Gill (Senior), Green, Jelleyman (Shields), Rea, Oldfield, Wicks***

Although Atkins was the supporters' choice to be in charge for Chester's first season in the Conference he turned down the offer of a one-year contract. However Smith went some way to appease the fans by appointing former favourite Graham Barrow for his second spell in charge.

During the summer, coaches Gary Shelton and Shaun Reid both left the club while out of contract Luke Beckett signed for Chesterfield. Beckett's transfer fee was set at £150,000 but it was later revealed that Chesterfield had misled the transfer tribunal and not only was the fee increased by £25,000 but the Spireites had nine points deducted and were fined £10,000. Many of the players brought in on short- term contracts by Atkins also left with only Paul Carden remaining although Andy Porter, who had previously been on loan, signed permanently in October.

*A frustrated Luke Beckett in the crucial relegation battle against Peterborough.*

Barrow set about building a new team for the Conference by signing Mark Beesley (Barnsley) Carl Ruffer (Runcorn), Scott Ruscoe (Newtown), David Kerr (Mansfield) and Craig Gaunt, a former Arsenal trainee who had been playing in Singapore. Also into the squad came experienced 35-year-old former Leeds and Sheffield United defender, Paul Beesley, who joined from Blackpool as Barrow's assistant.

Chester kicked off the 2000/01 season with an away fixture at promotion favourites Rushden and Diamonds, but they were comfortably beaten 2-0. The following Tuesday the Blues picked up their first points in the Conference with an entertaining 3-0 victory over Doncaster Rovers at the Deva Stadium. Mark Beesley had the honour of scoring the club's first goal after only 45 seconds. Chester settled comfortably into the Conference and by Christmas lay 8th in the table having only lost four games. However, too many games were being drawn, especially at home, and with only one side being promoted attention switched to Cup competitions where Chester were making significant progress.

The FA Cup campaign had started in the Fourth Qualifying Round, at the exposed ground of Easington Colliery on the North Sea coast. On a wet and windy day, goals from Mark Beesley and experienced campaigner Steve Whitehall, a September signing from Oldham, saw Chester through to the First Round proper where they faced former League rivals Plymouth Argyle. A Darren Wright goal looked to be sending Chester through until Argyle responded with a late equaliser as both teams finished with 10 men – Paul Beesley being sent-off for the Blues.

In the replay, Chester secured their first ever win at Home Park, with a 2-1 victory, thanks to an extra-time goal from Scott Ruscoe. The reward was another home tie against League opposition in the form of third-tier strugglers Oxford United. In a thrilling encounter Chester trailed the U's 2-0 after 25 minutes but pulled themselves back into the game before half-time when Paul Beesley headed his first goal for the club. Early in the second-half, the game was turned on its head when Steve Whitehall scored twice in three minutes to put Chester in front. The game finished 3-2 which not only extended Chester's unbeaten record to 16 games but also earned a Third Round tie at Premier League Blackburn Rovers. An astonishing 4,000 away fans travelled to Ewood Park to see Graham Barrow's team give a creditable display before bowing out 2-0.

There was a third victory over League opposition in the Auto Windscreens Shield where Hull City were defeated by a single Paul Carden goal, before Port Vale prevented any more giant-killing with a 2-0 win at Vale Park.Chester's first experience of the FA Trophy saw them earn a semi-final tie with Canvey Island after home victories over Doncaster, St Albans, Blyth Spartans and Southport. Supporters travelled down to Essex for the first leg full of hope but, in one of the worst performances of the season , City were easily beaten 2-0. In the second leg, at the Deva, any hopes of an appearance at Villa Park in the final were killed off when the Islanders took the lead after 30 minutes and Mark Stimson's second-half goal merely rubbed salt into the wounds. Terry Smith later took much of the credit for the successful FA Trophy run explaining that not only were his scouting reports invaluable but it was he who had *"designed the winning goal in the Quarter-Final."*

Nevertheless, Chester did win silverware for the first time since 1977 when they lifted the Nationwide Variety Club Trophy. In a series of prolonged encounters, three of which went into extra-time, City defeated Hednesford (after a replay), Southport and Nuneaton Borough to face Kingstonian in the Final for what was their 18th Cup tie of the season. Success in the various Cups had left Chester with major fixture congestion and they travelled down to Kingstonian for an 8pm kick off on a Bank Holiday Monday only four days after the semi-final win over Nuneaton and two days after the last Conference game of the season against Rushden. The fact that Chester had played 11 games in 24 days clearly showed in a leaden display that finished goalless after extra-time with little for the 495 fans to cheer. In the penalty shoot-out, keeper Wayne Brown was the hero when he saved Kingstonian's fourth penalty after Porter, Whitehall, Wright and Fisher had scored for the Blues.

*Terry Smith watches the FA Cup tie at Easington Colliery from the social club roof in October 2000*

With an overcrowded fixture list and no hope of promotion, the season petered out with the Blues finishing in 8th position. The season finished, as it had started, with defeat to Rushden who collected the Championship trophy at the Deva Stadium backed by a large following. However of more concern was the complete breakdown of relations between Terry Smith and the supporters.

A series of incidents throughout the 2000/01 campaign had increased the tension surrounding the club and by the end of the season this had developed into a fully fledged crisis. Two of the ISA-backed directors had resigned over concerns about how the club was being run while the resignation of the Chief Safety Officer, after a disagreement with Smith, had led to the short notice postponement of the Hayes fixture and a fine from the FA. The players and management team were not immune from criticism and Paul Beesley had been suspended from playing for standing in the wrong position for set pieces against Canvey with Smith claiming: *"We had practised, as in American football, tactics of where to stand and done scrimmages between the first team and reserves. In training the first team had scored 10 goals. But Beesley stood in the wrong place, ruining it for everybody."*

The treatment of Beesley led to an open revolt by the players who spoke out, despite being banned from talking to the press, and when eleven of them were asked to take part in an end of season training camp, none of them attended. Beesley, who won the Player of the Year award, was later sacked, along with England semi-professionals Wayne Brown and Carl Ruffer, for "gross misconduct" All three players were re-instated just before their case went to a tribunal but Beesley was later sacked for a second time.

The final straw was the banning of well-respected supporter Barrie Hipkiss who had worked in a voluntary capacity for the club for 30 years, after he spoke out against Smith's plans to form the "Chester City Democratic Supporters Association." Prior to the Rushden game an ISA-arranged funeral march to the ground took place with supporters carrying a coffin to symbolise what they believed was the slow death of the club and this was followed by a mass resignation of stewards after the match. The mood was not helped by the programme notes for the game which contained an extraordinary diatribe from Smith in which he defended his own record and attacked his critics, including the local press, with whom relations had deteriorated badly and with whom he had taken to regularly contact by fax.

As the season had reached a climax it had appeared as though the club was on the verge of being sold to a Liverpool-based consortium led by Phil Davies. However this deal collapsed as Smith gave every indication that he intended to stay on by appointing former music promoter, Gareth Evans, as Managing Director in May. The appointment was swiftly followed by the sacking of two members of the backroom staff, as well as physio Joe Hinnigan, in acrimonious circumstances. When former Manchester United and England winger, Gordon Hill, was elevated to Director of Football it was clear that the writing was also on the wall for Barrow and the popular leader was duly axed in June.

Hill, who had been in charge of the youth development programme, appealed for the fans to rally around but his pleas largely fell on deaf ears. At the same time as Hill was settling into his new job, ISA chairman, George Rogers, had stood as a candidate in the General Election for FANS – For A New Start for Chester City FC - in order to raise awareness of the problems affecting the club. By the end of June fans were picketing the Deva Stadium and, with many supporters refusing to attend home games until Smith departed, it was clear that the club was in for a difficult, short-term future.

With Kevin Ratcliffe stepping up his efforts to claim the £200,000 he was owed, by threatening a winding-up order, the pre-season was thrown into further chaos when home friendlies against Tranmere and Everton were called off because of a lack of stewards.

On the playing front, a transfer embargo was lifted when Chester paid Ilkeston Town £3,000 they owed for Tony Hemmings. Hill brought in brothers Michael and Stephen Rose from Manchester United while former Tranmere and Telford striker, Chris Malkin, signed up in the dual role as player and physio. The only other new signing was Hill's own son, Sam. Amongst the summer departures were Steve Whitehall, Matt Woods, Paul Carden and Neil Fisher while two of the club's brightest prospects, Darren Moss and Matt Doughty moved on free transfers to Shrewsbury and Rochdale respectively.

It was an ill-prepared Chester team that took to the field for the first home game of the season, against Woking, and the combination of a picket and fans' boycott restricted the attendance to 745. Within 51 seconds the Blues were trailing 1-0 and a second goal, just before the break, condemned Hill's side to a 2-0 defeat.

Successive victories over Hayes and Nuneaton briefly lifted the side but with Hill having few players at his disposal, Chester failed to win all eight Conference games in September as youngsters Wes Kilgannon, Paul Roberts and Chris Hopwood made their debuts. The short-term signings of Dave Linighan (Southport) and David McNiven (York) also failed to raise the team and Chester ended September in the lower reaches of the table with attendances averaging around 700.

However, after a number of false alarms, Smith finally sold the club at the start of October to Liverpool boxing promoter, Stephen Vaughan and his company Vaughan Promotions Ltd. Vaughan had previously been owner at Barrow where his spell in charge had ended in acrimonious circumstances as the club were placed in liquidation leaving a question mark over the ownership of their Holker Street ground. Vaughan, who bought Smith's 98% shareholding, stated his wish to *"stabilise the club and then take us back into the Football League."*

After announcing that all players on the transfer list would be taken off it, Vaughan sanctioned the signing of four new players Brett Baxter (Accrington), Chris O'Brien (on loan from Liverpool), Mick O'Brien (Droylsden) and Steve Halford (Bury) with the quartet all making debuts in the home game against Margate. A humiliating 3-0 defeat left Chester bottom of the Conference and marked the last game in charge for Gordon Hill who, as an associate of Terry Smith, had never won over the City fans.

Former Tranmere Rovers stalwart, Steve Mungall, took the role of caretaker manager and his first match in charge resulted in a 2-0 win over Hereford with Jimmy Haarhoff and Scott Ruscoe on the scoresheet. The attendance also topped 1,000 for the first time as supporters slowly returned to the Deva after the departure of Smith. An excellent 3-0 win at Morecambe, followed by a battling home draw with Doncaster, saw Mungall awarded the job until the end of the season. His first match in permanent control threw up an interesting encounter as Chester travelled to Stephen Vaughan's old club Barrow for an FA Cup Fourth Qualifying Round tie. The match was initially put in doubt because Vaughan was still the major creditor at the Cumbrian club and FA rules forbade anyone from having a financial interest in more than one club. A few days before the tie, Vaughan transferred his Barrow shares to a local painter and decorator and the match was given the go-ahead. Much to the delight of the Barrow supporters, a single goal from Grant Holt was enough to eliminate their former owner's side as Chester were knocked out in the qualifying stages of the FA Cup for the first time since 1930.

The following week a Mark Beesley goal, against Yeovil, gave Chester their third win in four games. However, the mini-revival under Mungall came grinding to a halt as the Blues lost five out of the next six Conference games culminating in defeat at local rivals, Northwich Victoria, on Boxing Day. During this period two familiar faces returned to the Deva Stadium in the form of Paul Carden and Iain Jenkins. Carden, who had joined Doncaster Rovers for £3,000 during the summer, had struggled to establish himself with the Yorkshire team and was delighted to return to the city while Jenkins signed from Shrewsbury. Short-term loan signing, Gary Williams from Accrington, scored on his debut in the JC Thompson Championship Shield defeat to Rushden and Diamonds. The match, between the previous seasons Conference Champions and League Cup winners, saw Chester lose out 4-3 on penalties with keeper Wayne Brown on target from one of the spot kicks.

The Boxing Day defeat against Northwich had left Chester propping up the table, alongside Scarborough, and Vaughan reacted by sacking Mungall after only 79 days in charge. Former Chester player and Barrow manager, Owen Brown, took control for the next game, against Hayes, as the poor run was ended with a 3-1 victory.

There was plenty of interest in the manager's job with Graham Barrow and Mark Wright emerging as favourites. In the end it was Wright, the former Liverpool and England defender, who got the nod and he watched from the stand as Northwich completed the double over Chester with a 2-1 win at the Deva in the first game of 2002. Wright, who had previous experience managing in the Conference with Southport, was under no illusion of the task ahead and after the Northwich game expressed his desire to bring in at least five new players in order to guide the club away from relegation to the Unibond League. Vaughan had already made his intentions clear to spend his way out of trouble with a £40,000 bid for Telford's Neil Moore that was turned down and offers for other Telford players Jim Bentley, Jake Edwards, Gary Fitzpatrick and Mark Albrighton were also unsuccessful.

However, there were new faces in the form of combative scouse midfielder Gary Brabin from Torquay, who had joined just before the arrival of the new manager, while Wright's first signings were Phil Bolland, on loan from Oxford, and Stuart Whittaker (Southport). Bolland, a 6ft 4ins centre-half, who had played under Wright at both Southport and Oxford, added immediate authority to the defence and the goals against column improved significantly after his arrival.

Bolland and Whittaker made their debuts in a 1-0 win over Barnet, where Andy Porter scored from the spot, as Chester started their climb away from the relegation zone. Another former Southport player, Brian McGorry, joined at the end of January while Mark Williams (Hereford), Michael McElhatton (Rushden) and former Republic of Ireland Under-21 international Shaun Carey (Rushden) all made their debuts in a 3-1 win at Nuneaton Borough. A convincing 4-0 triumph at Stalybridge, with goals from Mark Beesley, Chris Tate (on loan from Leyton Orient) and two from McElhatton, showed that the new look Chester were going places and only three defeats in the last 10 games saw City finish the season comfortably in 14th place.

The last home game of the season saw Chester beat Stevenage Borough 5-1 as Stuart Whittaker scored a hat-trick in a game where Danny Collins made his second start for the club. Highly-rated Collins had signed from Cymru Alliance side Buckley Town as a striker in December and, after making his Conference debut as a substitute at Northwich, went on to score 19 goals in 12 games for the Reserves.

Away from the Conference, Chester had reached the Sixth Round of the FA Trophy after victories over Stourport Swifts, Solihull Borough and Hereford. The victories at Stourport and Solihull both came after disappointing draws at the Deva and the 4-2 win at Solihull saw Dean Spink score the first hat-trick for Chester since Andy Milner scored four against Doncaster in 1997. In the Sixth Round Chester were comfortably beaten 2-0 by Burton Albion, but the performances in the second half of the season gave everyone hope for 2002/03 after four difficult seasons.

During the summer Mark Wright performed a complete overhaul of the squad as he attempted to push for promotion back into the Football League boosted by the news that a second promotion place had been approved through a play-off spot. Dean Spink, the Rose brothers, Mick O'Brien, Richard Peacock and Brett Baxter were all released at the end of their contracts while Brian McGorry, Andy Porter and David Brown were all put on the transfer list. Meanwhile Iain Jenkins finished his playing career but took the role as coach of the youth team. The influential Gary Brabin, who had been awarded the Player of the Season despite playing in only 16 games, also left the club after being unable to agree on a new contract.

Into the team came young midfielder Ben Davies from Kidderminster, Dave Cameron (Lincoln), Ryan Sugden (Scarborough) as well as Kevin McIntyre and Jimmy Kelly from Doncaster. Winger Michael Brown, the player who scored the goal that rescued Shrewsbury at the expense of Chester on the last day of the 1999/ 2000 season, also signed from Boston United. Two other players, who had impressed when playing against Chester, also moved to the Deva Stadium. Striker Steve Brodie arrived from Swansea while former Manchester United trainee Michael Twiss, who had been sought by several clubs, was seen as a significant signing. The talented Twiss had been playing for Leigh RMI where he finished as leading scorer in 2001/02 with three of his 15 goals being scored against Chester. The influx continued in July with the arrival of goalkeeper Jon Worsnop from Bradford City together with experienced former Carlisle, Liverpool and Sheffield Wednesday defender, Steve Harkness.

In addition, the signings of Wayne Hatswell and Scott Guyett from Oxford meant that Wright had signed three central defenders from his former club in six months. Guyett had been on the verge of a move back to Australia before agreeing a deal with Chester at the last moment.

With so many new signings, Chris O'Brien and Jimmy Haarhoff were allowed out on loan to Droylsden with the moves later being made permanent. The path to Droylsden became well trodden over the next few seasons with several players making the move to the Manchester team where Stephen Vaughan had a shareholding until he severed all financial links in July. Another player to move out on loan was Danny Collins who signed for Vauxhall Motors and was a member of their side that knocked QPR out of the FA Cup in November. By now Collins had been converted to a defender and the experience gained in this new role proved invaluable when he returned to the Deva in January.

Wright, aware of the fact that he had to mould all his new signings into an efficient unit, played down prospects for the new season by dismissing talk of the Championship while aiming for a top-six finish. However, there was a new-found optimism surrounding the club and this was increased when more than 5,000 saw a Chris Blackburn goal defeat an experienced Liverpool X1, including the likes of Jamie Carragher and Patrik Berger, in the last pre-season friendly.

The 2002/03 season opened with an anti-climatic goalless draw at home to Kettering Town and the newly structured defence remained impregnable in the first five games, even without the injured Phil Bolland. However, despite the abundance of strikers, Chester were struggling to find the back of the net. When Chester played Morecambe at the start of September goals from Sugden and Twiss were the first at the Deva while the Shrimpers' strike, from future City player Stewart Drummond, was the first conceded by Wayne Brown.

Goalless draws at Hereford and Halifax maintained Chester's unbeaten run and they went top of the table in the middle of September after a thrilling encounter with Dagenham and Redbridge at the Deva. Despite falling a goal behind after 30 seconds, Chester eventually won the game 5-2 with a brace from Ryan Sugden, a penalty from Jimmy Kelly and two from central defenders Bolland and Guyett. This came after both sides had a player dismissed. Wayne Brown had been sent-off for the Blues but replacement Chris Blackburn kept a clean sheet for the final 25 minutes. Sugden was again on target with both goals as Chester recovered from 1-0 down to beat Burton, and another goalless draw at promotion challengers Doncaster, followed by Dave Cameron's winner at Margate, kept the pressure on new leaders Yeovil. The Margate game saw Australian winger Jon Brady make his debut after signing from Woking, while Steve Harkness played for the last time before leaving the game to concentrate on his business interests.

October saw a blip in results as Chester suffered their first home defeat of the season, in a live televised game at home to Nuneaton. Points were then dropped in a home draw with Gravesend, followed by defeat at Woking where Hatswell and McIntyre were both dismissed. Although the defence was solid Wright made no secret of the fact that he was looking to improve the strike force which was failing to take the many chances that were being created. Both Cameron and Brodie had been unable to make an impression and were placed on the transfer list while Twiss had only scored twice and Mark Beesley failed to reproduce the form of the previous campaign. Only Ryan Sugden had produced a return, with 10 goals and an FA Cup hat-trick at Radcliffe Borough. At the end of October Wright finally got his man when he clinched the signing of Daryl Clare from Boston for a club record £95,000. Clare had been the Conference's leading scorer in 2001/02, as the Lincolnshire side gained promotion, and the Republic of Ireland Under-21 international arrived with a reputation as a proven goalscorer. The likeable Clare became an instant hero at the Deva when he scored two sensational goals on his debut, including a last-minute equaliser, in the thrilling top of the table clash with Yeovil that finished 2-2. On his next appearance at the Deva, Clare went one better with a hat-trick in a 5-0 thrashing of Margate and he went on to bag 15 goals in his first 12 Conference games.

The record signing of Clare highlighted the remarkable change in fortunes at the club over the previous 12 months. Vaughan had cleared the debts, including the outstanding claims of Kevin Ratcliffe, and made funds available to Wright who had created a promotion-challenging squad. However, there was controversy under the surface as stories emerged that the chairman's company, Vaughan Promotions, had offered to buy rivals Tranmere Rovers and build a new ground for them on the Wirral. Despite extensive negotiations the deal was scrapped at the end of January.

The signing of Clare put Chester back on track in November and three Conference wins and a draw, coupled with an FA Cup giant-killing act at third-tier League side Colchester United, earned Wright a Manager of the Month award. The win at Layer Road came courtesy of loan signing Chris Tate, who joined the club from Leyton Orient for a second loan spell. By the time that Chester played fellow Conference side Morecambe, in the Second Round, Tate had returned to London and Chester were eliminated by the odd goal in five with the game hinging on the first-half dismissal of Ryan Sugden with the score at 2-2.

By the end of the year Chester stood in third place, six points behind leaders Yeovil, but 2003 started off on the wrong foot when the Blues inexplicably threw away a two-goal lead against Northwich by conceding three second-half goals in the space of 10 minutes. The winning goal for Vics was scored by future City man Gregg Blundell and it was the only time that Chester conceded more than three goals in the Conference all season. Although Daryl Clare continued to score goals in January, his scoring- rate tailed off dramatically in the latter part of the season as he struggled with a knee injury that resulted in an operation during the summer. Although another striker, Mark Quayle, was brought in on loan from Nuneaton in February, Chester failed to score more than two goals in a game after the turn of the year. With Yeovil in unstoppable form it soon became clear that the Blues would have to settle for a play-off place.

*Daryl Clare celebrates scoring against Halifax in March 2003*

In mid-March Chester conquered a long-standing hoodoo when a Michael Twiss goal settled the promotion encounter with Doncaster, the first time they had won in front of the live television cameras. April began with an eleventh away win of the season thanks to Mark Beesley's solo goal in a game notable for the fact that Chester finished with 9 men after Mark Quayle and Carl Ruffer had been sent-off. A play-off place was secured at the Deva in dramatic style against relegation-threatened Woking. In a desperately poor performance Chester trailed 2-0 after 87 minutes when they pulled a goal back through Carl Ruffer. Almost immediately Woking had the chance to extend their two-goal advantage, but missed a penalty, prompting Chester to immediately go down to the other end and secure a barely deserved point through Michael Twiss.

The season ended at Yeovil where the home side celebrated the Championship in front of more than 8,000 fans, although Chester put a dampener on the party by coming away with a 1-1 draw through Kevin McIntyre's first goal of the season. A fourth-place finish secured Chester a play-off fixture against Doncaster Rovers. In the first leg, at Belle Vue, Chester controlled the game with McIntyre again on target to give the Blues a first-half lead. However, with five minutes remaining, substitute Mark Quayle received a harsh red card and in the fourth minute of injury-time Tristram Whitman snatched a vital equaliser. In the second leg, in front of a near full-house, it was Wayne Hatswell who put Chester in the lead before Paul Barnes equalised to send the game into sudden death extra-time. With the prospect of one mistake costing the game, it proved a nervous and cagey extra thirty minutes and the game went into penalties. Both sides had their first penalty saved with the normally prolific Daryl Clare failing for Chester. Mark Quayle, Ben Davies and Kevin McIntyre than all scored for City, but they were matched in turn by Doncaster to leave the sides level. Future City player, Tim Ryan, then scored for Rovers to put the pressure on Dave Cameron whose shot was saved by Andy Warrington. It was a sad way to lose out on the play-off place but made everyone at the club determined to secure a place back in the Football League in 2003/04.

There had been further semi-professional international honours for Chester players during the season, Danny Collins (who later became a Wales full international), Wayne Brown and Scott Guyett had all featured for the England National Game X1 against Holland in March and Guyett captained the England team that won the Four Nations Trophy in May. Wayne Hatswell also represented England in this tournament while Ben Davies played for Wales.

During the summer, semi-professional internationals Chris Blackburn (England) and Lee Woodyatt (Wales) were both released having both graduated from the youth team in the late 1990s. Jimmy Kelly, Jon Worsnop, Steve Brodie and Dave Cameron were also released, while Ryan Sugden was allowed to join Burton Albion as new strikers Ian Foster (Kidderminster) and Kevin Rapley (Colchester) moved to the Deva Stadium. Other new arrivals included midfielder Andy Harris (Leyton Orient), former loan goalkeeper Ian McCaldon (Oxford) and winger Jamie Heard (Hull).

The 2003/04 season kicked off with a goalless draw at Stevenage Borough where both sides struggled in stifling heat. Kevin Rapley was accompanied up front by Robert Gill, a loan signing from Doncaster, who played in the first three games before Mark Wright made the key signing of Darryn Stamp from Northampton. Stamp went on to form a prolific partnership with Daryl Clare, who missed the first two months of the season recovering from his knee operation. The defensive partnership of Bolland and Guyett also missed the Stevenage game through injury and it was October before the dominant Guyett could return to the team. Meanwhile, the third member of the former Oxford triumvirate, Wayne Hatswell, had asked to be put on the transfer list, for personal reasons, and after featuring in the first eight games was transferred to Kidderminster in September. There was compensation for the breakup of the trio with the further emergence of young Danny Collins who stepped into the breach and went on to play in all but the last fixture of the season.

After 1-0 home victories over Tamworth and Forest Green, the Blues suffered defeat at Exeter, despite going in front through Ian Foster's penalty. The Exeter game marked Darryn Stamp's debut and the big striker opened his account in the next game against one of the promotion favourites, Shrewsbury Town. Chester defeated their close rivals 2-1, but it took a dramatic 89th winner from Phil Bolland to secure the points. The following five games also resulted in victory, including a 4-0 win over Gravesend with substitute Michael Twiss scoring twice in injury-time. Danny Collins and Kevin Rapley both scored their first goals in a 4-0 win over neighbours Northwich while influential midfielder Paul Carden also found the back of the net. The month ended with a goalless draw against Telford when Daryl Clare made his long-awaited return to the side as a substitute.

Following another goalless draw, at Dagenham, there was an appearance in front of the Sky cameras at Burton Albion. Although Chester dominated the game, and took the lead through Stamp, they conceded a penalty equaliser in the third minute of injury-time. Despite these three successive draws, a 2-1 win over Woking left the Blues two points behind table-toppers Hereford United and the two sides met in October in front of more than 4,000 at the Deva. An entertaining game finished goalless, but Chester were left to rue a missed penalty from Ian Foster and finished with 10 men when Jamie Heard was sent-off in injury-time.

November opened with a 2-2 draw at Scarborough, when Clare scored his first goal since returning from injury, and he also struck in a 1-0 triumph at Morecambe when Chester went top of the Conference for the first time. The Morecambe game also saw Alex Smith return to the club, four years after his transfer to Port Vale. The enigmatic winger, who signed from Reading, added another dimension to a side that had proved resolute in defence but sometimes struggled to kill off games. Smith scored the only goal against Barnet, in his first home game, and was at his best in a thrilling 3-3 draw with Accrington, who became the only side to score three against the Blues all season.

A surprise 2-1 home defeat to Stevenage, only the second of the campaign, proved merely a blip as the Clare\ Stamp partnership, aided by new man Smith, moved into overdrive over the Christmas period. Clare banged in a hat-trick in a 5-1 thrashing of Tamworth, while Stamp hit a treble in the Boxing Day encounter with Leigh RMI at the Deva Stadium that finished 5-0. On New Year's Day 1,500 Chester fans made the short journey to Leigh for the return fixture and were rewarded with a remarkable game where Clare scored another hat-trick and missed a penalty in a 6-2 victory.

The three successive hat-tricks was the first time Chester had achieved this feat since 1936. Victory over Leigh left the Blues six points clear over Hereford at the top of the Conference, and early elimination from the FA Trophy, at the hands of Halifax, left them free to concentrate on the league. In the first home game of 2004 a first-half brace from Daryl Clare was cancelled out, after the break, by a battling Gravesend side that had also removed Chester from the FA Cup.

Points were also dropped in the next away game, where bogey side Forest Green Rovers won 2-1, but this defeat heralded a blistering run of form that saw City win nine and draw two of the next 11 games.

The sequence began with a comfortable 4-0 win at Northwich, where the consistent Kevin McIntyre scored his only goal of the season and Darryn Stamp netted twice. Everton's promising Scottish goalkeeper, Iain Turner, joined Chester on loan at the start of February as a replacement for Wayne Brown, who was struggling with a foot injury, and Ian McCaldon who had emigrated to Australia. Turner made his debut in the 3-2 home win over Farnborough where Daryl Clare scored a brilliant decider in the 88th minute. Chester left it even later in the next game, when a Darryn Stamp header, deep into injury-time, defeated Dagenham by the odd goal in three. That win put Chester eight points clear of Hereford, who were about to embark on a run of 11 successive victories to apply the pressure right until the end of the season.

A televised encounter with Woking saw Chester recover from 1-0 down to win 2-1. The deciding goal -a stunning 30-yard strike from Michael Twiss - was later voted Conference goal of the season. That victory earned Mark Wright another Manager of the Month award, and there were no slip ups at the start of March as Burton and Morecambe were both beaten at the Deva Stadium. The sequence of wins was broken with a goalless draw at Barnet in gale-force conditions.

Despite this formidable run of results, Chester briefly lost pole position at the end of the month when Hereford went top on goal difference, although the Bulls had played an extra two games. The Blues re-gained top spot in front of a large Chester following at Telford thanks to two late goals from Daryl Clare, and the in-form striker was again on target the following week as the 2-0 score-line was repeated at play-off chasing Accrington Stanley. A thrilling 4-2 win over Aldershot, including two goals in the first 10 minutes from Clare and Bolland and a second-half red card for Kevin McIntyre, left Chester needing seven points from the last four games to secure promotion back to the Football League. There was certainly no room for complacency as the last game of the season was at rivals Hereford, leaving the possibility of a winner-take-all clash at Edgar Street.

On April 10th Chester were back in front of the TV cameras for an evening clash with Exeter and it was Michael Twiss who repeated his Woking heroics for the viewers, with another Man of the Match performance. After a goalless first-half, the visitors took the lead through Sean Devine but goals from Twiss and Bolland put the Blues in command. With five minutes remaining, Twiss turned on the style to score a brilliant individual goal and, despite a late Exeter fightback, Chester held on to win 3-2.

Three days later a thoroughly professional performance at Shrewsbury saw City come away with a point in a tense goalless draw. This left Chester needing to beat Scarborough at the Deva Stadium in the penultimate game of the season. A capacity crowd saw Darryn Stamp's first-half goal settle the game and send Chester back into the Football League after four seasons in the Conference.

With promotion secured, Chester fans travelled down to Hereford for the last game of the season in party mood. A weakened City team, missing Collins, McIntyre, Carden and Clare, went down 2-1 to the team that had challenged valiantly for the title but the result failed to put a dampener on the celebrations. After the problems of the Terry Smith era, the last two seasons had proved a welcome relief as the focus had switched back to events on the field.

In the non-League end of season awards, Mark Wright was elected Manager of the Year while Daryl Clare and Danny Collins were both selected for the Non-League Team of the Year. Meanwhile Clare won the award for Best Player and his 29 goals earned him the Golden Boot as top scorer. Fast-improving midfielder, Ben Davies, also added three more Wales semi-professional caps to his total and captained the side that beat the Republic of Ireland to clinch the Four Nations Trophy. Goalkeeper Wayne Brown also became the first Chester player since Terry Carling, in 1971, to be awarded a benefit match.

**MATCH TO REMEMBER**
**CHESTER CITY 1 SCARBOROUGH 0**
**NATIONWIDE CONFERENCE – APRIL 17TH 2004**

***Four years after relegation Chester returned to the Football League after a tense encounter against Scarborough. In front of a capacity crowd, with many people locked out, Mark Wright's team secured the three points they needed to cap a remarkable turnaround in the club's fortunes.***

***In a scrappy encounter City's first chance fell to leading scorer Daryl Clare whose close-range effort was brilliantly saved by Leigh Walker while, at the other end, Iain Turner did well to scoop away a Tony Hackworth header. In the 19th minute Chester scored the vital breakthrough goal to help calm ragged nerves. Good work by Clare, on the left, resulted in a low near post cross which Glen Downey failed to control. Darryn Stamp nipped in to rob the ball from Downey and drilled the ball into the bottom right-hand corner of the net from the corner of the six-yard box. Ben Davies almost added a second but his long-range effort just cleared the bar. However Chester didn't have it all their own way and on 25 minutes Scarborough's Wayne Gill hit the base of the post with Turner beaten.***

***In the second-half Chester almost added a second when Ben Davies' 20 yard free kick was tipped over the bar by Walker while, ten minutes from time, Scarborough's former Chester midfielder, Jimmy Kelly, put hearts in mouths when his free kick flew just wide of Turner's right-hand post. With three minutes remaining Davies almost put the seal on promotion but once again Walker was equal to his shot from the edge of the box.***

***After an anxious three minutes' injury-time referee Turner blew for time to signal the start of the celebrations as Chester lifted their first Championship trophy since 1927.***

***Chester – Turner, Collins (Elam), McIntyre, Carden, Bolland, Guyett, Heard, Davies, Stamp, Clare (Rapley), Twiss (Harris)***
***Scarborough – Walker, Hotte, Gilroy, Kerr, Rose (Marcelle), Downey, Gill, Hackworth, Lyth, Kelly, Nicholson***

Darryn Stamp scores the vital goal against Scarborough.

Despite the success of the promotion-winning team there were a surprising number of arrivals and departures during the summer of 2004. Scott Guyett moved on to Yeovil Town while fellow central defender, Carl Ruffer, signed for Morecambe having spent time on loan with Droylsden in the latter part of the campaign. Michael Twiss, who had displayed his best form in the promotion run, also stayed in the Conference with Morecambe as did winger Jamie Heard.

Two other regular midfielders, Alex Smith and Shaun Carey, were also shown the exit door along with striker Ian Foster and part-time keeper Andy Woods. It wasn't only players who left the Deva Stadium, as assistant manager Steve Bleasdale and physio Joe Hinnigan also departed the club.

The rebuilding began with the signing of midfielder Stewart Drummond from

Morecambe, a long-time target of Wright, and continued with the arrival of goalkeeper Chris MacKenzie from Telford. Striker Michael Branch, an outstanding prospect as a youngster at Everton, was seen as a quality signing from Bradford City while the defence was bolstered with the arrival of Richard Hope and Darren Edmondson from York and Sean Hessey (Blackpool). Injury-troubled midfielder Andy Watson came in from Farsley Celtic while big, bruising striker Cortez Belle joined from Merthyr Tydfil, after being recommended to the club by QPR. The chairman's own son Stephen Vaughan junior, a former England schoolboy international, also signed on the dotted line and the arrivals were completed by attacking midfielder Kevin Ellison from Stockport.

*Manager Ian Rush with Paul Gascoigne prior to his first match in charge at Boston in August 2004.*

An unbeaten pre-season boosted prospects for the 2004/05 campaign at the newly sponsored Saunders Honda Stadium, but the club was thrust into turmoil the day before the opening fixture at Notts County when Mark Wright handed in his shock resignation. Vaughan was initially bullish about the departure claiming to the press that: *"The manager's resignation is not a disappointment, not at all. No individual is bigger than this club...... It will be business as usual this club is used to drama. The fans do not have to worry, because I, Stephen Vaughan, will remain at this club and continue to invest in the club financially. The time for fans to worry is when Stephen Vaughan leaves this club."*

In an increasingly acrimonious split Wright claimed his departure was for football reasons, while the Chester board reacted by launching a blistering statement refuting these claims and attacking Wright for his conduct which included his refusal to sign a new contract and over-commitment of the 2004/05 budget.

At short notice, former Tranmere stalwart Ray Matthias took the reins for the trip to Meadow Lane, where five players made their debuts including Stephen Vaughan junior. Newly-relegated Notts County took a second-half lead through a Baudet penalty but with three minutes remaining a Daryl Clare shot was handled in the penalty area by Whitlow. Clare himself took responsibility from the spot and although his penalty was saved by Mildenhall, substitute Kevin Rapley scrambled in the rebound with Clare himself on hand to make sure.

After a turbulent few days it was a subdued home crowd that welcomed League football back to the city the following Tuesday. On a wet evening Chester were no match for Wycombe Wanderers who secured an easy 2-0 victory, and the mood remained bleak after the next game when Mansfield scored three second-half goals to condemn City to another home defeat. Caretaker manager Ray Matthias was hardly helped by injuries to his main strikers with Darryn Stamp suffering an ankle injury and Daryl Clare requiring a hernia operation after the Mansfield game. The partnership that had fired City out of the Conference, with 49 goals between them, never had the chance to prove themselves in the League as Clare was transferred back to his former club Boston United in November after recovering from surgery. Meanwhile Stamp lost his place to Cortez Belle and signed for Stevenage the following January after only two starts.

Michael Branch scored his first goal in a 1-1 draw at Bury, while another heavy home defeat, 3-0 to Darlington, saw Chester bottom of the table after only five games. Speculation about the managerial situation was ended over the August Bank Holiday weekend when the club's most famous export, Ian Rush, was appointed manager with Mark Aizlewood as his assistant. Ray Matthias took the role as Director of Football.

Although this was the first managerial appointment role for Rush, who had made his debut as a Chester player in 1979, the Welshman had coaching experience with both Liverpool and the Wales Under-17s and he relished the opportunity of managing his former club. His first match in charge, at Boston United, saw another famous name make his bow as former England star, Paul Gascoigne, made his debut for the home side. It was Gascoigne who had the last laugh as Chester were again well beaten 3-1. The arrival of Rush prompted an improvement in performances and his first home game in charge resulted in a 1-0 win over Macclesfield courtesy of an injury-time goal for Danny Collins.

For Collins it was one of his last displays for the club as the highly-rated youngster was transferred to Sunderland the following month for £140,000. The Macclesfield victory prompted a run of nine unbeaten League games as Chester hauled themselves to mid-table. Such was the impact of the new appointment that October ended with Rush being strongly linked with the job in charge of the Wales national team as well as a Manager of the Month award. In the end Rush elected to stay with Chester and was rewarded with a contract extension to 2007. While Rush was starting his managerial career there was sad news in December when the death of Harry McNally was announced. Two years later the North Terrace was renamed in memory of the legendary manager.

Chester's unbeaten run ended with a heavy 4-1 defeat at Yeovil, where Daryl Clare scored his last goal for the club. This result marked the start of a slump with only one win in the next 15 games as the threat of relegation re-surfaced. Ray Matthias left the club in November and after another crushing defeat, 4-1 at Bristol Rovers, there was an ill-tempered encounter when Shrewsbury were the visitors. The match finished 1-1 but Kevin Ellison and former Blues defender, Darren Moss, were both sent-off. Chester's poor disciplinary record was earning them a reputation and by the end of the season they had accumulated more than 100 bookings as well as 11 red cards. One of the main culprits was uncompromising striker Cortez Belle, who was sent-off on three occasions.

Belle had been on the score-sheet in the FA Cup when Chester won 2-0 at Stafford Rangers at the first stage. Two Michael Branch goals, in a 3-1 Second Round victory over non-League Halifax, earned a long trip to AFC Bournemouth where the Blues lost 2-1 despite a gallant display. Chester's consolation strike came from winger Kevin Ellison who had hit a rich vein of goalscoring form with some stunning long-range efforts in his total of eleven goals. His performances earned a £100,000 move to Hull City after the Bournemouth tie. In the LDV Trophy, Chester reserved one of their best displays of the season for a 2-1 win at Sheffield Wednesday where Richard Hope scored on his first start. Sean Hessey's goal against Rochdale then saw Chester face local rivals Wrexham for the first time since 1997 in the Quarter Final. A crowd of over 5,000 at the Saunders Honda Stadium saw the Welsh side come out on top by a single goal.

Back in the League, Chester came from behind to score twice in four minutes in atrocious conditions at Macclesfield for a rare win but this was followed by five League games without a goal. The last of these, an embarrassing 3-0 home defeat to Cheltenham, was watched by just over 1,600 as the euphoria of promotion had well and truly worn off. Rush was struggling to make do with loan signings and, at the time of the Cheltenham game, there were no fewer than six loanees at the club. One of these, Dave Bayliss from Luton, was red-carded in what was his final match.

Wins against relegation rivals, Rushden and Kidderminster, provided a brief respite but any hope that a corner had been turned were firmly dispelled in another bruising clash with Shrewsbury where Chester were crushed 5-0 and had another player sent-off. Giant defender George Elokobi, on loan from Colchester, was the man who saw red. It was an unfortunate loan spell for Elokobi who went on to play Premiership football with Wolves. In the five games in which he featured, Chester failed to score and conceded 14 goals.

The Shrewsbury defeat left the club hovering in 21st place and prompted chairman Vaughan to offer a severance payment to Rush and Aizlewood to leave the club, which was rejected. Despite the air of uncertainty surrounding the management duo, Chester were beaten only once in March picking up vital home wins over Notts County and Bury in the process. Both goals in the home win over Bury were scored by Ryan Lowe who signed from Shrewsbury two days before the transfer deadline.

April started with a first visit to Darlington's cavernous Williamson Motors Stadium and the 1-0 defeat marked the last match in charge for Ian Rush. The following day assistant Mark Aizlewood had his contract terminated and an unhappy Rush resigned stating: *"Unfortunately, throughout my tenure, various events have gradually made it impossible for me to carry on. The club's decision to terminate the contract of my assistant, Mark Aizlewood, without my consent was the final straw".*

Rush left the club on the verge of safety and David Bell, who held the role of "technical co-ordinator", took over as caretaker manager. In his first game in charge, goals from Ryan Lowe and youngster Robbie Booth, helped defeat Boston 2-1 after Chester had trailed to an early goal. The following week, safety was assured when the Blues clawed back a two-goal deficit against Bristol Rovers in a 2-2 draw, with Stewart Drummond scoring twice.

Attention now turned to the appointment of a new manager, but any chance of a return for Mark Wright was firmly scotched by Vaughan who stated: *"While I'm in charge at Chester Mark Wright will never return as manager."* In the end it was another former England international defender, Keith Curle, who was unveiled as manager and he was introduced to the crowd before the final home game of the season, against Northampton. Curle, who played more than 700 League games for several clubs including Wimbledon, Manchester City and Wolves, had previous managerial experience with Mansfield Town whom he had taken to a play-off final in 2004.

Curle immediately started to remould the squad and, in a major clearout, released 20 players including Player of the Year and club captain Paul Carden, as well as long serving keeper Wayne Brown who joined Hereford on a 12-month loan deal before making the move permanent the following summer. Into the squad came four players who had been managed by Curle at Mansfield; Scott McNiven, Dave Artell, Tom Curtis and Maltese international defender Luke Dimech. Big striker, Marcus Richardson came in from Yeovil while two midfielders, Justin Walker and French-Moroccan Abdou El-Kholti, signed from relegated Cambridge United. Keith Curle's own son, Tom, also joined from Bradford PA while defender Carl Regan, who had been playing on non-contract terms, signed a one-year deal from Droylsden. The pre-season signings were completed with the signature of Craig Dove from Rushden while the transfer record was broken with the £100,000 signing of 29-year-old striker Gregg Blundell from Doncaster Rovers. Blundell, had often been a thorn in Chester's side having scored against them for both Doncaster, in the Conference penalty shoot-out in 2003, and Northwich Victoria.

The arrival of Blundell came shortly after Vaughan had revealed that he had invested £4 million into the club and the worsening financial situation was again at the forefront during the summer. In May the club had faced a court hearing for an outstanding payment of £180,000 to the Inland Revenue. This was eventually settled in September but not until the Inland Revenue had filed a petition to wind up the club. This had not been the club's only court appearance in the previous 12 months. The previous July the club had faced a winding-up order from HM Customs and Excise over an unpaid VAT bill from the previous regime and York-based Goldcrest Finance Corporation had served a winding-up notice to Vaughan Trading co Ltd for non-payment of funds in October 2004. An out-of-court settlement was agreed in the latter case but not before the club had considered going into administration. Legal proceedings were also taken against the club by the City council in September over rent arrears of £46,000, and £18,000 had also been paid to bailiffs from Flintshire County Council in the same month.

In order to ease the financial problems, and help recoup the £4 million he had loaned the club, Vaughan proposed the creation of four million shares at £1 each but this was met with little enthusiasm by the supporters. Despite the financial problems at Chester, Vaughan invested a substantial stake in Widnes Vikings Rugby League club at the end of the year having previously shown an interest in both Tranmere Rovers and Everton.

There were also problems over Ground Safety requirements which meant that the club was prohibited from holding any home pre-season friendlies. When a license was eventually granted in July the ground capacity was reduced from 6,099 to 5,489.

The start of the 2005/06 season commenced with a fixture at Peterborough United, now managed by Mark Wright and with Paul Carden in their team. Twelve months after Wright had walked out on the club this was seen as a grudge encounter and the large away support was delighted when Stewart Drummond settled the game in Chester's favour. Three days later, in the season's first home game, the Blues recovered a two-goal half- time deficit against Lincoln with goals from Ben Davies and a Michael Branch penalty in the fourth minute of injury-time.

The early season displays, under the likeable Curle, provided plenty of entertainment for supporters as Chester only lost one of the first 12 games and thrived on late goals. Gregg Blundell finally made his debut, after recovering from a knee injury, in the home game against Darlington and scored twice in a thrilling 4-4 draw with Marcus Richardson also grabbing his first two for the club. In a dramatic finale the Blues scored twice in the last two minutes in a game where New Zealand international Leo Bertos also made his debut. There was also a late winner in the next fixture, at Torquay on Bank Holiday Monday, where Ryan Lowe finally broke down a stubborn home defence after almost constant pressure from the attack-minded Blues.

Comfortable home wins over Bristol Rovers and Carlisle left Chester in third place at the end of September, and October opened with a breathtaking end-to-end encounter at second-placed Wycombe Wanderers which finished 3-3. Michael Branch, who had his best game in a Chester shirt,

*Record signing Gregg Blundell scores on his debut against Darlington in August 2005.*

scored twice and almost completed a hat-trick but his last-minute shot hit the crossbar. The exciting football on display attracted over 4,000 for the next game against Rochdale but despite another thrilling performance it was Chester's turn to be on the end of a late goal as they narrowly lost 3-2. There was also bad news as Gregg Blundell was stretchered off with a neck injury which kept him out for the next three months. After six goals in 10 games it was a blow for the Liverpudlian who struggled to regain his form when he returned to the team in the second half of the season.

A 3-1 win at Barnet, despite a red card for Stewart Drummond, prompted a run of seven games with only one defeat and by the time Chester beat Leyton Orient 1-0, at the start of December, they were 4th in the table and looking forward to an appearance in the Third Round of the FA Cup. The Blues had reached that stage after beating Folkestone Invicta and Nottingham Forest. The 3-0 win over Forest, with a brace from Ryan Lowe and one from Marcus Richardson, saw Chester outplay their illustrious opponents and was the high point of a season that started to collapse spectacularly in mid- December. The slump began at Lincoln City where keeper Chris MacKenzie suffered a broken thumb early in the second half and was replaced by debutant Ryan Brookfield. Despite Marcus Richardson then giving Chester the lead, and the Imps being reduced to 10 men with a red card for Dean Keates, the home side recovered to win the game 3-1. The injury to MacKenzie kept him out for the next 16 games during which time Chester only picked up one win and one draw and plummeted from a play-off position to bottom of the table. MacKenzie was initially replaced by John Ruddy, on loan from Everton, before Luxembourg international goalkeeper, Stephane Gillet, signed at the start of January. Ruddy made his debut against struggling Rushden where a City team, missing nine players through injury and suspension lost 2-1.

The year ended in controversial circumstances when the border clash with rivals Wrexham was re-arranged for midday on a normal working day over the Christmas period on safety advice. The change prompted Vaughan to ask permission for the fixture to be moved to the Halton Stadium, home of Widnes Vikings, but his request was turned down by the Football League. Vaughan was growing increasingly frustrated by the restrictions on the lease arrangement at the ground and what he considered an obstructive council. However, in his attempts to put pressure on the council, he angered the fan-base by refusing to rule out the possibility of moving other matches to Widnes at some point in the future. In the event the game was postponed because of the weather but the whole affair created an uneasy atmosphere. The following March the matter resurfaced when it was revealed that Vaughan had made enquiries to the FA about the possibility of changing the club's name to Chester-Halton although he denied that he intended to move the whole club to Widnes.

Memories of early season were recalled in the FA Cup at Cheltenham where Stephane Gillet made his debut and produced an outstanding performance to keep the home side at bay. In a pulsating Cup tie Chester fell behind to two penalties but Marcus Richardson pulled a goal back with 14 minutes remaining and the comeback was completed when Stewart Drummond scored from eight yards. More than 5,000 hopeful fans attended the replay at Bumpers Lane to see who would earn a bumper £250,000 payday with a televised tie against Newcastle United. In the event Chester surrendered meekly and succumbed to a single Odejayi goal.

Back in the League, Curle turned to two of his former Mansfield players in an attempt to halt the slide. Wayne Corden came from Scunthorpe while Derek Asamoah, who had scored for Lincoln against Chester in December, arrived from Sincil Bank. After seven straight defeats the Blues finally gained three points, ironically at Mansfield, when two former Stags players Scott McNiven and Asamoah both scored in a 2-1 victory. The win proved only a temporary respite and after Dave Artell was sent-off, in a 2-0 home defeat to Notts County, Curle brought in three new players on loan for the next game at Carlisle. Young Sheffield United pair Chris Robertson and Evan Horwood were joined by Mark Roberts (Crewe), but all three returned to their parent clubs after a humiliating 5-0 defeat that also resulted in the sacking of Curle's assistants John Gannon and David Bell along with physio Clive Goodyear. The writing was now on the wall for Curle and home defeats, to bottom-of-the-table Stockport County followed by Leyton Orient, proved to be his last in charge amidst stories of dressing room discontent. Curle, like Ian Rush before him, had started well and his leadership had attracted interest from other clubs including Bristol Rovers. Unfortunately, an astonishing turn around in fortunes over a mere two months led to his sacking and Vaughan was faced with looking for yet another manager.

When an appointment was made it came as a major surprise to everyone as Mark Wright returned to the club he had walked out on two years earlier. Wright, who had been dismissed by Peterborough at the end of January, immediately brought in two experienced defenders on loan in the form of Paul Ellender (Boston) and Mark Albrighton (Doncaster) followed by striker Jake Edwards from Exeter. Despite the change at the top, Chester only picked up one point from the next five games and the 2-1 defeat at Wrexham, where Jake Edwards scored on his debut, left the Blues two points adrift of safety.

However the Wrexham defeat marked another turning point for the club with Ryan Lowe and Michael Branch both dropped from the squad after a dressing room dispute. Lowe joined Crewe the following week while Branch, who never fulfilled his potential at Chester, had his contract cancelled later in the year without playing for the club again.

Their departure prompted a reshuffle of the side for the away trip to Boston and the out-of-favour Derek Asamoah was paired with Jake Edwards up front as Chris MacKenzie made his long awaited return from injury. Asamoah responded with a hat-trick in a 3-1 win in Lincolnshire and went on to score seven goals in the next five games as Chester recorded five straight wins in an astonishing turnaround of form. The run included a 2-1 win in the return match against Wrexham where Asamoah and Ben Davies, from the penalty spot, were the scorers. Goalless draws, against Bury and Barnet, virtually assured safety and City finished the season in 15th place and five points clear of relegation despite single goal defeats in the last two games against Northampton and Shrewsbury.

During the summer there was another huge turnover of playing staff as Mark Wright started his own restructuring of the team. The manager himself signed a two-year contract as Graham Barrow returned to the club for a third time, this time as assistant manager. Ben Davies, Stewart Drummond and Chris MacKenzie were all offered new contracts, but turned them down, and the trio signed for Shrewsbury Town. In total 16 players exited the club to make way for the new arrivals, with Wright concentrating on strengthening the defence.

The first signing was young goalkeeper John Danby from Kidderminster Harriers who went on to become a virtual ever present until the club's demise in 2010. During this period he broke Mike Metcalf's club record of 127 consecutive League starts. Danby started 133 games before picking up a shoulder injury, at Notts County, in April 2009. Kevin Sandwith (Macclesfield) and Laurence Wilson (Everton) came in to cover the left side of defence, while Simon Marples (Doncaster) challenged Stephen Vaughan for a place on the right. No fewer than four central defenders came to the club, Paul Linwood (Tranmere), Graham Allen (Rushden), Ashley Westwood (Northampton) and Phil Bolland, who was once again reunited with Wright after a short spell with Peterborough. Allen and Westwood both arrived at Chester having struggled with injury the previous season, while a fee of £15,000 was set on Linwood by a tribunal in September. Midfielders Glenn Cronin (Exeter) and Dean Bennett (Wrexham) also arrived at Chester with questionable fitness issues and the battling Cronin was unfortunate to miss most of the season after suffering a pre-season metatarsal injury.

Meanwhile Bennett continued to struggle with intermittent back problems which prevented him from having an extensive run in the side. The midfield was further bolstered with the arrival of Jamie Hand (Watford), but winger Jermaine McSporran (Doncaster) was released after one substitute appearance. There were two new strikers in the form of relegated Rushden's leading scorer, Drewe Broughton, and Jon Walters who had been released by Wrexham. The move to Chester helped revitalise Walters' career and his goals quickly started to attract the attention of bigger clubs. There was also a key signing in the form of well-respected Swansea midfielder Roberto Martinez. The Spaniard, a close friend of Assistant Manager Graham Barrow, won many friends in his short spell at Chester where his creativity and experience proved of great benefit to the team. His presence was sorely missed when he returned to South Wales to take the job as manager of Swansea in February.

Attempts were also made to re-sign Kevin Ellison, who was now at Hull, as well as winger Richie Partridge from Sheffield Wednesday. Chester did succeed in signing Doncaster midfielder Ricky Ravenhill on loan, but he returned to Rovers after receiving a red card in his only start, against Wrexham. Chester had originally intended to sign Ravenhill on a permanent basis but the deal fell through after the club were warned by the Football League that they had exceeded the salary cap which was set at 60% of turnover.

Despite all the new signings, the pre-season friendlies were poorly attended by supporters reluctant to pay regular League prices. When only 269 turned up from a game against Belgian side Cercle Brugge, a disillusioned Vaughan again spoke out about the level of support calling the attendance disgraceful. He stated: *"I've put a freeze on putting any more money for transfers and I'm going to take stock over the weekend. If there is anyone else out there with ideas of how they can take this club further then they can give me a call. And if they want to buy it they'll need £5 million."*

The 2006/07 season kicked off with a home game against League newcomers Accrington Stanley and no fewer than 11 players made their first appearance in a Chester shirt. Only Stephen Vaughan junior, who captained the side, Dave Artell and Gregg Blundell remained from the previous campaign. There was no fairy-tale return to the Football League for the Lancashire side as a workmanlike Chester secured a comfortable win with goals from Drewe Broughton and a Blundell penalty. A few days later two goals from Jon Walters and an own goal from former City full-back Colin Woodthorpe gave the Blues a 3-1 win at Bury but this was followed by exit from the Carling Cup, at the hands of Leeds United, and a run of seven League games without a win.

Nevertheless, Wright's use of three central defenders, which had worked successfully in 2003/04 gave the defence a solidity that had been lacking since the return to the Football League. Unfortunately there was no Daryl Clare or Darryn Stamp to score goals at the other end, and there was little to excite the supporters and attendances dwindled as the season progressed. Although Chester only conceded three goals on three occasions in the League, they only managed to score more than two against Bury, Boston and Lincoln.

A win at the National Hockey Stadium, in the first game against MK Dons, was followed by a goalless draw at Rochdale and a 2-0 win over Bristol Rovers, in one of the best performances of the season. Chester's last ever visit to Gay Meadow, the home of Shrewsbury, proved to be another feisty encounter in what was proving to be an increasingly bitter rivalry. The presence of six former Blues in the Shrews squad helped spice up the game and all was going well at half-time after Gregg Blundell had given City the lead. However an equaliser from former Chester star Ben Davies and a controversial last-minute penalty settled the game in the home side's favour. A match where six Chester players were booked ended in a mass brawl, the second of the game, after the dismissal of Shrewsbury's Sagi Burton. As a result both clubs were fined £3,000 for failing to keep their players under control while chairman Vaughan also faced a charge for his role in the incident. Appearances before the FA became a regular occurrence as Chester were also fined £1,000 for a similar incident against Barnet in October and £8,000 after the Christmas match with MK Dons. The poor disciplinary record continued to let Chester down throughout the season with the club yet again recording more than 100 bookings and eight red cards .

In the Johnstone's Paint Trophy a 3-0 win over Stockport was followed by an uncharacteristically high-scoring encounter with higher division Chesterfield in the next round. Eight goals were shared in a game that went into extra-time, but Chester were eliminated in a penalty shoot-out after missing three of their spot kicks. In the FA Cup there was another appearance in the Third Round but it came in unusual circumstances. A comfortable 4-1 win in the First Round at Clevedon Town was followed by a trip to Bury. Lee Steele, on loan from Leyton Orient, scored twice in a 2-2 draw at Gigg Lane but was red-carded for jumping into the crowd celebrating his second goal. Bury won the replay 3-1 but were subsequently removed from the competition when it was revealed they had fielded an ineligible player in the form of Lee Turnbull. Chester benefitted from this good fortune with the award of £24,000 Second Round prize money and a tie against Ipswich Town. After a goalless draw at the Saunders Honda Stadium, City were knocked out of the competition for a second time when the Tractor Boys went through by a single goal.

The Ipswich Cup tie also proved beneficial to striker Jon Walters who was transferred to the Suffolk side a week after the game. The initial fee was set at £100,000 with further payments based on appearances as well as a sell-on clause. Although Walters later moved to Premiership side Stoke City in August 2010, for £2.75 million, Chester never benefitted from the transfer as they had gone into liquidation. The transfer window also saw fellow striker Gregg Blundell transferred to Darlington for a five figure sum. Having allowed Drewe Broughton to join Boston, on loan in October, it meant that Chester were now without the three strikers who had started the season. This created a big impact in the second half of the campaign as Chester relied on two 33-year-olds, Lee Steele and Simon Yeo, along with youngster Chris Holroyd. Yeo signed from Peterborough in January while Steele made his loan move permanent but the Blues only managed to score 10 goals in the last 18 games after the transfer of Walters.

A series of dour encounters was best summarised by the home game against doomed Torquay at the start of March. After taking the lead through Dean Bennett, Chester seemed content to play out the game and paid the price when the visitors, managed by Keith Curle, equalised from the penalty spot with their first shot of the game in injury-time.

A 2-0 home win over Barnet saw another member of the Vaughan family, James, make his League debut at full-back although his brother Stephen was no longer in the side having signed for Boston United in January. The Barnet victory was the only win for Chester in the last 14 games as they slid down the table to finish in 18th place, seven points clear of relegation. However Wright and Barrow were no longer in charge for the final game of the season at Lincoln as they were sacked by Vaughan at the end of April after the poor run of results. Youth team manager Simon Davies took control for the 2-0 defeat at Sincil Bank as the 2006/07 season again ended with a search for yet another new manager.

An appointment was made quickly and former Kilmarnock, Hibernian and Plymouth manager, Bobby Williamson, was in place by the middle of May. Williamson, a former player with Rangers and West Bromwich Albion, had the distinction of featuring in the final game at Sealand Road when he was a member of the Rotherham team that lost 2-0. On his arrival at Chester Williamson acknowledged the budget limitations, stating that he would not put pressure on the board to spend money. He also expressed a desire to give a chance to players who had developed through the youth system. The previous season Chester had reached the last 32 of the Youth Cup having defeated Tottenham Hotspur on the way.

Once again the arrival of a new manager heralded a summer of changes with centre-half Dave Artell, Alex Meechan and Drewe Broughton the first players to leave. Williamson's first signing was forward Nathan Lowndes from Port Vale, a player he had previously managed at Plymouth. Lowndes, who had missed a large part of the previous season through injury, signed a two-year contract. However a recurrence of a back injury saw the 30-year-old striker's contract paid up after only eight League starts, and he was forced into retirement.

Two players who had frequently been targeted by Chester were also recruited during the summer with Kevin Ellison (Tranmere) re-signing on a three-year contract and Richie Partridge (Rotherham) joining on a two-year deal.

Meanwhile John Murphy, another player that had attracted Chester's attention in the past, also returned to the Deva Stadium from Macclesfield on a two-year contract having last played for the club in 1999. Further experience was added in the form of 37-year-old goalkeeper Gavin Ward from Tranmere while the 34-year-old ex-Sunderland, Wolves and Leeds centre-half Paul Butler arrived from MK Dons and was appointed captain. Former Everton and England Under-21 midfielder, Tony Grant from Accrington, became the seventh signing but the influx of players resulted in Chester once again coming under scrutiny from the Football League for exceeding the salary cap. Nevertheless the release of Lee Steele did allow Williamson to bring in hard-working midfielder Mark Hughes from Stevenage. Meanwhile Ashley Westwood (Port Vale) and Dean Bennett (Kidderminster) were both sent out on loan in August while midfielder Jamie Hand moved to Lincoln after appearing in the first game.

The 2007/08 season commenced with a goalless draw at home to relegated Chesterfield as seven players made their debut. However, an excellent 2-1 victory at Rochdale, where youngster Kevin Roberts made his first appearance, was followed by a 4-0 win over Football League newcomers Dagenham and Redbridge as Simon Yeo and John Murphy both scored twice. The versatile Roberts, a product of Chester's youth policy, was one of the successes of the season and scored his first goal for the club after coming off the bench in a 1-1 draw at Rotherham. Roberts was not the only youngster to be given a chance by Williamson as Neil Carroll, Paul McManus, Glenn Rule, Sean Newton and Shaun Kelly were all given debuts with varying degrees of success.

Chester's bright start to the season continued throughout September and an unbeaten October as Williamson's team won five successive away games and challenged at the top of the table. At Bury, Paul Butler scored his first Chester goal as City won 2-0 against his old side and John Murphy also had the distinction of netting against his former charges as the Blues secured a fortuitous 2-1 win at Macclesfield. An inspired performance by Richie Partridge, who scored two superb long-range goals in a 2-1 win at Stockport, was followed by a 2-2 home draw with Wycombe where young striker Chris Holroyd scored his first goal as Chester ended October in second place.

On the transfer front another experienced campaigner, Tony Dinning, signed from Stockport in October. The 32-year-old former Wolves and Wigan midfielder was on target from the penalty spot in a single goal victory at Lincoln in November where Chester arrived 30 minutes late after getting stuck in traffic. Less successful was an audacious bid to sign former Welsh international John Hartson on loan from West Bromwich Albion with the former Celtic star reluctant to drop down to Division Two.

In Cup competitions Chester put in a spirited performance in the First Round of the Carling Cup with a goalless draw against League One promotion favourites Nottingham Forest. Unfortunately they lost out in a penalty shoot-out but were more successful from the spot in the Johnstone's Paint Trophy against another League One side, Crewe Alexandra. After a 1-1 draw in 90 minutes Chester won the penalty decider 4-2 against their Cheshire rivals but there was no further progress after a 4-2 defeat at Carlisle in Round Two. In the FA Cup Chester were beaten at the opening stage by a single goal at Bradford City. This came only four days after they had received their first away League defeat of the season at the same ground.

Chester had started the Bradford City League game knowing that a win could potentially take them top of the table. Despite that defeat, followed by a setback at home to top of the table MK Dons, the Blues remained in promotion contention with home wins over Barnet and Bury in December. Unfortunately, in a collapse reminiscent of the Keith Curle era, the wheels came off in spectacular style after Christmas. The slide started with an astonishing 5-3 defeat at Morecambe on Boxing Day where the main tormenter was the former hero of the 2004 promotion team, Michael Twiss. Despite taking the lead through Kevin Ellison a woeful defensive performance saw Chester concede four identical first-half goals from Michael Twiss right-wing corners. This defeat marked the start of a dreadful run as Chester only won two of the last 26 games

Bobby Williamson was hardly helped by the departure of several fringe players from an already stretched squad affected by injury and loss of form. Nathan Lowndes' season and career ended in December and this followed on from the release of long-term casualty, Glenn Cronin, who only ever started one game in 18 months at the club. Sean Hessey spent most of the season on loan at Macclesfield while Ashley Westwood was transferred to Stevenage after his loan spell ended at Port Vale. In the January transfer window Phil Bolland and Gavin Ward both made the short journey down the road to Wrexham and Simon Yeo joined Bury on loan until the end of the season. At the same time Tony Dinning missed three months with knee ligament damage while Paul Butler, Richie Partridge and Tony Grant all suffered with intermittent injury problems and failed to regain their early season form on their return.

Williamson also lost his assistant Malcolm Thompson who returned to Scotland with Inverness CT. Thompson was briefly replaced by another Scot, Jimmy Bone, who lasted a mere two months while his successor, former manager Steve Mungall, fared even worse and was gone within three weeks . Meanwhile the only player arrivals in January were loan signings John Welsh from Hull and young striker Craig Lindfield from Liverpool, with neither making an impression.

The many departures accompanied more turmoil behind the scenes as Stephen Vaughan stepped down as both chairman and director in December amidst speculation that a number of parties had expressed an interest in taking a major shareholding in the club. In the end the talks came to nothing and attention switched back to on-the-field matters.

January ended in disastrous style as Rochdale won 4-0 at the Deva Stadium and both Kevin Ellison and Laurence Wilson were sent-off. Chester were also defeated in the next home game, against Accrington Stanley, when they threw away a half-time lead and conceded an injury-time goal to lose 3-2. Worse was to come three days later when another woeful performance resulted in a 6-2 thrashing at Dagenham and Redbridge. Two goals from Kevin Ellison and a Tony Dinning penalty gave Chester a first win in 13 games as they beat Mansfield 3-1, a result that proved crucial in the final analysis. Despite this result, Williamson became yet another victim of the axe the following week when he was dismissed after a single goal defeat at MK Dons at the start of March. Like Keith Curle before him the Scot had experienced an excellent start at Chester followed by a post-Christmas collapse under trying circumstances.

Youth team manager Simon Davies took charge for his second spell as caretaker manager but his first match in control resulted in another single goal defeat at Darlington. With no resources available, the former Manchester United midfielder could only shuffle the cards he had been dealt and youngsters Paul Rutherford, Paul McManus and Shaun Kelly were all given extended runs in the closing weeks of the season.

Davies' first match in charge at the Deva Stadium saw Chester lose their seventh successive home fixture as relegation-bound Wrexham won 2-0. The home hoodoo was finally broken at the ninth attempt when goals from Paul Rutherford and Richie Partridge helped defeat Darlington 2-1. Another unwanted record was ended with a battling goalless draw at Shrewsbury as Chester kept their first clean sheet in 25 games, their worst run in the Football League. Prior to the Shrewsbury game Davies was awarded a two-year contract, despite losing seven out of his nine games in charge. With Chester grateful for the points accumulated before Christmas, safety was eventually assured in a goalless draw against Stockport thanks to an outstanding performance from keeper John Danby. Another campaign of two halves ended with a third consecutive goalless draw against Macclesfield as the Blues finished one place above the relegation zone and five points clear of Mansfield.

After another trying season Simon Davies announced that the club would no longer be running a reserve team and relying on a younger squad for the 2008/09 campaign. The squad had already been reduced over the previous six months and the restructuring continued with the release of Sean Hessey, Simon Yeo and Dean Bennett who had al been on long term loan deals at other clubs. In additior reserve goalkeeper Phil Palethorpe, Tony Grant anc defender Simon Marples all departed while Kevin Sandwitl refused a new contract and joined Weymouth. In the closing weeks of the summer break John Murphy completed a move to Irish side St Patricks Athletic while fellow striker Chris Holroyd had his contract terminatec and signed for Cambridge United. Mark Hughes and Pau Rutherford, who had attracted interest from Barnet anc Bournemouth respectively, were both made available fo transfer but in the event remained at the club.

Simon Davies' first signings were all midfielders with Liverpool-born Anthony Barry, from Yeovil Town, the first to put pen to paper. Barry was followed by Accrington pair Jay Harris and David Mannix. Diminutive Harris was a fellow Liverpudlian while Mannix had been a former colleague of Richie Partridge and Stephen Vaughan junior in the Liverpool Reserve team . Vaughan himself had rejoined the club in February after suffering an Achilles injury at Boston which had kept him out of the game for 12 months. The fourth midfielder to sign was skilful Frenchman Damien Mozika who made a tremendous early impact before succumbing to a series of injuries.

Crowd favourite Ryan Lowe also returned to the club after two seasons at Crewe while an agreement was struck with Vauxhall Motors for the transfer of Paul Taylor. Chester had failed with a £50,000 bid for the Liverpool-born striker the previous December, but a six-month loan deal was eventually agreed with the move set to become permanent in January. Unfortunately the talented Taylor experienced disciplinary issues at Chester and after his contract was terminated in October it was revealed he had failed a random drugs test at the start of the month. As a result Taylor was suspended from football for six months although he later revived his career in Belgium before returning to England with Peterborough United.

The comings and goings left Chester with a squad of 22 at the start of the 2008/09 season which included youngsters Glenn Rule and Andy Mitchell who both signed one-year professional contracts. In addition two senior members of the squad, Paul Butler and Tony Dinning, signed one-year contract extensions. Both players had been in dispute with the club after receiving suspensions for a breach of club discipline and although the dispute appeared to have been resolved it proved to be an uneasy truce. The net result of the changes was a squad lacking in defenders and strikers but top heavy with midfielders.

For the first game of the 2008/09 campaign, at Dagenham and Redbridge, Davies gave Paul Butler a chance to re-establish himself at centre-half but with captain Paul Linwood out injured it was an inadequate defence that took to the field. The deficiencies of the squad were quickly made apparent as Chester suffered an embarrassing 6-0 defeat, the second season in succession that they had conceded six goals at Victoria Road. There was further humiliation a few days later when City's Carling Cup tie, against Leeds United was shown live on Sky television and the defence shipped another five goals in the first 35 minutes with Jermaine Beckford scoring a hat-trick. Although the team recovered some respect after the break, with two Ryan Lowe goals, it was the worst possible start and it was evident that the club were in for a season of struggle. To compound the problems, assistant manager Huw Griffiths was dismissed after the game following an alleged half- time incident with one of the players. Griffiths was replaced by former Tranmere striker Wayne Allison and the 39-year-old was also given a playing contract although he never played a game.

Davies reacted by starting young Shaun Kelly alongside Paul Linwood for the first home League game against Wycombe Wanderers. Kelly had replaced Paul Butler at half- time against Leeds and although the tide of goals was stemmed, Chester were beaten 2-0. In the next game, against Rotherham, Kevin Ellison had the distinction of scoring the opening goal of the League campaign but the Blues were still defeated 3-1 in their first visit to the Don Valley Stadium. Rotherham were one of three clubs in League Two who had started the season with large point deductions but despite this relegation cushion the gap was already being eroded. The Millers and AFC Bournemouth had both been deducted 17 points while Luton Town had suffered an insurmountable 30 point penalty.

After such a disastrous start to the season Mark Hughes, Stephen Vaughan and Paul Taylor were all given a chance in the starting line-up and Chester responded in spectacular style with an unexpected 5-1 hammering of Barnet as Ryan Lowe scored twice. The Barnet game was the first time that both Vaughan brothers had appeared in the starting eleven and heralded a run of five games without defeat including an emphatic 3-1 win at Grimsby where Kevin Ellison scored a hat-trick. At Luton Paul McManus netted an equaliser to secure a point against the bottom of the table team despite Chester finishing with 10 men after having Kevin Roberts sent-off. The draw left Chester in 13th place, the high point of the season.

Although Chester had once again been under scrutiny for breaching the salary-cap they were able to sign Eddie Johnson during October after another drawn-out saga. Chester-born Johnson had been training with the club after his release by Bradford City in the summer but transfer restrictions had prevented the former England youth international from formally signing. Johnson finally made his debut in the home defeat to Port Vale but he proved to be the last outfield player signed by the club until the following summer as a transfer embargo was placed on the club for late payment of wages shortly afterwards. In the next game, Chester suffered a crushing 6-1 defeat at the hands of Rochdale where they were hampered by Glenn Rule's first-half red card. The Rochdale game was the last of the season for Stephen Vaughan junior who suffered a recurrence of his Achilles injury while fringe player David Mannix suffered a broken jaw in a training ground incident later in the same month.

The slide back down the table continued with a 2-0 defeat at Gillingham but the Blues upset the form book in the next game with their best performance of the season as they beat champions-elect Brentford 3-0. Ryan Lowe continued to prove himself the best of the summer signings by scoring twice while the fast-maturing Kevin Roberts scored the other goal in front of a small home crowd of 1,301. Following a 2-0 defeat at Exeter, the Blues faced League One side Millwall in the FA Cup but once again were lax in defence and conceded three goals in the last fifteen minutes to lose 3-0. This meant that Chester had been eliminated from all three Cup competitions at the first stage. With the club having already conceded 40 goals in 18 games, and struggling in 19th place, Davies was sacked and returned to his role as youth team manager.

It was no surprise when Mark Wright was appointed as Davies' successor for his third spell in charge. Owner Stephen Vaughan had held well-publicised talks with Wright during the summer over the possibility of investing in the club and taking the position of Director of Football. Wright arrived back at the Deva Stadium, with former assistant Steve Bleasdale, keen to reproduce the formula that had taken Chester out of the Conference in 2004. Unfortunately, although Wright expressed his desire to change the personnel, there was no open cheque book this time around and the transfer embargo severely limited options. In addition, only two weeks after the appointment, Wright's cause was hardly helped by the news that Vaughan had put the club up for sale stating: "*...with the attendances dropping alarmingly and the level of commercial income also reducing, it is becoming more and more difficult to sustain a club at this level of football.*" Within a week Vaughan revealed that three parties had shown an interest in buying the club including Liverpool-based property company Property First Asset Management Ltd, who had been in discussions with the club about ambitious plans to develop the Deva Stadium. Meanwhile news that one of the bids came from John Batchelor, a previous owner of York City, met with little enthusiasm from fans when he revealed his plans to: *"change the identity, colours and name of the stadium"*.

Back on the playing field, Wright's first game in charge resulted in a 2-1 home defeat to Morecambe and a red card for Kevin Ellison saw the midfielder miss the next three games. A first win for Wright came at the expense of Darlington, at the end of November, where Ryan Lowe scored with a stunning volley from the corner of the penalty area to help City to a 2-1 victory. Tony Dinning was given another chance to resurrect his Chester career in the fixture at relegation rivals Bournemouth, but did himself no favours by coming off the bench and getting sent-off for violent conduct within 15 minutes. With only seven minutes of the game remaining former Tottenham and England player, Darren Anderton, scored a 25-yard winner in what was his last ever match. An away draw at Bradford City, sandwiched between two 2-0 home victories over Notts County and Accrington Stanley pulled Chester up to 17th but, not for the first time, the Christmas period marked another spectacular downturn in results as the Blues won only two of the next 24 games. In previous seasons Chester had been fortunate to build a cushion of points in the early part of the season but this time there was no leeway with both Rotherham and Bournemouth fast closing in on the Blues.

Mark Wright hoped to be able to bring in players during the January transfer window but the embargo remained in place. Instead, the squad was further weakened by departures as well as injuries and suspensions. Vaughan himself stated: *"Mark Wright has identified a number of players to bring in to strengthen the squad. It would be nice to strengthen what we already have, but I'm afraid we're not in a position to do that at the moment and I will ensure the embargo on us is enforced. I have to look at paying the club's bills and propping up any shortfalls which are haemorrhaging away any money we have at the football club".* As a result youngsters Paul McManus and Andy Mitchell both left the club and signed for Bangor City while Eddie Johnson had his contract terminated and moved to America with Austin Aztex. The biggest loss was that of midfielder Mark Hughes who joined relegation rivals Barnet while Paul Butler had his contract terminated. Meanwhile Tony Dinning was made available for transfer and spent time on loan at Grays and Gateshead but David Mannix, who had been on "gardening leave" after the training ground incident, was welcomed back to the fold.

With the squad down to the bare bones Wright was forced to fill the bench with untried youth team players and 16-year-old striker, Ben Jones came on as a substitute in the 2-2 draw against Luton, while James Owen, Lloyd Ellams, Paul Smith and Kristian Platt were all given debuts in the remaining months of the season. Despite some battling performances the first three months of 2009 saw the beleaguered Blues fail to win a game, and there was a further blow in February when assistant manager Steve Bleasdale departed the club under a cloud to be replaced by Simon Davies. In March, Chester faced three of their relegation rivals in successive games, but a 3-1 defeat at Barnet was followed by a humiliating 5-1 home defeat to Rotherham. A Ryan Lowe equaliser secured Chester a home point against 23rd placed Grimsby and the same player was on target the following week when his goal in the dying seconds won another point at Bury. Unfortunately, a surprise win for Grimsby at promotion-chasing Gillingham propelled Chester into the bottom two for the first time and Mark Wright considered his own future stating:

*"At this moment in time I think I have done all I can do for the players and for the club, and I can do no more.... I arrived at Chester after being told I could bring five players in. I haven't brought in one new player, but we've got rid of six players."*

A goalless draw, at home to play-off chasing Bradford City, was followed by Chester's first win since Boxing Day and it came in dramatic fashion at Notts County. Despite losing the consistent Laurence Wilson to injury, in the first 15 minutes, goals from David Mannix and Ryan Lowe gave Chester a deserved 2-0 lead. However, with three minutes remaining, keeper John Danby tore ligaments in his shoulder and had to be replaced by Lowe. Although the striker conceded one goal the defence held out for the additional seven minutes' injury-time. With Danby's long run of consecutive games at an end, the Football League gave Chester special dispensation to bring in a goalkeeper on emergency loan and Rochdale third choice, Jamie Spencer, came in for the remainder of the campaign.

Chester failed to build on their win at Notts County and meekly surrendered to Macclesfield in the next home game with a 2-0 defeat. The club was further rocked with the news that two players, Jay Harris and David Mannix had been charged by the FA for breaching betting rules when playing for Accrington Stanley. By a quirk of fate Chester's next away game was at Accrington and although Harris started, and put in a fine performance, Mannix remained on the bench. A Ryan Lowe penalty settled the game in Chester's favour and with three games to go the Blues remained in 23rd place, a point behind Grimsby and Bournemouth. However, with Bournemouth scheduled as the next visitors to the Deva Stadium, Chester's destiny still remained in their own hands if they could win the last three games. Nevertheless there was little belief amongst the supporters that a second great escape was on the cards and Chester's threadbare team were no match for the ruthless Cherries who comfortably won the game 2-0. With Grimsby also beating Port Vale it left Chester needing to win their last two games and rely on other results to avoid relegation. For the penultimate game, at Aldershot, the Blues travelled without Damien Mozika who had only played one game since January but was suspended for "serious breaches of club discipline." The absence of the Frenchman, who had looked such a promising prospect at the start of the campaign, merely underlined the problems behind the scenes that had affected the club throughout the season.

Although Ryan Lowe's 16th League goal of the season put Chester ahead in the first minute at Aldershot, the final score of 2-2 effectively relegated Chester back to the Conference after a five year absence. Lloyd Ellams had the distinction of being the last Chester player to score in the Football League with his first senior goal. A week later there were only 1,945 present to see if Chester could win their first home game since Boxing Day.

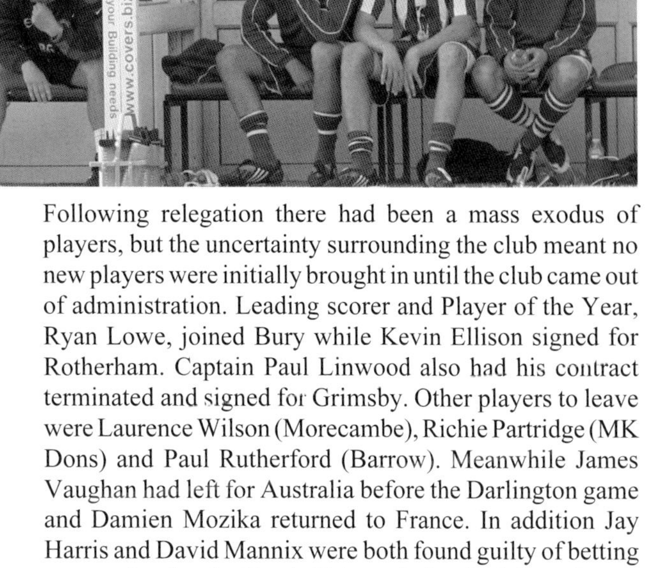


*Mark Wright (standing left) and the Chester bench face relegation at Aldershot in April 2009.*

Darlington visited the Deva Stadium for the final Football League match. Pavel Abbott put the visitors ahead, midway through the second period, but in the last minute Quakers' defender Ian Miller spectacularly headed the ball into his own net from an Anthony Barry cross. However, deep into injury-time, Abbott scored his second goal to give Darlington a 2-1 win and put the seal on relegation.

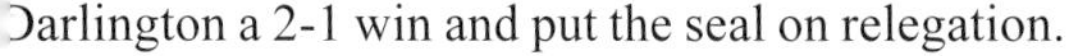

It had been a grim season for a club racked with problems, both on and off the field, and the situation worsened in the summer as the club entered into voluntary administration on May 14th. Only two months previously a press conference had been staged at the Deva Stadium where Liverpool-based property developer, Gary Metcalfe, had been revealed as the new owner of the club. Metcalfe was the managing director of First Property, the company at the forefront of plans to extend the ground, but despite the official unveiling the takeover never actually took place. It was later revealed that ownership of Stephen Vaughan's shares had passed into the hands of his son, Stephen Vaughan junior.

The move into administration started a catalogue of events that descended into a summer of chaos and the death of the club nine months later. On June 11th a creditors' meeting was held at the Deva Stadium where the administrators, Refresh Recovery Ltd, revealed that that the creditors were owed £7 million of which £4 million was made up of secured debts in the name of Vaughan and his company, Cestrian Trading. Meanwhile HM Revenue and Customs (HMRC) were owed £982,743 and the football debts amounted to £72,143. The administrators also revealed there had only been one viable bid for the club in the form of a £290,000 offer from Chester City Football Club Ltd (2004), a company owned by Stephen Vaughan. With the club virtually worthless the administrator recommended that the creditors accept Vaughan's offer for the club and a payment of 15p in the pound.

The bid to buy back the club proved successful and the Conference formally accepted the club into the League although they were given a 10 point deduction for going into administration. In an attempt to raise money Vaughan offered supporters' groups a seat on the board for £25,000 a year and set about putting a Company Voluntary Arrangement (CVA) in place while also looking to build a squad for the new season.

Following relegation there had been a mass exodus of players, but the uncertainty surrounding the club meant no new players were initially brought in until the club came out of administration. Leading scorer and Player of the Year, Ryan Lowe, joined Bury while Kevin Ellison signed for Rotherham. Captain Paul Linwood also had his contract terminated and signed for Grimsby. Other players to leave were Laurence Wilson (Morecambe), Richie Partridge (MK Dons) and Paul Rutherford (Barrow). Meanwhile James Vaughan had left for Australia before the Darlington game and Damien Mozika returned to France. In addition Jay Harris and David Mannix were both found guilty of betting on matches by the Football Association in July and were released by the club. Mannix was fined and banned for 10 months while Harris, who had also bet on Chester's away trip to Bournemouth, was fined and banned for 12 months.

It wasn't just players leaving the club as manager Mark Wright departed on June 22nd by mutual consent which meant that for the seventh season in succession the club would play the first game of the new campaign with a new man in charge. A replacement was quickly found in the shape of former, Huddersfield, Carlisle and Scarborough manager Mick Wadsworth. The 58-year-old Yorkshireman had an impressive CV that included extensive coaching experience with the FA, time on the England backroom staff under Bobby Robson and Graham Taylor and spells as assistant manager at both Newcastle and Southampton.

Wadsworth enthusiastically set about his new job with Neil Ashton (Shrewsbury), Michael Lea (Scunthorpe) and experienced defender Tim Ryan (Darlington) the first to move to the Deva Stadium. In addition Rhys Meynell (Stalybridge) was signed from under the noses of AFC Telford, while Uruguayan Fabian Yantorno, who had played for Wadsworth at Gretna, was seen as a flagship signing. In the event Yantorno continued to be troubled by a knee injury and was released at the start of September without ever playing a game for Chester. Gregg Blundell also rejoined the club from troubled Darlington and Andrew Murphy (Preston) was signed as backup to John

Danby who had signed a new contract. The pre-season signings were completed by veteran striker Glynn Hurst (Bury) and midfielder Ben Wilkinson (York).

On July 13th a Chester team, predominantly made up of youth team players, took to the field at Holywell for a pre-season fixture against Connah's Quay Nomads. Although the youngsters won the game 3-1, Wadsworth's plans were thrown into complete disarray only four days later when the FA prevented the club from playing any more pre-season friendlies. The Football Association's compliance unit advised that the club had not been affiliated to the FA since leaving administration because of concerns about the transfer of ownership from the old company to the new Chester City. Friendlies against a Liverpool X1, Airbus UK, AFC Telford and Burnley were all called off and the problems escalated still further on July 28th when the CVA was revoked at Manchester High Court after HMRC filed a successful appeal.

Special dispensation was given by the FA for Chester to play a match at Droylsden in memory of a soldier killed in Afghanistan, but this was the only public warm-up match that was played as the whole future of the club remained in doubt. With less than a week to go, before the season opener at Grays on August 8th, the club entered prolonged discussions with both the FA and Conference officials in order to satisfy the rules for affiliation. Two days before the Grays game an interim statement was issued by the Football Conference, in an attempt to remove some of the uncertainty surrounding the club. The statement accepted Chester into the Blue Square Premier but deducted a further 15 points for failing to agree on a CVA. However this arrangement did not satisfy the FA, who claimed that the Football Conference would be breaking their own rules by accepting Chester into the League and it was clear that football's governing body were still unhappy with the transfer of ownership and were holding back on affiliating the club. With the future still unclear the Grays game was postponed.

Over the weekend the Conference announced: *"The board made a decision to permit Chester City to enter the competition via a new company, Chester City Football Club (2004) Ltd. The new company does not tick all the boxes of transfer of membership rule 2.7, in particular: neither have all football creditors been paid nor have all other creditors been satisfied."* This damning statement prompted a response from the FA who declared that they would not consent to the affiliation unless all the Conference clubs accepted the decision to allow Chester's entry despite the breach of rules. A vote was therefore held on the Monday morning when the clubs unanimously elected to accept Chester into the Blue Square Premier. Despite this backing, the FA continued to express their dissatisfaction with the arrangements and scheduled the Football Conference to appear before a Commission of the FA's Sanctions and Registrations Committee three days later, which resulted in the postponement of the midweek home fixture against Gateshead. The club themselves issued a statement after the Gateshead postponement expressing their *"shock and amazement"* about the delay in accepting affiliation insisting they had met all the FA's requirements. On Thursday 13th August an agreement was finally reached and the Blues were given permission to start the season. After the meeting the FA released a statement in which they declared: *"The Commission found that the proposed arrangement whereby the new company running Chester City would be granted membership of the Conference by accepting a deduction of a further 15 points was a clear breach of Conference rules. As a result, the Commission has fined the Conference £5,000, suspended until the start of the 2010/11 season. It has also ordered that the Conference review their insolvency rules in conjunction with the FA by 31 December 2009*".

Although the club's short-term future had been resolved, manager Mick Wadsworth was faced with the prospect of lifting a team firmly entrenched at the bottom of the table on minus 25 points and already facing almost certain relegation. Having had an inadequate pre-season, Wadsworth also lost Glynn Hurst, who had departed for Gainsborough Trinity without kicking a ball in anger, although former Everton and Plymouth striker, Nick Chadwick, came in as a late replacement.

Chester belatedly kicked off the season with a home fixture against Cambridge United. Within a minute Ben Wilkinson had put the Blues ahead and substitute Chadwick extended the lead on 19 minutes. Unfortunately Wadsworth's team quickly ran out of steam and former striker, Chris Holroyd, punished the Blues with a hat-trick as Cambridge ran out 4-2 winners. Three days later another four goals were conceded at Oxford, with all the goals in the second-half, as James Constable became the second player to score a trio against a Blues side struggling to reach match fitness. Three players were brought in on loan before the next game with central defender Chris Lynch and midfielder Adam Kay arriving from Burnley, while striker Lewis Alessandra, who had played and scored in the only friendly at Droylsden, came in from Oldham. The newcomers helped Chester pick up an unexpected first point of the season with a goalless draw at pre-season promotion favourites Luton.

Gregg Blundell came off the bench for his first appearance in a 1-0 home defeat to Mansfield before Ben Wilkinson helped Chester to a second point of the season at Altrincham. However, after five games, no real impression had been made into the deduction and this was reflected in an attendance of only 1,171 for the next home game against Histon. The fixture saw James Vaughan make a surprise return to the side after his spell in Australia and he lined up alongside his brother Stephen who had been a regular in the side since the start of the campaign.

After the problems of the summer their joint appearance met with little enthusiasm and this was the last time the brothers featured in a Chester side with James moving on to Droylsden and Stephen joining Northwich on loan. Nevertheless goals from Kevin Roberts and Nick Chadwick gave Chester their first home victory since Boxing Day and the first three points of the season.

There was another home victory against ten-man Gateshead in the middle of September with Gregg Blundell, from the penalty spot, and Nick Chadwick scoring in a 2-1win. However, the attendance sunk below 1,000 for the first time since 2001. The Gateshead game was sandwiched between home defeats to Tamworth and Stevenage, but Chester were proving more resilient away from home where they had been unbeaten since the opening trip to Oxford. A dull goalless draw at Wrexham, in what proved to be the last border derby, saw loan signing Clark Keltie make his debut from Rochdale, but it also marked the last game for Chris Lynch who picked up a knee injury and returned to Burnley.

September ended with another home defeat, 2-1 to Forest Green, and it marked the last match in charge for Mick Wadsworth who was sacked by Stephen Vaughan, along with assistant manager Simon Davies, after only 13 games. It had been a thankless task for Wadsworth who expressed the feeling of many people when he departed by stating: *"This place is full of negativity and I've never known an environment like it and it's wearing. A lot of supporters won't come because they don't think we've got a cat in hell's chance of getting out of trouble, but all the players can do is fight."* Meanwhile Vaughan, who had now appointed nine managers in eight years, expressed his frustration at the situation by saying: *"Previous managers have also struggled at this club in recent years and I'm lost for words when I'm asked why that should be"*

Experienced defender Tim Ryan and coach Billy Gerrard took temporary charge for the next game, at Hayes and Yeading , where Chester came away with a goalless draw against a team that played with nine men for the last 20 minutes after having two players sent-off. There was a new man at the helm for the next game, and it proved a popular appointment with former Tranmere midfielder Jim Harvey taking the manager's role. The Irishman, who had most recently been managing Forest Green Rovers, immediately brought in Mark Beesley on loan from Cambridge and both men made their bow in the home game against Rushden. Unfortunately Chester slumped to a 1-0 defeat and had Glenn Rule and Nick Chadwick dismissed.

Nevertheless the arrival of Harvey revitalised the team and the addition of two more loan signings, Michael Coulson (Barnsley) and Jonathan Flynn (Blackburn), spurred Chester on to win the next three Blue Square Premier games and briefly raise hopes that the new manager could turn things around.

A Mark Beesley goal gave City a 1-0 win at Gateshead and this was followed by impressive 3-1 victories over both AFC Wimbledon and Grays as Chester raised their points tally to minus four points. However, as results improved on the field, the club was starting to unravel spectacularly off the pitch and the win at Grays marked the club's last ever victory.

On October 19th the Football Conference issued a transfer embargo and threatened to expel Chester from the league unless they paid off their football creditors within seven days. In an official statement the Conference declared that the club had *"not complied with the terms of the compromise agreement set by the Football Conference to allow the club to participate in the competition at the commencement of the current season"* In addition they were cited for failing to pay Vauxhall Motors, for money owed in relation to the loan of Paul Taylor, as well as failure to pay Wrexham for tickets sold for the recent fixture between the clubs. Stephen Vaughan went on the attack insisting that he would pay the money when he received money owed to the club by the Football League and the Conference. Once again Vaughan found himself at loggerheads with the authorities and once again negotiation took place between the club, the Conference, the Football League and Professional Footballers Association (PFA) in an attempt to resolve the situation. With discussions actively taking place, the deadline was extended to November 16th and then further drawn out to November 30th after the Football League issued notification that they required more time to seek legal advice over the award and distribution of money to the club. In the midst of these discussions Vaughan himself was disqualified from acting as a company director, or actively controlling a company, for 11 years following his involvement in an alleged VAT fraud at Widnes Vikings Rugby League club.

At the start of December, with Chester City now back under the ownership of Stephen Vaughan junior, the club once again stepped away from the brink when it was announced that football debts of £36,600 had been paid off. Managing director Bob Gray confirmed to the BBC: *"We've raised the capital to pay the creditors. Stephen's loaned it to his son. That has kept the club afloat. And now we should be all right."* The Conference themselves explained that Chester had agreed to lodge payment of the potential shortfall between funding due and football creditors which had allowed them to withdraw the threat of expulsion.

Meanwhile, on the pitch, results had taken another turn for the worse as Jim Harvey battled with the transfer embargo. In the FA Cup Chester were drawn against Barrow in the Fourth Qualifying Round. The Blues looked to be heading for the next round when Jonathan Flynn opened the scoring but the Cumbrians struck back and former Blues winger, Paul Rutherford, equalised to force a replay. Any hope of a money-spinning FA Cup run were firmly dismissed in the replay as Chester were trounced 4-0 at the Deva Stadium.

In the Blue Square Premier, Chester suffered five successive defeats after the Grays victory and by the end of November loan signings Mark Beesley, Clark Keltie, Jonathan Flynn, Michael Coulson and Adam Kay had all returned to their host clubs. The additional departure of Gregg Blundell, on loan to Barrow, left a squad painfully lacking in experience and Harvey was increasingly forced to rely on youth team players.

November ended with a home game against Eastbourne Borough. In front of a small crowd of 869 the match was abandoned in the second-half, with Chester leading 3-2, following two pitch invasions in protest about the Vaughan family's ownership of the club. On December 5th Chester City won their last ever point when they drew 0-0 with Luton Town. Under the circumstances it was an astonishing performance by a young team that had to contend with a first-half red card for Kevin Roberts. The side included two 17-year olds, Jack Rea and Jordan Freeman making their debuts as well as 18-year old James Owen and Lloyd Ellams. In addition 17-year-old Ryan Davidson came off the bench for his debut and 18-year-old Connell Rawlinson made only his third substitute appearance.

Another low was reached when only 518 fans attended the FA Trophy fixture against Fleetwood Town with the Blue Square North side qualifying for the next round by a single goal victory. The defeat was quickly followed by news that the players were refusing to train and threatening to go on strike for the next fixture at Rushden after their November wages had remained unpaid. In the event, discussions took place with the PFA and the players returned to training although the Rushden game was called off because of a frozen pitch.

On Boxing Day proceedings took another unexpected turn when Morrell Maison was appointed Director of Football before the fixture at Kidderminster. The controversial former Kettering manager arrived with a chequered past having most recently been owner and manager at troubled Halesowen Town, who had been forced into administration in September. The arrival of Maison came as news to manager Jim Harvey who only became aware of the appointment half an hour before the game at Kidderminster kicked off. Chester lost the game 2-0 and entered 2010 firmly entrenched at the bottom of the table on minus three points,

Frozen pitches resulted in the postponement of the next three games and by time that Chester took to the field for the next game, against Salisbury City, Jim Harvey had departed the club and an already grim situation had deteriorated still further. The well-respected Harvey, who had been working without a contract, left the club after being informed that Maison wanted to bring in his own team. Maison himself took charge of team affairs despite the fact that he was under a 12-month touchline ban after an incident involving one of his own players at Halesowen Meanwhile, Gregg Blundell had signed a permanent deal with Barrow and Anthony Barry, along with promising former Wales-Under-17 midfielder James Owen, had their contracts terminated. Even worse news was to come when it was announced that HMRC had submitted a winding-up order over an unpaid £26,000 tax bill which was due to be heard on January 27th.

There were only 425 present to watch Chester host Salisbury and the sparse crowd saw the Blues fail to score for the fifth consecutive game and lose to a Matt Tubbs penalty five minutes from time. Nick Chadwick became the next departure when he signed for Barrow and the club further angered the powers-that-be when they failed to send any decision makers to an EGM called by the Conference on January 21st. A bemused Conference general manager, Dennis Strudwick, declared: "*We were looking to meet senior personnel in a decision-making capacity, but, without wishing to sound condescending, they sent Bob Gray. Nobody else turned up. We can't deal with the club's former chairman Stephen Vaughan as he is a banned director after failing the fit and proper person's test. But his son is now the named chairman and they also have a new director of football in Morell Maison. We are trying to help the club. We have done our utmost in that respect this season, but we need to speak to them about issues such as whether they have yet paid the wages they owe for November and December.*"

On January 23rd Chester travelled to Mansfield where, despite a battling performance, a young side was completely outclassed by the dominant Stags and were comfortably beaten 4-0. Despite unfolding events and the imminent winding-up order an optimistic Morell Maison stated:" *I'm confident. I'm not in control of the situation, so I'm as confident as I can be without being in control of the situation. Assurances have been given, and negotiations and discussions are going on with HMRC. I'm very confident they will get to the place both sides need to be.*" On the eve of the winding-up order, a statement was issued by the club declaring that Stephen Vaughan junior was prepared to sell the club for £1. However, the offer was dampened by the news that any new owners would have to guarantee all existing creditors. In the event the winding-up order was adjourned until March 10th although it was stated that Chester City Football Club (2004) Ltd were seeking a CVA.

The weather forced the postponement of the re-arranged home fixture against Grays and Chester City took to the field for the last time when they faced Ebbsfleet United at the Deva Stadium. Although Jack Rea scored Chester's first goal since November, the visitors took all three points with a 2-1 win. By now the end game was fast approaching and the writing was on the wall when the forthcoming home fixture against Wrexham was postponed with less than a week to go.

***MATCH TO REMEMBER***
***CHESTER CITY 1 EBBSFLEET UNITED 2***
***BLUE SQUARE PREMIER – FEBRUARY 6TH 2010***

*One hundred and twenty five years of history came to a sad end when Chester City played their last ever game against Ebbsfleet United. With the club sinking fast under a weight of problems, both on and off the field, the Blues looked to end a run that had seen them lose ten of the previous eleven competitive games. With many fans boycotting the game there were less than 400 Chester supporters present in a paltry crowd of 460.*

*Morrell Maison was the man in charge of a youthful, unpaid team containing only two players over 21, and it was the youngsters who went ahead on 30 minutes against the run of play. Seventeen-year-old Jack Rea had the distinction of scoring Chester's final goal, and the first of his senior career, when he latched on to a partially cleared Glenn Rule cross and superbly let fly with a 20 yard volley into the top corner of the net. The Chester-born midfielder's goal was the first scored by the club in 687 minutes football.*

*The lead lasted for only ten minutes when Magno Vieira finished a flowing Ebbsfleet move and the Brazilian added a second, only three minutes later, when he scored from the edge of the area after good work by Moses Ashikodi.*

*In the second-half the visitors continued to put pressure on the battling Blues and it was left to keeper John Danby to keep the visitors at bay. Chester created few opportunities but the best fell to substitute Ryan Davidson who shot narrowly wide of the far post in the closing stages. The 2-1 defeat left Chester on minus three points, 31 points from safety.*

*Chester – Danby, Rule, Lea, Roberts, Kelly, Meynell, Rea, Coulter, Jones (Davidson), Ellams (Rawlinson), Wilkinson*
*Ebbsfleet United – Cronin, Salmon, Charles, Crooks, Easton, Shakes, Holmes, Stavrinou (Welsh), Bailey, Vieira (Ginty), Ashikodi*

he council issued a prohibition order n the ground when the police withdrew eir services after the club failed to pay olicing costs. Mean-while there were rcical scenes on February 9th when the xture at Forest Green Rovers had to be ostponed less than three hours before ick-off. With supporters and players aiting in the car park the coach ompany refused to depart until they ad received up-front payment from the lub.

n February 11th the Conference uspended Chester for seven days and rdered the club to attend a meeting in irmingham to answer five charges elating to breach of Conference rules ncluding failing to fulfil the fixtures gainst Forest Green and Wrexham. The ollowing week Chester pleaded guilty o all charges and the Conference ecommended that member clubs vote or expulsion amidst concerns that the lub would be unable to fulfil their ixtures.

A last-minute attempt to sell the club to an internet-based Danish Consortium came to nothing and on February 26th the member clubs met at Rushden and Diamonds ground and voted to throw the club out of the Blue Square Premier. In a brief statement the Conference announced:
"*Member clubs of the Football Conference, at a general meeting held today, voted in support of the Board of Director's recommendation to erase Chester City (2004) FC Ltd from membership in accordance with Article 5.2. Chester City did not attend the meeting.*"

On March 8th Chester were formally expelled from the Blue Square Premier and their record expunged as no appeal was lodged against their removal from the competition. Two days later, on March 10th, the final nail was put in the coffin when HMRC's case to wind up the club was heard in Court 76 of the High Courts of Justice in London. In a brief meeting, lasting less than a minute and with no club officials in attendance, the club was formally wound up. After 125 years of ups and downs, Chester City had ceased to exist.

*Above) Jack Rea elebrates scoring he last ever Chester goal ,with Ben Wilkinson, against Ebbsfleet.*

*(Left) A sparsely populated main stand for the last ever game, against Ebbsfleet.*

# CHESTER FC – "OUR CITY. OUR COMMUNITY. OUR CLUB."

At the same time as Chester City were falling apart the supporters were grouping together to prepare for the worst. City Fans United (CFU) was formed in October 2009 and on February 18th 2010, supporters packed the Guildhall to hear the board's plans to form a new club as Chester City teetered on the brink. The next three months saw huge activity as the board put a business plan together with assistance from Supporters Direct and three supporter-owned clubs: FC United of Manchester, AFC Wimbledon and AFC Telford United. Their guidance and support enabled CFU to put the structure in place to form a new club and when Chester City was wound up on March 10th they were already in a strong position to step into the breach.

The lease to the Deva Stadium was secured from Cheshire West & Chester Council on May 6th and the newly named Chester Football Club was formally re-launched at the Guildhall on May 20th. The day after the launch, Neil Young was unveiled as the new manager and started the task of building a squad capable of promotion. Young arrived at the Deva, with his assistant Gary Jones, having experienced two successful years at Colwyn Bay which had ended with promotion to the Evo-Stik Premier League a few weeks earlier. There was an immediate boost for the new Chester FC when a successful appeal was made against the decision by the FA Leagues Committee to place the club in the North West Counties Premier League. As a result Chester were placed in the Evo-Stik Division One North.

MBNA, the largest employer in Chester, were secured as shirt sponsors and many other local businesses were attracted by the fresh approach and commercial acumen shown by the board of directors led by Chairman, Chris Pilsbury and chief executive, Steve Ashton. Supporters themselves were quick to rally around with many volunteering their services and more than 1,000 season tickets were sold in the run up to the 2010/2011 season.

Chester FC took to the field for the first time in a pre-season friendly, against Colwyn Bay, on July10th and the first competitive fixture was staged at Warrington Town on August 24th. Over 1,200 supporters travelled from the city to witness Rob Hopley earn the distinction of scoring Chester FC's first league goal after only five minutes. Although Warrington fought back to equalise, the new club was up and running and on September 8th the first competitive home game was staged at the Deva Stadium. A crowd of 2,734 were treated to a goal feast and found themselves a new hero as striker Michael Wilde netted three goals in a 6-0 crushing defeat of Trafford. Wilde went on to score 36 league goals, including five hat-tricks in Chester's total of 107.

One defeat in the first thirteen games saw Chester go top of the table at the end of October when they won 2-1 at Cammell Laird with a brace from Wilde, and they maintained this position until the end of the campaign. A 3-1 win at AFC Fylde, on the penultimate game of the season, virtually assured promotion as goals from Wilde, Michael Powell and Robbie Booth overturned a half-time deficit. Four days later Chester travelled to Garforth Town for the final game with a three-point lead and a superior goal difference of eight over second-placed Skelmersdale United. On the stroke of half-time Michael Powell put Chester on the verge of promotion, despite the news that Skelmersdale were beating Ossett Albion 3-1. However, events unfolded in remarkable fashion after the break as Chester conceded two goals to lose 2-1 and Skelmersdale went on a scoring spree to thrash Ossett 7-2. With the match at Garforth finishing first, more than 2,000 Chester fans had to wait anxiously for confirmation of the result on the other side of the Pennines. When the dust settled promotion was secured by the narrow margin of two goals and Chester-born captain George Horan lifted the Evo-Stik North trophy amidst unforgettable scenes at Garforth.

It had been a fantastic first season for Chester FC as supporters reclaimed their club after years of neglect. Thanks to the hard work of the CFU off the pitch and Neil Young, his management team and the squad on the pitch, a sense of pride had been injected back into the club.

**This time Chester FC can really look forward to the future.**

# THE GROUNDS
# CHAPTER 16

## FAULKNER STREET (1885-1898)

Chester's first ground was located to the North-East of the city centre in an area of Hoole more commonly known as Flookersbrook. The playing area, located in Bishop's Field, initially took the name Weaver's Field, after the coach and cab owners who rented it from the Earl of Kilmorey on behalf of the club.

The ground was first used by Chester Rovers in 1884, with the initial game believed to be an 11-2 victory over Nantwich. When Rovers transformed into Chester F.C., the opening fixture was played against Northwich on September 26th 1885.

At first the main entrance to the ground was along Faulkner Street, which, at the time, terminated near to where Prescot Street now stands. Contemporary reports indicate that the playing surface ran North to South, with one end described as the Faulkner Street or Hoole village end, and the other as the Railway or Station End. Although the ground suffered drainage problems, and lay on a slope, it was frequently used as a neutral venue for Welsh Cup and Cheshire Senior Cup-ties.

The ground was not fully enclosed, and supporters could easily avoid the pay boxes through neighbouring houses. The dressing rooms were located some distance away at the Ermine Hotel in Hoole Road, although, at a later date, a shed at the back of the Bromfield Arms in Faulkner Street was used.

The playing field was initially surrounded by rope which was replaced by wire in 1887. In March 1888 a concert was held on behalf of the club at the Royalty Theatre. Fifteen pounds was raised and used to build a 66 yard (c.60 metres) 'grandstand', an extension to the existing three-tiered plank erection. Reports suggest that this stand was at least partially covered. In the houses behind the stand, the owners kept ducks and hens and they were among the most interested spectators at home matches! In a game against Everton, it was reported that they wandered onto the pitch and became entangled with the players.

In the 1890s it became possible to gain entrance to the ground along Tomkinson Street with access to Hoole Road alongside the Beehive Hotel. Throughout the 1890s the ground was known under two names, either Faulkner Street or Tomkinson Street.

In August 1897, building work began to swallow up the area and the club was faced with moving the hoardings closer to the playing area. Although alternative grounds were considered the cost of the move was prohibitive, and Chester remained at Faulkner Street for another season. By the end of the 1897/98 campaign, finances had improved considerably, and Chester played their last game at the ground, against Liverpool, on April 20th 1898.

At the start of the 1898/99 season the reformed Chester St.Oswalds moved to Faulkner Street, although the new housing meant that the playing pitch had to be moved closer to the cottages in Peploe Street (now Westminster Road). Houses soon encroached upon the rest of the land, and the ground is now covered by the residences of Faulkner Street, Prescot Street and Edna Street.

## THE OLD SHOWGROUND (1898-1899)

In June 1893, the Royal Agricultural Show was held in Chester on land between Hoole Road and Hoole Lane. The week-long festival attracted huge crowds and was attended by the Prince of Wales. The Football Club moved the short distance to this site in 1898, which became more commonly known as the Enclosed Ground, Hoole. As with Faulkner Street the ground was on prime building land and it was clear that the stay would be brief as the club only took out a 12 month lease.

Reports of the troubled Cheshire Senior cup-tie with Crewe describe a pond behind the hoardings, and fans leaving the ground along Vicarage Road. At the time Vicarage Road barely extended beyond Panton Road and the description would place the ground in an area behind Panton Road and to the east of Panton Place, where houses already existed. This area is now covered by the extension to Vicarage Road, Burges Street, and Hewitt Street.

The new ground cost £120 to prepare as hoardings were erected to fully enclose the area. For the first time spectators were unable to get in free as had been the case at Faulkner Street. Stands were erected, probably of very simple construction, and there was also a press box. There appeared to be no dressing room accommodation and it seems likely that the Beehive Hotel in Hoole Road was used.

The first game at the ground was played between Chester Reserves and Chester Garrison, with the inaugural first team game against Everton Reserves on September 10th 1898. In 1899 the hoardings and stand were destroyed by gales on three separate occasions. After the last incident, in April, the committee decided it was not worth re-erecting the hoardings for the final game on the ground, a friendly against the Chester Junior League. Instead the timber and galvanised steel were sold at auction and raised £58 14s. Meanwhile the owners of the land, on hearing of the problems caused by the gales, waived the £10 land rental which left the club in profit when they temporarily disbanded. As with Faulkner Street no trace remains of this short-lived ground which was quickly covered by houses.

## WHIPCORD LANE (1901-1906)

When Chester reformed in 1901, a ground was secured in Whipcord Lane, thanks to the efforts of Messrs Hallmark, Fletcher and Coventry, who guaranteed an overdraft at the bank of £150. By August the ground had been fully enclosed and an uncovered stand for 500 constructed. The pitch was enclosed by wire until 1903, when it was railed. Dressing room accommodation was provided for the visitors and referee but, for the first season, it appears as though Chester had to use the Victoria Road cricket pavilion some distance away. Although a press box was provided it soon drew complaints because the view was restricted by spectators standing directly in front of it.

The new ground was opened with a friendly against Everton on September 4th 1901, and the local press were initially enthusiastic, despite the problematical press box. The drawbacks to the new ground soon became apparent however, when Chester were disqualified from the 1901/02 FA Cup competition because the pitch was too short. The meagre proportions of the ground effectively excluded Chester from the FA Cup and Welsh Cup. To make matters worse the location of the ground, on a slope close to Finchett's Gutter, meant that the pitch resembled a quagmire for most of the season as games were played ankle deep in mud. Bark and sawdust were both spread on the pitch to absorb water but this only ever provided a temporary respite. The lower end of the pitch was described as a bog dotted with puddles of water while the centre of the field, and both flanks, frequently formed miniature lakes.

By 1905 an Improvement committee had been set up to develop the ground but attempts to enlarge the playing area and erect larger stands were rejected by the Earl of Crewe, the owner of the land. It appears as though some material improvements were permitted with the construction of a new exit gate and possibly some cover on the reserved side.

The limitations of Whipcord Lane made a switch inevitable and the club made the short move to Sealand Road in 1906. An idea of the scale of Whipcord Lane can be gauged by the fact that the new ground was described as 17 yards wider and 20 yards longer than the old one. The last game at Whipcord Lane was played against Birkenhead on November 10th 1906.

This ill-equipped ground was located at the northern end of Whipcord Lane, which used to run directly into Cheyney Road before the construction of Stadium Way and Saughall Road. The ground itself is now covered by the allotments which lie at the corner of those two thoroughfares.

## THE STADIUM, SEALAND ROAD (1906-1990)

It was local MP Alfred Mond who helped acquire the land for the Sealand Road ground by negotiating a 10 year lease from the Earl of Crewe and renting it to the club. Mond had intervened after the club had experienced difficulties in expanding the Whipcord Lane ground, which was also owned by the Earl. In order to finance the ground a limited company was formed with initial capital of £1,000.

Elaborate plans were drawn up for a stadium, with stand accommodation for 5,000, but by October 1906 the scheme had been scaled down considerably due to escalating costs. In November a tender for £725, the lowest on offer, was accepted from constructors Messrs. Vernon and Sons, and work started immediately. The first game was held against Bangor City on December 15th 1906, but the ground was by no means complete and it was the following month before a 1,000 capacity covered stand was opened. By the start of the 1908/09 season an open stand, also accommodating 1000, had been built on the reserved side, while a raised platform had been constructed on the unreserved side. Alfred Mond meanwhile had provided hot water baths at a cost of £50, a reward for winning the 1908 Welsh Cup.

When the club disbanded in 1915, the directors were obliged to sell the timber that made up the stands and close the ground. After the war the club had to start again from scratch, and army huts were used for dressing room accommodation while the corporation helped the club by loaning back the timber which had last been used to build stands for a Royal visit. A lack of funds meant that the stands could not be immediately re-erected, but rising attendances saw the construction of an uncovered stand at the Sealand Road End in 1920. The stand was initially built for 750, but was soon extended to hold 1500. This was quickly followed by a covered stand holding 700 which was opened at the home game against Winsford in December 1920.

In 1926, a small covered stand was completed on the popular side while, at the end of the 1926/27 season, dressing room accommodation was improved and the Sealand Road end partially covered. The 1930/31 season saw Chester make a concerted effort for League status and considerable improvements were made to the ground which became known as the Stadium in 1931. The first change was to the Sealand Road End which was completely covered at a cost of £300. The barrel roof supported by 16 pillars became known as the Barn, and remained unchanged until 1987 when the roof was finally replaced. Later in the 1930/31 season an extension was built to the main stand, at a cost of £1,000, and opened in time for the game against Port Vale Reserves in April. Within 3 months the stand had been further extended to cover the whole side and increase the seating capacity to 4,500. At about the same time Chester became one of the first clubs to install a public address system, and for many years the announcer would open up with the words *'Hello Spion Kop, Hello Albert'*, addressing a long-time supporter in the ground.

After record figures were announced at the end of the first season of League football, the club took the far-sighted decision to buy the ground and the adjacent land.

At the end of the 1934/35 season the railings around the ground were replaced by a concrete wall on the popular side and behind the goals. The paddock in front of the main stand also disappeared as a cinder track was placed around the perimeter of the pitch. The terracing on the popular side was also extended to span the length of the pitch, although supporters had to wait until 1966 until the side was completely covered. Finally terracing was extended on the Kop, or Saughall Road End, which had gradually been banked since 1931.

As with their previous grounds, the Stadium suffered serious drainage problems and these were made worse by the construction of the terracing and concrete wall. In 1936, £500 was spent on a drainage system planned by long-time supporter and engineer Captain Wright. The system made the Sealand Road surface one of the best in the Football League.

The ground remained unchanged for the next 25 years, when floodlights were erected and switched on for the League Cup game against Leyton Orient in October 1960. The angled floodlights, on 126ft pylons, were built by a Scottish company to a design already implemented at many Scottish grounds, including Hibs, Hearts and Motherwell. A large percentage of the money required was raised by the Supporters Association who also paid for a scoreboard on the Kop. In 1973 the land behind the main stand was sold and after the League Cup run of 1974/75 new offices were built at the corner of the Sealand Road end.

In 1979 the last major change was made to the ground when the cramped main stand was replaced by a new 2874 capacity structure costing more than £600,000. The new stand was built directly behind the old one but once the original structure was demolished a vast expanse was created in front which robbed the ground of much of its atmosphere. However the new stand offered a much better perspective, and it is unlikely that the old wooden structure, housing Jackie's bar and a tiny gymnasium underneath, would have survived the stricter safety regulations of the 1980s. During the final decade at the Stadium the wooden floor and the roof were replaced at the Sealand Road End, and £40,000 was spent on the Kop End. Despite this expenditure a safety certificate was refused for the Kop and covered visitors section, bringing the capacity below 6,000 for the 1989/90 season.

The final League game at the Stadium was played against Rotherham United on April 28th 1990, although the last ever match was a 3-3 draw with Tranmere in the Midland Senior League on May 3rd. When the ground was demolished the stand roof was sold to Port Vale, while some of the seats went to Ellesmere Port. No trace of the ground remains and the Stadium, which once held over 20,000 for an FA Cup-tie with Chelsea, is now covered by a retail park.

# MOSS ROSE, MACCLESFIELD (1990-1992)

Football was first played at the Moss Rose in 1891, and Chester first visited the ground in their Combination days. Floodlights were installed in 1965 while the 650 capacity main stand was erected in 1968. When Chester moved to Macclesfield, for their 2 years in exile, few changes were required to bring the ground up to League standard. The perimeter walls were strengthened and segregation fences erected to bring the capacity up to 6,000.

The first League game at Macclesfield was played against Exeter City on September 1st 1990 with the last, against Leyton Orient, on May 2nd 1992. The highest (Chester) attendance was 4,895 for the League encounter against Birmingham City on April 11th 1992, which contrasted sharply with the 409 who attended the Leyland Daf Cup game against Bury on November 27th 1990.

Unfortunately, when Macclesfield won the Vauxhall Conference in 1994/95, the guidelines for entry to the Football League had been tightened up and Moss Rose was deemed unfit for entry. Although Chester offered Macclesfield the chance of sharing the Deva Stadium it was to no avail. Happily justice was done at the end of the 1996/97 season when Macclesfield again won the Conference and replaced Hereford in the Football League.

# DEVA STADIUM (1992-Present day)

It took just 30 weeks to construct the Deva Stadium from the turf cutting ceremony on January 28th 1992 to the official opening of the ground by Lord Aberdare, chairman of the Football Trust, on August 24th 1992. The ground cost £3 million to build, including £500,000 donated by the Football Trust, and was originally designed with a capacity of 6,000. Following the installation of seats in the South Stand it currently has the potential to hold a maximum of 5,536 spectators, subject to ground grading regulations.

The Deva Stadium took its name from the Roman name for Chester and became the third new league ground of the modern era following on from Scunthorpe United and Walsall. It became the first ground in the country to comply with all the recommendations put forward by the Taylor report, set up after the Hillsborough disaster of 1989. Between 2004 and 2007 a sponsorship deal saw it re-named the Saunders Honda Stadium and when that arrangement ended it reverted to the Deva Stadium for the 2007/08 campaign. In 2008 it was announced that Stephen Vaughan's own company would be sponsoring the ground under the name Cestrian Trading Stadium. The collapse of Chester City, and subsequent formation of Chester FC in 2010, saw a new sponsorship deal established and it is now known as the Exacta Stadium.

The ground was designed by Scottish architects Percy Johnson-Marshall who were also involved in building similar style stadiums at Stirling Albion (1993) and Livingston (1995). The main East Stand currently seats a maximum of 2,108 spectators and contains the offices, hospitality area and changing room facilities. The smaller West Stand currently seats up to 1,253 while the North Terrace has a maximum capacity of 1,386 and was renamed the Harry McNally Terrace in memory of the former manager in December 2006. The South Stand was converted to seating in 2007 which reduced the capacity to 789.

The one feature that makes the Deva Stadium unique among football grounds is that it straddles a national border. It is normal for new grounds to have the main stand located on the west side, but at the Deva Stadium it is situated to the east. Most of the stadium, including the pitch itself, is in Wales and the border runs through the corner of the office block, in the Main Stand. The location of the offices, in England, ensures that Chester remains affiliated to the English FA.

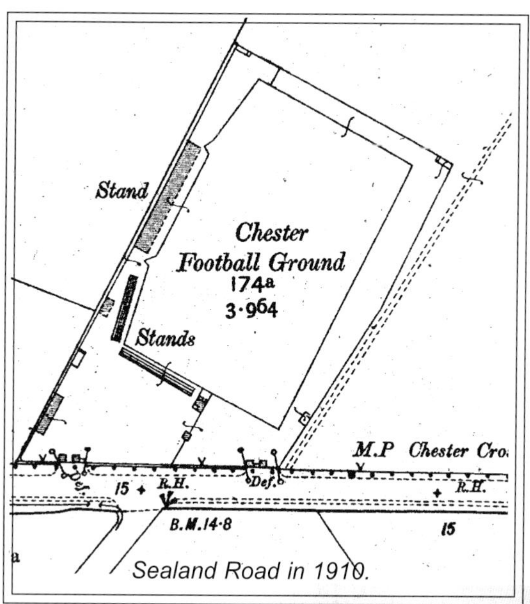


Sealand Road in 1910.

(Right) Site of Whipcord Lane Ground (Field 236) early 20th century.

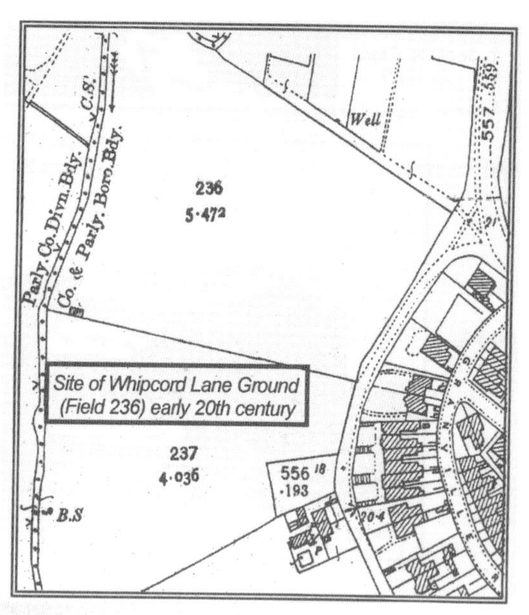


Site of Whipcord Lane Ground (Field 236) early 20th century

Sealand Road in 1931, just prior to joining the Football League.

*Sealand Road.*

*Moss Rose, Macclesfield.*

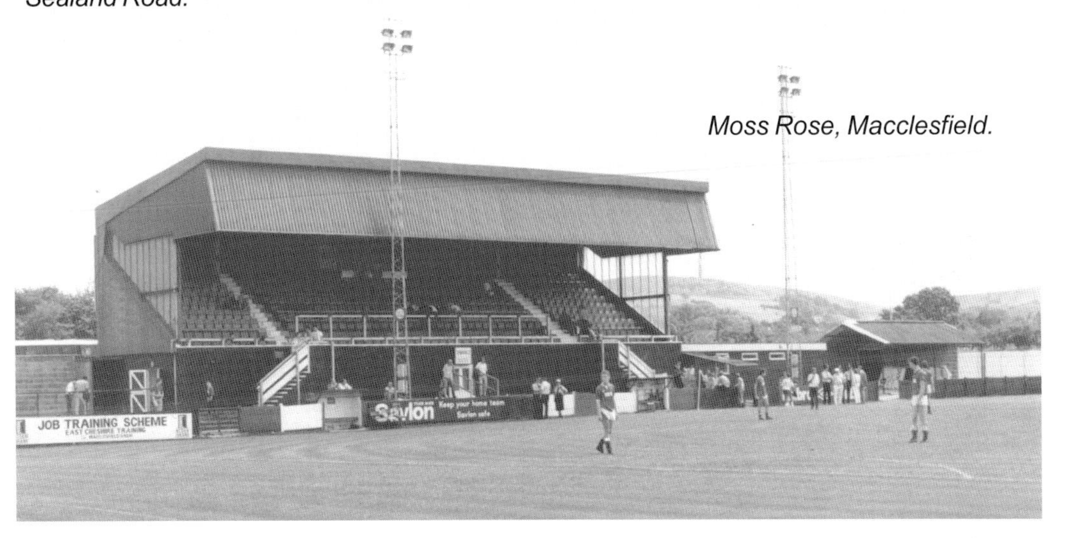


*Deva Stadium in mid-construction - 1992*

# HONOURS

**FOOTBALL LEAGUE**
Division 3N Runners-up 1935/36
Division 4 Runners-up 1985/86
Division 3 Runners-up 1993/94
**NATIONWIDE CONFERENCE**
Champions 2003/04
**FA CUP BEST**
Last 16 1890/91,1976/77,1979/80
LEAGUE CUP BEST
Semi-Finalists 1974/75
ASSOCIATE MEMBERS CUP BEST
Northern Finalists 1986/87
WELSH CUP
Winners 1907/08,1932/33,1946/47
Runners-up 1908/09,1909/10,1934/35,1935/36,1952/53, 1953/54,1954/55,1957/58,1965/66,1969/70
DEBENHAMS CUP
Winners 1976/77
DIVISION 3N CUP
Winners 1935/36,1936/37
Runners-up 1945/46
CHESHIRE COUNTY LEAGUE
Winners 1921/22,1925/26,1926/27
Runners-up 1930/31
THE COMBINATION
Winners 1908/09
Runners-up 1903/04,1904/05,1905/06, 1906/07,1907/08
NATIONWIDE VARIETY CLUB TROPHY
Winners 2000/01
J.C. THOMPSON CHAMPIONSHIP SHIELD
Runners-up 2001/02
CHESHIRE SENIOR CUP
Winners 1894/95,1896/97,1903/04,1907/08,1908/09,1930/31,1931/32
Runners-up 1887/88,1892/93,1893/94, 1904/05,1910/11,1928/29
LANCASHIRE CUP
Winners 1956/57
Runners-up 1952/53
LIVERPOOL SENIOR CUP
Runners-up 1895/96
**CHESHIRE LEAGUE CHALLENGE CUP**
Winners 1923/24 (shared)
Runners-up 1930/31
CHESHIRE SENIOR MEDALS
Winners 1926/27
Runners-up 1931/32
CHESHIRE BOWL
Winners 1932/33,1934/35,1936/37, 1940/41,1943/44,1944/45,1945/46, 1953/54,1964/65
Runners-up 1933/34,1938/39,1947/48, 1952/53,1953/54,1954/55
CHESHIRE PREMIER CUP
Winners 1977/78,1978/79,1980/81
Runners-up 1970/71,1972/73,1976/77,1979/80,1981/82
MINOR CUPS
**YERBURGH CHARITY CUP**
Winners 1889/90,1909/10,1910/11 (shared)
SIR OWEN PHILLIPS CUP
Winners 1921/22,1922/23
CAMBRIDGESHIRE PROFESSIONAL CUP
Winners 1992/93
**HEREFORDSHIRE SENIOR CUP**
Winners 1991/92 (shared)

# MANAGERS

| | |
|---|---|
| Pre-1930 | Selection committee |
| May 1930 - Apr 1936 | Charlie Hewitt |
| Apr 1936 - Jun 1936 | Harry Mansley (caretaker manager) |
| Jun 1936 - May 1938 | Alex Raisbeck |
| May 1938 - May 1953 | Frank Brown |
| May 1953 – May 1956 | Louis Page |
| Jun 1956 – Apr 1959 | John Harris |
| Apr 1959 - Nov 1961 | Stan Pearson |
| Nov 1961 - Jan 1962 | Selection committee |
| Jan 1962 - Jul 1963 | Bill Lambton |
| Aug 1963 - Feb 1968 | Peter Hauser |
| Feb 1968 - Mar 1968 | Selection committee |
| Mar 1968 - Sep 1976 | Ken Roberts |
| Sep 1976 - Mar 1982 | Alan Oakes |
| Mar 1982 - Jun 1982 | Cliff Sear (caretaker manager) |
| Jun 1982 - Nov 1982 | Cliff Sear |
| Nov 1982 – Nov 1983 | John Sainty |
| Nov 1983 - Jan 1984 | Trevor Storton (caretaker manager) |
| Jan 1984 - Jan 1984 | Cliff Sear (caretaker manager) |
| Jan 1984 - Dec 1984 | John McGrath |
| Dec 1984 - Mar 1985 | Mick Speight (caretaker manager) |
| Mar 1985 - Jul 1985 | Mick Speight |
| Jul 1985 – Oct 1992 | Harry McNally |
| Oct 1992 - Nov 1992 | Graham Barrow (caretaker manager) |
| Nov 1992 - Jun 1994 | Graham Barrow |
| Jul 1994 - Jan 1995 | Mike Pejic |
| Jan 1995 - Mar 1995 | Derek Mann (caretaker manager) |
| Mar 1995 - Apr 1995 | Derek Mann |
| Apr 1995 – May 1995 | Kevin Ratcliffe (caretaker manager) |
| May 1995 – Aug 1999 | Kevin Ratcliffe |
| Aug 1999 – Jan 2000 | Terry Smith |
| Jan 2000 – May 2000 | Ian Atkins |
| May 2000 – Jun 2001 | Graham Barrow |
| Jun 2001 – Oct 2001 | Gordon Hill |
| Oct 2001 – Oct 2001 | Steve Mungall (caretaker manager) |
| Oct 2001 – Dec 2001 | Steve Mungall |
| Dec 2001 – Jan 2001 | Owen Brown (caretaker manager) |
| Jan 2002 – Aug 2004 | Mark Wright |
| Aug 2004 - Aug 2004 | Ray Matthias (caretaker manager) |
| Aug 2004 - Apr 2005 | Ian Rush |
| Apr 2005 – Apr 2005 | David Bell (caretaker manager) |
| Apr 2005 - Feb 2006 | Keith Curle |
| Feb 2006 – Apr 2007 | Mark Wright |
| Apr 2007 – May 2007 | Simon Davies (caretaker manager) |
| May 2007 – Mar 2008 | Bobby Williamson |
| Mar 2008 – Apr 2008 | Simon Davies (caretaker manager) |
| Apr 2008 – Nov 2008 | Simon Davies |
| Nov 2008 – Nov 2008 | Wayne Allison (caretaker manager) |
| Nov 2008 – Jun 2009 | Mark Wright |
| Jun 2009 – Sept 2009 | Mick Wadsworth |
| Sep 2009 – Oct 2009 | Tim Ryan\Billy Gerrard (caretaker managers) |
| Oct 2009 – Jan 2010 | Jim Harvey |
| Jan 2010 – Feb 2010 | Morrell Maison |

# FULL INTERNATIONALS

| | | | |
|---|---|---|---|
| **CANADA** | MARTIN NASH (2) | V. | Trinidad & Tobago, Bermuda (2000) |
| **LUXEMBOURG** | STEPHANE GILLET (1) | V. | Belgium (2006) |
| **MALTA** | LUKE DIMECH (2) | V. | Northern Ireland (2005) Georgia (2006) |
| **NORTH. IRELAND** | IAIN JENKINS (3) | V | Armenia, Thailand (1997), Slovakia (1998) |
| **REP. OF IRELAND** | PETER FITZGERALD (2) | V | Czechoslovakia (1962 x 2) |
| **TRINIDAD & TOBAGO** | ANGUS EVE (35) | V | Canada (x2), Morocco, Mexico, Guatemala, Costa Rica, Netherlands Ant., Dominican Rep (x2), Haiti (x2) (2000) |

The following caps were awarded while on long term loan to Joe Public (Trinidad)
Cuba, Jamaica, Canada (x2), Mexico (x2), Guyana, Panama (x2) (2000), Grenada (x3), Cayman Island, Jamaica (x3), Guatemala, Costa Rica, Mexico, Barbados, Cuba, Panama, USA, Bermuda (2001)

| | | | |
|---|---|---|---|
| **WALES** | TOMMY ASTBURY (2) | V | England (x2) (1945) – (Wartime Internationals) |
| | IAN EDWARDS (3) | V | Kuwait (1978), Malta, West Germany (1979) |
| | ALBERT GRAY (6) | V | England, Scotland, Ireland (1937), Scotland, England, Ireland (1938) |
| | ANDY HOLDEN (1) | V | Israel (1984) |
| | SAM JONES (1) | V | Scotland (1890) |
| | BEN LEWIS (1) | V | Ireland (1891) |
| | WILLIAM LEWIS (13) | V | Ireland, England, Scotland (1892), Ireland, England, Scotland (1894), Ireland, England, Scotland (1895), Ireland, England, Scotland (1896), Ireland (1898) |

Lewis was also registered with Crewe Alex when awarded caps in 1892 and 1894

| | | | |
|---|---|---|---|
| | WILLIAM MATTHEWS (2) | V | Ireland (1905), England (1908) |
| | BOB ROBERTS (1) | V | Ireland (1890) |

## Club Leading Scorers: (Football League only)

135 - Stuart Rimmer
87 - Gary Talbot
73 - Frank Wrightson
69 - Elfed Morris
68 - Mike Metcalf
64 - Albert Burgess
63 - Gary Bennett
63 - Joe Mantle
57 - Frank Cresswell
54 - Derek Draper

## Most League Appearances:

406 - Ray Gill
399 - Ron Hughes
396 - Trevor Storton
363 - Eric Lee
361 - Stuart Rimmer
322 - Derek Draper
317 - Billy Stewart
303 - Tommy Astbury
299 - Nigel Edwards
296 - Graham Abel
296 - Billy Foulkes
290 - Grenville Millington

## Other Player Records

**Most goals in a match (pre-League)**
8 — Arthur Gale v Whitchurch,
Cheshire County League, Oct 1st 1930

**Most goals in a match (Football League)**
5 - Tommy Jennings v Walsall,
Division 3N, Jan 30th 1932
5 - Barry Jepson v York City,
Division 3N, Feb 8th 1958

**Most league goals in a season (pre-League)**
73 — Arthur Gale,
Cheshire County League, 1930/31

**Most league goals in a season (Football League)**
36 - Dick Yates,
Division 3N, 1946/47

**Record transfer fee received**
£300,000 from Liverpool
for Ian Rush, Apr 1980

**Record transfer fee paid**
£100,000 to Doncaster Rovers
for Gregg Blundell, Jul 2005

**Oldest player (Football League)**
40 yrs 101 days, Stan Pearson
v Crewe Alex. Apr 22nd 1959

**Youngest player (Football League)**
15 yrs 350 days, Aidan Newhouse
v Bury, May 7th 1988

# MISCELLANEOUS COMPETITIONS

This is a list of all other first team games played by Chester since their formation. As with the FA Cup and Welsh Cup, Chester did not enter these competitions on a regular basis, especially in pre-League days. When the first team entered the League in 1931, the Reserves took over in the Cheshire Senior Cup and the Cheshire League Challenge Cup. However it was predominantly the first team that beat Crewe Alexandra 1-0 in the 1931/32 Cheshire Senior Cup Final. Although Chester returned to non-league football in 2000, results in the Cheshire Senior Cup have not been included as the club continued to field a mainly Reserve team. The Cheshire Seniors medals was superseded by the Cheshire Bowl, which in turn was replaced by the Cheshire Premier Cup. From 1977/78 to 1980/81 the Premier Cup was played on a League basis.

## CENTRAL LEAGUE

| Date | Opponents | | Score | Scorers |
|---|---|---|---|---|
| 1896/97 | | | | |
| Oct 24 | Macclesfield | A | 1-1 | Blakeman |
| Nov 21 | Crewe Alex. | H | 1-0 | Turner |
| Apr 10 | Crewe Alex. | A | 0-1 | |
| Apr 16 | Dresden United | H | 4-1 | Gordon, Catherall(2), Unknown |
| Apr 24 | Macclesfield | H | 6-1 | Spencer, Lewis, Lipsham, Barker, Blakeman, og |
| Apr 26 | Walsall | H | 1-2 | Unknown |

Return matches against Walsall and Dresden not played

## CHESHIRE BOWL

| Date | Rd | Opponents | | Score | Scorers |
|---|---|---|---|---|---|
| 1932/33 | | | | | |
| Sep 28 | F | Crewe Alex. | H | 3-1 | Mantle, Stevenson, Cresswell |
| 1933/34 | | | | | |
| Sep 20 | SF | Crewe Alex. | H | 3-1 | Mantle, Mercer (2) |
| Oct 4 | F | Stockport County | H | 1-1 | Mercer |
| May 7 | Fr | Stockport County | A | 0-2 | |
| 1934/35 | | | | | |
| Sep 26 | SF | Tranmere Rovers | H | 2-0 | Newton (og), Sargeant |
| Oct 3 | F | Stockport County | H | 4-2 | Sargeant (2), Cresswell, Wallbanks |
| 1935/36 | | | | | |
| May 2 | SF | Crewe Alex. | H | 0-3 | |
| 1936/37 | | | | | |
| Sep 23 | SF | Crewe Alex. | H | 3-1 | Wrightson, Sargeant(2) |
| May1 | F | Tranmere Rovers | H | 1-0 | Wrightson |
| 1938/39 | | | | | |
| Apr 19 | F | Crewe Alex. | A | 1-2 | Warburton |
| 1945/46 | | | | | |
| May 6 | SF1 | Tranmere Rovers | A | 1-2 | Bett |
| May 8 | SF2 | Tranmere Rovers | H | 6-2 | Burden (3), Bett (2), Astbury |
| May 11 | F | Crewe Alex. | H | 3-1 | Burden, Marsh, Astbury |
| 1947/48 | | | | | |
| Apr 28 | F | Tranmere Rovers | H | 0-1 | |
| 1948/49 | | | | | |
| Apr 30 | SF | Tranmere Rovers | H | 1-3 | Westwood |
| 1949/50 | | | | | |
| Apr 19 | SF | Tranmere Rovers | H | 2-3 | Lee, Coffin |
| 1952/53 | | | | | |
| Jan 10 | SF | Crewe Alex. | A | 4-2 | Tomlinson (2), Travis, Astbury |
| May 2 | F | Stockport County | A | 1-3 | Travis |
| 1953/54 | | | | | |
| May 5 | F | Tranmere Rovers | H | 1-1 | Travis |
| May 8 | Fr | Tranmere Rovers | A | 2-1 | Windle, Gill |
| 1954/55 | | | | | |
| Apr 27 | SF | Stockport County | H | 2-1 | Windle, Whitlock |
| May14 | F | Tranmere Rovers | A | 2-3 | Coffin (2) |
| 1955/56 | | | | | |
| Oct 5 | SF | Stockport County | H | 0-1 | |
| 1956/57 | | | | | |
| Dec 8 | SF | Tranmere Rovers | A | 0-3 | |
| 1957/58 | | | | | |
| Apr 28 | SF | Crewe Alex. | A | 1-2 | Ireland |
| 1958/59 | | | | | |
| Mar 11 | SF | Stockport County | H | 2-5 | Richards(2) |
| 1959/60 | | | | | |
| Mar 23 | SF | Stockport County | H | 0-1 | |
| 1960/61 | | | | | |
| Apr 12 | SF | Crewe Alex. | A | 1-2 | Hughes |
| 1961/62 | | | | | |
| Oct 18 | SF | Stockport County | H | 1-1 | Clarke |
| Mar 5 | SFr | Stockport County | A | 0-1 | |
| 1962/63 | | | | | |
| Apr 9 | SF | Tranmere Rovers | H | 1-2 | Jones |
| 1963/64 | | | | | |
| Nov 4 | SF | Tranmere Rovers | A | 1-2 | Humes |
| 1964/65 | | | | | |
| Nov 2 | SF | Stockport County | A | 2-1 | Morris, Metcalf |
| Mar 22 | F | Tranmere Rovers | A | 2-0 | Bennion(2) |
| 1965/66 | | | | | |
| Oct 20 | SF | Tranmere Rovers | H | 1-3 | Lee |
| 1966/67 | | | | | |
| Mar 8 | SF | Crewe Alex. | H | 0-2 | |
| 1967/68 | | | | | |
| Feb 28 | SF | Crewe Alex. | H | 2-3 | Jones, Gannon (og) |

## CHESHIRE LEAGUE CHALLENGE CUP

| Date | Rd | Opponents | | Score | Scorers |
|---|---|---|---|---|---|
| 1920/21 | | | | | |
| Feb 5 | 1R | Crichton's A. | H | 1-2 | L Jones |
| 1921/22 | | | | | |
| Sep 7 | 1R | Whitchurch | A | 2-1 | Timmis, Pryde |
| Sep 28 | 2R | Connah's Duay | H | 3-2 | Butterton, Tr. Jones, Timmis |
| Apr 5 | 3R | Winsford United | H | 1-1 | Pimlott |
| Apr 19 | 3Rr | Winsford United | A | 0-7 | |
| 1922/23 | | | | | |
| Sep 6 | 1R | Middlewich | A | 0-1 | |
| 1923/24 | | | | | |
| Sep 5 | 1R | Wallasey United | A | 1-0 | McGivney |
| Sep 26 | 2R | Whitchurch | A | 2-1 | Parton, Cunlilfe |
| Apr 15 | SF | Congleton | A | 3-1 | Milne, Lydiate, Mokhtar |
| May 2 | F | Stockport County | H | 0-0 | |
| | | No replay played | | | |
| 1928/29 | | | | | |
| Aug 30 | 1R | Whitchurch | H | 4-0 | Peters (3), Burley |
| Feb 16 | 2R | Sandbach | H | 1-1 | Birtles |
| Mar 23 | 2Rr | Sandbach | A | 1-2 | Burke (og) |
| 1929/30 | | | | | |
| Sep 7 | 1R | Connah's Quay & S | H | 1-1 | Downey |
| Sep 25 | 1Rr | Connah's Quay & S | A | 1-1 | Williams |
| Oct 16 | 1R2r | Connah's Quay & S | A | 2-1 | Peters, Hopkins |
| Feb 27 | 2R | Tranmere Rovers | A | 2-4 | Hopkins, King |
| 1930/31 | | | | | |
| Apr 1 | 1R | Runcorn | H | 3-2 | Hart (2), Dickie |
| Apr 23 | 2R | Witton Albion | H | 8-0 | Gale(3), Atkinson, Clifford, Cresswell, Dickie, Burke(og) |
| Apr 27 | SF | Ashton National | H | 6-1 | Clifford (2), Morris, Irvine, Gale, Stevens (og) |
| May 2 | F | Port Vale Res. | H | 2-3 | Cresswell (2) |

## CHESHIRE PREMIER CUP

1968/69
Oct 14 SF Stockport County A 1-3 Dearden
1969/70
Sep 10 SF Crewe Alex. A 1-3 Chapman
1970/71
Oct 14 SF Crewe Alex. H 0-0
May 7 SFr Crewe Alex. A 2-0 Kennedy, Tarbuck
Aug 4 F Stockport County H 0-1
1972/73
Jul 29 SF Tranmere Rovers H 3-2 Wallace (2). Owen
Aug 8 F Crewe Alex. A 1-2 Hollis
1973/74
May 8 '73 SF Crewe Alex. A 1-3 Davies
1974/75
Aug 7 SF Tranmere Rovers A 1-2 Moore (og)
1975/76
Aug 9 SF Tranmere Rovers A 0-0
Oct 8 SFr Tranmere Rovers H 0-1
1976/77
Aug 7 SF Tranmere Rovers H 1-0 Philpotts (og)
Apr 26 F Crewe Alex. A 0-1
1977/78
Aug 1 Stockport County H 2-0 Kearney, N Edwards
Aug 3 Tranmere Rovers H 2-1 Kearney, I Edwards
Aug 6 Crewe Alex. A 2-0 I Edwards (2)
1978/79
Jul 29 Stockport County H 2-0 Howat, Jones
Aug 2 Tranmere Rovers A 2-1 Livermore, Phillips
Sep 20 Crewe Alex. H 1-0 Livermore
1979/80
Aug 1 Stockport County A 2-0 Edwards (2)
Aug 4 Tranmere Rovers A 0-1
1980/81
Jul 26 Crewe Alex. H 1-0 Kearney
Jul 30 Stockport County H 4-1 Birch (2), Anderson, Jones
Aug 2 Tranmere Rovers A 1-0 Ludlam
1981/82
Aug 12 F Tranmere Rovers H 2-2 Jones, Phillips
(Tranmere won 4-3 on penalties)

## CHESHIRE SENIOR CUP

1885/86
Dec12 1R Middlewich A 1-3 Southworth
1886/87
Dec 11 1R Crewe Steam Sheds H 2-1 McMillan, Hughes
Jan 22 2R Bollington A 3-1 Clare, Turner, Hughes
Mar 5 3R Davenham H 1-6 Turner
1887/88
Oct 29 1R Crewe Steam Sheds H (Crewe scratched)
Jan 21 2R Bollington A 3-2 Walley (2), Turner
Feb 25 SF Northwich Vics. N 1-0 Brierley
(Played at Crewe)
Mar 24 F Crewe Alex A 0-9
1888/89
Nov 24 1R Nantwich H 3-0 Turner (2), Lewis
Jan 5 2R Davenham H 2-1 Davies (2)
Feb 23 SF Northwich Vics. N 1-1 Turner
(Played at Crewe)
Mar 2 SFr Northwich Vics. N 0-1
(Played at Macclesfield)
1891/92
Nov 21 1R Tranmere Rovers H 8-1 Walker(2),Carter(2),Lewis,Dawes,Jones,Garner
Feb 20 SF Crewe Alex. N 0-5
(Played at Northwich)
1892/93
Nov 12 1R Marple A 4-3 Ashton, Browne, Unknown (2)
Mar 11 SF Northwich Vics. N 4-2 Porter (2), Lewis, Ashton
(Played at Crewe)
Apr 8 F Crewe Alex. N 0-0
(Played at Macclesfield)
Apr 22 Fr Crewe Alex. N 1-3 Heyes
(Played at Northwich)
1893/94
Mar 17 SF Northwich Vics. N 3-0 Heyes, Grewcock, Bull
(Played at Crewe)
Apr 14 F Macclesfield N 1-1 Heyes
(Played at Northwich)
Apr 21 Fr Macclesfield N 1-2 Lewis
(Played at Crewe)
1894/95
Mar 2 SF Northwich Vics. N 3-1 Brown, H Bull, Farrell
(Played at Crewe)
Mar 30 F Macclesfield N 2-1 Brown (2)
(Played at Northwich)
1895/96
Dec 7 1R Sandbach St Marys H (Sandbach scratched)
Jan 18 2R Macclesfield H 0-0
Feb 15 2Rr Macclesfield A 0-1
1896/97
Dec 5 1R Saltney Borderers A 2-1 Lipsham, Spencer
Jan16 2R Port Sunlight H 5-1 Barker, Gordon, Lipsham (2), Porter
Mar 6 SF Congleton Hornets A 1-1 Speakman
Mar 13 SFr Congleton Hornets H 1-0 Lewis
Mar 27 F Northwich Vics. N 1-1 Gordon
(Played at Macclesfield)
Apr 3 Fr Northwich Vics. N 2-1 Speakman, Hargreaves (og)
(Played at Macclesfield)
1897/98
Nov 27 1R Birkenhead Locos H 2-0 Blakeman, Lewis
Jan 15 2R Tranmere Rovers A 2-1 Speakman, Lewis
Mar 5 SF Nantwich A 0-3
1898/99
Nov 26 1R Wirral Railway Ath. H 2-0 Delaney, Marshall
Feb 11 2R Crewe Alex. H 1-4 Unknown
1901/02
Jan 18 1R Birkenhead H 3-0 Davies, Cooke, Griffiths
2R Bye
Feb 15 3R Sale Holmfield H 1-2 Griffiths
1902/03
Nov 22 1R Birkenhead A 2-2 Riley (2)
Dec 20 1Rr Birkenhead H 3-1 Delaney (3)
Jan 17 2R Tranmere Rovers H 1-2 Kelly
(Tranmere played ineligible player - Chester went through to next round)
Feb 14 3R Helsby A 3-1 Riley, Kelly, Delaney
Mar 28 SF Sale Holmfield H 1-1 Unknown
Apr 4 SFr Sale Holmfield A 1-3 Kelly
1903/04
Jan 16 2R Wirral Railway H 7-0 Bell (2), Smith, Jones, Delaney, Hall, Matthews
Feb 13 3R Witton Albion H 1-0 T Lipsham
Mar 12 SF Tranmere Rovers A 2-2 Bell, J Lipsham
Mar 30 SFr Tranmere Rovers H 3-2 Delaney (2),T Lipsham
Apr 16 F Nantwich N 1-1 Delaney
(Played at Northwich)
Apr 23 Fr Nantwich N 2-1 Barnes (og), Delaney
(Played at Crewe)
1904/05
Feb 11 3R Sale Holmfield H 3-1 Matthews (2), Delaney
Mar 4 4R Tranmere Rovers A 4-0 Matthews (2), J Lipsham (2)
Mar 11 SF Congleton A 0-0
Mar 25 SFr Congleton H 5-1 Evans, Dawson, J Lipsham, Case, Jones

Apr 8 F Altrincham N 1-2 J Lipsham
(Played at Northwich)
1905/06
Jan 6 3R Congleton A 0-0
Jan 13 3Rr Congleton H 0-0
Feb 3 3R2r Congleton N 3-0 J Jones (3)
(Played at Northwich)
Feb 10 4R Crewe Alex. H 2-3 H Jones, J Jones
1906/07
Jan 5 3R Port Sunlight A 2-3 W Jones, Evans
1907/08
Jan 4 3R Birkenhead N.E. H 4-0 Lees, Freeman (2), Jones
Feb 1 4R Lostock Gralam H 4-1 Freeman (3), Jones
Mar 7 SF Hyde N 5-1 Freeman, Lipsham, Lees(2), Jones
(Played at Northwich)
Apr 11 F Altrincham N 4-2 Freeman, Jones, Lees (2)
(Played at Crewe)
1908/09
Jan 2 3R Helsby H 5-0 Freeman (2),Lappin (2), Bentley
Jan 30 4R Crewe Alex. H 1-1 Lappin
Feb 27 4Rr Crewe Alex. A 1-0 Freeman
Mar 13 SF Macclesfield N 2-0 Bentley (2)
(Played at Crewe)
Apr 10 F Northwich Vics. N 1-1 Matthews
(Played at Crewe)
Apr 24 Fr Northwich Vics. N 3-0 Lappin (2), Jones
(Played at Crewe)
1909/10
Jan 1 3R Tranmere Rovers A 2-1 Winnington, Rainford
Feb 26 4R Stockport County H 0-0
4Rr Stockport County A 1-3 Rainford
1910/11
Dec 31 1R Tranmere Rovers H 4-1 Riley (2), Chetwood (2)
Jan 28 2R Crewe Alex. H 1-0 Riley
Mar 4 SF Altrincham N 2-0 Matthews, Holmes
(Played at Northwich)
Apr 8 F Macclesfield N 0-1
(Played at Crewe)
1911/12
Jan 20 1R Witton Albion A 1-1 Jordan
1Rr Witton Albion H (Witton scratched)
Feb 24 2R Crewe Alex. A 1-3 Jordan
1912/13
Jan 18 1R Crewe Alex. A 2-2 Jordan, Lipsham
Feb 5 1Rr Crewe Alex. H 1-2 Sheargold
1913/14
Jan 10 1R Macclesfield A 3-2 McCarthy (2), Cook
Feb 7 2R Stalybridge Celtic A 0-5
1914/15
Jan 9 1R Crewe Alex. H 1-2 Wood
1919/20
Jan 3 1R Sandbach Ramblers A 4-2 Jenkins (3), Lewis
Feb 10 2R Northwich Vics. H 2-2 Lewis, Smith
Mar 6 2Rr Northwich Vlcs A 3-2 Lewis, Jenkins, Roberts
Mar 13 SF Crichton's Ath. H 2-3 Lewis (2)
1920/21
Jan 15 1R Kinderton H 2-0 Hughes, Murray
Feb 12 2R Congleton A 0-1
1921/22

Jan 14 Q4 Runcorn A 2-1 Timmis, Phoenix
Feb 11 1R Stalybridge Celtic H 1-3 Pimlott
1922/23
Dec16 1R Sale Holmfield H 3-1 Howarth, Pryde, Donnachie
Jan 6 2R Barnton Victoria H 2-0 Rothwell, Pryde
Feb 10 3r Altrincham H 1-2 Nuttall

1923/24
Dec 15 1R Northwich Vics A 2-1 Lydiate,McGivney
Jan 12 2R Runcom H 0-0
Jan 16 2Rr Runcom A 1-0 Kearslake
Feb 9 3R Nantwich A 0-1
1924/25
Dec 20 1R Stalybridge Celtic A 2-1 J. Shaw, Healey
Jan 21 2R Northern Nomads H 5-2 Lightburn (2), Ankers (2), J Shaw
Feb 7 3R Crewe Alex. Res. H 2-2 Ankers, J Johnson
Feb 18 3Rr Crewe Alex. Res. A 0-3
1925/26
Dec 19 1R Northern Nomads H 3-3 Bingham (2), Peters
Dec 30 1Rr Northern Nomads H 9-1 Parkin(4), Bingham(2), Rothwell, Peters, Robertson(og)
Jan 23 2R Middlewich H 2-3 Rothwell, Bingham
1926/27
Dec 11 1R Winnington Park H 6-0 Yearsley (2), Bingham (3), Peters
Jan 22 2R Frodsham H 9-1 Hughes(4), Ankers(2), Peters, Rothwell, Tootle
Feb 19 3R Macclesfield H 2-3 Peters, Bingham
1927/28
Dec 10 1R Hyde United H 2-2 Boardman, Yearsley
Dec 15 1Rr Hyde United A 4-1 Yearsley (3), Boardman
Jan 7 2R Sandbach A 3-0 Yearsley, Etherington, Peters
Feb 11 3R Ashton Bros. H 3-1 Pollock, Yearsley, Peters
Mar 10 SF Witton Albion N 0-1
(Played at Crewe)
1928/29
Dec 8 1R Runcom A 2-2 Ankers (2)
Dec 12 1Rr Runcom H 4-1 Peters, Birtles (2), Ankers
Jan 12 2R Sandbach H 2-1 Ankers, Schofield
Mar 2 SF Tranmere Rovers N 3-2 Ramage (2),Birtles
(Played at Runcom)
Apr 13 F Northwich Vics. N 0-2
(Played at Crewe)
1929/30
Jan 4 1R Ellesmere Port T. H 6-2 Broome(2),Bradbury(2),Jenkins,Broma
Feb 1 2R Shell Mex H 5-3 Hopkins (2), Broome (?), Jenkins
Feb 22 3R Winsford United A 2-4 Bromage (2)
1930/31
Jan 7 1R Stalyhridge Celtic H 3-1 Clifford (2), Gale
Jan 31 2R Winsford United H 4-2 Gale (3), Wilkinson (og)
Feb 21 3R Nantwich H 3-0 Gale (3)
Mar 14 SF Congleton N 8-1 Gale (6), Burgess, Cresswell
(Played at Witton)
Apr 11 F Crewe Alex. N 6-1 Gale (4), Irvine, Dickie
(Played at Northwich)

## CHESHIRE SENIOR MEDALS

1926/27
Sep 15 SF Tranmere Rovers H 1-0 Duckworth
May 14 F Stockport County H 3-0 Bingham (2), Yearsley
1927/28
Sep 14 SF Stockport County A 1-5 Peters
1928/29
Sep12 SF Tranmere Rovers H 2-2 Burley (2)
Sep 20 SFr Tranmere Rovers A 1-4 Birtles
1931/32
Sep 23 SF Stockport County H 4-1 Jennings (2), Hedley (2)
Apr 21 F Tranmere Rovers A 0-2

## FLINTSHIRE & DENBIGHSHIRE CUP

1902/03
Nov 1 1R Colwyn Bay H 7-1 Delaney (3), Dryland (2), Kelly (2)
No record of any further matches in this competition

## FLINTSHIRE CHARITY CUP

1920/21
Mar 9 1R Buckley H 0-1

## ANCASHIRE CUP

945/46

ug 28 PR1L Wrexham H 2-2 Steele, Astbury
ep 5 PR2L Wrexham A 3-2 Astbury, Black, Bainbridge
ep 12 1R1L Crewe Alex. H 5-1 Dewar, Black (3), Astbury
ep 19 1R2L Crewe Alex. A 1-3 Steele
lar 11 2R1L Burnley A 1-2 Black
lar 16 2R2L Burnley H 0-2

946/47

)ct16 1R1L Rochdale H 2-0 Yates, Arthur
)ct 22 1R2L Rochdale A 1-0 Arthur
)ec 4 2R1L Bolton WanderersH 1-2 McNeil
)ec 11 2R2L Bolton WanderersA 0-3

947/48

)ct 23 1R Blackburn Rovers A 1-2 Yates

948/49

iep 22 1R Everton H 1-1 Best
iep 29 1Rr Everton A 0-4

1949/50

)ct 26 1R Blackburn Rovers H 3-0 Burgess, Davies, Coffin
Nov 29 2R Burnley A 4-4 Burgess (2), Jones, Foulkes
an 18 2Rr Burnley H 3-4 Burgess, Jackson, Astbury

1950/51

iep 26 1R Southport A 1-1 Morement
)ct 4 1Rr Southport H 0-2

1951/52

Oct 17 1R Oldham Athletic H 2-0 Yates, Windle
Mar 19 2R Blackburn Rovers A 2-3 Travis (2)

1952/53

Oct15 1R Barrow H 2-2 Travis (2)
Oct 23 1Rr Barrow A 1-0 Richardson
Mar 4 2R Accrington Stanley H 3-1 Coffin, Bullock, Morement
Apr 8 SF Manchester United H 3-2 Travis (3)
May 6 F Manchester City H 1-5 Travis

1953/54

Nov 4 1R Manchester United H 1-0 Molyneux
Mar 31 2R Liverpool A 2-4 Basford, Travis

1954/55

Oct 27 1R Liverpool A 0-3

1955/56

Oct 17 1R Accrington Stanley A 3-2 Pye, Collins, Allman
Mar 25 2R Preston North End A 0-2

1956/57

Nov 7 1R Rochdale A 3-0 Fields (2), Bullock
Apr 1 2R Accrington Stanley A 1-0 Bullock
May 1 SF Liverpool H 2-1 Foulkes, Fields
Oct 2 F Burnley H 1-0 Fields

1957/58

Feb 10 1R Accrington Stanley A 0-3

1958/59

Nov 19 1R Everton H 1-4 Hughes

1959/60

Oct 19 1R Blackpool A 2-2 Pimlott, Richards
Oct 28 1Rr Blackpool H 2-0 Foulkes, Richards
Jan 13 2R Burnley H 1-3 Hughes

1960/61

Oct 26 1R Blackburn Rovers H 1-4 Davies

1961/62

Oct 23 1R Liverpool A 0-4

1962/63

Oct 24 1R Blackburn Rovers H 3-2 Pritchard (3)
Nov 28 2R Manchester United H 0-5

1963/64

Nov 27 1R Rochdale H 2-0 Humes, Lee
Jan 15 2R Manchester City H 0-0
Jan 22 2Rr Manchester City A 0-3

1964/65

Oct 28 1R Burnley H 0-0
Dec15 1Rr Burnley A 1-8 Morris

1965/66

Nov 17 1R Oldham Athletic A 3-2 Chadwick (2), Corbishley
Feb 23 2R Rochdale H 1-3 L Jones

## LIVERPOOL SENIOR CUP

1892/93

Mar 22 1R Liverpool A 0-4

1893/94

Mar 31 1R Aintree Church H 3-1 Astbury, Grewcock (2)
Apr 16 SF Everton Res. N 1-5 Unknown
(Played at Birkenhead)

1894/95

Mar 18 1R Liverpool A 2-5 Spencer, Dunlop (og)

1895/96

SF Liverpool (Liverpool scratched)
Mar 28 F Everton Res. A 0-4

1901/02

Mar 12 1R Liverpool Police H 6-1 Griffiths (3), Rogers (2), Miller
Mar 31 2R Skelmersdale H 2-4 Delaney, Lipsham

## ABANDONED GAMES

Nov 14 1896 Wrexham A 0-2 (Comb. 45 mins rain)
Oct 26 1912 Walkden C. A 1-0 Jordan (Lancs. Comb. 45 mins rain)
Jan 22 1913 Crewe Alex. H 1-1 Matthews (CSC1Rr 90 mins bad light)
Dec 25 1923 Ellesmere Port C. H 1-0 Kearslake (CCL 45 mins snow)
Nov 27 1926 Altrincham A 1-4 Wagstaffe (CCL 85 mins fog)
Mar 15 1930 Colwyn Bay H 2-2 OG, Peters (WC 4Rr 40 mins snow)
Jan 3 1931 Stalybridge Celtic H 1-0 Gale (CCL 10 mins fog)
Mar 11 1931 New Brighton H 0-0 (WC 5Rr 100 mins bad light)
Jan 19 1933 Doncaster R. A 0-1 (League 41 mins snow/fog)
Feb 27 1937 Gateshead H 1-0 Gale (League 45 mins rain/snow)
Mar 5 1949 Tranmere R. A 1-0 Davies (League 45 mins blizzard)
May 11 1966 Luton Town H 0-2 (League 47 mins rain)
Oct 26 1976 Gillingham H 2-1 Delgado,Owen (League 52 mins fog)
Sep 2 1981 Plymouth A. H 2-2 Ludlam(2) (LC1R1L 78 mins broken goalpost)
Feb 23 1982 Carlisle U. H 1-1 Oakes (League 56 mins fog)
Jan 14 1992 Rotherham U. A 0-2 (Autoglass 1R 66 mins fog)
Jan 11 2003 Worksop T. H 0-0 (FA Trophy 3 26 mins frozen pitch)
Mar 29 2008 Stockport C. H 0-0 (League 59 mins rain)
Nov 28 2009 Eastbourne B. H 3-2 Barry, Ellams, Chadwick (Conference 72 mins pitch invasion)

# CHESTER CITY PLAYERS WHO'S WHO 1931/32 TO 1999/00 AND 2004/05 TO 2008/09

| Player | | Date of Birth | Place of Birth | First Season | Last Season | Previous Club | Next Club | League Apps | League G'ls | FA Cup Apps | FA Cup G'ls | League Cup Apps | League Cup G'ls | Others Apps | Others G'ls |
|---|---|---|---|---|---|---|---|---|---|---|---|---|---|---|---|
| ABEL | Graham | 17/09/60 | Runcorn | 1985/86 | 1992/93 | Northwich Vic. | Crewe Alexandra | 287/9 | 30 | 22 | 2 | 18 | 1 | 23/1 | 0 |
| ADAMS | Frank | 08/02/33 | Liverpool | 1963/64 | 1963/64 | Bury | Tranmere Rovers | 8 | 0 | 0 | 0 | 2 | 0 | 0 | 0 |
| AGOGO | Manuel | 01/08/79 | Accra, Ghana | 1999/00 | 1999/00 | Sheff. Wed. (loan) | | 10 | 6 | 0 | 0 | 0 | 0 | 0 | 0 |
| AISTON | Sam | 21/11/76 | Newcastle | 1996/97 | 1996/97 | Sunderland (loan) | | 25 | 0 | 0 | 0 | 0 | 0 | 3 | 0 |
| | | | | 1998/99 | 1998/99 | Sunderland (loan) | | | | | | | | | |
| ALBISTON | Arthur | 14/07/57 | Edinburgh | 1991/92 | 1992/93 | Dundee | Molde (Norway) | 67/1 | 0 | 2 | 0 | 4 | 0 | 3 | 0 |
| ALBRIGHTON | Mark | 06/03/76 | Nuneaton | 2005/06 | 2005/06 | Doncaster R (loan) | | 9 | 0 | 0 | 0 | 0 | 0 | 0 | 0 |
| ALDERSON | Tom | 01/04/09 | West Auckland | 1936/37 | 1937/38 | Darlington | Darlington | 44 | 4 | 2 | 1 | 0 | 0 | 6 | 2 |
| ALLEN | Andy | 04/09/74 | Liverpool | 1991/92 | 1991/92 | Trainee | Colwyn Bay | 0/1 | 0 | 0 | 0 | 0 | 0 | 0 | 0 |
| ALLEN | Graham | 08/04/77 | Bolton | 2006/07 | 2006/07 | Rushden & D. | Bradford PA | 2/1 | 0 | 0 | 0 | 0 | 0 | 0 | 0 |
| ALLEN | John | 14/11/64 | Mancot | 1981/82 | 1983/84 | Apprentice | Mansfield Town | 67/12 | 5 | 2 | 0 | 4 | 0 | 3 | 0 |
| ALLMAN | George | 23/07/30 | Stockport | 1955/56 | 1956/57 | Holywell Town | Ashton United | 49 | 13 | 2 | 0 | 0 | 0 | 2 | 0 |
| ALSFORD | Julian | 24/12/72 | Poole | 1994/95 | 1997/98 | Watford | Dundee United | 145/6 | 7 | 8 | 1 | 8/1 | 0 | 8 | 0 |
| | | | | 1998/99 | 1998/99 | Dundee United | Dorchester Town | | | | | | | | |
| ANACLET | Eddie | 31/08/85 | Arusha, Tanzania | 2004/05 | 2004/05 | Southampt'n(loan) | | 0 | 0 | 0/1 | 0 | 0 | 0 | 0 | 0 |
| ANDERSON | Jimmy | 25/12/32 | Glasgow | 1957/58 | 1959/60 | Bristol Rovers | Rhyl | 62 | 0 | 3 | 0 | 0 | 0 | 6 | 0 |
| ANDERSON | John | 05/04/28 | Glasgow | 1960/61 | 1960/61 | Rochdale | Wrexham | 17 | 2 | 0 | 0 | 1 | 0 | 2 | 0 |
| ANDERSON | John | | | 1980/81 | 1980/81 | Everton | Northwich Vic. | 0 | 0 | 0 | 0 | 1 | 0 | 0 | 0 |
| ANDERSON | Ted | 17/07/11 | Newcastle | 1935/36 | 1936/37 | West Ham United | Tranmere Rovers | 23 | 0 | 0 | 0 | 0 | 0 | 2 | 0 |
| ANTHROBUS | Steve | 10/11/68 | Lewisham | 1994/95 | 1994/95 | Wimbledon (loan) | | 7 | 0 | 0 | 0 | 0 | 0 | 0 | 0 |
| APPLEBY | Jim | 15/06/34 | Shotton Colliery | 1962/63 | 1962/63 | Southport | Horden C. W. | 1 | 0 | 0 | 0 | 0 | 0 | 0 | 0 |
| ARMES | Sammy | 30/03/08 | New Seaham | 1932/33 | 1933/34 | Carlisle United | Blackpool | 31 | 13 | 4 | 3 | 0 | 0 | 0 | 0 |
| ARTELL | Dave | 22/11/80 | Rotherham | 2005/06 | 2006/07 | Mansfield Town | Morecambe | 76/4 | 3 | 9 | 0 | 1 | 0 | 1 | 0 |
| ARTHUR | Jackie | 14/12/17 | Edenfield | 1946/47 | 1946/47 | Everton | Rochdale | 24 | 3 | 2 | 0 | 0 | 0 | 1 | 0 |
| ASAMOAH | Derek | 01/05/81 | Ghana | 2005/06 | 2005/06 | Lincoln City (loan) | | 14/3 | 8 | 0 | 0 | 0 | 0 | 0 | 0 |
| ASHFIELD | George | 07/04/34 | Manchester | 1958/59 | 1959/60 | Aston Villa | Rhyl | 5 | 0 | 0 | 0 | 0 | 0 | 1 | 0 |
| ASHWORTH | Barry | 18/08/42 | Stockport | 1967/68 | 1969/70 | Tranmere Rovers | Altrincham | 116/3 | 12 | 5 | 0 | 5 | 1 | 10 | 1 |
| ASHWORTH | Joe | 06/01/43 | Huddersfield | 1971/72 | 1971/72 | Rochdale | Stockport Co. | 5 | 0 | 0 | 0 | 0 | 0 | 1 | 0 |
| ASTBURY | Mick | 22/01/64 | Kippax | 1987/88 | 1987/88 | Darlington | Chesterfield | 5 | 0 | 0 | 0 | 0 | 0 | 0 | 0 |
| ASTBURY | Tommy | 09/02/20 | Buckley | 1946/47 | 1954/55 | Mold Alexandra | Retired | 303 | 38 | 15 | 2 | 0 | 0 | 22 | 5 |
| ATIENO | Taiwo | 06/08/85 | Brixton | 2004/05 | 2004/05 | Walsall (loan) | | 3/1 | 1 | 0 | 0 | 0 | 0 | 0 | 0 |
| ATKINSON | Josh | 28/03/02 | Blackpool | 1931/32 | 1931/32 | Barnsley | Fleetwood Town | 7 | 0 | 0 | 0 | 0 | 0 | 0 | 0 |
| AUNGER | Geoff | 04/02/68 | Red Deer, Canada | 1994/95 | 1994/95 | Luton Town | Vancouver 86(Can) | 1/4 | 0 | 0 | 0 | 0 | 0 | 0 | 0 |
| BADES | Brian | 03/07/39 | Blackburn | 1963/64 | 1963/64 | Stockport Co. | Runcorn | 15 | 1 | 2 | 0 | 0 | 0 | 0 | 0 |
| BAGNALL | John | 23/11/73 | Southport | 1993/94 | 1993/94 | Preston N. E. | Wigan Athletic | 0 | 0 | 0 | 0 | 0 | 0 | 1 | 0 |
| BAILEY | Ian | | | 1985/86 | 1985/86 | Juniors | | 0 | 0 | 0 | 0 | 0 | 0 | 1/1 | 0 |
| BANKS | Jason | 16/11/68 | Farnworth | 1987/88 | 1987/88 | Wigan Athletic | Atherton Collieries | 1/1 | 0 | 1 | 0 | 0 | 0 | 0 | 0 |
| BARBER | Fred | 26/08/63 | Ferryhill | 1990/91 | 1990/91 | Walsall (loan) | | 8 | 0 | 0 | 0 | 0 | 0 | 0 | 0 |
| BARLOW | Brett | 06/09/77 | | 1995/96 | 1995/96 | Trainee | Barry Town | 0 | 0 | 0 | 0 | 0/1 | 0 | 0 | 0 |
| BARRETT | Earl | 28/04/67 | Rochdale | 1985/86 | 1985/86 | Man City (loan) | | 12 | 0 | 0 | 0 | 0 | 0 | 0 | 0 |
| BARRETT | Tom | 16/03/34 | Salford | 1960/61 | 1960/61 | Plymouth Argyle | Oldham Athletic | 39 | 2 | 1 | 0 | 2 | 0 | 2 | 0 |
| BARROW | Graham | 13/06/54 | Chorley | 1986/87 | 1993/94 | Wigan Athletic | Wigan (Manager) | 244/4 | 18 | 17/1 | 1 | 14 | 2 | 18 | 2 |
| BARRY | Anthony | 29/05/86 | Liverpool | 2008/09 | 2009/10 | Yeovil Town | Fleetwood Town | 38/5 | 1 | 1 | 0 | 1 | 0 | 1 | 0 |
| BARTON | Reg | 04/03/42 | Chester | 1961/62 | 1964/65 | Juniors | Nantlle Vale | 14 | 0 | 0 | 0 | 0 | 0 | 2 | 0 |
| BASFORD | Jock | 24/07/25 | Crewe | 1953/54 | 1953/54 | Crewe Alexandra | Guildford City | 10 | 1 | 0 | 0 | 0 | 0 | 3 | 1 |
| BAYLISS | David | 08/06/76 | Liverpool | 2004/05 | 2004/05 | Luton Town (loan) | | 9 | 0 | 1 | 0 | 0 | 0 | 0 | 0 |
| BEAUMONT | Alan | 09/01/27 | Liverpool | 1948/49 | 1948/49 | South Liverpool | New Brighton | 5 | 0 | 0 | 0 | 0 | 0 | 0 | 0 |
| BECKETT | Luke | 25/11/76 | Sheffield | 1998/99 | 1999/00 | Barnsley | Chesterfield | 70/4 | 25 | 4 | 2 | 5 | 5 | 1 | 0 |
| BELL | Billy | 09/12/06 | Prestwich | 1932/33 | 1934/35 | Portsmouth | | 46 | 2 | 7 | 0 | 0 | 0 | 4 | 0 |
| BELLE | Cortez | 27/08/83 | Coventry | 2004/05 | 2004/05 | Merthyr Tydfil | Newport County | 17/5 | 1 | 1/1 | 1 | 1 | 0 | 0 | 0 |
| BELLETT | Wally | 14/11/33 | Stratford | 1961/62 | 1961/62 | Leyton Orient | Wrexham | 12 | 1 | 0 | 0 | 0 | 0 | 1 | 0 |
| BENJAMIN | Ian | 11/12/61 | Nottingham | 1988/89 | 1988/89 | Cambridge Utd | Exeter City | 18/4 | 2 | 2 | 1 | 2 | 0 | 2 | 1 |
| BENNETT | Dean | 12/12/77 | Wolverhampton | 2006/07 | 2006/07 | Wrexham | Kidderminster H. | 27/5 | 1 | 2/2 | 0 | 0 | 0 | 2 | 0 |
| BENNETT | Fred | 02/10/06 | Bristol | 1931/32 | 1935/36 | Bristol Rovers | Nantwich | 158 | 1 | 12 | 1 | 0 | 0 | 21 | 0 |
| BENNETT | Gary | 20/09/62 | Kirkby | 1985/86 | 1988/89 | Wigan Athletic | Southend United | 222/32 | 63 | 15/1 | 6 | 17/5 | 3 | 14/1 | 6 |
| | | | | 1989/90 | 1991/92 | Southend United | Wrexham | | | | | | | | |
| | | | | 1997/98 | 1998/99 | Wrexham | Retired | | | | | | | | |
| BENNETT | John | 27/03/46 | Liverpool | 1966/67 | 1968/69 | Liverpool | Macclesfield T. | 72/4 | 0 | 3/1 | 0 | 3/1 | 0 | 8 | 2 |
| BENNION | Stan | 09/02/38 | Blacon | 1963/64 | 1964/65 | Wrexham | New Brighton | 20 | 3 | 0 | 0 | 1 | 0 | 1 | 0 |
| BERRY | Dave | 01/06/45 | Newton-Le-Willows | 1964/65 | 1966/67 | Blackpool | Macclesfield T. | 0/1 | 0 | 0 | 0 | 0 | 0 | 1 | 0 |
| BERRY | Paul | 06/12/78 | Warrington | 1999/00 | 2001/02 | Warrington Town | Leek Town | 0/9 | 1 | 0/1 | 0 | 0/2 | 0 | 0 | 0 |
| BERTOS | Leo | 20/12/81 | Wellington (NZ) | 2005/06 | 2005/06 | Rochdale | York City | 2/3 | 0 | 0 | 0 | 0/1 | 0 | 1 | 0 |
| BERTSCHIN | Keith | 25/08/56 | Enfield | 1990/91 | 1990/91 | Walsall | Aldershot | 14/5 | 0 | 3 | 1 | 0 | 0 | 0 | 0 |
| BEST | Tommy | 23/12/20 | Milford Haven | 1947/48 | 1948/49 | Milford Haven Utd | Cardiff City | 40 | 14 | 1 | 0 | 0 | 0 | 1 | 0 |

| Player | | Date of Birth | Place of Birth | First Season | Last Season | Previous Club | Next Club | League Apps | League G'ls | FA Cup Apps | FA Cup G'ls | League Cup Apps | League Cup G'ls | Others Apps | Others G'ls |
|---|---|---|---|---|---|---|---|---|---|---|---|---|---|---|---|
| BETTERIDGE | R. Mike | 11/08/24 | Alcester | 1953/54 | 1953/54 | Swindon Town | Leek Town | 8 | 1 | 0 | 0 | 0 | 0 | 1 | 0 |
| BEYNON | David | 1914 | New Tredegar | 1937/38 | 1938/39 | Watford | Killed in war | 13 | 0 | 0 | 0 | 0 | 0 | 3 | 0 |
| BIGGINS | Brian | 19/05/40 | Ellesmere Port | 1957/58 | 1959/60 | Juniors | Pwllheli | 5 | 0 | 0 | 0 | 0 | 0 | 3 | 0 |
| BINGHAM | John | 23/09/49 | Ripley | 1971/72 | 1971/72 | Mansfield T. (loan) | | 7 | 1 | 0 | 0 | 0 | 0 | 0 | 0 |
| BIRCH | Trevor | 16/02/58 | Ormskirk | 1980/81 | 1980/81 | Shrewsbury Town | Marine | 30/1 | 0 | 1 | 1 | 2 | 0 | 0 | 0 |
| BIRKS | Graham | 25/01/42 | Sheffield | 1969/70 | 1971/72 | Southend United | Port Elizabeth(SA) | 71/2 | 0 | 11 | 0 | 3 | 0 | 5 | 0 |
| BISHOP | Eddie | 28/11/62 | Liverpool | 1990/91 | 1995/96 | Tranmere Rovers | Northwich Vic. | 97/18 | 26 | 3/3 | 0 | 14 | 4 | 4/2 | 0 |
| BLACKBURN | Chris | 02/08/82 | Crewe | 1999/00 | 2002/03 | Trainee | Nevada Won. (USA) | 0/1 | 0 | 0 | 0 | 0 | 0 | 0 | 0 |
| BLACKWELL | Paul | 13/01/63 | Mancot | 1981/82 | 1984/85 | Local | Rhyl | 89/5 | 3 | 2/1 | 0 | 2/1 | 0 | 2 | 0 |
| BLACKWOOD | Michael | 30/09/79 | Birmingham | 1999/00 | 1999/00 | Aston Villa (loan) | | 9 | 2 | 0 | 0 | 0 | 0 | 0 | 0 |
| BLEARS | Brian | 18/11/33 | Prestatyn | 1954/55 | 1955/56 | Everton | Northwich Vic. | 2 | 0 | 0 | 0 | 0 | 0 | 0 | 0 |
| BLEASE | Rory | 16/08/60 | Bebington | 1984/85 | 1984/85 | Caernarfon Town | Northwich Vic. | 4 | 0 | 0 | 0 | 0 | 0 | 0 | 0 |
| BLUNDELL | Gregg | 03/10/77 | Liverpool | 2005/06 | 2006/07 | Doncaster Rovers | Darlington | 44/13 | 13 | 5/1 | 1 | 1/1 | 0 | 2 | 2 |
| BOLLAND | Phil | 26/08/76 | Liverpool | 2001/02 | 2005/06 | Oxford United | Peterborough U. | 79/7 | 3 | 6/1 | 0 | 2 | 0 | 7 | 1 |
| | | | | 2006/07 | 2007/08 | Peterborough U. | Wrexham | | | | | | | | |
| BOOTH | Grenville | 02/04/25 | Chester | 1948/49 | 1949/50 | Juniors | Colwyn Bay | 8 | 0 | 1 | 0 | 0 | 0 | 0 | 0 |
| BOOTH | Robbie | 30/12/85 | Liverpool | 2004/05 | 2004/05 | Trainee | Southport | 7/4 | 1 | 1/1 | 0 | 0 | 0 | 2/1 | 0 |
| BRADBURY | Terry | 15/11/39 | Paddington | 1969/70 | 1970/71 | Wrexham | Weymouth | 90 | 2 | 10 | 0 | 4 | 0 | 11 | 0 |
| BRADLEY | Noel | 17/12/57 | Manchester | 1982/83 | 1982/83 | Bury | Mossley | 27/4 | 0 | 2 | 0 | 2 | 0 | 5 | 0 |
| BRAMHALL | John | 20/11/56 | Warrington | 1985/86 | 1985/86 | Bury (loan) | | 4 | 0 | 0 | 0 | 0 | 0 | 0 | 0 |
| BRANCH | Michael | 18/10/78 | Liverpool | 2004/05 | 2005/06 | Bradford City | Halifax Town | 54/6 | 16 | 3 | 3 | 2 | 0 | 0/1 | 0 |
| BRANDON | Ken | 08/02/34 | Birmingham | 1953/54 | 1955/56 | Swindon Town | Leicester City | 39 | 7 | 2 | 0 | 0 | 0 | 6 | 4 |
| BRENCHLEY | Scott | 22/11/76 | Hull | 1995/96 | 1995/96 | Liverpool | Witton Albion | 0 | 0 | 0 | 0 | 0/1 | 0 | 0 | 0 |
| BRETT | David | 08/04/61 | Chester | 1983/84 | 1985/86 | Colwyn Bay | Colwyn Bay | 52/15 | 6 | 2 | 0 | 1/1 | 0 | 4/2 | 1 |
| BRIEN | Tony | 10/02/69 | Dublin | 1995/96 | 1995/96 | W.B.A. (loan) | | 8 | 0 | 0 | 0 | 0 | 0 | 0 | 0 |
| BRIGHTWELL | David | 07/01/71 | Lutterworth | 1990/91 | 1990/91 | Man City (loan) | | 6 | 0 | 0 | 0 | 0 | 0 | 0 | 0 |
| BRODIE | Eric | 08/11/40 | Blairgowrie | 1968/69 | 1969/70 | Shrewsbury Town | Tranmere Rovers | 43/1 | 4 | 2 | 0 | 5 | 0 | 2 | 0 |
| BROOKFIELD | Ryan | 10/05/87 | Liverpool | 2005/06 | 2005/06 | Trainee | Colwyn Bay | 0/1 | 0 | 0 | 0 | 0 | 0 | 0 | 0 |
| BROUGHTON | Drewe | 25/10/78 | Hitchin | 2006/07 | 2006/07 | Rushden & D. | MK Dons | 9/5 | 2 | 0 | 0 | 1 | 0 | 0 | 0 |
| BROWN | Bill | 25/11/38 | Clydebank | 1960/61 | 1960/61 | Accrington S. | Morton | 41 | 0 | 0 | 0 | 2 | 0 | 2 | 0 |
| BROWN | Greg | 31/07/78 | Manchester | 1995/96 | 1996/97 | Trainee | Macclesfield T. | 1/3 | 0 | 0/1 | 0 | 0 | 0 | 0/1 | 0 |
| BROWN | Joe | 07/05/20 | Bebington | 1946/47 | 1947/48 | Port Sunlight | Runcorn | 15 | 2 | 2 | 0 | 0 | 0 | 1 | 1 |
| BROWN | Michael | 27/02/85 | Preston | 2004/05 | 2004/05 | Preston NE (loan) | | 11/7 | 0 | 1 | 0 | 0 | 0 | 0 | 0 |
| BROWN | Owen | 04/09/60 | Liverpool | 1984/85 | 1984/85 | Tranmere Rovers | Hyde United | 9/1 | 3 | 0 | 0 | 1 | 0 | 0 | 0 |
| BROWN | Wayne | 14/01/77 | Southampton | 1996/97 | 2004/05 | Weston Super Mare | Hereford United | 107 | 0 | 7 | 0 | 8 | 0 | 3 | 0 |
| BROWNLIE | Royce | 28/01/80 | Coffs Harb'r - Aus | 2006/07 | 2006/07 | Swindon T. (loan) | | 3/1 | 0 | 0 | 0 | 0 | 0 | 0 | 0 |
| BRYAN | Ernie | 06/06/26 | Hawarden | 1948/49 | 1948/49 | Juniors | Colwyn Bay | 1 | 0 | 0 | 0 | 0 | 0 | 0 | 0 |
| BULLOCK | Norman | 26/03/32 | Nuneaton | 1952/53 | 1959/60 | Aston Villa | Rhyl | 187 | 41 | 9 | 1 | 0 | 0 | 15 | 5 |
| BULMER | Peter | 31/08/65 | Liverpool | 1982/83 | 1984/85 | Apprentice | Rhyl | 56/15 | 2 | 1 | 0 | 2/2 | 0 | 2 | 0 |
| BURDEN | Tommy | 21/02/24 | Andover | 1946/47 | 1947/48 | Wolves | Leeds United | 82 | 40 | 7 | 4 | 0 | 0 | 3 | 3 |
| BURGESS | Albert | 21/09/19 | Birkenhead | 1948/49 | 1951/52 | Bolton Wanderers | Crystal Palace | 111 | 64 | 5 | 1 | 0 | 0 | 9 | 5 |
| BURKE | Denis | 05/05/63 | Birmingham | 1983/84 | 1983/84 | Birmingham City | Walsall | 0 | 0 | 0 | 0 | 0 | 0 | 1 | 0 |
| BURKE | John | 10/08/62 | Motherwell | 1983/84 | 1983/84 | Exeter City | Motherwell | 3 | 0 | 0 | 0 | 0 | 0 | 0 | 0 |
| BURKE | John J. | 28/06/11 | Dublin | 1931/32 | 1935/36 | Shelbourne | Millwall | 91 | 0 | 6 | 0 | 0 | 0 | 23 | 0 |
| BURNHAM | Jason | 08/05/73 | Mansfield | 1994/95 | 1995/96 | Northampton T. | Worcester City | 62/2 | 1 | 2 | 0 | 6 | 0 | 4 | 0 |
| BURNS | David | 12/11/58 | Ellesmere Port | 1976/77 | 1981/82 | Apprentice | Scarborough | 66/12 | 2 | 2 | 0 | 2 | 0 | 6 | 2 |
| BUTCHER | John | 27/05/56 | Newcastle | 1984/85 | 1986/87 | Oxford United | Altrincham | 84 | 0 | 4 | 0 | 5 | 0 | 2 | 0 |
| BUTCHER | Reg | 13/02/16 | Liverpool | 1938/39 | 1949/50 | Liverpool | Retired | 155 | 1 | 16 | 0 | 0 | 0 | 8 | 0 |
| BUTLER | Barry | 04/06/62 | Farnworth | 1985/86 | 1992/93 | Atherton L. R. | Barrow | 255/13 | 15 | 21 | 1 | 11/2 | 0 | 25/1 | 0 |
| BUTLER | Herbert | 11/07/06 | Atherton | 1932/33 | 1932/33 | Crystal Palace | Crewe Alexandra | 2 | 1 | 0 | 0 | 0 | 0 | 1 | 1 |
| BUTLER | John | 10/03/37 | Birmingham | 1962/63 | 1967/68 | Notts County | Retired | 220/2 | 0 | 10 | 0 | 11 | 0 | 19 | 0 |
| BUTLER | Paul | 02/11/72 | Manchester | 2007/08 | 2008/09 | MK Dons | Retired | 36 | 2 | 1 | 0 | 2 | 0 | 1 | 0 |
| CALDWELL | Tony | 21/03/58 | Salford | 1987/88 | 1987/88 | Bristol City (loan) | | 4 | 0 | 0 | 0 | 0 | 0 | 0 | 0 |
| CAMDEN | Chris | 28/05/63 | Birkenhead | 1983/84 | 1983/84 | Tranmere Rovers | Oswestry Town | 9 | 2 | 1 | 0 | 0 | 0 | 0 | 0 |
| CAME | Mark | 14/09/61 | Exeter | 1992/93 | 1993/94 | Bolton Wanderers | Exeter City | 47 | 1 | 3 | 0 | 2 | 0 | 6 | 1 |
| CAPPER | Jack | 23/07/31 | Wrexham | 1959/60 | 1960/61 | Lincoln City | Retired | 37 | 0 | 1 | 0 | 2 | 0 | 1 | 0 |
| CARDEN | Paul | 29/03/79 | Liverpool | 1999/00 | 2000/01 | Rochdale | Doncaster Rovers | 45/6 | 0 | 3 | 0 | 0/1 | 0 | 3 | 0 |
| | | | | 2001/02 | 2004/05 | Doncaster Rovers | Peterborough U. | | | | | | | | |
| CARLING | Terry | 26/02/39 | Otley | 1966/67 | 1970/71 | Walsall | Macclesfield T. | 199 | 0 | 14 | 0 | 9 | 0 | 19 | 0 |
| CARROLL | Neil | 21/09/88 | Liverpool | 2007/08 | 2007/08 | Trainee | Caernarfon Town | 1 | 0 | 0 | 0 | 0 | 0 | 0 | 0 |
| CARSON | Danny | 02/02/81 | Huyton | 1998/99 | 1999/00 | Trainee | Winsford United | 1/1 | 0 | 0 | 0 | 0/1 | 0 | 0 | 0 |
| CARTER | Ray | 01/05/51 | Chester | 1971/72 | 1973/74 | Wrexham | Crewe Alexandra | 56/6 | 0 | 3 | 0 | 1 | 0 | 4 | 0 |
| CARTLIDGE | David | 09/04/40 | Leicester | 1961/62 | 1962/63 | Bradford City | | 20 | 0 | 2 | 0 | 1 | 0 | 0 | 0 |
| CARVER | Joe | 11/06/71 | New York, USA | 1999/00 | 1999/00 | Hampt'n R. M..(US) | Chicago Sock. (US) | 1/1 | 0 | 0 | 0 | 0 | 0 | 0 | 0 |
| CASHLEY | Ray | 23/10/51 | Bristol | 1985/86 | 1985/86 | Trowbridge Town | East Worle | 9 | 0 | 0 | 0 | 0 | 0 | 1 | 0 |

| Player | | Date of Birth | Place of Birth | First Season | Last Season | Previous Club | Next Club | League | | FA Cup | | League Cup | | Others | |
|---|---|---|---|---|---|---|---|---|---|---|---|---|---|---|---|
| | | | | | | | | Apps | G'ls | Apps | G'ls | Apps | G'ls | Apps | G'ls |
| CAUGHTER | Allan | 19/02/46 | Bangor | 1969/70 | 1969/70 | Juniors | Runcorn | 1/1 | 0 | 0 | 0 | 0 | 0 | 0 | 0 |
| CHADWICK | Graham | 08/04/42 | Oldham | 1965/66 | 1966/67 | Walsall | New Brighton | 11/1 | 0 | 0 | 0 | 0 | 0 | 2 | 0 |
| CHAMBERS | Bill | 10/08/06 | Wednesbury | 1936/37 | 1937/38 | Oldham Athletic | Bath City | 48 | 18 | 1 | 0 | 0 | 0 | 11 | 7 |
| CHAMBERS | Leroy | 25/10/72 | Sheffield | 1994/95 | 1995/96 | Sheffield Wed. | Boston United | 8/13 | 1 | 0 | 0 | 2 | 1 | 2/1 | 0 |
| CHAPMAN | Roy | 18/03/34 | Birmingham | 1969/70 | 1969/70 | Port Vale | Stafford Rangers | 9 | 3 | 0 | 0 | 1 | 0 | 0 | 0 |
| CHEETHAM | Roy | 02/12/39 | Eccles | 1968/69 | 1971/72 | Charlton Athletic | Great Harwood | 122/2 | 8 | 11 | 1 | 6 | 1 | 9 | 0 |
| CITRON | Gerry | 08/04/35 | Manchester | 1959/60 | 1959/60 | Corinthian Cas. | Rhyl | 2 | 0 | 0 | 0 | 0 | 0 | 1 | 0 |
| CLAPHAM | Graham | 23/09/47 | Lincoln | 1971/72 | 1972/73 | Shrewsbury Town | Grantham Town | 37/4 | 5 | 0 | 0 | 1/1 | 0 | 1 | 0 |
| CLARE | Daryl | 01/08/78 | Jersey | 2002/03 | 2004/05 | Boston United | Boston United | 3/4 | 1 | 1 | 0 | 0 | 0 | 1 | 0 |
| CLARKE | Bobby | 13/10/41 | Liverpool | 1961/62 | 1962/63 | Liverpool | Witton Albion | 30 | 5 | 1 | 0 | 3 | 1 | 2 | 0 |
| CLEMPSON | Frank | 27/05/30 | Salford | 1959/60 | 1960/61 | Stockport Co. | Hyde United | 67 | 8 | 3 | 0 | 1 | 0 | 3 | 1 |
| CLUTTON | Nigel | 12/02/54 | Chester | 1977/78 | 1977/78 | Blacon | | 1 | 0 | 0 | 0 | 0 | 0 | 0 | 0 |
| COATES | John | 03/06/44 | Birkdale | 1966/67 | 1966/67 | Southport | Tranmere Rovers | 1 | 0 | 0 | 0 | 0 | 0 | 0 | 0 |
| COFFIN | Geoff | 17/08/24 | Chester | 1947/48 | 1954/55 | Heath Rangers | Winsford United | 151 | 35 | 6 | 3 | 0 | 0 | 12 | 5 |
| COLE | Doug | 02/07/16 | Heswall | 1946/47 | 1947/48 | Sheffield United | Stalybridge C. | 20 | 0 | 0 | 0 | 0 | 0 | 3 | 0 |
| COLE | Jim | 14/08/25 | Wrexham | 1949/50 | 1949/50 | Bolton Wanderers | | 1 | 0 | 0 | 0 | 0 | 0 | 0 | 0 |
| COLLINS | Danny | 06/08/80 | Chester | 2001/02 | 2004/05 | Buckley Town | Sunderland | 12 | 1 | 0 | 0 | 1 | 0 | 0 | 0 |
| COLLINS | Jim | 07/11/23 | Colne | 1955/56 | 1956/57 | Barrow | Winsford United | 48 | 11 | 1 | 0 | 0 | 0 | 1 | 0 |
| COLVILLE | Harry | 12/12/24 | Kirkcaldy | 1947/48 | 1947/48 | Raith Rovers | Raith Rovers | 4 | 1 | 2 | 0 | 0 | 0 | 0 | 0 |
| COMMON | Ted | 25/01/07 | Seaton Delaval | 1935/36 | 1938/39 | Preston N.E. | Retired | 142 | 0 | 13 | 0 | 0 | 0 | 21 | 0 |
| COMSTIVE | Paul | 25/11/61 | Southport | 1991/92 | 1992/93 | Bolton Wanderers | Southport | 54/2 | 6 | 3 | 0 | 2 | 1 | 3 | 0 |
| CONROY | Mike | 31/12/65 | Glasgow | 1998/99 | 1998/99 | Blackpool (loan) | | 11/4 | 3 | 0 | 0 | 0 | 0 | 0 | 0 |
| COOKE | Terry | 21/02/62 | Wrexham | 1980/81 | 1982/83 | Apprentice | Bangor City | 37/12 | 11 | 1 | 0 | 2/1 | 0 | 4/2 | 0 |
| COOPER | Jimmy | 19/01/42 | Hoole | 1959/60 | 1961/62 | Juniors | Southport | 91 | 17 | 3 | 0 | 3 | 2 | 0 | 0 |
| CORBISHLEY | Colin | 13/06/39 | Stoke-on-Trent | 1962/63 | 1964/65 | Port Vale | Stafford Rangers | 83 | 11 | 3 | 0 | 5 | 1 | 2 | 0 |
| CORDEN | Wayne | 01/11/75 | Leek | 2005/06 | 2005/06 | Scunthorpe (loan) | | 2 | 0 | 0 | 0 | 0 | 0 | 0 | 0 |
| COSTELLO | Matt | 04/08/24 | Airdrie | 1952/53 | 1952/53 | Chesterfield | Clay Cross M. W. | 9 | 2 | 0 | 0 | 0 | 0 | 0 | 0 |
| COTTAM | John | 05/06/50 | Worksop | 1979/80 | 1981/82 | Chesterfield | Scarborough | 117/3 | 1 | 6 | 0 | 8 | 0 | 4/1 | 0 |
| COULTER | Jackie | 26/03/05 | Whiteabbey | 1938/39 | 1938/39 | Chelmsford City | Swansea Town | 4 | 0 | 0 | 0 | 0 | 0 | 0 | 0 |
| COY | Bobby | 30/11/61 | Birmingham | 1983/84 | 1985/86 | Wolves | Northampton T. | 93 | 2 | 1 | 0 | 6 | 0 | 4 | 0 |
| CRAVEN | Mike | 20/11/57 | Birkenhead | 1975/76 | 1976/77 | Cadburys | Bangor City | 4 | 0 | 0 | 0 | 1 | 0 | 3 | 0 |
| CRESSWELL | Frank | 05/09/08 | South Shields | 1931/32 | 1933/34 | W.B.A. | Notts County | 173 | 57 | 15 | 7 | 0 | 0 | 20 | 6 |
| | | | | 1934/35 | 1937/38 | Notts County | Retired | | | | | | | | |
| CROFT | Alec | 17/06/37 | Chester | 1957/58 | 1960/61 | Juniors | Sankeys | 53 | 3 | 0 | 0 | 2 | 0 | 3 | 0 |
| CROFT | Brian | 27/09/67 | Chester | 1985/86 | 1987/88 | Apprentice | | 126/47 | 6 | 11/3 | 4 | 8/1 | 2 | 16/4 | 0 |
| | | | | 1989/90 | 1991/92 | Cambridge Utd | QPR | | | | | | | | |
| CRONIN | Glenn | 14/09/81 | Dublin | 2006/07 | 2006/07 | Exeter City | Bohemians | 1/3 | 0 | 0 | 0 | 0 | 0 | 0 | 0 |
| CROSBY | Andy | 03/03/73 | Rotherham | 1998/99 | 1998/99 | Darlington | Brighton & H. A. | 41 | 4 | 1 | 0 | 3 | 0 | 1 | 0 |
| CROSS | Jonathan | 02/03/75 | Wallasey | 1998/99 | 1999/00 | Wrexham | Colwyn Bay | 46/6 | 1 | 3/1 | 3 | 6 | 0 | 2 | 0 |
| CROSSLEY | Paul | 14/07/48 | Rochdale | 1975/76 | 1977/78 | Tranmere Rovers | Seattle Sound(US) | 93/6 | 26 | 7/2 | 4 | 3 | 3 | 7 | 2 |
| CULLERTON | Mike | 25/11/48 | Edinburgh | 1968/69 | 1968/69 | Port Vale (loan) | | 5/2 | 0 | 0 | 0 | 0 | 0 | 0 | 0 |
| CURLE | Tom | 03/03/86 | Bristol | 2005/06 | 2005/06 | Bradford PA | | 0/2 | 0 | 0 | 0 | 0 | 0 | 1 | 0 |
| CURRIE | John | 07/04/39 | Dumfries | 1963/64 | 1963/64 | Workington | Rhyl | 2 | 0 | 0 | 0 | 0 | 0 | 0 | 0 |
| CURTIS | Tom | 01/03/73 | Exeter | 2005/06 | 2005/06 | Mansfield Town | Notts County | 34/6 | 1 | 4 | 0 | 1 | 0 | 0 | 0 |
| CUTLER | Neil | 03/09/76 | Birmingham | 1995/96 | 1995/96 | W.B.A. (loan) | | 29 | 0 | 1 | 0 | 1 | 0 | 1 | 0 |
| | | | | 1996/97 | 1996/97 | Crewe Alex. (loan) | | | | | | | | | |
| | | | | 1998/99 | 1999/00 | Crewe Alexandra | Aston Villa | | | | | | | | |
| DALE | Carl | 29/04/66 | Colwyn Bay | 1988/89 | 1990/91 | Bangor City | Cardiff City | 106/10 | 40 | 9 | 5 | 7/1 | 0 | 6 | 2 |
| DANBY | John | 20/09/83 | Stoke | 2006/07 | 2009/10 | Kidderminster H. | Eastwood Town | 133 | 0 | 7 | 0 | 3 | 0 | 5 | 0 |
| DANIELS | Barney | 24/11/50 | Salford | 1975/76 | 1975/76 | Manchester City | Stockport Co. | 8/1 | 1 | 0 | 0 | 1/1 | 0 | 2 | 1 |
| DANZEY | Mike | 08/02/71 | Widnes | 1989/90 | 1989/90 | Nott'ham F (loan) | | 0/2 | 0 | 0 | 0 | 0 | 0 | 0 | 0 |
| DAVIDSON | Ross | 13/11/73 | Chertsey | 1995/96 | 1999/00 | Sheffield United | Barnet | 132 | 6 | 3/1 | 0 | 11 | 0 | 4 | 0 |
| DAVIES | Ben | 27/05/81 | Birmingham | 2002/03 | 2005/06 | Kidderminster H. | Shrewsbury Town | 80/9 | 9 | 6 | 0 | 1/1 | 1 | 1/2 | 0 |
| DAVIES | Geoff | 01/07/47 | Ellesmere Port | 1972/73 | 1973/74 | Wigan Athletic | Wrexham | 18/14 | 5 | 1 | 0 | 1 | 0 | 3 | 1 |
| DAVIES | George | 01/03/27 | Rednall | 1956/57 | 1957/58 | Sheffield Wed. | Wellington Town | 35 | 4 | 0 | 0 | 0 | 0 | 3 | 1 |
| DAVIES | Gordon | 04/09/32 | Ardwick | 1957/58 | 1958/59 | Manchester City | Southport | 22 | 5 | 2 | 0 | 0 | 0 | 1 | 0 |
| DAVIES | Jack | 14/11/16 | Denbigh | 1935/36 | 1936/37 | Ruthin Town | Everton | 18 | 1 | 0 | 0 | 0 | 0 | 5 | 2 |
| DAVIES | Joe | 30/01/26 | Birkenhead | 1947/48 | 1951/52 | Bromborough | | 55 | 10 | 2 | 0 | 0 | 0 | 1 | 0 |
| DAVIES | Maldwyn | | | 1946/47 | 1946/47 | Juniors | | 0 | 0 | 0 | 0 | 0 | 0 | 1 | 1 |
| DAVIES | Ron | 25/05/42 | Holywell | 1959/60 | 1962/63 | Juniors | Luton Town | 94 | 44 | 3 | 2 | 5 | 4 | 3 | 0 |
| DAVIS | Eric | 26/02/32 | Stonehouse | 1958/59 | 1959/60 | Scunthorpe Utd | Oldham Athletic | 31 | 11 | 1 | 0 | 0 | 0 | 0 | 0 |
| DEAKIN | Bill | 19/01/25 | Maltby | 1952/53 | 1952/53 | Barnsley | Corby Town | 27 | 5 | 1 | 0 | 0 | 0 | 2 | 1 |
| DEAKIN | George | 21/02/15 | Holywell | 1937/38 | 1937/38 | Caergwrle | | 1 | 0 | 0 | 0 | 0 | 0 | 0 | 0 |
| DEAN | Mark | 18/11/64 | Northwich | 1981/82 | 1982/83 | Apprentice | Northwich Vic. | 23/2 | 0 | 0 | 0 | 1 | 0 | 3 | 0 |
| DEARDEN | Billy | 11/02/44 | Oldham | 1968/69 | 1969/70 | Crewe Alexandra | Sheffield United | 120/1 | 29 | 13 | 5 | 6 | 2 | 9 | 5 |
| | | | | 1975/76 | 1976/77 | Sheffield United | Chesterfield | | | | | | | | |

| Player | | Date of Birth | Place of Birth | First Season | Last Season | Previous Club | Next Club | League Apps | League G'ls | FA Cup Apps | FA Cup G'ls | League Cup Apps | League Cup G'ls | Others Apps | Others G'ls |
|---|---|---|---|---|---|---|---|---|---|---|---|---|---|---|---|
| DELGADO | Bob | 29/01/49 | Cardiff | 1975/76 | 1978/79 | Rotherham Utd | Port Vale | 125/3 | 8 | 12 | 0 | 7 | 0 | 9 | 1 |
| DEVINE | John | 09/07/33 | Liverpool | 1955/56 | 1955/56 | Rhyl | New Brighton | 1 | 0 | 0 | 0 | 0 | 0 | 0 | 0 |
| DEVONSHIRE | Les | 13/06/26 | Acton | 1950/51 | 1950/51 | Brentford | Crystal Palace | 44 | 4 | 1 | 0 | 0 | 0 | 2 | 1 |
| DICKENS | Leo | 16/03/27 | Hemsworth | 1952/53 | 1952/53 | Rotherham Utd | | 7 | 0 | 0 | 0 | 0 | 0 | 0 | 0 |
| DICKIE | Jim | 22/09/03 | Montrose | 1932/33 | 1932/33 | Bristol City | New Brighton | 1 | 0 | 0 | 0 | 0 | 0 | 0 | 0 |
| DIMECH | Luke | 11/01/77 | Malta | 2005/06 | 2005/06 | Mansfield Town | Marsaxlokk (Malta) | 27/3 | 0 | 4 | 0 | 1 | 0 | 0 | 0 |
| DINNING | Tony | 12/04/75 | Wallsend | 2007/08 | 2008/09 | Stockport Co. | Stafford Rangers | 23/1 | 2 | 1 | 0 | 0 | 0 | 1 | 0 |
| DIXON | Lee | 17/03/64 | Manchester | 1983/84 | 1984/85 | Burnley | Bury | 56/1 | 1 | 1 | 0 | 2 | 0 | 3 | 0 |
| DOBSON | Ryan | 24/09/78 | Wellington | 1997/98 | 1997/98 | Trainee | Telford United | 6 | 0 | 0 | 0 | 0 | 0 | 0 | 0 |
| DONALDSON | Fred | 07/04/37 | Stoke-on-Trent | 1961/62 | 1961/62 | Exeter City | Macclesfield T. | 21 | 0 | 2 | 0 | 1 | 0 | 1 | 0 |
| DONE | Bob | 27/04/04 | Runcorn | 1937/38 | 1937/38 | Reading | Accrington S. | 37 | 0 | 1 | 0 | 0 | 0 | 5 | 0 |
| DONNELLY | Darren | 28/12/71 | Liverpool | 1993/94 | 1993/94 | Blackburn Rovers | Holywell Town | 0/9 | 0 | 0 | 0 | 0/1 | 0 | 0 | 0 |
| DONNELLY | Peter | 11/05/65 | Chester | 1983/84 | 1983/84 | Local | Oswestry Town | 1 | 0 | 0 | 0 | 0 | 0 | 0 | 0 |
| DOUGHTY | Matt | 02/11/81 | Warrington | 1999/00 | 2000/01 | Trainee | Rochdale | 19/14 | 1 | 4 | 0 | 2 | 0 | 0 | 0 |
| DOVE | Craig | 16/08/83 | Hartlepool | 2005/06 | 2005/06 | Rushden & D | Buxton | 2/3 | 0 | 0/1 | 0 | 0 | 0 | 1 | 0 |
| DOYLE | Colin | 12/08/85 | Cork | 2004/05 | 2004/05 | Birmingham (loan) | | 0 | 0 | 0 | 0 | 0 | 0 | 1 | 0 |
| DRAPER | Derek | 11/05/43 | Swansea | 1968/69 | 1976/77 | Bradford P.A. | Retired | 316/6 | 54 | 20 | 2 | 20 | 7 | 24 | 6 |
| DRUMMOND | Stewart | 11/12/75 | Preston | 2004/05 | 2005/06 | Morecambe | Shrewsbury Town | 85/2 | 12 | 6 | 1 | 2 | 0 | 1/2 | 0 |
| DUCKWORTH | Dick | 06/06/06 | Harpurhey | 1932/33 | 1933/34 | Southport | Rotherham Utd | 30 | 0 | 2 | 0 | 0 | 0 | 5 | 0 |
| DUFF | Stan | 02/04/05 | Liverpool | 1938/39 | 1938/39 | Waterford | New Brighton | 2 | 0 | 0 | 0 | 0 | 0 | 0 | 0 |
| DUNLEAVY | Chris | 30/12/49 | Liverpool | 1973/74 | 1976/77 | Southport | Halifax Town | 74/2 | 0 | 3 | 0 | 6/1 | 0 | 6 | 0 |
| DURIE | Dave | 13/08/31 | Blackpool | 1964/65 | 1966/67 | Blackpool | Fleetwood | 87/2 | 4 | 6 | 0 | 2 | 0 | 8 | 0 |
| DUTTON | Reg | | | 1946/47 | 1946/47 | Amateur | Ellesmere Port | 0 | 0 | 0 | 0 | 0 | 0 | 1 | 0 |
| EADIE | Jim | 04/02/47 | Kirkintilloch | 1972/73 | 1972/73 | Cardiff C. (loan) | | 6 | 0 | 0 | 0 | 2 | 0 | 0 | 0 |
| EDMONDSON | Darren | 04/11/71 | Ulverston | 2004/05 | 2004/05 | York City | Barrow | 26/1 | 0 | 2 | 0 | 0 | 0 | 0 | 0 |
| EDWARDS | Ian | 30/01/55 | Rossett | 1976/77 | 1979/80 | W.B.A. | Wrexham | 104 | 36 | 6 | 4 | 10 | 3 | 9 | 2 |
| EDWARDS | Jake | 11/05/76 | Prestwich | 2005/06 | 2005/06 | Exeter City (loan) | | 10 | 1 | 0 | 0 | 0 | 0 | 0 | 0 |
| EDWARDS | John | | | 1937/38 | 1937/38 | Buckley | | 1 | 0 | 0 | 0 | 0 | 0 | 0 | 0 |
| EDWARDS | Keith | 10/06/44 | Chester | 1965/66 | 1966/67 | Buckley Wands. | | 3 | 0 | 1 | 0 | 0 | 0 | 0 | 0 |
| EDWARDS | Malcolm | 25/10/39 | Wrexham | 1960/61 | 1961/62 | Bolton Wanderers | Tranmere Rovers | 43 | 5 | 0 | 0 | 1 | 0 | 1 | 0 |
| EDWARDS | Nigel | 31/12/50 | Wrexham | 1968/69 | 1977/78 | Johnstown RGA | Aldershot | 289/10 | 16 | 16/2 | 2 | 22 | 1 | 28/1 | 4 |
| | | | | 1982/83 | 1982/83 | Aldershot | Oswestry Town | | | | | | | | |
| EL KHOLTI | Abdou | 17/10/80 | Annemasse (Fr) | 2005/06 | 2005/06 | Cambridge Utd | Weymouth | 7/15 | 0 | 0/4 | 0 | 0 | 0 | 1 | 0 |
| ELLAMS | Lloyd | 11/01/91 | Chester | 2008/09 | 2009/10 | Trainee | Marine | 2/2 | 1 | 0 | 0 | 0 | 0 | 0 | 0 |
| ELLENDER | Paul | 21/10/74 | Scunthorpe | 2005/06 | 2005/06 | Boston U. (loan) | | 5 | 0 | 0 | 0 | 0 | 0 | 0 | 0 |
| ELLIOTT | Andy | 21/11/63 | Ashton-u-Lyne | 1983/84 | 1983/84 | Sligo Rovers | Mossley | 24/8 | 3 | 0/1 | 0 | 4 | 1 | 1 | 0 |
| ELLIOTT | Ted | 24/05/19 | Carlisle | 1948/49 | 1950/51 | Wolves | Halifax Town | 59 | 0 | 4 | 0 | 0 | 0 | 5 | 0 |
| ELLIS | Ken | 22/01/28 | Buckley | 1946/47 | 1946/47 | Amateur | Wrexham | 1 | 0 | 0 | 0 | 0 | 0 | 0 | 0 |
| ELLIS | Neil | 30/04/69 | Chester | 1990/91 | 1990/91 | Bangor City | Maidstone Utd | 13/8 | 1 | 1/1 | 0 | 2/2 | 1 | 1 | 0 |
| ELLISON | Kevin | 23/02/79 | Liverpool | 2004/05 | 2004/05 | Stockport Co. | Hull City | 99 | 28 | 5 | 1 | 3 | 0 | 4 | 2 |
| | | | | 2007/08 | 2008/09 | Tranmere Rovers | Rotherham Utd | | | | | | | | |
| ELOKOBI | George | 31/01/86 | Cameroon | 2004/05 | 2004/05 | Colchester U. (loan) | | 4/1 | 0 | 0 | 0 | 0 | 0 | 0 | 0 |
| EVANS | David | 04/04/67 | Chester | 1983/84 | 1984/85 | Apprentice | Bangor City | 15/1 | 1 | 0 | 0 | 1 | 0 | 1 | 0 |
| EVANS | George | 26/07/35 | Rhostyllen | 1963/64 | 1968/69 | Wrexham | Bethesda Ath. | 109/4 | 0 | 3 | 0 | 4 | 0 | 13/1 | 1 |
| EVANS | John | 24/03/41 | Chester | 1961/62 | 1964/65 | Juniors | Rhyl | 40 | 0 | 2 | 0 | 0 | 0 | 2 | 0 |
| EVANS | Spencer | 24/09/11 | St.Asaph | 1931/32 | 1931/32 | Rhyl | Altrincham | 1 | 0 | 0 | 0 | 0 | 0 | 0 | 0 |
| EVANS | Royson | 09/02/39 | Lampeter | 1957/58 | 1959/60 | Wrexham | Sankeys | 23 | 3 | 0 | 0 | 0 | 0 | 6 | 1 |
| EVE | Angus | 23/02/72 | Port of Spain,Trin. | 1999/00 | 1999/00 | Joe Public (Trin.) | Jabloteh (Trin.) | 9/5 | 4 | 0 | 0 | 0 | 0 | 0/1 | 0 |
| EYJOLFSSON | Siggi | 01/12/73 | Reykjavik, Iceland | 1999/00 | 1999/00 | Walsall (loan) | | 9 | 3 | 0 | 0 | 0 | 0 | 1 | 0 |
| FANTHAM | John | 1908 | Sheffield | 1934/35 | 1934/35 | Rotherham Utd | Exeter City | 15 | 0 | 1 | 0 | 0 | 0 | 0 | 0 |
| FAZACKERLEY | Derek | 05/11/51 | Preston | 1986/87 | 1987/88 | Blackburn Rovers | York City | 66 | 0 | 3 | 0 | 2 | 0 | 8 | 1 |
| FEAR | Keith | 08/05/52 | Bristol | 1979/80 | 1980/81 | Plymouth Argyle | Bangor City | 41/3 | 3 | 0 | 0 | 0 | 0 | 1 | 0 |
| FEENEY | Joe | 21/07/26 | Glasgow | 1951/52 | 1951/52 | Rhyl | | 5 | 0 | 0 | 0 | 0 | 0 | 0 | 0 |
| FEENEY | Tom | 26/08/10 | Grangetown | 1937/38 | 1937/38 | Halifax Town | Darlington | 5 | 0 | 0 | 0 | 0 | 0 | 1 | 0 |
| FELGATE | David | 04/03/60 | Blaenau Ffestiniog | 1993/94 | 1994/95 | Wolves | Wigan Athletic | 71/1 | 0 | 6 | 0 | 2 | 0 | 5 | 0 |
| FELIX | Gary | 31/10/57 | Manchester | 1978/79 | 1978/79 | Leeds United | Witton Albion | 8 | 0 | 0 | 0 | 0 | 0 | 1 | 1 |
| FERGUSON | Archie | | | 1931/32 | 1931/32 | Rhyl | Rhyl | 1 | 1 | 0 | 0 | 0 | 0 | 1 | 0 |
| FERGUSON | Danny | 25/01/03 | Flint | 1931/32 | 1932/33 | Accrington S. | Halifax Town | 29 | 3 | 0 | 0 | 0 | 0 | 2 | 0 |
| FIELD | Tony | 23/05/42 | Chester | 1960/61 | 1960/61 | Juniors | Southport | 2 | 0 | 0 | 0 | 0 | 0 | 0 | 0 |
| FIELDS | Mike | 12/08/35 | Chester | 1955/56 | 1957/58 | Local | Borough United | 22 | 1 | 0 | 0 | 0 | 0 | 1 | 0 |
| FINNEY | Steve | 31/10/73 | Hexham | 1999/00 | 2000/01 | Barrow | Altrincham | 4/9 | 0 | 0 | 0 | 0 | 0 | 0 | 0 |
| FINNIGAN | Richard | 16/05/04 | Wrexham | 1932/33 | 1933/34 | Colwyn Bay Utd. | Stockport Co. | 13 | 0 | 0 | 0 | 0 | 0 | 0 | 0 |
| FISHER | Neil | 07/11/70 | St.Helens | 1995/96 | 1997/98 | Bolton Wanderers | Bangor City | 132/25 | 5 | 10 | 0 | 12 | 0 | 4 | 0 |
| | | | | 1998/99 | 2000/01 | Connahs Quay N. | Leigh RMI | | | | | | | | |
| FITZGERALD | Peter | 17/06/37 | Waterford | 1961/62 | 1963/64 | Leeds United | Waterford | 80 | 12 | 3 | 0 | 5 | 1 | 1 | 1 |

| Player | | Date of Birth | Place of Birth | First Season | Last Season | Previous Club | Next Club | League Apps | League G'ls | FA Cup Apps | FA Cup G'ls | League Cup Apps | League Cup G'ls | Others Apps | Others G'ls |
|---|---|---|---|---|---|---|---|---|---|---|---|---|---|---|---|
| FLEMING | Bernard | 08/01/37 | Middlesbrough | 1962/63 | 1963/64 | Workington | Winsford United | 64 | 0 | 1 | 0 | 6 | 0 | 2 | 0 |
| FLETCHER | James | 23/12/26 | Brentwood | 1951/52 | 1951/52 | Birmingham City | Wellington Town | 23 | 9 | 4 | 1 | 0 | 0 | 1 | 2 |
| FLETCHER | Ken | 31/12/31 | Liverpool | 1953/54 | 1955/56 | Everton | Prescot Cables | 34 | 0 | 1 | 0 | 0 | 0 | 5 | 1 |
| FLITCROFT | David | 14/01/74 | Bolton | 1993/94 | 1998/99 | Preston N. E. | Rochdale | 146/21 | 18 | 7 | 0 | 10/1 | 0 | 8 | 1 |
| FORSYTH | John | 20/12/18 | Dumbarton | 1948/49 | 1948/49 | New Brighton | | 32 | 1 | 2 | 1 | 0 | 0 | 0 | 0 |
| FOULDS | Albert | 08/08/19 | Salford | 1948/49 | 1948/49 | Altrincham | Yeovil Town | 31 | 14 | 2 | 0 | 0 | 0 | 0 | 0 |
| FOULKES | Billy | 29/05/26 | Merthyr Tydfil | 1948/49 | 1951/52 | Cardiff City | Newcastle Utd | 296 | 37 | 15 | 1 | 0 | 0 | 15 | 0 |
| | | | | 1956/57 | 1960/61 | Winsford United | Hyde United | | | | | | | | |
| FOX | Steve | 17/02/58 | Tamworth | 1984/85 | 1985/86 | Port Vale | Tamworth | 29/4 | 4 | 1 | 1 | 2 | 0 | 0/1 | 0 |
| FOY | Robbie | 28/10/85 | Edinburgh | 2004/05 | 2004/05 | Liverpool (loan) | | 13 | 0 | 0 | 0 | 0 | 0 | 0 | 0 |
| FREEMAN | Tom | 26/01/07 | Brandon | 1933/34 | 1933/34 | Middlesbrough | Blyth Spartans | 17 | 0 | 0 | 0 | 0 | 0 | 2 | 0 |
| FUTCHER | Graham | 15/06/53 | Chester | 1971/72 | 1972/73 | Apprentice | Skelmersdale U. | 5/5 | 0 | 0 | 0 | 1 | 0 | 0/2 | 0 |
| FUTCHER | Paul | 25/09/56 | Chester | 1972/73 | 1973/74 | Apprentice | Luton Town | 20 | 0 | 1 | 0 | 0 | 0 | 1/1 | 0 |
| FUTCHER | Ron | 25/09/56 | Chester | 1973/74 | 1973/74 | Apprentice | Luton Town | 4 | 0 | 0 | 0 | 0 | 0 | 2 | 0 |
| GAGE | Wakeley | 05/05/58 | Northampton | 1985/86 | 1985/86 | Northampton T. | Peterborough U. | 17 | 1 | 1 | 0 | 3 | 0 | 0 | 0 |
| GALE | Arthur | 16/11/04 | Salford | 1936/37 | 1938/39 | W.B.A. | Macclesfield T. | 35 | 16 | 3 | 2 | 0 | 0 | 2 | 1 |
| GARDINER | Mark | 25/12/66 | Cirencester | 1994/95 | 1994/95 | Crewe Alex (loan) | | 2/1 | 0 | 0 | 0 | 0 | 0 | 0 | 0 |
| GARNETT | Shaun | 22/11/69 | Wallasey | 1992/93 | 1992/93 | Tranmere R. (loan) | | 9 | 0 | 0 | 0 | 0 | 0 | 0 | 0 |
| GENDALL | Richie | 25/09/60 | Wrexham | 1980/81 | 1980/81 | Apprentice | Bangor City | 4/1 | 0 | 0 | 0 | 0 | 0 | 0 | 0 |
| GILES | Martin | 01/01/79 | Shrewsbury | 1996/97 | 1997/98 | Trainee | Telford United | 8/2 | 0 | 0/1 | 0 | 0 | 0 | 0 | 0 |
| GILL | Ray | 08/12/24 | Manchester | 1951/52 | 1961/62 | Manchester City | Hyde United | 406 | 3 | 15 | 0 | 0 | 0 | 28 | 1 |
| GILLET | Stephane | 20/08/77 | Luxembourg | 2005/06 | 2005/06 | Racing Union (Lux) | Racing Union (Lux) | 8 | 0 | 2 | 0 | 0 | 0 | 0 | 0 |
| GLENN | David | 30/11/62 | Wigan | 1985/86 | 1988/89 | Blackburn Rovers | Fleetwood T. | 70/3 | 1 | 1/1 | 0 | 9 | 0 | 3 | 0 |
| GOODWIN | Craig | 12/02/74 | Wrexham | 1992/93 | 1992/93 | Aston Villa | Holywell Town | 3/2 | 0 | 0/1 | 0 | 0/1 | 0 | 0 | 0 |
| GRAHAM | Milton | 02/11/62 | Tottenham | 1985/86 | 1988/89 | Bournemouth | Peterborough U. | 123/6 | 11 | 8 | 1 | 7 | 0 | 8 | 0 |
| GRANT | Tony | 14/11/74 | Liverpool | 2007/08 | 2007/08 | Accrington Stanley | Huddersfield Town | 15/4 | 1 | 1 | 0 | 1 | 0 | 1 | 0 |
| GRAY | Bert | 23/09/00 | Tredegar | 1936/37 | 1937/38 | Tranmere Rovers | Congleton Town | 73 | 0 | 3 | 0 | 0 | 0 | 10 | 0 |
| GRAY | Bob | 17/10/03 | Cowpen | 1932/33 | 1932/33 | Rotherham Utd | Southport | 6 | 1 | 0 | 0 | 0 | 0 | 0 | 0 |
| GREENALL | Colin | 30/12/63 | Billinge | 1993/94 | 1993/94 | Preston N.E. | Lincoln City | 42 | 1 | 4 | 0 | 2 | 0 | 4 | 1 |
| GREENHOUGH | Ricky | 30/05/61 | Mexborough | 1984/85 | 1987/88 | Alfreton Town | Scarborough | 123/9 | 16 | 7 | 0 | 3 | 0 | 13/1 | 0 |
| GREENWOOD | Peter | 11/09/24 | Todmorden | 1948/49 | 1951/52 | Burnley | Witton Albion | 62 | 3 | 5 | 1 | 0 | 0 | 10 | 1 |
| GREER | Ross | 23/09/67 | Perth, Australia | 1989/90 | 1989/90 | Floreat Ath. (Aus) | Instant Dict (HK) | 2 | 0 | 1 | 0 | 0 | 0 | 1 | 0 |
| GREGG | Willis | 21/07/08 | Woodhouse | 1938/39 | 1938/39 | Manchester City | Buxton | 29 | 2 | 7 | 1 | 0 | 0 | 2 | 0 |
| GREGSON | John | 17/05/39 | Skelmersdale | 1962/63 | 1962/63 | Blackpool | Shrewsbury Town | 32 | 5 | 1 | 0 | 4 | 0 | 1 | 0 |
| GRIFFITHS | Bob | 15/09/42 | Birmingham | 1962/63 | 1962/63 | Stoke City | Bangor City | 2 | 0 | 0 | 0 | 0 | 0 | 0 | 0 |
| GRIFFITHS | Brian | 21/11/33 | Penycae | 1958/59 | 1958/59 | Wrexham | Caernarvon Town | 2 | 1 | 0 | 0 | 0 | 0 | 1 | 1 |
| GRIFFITHS | George | | | 1938/39 | 1938/39 | Hoole Alexandra | | 6 | 0 | 0 | 0 | 0 | 0 | 1 | 0 |
| GRIFFITHS | Ivor | 19/06/18 | Port Talbot | 1946/47 | 1946/47 | Tottenham H. | Oswestry Town | 1 | 0 | 0 | 0 | 0 | 0 | 0 | 0 |
| GRIFFITHS | Keith | 30/12/27 | Chester | 1955/56 | 1958/59 | Rhyl | | 54 | 0 | 2 | 0 | 0 | 0 | 5 | 0 |
| GRIFFITHS | Neil | 12/10/51 | Stoke-on-Trent | 1970/71 | 1973/74 | St. Lukes YC | Port Vale | 89/1 | 5 | 3 | 0 | 3 | 0 | 7 | 0 |
| GRIFFITHS | Ray | 26/09/31 | Llanelli | 1955/56 | 1959/60 | Stockton Heath N | | 18 | 0 | 0 | 0 | 0 | 0 | 0 | 0 |
| GROVES | Alan | 24/10/48 | Ainsdale | 1970/71 | 1970/71 | Southport | Shrewsbury Town | 21/1 | 3 | 4 | 0 | 3 | 0 | 1 | 0 |
| GRUMMETT | Jim | 11/07/45 | Barnsley | 1973/74 | 1973/74 | Aldershot | Rochdale | 15/1 | 0 | 1 | 1 | 1 | 0 | 0 | 0 |
| GURRY | John | 17/07/07 | Barking | 1936/37 | 1936/37 | Southampton | | 6 | 3 | 0 | 0 | 0 | 0 | 2 | 0 |
| HACKETT | Bernard | 07/09/33 | Ramsbotton | 1955/56 | 1956/57 | Aston Villa | Lockheed Leam. | 21 | 4 | 0 | 0 | 0 | 0 | 2 | 2 |
| HACKETT | Gary | 11/10/62 | Stourbridge | 1994/95 | 1994/95 | Peterborough U. | Halesowen Town | 30/5 | 5 | 2 | 0 | 0 | 0 | 2 | 0 |
| HADDOCK | Andy | 05/05/46 | Edinburgh | 1963/64 | 1963/64 | Edinburgh Boys | Crewe Alexandra | 22 | 1 | 1 | 0 | 1 | 0 | 1 | 0 |
| | | | | 1967/68 | 1967/68 | Bradford PA | Fleetwood Town | | | | | | | | |
| HAINES | John | 24/04/20 | Wickhamford | 1955/56 | 1956/57 | Rochdale | Wellington Town | 46 | 8 | 3 | 0 | 0 | 0 | 2 | 0 |
| HALL | Ernie | 23/02/04 | Nuneaton | 1934/35 | 1937/38 | Q.P.R. | (Trainer) | 118 | 0 | 8 | 0 | 0 | 0 | 20 | 0 |
| HALSTEAD | Roy | 26/07/31 | Whitworth | 1954/55 | 1954/55 | Burnley | Winsford United | 21 | 4 | 0 | 0 | 0 | 0 | 0 | 0 |
| HAMILTON | Bobby | 25/04/24 | Edinburgh | 1946/47 | 1947/48 | Hearts | Yeovil Town | 68 | 10 | 7 | 1 | 0 | 0 | 2 | 1 |
| HAMILTON | David | 07/11/60 | South Shields | 1989/90 | 1989/90 | Wigan Athletic | Burnley | 26/2 | 0 | 3 | 0 | 1 | 0 | 4 | 0 |
| HANCOX | David | 02/10/47 | Conisbrough | 1967/68 | 1967/68 | Sheffield United | Runcorn | 17/2 | 4 | 2 | 1 | 0 | 0 | 2 | 1 |
| HAND | Jamie | 07/02/84 | Uxbridge | 2006/07 | 2007/08 | Watford | Lincoln City | 43/1 | 2 | 5 | 1 | 2 | 0 | 1 | 1 |
| HANDSCOMBE | Mal | 29/06/34 | Normanton | 1957/58 | 1957/58 | Amateur | Cambridge Utd | 4 | 0 | 0 | 0 | 0 | 0 | 1 | 0 |
| HANKINSON | Jim | 01/07/28 | Preston | 1950/51 | 1950/51 | Preston N.E. | | 15 | 1 | 1 | 0 | 0 | 0 | 0 | 0 |
| HANSELL | Ron | 03/10/30 | Norwich | 1956/57 | 1956/57 | Norwich City | Great Yarmouth | 36 | 9 | 1 | 0 | 0 | 0 | 3 | 0 |
| HARDIE | John | 07/02/38 | Edinburgh | 1961/62 | 1962/63 | Oldham Athletic | Bradford P.A. | 84 | 0 | 3 | 0 | 4 | 0 | 2 | 0 |
| HARLEY | Albert | 17/04/40 | Chester | 1969/70 | 1969/70 | Stockport Co. | Connah's Quay | 3 | 1 | 0 | 0 | 0 | 0 | 0 | 0 |
| HARLEY | Lee | 07/07/67 | Crewe | 1985/86 | 1985/86 | Local | Rhyl | 0/1 | 0 | 0 | 0 | 0 | 0 | 0 | 0 |
| HARLEY | Les | 26/09/46 | Chester | 1964/65 | 1966/67 | Juniors | Blackpool | 22/3 | 3 | 0 | 0 | 0 | 0 | 5 | 0 |
| HARRIGAN | Duncan | 26/06/21 | Paisley | 1948/49 | 1948/49 | Aston Villa | Colwyn Bay | 20 | 4 | 2 | 1 | 0 | 0 | 1 | 0 |
| HARRINGTON | Phil | 20/11/63 | Bangor | 1981/82 | 1984/85 | Apprentice | Blackpool | 76 | 0 | 1 | 0 | 4 | 0 | 6 | 0 |
| HARRIS | Andy | 26/02/77 | Springs, SA | 2003/04 | 2004/05 | Leyton Orient | Weymouth | 9/10 | 0 | 1/1 | 0 | 0 | 0 | 3 | 0 |

| Player | | Date of Birth | Place of Birth | First Season | Last Season | Previous Club | Next Club | League Apps | League G'ls | FA Cup Apps | FA Cup G'ls | League Cup Apps | League Cup G'ls | Others Apps | Others G'ls |
|---|---|---|---|---|---|---|---|---|---|---|---|---|---|---|---|
| HARRIS | Jay | 15/04/87 | Liverpool | 2008/09 | 2008/09 | Accrington Stanley | Enkopings SK(Swe) | 24/7 | 0 | 1 | 0 | 0/1 | 0 | 0 | 0 |
| HARRIS | John | 30/06/17 | Glasgow | 1956/57 | 1956/57 | Chelsea | (Manager) | 27 | 1 | 2 | 0 | 0 | 0 | 0 | 0 |
| HARRISON | Paul | | | 1982/83 | 1982/83 | Juniors | | 0 | 0 | 0 | 0 | 0 | 0 | 0/1 | 0 |
| HARRISON | Paul | 18/12/84 | Liverpool | 2005/06 | 2005/06 | Wolverhampton W. | Hereford United | 4 | 0 | 0 | 0 | 0 | 0 | 0 | 0 |
| HARVEY | Brian | 12/01/47 | Liverpool | 1964/65 | 1964/65 | Sheffield Wed. | Rhyl | 1 | 0 | 0 | 0 | 0 | 0 | 0 | 0 |
| HAUSER | Peter | 20/04/34 | Kimberley, SA | 1963/64 | 1966/67 | Cheltenham | Highland Park SA | 117/4 | 3 | 9 | 0 | 7 | 0 | 11 | 0 |
| HAWKINS | Dennis | 22/10/47 | Swansea | 1970/71 | 1970/71 | Shrewsbury (loan) | | 6/1 | 1 | 0 | 0 | 0 | 0 | 0 | 0 |
| HAWTIN | Craig | 29/03/70 | Buxton | 1987/88 | 1988/89 | Apprentice | Burnley | 6/1 | 1 | 0/1 | 0 | 0/1 | 0 | 0 | 0 |
| HAYDE | Mick | 20/06/71 | St. Helens | 1989/90 | 1989/90 | Liverpool | St. Helens Town | 0/1 | 0 | 0 | 0 | 0 | 0 | 0 | 0 |
| HEDLEY | Foster | 06/01/08 | Monkseaton | 1931/32 | 1933/34 | Manchester City | Tottenham H. | 88 | 29 | 7 | 8 | 0 | 0 | 8 | 3 |
| HEGGS | Carl | 11/10/70 | Leicester | 1999/00 | 1999/00 | Rushden (loan) | | 11 | 2 | 0 | 0 | 0 | 0 | 0 | 0 |
| HELLIWELL | Ian | 07/11/62 | Rotherham | 1996/97 | 1996/97 | Burnley (loan) | | 8/1 | 1 | 0 | 0 | 0 | 0 | 0 | 0 |
| HEMMINGS | Tony | 21/09/67 | Burton on Trent | 1999/00 | 1999/00 | Ilkeston Town | Carlisle United | 19 | 2 | 0 | 0 | 0 | 0 | 0 | 0 |
| HENDERSON | Peter | 29/09/52 | Berwick-on-Tweed | 1978/79 | 1979/80 | Witton Albion | Gillingham | 87/5 | 15 | 4 | 3 | 4 | 2 | 3 | 0 |
| | | | | 1981/82 | 1981/82 | Gillingham | Telford United | | | | | | | | |
| HENNIN | Derek | 28/12/31 | Prescot | 1960/61 | 1961/62 | Bolton Wanderers | Wigan Athletic | 54 | 4 | 2 | 0 | 1 | 0 | 0 | 0 |
| HEROD | Baden | 16/05/00 | Ilford | 1931/32 | 1932/33 | Tottenham H. | Swindon Town | 79 | 1 | 7 | 0 | 0 | 0 | 8 | 0 |
| HESSEY | Sean | 19/09/78 | Liverpool | 2004/05 | 2006/07 | Blackpool | Macclesfield T. | 70/9 | 1 | 6 | 0 | 2 | 0 | 5 | 1 |
| HETZKE | Steve | 03/06/55 | Marlborough | 1987/88 | 1987/88 | Sunderland | Colchester Utd | 14 | 0 | 0 | 0 | 2 | 0 | 1 | 0 |
| HEWITT | Ron | 21/06/28 | Flint | 1961/62 | 1962/63 | Coventry City | Hereford United | 29 | 6 | 0 | 0 | 1 | 0 | 1 | 0 |
| HICKS | Stuart | 30/05/67 | Peterborough | 1999/00 | 1999/00 | Leyton Orient | Mansfield Town | 13 | 0 | 0 | 0 | 0 | 0 | 0 | 0 |
| HIGGINS | Andy | 12/02/60 | Bolsover | 1984/85 | 1984/85 | Rochdale | Hellenic (SA) | 16/3 | 1 | 1 | 0 | 1/1 | 0 | 0 | 0 |
| HIGGINS | Charles | 12/05/21 | Bellshill | 1946/47 | 1946/47 | Arbroath | Airdrie | 11 | 0 | 0 | 0 | 0 | 0 | 2 | 0 |
| HIGNETT | Alan | 01/11/46 | Liverpool | 1966/67 | 1966/67 | Liverpool | Pan Hellenic (Aus) | 6 | 0 | 0 | 0 | 0 | 0 | 0 | 0 |
| HILDERSLEY | Ronnie | 06/04/65 | Kirkcaldy | 1983/84 | 1984/85 | Manchester City | Rochdale | 14/4 | 0 | 1 | 0 | 0 | 0 | 1 | 0 |
| HILLIER | Ian | 26/12/79 | Neath | 2004/05 | 2004/05 | Luton Town (loan) | | 7/1 | 0 | 0 | 0 | 0 | 0 | 0 | 0 |
| HILLIER | Jack | 10/09/33 | Halsall | 1954/55 | 1954/55 | Bootle | | 6 | 0 | 0 | 0 | 0 | 0 | 2 | 0 |
| HILTON | Joe | 20/07/31 | Bromborough | 1950/51 | 1953/54 | Leeds United | Goole Town | 61 | 9 | 3 | 0 | 0 | 0 | 7 | 2 |
| HINDLE | Frank | 22/06/25 | Blackburn | 1949/50 | 1950/51 | Blackburn Rovers | Bradford P.A. | 81 | 0 | 3 | 0 | 0 | 0 | 8 | 0 |
| HINNIGAN | Joe | 03/12/55 | Liverpool | 1988/89 | 1989/90 | Wrexham | (Physio) | 52/2 | 2 | 2 | 0 | 4 | 0 | 3 | 1 |
| HOBSON | Alf | 09/09/13 | Co. Durham | 1938/39 | 1938/39 | Liverpool | South Liverpool | 17 | 0 | 0 | 0 | 0 | 0 | 0 | 0 |
| HOBSON | Gary | 12/11/72 | Hull | 1999/00 | 1999/00 | Brighton & HA | York City | 20 | 0 | 0 | 0 | 0 | 0 | 0 | 0 |
| HOLDEN | Andy | 14/09/62 | Flint | 1983/84 | 1986/87 | Rhyl | Wigan Athletic | 100 | 16 | 2 | 2 | 8 | 1 | 4 | 2 |
| HOLLAND | Reg | 23/01/40 | Sutton-in-Ashfield | 1965/66 | 1966/67 | Wrexham | Altrincham | 5/1 | 0 | 0 | 0 | 0 | 0 | 2 | 0 |
| HOLLIS | Mike | 14/11/49 | Loughborough | 1972/73 | 1972/73 | Barrow | Stockport Co. | 34/3 | 8 | 2 | 1 | 4 | 2 | 3 | 0 |
| HOLROYD | Chris | 24/10/86 | Nantwich | 2006/07 | 2007/08 | Crewe Alexandra | Cambridge Utd | 21/26 | 4 | 0/1 | 0 | 0/2 | 0 | 0/2 | 1 |
| HOPE | Richard | 22/06/78 | Middlesbrough | 2004/05 | 2004/05 | York City | Shrewsbury Town | 26/2 | 0 | 2 | 0 | 0 | 0 | 1/2 | 1 |
| HORNE | Stan | 17/12/44 | Clanfield | 1973/74 | 1973/74 | Fulham | Rochdale | 17/1 | 0 | 1 | 0 | 1 | 0 | 0 | 0 |
| HORNSBY | Brian | 10/09/54 | Great Shelford | 1981/82 | 1981/82 | Sheff Wed (loan) | | 4 | 0 | 0 | 0 | 0 | 0 | 0 | 0 |
| HORSMAN | Bill | 18/12/08 | Doncaster | 1935/36 | 1938/39 | Birmingham | Chester Nomads | 151 | 34 | 13 | 3 | 0 | 0 | 24 | 10 |
| HORWOOD | Evan | 10/03/86 | Billingham | 2005/06 | 2005/06 | Sheffield U. (loan) | | 1 | 0 | 0 | 0 | 0 | 0 | 0 | 0 |
| HOUGHTON | Peter | 30/11/54 | Liverpool | 1985/86 | 1987/88 | Preston N.E. | Runcorn | 78/7 | 13 | 7 | 1 | 6 | 1 | 2/3 | 0 |
| HOUNSLEA | Bill | 15/08/26 | Liverpool | 1948/49 | 1948/49 | New Brighton | Winsford United | 1 | 0 | 0 | 0 | 0 | 0 | 0 | 0 |
| HOWARD | Richard | 10/06/43 | Birkenhead | 1965/66 | 1965/66 | Chester T. C. | Hyde United | 1 | 0 | 0 | 0 | 0 | 0 | 1 | 0 |
| HOWARD | Terry | 26/02/66 | Stepney | 1986/87 | 1986/87 | Chelsea (loan) | | 2 | 0 | 2 | 0 | 0 | 0 | 0 | 0 |
| HOWARTH | Harold | 25/11/08 | Little Hulton | 1934/35 | 1938/39 | Bolton Wanderers | Southport | 175 | 7 | 11 | 0 | 0 | 0 | 26 | 0 |
| HOWAT | Ian | 29/07/58 | Wrexham | 1976/77 | 1981/82 | Apprentice | Crewe Alexandra | 48/9 | 10 | 7/4 | 3 | 2/2 | 0 | 6/2 | 2 |
| HOWELLS | Ron | 12/01/27 | Ponthenry | 1958/59 | 1959/60 | Worcester City | Barry Town | 80 | 0 | 5 | 0 | 0 | 0 | 0 | 0 |
| HOWLETT | Gary | 02/04/63 | Dublin | 1987/88 | 1987/88 | Bournem'th (loan) | | 6 | 1 | 0 | 0 | 0 | 0 | 0 | 0 |
| HUGHES | Alan | 05/10/48 | Wallasey | 1967/68 | 1967/68 | Liverpool (loan) | | 9 | 2 | 2 | 0 | 0 | 0 | 1 | 1 |
| HUGHES | Jack | 25/09/12 | Oswestry | 1933/34 | 1935/36 | Bolton Wanderers | Chesterfield | 82 | 21 | 4 | 0 | 0 | 0 | 17 | 6 |
| HUGHES | John | 18/02/42 | Prestatyn | 1962/63 | 1962/63 | Rhyl | | 2 | 0 | 0 | 0 | 0 | 0 | 0 | 0 |
| HUGHES | Mark | 16/09/83 | Dungannon | 2007/08 | 2008/09 | Stevenage B. | Barnet | 64/5 | 4 | 2 | 0 | 1 | 0 | 3 | 0 |
| HUGHES | Ron | 01/07/30 | Mold | 1951/52 | 1961/62 | Mold Alexandra | Holywell Town | 399 | 21 | 16 | 1 | 3 | 0 | 28 | 4 |
| HULME | Kevin | 02/12/67 | Farnworth | 1989/90 | 1989/90 | Bury (loan) | | 4 | 0 | 0 | 0 | 0 | 0 | 0 | 0 |
| HUMES | Jimmy | 06/08/42 | Carlisle | 1963/64 | 1966/67 | Bristol Rovers | Barnsley | 124 | 31 | 8 | 4 | 5 | 2 | 14/1 | 6 |
| HUNT | Bobby | 04/09/34 | Liverpool | 1958/59 | 1960/61 | Wrexham | Pwllheli | 84 | 2 | 6 | 1 | 2 | 0 | 2 | 0 |
| IRELAND | Jerry | 14/09/38 | Chester | 1957/58 | 1961/62 | Juniors | Altrincham | 40 | 8 | 0 | 0 | 0 | 0 | 5 | 2 |
| ISHERWOOD | Dennis | 09/01/24 | Northwich | 1946/47 | 1946/47 | Wrexham | Northwich Vic. | 3 | 0 | 0 | 0 | 0 | 0 | 2 | 1 |
| JACKSON | Harry | 30/12/18 | Blackburn | 1949/50 | 1949/50 | Blackburn Rovers | Hyde United | 21 | 10 | 2 | 3 | 0 | 0 | 1 | 1 |
| JACKSON | Peter | 06/04/61 | Shelf | 1994/95 | 1996/97 | Huddersfield T. | Halifax Town | 100 | 3 | 4 | 0 | 5 | 0 | 3 | 0 |
| JAKUB | Joe | 07/12/56 | Falkirk | 1988/89 | 1988/89 | AZ Alkmaar (Holl) | Burnley | 77/1 | 1 | 6 | 0 | 6 | 0 | 6 | 0 |
| | | | | 1993/94 | 1993/94 | Burnley | Wigan Athletic | | | | | | | | |
| JAMES | John | 24/10/48 | Stoke-on-Trent | 1972/73 | 1975/76 | Port Vale | Tranmere Rovers | 97/1 | 40 | 4 | 2 | 10 | 4 | 2 | 1 |
| JEFFRIES | Derek | 22/03/51 | Longsight | 1977/78 | 1980/81 | Crystal Palace | Telford United | 116/5 | 2 | 8/1 | 0 | 10 | 0 | 5 | 0 |

| Player | | Date of Birth | Place of Birth | First Season | Last Season | Previous Club | Next Club | League Apps | League G'ls | FA Cup Apps | FA Cup G'ls | League Cup Apps | League Cup G'ls | Others Apps | Others G'ls |
|---|---|---|---|---|---|---|---|---|---|---|---|---|---|---|---|
| JENKINS | Iain | 24/11/72 | Prescot | 1993/94 | 1997/98 | Everton | Dundee United | 155/5 | 1 | 11/1 | 0 | 7/2 | 0 | 12 | 0 |
| JENNINGS | Tommy | 08/03/02 | Strathaven | 1931/32 | 1932/33 | Leeds United | Bangor City | 48 | 33 | 1 | 0 | 0 | 0 | 6 | 5 |
| JEPSON | Barry | 29/12/29 | Alfreton | 1956/57 | 1959/60 | Mansfield Town | Southport | 89 | 42 | 3 | 5 | 0 | 0 | 9 | 3 |
| JOHNSON | Arthur | 23/01/33 | Liverpool | 1962/63 | 1962/63 | Wrexham (loan) | | 3 | 0 | 0 | 0 | 1 | 0 | 0 | 0 |
| JOHNSON | Bill | | Sheffield | 1931/32 | 1932/33 | Leeds United | Crewe Alexandra | 54 | 0 | 5 | 0 | 0 | 0 | 3 | 0 |
| JOHNSON | Eddie | 20/09/84 | Chester | 2008/09 | 2008/09 | Bradford City | Austin Aztex (US) | 7/3 | 1 | 1 | 0 | 0 | 0 | 0 | 0 |
| JOHNSON | Paul | 19/09/55 | Stoke-on-Trent | 1982/83 | 1982/83 | Stoke City | Altrincham | 18/1 | 0 | 1 | 0 | 2 | 0 | 2/1 | 0 |
| JOHNSON | Steve | 23/06/57 | Liverpool | 1985/86 | 1985/86 | Bristol City (loan) | | 45/3 | 16 | 2 | 0 | 4 | 0 | 2 | 0 |
| | | | | 1988/89 | 1988/89 | Scunthorpe Utd | Huskvarna (Swe) | | | | | | | | |
| JOLLEY | Charlie | 03/03/36 | Liverpool | 1955/56 | 1955/56 | Tranmere Rovers | Oswestry Town | 7 | 3 | 0 | 0 | 0 | 0 | 0 | 0 |
| JOLLY | Henry | 05/04/08 | Ushaw Moor | 1932/33 | 1932/33 | Leeds United | Southport | 9 | 0 | 0 | 0 | 0 | 0 | 0 | 0 |
| JONES | Ben | 07/07/92 | Wrexham | 2008/09 | 2009/10 | Trainee | Colwyn Bay | 2/13 | 0 | 0 | 0 | 0 | 0 | 0 | 0 |
| JONES | Bill | 06/06/24 | Liverpool | 1951/52 | 1951/52 | Manchester City | Wellington Town | 29 | 4 | 2 | 1 | 0 | 0 | 3 | 0 |
| JONES | Bobby | 28/03/33 | Walton | 1953/54 | 1957/58 | Southport | Blackburn Rovers | 166 | 0 | 5 | 0 | 0 | 0 | 13 | 0 |
| JONES | Bryn | 26/05/39 | Bagillt | 1964/65 | 1966/67 | Watford | New Brighton | 30 | 0 | 2 | 0 | 0 | 0 | 1 | 0 |
| JONES | Brynley | 16/05/59 | St. Asaph | 1976/77 | 1981/82 | Apprentice | Scarborough | 149/13 | 17 | 9 | 2 | 5/1 | 1 | 8 | 1 |
| JONES | Colin | 08/09/40 | Chester | 1959/60 | 1959/60 | Juniors | Wrexham | 3 | 0 | 0 | 0 | 0 | 0 | 0 | 0 |
| JONES | Ernie | 09/12/19 | Ruabon | 1949/50 | 1950/51 | Bangor City | | 6 | 1 | 0 | 0 | 0 | 0 | 1 | 0 |
| JONES | Harvey | 16/08/36 | Rhos | 1960/61 | 1960/61 | Wrexham | Ellesmere Port | 19 | 0 | 0 | 0 | 0 | 0 | 0 | 0 |
| JONES | Henry | 1909 | Bangor | 1933/34 | 1933/34 | Bangor City | | 8 | 0 | 0 | 0 | 0 | 0 | 1 | 0 |
| JONES | Jonathan | 27/10/78 | Wrexham | 1996/97 | 1999/00 | Trainee | TNS | 11/27 | 2 | 0/3 | 0 | 1/3 | 1 | 1/2 | 0 |
| JONES | Les | 09/11/40 | Wrexham | 1965/66 | 1968/69 | Tranmere Rovers | Runcorn | 132/3 | 35 | 5/1 | 1 | 6 | 0 | 13 | 8 |
| JONES | Mervyn | 30/04/31 | Bangor | 1961/62 | 1962/63 | Crewe Alexandra | Lincoln City | 63 | 10 | 2 | 1 | 4 | 1 | 2 | 0 |
| JONES | Ray | 04/06/44 | Chester | 1962/63 | 1968/69 | Juniors | Runcorn | 169/1 | 0 | 10 | 0 | 9 | 0 | 11/1 | 0 |
| JONES | Simon | 16/05/45 | Nettleham | 1967/68 | 1967/68 | Bangor City | Stalybridge C. | 3 | 0 | 1 | 0 | 0 | 0 | 0 | 0 |
| JONES | Walter | | | 1931/32 | 1931/32 | Buckley | | 2 | 0 | 0 | 0 | 0 | 0 | 0 | 0 |
| KAY | John | 1908 | Dalmellington | 1933/34 | 1933/34 | Dundee United | Dundee United | 2 | 0 | 0 | 0 | 0 | 0 | 1 | 0 |
| KAYE | David | 14/11/59 | Huddersfield | 1984/85 | 1985/86 | Mexborough T. | Denaby United | 10 | 0 | 0 | 0 | 1 | 0 | 0 | 0 |
| KEARNEY | Alan | 22/09/87 | Cork | 2006/07 | 2006/07 | Everton (loan) | | 4/2 | 0 | 0 | 0 | 0 | 0 | 0 | 0 |
| KEARNEY | Mike | 18/02/53 | Glasgow | 1976/77 | 1977/78 | Shrewsbury Town | Reading | 46/1 | 5 | 2 | 1 | 4 | 1 | 2 | 0 |
| | | | | 1980/81 | 1980/81 | Reading | Reading | | | | | | | | |
| KEATING | Dennis | 18/10/40 | Cork | 1962/63 | 1962/63 | Saltney Juniors | Wellington Town | 1 | 0 | 1 | 0 | 0 | 0 | 0 | 0 |
| KEELEY | Arthur | 29/03/05 | Ellesmere Port | 1938/39 | 1938/39 | Bournemouth | Portsmouth | 36 | 18 | 7 | 0 | 0 | 0 | 2 | 2 |
| KEELEY | Ernest | 01/10/08 | Ellesmere Port | 1931/32 | 1931/32 | Ellesmere Port | Leicester City | 19 | 0 | 2 | 0 | 0 | 0 | 1 | 0 |
| KEELEY | John | 27/07/61 | Plaistow | 1992/93 | 1992/93 | Oldham A. (loan) | | 4 | 0 | 0 | 0 | 0 | 0 | 0 | 0 |
| KEISTER | John | 11/11/70 | Manchester | 1999/00 | 1999/00 | Walsall | Shrewsbury Town | 8/2 | 0 | 0 | 0 | 0 | 0 | 1 | 0 |
| KELLY | Gerry | 18/09/08 | Hylton | 1932/33 | 1935/36 | Charlton Athletic | Port Vale | 73 | 27 | 3 | 2 | 0 | 0 | 16 | 8 |
| KELLY | John | 20/10/60 | Bebington | 1985/86 | 1986/87 | Preston N.E. | Swindon Town | 109/7 | 18 | 9 | 2 | 6 | 0 | 7/1 | 1 |
| | | | | 1992/93 | 1992/93 | Huddersfield Town | Rhyl | | | | | | | | |
| KELLY | Shaun | 11/12/88 | Liverpool | 2006/07 | 2009/10 | Trainee | Burton Albion | 30/9 | 1 | 0 | 0 | 0/1 | 0 | 0 | 0 |
| KELLY | Tony | 01/10/64 | Prescot | 1988/89 | 1988/89 | W.B.A. (loan) | | 5 | 0 | 0 | 0 | 2 | 0 | 0 | 0 |
| KELLY | Walter | 15/04/29 | Cowdenbeath | 1959/60 | 1960/61 | Stockport Co. | Rhyl | 56 | 24 | 3 | 1 | 0 | 0 | 2 | 1 |
| KENNEDY | Dave | 14/02/49 | Birkenhead | 1970/71 | 1973/74 | Tranmere Rovers | Torquay United | 79/8 | 9 | 4 | 1 | 6/1 | 0 | 8 | 0 |
| KENNEDY | Joe | 15/11/25 | Cleator Moor | 1961/62 | 1961/62 | W.B.A. | Stourbridge | 35 | 0 | 0 | 0 | 1 | 0 | 1 | 0 |
| KENWORTHY | Jon | 18/08/74 | St. Asaph | 1995/96 | 1995/96 | Tranmere R. (loan) | | 5/2 | 1 | 0 | 0 | 0 | 0 | 0 | 0 |
| KILCAR | Steve | 22/12/07 | Bo'ness | 1934/35 | 1934/35 | Mansfield Town | Burnley | 3 | 4 | 0 | 0 | 0 | 0 | 1 | 0 |
| KINSEY | Steve | 02/01/63 | Manchester | 1982/83 | 1982/83 | Man City (loan) | | 3 | 1 | 0 | 0 | 0 | 0 | 0 | 0 |
| KIRKPATRICK | Roger | 29/05/23 | Chester | 1947/48 | 1952/53 | Juniors | Altrincham | 111 | 26 | 2 | 1 | 0 | 0 | 3 | 0 |
| KITCHEN | Peter | 16/02/52 | Mexborough | 1984/85 | 1984/85 | Dagenham | Dagenham | 3/2 | 1 | 0 | 0 | 0 | 0 | 0 | 0 |
| KNOWLES | Chris | 04/02/78 | Stoke | 1996/97 | 1996/97 | Peterborough U. | Hereford United | 2 | 0 | 0 | 0 | 1 | 0 | 0 | 0 |
| LACEY | Des | 03/08/25 | Dublin | 1946/47 | 1946/47 | Amateur | Witton Albion | 1 | 0 | 0 | 0 | 0 | 0 | 1 | 0 |
| LAIRD | Kamu | 23/12/75 | Port of Spain,Trin. | 1999/00 | 1999/00 | Augusta Uni. (US) | Dulwich Hamlet | 2/1 | 1 | 0 | 0 | 0 | 0 | 0 | 0 |
| LAMBIE | Alex | 15/4/1897 | Troon | 1931/32 | 1931/32 | Partick Thistle | Swindon Town | 1 | 0 | 0 | 0 | 0 | 0 | 0 | 0 |
| LANCASHIRE | Graham | 19/10/72 | Blackpool | 1993/94 | 1993/94 | Burnley (loan) | | 10/1 | 7 | 0 | 0 | 0 | 0 | 0 | 0 |
| LANCASTER | Martyn | 10/11/80 | Wigan | 1998/99 | 2002/03 | Trainee | Leigh RMI | 22/6 | 0 | 1/2 | 0 | 3 | 0 | 1/1 | 0 |
| LANE | Martin | 12/04/61 | Altrincham | 1982/83 | 1986/87 | Manchester Utd | Coventry City | 272/2 | 3 | 17 | 1 | 20 | 0 | 19 | 0 |
| | | | | 1988/89 | 1990/91 | Coventry City | Walsall | | | | | | | | |
| LANG | Gavan | 21/03/26 | Lanark | 1956/57 | 1956/57 | Spalding United | | 3 | 0 | 0 | 0 | 0 | 0 | 0 | 0 |
| LANG | Gavin | 10/11/51 | Hereford | 1969/70 | 1969/70 | Newcastle United | Crewe Alexandra | 0 | 0 | 1 | 1 | 0 | 0 | 0 | 0 |
| LANGLEY | Kevin | 24/05/64 | St. Helens | 1987/88 | 1987/88 | Man City (loan) | | 9 | 0 | 0 | 0 | 0 | 0 | 0 | 0 |
| LAWTON | Bill | 04/06/20 | Ashton-U-Lyne | 1949/50 | 1949/50 | Oldham Athletic | Bacup Borough | 0 | 0 | 0 | 0 | 0 | 0 | 1 | 0 |
| LEE | Eric | 18/10/22 | Chester | 1946/47 | 1956/57 | Amateur | Retired | 363 | 10 | 19 | 0 | 0 | 0 | 28 | 0 |
| LEE | Garth | 30/09/43 | Sheffield | 1963/64 | 1964/65 | Sheffield United | New Brighton | 28 | 7 | 2 | 2 | 0 | 0 | 1 | 1 |
| LENNARD | Dave | 31/12/44 | Manchester | 1974/75 | 1975/76 | Cambridge Utd | Stockport Co. | 73/2 | 11 | 4 | 0 | 8 | 1 | 5 | 2 |
| LEONARD | Mark | 27/09/62 | St. Helens | 1993/94 | 1993/94 | Preston N.E. | Wigan Athletic | 28/4 | 9 | 3 | 1 | 2 | 0 | 3 | 0 |
| LEONARD | Stan | 08/10/24 | Hawarden | 1946/47 | 1946/47 | Amateur | | 1 | 0 | 0 | 0 | 0 | 0 | 0 | 0 |

| Player | | Date of Birth | Place of Birth | First Season | Last Season | Previous Club | Next Club | League | | FA Cup | | League Cup | | Others | |
|---|---|---|---|---|---|---|---|---|---|---|---|---|---|---|---|
| | | | | | | | | Apps | G'ls | Apps | G'ls | Apps | G'ls | Apps | G'ls |
| LEWIS | Paul | | | 1979/80 | 1979/80 | Apprentice | Newport County | 0 | 0 | 0 | 0 | 0 | 0 | 1/1 | 0 |
| LIGHTFOOT | Chris | 01/04/70 | Winwick | 1987/88 | 1994/95 | Trainee | Wigan Athletic | 263/14 | 31 | 16/2 | 1 | 15/2 | 1 | 14/2 | 5 |
| LIMBERT | Mark | 03/10/73 | Hawarden | 1992/93 | 1992/93 | Trainee | Connah's Quay N. | 12/2 | 0 | 0 | 0 | 0 | 0 | 0 | 0 |
| LINDFIELD | Craig | 07/09/88 | Wirral | 2007/08 | 2007/08 | Liverpool (loan) | | 5/2 | 0 | 0 | 0 | 0 | 0 | 0 | 0 |
| LINWOOD | Paul | 24/10/83 | Birkenhead | 2006/07 | 2008/09 | Tranmere Rovers | Grimsby Town | 118/4 | 4 | 3/1 | 0 | 3 | 0 | 4 | 1 |
| LITTLE | Jack | 18/09/04 | Dunston-on-Tyne | 1933/34 | 1934/35 | Southport | Le Havre (France) | 36 | 0 | 2 | 0 | 0 | 0 | 3 | 0 |
| LIVERMORE | Doug | 27/12/47 | Liverpool | 1977/78 | 1978/79 | Cardiff City | Cardiff (Res. Man) | 71 | 6 | 5 | 0 | 4 | 1 | 3 | 0 |
| LIVSEY | Gordon | 24/01/47 | Keighley | 1971/72 | 1971/72 | Wrexham | Kettering Town | 44 | 0 | 2 | 0 | 2 | 0 | 3 | 0 |
| LLOYD | Brian | 18/03/48 | St. Asaph | 1977/78 | 1979/80 | Wrexham | Stockport Co. | 94 | 0 | 5 | 0 | 8 | 0 | 5 | 0 |
| LLOYD | John | 20/06/16 | Brymbo | 1937/38 | 1937/38 | Local | Wrexham | 1 | 0 | 0 | 0 | 0 | 0 | 0 | 0 |
| LOSKA | Tony | 11/02/50 | Chesterton | 1973/74 | 1976/77 | Port Vale | Halifax Town | 103/7 | 5 | 4 | 0 | 12 | 0 | 6 | 1 |
| LOWE | Ryan | 18/09/78 | Liverpool | 2004/05 | 2005/06 | Shrewsbury Town | Crewe Alexandra | 81/4 | 30 | 3 | 3 | 1 | 2 | 0/1 | 0 |
| | | | | 2008/09 | 2008/09 | Crewe Alexandra | Bury | | | | | | | | |
| LOWEY | John | 07/03/58 | Manchester | 1987/88 | 1987/88 | Preston N.E. | Brisbane L'ns (Aus) | 9 | 0 | 0 | 0 | 0 | 0 | 0 | 0 |
| LOWNDES | Nathan | 02/06/77 | Salford | 2007/08 | 2007/08 | Port Vale | Retired | 8/4 | 0 | 1 | 0 | 1 | 0 | 0/1 | 0 |
| LOYDEN | Eddie | 22/12/45 | Liverpool | 1967/68 | 1967/68 | Carlisle United | Shrewsbury Town | 99 | 48 | 8 | 2 | 3 | 0 | 9 | 5 |
| | | | | 1970/71 | 1971/72 | Barnsley | Tranmere Rovers | | | | | | | | |
| LUDLAM | Steve | 18/10/55 | Chesterfield | 1980/81 | 1982/83 | Carlisle United | Ilves (Finland) | 100/2 | 12 | 4 | 0 | 5 | 0 | 5/1 | 0 |
| LUNDON | Sean | 07/03/69 | Liverpool | 1986/87 | 1990/91 | Everton | Bath City | 48/8 | 4 | 5 | 0 | 3/1 | 0 | 5 | 0 |
| LUNN | Phil | | | 1974/75 | 1974/75 | Bangor City | Bangor City | 0 | 0 | 0 | 0 | 0 | 0 | 1 | 1 |
| LYNCH | Gavin | 07/09/85 | Liverpool | 2004/05 | 2004/05 | Trainee | Marine | 0/1 | 0 | 0/1 | 0 | 0 | 0 | 0 | 0 |
| MACKIE | Tom | 30/03/18 | Burntisland | 1948/49 | 1948/49 | New Brighton | Runcorn | 5 | 0 | 2 | 0 | 0 | 0 | 0 | 0 |
| MADDY | Paul | 17/08/62 | Cwmcarn | 1987/88 | 1987/88 | Brentford | Hereford United | 17/1 | 1 | 0 | 0 | 0 | 0 | 3 | 0 |
| MALONE | Steve | 28/04/78 | Glasgow | 1999/00 | 1999/00 | Knightswood | Glencairn | 0 | 0 | 1 | 0 | 0 | 0 | 0 | 0 |
| MANNION | Gerry | 21/12/39 | Burtonwood | 1967/68 | 1967/68 | Norwich City | Kidderminster H. | 6 | 0 | 0 | 0 | 0 | 0 | 1 | 0 |
| MANNIX | David | 24/09/85 | Winsford | 2008/09 | 2008/09 | Accrington S. | Vauxhall Motors | 10/3 | 2 | 0 | 0 | 1 | 0 | 0 | 0 |
| MANNS | Paul | 15/04/61 | Stafford | 1982/83 | 1983/84 | Notts County | Brereton Social | 28 | 3 | 1 | 3 | 2 | 0 | 0 | 0 |
| MANSLEY | Cliff | 05/04/21 | Skipton | 1948/49 | 1948/49 | Barnsley | Yeovil Town | 22 | 0 | 0 | 0 | 0 | 0 | 1 | 0 |
| MANSLEY | Eric | 28/02/17 | Chester | 1936/37 | 1938/39 | Llanerch Celts | Liverpool | 9 | 0 | 0 | 0 | 0 | 0 | 2 | 0 |
| MANTLE | Joe | 09/05/08 | Hetton-le-Hole | 1932/33 | 1934/35 | Plymouth Argyle | Carlisle United | 74 | 63 | 7 | 5 | 0 | 0 | 12 | 6 |
| MARPLES | Simon | 30/07/75 | Sheffield | 2006/07 | 2007/08 | Doncaster Rovers | Alfreton Town | 40/6 | 0 | 4 | 0 | 0 | 0 | 2 | 0 |
| MARSH | Frank | 07/06/16 | Bolton | 1946/47 | 1947/48 | Bolton Wanderers | Macclesfield T. | 69 | 2 | 3 | 0 | 0 | 0 | 5 | 0 |
| MARTINEZ | Roberto | 13/07/73 | Balaguer - Spain | 2006/07 | 2006/07 | Swansea City | Swansea City (man) | 31 | 3 | 5 | 0 | 1 | 0 | 1 | 0 |
| MASON | Jimmy | 17/04/33 | Glasgow | 1957/58 | 1958/59 | Accrington S. | Chelmsford City | 64 | 7 | 5 | 1 | 0 | 0 | 2 | 0 |
| MASON | Stuart | 02/06/48 | Whitchurch | 1973/74 | 1977/78 | Wrexham | Rochdale | 132/5 | 7 | 6 | 0 | 12/1 | 1 | 8/1 | 2 |
| MATTHEWS | Cyril | 01/12/01 | Cowes | 1931/32 | 1931/32 | Stockport Co. | Hyde United | 9 | 1 | 0 | 0 | 0 | 0 | 1 | 0 |
| MATTHEWS | Billy | 04/04/1897 | Plas Bennion | 1931/32 | 1931/32 | New Brighton | Oswestry Town | 5 | 0 | 0 | 0 | 0 | 0 | 1 | 0 |
| MATTHEWSON | Reg | 06/08/39 | Sheffield | 1972/73 | 1975/76 | Fulham | Bangor City | 86/1 | 1 | 3 | 0 | 9 | 0 | 4 | 0 |
| MAYERS | Alan | 20/04/37 | Chester | 1954/55 | 1955/56 | Local | Llandudno | 1 | 0 | 0 | 0 | 0 | 0 | 1 | 0 |
| MAYLETT | Brad | 24/12/80 | Manchester | 2006/07 | 2006/07 | Boston U. (loan) | | 3/2 | 1 | 0 | 0 | 0 | 0 | 0 | 0 |
| McCARTHY | Bernard | | | 1937/38 | 1937/38 | Bangor City | Wolves | 1 | 0 | 0 | 0 | 0 | 0 | 0 | 0 |
| McCARTHY | Paddy | 02/02/14 | Liverpool | 1937/38 | 1937/38 | Southport | Retired | 2 | 0 | 0 | 0 | 0 | 0 | 0 | 0 |
| McCREARY | John | 18/01/09 | Shotts | 1937/38 | 1938/39 | Bury | | 56 | 2 | 1 | 0 | 0 | 0 | 8 | 2 |
| McDONALD | Rod | 20/03/67 | London | 1996/97 | 1997/98 | Southport | Barrow | 43/10 | 11 | 1 | 0 | 1 | 0 | 3 | 1 |
| McGILL | Jimmy | 02/10/39 | Bellshill | 1962/63 | 1963/64 | Crewe Alexandra | Wrexham | 32 | 0 | 0 | 0 | 2 | 0 | 1 | 0 |
| McGOUGH | Joe | 27/10/09 | Tow Law | 1938/39 | 1938/39 | Reading | Southport | 34 | 4 | 7 | 0 | 0 | 0 | 0 | 0 |
| McGOWAN | George | 30/11/43 | Carluke | 1962/63 | 1963/64 | Preston N.E. | Stockport Co. | 18 | 3 | 0 | 0 | 1 | 0 | 0 | 0 |
| McGUINNESS | Paul | 02/03/66 | Manchester | 1991/92 | 1991/92 | Manchester Utd | Man U (Youth C) | 3/4 | 0 | 0 | 0 | 2/2 | 0 | 0 | 0 |
| McHALE | Kevin | 01/10/39 | Darfield | 1970/71 | 1971/72 | Crewe Alexandra | Hastings United | 61/3 | 4 | 6 | 1 | 1 | 0 | 5 | 0 |
| McILHARGEY | Steve | 28/08/63 | Ferryhill | 1993/94 | 1993/94 | Blackpool (loan) | | 1 | 0 | 0 | 0 | 0 | 0 | 0 | 0 |
| McINTYRE | Kevin | 23/12/77 | Liverpool | 2002/03 | 2004/05 | Doncaster Rovers | Macclesfield T. | 9/1 | 0 | 1/1 | 0 | 1 | 0 | 3 | 0 |
| McKAY | Matt | 21/01/81 | Warrington | 1997/98 | 1997/98 | Trainee | Everton | 3/2 | 0 | 0 | 0 | 0 | 0 | 0 | 0 |
| MacKENZIE | Chris | 14/05/72 | Northampton | 2004/05 | 2005/06 | Telford United | Shrewsbury Town | 53/1 | 0 | 4 | 0 | 1 | 0 | 2 | 0 |
| McLACHLAN | George | 21/09/02 | Glasgow | 1933/34 | 1933/34 | Manchester Utd | Le Havre (France) | 29 | 7 | 2 | 0 | 0 | 0 | 2 | 0 |
| MacLAREN | Jimmy | 26/11/21 | Crieff | 1946/47 | 1948/49 | Berwick Rangers | Carlisle United | 30 | 0 | 2 | 0 | 0 | 0 | 3 | 0 |
| McLAUGHLIN | Tony | 24/09/46 | Liverpool | 1967/68 | 1967/68 | Wrexham | Wigan Athletic | 2/2 | 0 | 0 | 0 | 0 | 0 | 0 | 0 |
| McMANUS | Paul | 22/04/90 | Liverpool | 2007/08 | 2008/09 | Trainee | Bangor City | 15/13 | 3 | 0/1 | 0 | 0 | 0 | 2 | 0 |
| McMILLAN | Sammy | 29/09/41 | Belfast | 1969/70 | 1969/70 | Southend United | Stockport Co. | 16/2 | 0 | 0 | 0 | 0 | 0 | 5 | 0 |
| McNEIL | Dave | 14/05/21 | Chester | 1946/47 | 1950/51 | Hoole Alexandra | Holywell Town | 114 | 1 | 9 | 0 | 0 | 0 | 3 | 0 |
| McNIVEN | Scott | 27/05/78 | Leeds | 2005/06 | 2005/06 | Mansfield Town | Morecambe | 41 | 1 | 4 | 0 | 1 | 0 | 0/1 | 0 |
| McSPORRAN | Jermaine | 01/01/77 | Manchester | 2006/07 | 2006/07 | Doncaster Rovers | Kidlington Town | 0/1 | 0 | 0 | 0 | 0 | 0 | 0 | 0 |
| MEECHAN | Alex | 29/01/80 | Plymouth | 2006/07 | 2006/07 | Forest Green Rovers | York City | 2/6 | 0 | 0 | 0 | 0 | 0 | 0 | 0 |
| MELLOR | Ian | 19/02/50 | Sale | 1977/78 | 1978/79 | Brighton & H.A. | Sheffield Wed. | 38/2 | 11 | 3 | 3 | 4 | 1 | 0/1 | 0 |
| MERCER | Arthur | 17/03/05 | St. Helens | 1931/32 | 1933/34 | Bristol City | Halifax Town | 63 | 18 | 7 | 1 | 0 | 0 | 7 | 2 |
| METCALF | Mike | 24/05/39 | Liverpool | 1963/64 | 1968/69 | Wrexham | Altrincham | 221 | 68 | 12 | 8 | 10 | 7 | 22 | 3 |
| MIDDLETON | Bob | 15/01/03 | Brechin | 1933/34 | 1937/38 | Burton Town | Congleton Town | 56 | 0 | 4 | 0 | 0 | 0 | 5 | 0 |

| Player | | Date of Birth | Place of Birth | First Season | Last Season | Previous Club | Next Club | League | | FA Cup | | League Cup | | Others | |
|---|---|---|---|---|---|---|---|---|---|---|---|---|---|---|---|
| | | | | | | | | Apps | G'ls | Apps | G'ls | Apps | G'ls | Apps | G'ls |
| MILLINGTON | Grenville | 10/12/51 | Queensferry | 1968/69 | 1968/69 | Rhyl | Rhyl | 290 | 0 | 19 | 0 | 20 | 0 | 16 | 0 |
| | | | | 1973/74 | 1982/83 | Brighton & HA | Oswestry Town | | | | | | | | |
| MILLS | John | 19/12/20 | Bagillt | 1946/47 | 1946/47 | Juniors | Altrincham | 3 | 0 | 0 | 0 | 0 | 0 | 1 | 0 |
| MILLSOM | Ernie | 27/08/01 | Old Brumby | 1931/32 | 1931/32 | Charlton Athletic | | 11 | 0 | 1 | 0 | 0 | 0 | 1 | 0 |
| MILNER | Andy | 10/02/67 | Kendal | 1994/95 | 1997/98 | Rochdale | Morecambe | 106/19 | 24 | 5/1 | 4 | 5/3 | 3 | 4/1 | 0 |
| MILOSAVIJEVIC | Goran | 11/04/67 | Kraljevo,Serbia | 1999/00 | 1999/00 | Montelimar (Fra) | China (trial) | 11/1 | 0 | 3 | 0 | 2 | 0 | 1 | 0 |
| MITCHELL | Andy | 18/04/90 | Liverpool | 2007/08 | 2007/08 | Trainee | Bangor City | 0/4 | 0 | 0 | 0 | 0 | 0 | 0 | 0 |
| MOFFATT | Greg | 08/01/64 | Liverpool | 1982/83 | 1982/83 | Apprentice | Olympiakos (Cyp) | 6/1 | 0 | 0 | 0 | 0 | 0 | 0 | 0 |
| MOIR | Ian | 30/06/43 | Aberdeen | 1967/68 | 1967/68 | Blackpool | Wrexham | 25 | 3 | 2 | 0 | 1 | 0 | 0 | 0 |
| MOLYNEUX | Geoff | 23/01/43 | Warrington | 1962/63 | 1962/63 | Rylands Y. C. | New Brighton | 1 | 0 | 0 | 0 | 1 | 0 | 0 | 0 |
| MOLYNEUX | John | 03/02/31 | Warrington | 1949/50 | 1954/55 | Juniors | Liverpool | 245 | 1 | 12 | 1 | 6 | 0 | 21 | 1 |
| | | | | 1962/63 | 1964/65 | Liverpool | New Brighton | | | | | | | | |
| MOORE | Gary | 04/11/45 | Sunderland | 1974/75 | 1975/76 | Southend United | Swansea City | 29/14 | 4 | 2 | 1 | 1/2 | 1 | 1/1 | 0 |
| MOORE | Tony | 04/09/47 | Scarborough | 1971/72 | 1971/72 | Chesterfield | Retired | 9/4 | 3 | 0 | 0 | 0 | 0 | 1 | 0 |
| MOORE | Steve | 17/12/69 | Chester | 1987/88 | 1987/88 | Apprentice | Rhyl | 0/1 | 0 | 0 | 0 | 1 | 0 | 0 | 0 |
| MOREMENT | Ralph | 24/09/24 | Sheffield | 1950/51 | 1952/53 | Sheffield United | Rochdale | 121 | 19 | 4 | 1 | 0 | 0 | 8 | 3 |
| MORREY | Bernard | 08/04/27 | Liverpool | 1953/54 | 1954/55 | Newport County | Ellesmere Port | 30 | 6 | 0 | 0 | 0 | 0 | 6 | 1 |
| MORRIS | Alan | 15/07/54 | Chester | 1974/75 | 1974/75 | Juniors | | 0/1 | 0 | 0 | 0 | 0 | 0 | 1 | 0 |
| | | | | 1984/85 | 1984/85 | Bangor City | Bangor City | | | | | | | | |
| MORRIS | Eric | 15/04/40 | Mold | 1960/61 | 1960/61 | Local | Ellesmere Port | 1 | 0 | 0 | 0 | 0 | 0 | 0 | 0 |
| MORRIS | Elfed | 09/06/42 | Colwyn Bay | 1962/63 | 1967/68 | Wrexham | Halifax Town | 164/3 | 69 | 9 | 5 | 3 | 1 | 18 | 9 |
| MORRIS | Fred | 15/06/29 | Oswestry | 1961/62 | 1961/62 | Gillingham | Altrincham | 29 | 3 | 2 | 1 | 1 | 0 | 1 | 0 |
| MORRIS | Sam | 12/02/30 | Warrington | 1951/52 | 1956/57 | Stockton Heath | Retired | 90 | 0 | 6 | 0 | 0 | 0 | 12 | 1 |
| MORRIS | Sam W. | 16/04/07 | Prescot | 1933/34 | 1933/34 | Charlton Athletic | Bath City | 5 | 0 | 0 | 0 | 0 | 0 | 1 | 0 |
| MORRISSEY | Pat | 23/02/48 | Enniscorthy | 1971/72 | 1971/72 | Crewe Alexandra | Watford | 9 | 1 | 2 | 0 | 0 | 0 | 0 | 0 |
| MORTON | Neil | 21/12/68 | Congleton | 1990/91 | 1992/93 | Northwich Vic.. | Wigan Athletic | 63/32 | 13 | 2/4 | 0 | 2/2 | 0 | 6/1 | 2 |
| MOSS | Darren | 24/05/81 | Wrexham | 1998/99 | 2000/01 | Trainee | Shrewsbury Town | 33/9 | 0 | 4 | 0 | 1/1 | 0 | 1 | 0 |
| MOZIKA | Damien | 15/04/87 | Corbeil-Ess.,France | 2008/09 | 2008/09 | AS Nancy | Tarbiat Yazd (Iran) | 21/1 | 2 | 1 | 0 | 1 | 0 | 1 | 0 |
| MULHOLLAND | John | 20/01/32 | Dumbarton | 1956/57 | 1956/57 | Southampton | Halifax Town | 8 | 1 | 0 | 0 | 0 | 0 | 1 | 0 |
| MURPHY | John | 18/10/76 | Whiston | 1994/95 | 1998/99 | Trainee | Blackpool | 104/38 | 29 | 1/2 | 0 | 7/3 | 1 | 4/1 | 0 |
| | | | | 2007/08 | 2007/08 | Macclesfield T. | St Patrick's Ath. | | | | | | | | |
| MURRAY | David | 30/09/67 | Chorley | 1985/86 | 1985/86 | Wigan Athletic | Witton Albion | 3/3 | 1 | 0 | 0 | 1 | 1 | 1 | 0 |
| MYERSCOUGH | Bill | 22/06/30 | Bolton | 1961/62 | 1962/63 | Coventry City | Wrexham | 36 | 10 | 1 | 0 | 3 | 2 | 1 | 0 |
| NASH | Martin | 27/12/75 | Victoria, Canada | 1999/00 | 1999/00 | Vancouver 86(Can) | Rochester Rhinos | 12/4 | 0 | 3/1 | 0 | 0 | 0 | 0 | 0 |
| NASSARI | Derek | 20/10/71 | Salford | 1989/90 | 1989/90 | Apprentice | Northwich Vic. | 0/1 | 0 | 0 | 0 | 0 | 0 | 0 | 0 |
| NAVARRO | Alan | 31/05/81 | Liverpool | 2004/05 | 2004/05 | Tranmere R. (loan) | | 3 | 0 | 0 | 0 | 1 | 0 | 0 | 0 |
| NEEDHAM | Paul | 15/06/61 | Buxton | 1980/81 | 1982/83 | Apprentice | Oswestry Town | 55/2 | 1 | 2 | 0 | 2 | 0 | 3 | 0 |
| NEWHOUSE | Aidan | 23/05/72 | Wallasey | 1987/88 | 1989/90 | Trainee | Wimbledon | 29/15 | 6 | 0/2 | 0 | 5/1 | 0 | 2/3 | 1 |
| NEWLAND | Ray | 19/07/71 | Liverpool | 1994/95 | 1995/96 | Plymouth Argyle | Torquay United | 9/1 | 0 | 0 | 0 | 0 | 0 | 2 | 0 |
| NEWTON | Sean | 23/09/88 | Liverpool | 2007/08 | 2007/08 | Trainee | Droylsden | 2 | 0 | 0 | 0 | 0 | 0 | 0 | 0 |
| NICKEAS | Mark | 20/10/56 | Southport | 1975/76 | 1978/79 | Plymouth Argyle | Vancouver W (Can) | 58/2 | 1 | 4 | 0 | 1 | 0 | 5 | 0 |
| NICHOLAS | Andy | 10/10/83 | Liverpool | 2004/05 | 2004/05 | Swindon T. (loan) | | 5 | 0 | 0 | 0 | 0 | 0 | 0 | 0 |
| NOLAN | David | 24/02/68 | Liverpool | 1991/92 | 1991/92 | Bromborough Pool | Barrow | 1 | 0 | 0 | 0 | 0 | 0 | 1 | 0 |
| NOTEMAN | Kevin | 15/10/69 | Preston | 1995/96 | 1996/97 | Doncaster Rovers | Rushden & D. | 57/11 | 18 | 3/1 | 0 | 0/1 | 1 | 1/2 | 0 |
| O'BERG | Paul | 08/05/58 | Hull | 1984/85 | 1984/85 | Wimbledon (loan) | | 5 | 1 | 0 | 0 | 0 | 0 | 2 | 0 |
| O'KEEFE | Eamon | 13/03/53 | Manchester | 1988/89 | 1989/90 | St. Patrick's Ath. | Retired | 12/5 | 4 | 0 | 0 | 0 | 0 | 0 | 0 |
| O'NEILL | Joe | 28/10/82 | Blackburn | 2004/05 | 2004/05 | Preston North End | York City | 5/6 | 1 | 0 | 0 | 0 | 0 | 0 | 0 |
| O'ROURKE | Billy | 02/04/60 | Nottingham | 1983/84 | 1983/84 | Burnley | Blackpool | 5 | 0 | 0 | 0 | 0 | 0 | 0 | 0 |
| OAKES | Alan | 01/09/42 | Winsford | 1976/77 | 1981/82 | Manchester City | Port Vale | 211 | 15 | 13 | 0 | 17 | 1 | 12 | 0 |
| OWEN | Cliff | 25/03/05 | Barry | 1938/39 | 1938/39 | Halifax Town | Accrington S. | 21 | 0 | 7 | 0 | 0 | 0 | 2 | 0 |
| OWEN | Derek | 25/09/38 | Ellesmere Port | 1958/59 | 1960/61 | Ellesmere Port | Runcorn | 7 | 0 | 1 | 0 | 0 | 0 | 0 | 0 |
| OWEN | James | 14/01/91 | Caernarfon | 2008/09 | 2009/10 | Trainee | Barrow | 4/3 | 0 | 0 | 0 | 0 | 0 | 0 | 0 |
| OWEN | Les | 11/04/33 | Saltney | 1956/57 | 1956/57 | Saltney Juniors | Runcorn | 1 | 0 | 0 | 0 | 0 | 0 | 0 | 0 |
| OWEN | Terry | 11/09/49 | Liverpool | 1972/73 | 1976/77 | Bradford City | Cambridge Utd | 161/15 | 41 | 9/1 | 1 | 10/2 | 2 | 11 | 4 |
| PAGE | Don | 18/01/64 | Manchester | 1994/95 | 1994/95 | Doncaster Rovers | Scarborough | 22/8 | 5 | 2 | 1 | 2 | 0 | 3 | 2 |
| PAINTER | Robbie | 26/01/71 | Ince | 1987/88 | 1990/91 | Trainee | Maidstone Utd | 58/26 | 8 | 7/1 | 3 | 2/2 | 0 | 3/4 | 0 |
| PALETHORPE | Phil | 17/09/86 | Wallasey | 2007/08 | 2007/08 | Tranmere Rovers | Airbus UK Brough. | 0/1 | 0 | 0 | 0 | 0 | 0 | 0 | 0 |
| PALMER | Richie | | | 1985/86 | 1985/86 | Juniors | | 0 | 0 | 0 | 0 | 0 | 0 | 1 | 0 |
| PARKER | Stuart | 16/02/54 | Preston | 1983/84 | 1983/84 | Preston N.E. | Blackpool | 9 | 5 | 0 | 0 | 2 | 0 | 0 | 0 |
| PARRY | Mark | 21/05/70 | Wrexham | 1987/88 | 1987/88 | Apprentice | Northwich Vic. | 4/1 | 1 | 0 | 0 | 1 | 0 | 0 | 0 |
| PARSLEY | Neil | 25/04/66 | Liverpool | 1989/90 | 1989/90 | Leeds Utd (loan) | | 6 | 0 | 0 | 0 | 0 | 0 | 0 | 0 |
| PARTRIDGE | Richie | 12/09/80 | Dublin | 2007/08 | 2008/09 | Rotherham Utd | MK Dons | 49/15 | 5 | 0 | 0 | 1 | 0 | 3 | 2 |
| PEARSON | Billy | 23/10/21 | Clonmel | 1949/50 | 1949/50 | Grimsby Town | Retired | 12 | 3 | 1 | 0 | 0 | 0 | 3 | 1 |
| PEARSON | Stan | 11/01/19 | Salford | 1957/58 | 1958/59 | Bury | (Manager) | 57 | 16 | 5 | 2 | 0 | 0 | 5 | 0 |
| PENDERGAST | Bill | 13/04/15 | Pen-y-groes | 1938/39 | 1938/39 | Colchester Utd | New Brighton | 34 | 26 | 7 | 2 | 0 | 0 | 2 | 1 |
| PERCIVAL | Peter | 23/02/11 | Reddish | 1936/37 | 1936/37 | Sheffield Wed | Hurst | 2 | 0 | 0 | 0 | 0 | 0 | 0 | 0 |

| Player | | Date of Birth | Place of Birth | First Season | Last Season | Previous Club | Next Club | League Apps | League G'ls | FA Cup Apps | FA Cup G'ls | League Cup Apps | League Cup G'ls | Others Apps | Others G'ls |
|---|---|---|---|---|---|---|---|---|---|---|---|---|---|---|---|
| PHILLIPS | Ron | 30/03/47 | Worsley | 1977/78 | 1980/81 | Bury | Chorley | 128/2 | 21 | 10 | 2 | 8/2 | 1 | 8 | 2 |
| PHILLIPS | Trevor | 18/09/52 | Rotherham | 1979/80 | 1981/82 | Hull City | Stockport Co. | 66/8 | 12 | 2 | 0 | 3 | 1 | 3 | 0 |
| | | | | 1983/84 | 1983/84 | Stockport Co. | Oswestry Town | | | | | | | | |
| PICKERING | Ally | 22/06/67 | Manchester | 1999/00 | 1999/00 | Altrincham | Hyde United | 7 | 1 | 0 | 0 | 0 | 0 | 0 | 0 |
| PILKINGTON | George | 03/06/26 | Hemsworth | 1952/53 | 1952/53 | Rotherham Utd | Stockport Co. | 16 | 0 | 1 | 0 | 0 | 0 | 3 | 0 |
| PIMLOTT | John | 21/01/39 | Radcliffe | 1959/60 | 1960/61 | Bury | Hyde United | 41 | 11 | 2 | 0 | 0 | 0 | 0 | 0 |
| PITCAIRN | John | 29/01/04 | Kelvinside | 1932/33 | 1936/37 | Charlton Athletic | Wigan Athletic | 135 | 0 | 15 | 0 | 0 | 0 | 19 | 1 |
| PLATT | Kristian | 15/12/91 | Rock Ferry | 2008/09 | 2009/10 | Trainee | Stalybridge C. | 0/1 | 0 | 0 | 0 | 0 | 0 | 0 | 0 |
| PORT | Bernard | 14/12/25 | Burton-on-Trent | 1951/52 | 1952/53 | Hull City | Bangor City | 9 | 0 | 0 | 0 | 0 | 0 | 1 | 0 |
| PORTER | Andy | 17/09/68 | Holmes Chapel | 1999/00 | 1999/00 | Wigan Ath.(loan) | | 16 | 0 | 0 | 0 | 0 | 0 | 0 | 0 |
| POTTER | Gary | 06/08/52 | Chester | 1972/73 | 1974/75 | Juniors | | 11 | 0 | 0 | 0 | 0 | 0 | 2 | 0 |
| POUNTNEY | Dave | 12/10/39 | Baschurch | 1970/71 | 1972/73 | Shrewsbury Town | Oswestry Town | 135 | 1 | 8 | 0 | 9 | 1 | 11 | 0 |
| PREECE | Roger | 09/06/69 | Much Wenlock | 1990/91 | 1995/96 | Wrexham | Southport | 165/5 | 4 | 8 | 1 | 10 | 0 | 11 | 0 |
| PRIEST | Chris | 18/10/73 | Leigh | 1994/95 | 1998/99 | Everton | Macclesfield T. | 162/5 | 26 | 6 | 1 | 6 | 0 | 8 | 0 |
| PRITCHARD | Alan | 24/08/43 | Chester | 1960/61 | 1963/64 | Juniors | Ellesmere Port | 19 | 6 | 0 | 0 | 2 | 1 | 0 | 0 |
| PROUT | Stan | 25/03/05 | Fulham | 1936/37 | 1936/37 | Bristol Rovers | Dartford | 2 | 1 | 0 | 0 | 0 | 0 | 0 | 0 |
| PROVAN | Andy | 01/01/44 | Greenock | 1968/69 | 1969/70 | York City | Wrexham | 78/4 | 18 | 9 | 1 | 1 | 0 | 7 | 4 |
| PUGH | David | 19/09/64 | Liverpool | 1989/90 | 1993/94 | Runcorn | Bury | 168/11 | 23 | 11/1 | 0 | 13 | 0 | 9 | 0 |
| PUGH | Graham | 12/02/48 | Hoole | 1974/75 | 1976/77 | Huddersfield T. | Barnsley | 67/2 | 3 | 3 | 0 | 5 | 0 | 4 | 0 |
| PURDIE | Bernard | 20/04/49 | Wrexham | 1971/72 | 1972/73 | Wrexham | Crewe Alexandra | 54/9 | 14 | 2/1 | 0 | 6 | 1 | 3/1 | 2 |
| PYE | Billy | 08/11/30 | St. Helens | 1953/54 | 1955/56 | Stockport Co. | Prescot Cables | 28 | 11 | 0 | 0 | 0 | 0 | 6 | 4 |
| QUINN | Philip | 05/10/78 | Wallasey | 1995/96 | 1995/96 | Apprentice | | 0 | 0 | 0 | 0 | 0/1 | 0 | 0 | 0 |
| RAMPLING | Eddie | 17/02/48 | Wigan | 1967/68 | 1967/68 | Newton Le Will..YC | Stalybridge C. | 2/1 | 0 | 0 | 0 | 0 | 0 | 0 | 0 |
| RANSON | John | 01/04/09 | Norwich | 1931/32 | 1931/32 | Swansea Town | Colwyn Bay | 8 | 1 | 0 | 0 | 0 | 0 | 0 | 0 |
| RAPLEY | Kevin | 21/09/77 | Reading | 2003/04 | 2004/05 | Colchester United | Droylsden | 12/9 | 2 | 1/2 | 2 | 0 | 0 | 3 | 0 |
| RATCLIFFE | Kevin | 12/11/60 | Mancot | 1994/95 | 1994/95 | Derby County | (Manager) | 23 | 0 | 1 | 0 | 2 | 0 | 2/1 | 0 |
| RAVENHILL | Ricky | 16/01/81 | Doncaster | 2006/07 | 2006/07 | Doncaster R (loan) | | 1/2 | 0 | 0 | 0 | 0 | 0 | 0 | 0 |
| RAYBOULD | Eric | 08/12/40 | Manchester | 1960/61 | 1961/62 | Juniors | Mossley | 10 | 0 | 1 | 0 | 0 | 0 | 0 | 0 |
| RAYNOR | Paul | 03/09/57 | Chester | 1974/75 | 1981/82 | Apprentice | Oswestry Town | 199/1 | 9 | 7/1 | 1 | 12 | 0 | 9/1 | 0 |
| | | | | 1983/84 | 1983/84 | Oswestry Town | | | | | | | | | |
| READ | David | 15/01/41 | West Bromwich | 1962/63 | 1966/67 | Wolves | Wellington Town | 68/4 | 6 | 1 | 0 | 3 | 0 | 5 | 0 |
| REDFERN | Jimmy | 01/08/52 | Kirkby | 1973/74 | 1976/77 | Bolton Wanderers | Washington Dip (US) | 98/8 | 15 | 7 | 1 | 3 | 0 | 4 | 1 |
| REEVES | Alan | 19/11/67 | Birkenhead | 1989/90 | 1990/91 | Norwich City | Rochdale | 31/9 | 2 | 3 | 0 | 1/1 | 0 | 3 | 0 |
| REEVES | Dennis | 01/12/44 | Lochmaben | 1963/64 | 1966/67 | Juniors | Wrexham | 139 | 0 | 9 | 0 | 5 | 0 | 12 | 0 |
| REGAN | Carl | 14/01/80 | Liverpool | 2004/05 | 2005/06 | Droylsden | Macclesfield T. | 43/4 | 0 | 4 | 0 | 1 | 0 | 0 | 0 |
| REGIS | Cyrille | 09/02/58 | Mariap'la,(Fr Guia) | 1995/96 | 1995/96 | Wycombe Wands. | W.B.A (Coach) | 29 | 7 | 1 | 0 | 3 | 0 | 0 | 0 |
| REID | Shaun | 13/10/65 | Huyton | 1996/97 | 1999/00 | Bury | Leigh RMI | 53/9 | 2 | 3 | 0 | 4 | 0 | 4 | 0 |
| REILLY | William | 24/12/02 | Lanark | 1931/32 | 1931/32 | Gateshead | Southend United | 35 | 1 | 2 | 0 | 0 | 0 | 4 | 0 |
| RELISH | John | 05/10/53 | Huyton | 1972/73 | 1973/74 | Apprentice | Newport County | 10/1 | 1 | 0 | 0 | 3 | 0 | 3 | 0 |
| RICHARDS | Gordon | 23/10/33 | Rhos | 1957/58 | 1960/61 | Wrexham | Sankeys | 74 | 16 | 5 | 0 | 0 | 0 | 1 | 0 |
| RICHARDSON | Fred | 18/08/25 | Middlestone Moor | 1951/52 | 1952/53 | W.B.A. | Hartlepools Utd | 23 | 6 | 0 | 0 | 0 | 0 | 0 | 0 |
| RICHARDSON | Harry | | | 1949/50 | 1949/50 | | | 0 | 0 | 0 | 0 | 0 | 0 | 1 | 0 |
| RICHARDSON | Ian | 09/05/64 | Ely | 1985/86 | 1986/87 | Watford | Scunthorpe Utd | 31/4 | 10 | 0 | 0 | 1/1 | 0 | 0 | 0 |
| RICHARDSON | Marcus | 31/08/77 | Reading | 2005/06 | 2005/06 | Yeovil Town | Weymouth | 22/12 | 4 | 3/1 | 2 | 0 | 0 | 1 | 0 |
| RICHARDSON | Nick | 11/04/67 | Halifax | 1994/95 | 1994/95 | Cardiff C.(loan) | | 164/11 | 12 | 8 | 2 | 11 | 1 | 5 | 1 |
| | | | | 1995/96 | 2000/01 | Bury | York City | | | | | | | | |
| RICHARDSON | Paul | 25/10/49 | Shirebrook | 1976/77 | 1976/77 | Nottingham F. | Stoke City | 28 | 2 | 5 | 0 | 0 | 0 | 1 | 0 |
| RIGBY | Bill | 09/06/21 | Chester | 1946/47 | 1946/47 | Juniors | | 1 | 0 | 0 | 0 | 0 | 0 | 0 | 0 |
| RIMMER | Stuart | 12/10/64 | Southport | 1984/85 | 1987/88 | Everton | Watford | 323/38 | 135 | 14/6 | 2 | 20/2 | 9 | 21/4 | 4 |
| | | | | 1991/92 | 1997/98 | Barnsley | Marine | | | | | | | | |
| ROBERTS | Charlie | 28/02/01 | Halesowen | 1933/34 | 1933/34 | Crystal Palace | Rotherham Utd | | | | | | | | |
| ROBERTS | Kevin | 17/08/89 | Liverpool | 2007/08 | 2009/10 | Trainee | Cambridge Utd | 74/7 | 7 | 1 | 0 | 0/1 | 0 | 1/1 | 0 |
| ROBERTS | Mark | 16/10/83 | Northwich | 2005/06 | 2005/06 | Crewe Alex. (loan) | | 1 | 0 | 0 | 0 | 0 | 0 | 0 | 0 |
| ROBERTS | Norman | 1915 | Penmachno | 1933/34 | 1933/34 | Penmachno | Bangor City | 1 | 1 | 0 | 0 | 0 | 0 | 2 | 0 |
| ROBERTS | Syd | 25/03/05 | Bootle | 1937/38 | 1938/39 | Shrewsbury Town | Northfleet Utd. | 29 | 6 | 0 | 0 | 0 | 0 | 5 | 1 |
| ROBERTS | Tom | 28/07/27 | Liverpool | 1955/56 | 1955/56 | Watford | Skelmersdale U. | 5 | 0 | 0 | 0 | 0 | 0 | 0 | 0 |
| ROBERTSON | Chris | 29/03/05 | Mablethorpe | 1938/39 | 1938/39 | Grimsby Town | Hereford United | 13 | 0 | 0 | 0 | 0 | 0 | 0 | 0 |
| ROBERTSON | Chris | 11/10/86 | Dundee | 2005/06 | 2005/06 | Sheffield U. (loan) | | 0/1 | 0 | 0 | 0 | 0 | 0 | 0 | 0 |
| ROBINSON | Albert | 01/06/48 | Chester | 1967/68 | 1968/69 | Juniors | Runcorn | 4/1 | 0 | 0 | 0 | 0 | 0 | 0 | 0 |
| ROBINSON | Jamie | 26/02/72 | Liverpool | 1999/00 | 1999/00 | Exeter City | Retired | 9 | 0 | 0 | 0 | 0 | 0 | 0 | 0 |
| ROBINSON | Matthew | 21/04/07 | Felling | 1931/32 | 1931/32 | Manchester Utd | Barrow | 6 | 1 | 0 | 0 | 0 | 0 | 0 | 0 |
| ROBSON | Cud | 19/10/00 | High Wheatley | 1931/32 | 1931/32 | Bristol City | | 13 | 4 | 2 | 0 | 0 | 0 | 1 | 0 |
| ROGERS | Dave | 25/08/75 | Liverpool | 1995/96 | 1996/97 | Tranmere Rovers | Southport | 18/7 | 1 | 0/1 | 0 | 2/2 | 0 | 1 | 0 |
| ROGERS | Joe | 29/03/05 | Normanton | 1938/39 | 1938/39 | Manchester City | Shrewsbury Town | 8 | 1 | 3 | 0 | 0 | 0 | 0 | 0 |
| ROLFE | Jimmy | 08/02/32 | Liverpool | 1953/54 | 1954/55 | Liverpool | Crewe Alexandra | 50 | 4 | 1 | 0 | 0 | 0 | 7 | 3 |
| ROSCOE | Jack | 28/01/06 | Oldham | 1932/33 | 1932/33 | Oldham Athletic | Macclesfield T. | 1 | 1 | 0 | 0 | 0 | 0 | 0 | 0 |
| ROSS | Albert | 07/10/16 | York | 1938/39 | 1938/39 | Bradford P. A. | | 1 | 0 | 0 | 0 | 0 | 0 | 0 | 0 |

| Player | | Date of Birth | Place of Birth | First Season | Last Season | Previous Club | Next Club | League | | FA Cup | | League Cup | | Others | |
|---|---|---|---|---|---|---|---|---|---|---|---|---|---|---|---|
| | | | | | | | | Apps | G'ls | Apps | G'ls | Apps | G'ls | Apps | G'ls |
| ROWLANDS | Colin | | | 1974/75 | 1974/75 | Juniors | | 0 | 0 | 0 | 0 | 0 | 0 | 1 | 0 |
| ROWLEY | Bill | 10/11/12 | Chester | 1934/35 | 1935/36 | Ellesmere Port | | 2 | 0 | 0 | 0 | 0 | 0 | 1 | 0 |
| RUDDY | John | 24/10/86 | St Ives | 2005/06 | 2005/06 | Everton (loan) | | 4 | 0 | 0 | 0 | 0 | 0 | 0 | 0 |
| RUGGIERO | John | 26/11/54 | Stoke-on-Trent | 1979/80 | 1979/80 | Brighton & H.A. | Telford United | 9/3 | 1 | 0 | 0 | 3 | 0 | 0 | 0 |
| RULE | Glenn | 30/11/89 | Birkenhead | 2007/08 | 2009/10 | Trainee | Colwyn Bay | 20/6 | 0 | 0 | 0 | 0 | 0 | 0/1 | 0 |
| RUSH | Ian | 20/10/61 | St. Asaph | 1978/79 | 1979/80 | Apprentice | Liverpool | 33/1 | 14 | 5 | 4 | 0 | 0 | 2 | 1 |
| RUTHERFORD | Paul | 10/07/87 | Moreton | 2005/06 | 2008/09 | Greenleas | Barrow | 22/35 | 1 | 0/2 | 0 | 0/2 | 0 | 1/2 | 0 |
| RYAN | Darren | 03/07/72 | Oswestry | 1992/93 | 1992/93 | Shrewsbury Town | Stockport Co. | 7/14 | 3 | 1/1 | 1 | 2 | 0 | 1/1 | 0 |
| | | | | 1995/96 | 1995/96 | Rochdale | Barry Town | | | | | | | | |
| RYAN | John | 20/07/47 | Lewisham | 1983/84 | 1983/84 | Stockport Co. | Cambridge Utd | 4 | 0 | 0 | 0 | 0 | 0 | 0 | 0 |
| RYDEN | Hugh | 07/04/43 | Dumbarton | 1964/65 | 1967/68 | Stockport Co. | Halifax Town | 140/1 | 44 | 7 | 0 | 6 | 1 | 16 | 5 |
| SALMON | Mike | 14/07/64 | Leyland | 1982/83 | 1982/83 | Blackbrn R (loan) | | 16 | 0 | 2 | 0 | 0 | 0 | 0 | 0 |
| SANDERS | Bob | 20/08/13 | Leeswood | 1935/36 | 1938/39 | Brickfields Ath | | 44 | 23 | 4 | 1 | 0 | 0 | 8 | 2 |
| SANDERSON | Paul | 16/12/66 | Blackpool | 1983/84 | 1983/84 | Manchester City | Halifax Town | 24 | 3 | 0 | 0 | 0 | 0 | 2 | 0 |
| SANDWITH | Kevin | 30/04/78 | Workington | 2006/07 | 2007/08 | Macclesfield T. | Weymouth | 39/15 | 3 | 3 | 0 | 0 | 0 | 2 | 0 |
| SARGEANT | Charlie | 02/02/09 | Cornsay | 1933/34 | 1937/38 | Hull City | Stockport Co. | 153 | 51 | 9 | 1 | 0 | 0 | 27 | 19 |
| SAUNDERS | Jack | 24/08/24 | Middlesbrough | 1957/58 | 1958/59 | Crystal Palace | Hyde United | 67 | 3 | 4 | 0 | 0 | 0 | 5 | 0 |
| SAYER | Peter | 02/05/55 | Cardiff | 1984/85 | 1984/85 | Preston N.E. | Morecambe | 35/1 | 6 | 0/1 | 0 | 2 | 0 | 0/1 | 0 |
| SCALES | George | 14/03/23 | Northwich | 1946/47 | 1948/49 | Manchester City | Rhyl | 81 | 0 | 5 | 0 | 0 | 0 | 3 | 0 |
| SCONCE | Mark | 18/02/68 | Wrexham | 1985/86 | 1986/87 | School | Rhyl | 1/1 | 0 | 0 | 0 | 0 | 0 | 2/1 | 0 |
| SEALEY | John | 27/12/45 | Wallasey | 1966/67 | 1967/68 | Liverpool | Wigan Athletic | 3/1 | 0 | 0 | 0 | 0 | 0 | 0/1 | 0 |
| SEAR | Cliff | 22/09/36 | Rhostyllen | 1968/69 | 1969/70 | Manchester City | (Coach) | 48/1 | 1 | 4 | 0 | 4 | 0 | 2 | 0 |
| SEARLE | Frank | 30/01/06 | Hednesford | 1932/33 | 1932/33 | Charlton Athletic | Watford | 4 | 0 | 0 | 0 | 0 | 0 | 0 | 0 |
| SEATON | Gordon | 01/09/45 | Wick | 1966/67 | 1967/68 | Rhyl | Runcorn | 46/3 | 2 | 2 | 0 | 1 | 0 | 0/1 | 0 |
| SEDDON | Ian | 14/10/50 | Prestbury | 1973/74 | 1975/76 | Bolton Wanderers | Stockport Co. | 62/11 | 7 | 1/1 | 0 | 9 | 0 | 2 | 0 |
| SELBY | Dennis | 15/10/20 | Broughton | 1946/47 | 1946/47 | Amateur | Altrincham | 5 | 1 | 1 | 0 | 0 | 0 | 0 | 0 |
| SEMPLE | Ryan | 04/07/85 | Belfast | 2006/07 | 2006/07 | Lincoln City (loan) | | 0/3 | 0 | 1/1 | 0 | 0 | 0 | 1 | 0 |
| SENIOR | Karl | 03/09/72 | Northwich | 1989/90 | 1989/90 | School | Northwich Vic. | 0/1 | 0 | 0 | 0 | 0 | 0 | 0 | 0 |
| SESTANOVICH | Ashley | 18/09/81 | Lambeth | 2004/05 | 2004/05 | Sheffield United | Gravesend & N. | 3/4 | 0 | 0 | 0 | 0 | 0 | 0 | 0 |
| SHELTON | Andy | 19/06/80 | Sutton Coldfield | 1997/98 | 2000/01 | Trainee | Harrogate Town | 14/21 | 1 | 1/2 | 0 | 5 | 1 | 0/1 | 0 |
| SHELTON | Gary | 21/03/58 | Nottingham | 1994/95 | 1997/98 | Bristol City | (Assistant Man.) | 62/7 | 5 | 3 | 0 | 4/1 | 0 | 2 | 2 |
| SHEPPARD | Bill | 21/03/05 | Ferryhill | 1934/35 | 1934/35 | Walsall | Walsall | 1 | 0 | 0 | 0 | 0 | 0 | 0 | 0 |
| SIBLEY | Eric | 17/11/15 | Christchurch | 1949/50 | 1949/50 | Grimsby Town | Lytham | 7 | 0 | 0 | 0 | 0 | 0 | 0 | 0 |
| SIDDALL | Barry | 12/09/54 | Ellesmere Port | 1991/92 | 1991/92 | Carlisle United | Preston N.E. | 9 | 0 | 1 | 0 | 1 | 0 | 1 | 0 |
| SIMMS | Hedley | 04/06/13 | Jackswood | 1934/35 | 1934/35 | Northern Nomads | Northern Nomads | 1 | 1 | 0 | 0 | 0 | 0 | 1 | 0 |
| SIMPSON | Gary | 10/06/59 | Chesterfield | 1981/82 | 1982/83 | Chesterfield | Oswestry Town | 57/6 | 18 | 2 | 0 | 4 | 0 | 7 | 2 |
| SINCLAIR | Ronnie | 19/11/64 | Stirling | 1996/97 | 1997/98 | Stoke City | Cardiff City | 70 | 0 | 3 | 0 | 3 | 0 | 1 | 0 |
| SINCLAIR | Roy | 10/12/44 | Liverpool | 1971/72 | 1971/72 | Watford (loan) | | 5 | 2 | 0 | 0 | 0 | 0 | 1 | 0 |
| SINGLETON | Tom | 08/09/40 | Blackpool | 1965/66 | 1967/68 | Peterborough U. | Bradford P.A. | 87/1 | 1 | 2 | 0 | 3 | 0 | 11 | 0 |
| SKINNER | David | | | 1946/47 | 1946/47 | Park Villa | Ellesmere Port | 0 | 0 | 0 | 0 | 0 | 0 | 1 | 0 |
| SKITT | Harry | 26/06/01 | Portobello, Staffs | 1931/32 | 1935/36 | Tottenham H. | Congleton Town | 101 | 0 | 9 | 0 | 0 | 0 | 12 | 0 |
| SLOAN | Tom | 10/07/59 | Ballymena | 1982/83 | 1982/83 | Manchester Utd | Linfield | 44 | 3 | 2 | 0 | 2 | 1 | 5 | 2 |
| SMALLWOOD | Fred | 24/03/05 | Brynteg | 1934/35 | 1934/35 | Wrexham | Macclesfield T. | 1 | 0 | 0 | 0 | 0 | 0 | 0 | 0 |
| SMEETS | Jorg | 05/11/70 | Bussum | 1998/99 | 1998/99 | Wigan A. (loan) | | 1/2 | 0 | 0 | 0 | 0 | 0 | 0 | 0 |
| SMITH | Alex | 15/02/76 | Liverpool | 1998/99 | 1998/99 | Huddersfield Town | Port Vale | 32 | 2 | 0 | 0 | 4 | 1 | 1 | 0 |
| SMITH | Bobby | 14/03/44 | Prestbury | 1971/72 | 1971/72 | Brighton & H.A. | Hartlepool | 2 | 0 | 0 | 0 | 0 | 0 | 0 | 0 |
| SMITH | Clem | 26/03/05 | Wath-on-Dearne | 1937/38 | 1937/38 | Halifax Town | Stoke City | 26 | 3 | 1 | 0 | 0 | 0 | 3 | 1 |
| SMITH | Harry | 27/08/30 | Chester | 1952/53 | 1957/58 | Connah's Quay N | Flint Town | 73 | 7 | 0 | 0 | 0 | 0 | 8 | 6 |
| SMITH | Paul | 17/11/91 | Liverpool | 2008/09 | 2008/09 | Trainee | Rhyl | 0/5 | 0 | 0 | 0 | 0 | 0 | 0 | 0 |
| SMYTH | Gerry | 05/11/31 | Belfast | 1951/52 | 1951/52 | Cardiff City | | 2 | 0 | 0 | 0 | 0 | 0 | 0 | 0 |
| SOUTER | Bill | 03/03/31 | Dundee | 1957/58 | 1959/60 | Burnley | Bangor City | 51 | 1 | 4 | 0 | 0 | 0 | 4 | 0 |
| SPEIGHT | Mick | 01/11/51 | Upton | 1984/85 | 1985/86 | Grimsby Town | Flekkeflord (Nw) | 40 | 1 | 2 | 0 | 3 | 0 | 0 | 0 |
| SPENCE | Alan | 07/02/40 | Seaham | 1969/70 | 1969/70 | Oldham Athletic | Southport | 5/4 | 2 | 2 | 0 | 0 | 0 | 2 | 1 |
| SPENCER | James | 11/04/85 | Stockport | 2008/09 | 2008/09 | Rochdale (loan) | | 5 | 0 | 0 | 0 | 0 | 0 | 0 | 0 |
| SPINK | Tony | 16/11/29 | Doncaster | 1951/52 | 1952/53 | Sheffield Wed | Weymouth | 13 | 3 | 1 | 0 | 0 | 0 | 0 | 0 |
| SPOONER | Nicky | 05/06/71 | Manchester | 1999/00 | 1999/00 | Charl'n B(US)(loan) | | 9 | 0 | 2 | 0 | 0 | 0 | 0 | 0 |
| SPRUCE | George | 03/04/23 | Chester | 1958/59 | 1960/61 | Barnsley | Runcorn | 63 | 0 | 4 | 0 | 1 | 0 | 2 | 0 |
| STACEY | Steve | 27/08/44 | Bristol | 1969/70 | 1969/70 | Ipswich T. (loan) | | 1 | 0 | 0 | 0 | 0 | 0 | 0 | 0 |
| STAMP | Darryn | 21/09/78 | Beverley | 2003/04 | 2004/05 | Northampton T. | Stevenage B. | 2/2 | 0 | 0 | 0 | 0 | 0 | 1 | 0 |
| STARKEY | Malcolm | 25/01/36 | Bulwell | 1962/63 | 1966/67 | Shrewsbury Town | Retired | 109 | 1 | 3 | 0 | 3 | 0 | 14 | 0 |
| STEELE | Lee | 07/12/73 | Liverpool | 2006/07 | 2006/07 | Leyton Orient | Northwich Vic. | 11/9 | 1 | 1/2 | 2 | 0 | 0 | 1 | 0 |
| STEVENSON | John | 27/02/1898 | Wigan | 1932/33 | 1932/33 | Falkirk | Bristol Rovers | 11 | 2 | 0 | 0 | 0 | 0 | 0 | 0 |
| STEWART | Billy | 01/01/65 | Liverpool | 1986/87 | 1993/94 | Wigan Athletic | Northampton T. | 317 | 0 | 20 | 0 | 25 | 0 | 21 | 0 |
| | | | | 1995/96 | 1995/96 | Northampton T. | Southport | | | | | | | | |
| STIFFLE | Nelson | 30/07/28 | India | 1951/52 | 1951/52 | Ashton United | Altrincham | 7 | 2 | 0 | 0 | 0 | 0 | 3 | 0 |
| STOPFORD | Les | 09/05/42 | Manchester | 1959/60 | 1961/62 | Juniors | Northwich Vic. | 6 | 1 | 0 | 0 | 0 | 0 | 0 | 0 |

| Player | | Date of Birth | Place of Birth | First Season | Last Season | Previous Club | Next Club | League | | FA Cup | | League Cup | | Others | |
|---|---|---|---|---|---|---|---|---|---|---|---|---|---|---|---|
| | | | | | | | | Apps | G'ls | Apps | G'ls | Apps | G'ls | Apps | G'ls |
| STORTON | Trevor | 26/11/49 | Keighley | 1974/75 | 1983/84 | Liverpool | Oswestry Town | 396 | 17 | 23 | 1 | 28 | 1 | 21 | 0 |
| STOWELL | Mike | 19/04/65 | Preston | 1987/88 | 1987/88 | Everton (loan) | | 14 | 0 | 0 | 0 | 0 | 0 | 2 | 0 |
| SUMMERBEE | George | 22/10/14 | Winchester | 1946/47 | 1946/47 | Preston N.E. | Barrow | 9 | 0 | 0 | 0 | 0 | 0 | 1 | 0 |
| SUTCLIFFE | Fred | 29/05/31 | Knottingley | 1952/53 | 1954/55 | Birmingham City | Winsford United | 50 | 2 | 1 | 0 | 0 | 0 | 8 | 1 |
| SUTCLIFFE | Peter | 25/01/57 | Manchester | 1978/79 | 1981/82 | Port Vale | Bangor City | 114/6 | 7 | 7 | 1 | 4 | 1 | 4 | 0 |
| | | | | 1983/84 | 1983/84 | Bangor City | Stockport Co. | | | | | | | | |
| SUTTON | Mike | 05/10/44 | Norwich | 1967/68 | 1969/70 | Norwich City | Carlisle United | 137/1 | 9 | 10 | 0 | 6 | 1 | 11 | 0 |
| TAIT | Paul | 24/10/74 | Newcastle | 2005/06 | 2005/06 | Rochdale | Boston United | 3/6 | 0 | 0 | 0 | 0 | 0 | 0 | 0 |
| TALBOT | Gary | 15/12/37 | Blackburn | 1963/64 | 1966/67 | Amateur | Crewe Alexandra | 153/1 | 83 | 8 | 4 | 9 | 6 | 12 | 13 |
| | | | | 1968/69 | 1968/69 | Crewe Alexandra | Drumcondra | | | | | | | | |
| TALLON | Gary | 05/09/73 | Drogheda | 1996/97 | 1996/97 | Kilmarnock (loan) | | 1 | 0 | 0 | 0 | 0 | 0 | 0 | 0 |
| TARBUCK | Alan | 10/10/48 | Liverpool | 1969/70 | 1971/72 | Crewe Alexandra | Preston N.E. | 69 | 24 | 8 | 4 | 5 | 1 | 8 | 1 |
| TAYLOR | John | 25/06/49 | Birmingham | 1970/71 | 1974/75 | Pwllheli | Stockport Co. | 70 | 0 | 2 | 0 | 3 | 0 | 7 | 0 |
| TAYLOR | Paul | 04/10/87 | Liverpool | 2008/09 | 2008/09 | Vauxhall M. (loan) | | 2/7 | 0 | 0 | 0 | 0 | 0 | 0/1 | 0 |
| THOMAS | John | 05/08/58 | Wednesbury | 1982/83 | 1982/83 | Bolton Wanderers | Lincoln City | 44 | 20 | 2 | 0 | 2 | 1 | 4 | 3 |
| THOMAS | John W. | 23/12/26 | Liverpool | 1953/54 | 1953/54 | Headington Utd | Stockport Co. | 29 | 5 | 1 | 0 | 0 | 0 | 2 | 0 |
| THOMAS | Rod | 10/10/70 | Harlesden | 1997/98 | 1998/99 | Carlisle United | Brighton & H. A. | 28/16 | 7 | 2 | 0 | 3/2 | 0 | 0 | 0 |
| THOMPSON | Andy | 21/01/1899 | Newcastle | 1931/32 | 1931/32 | Tottenham H. | Norwich City | 7 | 2 | 0 | 0 | 0 | 0 | 0 | 0 |
| THOMPSON | David | 27/05/62 | Manchester | 1992/93 | 1993/94 | Preston N.E. | Rochdale | 70/10 | 9 | 5 | 0 | 4 | 0 | 4 | 0 |
| THREADGOLD | Harry | 06/11/24 | Tattenhall | 1949/50 | 1951/52 | Tarvin United | Sunderland | 83 | 0 | 5 | 0 | 0 | 0 | 7 | 0 |
| TILSTON | Tommy | 19/02/26 | Chester | 1948/49 | 1950/51 | Local | Tranmere Rovers | 22 | 7 | 0 | 0 | 0 | 0 | 3 | 0 |
| TINNION | Brian | 11/06/48 | Workington | 1971/72 | 1971/72 | Wrexham (loan) | | 3 | 0 | 0 | 0 | 0 | 0 | 0 | 0 |
| TOLSON | Neil | 25/10/73 | Wordsley | 1994/95 | 1994/95 | Bradford C. (loan) | | 3/1 | 0 | 0 | 0 | 0 | 0 | 0 | 0 |
| TOMLEY | Fred | 11/07/31 | Liverpool | 1955/56 | 1955/56 | Liverpool | Witton Albion | 1 | 0 | 0 | 0 | 0 | 0 | 0 | 0 |
| TOMLINSON | Frank | 23/10/25 | Manchester | 1952/53 | 1952/53 | Rochdale | Ashton National | 11 | 0 | 0 | 0 | 0 | 0 | 3 | 2 |
| TRAVIS | Don | 21/01/24 | Moston | 1951/52 | 1953/54 | Oldham Athletic | Oldham Athletic | 99 | 45 | 2 | 0 | 0 | 0 | 9 | 9 |
| TREVIS | Arthur | 24/03/05 | Blackheath,Worcs | 1936/37 | 1938/39 | W.B.A. | Worcester City | 29 | 2 | 0 | 0 | 0 | 0 | 8 | 0 |
| TURNER | Graham | 05/10/47 | Ellesmere Port | 1967/68 | 1972/73 | Wrexham | Shrewsbury Town | 215/3 | 5 | 15 | 1 | 14 | 0 | 19 | 3 |
| TURNER | John | 29/03/05 | Wednesbury | 1936/37 | 1937/38 | B'mouth & B.A. | Bristol City | 4 | 0 | 0 | 0 | 0 | 0 | 2 | 0 |
| TURNER | Phil | 20/02/27 | Chester | 1946/47 | 1947/48 | Juniors | Carlisle United | 43 | 9 | 2 | 1 | 0 | 0 | 4 | 1 |
| | | | | 1956/57 | 1956/57 | Accrington S. | Winsford United | | | | | | | | |
| UPTON | Billy | | Coatbridge | 1933/34 | 1933/34 | Blackpool | Albion Rovers | 2 | 0 | 0 | 0 | 0 | 0 | 0 | 0 |
| VALENTINE | Albert | 03/06/07 | Higher Ince | 1931/32 | 1931/32 | Wigan Borough | Crewe Alexandra | 2 | 1 | 1 | 1 | 0 | 0 | 0 | 0 |
| VAUGHAN | James | 06/12/86 | Liverpool | 2006/07 | 2008/09 | Tranmere Rovers | Wollongong (Aus) | 76/2 | 0 | 1 | 0 | 2 | 0 | 2/1 | 0 |
| VAUGHAN | Stephen | 22/01/85 | Liverpool | 2004/05 | 2006/07 | Liverpool | Boston United | 48/18 | 0 | 4/4 | 0 | 2/1 | 0 | 5 | 0 |
| | | | | 2008/09 | 2009/10 | Boston United | Marine | | | | | | | | |
| VAUGHAN | Tommy | 27/09/08 | Cardiff | 1932/33 | 1933/34 | Treorchy | Cardiff City | 2 | 0 | 0 | 0 | 0 | 0 | 2 | 1 |
| VINER | Ron | 1904 | Reading | 1932/33 | 1932/33 | Accrington S. | Barrow | 1 | 0 | 0 | 0 | 0 | 0 | 0 | 0 |
| WAINWRIGHT | Tony | | | 1959/60 | 1959/60 | Juniors | | 0 | 0 | 0 | 0 | 0 | 0 | 1 | 0 |
| WALKER | Jim | 10/06/47 | Northwich | 1976/77 | 1980/81 | Peterborough U. | (Coach) | 171/1 | 4 | 12/2 | 0 | 12 | 0 | 10 | 0 |
| WALKER | Justin | 06/09/75 | Nottingham | 2005/06 | 2005/06 | Cambridge Utd | Ilkeston Town | 13/8 | 0 | 3 | 0 | 1 | 0 | 1 | 0 |
| WALKER | Nigel | 07/04/59 | Gateshead | 1984/85 | 1984/85 | Sunderland | Hartlepool Utd | 41 | 9 | 1 | 0 | 2 | 0 | 2 | 0 |
| WALLACE | Bob | 14/02/48 | Huddersfield | 1972/73 | 1972/73 | Halifax Town | Aldershot | 41 | 9 | 2 | 0 | 4 | 1 | 3 | 1 |
| WALLBANKS | John | 07/07/05 | Hindley | 1933/34 | 1934/35 | Portsmouth | Bradford P.A. | 38 | 36 | 3 | 2 | 0 | 0 | 2 | 4 |
| WALSH | Michael | 30/05/86 | Liverpool | 2004/05 | 2004/05 | Rhyl | Rhyl | 2/3 | 1 | 0/1 | 0 | 0 | 0 | 0 | 0 |
| WALTERS | Jon | 20/09/83 | Birkenhead | 2006/07 | 2006/07 | Wrexham | Ipswich Town | 24/2 | 9 | 5 | 1 | 1 | 0 | 0/1 | 0 |
| WALTERS | Trevor | 13/01/16 | Aberdare | 1937/38 | 1948/49 | Aberaman | Caernarvon Town | 151 | 1 | 12 | 0 | 0 | 0 | 11 | 0 |
| WALTON | John | 21/03/28 | Horwich | 1959/60 | 1959/60 | Kettering Town | | 1 | 0 | 0 | 0 | 0 | 0 | 0 | 0 |
| WANN | Dennis | 17/11/50 | Blackpool | 1983/84 | 1983/84 | Workington | Workington | 2/1 | 0 | 0 | 0 | 1 | 0 | 0 | 0 |
| WARBURTON | George | 30/03/05 | Holland | 1938/39 | 1938/39 | Preston N.E. | Morecambe | 10 | 2 | 0 | 0 | 0 | 0 | 2 | 0 |
| WARD | Gavin | 30/06/70 | Sutton Coldfield | 2007/08 | 2007/08 | Tranmere Rovers | Wrexham | 0 | 0 | 0 | 0 | 0 | 0 | 0/1 | 0 |
| WATFORD | Albert | 12/02/17 | Chesterfield | 1938/39 | 1938/39 | Mosborough | Bradford P. A. | 1 | 0 | 0 | 0 | 0 | 0 | 0 | 0 |
| WATLING | Barry | 16/07/46 | Walthamstow | 1975/76 | 1975/76 | Hartlepool (loan) | | 5 | 0 | 0 | 0 | 0 | 0 | 0 | 0 |
| WATSON | Andy | 13/11/78 | Leeds | 2004/05 | 2004/05 | Farsley Celtic | Farsley Celtic | 0 | 0 | 0 | 0 | 0 | 0 | 1 | 0 |
| WATSON | John | 02/05/42 | Wrexham | 1960/61 | 1961/62 | Everton | Wrexham | 25 | 0 | 0 | 0 | 2 | 0 | 2 | 0 |
| WAYMAN | Frank | 30/12/31 | Bishop Auckland | 1955/56 | 1955/56 | Preston N.E. | Darlington | 30 | 2 | 1 | 0 | 0 | 0 | 2 | 0 |
| WEBBER | Keith | 05/01/43 | Cardiff | 1969/70 | 1970/71 | Doncaster Rovers | Stockport Co. | 66/8 | 14 | 6/3 | 3 | 3/1 | 0 | 9 | 5 |
| WEBSTER | Harry | 22/08/30 | Sheffield | 1958/59 | 1959/60 | Bolton Wanderers | Chorley | 34 | 11 | 2 | 1 | 0 | 0 | 0 | 0 |
| WELSH | John | 10/01/84 | Liverpool | 2007/08 | 2007/08 | Hull City (loan) | | 6 | 0 | 0 | 0 | 0 | 0 | 0 | 0 |
| WESTON | Don | 06/03/36 | New Houghton | 1968/69 | 1968/69 | Wrexham | Altrincham | 1/2 | 0 | 0 | 0 | 1 | 0 | 0 | 0 |
| WESTWOOD | Ashley | 31/08/76 | Bridgnorth | 2006/07 | 2006/07 | Northampton T. | Stevenage B. | 21 | 3 | 2 | 0 | 1 | 0 | 1 | 0 |
| WESTWOOD | Ray | 14/04/12 | Brierley Hill | 1947/48 | 1948/49 | Bolton Wanderers | Darwen | 38 | 13 | 2 | 0 | 0 | 0 | 0 | 0 |
| WHALLEY | Shaun | 07/08/87 | Whiston | 2004/05 | 2004/05 | Southport | Runcorn FC Halton | 0/3 | 0 | 0 | 0 | 0 | 0 | 0/2 | 0 |
| WHARTON | Andy | 21/12/61 | Bacup | 1983/84 | 1984/85 | Burnley | Rossendale Utd | 19/4 | 2 | 0 | 0 | 0 | 0 | 2 | 0 |
| WHARTON | Guy | 05/12/16 | Broomfield | 1934/35 | 1935/36 | Broomhill | Wolves | 12 | 5 | 1 | 0 | 0 | 0 | 11 | 4 |
| WHEATON | Gil | 01/11/41 | Newcastle | 1963/64 | 1963/64 | Grimsby Town | Rhyl | 1 | 0 | 0 | 0 | 0 | 0 | 0 | 0 |

| Player | | Date of Birth | Place of Birth | First Season | Last Season | Previous Club | Next Club | League Apps | League G'ls | FA Cup Apps | FA Cup G'ls | League Cup Apps | League Cup G'ls | Others Apps | Others G'ls |
|---|---|---|---|---|---|---|---|---|---|---|---|---|---|---|---|
| WHEELER | Paul | 03/01/65 | Caerphilly | 1992/93 | 1993/94 | Stockport Co. | Stalybridge C. | 35/5 | 7 | 4 | 0 | 0 | 0 | 4 | 0 |
| WHELAN | Spencer | 17/09/71 | Liverpool | 1990/91 | 1997/98 | Liverpool | Shrewsbury Town | 196/19 | 8 | 9/3 | 0 | 11/1 | 2 | 5/2 | 0 |
| WHITE | Billy | 13/10/36 | Liverpool | 1961/62 | 1961/62 | Wrexham | Halifax Town | 13 | 3 | 1 | 0 | 0 | 0 | 0 | 0 |
| WHITE | Tommy | | | 1938/39 | 1938/39 | Skelmersdale U. | | 1 | 0 | 0 | 0 | 0 | 0 | 0 | 0 |
| WHITEHEAD | Norman | 22/04/48 | Fazakerley | 1973/74 | 1975/76 | Rotherham Utd | Grimsby Town | 66/8 | 5 | 4 | 0 | 9 | 1 | 6 | 0 |
| WHITLOCK | Phil | 01/05/30 | Llanhilleth | 1950/51 | 1958/59 | Cardiff City | Caernarvon Town | 142 | 3 | 8 | 0 | 0 | 0 | 13 | 0 |
| WHITTAM | Ernie | 07/01/11 | Wealdstone | 1933/34 | 1934/35 | Huddersfield T. | Mansfield Town | 54 | 20 | 4 | 1 | 0 | 0 | 6 | 0 |
| WILLCOX | Fred | 23/10/22 | St. Helens | 1947/48 | 1947/48 | Everton | South Liverpool | 16 | 0 | 3 | 0 | 0 | 0 | 1 | 0 |
| WILLDER | Fred | 20/03/44 | Lytham St. Annes | 1964/65 | 1965/66 | Preston N.E. | Fleetwood | 1/1 | 0 | 0 | 0 | 0 | 0 | 1 | 1 |
| WILLIAMS | Aled | 14/06/33 | Holywell | 1957/58 | 1957/58 | Burnley | Stalybridge C. | 33 | 1 | 2 | 0 | 0 | 0 | 3 | 0 |
| WILLIAMS | Bobby | 24/11/32 | Chester | 1951/52 | 1959/60 | Saltney Juniors | Runcorn | 37 | 3 | 1 | 0 | 0 | 0 | 2 | 0 |
| WILLIAMS | Derek | 09/12/22 | Ellesmere Port | 1946/47 | 1946/47 | Little Sutton J. | Oldham Athletic | 2 | 0 | 0 | 0 | 0 | 0 | 1 | 0 |
| WILLIAMS | Mike | 06/02/65 | Mancot | 1981/82 | 1983/84 | Apprentice | Wrexham | 31/4 | 4 | 1/1 | 1 | 4 | 0 | 1 | 0 |
| WILLIAMS | Phil J. | 07/02/63 | Swansea | 1983/84 | 1983/84 | Wigan Ath. (loan) | | 5/1 | 0 | 0 | 0 | 1 | 0 | 0 | 0 |
| WILLIAMS | Phil L. | 05/04/58 | Birkenhead | 1976/77 | 1976/77 | Juniors | | 1 | 0 | 0 | 0 | 0 | 0 | 0 | 0 |
| WILLIAMS | Ronnie | 23/01/17 | Llansamlet | 1935/36 | 1935/36 | Newcastle Utd | Swansea Town | 24 | 15 | 2 | 0 | 0 | 0 | 0 | 0 |
| WILLIAMSON | George | 13/09/25 | Newcastle | 1947/48 | 1949/50 | Middlesbrough | Bradford City | 75 | 4 | 6 | 1 | 0 | 0 | 4 | 1 |
| WILSON | Arthur | 06/10/08 | Newcastle | 1933/34 | 1937/38 | West Ham United | Wolves | 136 | 6 | 8 | 0 | 0 | 0 | 23 | 0 |
| WILSON | Bobby | 29/06/34 | Musselburgh | 1962/63 | 1962/63 | Accrington S. | Sankeys | 15 | 0 | 0 | 0 | 3 | 0 | 0 | 0 |
| WILSON | Clive | 13/11/61 | Manchester | 1982/83 | 1982/83 | Man City (loan) | | 21 | 2 | 0 | 0 | 0 | 0 | 2 | 0 |
| WILSON | Laurence | 10/10/86 | Liverpool | 2006/07 | 2008/09 | Everton | Morecambe | 108/7 | 4 | 6/1 | 2 | 3 | 0 | 5 | 2 |
| WINDLE | Billy | 09/07/20 | Maltby | 1951/52 | 1954/55 | Lincoln City | Caernarvon Town | 127 | 20 | 6 | 1 | 0 | 0 | 11 | 1 |
| WINTERSGILL | David | 19/09/65 | Northallerton | 1983/84 | 1983/84 | Wolves (loan) | | 5 | 0 | 0 | 0 | 0 | 0 | 1 | 0 |
| WITHE | Chris | 25/09/62 | Liverpool | 1990/91 | 1990/91 | Bury (loan) | | 2 | 0 | 0 | 0 | 0 | 0 | 0 | 0 |
| WOODALL | Brian | 06/06/48 | Chester | 1970/71 | 1970/71 | Sheffield Wed. | Oswestry Town | 11/2 | 2 | 0 | 0 | 3 | 1 | 1 | 0 |
| WOODS | Matt | 09/09/76 | Gosport | 1996/97 | 2000/01 | Everton | Stalybridge C. | 114/21 | 4 | 6/1 | 0 | 8/3 | 0 | 3/1 | 0 |
| WOODTHORPE | Colin | 13/01/69 | Ellesmere Port | 1985/86 | 1989/90 | Apprentice | Norwich City | 154/1 | 6 | 8/1 | 0 | 10 | 0 | 18 | 1 |
| WORKMAN | Ian | 13/11/62 | Liverpool | 1982/83 | 1982/83 | Southport | Southport | 3 | 0 | 0 | 0 | 0 | 0 | 2 | 0 |
| WORSWICK | Randall | 28/12/11 | Wavertree | 1938/39 | 1938/39 | Northwich Vic. | Prescot Cables | 8 | 4 | 0 | 0 | 0 | 0 | 0 | 0 |
| WRIGHT | Barry | 23/07/39 | Wrexham | 1962/63 | 1962/63 | Wrexham | Bangor City | 1 | 0 | 0 | 0 | 0 | 0 | 0 | 0 |
| WRIGHT | Billy | 28/04/58 | Liverpool | 1985/86 | 1985/86 | Birmingham (loan) | | 6 | 1 | 0 | 0 | 0 | 0 | 0 | 0 |
| WRIGHT | Darren | 07/09/79 | Warrington | 1997/98 | 2001/02 | Trainee | Droylsden | 24/24 | 2 | 4 | 0 | 4/1 | 0 | 0/2 | 0 |
| WRIGHT | Dick | 05/12/31 | Mexborough | 1952/53 | 1954/55 | Leeds United | Bradford City | 52 | 0 | 2 | 0 | 0 | 0 | 5 | 0 |
| WRIGHT | H Monty | 29/05/31 | Shirebrook | 1954/55 | 1954/55 | Stockport Co. | Retired | 21 | 4 | 0 | 0 | 0 | 0 | 0 | 0 |
| WRIGHTSON | Frank | 09/01/06 | Shildon | 1935/36 | 1938/39 | Exeter City | | 89 | 73 | 4 | 2 | 0 | 0 | 14 | 13 |
| WYNESS | George | 12/08/07 | Monkwearmouth | 1933/34 | 1933/34 | Southport | Rochdale | 8 | 0 | 0 | 0 | 0 | 0 | 1 | 0 |
| WYNNE | Darren | 12/10/70 | St. Asaph | 1988/89 | 1989/90 | Trainee | Connah's Quay N | 0/12 | 0 | 0 | 0 | 0 | 0 | 0 | 0 |
| WYPER | Tommy | 08/10/00 | Calton | 1931/32 | 1932/33 | Q.P.R. | Bristol Rovers | 24 | 7 | 2 | 2 | 0 | 0 | 1 | 0 |
| YATES | Dick | 06/06/21 | Queensferry | 1946/47 | 1947/48 | Wolves | Wrexham | 52 | 37 | 4 | 3 | 0 | 0 | 5 | 6 |
| YATES | John | 18/11/29 | Rotherham | 1951/52 | 1951/52 | Sheffield United | | 2 | 0 | 0 | 0 | 0 | 0 | 0 | 0 |
| YEO | Simon | 20/10/73 | Stockport | 2006/07 | 2007/08 | Peterborough U. | Macclesfield T. | 21/15 | 8 | 1 | 0 | 1 | 0 | 2 | 0 |
| ZELEM | Peter | 13/01/62 | Manchester | 1980/81 | 1984/85 | Apprentice | Wolves | 124/5 | 15 | 5 | 0 | 8 | 2 | 10 | 1 |

# CHESTER CITY PLAYERS WHO'S WHO 2000/01 TO 2003/04 AND 2009/10

| Player | | Date of Birth | Place of Birth | First Season | Last Season | Previous Club | Next Club | Conference Apps | Conference G'ls | FA Cup Apps | FA Cup G'ls | FA Trophy Apps | FA Trophy G'ls | Others Apps | Others G'ls |
|---|---|---|---|---|---|---|---|---|---|---|---|---|---|---|---|
| ALESSANDRA | Lewis | 08/02/89 | Bury | 2009/10 | 2009/10 | Oldham Ath.(loan) | | *4* | *0* | 0 | 0 | 0 | 0 | 0 | 0 |
| ASHTON | Neil | 15/01/85 | Liverpool | 2009/10 | 2009/10 | Shrewsbury Town | Wrexham | *19* | *0* | 2 | 0 | 0 | 0 | 0 | 0 |
| BARRY | Anthony | 29/05/86 | Liverpool | 2008/09 | 2009/10 | Yeovil Town | Fleetwood Town | *11/3* | *1* | 2 | 0 | 1 | 0 | 0 | 0 |
| BAXTER | Brett | 12/05/79 | Oldham | 2001/02 | 2001/02 | Accrington S. | Rossendale United | 1/1 | 0 | 0 | 0 | 0 | 0 | 0/1 | 0 |
| BEESLEY | Mark | 10/11/81 | Burscough | 2000/01 | 2003/04 | Preston N. E. | Hereford United | 80/17 | 33 | 5/1 | 1 | 12 | 3 | 8/1 | 4 |
| | | | | 2009/10 | 2009/10 | Cambridge U. (loan) | | *8* | *2* | 2 | 0 | 0 | 0 | 0 | 0 |
| BEESLEY | Paul | 21/07/65 | Liverpool | 2000/01 | 2000/01 | Blackpool | Kilkenny City | 32 | 0 | 5 | 1 | 5 | 1 | 2 | 0 |
| BERRY | Paul | 06/12/78 | Warrington | 1999/00 | 2000/01 | Warrington Town | Leek Town | 0/1 | 0 | 0 | 0 | 0 | 0 | 0/1 | 0 |
| BOLLAND | Phil | 26/08/76 | Liverpool | 2001/02 | 2005/06 | Oxford United | Peterborough U. | 74/5 | 5 | 5 | 1 | 5 | 3 | 3 | 0 |
| BLACKBURN | Chris | 02/08/82 | Crewe | 1999/00 | 2002/03 | Trainee | Nevada Won. (USA) | 70/12 | 7 | 7/1 | 0 | 7/1 | 1 | 8 | 2 |
| BLUNDELL | Gregg | 03/10/77 | Liverpool | 2009/10 | 2009/10 | Darlington | Barrow | *10/9* | *3* | 0 | 0 | 0 | 0 | 0 | 0 |
| BRABIN | Gary | 09/12/70 | Liverpool | 2001/02 | 2001/02 | Torquay United | TNS | 16 | 3 | 0 | 0 | 4 | 0 | 0 | 0 |
| BRADY | Jon | 14/01/75 | Newcastle (Aus) | 2002/03 | 2003/04 | Woking | Stevenage B. | 30/4 | 2 | 3/2 | 0 | 0/1 | 0 | 4 | 0 |
| BRODIE | Steve | 14/01/73 | Sunderland | 2002/03 | 2003/04 | Swansea City | Droylsden | 3/3 | 0 | 0 | 0 | 0 | 0 | 0 | 0 |
| BROWN | David | 02/10/78 | Bolton | 2001/02 | 2001/02 | Torquay United | Telford United | 11/2 | 2 | 0 | 0 | 3/2 | 1 | 0 | 0 |
| BROWN | Michael | 08/02/68 | Birmingham | 2002/03 | 2002/03 | Boston United | Nuneaton Borough | 6/17 | 0 | 0/3 | 0 | 1 | 0 | 0/1 | 0 |
| BROWN | Wayne | 14/01/77 | Southampton | 1996/97 | 2004/05 | Weston Super Mare | Hereford United | 131/1 | 0 | 15 | 0 | 13 | 0 | 10 | 0 |
| BUCKLEY | Dean | 31/07/85 | Liverpool | 2003/04 | 2003/04 | Trainee | Caernarfon Town | 0 | 0 | 0 | 0 | 0 | 0 | 0/1 | 0 |
| BYRNE | Danny | 17/03/83 | Crosby, Liverpool | 2002/03 | 2002/03 | Southport | Droylsden | 0 | 0 | 0 | 0 | 0/1 | 0 | 0 | 0 |
| CAMERON | David | 24/08/75 | Bangor | 2002/03 | 2002/03 | Lincoln City | Droylsden | 7/8 | 2 | 0/1 | 1 | 0/1 | 0 | 0/2 | 0 |

| Player | | Date of Birth | Place of Birth | First Season | Last Season | Previous Club | Next Club | Conference | | FA Cup | | FA Trophy | | Others | |
|---|---|---|---|---|---|---|---|---|---|---|---|---|---|---|---|
| | | | | | | | | Apps | G'ls | Apps | G'ls | Apps | G'ls | Apps | G'ls |
| CARDEN | Paul | 29/03/79 | Liverpool | 1999/00 | 2000/01 | Rochdale | Doncaster Rovers | 113/4 | 4 | 9 | 0 | 12 | 0 | 7/1 | 3 |
| | | | | 2001/02 | 2004/05 | Doncaster Rovers | Peterborough U. | | | | | | | | |
| CAREY | Shaun | 13/05/76 | Kettering | 2001/02 | 2003/04 | Rushden & D. | Hornchurch | 47/4 | 2 | 3 | 0 | 2 | 0 | 1 | 0 |
| CHADWICK | Nick | 26/10/82 | Stoke | 2009/10 | 2009/10 | Shrewsbury Town | Barrow | 21/2 | 7 | 0 | 0 | 1 | 0 | 0 | 0 |
| CLARE | Daryl | 01/08/78 | Jersey | 2002/03 | 2004/05 | Boston United | Boston United | 50/3 | 46 | 4 | 2 | 0 | 0 | 2 | 0 |
| CLIFFORD | Mark | 11/09/77 | Nottingham | 2002/03 | 2002/03 | Boston U. (loan) | | 1 | 0 | 0 | 0 | 0 | 0 | 0 | 0 |
| COLLINS | Danny | 06/08/80 | Chester | 2001/02 | 2004/05 | Buckley Town | Sunderland | 54/5 | 3 | 2 | 0 | 1 | 0 | 3 | 0 |
| COULSON | Michael | 04/04/88 | Scarborough | 2009/10 | 2009/10 | Barnsley (loan) | | 5 | 1 | 2 | 0 | 0 | 0 | 0 | 0 |
| COULTER | Sam | 13/11/91 | Liverpool | 2009/10 | 2009/10 | Trainee | Colwyn Bay | 2/1 | 0 | 0 | 0 | 0 | 0 | 0 | 0 |
| DANBY | John | 20/09/83 | Stoke | 2006/07 | 2009/10 | Kidderminster H. | Eastwood Town | 28 | 0 | 2 | 0 | 1 | 0 | 0 | 0 |
| DAVIDSON | Ryan | 12/04/92 | Chester | 2009/10 | 2009/10 | Trainee | Prestatyn Town | 2/3 | 0 | 0 | 0 | 0 | 0 | 0 | 0 |
| DAVIES | Ben | 27/05/81 | Birmingham | 2002/03 | 2005/06 | Kidderminster H. | Shrewsbury Town | 50/14 | 7 | 5 | 0 | 0/1 | 0 | 3 | 0 |
| DOGUN | Peter | 25/01/85 | Liverpool | 2003/04 | 2003/04 | Trainee | Droylsden | 0 | 0 | 0 | 0 | 0 | 0 | 0/1 | 0 |
| DOUGHTY | Matt | 02/11/81 | Warrington | 1999/00 | 2000/01 | Trainee | Rochdale | 35/5 | 1 | 5 | 0 | 5 | 0 | 6 | 0 |
| ELAM | Lee | 24/09/76 | Bradford | 2003/04 | 2003/04 | Yeovil Town (loan) | | 1/3 | 0 | 0 | 0 | 0 | 0 | 0 | 0 |
| ELLAMS | Lloyd | 11/01/91 | Chester | 2008/09 | 2009/10 | Trainee | Marine | 9/8 | 0 | 0/2 | 0 | 1 | 0 | 0 | 0 |
| EVANS | Andy | 25/11/75 | Aberystwyth | 2000/01 | 2000/01 | Barnsley (loan) | | 5/3 | 2 | 0 | 0 | 0 | 0 | 0 | 0 |
| FINNEY | Steve | 31/10/73 | Hexham | 1999/00 | 2000/01 | Barrow | Altrincham | 4/5 | 0 | 0 | 0 | 0 | 0 | 1 | 0 |
| FISHER | Neil | 07/11/70 | St Helens | 1998/99 | 2000/01 | Connahs Quay N. | Leigh RMI | 31/5 | 4 | 4/1 | 0 | 5 | 0 | 5/1 | 0 |
| FLYNN | Jonathan | 18/11/89 | Ballymena | 2009/10 | 2009/10 | Blackburn R. (loan) | | 3 | 0 | 2 | 1 | 0 | 0 | 0 | 0 |
| FOSTER | Ian | 11/11/76 | Liverpool | 2003/04 | 2003/04 | Kidderminster H. | Kidderminster H. | 10/10 | 2 | 2 | 0 | 1 | 0 | 1 | 0 |
| FREEMAN | Jordan | 08/07/92 | Chester | 2009/10 | 2009/10 | Trainee | GAP Connah's Quay | 1 | 0 | 0 | 0 | 1 | 0 | 0 | 0 |
| GAUNT | Craig | 31/03/74 | Sutton | 2000/01 | 2000/01 | Woodlands W(Sing) | Moor Green | 21/4 | 1 | 0/1 | 0 | 2/2 | 0 | 4 | 0 |
| GILL | Robert | 10/02/82 | Nottingham | 2003/04 | 2003/04 | Doncaster R. (loan) | | 3/1 | 0 | 0 | 0 | 0 | 0 | 0 | 0 |
| GREYGOOSE | Dean | 18/12/64 | Thetford | 2000/01 | 2000/01 | Altrincham | Witton Albion | 3 | 0 | 0 | 0 | 0 | 0 | 0 | 0 |
| GRIFFIN | Adam | 28/08/84 | Manchester | 2002/03 | 2002/03 | Oldham A. (loan) | | 0/1 | 0 | 0 | 0 | 0 | 0 | 0 | 0 |
| GUYETT | Scott | 20/01/76 | Ascot | 2002/03 | 2003/04 | Oxford United | Yeovil Town | 56/3 | 4 | 3/1 | 0 | 1 | 0 | 4 | 1 |
| HAARHOFF | Jimmy | 27/05/81 | Lusaka (Zambia) | 2000/01 | 2001/02 | Birmingham City | Droylsden | 12/25 | 2 | 1 | 0 | 2/6 | 3 | 1/2 | 0 |
| HALFORD | Steve | 21/09/80 | Bury | 2001/02 | 2001/02 | Bury | Accrington S. | 10 | 0 | 1 | 0 | 0 | 0 | 1 | 0 |
| HARKNESS | Steve | 27/08/71 | Carlisle | 2002/03 | 2002/03 | Sheffield Wed. | Retired | 10 | 0 | 0 | 0 | 0 | 0 | 0 | 0 |
| HARRIS | Andy | 26/02/77 | Springs (S. Africa) | 2003/04 | 2004/05 | Leyton Orient | Weymouth | 10/4 | 0 | 0 | 0 | 0 | 0 | 1 | 0 |
| HATSWELL | Wayne | 08/02/79 | Swindon | 2002/03 | 2003/04 | Oxford United | Kidderminster H. | 35/2 | 2 | 3 | 0 | 0 | 0 | 3 | 1 |
| HEARD | Jamie | 11/08/83 | Sheffield | 2003/04 | 2003/04 | Hull City | Morecambe | 24/1 | 0 | 2 | 0 | 0 | 0 | 1 | 0 |
| HIGGINS | Alex | 22/07/81 | Sheffield | 2001/02 | 2001/02 | QPR | Ilkeston Town | 0/1 | 0 | 0 | 0 | 0 | 0 | 0 | 0 |
| HILL | Sam | 02/12/80 | Ascot | 2001/02 | 2001/02 | Crewe Alexandra | Droylsden | 13 | 1 | 0 | 0 | 0 | 0 | 0 | 0 |
| HOPWOOD | Chris | 05/07/83 | Wrexham | 2001/02 | 2001/02 | Trainee | Oswestry Town | 0/4 | 0 | 0 | 0 | 0 | 0 | 0 | 0 |
| JENKINS | Iain | 24/11/72 | Liverpool | 2001/02 | 2001/02 | Shrewsbury Town | (Youth team man.) | 5/1 | 0 | 0 | 0 | 2 | 0 | 0 | 0 |
| JONES | Ben | 07/07/92 | Wrexham | 2008/09 | 2009/10 | Trainee | Colwyn Bay | 4 | 0 | 0 | 0 | 0/1 | 0 | 0 | 0 |
| JOY | Ian | 14/07/81 | San Diego (USA) | 2002/03 | 2002/03 | Columbus Crew(US) | Hamburg SV (Ger) | 3 | 0 | 0 | 0 | 0 | 0 | 0 | 0 |
| KAY | Adam | 05/03/90 | Burnley | 2009/10 | 2009/10 | Burnley (loan) | | 13/3 | 0 | 2 | 0 | 0 | 0 | 0 | 0 |
| KELLY | Jimmy | 14/02/73 | Liverpool | 2002/03 | 2002/03 | Doncaster Rovers | Scarborough | 29/3 | 1 | 0/1 | 0 | 1 | 0 | 0 | 0 |
| KELLY | Shaun | 11/12/88 | Liverpool | 2006/07 | 2009/10 | Trainee | Burton Albion | 15/3 | 1 | 0/1 | 0 | 1 | 0 | 0 | 0 |
| KELTIE | Clark | 31/08/83 | Newcastle | 2009/10 | 2009/10 | Rochdale (loan) | | 11 | 0 | 2 | 0 | 0 | 0 | 0 | 0 |
| KERR | David | 06/09/74 | Dumfries | 2000/01 | 2001/02 | Mansfield Town | Droylsden | 13/7 | 0 | 1 | 0 | 0 | 0 | 1/3 | 0 |
| KILGANNON | Wes | 08/04/82 | Chester | 2001/02 | 2001/02 | Trainee | Caernarfon Town | 8/4 | 0 | 0 | 0 | 0 | 0 | 0 | 0 |
| LANCASTER | Martyn | 10/11/80 | Wigan | 1998/99 | 2002/03 | Trainee | Leigh RMI | 74/3 | 2 | 6 | 0 | 12 | 0 | 6/1 | 0 |
| LANE | Chris | 25/05/79 | Liverpool | 2003/04 | 2003/04 | Leigh RMI | Leigh RMI | 1/3 | 0 | 0 | 0 | 0 | 0 | 0 | 0 |
| LEA | Michael | 04/11/87 | Salford | 2009/10 | 2009/10 | Scunthorpe United | Hyde United | 18/1 | 0 | 1 | 0 | 0/1 | 0 | 0 | 0 |
| LINIGHAN | David | 09/01/65 | Hartlepool | 2001/02 | 2001/02 | Southport | Hyde United | 3 | 0 | 0 | 0 | 0 | 0 | 0 | 0 |
| LOPEZ | Carlos | 18/04/70 | Mexico City | 2001/02 | 2001/02 | Cambridge U. (trial) | Wycombe Wands. | 0/2 | 0 | 0 | 0 | 0 | 0 | 0 | 0 |
| LYNCH | Chris | 31/01/91 | Blackburn | 2009/10 | 2009/10 | Burnley (loan) | | 10 | 0 | 0 | 0 | 0 | 0 | 0 | 0 |
| MACKEN | Louis | 29/02/84 | Chester | 2000/01 | 2000/01 | Trainee | Caernarfon Town | 0 | 0 | 0 | 0 | 0 | 0 | 0/1 | 0 |
| MALKIN | Chris | 04/06/67 | Hoylake | 2001/02 | 2001/02 | Telford United | Oswestry Town | 5/4 | 0 | 0 | 0 | 0 | 0 | 1 | 0 |
| McCALDON | Ian | 14/09/74 | Liverpool | 2002/03 | 2002/03 | Oxford U. (loan) | | 15 | 0 | 2 | 0 | 1 | 0 | 1 | 0 |
| | | | | 2003/04 | 2003/04 | Oxford United | Ross County | | | | | | | | |
| McELHATTON | Michael | 16/04/75 | Co Kerry | 2001/02 | 2001/02 | Rushden (loan) | | 8 | 2 | 0 | 0 | 1 | 0 | 0 | 0 |
| McGORRY | Brian | 16/04/70 | Liverpool | 2001/02 | 2001/02 | Southport | Tamworth | 14 | 0 | 0 | 0 | 4 | 0 | 0 | 0 |
| McINTYRE | Kevin | 23/12/77 | Liverpool | 2002/03 | 2004/05 | Doncaster Rovers | Macclesfield T. | 79/1 | 2 | 4 | 0 | 1 | 0 | 4 | 1 |
| McNIVEN | David | 27/05/78 | Stonehouse | 2001/02 | 2001/02 | York City | Hamilton A. | 3 | 0 | 0 | 0 | 0 | 0 | 0 | 0 |
| MEYNELL | Rhys | 17/08/88 | Barnsley | 2009/10 | 2009/10 | Stalybridge C. | Galway United | 11/5 | 0 | 0 | 0 | 0 | 0 | 0 | 0 |
| MOSS | Darren | 24/05/81 | Wrexham | 1998/99 | 2000/01 | Trainee | Shrewsbury Town | 16/5 | 0 | 0/1 | 0 | 2/3 | 0 | 3/2 | 0 |
| MURPHY | Andrew | 22/09/88 | Liverpool | 2009/10 | 2009/10 | Preston N E | Kendal Town | 0/1 | 0 | 0 | 0 | 0 | 0 | 0 | 0 |
| O'BRIEN | Chris | 13/01/82 | Liverpool | 2001/02 | 2001/02 | Liverpool | Droylsden | 9 | 0 | 0 | 0 | 0 | 0 | 1 | 0 |
| O'BRIEN | Mick | 25/09/79 | Liverpool | 2001/02 | 2001/02 | Droylsden | Droylsden | 8/2 | 2 | 0 | 0 | 2 | 0 | 0 | 0 |
| OWEN | James | 14/01/91 | Caernarfon | 2008/09 | 2009/10 | Trainee | Barrow | 7/5 | 0 | 0/2 | 0 | 1 | 0 | 0 | 0 |

| Player | | Date of Birth | Place of Birth | First Season | Last Season | Previous Club | Next Club | Conference Apps | Conference G'ls | FA Cup Apps | FA Cup G'ls | FA Trophy Apps | FA Trophy G'ls | Others Apps | Others G'ls |
|---|---|---|---|---|---|---|---|---|---|---|---|---|---|---|---|
| PEACOCK | Richard | 29/10/72 | Sheffield | 2001/02 | 2001/02 | Stalybridge C. | Worksop Town | 6 | 0 | 0 | 0 | 0 | 0 | 0 | 0 |
| PLATT | Kristian | 15/12/91 | Rock Ferry | 2008/09 | 2009/10 | Trainee | Stalybridge C. | *2/3* | *0* | 0 | 0 | 0 | 0 | 0 | 0 |
| PORTER | Andy | 17/09/68 | Holmes Chapel | 2000/01 | 2001/02 | Wigan Athletic | Kidsgrove Athletic | 34/4 | 4 | 6 | 0 | 4/3 | 0 | 4/1 | 0 |
| PRICE | Michael | 28/05/81 | Wrexham | 2000/01 | 2000/01 | Aston Villa | Brymbo Broughton | 0 | 0 | 0 | 0 | 0 | 0 | 1 | 0 |
| PRIESTLEY | Phil | 30/03/76 | Wigan | 2000/01 | 2000/01 | Rochdale (loan) | | 5/1 | 0 | 0 | 0 | 0 | 0 | 0 | 0 |
| QUAYLE | Mark | 02/10/78 | Liverpool | 2002/03 | 2002/03 | Nuneaton B. (loan) | | 6/3 | 1 | 0 | 0 | 0 | 0 | 0/2 | 0 |
| RAPLEY | Kevin | 21/09/77 | Reading | 2003/04 | 2004/05 | Colchester United | Droylsden | 9/17 | 2 | 0/2 | 0 | 0/1 | 0 | 1 | 0 |
| RAWLINSON | Connell | 22/09/91 | Wrexham | 2009/10 | 2009/10 | Trainee | TNS | *0/3* | *0* | 0 | 0 | 0 | 0 | 0 | 0 |
| REA | Jack | 15/04/92 | Chester | 2009/10 | 2009/10 | Trainee | Stalybridge C. | *3/1* | *1* | 0 | 0 | 1 | 0 | 0 | 0 |
| REGAN | Carl | 14/01/80 | Liverpool | 2003/04 | 2003/04 | Hull City (loan) | | 4 | 0 | 0 | 0 | 1 | 0 | 0 | 0 |
| RICHARDSON | Nick | 11/04/67 | Halifax | 1995/96 | 2000/01 | Bury | York City | 1/4 | 0 | 0 | 0 | 0 | 0 | 1 | 0 |
| ROBERTS | Kevin | 17/08/89 | Liverpool | 2007/08 | 2009/10 | Trainee | Cambridge Utd | *27/1* | *2* | 2 | 0 | 0 | 0 | 0 | 0 |
| ROBERTS | Paul | 08/08/82 | Whiston | 2001/02 | 2001/02 | Trainee | Caernarfon Town | 1/5 | 0 | 0 | 0 | 0 | 0 | 0 | 0 |
| ROSE | Michael | 28/07/82 | Salford | 2001/02 | 2001/02 | Manchester United | Hereford United | 33/1 | 4 | 1 | 0 | 4 | 0 | 1 | 0 |
| ROSE | Stephen | 23/11/80 | Salford | 2001/02 | 2001/02 | Bristol Rovers | Altrincham | 8/3 | 0 | 0 | 0 | 0 | 0 | 0 | 0 |
| RUFFER | Carl | 20/12/74 | Chester | 2000/01 | 2003/04 | Runcorn | Morecambe | 79/14 | 6 | 8/3 | 0 | 6 | 1 | 6 | 1 |
| RULE | Glenn | 30/11/89 | Birkenhead | 2007/08 | 2009/10 | Trainee | Colwyn Bay | *14/3* | *1* | 0 | 0 | 1 | 0 | 0 | 0 |
| RUSCOE | Scott | 15/12/77 | Shrewsbury | 2000/01 | 2001/02 | Newtown | TNS | 37/13 | 5 | 1/3 | 1 | 6 | 1 | 7/1 | 0 |
| RYAN | Tim | 10/12/74 | Stockport | 2009/10 | 2009/10 | Darlington | Stalybridge C. | *24* | *0* | 2 | 0 | 1 | 0 | 0 | 0 |
| SHELTON | Andy | 19/06/80 | Sutton Coldfield | 1997/98 | 2000/01 | Trainee | Harrogate Town | 0/3 | 0 | 0 | 0 | 0 | 0 | 0 | 0 |
| SMITH | Alex | 15/02/76 | Liverpool | 2003/04 | 2003/04 | Reading | Wrexham | 20 | 4 | 0 | 0 | 1 | 0 | 0 | 0 |
| SPINK | Dean | 22/01/67 | Birmingham | 2001/02 | 2001/02 | Wrexham | Telford United | 19/2 | 2 | 1 | 0 | 4/1 | 3 | 0/1 | 0 |
| STAMP | Darryn | 21/09/78 | Beverley | 2003/04 | 2004/05 | Northampton T. | Stevenage B. | 35/3 | 20 | 2 | 0 | 1 | 0 | 0 | 0 |
| SUGDEN | Ryan | 26/12/80 | Bradford | 2002/03 | 2002/03 | Scarborough | Burton Albion | 26/7 | 12 | 2 | 3 | 1 | 0 | 2/1 | 0 |
| TATE | Chris | 27/12/77 | York | 2001/02 | 2001/02 | Leyton O. (loan) | | 4/2 | 1 | 2 | 1 | 1 | 0 | 0 | 0 |
| | | | | 2002/03 | 2002/03 | Leyton O. (loan) | | | | | | | | | |
| TURNER | Iain | 26/01/84 | Stirling | 2003/04 | 2003/04 | Everton (loan) | | 12 | 0 | 0 | 0 | 0 | 0 | 0 | 0 |
| TWISS | Michael | 26/12/77 | Salford | 2002/03 | 2003/04 | Leigh RMI | Morecambe | 31/36 | 13 | 1/1 | 0 | 2 | 1 | 2 | 0 |
| VAUGHAN | James | 06/12/86 | Liverpool | 2009/10 | 2009/10 | Wollongong (Aus) | Droylsden | *1* | *0* | 0 | 0 | 0 | 0 | 0 | 0 |
| VAUGHAN | Stephen | 22/01/85 | Liverpool | 2008/09 | 2009/10 | Boston United | Marine | *6* | *0* | 0 | 0 | 0 | 0 | 0 | 0 |
| WHITEHALL | Steve | 08/12/66 | Bromborough | 2000/01 | 2000/01 | Oldham Athletic | Nuneaton Borough | 26/3 | 9 | 5 | 4 | 3/2 | 3 | 3 | 0 |
| WHITTAKER | Stuart | 02/01/75 | Liverpool | 2001/02 | 2001/02 | Southport | Leigh RMI | 6/1 | 4 | 0 | 0 | 3 | 0 | 0 | 0 |
| WILKINSON | Ben | 25/04/87 | Sheffield | 2009/10 | 2009/10 | York City | Tamworth | *19/7* | *3* | 1 | 0 | 1 | 0 | 0 | 0 |
| WILLIAMS | Danny | 12/07/79 | Wrexham | 2003/04 | 2003/04 | Kidderm'r H (loan) | | 5 | 0 | 0 | 0 | 0 | 0 | 0 | 0 |
| WILLIAMS | Gary | 19/07/79 | Burnley | 2001/02 | 2001/02 | Accrington (loan) | | 1/2 | 0 | 0 | 0 | 0 | 0 | 1 | 1 |
| WILLIAMS | Mark | 10/11/78 | Liverpool | 2001/02 | 2001/02 | Hereford United | BAFA (Brunei) | 5/3 | 0 | 0 | 0 | 0 | 0 | 0 | 0 |
| WOODS | Andy | 15/01/76 | Colchester | 2003/04 | 2003/04 | Northwich Vic. | Farsley Celtic | 1/1 | 0 | 0 | 0 | 0 | 0 | 0 | 0 |
| WOODS | Matt | 09/09/76 | Gosport | 1996/97 | 2000/01 | Everton | Stalybridge C. | 33/3 | 5 | 1/2 | 0 | 4/2 | 1 | 3/2 | 1 |
| WOODYATT | Lee | 16/07/83 | Bangor | 2000/01 | 2002/03 | Trainee | Northwich Vic. | 32/14 | 2 | 0 | 0 | 6/3 | 0 | 3/3 | 0 |
| WORSNOP | Jon | 13/01/83 | Bradford | 2002/03 | 2002/03 | Bradford City | Aberystwyth Town | 1 | 0 | 0 | 0 | 0 | 0 | 0 | 0 |
| WRIGHT | Darren | 07/09/79 | Warrington | 1997/98 | 2001/02 | Trainee | Droylsden | 16/24 | 5 | 0/5 | 1 | 0/3 | 0 | 2/5 | 1 |

## KEY TO WHO'S WHO SECTION

This section includes all players who appeared in competitive first team matches for the club between 1931 and 2010. The first table covers the Football League years while the second table shows the Conference years. Note that some players appear in both tables and although their first and last season's reflect the full time they spent at Chester there is no overlap between the appearances in the two tables. In other words, to find the total appearances made by a player like Paul Carden , who played in both the Football League and Conference you need to add the totals in both tables. Players who featured in the aborted 2009/10 Blue Square Premier season have been included in the second table but their league appearances are italicised as technically these appearances were later expunged. The second figure in the Apps. columns indicates number of substitute appearances. The appearances and goals in the Football League 'Other' columns apply to matches in Play-offs, Associate Members Cup (and later sponsors' named competitions), Welsh Cup, Division 3 North Cup and Debenhams Cup, The appearances and goals in the Conference 'Other' columns apply to match in the Play-offs, Associate Members Cup, Nationwide Variety Trophy and JC Thompson Championship Shield. Any blank entries indicate that the information is unknown.

## KEY TO SEASONAL STATISTICS RECORDS

The pages that follow have been designed for easy reference and are generally self-explanatory. The left hand column signifies the match number or the round number in a cup competition, e.g. 4Q = 4th qualifying round, 2R = 2nd round, 3Rr = 3rd round replay, 1R2 = 1st round second leg, SF = Semi-final, etc. The second column indicates the date. The third column shows the opposition team (upper case - capital letters - a Chester home match, lower case - away match). Neutral, or alternative venues are indicated otherwise. The fourth column shows the result (W = Won, D = Drawn, L = Lost), while the fifth and sixth columns show the full-time and the half-time result with the Chester score first. The seventh column shows the attendance, where known. The eighth column shows the Chester goalscorers, where known. A number in brackets is the number of goals scored by that player, (og) signifies an own goal (i.e. credited to an opposition player) and (p) or (pen) indicates a penalty. The numbers refer to the shirt number worn by that player in the starting line-up (or the accepted position in pre-War seasons, i.e. 1 = goalkeeper, 2 = right-back, 10 = inside-left, etc.) - where known. Unused substitutes have not been included. Used substitutes - no.12 replaced player suffixed *, no.13 replaced player suffixed ', no.14 replaced player suffixed ", no. 15 replaced player suffixed + no.16 replaced player suffixed ~ . The introduction of squad numbers in the Football League in 1999/2000 sees a reversion to numbering based on accepted position while the substitute numbers reflect the order of the substitutions. Number 12 is therefore the first substitute and he replaced the player suffixed * , number 13 is the second substitute and he replaced the player suffixed ' and so on. This system is also used in the Conference seasons. Any additional players are shown at the end of the appropriate table, the first number/letters indicating the match or round number, the second number, that player's position/shirt number. Appearances and goals relating to matches where the opposition's results were subsequently expunged have not been included.

# SEASON 1885-86

## WELSH CUP

| | Date | Opposition | | FT | HT | Att. | Goalscorers |
|---|---|---|---|---|---|---|---|
| 1R | Nov 7 | Crewe Brittania | L | 0-3 | 0-1 | | |

## FRIENDLIES

| | Date | Opposition | | FT | HT | Att. | Goalscorers |
|---|---|---|---|---|---|---|---|
| 1 | Sep 15 | Earlestown | L | | | | |
| 2 | 19 | Oswestry | L | 0-10 | 0-4 | | |
| 3 | 26 | NORTHWICH VICS. | L | 0-3 | 0-2 | 750 | |
| 4 | Oct 3 | CHESTER COLLEGE * | W | 1-0 | 0-0 | | Lockwood |
| 5 | 10 | Hartford St. Johns | D | 1-1 | 0-1 | | Unknown |
| 6 | 17 | Crewe Alex. | D | 2-2 | 2-1 | 1200 | Turner, Hack |
| 7 | 24 | Chester St. Oswalds | L | 1-2 | 1-1 | | Maddocks |
| 8 | 31 | Liverpool Ramblers | W | 6-1 | | | Unknown (6) |
| 9 | Nov 14 | NANTWICH | W | 4-1 | 3-0 | | Roberts, Southworth (2), Turner |
| 10 | 28 | Wrexham Olympic | D | 5-5 | 5-0 | | Unknown (5) |
| 11 | Dec 5 | BOOTLE | L | 2-4 | 1-3 | | McMillan, Unknown |
| 12 | 19 | CHESTER ST. OSWALDS | W | 2-1 | 2-1 | | Tomkinson, Lockwood |
| 13 | 26 | Chirk | D | 4-4 | 1-4 | | Lockwood, Unknown (3) |
| 14 | Jan 2 | CREWE BRITTANIA | D | 1-1 | 0-0 | 500 | James |
| 15 | 9 | OSWESTRY | L | 2-6 | 0-5 | 500 | Unknown (2) |
| 16 | 16 | BROUGHTON & DISTRICT | W | 7-2 | 2-1 | | Tomkinson, Turner, Unknown (5) |
| 17 | 30 | HARTFORD ST. JOHNS | L | 2-3 | 1-1 | 400 | Unknown (2) |
| 18 | Feb 6 | CHIRK | W | 6-1 | 2-1 | 300 | Haswell (3), Clare (2), Maddocks |
| 19 | 27 | Chester College | L | 0-4 | 0-1 | | |
| 20 | Mar 6 | Bootle | D | 4-4 | 1-1 | | Clare, Turner (2), McMillan |
| 21 | 13 | NORTHWICH VICS. | L | 0-5 | | | |
| 22 | 20 | EARLESTOWN | W | 2-1 | 2-0 | | Unknown (2) |
| 23 | 27 | WIRRAL & DISTRICT | W | 6-0 | 4-0 | | Unknown (6) |
| 24 | Apr 3 | CHESTER ST. OSWALDS @ | W | 4-1 | 2-0 | 1500 | Turner (3), Unknown |
| 25 | 10 | WREXHAM OLYMPIC | L | 0-1 | 0-1 | | |
| 26 | 17 | CREWE ALEX. | L | 2-3 | 1-2 | | Clare, Lockwood |
| 27 | 24 | DRUIDS | W | 6-0 | | | Unknown (6) |
| 28 | 26 | Nantwich | W | 4-1 | | | Unknown (4) |
| 29 | May 1 | CHESTER ST. OSWALDS # | W | 4-2 | | | Unknown (4) |

* Goal disputed College left pitch 7 minutes from time @ James Southworth Benefit # Chester Infirmary Benefit

# SEASON 1886-87

## FA CUP

| | Date | Opposition | | FT | HT | Att. | Goalscorers |
|---|---|---|---|---|---|---|---|
| 1R | Nov 20 | GOLDENHILL * | W | 1-0 | 0-0 | 1500 | Turner |

* Chester disqualified for playing 4 unregistered players

## WELSH CUP

| | Date | Opposition | | FT | HT | Att. | Goalscorers |
|---|---|---|---|---|---|---|---|
| 1R | Nov 6 | HARTFORD ST. JOHNS | W | 4-2 | 2-1 | 450 | Turner, Fleming, Hughes, Unknown |
| 2R | Dec 18 | Davenham | D | 0-0 | 0-0 | 120 | |
| 2Rr | Jan 1 | DAVENHAM | L | 1-2 | 1-0 | | Turner |

## FRIENDLIES

| | Date | Opposition | | FT | HT | Att. | Goalscorers |
|---|---|---|---|---|---|---|---|
| 1 | Sep 18 | DAVENHAM | L | 1-4 | 1-3 | | Turner |
| 2 | 25 | Chirk * | L | 2-3 | 0-2 | | McMillan (2) |
| 3 | Oct 2 | HOLYWELL | W | 15-1 | 6-0 | | Unknown (15) |
| 4 | 9 | Rhyl | W | 6-3 | 4-0 | | James Southworth, McMillan (4), Hughes |
| 5 | 16 | FLINT | W | 10-0 | | | Turner(3),Hughes(3),McMillan(2),Rogers,Clare |
| 6 | 23 | OSWESTRY | W | 5-0 | 5-0 | | McMillan (3), Higginson, Fleming |
| 7 | 30 | Walsall Swifts | L | 0-5 | 0-2 | | |
| 8 | Nov 13 | Wrexham Olympic | L | 1-6 | | | John Southworth |
| 9 | 27 | CREWE ALEX. | D | 1-1 | 0-0 | 900 | Turner |
| 10 | Dec 4 | CHIRK | L | 0-1 | 0-1 | | |
| 11 | 27 | Crewe Alex. | L | 0-8 | | | |
| 12 | Jan 15 | Earlestown | L | 0-6 | 0-5 | | |
| 13 | 29 | Chester St Oswalds | W | 4-1 | 2-0 | 1500 | Clare, Turner (2), Hughes |
| 14 | Feb 5 | Oswestry | L | 0-9 | 0-3 | | |
| 15 | 12 | Crewe Alex. | D | 1-1 | 1-0 | | Jones |
| 16 | 26 | Preston Old Wanderers | W | 4-0 | 2-0 | 2000 | Turner (2), McMillan (2) |
| 17 | Mar 12 | CHIRK | L | 2-4 | 1-1 | 300 | Turner, Fleming |
| 18 | 19 | HARTFORD ST. JOHNS | W | 8-0 | 4-0 | | Turner (3), McMillan (2), Clare (2), Jones |
| 19 | 26 | CHESTER ST OSWALDS | W | 4-1 | 1-0 | 1000 | McMillan (2), Turner, Unknown |
| 20 | Apr 9 | Haydock | L | 1-3 | | | Unknown |
| 21 | 11 | HAYDOCK | D | 1-1 | 0-1 | 2500 | Fleming |
| 22 | 16 | CHESTER ST OSWALDS @ | W | 3-1 | 0-1 | 1500 | Coppack, Fleming, McMillan |

* Abandoned 7 minutes from time, unfair referee @ Chester Infirmary Benefit

# SEASON 1887-88

## FA CUP

| | Date | Opposition | | FT | HT | Att. | Goalscorers |
|---|---|---|---|---|---|---|---|
| 1R | Oct 15 | DAVENHAM * | L | 2-3 | 2-1 | 4000 | Higginson, Unknown |

* Extra time played following score of 2-2 after 90 minutes

## FRIENDLIES

| | Date | Opposition | | FT | HT | Att. | Goalscorers |
|---|---|---|---|---|---|---|---|
| 1 | Sep 10 | BLACKBURN OLYMPIC | L | 0-1 | 0-0 | 2500 | |
| 2 | 17 | Crewe Steam Shed | L | 1-3 | 0-1 | | Lee (og) |
| 3 | 24 | Earlestown | D | 2-2 | 2-1 | | Carty, McMillan |
| 4 | Oct 1 | CHIRK | L | 1-4 | 0-1 | | Unknown |
| 5 | 8 | CHESTER COLLEGE | W | 6-0 | 3-0 | | Unknown (6) |
| 6 | 22 | Chester College | W | 2-0 | 1-0 | | Carty, Howarth (og) |
| 7 | 29 | Crewe Alex. * | L | 1-2 | | | McMillan |
| 8 | Nov 12 | CREWE STEAM SHED | W | 8-1 | 5-1 | | Turner (4), Fleming, Higginson, Hughes (2) |
| 9 | 19 | NORTHWICH VICS. | L | 2-4 | 1-3 | | Unknown (2) |
| 10 | 26 | WREXHAM OLYMPIC | W | 3-1 | 2-0 | 1500 | Fleming, Turner, McMillan |
| 11 | Dec 10 | DAVENHAM | L | 3-4 | 1-3 | | Taylor (2), Walker |
| 12 | 28 | CREWE ALEX. | W | 1-0 | 0-0 | | Walley |
| 13 | Jan 7 | OSWESTRY @ | W | 2-1 | 1-1 | | Thompson, McMillan |
| 14 | 28 | HASLINGDEN CHURCH INS. | W | 1-0 | | 300 | Unknown |
| 15 | Feb 4 | Chirk | L | 2-7 | 0-4 | | Clare, Turner |
| 16 | 11 | HAYDOCK CENTRAL | W | 17-0 | 5-0 | | Unknown (17) |
| 17 | 18 | PRESTON NORTH END RES. | L | 1-4 | 0-2 | 3000 | Brierley |
| 18 | Mar 10 | EARLESTOWN | W | 4-1 | 1-1 | 800 | McMillan (2), Turner, Higginson |
| 19 | 17 | Gorton Villa | W | 4-2 | | | Unknown (4) |
| 20 | 30 | MITCHELL ST. GEORGES | D | 1-1 | 1-1 | 1000 | Brierley |
| 21 | 31 | Davenham | L | 1-5 | 1-3 | | Unknown |
| 22 | Apr 2 | GORTON VILLA | W | 5-0 | 4-0 | | Townsend, Unknown (4) |
| 23 | 21 | CHIRK # | L | 2-3 | 2-1 | | Brierley, Turner |
| 24 | 28 | STAFFORD RANGERS | W | 5-1 | 1-1 | | Fleming (3), Dickenson, Unknown |

* Abandoned 15 minutes from time, Chester walked off after dispute.

@ Benefit for Chester School of Science and Art

# Chester Infirmary Benefit

# SEASON 1888-89

## FA CUP

| | Date | Opposition | | FT | HT | Att. | Goalscorers |
|---|---|---|---|---|---|---|---|
| Q1 | Oct 6 | MACCLESFIELD * | W | 3-2 | 1-1 | | Walker, Turner, Unknown |
| Q2 | 27 | OVER WANDERERS | W | 5-1 | 1-0 | | Lowe, Davies, Turner, Unknown (2) |
| Q3 | Nov 17 | VALE OF LLANGOLLEN | W | 5-1 | 2-0 | 2000 | Lowe, Davies (2), Higginson, og |
| Q4 | Dec 8 | WREXHAM | L | 2-3 | 1-3 | 4000 | Turner (2) |

* Extra time played following score of 2-2 after 90 minutes

## FRIENDLIES

| | Date | Opposition | | FT | HT | Att. | Goalscorers |
|---|---|---|---|---|---|---|---|
| 1 | Sep 1 | Haydock | W | 7-3 | 5-2 | 300 | Lewis, Unknown (6) |
| 2 | 8 | NEWTON HEATH CENTRAL | W | 6-1 | 2-0 | | Higginson, Turner, Jowett (og), Unknown (3) |
| 3 | 15 | NOTTS JARDINES | D | 2-2 | 0-1 | 900 | Turner, Higginson |
| 4 | 22 | Northwich Vics. | L | 0-1 | 0-1 | 500 | |
| 5 | 29 | DAVENHAM | D | 1-1 | 0-1 | | Turner |
| 6 | Oct 13 | STAFFORD RANGERS | D | 1-1 | 1-0 | | Carty |
| 7 | 20 | EARLESTOWN | W | 3-2 | 1-2 | | Davies, Cooper, Walker |
| 8 | Nov 3 | Wrexham | D | 1-1 | 0-0 | | Turner |
| 9 | 10 | MANCHESTER WELSH | W | 5-1 | 1-1 | | Turner (2), Lee, Unknown (2) |
| 10 | Dec 1 | Manchester Welsh | D | 0-0 | 0-0 | | |
| 11 | 22 | Stafford Rangers | L | 0-2 | | | |
| 12 | 26 | STOKE | L | 1-3 | 1-3 | 4500 | Davies |
| 13 | 29 | WITTON | W | 3-1 | 2-1 | 2500 | Turner (2), Baker |
| 14 | Jan 12 | LIVERPOOL STANLEY | W | 3-1 | 1-0 | 1000 | Townsend, Turner, Carty |
| 15 | 19 | Mitchell's St. Georges | W | 4-1 | 2-0 | | Unknown (4) |
| 16 | 26 | CREWE ALEX. | L | 0-2 | 0-1 | 2500 | |
| 17 | Feb 16 | Chirk | L | 1-2 | | | Turner |
| 18 | Mar 9 | Newton Heath Central | L | 1-4 | | | Unknown |
| 19 | 16 | CHIRK * | W | 3-2 | 1-1 | | Turner (2), Davies |
| 20 | 30 | HIGHER WALTON | D | 2-2 | 1-0 | | Lowe, og |
| 21 | Apr 6 | Bootle | L | 2-4 | 1-2 | 1500 | Turner, Lowe |
| 22 | 13 | GORTON VILLA | L | 1-4 | 1-0 | | Turner |
| 23 | 19 | MITCHELL'S ST. GEORGES | L | 0-2 | 0-1 | 2000 | |
| 24 | 20 | Earlestown | L | 2-3 | 1-0 | | Turner, Unknown |
| 25 | 22 | DENTON * | W | 6-1 | 2-0 | 2000 | Turner (2), Davies, Owen, Lowe (2) |
| 26 | 27 | Gorton Villa | W | 3-1 | | | Unknown (3) |
| 27 | May 4 | NORTHWICH VICS. | D | 1-1 | 0-1 | 1500 | Fleming |
| 28 | 25 | BOOTLE | L | 4-6 | 1-5 | | Fleming, Southworth (3) |

* Chester Infirmary Benefit

# SEASON 1889-90

## FA CUP

| | Date | Opposition | | FT | HT | Att. | Goalscorers |
|---|---|---|---|---|---|---|---|
| Q1 | Oct 5 | OVER WANDERERS | W | 2-0 | 0-0 | 1500 | Fleming (2) |
| Q2 | 26 | BURSLEM PORT VALE | W | 1-0 | 0-0 | | R Davies |
| Q3 | Nov 16 | Chester St. Oswalds | W | 3-0 | 1-0 | 3500 | J Davies, Turner, Unknown |
| Q4 | Dec 7 | CREWE ALEX. | W | 2-1 | 2-0 | 3000 | Fleming, Lewis |
| 1R | Jan 18 | Lincoln City | L | 0-2 | 0-0 | 2500 | |

## FRIENDLIES

| | | | | | | | |
|---|---|---|---|---|---|---|---|
| 1 | Sep 7 | Earlestown | L | 2-3 | | | Unknown (2) |
| 2 | 14 | NEWTON HEATH CENTRAL | W | 6-1 | 2-1 | 1500 | Higginson, Owen, R Davies (2), Turner, Unknown |
| 3 | 16 | BOLTON WANDERERS | L | 0-3 | 0-1 | 2000 | |
| 4 | 21 | Gorton Villa | D | 2-2 | 2-0 | | Turner, Unknown |
| 5 | 28 | MACCLESFIELD | W | 3-1 | 1-0 | | Turner (2), Lowe |
| 6 | Oct 12 | Burslem Port Vale | L | 1-3 | 1-1 | 2000 | R Davies |
| 7 | 19 | GOLBORNE | W | 7-0 | 2-0 | 500 | R Davies(3), Turner, J Davies, Fleming, Unknown |
| 8 | Nov 2 | Blackpool | L | 0-4 | 0-1 | | |
| 9 | 9 | CHIRK | W | 4-2 | 1-2 | 1000 | Dickenson, Unknown (3) |
| 10 | 23 | GORTON VILLA | W | 1-0 | 0-0 | | Unknown |
| 11 | Dec 14 | Chirk | D | 0-0 | 0-0 | | |
| 12 | 21 | OSWESTRY | D | 1-1 | 0-1 | | R Davies |
| 13 | 26 | STOKE | D | 2-2 | 1-2 | 3500 | Fleming, R Davies |
| 14 | 28 | ROTHERHAM SWIFTS | L | 2-3 | | | Unknown (2) |
| 15 | Jan 4 | WREXHAM | W | 7-0 | 3-0 | | R Davies, Fleming, Morgan (2), Turner, Lewis (2) |
| 16 | 11 | WITTON | W | 7-0 | 2-0 | 1000 | Turner (2), Lewis (2), R Davies (2), Fleming |
| 17 | Feb 1 | Wrexham | L | 1-3 | 1-3 | | Fleming |
| 18 | 15 | HARTFORD & DAVENHAM | W | 4-2 | 2-1 | | Lewis (2), Turner, Unknown |
| 19 | Mar 1 | DARWEN DIMMOCKS | W | 13-0 | | | Unknown (13) |
| 20 | 8 | Hartford & Davenham | L | 1-2 | 1-0 | | C Jones |
| 21 | 15 | BURSLEM PORT VALE | W | 2-1 | 2-0 | | Owen, Bateman (og) |
| 22 | 22 | RHOSLLANERCRUGOG * | W | 2-0 | 2-0 | | Turner, C Jones |
| 23 | 29 | Macclesfield | L | 1-2 | 0-2 | | Lee |
| 24 | Apr 4 | HURST | W | 4-3 | 2-2 | 2000 | Pooley (2), R Davies, Unknown |
| 25 | 5 | Denton | L | 1-4 | 0-3 | | Unknown |
| 26 | 7 | NOTTS JARDINES | D | 0-0 | 0-0 | | |
| 27 | 12 | Oswestry | D | 0-0 | 0-0 | | |
| 28 | 19 | EARLESTOWN | W | 7-0 | 5-0 | | Fleming (2), C Jones (2), Turner (2), Unknown |
| 29 | 26 | DENTON @ | W | 2-0 | 0-0 | | Unknown (2) |
| 30 | May 3 | NORTHWICH VICS * | W | 5-0 | 2-0 | 2500 | Turner, Fleming (2), C Jones (2) |

* Yerburgh Charity Cup @ Arthur Turner Benefit

**1889/90** Back - Fleming, Lee, Roberts, E McCarthy, Dickson, S Jones, T McCarthy, Davies.
Middle - Wray (Secretary), Yerburgh Charity Cup, Paris (Chairman).
Front - Lowe, Turner, Lewis

# SEASON 1890-91

## THE COMBINATION

| | Date | Opposition | | FT | HT | Att. | Goalscorers |
|---|---|---|---|---|---|---|---|
| 1 | Sep 13 | Wrexham | W | 1-0 | 0-0 | 500 | Mitchell |
| 2 | 27 | STAFFORD COUNTY * | W | 14-1 | 9-1 | | C Jones, R Davies(2), Lewis(2), Morgan(2), Williams, Unknown(6) |
| 3 | Oct 11 | Northwich Vics. | D | 1-1 | 1-1 | 2000 | C Jones |
| 4 | 18 | Witton (Blackburn) * | W | 4-3 | 1-1 | | C Jones(2), Lowe, Unknown |
| 5 | Nov 8 | Gorton Villa | W | 1-0 | 1-0 | | Lewis |
| 6 | 22 | Macclesfield | W | 3-2 | 2-0 | | C Jones (2), Lewis |
| 7 | 29 | HYDE | W | 3-0 | 1-0 | | Fleming, R Davies, C Jones |
| 8 | Dec 26 | BURTON SWIFTS | W | 6-3 | | | R Davies (2), Unknown (4) |
| 9 | 27 | Derby St Lukes * | L | 1-2 | 0-2 | 100 | Townsend |
| 10 | Jan 3 | WITTON (BLACKBURN)* | W | 6-0 | 1-0 | | Lewis (2), R Davies, Fleming, C Jones (2) |
| 11 | 24 | WREXHAM | L | 2-4 | 1-2 | 1000 | Lewis, Williams |
| 12 | Feb 7 | DENTON | W | 4-3 | 2-2 | | R Davies (2), Fleming, Ashton |
| 13 | 14 | Burton Swifts | L | 0-1 | 0-0 | | |
| 14 | 21 | GORTON VILLA | D | 3-3 | 3-2 | | Murray, R Davies, C Jones |
| 15 | 28 | MACCLESFIELD | D | 1-1 | 1-0 | | C Jones |
| 16 | Mar 7 | Denton | L | 4-5 | 2-4 | | Maddocks, C Jones (2), Unknown |
| 17 | 14 | Leek | L | 1-3 | 1-2 | | C Jones |
| 18 | 21 | Hyde @ | D | 3-3 | 0-1 | | Lewis, Fleming, Maddocks |
| 19 | 27 | LEEK | W | 7-1 | 2-0 | | C Jones (2), Fleming, Lewis, H Lee, Maddocks, Unknown |
| 20 | 30 | NORTHWICH VICS. | W | 2-0 | 1-0 | 2000 | H Lee, Thompson |

* Stafford County, Witton (Blackburn) and Derby St Lukes all withdrew during the season.
In all cases their records were expunged.
@ Only played 10 men

## F.A. CUP

| | | | | | | | |
|---|---|---|---|---|---|---|---|
| Q1 | Oct 4 | Chester St Oswalds | W | 6-0 | 2-0 | 4000 | C Jones (3), R Davies, Fleming, Townsend |
| Q2 | 25 | NORTHWICH VICS | W | 2-0 | 2-0 | 1500 | C Jones, Townsend |
| Q3 | Nov 15 | Nantwich | W | 5-4 | 4-4 | 2000 | C Jones (2), Fleming, Lewis, Townsend |
| Q4 | Dec 6 | CLIFTONVILLE | | | | | Cliftonville scratched |
| 1R | Jan 17 | LINCOLN CITY | W | 1-0 | 1-0 | | Roberts |
| 2R | 31 | Blackburn Rovers | L | 0-7 | 0-3 | 2000 | |

## FRIENDLIES

| | | | | | | | |
|---|---|---|---|---|---|---|---|
| 1 | Sep 1 | Everton | L | 0-11 | 0-6 | 5000 | |
| 2 | Sep 6 | HALLIWELL | W | 3-1 | 2-0 | 1000 | Unknown (3) |
| 3 | Sep 20 | South Shore | L | 1-3 | 1-1 | 1000 | Lee |
| 4 | Oct 16 | EVERTON | L | 0-4 | 0-2 | | |
| 5 | Nov 1 | OVER WANDERERS | W | 9-1 | 4-0 | | Townsend, R Davies (2), Lewis (2), C Jones (4) |
| 6 | Dec 6 | MANCHESTER ASSOC. | W | 3-2 | 2-0 | | C Jones, Lewis, Fleming |
| 7 | Dec 20 | HURST | W | 11-1 | 5-0 | 12 | C Jones(3), Maddocks(2), R Davies(2), Lewis, Fleming, og, Unknown |
| 8 | Jan 10 | Darwen | L | 1-4 | 0-3 | | Lewis |
| 9 | Apr 11 | SOUTH SHORE | D | 2-2 | 2-0 | | C Jones, Fleming |
| 10 | Apr 18 | DARWEN | D | 2-2 | 1-2 | | Lewis, C Jones |
| 11 | Apr 25 | Chester St. Oswalds * | L | 0-2 | 0-2 | | |

* Hospital Charity Cup

Final League Table: 1890-91

| | P | W | D | L | F | A | Pts |
|---|---|---|---|---|---|---|---|
| 1 Gorton Villa | 16 | 10 | 2 | 4 | 47 | 26 | 22 |
| 2 Macclesfield | 16 | 9 | 3 | 4 | 44 | 27 | 21 |
| **3 Chester** | **16** | **8** | **4** | **4** | **42** | **30** | **20** |
| 4 Burton Swifts | 14 | 9 | 0 | 5 | 55 | 28 | 18 |
| 5 Denton | 16 | 8 | 1 | 7 | 39 | 32 | 17 |
| 6 Northwich Victoria | 16 | 5 | 7 | 4 | 28 | 30 | 17 |
| 7 Hyde | 14 | 3 | 4 | 7 | 25 | 39 | 10 |
| 8 Wrexham | 16 | 4 | 4 | 8 | 25 | 47 | 10 |
| 9 Leek | 16 | 1 | 1 | 14 | 18 | 60 | 3 |

* 2 points deducted for playing an ineligible player

# SEASON 1891-92

## THE COMBINATION

| | Date | Opposition | | FT | HT | Att. | Goalscorers |
|---|---|---|---|---|---|---|---|
| 1 | Sep 5 | NORTHWICH VICS. | L | 1-4 | 0-0 | | Ashton |
| 2 | 12 | DENTON | D | 3-3 | 2-1 | | Morris, Dawes, Unknown |
| 3 | 19 | Stoke Swifts | L | 1-9 | 0-4 | | Fleming |
| 4 | 26 | WREXHAM | L | 2-3 | 0-2 | 1000 | Dawes, Stoneley |
| 5 | Oct 31 | Everton Res. | L | 0-6 | 0-5 | 3000 | |
| 6 | Nov 7 | Gorton Villa | L | 1-4 | 0-1 | 3000 | Morris |
| 7 | 28 | MACCLESFIELD | L | 2-4 | 2-2 | | Carter, Maddocks |
| 8 | Dec 12 | Wrexham | W | 3-1 | 2-0 | | E Jones, Walker, Lewis |
| 9 | 26 | GORTON VILLA | W | 6-1 | 6-0 | | Carter (2), Lewis (2), Morris, Unknown |
| 10 | Jan 1 | Chirk | D | 3-3 | 2-1 | | Unknown (3) |
| 11 | 2 | Northwich Vics. | L | 1-8 | 1-2 | | Morris |
| 12 | Feb 6 | STOKE SWIFTS | W | 4-1 | 3-0 | | Dawes, Walker, Rogers, Unknown |
| 13 | 13 | LEEK | L | 1-2 | 1-0 | | Walker |
| 14 | 27 | BUXTON | L | 0-1 | 0-1 | | |
| 15 | Mar 5 | Stockport County | L | 0-1 | 0-1 | | |
| 16 | 7 | CHIRK * | W | 3-0 | 2-0 | | Carter (2), Fleming |
| 17 | 19 | Leek | W | 3-2 | 2-0 | | Unknown (3) |
| 18 | Apr 2 | Denton | W | 5-1 | 1-1 | | Unknown (5) |
| 19 | 9 | Macclesfield | L | 2-3 | 1-0 | | Lewis (2) |
| 20 | 16 | EVERTON RES. | W | 6-2 | 2-2 | | Carter,Fleming,Lewis,Ashton,Unknown(2) |
| 21 | 23 | STOCKPORT COUNTY | W | 3-0 | 1-0 | | Morris, Carter, Unknown |
| 22 | 30 | Buxton | D | 2-2 | 1-1 | 1200 | Ashton, Unknown |

* Only 35 minutes each way played

## F.A. CUP

| | Date | Opposition | | FT | HT | Att. | Goalscorers |
|---|---|---|---|---|---|---|---|
| Q1 | Oct 3 | Rhosllanerchrugog | W | 1-0 | 1-0 | | Dawes |
| Q2 | 24 | WREXHAM | L | 2-4 | 0-1 | 2000 | Thompson, Browne |

## FRIENDLIES

| | Date | Opposition | | FT | HT | Att. | Goalscorers |
|---|---|---|---|---|---|---|---|
| 1 | Sep 23 | BLACKBURN ROVERS | L | 1-6 | 0-4 | | Dawes |
| 2 | Oct 17 | TRANMERE ROVERS | W | 5-2 | 3-2 | | Dawes, Thompson (2), Crump, Morris |
| 3 | 24 | HALLIWELL | W | 8-2 | 3-1 | | T Carty(3),Morris(2),Carter,Walker(2) |
| 4 | Nov 14 | Witton | D | 2-2 | 0-1 | | Unknown (2) |
| 5 | Dec 5 | West Manchester | D | 3-3 | 1-2 | | Morris, Carter, Unknown |
| 6 | 19 | NANTWICH | D | 1-1 | 0-1 | | Maddocks |
| 7 | 28 | CANADIAN X1 | D | 3-3 | 2-3 | | Lewis, Morris (2) |
| 8 | 23 | CHESTER ST OSWALDS | W | 7-0 | 3-0 | | Whittingham,Lewis,Carter,Morris,Unknown(3) |
| 9 | 30 | WEST MANCHESTER | L | 1-2 | 0-2 | | Dawes |
| 10 | Mar 12 | NORTHWICH VICS. | D | 2-2 | 1-1 | | Morris, Carter |
| 11 | 26 | STAFFORD | W | 2-1 | 0-1 | | Morris, Unknown |
| 12 | Apr 8 | SALTNEY | W | 2-0 | 1-0 | | Lewis, Fleming |
| 13 | 18 | WITTON | W | 5-0 | 0-0 | | Unknown (5) |

Final League Table

| | P | W | D | L | F | A | Pts |
|---|---|---|---|---|---|---|---|
| 1 Everton Reserves | 22 | 17 | 2 | 3 | 99 | 20 | 36 |
| 2 Northwich Victoria | 22 | 15 | 1 | 6 | 84 | 25 | 31 |
| 3 Macclesfield | 22 | 15 | 0 | 7 | 52 | 38 | 30 |
| 4 Stoke Swifts | 22 | 13 | 1 | 8 | 49 | 29 | 27 |
| 5 Buxton | 22 | 11 | 3 | 8 | 35 | 30 | 25 |
| 6 Wrexham | 22 | 9 | 2 | 11 | 45 | 65 | 20 |
| 7 Chirk | 22 | 7 | 5 | 10 | 48 | 56 | 19 |
| **8 Chester** | **22** | **8** | **3** | **11** | **52** | **61** | **19** |
| 9 Gorton Villa | 22 | 8 | 3 | 11 | 41 | 51 | 19 |
| 10 Leek | 22 | 8 | 0 | 14 | 46 | 62 | 16 |
| 11 Stockport County | 22 | 7 | 2 | 13 | 29 | 44 | 16 |
| 12 Denton | 22 | 2 | 2 | 18 | 25 | 124 | 6 |

# SEASON 1892-93

## THE COMBINATION

| | Date | Opposition | | FT | HT | Att. | Goalscorers |
|---|---|---|---|---|---|---|---|
| 1 | Sep 10 | Everton Res. | L | 1-10 | 0-5 | 3000 | Lewis |
| 2 | 17 | STOKE SWIFTS | L | 1-2 | 1-1 | | Fleming |
| 3 | 24 | Wrexham | L | 0-3 | 0-1 | 1000 | |
| 4 | Oct 1 | Macclesfield | L | 1-3 | 0-1 | 1000 | Carter |
| 5 | 8 | NANTWICH | W | 4-1 | 2-1 | | Whittingham (2), Lewis, Unknown |
| 6 | 22 | Leek | W | 4-2 | 1-1 | | Porter, Unknown (3) |
| 7 | Nov 5 | BUXTON | D | 3-3 | 3-1 | | Browne (2), Ashton |
| 8 | Dec 3 | WREXHAM | W | 5-1 | 4-0 | | Ashton (3), Malcolm, Unknown |
| 9 | 10 | Stockport County | D | 2-2 | 2-0 | 1000 | Lewis, Ashton |
| 10 | 24 | EVERTON RES. | W | 3-2 | 3-1 | | Heyes, Morris, Fleming |
| 11 | 26 | GORTON VILLA | W | 2-1 | 1-0 | | Fleming, Heyes |
| 12 | 31 | Dresden United | W | 2-0 | 1-0 | | Ashton, Morris |
| 13 | Jan 7 | STOCKPORT COUNTY | W | 4-2 | 0-1 | | Lewis, Heyes, Gittins (og), Unknown |
| 14 | 14 | Chirk | L | 0-2 | 0-1 | | |
| 15 | 28 | CHIRK | W | 3-0 | 1-0 | | Fleming (2), Heyes |
| 16 | Feb 4 | Nantwich | L | 2-4 | 0-1 | | Fleming, Morris |
| 17 | 18 | MACCLESFIELD * | W | 1-0 | 1-0 | | Fleming |
| 18 | Mar 4 | DRESDEN UNITED | W | 3-0 | 2-0 | | Heyes (2), Astbury |
| 19 | 18 | Buxton | L | 0-1 | 0-0 | | |
| 20 | 25 | Gorton Villa # | W | 6-0 | 3-0 | | Dawes (2), Ashton, Astbury, Wilson (2) |
| 21 | Apr 1 | Stoke Swifts | L | 1-2 | 0-1 | | Ashton |
| 22 | 3 | LEEK | W | 4-0 | 3-0 | | Fleming, Porter, Heyes (2) |

* Only 60 minutes played

# Match switched to Chester because of clash with Cup Final in Manchester

## F.A. CUP

| | Date | Opposition | | FT | HT | Att. | Goalscorers |
|---|---|---|---|---|---|---|---|
| Q1 | Oct 15 | STANLEY | W | 11-0 | 4-0 | | Browne(2),Ashton,Fleming,Morris,Lewis,Unknown(5) |
| Q2 | 29 | PRESCOT | W | 2-1 | 1-0 | | Fleming, Lewis |
| Q3 | Nov 19 | Liverpool Caledonians | L | 2-3 | 1-1 | 1000 | Lewis (2) |

## FRIENDLIES

| | Date | Opposition | | FT | HT | Att. | Goalscorers |
|---|---|---|---|---|---|---|---|
| 1 | Sep 3 | STOCKPORT ASSOC. | W | 4-3 | 3-1 | | Carter, Morris, Lee, Lewis |
| 2 | Nov 14 | Wrexham * | D | 2-2 | 0-1 | | Browne, Unknown |
| 3 | Nov 26 | HANLEY TOWN | W | 11-1 | 6-1 | | Ashton(4),Lewis(3),Browne,Malcolm,Morris,Unknown |
| 4 | Dec 17 | CHIRK | L | 2-4 | 2-2 | | Lewis, Fleming |
| 5 | 27 | SHREWSBURY TOWN | W | 3-2 | 1-2 | | Heyes, Unknown (2) |
| 6 | Jan 21 | CREWE ALEX | L | 0-1 | 0-1 | | |
| 7 | Feb 11 | EVERTON RES. | W | 1-0 | 1-0 | | Unknown |
| 8 | 25 | NEWTOWN | W | 4-1 | 1-1 | | Heyes, Morris (2), Fleming |
| 9 | Mar 31 | HIGHER WALTON | W | 8-0 | 4-0 | 1500 | Lewis (3), Heyes (2), Morris (2), Unknown |
| 10 | Apr 15 | DRUIDS | W | 3-1 | 1-1 | 1000 | Morris (2), Fleming |

* Frank Stones benefit

Final League Table

| | P | W | D | L | F | A | Pts |
|---|---|---|---|---|---|---|---|
| 1 Everton Reserves | 22 | 18 | 2 | 2 | 107 | 13 | 38 |
| 2 Stoke Swifts | 22 | 14 | 4 | 4 | 48 | 23 | 32 |
| **3 Chester** | **22** | **12** | **2** | **8** | **52** | **41** | **26** |
| 4 Chirk | 22 | 10 | 3 | 9 | 63 | 43 | 23 |
| 5 Buxton | 22 | 8 | 7 | 7 | 37 | 33 | 23 |
| 6 Stockport County | 22 | 8 | 6 | 8 | 38 | 35 | 22 |
| 7 Wrexham | 22 | 9 | 1 | 12 | 41 | 66 | 19 |
| 8 Dresden United | 22 | 8 | 3 | 11 | 34 | 43 | 19 |
| 9 Macclesfield | 22 | 6 | 6 | 10 | 45 | 55 | 18 |
| 10 Leek | 22 | 6 | 3 | 13 | 31 | 60 | 15 |
| 11 Nantwich | 22 | 6 | 3 | 13 | 36 | 81 | 15 |
| 12 Gorton Villa | 22 | 6 | 2 | 14 | 29 | 68 | 14 |

# SEASON 1893-94

## THE COMBINATION

| | Date | Opposition | | FT | HT | Att. | Goalscorers |
|---|---|---|---|---|---|---|---|
| 1 | Sep 9 | Nantwich | D | 0-0 | 0-0 | | |
| 2 | 16 | WREXHAM | L | 1-2 | 0-2 | 2500 | Porter |
| 3 | Oct 7 | Stockport County | D | 1-1 | 1-0 | 3000 | Lewis |
| 4 | 28 | Wrexham | W | 1-0 | 1-0 | | Turner |
| 5 | Nov 18 | STOCKPORT COUNTY | D | 1-1 | 1-1 | | Heyes |
| 6 | Dec 9 | NANTWICH | W | 4-2 | 3-1 | | Lewis (2), Heyes, Bull |
| 7 | 23 | EVERTON RES. | L | 0-3 | 0-0 | | |
| 8 | 30 | Macclesfield | D | 1-1 | 1-1 | 3000 | Heyes |
| 9 | Jan 13 | STOKE SWIFTS | W | 4-2 | 2-2 | 1500 | Bull (3), Lewis |
| 10 | 27 | MACCLESFIELD | D | 1-1 | 1-1 | | Carter |
| 11 | Feb 3 | Dresden United | L | 2-3 | 2-1 | | Bull, Unknown |
| 12 | 10 | BUXTON | W | 3-0 | 1-0 | | Grewcock, Lewis, Heyes |
| 13 | 17 | Stoke Swifts | L | 0-1 | 0-0 | | |
| 14 | 24 | LEEK | W | 1-0 | 1-0 | | Heyes |
| 15 | Mar 3 | Everton Res. | L | 1-7 | 0-3 | | Lewis |
| 16 | 10 | Leek | L | 0-1 | 0-1 | | |
| 17 | 26 | DRESDEN UNITED | D | 0-0 | 0-0 | | |
| 18 | Apr 7 | Buxton | W | 3-1 | 1-1 | | Heyes, Pickering, Fleming |

## F.A. CUP

| | Date | Opposition | | FT | HT | Att. | Goalscorers |
|---|---|---|---|---|---|---|---|
| Q2 | Nov 4 | Macclesfield | L | 1-6 | 1-3 | 3500 | Fleming |

## FRIENDLIES

| | Date | Opposition | | FT | HT | Att. | Goalscorers |
|---|---|---|---|---|---|---|---|
| 1 | Sep 2 | CHIRK | W | 1-0 | 1-0 | | Grewcock |
| 2 | 6 | Northwich Vics. | D | 1-1 | 1-1 | | Lewis |
| 3 | 20 | NORTHWICH VICS. | W | 4-1 | 2-0 | | Bull (2), Turner, Heyes |
| 4 | 23 | Notts County | L | 1-5 | 1-4 | 1500 | Lewis |
| 5 | 30 | NEWTOWN | W | 5-2 | 3-2 | | Heyes, Bull, Pickering (3) |
| 6 | Oct 14 | Crewe Alex. | L | 1-3 | 0-1 | | Lewis |
| 7 | 21 | EVERTON RES. | L | 1-2 | 0-1 | 2000 | Lewis |
| 8 | Nov 11 | DRESDEN UNITED | W | 1-0 | 1-0 | | Turner |
| 9 | 25 | NORTHWICH VICS. | W | 3-1 | 1-1 | 300 | Lewis (2), Heyes |
| 10 | Dec 2 | OSWESTRY UNITED | W | 6-0 | 2-0 | | Heyes (3), Lewis, Astbury, Grewcock |
| 11 | 16 | Northwich Vics. | W | 2-1 | 1-1 | | Heyes, Lewis |
| 12 | 26 | RAMSBOTTOM | W | 6-1 | | | Unknown (6) |
| 13 | Jan 6 | Sandbach St Marys | W | 2-1 | | | Unknown (2) |
| 14 | Mar 24 | Wrexham | D | 1-1 | 0-1 | | Unknown |
| 15 | 30 | LONDON WELSH | W | 5-0 | 1-0 | 4000 | Brown (3), Heyes, Unknown |
| 16 | Apr 11 | LIVERPOOL & DISTRICT | D | 2-2 | | | Unknown (2) |

Final League Table

| | P | W | D | L | F | A | Pts |
|---|---|---|---|---|---|---|---|
| 1 Everton Reserves | 18 | 15 | 2 | 1 | 77 | 19 | 32 |
| 2 Stoke Swifts | 18 | 10 | 1 | 7 | 57 | 31 | 21 |
| 3 Leek | 18 | 9 | 2 | 7 | 32 | 27 | 20 |
| 4 Stockport County | 18 | 7 | 6 | 5 | 33 | 32 | 20 |
| 5 Dresden United | 18 | 7 | 5 | 6 | 34 | 28 | 19 |
| **6 Chester** | **18** | **6** | **6** | **6** | **24** | **26** | **18** |
| 7 Macclesfield | 18 | 5 | 7 | 6 | 36 | 35 | 17 |
| 8 Wrexham | 18 | 5 | 6 | 7 | 36 | 46 | 16 |
| 9 Buxton | 18 | 5 | 4 | 9 | 28 | 41 | 14 |
| 10 Nantwich | 18 | 1 | 1 | 16 | 12 | 84 | 3 |

# SEASON 1894-95

## THE COMBINATION

| | Date | Opposition | | FT | HT | Att. | Goalscorers |
|---|---|---|---|---|---|---|---|
| 1 | Sep 8 | STALYBRIDGE ROVERS | W | 1-0 | 0-0 | | Lewis |
| 2 | 15 | LEEK | W | 4-1 | 2-1 | | Astbury (3), Pickering |
| 3 | 22 | Macclesfield | L | 2-4 | 1-3 | 3000 | Hewitt, Unknown |
| 4 | 29 | Buxton | W | 2-0 | 1-0 | | Lewis, Farrell |
| 5 | Oct 27 | Hurst Ramblers | W | 3-1 | 2-0 | | Pickering, Brown, Moore |
| 6 | Nov 17 | Northwich Vics. | D | 0-0 | 0-0 | | |
| 7 | 24 | Ashton North End | L | 4-6 | 3-0 | 4000 | H Bull, Lewis, Unknown (2) |
| 8 | Dec 22 | NORTHWICH VICS. | W | 4-1 | 3-0 | | Lewis, R Bull (2), Brown |
| 9 | 25 | HURST RAMBLERS | W | 6-2 | | | Unknown (6) |
| 10 | 26 | GLOSSOP NORTH END | W | 3-2 | | | Unknown (3) |
| 11 | Feb 2 | Dresden United | L | 2-5 | 0-2 | | Lewis, H Bull |
| 12 | 9 | Hanley Town | L | 4-5 | 2-1 | | H Bull, Spencer, Brown, Unknown |
| 13 | 23 | MACCLESFIELD | W | 2-0 | 0-0 | | Spencer, Lewis |
| 14 | Mar 9 | Leek | W | 3-0 | 0-0 | | Unknown (3) |
| 15 | 23 | HANLEY TOWN | W | 4-1 | 1-1 | | H Bull, Brown, Spencer (2) |
| 16 | Apr 6 | BUXTON | W | 3-1 | 1-0 | | R Bull, Brown (2) |
| 17 | 13 | ASHTON NORTH END | D | 0-0 | 0-0 | | |
| 18 | 15 | DRESDEN UNITED | W | 2-0 | 1-0 | | Brown, Lewis |
| 19 | 20 | Glossop North End | L | 2-3 | 0-2 | | Unknown (2) |
| 20 | 27 | Stalybridge Rovers | L | 2-3 | 0-2 | 2000 | Unknown (2) |

## F.A. CUP

| | Date | Opposition | | FT | HT | Att. | Goalscorers |
|---|---|---|---|---|---|---|---|
| Q1 | Oct 13 | MACCLESFIELD | L | 1-2 | 1-1 | 1000 | Astbury |

## FRIENDLIES

| | Date | Opposition | | FT | HT | Att. | Goalscorers |
|---|---|---|---|---|---|---|---|
| 1 | Sep 1 | WREXHAM | L | 1-3 | 1-3 | | Pickering |
| 2 | Oct 20 | Stoke Swifts | D | 3-3 | 2-3 | | Lewis (2), Unknown |
| 3 | Nov 3 | TONGE | W | 3-0 | 2-0 | | Lewis (2), Spencer |
| 4 | 10 | Wrexham | L | 2-4 | 2-2 | | Lewis (2) |
| 5 | Dec 1 | WREXHAM | D | 1-1 | 1-0 | | R Bull |
| 6 | 15 | CREWE ALEX. | W | 4-1 | 4-0 | | Lewis (2), Brown, Brett |
| 7 | Jan 5 | Stalybridge Rovers | L | 2-3 | 0-3 | 1500 | Lewis, Pickering |
| 8 | 19 | EVERTON RES. * | L | 1-2 | 1-1 | | Turner |
| 9 | 26 | STOKE SWIFTS | W | 3-1 | 2-1 | | Brown, R Bull, Spencer |
| 10 | Feb 16 | SOUTHPORT CENTRAL | D | 1-1 | 0-1 | | H Bull |
| 11 | Mar 16 | Southport Central | L | 1-5 | 0-4 | | R Bull |
| 12 | Apr 12 | EVERTON RES. | W | 3-1 | 1-0 | 2000 | H Bull, Webster (2) |

* In aid of Chester professionals

Final League Table

| | P | W | D | L | F | A | Pts |
|---|---|---|---|---|---|---|---|
| 1 Ashton North End | 20 | 14 | 3 | 3 | 62 | 32 | 31 |
| 2 Glossop North End | 20 | 14 | 2 | 4 | 49 | 19 | 30 |
| **3 Chester** | **20** | **12** | **2** | **6** | **53** | **35** | **26** |
| 4 Dresden United | 20 | 9 | 7 | 4 | 52 | 25 | 25 |
| 5 Stalybridge Rovers | 20 | 8 | 5 | 7 | 41 | 35 | 21 |
| 6 Macclesfield | 20 | 8 | 3 | 9 | 44 | 38 | 19 |
| 7 Leek | 20 | 7 | 4 | 9 | 36 | 47 | 18 |
| 8 Hurst Ramblers | 20 | 7 | 1 | 12 | 35 | 61 | 15 |
| 9 Hanley Town | 20 | 6 | 2 | 12 | 37 | 62 | 12 |
| 10 Buxton | 20 | 4 | 3 | 13 | 22 | 48 | 11 |
| 11 Northwich Victoria | 20 | 4 | 2 | 14 | 26 | 55 | 10 |

* 2 points deducted for playing an ineligible player

## EASON 1895-96

### IE COMBINATION

| Date | Opposition | | FT | HT | Att. | Goalscorers |
|---|---|---|---|---|---|---|
| Sep 14 | NORTHWICH VICS. | W | 3-1 | 1-1 | | Bull, Worgan, Spencer |
| 21 | Glossop North End | L | 1-4 | 0-0 | 2000 | Spencer |
| 28 | LEEK | W | 5-1 | 2-0 | | Spencer (3), Unknown (2) |
| Oct 5 | Buxton | L | 1-4 | 0-1 | | Unknown |
| 26 | Everton Res. | L | 1-4 | 1-0 | | Worgan |
| Nov 9 | Macclesfield | L | 1-2 | 0-2 | | Unknown |
| 16 | EVERTON RES. | L | 0-3 | 0-2 | | |
| 30 | BUXTON | D | 1-1 | 0-1 | | Jones |
| Dec 26 | GLOSSOP NORTH END | W | 5-1 | 1-0 | | Webster, B Lewis, Unknown (3) |
| 28 | Northwich Vics. | L | 0-1 | 0-0 | | |
| Jan 4 | Oldham County | L | 1-2 | 0-0 | | Unknown |
| 11 | MACCLESFIELD | L | 2-3 | 2-2 | | Lipsham, B Lewis |
| Feb 22 | OLDHAM COUNTY | W | 4-0 | 3-0 | | Turner, Worgan (2), W Lewis |
| 29 | Leek | D | 2-2 | 1-0 | | Unknown (2) |

### A. CUP

| Date | Opposition | | FT | HT | Att. | Goalscorers |
|---|---|---|---|---|---|---|
| Oct 12 | Port Sunlight | W | 5-1 | 2-1 | 2000 | W Lewis (2), Unknown (3) |
| Nov 2 | MIDDLETON | L | 0-3 | 0-2 | | |

### RIENDLIES

| Date | Opposition | | FT | HT | Att. | Goalscorers |
|---|---|---|---|---|---|---|
| Sep 7 | Wrexham | W | 5-2 | 2-1 | | Spencer, Turner, Unknown (3) |
| Oct 19 | WREXHAM | W | 2-0 | 2-0 | | Farrall, W Lewis |
| Nov 23 | Southport Central | L | 1-4 | 1-3 | | Spencer |
| Dec 25 | LIVERPOOL & DISTRICT | W | 3-0 | 3-0 | | W Lewis, Unknown (2) |
| Jan 25 | Macclesfield | L | 1-3 | 1-1 | 2000 | Turner |
| Feb 1 | BURSLEM PORT VALE | L | 0-2 | 0-0 | | |
| 8 | Liverpool South End | L | 0-5 | 0-2 | | |
| Mar 7 | CHESTER COLLEGE | D | 1-1 | 0-1 | | Lipsham |
| Apr 3 | NORTHWICH VICS. | D | 1-1 | 1-0 | | W Lewis |
| 4 | CHIRK | W | 5-1 | 3-1 | 500 | Worgan (2), W Lewis, Jones, Spencer |
| 6 | CREWE ALEX. | W | 3-1 | 0-1 | | Worgan, W Lewis, Jones |
| 25 | SALTNEY BORDERERS | W | 3-0 | | | Unknown (3) |

## SEASON 1896-97

### HE COMBINATION

| | Date | Opposition | | FT | HT | Att. | Goalscorers |
|---|---|---|---|---|---|---|---|
| 1 | Sep 12 | Everton Res. | L | 1-3 | 1-1 | 3000 | Worgan |
| 2 | 19 | Northwich Vics. | D | 1-1 | 0-1 | | Spencer |
| 3 | Oct 3 | BARNTON ROVERS | W | 7-0 | 5-0 | 1000 | Blakeman (3), Worgan (3), Speakman |
| 4 | Nov 7 | WREXHAM | W | 3-2 | 1-1 | | Blakeman, Spencer, Taylor (og) |
| 5 | 28 | Rockferry | L | 0-3 | 0-0 | 1500 | |
| 6 | Dec 19 | EVERTON RES. | L | 1-2 | 0-2 | | Turner |
| 7 | 26 | MACCLESFIELD | W | 5-1 | 2-1 | | Gordon, Spencer (2), Porter, Barker |
| 8 | Jan 2 | ROCKFERRY | W | 2-1 | 1-0 | | Spencer, Porter |
| 9 | 9 | Barnton Rovers | W | 2-1 | 2-0 | 20 | Blakeman, Spencer |
| 10 | 23 | BUXTON | W | 3-0 | 2-0 | | Lipsham, Speakman, Unknown |
| 11 | 30 | Middleton | L | 3-4 | 2-3 | | Spencer, Unknown (2) |
| 12 | Feb 20 | Macclesfield | D | 2-2 | 1-0 | | Speakman, Spencer |
| 13 | 27 | MIDDLETON | D | 2-2 | 1-1 | | Spencer, Gordon |
| 14 | Mar 20 | Buxton | W | 2-1 | 1-1 | | Unknown (2) |
| 15 | Apr 12 | Wrexham | W | 2-0 | 2-0 | | Coventry, Barker |
| 16 | 17 | CREWE ALEX. | W | 3-2 | 1-1 | | Speakman (2), Porter |
| 17 | 19 | NORTHWICH VICS. | W | 1-0 | 1-0 | | Lewis |
| 18 | 27 | Crewe Alex. | W | 1-0 | 1-0 | | Spencer |

### F.A. CUP

| | Date | Opposition | | FT | HT | Att. | Goalscorers |
|---|---|---|---|---|---|---|---|
| Q1 | Oct 31 | Middleton | L | 2-3 | 2-2 | 1500 | Barker, Seddon (og) |

### FRIENDLIES

| | Date | Opposition | | FT | HT | Att. | Goalscorers |
|---|---|---|---|---|---|---|---|
| 1 | Sep 5 | LIVERPOOL CASUALS | W | 6-1 | 1-0 | | Speakman, Lipsham, Spencer (3), Blakeman |
| 2 | Oct 10 | Rockferry | L | 3-4 | 1-2 | 1000 | Worgan, Unknown (2) |
| 3 | Dec 25 | BUCKLEY TOWN | L | 1-3 | 1-1 | | Unknown |
| 4 | Feb 13 | EVERTON RES. | W | 2-0 | 1-0 | | Gordon (2) |

## SEASON 1897-98

### THE COMBINATION

| | Date | Opposition | | FT | HT | Att. | Goalscorers |
|---|---|---|---|---|---|---|---|
| 1 | Sep 4 | NORTHWICH VICS. | D | 0-0 | 0-0 | | |
| 2 | 11 | Chirk | L | 1-3 | 0-3 | | Catherall |
| 3 | 18 | ROCKFERRY | D | 1-1 | 0-0 | | Spencer |
| 4 | Oct 2 | EVERTON RES. | D | 1-1 | 0-1 | 2000 | Lewis |
| 5 | 9 | Crewe Alex. | L | 1-2 | 1-2 | | Blakeman |
| 6 | 16 | DRESDEN UNITED * | W | 5-0 | 4-0 | | Blakeman (3), Lewis (2) |
| 7 | 23 | Everton Res. | L | 1-4 | 1-4 | | Lewis |
| 8 | Nov 6 | CHIRK | W | 1-0 | 1-0 | | Wilson |
| 9 | 20 | DRUIDS | W | 1-0 | 0-0 | | Gordon |
| 10 | Dec 4 | Garston Copper Works | L | 4-7 | 3-2 | | Gordon, Spencer, Lewis, Roberts |
| 11 | 11 | TRANMERE ROVERS | W | 6-0 | 2-0 | | Lewis (4), Speakman, Gordon |
| 12 | 18 | Northwich Vics. | L | 2-5 | 0-1 | | Spencer, Gordon |
| 13 | 26 | Wrexham | W | 3-1 | 1-0 | 3000 | Lewis, Spencer, Webster |
| 14 | Jan 8 | Rockferry | L | 0-4 | 0-0 | 3000 | |
| 15 | 22 | Tranmere Rovers | L | 2-3 | 0-2 | 1000 | Unknown, og |
| 16 | 29 | WHITE STAR WANDERERS | D | 2-2 | 2-1 | | Spencer, Speakman |
| 17 | Feb 5 | GARSTON COPPER WORKS | W | 5-0 | 3-0 | | Lewis (2), Hales (2), Catherall |
| 18 | 19 | Druids | L | 1-4 | 0-3 | | Hales |
| 19 | 26 | STOKE SWIFTS | L | 0-2 | 0-1 | | |
| 20 | Mar 12 | Stoke Swifts | L | 0-3 | 0-2 | | |
| 21 | 26 | BUXTON | W | 3-1 | 1-0 | | Spencer (2), Lewis |
| 22 | Apr 2 | Buxton | L | 3-4 | 2-1 | | Spencer, Catherall, Gordon |
| 23 | 8 | WREXHAM | W | 1-0 | 1-0 | 3000 | Lewis |
| 24 | 11 | CREWE ALEX. | D | 0-0 | 0-0 | | |
| 25 | 23 | White Star Wanderers | L | 0-3 | 0-1 | | |

* Dresden United withdrew from League, record expunged

### F.A. CUP

| | Date | Opposition | | FT | HT | Att. | Goalscorers |
|---|---|---|---|---|---|---|---|
| Q1 | Sep 25 | Stockport County | L | 1-2 | 0-2 | | Lewis |

### FRIENDLIES

| | Date | Opposition | | FT | HT | Att. | Goalscorers |
|---|---|---|---|---|---|---|---|
| 1 | Oct 30 | OSWESTRY | W | 5-2 | 5-1 | | Speakman(2), Spencer, Blakeman, Unknown |
| 2 | Dec 25 | RAWTENSTALL | W | 7-0 | 2-0 | | Gordon (3), Spencer (2), Speakman, Lewis |
| 3 | Feb 12 | CHESTER & DISTRICT | W | 4-1 | 1-0 | | Lewis, Hales, Lipsham, Unknown |
| 4 | Mar 19 | EVERTON RES. | W | 4-1 | 1-0 | | Spencer (2), Blakeman, Lewis |
| 5 | Apr 20 | LIVERPOOL | L | 1-3 | 0-0 | | Wilson |

### Final League Tables

#### 1895-96

| | P | W | D | L | F | A | Pts |
|---|---|---|---|---|---|---|---|
| 1 Everton Reserves | 14 | 11 | 2 | 1 | 54 | 12 | 24 |
| 2 Macclesfield | 14 | 11 | 2 | 1 | 37 | 13 | 24 |
| 3 Glossop North End | 14 | 9 | 3 | 2 | 33 | 13 | 21 |
| 4 Oldham County | 14 | 5 | 1 | 8 | 24 | 39 | 11 |
| **5 Chester** | **14** | **4** | **2** | **8** | **27** | **29** | **10** |
| 6 Northwich Victoria | 14 | 4 | 1 | 9 | 14 | 35 | 9 |
| 7 Leek | 14 | 3 | 3 | 8 | 15 | 35 | 7 |
| 8 Buxton | 14 | 1 | 2 | 11 | 15 | 43 | 4 |

* 2 points deducted for playing an ineligible player.

#### 1896-97

| | P | W | L | D | F | A | Pts |
|---|---|---|---|---|---|---|---|
| 1 Everton Reserves | 18 | 14 | 3 | 1 | 61 | 14 | 31 |
| 2 Rockferry | 18 | 12 | 3 | 3 | 57 | 18 | 27 |
| **3 Chester** | **18** | **11** | **3** | **4** | **41** | **25** | **25** |
| 4 Northwich Victoria | 18 | 8 | 2 | 8 | 31 | 41 | 18 |
| 5 Buxton | 18 | 7 | 3 | 8 | 39 | 34 | 17 |
| 6 Wrexham | 18 | 7 | 2 | 9 | 41 | 40 | 16 |
| 7 Middleton | 18 | 7 | 3 | 8 | 40 | 32 | 15 |
| 8 Macclesfield | 18 | 5 | 2 | 11 | 34 | 60 | 12 |
| 9 Crewe Alexandra | 18 | 5 | 1 | 12 | 35 | 50 | 9 |
| 10 Barnton Victoria | 18 | 2 | 2 | 14 | 18 | 80 | 4 |

* 2 points deducted for playing an ineligible player.

#### 1897-98

| | P | W | D | L | F | A | Pts |
|---|---|---|---|---|---|---|---|
| 1 Everton Reserves | 24 | 15 | 5 | 4 | 65 | 25 | 35 |
| 2 Crewe Alexandra | 24 | 12 | 6 | 6 | 53 | 34 | 30 |
| 3 Chirk | 24 | 11 | 4 | 9 | 38 | 27 | 26 |
| 4 Wrexham | 24 | 10 | 6 | 8 | 45 | 44 | 26 |
| 5 Stoke Swifts | 24 | 10 | 5 | 9 | 42 | 35 | 25 |
| 6 Buxton | 24 | 9 | 7 | 8 | 44 | 44 | 25 |
| 7 Rockferry | 24 | 8 | 8 | 8 | 34 | 30 | 24 |
| 8 White Star Wanderers | 24 | 8 | 7 | 9 | 41 | 42 | 23 |
| 9 Garston Copper Works | 24 | 8 | 7 | 9 | 37 | 60 | 23 |
| 10 Druids | 24 | 9 | 3 | 12 | 43 | 46 | 21 |
| **11 Chester** | **24** | **7** | **5** | **12** | **39** | **50** | **19** |
| 12 Tranmere Rovers | 24 | 9 | 3 | 12 | 35 | 45 | 19 |
| 13 Northwich Victoria | 24 | 6 | 2 | 16 | 40 | 74 | 14 |

* 2 points deducted for playing an ineligible player.
Dresden United withdrew - record expunged.

# SEASON 1898-99

## THE COMBINATION

| | Date | Opposition | | FT | HT | Att. | Goalscorers |
|---|---|---|---|---|---|---|---|
| 1 | Sep 3 | Tranmere Rovers | L | 0-4 | 0-2 | 500 | |
| 2 | 10 | EVERTON RES. | L | 1-3 | 0-1 | | Unknown |
| 3 | 17 | DRUIDS | W | 1-0 | 1-0 | | Speakman |
| 4 | 24 | WREXHAM | W | 3-1 | 1-0 | | Hales (2), Delaney |
| 5 | Oct 8 | CHIRK | W | 1-0 | 0-0 | | Delaney |
| 6 | 22 | Druids | L | 0-5 | 0-4 | | |
| 7 | 29 | TRANMERE ROVERS | W | 3-1 | 1-0 | 2500 | Donoghue, Bennion, Gordon |
| 8 | Nov 5 | Liverpool Res. | L | 0-2 | 0-0 | | |
| 9 | 12 | Everton Res. | L | 0-4 | 0-2 | 3000 | |
| 10 | 19 | Wrexham | L | 0-1 | 0-1 | | |
| 11 | Dec 3 | BUXTON | W | 4-0 | 0-0 | | Lewis (2), Delaney, Carter |
| 12 | 10 | White Star Wanderers | D | 3-3 | 3-1 | | Gordon, Carroll, Speakman |
| 13 | 24 | Chirk | L | 2-4 | 1-4 | | Lewis, Delaney |
| 14 | 31 | LLANDUDNO SWIFTS | W | 4-2 | 2-1 | | Delaney, Whitehouse (2), Speakman |
| 15 | Jan 7 | OSWESTRY UNITED | W | 1-0 | 0-0 | | Donoghue |
| 16 | 14 | Garston Copper Works | W | 4-2 | 2-1 | | Donoghue (3), Poutney |
| 17 | 28 | WHITE STAR WANDERERS | W | 4-1 | 2-1 | | Donoghue (2), Lewis, Poutney |
| 18 | Feb 4 | LIVERPOOL RES. | D | 0-0 | 0-0 | | |
| 19 | 18 | Bangor | D | 4-4 | 2-3 | | Spencer, Donoghue, Gordon, Poutney |
| 20 | 25 | GARSTON COPPER WORKS | W | 2-1 | 0-1 | | Donoghue, Spencer |
| 21 | Mar 4 | Rhyl | W | 5-3 | 3-2 | | Spencer(2),Lewis, Poutney, Whitehouse |
| 22 | 18 | Oswestry United | L | 3-6 | 2-3 | | Spencer, Lewis, Gordon |
| 23 | 25 | BANGOR | D | 3-3 | 1-2 | | Spencer, Poutney, Unknown |
| 24 | 31 | RHYL | W | 5-0 | 4-0 | | Poutney, Spencer, Gordon,Unknown (2) |
| 25 | Apr 3 | SOUTH LIVERPOOL | W | 5-1 | 2-0 | | Poutney (2), Donoghue (2), Lewis |
| 26 | 15 | Buxton | D | 2-2 | 2-1 | | Poutney, Gordon |
| 27 | 22 | Llandudno Swifts | L | 0-3 | 0-2 | | |
| 28 | 29 | South Liverpool | L | 0-1 | 0-1 | | |

## F.A. CUP

| | | | | | | |
|---|---|---|---|---|---|---|
| Q1 | Oct 1 | Wrexham | L | 2-3 | 1-2 | Lewis, Unknown |

## FRIENDLIES

| | | | | | | | |
|---|---|---|---|---|---|---|---|
| 1 | Oct 15 | Crewe Alex. | L | 1-7 | 1-0 | | Donoghue |
| 2 | Dec 26 | MANCHESTER CITY RES. | L | 1-2 | 1-0 | 2000 | Delaney |
| 3 | 27 | CHESTER JUNIOR LEAGUE | W | 3-1 | | | Unknown (3) |
| 4 | Apr 1 | CREWE ALEX. | D | 0-0 | 0-0 | | |
| 5 | 8 | CHESTER JUNIOR LEAGUE * | W | 4-3 | 4-0 | | Spencer (2), Powell, Unknown |

* In aid of Chester F. C.

Final League Table

| | P | W | D | L | F | A | Pts |
|---|---|---|---|---|---|---|---|
| 1 Everton Reserves | 28 | 23 | 4 | 1 | 112 | 18 | 50 |
| 2 Liverpool Res. | 28 | 21 | 3 | 4 | 87 | 22 | 45 |
| 3 Tranmere Rovers | 28 | 15 | 4 | 9 | 54 | 33 | 34 |
| 4 Druids | 28 | 16 | 1 | 11 | 64 | 31 | 33 |
| 5 Wrexham | 28 | 15 | 3 | 10 | 55 | 48 | 33 |
| 6 Chester | 28 | 13 | 5 | 10 | 60 | 57 | 31 |
| 7 Bangor | 28 | 12 | 6 | 10 | 63 | 78 | 30 |
| 8 Chirk | 28 | 12 | 3 | 13 | 44 | 48 | 27 |
| 9 Llandudno Swifts | 28 | 12 | 3 | 13 | 48 | 58 | 27 |
| 10 White Star Wanderers* | 28 | 11 | 6 | 11 | 68 | 54 | 26 |
| 11 South Liverpool | 28 | 9 | 4 | 15 | 36 | 52 | 22 |
| 12 Oswestry United | 28 | 9 | 2 | 17 | 49 | 73 | 20 |
| 13 Buxton | 28 | 7 | 2 | 19 | 43 | 102 | 16 |
| 14 Garston Copper Works | 28 | 5 | 2 | 21 | 31 | 77 | 12 |
| 15 Rhyl | 28 | 6 | 0 | 22 | 35 | 98 | 12 |

*2 points deducted for playing an ineligible player

**1898/99 Season**

Back - Dr Butt, Carter, Halliday, Eardley, Jones, Fletcher, Coventry

Middle - Delaney, Marshall, Atherton, Barker, Lewis

Front - Gordon, Spencer, Poutney, Donoghue, Speakman, Whitehouse

**SEASONS 1899-1900 - 1900-01**

**CLUB DISBANDED.**

**1896/97 Season with Cheshire Cup**

(Back) Barnes, Porter, Butt, Coventry, Clarke.

(Middle) Blakeman, Catherall, Carter.

(Front) Gordon, Spencer, Lewis, Speakman, Lipsham

# SEASON 1901-02

## THE COMBINATION

| | Date | Opposition | | FT | HT | Att. | Goalscorers |
|---|---|---|---|---|---|---|---|
| 1 | Sep 7 | White Star Wanderers | L | 3-6 | 2-3 | | Gibbs, Farrell, Davies |
| 2 | 14 | NANTWICH | W | 3-1 | 0-0 | 1000 | Delaney (2), Brown |
| 3 | 21 | Chirk | L | 1-2 | 1-1 | | Spencer |
| 4 | 28 | WREXHAM | D | 2-2 | 1-1 | 2000 | Brown, Griffiths |
| 5 | Oct 12 | WELLINGTON TOWN | L | 1-2 | 0-2 | | Davies |
| 6 | 19 | Burslem Port Vale Res. | L | 1-6 | 1-4 | | Griffiths |
| 7 | 26 | BANGOR | D | 1-1 | 0-0 | | Delaney |
| 8 | Nov 16 | WITTON ALBION | L | 2-3 | 1-2 | | Griffiths (2) |
| 9 | 30 | TRANMERE ROVERS | L | 1-3 | 0-0 | | Delaney |
| 10 | Dec 21 | Birkenhead | L | 3-4 | 1-4 | | Griffiths, Unknown (2) |
| 11 | 28 | RHYL | D | 1-1 | 0-1 | | Rogers |
| 12 | Jan 4 | TRANMERE ROVERS | D | 3-3 | 2-1 | | Griffiths, Woods, Rogers |
| 13 | 11 | NEWTON LE WILLOWS * | W | 5-1 | 1-0 | | Lipsham (2), Griffiths (2), Cooke |
| 14 | 25 | OSWESTRY UNITED | L | 1-8 | 0-6 | | Davies |
| 15 | Feb 1 | Wellington Town | D | 1-1 | 1-0 | | Griffiths |
| 16 | 22 | Oswestry United | L | 0-3 | 0-2 | | |
| 17 | Mar 8 | Bangor | D | 1-1 | 1-0 | | Griffiths |
| 18 | 22 | WHITE STAR WANDERERS | W | 4-1 | 1-1 | | Foote (og), Miller (2), Spencer |
| 19 | 28 | Rhyl | W | 2-1 | 1-1 | | Spencer, Delaney |
| 20 | 29 | CHIRK | W | 3-1 | 3-0 | | Delaney, Cooke, Wakefield |
| 21 | 31 | BIRKENHEAD | L | 0-2 | 0-2 | | |
| 22 | Apr 5 | BURSLEM PORT VALE RES. | D | 2-2 | 1-2 | | Spencer, Barker |
| 23 | 12 | Newton Le Willows | L | 1-2 | 0-2 | | Lloyd |
| 24 | 16 | Witton Albion | L | 1-6 | 0-3 | | Miller |
| 25 | 23 | Wrexham | L | 0-3 | 0-1 | | |
| 26 | 26 | Nantwich | W | 3-1 | 1-1 | | Cooke, Riley, Unknown |

* Only 30 minutes played each way

## F.A. CUP

| | Date | Opposition | | FT | HT | Att. | Goalscorers |
|---|---|---|---|---|---|---|---|
| Q1 | Oct 5 | Birkenhead | D | 1-1 | 1-0 | | Griffiths |
| Q1r | 9 | BIRKENHEAD * | W | 5-4 | 2-3 | | Spencer(2), Griffiths, Prescott, Davies |

* Extra time played following score of 3-3 after 90 minutes
Chester disqualified - pitch too short

## WELSH CUP

| | Date | Opposition | | FT | HT | Att. | Goalscorers |
|---|---|---|---|---|---|---|---|
| 2R | | BROUGHTON UNITED | | | | | Chester scratched |

## FRIENDLIES

| | Date | Opposition | | FT | HT | Att. | Goalscorers |
|---|---|---|---|---|---|---|---|
| 1 | Sep 4 | EVERTON | L | 1-4 | 0-0 | 1000 | Griffiths |
| 2 | Nov 9 | WHITE STAR WANDERERS | W | 3-1 | 2-1 | | Farrell, Bayley (og), Spencer |
| 3 | Dec 14 | BOLTON WANDERERS RES. | L | 0-1 | 0-0 | 300 | |
| 4 | Apr 19 | CHESTER & DISTRICT L. * | W | 3-1 | 1-1 | | Cooke, Spencer, Wakefield |
| 5 | May 3 | SALTNEY & NEWTON @ | D | 3-3 | 2-0 | 400 | Miller, Lipsham, Poutney |

* In aid of Chester F. C.
@ In aid of Ibrox disaster

### Final League Table

| | P | W | D | L | F | A | Pts |
|---|---|---|---|---|---|---|---|
| 1 Wrexham | 26 | 17 | 7 | 2 | 80 | 21 | 41 |
| 2 Burslem Port Vale Res. | 26 | 14 | 7 | 5 | 61 | 43 | 33 * |
| 3 Oswestry United | 26 | 12 | 6 | 8 | 55 | 33 | 30 |
| 4 Nantwich | 26 | 13 | 4 | 9 | 68 | 47 | 30 |
| 5 Wellington | 26 | 11 | 5 | 10 | 39 | 36 | 27 |
| 6 Bangor | 26 | 11 | 5 | 10 | 51 | 74 | 27 |
| 7 Birkenhead | 26 | 9 | 8 | 9 | 42 | 40 | 26 |
| 8 Witton Albion | 26 | 11 | 3 | 12 | 47 | 52 | 25 |
| 9 Newton Le Willows | 26 | 9 | 6 | 11 | 40 | 71 | 24 |
| 10 Tranmere Rovers | 26 | 8 | 7 | 11 | 46 | 49 | 23 |
| 11 Rhyl | 26 | 6 | 8 | 12 | 45 | 53 | 20 |
| 12 White Star Wanderers | 26 | 9 | 2 | 15 | 50 | 63 | 20 |
| 13 Chirk | 26 | 8 | 1 | 17 | 48 | 69 | 17 |
| **14 Chester** | **26** | **6** | **7** | **13** | **46** | **67** | **17** * |

* 2 points deducted for playing an ineligible player

# SEASON 1902-03

## THE COMBINATION

| | Date | Opposition | | FT | HT | Att. | Goalscorers |
|---|---|---|---|---|---|---|---|
| 1 | Sep 6 | White Star Wanderers * | L | 1-2 | 0-0 | | Turner |
| 2 | 13 | WITTON ALBION | L | 1-3 | 0-1 | | Delaney |
| 3 | 27 | Chirk | W | 1-0 | 0-0 | | Griffiths |
| 4 | Oct 4 | BURSLEM PORT VALE RES. | D | 2-2 | 1-2 | 700 | Delaney, Kelly |
| 5 | 11 | MIDDLEWICH | D | 1-1 | 0-1 | | Delaney |
| 6 | 18 | TRANMERE ROVERS | W | 5-0 | 3-0 | | Hodnett, Delaney, Riley, Kelly (2) |
| 7 | 25 | Middlewich | D | 2-2 | 1-1 | | Hodnett (2) |
| 8 | Nov 8 | OSWESTRY UNITED | D | 1-1 | 0-1 | | Delaney |
| 9 | 15 | Witton Albion | W | 2-0 | 1-0 | | Hodnett, Kelly |
| 10 | 29 | WINSFORD UNITED | W | 6-0 | 2-0 | | Delaney (2), Riley (2), Kelly (2) |
| 11 | Dec 13 | Oswestry United | L | 2-5 | 0-2 | | Delaney, Turner |
| 12 | 25 | Wrexham | L | 1-3 | 0-0 | | Delaney |
| 13 | 26 | WHITE STAR WANDERERS* | L | 1-2 | 0-0 | | Delaney |
| 14 | 27 | RHYL | W | 4-3 | 4-2 | 550 | Kelly, Sherman, Turner, Riley |
| 15 | Jan 3 | Rhyl | D | 2-2 | 2-2 | | Kelly, Turner |
| 16 | 10 | Tranmere Rovers | D | 0-0 | 0-0 | | |
| 17 | Feb 28 | NEWTON LE WILLOWS | W | 2-0 | 1-0 | | Riley, Delaney |
| 18 | Mar 7 | BANGOR | W | 6-0 | 4-0 | | Delaney (2), Turner, Lewis, Kelly (2) |
| 19 | 14 | Nantwich | L | 1-9 | | | Unknown |
| 20 | 21 | Burslem Port Vale Res. | W | 1-0 | 1-0 | | Kelly |
| 21 | Apr 1 | NANTWICH | D | 1-1 | 1-0 | | Riley |
| 22 | 10 | WREXHAM | L | 0-4 | 0-1 | | |
| 23 | 11 | Bangor | L | 0-1 | 0-1 | | |
| 24 | 13 | CHIRK | D | 2-2 | 2-1 | | McGuffie, Hardacre |
| 25 | 18 | Winsford United | L | 0-3 | 0-1 | | |
| 26 | 20 | Newton Le Willows | W | 3-1 | 1-1 | | Hardacre (2), Delaney |
| 27 | 25 | Birkenhead | L | 1-4 | 0-3 | | Turner |
| 28 | 29 | BIRKENHEAD | L | 1-2 | 1-0 | | Kelly |

* White Star Wanderers resigned from League, record expunged

## WELSH CUP

| | Date | Opposition | | FT | HT | Att. | Goalscorers |
|---|---|---|---|---|---|---|---|
| 3R | Dec 6 | WREXHAM | L | 0-2 | 0-1 | 2000 | |

* Match switched to Wrexham - pitch too short

## FRIENDLIES

| | Date | Opposition | | FT | HT | Att. | Goalscorers |
|---|---|---|---|---|---|---|---|
| 1 | Sep 3 | EVERTON | L | 0-4 | 0-3 | | |
| 2 | 20 | Connah's Quay | W | 2-1 | 1-1 | | Delaney, Kelly |
| 3 | Feb 7 | MANCHESTER CITY RES. | W | 3-2 | 2-2 | | Delaney (2), Lewis |

### Final League Table

| | P | W | D | L | F | A | Pts |
|---|---|---|---|---|---|---|---|
| 1 Wrexham | 26 | 19 | 5 | 2 | 80 | 23 | 43 |
| 2 Nantwich | 26 | 15 | 4 | 7 | 69 | 43 | 34 |
| 3 Birkenhead | 26 | 15 | 4 | 7 | 53 | 36 | 34 |
| 4 Burslem Port Vale Res. | 26 | 12 | 7 | 7 | 63 | 35 | 31 |
| 5 Oswestry United | 26 | 14 | 2 | 10 | 57 | 42 | 30 |
| 6 Witton Albion | 26 | 11 | 8 | 7 | 52 | 49 | 30 |
| **7 Chester** | **26** | **9** | **8** | **9** | **48** | **49** | **26** |
| 8 Middlewich | 26 | 9 | 8 | 9 | 43 | 62 | 26 |
| 9 Bangor | 26 | 9 | 8 | 9 | 53 | 72 | 24 * |
| 10 Winsford United | 26 | 8 | 5 | 13 | 51 | 54 | 19 * |
| 11 Newton Le Willows | 26 | 8 | 3 | 15 | 52 | 74 | 19 |
| 12 Rhyl | 26 | 8 | 4 | 14 | 52 | 64 | 18 * |
| 13 Tranmere Rovers | 26 | 4 | 5 | 17 | 30 | 64 | 13 |
| 14 Chirk | 26 | 4 | 3 | 19 | 34 | 70 | 11 |

* 2 points deducted for playing an ineligible player.
White Star Wanderers resigned March 1903 - record expunged.

# SEASON 1903-04

## THE COMBINATION

| | Date | Opposition | | FT | HT | Att. | Goalscorers |
|---|---|---|---|---|---|---|---|
| 1 | Sep 5 | WITTON ALBION | W | 5-0 | 2-0 | | J Lipsham, Smith (2), Matthews, T Lipsham |
| 2 | 12 | BIRKENHEAD | L | 1-2 | 0-1 | | T Lipsham |
| 3 | 19 | Birkenhead | W | 2-1 | 2-1 | | Smith, T Delaney |
| 4 | 26 | TRANMERE ROVERS | W | 3-2 | 2-2 | | Matthews (2), Smith |
| 5 | Oct 3 | WINSFORD UNITED | W | 4-2 | 2-2 | | Bell, J Lipsham, Smith, T Lipsham |
| 6 | 10 | MIDDLEWICH | W | 2-1 | 1-1 | | T Delaney, T Lipsham |
| 7 | 24 | Chirk | W | 7-2 | 2-1 | | Bell, T Lipsham, Smith (2), T Delaney (3) |
| 8 | 31 | BANGOR | W | 7-0 | 3-0 | | Smith (4), T Lipsham, Bell, Matthews |
| 9 | Nov 7 | Winsford United | W | 3-2 | 1-1 | | Bell, Smith (2) |
| 10 | 14 | Broughton United | D | 1-1 | 1-1 | 2000 | T Lipsham |
| 11 | 21 | Oswestry United | L | 1-2 | 0-0 | | Unknown |
| 12 | Dec 5 | Rhyl | L | 1-2 | 0-1 | | T Lipsham |
| 13 | 25 | Wrexham | W | 3-1 | 2-1 | 2500 | T Delaney, T Lipsham (2) |
| 14 | 26 | BROUGHTON UNITED | W | 3-1 | 1-1 | 4000 | Matthews, Unknown (2) |
| 15 | Jan 23 | CHIRK | W | 7-1 | 4-1 | | T Delaney, Barker, Bell (3), Smith (2) |
| 16 | 30 | Tranmere Rovers | L | 0-1 | 0-0 | | |
| 17 | Feb 20 | NANTWICH | L | 1-4 | 1-0 | | Bell |
| 18 | Mar 5 | Middlewich | D | 1-1 | 0-0 | | T Delaney |
| 19 | 19 | Nantwich | L | 0-1 | 0-1 | | |
| 20 | Apr 1 | WREXHAM | D | 1-1 | 0-0 | | J Lipsham |
| 21 | 2 | Bangor | W | 1-0 | 1-0 | | Barker |
| 22 | 4 | Witton Albion | W | 1-0 | 1-0 | | T Lipsham |
| 23 | 27 | OSWESTRY UNITED | W | 7-1 | 3-0 | | T Lipsham, Matthews(3), T Delaney, J Lipsham(2) |
| 24 | 30 | RHYL | W | 3-0 | 0-0 | | Matthews, Delaney, T Lipsham |

## WELSH CUP

| | | | | | | | |
|---|---|---|---|---|---|---|---|
| 3R | Dec 12 | Druids | L | 0-1 | 0-0 | | |

## FRIENDLIES

| | | | | | | | |
|---|---|---|---|---|---|---|---|
| 1 | Sep 16 | EVERTON | L | 1-6 | 1-4 | | Hardacre |
| 2 | Oct 17 | KIRKDALE | W | 6-0 | 4-0 | | T Delaney (2), Breen, Bell (2), Smith |

Final League Table

| | P | W | D | L | F | A | Pts |
|---|---|---|---|---|---|---|---|
| 1 Birkenhead | 24 | 17 | 3 | 4 | 49 | 22 | 37 |
| **2 Chester** | **24** | **15** | **3** | **6** | **65** | **29** | **33** |
| 3 Nantwich | 24 | 14 | 3 | 7 | 60 | 30 | 31 |
| 4 Tranmere Rovers | 24 | 14 | 1 | 9 | 54 | 42 | 29 |
| 5 Wrexham | 24 | 12 | 4 | 8 | 54 | 34 | 28 |
| 6 Bangor | 24 | 12 | 2 | 10 | 60 | 55 | 26 |
| 7 Oswestry United | 24 | 11 | 2 | 11 | 42 | 55 | 24 |
| 8 Rhyl | 24 | 10 | 1 | 13 | 52 | 52 | 21 |
| 9 Middlewich | 24 | 7 | 5 | 12 | 40 | 63 | 19 |
| 10 Broughton United | 24 | 8 | 3 | 13 | 38 | 55 | 19 |
| 11 Winsford United | 24 | 6 | 6 | 12 | 40 | 46 | 18 |
| 12 Witton Albion | 24 | 4 | 8 | 12 | 30 | 61 | 16 |
| 13 Chirk | 24 | 3 | 5 | 16 | 36 | 76 | 11 |

# SEASON 1904-05

## THE COMBINATION

| | Date | Opposition | | FT | HT | Att. | Goalscorers |
|---|---|---|---|---|---|---|---|
| 1 | Sep 3 | Tranmere Rovers | L | 0-3 | 0-2 | | |
| 2 | 10 | DRUIDS | W | 6-0 | 4-0 | | Delaney (2), Matthews (2), Lewis, T Lipsham |
| 3 | 17 | BIRKENHEAD | L | 0-1 | 0-0 | | |
| 4 | 24 | Chirk | W | 6-3 | 4-0 | | Case (3), Matthews, Delaney, J Lipsham |
| 5 | Oct 1 | Rhyl | W | 4-0 | 3-0 | | T Lipsham (2), Case, J Lipsham |
| 6 | 8 | Whitchurch | W | 4-1 | 3-1 | | White, Case (2), T Lipsham |
| 7 | 22 | BANGOR | W | 4-2 | 2-0 | | Delaney, Matthews, J Lipsham (2) |
| 8 | 29 | MIDDLEWICH | W | 2-1 | 1-1 | | Delaney, Matthews |
| 9 | Nov 5 | Birkenhead | W | 3-1 | 1-0 | | J Lipsham, T Lipsham, Matthews |
| 10 | 12 | BROUGHTON UNITED | W | 4-0 | 1-0 | | Delaney (2), Evans, Case |
| 11 | 19 | Nantwich | D | 1-1 | 1-1 | 1000 | Case |
| 12 | 26 | Broughton United | L | 1-2 | 0-1 | | T Lipsham |
| 13 | Dec 3 | Wrexham | L | 2-3 | 1-0 | 2000 | T Lipsham, Case |
| 14 | 26 | CHIRK | W | 1-0 | 0-0 | | White |
| 15 | 27 | OSWESTRY UNITED | W | 4-1 | 3-1 | | Perry (og), Case, Delaney, J Jones |
| 16 | 31 | RHYL | W | 1-0 | 0-0 | | White |
| 17 | Jan 14 | Oswestry United | L | 1-3 | 1-2 | | Delaney |
| 18 | 21 | Bangor | W | 5-3 | 2-2 | | Case, J Jones, J Lipsham (2), Matthews |
| 19 | Feb 18 | Port Sunlight | W | 3-2 | 2-1 | 1500 | Case, Matthews, J Jones |
| 20 | 25 | Middlewich | W | 3-1 | 2-1 | | White (2), Evans |
| 21 | Mar 18 | NANTWICH * | W | 4-2 | 2-1 | | Case (2), J Jones, J Lipsham |
| 22 | Apr 1 | WREXHAM | D | 1-1 | 1-1 | 4000 | Delaney |
| 23 | 15 | PORT SUNLIGHT | W | 5-1 | 3-1 | | Matthews, J Lipsham (2), O O'Neil (2) |
| 24 | 21 | WHITCHURCH | D | 1-1 | 0-1 | 4000 | Matthews |
| 25 | 24 | TRANMERE ROVERS | W | 2-0 | 2-0 | | Matthews, J Jones |
| 26 | 26 | Druids | L | 1-2 | 0-1 | | Case |

* Tommy Delaney Benefit

## WELSH CUP

| | | | | | | | |
|---|---|---|---|---|---|---|---|
| 3R | Jan 7 | Wrexham | L | 0-2 | 0-0 | | |

## FRIENDLIES

| | | | | | | | |
|---|---|---|---|---|---|---|---|
| 1 | Dec 24 | BIRKENHEAD | W | 3-0 | 1-0 | | Jones, J Lipsham, White |
| 2 | Jan 28 | EVERTON RES. | W | 2-1 | 1-0 | | J Lipsham, Case |
| 3 | Feb 4 | Cheshire Regiment | W | 3-2 | 1-2 | | Delaney, Case, E O'Neil |
| 4 | Mar 8 | CHESTER WEDNESDAY * | W | 9-0 | | | Unknown (9) |
| 5 | Apr 29 | Crewe Alex. | L | 2-3 | 2-2 | | Matthews, Case |

* Harry Astbury Benefit

Final League Table

| | P | W | D | L | F | A | Pts |
|---|---|---|---|---|---|---|---|
| 1 Wrexham | 26 | 21 | 1 | 4 | 70 | 16 | 43 |
| **2 Chester** | **26** | **17** | **3** | **6** | **69** | **35** | **37** |
| 3 Broughton United | 26 | 14 | 5 | 7 | 43 | 44 | 33 |
| 4 Nantwich | 26 | 11 | 7 | 8 | 66 | 39 | 29 |
| 5 Port Sunlight | 26 | 11 | 5 | 10 | 56 | 50 | 27 |
| 6 Tranmere Rovers | 26 | 10 | 7 | 9 | 41 | 37 | 27 |
| 7 Rhyl | 26 | 11 | 5 | 10 | 40 | 44 | 27 |
| 8 Whitchurch | 26 | 11 | 4 | 11 | 60 | 58 | 26 |
| 9 Middlewich | 26 | 10 | 2 | 14 | 44 | 55 | 22 |
| 10 Oswestry United | 26 | 10 | 2 | 14 | 43 | 62 | 22 |
| 11 Birkenhead | 26 | 7 | 6 | 13 | 35 | 47 | 20 |
| 12 Bangor | 26 | 8 | 3 | 15 | 55 | 61 | 19 |
| 13 Druids | 26 | 7 | 5 | 14 | 29 | 54 | 19 |
| 14 Chirk | 26 | 4 | 5 | 17 | 32 | 81 | 13 |

1904/05 Season
Back - Fletcher (Secretary), Hallmark, Delaney, Coventry, Barker, Coventry (Treasurer)
Middle - Matthews, E O'Neil, Case, White, Lipsham, Eardley (Trainer)
Front - Hughes, Jones, Dawson

# SEASON 1905-06

## THE COMBINATION

| | Date | Opposition | | FT | HT | Att. | Goalscorers |
|---|---|---|---|---|---|---|---|
| 1 | Sep 2 | Bangor | D | 1-1 | 1-0 | | J Jones |
| 2 | 9 | CHIRK | W | 9-0 | 5-0 | | Marshall(3),Delaney(3),Matthews(2),J Lipsham |
| 3 | 16 | Crewe Alex Res. | L | 1-2 | 1-0 | | Matthews |
| 4 | 23 | NANTWICH | W | 3-1 | 2-0 | | Warren, J Lipsham (2) |
| 5 | 30 | Middlewich | W | 3-0 | 2-0 | | J Lipsham (2), Matthews |
| 6 | Oct 14 | Tranmere Rovers | L | 0-3 | 0-1 | | |
| 7 | 21 | RHYL | W | 8-0 | 4-0 | | Delaney (4), J Jones, Galley, Matthews (2) |
| 8 | Nov 11 | Druids | D | 1-1 | 1-0 | | Matthews |
| 9 | 25 | Oswestry United | W | 2-0 | 1-0 | | Galley, J Jones |
| 10 | Dec 2 | BIRKENHEAD | W | 2-0 | 1-0 | | Jackson, Dodd |
| 11 | 16 | MIDDLEWICH | W | 8-0 | 5-0 | | H Jones(4),J Jones,Jackson(2),J Lipsham |
| 12 | 23 | Birkenhead | D | 1-1 | 0-1 | | Delaney |
| 13 | 25 | GLOSSOP RES. | W | 3-1 | 2-1 | | H Jones, J Lipsham (2) |
| 14 | 26 | CREWE ALEX. RES. | W | 3-0 | 2-0 | | Jackson, J Lipsham, Delaney |
| 15 | 30 | BANGOR | W | 5-0 | 2-0 | | Delaney,J Lipsham (2),Jackson,Matthews |
| 16 | Jan 27 | Nantwich | L | 0-3 | 0-3 | | |
| 17 | Feb 17 | TRANMERE ROVERS | W | 1-0 | 0-0 | | H Jones |
| 18 | 24 | Rhyl | W | 2-1 | 0-0 | | J Lipsham, Galley |
| 19 | Mar 10 | Glossop Res. | L | 0-3 | 0-1 | | |
| 20 | 24 | Whitchurch | L | 0-2 | 0-1 | | |
| 21 | 31 | OSWESTRY UNITED | W | 6-1 | 2-0 | | J Jones(2),Jackson,Delaney(2),Matthews |
| 22 | Apr 7 | PORT SUNLIGHT | W | 3-0 | 1-0 | | W Jones, Williams (2) |
| 23 | 13 | WHITCHURCH | D | 2-2 | 2-0 | 4000 | H Jones, J Lipsham |
| 24 | 16 | DRUIDS | W | 6-0 | 2-0 | | W Jones,R Jones,J Jones (2),Williams,Dodd |
| 25 | 18 | BROUGHTON UNITED * | W | 1-0 | 1-0 | | Evans |
| 26 | 21 | Chirk | L | 1-3 | 1-2 | | Walker |
| 27 | 28 | Port Sunlight | L | 0-1 | 0-1 | | |
| 28 | 30 | Broughton United @ | L | 0-4 | 0-3 | | |

* Only 35 minutes played each way
@ Played at Wrexham

### F.A. CUP

| | | | | | | | |
|---|---|---|---|---|---|---|---|
| Q1 | Oct 7 | NORTHERN NOMADS | W | 2-0 | 2-0 | | Matthews, J Jones |
| Q2 | 28 | Chirk | L | 0-2 | 0-1 | | |

### WELSH CUP

| | | | | | | | |
|---|---|---|---|---|---|---|---|
| 4R | | RHYL | | | | | Chester scratched |

### FRIENDLIES

| | | | | | | | |
|---|---|---|---|---|---|---|---|
| 1 | Nov 18 | Flint United * | W | 1-0 | 1-0 | | Unknown |
| 2 | Dec 9 | Northwich Vics. | L | 0-3 | 0-1 | | |
| 3 | Mar 17 | Connah's Quay Twenties | L | 1-2 | 1-2 | | H Jones |

* In aid of Flint United

Final League Table

| | P | W | D | L | F | A | Pts |
|---|---|---|---|---|---|---|---|
| 1 Whitchurch | 28 | 18 | 5 | 5 | 87 | 32 | 41 |
| **2 Chester** | **28** | **16** | **4** | **8** | **72** | **29** | **36** |
| 3 Glossop Reserves | 28 | 15 | 4 | 9 | 53 | 37 | 34 |
| 4 Druids | 28 | 14 | 5 | 9 | 52 | 46 | 33 |
| 5 Tranmere Rovers | 28 | 13 | 8 | 7 | 40 | 36 | 32 |
| 6 Crewe Alexandra Res. | 28 | 14 | 3 | 11 | 53 | 42 | 31 |
| 7 Nantwich | 28 | 14 | 2 | 12 | 47 | 53 | 30 |
| 8 Port Sunlight | 28 | 11 | 6 | 11 | 43 | 42 | 28 |
| 9 Oswestry United | 28 | 13 | 1 | 14 | 72 | 56 | 27 |
| 10 Bangor | 28 | 9 | 6 | 13 | 38 | 63 | 24 |
| 11 Rhyl | 28 | 10 | 3 | 15 | 61 | 70 | 23 |
| 12 Chirk | 28 | 8 | 7 | 13 | 48 | 71 | 23 |
| 13 Broughton United | 28 | 11 | 2 | 15 | 46 | 61 | 22 |
| 14 Birkenhead | 28 | 9 | 3 | 16 | 38 | 54 | 21 |
| 15 Wigan Town | 28 | 4 | 3 | 21 | 32 | 90 | 7 ** |

* 2 points deducted for playing an ineligible player
** 4 points deducted for playing an ineligible player.
Middlewich resigned in January 1906. Their place and record were taken over by Wigan Town.

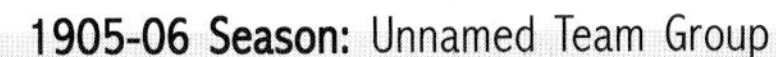

**1905-06 Season:** Unnamed Team Group

# SEASON 1906-07

## THE COMBINATION

| | Date | Opposition | | FT | HT | Att. | Goalscorers |
|---|---|---|---|---|---|---|---|
| 1 | Sep 1 | NANTWICH | W | 7-1 | 4-1 | | W Jones(2),Williams(2),Walker(2),Lees |
| 2 | 15 | Tranmere Rovers | W | 4-0 | 3-0 | | Lees, W Jones, Schofield, Walker |
| 3 | 22 | Birkenhead | W | 4-0 | 3-0 | | Walker, R Jones, Schofield, Williams |
| 4 | 29 | WREXHAM VICTORIA | W | 2-0 | 2-0 | | Schofield, W Jones |
| 5 | Oct 13 | CREWE ALEX. RES. | W | 7-1 | 3-1 | | Walker (3), W Jones (3), McFarlane |
| 6 | 20 | Chirk | W | 4-1 | 0-0 | | Walker, W Jones (2), Lees |
| 7 | 27 | WREXHAM RES. | W | 2-0 | 2-0 | 3000 | Walker, Williams |
| 8 | Nov 3 | Wigan Town | D | 1-1 | 1-1 | | Williams |
| 9 | 10 | BIRKENHEAD | W | 4-0 | 1-0 | | W Jones (2), Williams, Riding |
| 10 | Dec 8 | Oswestry United | W | 1-0 | 1-0 | | Williams |
| 11 | 15 | BANGOR | W | 4-0 | 2-0 | | Jenkins, Walker, Williams, W Jones |
| 12 | 22 | Rhyl | W | 2-1 | 0-0 | | W Jones, Lees |
| 13 | 25 | DRUIDS | W | 7-0 | 1-0 | 5000 | Lees (4), Walker (3) |
| 14 | Jan 26 | Bangor | D | 2-2 | 0-1 | | W Jones (2) |
| 15 | Feb 9 | TRANMERE ROVERS | W | 3-2 | 0-1 | | Williams, Walker, W Jones |
| 16 | 23 | Nantwich | L | 1-4 | 1-3 | | Walker |
| 17 | Mar 16 | CHIRK | W | 3-1 | 1-1 | | Williams (3) |
| 18 | 29 | WHITCHURCH | D | 1-1 | 0-1 | 6670 | Hallam |
| 19 | 30 | Druids | W | 3-0 | 2-0 | | Grainger, Unknown (2) |
| 20 | Apr 1 | WIGAN TOWN | W | 3-0 | 1-0 | 5000 | Lewis (2), W Jones |
| 21 | 6 | RHYL | W | 4-2 | 2-2 | | Walker (2), Lees (2) |
| 22 | 13 | Whitchurch | L | 0-4 | 0-3 | 1500 | |
| 23 | 20 | Crewe Alex. Res. | L | 1-5 | 1-3 | | Evans |
| 24 | 24 | Wrexham Res. | L | 0-1 | 0-0 | | |
| 25 | 27 | OSWESTRY UNITED | W | 3-0 | 2-0 | | Lewis (2), W Jones |
| 26 | 29 | Wrexham Victoria | W | 2-0 | 1-0 | | Williams, Unknown |

### WELSH CUP

| | | | | | | | |
|---|---|---|---|---|---|---|---|
| 3R | Jan 12 | BANGOR | W | 4-0 | 0-0 | | Riding, Lees, W Jones, Walker |
| 4R | Feb 2 | MILFORD HAVEN UTD. | W | 5-1 | 1-1 | | W Jones (2), Lees (2), Riding |
| SF | Feb 16 | Oswestry United * | D | 2-2 | 2-2 | 3689 | W Jones, Walker |
| SFr | Mar 2 | Oswestry United * | L | 0-1 | 0-0 | 4000 | |

* Played at Wrexham

### FRIENDLIES

| | | | | | | | |
|---|---|---|---|---|---|---|---|
| 1 | Sep 8 | WHITCHURCH | D | 4-4 | 1-1 | | Walker (3), W Jones |
| 2 | Oct 6 | Liverpool Res. | L | 0-1 | 0-1 | | |
| 3 | Dec 1 | Macclesfield | W | 3-2 | 1-0 | | Lees, W Jones, Walker |
| 4 | Jan 19 | MACCLESFIELD | W | 6-2 | 2-1 | | Riding,W Jones,Walker,Lees,Unknown(2) |
| 5 | Mar 23 | CHESHIRE REGIMENT | W | 2-0 | 1-0 | | Hallam, W Jones |
| 6 | Apr 17 | WREXHAM * | L | 0-2 | 0-1 | | |

* Billy Lewis Benefit

Final League Table

| | P | W | D | L | F | A | Pts |
|---|---|---|---|---|---|---|---|
| 1 Whitchurch | 26 | 20 | 5 | 1 | 84 | 30 | 45 |
| **2 Chester** | **26** | **19** | **3** | **4** | **75** | **27** | **41** |
| 3 Wigan Town | 26 | 12 | 6 | 8 | 44 | 45 | 30 |
| 4 Nantwich | 26 | 12 | 3 | 11 | 49 | 46 | 27 |
| 5 Wrexham Reserves | 26 | 11 | 4 | 11 | 50 | 45 | 26 |
| 6 Birkenhead | 26 | 12 | 4 | 10 | 64 | 63 | 26* |
| 7 Crewe Alexandra Res. | 26 | 10 | 5 | 11 | 66 | 61 | 25 |
| 8 Tranmere Rovers | 26 | 10 | 5 | 11 | 35 | 39 | 25 |
| 9 Oswestry United | 26 | 9 | 6 | 11 | 49 | 41 | 24 |
| 10 Bangor | 26 | 8 | 5 | 13 | 36 | 51 | 21 |
| 11 Chirk | 26 | 8 | 4 | 14 | 39 | 61 | 20 |
| 12 Rhyl | 26 | 8 | 2 | 16 | 38 | 64 | 18 |
| 13 Druids | 26 | 6 | 6 | 14 | 29 | 70 | 18 |
| 14 Wrexham Victoria | 26 | 8 | 0 | 18 | 29 | 44 | 16 |

* 2 points deducted for playing an ineligible player

**1906/07 Season:** Back - Roberts (Referee), Fletcher (Secretary), R Jones, Keeley, Russell, J Jones, Eardley (Trainer), Evans, Davies (Director), Reeves (Director)
Front - Grainger, Williams, Lees, Walker, W Jones, Jenkins

# SEASON 1907-08

## THE COMBINATION

| | Date | Opposition | | FT | HT | Att. | Goalscorers |
|---|---|---|---|---|---|---|---|
| 1 | Sep 7 | WREXHAM RES. | W | 5-3 | 2-1 | | Gordon, Lees, Lipsham, Freeman (2) |
| 2 | 14 | Chirk | W | 3-0 | 2-0 | | Matthews, Freeman, Jones |
| 3 | 28 | Wrexham Res. | D | 2-2 | 1-0 | | Jones, Grainger |
| 4 | Oct 12 | BIRKENHEAD | W | 8-0 | 3-0 | | Jones (3), Freeman (3), Lipsham, Williams |
| 5 | 19 | Nantwich | W | 4-3 | 2-3 | | Lipsham, Freeman, Williams, Lees |
| 6 | 26 | OSWESTRY UNITED | L | 2-3 | 1-1 | | Jones, Lipsham |
| 7 | Nov 9 | RHYL | W | 6-0 | 3-0 | | Williams (2), Jones (2), Matthews, Freeman |
| 8 | 16 | Connah's Quay Utd. | L | 1-2 | 1-1 | | Matthews |
| 9 | 23 | NANTWICH | W | 2-1 | 1-0 | | Lipsham, Grainger |
| 10 | Dec 7 | Welshpool | W | 5-1 | 1-1 | | Williams, Freeman (2), Lipsham (2) |
| 11 | 21 | Druids | W | 4-0 | 2-0 | | Lipsham (2), Freeman (2) |
| 12 | 25 | DRUIDS | W | 4-2 | 1-0 | | Williams, Jones, Goode (2) |
| 13 | 26 | TRANMERE ROVERS | W | 2-0 | 0-0 | | Freeman, Goode |
| 14 | 28 | Oswestry United | L | 0-1 | 0-1 | | |
| 15 | Jan 25 | Crewe Alex Res. | W | 3-1 | 1-1 | | Lipsham (2), Freeman |
| 16 | Feb 15 | CHIRK | W | 3-1 | 3-1 | | Goode (2), Freeman |
| 17 | 22 | BANGOR | W | 5-1 | 2-0 | | Freeman, Lipsham, Goode, Matthews (2) |
| 18 | 29 | Tranmere Rovers | D | 2-2 | 1-2 | | Goode, Freeman |
| 19 | Mar 14 | Rhyl | W | 3-2 | 2-2 | | Gordon, Matthews, Goode |
| 20 | 21 | CONNAH'S QUAY UTD. | W | 6-1 | 2-0 | 5000 | Lees, Goode, Matthews (2), Freeman, Grainger |
| 21 | Apr 4 | Bangor | W | 3-1 | 1-1 | | Goode, Williams, Freeman |
| 22 | 8 | WELSHPOOL | W | 4-1 | 0-1 | | Lipsham (2), Lees, Jones |
| 23 | 17 | WHITCHURCH | W | 2-0 | 1-0 | 5650 | Freeman, Lipsham |
| 24 | 18 | CREWE ALEX RES. | W | 4-0 | 2-0 | | Williams, Freeman, Lipsham, Goode |
| 25 | 25 | Whitchurch | W | 2-0 | 1-0 | | Goode (2) |
| 26 | 30 | Birkenhead | W | 2-1 | 1-1 | | Lees (2) |

Final League Table

| | P | W | D | L | F | A | Pts |
|---|---|---|---|---|---|---|---|
| 1 Tranmere Rovers | 26 | 20 | 4 | 2 | 83 | 21 | 44 |
| **2 Chester** | **26** | **21** | **2** | **3** | **87** | **29** | **44** |
| 3 Oswestry United | 26 | 16 | 4 | 6 | 62 | 38 | 36 |
| 4 Crewe Alexandra Res. | 26 | 14 | 3 | 9 | 69 | 50 | 31 |
| 5 Whitchurch | 26 | 13 | 4 | 9 | 66 | 42 | 30 |
| 6 Nantwich | 26 | 12 | 5 | 9 | 65 | 57 | 29 |
| 7 Connah's Quay United | 26 | 13 | 3 | 10 | 55 | 57 | 29 |
| 8 Druids | 26 | 9 | 5 | 12 | 53 | 58 | 23 |
| 9 Bangor | 26 | 8 | 3 | 15 | 38 | 68 | 19 |
| 10 Chirk | 26 | 9 | 0 | 17 | 41 | 63 | 18 |
| 11 Rhyl | 26 | 7 | 2 | 17 | 49 | 80 | 16 |
| 12 Wrexham Reserves | 26 | 6 | 4 | 16 | 42 | 74 | 16 |
| 13 Birkenhead | 26 | 5 | 5 | 16 | 33 | 61 | 15 |
| 14 Welshpool | 26 | 5 | 4 | 17 | 34 | 79 | 14 |

## F.A. CUP

| | | | | | | | |
|---|---|---|---|---|---|---|---|
| Q1 | Oct 5 | TRANMERE ROVERS | L | 0-4 | 0-1 | 3000 | |

## WELSH CUP

| | | | | | | | |
|---|---|---|---|---|---|---|---|
| 3R | Jan 11 | Tranmere Rovers | D | 1-1 | 0-0 | | Goode |
| 3Rr | 18 | TRANMERE ROVERS | W | 2-1 | 1-1 | | Lipsham, Freeman |
| 4 | Feb 8 | Druids | W | 6-1 | 4-0 | 3000 | Lipsham (2), Lees (2), Goode (2) |
| SF | Mar 28 | Aberystwyth * | W | 4-2 | 3-0 | 3000 | Freeman, Lees, Williams, Goode |
| F | Apr 20 | Connah's Quay Utd. # | W | 3-1 | 1-1 | 8000 | Goode (2), Lees |

* Played at Welshpool
# Played at Wrexham

## FRIENDLIES

| | | | | | | | |
|---|---|---|---|---|---|---|---|
| 1 | Sep 2 | NEWTON LE WILLOWS | W | 4-3 | 1-0 | | Freeman (4) |
| 2 | 21 | CHESTERFIELD | W | 4-2 | 2-1 | | Lipsham, Williams (2), Grundy |
| 3 | Nov 2 | BARNSLEY | L | 3-6 | 0-3 | | Lipsham, Freeman (2) |
| 4 | Dec 14 | PRESTON NORTH END RES. | W | 2-0 | 1-0 | | Freeman, Grainger |
| 16 | Jan 1 | WEST CHESHIRE LEAGUE | L | 1-4 | 0-2 | | Unknown |

Back - Webster, Johnson, Dodd, Davies, Wildgoose, Reeves
Standing - Jepson, Russell, Fletcher (Secretary), Keeley, Hallmark (Chairman), Grundy, Hales
Sitting - Eardley (Trainer), Matthews, Grainger, Cheshire Cup, Welsh Cup, T Gordon (Captain), Appleton
Front - Williams, Lees, Freeman, Jones, Goode, Lipsham

# SEASON 1908-09

## THE COMBINATION

| | Date | Opposition | | FT | HT | Att. | Goalscorers |
|---|---|---|---|---|---|---|---|
| 1 | Sep 5 | BIRKENHEAD | W | 5-1 | 3-0 | | Lappin, Roberts, Freeman, Lipsham, Matthews |
| 2 | 12 | Nantwich | D | 2-2 | 0-2 | | Roberts, Freeman |
| 3 | 19 | Chirk | W | 2-1 | 1-0 | | Lappin, Roberts |
| 4 | 26 | BANGOR | W | 7-0 | 4-0 | | Freeman(2),Roberts,Lipsham,Lappin,Jones,Unknown |
| 5 | Oct 10 | RHYL | W | 5-0 | 4-0 | | Matthews (2), Roberts (2), Lappin |
| 6 | 24 | Birkenhead | W | 2-1 | 0-0 | 3000 | Roberts (2) |
| 7 | 31 | CONNAH'S QUAY UTD. | D | 1-1 | 0-0 | | Lipsham |
| 8 | Nov 14 | Druids | W | 3-1 | 1-0 | | Matthews, Freeman, Lappin |
| 9 | 21 | Rhyl | W | 3-0 | 1-0 | | Freeman (2), Lappin |
| 10 | 28 | MIDDLEWICH | W | 3-2 | 2-1 | | Freeman, Lappin, Matthews |
| 11 | Dec 5 | WELSHPOOL | W | 5-1 | 2-1 | | Roberts (3), Lipsham, Stockton |
| 12 | 12 | Crewe Alex. Res. | D | 3-3 | 1-2 | 1500 | Freeman (2), Lipsham |
| 13 | 19 | NANTWICH | W | 4-0 | 0-0 | | Lappin, Freeman, Roberts, Lipsham |
| 14 | 25 | DRUIDS | W | 2-1 | 1-1 | | Matthews (2) |
| 15 | 26 | TRANMERE ROVERS | D | 2-2 | 1-1 | | Matthews, Roberts |
| 16 | Jan 16 | WREXHAM RES. | W | 3-1 | 0-0 | | Roberts, Freeman, Lipsham |
| 17 | 23 | Whitchurch | D | 0-0 | 0-0 | | |
| 18 | Feb 6 | CREWE ALEX. RES. | W | 2-1 | 1-1 | | Matthews, Roberts |
| 19 | 20 | SALTNEY | D | 3-3 | 0-1 | 6000 | Matthews, Roberts, Freeman |
| 20 | Mar 6 | Bangor | L | 2-3 | 1-3 | | Bentley (2) |
| 21 | 20 | Wrexham Res. | W | 4-0 | 3-0 | | Roberts, Freeman (2), Lipsham |
| 22 | 25 | Tranmere Rovers | L | 0-2 | 0-0 | 2000 | |
| 23 | 27 | Oswestry United | W | 4-2 | 3-0 | | Bradshaw (3), Freeman |
| 24 | 29 | Connah's Quay Utd. | W | 7-0 | 0-0 | | Brett (2), Freeman (3), Lappin, Lipsham |
| 25 | Apr 9 | OSWESTRY UNITED | W | 4-2 | 2-1 | | Lipsham, Brett (2), Freeman |
| 26 | 17 | Middlewich | D | 2-2 | 1-0 | | Roberts, Brett |
| 27 | 21 | Saltney | W | 2-1 | 0-1 | 4500 | Jones, Hewitt (og) |
| 28 | 26 | CHIRK | W | 2-1 | 0-1 | | Roberts (2) |
| 29 | 28 | WHITCHURCH | W | 3-0 | 2-0 | | Freeman (3) |
| 30 | 29 | Welshpool | W | 4-0 | 4-0 | | Freeman (2), Bradshaw, Stockton |

Final League Table

| | P | W | D | L | F | A | Pts |
|---|---|---|---|---|---|---|---|
| **1 Chester** | **30** | **21** | **7** | **2** | **91** | **34** | **49** |
| 2 Saltney | 30 | 16 | 9 | 5 | 93 | 42 | 41 |
| 3 Tranmere Rovers | 30 | 15 | 5 | 10 | 86 | 48 | 35 |
| 4 Welshpool | 30 | 13 | 8 | 9 | 63 | 53 | 34 |
| 5 Crewe Alexandra Res. | 30 | 13 | 7 | 10 | 95 | 56 | 33 |
| 6 Connah's Quay United | 30 | 13 | 7 | 10 | 60 | 63 | 33 |
| 7 Bangor | 30 | 13 | 6 | 11 | 71 | 81 | 32 |
| 8 Nantwich | 30 | 12 | 7 | 11 | 59 | 61 | 31 |
| 9 Oswestry United | 30 | 13 | 4 | 13 | 74 | 55 | 30 |
| 10 Whitchurch | 30 | 11 | 8 | 11 | 53 | 64 | 30 |
| 11 Wrexham Reserves | 30 | 10 | 6 | 14 | 48 | 59 | 26 |
| 12 Chirk | 30 | 9 | 8 | 13 | 48 | 62 | 26 |
| 13 Middlewich | 30 | 8 | 8 | 14 | 67 | 84 | 24 |
| 14 Druids | 30 | 10 | 4 | 16 | 51 | 74 | 24 |
| 15 Birkenhead | 30 | 7 | 2 | 21 | 48 | 95 | 16 |
| 16 Rhyl | 30 | 6 | 4 | 20 | 37 | 113 | 16 |

## F.A. CUP

| | Date | Opposition | | FT | HT | Att. | Goalscorers |
|---|---|---|---|---|---|---|---|
| Q1 | Oct 3 | DRUIDS | W | 4-1 | 1-0 | | Freeman, Lappin, Roberts, Matthews |
| Q2 | 17 | WELLINGTON TOWN | W | 3-1 | 2-0 | | Roberts, Lappin, Matthews |
| Q3 | Nov 7 | WREXHAM | L | 1-3 | 1-1 | 4000 | Roberts |

## WELSH CUP

| | Date | Opposition | | FT | HT | Att. | Goalscorers |
|---|---|---|---|---|---|---|---|
| 3R | Jan 9 | NANTWICH | W | 8-2 | 2-2 | | Freeman (4), Lappin, Roberts (2), Lipsham |
| 4R | Feb 13 | Aberystwyth | W | 2-0 | 1-0 | | Matthews, Lappin |
| SF | Apr 3 | Wellington St George * | W | 2-1 | 2-0 | | Bentley, Freeman |
| F | 12 | Wrexham | L | 0-1 | 0-0 | 9000 | |

* Played at Wrexham

## FRIENDLIES

| | Date | Opposition | | FT | HT | Att. | Goalscorers |
|---|---|---|---|---|---|---|---|
| 1 | Apr 30 | THE COMBINATION | W | 4-1 | 2-1 | | Freeman (3), Matthews |

Back - Blaylock, Jepson, Wildgoose, Davies, Reeves, Webster, Johnson
Standing - Hallmark, Brett, Russell, Keeley, Grainger, Davies,
Gordon, Bradshaw, Fletcher (Secretary)
Sitting - Eardley (Trainer), Stockton, Jones, Lappin, Lipsham
Front - Roberts, Freeman, Matthews

# SEASON 1909-10

## THE COMBINATION

| | Date | Opposition | | FT | HT | Att. | Goalscorers |
|---|---|---|---|---|---|---|---|
| 1 | Sep 4 | Oswestry United | L | 2-4 | 1-1 | | Graham, Unknown |
| 2 | 11 | OSWESTRY UNITED | W | 3-0 | 2-0 | | Roberts (2), Lipsham |
| 3 | 15 | DENBIGH | W | 4-1 | 2-0 | | Roberts, Matthews (2), Lipsham |
| 4 | 25 | Nantwich | W | 4-1 | 3-1 | | Graham (2), Roberts, Bradshaw |
| 5 | Oct 2 | MIDDLEWICH | W | 4-1 | 3-0 | | Graham, Roberts, Bradshaw, Wright |
| 6 | 9 | Druids | W | 4-0 | 0-0 | | Roberts (3), Lipsham |
| 7 | 16 | BANGOR | W | 7-3 | 4-0 | | Graham (2), Winnington (2), Lipsham (2), Bradshaw |
| 8 | 23 | Crewe Alex. Res. | L | 1-3 | 1-1 | | Lipsham |
| 9 | 30 | Saltney | L | 0-1 | 0-0 | | |
| 10 | Nov 6 | Bangor | L | 3-5 | 2-4 | | Graham, Russell, Jones (og) |
| 11 | 13 | Rhyl | L | 0-2 | 0-1 | | |
| 12 | 20 | SALTNEY | W | 3-0 | 2-0 | | Graham (2), O Jones |
| 13 | 27 | Whitchurch | D | 2-2 | 1-2 | | O Jones (2) |
| 14 | Dec 4 | Birkenhead * | W | 6-1 | 5-0 | | O Jones (2), Matthews (2), Graham (2) |
| 15 | 11 | Wrexham Res. | D | 3-3 | 1-2 | 1000 | Matthews, Graham, Lipsham |
| 16 | 18 | CREWE ALEX. RES. | W | 2-0 | 0-0 | | Matthews, Yuill |
| 17 | 25 | DRUIDS | W | 4-2 | 0-1 | | Grainger, Lipsham, Graham, Matthews |
| 18 | 27 | TRANMERE ROVERS | L | 1-7 | 0-1 | | Lipsham |
| 19 | Jan 15 | BRYMBO VICTORIA | W | 4-0 | 2-0 | | O Jones (2), T Jones, Lipsham |
| 20 | 22 | WREXHAM RES. | W | 2-1 | 2-0 | | Graham (2) |
| 21 | Feb 5 | Tranmere Rovers | W | 5-1 | 2-1 | | Graham (2), Roberts (2), Matthews |
| 22 | 19 | CONNAH'S QUAY UTD. | W | 3-2 | 0-1 | | O Jones, Rainford, Matthews |
| 23 | Mar 12 | Denbigh | W | 4-2 | 0-1 | | Gordon, Riley, Winnington, Smith (og) |
| 24 | 25 | WHITCHURCH | W | 4-0 | 2-0 | | Rainford, Graham, O Jones (2) |
| 25 | 26 | Connah's Quay Utd. | W | 1-0 | 0-0 | | Roberts |
| 26 | Apr 2 | CHIRK | W | 5-0 | 1-0 | | Riley (3), Matthews, Gordon |
| 27 | 20 | Chirk | L | 1-2 | 1-2 | | Unknown |
| 28 | 23 | NANTWICH | W | 2-0 | 1-0 | | Matthews (2) |
| 29 | 27 | RHYL | W | 1-0 | 0-0 | | Unknown |
| 30 | 30 | Middlewich | L | 0-3 | 0-0 | | |

* Birkenhead resigned from the League and their fixtures were taken over by Brymbo Victoria

## F.A. CUP

| | Date | Opposition | | FT | HT | Att. | Goalscorers |
|---|---|---|---|---|---|---|---|
| PQ | Sep 18 | Tranmere Rovers | L | 0-6 | 0-3 | 4000 | |

## WELSH CUP

| | Date | Opposition | | FT | HT | Att. | Goalscorers |
|---|---|---|---|---|---|---|---|
| 3R | Jan 8 | Rhyl | W | 6-2 | 1-2 | | Graham (3), Rainford (2), O Jones |
| 4R | Feb 12 | DRUIDS | W | 3-1 | 1-1 | 2000 | O Jones, Winnington, Roberts |
| SF | Mar 7 | Milford Haven Utd. * | D | 0-0 | 0-0 | 3500 | |
| F | 28 | Wrexham | L | 1-2 | 1-1 | 10000 | O Jones |

* Played at Merthyr Tydfil. Milford Haven refused to play the replay, tie awarded to Chester

## FRIENDLIES

| | Date | Opposition | | FT | HT | Att. | Goalscorers |
|---|---|---|---|---|---|---|---|
| 1 | Apr 16 | Chester & District League | D | 1-1 | 0-0 | | Grainger |
| 2 | 18 | SALTNEY * | W | 4-0 | 1-0 | | Wright, Grainger, Lipsham, Matthews |
| 3 | 25 | LIVERPOOL | W | 4-3 | 1-1 | | Riley (3), Roberts |

* Yerburgh Charity Cup

### Final League Table

| | P | W | D | L | F | A | Pts |
|---|---|---|---|---|---|---|---|
| 1 Crewe Alexandra Res. | 30 | 24 | 3 | 3 | 105 | 33 | 51 |
| 2 Saltney | 30 | 22 | 4 | 4 | 81 | 32 | 48 |
| **3 Chester** | **30** | **20** | **2** | **8** | **85** | **47** | **42** |
| 4 Tranmere Rovers | 30 | 18 | 2 | 10 | 92 | 50 | 38 |
| 5 Bangor | 30 | 16 | 3 | 11 | 79 | 66 | 35 |
| 6 Whitchurch | 30 | 16 | 3 | 11 | 61 | 53 | 35 |
| 7 Wrexham Reserves | 30 | 15 | 5 | 10 | 64 | 58 | 35 |
| 8 Nantwich | 30 | 14 | 4 | 12 | 57 | 56 | 32 |
| 9 Connah's Quay United | 30 | 14 | 1 | 15 | 65 | 67 | 29 |
| 10 Middlewich | 30 | 12 | 3 | 15 | 58 | 61 | 27 |
| 11 Oswestry United | 30 | 9 | 7 | 14 | 44 | 62 | 25 |
| 12 Rhyl | 30 | 7 | 6 | 17 | 54 | 83 | 20 |
| 13 Chirk | 30 | 8 | 3 | 19 | 57 | 91 | 19 |
| 14 Druids | 30 | 7 | 3 | 20 | 44 | 83 | 17 |
| 15 Denbigh | 30 | 6 | 4 | 20 | 52 | 93 | 16 |
| 16 Brymbo Victoria | 30 | 5 | 1 | 24 | 42 | 105 | 11 |

From the 1909-10 Season:
(Left) Lipsham
(Right) Yuill

# SEASON 1910-11

## LANCASHIRE COMBINATION DIVISION 2

| | Date | Opposition | | FT | HT | Att. | Goalscorers |
|---|---|---|---|---|---|---|---|
| 1 | Sep 3 | Atherton | W | 3-0 | 1-0 | | Yuill, Blackburn, Chetwood |
| 2 | 5 | Hyde | L | 3-5 | 1-1 | 3000 | Blackburn, Yuill, Chetwood |
| 3 | 7 | ASHTON TOWN * | W | 6-0 | 4-0 | | Chetwood (3), Yuill, W Smith (2) |
| 4 | 10 | BARROW | W | 3-0 | 2-0 | | Matthews, Blackburn, Lipsham |
| 5 | 14 | Ashton Town * | D | 2-2 | 1-2 | | Blackurn, Brennan |
| 6 | 24 | FLEETWOOD | W | 4-0 | 3-0 | | Yuill, Lipsham, Blackburn (2) |
| 7 | Oct 8 | ST HELENS TOWN | D | 2-2 | 2-0 | | W Smith, Blackburn |
| 8 | 22 | HASLINGDEN | W | 5-3 | 2-2 | | W Smith, Tremlett, Riley (2), Matthews |
| 9 | 29 | HEYWOOD UNITED | W | 2-1 | 1-1 | | Dargie, Lipsham |
| 10 | Nov 12 | Denton | L | 2-4 | 1-1 | | Blackburn, W Smith |
| 11 | 26 | TRANMERE ROVERS | W | 1-0 | 0-0 | 2000 | Blackburn |
| 12 | Dec 3 | Great Harwood | L | 1-2 | 1-1 | | Blackburn |
| 13 | 10 | Earlestown | W | 4-3 | 3-1 | | Dargie (2), Yuill, Lipsham |
| 14 | 17 | ROSSENDALE UNITED | W | 4-2 | 4-2 | | Jordan (2), W Smith, Chetwood |
| 15 | 24 | DENTON | W | 4-1 | 1-0 | | Chetwood, Yuill, Riley (2) |
| 16 | 26 | ECCLES BOROUGH | W | 3-1 | 2-1 | | Jordan (2), Dargie |
| 17 | 27 | HINDLEY CENTRAL | W | 1-0 | 1-0 | | W Smith |
| 18 | 31 | St Helens Town | D | 0-0 | 0-0 | | |
| 19 | Jan 14 | DARWEN | W | 3-0 | 1-0 | | Holmes, Yuill (2) |
| 20 | 21 | Heywood United | D | 2-2 | 1-1 | | Jordan (2) |
| 21 | 28 | Hindley Central | W | 2-1 | 0-0 | | Jordan, Holmes |
| 22 | Feb 4 | EARLESTOWN | W | 3-0 | 2-0 | | W Smith, Matthews, Holmes |
| 23 | 11 | Barrow | L | 1-4 | 0-2 | 6000 | Gordon |
| 24 | 18 | WALKDEN CENTRAL | W | 7-0 | 3-0 | | W Smith (2), Holmes, Yuill, Lipsham (3) |
| 25 | 25 | Padiham | W | 6-0 | 0-0 | | Dargie (3), W Smith (2), Yuill |
| 26 | 28 | Darwen | L | 1-5 | 0-4 | | Lipsham |
| 27 | Mar 11 | Walkden Central | W | 1-0 | 1-0 | | Chetwood |
| 28 | 18 | Haslingden | W | 2-0 | 0-0 | | W Smith, Dargie |
| 29 | 25 | Fleetwood | W | 2-1 | 1-0 | | A Smith, Chetwood |
| 30 | Apr 1 | Rossendale United | W | 2-1 | 0-1 | | Jordan, Yuill |
| 31 | 3 | Tranmere Rovers | L | 0-4 | 0-1 | | |
| 32 | 5 | HYDE | W | 4-0 | 0-0 | | W Smith, Yuill (2), Chetwood |
| 33 | 10 | BACUP | W | 5-3 | 3-2 | 4000 | W Smith(2), Chetwood, Lipsham, Jordan |
| 34 | 12 | Eccles Borough | L | 1-2 | 0-2 | | Jordan |
| 35 | 14 | ATHERTON | W | 1-0 | 1-0 | 5000 | Jordan |
| 36 | 17 | PADIHAM | W | 7-1 | 3-0 | | Yuill, Jordan(2), W Smith(2), Chetwood(2) |
| 37 | 26 | GREAT HARWOOD | W | 4-0 | 1-0 | | Jordan (4) |
| 38 | 29 | Bacup | L | 0-1 | 0-1 | | |

* Ashton Town resigned from the League and their fixtures were taken over by Tyldesley Albion

## F.A. CUP

| | Date | Opposition | | FT | HT | Att. | Goalscorers |
|---|---|---|---|---|---|---|---|
| PQ | Sep 17 | Druids | W | 3-1 | 1-1 | | Blackburn (2), Chetwood |
| Q1 | Oct 1 | WREXHAM | W | 1-0 | 1-0 | 5300 | Lipsham |
| Q2 | 15 | New Brighton Tower * | W | 3-0 | 1-0 | | Riley, Smith, McCarthy |
| Q3 | Nov 5 | WITTON ALBION | W | 7-1 | 2-1 | | Dargie(3),Blackburn(2),Matthews,Lipsham |
| Q4 | 19 | Crewe Alex. | L | 3-4 | 3-1 | 5500 | Dargie (2), Lipsham |

* Match switched to Chester

## WELSH CUP

| | Date | Opposition | | FT | HT | Att. | Goalscorers |
|---|---|---|---|---|---|---|---|
| 3R | Jan 7 | MOLD TOWN | D | 1-1 | 1-1 | | Jordan |
| 3Rr | 12 | Mold Town | L | 0-2 | 0-2 | | |

## FRIENDLIES

| | Date | Opposition | | FT | HT | Att. | Goalscorers |
|---|---|---|---|---|---|---|---|
| 1 | Apr 22 | WREXHAM * | D | 3-3 | 2-2 | | W Smith (2), Yuill |

* Yerburgh Charity Cup

### Final League Table

| | P | W | D | L | F | A | Pts |
|---|---|---|---|---|---|---|---|
| 1 Haslingden | 38 | 26 | 5 | 7 | 98 | 47 | 57 |
| 2 Barrow | 38 | 27 | 2 | 9 | 102 | 47 | 56 |
| **3 Chester** | **38** | **26** | **4** | **8** | **104** | **51** | **56** |
| 4 St Helens Town | 38 | 25 | 4 | 8 | 89 | 38 | 54 |
| 5 Hyde | 38 | 24 | 5 | 9 | 99 | 49 | 53 |
| 6 Bacup | 38 | 17 | 12 | 9 | 98 | 70 | 46 |
| 7 Rossendale United | 38 | 19 | 7 | 12 | 124 | 64 | 45 |
| 8 Denton | 38 | 21 | 3 | 14 | 100 | 76 | 45 |
| 9 Earlestown | 38 | 15 | 8 | 15 | 73 | 76 | 38 |
| 10 Walkden Central | 38 | 14 | 9 | 15 | 72 | 71 | 37 |
| 11 Eccles Borough | 38 | 13 | 9 | 16 | 67 | 81 | 35 |
| 12 Heywood United | 38 | 14 | 6 | 18 | 75 | 73 | 34 |
| 13 Tranmere Rovers | 38 | 14 | 6 | 18 | 60 | 69 | 34 |
| 14 Fleetwood | 38 | 14 | 6 | 18 | 72 | 83 | 34 |
| 15 Great Harwood | 38 | 12 | 6 | 20 | 54 | 78 | 30 |
| 16 Atherton | 38 | 11 | 7 | 20 | 55 | 73 | 29 |
| 17 Darwen | 38 | 13 | 3 | 22 | 59 | 91 | 29 |
| 18 Hindley Central | 38 | 9 | 4 | 25 | 48 | 103 | 22 |
| 19 Padiham | 38 | 5 | 5 | 28 | 31 | 120 | 15 |
| 20 Tyldesley Albion | 38 | 2 | 7 | 29 | 21 | 141 | 11 |

**1910-11 Season:**
(Back) Dorset, Hallmark (Dir.), Jones (Dir.), Simpson, Bancroft, Wright, Davies (Dir.), Reeves (Dir.).
(Middle) Slyfield (Trainer), Yuill, Smith, Blackburn, Chetwood, Lipsham, Fletcher (Secretary).
(Front) Matthews, Tremlett, Gordon.

**1911-12 Season:**
(Back) Matthias, W.Jones, Simpson, Wildgoose, Spencer
(Centre) J.Jones (Secretary), Matthews, G.Jones, Williams, Bancroft, A.Smith, Grundy, Riley, Hallmark (Chairman)
(Front) Langdford, W.Smith, Cook, Jordan, Lipsham, Riley (Trainer)

# SEASON 1911-12

## LANCASHIRE COMBINATION DIVISION 1

| | Date | Opposition | | FT | HT | Att. | Goalscorers |
|---|---|---|---|---|---|---|---|
| 1 | Sep 2 | Colne | L | 2-3 | 0-2 | | Cook, Hannaby |
| 2 | 4 | ECCLES BOROUGH | W | 4-1 | 2-1 | | W Smith (2), Cook (2) |
| 3 | 9 | ST HELENS TOWN | D | 1-1 | 1-0 | | Cook |
| 4 | 11 | Accrington | L | 2-3 | 2-3 | | Matthews, Cook |
| 5 | 16 | Nelson | L | 2-3 | 1-2 | | Langford, Cook |
| 6 | 23 | HASLINGDEN | W | 3-2 | 0-2 | | Cook (2), Jordan |
| 7 | Oct 7 | BACUP | W | 3-0 | 2-0 | | Cook (2), W Smith |
| 8 | 21 | WALKDEN CENTRAL | W | 6-1 | 3-1 | | Hughes, Cook (3), W Smith, Jordan |
| 9 | 28 | HEYWOOD UNITED | W | 4-1 | 2-0 | | Cook, W Smith, Jordan, Lipsham |
| 10 | Nov 11 | DENTON | W | 3-0 | 2-0 | | W Smith, Cook, Yuill |
| 11 | 25 | St Helens Recs. | L | 1-2 | 0-0 | | Lipsham |
| 12 | Dec 9 | ROSSENDALE UNITED | W | 1-0 | 0-0 | | Cook |
| 13 | 16 | Hyde | W | 2-1 | 2-0 | | W Smith (2) |
| 14 | 25 | Barrow | D | 1-1 | 0-1 | 6000 | Cook |
| 15 | 26 | ROCHDALE | W | 3-1 | 1-1 | 5000 | Cook (3) |
| 16 | 30 | COLNE | D | 1-1 | 0-1 | | Matthias |
| 17 | Jan 1 | Rochdale | L | 0-3 | 0-0 | | |
| 18 | Feb 3 | Chorley | D | 2-2 | 2-1 | | Lipsham, Cook |
| 19 | 10 | Bacup | W | 7-0 | 3-0 | | Jordan, Cook (4), Hughes, Grundy |
| 20 | 17 | NELSON | W | 6-2 | 2-0 | | Cook (3), Jordan, Hughes, Yuill |
| 21 | Mar 2 | Heywood United | L | 1-2 | 0-0 | | Cook |
| 22 | 9 | Haslingden | W | 2-0 | 2-0 | | Cook, Jordan |
| 23 | 16 | Denton | W | 3-1 | 2-0 | | Brooks, Yuill, Jordan |
| 24 | 30 | ST HELENS RECS. | W | 3-2 | 2-0 | | Yuill, Cook (2) |
| 25 | Apr 5 | BARROW | D | 1-1 | 1-1 | 5000 | Brooks |
| 26 | 6 | ACCRINGTON | D | 2-2 | 1-0 | | Cook, Jordan |
| 27 | 8 | CHORLEY | W | 2-0 | 1-0 | | Cook (2) |
| 28 | 13 | Rossendale United | L | 1-5 | | | Unknown |
| 29 | 17 | Walkden Central | L | 2-3 | 1-2 | 1000 | Lipsham, Matthews |
| 30 | 20 | HYDE | L | 0-1 | 0-0 | | |
| 31 | 25 | St Helens Town | D | 1-1 | 0-1 | | Matthias |
| 32 | 27 | Eccles Borough | L | 2-4 | 1-3 | | Cook, Matthews |

### F.A. CUP

| | Date | Opposition | | FT | HT | Att. | Goalscorers |
|---|---|---|---|---|---|---|---|
| Q1 | Sep 30 | SHREWSBURY TOWN | W | 6-1 | 2-0 | | Jordan, Lipsham, Cook (3), W Smith |
| Q2 | Oct 14 | NORTHERN NOMADS | W | 4-1 | 1-1 | | W Smith (2), Cook (2) |
| Q3 | Nov 4 | Wrexham | W | 4-1 | 1-0 | 7500 | Cook, Yuill (2), Jordan |
| Q4 | 18 | STOCKPORT COUNTY | L | 1-4 | 1-2 | 4500 | Lipsham |

### WELSH CUP

| | Date | Opposition | | FT | HT | Att. | Goalscorers |
|---|---|---|---|---|---|---|---|
| 1R | Nov 8 | RHYL | W | 9-0 | 4-0 | | Jordan(2),Yuill,W Smith(2),A Smith(2),Cook,Matthews |
| 2R | Dec 2 | Saltney | D | 1-1 | 0-1 | | Cook |
| 2Rr | 13 | SALTNEY | W | 4-1 | 2-0 | | Yuill, Grundy, Jordan, Matthias |
| 3R | Jan 8 | Oswestry United | W | 3-1 | 0-0 | | Matthias, Hughes, Cook |
| 4R | 27 | Rhos | W | 2-0 | 1-0 | 3000 | Jordan, Cook |
| SF | Mar 23 | Cardiff City | D | 1-1 | 0-1 | | Matthias |
| SFr | 27 | Cardiff City * | L | 1-2 | 1-0 | 5000 | Matthias |

* Played at Wrexham. Extra time played following score of 1-1 after 90 minutes

### Final League Table

| | P | W | D | L | F | A | Pts |
|---|---|---|---|---|---|---|---|
| 1 Rochdale | 32 | 23 | 4 | 5 | 81 | 24 | 50 |
| 2 St Helens Recreation | 32 | 19 | 6 | 7 | 69 | 42 | 44 |
| 3 Hyde | 32 | 17 | 5 | 10 | 68 | 41 | 39 |
| 4 Barrow | 32 | 15 | 9 | 8 | 66 | 48 | 39 |
| 5 Colne | 32 | 16 | 6 | 10 | 59 | 42 | 38 |
| **6 Chester** | **32** | **15** | **7** | **10** | **74** | **50** | **37** |
| 7 Chorley | 32 | 14 | 7 | 11 | 50 | 43 | 35 |
| 8 Rossendale United | 32 | 12 | 9 | 11 | 58 | 48 | 33 |
| 9 Accrington Stanley | 32 | 12 | 6 | 14 | 70 | 66 | 30 |
| 10 Haslingden | 32 | 11 | 8 | 13 | 54 | 53 | 30 |
| 11 Eccles Borough | 32 | 12 | 6 | 14 | 49 | 51 | 30 |
| 12 Heywood United | 32 | 11 | 5 | 16 | 40 | 68 | 27 |
| 13 St Helens Town | 32 | 9 | 8 | 15 | 45 | 56 | 26 |
| 14 Nelson | 32 | 9 | 7 | 16 | 58 | 66 | 25 |
| 15 Denton | 32 | 11 | 3 | 18 | 52 | 78 | 25 |
| 16 Walkden Central | 32 | 6 | 7 | 19 | 37 | 75 | 19 |
| 17 Bacup | 32 | 6 | 5 | 21 | 41 | 114 | 17 |

# SEASON 1912-13

## LANCASHIRE COMBINATION DIVISION 1

| | Date | Opposition | | FT | HT | Att. | Goalscorers |
|---|---|---|---|---|---|---|---|
| 1 | Sep 4 | Chorley | W | 3-1 | 2-1 | | Jordan, Matthews, Lipsham |
| 2 | 7 | ST HELENS TOWN | W | 8-1 | 4-1 | | Ralphs(2),Wynn(2),Sheargold,Jordan,Ritchie,Lipsham |
| 3 | 14 | ST HELENS RECS. | W | 3-1 | 1-0 | | Ritchie (2), Hamlet (og) |
| 4 | 21 | Barrow | L | 0-4 | 0-2 | 7500 | |
| 5 | Oct 5 | COLNE | W | 5-1 | 1-1 | | Jordan (3), Wynn (2) |
| 6 | 19 | ECCLES BOROUGH | W | 2-1 | 1-1 | | Ritchie, Lipsham |
| 7 | Nov 2 | Accrington | D | 2-2 | 2-2 | | Wynn (2) |
| 8 | 9 | FLEETWOOD | D | 3-3 | 1-3 | | Jordan, Ritchie (2) |
| 9 | 16 | HASLINGDEN | L | 2-3 | 0-2 | | Ritchie (2) |
| 10 | 23 | ACCRINGTON | L | 1-2 | 0-1 | | Matthews |
| 11 | 30 | Rossendale United | D | 3-3 | 2-2 | | Winnington (2), Ritchie |
| 12 | Dec 7 | TRANMERE ROVERS | D | 2-2 | 0-1 | | Lipsham, og |
| 13 | 14 | HEYWOOD UNITED | W | 4-0 | 3-0 | | Best (3), Ritchie |
| 14 | 21 | Denton | D | 1-1 | 0-0 | | Winnington |
| 15 | 25 | ALTRINCHAM | D | 2-2 | 1-0 | | Winnington, Porter |
| 16 | 26 | NELSON | W | 9-2 | 7-0 | | Best (4), Jordan (3), Bourne (og), R. Griffiths |
| 17 | 28 | Hyde | D | 2-2 | 0-2 | | Porter, Jordan |
| 18 | Jan 1 | Altrincham | D | 1-1 | 1-1 | | Jordan |
| 19 | 11 | Eccles Borough | L | 1-2 | 1-0 | | Lipsham |
| 20 | Feb 1 | Nelson | L | 2-4 | 2-1 | | Best, Porter |
| 21 | 8 | Tranmere Rovers | L | 0-3 | 0-2 | 5000 | |
| 22 | 15 | Heywood United | D | 1-1 | 0-1 | | Best |
| 23 | Mar 1 | HYDE * | W | 4-0 | 4-0 | | Wynn (2), Anderton, R. Griffiths |
| 24 | 15 | St Helens Recs. | W | 1-0 | 1-0 | | Jordan |
| 25 | 21 | BARROW | D | 2-2 | 1-0 | 3000 | Sheargold, Winnington |
| 26 | 22 | Walkden Central | L | 1-6 | 1-2 | | Best |
| 27 | 24 | CHORLEY | L | 0-1 | 0-0 | | |
| 28 | 29 | Fleetwood | W | 2-1 | 1-0 | | Matthews, Owens |
| 29 | Apr 5 | St Helens Town | D | 1-1 | 1-0 | | Porter |
| 30 | 12 | ROSSENDALE UNITED | D | 4-4 | 2-0 | | Walker, Jordan, Brogden, Owens |
| 31 | 16 | WALKDEN CENTRAL | W | 7-0 | 3-0 | | Brogden (3), Sheargold (3), Lloyd |
| 32 | 19 | Colne | D | 2-2 | 0-0 | | Owens (2) |
| 33 | 23 | DENTON | W | 8-1 | 4-0 | | Wynn(2),Lloyd(2),Jordan(2),Sheargold,Brogden |
| 34 | 26 | Haslingden | L | 0-4 | 0-2 | | |

* Jack Lipsham/Billy Matthews Bene...

### F.A. CUP

| | Date | Opposition | | FT | HT | Att. | Goalscorers |
|---|---|---|---|---|---|---|---|
| Q1 | Sep 28 | Wrexham | L | 0-2 | 0-1 | 5000 | |

### WELSH CUP

| | Date | Opposition | | FT | HT | Att. | Goalscorers |
|---|---|---|---|---|---|---|---|
| 3R | Jan 4 | OSWESTRY UNITED | D | 1-1 | 0-0 | | Best |
| 3Rr | 14 | Oswestry United | W | 2-1 | 1-0 | | Jordan (2) |
| 4R | 25 | TROEDYRHIW | W | 1-0 | 0-0 | | Best |
| SF | Mar 8 | Pontypridd * | L | 0-3 | 0-0 | 5000 | |

* Played at Cardiff

### FRIENDLIES

| | Date | Opposition | | FT | HT | Att. | Goalscorers |
|---|---|---|---|---|---|---|---|
| 1 | Oct 12 | WALSALL | W | 3-1 | 2-1 | | Jordan, Ritchie, Lipsham |
| 2 | Feb 22 | ST HELENS TOWN | W | 6-1 | 1-1 | | Anderton (3), Matthews, Brogden, Polding (og) |

### Final League Table

| | P | W | D | L | F | A | Pts |
|---|---|---|---|---|---|---|---|
| 1 Eccles Borough | 34 | 23 | 4 | 7 | 96 | 49 | 50 |
| 2 Accrington Stanley | 34 | 21 | 3 | 10 | 75 | 54 | 45 |
| 3 Nelson | 34 | 19 | 4 | 11 | 82 | 59 | 42 |
| 4 Chorley | 34 | 18 | 5 | 11 | 67 | 51 | 41 |
| 5 Barrow | 34 | 17 | 6 | 11 | 73 | 34 | 40 |
| 6 Tranmere Rovers | 34 | 16 | 6 | 12 | 92 | 58 | 38 |
| **7 Chester** | **34** | **12** | **13** | **9** | **89** | **64** | **37** |
| 8 St Helens Recreation | 34 | 16 | 4 | 14 | 72 | 56 | 36 |
| 9 Fleetwood | 34 | 14 | 7 | 13 | 71 | 69 | 35 |
| 10 Haslingden | 34 | 16 | 2 | 16 | 77 | 78 | 34 |
| 11 Altrincham | 34 | 13 | 6 | 15 | 81 | 84 | 32 |
| 12 Hyde | 34 | 13 | 5 | 16 | 76 | 70 | 31 |
| 13 Walkden Central | 34 | 13 | 5 | 16 | 54 | 80 | 31 |
| 14 St Helens Town | 34 | 12 | 5 | 17 | 49 | 75 | 29 |
| 15 Heywood United | 34 | 13 | 2 | 19 | 76 | 100 | 28 |
| 16 Denton | 34 | 9 | 6 | 19 | 55 | 101 | 24 |
| 17 Rossendale United | 34 | 8 | 7 | 19 | 63 | 105 | 23 |
| 18 Colne | 34 | 6 | 4 | 24 | 49 | 110 | 16 |

**1912-13 season:**

(Back) Griffiths, Hughes, Reeves (Dir.), Gardner (Dir.), Matthews, Jones, Pate, Sheargold, Fletcher, Davies(Dir.), Balmer, Wildgoose (Dir.), Grundy, Hallmark (Ex-Chair.), Blaylock (Dir.).
(Front) Riley (Trainer), Ralphs, Winnington, Ritchie, Wynn, Jordan, Lipsham, Jones (Secretary).

# SEASON 1913-14

## LANCASHIRE COMBINATION DIVISION 1

| | Date | Opposition | | FT | HT | Att. | Goalscorers |
|---|---|---|---|---|---|---|---|
| 1 | Sep 6 | St Helens Town | L | 1-2 | 0-1 | | McCarthy |
| 2 | 13 | ST HELENS TOWN | W | 4-0 | 1-0 | | McCarthy, Flannery, Cook (2) |
| 3 | 20 | ACCRINGTON STANLEY | W | 4-1 | 2-1 | | Cook (2), McCarthy, Lloyd |
| 4 | Oct 4 | HYDE | D | 1-1 | 0-0 | | McCarthy |
| 5 | 18 | NORTHWICH VICS. | L | 1-2 | 1-1 | | Cook |
| 6 | 25 | Accrington Stanley | L | 1-3 | 1-2 | | Wolstenholme |
| 7 | Nov 8 | Hyde | D | 2-2 | 2-2 | | Matthews, McCarthy |
| 8 | 15 | ECCLES BOROUGH | D | 3-3 | 2-1 | | McCarthy, Hughes (2) |
| 9 | 22 | Northwich Vics. | L | 0-3 | 0-1 | | |
| 10 | 29 | ALTRINCHAM | W | 5-1 | 3-0 | | Matthews, Wynn, McCarthy (2), Hughes |
| 11 | Dec 6 | HEYWOOD UNITED | W | 1-0 | 0-0 | | Wolstenholme |
| 12 | 13 | Hurst | L | 1-2 | 1-2 | | Cook |
| 13 | 20 | Barrow | L | 1-3 | 1-1 | | McCarthy |
| 14 | 25 | FLEETWOOD | W | 3-1 | 0-1 | | McCarthy (2), Matthews |
| 15 | 26 | NELSON | W | 3-0 | 3-0 | | R. Griffiths, McCarthy, Hodgkinson |
| 16 | Jan 1 | South Liverpool | L | 3-4 | 3-1 | | McCarthy, Wolstenholme, Hodgkinson |
| 17 | 17 | Walkden Central | D | 2-2 | 1-1 | | Cook (2) |
| 18 | 31 | Altrincham | W | 2-1 | 2-0 | | Matthews, Cook |
| 19 | Feb 14 | Chorley | D | 1-1 | 1-0 | | Mason |
| 20 | 21 | TRANMERE ROVERS | L | 1-3 | 0-2 | 4000 | Matthews |
| 21 | 28 | Heywood United | L | 1-3 | 1-2 | 2000 | R. Anderson |
| 22 | Mar 7 | Fleetwood | D | 1-1 | 1-0 | | Cook |
| 23 | 14 | CHORLEY | D | 2-2 | 0-1 | | Wolstenholme, R. Griffiths |
| 24 | 21 | Eccles Borough | L | 0-2 | 0-1 | | |
| 25 | 25 | ATHERTON | D | 1-1 | 1-0 | | Hughes |
| 26 | 28 | Tranmere Rovers | L | 0-2 | 0-2 | 6000 | |
| 27 | Apr 4 | Atherton | L | 0-3 | 0-1 | | |
| 28 | 10 | BARROW | W | 2-1 | 1-0 | 7000 | R. Anderson, McIlwraith (og) |
| 29 | 11 | Haslingden | D | 1-1 | 0-1 | | Matthews |
| 30 | 13 | SOUTH LIVERPOOL | L | 1-4 | 1-1 | 8000 | Matthews |
| 31 | 18 | Nelson | L | 1-2 | 1-1 | | Ankers |
| 32 | 22 | WALKDEN CENTRAL | W | 6-0 | 3-0 | | Matthews,Ankers(2),McCarthy(2),Pearce |
| 33 | 25 | HURST | D | 1-1 | 1-1 | | McCarthy |
| 34 | 29 | HASLINGDEN | L | 2-4 | 1-3 | | Matthews, Unknown |

## F.A. CUP

| | | | | | | | |
|---|---|---|---|---|---|---|---|
| PQ | Sep 27 | NANTWICH | W | 5-3 | 3-3 | | Flannery (3), McCarthy, Cook |
| Q1 | Oct 11 | TRANMERE ROVERS | W | 2-1 | 1-1 | 4000 | Cook (2) |
| Q2 | Nov 1 | PORT VALE | L | 2-5 | 0-4 | | Pugh, Cook |

## WELSH CUP

| | | | | | | | |
|---|---|---|---|---|---|---|---|
| Q3 | Jan 3 | Swansea Town | L | 0-1 | | 9000 | |

## FRIENDLIES

| | | | | | | | |
|---|---|---|---|---|---|---|---|
| 1 | Jan 24 | NORTHERN NOMADS | W | 4-1 | 3-0 | | McCarthy (2), Matthews, Wolstenholme |

### Final League Table

| | P | W | D | L | F | A | Pts |
|---|---|---|---|---|---|---|---|
| 1 Tranmere Rovers | 34 | 25 | 4 | 5 | 85 | 32 | 54 |
| 2 Barrow | 34 | 21 | 5 | 8 | 92 | 39 | 47 |
| 3 Northwich Victoria | 34 | 21 | 5 | 8 | 65 | 36 | 47 |
| 4 Eccles Borough | 34 | 19 | 5 | 10 | 70 | 49 | 43 |
| 5 Atherton | 34 | 18 | 6 | 10 | 82 | 57 | 42 |
| 6 South Liverpool | 34 | 17 | 7 | 10 | 78 | 62 | 41 |
| 7 Accrington Stanley | 34 | 15 | 8 | 11 | 76 | 66 | 38 |
| 8 Hurst | 34 | 12 | 8 | 14 | 58 | 54 | 32 |
| 9 Chorley | 34 | 12 | 8 | 14 | 48 | 60 | 32 |
| 10 Nelson | 34 | 14 | 4 | 16 | 47 | 64 | 32 |
| 11 Fleetwood | 34 | 10 | 9 | 15 | 54 | 57 | 29 |
| **12 Chester** | **34** | **9** | **10** | **15** | **59** | **62** | **28** |
| 13 Altrincham | 34 | 10 | 7 | 17 | 61 | 80 | 27 |
| 14 Hyde | 34 | 10 | 7 | 17 | 59 | 82 | 27 |
| 15 Heywood United | 34 | 10 | 6 | 18 | 41 | 57 | 26 |
| 16 Haslingden | 34 | 11 | 4 | 19 | 52 | 77 | 26 |
| 17 St Helens Town | 34 | 9 | 8 | 17 | 47 | 83 | 26 |
| 18 Walkden Central | 34 | 5 | 5 | 24 | 40 | 97 | 15 |

From the 1913-14 Season:
(Letf) Matthews, (right) Wolstenholme

# SEASON 1914-15

## LANCASHIRE COMBINATION DIVISION 1

| | Date | Opposition | | FT | HT | Att. | Goalscorers |
|---|---|---|---|---|---|---|---|
| 1 | Sep 2 | HYDE | W | 3-1 | 2-1 | | Brindley, Billings, Ankers |
| 2 | 5 | South Liverpool | W | 3-2 | 1-1 | | Ankers, Brindley, Billings |
| 3 | 12 | NORTHWICH VICS. | W | 4-1 | 3-1 | | Hughes (2), Ankers, Brindley |
| 4 | 16 | ATHERTON | W | 2-1 | 0-0 | | Hughes, Ankers |
| 5 | 19 | Macclesfield | W | 4-1 | 1-1 | | Billings (2), Ankers, Smith |
| 6 | Oct 3 | ALTRINCHAM | W | 3-1 | 1-1 | | Ankers, Brindley (2) |
| 7 | 17 | MACCLESFIELD | W | 3-2 | 2-1 | | Hughes, Smith, Kirby |
| 8 | 31 | TRANMERE ROVERS | L | 0-2 | 0-1 | 5000 | |
| 9 | Nov 14 | WITTON ALBION | W | 8-2 | 3-1 | | Brindley(2),Ankers(2),Moorcroft(2) |
| 10 | 28 | Fleetwood | D | 2-2 | 0-1 | | Unknown (2) |
| 11 | Dec 5 | Hyde | D | 1-1 | 1-0 | | Wood |
| 12 | 12 | HURST | D | 2-2 | 1-2 | | Ankers, Wood |
| 13 | 19 | Northwich Vics. | L | 2-3 | 1-1 | | Wood, Smith |
| 14 | 25 | FLEETWOOD | L | 0-2 | 0-2 | | |
| 15 | 26 | ACCRINGTON STANLEY | L | 1-2 | 1-0 | | Billings |
| 16 | Feb 6 | NELSON | L | 2-3 | 1-1 | | Matthews, Fuller |
| 17 | 20 | DENTON | W | 4-2 | 2-1 | | Lennard (2), Settle, Wood |
| 18 | 27 | Tranmere Rovers | L | 1-8 | 0-7 | | Lennard |
| 19 | Mar 6 | ECCLES BOROUGH | L | 0-6 | 0-3 | | |

Chester withdrew from League, record expunged

## F.A. CUP

| | | | | | | | |
|---|---|---|---|---|---|---|---|
| PQ | Sep 26 | LOSTOCK GRALAM | | | | | Lostock Gralam scratched |
| Q1 | Oct 10 | ORMSKIRK | W | 2-0 | 1-0 | 3000 | Brindley, Billings |
| Q2 | 24 | Tranmere Rovers | L | 1-5 | 1-2 | 8000 | Brindley |

## WELSH CUP

| | | | | | | | |
|---|---|---|---|---|---|---|---|
| 3R | Jan 2 | OSWESTRY UNITED | W | 5-3 | 3-2 | | Wood (2), Hughes, Unknown (2) |
| 4R | 23 | LLANDUDNO | D | 2-2 | 1-1 | | Kirby, Brindley |
| 4Rr | 30 | Llandudno | L | 0-1 | | | |

## FRIENDLIES

| | | | | | | | |
|---|---|---|---|---|---|---|---|
| 1 | Nov 7 | CREWE ALEX. | L | 2-4 | 0-2 | 1000 | Smith, Billings |
| 2 | 21 | Witton Albion | L | 1-3 | 1-3 | | Billings |

### Final League Table

| | P | W | D | L | F | A | Pts |
|---|---|---|---|---|---|---|---|
| 1 Eccles Borough | 32 | 18 | 8 | 6 | 77 | 41 | 44 |
| 2 Hurst | 32 | 17 | 8 | 7 | 76 | 48 | 42 |
| 3 Tranmere Rovers | 32 | 19 | 3 | 10 | 84 | 52 | 41 |
| 4 Macclesfield | 32 | 19 | 3 | 10 | 68 | 49 | 41 |
| 5 Northwich Victoria | 32 | 16 | 6 | 10 | 71 | 50 | 38 |
| 6 Accrington Stanley | 32 | 15 | 7 | 10 | 75 | 59 | 37 |
| 7 Altrincham | 32 | 15 | 4 | 13 | 68 | 55 | 34 |
| 8 Atherton | 32 | 15 | 4 | 13 | 69 | 59 | 34 |
| 9 South Liverpool | 32 | 13 | 7 | 12 | 72 | 67 | 33 |
| 10 Witton Albion | 32 | 13 | 6 | 13 | 61 | 63 | 32 |
| 11 Nelson | 32 | 13 | 4 | 15 | 66 | 64 | 30 |
| 12 Denton | 32 | 13 | 2 | 17 | 72 | 98 | 28 |
| 13 Barrow | 32 | 11 | 6 | 15 | 59 | 89 | 28 |
| 14 Fleetwood | 32 | 9 | 5 | 18 | 65 | 94 | 23 |
| 15 Rossendale United | 32 | 11 | 0 | 21 | 42 | 64 | 22 |
| 16 Hyde | 32 | 8 | 5 | 19 | 65 | 93 | 21 |
| 17 Chorley | 32 | 6 | 4 | 22 | 46 | 91 | 16 |

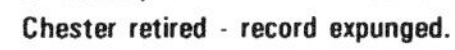
Chester retired - record expunged.

# SEASON 1919-20

## CHESHIRE COUNTY LEAGUE

| | Date | Opposition | | FT | HT | Att. | Goalscorers |
|---|---|---|---|---|---|---|---|
| 1 | Sep 6 | ALTRINCHAM | L | 2-4 | 1-0 | | Riley, Lipsham |
| 2 | 13 | Witton Albion | L | 3-4 | 2-0 | | Gleave, Settle, Petrie |
| 3 | 20 | MOSSLEY | W | 5-2 | 4-1 | | Cordall, G Jones (2), Tremlett, Lipsham |
| 4 | Oct 4 | NANTWICH | W | 2-1 | 0-0 | | Lipsham, Lawson |
| 5 | 11 | Tranmere Rovers * | L | 1-8 | 1-5 | 2000 | Lawson |
| 6 | 18 | WITTON ALBION | W | 5-1 | 2-1 | | Roberts, Jenkins (2), Lewis (2) |
| 7 | Nov 1 | Crichton's Athletic | D | 1-1 | 1-1 | 3000 | Lewis |
| 8 | 8 | NORTHWICH VICS. | W | 5-1 | 1-1 | | Roberts, Settle, Lewis (2), Lipsham |
| 9 | 15 | Mossley | L | 3-6 | 2-2 | | Lewis (2), Burman (og) |
| 10 | 22 | Winsford United | L | 0-5 | 0-2 | | |
| 11 | 29 | CRICHTON'S ATHLETIC | W | 3-1 | 3-1 | | Lewis (3) |
| 12 | Dec 6 | Altrincham | L | 2-3 | 1-2 | | Lewis, Spencer |
| 13 | 13 | CREWE ALEX RES. | W | 2-0 | 0-0 | | Lipsham, Spencer |
| 14 | 20 | Macclesfield | L | 0-2 | 0-2 | | |
| 15 | 27 | Runcorn | L | 0-6 | 0-3 | | |
| 16 | Jan 10 | Monk's Hall | D | 2-2 | 1-0 | | Lewis, Unknown |
| 17 | 24 | Northwich Vics. | W | 3-2 | 0-1 | | Lewis, Roberts, Jenkins |
| 18 | 31 | MONK'S HALL | W | 4-0 | 2-0 | | Lipsham (3), Smith |
| 19 | Mar 20 | Crewe Alex Res. | W | 3-0 | 0-0 | | Lewis, Hardman, Roberts |
| 20 | 27 | Nantwich | L | 3-5 | 0-3 | | Jenkins (2), Lloyd |
| 21 | Apr 14 | MACCLESFIELD | D | 3-3 | 3-2 | 1200 | Jenkins, Lloyd, Shaw (og) |
| 22 | 21 | RUNCORN | L | 2-4 | 1-4 | 1300 | Settle, Johnson |
| 23 | 24 | WINSFORD UNITED | D | 2-2 | 2-2 | | Lipsham (2) |

* Tranmere withdrew to join Central League, record expunged

## CHESHIRE LEAGUE SUBSIDIARY COMPETITION (SECTION B)

| | Date | Opposition | | FT | HT | Att. | Goalscorers |
|---|---|---|---|---|---|---|---|
| 1 | Dec 25 | Crichton's Athletic | L | 2-4 | | | Unknown (2) |
| 2 | Jan 17 | CREWE ALEX RES. | L | 3-6 | 3-3 | | Smith, Roberts, Cordall |
| 3 | Feb 21 | NANTWICH | W | 7-3 | 2-2 | | Lewis, Roberts, Settle, Jenkins (4) |
| 4 | 28 | Runcorn | L | 1-2 | 1-0 | | Lewis |
| 5 | Apr 2 | CRICHTON'S ATHLETIC | L | 1-2 | 0-1 | 3050 | Jenkins |
| 6 | 3 | Nantwich | L | 1-4 | 1-3 | | Lloyd |
| 7 | 10 | RUNCORN | D | 3-3 | 0-2 | | Jenkins (2), Lloyd |
| 8 | 17 | Monk's Hall | L | 0-7 | 0-2 | | |
| 9 | 26 | Crewe Alex Res. | L | 2-5 | 0-2 | 700 | Lewis, Emery (og) |
| 10 | 28 | MONK'S HALL | W | 3-1 | 1-0 | | Jenkins, Lewis, Lloyd |

## F.A. CUP

| | Date | Opposition | | FT | HT | Att. | Goalscorers |
|---|---|---|---|---|---|---|---|
| PQ | Sep 27 | Nantwich | L | 0-5 | 0-2 | | |

## WELSH CUP

| | Date | Opposition | | FT | HT | Att. | Goalscorers |
|---|---|---|---|---|---|---|---|
| 3R | Jan 17 | TRANMERE ROVERS | | | | | Tranmere Rovers scratched |
| 4R | Feb 7 | Cardiff City | L | 0-5 | 0-3 | 3000 | |

## FRIENDLIES

| | Date | Opposition | | FT | HT | Att. | Goalscorers |
|---|---|---|---|---|---|---|---|
| 1 | Dec 26 | PORT VALE | W | 3-1 | 2-0 | | Roberts (2), Settle |
| 2 | Feb 14 | EVERTON X1 | W | 3-2 | 1-1 | | Lewis, Jenkins, Roberts |
| 3 | Apr 5 | EVERTON X1 | W | 6-1 | 2-0 | 3000 | Jenkins(2), Settle(2), Brownbill, Roberts |

Final League Table

| | | P | W | D | L | F | A | Pts |
|---|---|---|---|---|---|---|---|---|
| 1 | Runcorn | 22 | 17 | 2 | 3 | 57 | 19 | 36 |
| 2 | Mossley | 22 | 11 | 3 | 8 | 41 | 43 | 25 |
| 3 | Witton Albion | 22 | 10 | 4 | 8 | 41 | 38 | 24 |
| 4 | Crewe Alexandra Res. | 22 | 10 | 3 | 9 | 45 | 45 | 23 |
| 5 | Crichton's Athletic | 22 | 9 | 4 | 9 | 48 | 38 | 22 |
| **6** | **Chester** | **22** | **9** | **4** | **9** | **55** | **55** | **22** |
| 7 | Winsford United | 22 | 10 | 1 | 11 | 45 | 34 | 21 |
| 8 | Altrincham | 22 | 7 | 6 | 9 | 38 | 47 | 20 |
| 9 | Macclesfield | 22 | 8 | 4 | 10 | 36 | 54 | 20 |
| 10 | Monk's Hall | 22 | 8 | 2 | 12 | 47 | 54 | 18 |
| 11 | Nantwich | 22 | 8 | 2 | 12 | 39 | 54 | 18 |
| 12 | Northwich Victoria | 22 | 5 | 5 | 12 | 33 | 44 | 15 |

(Subsidiary Competition Final League Table)

| | | P | W | D | L | F | A | Pts |
|---|---|---|---|---|---|---|---|---|
| 1 | Crewe Alexandra Res. | 10 | 7 | 1 | 2 | 33 | 13 | 15 |
| 2 | Runcorn | 10 | 5 | 4 | 1 | 20 | 15 | 14 |
| 3 | Monk's Hall | 10 | 5 | 1 | 4 | 26 | 19 | 11 |
| 4 | Crichton's Athletic | 10 | 5 | 0 | 5 | 15 | 21 | 10 |
| **5** | **Chester** | **10** | **2** | **1** | **7** | **23** | **37** | **5** |
| 6 | Nantwich | 10 | 2 | 1 | 7 | 14 | 26 | 5 |

# SEASON 1920-21

## CHESHIRE COUNTY LEAGUE

| | Date | Opposition | | FT | HT | Att. | Goalscorers |
|---|---|---|---|---|---|---|---|
| 1 | Aug 28 | Mossley | L | 2-4 | 1-3 | | Williams, Settle |
| 2 | Sep 4 | Northwich Vics. | W | 4-1 | 1-0 | 2400 | Murray (2), Williams, Jenkins |
| 3 | 11 | NORTHWICH VICS. | W | 2-1 | 2-1 | 3148 | Jenkins, Lipsham |
| 4 | 18 | Winsford United | L | 3-4 | 2-0 | 2000 | Williams, Murray, Settle |
| 5 | 25 | ASHTON NATIONAL | W | 4-1 | 1-1 | 3000 | Jenkins (2), Lipsham, Murray |
| 6 | Oct 2 | MOSSLEY | W | 5-1 | 2-1 | | Jenkins (2), Settle (2), Murray |
| 7 | 9 | TRANMERE R. RES. | W | 5-3 | 2-2 | 4000 | Murray, Settle (3), Jenkins |
| 8 | 16 | Sandbach Ramblers | L | 1-3 | 1-1 | | Jenkins |
| 9 | 23 | ALTRINCHAM | D | 1-1 | 0-1 | 4000 | Murray |
| 10 | Nov 6 | RUNCORN | L | 0-3 | 0-1 | 3600 | |
| 11 | 13 | CONGLETON TOWN | D | 1-1 | 1-1 | | Jenkins |
| 12 | 20 | Congleton Town | L | 1-3 | 0-1 | | Williams |
| 13 | 27 | WITTON ALBION | W | 5-2 | 3-2 | | Dawson (2), R Jones, Scholes, Settle |
| 14 | Dec 4 | Witton Albion | L | 1-4 | 1-0 | | Thornley |
| 15 | 18 | WINSFORD UNITED | D | 1-1 | 1-0 | | Thornley |
| 16 | 25 | Connah's Quay | W | 3-1 | 3-1 | 3500 | Hughes, Jenkins, L Jones |
| 17 | 27 | CONNAH'S QUAY | D | 4-4 | 1-2 | 5000 | Thornley, Scholes, Jenkins, Settle |
| 18 | Jan 1 | Stalybridge C. Res. | L | 1-2 | 0-1 | | Jenkins |
| 19 | 3 | Ashton National | L | 2-5 | 1-3 | 3500 | Dawson, Hughes |
| 20 | 8 | MONKS HALL | D | 2-2 | 2-0 | 2500 | Thornley, Hughes |
| 21 | 22 | Tranmere R. Res. | W | 2-1 | 2-0 | 2000 | Scholes, Jenkins |
| 22 | 29 | Monks Hall | L | 1-2 | 1-1 | | Dawson |
| 23 | Feb 19 | Altrincham | L | 0-1 | 0-1 | | |
| 24 | 26 | SANDBACH RAMBLERS | W | 2-0 | 1-0 | 2500 | Burley, Settle |
| 25 | Mar 5 | Crewe Alex. Res. | L | 3-4 | 1-2 | | Leedham, Jenkins, Killeen (og) |
| 26 | 19 | Nantwich | L | 1-9 | 1-4 | | Matthews |
| 27 | 25 | CRICHTONS ATHLETIC | W | 3-0 | 1-0 | 5500 | Jenkins, Quinn, Connor |
| 28 | 26 | STALYBRIDGE C. RES. | L | 2-4 | 2-3 | 3000 | Roberts, Jenkins |
| 29 | 28 | Crichtons Athletic * | W | 1-0 | 0-0 | 4500 | Quinn |
| 30 | Apr 2 | Runcorn | W | 1-0 | 1-0 | | Johnson |
| 31 | 16 | CREWE ALEX. RES. | W | 1-0 | 1-0 | | Settle |
| 32 | 23 | MACCLESFIELD | W | 1-0 | 1-0 | | Roberts |
| 33 | 30 | NANTWICH | W | 6-2 | 3-2 | | Roberts(2), Jenkins(2), Settle, Lightburn |
| 34 | May 7 | Macclesfield | L | 0-5 | 0-3 | | |

* Played at Chester

## WELSH CUP

| | Date | Opposition | | FT | HT | Att. | Goalscorers |
|---|---|---|---|---|---|---|---|
| 1R | Oct 30 | CHIRK | D | 0-0 | 0-0 | 3700 | |
| 1Rr | Nov 4 | Chirk * | D | 2-2 | 1-0 | 1200 | Murray, Jenkins |
| 1R2r | 10 | CHIRK | L | 0-2 | 0-1 | 2500 | |

* Extra time played following score of 2-2 after 90 minutes

## FRIENDLIES

| | Date | Opposition | | FT | HT | Att. | Goalscorers |
|---|---|---|---|---|---|---|---|
| 1 | Dec 11 | EVERTON | L | 1-2 | 0-1 | | Jenkins |
| 2 | May 14 | CRICHTONS ATHLETIC * | L | 1-2 | 0-2 | | Roberts |

* Sir Owen Phillips Cup (Royal Infirmary Benefit)

Final League Table

| | | P | W | D | L | F | A | Pts |
|---|---|---|---|---|---|---|---|---|
| 1 | Winsford United | 34 | 19 | 6 | 9 | 67 | 48 | 44 |
| 2 | Congleton Town | 34 | 17 | 8 | 9 | 68 | 56 | 42 |
| 3 | Runcorn | 34 | 17 | 7 | 10 | 64 | 42 | 41 |
| 4 | Monk's Hall | 34 | 16 | 9 | 9 | 58 | 40 | 41 |
| 5 | Crewe Alexandra Res. | 34 | 15 | 9 | 10 | 80 | 51 | 39 |
| 6 | Macclesfield | 34 | 16 | 7 | 11 | 67 | 50 | 39 |
| 7 | Crichton's Athletic | 34 | 16 | 6 | 12 | 72 | 62 | 38 |
| 8 | Mossley | 34 | 14 | 8 | 12 | 49 | 48 | 36 |
| 9 | Altrincham | 34 | 14 | 8 | 12 | 59 | 70 | 36 |
| **10** | **Chester** | **34** | **15** | **5** | **14** | **72** | **75** | **35** |
| 11 | Nantwich | 34 | 14 | 6 | 14 | 82 | 72 | 34 |
| 12 | Ashton National | 34 | 14 | 5 | 15 | 69 | 64 | 33 |
| 13 | Northwich Victoria | 34 | 12 | 5 | 17 | 53 | 60 | 29 |
| 14 | Tranmere Rovers Res. | 34 | 13 | 3 | 18 | 52 | 69 | 29 |
| 15 | Stalybridge Celtic Res. | 34 | 11 | 5 | 18 | 61 | 74 | 27 |
| 16 | Sandbach Ramblers | 34 | 8 | 9 | 17 | 42 | 68 | 25 |
| 17 | Witton Albion | 34 | 10 | 3 | 21 | 48 | 77 | 23 |
| 18 | Connah's Quay | 34 | 6 | 9 | 19 | 44 | 82 | 21 |

# SEASON 1921-22

## CHESHIRE COUNTY LEAGUE

| | Date | Opposition | | FT | HT | Att. | Goalscorers |
|---|---|---|---|---|---|---|---|
| 1 | Aug 27 | SALTNEY ATHLETIC | D | 1-1 | 1-0 | 6000 | Cooper |
| 2 | Sep 3 | ALTRINCHAM | W | 2-1 | 0-1 | 5000 | Timmis, H Howarth |
| 3 | 17 | Ellesmere P. Cement | W | 1-0 | 0-0 | 4000 | Timmis |
| 4 | Oct 1 | CREWE ALEX. RES. | W | 3-0 | 1-0 | | Butterton (2), Tr Jones |
| 5 | 15 | ELLESMERE P. CEMENT | W | 2-1 | 1-0 | | Cooper (2) |
| 6 | 29 | Ashton National | L | 0-1 | 0-1 | 4000 | |
| 7 | Nov 12 | CONNAH'S QUAY | W | 2-1 | 1-0 | | Copper, Donnachie |
| 8 | 26 | STALYBRIDGE C. RES. | L | 2-4 | 0-2 | | H Howarth, Pryde |
| 9 | Dec 3 | Runcorn | W | 1-0 | 1-0 | | Tom Jones |
| 10 | 10 | MACCLESFIELD | W | 5-1 | 2-0 | | Butterton(2),Tr Jones,H Howarth,Pimlott |
| 11 | 17 | Connah's Quay | D | 1-1 | 1-1 | | Tr Jones |
| 12 | 24 | Saltney Athletic | D | 2-2 | 2-0 | | C. Jones, Butterton |
| 13 | 26 | TRANMERE R. RES. | W | 3-1 | 0-1 | 6000 | H Howarth (2), Carter |
| 14 | 27 | RUNCORN | W | 2-1 | 2-1 | 6000 | Pimlott, Carter |
| 15 | 31 | Mossley | W | 2-1 | 1-1 | | Timmis, Phoenix |
| 16 | Jan 2 | Altrincham | W | 2-1 | 0-0 | | Timmis, Carter |
| 17 | 7 | NORTHWICH VICS. | L | 3-4 | 3-0 | | Phoenix, Tr Jones, Pimlott |
| 18 | 21 | MOSSLEY | W | 1-0 | 1-0 | | Butterton |
| 19 | 28 | Macclesfield | L | 0-2 | 0-1 | | |
| 20 | Feb 4 | CONGLETON TOWN | W | 3-2 | 1-1 | 1800 | Phoenix, Tom Jones, H Howarth |
| 21 | 18 | Northwich Vics. | L | 1-4 | 0-0 | | Tom Jones |
| 22 | 25 | Sandbach Ramblers | L | 0-1 | 0-0 | | |
| 23 | Mar 4 | WINSFORD UNITED | W | 6-0 | 3-0 | 4000 | Pimlott, Taylor (2), Pryde, Virr (2) |
| 24 | 11 | ASHTON NATIONAL | W | 6-2 | 2-1 | | Virr (4), Timmis, H Howarth |
| 25 | 18 | Nantwich | L | 0-2 | 0-1 | | |
| 26 | 21 | Stalybridge C. Res. | L | 1-2 | 1-1 | | Donnachie |
| 27 | 25 | Witton Albion | L | 0-4 | 0-3 | | |
| 28 | 29 | NANTWICH | W | 2-0 | 1-0 | 4000 | H Howarth, Virr |
| 29 | Apr 1 | Congleton Town | L | 0-4 | 0-2 | | |
| 30 | 8 | STOCKPORT CO. RES. | W | 5-1 | 2-0 | | H Howarth, Pimlott, Tr Jones, Taylor (2) |
| 31 | 12 | Crewe Alex. Res. | W | 1-0 | 0-0 | | H Howarth |
| 32 | 14 | WHITCHURCH | W | 3-2 | 3-0 | 7000 | Pryde, Donnachie, Virr |
| 33 | 15 | Whitchurch | W | 2-0 | 1-0 | | Tr Jones, H Howarth |
| 34 | 17 | Tranmere R. Res. | W | 1-0 | 1-0 | 4500 | Taylor |
| 35 | 22 | Winsford United | W | 3-0 | 2-0 | | H Howarth, Virr (2) |
| 36 | 27 | Stockport Co. Res. | W | 3-0 | 2-0 | | Pimlott (2), Virr |
| 37 | May 3 | WITTON ALBION | W | 3-1 | 1-1 | 4000 | Donnachie, Virr, Pimlott |
| 38 | 6 | SANDBACH RAMBLERS | W | 3-2 | 3-1 | 3500 | Pimlott (2), Pryde |

## FA CUP

| | | | | | | | |
|---|---|---|---|---|---|---|---|
| EPQ | Sep 10 | MACHYNLLETH | W | 7-0 | 6-0 | | Tr Jones,Tom Jones(2),Butterton(2),Cooper(2) |
| PQ | 24 | Ellesmere Port T. | W | 3-1 | 1-1 | 4200 | Tom Jones, Cooper (2) |
| Q1 | Oct 8 | LOSTOCK GRALAM | W | 2-0 | 2-0 | 4000 | Cooper (2) |
| Q2 | 22 | Harrowby | W | 3-1 | 0-1 | 1500 | Cooper (3) |
| Q3 | Nov 5 | NORTHWICH VICS. | D | 3-3 | 1-2 | | Cooper (2), Tom Jones |
| Q3r | 9 | Northwich Vics. | W | 1-0 | 0-0 | | Tr Jones |
| Q4 | 19 | Crewe Alex. | D | 1-1 | 1-1 | 8000 | Cooper |
| Q4r | 23 | CREWE ALEX. * | L | 1-2 | 0-0 | 7000 | Howarth |

* Extra time played following score of 1-1 after 90 minutes

## FRIENDLIES

| | | | | | | | |
|---|---|---|---|---|---|---|---|
| 1 | Apr 29 | MANCHESTER CITY | W | 1-0 | 1-0 | | Pryde |
| 2 | May 10 | ELLESMERE P. CEMENT * | W | 2-1 | 2-0 | | Tom Jones, Virr |
| 3 | 13 | BUCKLEY * | W | 3-0 | 1-0 | | Virr, Pimlott (2) |

* Sir Owen Phillips Cup (Royal Infirmary Benefit)

### Final League Table

| | | P | W | D | L | F | A | Pts |
|---|---|---|---|---|---|---|---|---|
| **1** | **Chester** | **38** | **25** | **3** | **10** | **78** | **50** | **53** |
| 2 | Congleton Town | 38 | 22 | 6 | 10 | 82 | 49 | 50 |
| 3 | Ashton National | 38 | 23 | 2 | 13 | 78 | 63 | 48 |
| 4 | Witton Albion | 38 | 20 | 7 | 11 | 77 | 54 | 47 |
| 5 | Stalybridge Celtic Res. | 38 | 18 | 8 | 12 | 71 | 59 | 44 |
| 6 | Nantwich | 38 | 15 | 13 | 10 | 71 | 57 | 43 |
| 7 | Northwich Victoria | 38 | 15 | 10 | 13 | 62 | 40 | 40 |
| 8 | Macclesfield | 38 | 13 | 13 | 12 | 60 | 64 | 39 |
| 9 | Connah's Quay | 38 | 13 | 12 | 13 | 51 | 52 | 38 |
| 10 | Whitchurch | 38 | 16 | 6 | 16 | 65 | 71 | 38 |
| 11 | Winsford United | 38 | 13 | 12 | 13 | 53 | 64 | 38 |
| 12 | Altrincham | 38 | 13 | 9 | 16 | 75 | 70 | 35 |
| 13 | Sandbach Ramblers | 38 | 13 | 9 | 16 | 51 | 54 | 35 |
| 14 | Ellesmere Port Cement | 38 | 14 | 6 | 18 | 61 | 63 | 34 |
| 15 | Crewe Alexandra Res. | 38 | 13 | 8 | 17 | 61 | 70 | 34 |
| 16 | Saltney Athletic | 38 | 9 | 15 | 14 | 65 | 75 | 33 |
| 17 | Mossley | 38 | 11 | 7 | 20 | 54 | 84 | 29 |
| 18 | Stockport County Res. | 38 | 11 | 6 | 21 | 57 | 102 | 28 |
| 19 | Tranmere Rovers Res. | 38 | 10 | 7 | 21 | 59 | 66 | 27 |
| 20 | Runcorn | 38 | 10 | 7 | 21 | 56 | 80 | 27 |

1921-22 **Season**: Unnamed Team group

# SEASON 1922-23

## CHESHIRE COUNTY LEAGUE

| | Date | Opposition | | FT | HT | Att. | Goalscorers |
|---|---|---|---|---|---|---|---|
| 1 | Aug 26 | CREWE ALEX. RES. | L | 0-2 | 0-0 | | |
| 2 | 30 | NANTWICH | W | 3-0 | 2-0 | 4000 | Lea, Pimlott, R Taylor |
| 3 | Sep 2 | Crewe Alex. Res. | L | 0-2 | 0-0 | | |
| 4 | 9 | SANDBACH RAMBLERS | D | 2-2 | 1-2 | 3500 | Goode, T Jones |
| 5 | 16 | Ellesmere P. Cement | L | 0-2 | 0-0 | 3000 | |
| 6 | 30 | Northwich Vics. | L | 2-3 | 1-1 | | Gittens (2) |
| 7 | Oct 7 | Saltney | L | 1-2 | 0-1 | | Parton |
| 8 | 14 | SALTNEY | L | 1-2 | 1-1 | | McGovern |
| 9 | 21 | ALTRINCHAM | W | 2-1 | 1-1 | 4000 | Parton (2) |
| 10 | 28 | Tranmere R. Res. | W | 4-1 | 1-0 | 4000 | Rothwell, Twiss, T Jones, Mellor |
| 11 | Nov 4 | NORTHWICH VICS. | W | 1-0 | 1-0 | | Rothwell |
| 12 | 11 | Stalybridge C. Res. | L | 0-1 | 0-0 | 2000 | |
| 13 | 18 | Macclesfield | L | 0-2 | 0-0 | | |
| 14 | 25 | TRANMERE R. RES. | D | 1-1 | 0-0 | | Donnachie |
| 15 | Dec 2 | Stockport Co. Res. | L | 0-9 | 0-3 | | |
| 16 | 9 | Ashton National | W | 2-1 | 1-1 | | Donnachie, Howarth |
| 17 | 23 | Altrincham | L | 1-4 | 1-1 | | Rothwell |
| 18 | 25 | Middlewich | W | 1-0 | 1-0 | | Spencer |
| 19 | 26 | ELLESMERE P. CEMENT | L | 1-2 | 0-2 | 4000 | Donnachie |
| 20 | 30 | Whitchurch | L | 0-3 | 0-1 | 2000 | |
| 21 | Jan 1 | Runcorn | L | 0-2 | 0-1 | | |
| 22 | 13 | WINSFORD UNITED | W | 3-1 | 1-0 | | Howarth (2), P Jones |
| 23 | 20 | Witton Albion | D | 1-1 | 0-1 | 2000 | Nuttall |
| 24 | 27 | CONGLETON TOWN | W | 5-0 | 4-0 | 2813 | Rothwell, McGivney, P Jones (3) |
| 25 | Feb 3 | Sandbach Ramblers | D | 1-1 | 0-0 | | Nuttall |
| 26 | 17 | ASHTON NATIONAL | D | 2-2 | 1-0 | 2000 | Rothwell, McGivney |
| 27 | 24 | WHITCHURCH | D | 1-1 | 0-1 | 2000 | Howarth |
| 28 | Mar 3 | Congleton Town | L | 1-4 | 1-2 | | Parton |
| 29 | 10 | MACCLESFIELD | D | 1-1 | 1-1 | 2000 | Nuttall |
| 30 | 17 | Mossley | D | 1-1 | 0-1 | 2000 | Nuttall |
| 31 | 24 | MOSSLEY | W | 3-0 | 1-0 | 2500 | Nuttall (2), Donnachie |
| 32 | 30 | RUNCORN | W | 4-0 | 2-0 | | McGivney (3), Nuttall |
| 33 | 31 | MIDDLEWICH | W | 3-1 | 2-0 | | Sumner, Nuttall, Hough |
| 34 | Apr 2 | STALYBRIDGE C. RES. | W | 4-0 | 3-0 | | McGivney (2), Nuttall, Howarth |
| 35 | 14 | Winsford United | L | 0-2 | 0-2 | | |
| 36 | 21 | Nantwich | L | 1-2 | 1-2 | | Howarth |
| 37 | 28 | WITTON ALBION | L | 0-1 | 0-1 | 1500 | |
| 38 | May 5 | STOCKPORT CO. RES. | W | 6-0 | 5-0 | | Henderson(og),McGivney(3),Murphy,Howarth |

## F.A. CUP

| | Date | Opposition | | FT | HT | Att. | Goalscorers |
|---|---|---|---|---|---|---|---|
| PQ | Sep 23 | New Brighton | L | 2-4 | 1-2 | 9000 | Howarth, Gittens |

## FRIENDLIES

| | Date | Opposition | | FT | HT | Goalscorers |
|---|---|---|---|---|---|---|
| 1 | May 9 | SALTNEY ATHLETIC * | W | 2-1 | 2-0 | Ritches, Rothwell |
| 2 | 12 | ELLESMERE P. CEMENT * | W | 2-0 | 1-0 | Ritches (2) |

* Sir Owen Phillips Cup (Royal Infirmary Benefit)

### Final League Table

| | | P | W | D | L | F | A | Pts |
|---|---|---|---|---|---|---|---|---|
| 1 | Crewe Alexandra Res. | 38 | 27 | 6 | 5 | 102 | 42 | 60 |
| 2 | Stockport County Res. | 38 | 20 | 8 | 10 | 89 | 58 | 48 |
| 3 | Altrincham | 38 | 19 | 10 | 9 | 86 | 60 | 48 |
| 4 | Macclesfield | 38 | 18 | 10 | 10 | 84 | 52 | 46 |
| 5 | Ellesmere Port Cement | 38 | 18 | 7 | 13 | 69 | 48 | 43 |
| 6 | Saltney Athletic | 38 | 20 | 3 | 15 | 75 | 83 | 43 |
| 7 | Winsford United | 38 | 17 | 7 | 14 | 51 | 52 | 41 |
| 8 | Tranmere Rovers Res. | 38 | 16 | 9 | 13 | 69 | 71 | 41 |
| 9 | Mossley | 38 | 15 | 10 | 13 | 76 | 62 | 40 |
| 10 | Stalybridge Celtic Res. | 38 | 15 | 9 | 14 | 56 | 49 | 39 |
| 11 | Ashton National | 38 | 14 | 10 | 14 | 75 | 57 | 38 |
| 12 | Whitchurch | 38 | 14 | 9 | 15 | 66 | 78 | 37 |
| 13 | Congleton Town | 38 | 14 | 8 | 16 | 64 | 71 | 36 |
| 14 | Nantwich | 38 | 15 | 5 | 18 | 61 | 84 | 35 |
| **15** | **Chester** | **38** | **13** | **8** | **17** | **59** | **60** | **34** |
| 16 | Sandbach Ramblers | 38 | 10 | 10 | 18 | 53 | 81 | 30 |
| 17 | Runcorn | 38 | 11 | 5 | 22 | 56 | 85 | 27 |
| 18 | Northwich Victoria | 38 | 8 | 10 | 20 | 47 | 75 | 26 |
| 19 | Witton Albion | 38 | 9 | 7 | 22 | 43 | 83 | 25 |
| 20 | Middlewich | 38 | 8 | 7 | 23 | 40 | 70 | 23 |

# SEASON 1923-24

## CHESHIRE COUNTY LEAGUE

| | Date | Opposition | | FT | HT | Att. | Goalscorers |
|---|---|---|---|---|---|---|---|
| 1 | Aug 25 | MIDDLEWICH | D | 0-0 | 0-0 | | |
| 2 | 29 | Whitchurch | L | 1-4 | 0-3 | | McGivney |
| 3 | Sep 1 | Ellesmere P. Cement | D | 0-0 | 0-0 | | |
| 4 | 8 | MOSSLEY | W | 5-0 | 2-0 | | Parton, McGivney (2), Heath, Dempsey |
| 5 | 15 | Altrincham | W | 3-0 | 1-0 | | Dempsey, Parton, McGivney |
| 6 | 17 | Stalybridge Celtic | L | 0-2 | 0-1 | 1800 | |
| 7 | 29 | MACCLESFIELD | L | 1-3 | 1-1 | 3500 | Heath |
| 8 | Oct 13 | CONGLETON TOWN | D | 0-0 | 0-0 | 2500 | |
| 9 | 27 | NORTHWICH VICS. | D | 0-0 | 0-0 | | |
| 10 | Nov 3 | Stockport Co. Res. | L | 2-3 | 2-0 | | Gregory, Parton |
| 11 | 10 | Nantwich | L | 0-2 | 0-2 | | |
| 12 | 17 | ASHTON NATIONAL | D | 2-2 | 0-1 | | McGivney, Milne |
| 13 | Dec 1 | Macclesfield | L | 0-3 | 0-1 | | |
| 14 | 8 | PORT VALE RES. | L | 0-2 | 0-0 | | |
| 15 | 22 | WITTON ALBION | D | 0-0 | 0-0 | | |
| 16 | 26 | SANDBACH RAMBLERS | W | 4-0 | 2-0 | | Kearslake (2), Milne (2) |
| 17 | 29 | Hurst | L | 1-2 | 0-1 | | McGivney |
| 18 | Jan 1 | Runcorn | D | 1-1 | 1-0 | 4000 | McGivney |
| 19 | 5 | CREWE ALEX. RES. | L | 2-3 | 2-2 | 3000 | Lydiate, Kearslake |
| 20 | 19 | HURST | W | 5-1 | 4-0 | 2000 | Lydiate, Howarth (2), Kearslake (2) |
| 21 | 26 | WHITCHURCH | W | 1-0 | 1-0 | | Barton |
| 22 | Feb 2 | Ashton National | W | 2-1 | 1-1 | | Johnson, Barton |
| 23 | 16 | NANTWICH | D | 1-1 | 0-0 | | Howarth |
| 24 | 23 | WALLASEY UNITED | D | 0-0 | 0-0 | | |
| 25 | Mar 1 | Crewe Alex. Res. | L | 2-3 | 1-3 | | Sodun, Kearslake |
| 26 | 8 | Winsford United | L | 0-2 | 0-0 | | |
| 27 | 15 | Middlewich | L | 2-3 | 0-2 | | Lydiate (2) |
| 28 | 22 | ELLESMERE P. CEMENT | W | 2-1 | 1-0 | 2000 | Mokhtar, Milne |
| 29 | 26 | Northwich Vics. | D | 2-2 | 2-1 | | Mokhtar, Milne |
| 30 | 29 | ALTRINCHAM | W | 3-2 | 0-1 | 2000 | Lydiate, Swindells, Mokhtar |
| 31 | Apr 2 | STOCKPORT CO. RES. | D | 3-3 | 0-2 | 1500 | Swindells, Milne (2) |
| 32 | 3 | Witton Albion | L | 0-4 | 0-3 | | |
| 33 | 5 | Port Vale Res. | D | 2-2 | 1-2 | | Mokhtar, Lydiate |
| 34 | 9 | WINSFORD UNITED | L | 1-2 | 0-2 | | Mokhtar |
| 35 | 12 | Tranmere R. Res. | D | 0-0 | 0-0 | 3000 | |
| 36 | 18 | RUNCORN | W | 2-0 | 1-0 | 4398 | Mokhtar (2) |
| 37 | 19 | Wallasey United | L | 2-3 | 1-3 | | Milne (2) |
| 38 | 21 | STALYBRIDGE CELTIC | W | 1-0 | 0-0 | 5000 | Kearslake |
| 39 | 26 | Sandbach Ramblers | D | 2-2 | 1-1 | | Sodun, Sumner |
| 40 | 28 | TRANMERE R. RES. | W | 3-2 | 0-1 | | Hughes, Mokhtar, Lydiate |
| 41 | 29 | Mossley | D | 1-1 | | | Unknown |
| 42 | May 3 | Congleton Town | L | 0-4 | 0-2 | | |

## F.A. CUP

| | Date | Opposition | | FT | HT | Att. | Goalscorers |
|---|---|---|---|---|---|---|---|
| PQ | Sep 22 | ELLESMERE P. CEMENT | W | 1-0 | 0-0 | 4000 | Dempsey |
| Q1 | Oct 6 | LOSTOCK GRALAM | W | 5-1 | 1-0 | 2714 | Milne (3), McGivney, Heath |
| Q2 | 20 | Ellesmere Port | L | 1-2 | 1-0 | | Milne |

## FRIENDLIES

| | Date | Opposition | | FT | HT | Goalscorers |
|---|---|---|---|---|---|---|
| 1 | May 10 | ELLESMERE P. CEMENT * | L | 0-3 | 0-0 | |

* Sir Owen Phillips Cup (Royal Infirmary Benefit)

### Final League Table

| | | P | W | D | L | F | A | Pts |
|---|---|---|---|---|---|---|---|---|
| 1 | Crewe Alexandra Res. | 42 | 28 | 5 | 9 | 96 | 62 | 61 |
| 2 | Port Vale Res. | 42 | 24 | 10 | 8 | 109 | 60 | 58 |
| 3 | Whitchurch | 42 | 24 | 8 | 10 | 81 | 52 | 56 |
| 4 | Stalybridge Celtic | 42 | 24 | 6 | 12 | 93 | 50 | 54 |
| 5 | Stockport County Res. | 42 | 21 | 12 | 9 | 92 | 56 | 54 |
| 6 | Northwich Victoria | 42 | 18 | 10 | 14 | 85 | 77 | 46 |
| 7 | Congleton Town | 42 | 18 | 9 | 15 | 86 | 59 | 45 |
| 8 | Hurst | 42 | 19 | 7 | 16 | 78 | 76 | 45 |
| 9 | Macclesfield | 42 | 18 | 6 | 18 | 82 | 67 | 42 |
| 10 | Altrincham | 42 | 19 | 4 | 19 | 69 | 75 | 42 |
| 11 | Ashton National | 42 | 15 | 11 | 16 | 59 | 60 | 41 |
| 12 | Ellesmere Port Cement | 42 | 14 | 12 | 16 | 66 | 64 | 40 |
| 13 | Mossley | 42 | 16 | 8 | 18 | 77 | 90 | 40 |
| 14 | Winsford United | 42 | 17 | 5 | 20 | 56 | 77 | 39 |
| 15 | Wallasey United | 42 | 13 | 12 | 17 | 50 | 71 | 38 |
| **16** | **Chester** | **42** | **11** | **15** | **16** | **59** | **66** | **37** |
| 17 | Witton Albion | 42 | 14 | 9 | 19 | 55 | 67 | 37 |
| 18 | Tranmere Rovers Res. | 42 | 13 | 9 | 20 | 78 | 90 | 35 |
| 19 | Runcorn | 42 | 13 | 9 | 20 | 54 | 68 | 35 |
| 20 | Middlewich | 42 | 12 | 8 | 22 | 56 | 101 | 32 |
| 21 | Nantwich | 42 | 9 | 6 | 27 | 53 | 101 | 24 |
| 22 | Sandbach Ramblers | 42 | 7 | 9 | 26 | 41 | 85 | 23 |

# *SEASON 1924-25*

## CHESHIRE COUNTY LEAGUE

| | Date | Opposition | | FT | HT | Att. | Goalscorers |
|---|---|---|---|---|---|---|---|
| 1 | Aug 30 | ALTRINCHAM | W | 3-1 | 1-0 | 3000 | Mokhtar (2), Cordwell (og) |
| 2 | Sep 3 | MACCLESFIELD | L | 1-2 | 1-1 | | Mokhtar |
| 3 | 6 | Sandbach Ramblers | L | 0-1 | 0-1 | | |
| 4 | 10 | MIDDLEWICH | W | 2-0 | 1-0 | | Fleetwood (2) |
| 5 | 13 | Ellesmere P. Cement | L | 0-1 | 0-1 | | |
| 6 | 17 | MANCHESTER N. E. | W | 3-2 | 2-0 | | S. Hughes, Booth (2) |
| 7 | 22 | Stalybridge Celtic | L | 0-1 | 0-1 | 3000 | |
| 8 | 27 | WINSFORD UNITED | L | 0-2 | 0-0 | | |
| 9 | Oct 11 | Crewe Alex. Res. | L | 1-4 | 0-2 | | J Shaw |
| 10 | 18 | NANTWICH | W | 4-3 | 1-1 | | J Shaw(2),S Hughes,Small |
| 11 | 25 | NORTHWICH VICS. | D | 2-2 | 2-1 | | Small, J Shaw |
| 12 | Nov 1 | CONGLETON TOWN | D | 2-2 | 0-2 | | Russell, J. Shaw |
| 13 | 8 | Ellesmere Port Town | L | 0-3 | 0-0 | | |
| 14 | 15 | Manchester N. E. | W | 1-0 | 1-0 | | Smith |
| 15 | 22 | SANDBACH RAMBLERS | D | 1-1 | 1-1 | | J Shaw |
| 16 | 29 | Whitchurch | L | 1-3 | 1-1 | | Woods (og) |
| 17 | Dec 6 | WHITCHURCH | D | 2-2 | 0-2 | | J Shaw, Williams |
| 18 | 13 | ASHTON NATIONAL | W | 1-0 | 0-0 | 550 | Boyle |
| 19 | 25 | ELLESMERE P. CEMENT | D | 1-1 | | | Lightburn |
| 20 | 26 | TRANMERE R. RES. | W | 3-2 | 0-0 | | L Johnson,Ankers,S Hughes |
| 21 | 27 | Congleton Town | W | 2-0 | 1-0 | | Healey (2) |
| 22 | Jan 1 | Runcorn | D | 1-1 | 0-0 | | Boyle |
| 23 | 3 | Witton Albion | L | 0-4 | 0-2 | | |
| 24 | 10 | WITTON ALBION | W | 1-0 | 0-0 | | Phillips |
| 25 | 17 | Macclesfield | L | 2-5 | 2-2 | 5000 | Ankers, J Shaw |
| 26 | 24 | Hurst | L | 0-4 | 0-1 | | |
| 27 | 31 | CREWE ALEX. RES. | W | 2-1 | 0-1 | | Barton, Ankers |
| 28 | Feb 14 | PORT VALE RES. | L | 1-7 | 0-3 | | Ankers |
| 29 | 21 | Mossley | L | 1-4 | 1-2 | | Ankers |
| 30 | 28 | HURST | W | 2-1 | 1-1 | 1329 | L Johnson, Ellis |
| 31 | Mar 7 | ELLESMERE PORT TOWN | W | 4-0 | 3-0 | | L Johnson(2),Barton,Ankers |
| 32 | 14 | Tranmere R. Res. | L | 1-4 | 1-1 | 2000 | Barton |
| 33 | 21 | Ashton National | L | 3-5 | 2-4 | 3000 | Ankers, Healey, Bell |
| 34 | 28 | MOSSLEY | W | 3-2 | 2-1 | 2000 | Ellis, Lightburn, Barton |
| 35 | Apr 4 | Altrincham | L | 0-5 | 0-1 | | |
| 36 | 10 | RUNCORN | W | 3-1 | 1-1 | 4000 | S Hughes,L Johnson,Evans |
| 37 | 11 | Port Vale Res. | L | 0-7 | 0-2 | | |
| 38 | 13 | STALYBRIDGE CELTIC | L | 0-3 | 0-1 | | |
| 39 | 15 | Nantwich | D | 1-1 | 0-1 | | S. Hughes |
| 40 | 18 | Middlewich | L | 2-4 | 1-2 | | Clough (2) |
| 41 | 20 | Northwich Vics. | L | 2-7 | 0-4 | | Massey, Lightburn |
| 42 | 27 | Winsford United | L | 0-4 | 0-1 | | |

## F.A. CUP

| | Date | Opposition | | FT | HT | Att. | Goalscorers |
|---|---|---|---|---|---|---|---|
| PQ | Sep 20 | Witton Albion | L | 0-2 | 0-1 | | |

## FRIENDLIES

| | Date | Opposition | | FT | HT | Att. | Goalscorers |
|---|---|---|---|---|---|---|---|
| 1 | Oct 4 | BOLTON WANDERERS 'A' | L | 0-3 | | | |

Final League Table

| | | P | W | D | L | F | A | Pts |
|---|---|---|---|---|---|---|---|---|
| 1 | Port Vale Res. | 42 | 25 | 10 | 7 | 112 | 43 | 60 |
| 2 | Northwich Victoria | 42 | 25 | 6 | 11 | 94 | 58 | 56 |
| 3 | Stalybridge Celtic | 42 | 24 | 7 | 11 | 92 | 52 | 55 |
| 4 | Ashton National | 42 | 24 | 6 | 12 | 94 | 50 | 54 |
| 5 | Hurst | 42 | 22 | 10 | 10 | 101 | 61 | 54 |
| 6 | Macclesfield | 42 | 21 | 6 | 15 | 79 | 77 | 48 |
| 7 | Tranmere Rovers Res. | 42 | 21 | 5 | 16 | 106 | 79 | 47 |
| 8 | Crewe Alexandra Res. | 42 | 20 | 5 | 17 | 91 | 68 | 45 |
| 9 | Mossley | 42 | 17 | 8 | 17 | 85 | 83 | 42 |
| 10 | Winsford United | 42 | 18 | 6 | 18 | 85 | 87 | 42 |
| 11 | Middlewich | 42 | 18 | 6 | 18 | 67 | 71 | 42 |
| 12 | Altrincham | 42 | 16 | 7 | 19 | 70 | 93 | 39 |
| 13 | Manchester North End | 42 | 15 | 7 | 20 | 96 | 95 | 37 |
| 14 | Congleton Town | 42 | 14 | 8 | 20 | 77 | 93 | 36 |
| 15 | Whitchurch | 42 | 12 | 12 | 18 | 55 | 86 | 36 |
| 16 | Sandbach Ramblers | 42 | 12 | 11 | 19 | 57 | 81 | 35 |
| **17** | **Chester** | **42** | **14** | **7** | **21** | **59** | **103** | **35** |
| 18 | Witton Albion | 42 | 13 | 7 | 22 | 59 | 82 | 33 |
| 19 | Nantwich | 42 | 12 | 9 | 21 | 72 | 102 | 33 |
| 20 | Runcorn | 42 | 14 | 5 | 23 | 62 | 94 | 33 |
| 21 | Ellesmere Port Cement | 42 | 13 | 6 | 23 | 67 | 84 | 32 |
| 22 | Ellesmere Port Town | 42 | 12 | 6 | 24 | 56 | 88 | 30 |

# *SEASON 1925-26*

## CHESHIRE COUNTY LEAGUE

| | Date | Opposition | | FT | HT | Att. | Goalscorers |
|---|---|---|---|---|---|---|---|
| 1 | Aug 29 | MACCLESFIELD | W | 4-0 | 3-0 | 2000 | Peters, Regan, Jackson, Bingham |
| 2 | Sep 1 | Ashton National | L | 2-3 | 2-1 | 3000 | Rainford (og), Mills |
| 3 | 5 | NANTWICH | W | 2-1 | 1-0 | | Tilley, Ankers |
| 4 | 9 | WITTON ALBION | W | 4-0 | 1-0 | 1500 | Proctor, Tilley (2), Bingham |
| 5 | 12 | Nantwich | L | 1-2 | 1-2 | | Tilley |
| 6 | 16 | Witton Albion | L | 0-4 | 0-3 | | |
| 7 | 26 | Congleton Town | W | 2-1 | 1-1 | | Owens, Peters |
| 8 | Oct 10 | Port Vale Res. | D | 3-3 | 1-2 | 5000 | Owens, Peters, Bingham |
| 9 | 24 | Runcorn | L | 1-3 | 1-1 | | Rothwell |
| 10 | Nov 7 | MOSSLEY | D | 2-2 | 0-1 | 837 | Ankers, Caulfield |
| 11 | 14 | Ellesmere Port Town | W | 3-2 | 2-1 | | Parkin (2), Duckworth |
| 12 | 21 | CREWE ALEX. RES. | W | 2-1 | 1-1 | 2000 | Parkin, Peters |
| 13 | 28 | NORTHWICH VICS. | W | 3-0 | 2-0 | | Parkin, Rothwell, Peters |
| 14 | Dec 5 | Winsford United | W | 6-5 | 2-3 | | Duckworth,Bingham, Brittleton(og), Rothwell, Peters, Ankers |
| 15 | 12 | MANCHESTER N. E. | W | 5-2 | 2-2 | 1500 | Peters (2), Richardson, Parkin, Bingham |
| 16 | 25 | SANDBACH RAMBLERS | W | 3-1 | 2-0 | 3000 | Rothwell, Bingham, Peters |
| 17 | Jan 1 | Eccles United | W | 5-2 | 4-0 | | Rothwell (3), Parkin (2) |
| 18 | 2 | Tranmere R. Res. | W | 2-0 | 1-0 | | Ankers, Bingham |
| 19 | 9 | PORT VALE RES. | W | 3-1 | 3-0 | 6000 | Ankers, Peters, Bingham |
| 20 | 16 | Whitchurch | W | 3-1 | 1-1 | 1000 | Peters, Parkin (2) |
| 21 | 30 | TRANMERE R. RES. | W | 6-1 | 3-0 | 2000 | Rothwell(2), Ankers, Parkin, Duckworth, Bingham |
| 22 | Feb 6 | Manchester N. E. | W | 5-2 | 1-2 | | Bingham, Parkin (2), Peters, Rothwell |
| 23 | 13 | RUNCORN | W | 4-1 | 2-0 | 2500 | Parkin (2), Rothwell, Peters |
| 24 | 20 | Hurst | L | 0-3 | 0-3 | | |
| 25 | 24 | ELLESMERE PORT TOWN | W | 5-2 | 3-2 | | Peters (3), Parkin, Rothwell |
| 26 | 27 | HURST | D | 2-2 | 1-0 | 3000 | Peters, Jackson |
| 27 | Mar 6 | Middlewich | L | 0-1 | 0-1 | | |
| 28 | 13 | Northwich Vics. | W | 3-0 | 1-0 | 2000 | Owens (2), Parkin |
| 29 | 20 | MIDDLEWICH | W | 2-0 | 2-0 | | Owens, Duckworth |
| 30 | 24 | ALTRINCHAM | W | 4-0 | 2-0 | | Ankers, Peters, Barton, Rothwell |
| 31 | 27 | WINSFORD UNITED | W | 2-1 | 2-1 | | Ankers, Parkin |
| 32 | 30 | Stalybridge Celtic | L | 2-3 | 1-0 | | Owens, Jackson |
| 33 | Apr 2 | WHITCHURCH | W | 4-1 | 3-1 | 5964 | Rothwell, Peters, Bingham, Owens |
| 34 | 3 | Mossley | D | 0-0 | 0-0 | | |
| 35 | 5 | ECCLES UNITED | W | 3-0 | 1-0 | 5000 | Ankers, Jackson (2) |
| 36 | 10 | Sandbach Ramblers | W | 2-1 | 0-0 | | Rothwell, Bingham |
| 37 | 14 | Altrincham | W | 1-0 | 1-0 | | Parkin |
| 38 | 17 | CONGLETON TOWN | W | 2-0 | 1-0 | | Owens, Parkin |
| 39 | 21 | Macclesfield | L | 0-2 | 0-1 | | |
| 40 | 24 | ASHTON NATIONAL | D | 2-2 | 1-1 | | Owens, Ankers |
| 41 | 26 | Crewe Alex. Res. | W | 3-0 | 1-0 | 1500 | Richardson, Jones (og), Jackson |
| 42 | May 1 | STALYBRIDGE CELTIC | W | 2-1 | 1-1 | | Caulfield, Bingham |

## F.A. CUP

| | Date | Opposition | | FT | HT | Att. | Goalscorers |
|---|---|---|---|---|---|---|---|
| PQ | Sep 19 | Llandudno | D | 0-0 | 0-0 | 1500 | |
| PQr | 23 | LLANDUDNO | W | 2-1 | 1-1 | 2000 | Tilley, Peters |
| Q1 | Oct 3 | SANDBACH RAMBLERS | W | 2-0 | 1-0 | 3000 | Ankers, Peters |
| Q2 | 17 | WITTON ALBION | D | 2-2 | 0-1 | 3500 | Caulfield (2) |
| Q2r | 21 | Witton Albion | W | 4-2 | 3-1 | 2000 | Ankers, Rigg, Owens, Caulfield |
| Q3 | 31 | MOLD | D | 2-2 | 0-1 | 6500 | Caulfield, Jackson |
| Q3r | Nov 5 | Mold | L | 0-5 | 0-0 | 4000 | |

## FRIENDLIES

| | Date | Opposition | | FT | HT | Att. | Goalscorers |
|---|---|---|---|---|---|---|---|
| 1 | Dec 26 | ELLESMERE PORT TOWN | W | 3-0 | 2-0 | 3000 | Peters, Richardson, Bingham |
| 2 | Mar 10 | WREXHAM | W | 2-0 | 1-0 | | Rothwell, Caulfield |

Final League Table

| | | P | W | D | L | F | A | Pts |
|---|---|---|---|---|---|---|---|---|
| **1** | **Chester** | **42** | **29** | **5** | **8** | **110** | **57** | **63** |
| 2 | Port Vale Reserves | 42 | 26 | 6 | 10 | 115 | 58 | 58 |
| 3 | Congleton Town | 42 | 25 | 6 | 11 | 125 | 74 | 56 |
| 4 | Stalybridge Celtic | 42 | 24 | 4 | 14 | 133 | 77 | 52 |
| 5 | Witton Albion | 42 | 21 | 8 | 13 | 121 | 85 | 50 |
| 6 | Ashton National | 42 | 20 | 8 | 14 | 98 | 84 | 48 |
| 7 | Winsford United | 42 | 22 | 3 | 17 | 96 | 87 | 47 |
| 8 | Nantwich | 42 | 19 | 9 | 14 | 90 | 90 | 47 |
| 9 | Tranmere Rovers Res. | 42 | 17 | 11 | 14 | 104 | 97 | 45 |
| 10 | Manchester North End | 42 | 18 | 7 | 17 | 92 | 111 | 43 |
| 11 | Crewe Alexandra Res. | 42 | 18 | 6 | 18 | 96 | 75 | 42 |
| 12 | Runcorn | 42 | 19 | 4 | 19 | 79 | 92 | 42 |
| 13 | Hurst | 42 | 16 | 9 | 17 | 114 | 95 | 41 |
| 14 | Mossley | 42 | 14 | 8 | 20 | 80 | 106 | 36 |
| 15 | Ellesmere Port Town | 42 | 16 | 4 | 22 | 73 | 107 | 36 |
| 16 | Altrincham | 42 | 15 | 4 | 23 | 85 | 94 | 34 |
| 17 | Sandbach Ramblers | 42 | 14 | 6 | 22 | 81 | 92 | 34 |
| 18 | Northwich Victoria | 42 | 14 | 5 | 23 | 75 | 101 | 33 |
| 19 | Whitchurch | 42 | 14 | 4 | 24 | 85 | 124 | 32 |
| 20 | Macclesfield | 42 | 12 | 8 | 22 | 88 | 142 | 32 |
| 21 | Middlewich | 42 | 13 | 4 | 25 | 76 | 120 | 30 |
| 22 | Eccles United | 42 | 9 | 5 | 28 | 84 | 132 | 23 |

**1924-25 Season:**
(Back) Barton, Whitehead, Shaw, (Middle) Fleetwood, Hughes, Williams. (Front) Taylor, Booth, Mokhtar, Parker, Thompson.

**1925-26 Season:** Unnamed Team group

# SEASON 1926-27

## CHESHIRE COUNTY LEAGUE

| | Date | Opposition | | FT | HT | Att. | Goalscorers |
|---|---|---|---|---|---|---|---|
| 1 | Aug 28 | Tranmere R. Res. | W | 4-3 | 2-1 | 5000 | Burley (2), Bingham, Peers |
| 2 | 31 | Hurst | W | 4-0 | 0-0 | | Burley (2), Peters, Peers |
| 3 | Sep 4 | NANTWICH | W | 5-0 | 4-0 | 4000 | Burley (3), Jackson, Peters |
| 4 | 6 | Ashton National | L | 1-2 | 1-1 | | Bingham |
| 5 | 11 | CONGLETON TOWN | W | 3-0 | 3-0 | | Bingham, Burley, Peters |
| 6 | 22 | WITTON ALBION | W | 3-2 | 3-1 | | Burley (3) |
| 7 | 25 | MOSSLEY | W | 3-1 | 2-1 | | Bingham, Burley (2) |
| 8 | 29 | MIDDLEWICH | W | 8-3 | 3-2 | 3000 | Burley (5), Rothwell (2), Duckworth |
| 9 | Oct 2 | Macclesfield | L | 2-4 | 1-3 | 5000 | Burley, Blinko |
| 10 | 9 | ECCLES UNITED | W | 5-1 | 2-1 | | Burley (4), Peters |
| 11 | 16 | Northwich Vics. | W | 3-0 | 0-0 | 2500 | Burley (2), Buckley (og) |
| 12 | 23 | MANCHESTER N. E. | W | 4-1 | 2-1 | | Bingham, Blinko, Rothwell (2) |
| 13 | 30 | Eccles United | W | 4-3 | 0-0 | 1600 | Yearsley (3), Peters |
| 14 | Nov 6 | RUNCORN | W | 9-1 | 4-1 | 3000 | Yearsley (5), Peters (2), Wagstaffe, Bingham |
| 15 | 13 | Port Vale Res. | L | 5-6 | 3-4 | | Rothwell (2), Bingham, Ankers, Yearsley |
| 16 | 20 | SANDBACH RAMBLERS | W | 5-1 | 5-0 | | Yearsley (2), Bingham (2), Peters |
| 17 | Dec 4 | ASHTON NATIONAL | W | 3-0 | 0-0 | | Yearsley, Rothwell, Peel |
| 18 | 18 | Congleton Town | L | 0-4 | 0-2 | | |
| 19 | 25 | ELLESMERE PORT TOWN | W | 5-2 | 3-0 | 4000 | Bingham, Rigg, Yearsley, Rothwell, Peters |
| 20 | 27 | TRANMERE R. RES. | W | 3-1 | 3-0 | 4800 | Jackson, Bingham, Yearsley |
| 21 | Jan 1 | Runcorn | L | 1-5 | 1-1 | 6000 | Rothwell |
| 22 | 8 | MACCLESFIELD | W | 4-1 | 3-1 | | Yearsley (2), Rothwell, Bingham |
| 23 | 15 | Sandbach Ramblers | W | 2-1 | 0-1 | | Ankers, Rothwell |
| 24 | 29 | Manchester N. E. | L | 1-4 | 1-1 | 4000 | Tootle |
| 25 | Feb 5 | Crewe Alex. Res. | W | 2-1 | 1-1 | 5300 | Yearsley, Jackson |
| 26 | 12 | Middlewich | W | 3-0 | 1-0 | | Yearsley (2), Rothwell |
| 27 | 26 | CREWE ALEX RES. | W | 2-0 | 2-0 | 2000 | Yearsley, Peters |
| 28 | Mar 5 | Nantwich | W | 4-1 | 1-0 | | Yearsley (2), Ankers, Rothwell |
| 29 | 12 | Winsford United | W | 3-1 | 2-0 | | Yearsley (2), Peters |
| 30 | 19 | ALTRINCHAM | W | 4-2 | 3-0 | | Yearsley (2), Ankers, Peters |
| 31 | 26 | Stalybridge Celtic | L | 3-4 | 3-2 | | Yearsley, Davies, Peters |
| 32 | Apr 2 | STALYBRIDGE CELTIC | D | 1-1 | 1-1 | | Ankers |
| 33 | 6 | Altrincham | L | 1-2 | 1-1 | | Peters |
| 34 | 9 | Mossley | W | 3-2 | 0-0 | | Rothwell (2), Grimwood (og) |
| 35 | 15 | WHITCHURCH | W | 4-0 | 0-0 | 4000 | Rothwell (2), Ankers, Bingham |
| 36 | 16 | Ellesmere Port Town | W | 7-0 | 3-0 | | Yearsley (5), Pollock, Duckworth |
| 37 | 18 | HURST | D | 1-1 | 1-1 | 4000 | Yearsley |
| 38 | 20 | Witton Albion | W | 3-1 | 1-1 | | Yearsley (2), Pollock |
| 39 | 23 | WINSFORD UNITED | W | 4-1 | 1-0 | | Peers, Walsh (og), Yearsley (2) |
| 40 | 27 | Whitchurch | W | 5-0 | 0-0 | | Peers (2), Yearsley (2), Tootle |
| 41 | 30 | PORT VALE RES. | D | 3-3 | 3-2 | | Smith, Peers, Yearsley |
| 42 | May 7 | NORTHWICH VICS. | W | 7-1 | 0-1 | | Yearsley (5), Peters, Jackson |

## F.A. CUP

| | Date | Opposition | | FT | HT | Att. | Goalscorers |
|---|---|---|---|---|---|---|---|
| PQ | Sep 18 | LLANDUDNO | L | 0-2 | 0-0 | | |

## FRIENDLIES

| | Date | Opposition | | FT | HT | Att. | Goalscorers |
|---|---|---|---|---|---|---|---|
| 1 | May 4 | CONNAH'S QUAY * | L | 3-5 | | | Blinko (2), C Jones |

* Infirmary Benefit

**1926-27 Season:** Unnamed Team Group.

# SEASON 1927-28

## CHESHIRE COUNTY LEAGUE

| | Date | Opposition | | FT | HT | Att. | Goalscorers |
|---|---|---|---|---|---|---|---|
| 1 | Aug 27 | PORT VALE RES. | W | 4-1 | 2-1 | 3000 | Jackson, Rothwell, Roberts, Tootle |
| 2 | 29 | Port Vale Res. | L | 1-3 | 0-1 | | Ankers |
| 3 | Sep 3 | Witton Albion | L | 0-2 | 0-2 | 1000 | |
| 4 | 7 | Whitchurch | W | 1-0 | 1-0 | | Ankers |
| 5 | 10 | CONGLETON TOWN | D | 1-1 | 1-0 | | Yearsley |
| 6 | 21 | Ashton National | W | 2-1 | 1-1 | | Jenkins, Randles |
| 7 | 24 | STOCKPORT CO. RES. | L | 1-4 | 0-1 | | Jenkins |
| 8 | Oct 8 | Winsford United | W | 2-0 | 2-0 | | Bingham, Yearsley |
| 9 | 22 | Crewe Alex. Res. | L | 0-3 | 0-1 | | |
| 10 | 29 | SANDBACH RAMBLERS | W | 5-1 | 3-0 | | Yearsley (4), F Jones |
| 11 | Nov 5 | Hurst | L | 2-5 | 0-3 | | Pollock, Jenkins |
| 12 | 12 | NORTHWICH VICS. | W | 8-2 | 3-2 | | Yearsley, Jenkins, Pollock, Rothwell, Bingham, Bimson, F Jones (2) |
| 13 | 19 | Sandbach Ramblers | W | 3-1 | 1-0 | | Boardman, Yearsley (2) |
| 14 | 26 | ECCLES UNITED | W | 6-0 | 5-0 | | Bimson, Rothwell (2), Yearsley (3) |
| 15 | Dec 3 | Nantwich | W | 5-2 | 2-1 | | Yearsley (5) |
| 16 | 17 | WITTON ALBION | L | 1-3 | 0-0 | | Pollock |
| 17 | 24 | Eccles United | W | 3-1 | 0-0 | | Craig, Rothwell, Etherington |
| 18 | 26 | CREWE ALEX. RES. | W | 1-0 | 0-0 | | Tootle |
| 19 | 27 | RUNCORN | W | 5-2 | 3-0 | | Craig (2), Yearsley, Rothwell, Bimson |
| 20 | 31 | Northwich Vics. | L | 0-1 | 0-1 | | |
| 21 | Jan 2 | Runcorn | D | 1-1 | 1-1 | | Peters |
| 22 | 14 | Tranmere R. Res. | W | 6-1 | 4-1 | | Yearsley (2), Peters (2), Bimson, Etherington |
| 23 | 21 | WINSFORD UNITED | W | 7-3 | 3-2 | | Yearsley (4), Peters, Bimson (2) |
| 24 | 28 | Altrincham | W | 7-2 | 4-0 | | Yearsley (2), Pollock (2), Etherington (2), Bimson |
| 25 | Feb 4 | ALTRINCHAM | W | 4-2 | 0-2 | | Yearsley (2), Tootle, Johnson (og) |
| 26 | 18 | MOSSLEY | W | 4-1 | 1-0 | | Yearsley (2), Etherington (2) |
| 27 | 25 | NANTWICH | W | 6-3 | 2-1 | | Peters (3), Rothwell (2), Yearsley |
| 28 | Mar 3 | Middlewich | L | 1-4 | 0-1 | | Rothwell |
| 29 | 17 | STALYBRIDGE CELTIC | L | 0-1 | 0-0 | | |
| 30 | 24 | ASHTON NATIONAL | W | 7-3 | 3-1 | | Yearsley (3), Keedwell (2), Boardman, Peters |
| 31 | 31 | Stockport Co. Res. | D | 2-2 | 0-1 | | Keedwell, Boardman |
| 32 | Apr 6 | WHITCHURCH | W | 8-0 | 6-0 | | Keedwell (4), Yearsley (2), Boardman, Peters |
| 33 | 7 | Stalybridge Celtic | D | 1-1 | 1-1 | | Boardman |
| 34 | 9 | HURST | L | 1-2 | 1-0 | | Yearsley |
| 35 | 14 | Macclesfield | L | 0-2 | 0-2 | | |
| 36 | 18 | MANCHESTER N. E. | D | 1-1 | 0-1 | 877 | Peters |
| 37 | 21 | MACCLESFIELD | W | 4-1 | 4-0 | 819 | Tootle, Keedwell, Peters, Ankers |
| 38 | 23 | Congleton Town | W | 1-0 | 0-0 | | Ankers |
| 39 | 25 | MIDDLEWICH | W | 4-1 | 2-1 | | Rothwell (2), Yearsley (2) |
| 40 | 28 | Manchester N. E. | L | 2-6 | 1-2 | | Keedwell, Peters |
| 41 | May 2 | Mossley | L | 0-1 | 0-1 | | |
| 42 | 7 | TRANMERE R. RES. | D | 2-2 | 0-2 | | Yearsley, Ankers |

## F.A. CUP

| | Date | Opposition | | FT | HT | Att. | Goalscorers |
|---|---|---|---|---|---|---|---|
| PQ | Sep 17 | LOSTOCK GRALAM | W | 10-1 | 4-0 | | Yearsley (4), Peters (3), Davies (2), Ankers |
| Q1 | Oct 1 | WINSFORD UNITED | W | 4-0 | 1-0 | | Yearsley (3), Bimson |
| Q2 | 15 | Bangor City | L | 0-1 | 0-1 | | |

## Final League Table: 1926-27

| | | P | W | D | L | F | A | Pts |
|---|---|---|---|---|---|---|---|---|
| **1** | **Chester** | **42** | **31** | **3** | **8** | **147** | **67** | **65** |
| 2 | Ashton National | 42 | 29 | 4 | 9 | 119 | 63 | 62 |
| 3 | Tranmere Rovers Res. | 42 | 28 | 4 | 10 | 163 | 72 | 60 |
| 4 | Congleton Town | 42 | 27 | 5 | 10 | 125 | 59 | 59 |
| 5 | Stalybridge Celtic | 42 | 26 | 6 | 10 | 136 | 79 | 58 |
| 6 | Crewe Alexandra Res. | 42 | 26 | 6 | 10 | 118 | 81 | 58 |
| 7 | Port Vale Reserves | 42 | 24 | 5 | 13 | 119 | 74 | 53 |
| 8 | Manchester North End | 42 | 24 | 3 | 15 | 156 | 90 | 51 |
| 9 | Altrincham | 42 | 20 | 7 | 15 | 129 | 108 | 47 |
| 10 | Runcorn | 42 | 19 | 7 | 16 | 94 | 101 | 45 |
| 11 | Macclesfield | 42 | 19 | 5 | 18 | 113 | 112 | 43 |
| 12 | Nantwich | 42 | 16 | 10 | 16 | 95 | 86 | 42 |
| 13 | Winsford United | 42 | 18 | 5 | 19 | 120 | 97 | 41 |
| 14 | Middlewich | 42 | 15 | 6 | 21 | 99 | 132 | 36 |
| 15 | Witton Albion | 42 | 13 | 6 | 23 | 79 | 108 | 32 |
| 16 | Eccles United | 42 | 10 | 9 | 23 | 84 | 127 | 29 |
| 17 | Mossley | 42 | 11 | 7 | 24 | 88 | 146 | 29 |
| 18 | Northwich Victoria | 42 | 11 | 4 | 27 | 70 | 141 | 26 |
| 19 | Whitchurch | 42 | 10 | 6 | 26 | 62 | 134 | 26 |
| 20 | Hurst | 42 | 8 | 6 | 28 | 65 | 119 | 22 |
| 21 | Sandbach Ramblers | 42 | 7 | 7 | 28 | 59 | 124 | 21 |
| 22 | Ellesmere Port Town | 42 | 8 | 3 | 31 | 77 | 196 | 19 |

## Final League Table: 1927-28

| | | P | W | D | L | F | A | Pts |
|---|---|---|---|---|---|---|---|---|
| 1 | Port Vale Reserves | 42 | 31 | 5 | 6 | 147 | 48 | 67 |
| 2 | Stockport County Res. | 42 | 26 | 9 | 7 | 158 | 81 | 61 |
| 3 | Ashton National | 42 | 28 | 5 | 9 | 145 | 78 | 61 |
| 4 | Congleton Town | 42 | 26 | 7 | 9 | 105 | 60 | 59 |
| **5** | **Chester** | **42** | **23** | **6** | **13** | **120** | **73** | **52** |
| 6 | Winsford United | 42 | 21 | 9 | 12 | 122 | 101 | 51 |
| 7 | Stalybridge Celtic | 42 | 21 | 6 | 15 | 120 | 93 | 48 |
| 8 | Runcorn | 42 | 19 | 10 | 13 | 86 | 81 | 48 |
| 9 | Manchester North End | 42 | 20 | 7 | 15 | 133 | 101 | 47 |
| 10 | Hurst | 42 | 19 | 7 | 16 | 105 | 101 | 45 |
| 11 | Tranmere Rovers Res. | 42 | 21 | 3 | 18 | 104 | 101 | 45 |
| 12 | Crewe Alexandra Res. | 42 | 17 | 9 | 16 | 112 | 98 | 43 |
| 13 | Witton Albion | 42 | 18 | 7 | 17 | 89 | 98 | 43 |
| 14 | Middlewich | 42 | 15 | 8 | 19 | 87 | 102 | 38 |
| 15 | Sandbach Ramblers | 42 | 13 | 8 | 21 | 89 | 101 | 34 |
| 16 | Nantwich | 42 | 15 | 3 | 24 | 103 | 133 | 33 |
| 17 | Macclesfield | 42 | 13 | 5 | 24 | 75 | 117 | 31 |
| 18 | Northwich Victoria | 42 | 10 | 9 | 23 | 88 | 136 | 29 |
| 19 | Mossley | 42 | 12 | 5 | 25 | 86 | 138 | 29 |
| 20 | Altrincham | 42 | 10 | 4 | 28 | 77 | 146 | 24 |
| 21 | Whitchurch | 42 | 8 | 2 | 32 | 77 | 166 | 18 |
| 22 | Eccles United | 42 | 7 | 4 | 31 | 64 | 153 | 18 |

# SEASON 1928-29

## CHESHIRE COUNTY LEAGUE

| | Date | Opposition | | FT | HT | Att. | Goalscorers |
|---|---|---|---|---|---|---|---|
| 1 | Aug 23 | PORT VALE RES. | L | 0-2 | 0-2 | 2493 | |
| 2 | Sep 1 | Port Vale Res. | L | 2-3 | 2-1 | | Ecclestone (2) |
| 3 | 6 | Tranmere R. Res. | W | 2-0 | 1-0 | | Burley (2) |
| 4 | 8 | STALYBRIDGE CELTIC | W | 3-1 | 2-0 | 1472 | Burley (2), Pollock |
| 5 | 22 | MACCLESFIELD | W | 3-0 | 3-0 | 2142 | Burley (2), Birtles |
| 6 | 29 | Middlewich | L | 0-2 | 0-2 | | |
| 7 | Oct 6 | Stalybridge Celtic | L | 2-3 | 0-0 | | Birtles, Burley |
| 8 | 13 | ASHTON NATIONAL | W | 2-0 | 1-0 | 2363 | Peters, Burley |
| 9 | 20 | MANCHESTER N. E. | L | 3-4 | 3-0 | | Peters (2), Birtles |
| 10 | 27 | Crewe Alex. Res. | W | 3-0 | 2-0 | 2000 | Birtles (2), Burley |
| 11 | Nov 3 | ALTRINCHAM | W | 4-2 | 3-0 | | Burley (2), Walsh, Ankers |
| 12 | 10 | Winsford United | L | 1-4 | 0-4 | | Burley |
| 13 | 17 | MIDDLEWICH | W | 5-0 | 3-0 | | Ankers (3), Birtles, McConnachie |
| 14 | 24 | Northwich Vics. | D | 1-1 | 1-1 | | Lloyd (og) |
| 15 | Dec 1 | WINSFORD UNITED | W | 3-1 | 1-1 | | Schofield (2), Peters |
| 16 | 15 | Congleton Town | L | 1-5 | 1-2 | | Davies |
| 17 | 22 | Hurst | L | 3-6 | 1-6 | | Schofield, Peters, McConnachie |
| 18 | 25 | SANDBACH RAMBLERS | W | 4-3 | 1-1 | | Gregson, Schofield (2), Birtles |
| 19 | 26 | RUNCORN | W | 3-0 | 2-0 | | Schofield (2), Walsh |
| 20 | 29 | Witton Albion | L | 1-3 | 0-1 | | Schofield |
| 21 | Jan 1 | Runcorn | D | 2-2 | 1-0 | | Ankers, Peters |
| 22 | 5 | WITTON ALBION | W | 4-0 | 2-0 | | Schofield (2), Ankers, Tootle |
| 23 | 26 | Ashton National | L | 1-5 | 0-3 | 5000 | Ankers |
| 24 | Feb 1 | TRANMERE R. RES. | D | 5-5 | 2-3 | | Ankers,Tootle,Birtles,Rothwell,Davies |
| 25 | 23 | Macclesfield | L | 3-4 | 2-1 | | Davies, Birtles, Ankers |
| 26 | Mar 9 | NORTHWICH VICS. | W | 4-0 | 1-0 | | Southall (3), Ankers |
| 27 | 16 | Altrincham | D | 1-1 | 1-0 | | Walsh |
| 28 | 23 | NANTWICH | W | 6-0 | 2-0 | | Southall(2),Peters(2),Birtles,Ramage |
| 29 | 29 | WHITCHURCH | W | 3-0 | 1-0 | 3000 | Southall, Davies, Birtles |
| 30 | 30 | Mossley | W | 4-2 | 2-2 | | Peters (2), Southall, Birtles |
| 31 | Apr 1 | HURST | L | 0-2 | 0-2 | | |
| 32 | 6 | Manchester N. E. | D | 1-1 | 1-0 | | Ankers |
| 33 | 17 | Whitchurch | L | 1-5 | 0-1 | | Ankers |
| 34 | 20 | CREWE ALEX. RES. | W | 5-2 | 3-0 | | Walsh,Buckley,Ramage,Peters,Rose |
| 35 | 24 | CONGLETON TOWN | W | 6-2 | 2-2 | | Ankers (3), Peters, Ramage, Hopkins |
| 36 | 27 | MOSSLEY | W | 3-0 | 0-0 | | Ramage, Peters, Rose |
| 37 | May 1 | Nantwich | W | 4-1 | 1-1 | | Birtles, Buckley (2), Rose |
| 38 | 4 | Sandbach Ramblers | L | 0-3 | 0-2 | | |

### F.A. CUP

| | Date | Opposition | | FT | HT | Att. | Goalscorers |
|---|---|---|---|---|---|---|---|
| PQ | Sep 15 | Northwich Vics. | L | 1-3 | 0-1 | 2365 | Rothwell |

### WELSH CUP

| | Date | Opposition | | FT | HT | Att. | Goalscorers |
|---|---|---|---|---|---|---|---|
| 3R | Jan 19 | OSWESTRY TOWN | D | 1-1 | 0-1 | 3000 | Birtles |
| 3Rr | 24 | Oswestry Town * | W | 5-4 | 3-1 | 2000 | Ankers (3), Birtles, Schofield |
| 4R | Feb 19 | BUCKLEY | L | 2-5 | 1-1 | | Ankers, Birtles |

* Extra time played following score of 4-4 after 90 minutes

Final League Table

| | | P | W | D | L | F | A | Pts |
|---|---|---|---|---|---|---|---|---|
| 1 | Port Vale Reserves | 38 | 24 | 6 | 8 | 121 | 64 | 54 |
| 2 | Ashton National | 38 | 23 | 5 | 10 | 115 | 70 | 51 |
| 3 | Winsford United | 38 | 22 | 7 | 9 | 109 | 74 | 51 |
| 4 | Congleton Town | 38 | 21 | 7 | 10 | 97 | 76 | 49 |
| 5 | Manchester North End | 38 | 20 | 8 | 10 | 122 | 81 | 48 |
| 6 | Tranmere Rovers Res. | 38 | 18 | 8 | 12 | 128 | 88 | 44 |
| 7 | Stalybridge Celtic | 38 | 19 | 6 | 13 | 92 | 75 | 44 |
| **8** | **Chester** | **38** | **19** | **5** | **14** | **99** | **75** | **43** |
| 9 | Crewe Alexandra Res. | 38 | 18 | 5 | 15 | 92 | 84 | 41 |
| 10 | Macclesfield | 38 | 17 | 3 | 18 | 94 | 93 | 37 |
| 11 | Runcorn | 38 | 13 | 11 | 14 | 86 | 94 | 37 |
| 12 | Hurst | 38 | 14 | 8 | 16 | 126 | 119 | 36 |
| 13 | Mossley | 38 | 14 | 8 | 16 | 89 | 93 | 36 |
| 14 | Northwich Victoria | 38 | 13 | 7 | 18 | 85 | 90 | 33 |
| 15 | Sandbach Ramblers | 38 | 14 | 2 | 22 | 101 | 116 | 30 |
| 16 | Whitchurch | 38 | 13 | 4 | 21 | 96 | 115 | 30 |
| 17 | Witton Albion | 38 | 9 | 12 | 17 | 62 | 82 | 30 |
| 18 | Middlewich | 38 | 11 | 4 | 23 | 51 | 125 | 26 |
| 19 | Altrincham | 38 | 8 | 7 | 23 | 74 | 128 | 23 |
| 20 | Nantwich | 38 | 8 | 1 | 29 | 62 | 159 | 17 |

# SEASON 1929-30

## CHESHIRE COUNTY LEAGUE

| | Date | Opposition | | FT | HT | Att. | Goalscorers |
|---|---|---|---|---|---|---|---|
| 1 | Aug 31 | Stalybridge Celtic | L | 4-5 | 1-2 | 4000 | Downey (2), Hopkins, Hicks |
| 2 | Sep 4 | MANCHESTER CENTRAL | L | 0-3 | 0-2 | 3000 | |
| 3 | 11 | Runcorn | L | 0-2 | 0-0 | | |
| 4 | 14 | Tranmere R. Res. | D | 2-2 | 1-2 | | Peters, Downey |
| 5 | 18 | WITTON ALBION | L | 3-4 | 1-1 | | Downey (2), Walsh |
| 6 | 21 | MIDDLEWICH | W | 6-3 | 3-2 | | Prince (2), Williams (2), Broome, Peters |
| 7 | 28 | Winsford United | W | 4-2 | 2-0 | | Hopkins (3), Williams |
| 8 | Oct 5 | Mossley | L | 0-3 | 0-3 | | |
| 9 | 12 | SANDBACH RAMBLERS | L | 2-5 | 1-1 | | Peters, Walsh |
| 10 | 19 | WINSFORD UNITED | W | 4-0 | 1-0 | | Peters, Williams, Hopkins, Broome |
| 11 | 26 | Manchester Central | W | 2-1 | 1-0 | 500 | Williams, Cash |
| 12 | Nov 2 | NORTHWICH VICS. | L | 1-3 | 1-2 | 3000 | Parkin |
| 13 | 9 | Manchester N. E. | W | 4-1 | 1-1 | | Broome (2), Bromage, Parkin |
| 14 | 16 | CONGLETON TOWN | W | 3-1 | 0-1 | | Shaw (2), Broome |
| 15 | 23 | Whitchurch | D | 3-3 | 2-1 | | Parkin, Jenkins, Broome |
| 16 | 30 | ALTRINCHAM | W | 13-2 | 8-1 | | Peters(6), Broome(3), Bromage(2), Parkin(2) |
| 17 | Dec 7 | Sandbach Ramblers | L | 3-4 | 2-2 | | Jenkins, Hopkins, Walsh |
| 18 | 14 | MANCHESTER N. E. | W | 3-2 | 2-1 | 500 | Peters (2), Broome |
| 19 | 21 | Northwich Vics. | W | 4-0 | 2-0 | | Broome (2), Jenkins, Shaw |
| 20 | 25 | TRANMERE R. RES. | L | 3-4 | 2-2 | | Rowe, Bromage, Parkin |
| 21 | 26 | HURST | D | 3-3 | 2-2 | | Broome, Walsh, Rowe |
| 22 | 28 | WHITCHURCH | W | 4-1 | 0-1 | | Jenkins, Broome, Parkin, Hopkins |
| 23 | Jan 1 | Hurst | W | 2-0 | 1-0 | 1500 | Hopkins, Bromage |
| 24 | 11 | Witton Albion | L | 0-2 | 0-0 | | |
| 25 | 18 | PORT VALE RES. | W | 3-2 | 0-1 | | Walsh (2), Shaw |
| 26 | 25 | Port Vale Res. | L | 0-7 | 0-4 | | |
| 27 | Feb 9 | MOSSLEY | W | 6-1 | 3-0 | | King (3), Peters, Hopkins, Broome |
| 28 | 16 | Ashton National | L | 1-5 | 0-2 | | Bromage |
| 29 | Mar 1 | NANTWICH | W | 4-1 | 2-0 | | King (2), Parkin, Peters |
| 30 | 8 | ASHTON NATIONAL | W | 4-1 | 2-1 | | Bromage (2), King (2) |
| 31 | 15 | Altrincham | L | 0-1 | 0-1 | | |
| 32 | 29 | Middlewich | L | 0-4 | 0-2 | | |
| 33 | Apr 5 | Macclesfield | L | 2-4 | 0-3 | 3000 | King (2) |
| 34 | 9 | Crewe Alex. Res. | L | 2-4 | 0-2 | | Bromage, Parkin |
| 35 | 12 | CREWE ALEX. RES. | D | 5-5 | 3-2 | | King (3), Broome, Walsh |
| 36 | 18 | CONNAH'S QUAY & S. | L | 1-4 | 0-1 | 5311 | Bromage |
| 37 | 19 | Connah's Quay & S. | L | 0-4 | 0-0 | | |
| 38 | 21 | STALYBRIDGE CELTIC | W | 5-1 | 3-0 | | Basnett, Parkin, Walsh (2), Bromage |
| 39 | 23 | RUNCORN | W | 6-2 | 2-1 | 372 | Basnett, Peters (2), King (2), Parkin |
| 40 | 26 | MACCLESFIELD | W | 4-2 | 2-1 | | Walsh (3), Holt (og) |
| 41 | 30 | Nantwich | L | 2-3 | 0-0 | | King, Lane |
| 42 | May 3 | Congleton Town | D | 2-2 | 2-2 | | Bromage, King |

### WELSH CUP

| | Date | Opposition | | FT | HT | Att. | Goalscorers |
|---|---|---|---|---|---|---|---|
| 3R | Feb 5 | Holywell Arcadians * | W | 2-1 | 1-1 | | Peters, Broome |
| 4R | Mar 5 | Colwyn Bay | D | 4-4 | 3-2 | | Bromage, Hopkin, Jenkins (2) |
| 4Rr | 19 | COLWYN BAY @ | L | 2-4 | 2-1 | | Hopkin, King |

* Played at Chester

@ Extra time played following score of 2-2 after 90 minutes

Final League Table

| | | P | W | D | L | F | A | Pts |
|---|---|---|---|---|---|---|---|---|
| 1 | Port Vale Reserves | 42 | 29 | 6 | 7 | 146 | 49 | 64 |
| 2 | Connah's Quay & Shotton | 42 | 30 | 3 | 9 | 148 | 59 | 63 |
| 3 | Tranmere Rovers Res. | 42 | 26 | 6 | 10 | 154 | 90 | 58 |
| 4 | Macclesfield | 42 | 24 | 7 | 11 | 139 | 109 | 55 |
| 5 | Ashton National | 42 | 24 | 4 | 14 | 118 | 70 | 52 |
| 6 | Stalybridge Celtic | 42 | 25 | 2 | 15 | 136 | 109 | 52 |
| 7 | Runcorn | 42 | 23 | 5 | 14 | 123 | 98 | 51 |
| 8 | Sandbach Ramblers | 42 | 21 | 5 | 16 | 112 | 108 | 47 |
| **9** | **Chester** | **42** | **18** | **5** | **19** | **120** | **109** | **41** |
| 10 | Mossley | 42 | 18 | 5 | 19 | 99 | 126 | 41 |
| 11 | Crewe Alexandra Res. | 42 | 15 | 10 | 17 | 99 | 115 | 40 |
| 12 | Northwich Victoria | 42 | 19 | 2 | 21 | 95 | 111 | 40 |
| 13 | Witton Albion | 42 | 15 | 8 | 19 | 105 | 120 | 38 |
| 14 | Winsford United | 42 | 16 | 5 | 21 | 105 | 128 | 37 |
| 15 | Manchester Cent. Res. | 42 | 15 | 4 | 23 | 92 | 125 | 34 |
| 16 | Manchester North End | 42 | 14 | 4 | 24 | 115 | 130 | 32 |
| 17 | Congleton Town | 42 | 11 | 10 | 21 | 69 | 92 | 32 |
| 18 | Whitchurch | 42 | 14 | 4 | 24 | 86 | 122 | 32 |
| 19 | Hurst | 42 | 14 | 2 | 26 | 96 | 130 | 30 |
| 20 | Nantwich | 42 | 12 | 5 | 25 | 69 | 112 | 29 |
| 21 | Middlewich | 42 | 12 | 5 | 25 | 70 | 125 | 29 |
| 22 | Altrincham | 42 | 12 | 3 | 27 | 81 | 140 | 27 |

# SEASON 1930-31

## CHESHIRE COUNTY LEAGUE

| | Date | Opposition | | FT | HT | Att. | Goalscorers |
|---|---|---|---|---|---|---|---|
| 1 | Aug 30 | NORTHWICH VICS. | W | 5-1 | 3-0 | 5479 | Clifford, Gale, Wilson, Cresswell (2) |
| 2 | Sep 3 | WITTON ALBION | W | 3-2 | 2-1 | 5323 | Gale, Wilson, Cresswell |
| 3 | 8 | Port Vale Res. | L | 0-4 | 0-1 | 4000 | |
| 4 | 13 | MANCHESTER CENTRAL | W | 4-0 | 2-0 | 4083 | Morris, Clifford, Gale, Dickie |
| 5 | 17 | Runcorn | D | 3-3 | 0-1 | 3000 | Gale (2), Clifford |
| 6 | 20 | Crewe Alex Res. | D | 1-1 | 1-1 | 3750 | Gale |
| 7 | 24 | ALTRINCHAM | D | 5-5 | 3-1 | 4708 | Cresswell (3), Gale, Clifford |
| 8 | 27 | Ashton National | W | 1-0 | 0-0 | 5000 | Gale |
| 9 | Oct 1 | WHITCHURCH | W | 10-2 | 5-2 | 3740 | Gale (8), Clifford, Morris |
| 10 | 4 | CONGLETON TOWN | W | 9-1 | 5-0 | 6388 | Gale(3),Burgess(2),Neale,Dickie,Clifford,Cresswell |
| 11 | 6 | Macclesfield | D | 2-2 | 1-2 | 5000 | Burgess, Cresswell |
| 12 | 11 | Witton Albion | W | 2-0 | 1-0 | | Gale (2) |
| 13 | 18 | Hyde United | W | 1-0 | 0-0 | 7000 | Gale |
| 14 | 25 | RUNCORN | L | 1-5 | 0-4 | 3394 | Clifford |
| 15 | Nov 1 | Connah's Quay & S. | W | 4-1 | 4-1 | 5373 | Clifford, Gale (2), Cresswell |
| 16 | 8 | SANDBACH RAMBLERS | W | 8-2 | 1-0 | 5171 | Gale (5), Cresswell , Dickie (2) |
| 17 | 15 | Winsford United | W | 4-1 | 1-1 | 3000 | Morris, Clifford, Gale, Cresswell |
| 18 | 22 | CONNAH'S QUAY & S. | W | 7-1 | 3-1 | 8014 | Cresswell (2), Gale (2), Clifford (2), Atkinson |
| 19 | 29 | MOSSLEY | W | 4-2 | 1-1 | 4365 | Gale (2), Burgess, Cresswell |
| 20 | Dec 6 | MANCHESTER N. E. | W | 9-0 | 6-0 | 4033 | Gale (5), Dickie (2), Cresswell, Morris |
| 21 | 13 | Whitchurch | W | 4-0 | 2-0 | 2500 | Cresswell (2), Morris, Dickie |
| 22 | 20 | Nantwich | W | 4-0 | 1-0 | | Gale, Cresswell, Dickie, Harris (og) |
| 23 | 25 | HYDE UNITED | W | 7-1 | 3-1 | 8313 | Gale (5), Irvine, Dickie |
| 24 | 26 | TRANMERE R. RES. | W | 9-0 | 4-0 | 7111 | Gale (5), Clifford, Cresswell, Dickie (2) |
| 25 | 27 | Northwich Vics. | W | 5-0 | 2-0 | 7500 | Gale (2), Clifford (2), Burgess |
| 26 | Jan 10 | CREWE ALEX. RES. | L | 1-2 | 0-0 | 5749 | Gale |
| 27 | 17 | Hurst | W | 5-2 | 3-1 | 5000 | Irvine (3), Gale (2) |
| 28 | 24 | NANTWICH | W | 5-1 | 2-0 | 4043 | Gale (2), Morris, Clifford, Irvine |
| 29 | Feb 7 | Tranmere R. Res. | W | 3-1 | 1-0 | 4000 | Gale, Cresswell, Dickie |
| 30 | 14 | WINSFORD UNITED | W | 7-2 | 4-2 | 4491 | Gale (4), Dickie (2), Hart |
| 31 | Mar 7 | ASHTON NATIONAL | D | 1-1 | 0-0 | 3570 | Cresswell |
| 32 | 21 | HURST | W | 5-1 | 1-1 | 4073 | Hart (2), Cresswell (2), Morris |
| 33 | 28 | STALYBRIDGE CELTIC | W | 6-2 | 2-2 | 2754 | Gale (3), Dickie (3) |
| 34 | Apr 3 | PORT VALE RES. | W | 2-0 | 2-0 | 13150 | Clifford, Gale |
| 35 | 4 | Altrincham | W | 1-0 | 1-0 | 8000 | Morris |
| 36 | 6 | MACCLESFIELD | W | 7-3 | 1-1 | 7000 | Irvine (2), Dickie (2), Morris, Cresswell, Gale |
| 37 | 16 | Mossley | W | 4-2 | 3-2 | 2500 | Cresswell (2), Gale, Irvine |
| 38 | 18 | Stalybridge Celtic | W | 3-1 | 1-0 | | Gale (3) |
| 39 | 20 | Manchester Central | W | 5-0 | 4-0 | | Burgess, Clifford, Irvine, Gale (2) |
| 40 | 25 | Manchester N. E. | L | 0-3 | 0-2 | 8000 | |
| 41 | 29 | Sandbach Ramblers | D | 2-2 | 0-0 | | Clifford, Cresswell |
| 42 | May 1 | Congleton Town | L | 1-2 | 1-1 | | Crawford |

## F.A. CUP

| | | | | | | | |
|---|---|---|---|---|---|---|---|
| EP | Sep 6 | Rhyl | L | 2-4 | 1-2 | 2000 | Wilson, Cresswell |

## WELSH CUP

| | | | | | | | |
|---|---|---|---|---|---|---|---|
| 3R | Jan 14 | CROSS STREET | W | 9-1 | 4-1 | 2303 | Neale (6), Clifford (2), Cresswell |
| 4R | Feb 4 | Llanfairfechan * | W | 11-2 | 6-1 | 2187 | Gale(7),Bennett,Morris,Neale,Evans(og) |
| 5R | Mar 4 | NEW BRIGHTON | D | 1-1 | 0-1 | 7212 | MacDonald (og) |
| 5Rr | 18 | NEW BRIGHTON | W | 4-2 | 1-1 | 7869 | Clifford, Irvine, Gale, Cresswell |
| 6R | 25 | CARDIFF CITY | L | 0-1 | 0-1 | 11507 | |

* Played at Chester

## FRIENDLIES

| | | | | | | | |
|---|---|---|---|---|---|---|---|
| 1 | Feb 25 | CONNAH'S QUAY & S. * | W | 3-1 | 2-1 | 1189 | Hart, Cresswell, Dickie |

* In aid of Connah's Quay funds

Final League Table

| | | P | W | D | L | F | A | Pts |
|---|---|---|---|---|---|---|---|---|
| 1 | Port Vale Reserves | 42 | 33 | 5 | 4 | 163 | 48 | 71 |
| **2** | **Chester** | **42** | **31** | **6** | **5** | **170** | **59** | **68** |
| 3 | Hyde United | 42 | 25 | 6 | 11 | 133 | 84 | 56 |
| 4 | Altrincham | 42 | 22 | 8 | 12 | 123 | 96 | 52 |
| 5 | Runcorn | 42 | 20 | 9 | 13 | 129 | 83 | 49 |
| 6 | Stalybridge Celtic | 42 | 21 | 6 | 15 | 122 | 114 | 48 |
| 7 | Crewe Alexandra Res. | 42 | 19 | 8 | 15 | 132 | 104 | 46 |
| 8 | Ashton National | 42 | 18 | 8 | 16 | 114 | 90 | 44 |
| 9 | Macclesfield | 42 | 20 | 4 | 18 | 112 | 101 | 44 |
| 10 | Sandbach Ramblers | 42 | 19 | 4 | 19 | 123 | 124 | 42 |
| 11 | Witton Albion | 42 | 18 | 6 | 18 | 97 | 103 | 42 |
| 12 | Tranmere Rovers Res. | 42 | 18 | 6 | 18 | 105 | 120 | 42 |
| 13 | Manchester North End | 42 | 19 | 4 | 19 | 97 | 119 | 42 |
| 14 | Hurst | 42 | 18 | 5 | 19 | 132 | 115 | 41 |
| 15 | Congleton Town | 42 | 14 | 8 | 20 | 68 | 112 | 36 |
| 16 | Mossley | 42 | 12 | 10 | 20 | 104 | 124 | 34 |
| 17 | Northwich Victoria | 42 | 15 | 3 | 24 | 105 | 135 | 33 |
| 18 | Connah's Quay & Shotton | 42 | 15 | 2 | 25 | 96 | 122 | 32 |
| 19 | Winsford United | 42 | 13 | 4 | 25 | 98 | 151 | 30 |
| 20 | Whitchurch | 42 | 10 | 7 | 25 | 79 | 160 | 27 |
| 21 | Nantwich | 42 | 9 | 8 | 25 | 83 | 132 | 26 |
| 22 | Manchester Central | 42 | 7 | 5 | 30 | 51 | 140 | 19 |

(Back) Unknown, Unknown, Morris, McCloy, Jarvie, Hewitt (Manager), Bennett, Burgess, Neale, Simpson )Trainer)
(Front) Atkinson, Clifford, Irvine, Gale, Cresswell, Dickie, Unknown.

# SEASON 1931-32

## FOOTBALL LEAGUE DIVISION 3 (NORTH)

| | Date | Opposition | | FT | HT | Att. | Goalscorers |
|---|---|---|---|---|---|---|---|
| 1 | Aug 29 | WIGAN BOROUGH * | W | 4-0 | 0-0 | 12770 | Cresswell, Ranson, Jennings, Hedley |
| 2 | Sep 2 | Wrexham | D | 1-1 | 1-0 | 19000 | Jennings |
| 3 | 5 | Darlington | L | 1-4 | 1-4 | 4222 | Jennings |
| 4 | 9 | Hartlepools United | D | 2-2 | 1-1 | 4717 | Cresswell, Jennings |
| 5 | 12 | HALIFAX TOWN | W | 3-1 | 1-0 | 6824 | Hedley (2), A Ferguson |
| 6 | 16 | HARTLEPOOLS UNITED | L | 2-3 | 2-1 | 8417 | Ranson, Cresswell |
| 7 | 19 | Walsall | D | 1-1 | 0-1 | 4455 | Jennings |
| 8 | 26 | GATESHEAD | D | 1-1 | 1-1 | 10195 | C Matthews |
| 9 | 30 | WREXHAM | L | 2-5 | 0-3 | 13656 | Thompson, Jennings |
| 10 | Oct 3 | New Brighton | W | 1-0 | 0-0 | 5105 | Hedley |
| 11 | 10 | BARROW | W | 4-2 | 3-0 | 8322 | Cresswell, Thompson, Jennings (2) |
| 12 | 17 | ACCRINGTON STANLEY | W | 1-0 | 0-0 | 7094 | Jennings |
| 13 | 24 | Stockport County | D | 0-0 | 0-0 | 8811 | |
| 14 | 31 | ROTHERHAM UNITED | W | 2-1 | 1-0 | 6704 | Robson, Hedley |
| 15 | Nov 7 | Tranmere Rovers | D | 2-2 | 1-1 | 11578 | Jennings, Robson |
| 16 | 14 | YORK CITY | W | 3-0 | 0-0 | 7207 | Mercer, Hedley, Robson |
| 17 | 21 | Southport | D | 1-1 | 1-0 | 6023 | Valentine |
| 18 | Dec 5 | Rochdale | W | 3-0 | 1-0 | 3199 | Cresswell, Hedley, Jennings |
| 19 | 19 | Carlisle United | L | 3-4 | 2-1 | 4220 | Hedley, Robson, Mercer |
| 20 | 25 | LINCOLN CITY | W | 2-1 | 1-1 | 10184 | Cresswell, Reilly |
| 21 | 26 | Lincoln City | L | 0-4 | 0-1 | 12856 | |
| 22 | Jan 9 | DONCASTER ROVERS | D | 1-1 | 0-0 | 5466 | Bennett (pen) |
| 23 | 16 | DARLINGTON | W | 3-1 | 1-1 | 5460 | Jennings, Mercer (2) |
| 24 | 23 | Halifax Town | L | 1-2 | 0-1 | 3703 | Hedley |
| 25 | 30 | WALSALL | W | 5-1 | 3-0 | 5198 | Jennings (5) |
| 26 | Feb 6 | Gateshead | W | 2-1 | 1-0 | 7688 | Mercer, Jennings |
| 27 | 13 | NEW BRIGHTON | W | 2-0 | 2-0 | 6294 | Cresswell, Jennings |
| 28 | 20 | Barrow | L | 0-4 | 0-3 | 6557 | |
| 29 | 27 | Accrington Stanley | W | 3-2 | 3-0 | 3981 | Jennings (2), Cresswell |
| 30 | Mar 5 | STOCKPORT COUNTY | W | 2-1 | 2-0 | 6759 | Wyper (2) |
| 31 | 12 | Rotherham United | L | 0-3 | 0-1 | 4023 | |
| 32 | 19 | TRANMERE ROVERS | W | 3-1 | 2-1 | 8810 | Gray (og), Mercer, Herod (pen) |
| 33 | 25 | HULL CITY | W | 2-0 | 1-0 | 13648 | Jennings (2) |
| 34 | 26 | York City | L | 1-3 | 0-0 | 5388 | Cresswell |
| 35 | 28 | Hull City | W | 2-0 | 0-0 | 7914 | Robinson, Jennings |
| 36 | Apr 2 | SOUTHPORT | W | 4-0 | 2-0 | 7775 | Mercer, Jennings (2), Wyper |
| 37 | 6 | CREWE ALEX. | W | 1-0 | 1-0 | 6938 | Wyper |
| 38 | 9 | Doncaster Rovers | L | 0-3 | 0-2 | 4365 | |
| 39 | 16 | ROCHDALE | W | 7-2 | 4-0 | 4658 | Mercer, Williams(og), Jennings(4), Hedley |
| 40 | 23 | Crewe Alex. | L | 0-1 | 0-0 | 6823 | |
| 41 | 30 | CARLISLE UNITED | W | 4-1 | 1-0 | 4618 | Cresswell, Mercer, Jennings, Hedley |

* Wigan Borough resigned from the League, record expunged

| | Johnson W. | Herod B. | Jones W. | Keeley E. | Skitt H. | Reilly W. | Matthews C. | Ranson J. | Jennings T. | Cresswell F. | Hedley F. | Thompson A. | Bennett F. | Atkinson J. | Ferguson A. | Burke J. | Lambie A. | Millsom E. | Robson C. | Mercer A. | Valentine A. | Matthews W. | Wyper W. | Evans R. | Ferguson D. | Robinson M. |
|---|---|---|---|---|---|---|---|---|---|---|---|---|---|---|---|---|---|---|---|---|---|---|---|---|---|---|
| 1 | 1 | 2 | 3 | 4 | 5 | 6 | 7 | 8 | 9 | 10 | 11 | | | | | | | | | | | | | | | |
| 2 | 1 | 2 | 3 | 4 | 5 | 6 | | 8 | 9 | 10 | 11 | 7 | | | | | | | | | | | | | | |
| 3 | 1 | 3 | | 4 | 5 | 6 | | 8 | 9 | 10 | 11 | 7 | 2 | | | | | | | | | | | | | |
| 4 | 1 | 3 | | 4 | 5 | | | 8 | 9 | 10 | 11 | 7 | 2 | 6 | | | | | | | | | | | | |
| 5 | 1 | 3 | | 4 | 5 | | | 8 | 9 | 10 | 11 | | 2 | 6 | 7 | | | | | | | | | | | |
| 6 | 1 | 3 | | 4 | 5 | 6 | | 8 | 9 | 10 | 11 | | 2 | 7 | | | | | | | | | | | | |
| 7 | 1 | 3 | | 4 | 5 | | 7 | 8 | 9 | 10 | 11 | | 2 | 6 | | | | | | | | | | | | |
| 8 | 1 | 3 | | 4 | 5 | | 7 | 8 | 9 | 10 | 11 | | 2 | 6 | | | | | | | | | | | | |
| 9 | | 2 | 3 | | 5 | 6 | 7 | | 9 | 10 | 11 | 8 | | | | 1 | 4 | | | | | | | | | |
| 10 | | 3 | | 4 | 5 | 6 | 7 | 10 | 9 | | 11 | 8 | 2 | | | 1 | | | | | | | | | | |
| 11 | | 3 | | 4 | 5 | 6 | 7 | | 9 | 10 | 11 | 8 | 2 | | | 1 | | | | | | | | | | |
| 12 | | 3 | | | 5 | 6 | 7 | | 9 | 10 | 11 | 8 | 2 | 4 | | 1 | | | | | | | | | | |
| 13 | | 3 | | | 5 | 6 | | | 9 | 10 | 11 | | 2 | | | 1 | | 4 | 7 | 8 | | | | | | |
| 14 | | 3 | | 4 | | 6 | | | 9 | 10 | 11 | | 2 | 5 | | 1 | | | 7 | 8 | | | | | | |
| 15 | | 3 | | 4 | 5 | 6 | | | 9 | 10 | 11 | | 2 | | | 1 | | | 7 | 8 | | | | | | |
| 16 | | 3 | | 4 | 5 | 6 | | | 9 | 10 | 11 | | 2 | | | 1 | | | 7 | 8 | | | | | | |
| 17 | | 3 | | 4 | | 6 | | | | 10 | 11 | | 2 | | | 1 | | 5 | 7 | 8 | 9 | | | | | |
| 18 | 1 | 3 | | 4 | | 6 | | | 9 | 10 | 11 | | 2 | | | | | 5 | 7 | 8 | | | | | | |
| 19 | | 3 | | 4 | | 6 | | | 9 | 10 | 11 | | 2 | | | 1 | | 5 | 7 | 8 | | | | | | |
| 20 | | 3 | | | 4 | 6 | | | 9 | 10 | 11 | | 2 | | | 1 | | 5 | 7 | 8 | | | | | | |
| 21 | 1 | 3 | | 4 | | | | | 9 | 6 | 11 | | 2 | | | | | 5 | 7 | 8 | 10 | | | | | |
| 22 | 1 | 3 | | 4 | 5 | 6 | | | 9 | 10 | 11 | | 2 | | | | | | 7 | 8 | | | | | | |
| 23 | 1 | 3 | | | | 6 | | | 9 | 10 | 11 | | 2 | | | | | 4 | 7 | 8 | | 5 | | | | |
| 24 | 1 | 3 | | | | 6 | | | 9 | 10 | 11 | | 2 | | | | | 4 | 7 | 8 | | 5 | | | | |
| 25 | 1 | 3 | | | 4 | 6 | | | 9 | 10 | 11 | | 2 | | | | | | 7 | 8 | | 5 | | | | |
| 26 | 1 | 3 | | 5 | 4 | 6 | 7 | | 9 | 10 | 11 | | 2 | | | | | | | 8 | | | | | | |
| 27 | 1 | 3 | | 5 | 4 | 6 | 7 | | 9 | 10 | 11 | | 2 | | | | | | | 8 | | | | | | |
| 28 | 1 | 3 | | | 4 | 6 | 7 | | 9 | 10 | 11 | | 2 | | | | | 5 | | 8 | | | | | | |
| 29 | 1 | 3 | | | 4 | 6 | | | 9 | 10 | 11 | | 2 | | | | | 5 | | 8 | | | 7 | | | |
| 30 | 1 | 3 | | | 4 | 6 | | | 9 | 10 | 11 | | 2 | | | | | | | 8 | | | 7 | 5 | | |
| 31 | 1 | 3 | | | 5 | 6 | | | 9 | 10 | | | 2 | | | | | | | 8 | | | 7 | | 4 | 11 |
| 32 | 1 | 3 | | | 5 | 6 | | | 9 | 10 | 11 | | 2 | | | | | | | 8 | | | 7 | | 4 | |
| 33 | 1 | 3 | | | 5 | 6 | | | 9 | 10 | 11 | | 2 | | | | | | | 8 | | | 7 | | 4 | |
| 34 | 1 | 3 | | | | 6 | | | 9 | 10 | 11 | | 2 | | | | | 4 | | 8 | | 5 | 7 | | | |
| 35 | 1 | 3 | | | | 6 | | | 9 | 10 | | | 2 | | | | | | | 8 | | 5 | 7 | | 4 | 11 |
| 36 | 1 | 3 | | | 5 | 6 | | | 9 | 10 | | | 2 | | | | | | | 8 | | | 7 | | 4 | 11 |
| 37 | 1 | 3 | | | 5 | 6 | | | 9 | 10 | | | 2 | | | | | | | 8 | | | 7 | | 4 | 11 |
| 38 | 1 | 3 | | | 5 | 6 | | | 9 | 10 | | | 2 | | | | | | | 8 | | | 7 | | 4 | 11 |
| 39 | 1 | 3 | | | 5 | 6 | | | 9 | 10 | 11 | | 2 | | | | | | | 8 | | | 7 | | 4 | |
| 40 | 1 | 3 | | | 5 | 6 | | | 9 | 10 | 11 | | 2 | | | | | | | 8 | | | | | 4 | 7 |
| 41 | 1 | 3 | | | 5 | 6 | | | 9 | 10 | 11 | | 2 | | | | | | | 8 | | | 7 | | 4 | |
| Apps. | 29 | 40 | 2 | 19 | 31 | 35 | 9 | 8 | 39 | 39 | 35 | 7 | 38 | 7 | 1 | 11 | 1 | 11 | 13 | 29 | 2 | 5 | 12 | 1 | 10 | 6 |
| Goals | | 1 | | | | 1 | 1 | 1 | 30 | 9 | 10 | 2 | 1 | | 1 | | | | 4 | 9 | 1 | | 4 | | | 1 |

Own goals 2

## F.A. CUP

| | Date | Opposition | | FT | HT | Att. | Goalscorers |
|---|---|---|---|---|---|---|---|
| 1R | Nov 28 | HARTLEPOOLS UNITED | W | 4-1 | 2-0 | 8403 | Hedley (2), Valentine, Bennett |
| 2R | Dec 12 | Darwen | L | 1-2 | 1-0 | 6500 | Murray (og) |

| | Johnson W. | Herod B. | Jones W. | Keeley E. | Skitt H. | Reilly W. | Matthews C. | Ranson J. | Jennings T. | Cresswell F. | Hedley F. | Thompson A. | Bennett F. | Atkinson J. | Ferguson A. | Burke J. | Lambie A. | Millsom E. | Robson C. | Mercer A. | Valentine A. | Matthews W. | Wyper W. | Evans R. | Ferguson D. | Robinson M. |
|---|---|---|---|---|---|---|---|---|---|---|---|---|---|---|---|---|---|---|---|---|---|---|---|---|---|---|
| 1R | 1 | 3 | | 4 | 5 | 6 | | | | 10 | 11 | | 2 | | | | | | 7 | 8 | 9 | | | | | |
| 2R | 1 | 3 | | 4 | | 6 | | | 9 | 10 | 11 | | 2 | | | | | 5 | 7 | 8 | | | | | | |

## WELSH CUP

| | Date | Opposition | | FT | HT | Att. | Goalscorers |
|---|---|---|---|---|---|---|---|
| 5R | Feb 3 | OSWESTRY TOWN | D | 1-1 | 1-0 | 2000 | Jennings |
| 5Rr | 11 | Oswestry Town | W | 4-0 | 1-0 | 1500 | Hedley (2), Jennings (2) |
| 6 | Mar 2 | CARDIFF CITY | W | 2-1 | 1-1 | 9400 | Mercer, Jennings |
| SF | Apr 13 | SWANSEA TOWN | L | 0-2 | 0-1 | 10234 | |

| | Johnson W. | Herod B. | Jones W. | Keeley E. | Skitt H. | Reilly W. | Matthews C. | Ranson J. | Jennings T. | Cresswell F. | Hedley F. | Thompson A. | Bennett F. | Atkinson J. | Ferguson A. | Burke J. | Lambie A. | Millsom E. | Robson C. | Mercer A. | Valentine A. | Matthews W. | Wyper W. | Evans R. | Ferguson D. | Robinson M. |
|---|---|---|---|---|---|---|---|---|---|---|---|---|---|---|---|---|---|---|---|---|---|---|---|---|---|---|
| 5R | 1 | 3 | | | 4 | 6 | | | 9 | 10 | 11 | | 2 | | | | | | 7 | 8 | | 5 | | | | |
| 5Rr | 1 | 3 | | 4 | 5 | 6 | 7 | | 9 | 10 | 11 | | 2 | | | | | | | 8 | | | | | | |
| 6 | | 3 | | | 5 | 6 | | | 9 | 10 | 11 | | 2 | | 7 | 1 | | 4 | | 8 | | | | | | |
| SF | 1 | 3 | | | 5 | 6 | | | 9 | 10 | 11 | | 2 | | | | | | | 8 | | | 7 | | 4 | |

**Final League Table**

| | | Pl. | Home W | Home D | Home L | Home F | Home A | Away W | Away D | Away L | Away F | Away A | F. | A. | Pts |
|---|---|---|---|---|---|---|---|---|---|---|---|---|---|---|---|
| 1 | Lincoln City | 40 | 16 | 2 | 2 | 65 | 13 | 10 | 3 | 7 | 41 | 34 | 106 | 47 | 57 |
| 2 | Gateshead | 40 | 15 | 3 | 2 | 59 | 20 | 10 | 4 | 6 | 35 | 28 | 94 | 48 | 57 |
| ***3*** | ***Chester*** | ***40*** | ***16*** | ***2*** | ***2*** | ***54*** | ***22*** | ***5*** | ***6*** | ***9*** | ***24*** | ***38*** | ***78*** | ***60*** | ***50*** |
| 4 | Tranmere Rovers | 40 | 15 | 4 | 1 | 76 | 23 | 4 | 7 | 9 | 31 | 35 | 107 | 58 | 49 |
| 5 | Barrow | 40 | 16 | 1 | 3 | 59 | 23 | 8 | 0 | 12 | 27 | 36 | 86 | 59 | 49 |
| 6 | Crewe Alexandra | 40 | 15 | 3 | 2 | 64 | 24 | 6 | 3 | 11 | 31 | 42 | 95 | 66 | 48 |
| 7 | Southport | 40 | 14 | 5 | 1 | 44 | 15 | 4 | 5 | 11 | 14 | 38 | 58 | 53 | 46 |
| 8 | Hull City | 40 | 14 | 1 | 5 | 52 | 21 | 6 | 4 | 10 | 30 | 32 | 82 | 53 | 45 |
| 9 | York City | 40 | 14 | 3 | 3 | 49 | 24 | 4 | 4 | 12 | 27 | 57 | 76 | 81 | 43 |
| 10 | Wrexham | 40 | 14 | 2 | 4 | 42 | 25 | 4 | 5 | 11 | 22 | 44 | 64 | 69 | 43 |
| 11 | Darlington | 40 | 12 | 1 | 7 | 41 | 27 | 5 | 3 | 12 | 25 | 42 | 66 | 69 | 38 |
| 12 | Stockport County | 40 | 12 | 3 | 5 | 31 | 15 | 1 | 8 | 11 | 24 | 38 | 55 | 53 | 37 |
| 13 | Hartlepools United | 40 | 10 | 4 | 6 | 47 | 37 | 6 | 1 | 13 | 31 | 63 | 78 | 100 | 37 |
| 14 | Accrington Stanley | 40 | 14 | 4 | 2 | 56 | 20 | 1 | 2 | 17 | 19 | 60 | 75 | 80 | 36 |
| 15 | Doncaster Rovers | 40 | 12 | 3 | 5 | 38 | 27 | 4 | 1 | 15 | 21 | 53 | 59 | 80 | 36 |
| 16 | Walsall | 40 | 12 | 3 | 5 | 42 | 30 | 4 | 0 | 16 | 15 | 55 | 57 | 85 | 35 |
| 17 | Halifax Town | 40 | 11 | 6 | 3 | 36 | 18 | 2 | 2 | 16 | 25 | 69 | 61 | 87 | 34 |
| 18 | Carlisle United | 40 | 9 | 7 | 4 | 40 | 23 | 2 | 4 | 14 | 24 | 56 | 64 | 79 | 33 |
| 19 | Rotherham United | 40 | 10 | 3 | 7 | 41 | 23 | 4 | 1 | 15 | 22 | 49 | 63 | 72 | 32 |
| 20 | New Brighton | 40 | 8 | 5 | 7 | 25 | 23 | 0 | 3 | 17 | 13 | 53 | 38 | 76 | 24 |
| 21 | Rochdale | 40 | 4 | 2 | 14 | 33 | 63 | 0 | 1 | 19 | 15 | 72 | 48 | 135 | 11 |

(Back) Thompson, Johnson, Unknown, Ranson, Simpson, (Trainer), Millsom, Cresswell, Reilly
(Front) Hedley, Skitt, Herod, Jennings, Matthews.

# SEASON 1932-33

## FOOTBALL LEAGUE DIVISION 3 (NORTH)

| | Date | Opposition | | FT | HT | Att. | Goalscorers |
|---|---|---|---|---|---|---|---|
| 1 | Aug 27 | Mansfield Town | L | 0-1 | 0-0 | 8009 | |
| 2 | 31 | SOUTHPORT | D | 1-1 | 1-0 | 11210 | Jennings |
| 3 | Sep 3 | ROTHERHAM UNITED | W | 1-0 | 0-0 | 7657 | Ferguson |
| 4 | 6 | Southport | L | 1-2 | 1-1 | 6219 | Roscoe |
| 5 | 10 | Accrington Stanley | W | 4-1 | 2-0 | 5569 | Jennings, Wyper (2), Hedley |
| 6 | 14 | STOCKPORT COUNTY | D | 2-2 | 1-1 | 8031 | Hedley, Gray |
| 7 | 17 | NEW BRIGHTON | W | 3-0 | 3-0 | 9655 | Ferguson (pen), Hedley, Jennings |
| 8 | 21 | WALSALL | W | 1-0 | 1-0 | 5311 | Stevenson |
| 9 | 24 | Wrexham | W | 2-1 | 2-1 | 19649 | Mantle, Bell |
| 10 | Oct 1 | Barrow | W | 3-2 | 1-1 | 6414 | Ferguson, Bell, Cresswell |
| 11 | 8 | CARLISLE UNITED | W | 4-0 | 4-0 | 5732 | Mantle (2), Cresswell, Stevenson |
| 12 | 15 | York City | L | 1-3 | 0-3 | 5689 | Cresswell |
| 13 | 22 | TRANMERE ROVERS | L | 1-2 | 0-1 | 7773 | Hedley |
| 14 | 29 | Halifax Town | W | 2-0 | 2-0 | 4906 | Mantle (2) |
| 15 | Nov 5 | HARTLEPOOLS UNITED | D | 3-3 | 1-1 | 6947 | Cresswell, Mercer, Wyper (pen) |
| 16 | 12 | Barnsley | W | 3-0 | 1-0 | 6975 | Mantle, Hedley, Cresswell |
| 17 | 19 | HULL CITY | D | 1-1 | 1-0 | 10064 | Mantle |
| 18 | Dec 3 | DARLINGTON | W | 5-2 | 3-0 | 5558 | Hedley (2), Mantle (2), Mercer |
| 19 | 17 | GATESHEAD | W | 3-1 | 1-1 | 7030 | Cresswell, Hedley, Mantle |
| 20 | 24 | Walsall | L | 1-3 | 0-0 | 6606 | Mantle |
| 21 | 26 | CREWE ALEX. | W | 3-1 | 2-1 | 14000 | Hedley, Mantle (2) |
| 22 | 27 | Crewe Alex. | W | 1-0 | 0-0 | 11219 | Mantle |
| 23 | 31 | MANSFIELD TOWN | W | 5-2 | 4-2 | 6618 | Mantle(3),Cresswell,Anthoney(og) |
| 24 | Jan 7 | Rotherham United | W | 5-0 | 1-0 | 4724 | Armes, Mantle (4) |
| 25 | 21 | ACCRINGTON STANLEY | W | 4-2 | 4-2 | 4980 | Hedley (3), Armes |
| 26 | Feb 4 | WREXHAM | L | 0-3 | 0-0 | 16835 | |
| 27 | 8 | New Brighton | L | 1-3 | 0-1 | 3384 | Mantle |
| 28 | 11 | BARROW | W | 2-1 | 0-1 | 6268 | Hedley, Butler |
| 29 | 18 | Carlisle United | D | 1-1 | 1-1 | 4490 | Mantle |
| 30 | Mar 4 | Tranmere Rovers | D | 2-2 | 0-1 | 8649 | Mantle (2) |
| 31 | 11 | HALIFAX TOWN | W | 6-3 | 4-0 | 7287 | Cresswell,Mercer,Mantle(4,1 pen) |
| 32 | 18 | Hartlepools United | L | 1-3 | 0-0 | 5293 | Mantle |
| 33 | 25 | BARNSLEY | W | 3-1 | 1-0 | 6508 | Cresswell, Hedley, Mercer |
| 34 | 29 | YORK CITY | W | 5-0 | 3-0 | 4977 | Mantle (2), Mercer (3) |
| 35 | Apr 1 | Hull City | L | 0-2 | 0-1 | 20248 | |
| 36 | 8 | DONCASTER ROVERS | W | 2-0 | 0-0 | 5669 | Mantle, Hedley |
| 37 | 14 | ROCHDALE | W | 2-0 | 0-0 | 9870 | Cresswell, Hedley |
| 38 | 15 | Darlington | D | 1-1 | 1-0 | 3064 | Mantle |
| 39 | 17 | Rochdale | L | 0-2 | 0-1 | 3742 | |
| 40 | 27 | Doncaster Rovers | D | 3-3 | 0-2 | 4379 | Cresswell (2), Kelly |
| 41 | 29 | Gateshead | L | 0-3 | 0-2 | 1424 | |
| 42 | May 6 | Stockport County | L | 5-8 | 2-5 | 4255 | Kelly (4, 1 pen), Armes |

| | Johnson W. | Bennett F. | Herod B. | Skitt H. | Jolly H. | Cresswell F. | Armes S. | Stevenson J. | Jennings T. | Gray R. | Hedley F. | Ferguson D. | Bell W. | Wyper W. | Roscoe J. | Dickie J. | Mercer A. | Mantle J. | Pitcairn J. | Burke J. | Searle F. | Viner R. | Kelly G. | Butler H. | Duckworth R. | Finnigan R. | Vaughan T. |
|---|---|---|---|---|---|---|---|---|---|---|---|---|---|---|---|---|---|---|---|---|---|---|---|---|---|---|---|
| 1 | 1 | 2 | 3 | 4 | 5 | 6 | 7 | 8 | 9 | 10 | 11 | | | | | | | | | | | | | | | | |
| 2 | 1 | 2 | 3 | 4 | 5 | 6 | 7 | 10 | 9 | 8 | 11 | | | | | | | | | | | | | | | | |
| 3 | 1 | 2 | 3 | 5 | | 10 | 7 | | 9 | 8 | 11 | 4 | 6 | | | | | | | | | | | | | | |
| 4 | 1 | 2 | 3 | 4 | 5 | 10 | | | | | | 8 | 6 | 7 | 9 | 11 | | | | | | | | | | | |
| 5 | 1 | 2 | 3 | | 5 | 6 | | | 9 | 10 | 11 | 4 | | 7 | | | 8 | | | | | | | | | | |
| 6 | 1 | 2 | 3 | 4 | 5 | 6 | | | 9 | 10 | 11 | 8 | | 7 | | | | | | | | | | | | | |
| 7 | 1 | 2 | 3 | 5 | | 6 | 7 | 8 | 9 | 10 | 11 | 4 | | | | | | | | | | | | | | | |
| 8 | 1 | 2 | 3 | 5 | | 10 | 7 | 8 | 9 | | 11 | 4 | 6 | | | | | | | | | | | | | | |
| 9 | 1 | 2 | 3 | 5 | | 10 | 7 | 8 | | | 11 | 4 | 6 | | | | | 9 | | | | | | | | | |
| 10 | 1 | 2 | 3 | 5 | | 10 | | 8 | | | 11 | 4 | 6 | 7 | | | | 9 | | | | | | | | | |
| 11 | 1 | 2 | 3 | 5 | | 10 | | 8 | | | 11 | 4 | 6 | 7 | | | | 9 | | | | | | | | | |
| 12 | 1 | 2 | 3 | 5 | | 10 | 7 | 8 | | | 11 | 4 | 6 | | | | | 9 | | | | | | | | | |
| 13 | 1 | 2 | 3 | 5 | | 10 | 7 | 8 | | | 11 | 4 | | | | | | 9 | 6 | | | | | | | | |
| 14 | 1 | 2 | 3 | | 5 | 10 | | | | | 11 | | 6 | 7 | | | 8 | 9 | 4 | | | | | | | | |
| 15 | 1 | 2 | 3 | | 5 | 10 | | | | | 11 | | 6 | 7 | | | 8 | 9 | 4 | | | | | | | | |
| 16 | 1 | 2 | 3 | 5 | | 10 | | | | | 11 | | 6 | 7 | | | 8 | 9 | 4 | | | | | | | | |
| 17 | 1 | 2 | 3 | 5 | | 10 | | | | | 11 | | 6 | 7 | | | 8 | 9 | 4 | | | | | | | | |
| 18 | 1 | 2 | 3 | 5 | | 10 | | | | | 11 | | 6 | 7 | | | 8 | 9 | 4 | | | | | | | | |
| 19 | 1 | 2 | 3 | 5 | | 10 | 7 | | | | 11 | | 6 | | | | 8 | 9 | 4 | | | | | | | | |
| 20 | 1 | 2 | 3 | 5 | | 10 | | | | | 11 | | 6 | 7 | | | 8 | 9 | 4 | | | | | | | | |
| 21 | 1 | 2 | 3 | 5 | | 10 | | 8 | | | 11 | | 6 | 7 | | | | 9 | 4 | | | | | | | | |
| 22 | 1 | 2 | 3 | 5 | | 10 | 7 | | | | 11 | 4 | 6 | | | | 8 | 9 | | | | | | | | | |
| 23 | 1 | 2 | 3 | 5 | | 10 | 7 | | | | 11 | 4 | 6 | | | | 8 | 9 | | | | | | | | | |
| 24 | 1 | 2 | 3 | 5 | | 10 | 7 | | | | 11 | | 6 | | | | 8 | 9 | 4 | | | | | | | | |
| 25 | 1 | 2 | 3 | 5 | | 10 | 7 | | | | 11 | | 6 | | | | 8 | 9 | 4 | | | | | | | | |
| 26 | | 2 | 3 | | 5 | 10 | 7 | | | | 11 | 4 | 6 | | | | 8 | 9 | | 1 | | | | | | | |
| 27 | | 2 | | | 5 | | 7 | 10 | | | 11 | 4 | 6 | | | | 8 | 9 | | 1 | 3 | | | | | | |
| 28 | | 2 | 3 | | | | | | | | 11 | 4 | | | | | 8 | 9 | | 1 | 6 | 5 | 7 | 10 | | | |
| 29 | | 2 | 3 | 5 | | 10 | | | | | 11 | | | | | | 8 | 9 | 4 | 1 | | | 7 | | 6 | | |
| 30 | | 2 | 3 | 5 | | | | | 8 | | 11 | | | | | | | 9 | 4 | 1 | | | 7 | 10 | 6 | | |
| 31 | | 2 | 3 | 5 | | 10 | | | | | 11 | | | | | | 8 | 9 | 4 | | | | 7 | | 6 | 1 | |
| 32 | | 2 | 3 | 5 | | 10 | | | | | 11 | | | | | | 8 | 9 | 4 | 1 | | | 7 | | 6 | | |
| 33 | | 2 | 3 | 5 | | 10 | | | | | 11 | | | | | | 8 | 9 | 4 | 1 | | | 7 | | 6 | | |
| 34 | | 2 | 3 | 5 | | 10 | | | | | 11 | 4 | | | | | 8 | 9 | | 1 | | | 7 | | 6 | | |
| 35 | | 2 | 3 | 5 | | | | | 10 | | 11 | | | | | | 8 | 9 | 4 | 1 | | | 7 | | 6 | | |
| 36 | | 2 | 3 | 5 | | 10 | | | | | 11 | | | | | | 8 | 9 | 4 | 1 | | | 7 | | 6 | | |
| 37 | | 2 | 3 | 5 | | 10 | | | | | 11 | | | | | | | 9 | 4 | 1 | | | 7 | | 6 | | 8 |
| 38 | | 2 | 3 | 5 | | 10 | | | | | 11 | 4 | | | | | 8 | 9 | | 1 | | | 7 | | 6 | | |
| 39 | | 2 | 3 | 5 | | 10 | | | | | 11 | 4 | | | | | 8 | 9 | | 1 | | | 7 | | 6 | | |
| 40 | | 2 | | 5 | | 10 | | | | | 11 | | | | | | 8 | 9 | 4 | 1 | 3 | | 7 | | 6 | | |
| 41 | | 2 | | 5 | | 10 | | | | | 11 | | | | | | 8 | 9 | 4 | 1 | 3 | | 7 | | 6 | | |
| 42 | | 2 | 3 | 5 | | 10 | 7 | | | | 11 | | | | | | 8 | | 4 | 1 | | | 9 | | 6 | | |
| Apps. | 25 | 42 | 39 | 36 | 9 | 38 | 16 | 11 | 9 | 6 | 41 | 19 | 21 | 12 | 1 | 1 | 27 | 33 | 22 | 16 | 4 | 1 | 15 | 2 | 14 | 1 | 1 |
| Goals | | | | | | 12 | 3 | 2 | 3 | 1 | 16 | 3 | 2 | 3 | 1 | | 7 | 34 | | | | | 5 | 1 | | | |

Own goals 1

## F.A. CUP

| | Date | Opposition | | FT | HT | Att. | Goalscorers |
|---|---|---|---|---|---|---|---|
| 1R | Nov 26 | ROTHERHAM UNITED | W | 4-0 | 2-0 | 7000 | Mantle, Wyper (2), Hedley |
| 2R | Dec 10 | YEOVIL & PETTERS UTD | W | 2-1 | 1-0 | 8000 | Cresswell, Hedley |
| 3R | Jan 14 | FULHAM | W | 5-0 | 3-0 | 14328 | Mercer, Hedley (4) |
| 4R | 28 | HALIFAX TOWN | D | 0-0 | 0-0 | 10538 | |
| 4Rr | Feb 2 | Halifax Town * | L | 2-3 | 0-2 | 14224 | Mantle (2) |

| | Johnson W. | Bennett F. | Herod B. | Skitt H. | Jolly H. | Cresswell F. | Armes S. | Stevenson J. | Jennings T. | Gray R. | Hedley F. | Ferguson D. | Bell W. | Wyper W. | Roscoe J. | Dickie J. | Mercer A. | Mantle J. | Pitcairn J. | Burke J. | Searle F. | Viner R. | Kelly G. | Butler H. | Duckworth R. | Finnigan R. | Vaughan T. |
|---|---|---|---|---|---|---|---|---|---|---|---|---|---|---|---|---|---|---|---|---|---|---|---|---|---|---|---|
| 1R | 1 | 2 | 3 | 5 | | 10 | | | | | 11 | | 6 | 7 | | | 8 | 9 | 4 | | | | | | | | |
| 2R | 1 | 2 | 3 | 5 | | 10 | | | | | 11 | | 6 | 7 | | | 8 | 9 | 4 | | | | | | | | |
| 3R | 1 | 2 | 3 | 5 | | 10 | 7 | | | | 11 | | 6 | | | | 8 | 9 | 4 | | | | | | | | |
| 4R | | 2 | 3 | 5 | | 10 | 7 | | | | 11 | | 6 | | | | 8 | 9 | 4 | 1 | | | | | | | |
| 4Rr | | 2 | 3 | 5 | | 10 | | | | | 11 | | 6 | | | | 8 | 9 | 4 | 1 | | | 7 | | | | |

* After extra time following score of 2-2 after 90 minutes

## WELSH CUP

| | Date | Opposition | | FT | HT | Att. | Goalscorers |
|---|---|---|---|---|---|---|---|
| 7R | Feb 22 | Crewe Alex. | W | 5-3 | 1-3 | 2000 | Butler, Mantle (2), Kelly (2) |
| 8R | Mar 14 | Llanelli | W | 4-0 | 1-0 | 10500 | Kelly,Harris(og),Hedley,Jennings |
| SF | Apr 5 | CARDIFF CITY | W | 2-1 | 1-1 | 8000 | Mercer, Cresswell (pen) |
| F | May 3 | WREXHAM | W | 2-0 | 1-0 | 15000 | Kelly, Cresswell |

| | Johnson W. | Bennett F. | Herod B. | Skitt H. | Jolly H. | Cresswell F. | Armes S. | Stevenson J. | Jennings T. | Gray R. | Hedley F. | Ferguson D. | Bell W. | Wyper W. | Roscoe J. | Dickie J. | Mercer A. | Mantle J. | Pitcairn J. | Burke J. | Searle F. | Viner R. | Kelly G. | Butler H. | Duckworth R. | Finnigan R. | Vaughan T. |
|---|---|---|---|---|---|---|---|---|---|---|---|---|---|---|---|---|---|---|---|---|---|---|---|---|---|---|---|
| 7R | | 2 | 3 | 5 | | | | | 8 | | 11 | 4 | 6 | | | | | 9 | | 1 | | | 7 | 10 | | | |
| 8R | | 2 | 3 | 5 | | 10 | | | 9 | | 11 | | | | | | 8 | | 4 | 1 | | | 7 | | 6 | | |
| SF | | 2 | 3 | 5 | | 10 | | | | | 11 | | | | | | 8 | 9 | 4 | 1 | | | 7 | | 6 | | |
| F | | 2 | 3 | 5 | | 10 | | | | | 11 | | | | | | 8 | 9 | 4 | 1 | | | 7 | | 6 | | |

### Final League Table

| | | Pl. | Home W | D | L | F | A | Away W | D | L | F | A | F. | A. | Pts |
|---|---|---|---|---|---|---|---|---|---|---|---|---|---|---|---|
| 1 | Hull City | 42 | 18 | 3 | 0 | 69 | 14 | 8 | 4 | 9 | 31 | 31 | 100 | 45 | 59 |
| 2 | Wrexham | 42 | 18 | 2 | 1 | 75 | 15 | 6 | 7 | 8 | 31 | 36 | 106 | 51 | 57 |
| 3 | Stockport County | 42 | 16 | 2 | 3 | 69 | 30 | 5 | 10 | 6 | 30 | 28 | 99 | 58 | 54 |
| ***4*** | ***Chester*** | ***42*** | ***15*** | ***4*** | ***2*** | ***57*** | ***25*** | ***7*** | ***4*** | ***10*** | ***37*** | ***41*** | ***94*** | ***66*** | ***52*** |
| 5 | Walsall | 42 | 16 | 4 | 1 | 53 | 15 | 3 | 6 | 12 | 22 | 43 | 75 | 58 | 48 |
| 6 | Doncaster Rovers | 42 | 13 | 8 | 0 | 52 | 26 | 4 | 6 | 11 | 25 | 53 | 77 | 79 | 48 |
| 7 | Gateshead | 42 | 12 | 5 | 4 | 45 | 25 | 7 | 4 | 10 | 33 | 42 | 78 | 67 | 47 |
| 8 | Barnsley | 42 | 14 | 3 | 4 | 60 | 31 | 5 | 5 | 11 | 32 | 49 | 92 | 80 | 46 |
| 9 | Barrow | 42 | 12 | 3 | 6 | 41 | 24 | 6 | 4 | 11 | 19 | 36 | 60 | 60 | 43 |
| 10 | Crewe Alexandra | 42 | 16 | 3 | 2 | 57 | 16 | 4 | 0 | 17 | 23 | 68 | 80 | 84 | 43 |
| 11 | Tranmere Rovers | 42 | 11 | 4 | 6 | 49 | 31 | 6 | 4 | 11 | 21 | 35 | 70 | 66 | 42 |
| 12 | Southport | 42 | 15 | 3 | 3 | 54 | 20 | 2 | 4 | 15 | 16 | 47 | 70 | 67 | 41 |
| 13 | Accrington Stanley | 42 | 12 | 4 | 5 | 55 | 29 | 3 | 6 | 12 | 23 | 47 | 78 | 76 | 40 |
| 14 | Hartlepools United | 42 | 15 | 3 | 3 | 56 | 29 | 1 | 4 | 16 | 31 | 87 | 87 | 116 | 39 |
| 15 | Halifax Town | 42 | 12 | 4 | 5 | 39 | 23 | 3 | 4 | 14 | 32 | 67 | 71 | 90 | 38 |
| 16 | Mansfield Town | 42 | 13 | 4 | 4 | 57 | 22 | 1 | 3 | 17 | 27 | 78 | 84 | 100 | 35 |
| 17 | Rotherham United | 42 | 14 | 3 | 4 | 42 | 21 | 0 | 3 | 18 | 18 | 63 | 60 | 84 | 34 |
| 18 | Rochdale | 42 | 9 | 4 | 8 | 32 | 33 | 4 | 3 | 14 | 26 | 47 | 58 | 80 | 33 |
| 19 | Carlisle United | 42 | 8 | 7 | 6 | 34 | 25 | 5 | 0 | 16 | 17 | 50 | 51 | 75 | 33 |
| 20 | York City | 42 | 10 | 4 | 7 | 51 | 38 | 3 | 2 | 16 | 21 | 54 | 72 | 92 | 32 |
| 21 | New Brighton | 42 | 8 | 6 | 7 | 42 | 36 | 3 | 4 | 14 | 21 | 52 | 63 | 88 | 32 |
| 22 | Darlington | 42 | 9 | 6 | 6 | 42 | 32 | 1 | 2 | 18 | 24 | 77 | 66 | 109 | 28 |

**1932/33 Season**
(Back) Bennett, Pitcairn, Johnson, Latham (Trainer), Skitt, Bell.
(Front) Wyper, Mercer, Mantle, Herod, Cresswell, Hedley.

**1933/34 Season**
(Back) Pitcairn, Bennett, Burke, Skitt, McLachlan, Freeman, Latham (Trainer).
(Front) Mansley (Chairman), Kelly, Mercer, Mantle, Cresswell, Hedley, Hewitt (Manager).

# SEASON 1933-34

## FOOTBALL LEAGUE DIVISION 3 (NORTH)

| | Date | Opposition | | FT | HT | Att. | Goalscorers |
|---|---|---|---|---|---|---|---|
| 1 | Aug 26 | ROTHERHAM UNITED | W | 5-1 | 5-1 | 9616 | Kelly, Mantle, Mercer, Cresswell, Hedley |
| 2 | 30 | Halifax Town | L | 0-1 | 0-0 | 8517 | |
| 3 | Sep 2 | Walsall | L | 0-5 | 0-0 | 8786 | |
| 4 | 6 | HALIFAX TOWN | L | 1-2 | 1-1 | 8747 | Cresswell (pen) |
| 5 | 9 | YORK CITY | D | 1-1 | 1-0 | 7942 | Whittam |
| 6 | 16 | Wrexham | W | 3-0 | 1-0 | 18782 | Hedley (2), Mantle |
| 7 | 23 | Doncaster Rovers | L | 1-3 | 0-0 | 6057 | Mantle |
| 8 | 30 | BARROW | L | 1-3 | 0-1 | 6981 | Mercer |
| 9 | Oct 7 | Carlisle United | L | 0-1 | 0-0 | 5473 | |
| 10 | 14 | STOCKPORT COUNTY | D | 1-1 | 0-1 | 6153 | Kelly |
| 11 | 21 | HARTLEPOOLS UNITED | D | 3-3 | 3-0 | 6368 | Kelly, Whittam (2) |
| 12 | 28 | Mansfield Town | L | 1-2 | 1-0 | 4007 | Kelly |
| 13 | Nov 4 | BARNSLEY | W | 4-2 | 3-1 | 6501 | Whittam, Mantle (3) |
| 14 | 11 | Tranmere Rovers | L | 1-6 | 0-3 | 9005 | McLachlan |
| 15 | 18 | ROCHDALE | W | 7-1 | 3-1 | 4477 | Armes (4), McLachlan, Mantle (2) |
| 16 | Dec 2 | ACCRINGTON STANLEY | W | 7-0 | 3-0 | 4795 | Armes(2), Mantle(3), McLachlan, Cresswell |
| 17 | 16 | DARLINGTON | W | 8-0 | 5-0 | 3990 | Armes (3), Mantle (4, 1 pen), McLachlan |
| 18 | 23 | Southport | L | 1-3 | 0-1 | 3023 | Armes |
| 19 | 25 | NEW BRIGHTON | D | 0-0 | 0-0 | 8970 | |
| 20 | 26 | New Brighton | W | 2-0 | 1-0 | 6153 | Cresswell, Mantle |
| 21 | 30 | Rotherham United | W | 3-0 | 2-0 | 5132 | McLachlan (2), Cresswell |
| 22 | Jan 1 | Chesterfield | L | 1-6 | 0-1 | 10957 | Kelly |
| 23 | 6 | WALSALL | L | 0-1 | 0-0 | 5979 | |
| 24 | 20 | York City | L | 2-3 | 0-1 | 4171 | Hughes (2, 1 pen) |
| 25 | 27 | WREXHAM | L | 1-2 | 1-0 | 14481 | Mantle |
| 26 | Feb 3 | DONCASTER ROVERS | W | 3-1 | 1-0 | 4012 | C Roberts (2), Hughes (pen) |
| 27 | 10 | Barrow | L | 0-9 | 0-6 | 4091 | |
| 28 | 17 | CARLISLE UNITED | D | 3-3 | 0-3 | 4454 | Kelly, N Roberts, Mantle |
| 29 | 24 | Stockport County | L | 2-4 | 2-2 | 10973 | Kelly, Hughes |
| 30 | Mar 3 | Hartlepools United | L | 0-1 | 0-0 | 2900 | |
| 31 | 10 | MANSFIELD TOWN | D | 1-1 | 1-0 | 3728 | McLachlan |
| 32 | 17 | Barnsley | L | 0-2 | 0-0 | 8195 | |
| 33 | 24 | TRANMERE ROVERS | W | 4-2 | 1-1 | 6545 | Wallbanks (2), Whittam, Sargeant |
| 34 | 30 | Crewe Alex. | W | 5-3 | 3-1 | 7810 | Wallbanks (3), Hughes (2) |
| 35 | 31 | Rochdale | L | 0-6 | 0-2 | 2942 | |
| 36 | Apr 2 | CREWE ALEX. | W | 1-0 | 1-0 | 7874 | Wilson |
| 37 | 7 | CHESTERFIELD | W | 3-2 | 3-0 | 9051 | Wallbanks (2), Wilson |
| 38 | 14 | Accrington Stanley | L | 1-4 | 0-4 | 2096 | Wilson |
| 39 | 21 | GATESHEAD | W | 4-0 | 1-0 | 4564 | Whittam (3), Wallbanks |
| 40 | 25 | Gateshead | W | 3-1 | 1-0 | 1043 | Whittam (2), Wallbanks |
| 41 | 28 | Darlington | W | 4-0 | 2-0 | 2117 | Whittam, Hughes, Wallbanks (2) |
| 42 | May 5 | SOUTHPORT | W | 1-0 | 0-0 | 3768 | Wallbanks |

| | Burke J. | Bennett F. | Freeman T. | Pitcairn J. | Skitt H. | McLachlan G. | Kelly G. | Mercer A. | Mantle J. | Cresswell F. | Hedley F. | Wyness G. | Whittam E. | Vaughan T. | Finnigan R. | Armes S. | Little J. | Upton W. | Duckworth R. | Jones H. | Bell W. | Morris S. | Hughes J. | Roberts C. | Kay J. | Roberts N. | Middleton R. | Wallbanks J. | Wilson A. | Sargeant C. |
|---|---|---|---|---|---|---|---|---|---|---|---|---|---|---|---|---|---|---|---|---|---|---|---|---|---|---|---|---|---|---|
| 1 | 1 | 2 | 3 | 4 | 5 | 6 | 7 | 8 | 9 | 10 | 11 | | | | | | | | | | | | | | | | | | | |
| 2 | 1 | 2 | 3 | | 5 | 6 | 7 | 8 | | 10 | 11 | 4 | 9 | | | | | | | | | | | | | | | | | |
| 3 | 1 | 2 | 3 | 4 | 5 | 6 | 7 | 8 | | 10 | 11 | | | 9 | | | | | | | | | | | | | | | | |
| 4 | 1 | 2 | 3 | 4 | 5 | 6 | 7 | 8 | 9 | 10 | 11 | | | | | | | | | | | | | | | | | | | |
| 5 | | 2 | 3 | 4 | 5 | 6 | 7 | | 9 | 10 | 11 | | 8 | | 1 | | | | | | | | | | | | | | | |
| 6 | | 2 | 3 | 4 | 5 | 6 | | 8 | 9 | 10 | 11 | | | | 1 | 7 | | | | | | | | | | | | | | |
| 7 | | 2 | 3 | 4 | 5 | 6 | | 8 | 9 | | 11 | | 10 | | 1 | 7 | | | | | | | | | | | | | | |
| 8 | | 2 | 3 | 4 | 5 | 6 | | 8 | 9 | | 11 | | 10 | | 1 | 7 | | | | | | | | | | | | | | |
| 9 | 1 | | 2 | 4 | 5 | 6 | | | 9 | | 11 | | 10 | | | 7 | 3 | 8 | | | | | | | | | | | | |
| 10 | 1 | | 3 | 4 | 5 | 6 | 7 | | 9 | 10 | 11 | | | | | | 2 | 8 | | | | | | | | | | | | |
| 11 | 1 | | 3 | 4 | 5 | 6 | 9 | | | 10 | 11 | | 8 | | | 7 | 2 | | | | | | | | | | | | | |
| 12 | 1 | | 3 | 4 | 5 | 6 | 9 | | | 10 | 11 | | 8 | | | 7 | 2 | | | | | | | | | | | | | |
| 13 | 1 | 2 | 3 | 4 | 5 | 11 | 7 | | 9 | 10 | | | 8 | | | | | | 6 | | | | | | | | | | | |
| 14 | 1 | 2 | 3 | 4 | 5 | 11 | 7 | | 9 | 10 | | | 8 | | | | | | 6 | | | | | | | | | | | |
| 15 | 1 | 2 | | 4 | | 11 | | | 9 | 10 | | 5 | 8 | | | 7 | 3 | | 6 | | | | | | | | | | | |
| 16 | 1 | 2 | | 4 | 5 | 11 | | | 9 | 10 | | | 8 | | | 7 | 3 | | 6 | | | | | | | | | | | |
| 17 | | 2 | | 4 | | 11 | | | 9 | 10 | | 5 | 8 | | 1 | 7 | 3 | | 6 | | | | | | | | | | | |
| 18 | | 2 | | 4 | | 11 | | | 9 | 10 | | 5 | 8 | | 1 | 7 | 3 | | 6 | | | | | | | | | | | |
| 19 | | 2 | | 4 | 5 | 11 | | | 9 | 10 | | | 8 | | 1 | 7 | | | | 3 | 6 | | | | | | | | | |
| 20 | | 2 | | 4 | | 11 | | | 9 | 10 | | 5 | 8 | | 1 | 7 | | | | 3 | 6 | | | | | | | | | |
| 21 | | | | 4 | | 11 | | | 9 | 10 | | 5 | 8 | | 1 | 7 | 2 | | | 3 | 6 | | | | | | | | | |
| 22 | | | | | | 11 | 9 | | | 10 | | 5 | 8 | | 1 | 7 | 2 | | | 3 | 6 | 4 | | | | | | | | |
| 23 | | 2 | | 4 | | 11 | 9 | | | 10 | | 5 | 8 | | 1 | 7 | | | | 3 | 6 | | | | | | | | | |
| 24 | 1 | 2 | 3 | 4 | 5 | 11 | | | 9 | | | | 8 | | | | | | 6 | | | | 7 | 10 | | | | | | |
| 25 | 1 | 2 | 3 | 4 | 5 | 11 | | | 9 | | | | 8 | | | | | | 6 | | | | 7 | 10 | | | | | | |
| 26 | 1 | 2 | | | 5 | | 11 | | 9 | | | | 8 | | | | | | | 3 | 6 | 4 | 7 | 10 | | | | | | |
| 27 | 1 | 2 | 11 | 4 | 5 | | 9 | | | | | | 8 | | | | | | 6 | 3 | | | 7 | 10 | | | | | | |
| 28 | 1 | 2 | | 4 | | | 7 | | 9 | | | | | | | | | | 6 | 3 | | 5 | 8 | | 10 | 11 | | | | |
| 29 | | 2 | | 4 | 5 | 11 | 7 | | 9 | | | | | | 1 | | 3 | | 6 | | | | 8 | | 10 | | | | | |
| 30 | | 2 | | 4 | 5 | 6 | 7 | | 9 | | | | 8 | | | | 3 | | | | | | 11 | 10 | | | 1 | | | |
| 31 | | 2 | | 4 | 5 | 11 | 10 | | 9 | | | | 8 | | | | 3 | | 6 | | | | 7 | | | | 1 | | | |
| 32 | | 2 | | 4 | 5 | | 8 | | | | | | | | | | 3 | | 6 | | | | 7 | | | | 1 | 9 | 10 | 11 |
| 33 | | 2 | | 4 | 5 | | | | | | | | 8 | | | | 3 | | 6 | | | | 7 | | | | 1 | 9 | 10 | 11 |
| 34 | | 2 | | 4 | 5 | | | | | | | | 8 | | | | 3 | | 6 | | | | 7 | | | | 1 | 9 | 10 | 11 |
| 35 | | 2 | | 4 | 5 | | | | | | | | 8 | | | | 3 | | 6 | | | | 7 | | | | 1 | 9 | 10 | 11 |
| 36 | | 2 | | 4 | 5 | | | | | | | | 8 | | | | 3 | | | | 6 | | 7 | | | | 1 | 9 | 10 | 11 |
| 37 | | 2 | | | 5 | | | | | | | | 8 | | | | 3 | | | | 6 | 4 | 7 | | | | 1 | 9 | 10 | 11 |
| 38 | | 2 | | | 5 | | | | | | | | 8 | | | | 3 | | | | 6 | 4 | 7 | | | | 1 | 9 | 10 | 11 |
| 39 | | 2 | | 4 | 5 | 11 | | | | | | | 8 | | | | 3 | | | | 6 | | 7 | | | | 1 | 9 | 10 | |
| 40 | | 2 | | 4 | 5 | | | | | | | | 8 | | | | 3 | | | | 6 | | 7 | | | | 1 | 9 | 10 | 11 |
| 41 | | 2 | | 4 | 5 | | | | | | | | 8 | | | | 3 | | | | 6 | | 7 | | | | 1 | 9 | 10 | 11 |
| 42 | | 2 | | 4 | 5 | | | | | | | | 8 | | | | 3 | | | | 6 | | 7 | | | | 1 | 9 | 10 | 11 |
| Apps. | 17 | 36 | 17 | 37 | 34 | 29 | 19 | 7 | 24 | 20 | 12 | 8 | 34 | 1 | 12 | 15 | 24 | 2 | 16 | 8 | 13 | 5 | 19 | 5 | 2 | 1 | 13 | 11 | 11 | 10 |
| Goals | | | | | | 7 | 7 | 2 | 18 | 5 | 3 | | 11 | | | 10 | | | | | | | 7 | 2 | | 1 | | 12 | 3 | 1 |

## F.A. CUP

| | Date | Opposition | | FT | HT | Att. | Goalscorers |
|---|---|---|---|---|---|---|---|
| 1R | Nov 25 | DARLINGTON | W | 6-1 | 1-1 | 7000 | Mantle (2), Armes (3), Cresswell |
| 2R | Dec 9 | Southend United | L | 1-2 | 0-1 | 6900 | Cresswell |

| | Burke J. | Bennett F. | Freeman T. | Pitcairn J. | Skitt H. | McLachlan G. | Kelly G. | Mercer A. | Mantle J. | Cresswell F. | Hedley F. | Wyness G. | Whittam E. | Vaughan T. | Finnigan R. | Armes S. | Little J. | Upton W. | Duckworth R. | Jones H. | Bell W. | Morris S. | Hughes J. | Roberts C. | Kay J. | Roberts N. | Middleton R. | Wallbanks J. | Wilson A. | Sargeant C. |
|---|---|---|---|---|---|---|---|---|---|---|---|---|---|---|---|---|---|---|---|---|---|---|---|---|---|---|---|---|---|---|
| 1R | 1 | 2 | | 4 | 5 | 11 | | | 9 | 10 | | | 0 | | | 7 | 3 | | 6 | | | | | | | | | | | |
| 2R | 1 | 2 | | 4 | 5 | 11 | | | 9 | 10 | | | 8 | | | 7 | 3 | | 6 | | | | | | | | | | | |

## WELSH CUP

| | Date | Opposition | | FT | HT | Att. | Goalscorers |
|---|---|---|---|---|---|---|---|
| 6R | Feb 7 | SWANSEA TOWN | W | 2-1 | 1-1 | 4300 | Hughes (2 pens) |
| 7R | Mar 7 | Bangor City | L | 0-1 | 0-0 | 5500 | |

| | Burke J. | Bennett F. | Freeman T. | Pitcairn J. | Skitt H. | McLachlan G. | Kelly G. | Mercer A. | Mantle J. | Cresswell F. | Hedley F. | Wyness G. | Whittam E. | Vaughan T. | Finnigan R. | Armes S. | Little J. | Upton W. | Duckworth R. | Jones H. | Bell W. | Morris S. | Hughes J. | Roberts C. | Kay J. | Roberts N. | Middleton R. | Wallbanks J. | Wilson A. | Sargeant C. |
|---|---|---|---|---|---|---|---|---|---|---|---|---|---|---|---|---|---|---|---|---|---|---|---|---|---|---|---|---|---|---|
| 6R | 1 | 2 | 3 | | 5 | 6 | 11 | | 9 | | | | | 8 | | | | | | | | 4 | 7 | 10 | | | | | | |
| 7R | 1 | 2 | | 4 | 5 | | 7 | | 9 | | | | 8 | | | | 3 | | 6 | | | | 11 | 10 | | | | | | |

## DIVISION 3 NORTH CUP

| | Date | Opposition | | FT | HT | Att. | Goalscorers |
|---|---|---|---|---|---|---|---|
| 1R | Jan 30 | Southport | D | 1-1 | 0-0 | 1000 | Hughes (pen) |
| 1Rr | Feb 14 | SOUTHPORT | W | 3-2 | 2-1 | 2000 | Hughes (2, 1 pen), Vaughan |
| 2R | 28 | Wrexham | L | 0-2 | 0-1 | 10497 | |

| | Burke J. | Bennett F. | Freeman T. | Pitcairn J. | Skitt H. | McLachlan G. | Kelly G. | Mercer A. | Mantle J. | Cresswell F. | Hedley F. | Wyness G. | Whittam E. | Vaughan T. | Finnigan R. | Armes S. | Little J. | Upton W. | Duckworth R. | Jones H. | Bell W. | Morris S. | Hughes J. | Roberts C. | Kay J. | Roberts N. | Middleton R. | Wallbanks J. | Wilson A. | Sargeant C. |
|---|---|---|---|---|---|---|---|---|---|---|---|---|---|---|---|---|---|---|---|---|---|---|---|---|---|---|---|---|---|---|
| 1R | 1 | 2 | 3 | 4 | 5 | | 7 | | 9 | | | | 10 | | | | | | | | 6 | | 8 | | | 11 | | | | |
| 1Rr | 1 | 2 | | 4 | | | 7 | | | | | 5 | 10 | 9 | | | | | 6 | 3 | | | 8 | | | 11 | | | | |
| 2R | 1 | 2 | | 4 | 5 | 11 | 7 | | 9 | | | | | | | | 3 | | | | 6 | | 8 | | 10 | | | | | |

## FRIENDLIES

| | Date | Opposition | | FT | HT | Att. | Goalscorers |
|---|---|---|---|---|---|---|---|
| 1 | Apr 18 | Wrexham * | W | 3-2 | 3-0 | 2500 | C Roberts, Hughes (2) |

* Alf Jones Benefit

Final League Table

| | | Pl. | Home W | D | L | F | A | Away W | D | L | F | A | F. | A. | Pts |
|---|---|---|---|---|---|---|---|---|---|---|---|---|---|---|---|
| 1 | Barnsley | 42 | 18 | 3 | 0 | 64 | 18 | 9 | 5 | 7 | 54 | 43 | 118 | 61 | 62 |
| 2 | Chesterfield | 42 | 18 | 1 | 2 | 56 | 17 | 9 | 6 | 6 | 30 | 26 | 86 | 43 | 61 |
| 3 | Stockport County | 42 | 18 | 3 | 0 | 84 | 23 | 6 | 8 | 7 | 31 | 29 | 115 | 52 | 59 |
| 4 | Walsall | 42 | 18 | 2 | 1 | 66 | 18 | 5 | 5 | 11 | 31 | 42 | 97 | 60 | 53 |
| 5 | Doncaster Rovers | 42 | 17 | 1 | 3 | 58 | 24 | 5 | 8 | 8 | 25 | 37 | 83 | 61 | 53 |
| 6 | Wrexham | 42 | 14 | 1 | 6 | 68 | 35 | 9 | 4 | 8 | 34 | 38 | 102 | 73 | 51 |
| 7 | Tranmere Rovers | 42 | 16 | 2 | 3 | 57 | 21 | 4 | 5 | 12 | 27 | 42 | 84 | 63 | 47 |
| 8 | Barrow | 42 | 12 | 5 | 4 | 78 | 45 | 7 | 4 | 10 | 38 | 49 | 116 | 94 | 47 |
| 9 | Halifax Town | 42 | 15 | 2 | 4 | 57 | 30 | 5 | 2 | 14 | 23 | 61 | 80 | 91 | 44 |
| ***10*** | ***Chester*** | ***42*** | ***11*** | ***6*** | ***4*** | ***59*** | ***26*** | ***6*** | ***0*** | ***15*** | ***30*** | ***60*** | ***89*** | ***86*** | ***40*** |
| 11 | Hartlepools United | 42 | 14 | 3 | 4 | 54 | 24 | 2 | 4 | 15 | 35 | 69 | 89 | 93 | 39 |
| 12 | York City | 42 | 11 | 5 | 5 | 44 | 28 | 4 | 3 | 14 | 27 | 46 | 71 | 74 | 38 |
| 13 | Carlisle United | 42 | 11 | 6 | 4 | 43 | 23 | 4 | 2 | 15 | 23 | 58 | 66 | 81 | 38 |
| 14 | Crewe Alexandra | 42 | 12 | 3 | 6 | 54 | 38 | 3 | 3 | 15 | 27 | 59 | 81 | 97 | 36 |
| 15 | New Brighton | 42 | 13 | 3 | 5 | 41 | 25 | 1 | 5 | 15 | 21 | 62 | 62 | 87 | 36 |
| 16 | Darlington | 42 | 11 | 4 | 6 | 47 | 35 | 2 | 5 | 14 | 23 | 66 | 70 | 101 | 35 |
| 17 | Mansfield Town | 42 | 9 | 7 | 5 | 49 | 29 | 2 | 5 | 14 | 32 | 59 | 81 | 88 | 34 |
| 18 | Southport | 42 | 6 | 11 | 4 | 35 | 29 | 2 | 6 | 13 | 28 | 61 | 63 | 90 | 33 |
| 19 | Gateshead | 42 | 10 | 3 | 8 | 46 | 40 | 2 | 6 | 13 | 30 | 70 | 76 | 110 | 33 |
| 20 | Accrington Stanley | 42 | 10 | 6 | 5 | 44 | 38 | 3 | 1 | 17 | 21 | 63 | 65 | 101 | 33 |
| 21 | Rotherham United | 42 | 5 | 7 | 9 | 31 | 35 | 5 | 1 | 15 | 22 | 56 | 53 | 91 | 28 |
| 22 | Rochdale | 42 | 7 | 5 | 9 | 34 | 30 | 2 | 1 | 18 | 19 | 73 | 53 | 103 | 24 |

# SEASON 1934-35

## FOOTBALL LEAGUE DIVISION 3 (NORTH)

| | Date | Opposition | | FT | HT | Att. | Goalscorers | Middleton R. | Bennett F. | Hall E. | Pitcairn J. | Wilson A. | Fantham J. | Hughes J. | Whittam E. | Wallbanks J. | Cresswell F. | Sargeant C. | Bell W. | Sheppard W. | Little J. | Mantle J. | Kelly G. | Smallwood F. | Howarth H. | Burke J. | Simms H. | Kilcar S. | Rowley W. | Wharton G. |
|---|---|---|---|---|---|---|---|---|---|---|---|---|---|---|---|---|---|---|---|---|---|---|---|---|---|---|---|---|---|---|
| 1 | Aug 25 | Gateshead | W | 4-2 | 3-1 | 6532 | Sargeant (2), Whittam (2) | 1 | 2 | 3 | 4 | 5 | 6 | 7 | 8 | 9 | 10 | 11 | | | | | | | | | | | | |
| 2 | 29 | Hartlepools United | W | 2-0 | 0-0 | 5496 | Hughes (2) | 1 | 2 | 3 | 4 | 5 | 6 | 7 | 8 | 9 | 10 | 11 | | | | | | | | | | | | |
| 3 | Sep 1 | ACCRINGTON STANLEY | W | 4-0 | 3-0 | 8932 | Wallbanks, Cresswell (2), Hughes | 1 | 2 | 3 | 4 | 5 | 6 | 7 | 8 | 9 | 10 | 11 | | | | | | | | | | | | |
| 4 | 5 | HARTLEPOOLS UNITED | W | 4-1 | 3-1 | 8979 | Cresswell (3), Wallbanks | 1 | 2 | 3 | 4 | 5 | 6 | 7 | 8 | 9 | 10 | 11 | | | | | | | | | | | | |
| 5 | 8 | Darlington | L | 0-1 | 0-1 | 6991 | | 1 | 2 | 3 | 4 | 5 | | 7 | | 9 | 10 | 11 | 6 | 8 | | | | | | | | | | |
| 6 | 15 | YORK CITY | W | 5-1 | 3-1 | 8592 | Hughes (2, 1 pen), Whittam, Wallbanks (2) | 1 | | 3 | 4 | 5 | 6 | 7 | 8 | 9 | 10 | 11 | | | 2 | | | | | | | | | |
| 7 | 22 | New Brighton | W | 2-0 | 2-0 | 5249 | Wallbanks, Hughes | 1 | 2 | 3 | 4 | 5 | 6 | 7 | 8 | 9 | 10 | 11 | | | | | | | | | | | | |
| 8 | 29 | WREXHAM | W | 6-2 | 5-0 | 15106 | Wallbanks (4), Cresswell (2) | 1 | 2 | 3 | 4 | 5 | 6 | 8 | | 9 | 10 | 11 | | | | 7 | | | | | | | | |
| 9 | Oct 6 | SOUTHPORT | L | 0-2 | 0-0 | 5564 | | 1 | 2 | | 4 | 5 | 6 | 8 | | 9 | 10 | 11 | | | 3 | 7 | | | | | | | | |
| 10 | 13 | Doncaster Rovers | L | 0-3 | 0-0 | 10576 | | 1 | 2 | 3 | 4 | 5 | 6 | 7 | 8 | 9 | 10 | 11 | | | | | | | | | | | | |
| 11 | 20 | Halifax Town | L | 0-1 | 0-0 | 14488 | | 1 | 2 | 3 | 4 | 5 | 6 | 8 | | 9 | 10 | 11 | | | | | 7 | | | | | | | |
| 12 | 27 | ROTHERHAM UNITED | W | 4-1 | 3-0 | 5889 | Whittam (2), Sargeant, Wallbanks | 1 | 2 | 3 | 4 | 5 | 6 | | 8 | 9 | 10 | 11 | | | | 7 | | | | | | | | |
| 13 | Nov 3 | Walsall | D | 1-1 | 1-1 | 6721 | Kelly | 1 | 2 | 3 | 4 | 5 | 6 | | 8 | | 10 | 11 | | | | 9 | 7 | | | | | | | |
| 14 | 10 | CHESTERFIELD | D | 1-1 | 1-0 | 6230 | Hughes | 1 | 2 | 3 | 4 | 5 | 6 | 7 | 8 | 9 | 10 | 11 | | | | | | | | | | | | |
| 15 | 17 | Mansfield Town | D | 1-1 | 0-1 | 6402 | Wallbanks | 1 | 2 | 3 | 4 | 5 | 6 | | 8 | 9 | 10 | 11 | | | | | 7 | | | | | | | |
| 16 | Dec 1 | Carlisle United | W | 3-1 | 2-1 | 3711 | Wallbanks (3) | 1 | 2 | 3 | 4 | 5 | 6 | 8 | | 9 | 10 | 11 | | | | | 7 | | | | | | | |
| 17 | 15 | Lincoln City | D | 0-0 | 0-0 | 4394 | | 1 | 2 | 3 | 4 | 5 | | 8 | | 9 | 10 | 11 | 6 | | | | 7 | | | | | | | |
| 18 | 22 | TRANMERE ROVERS | D | 0-0 | 0-0 | 11217 | | 1 | 2 | 3 | 4 | 5 | | 8 | | 9 | 10 | 11 | 6 | | | | 7 | | | | | | | |
| 19 | 25 | STOCKPORT COUNTY | W | 5-1 | 1-1 | 7686 | Cresswell, Wallbanks (3), Kelly | 1 | 2 | 3 | 4 | 5 | | 8 | | 9 | 10 | 11 | 6 | | | | 7 | | | | | | | |
| 20 | 26 | Stockport County | W | 1-0 | 0-0 | 14196 | Wallbanks | 1 | 2 | 3 | 4 | 5 | | 8 | | 9 | 10 | 11 | 6 | | | | 7 | | | | | | | |
| 21 | 29 | GATESHEAD | D | 2-2 | 1-1 | 5419 | Wallbanks (2) | 1 | 2 | 3 | 4 | 5 | | 8 | | 9 | 10 | 11 | 6 | | | | 7 | | | | | | | |
| 22 | Jan 1 | Tranmere Rovers | D | 1-1 | 0-0 | 13054 | Cresswell | 1 | 2 | | 4 | 5 | | 7 | 8 | 9 | 10 | | 6 | | 3 | | | 11 | | | | | | |
| 23 | 5 | Accrington Stanley | D | 1-1 | 1-0 | 3733 | Whittam | 1 | 2 | | 4 | 5 | | 7 | 8 | 9 | 10 | 11 | 6 | | 3 | | | | | | | | | |
| 24 | 16 | BARROW | W | 6-2 | 5-1 | 3155 | Sargeant(2),Wallbanks(2),Cresswell,Whittam | 1 | 2 | 3 | 4 | 5 | | 7 | 8 | 9 | 10 | 11 | 6 | | | | | | | | | | | |
| 25 | 19 | DARLINGTON | W | 3-1 | 1-0 | 6892 | Cresswell (2), Mantle | 1 | 2 | 3 | 4 | 5 | | 7 | 8 | | 10 | 11 | 6 | | | 9 | | | | | | | | |
| 26 | 26 | York City | D | 1-1 | 1-1 | 2456 | Mantle | 1 | 2 | 3 | 4 | 5 | | 8 | | | 10 | 11 | 6 | | | 9 | 7 | | | | | | | |
| 27 | Feb 2 | NEW BRIGHTON | W | 5-4 | 3-1 | 6608 | Kelly (3), Hughes, Wilson (pen) | 1 | 2 | 3 | 4 | 5 | | 8 | | 9 | 10 | 11 | 6 | | | | 7 | | | | | | | |
| 28 | 9 | Wrexham | D | 2-2 | 1-1 | 18233 | Wallbanks, Cresswell | 1 | 2 | | 4 | 5 | | 8 | | 9 | 10 | 11 | | | 3 | | 7 | | 6 | | | | | |
| 29 | 16 | Southport | D | 1-1 | 0-1 | 1636 | Wallbanks | 1 | 2 | 3 | 4 | 5 | | | 8 | 9 | 10 | 11 | | | | | 7 | | 6 | | | | | |
| 30 | 23 | DONCASTER ROVERS | L | 1-3 | 0-1 | 9685 | Whittam | 1 | 2 | 3 | 4 | 5 | | | 8 | 9 | 10 | 11 | | | | | 7 | | 6 | | | | | |
| 31 | Mar 2 | HALIFAX TOWN | W | 5-0 | 4-0 | 5770 | Taylor (og), Cresswell (2), Mantle, Whittam | | 2 | | 4 | 5 | | | 8 | | 10 | 11 | | | 3 | 9 | 7 | | 6 | 1 | | | | |
| 32 | 9 | Rotherham United | L | 1-6 | 0-4 | 8182 | Sargeant | | 2 | | 4 | 5 | | | 8 | | 10 | 11 | | | 3 | 9 | 7 | | 6 | 1 | | | | |
| 33 | 16 | WALSALL | W | 2-1 | 2-0 | 4607 | Kelly, Simms | | 2 | 3 | 4 | 5 | | 8 | | | 10 | 11 | | | | | 7 | | 6 | 1 | 9 | | | |
| 34 | 23 | Chesterfield | W | 2-1 | 2-0 | 3479 | Kelly, Kilcar | | 2 | 3 | 4 | 5 | | 8 | | | | 11 | | | | 9 | 7 | | 6 | 1 | | 10 | | |
| 35 | 30 | MANSFIELD TOWN | W | 3-2 | 1-1 | 5160 | Kilcar (3) | | | 3 | 4 | 5 | | 8 | | | | 11 | | | 2 | 9 | 7 | | 6 | 1 | | 10 | | |
| 36 | Apr 3 | ROCHDALE | W | 1-0 | 0-0 | 3004 | Wilson (pen) | | | 3 | 4 | 5 | | 8 | | | | 11 | | | 2 | 9 | 7 | | 6 | 1 | | 10 | | |
| 37 | 6 | Barrow | L | 2-4 | 2-2 | 3544 | Mantle (2) | | | 3 | 4 | 5 | | 8 | | | 10 | 11 | | | 2 | 9 | 7 | | 6 | 1 | | | | |
| 38 | 13 | CARLISLE UNITED | W | 3-0 | 1-0 | 3986 | Sargeant, Henderson (og), Mantle | | 2 | 3 | 4 | 5 | | 8 | | | 10 | 11 | | | | 9 | 7 | | 6 | 1 | | | | |
| 39 | 19 | CREWE ALEX. | D | 2-2 | 1-0 | 10027 | Mantle, Kelly | | 2 | 3 | 4 | 5 | | 8 | | | 10 | 11 | | | | 9 | 7 | | 6 | 1 | | | | |
| 40 | 20 | Rochdale | D | 3-3 | 3-2 | 6933 | Mantle (3) | | 2 | | 4 | 5 | | 8 | | | 10 | 11 | | | 3 | 9 | 7 | | 6 | 1 | | | | |
| 41 | 22 | Crewe Alex. | D | 1-1 | 0-0 | 7761 | Mantle | | | 3 | 4 | 5 | | 7 | 8 | | 10 | 11 | | | | 9 | | | 6 | 1 | | | 2 | |
| 42 | 27 | LINCOLN CITY | L | 0-1 | 0-1 | 3733 | | | 2 | | 4 | 5 | | 8 | | | 10 | 11 | | | 3 | 9 | 7 | | 6 | 1 | | | | |
| | | | | | | | Apps. | 30 | 37 | 34 | 42 | 42 | 15 | 35 | 20 | 27 | 39 | 41 | 12 | 1 | 12 | 17 | 25 | 1 | 15 | 12 | 1 | 3 | 1 | |
| | | | | | | | Goals | | | | | 2 | | 8 | 9 | 24 | 15 | 7 | | | | 11 | 8 | | | | 1 | 4 | | |

Own Goals 2

## F.A. CUP

| | Date | Opposition | | FT | HT | Att. | Goalscorers | Middleton R. | Bennett F. | Hall E. | Pitcairn J. | Wilson A. | Fantham J. | Hughes J. | Whittam E. | Wallbanks J. | Cresswell F. | Sargeant C. | Bell W. | Sheppard W. | Little J. | Mantle J. | Kelly G. | Smallwood F. | Howarth H. | Burke J. | Simms H. | Kilcar S. | Rowley W. | Wharton G. |
|---|---|---|---|---|---|---|---|---|---|---|---|---|---|---|---|---|---|---|---|---|---|---|---|---|---|---|---|---|---|---|
| 1R | Nov 24 | DINNINGTON ATHLETIC | W | 3-1 | 2-0 | 6000 | Whittam, Kelly, Wallbanks | 1 | 2 | 3 | 4 | 5 | 6 | | 8 | 9 | 10 | 11 | | | | | 7 | | | | | | | |
| 2R | Dec 8 | Clapton Orient | W | 3-1 | 1-0 | 12350 | Cresswell, Kelly, Wallbanks | 1 | 2 | 3 | 4 | 5 | | 8 | | 9 | 10 | 11 | 6 | | | | 7 | | | | | | | |
| 3R | Jan 12 | NOTTINGHAM FOREST | L | 0-4 | 0-3 | 13127 | | 1 | 2 | 3 | 4 | 5 | | 7 | 8 | 9 | 10 | 11 | 6 | | | | | | | | | | | |

## WELSH CUP

| | Date | Opposition | | FT | HT | Att. | Goalscorers | Middleton R. | Bennett F. | Hall E. | Pitcairn J. | Wilson A. | Fantham J. | Hughes J. | Whittam E. | Wallbanks J. | Cresswell F. | Sargeant C. | Bell W. | Sheppard W. | Little J. | Mantle J. | Kelly G. | Smallwood F. | Howarth H. | Burke J. | Simms H. | Kilcar S. | Rowley W. | Wharton G. |
|---|---|---|---|---|---|---|---|---|---|---|---|---|---|---|---|---|---|---|---|---|---|---|---|---|---|---|---|---|---|---|
| 6R | Feb 13 | BANGOR CITY | W | 5-1 | 2-0 | 1000 | Wallbanks (3), Kelly, Pitcairn | 1 | 2 | | 4 | 5 | | 8 | | 9 | 10 | 11 | 6 | | 3 | | 7 | | | | | | | |
| 7R | Mar 27 | Cardiff City | D | 2-2 | 1-1 | | Mantle (2) | | 2 | 3 | 4 | 5 | | 8 | | | | 11 | | | | 9 | 7 | | 6 | 1 | | 10 | | |
| 7Rr | Apr 10 | CARDIFF CITY | W | 3-0 | 1-0 | 3000 | Sargeant (2), Mantle | | 2 | 3 | 4 | 5 | | 8 | | | 10 | 11 | | | | 9 | 7 | | 6 | 1 | | | | |
| SF | 24 | Swansea Town * | W | 5-0 | 4-0 | 5300 | Sargeant, Cresswell, Mantle, Hughes, Kelly | | 2 | 3 | 4 | 5 | | 8 | | | 10 | 11 | | | | 9 | 7 | | 6 | 1 | | | | |
| F | May 4 | TRANMERE ROVERS | L | 0-1 | 0-0 | 10000 | | | 2 | 3 | 4 | 5 | | 8 | | | 10 | 11 | | | | 9 | 7 | | 6 | 1 | | | | |

* Played at Wrexham

## DIVISION 3 NORTH CUP

| | Date | Opposition | | FT | HT | Att. | Goalscorers | Middleton R. | Bennett F. | Hall E. | Pitcairn J. | Wilson A. | Fantham J. | Hughes J. | Whittam E. | Wallbanks J. | Cresswell F. | Sargeant C. | Bell W. | Sheppard W. | Little J. | Mantle J. | Kelly G. | Smallwood F. | Howarth H. | Burke J. | Simms H. | Kilcar S. | Rowley W. | Wharton G. |
|---|---|---|---|---|---|---|---|---|---|---|---|---|---|---|---|---|---|---|---|---|---|---|---|---|---|---|---|---|---|---|
| 1R | Nov 14 | Wrexham | D | 1-1 | 0-0 | 6190 | Wallbanks | 1 | 2 | 3 | 4 | 5 | | 7 | 8 | 9 | 10 | 11 | | | | | | | | | | | | 6 |
| 1Rr | Feb 27 | WREXHAM | W | 1-0 | 0-0 | 2900 | Kelly | | 2 | 3 | | 5 | | | 8 | | 10 | 11 | | | | 9 | 7 | | 6 | 1 | | | | 4 |
| 3R | Mar 13 | CREWE ALEX. | L | 0-1 | 0-1 | 1598 | | | 2 | 3 | | 5 | | 7 | 8 | | 10 | 11 | | | | | | | 6 | 1 | 9 | | | 4 |

### Final League Table

| | | Pl. | Home W | Home D | Home L | Home F | Home A | Away W | Away D | Away L | Away F | Away A | F. | A. | Pts |
|---|---|---|---|---|---|---|---|---|---|---|---|---|---|---|---|
| 1 | Doncaster Rovers | 42 | 16 | 0 | 5 | 53 | 21 | 10 | 5 | 6 | 34 | 23 | 87 | 44 | 57 |
| 2 | Halifax Town | 42 | 17 | 2 | 2 | 50 | 24 | 8 | 3 | 10 | 26 | 43 | 76 | 67 | 55 |
| ***3*** | ***Chester*** | ***42*** | ***14*** | ***4*** | ***3*** | ***62*** | ***27*** | ***6*** | ***10*** | ***5*** | ***29*** | ***31*** | ***91*** | ***58*** | ***54*** |
| 4 | Lincoln City | 42 | 14 | 3 | 4 | 55 | 21 | 8 | 4 | 9 | 32 | 37 | 87 | 58 | 51 |
| 5 | Darlington | 42 | 15 | 5 | 1 | 50 | 15 | 6 | 4 | 11 | 30 | 44 | 80 | 59 | 51 |
| 6 | Tranmere Rovers | 42 | 15 | 4 | 2 | 53 | 20 | 5 | 7 | 9 | 21 | 35 | 74 | 55 | 51 |
| 7 | Stockport County | 42 | 15 | 2 | 4 | 57 | 22 | 7 | 1 | 13 | 33 | 50 | 90 | 72 | 47 |
| 8 | Mansfield Town | 42 | 16 | 3 | 2 | 55 | 25 | 3 | 6 | 12 | 20 | 37 | 75 | 62 | 47 |
| 9 | Rotherham United | 42 | 14 | 4 | 3 | 56 | 21 | 5 | 3 | 13 | 30 | 52 | 86 | 73 | 45 |
| 10 | Chesterfield | 42 | 13 | 4 | 4 | 46 | 21 | 4 | 6 | 11 | 25 | 31 | 71 | 52 | 44 |
| 11 | Wrexham | 42 | 12 | 5 | 4 | 47 | 25 | 4 | 6 | 11 | 29 | 44 | 76 | 69 | 43 |
| 12 | Hartlepools United | 42 | 12 | 4 | 5 | 52 | 34 | 5 | 3 | 13 | 28 | 44 | 80 | 78 | 41 |
| 13 | Crewe Alexandra | 42 | 12 | 6 | 3 | 41 | 25 | 2 | 5 | 14 | 25 | 61 | 66 | 86 | 39 |
| 14 | Walsall | 42 | 11 | 7 | 3 | 51 | 18 | 2 | 3 | 16 | 30 | 54 | 81 | 72 | 36 |
| 15 | York City | 42 | 12 | 5 | 4 | 50 | 20 | 3 | 1 | 17 | 26 | 62 | 76 | 82 | 36 |
| 16 | New Brighton | 42 | 9 | 6 | 6 | 32 | 25 | 5 | 2 | 14 | 27 | 51 | 59 | 76 | 36 |
| 17 | Barrow | 42 | 11 | 5 | 5 | 37 | 31 | 2 | 4 | 15 | 21 | 56 | 58 | 87 | 35 |
| 18 | Accrington Stanley | 42 | 11 | 5 | 5 | 44 | 36 | 1 | 5 | 15 | 19 | 53 | 63 | 89 | 34 |
| 19 | Gateshead | 42 | 12 | 4 | 5 | 36 | 28 | 1 | 4 | 16 | 22 | 68 | 58 | 96 | 34 |
| 20 | Rochdale | 42 | 9 | 5 | 7 | 39 | 35 | 2 | 6 | 13 | 14 | 36 | 53 | 71 | 33 |
| 21 | Southport | 42 | 6 | 6 | 9 | 27 | 36 | 4 | 6 | 11 | 28 | 49 | 55 | 85 | 32 |
| 22 | Carlisle United | 42 | 7 | 6 | 8 | 34 | 36 | 1 | 1 | 19 | 17 | 66 | 51 | 102 | 23 |

**1934/35 Season**

(Back) Pitcairn, Wilson, Bennett, Middleton, Hall, Fantham. (Front) Hughes, Kelly, Whittam, Wallbanks, Cresswell, Sargeant.

**1935/36 Season**

(Back) Wrightson, Pitcairn, Burke, Skitt, Hall, Ross (Trainer). (Front) Common, Horsman, Williams, Wilson, Cresswell, Sargeant.

# SEASON 1935-36

## FOOTBALL LEAGUE DIVISION 3 (NORTH)

| | Date | Opposition | | FT | HT | Att. | Goalscorers | Burke J. | Common E. | Hall E. | Anderson E. | Wilson A. | Howarth H. | Kelly G. | Wrightson F. | Williams R. | Cresswell F. | Sargeant C. | Horsman W. | Bennett F. | Pitcairn J. | Hughes J. | Wharton G. | Davies J. | Middleton R. | Sanders R. | Rowley W. | Skitt H. |
|---|---|---|---|---|---|---|---|---|---|---|---|---|---|---|---|---|---|---|---|---|---|---|---|---|---|---|---|---|
| 1 | Aug 31 | SOUTHPORT | W | 5-1 | 3-0 | 9444 | Williams (3), Grainger (og), Sargeant | 1 | 2 | 3 | 4 | 5 | 6 | 7 | 8 | 9 | 10 | 11 | | | | | | | | | | |
| 2 | Sep 2 | Accrington Stanley | W | 3-0 | 3-0 | 4227 | Williams, Kelly, Wrightson | 1 | 2 | 3 | 4 | 5 | 6 | 7 | 8 | 9 | 10 | 11 | | | | | | | | | | |
| 3 | 7 | Wrexham | L | 0-1 | 0-0 | 24690 | | 1 | 2 | 3 | 4 | 5 | 6 | 7 | 8 | 9 | 10 | 11 | | | | | | | | | | |
| 4 | 11 | ACCRINGTON STANLEY | W | 4-0 | 3-0 | 6521 | Sargeant (2), Williams, Wrightson | 1 | 2 | 3 | 4 | 5 | 6 | | 8 | 9 | 10 | 11 | 7 | | | | | | | | | |
| 5 | 14 | Lincoln City | D | 1-1 | 1-1 | 8051 | Williams | 1 | 2 | 3 | 4 | 5 | 6 | | 8 | 9 | 10 | 11 | 7 | | | | | | | | | |
| 6 | 18 | Crewe Alex. | D | 1-1 | 1-1 | 6976 | Williams | 1 | 2 | 3 | 4 | 5 | 6 | | 8 | 9 | 10 | 11 | 7 | | | | | | | | | |
| 7 | 21 | ROCHDALE | W | 5-2 | 4-1 | 6914 | Wrightson (2), Williams, Cresswell (2) | 1 | | 3 | 4 | 5 | 6 | | 8 | 9 | 10 | 11 | 7 | 2 | | | | | | | | |
| 8 | 25 | OLDHAM ATHLETIC | D | 1-1 | 1-0 | 8205 | Williams | 1 | | 3 | 4 | 5 | 6 | | 8 | 9 | 10 | 11 | 7 | | 2 | | | | | | | |
| 9 | 28 | York City | W | 2-1 | 1-1 | 4917 | Williams (2) | 1 | | 3 | 4 | 5 | 6 | | 8 | 9 | | 11 | 7 | 2 | | 10 | | | | | | |
| 10 | Oct 2 | CREWE ALEX. | L | 0-1 | 0-0 | 5470 | | 1 | | 3 | 4 | 5 | 6 | | 8 | 9 | | 11 | 7 | 2 | | 10 | | | | | | |
| 11 | 5 | BARROW | L | 1-2 | 1-1 | 5841 | Williams | 1 | | 3 | 4 | 5 | 6 | | 8 | 9 | 10 | 11 | 7 | 2 | | | | | | | | |
| 12 | 12 | New Brighton | D | 3-3 | 2-1 | 5065 | Cresswell, Howarth, Williams | 1 | | 3 | | 5 | 6 | | 8 | 9 | 10 | 11 | 7 | 2 | | | 4 | | | | | |
| 13 | 19 | ROTHERHAM UNITED | D | 0-0 | 0-0 | 5187 | | 1 | 2 | 3 | 4 | 5 | 6 | 7 | | 9 | 10 | | 11 | | | 8 | | | | | | |
| 14 | 26 | Mansfield Town | D | 0-0 | 0-0 | 5561 | | 1 | 2 | 3 | 4 | 5 | 6 | | 8 | 9 | 10 | 11 | 7 | | | | | | | | | |
| 15 | Nov 2 | HARTLEPOOLS UNITED | W | 4-0 | 1-0 | 5503 | Cresswell, Horsman, Hughes, Williams | 1 | 2 | 3 | | 5 | 6 | | | 9 | 10 | 11 | 7 | | 4 | 8 | | | | | | |
| 16 | 9 | Carlisle United | W | 3-1 | 1-1 | 8778 | Horsman, Cresswell, Sargeant | 1 | 2 | 3 | | 5 | 6 | | | 9 | 10 | 11 | 7 | | 4 | 8 | | | | | | |
| 17 | 16 | WALSALL | W | 2-0 | 2-0 | 6429 | Cresswell, Williams | 1 | 2 | 3 | | 5 | 6 | | | 9 | 10 | 11 | 7 | | 4 | 8 | | | | | | |
| 18 | 23 | Tranmere Rovers | L | 1-3 | 0-2 | 15457 | Hughes | 1 | 2 | 3 | | 5 | 6 | | | 9 | 10 | 11 | 7 | | 4 | 8 | | | | | | |
| 19 | Dec 7 | Darlington | D | 1-1 | 1-0 | 3906 | Hughes | 1 | 2 | 3 | | 5 | 6 | 9 | | 8 | 10 | | | | 4 | 7 | | 11 | | | | |
| 20 | 25 | CHESTERFIELD | D | 1-1 | 1-0 | 7880 | Cresswell | | 2 | 3 | | 5 | 6 | | | 9 | 10 | 11 | 7 | | 4 | 8 | | | 1 | | | |
| 21 | 26 | Chesterfield | L | 0-1 | 0-0 | 7310 | | | 2 | 3 | | 5 | 6 | | | 9 | 10 | 11 | 7 | | 4 | 8 | | | 1 | | | |
| 22 | 28 | Southport | L | 1-2 | 0-2 | 3000 | Horsman | 1 | 2 | 3 | | 5 | 6 | 9 | | 8 | 10 | | 11 | | 4 | 7 | | | | | | |
| 23 | Jan 4 | WREXHAM | D | 1-1 | 0-1 | 10511 | Sargeant | 1 | 2 | 3 | | 5 | 6 | | | 9 | 10 | 11 | 7 | | 4 | 8 | | | | | | |
| 24 | 11 | GATESHEAD | W | 4-0 | 1-0 | 3581 | Kelly (3), Cresswell | | 2 | 3 | | | 6 | 9 | | | 10 | 11 | 7 | | 4 | 8 | 5 | | 1 | | | |
| 25 | 25 | Rochdale | D | 1-1 | 1-0 | 4420 | Cresswell (pen) | | 2 | 3 | | | 6 | 9 | | | 10 | 11 | 7 | | 4 | 8 | 5 | | 1 | | | |
| 26 | Feb 1 | YORK CITY | W | 12-0 | 8-0 | 3775 | Sargeant (4), Wrightson (4), Cresswell (2), Horsman (2) | | 2 | 3 | | 5 | 6 | | 9 | | 10 | 11 | 7 | | | 8 | 4 | | 1 | | | |
| 27 | 8 | Barrow | W | 4-2 | 2-0 | 2930 | Wrightson (3), Cresswell (pen) | | 2 | 3 | | 5 | 6 | | 9 | | 10 | 11 | 7 | | | 8 | 4 | | 1 | | | |
| 28 | 15 | NEW BRIGHTON | W | 8-2 | 3-0 | 4860 | Wrightson (3), Cresswell (2,1 pen), Hughes (2), Horsman | | 2 | 3 | | 5 | 6 | | 9 | | 10 | 11 | 7 | | | 8 | 4 | | 1 | | | |
| 29 | 22 | Rotherham United | W | 2-1 | 2-1 | 5300 | Wrightson (2) | 1 | 2 | 3 | | 5 | 6 | | 9 | | 10 | 11 | 7 | | | 8 | 4 | | | | | |
| 30 | 25 | Oldham Athletic | W | 3-1 | 3-0 | 3361 | Wrightson, Hughes, Sargeant | 1 | 2 | 3 | | 5 | 6 | | 9 | | 10 | 11 | 7 | | | 8 | 4 | | | | | |
| 31 | 29 | CARLISLE UNITED | W | 3-2 | 2-1 | 3675 | Wrightson, Horsman, Cresswell | 1 | 2 | 3 | | 5 | 6 | | 9 | | 10 | 11 | 7 | | | 8 | 4 | | | | | |
| 32 | Mar 7 | Hartlepools United | W | 2-0 | 1-0 | 4167 | Wrightson (2) | 1 | 2 | 3 | 4 | 5 | 6 | | 9 | | 10 | 11 | 7 | | | 8 | | | | | | |
| 33 | 14 | MANSFIELD TOWN | W | 4-0 | 2-0 | 5533 | Kelly (2), Wrightson (2) | 1 | 2 | 3 | 4 | 5 | 6 | 11 | 9 | | 10 | | 7 | | | 8 | | | | | | |
| 34 | 21 | Walsall | L | 0-1 | 0-1 | 5489 | | 1 | 2 | 3 | 4 | 5 | 6 | | 9 | | 10 | 11 | 7 | | | 8 | | | | | | |
| 35 | 28 | TRANMERE ROVERS | D | 1-1 | 1-0 | 16375 | Horsman | 1 | 2 | 3 | | 5 | 6 | 10 | 9 | | | 11 | 7 | | 4 | 8 | | | | | | |
| 36 | Apr 4 | Gateshead | L | 0-2 | 0-0 | 3639 | | 1 | 2 | 3 | | 5 | 6 | 7 | 9 | 10 | | 11 | | | 4 | 8 | | | | | | |
| 37 | 10 | STOCKPORT COUNTY | W | 2-0 | 1-0 | 10500 | Wrightson (2) | 1 | 2 | 3 | | 5 | 6 | 7 | 9 | | | 11 | | | 4 | 8 | | | | 10 | | |
| 38 | 11 | DARLINGTON | W | 4-1 | 2-1 | 4829 | Coulthard (og), Wrightson (2), Kelly | 1 | 2 | 3 | | 5 | 6 | 7 | 9 | | | 11 | | | 4 | 8 | | | | 10 | | |
| 39 | 13 | Stockport County | L | 0-2 | 0-0 | 6750 | | 1 | 2 | 3 | | 5 | 6 | 9 | | | | 11 | | | 4 | 8 | | 7 | | 10 | | |
| 40 | 18 | Halifax Town | W | 3-2 | 2-1 | 5932 | Wharton (2), Sargeant | 1 | 2 | | | 5 | 6 | | 9 | | | 11 | 7 | | 4 | | 8 | | | 10 | 3 | |
| 41 | 22 | LINCOLN CITY | W | 4-2 | 3-0 | 4726 | Wharton (2), Horsman (2) | 1 | 2 | 3 | | 5 | 6 | | 9 | | | 11 | 7 | | 4 | | 8 | | | 10 | | |
| 42 | 29 | HALIFAX TOWN | W | 3-1 | 0-1 | 3973 | Wrightson, Wharton, Wilson | 1 | 2 | 3 | | 5 | 6 | | 9 | | | 11 | 7 | | 4 | | 8 | | | 10 | | |
| | | | | | | | Apps. | 35 | 36 | 41 | 16 | 40 | 42 | 14 | 29 | 24 | 32 | 38 | 34 | 5 | 20 | 28 | 12 | 2 | 7 | 6 | 1 | |
| | | | | | | | Goals | | | | | 1 | 1 | 7 | 27 | 15 | 15 | 11 | 10 | | | 6 | 5 | | | | | |

Own Goals 2

## F.A. CUP

| | Date | Opposition | | FT | HT | Att. | Goalscorers | Burke J. | Common E. | Hall E. | Anderson E. | Wilson A. | Howarth H. | Kelly G. | Wrightson F. | Williams R. | Cresswell F. | Sargeant C. | Horsman W. | Bennett F. | Pitcairn J. | Hughes J. | Wharton G. | Davies J. | Middleton R. | Sanders R. | Rowley W. | Skitt H. |
|---|---|---|---|---|---|---|---|---|---|---|---|---|---|---|---|---|---|---|---|---|---|---|---|---|---|---|---|---|
| 1R | Nov 30 | GATESHEAD | W | 1-0 | 0-0 | 6200 | Cresswell | 1 | 2 | 3 | | 5 | 6 | | | 9 | 10 | 11 | 7 | | 4 | 8 | | | | | | |
| 2R | Dec 14 | READING | D | 3-3 | 3-2 | 13000 | Cresswell (2), Wrightson | 1 | 2 | 3 | | 6 | | | 8 | 9 | 10 | 11 | 7 | | 4 | | | | | | | 5 |
| 2Rr | 18 | Reading | L | 0-3 | 0-1 | 10152 | | | 2 | 3 | | 5 | | | 9 | | 10 | 11 | 7 | | 4 | 8 | 6 | | 1 | | | |

## WELSH CUP

| | Date | Opposition | | FT | HT | Att. | Goalscorers | Burke J. | Common E. | Hall E. | Anderson E. | Wilson A. | Howarth H. | Kelly G. | Wrightson F. | Williams R. | Cresswell F. | Sargeant C. | Horsman W. | Bennett F. | Pitcairn J. | Hughes J. | Wharton G. | Davies J. | Middleton R. | Sanders R. | Rowley W. | Skitt H. |
|---|---|---|---|---|---|---|---|---|---|---|---|---|---|---|---|---|---|---|---|---|---|---|---|---|---|---|---|---|
| 7R | Feb 12 | SOUTHPORT | W | 2-1 | 1-1 | 2000 | Wrightson, Horsman | | 2 | 3 | | 5 | 6 | | 9 | | 10 | 11 | 7 | | | 8 | 4 | | 1 | | | |
| 8R | Mar 11 | SWANSEA TOWN | W | 4-1 | 1-1 | 5500 | Wrightson (2), Cresswell, Kelly | 1 | 2 | 3 | 4 | 5 | 6 | 11 | 9 | | 10 | | 7 | | | 8 | | | | | | |
| SF | Apr 16 | Rhyl | W | 3-0 | 1-0 | | Wharton (3) | 1 | 2 | | | 5 | 6 | | 9 | | | 11 | 7 | | 4 | | 8 | | | 10 | 3 | |
| F | 30 | Crewe Alex. * | L | 0-2 | 0-1 | 7000 | | 1 | 2 | 3 | | 5 | 6 | | 9 | | | 11 | 7 | | 4 | | 8 | | | 10 | | |

* Played at Wrexham

## DIVISION 3 NORTH CUP

| | Date | Opposition | | FT | HT | Att. | Goalscorers | Burke J. | Common E. | Hall E. | Anderson E. | Wilson A. | Howarth H. | Kelly G. | Wrightson F. | Williams R. | Cresswell F. | Sargeant C. | Horsman W. | Bennett F. | Pitcairn J. | Hughes J. | Wharton G. | Davies J. | Middleton R. | Sanders R. | Rowley W. | Skitt H. |
|---|---|---|---|---|---|---|---|---|---|---|---|---|---|---|---|---|---|---|---|---|---|---|---|---|---|---|---|---|
| 2R | Jan 29 | Wrexham | D | 2-2 | 1-0 | 2577 | Cresswell, Sargeant | | 2 | 3 | | | 6 | | 9 | | 10 | 11 | 7 | | 4 | 8 | 5 | | 1 | | | |
| 2Rr | Feb 19 | WREXHAM | W | 4-0 | 3-0 | | Wrightson, Cresswell, Sargeant (2) | 1 | 2 | 3 | | 5 | 6 | | 9 | | 10 | 11 | 7 | | | 8 | 4 | | | | | |
| 3R | Mar 25 | SOUTHPORT | W | 4-1 | 3-1 | 2000 | Wrightson (4) | 1 | 2 | 3 | | 10 | 6 | | 9 | | | 11 | 7 | | 4 | 8 | 5 | | | | | |
| SF | Apr 23 | Lincoln City | W | 3-2 | 2-1 | 1000 | Wharton, Wrightson, Sargeant | 1 | 2 | 3 | | 5 | 6 | | 9 | | | 11 | 7 | | 4 | | 8 | | | 10 | | |
| F | 27 | Darlington | W | 2-1 | 1-0 | 7820 | Horsman, Wrightson | 1 | 2 | 3 | | 5 | 6 | | 9 | | | 11 | 7 | | 4 | | 8 | | | 10 | | |

### Final League Table

| | | Pl. | Home W | Home D | Home L | Home F | Home A | Away W | Away D | Away L | Away F | Away A | F. | A. | Pts |
|---|---|---|---|---|---|---|---|---|---|---|---|---|---|---|---|
| 1 | Chesterfield | 42 | 15 | 3 | 3 | 60 | 14 | 9 | 9 | 3 | 32 | 25 | 92 | 39 | 60 |
| ***2*** | ***Chester*** | ***42*** | ***14*** | ***5*** | ***2*** | ***69*** | ***18*** | ***8*** | ***6*** | ***7*** | ***31*** | ***27*** | ***100*** | ***45*** | ***55*** |
| 3 | Tranmere Rovers | 42 | 17 | 2 | 2 | 75 | 28 | 5 | 9 | 7 | 18 | 30 | 93 | 58 | 55 |
| 4 | Lincoln City | 42 | 18 | 1 | 2 | 64 | 14 | 4 | 8 | 9 | 27 | 37 | 91 | 51 | 53 |
| 5 | Stockport County | 42 | 15 | 2 | 4 | 45 | 18 | 5 | 6 | 10 | 20 | 31 | 65 | 49 | 48 |
| 6 | Crewe Alexandra | 42 | 14 | 4 | 3 | 55 | 31 | 5 | 5 | 11 | 25 | 46 | 80 | 70 | 47 |
| 7 | Oldham Athletic | 42 | 13 | 5 | 3 | 60 | 25 | 5 | 4 | 12 | 26 | 48 | 86 | 73 | 45 |
| 8 | Hartlepools United | 42 | 13 | 6 | 2 | 41 | 18 | 2 | 6 | 13 | 16 | 43 | 57 | 61 | 42 |
| 9 | Accrington Stanley | 42 | 12 | 5 | 4 | 43 | 24 | 5 | 3 | 13 | 20 | 48 | 63 | 72 | 42 |
| 10 | Walsall | 42 | 15 | 2 | 4 | 58 | 13 | 1 | 7 | 13 | 21 | 46 | 79 | 59 | 41 |
| 11 | Rotherham United | 42 | 14 | 3 | 4 | 52 | 13 | 2 | 6 | 13 | 17 | 53 | 69 | 66 | 41 |
| 12 | Darlington | 42 | 16 | 3 | 2 | 60 | 26 | 1 | 3 | 17 | 14 | 53 | 74 | 79 | 40 |
| 13 | Carlisle United | 42 | 13 | 5 | 3 | 44 | 19 | 1 | 7 | 13 | 12 | 43 | 56 | 62 | 40 |
| 14 | Gateshead | 42 | 11 | 10 | 0 | 37 | 18 | 2 | 4 | 15 | 19 | 58 | 56 | 76 | 40 |
| 15 | Barrow | 42 | 9 | 9 | 3 | 33 | 16 | 4 | 3 | 14 | 25 | 49 | 58 | 65 | 38 |
| 16 | York City | 42 | 10 | 8 | 3 | 41 | 28 | 3 | 4 | 14 | 21 | 67 | 62 | 95 | 38 |
| 17 | Halifax Town | 42 | 12 | 3 | 6 | 34 | 22 | 3 | 4 | 14 | 23 | 39 | 57 | 61 | 37 |
| 18 | Wrexham | 42 | 12 | 3 | 6 | 39 | 18 | 3 | 4 | 14 | 27 | 57 | 66 | 75 | 37 |
| 19 | Mansfield Town | 42 | 13 | 5 | 3 | 55 | 25 | 1 | 4 | 16 | 25 | 66 | 80 | 91 | 37 |
| 20 | Rochdale | 42 | 8 | 10 | 3 | 35 | 26 | 2 | 3 | 16 | 23 | 62 | 58 | 88 | 33 |
| 21 | Southport | 42 | 9 | 8 | 4 | 31 | 26 | 2 | 1 | 18 | 17 | 64 | 48 | 90 | 31 |
| 22 | New Brighton | 42 | 8 | 5 | 8 | 29 | 33 | 1 | 1 | 19 | 14 | 69 | 43 | 102 | 24 |

# SEASON 1936-37

## FOOTBALL LEAGUE DIVISION 3 (NORTH)

| | Date | Opposition | | FT | HT | Att. | Goalscorers |
|---|---|---|---|---|---|---|---|
| 1 | Aug 29 | WREXHAM | W | 4-1 | 0-0 | 16004 | Wrightson, Chambers, Horsman (2) |
| 2 | Sep 2 | CREWE ALEX. | W | 5-0 | 2-0 | 8531 | Wrightson (2), Chambers (3) |
| 3 | 5 | Rochdale | W | 1-0 | 0-0 | 5806 | Horsman |
| 4 | 7 | Crewe Alex. | D | 1-1 | 1-0 | 7389 | Sargeant |
| 5 | 12 | BARROW | W | 6-0 | 5-0 | 6104 | Wrightson (2), Horsman (2), Trevis, Sargeant |
| 6 | 16 | TRANMERE ROVERS | W | 5-2 | 3-1 | 12579 | Sargeant, Wrightson(2), Alderson, Chambers (pen) |
| 7 | 19 | York City | W | 2-0 | 1-0 | 10629 | Wrightson, Sargeant |
| 8 | 26 | CARLISLE UNITED | W | 4-0 | 2-0 | 8932 | Horsman, Wrightson (3) |
| 9 | Oct 3 | Hartlepools United | W | 1-0 | 1-0 | 12220 | Sargeant |
| 10 | 10 | SOUTHPORT | L | 2-3 | 1-2 | 8639 | Sargeant, Wrightson |
| 11 | 17 | DARLINGTON | W | 2-1 | 2-1 | 6762 | Horsman, Wrightson |
| 12 | 24 | Gateshead | D | 1-1 | 1-0 | 3838 | Wrightson |
| 13 | 31 | HULL CITY | W | 3-1 | 3-0 | 10235 | Wrightson (2), Dimbleby (og) |
| 14 | Nov 7 | New Brighton | L | 0-1 | 0-0 | 8435 | |
| 15 | 14 | LINCOLN CITY | W | 7-3 | 4-1 | 8343 | Gurry (3), Wrightson (3), Sargeant |
| 16 | 21 | Accrington Stanley | L | 1-2 | 1-0 | 4727 | Wrightson |
| 17 | 28 | PORT VALE | D | 0-0 | 0-0 | 7616 | |
| 18 | Dec 5 | Port Vale | L | 0-4 | 0-1 | 12950 | |
| 19 | 12 | ROTHERHAM UNITED | W | 2-1 | 2-1 | 4076 | Wrightson, Sanders |
| 20 | 19 | Stockport County | L | 0-4 | 0-1 | 6953 | |
| 21 | 25 | HALIFAX TOWN | D | 1-1 | 1-0 | 11241 | Wrightson |
| 22 | 26 | Wrexham | W | 2-1 | 1-0 | 29261 | Wrightson, Sanders |
| 23 | 28 | Halifax Town | L | 0-1 | 0-1 | 6290 | |
| 24 | Jan 1 | Tranmere Rovers | L | 0-5 | 0-3 | 13051 | |
| 25 | 2 | ROCHDALE | D | 2-2 | 1-1 | 4514 | Wrightson, Davies |
| 26 | 9 | Barrow | W | 2-1 | 1-0 | 4103 | Wrightson, Sargeant |
| 27 | 23 | YORK CITY | W | 3-1 | 1-1 | 4235 | Alderson, Legge (og), Sargeant |
| 28 | Feb 4 | Carlisle United | D | 1-1 | 0-1 | 3362 | Alderson |
| 29 | 6 | HARTLEPOOLS UNITED | W | 3-0 | 1-0 | 5444 | Alderson, Wrightson, Gale |
| 30 | 13 | Southport | W | 2-1 | 1-0 | 6953 | Horsman, Prout |
| 31 | 20 | Darlington | W | 3-1 | 1-1 | 6646 | Wrightson (2), Gale |
| 32 | Mar 6 | Hull City | D | 1-1 | 1-1 | 7986 | Sargeant |
| 33 | 13 | NEW BRIGHTON | W | 4-1 | 2-1 | 5755 | Wrightson (2), Gale, Sargeant |
| 34 | 20 | Lincoln City | L | 0-3 | 0-1 | 11498 | |
| 35 | 26 | Mansfield Town | L | 0-5 | 0-0 | 6920 | |
| 36 | 27 | ACCRINGTON STANLEY | D | 1-1 | 1-0 | 6197 | Chambers |
| 37 | 29 | MANSFIELD TOWN | W | 5-1 | 2-0 | 9448 | Horsman (2), Gale, Sargeant, Chambers |
| 38 | Apr 3 | Oldham Athletic | L | 0-1 | 0-1 | 9899 | |
| 39 | 14 | OLDHAM ATHLETIC | W | 2-1 | 1-0 | 2707 | Gale, Hilton (og) |
| 40 | 17 | Rotherham United | L | 1-2 | 0-1 | 4054 | Chambers |
| 41 | 21 | GATESHEAD | W | 6-0 | 3-0 | 1765 | Sargeant (3), Wrightson (2), Chambers |
| 42 | 24 | STOCKPORT COUNTY | D | 1-1 | 1-0 | 15255 | Sargeant |

| | Gray A. | Common E. | Hall E. | Trevis A. | Wilson A. | Howarth H. | Horsman W. | Chambers W. | Wrightson F. | Alderson T. | Sargeant C. | Pitcairn J. | Mansley E. | Anderson E. | Gurry J. | Percival P. | Sanders R. | Gale A. | Davies J. | Prout S. | Turner J. | Middleton R. |
|---|---|---|---|---|---|---|---|---|---|---|---|---|---|---|---|---|---|---|---|---|---|---|
| 1 | 1 | 2 | 3 | 4 | 5 | 6 | 7 | 8 | 9 | 10 | 11 | | | | | | | | | | | |
| 2 | 1 | 2 | 3 | 4 | 5 | 6 | 7 | 8 | 9 | 10 | 11 | | | | | | | | | | | |
| 3 | 1 | 2 | 3 | 4 | 5 | 6 | 7 | 8 | 9 | 10 | 11 | | | | | | | | | | | |
| 4 | 1 | 2 | 3 | 4 | 5 | 6 | 7 | 8 | 9 | 10 | 11 | | | | | | | | | | | |
| 5 | 1 | 2 | 3 | 4 | 5 | 6 | 7 | 8 | 9 | 10 | 11 | | | | | | | | | | | |
| 6 | 1 | 2 | 3 | 4 | 5 | 6 | 7 | 8 | 9 | 10 | 11 | | | | | | | | | | | |
| 7 | 1 | 2 | 3 | 4 | 5 | 6 | 7 | 8 | 9 | 10 | 11 | | | | | | | | | | | |
| 8 | 1 | 2 | 3 | 4 | 5 | 6 | 7 | 8 | 9 | 10 | 11 | | | | | | | | | | | |
| 9 | 1 | 2 | 3 | 4 | 5 | 6 | 7 | 8 | 9 | 10 | 11 | | | | | | | | | | | |
| 10 | 1 | 2 | 3 | | 5 | 6 | 7 | 8 | 9 | 10 | 11 | 4 | | | | | | | | | | |
| 11 | | 2 | 3 | | 5 | 6 | 7 | 8 | 9 | 10 | 11 | | 1 | 4 | | | | | | | | |
| 12 | 1 | 2 | 3 | | 5 | 6 | 7 | 8 | 9 | | 11 | | | 4 | 10 | | | | | | | |
| 13 | 1 | 2 | 3 | | 5 | 6 | 7 | 8 | 9 | 10 | 11 | | | 4 | | | | | | | | |
| 14 | 1 | 2 | 3 | | 5 | 6 | 7 | | 9 | 10 | 11 | | | 4 | 8 | | | | | | | |
| 15 | 1 | 2 | 3 | | 5 | 6 | 7 | | 9 | 10 | 11 | | | 4 | 8 | | | | | | | |
| 16 | 1 | 2 | 3 | | 5 | 6 | | | 9 | 10 | 11 | | | 4 | 8 | 7 | | | | | | |
| 17 | 1 | 2 | 3 | | 5 | 6 | 7 | | 9 | 10 | 11 | | | 4 | 8 | | | | | | | |
| 18 | 1 | 2 | 3 | | 5 | 6 | 7 | 9 | | 10 | 11 | 4 | | | 8 | | | | | | | |
| 19 | 1 | 2 | 3 | | 5 | 6 | 7 | | 9 | 10 | 11 | 4 | | | | | 8 | | | | | |
| 20 | 1 | 2 | 3 | | 5 | 6 | 7 | | 9 | 10 | 11 | 4 | | | | | 8 | | | | | |
| 21 | 1 | 2 | 3 | | 5 | 6 | 7 | | 9 | 10 | 11 | 4 | | | | | | 8 | | | | |
| 22 | 1 | 2 | 3 | | 5 | 6 | 7 | | 9 | | 11 | 4 | | | | | 10 | 8 | | | | |
| 23 | 1 | 2 | 3 | | 5 | 6 | 7 | | 9 | | 11 | 4 | | | | | 10 | 8 | | | | |
| 24 | 1 | 2 | 3 | | 5 | 6 | | 8 | 9 | 10 | 11 | 4 | | | | | | 7 | | | | |
| 25 | 1 | 2 | 3 | | 5 | 6 | 7 | | 9 | 10 | | 4 | | | | | | 8 | 11 | | | |
| 26 | 1 | 2 | 3 | | 5 | | | | 9 | 10 | 11 | 4 | | | | 7 | | 8 | 6 | | | |
| 27 | 1 | 2 | 3 | | 5 | 6 | | | 9 | 10 | 11 | 4 | | | | | | 8 | 7 | | | |
| 28 | 1 | 2 | 3 | | 5 | 6 | 7 | 8 | 9 | 10 | | 4 | | | | | | | 11 | | | |
| 29 | 1 | 2 | 3 | | 5 | 6 | | 8 | 9 | 10 | | 4 | | | | | | 7 | | 11 | | |
| 30 | 1 | 2 | 3 | | 5 | 4 | 7 | | 9 | 10 | | | | | | | | 8 | 6 | 11 | | |
| 31 | 1 | 2 | 3 | | 5 | 4 | 7 | | 9 | 10 | 11 | | | | | | | 8 | 6 | | | |
| 32 | 1 | 2 | 3 | | 5 | 4 | 7 | | 9 | 10 | 11 | | | | | | | 8 | 6 | | | |
| 33 | 1 | 2 | 3 | | 5 | 4 | 7 | | 9 | 10 | 11 | | | | | | | 8 | 6 | | | |
| 34 | 1 | 2 | 3 | | 5 | 4 | 7 | | 9 | 10 | 11 | | | | | | | 8 | 6 | | | |
| 35 | 1 | 2 | 3 | | 5 | 6 | 7 | | 9 | 10 | 11 | 4 | | | | | | 8 | | | | |
| 36 | 1 | 2 | 3 | | 5 | 4 | | 8 | 9 | 10 | 11 | | | | | | | 7 | 6 | | | |
| 37 | 1 | 2 | | | 5 | 4 | 7 | 8 | | 10 | 11 | | | | | | | 9 | 6 | | 3 | |
| 38 | 1 | 2 | | | 5 | 4 | 7 | 8 | | 10 | 11 | | | | | | | 9 | 6 | | 3 | |
| 39 | 1 | 2 | | | 5 | 4 | 7 | 8 | | 10 | 11 | | | | | | | 9 | 6 | | 3 | |
| 40 | 1 | 2 | 3 | | 5 | 4 | 7 | 8 | 9 | 10 | 11 | | | | | | | | 6 | | | |
| 41 | 1 | 2 | 3 | 4 | 5 | | 7 | 8 | 9 | 10 | 11 | | | | | | | | 6 | | | |
| 42 | 1 | 2 | 3 | | 5 | 4 | 7 | 8 | 9 | 10 | 11 | | | | | | | | 6 | | | |
| Apps. | 41 | 42 | 39 | 10 | 42 | 40 | 36 | 24 | 38 | 39 | 38 | 14 | 1 | 7 | 6 | 2 | 4 | 18 | 16 | 2 | 3 | |
| Goals | | | | 1 | | | 10 | 9 | 32 | 4 | 16 | | | | 3 | | 2 | 5 | 1 | 1 | | |

Own goals 3

## F.A. CUP

| | Date | Opposition | | FT | HT | Att. | Goalscorers | Gray A. | Common E. | Hall E. | Trevis A. | Wilson A. | Howarth H. | Horsman W. | Chambers W. | Wrightson F. | Alderson T. | Sargeant C. | Pitcairn J. | Mansley E. | Anderson E. | Gurry J. | Percival P. | Sanders R. | Gale A. | Davies J. | Prout S. | Turner J. | Middleton R. |
|---|---|---|---|---|---|---|---|---|---|---|---|---|---|---|---|---|---|---|---|---|---|---|---|---|---|---|---|---|---|
| 3R | Jan 16 | DONCASTER ROVERS | W | 4-0 | 1-0 | 9600 | Gale, Alderson, Sargeant, Wrightson | 1 | 2 | 3 | | 5 | 6 | 7 | | 9 | 10 | 11 | 4 | | | | | | 8 | | | | |
| 4R | 30 | Coventry City | L | 0-2 | 0-1 | 21605 | | 1 | 2 | 3 | | 5 | 6 | 7 | | 9 | 10 | 11 | 4 | | | | | | 8 | | | | |

## WELSH CUP

| | Date | Opposition | | FT | HT | Att. | Goalscorers | Gray A. | Common E. | Hall E. | Trevis A. | Wilson A. | Howarth H. | Horsman W. | Chambers W. | Wrightson F. | Alderson T. | Sargeant C. | Pitcairn J. | Mansley E. | Anderson E. | Gurry J. | Percival P. | Sanders R. | Gale A. | Davies J. | Prout S. | Turner J. | Middleton R. |
|---|---|---|---|---|---|---|---|---|---|---|---|---|---|---|---|---|---|---|---|---|---|---|---|---|---|---|---|---|---|
| 6R | Feb 24 | SOUTHPORT | W | 4-1 | 2-0 | | Chambers (2), Wrightson, Sargeant | 1 | 2 | 3 | | 5 | 4 | 7 | 8 | 9 | 10 | 11 | | | | | | | | 6 | | | |
| 7R | Mar 17 | Crewe Alex. | L | 1-2 | 1-2 | 1040 | Chambers | | 2 | 3 | | 5 | 4 | 7 | 9 | | 10 | 11 | | | | 8 | | | | 6 | | | 1 |

## DIVISION 3 NORTH CUP

| | Date | Opposition | | FT | HT | Att. | Goalscorers | Gray A. | Common E. | Hall E. | Trevis A. | Wilson A. | Howarth H. | Horsman W. | Chambers W. | Wrightson F. | Alderson T. | Sargeant C. | Pitcairn J. | Mansley E. | Anderson E. | Gurry J. | Percival P. | Sanders R. | Gale A. | Davies J. | Prout S. | Turner J. | Middleton R. |
|---|---|---|---|---|---|---|---|---|---|---|---|---|---|---|---|---|---|---|---|---|---|---|---|---|---|---|---|---|---|
| 1R | Oct 14 | Tranmere Rovers | W | 1-0 | 1-0 | 3000 | Amery (og) | 1 | 2 | | | 5 | 6 | 7 | 8 | 9 | | 11 | | | 4 | 10 | | | | | | 3 | |
| 3R | Mar 10 | NEW BRIGHTON | W | 9-2 | 4-0 | | Sargeant(5,1 pen),Alderson,Wrightson(2),Davies | 1 | 2 | | 4 | 5 | | 7 | 8 | 9 | 10 | 11 | | | | | | | | 6 | | 3 | |
| SF | Apr 10 | PORT VALE | W | 3-0 | 0-0 | | Horsman, Chambers, Gale | 1 | 2 | 3 | | 5 | 4 | 7 | 8 | | 10 | 11 | | | | | | | 9 | 6 | | | |
| F | 27 | Southport | W | 3-1 | 2-1 | 6000 | Frame (og), Davies, Horsman | 1 | 2 | 3 | | 5 | 4 | 7 | 8 | 9 | 10 | 11 | | | | | | | | 6 | | | |

Chester were awarded a bye in the 2nd Round

### Final League Table

| | | Pl. | Home W | Home D | Home L | Home F | Home A | Away W | Away D | Away L | Away F | Away A | F. | A. | Pts |
|---|---|---|---|---|---|---|---|---|---|---|---|---|---|---|---|
| 1 | Stockport County | 42 | 17 | 3 | 1 | 59 | 18 | 6 | 11 | 4 | 25 | 21 | 84 | 39 | 60 |
| 2 | Lincoln City | 42 | 18 | 1 | 2 | 65 | 20 | 7 | 6 | 8 | 38 | 37 | 103 | 57 | 57 |
| ***3*** | ***Chester*** | ***42*** | ***15*** | ***5*** | ***1*** | ***68*** | ***21*** | ***7*** | ***4*** | ***10*** | ***19*** | ***36*** | ***87*** | ***57*** | ***53*** |
| 4 | Oldham Athletic | 42 | 13 | 7 | 1 | 49 | 25 | 7 | 4 | 10 | 28 | 34 | 77 | 59 | 51 |
| 5 | Hull City | 42 | 13 | 6 | 2 | 39 | 22 | 4 | 6 | 11 | 29 | 47 | 68 | 69 | 46 |
| 6 | Hartlepools United | 42 | 16 | 1 | 4 | 53 | 21 | 3 | 6 | 12 | 22 | 48 | 75 | 69 | 45 |
| 7 | Halifax Town | 42 | 12 | 4 | 5 | 40 | 20 | 6 | 5 | 10 | 28 | 43 | 68 | 63 | 45 |
| 8 | Wrexham | 42 | 12 | 3 | 6 | 41 | 21 | 4 | 9 | 8 | 30 | 36 | 71 | 57 | 44 |
| 9 | Mansfield Town | 42 | 13 | 1 | 7 | 64 | 35 | 5 | 7 | 9 | 27 | 41 | 91 | 76 | 44 |
| 10 | Carlisle United | 42 | 13 | 6 | 2 | 42 | 19 | 5 | 2 | 14 | 23 | 49 | 65 | 68 | 44 |
| 11 | Port Vale | 42 | 12 | 6 | 3 | 39 | 23 | 5 | 4 | 12 | 19 | 41 | 58 | 64 | 44 |
| 12 | York City | 42 | 13 | 3 | 5 | 54 | 27 | 3 | 8 | 10 | 25 | 43 | 79 | 70 | 43 |
| 13 | Accrington Stanley | 42 | 14 | 2 | 5 | 51 | 26 | 2 | 7 | 12 | 25 | 43 | 76 | 69 | 41 |
| 14 | Southport | 42 | 10 | 8 | 3 | 39 | 28 | 2 | 5 | 14 | 34 | 59 | 73 | 87 | 37 |
| 15 | New Brighton | 42 | 10 | 8 | 3 | 36 | 16 | 3 | 3 | 15 | 19 | 54 | 55 | 70 | 37 |
| 16 | Barrow | 42 | 11 | 5 | 5 | 42 | 25 | 2 | 5 | 14 | 28 | 61 | 70 | 86 | 36 |
| 17 | Rotherham United | 42 | 11 | 7 | 3 | 52 | 28 | 3 | 0 | 18 | 26 | 63 | 78 | 91 | 35 |
| 18 | Rochdale | 42 | 12 | 3 | 6 | 44 | 27 | 1 | 6 | 14 | 25 | 59 | 69 | 86 | 35 |
| 19 | Tranmere Rovers | 42 | 10 | 8 | 3 | 52 | 30 | 2 | 1 | 18 | 19 | 58 | 71 | 88 | 33 |
| 20 | Crewe Alexandra | 42 | 6 | 8 | 7 | 31 | 31 | 4 | 4 | 13 | 24 | 52 | 55 | 83 | 32 |
| 21 | Gateshead | 42 | 9 | 8 | 4 | 40 | 31 | 2 | 2 | 17 | 23 | 67 | 63 | 98 | 32 |
| 22 | Darlington | 42 | 6 | 8 | 7 | 42 | 46 | 2 | 6 | 13 | 24 | 50 | 66 | 96 | 30 |

**1936/37 Season**
Back - Gurry, Pitcairn, Chambers, Hall, Wilson, Howarth, Trevis, Collins (Trainer).
Front - Horsman, Sanders, Wrightson, Common, Alderson, Sargeant.

**1937/38 Season**
(Back) Beaumont (Asst. Trainer), Common, Howarth, Wilson, Gray, Hall, Feeney, Trevis, Collins, (Trainer)
(Front) Raisbeck (Manager), Horsman, Smith, Wrightson, Alderson, Sargeant, Peters )Secretary)

# SEASON 1937-38

## FOOTBALL LEAGUE DIVISION 3 (NORTH)

| | Date | Opposition | | FT | HT | Att. | Goalscorers | Gray A. | Common E. | Hall E. | Trevis A. | Wilson A. | Howarth H. | Horsman W. | Smith C. | Wrightson F. | Alderson T. | Sargeant C. | Feeney T. | Walters T. | Chambers W. | Turner J. | Done R. | McCreary J. | Gale A. | Sanders R. | McCarthy P. | Middleton R. | Lloyd J. | Roberts S. | Mansley E. | Cresswell F. | McCarthy B. | Deakin G. | Beynon D. | Edwards J. |
|---|---|---|---|---|---|---|---|---|---|---|---|---|---|---|---|---|---|---|---|---|---|---|---|---|---|---|---|---|---|---|---|---|---|---|---|---|
| 1 | Aug 28 | HALIFAX TOWN | D | 1-1 | 1-1 | 8328 | Wrightson |1|2|3|4|5|6|7|8|9|10|11||||||||||||||||||
| 2 | Sep 2 | Carlisle United | W | 3-1 | 2-1 | 11377 | Sargeant, Wrightson (2) |1|2|3|||6|7|10|9||11|4|5|8|||||||||||||||
| 3 | 4 | Tranmere Rovers | D | 0-0 | 0-0 | 14618 | |1|2|3|||6|7|10|9||11|4|5|8|||||||||||||||
| 4 | 8 | CARLISLE UNITED | W | 1-0 | 0-0 | 5372 | Chambers |1|2|3|||6|7|10|9||11|4|5|8|||||||||||||||
| 5 | 11 | YORK CITY | W | 4-3 | 2-2 | 7284 | Wrightson (2), Smith, Horsman |1|||||6|7|8|9|10|11||5||2|3|4||||||||||||
| 6 | 18 | Bradford City | D | 2-2 | 1-1 | 6010 | Wrightson (2) |1|2||||6|7|10|9||11||5|8||3|4||||||||||||
| 7 | 25 | SOUTHPORT | W | 2-1 | 1-1 | 7401 | Gale, Sargeant (pen) |1|2||||6|7||9|10|11||5|||3|4|8|||||||||||
| 8 | 28 | Accrington Stanley | D | 0-0 | 0-0 | 6442 | |1|2||||6|7|10|9||11||5|8||3|4||||||||||||
| 9 | Oct 2 | Doncaster Rovers | L | 1-2 | 0-1 | 16391 | Chambers |1|2||||6|7|10|9||11||5|8||3|4||||||||||||
| 10 | 9 | ROCHDALE | W | 4-1 | 1-1 | 5913 | Sargeant (2), Wrightson, Sanders |1|2||||6|7||9||11||5|8||3|4||10|||||||||||
| 11 | 16 | Hartlepools United | W | 1-0 | 1-0 | 5955 | Wrightson |1|2||||6|7||9||11|8|5|||3|4||10|||||||||||
| 12 | 23 | LINCOLN CITY | D | 1-1 | 1-1 | 6507 | Wrightson |1|2||4|||7|8|9|10|11||5|||3|6||||||||||||
| 13 | 30 | Hull City | D | 2-2 | 1-0 | 11383 | McCreary, Wrightson ||2||4||6|7|8|9||11||5|||3|10||||1|||||||||
| 14 | Nov 6 | NEW BRIGHTON | L | 1-2 | 0-0 | 6924 | McCreary |1|2||4||6|7|8|9||11||5|||3|10||||||||||||
| 15 | 13 | Gateshead | L | 1-3 | 0-2 | 13170 | Wrightson |1|2||4||6|7|8|9||||5|||3|10|||11||||||||||
| 16 | 20 | OLDHAM ATHLETIC | D | 3-3 | 1-0 | 6354 | Wrightson, Horsman, Gale |1|2||||4|7|10|9||||5|||3|6|8||11||||||||||
| 17 | Dec 4 | PORT VALE | W | 7-2 | 4-2 | 3849 | Horsman, Howarth, Chambers, * |1|2||||6|7|8|||11||5|9||3|4||10|||||||||||
| 18 | 11 | Oldham Athletic | L | 2-3 | 2-1 | 5283 | Smith, Sanders |1|2||||6|7|8|||11||5|9||3|4||10|||||||||||
| 19 | 18 | BARROW | W | 3-1 | 2-1 | 3201 | Sanders (2), Gale |1|2||||6|7|8|||||5|9||3|4|11|10|||||||||||
| 20 | 25 | ROTHERHAM UNITED | L | 2-3 | 2-0 | 6105 | Chambers, Horsman |1|2||||6|7||||||5|9||3|4|8|10|||11||||||||
| 21 | 27 | Rotherham United | L | 1-4 | 1-2 | 11394 | Wrightson (pen) ||2||5||6|7|10|9|||||||3|4|8|11||1|||||||||
| 22 | Jan 1 | Halifax Town | D | 1-1 | 1-1 | 6594 | Gale |1|2||||6|7|10|||11||5|8||3|4|9||||||||||||
| 23 | 15 | TRANMERE ROVERS | D | 1-1 | 1-1 | 5043 | Smith |1|2||||6|7|8|||11|9|5|||3|4||10|||||||||||
| 24 | 26 | York City | L | 0-4 | 0-2 | 3380 | |1|2||||6|7|8||10|11||5|9||3|4||||||||||||
| 25 | 29 | BRADFORD CITY | W | 3-1 | 3-0 | 3320 | Chambers, Sargeant, Roberts |1|2||||6|7|8|||11||5|9||3|4||||||10|||||||
| 26 | Feb 5 | Southport | D | 2-2 | 0-2 | 5198 | Sargeant, Chambers |1|2||||6|7|8|||11||5|9||3|4||||||10|||||||
| 27 | 12 | DONCASTER ROVERS | W | 4-0 | 2-0 | 5188 | Sanders, Sargeant (3, 1 pen) |1|2||||6|7|8|9||11||5|||3|4||10|||||||||||
| 28 | 19 | Rochdale | L | 0-4 | 0-1 | 5728 | |1|2||||6|7|8|||11||5|||3|4|9|||||10|||||||
| 29 | 26 | HARTLEPOOLS UNITED | W | 6-0 | 2-0 | 3723 | Sargeant(4,1 pen),Sanders,Roberts ||2||5||6|7|8|||11|||||3|4||10||||9|1||||||
| 30 | Mar 5 | Lincoln City | D | 1-1 | 1-0 | 10157 | Sargeant ||2||5||6|7|8|||11|||||3|4||10||||9|1||||||
| 31 | 12 | HULL CITY | L | 1-3 | 0-1 | 6864 | Sargeant ||2||5||6|7||9||11|||||3|4|8|||||10|1||||||
| 32 | 19 | New Brighton | L | 0-4 | 0-1 | 4629 | ||2||||6|||9||||5|8||3|4|7|11||||10|1||||||
| 33 | 26 | GATESHEAD | W | 2-1 | 1-0 | 3154 | Chambers (2, 1 pen) |1|2||4||6|||||||5|9||3|8|7|||||10||11|||||
| 34 | Apr 6 | Crewe Alex. | L | 0-1 | 0-0 | 3312 | |1|2||||6|7||9||||5|||3|4||||||10|||8|11|||
| 35 | 9 | DARLINGTON | W | 3-2 | 2-1 | 3024 | Roberts, Gale (2) |1|2||6|||7||||||5|8||3|4|9|||||10||11|||||
| 36 | 15 | WREXHAM | W | 2-1 | 1-0 | 10892 | Cresswell, Gale |1|2||||6|7||||||5|8||3|4|9|||||10||11|||||
| 37 | 16 | Port Vale | D | 2-2 | 1-1 | 6695 | Gale (2) ||2||||6|7||||||5|8||3|4|9|||1||10||11|||||
| 38 | 18 | Wrexham | L | 1-3 | 1-2 | 11480 | Gale |1|2||4||6|7||||||5|8||||9|||||10||11|||3||
| 39 | 23 | CREWE ALEX. | L | 0-3 | 0-1 | 3379 | ||2||4||6|7||||||5|||3|8|9|11||1||10|||||||
| 40 | 27 | Darlington | L | 1-2 | 0-2 | 4359 | Walters ||2||5||6|7||||||11|8||3|||10||1||9||||||4|
| 41 | 30 | Barrow | W | 2-0 | 0-0 | 3324 | Trevis, Sanders ||2||5||6|7||||||11|8||3|4||10||1||9|||||||
| 42 | May 7 | ACCRINGTON STANLEY | W | 3-1 | 2-1 | 1940 | Gale, Sanders, Chambers |1|2||5||6|7|||||||9||3|4|8|10||||11|||||||
| | | | | | | | Apps. |32|41|4|16|1|40|40|26|21|5|26|5|36|24|1|37|36|16|16|2|6|1|17|4|5|1|1|1|1|
| | | | | | | | Goals ||||1||1|4|3|14||16||1|9|||2|11|10||||3||1|||||

* Other goalscorers:Sargeant, Sanders (2), Johnson(og)

Own goals 1

## F.A. CUP

| | Date | Opposition | | FT | HT | Att. | Goalscorers | Gray A. | Common E. | Hall E. | Trevis A. | Wilson A. | Howarth H. | Horsman W. | Smith C. | Wrightson F. | Alderson T. | Sargeant C. | Feeney T. | Walters T. | Chambers W. | Turner J. | Done R. | McCreary J. | Gale A. | Sanders R. | McCarthy P. | Middleton R. | Lloyd J. | Roberts S. | Mansley E. | Cresswell F. | McCarthy B. | Deakin G. | Beynon D. | Edwards J. |
|---|---|---|---|---|---|---|---|---|---|---|---|---|---|---|---|---|---|---|---|---|---|---|---|---|---|---|---|---|---|---|---|---|---|---|---|---|
| 3R | Jan 8 | Leeds United | L | 1-3 | 1-2 | 37155 | Gale |1|2||||6|7|8|||11||5|10||3|4|9|||||||||||

## WELSH CUP

| | Date | Opposition | | FT | HT | Att. | Goalscorers | Gray A. | Common E. | Hall E. | Trevis A. | Wilson A. | Howarth H. | Horsman W. | Smith C. | Wrightson F. | Alderson T. | Sargeant C. | Feeney T. | Walters T. | Chambers W. | Turner J. | Done R. | McCreary J. | Gale A. | Sanders R. | McCarthy P. | Middleton R. | Lloyd J. | Roberts S. | Mansley E. | Cresswell F. | McCarthy B. | Deakin G. | Beynon D. | Edwards J. |
|---|---|---|---|---|---|---|---|---|---|---|---|---|---|---|---|---|---|---|---|---|---|---|---|---|---|---|---|---|---|---|---|---|---|---|---|---|
| 6R | Feb 23 | New Brighton | W | 5-1 | 2-1 | 1081 | Sanders (2), Sargeant (3) ||2||5||6|7|8|||11|||9|||4||10|||||1||||3||
| 7R | Mar 9 | SHREWSBURY TOWN | D | 0-0 | 0-0 | 3600 | |1|2||5||6|7|8|||11|||9||3|4||10|||||||||||
| 7Rr | Apr 2 | Shrewsbury Town * | L | 1-2 | 0-1 | 8000 | McCreary |1|2||4||6|11||||||5|9||3|8|7|10|||||||||||

* Extra time played following score of 1-1 after 90 minutes

## DIVISION 3 NORTH CUP

| | Date | Opposition | | FT | HT | Att. | Goalscorers | Gray A. | Common E. | Hall E. | Trevis A. | Wilson A. | Howarth H. | Horsman W. | Smith C. | Wrightson F. | Alderson T. | Sargeant C. | Feeney T. | Walters T. | Chambers W. | Turner J. | Done R. | McCreary J. | Gale A. | Sanders R. | McCarthy P. | Middleton R. | Lloyd J. | Roberts S. | Mansley E. | Cresswell F. | McCarthy B. | Deakin G. | Beynon D. | Edwards J. |
|---|---|---|---|---|---|---|---|---|---|---|---|---|---|---|---|---|---|---|---|---|---|---|---|---|---|---|---|---|---|---|---|---|---|---|---|---|
| 1R | Oct 20 | CREWE ALEX. | W | 4-2 | 2-1 | 1100 | Chambers (2), Alderson, Sargeant |1|2|3|4|5|6|7|||10|11|8||9||||||||||||||||
| 2R | Feb 9 | New Brighton | W | 5-0 | 3-0 | | Horsman (3), Sargeant (pen), Smith |1|||6|||7|8|||11||5|||3|4||||||9||10|||2||
| 3R | Mar 16 | TRANMERE ROVERS | D | 2-2 | 1-1 | 1700 | Horsman, Sargeant ||||6|||7||9||11||5|||3|4||10||||8|1||||2||
| 3Rr | 30 | Tranmere Rovers | L | 2-3 | 2-3 | 1300 | McCreary, Chambers |1|2||4||6|7||||||5|9||3|8||||||10||11|||||

## FRIENDLIES

| | Date | Opposition | | FT | HT | Att. | Goalscorers |
|---|---|---|---|---|---|---|---|
| 1 | Nov 27 | Millwall | L | 2-3 | 1-1 | 10000 | Smith, Sargeant |
| 2 | May 14 | MILLWALL * | W | 3-1 | 1-0 | 2906 | Chambers (2), Trevis |

* Royal Infirmary & British Empire Cancer Campaign charity match

### Final League Table

| | | Pl. | Home W | D | L | F | A | Away W | D | L | F | A | F. | A. | Pts |
|---|---|---|---|---|---|---|---|---|---|---|---|---|---|---|---|
| 1 | Tranmere Rovers | 42 | 15 | 4 | 2 | 57 | 21 | 8 | 6 | 7 | 24 | 20 | 81 | 41 | 56 |
| 2 | Doncaster Rovers | 42 | 15 | 4 | 2 | 48 | 16 | 6 | 8 | 7 | 26 | 33 | 74 | 49 | 54 |
| 3 | Hull City | 42 | 11 | 8 | 2 | 51 | 19 | 9 | 5 | 7 | 29 | 24 | 80 | 43 | 53 |
| 4 | Oldham Athletic | 42 | 16 | 4 | 1 | 48 | 18 | 3 | 9 | 9 | 19 | 28 | 67 | 46 | 51 |
| 5 | Gateshead | 42 | 15 | 5 | 1 | 53 | 20 | 5 | 6 | 10 | 31 | 39 | 84 | 59 | 51 |
| 6 | Rotherham United | 42 | 13 | 6 | 2 | 45 | 21 | 7 | 4 | 10 | 23 | 35 | 68 | 56 | 50 |
| 7 | Lincoln City | 42 | 14 | 3 | 4 | 48 | 17 | 5 | 5 | 11 | 18 | 33 | 66 | 50 | 46 |
| 8 | Crewe Alexandra | 42 | 14 | 3 | 4 | 47 | 17 | 4 | 6 | 11 | 24 | 36 | 71 | 53 | 45 |
| ***9*** | ***Chester*** | ***42*** | ***13*** | ***4*** | ***4*** | ***54*** | ***31*** | ***3*** | ***8*** | ***10*** | ***23*** | ***41*** | ***77*** | ***72*** | ***44*** |
| 10 | Wrexham | 42 | 14 | 4 | 3 | 37 | 15 | 2 | 7 | 12 | 21 | 48 | 58 | 63 | 43 |
| 11 | York City | 42 | 11 | 4 | 6 | 40 | 25 | 5 | 6 | 10 | 30 | 43 | 70 | 68 | 42 |
| 12 | Carlisle United | 42 | 11 | 5 | 5 | 35 | 19 | 4 | 4 | 13 | 22 | 48 | 57 | 67 | 39 |
| 13 | New Brighton | 42 | 12 | 5 | 4 | 43 | 18 | 3 | 3 | 15 | 17 | 43 | 60 | 61 | 38 |
| 14 | Bradford City | 42 | 12 | 6 | 3 | 46 | 21 | 2 | 4 | 15 | 20 | 48 | 66 | 69 | 38 |
| 15 | Port Vale | 42 | 11 | 8 | 2 | 45 | 27 | 1 | 6 | 14 | 20 | 46 | 65 | 73 | 38 |
| 16 | Southport | 42 | 8 | 8 | 5 | 30 | 26 | 4 | 6 | 11 | 23 | 56 | 53 | 82 | 38 |
| 17 | Rochdale | 42 | 7 | 10 | 4 | 38 | 27 | 6 | 1 | 14 | 29 | 51 | 67 | 78 | 37 |
| 18 | Halifax Town | 42 | 9 | 7 | 5 | 24 | 19 | 3 | 5 | 13 | 20 | 47 | 44 | 66 | 36 |
| 19 | Darlington | 42 | 10 | 4 | 7 | 37 | 31 | 1 | 6 | 14 | 17 | 48 | 54 | 79 | 32 |
| 20 | Hartlepools United | 42 | 10 | 8 | 3 | 36 | 20 | 0 | 4 | 17 | 17 | 60 | 53 | 80 | 32 |
| 21 | Barrow | 42 | 9 | 6 | 6 | 28 | 20 | 2 | 4 | 15 | 13 | 51 | 41 | 71 | 32 |
| 22 | Accrington Stanley | 42 | 9 | 2 | 10 | 31 | 32 | 2 | 5 | 14 | 14 | 43 | 45 | 75 | 29 |

# SEASON 1938-39

## FOOTBALL LEAGUE DIVISION 3 (NORTH)

| | Date | Opposition | | FT | HT | Att. | Goalscorers | Owen C. | Common E. | Beynon D. | Trevis A. | Walters T. | Howarth H. | Horsman W. | McGough J. | Keeley A. | Roberts S. | Rogers J. | Wrightson F. | McCreary J. | Robertson A. | Gale A. | Pendergast W. | Sanders R. | Mansley E. | Hobson A. | Griffiths G. | Gregg W. | Warburton G. | Butcher R. | Ross A. | Duff S. | White T. | Worswick R. | Watford A. | Coulter J. |
|---|---|---|---|---|---|---|---|---|---|---|---|---|---|---|---|---|---|---|---|---|---|---|---|---|---|---|---|---|---|---|---|---|---|---|---|---|
| 1 | Aug 27 | HULL CITY | D | 1-1 | 1-1 | 8986 | Howarth (pen) | 1 | 2 | 3 | 4 | 5 | 6 | 7 | 8 | 9 | 10 | 11 | | | | | | | | | | | | | | | | | | |
| 2 | 31 | NEW BRIGHTON | L | 1-3 | 0-1 | 6306 | Roberts | 1 | 2 | 3 | 4 | 5 | 6 | 7 | 8 | | 10 | 11 | 9 | | | | | | | | | | | | | | | | | |
| 3 | Sep 3 | Lincoln City | W | 3-0 | 2-0 | 4544 | Pendergast, Horsman, Howarth | 1 | | 2 | | 3 | 6 | 7 | 8 | | | 11 | | 4 | 5 | 9 | 10 | | | | | | | | | | | | | |
| 4 | 5 | Bradford City | L | 0-1 | 0-0 | 6229 | | 1 | | 2 | | 3 | 6 | 7 | 8 | 9 | | | | 4 | 5 | | 10 | 11 | | | | | | | | | | | | |
| 5 | 10 | STOCKPORT COUNTY | W | 4-3 | 1-1 | 9779 | Pendergast (3), Keeley | 1 | | 2 | | 3 | 6 | 7 | 8 | 9 | | | | 4 | 5 | | 10 | 11 | | | | | | | | | | | | |
| 6 | 17 | Accrington Stanley | W | 3-2 | 1-1 | 4728 | Keeley, Pendergast, Sanders | 1 | | 2 | | 3 | 6 | 7 | 8 | 9 | | | | 4 | 5 | | 10 | 11 | | | | | | | | | | | | |
| 7 | 24 | BARNSLEY | W | 2-1 | 0-0 | 9479 | Horsman, Pendergast | 1 | | 2 | | 3 | 6 | 7 | 8 | 9 | | | | 4 | 5 | | 10 | 11 | | | | | | | | | | | | |
| 8 | Oct 1 | Oldham Athletic | W | 3-1 | 1-1 | 12144 | Pendergast (2), Rogers | 1 | | 2 | | 3 | 6 | 7 | 8 | 9 | | 11 | | 4 | 5 | | 10 | | | | | | | | | | | | | |
| 9 | 8 | HALIFAX TOWN | W | 5-1 | 0-1 | 6792 | Keeley (3), Pendergast, Horsman (pen) | 1 | | 2 | | 3 | 6 | 7 | 8 | 9 | | 11 | | 4 | 5 | | 10 | | | | | | | | | | | | | |
| 10 | 15 | GATESHEAD | D | 2-2 | 0-0 | 9033 | Pendergast, McGough | 1 | | 2 | | 3 | 6 | 7 | 8 | 9 | | 11 | | 4 | 5 | | 10 | | | | | | | | | | | | | |
| 11 | 22 | Wrexham | L | 2-3 | 1-1 | 15785 | Pendergast, Keeley | | | 2 | | 3 | 6 | 7 | 8 | 9 | | 11 | | 4 | 5 | | 10 | | 1 | | | | | | | | | | | |
| 12 | 29 | YORK CITY | W | 5-1 | 2-1 | 7315 | Wass (og), Pendergast, Sanders (2), Keeley | | | | | 3 | 6 | 7 | 8 | 9 | | | | 4 | 5 | | 10 | 11 | | 1 | 2 | | | | | | | | | |
| 13 | Nov 5 | Rochdale | L | 2-5 | 2-3 | 6732 | Howarth, Pendergast | | | 2 | | 3 | 6 | 7 | 8 | 9 | | | | 4 | 5 | | 10 | 11 | | 1 | | | | | | | | | | |
| 14 | 12 | ROTHERHAM UNITED | L | 1-4 | 1-2 | 7082 | Pendergast | | | | | 3 | 6 | 7 | 8 | 9 | | | | 4 | 5 | | 10 | | | 1 | | 2 | 11 | | | | | | | |
| 15 | 19 | Doncaster Rovers | L | 1-4 | 0-2 | 14675 | Pendergast | | | | | 3 | | 7 | 8 | | 10 | | | 4 | 5 | | 9 | | | 1 | | 2 | 11 | 6 | | | | | | |
| 16 | Dec 3 | Crewe Alex. | W | 2-0 | 1-0 | 7431 | Keeley, Pendergast | 1 | 3 | | | 5 | 4 | | 8 | 9 | | 11 | | | | | 10 | | | | | 2 | 7 | 6 | | | | | | |
| 17 | 17 | Darlington | D | 3-3 | 0-3 | 2647 | Keeley, McGough (2) | 1 | | | | 5 | | 7 | 8 | 9 | | | | 4 | | | 10 | 11 | | | | 3 | | 6 | 2 | | | | | |
| 18 | 24 | Hull City | L | 0-3 | 0-0 | 5911 | | | 3 | | | 5 | 4 | 7 | 8 | 9 | | | | | | | 10 | | | 1 | | 2 | | 6 | | 11 | | | | |
| 19 | 26 | Hartlepools United | W | 5-2 | 2-0 | 5177 | Pendergast (2), Horsman (2), Keeley | | | | | 5 | | 7 | 8 | 9 | | | | 4 | | | 10 | | | 1 | 3 | 2 | | 6 | | 11 | | | | |
| 20 | 27 | HARTLEPOOLS UNITED | W | 8-2 | 3-2 | 7748 | Keeley(2), Pendergast(2,1pen), Sanders(3),Gregg(pen) | | 3 | | | 5 | 4 | 7 | 8 | 9 | | | | | | | 10 | 11 | | 1 | | 2 | | 6 | | | | | | |
| 21 | 31 | LINCOLN CITY | D | 0-0 | 0-0 | 6079 | | | 3 | | | | 4 | 7 | 8 | | | | | | | | 10 | 11 | 1 | | | 2 | | 6 | | | 5 | 9 | | |
| 22 | Jan 14 | Stockport County | D | 0-0 | 0-0 | 10781 | | | 3 | | | 5 | 4 | 7 | 8 | 9 | | | | 6 | | | 10 | 11 | 1 | | | 2 | | | | | | | | |
| 23 | 28 | Barnsley | L | 0-3 | 0-3 | 13161 | | | | | 8 | 5 | | 7 | | 9 | | | | | | | 10 | 11 | 1 | | 3 | 2 | | 6 | | | | | 4 | |
| 24 | Feb 4 | OLDHAM ATHLETIC | W | 4-2 | 2-1 | 5983 | Pendergast, Roberts, Keeley, Sanders | 1 | 3 | | | 5 | 4 | 7 | | 9 | 8 | | | 6 | | | 10 | 11 | | | | 2 | | | | | | | | |
| 25 | 11 | Halifax Town | D | 1-1 | 0-1 | 5217 | Pendergast | 1 | 3 | | | 5 | 4 | 7 | | 9 | 8 | | | | | | 10 | 11 | | | | 2 | | 6 | | | | | | |
| 26 | 15 | ACCRINGTON STANLEY | W | 1-0 | 0-0 | 1728 | McGough | 1 | 3 | | | 5 | 4 | 7 | 8 | 9 | | | | | | | 10 | 11 | | | | 2 | | 6 | | | | | | |
| 27 | 18 | Gateshead | L | 0-3 | 0-1 | 4492 | | 1 | 3 | | | 5 | 4 | 7 | 8 | 9 | 11 | | | | | | 10 | | | | | 2 | | 6 | | | | | | |
| 28 | 25 | WREXHAM | W | 4-2 | 1-1 | 10364 | Keeley (2), Sanders, Pendergast | 1 | 3 | | | 5 | 4 | 7 | 8 | 9 | | | | | | | 10 | 11 | | | | 2 | | 6 | | | | | | |
| 29 | Mar 1 | CARLISLE UNITED | W | 6-1 | 2-0 | 1735 | Sanders (3), Pendergast (2), Keeley | 1 | | | | 5 | 4 | 7 | | 9 | 8 | | | | | | 10 | 11 | | | 3 | 2 | | 6 | | | | | | |
| 30 | 4 | York City | D | 2-2 | 0-2 | 4106 | Pendergast, Horsman | 1 | | | | 5 | 4 | 7 | | 9 | 8 | | | | | | 10 | 11 | | | 3 | 2 | | 6 | | | | | | |
| 31 | 11 | ROCHDALE | D | 0-0 | 0-0 | 4375 | | 1 | 3 | | | 5 | 4 | 7 | | 9 | 8 | | | | | | 10 | | | | | 2 | | 6 | | | | | | 11 |
| 32 | 18 | Rotherham United | L | 0-2 | 0-0 | 5317 | | 1 | 3 | | | 5 | 4 | 7 | | 9 | 8 | | | | | | 10 | 11 | | | | 2 | | 6 | | | | | | |
| 33 | 25 | DONCASTER ROVERS | L | 0-4 | 0-2 | 4982 | | | 3 | | | 5 | 4 | 7 | 8 | 9 | | | | | | | 10 | | | 1 | | 2 | | 6 | | | | | | 11 |
| 34 | Apr 1 | Southport | L | 0-2 | 0-2 | 4257 | | | 3 | | | 5 | 4 | 7 | 8 | | 10 | | | | | | 9 | | | 1 | | 2 | | 6 | | | | | | 11 |
| 35 | 7 | BARROW | L | 1-2 | 1-2 | 6057 | Howarth | | | | | 5 | 4 | 7 | 8 | | 10 | | | | | | | | | 1 | 3 | 2 | | 6 | | | | 9 | | 11 |
| 36 | 8 | CREWE ALEX. | W | 4-0 | 2-0 | 4235 | Horsman, Gregg (pen), Worswick (2) | | 3 | | | 5 | 4 | 7 | 8 | 9 | | | | 6 | | | | | | 1 | | 2 | 11 | | | | | 10 | | |
| 37 | 10 | Barrow | W | 1-0 | 0-0 | 8977 | Warburton | | 3 | | | 5 | 4 | 7 | 8 | 9 | | | | 6 | | | | | | 1 | | 2 | 11 | | | | | 10 | | |
| 38 | 15 | Carlisle United | W | 3-1 | 3-1 | 2601 | Horsman (3) | | 3 | | | 5 | 4 | 7 | 8 | 9 | | | | 6 | | | | | | 1 | | 2 | 11 | | | | | 10 | | |
| 39 | 22 | DARLINGTON | D | 0-0 | 0-0 | 2406 | | | 3 | | | 5 | 4 | 7 | 8 | 9 | | | | | | | 10 | | | 1 | | 2 | 11 | 6 | | | | | | |
| 40 | 26 | SOUTHPORT | W | 2-0 | 2-0 | 1727 | Worswick, Pendergast | | 3 | | | 5 | 4 | 7 | | 9 | | | | | | | 8 | | | 1 | | 2 | 11 | 6 | | | | 10 | | |
| 41 | 29 | New Brighton | W | 3-1 | 2-0 | 2553 | Howarth, Bulloch (og), Keeley | | 3 | | | 5 | 4 | 7 | 8 | 9 | | | | | | | | | | 1 | | 2 | 11 | 6 | | | | 10 | | |
| 42 | May 6 | BRADFORD CITY | W | 3-2 | 2-0 | 3033 | Warburton, Worswick, Keeley | | 3 | | | 5 | 4 | 7 | 8 | 9 | | | | | | | | | | 1 | | 2 | 11 | 6 | | | | 10 | | |
| | | | | | | | Apps. | 21 | 23 | 12 | 3 | 41 | 38 | 41 | 34 | 36 | 12 | 8 | 1 | 20 | 13 | 1 | 34 | 18 | 4 | 17 | 6 | 29 | 10 | 23 | 1 | 2 | 1 | 8 | 1 | 4 |
| | | | | | | | Goals | | | | | | 5 | 10 | 4 | 18 | 3 | 1 | | | | | 26 | 11 | | | | 2 | 2 | | | | | 4 | | |

Own goals 2

## F.A. CUP

| | Date | Opposition | | FT | HT | Att. | Goalscorers | Owen C. | Common E. | Beynon D. | Trevis A. | Walters T. | Howarth H. | Horsman W. | McGough J. | Keeley A. | Roberts S. | Rogers J. | Wrightson F. | McCreary J. | Robertson A. | Gale A. | Pendergast W. | Sanders R. | Mansley E. | Hobson A. | Griffiths G. | Gregg W. | Warburton G. | Butcher R. | Ross A. | Duff S. | White T. | Worswick R. | Watford A. | Coulter J. |
|---|---|---|---|---|---|---|---|---|---|---|---|---|---|---|---|---|---|---|---|---|---|---|---|---|---|---|---|---|---|---|---|---|---|---|---|---|
| 1R | Nov 26 | BRADFORD CITY | W | 3-1 | 2-0 | 6672 | Horsman, Pendergast, Hinsley (og) | 1 | 3 | | | 5 | 4 | 7 | 8 | 9 | | 11 | | | | | 10 | | | | | 2 | | 6 | | | | | | |
| 2R | Dec 10 | HULL CITY | D | 2-2 | 1-2 | 9905 | Horsman, Gregg (pen) | 1 | 3 | | | 5 | 4 | 7 | 8 | 9 | | 11 | | | | | 10 | | | | | 2 | | 6 | | | | | | |
| 2Rr | 15 | Hull City | W | 1-0 | 0-0 | 8184 | Horsman | 1 | 3 | | | 5 | 4 | 7 | 8 | 9 | | 11 | | | | | 10 | | | | | 2 | | 6 | | | | | | |
| 3R | Jan 7 | COVENTRY CITY | W | 1-0 | 0-0 | 11248 | Pendergast | 1 | 3 | | | 5 | 4 | 7 | 8 | 9 | | | | | | | 10 | 11 | | | | 2 | | 6 | | | | | | |
| 4R | 21 | Sheffield Wednesday | D | 1-1 | 0-1 | 29237 | Sanders | 1 | 3 | | | 5 | 4 | 7 | 8 | 9 | | | | | | | 10 | 11 | | | | 2 | | 6 | | | | | | |
| 4Rr | 25 | SHEFFIELD WEDNESDAY * | D | 1-1 | 0-0 | 18816 | Hanford (og) | 1 | 3 | | | 5 | 4 | 7 | 8 | 9 | | | | | | | 10 | 11 | | | | 2 | | 6 | | | | | | |
| 4R2r | 30 | Sheffield Wednesday @ | L | 0-2 | 0-0 | 15321 | | 1 | 3 | | | 5 | 4 | 7 | 8 | 9 | | | | | | | 10 | 11 | | | | 2 | | 6 | | | | | | |

* Extra time played following score of 1-1 after 90 minutes @ Played at Manchester City

## WELSH CUP

| | Date | Opposition | | FT | HT | Att. | Goalscorers | Owen C. | Common E. | Beynon D. | Trevis A. | Walters T. | Howarth H. | Horsman W. | McGough J. | Keeley A. | Roberts S. | Rogers J. | Wrightson F. | McCreary J. | Robertson A. | Gale A. | Pendergast W. | Sanders R. | Mansley E. | Hobson A. | Griffiths G. | Gregg W. | Warburton G. | Butcher R. | Ross A. | Duff S. | White T. | Worswick R. | Watford A. | Coulter J. |
|---|---|---|---|---|---|---|---|---|---|---|---|---|---|---|---|---|---|---|---|---|---|---|---|---|---|---|---|---|---|---|---|---|---|---|---|---|
| 6R | Feb 8 | RHYL | W | 4-0 | 2-0 | 1558 | Horsman, Roberts, Keeley, Pendergast | 1 | | | | 5 | 4 | 7 | | 9 | 8 | | | 6 | | | 10 | | | | 3 | 2 | 11 | | | | | | | |
| SF | Mar 22 | South Liverpool * | L | 2-5 | 1-3 | | Horsman, Keeley | 1 | 3 | | | 5 | | 7 | | 9 | 8 | | | 4 | | | 10 | | | | | 2 | 11 | 6 | | | | | | |

* Played at Everton. Chester were awarded a bye in the 7th Round

## FRIENDLIES

| | Date | Opposition | | FT | HT | Att. | Goalscorers |
|---|---|---|---|---|---|---|---|
| 1 | Aug 20 | WREXHAM * | W | 4-2 | 1-1 | 5086 | McGough, Keeley (2), Rogers |

* Jubilee Fund match

Final League Table

| | | Pl. | Home W | D | L | F | A | Away W | D | L | F | A | F. | A. | Pts |
|---|---|---|---|---|---|---|---|---|---|---|---|---|---|---|---|
| 1 | Barnsley | 42 | 18 | 2 | 1 | 60 | 12 | 12 | 5 | 4 | 34 | 22 | 94 | 34 | 67 |
| 2 | Doncaster Rovers | 42 | 12 | 5 | 4 | 47 | 21 | 9 | 9 | 3 | 40 | 26 | 87 | 47 | 56 |
| 3 | Bradford City | 42 | 16 | 2 | 3 | 59 | 21 | 6 | 6 | 9 | 30 | 35 | 89 | 56 | 52 |
| 4 | Southport | 42 | 14 | 5 | 2 | 47 | 16 | 6 | 5 | 10 | 28 | 38 | 75 | 54 | 50 |
| 5 | Oldham Athletic | 42 | 16 | 1 | 4 | 51 | 21 | 6 | 4 | 11 | 25 | 38 | 76 | 59 | 49 |
| ***6*** | ***Chester*** | ***42*** | ***12*** | ***5*** | ***4*** | ***54*** | ***31*** | ***8*** | ***4*** | ***9*** | ***34*** | ***39*** | ***88*** | ***70*** | ***49*** |
| 7 | Hull City | 42 | 13 | 5 | 3 | 57 | 25 | 5 | 5 | 11 | 26 | 49 | 83 | 74 | 46 |
| 8 | Crewe Alexandra | 42 | 12 | 5 | 4 | 54 | 23 | 7 | 1 | 13 | 28 | 47 | 82 | 70 | 44 |
| 9 | Stockport County | 42 | 13 | 6 | 2 | 57 | 24 | 4 | 3 | 14 | 34 | 53 | 91 | 77 | 43 |
| 10 | Gateshead | 42 | 11 | 6 | 4 | 45 | 24 | 3 | 8 | 10 | 29 | 43 | 74 | 67 | 42 |
| 11 | Rotherham United | 42 | 12 | 4 | 5 | 45 | 21 | 5 | 4 | 12 | 19 | 43 | 64 | 64 | 42 |
| 12 | Halifax Town | 42 | 9 | 10 | 2 | 33 | 22 | 4 | 6 | 11 | 19 | 32 | 52 | 54 | 42 |
| 13 | Barrow | 42 | 11 | 5 | 5 | 46 | 22 | 5 | 4 | 12 | 20 | 43 | 66 | 65 | 41 |
| 14 | Wrexham | 42 | 15 | 2 | 4 | 46 | 28 | 2 | 5 | 14 | 20 | 51 | 66 | 79 | 41 |
| 15 | Rochdale | 42 | 10 | 5 | 6 | 58 | 29 | 5 | 4 | 12 | 34 | 53 | 92 | 82 | 39 |
| 16 | New Brighton | 42 | 11 | 2 | 8 | 46 | 32 | 4 | 7 | 10 | 22 | 41 | 68 | 73 | 39 |
| 17 | Lincoln City | 42 | 9 | 6 | 6 | 40 | 33 | 3 | 3 | 15 | 26 | 59 | 66 | 92 | 33 |
| 18 | Darlington | 42 | 12 | 2 | 7 | 43 | 30 | 1 | 5 | 15 | 19 | 62 | 62 | 92 | 33 |
| 19 | Carlisle United | 42 | 10 | 5 | 6 | 44 | 33 | 3 | 2 | 16 | 22 | 78 | 66 | 111 | 33 |
| 20 | York City | 42 | 8 | 5 | 8 | 37 | 34 | 4 | 3 | 14 | 27 | 58 | 64 | 92 | 32 |
| 21 | Hartlepools United | 42 | 10 | 4 | 7 | 36 | 33 | 2 | 3 | 16 | 19 | 61 | 55 | 94 | 31 |
| 22 | Accrington Stanley | 42 | 6 | 5 | 10 | 30 | 39 | 1 | 1 | 19 | 19 | 64 | 49 | 103 | 20 |

**1938/39 Season**: (Back) Trevis, Common, Owen, Brown (Manager), Walters, Howarth, Beynon. (Sitting) Peters (Secretary), McGough, Keeley, Roberts, Atterbury (Trainer). (Front) Horsman, Roberts.

**1939/40 Season**: (Back) Atterbury (Trainer), Law, Butcher, Hobson, Walters, Brown, Hall (Asst. Trainer). (Front) Horsman, McGough, Howarth, Perndergast, Gregg, Warburton.

# SEASON 1939-40

## FOOTBALL LEAGUE (Abandoned)

| | Date | Opposition | | FT | HT | Att. | Goalscorers | | | | | | | | | | | |
|---|---|---|---|---|---|---|---|---|---|---|---|---|---|---|---|---|---|---|
| 1 | Aug 26 | York City | D | 2-2 | 1-1 | 6516 | Pendergast, Warburton | A.Hobson | V.Brown | W.Gregg | H.Howarth | T.Walters | R.Butcher | W.Horsman | J.McGough | R.Worswick | W.Pendergast | G.Warburton |
| 2 | 30 | DONCASTER R. | W | 1-0 | 1-0 | 6463 | McGough | " | " | " | " | " | " | " | " | A.Law | " | F.Marsh |
| 3 | Sep 2 | TRANMERE ROVERS | W | 2-0 | 1-0 | 6618 | Law, McGough | " | " | " | " | " | " | " | " | " | " | " |

## REGIONAL LEAGUE (WESTERN SECTION)

| | Date | Opposition | | FT | HT | Att. | Goalscorers | | | | | | | | | | | |
|---|---|---|---|---|---|---|---|---|---|---|---|---|---|---|---|---|---|---|
| 1 | Oct 21 | Tranmere Rovers | W | 2-1 | 0-0 | 5000 | Yates, Astbury | W.Shortt | V.Brown | E.Common | H.Howarth | T.Walters | R.Butcher | W.Horsman | T.Astbury | R.Yates | C.Leyfield | E.Stubbs |
| 2 | 28 | MANCHESTER UTD. | L | 0-4 | 0-1 | 5000 | | " | " | " | " | " | " | " | " | F.Marsh | " | " |
| 3 | Nov 11 | Wrexham | D | 2-2 | 1-0 | 4500 | Leyfield, Dickinson | " | " | " | " | J.Rogers | " | " | " | A.Dickinson | " | R.Sanders |
| 4 | 18 | EVERTON | W | 3-2 | 3-2 | 6000 | Sanders, McMahon, og | " | " | " | " | T.Walters | D.Cole | " | " | D.McMahon | " | " |
| 5 | 25 | Stoke City | L | 0-2 | 0-0 | 2000 | | " | " | " | " | " | " | " | J.McGough | " | " | " |
| 6 | Dec 2 | NEW BRIGHTON | D | 1-1 | 0-1 | 1500 | McGough | " | G.Griffiths | " | " | " | " | " | " | " | " | " |
| 7 | 9 | Manchester City | L | 1-4 | 1-3 | 3000 | McMahon | " | " | " | " | " | R.Butcher | " | T.Astbury | " | " | " |
| 8 | 23 | STOCKPORT C. | W | 8-1 | 2-0 | 800 | McMahon(6), og, Sanders | " | V.Brown | " | R.Butcher | " | H.Howarth | " | J.McGough | " | T.Astbury | " |
| 9 | Jan 6 | CREWE ALEX. | W | 1-0 | 0-0 | | Yates | " | " | " | H.Howarth | " | R.Butcher | " | N.Forgham | R.Yates | " | " |
| 10 | 20 | Liverpool | D | 1-1 | 0-0 | 2000 | Astbury | " | " | " | R.Butcher | " | H.Howarth | A.Williams | J.McGough | " | " | " |
| 11 | Feb 24 | Manchester United | L | 1-5 | 0-3 | 6000 | Howarth(pen) | " | " | " | D.Cole | " | " | " | " | " | " | " |
| 12 | Mar 2 | PORT VALE | L | 0-3 | 0-0 | 1000 | | " | " | " | H.Howarth | J.Rogers | R.Butcher | W.Horsman | T.Astbury | " | A.Williams | " |
| 13 | 9 | WREXHAM | W | 4-1 | 1-1 | 1400 | Yates,Astbury,Sanders,Pendergast | " | " | D.McNeil | " | G.Chiverton | " | " | " | " | W.Pendergast | " |
| 14 | 16 | Everton | L | 0-5 | 0-4 | | | " | " | T.Walters | " | " | D.Cole | " | " | J.McIntosh | G.Booth | " |
| 15 | 23 | STOKE CITY | D | 3-3 | 1-1 | 3830 | Yates, Horsman, Sanders | " | H.Hollis | V.Brown | " | T.Walters | R.Butcher | " | " | R.Yates | W.Pendergast | " |
| 16 | 25 | TRANMERE ROVERS | D | 2-2 | 0-1 | 2124 | Horsman, Yates | " | " | " | " | " | " | " | " | " | " | A.Williams |
| 17 | 30 | New Brighton | L | 2-4 | 0-1 | 2997 | Yates(2) | " | " | " | " | K.Hollis | " | " | " | " | J.McGough | " |
| 18 | Apr 6 | MANCHESTER CITY | L | 0-3 | 0-2 | 2500 | | " | " | " | " | T.Walters | D.Cole | " | " | " | J.Devlin | E.Stubbs |
| 19 | May 4 | Port Vale | L | 1-3 | 0-2 | | og | " | " | K.Hollis | " | " | " | A.Williams | J.McGough | A.Keeley | T.Astbury | G.Warburton |
| 20 | 18 | LIVERPOOL | W | 4-0 | 1-0 | 1500 | McIntosh, Astbury(2), Rogers | " | V.Brown | W.Cook | " | " | " | J.Rogers | J.Hughes | R.Yates | " | J.McIntosh |
| 21 | 25 | Stockport County | W | 3-1 | 2-0 | 750 | Simms, Astbury, Yates | " | " | K.Hollis | " | " | " | H.Simms | " | " | " | R.Sanders |
| 22 | Jun 1 | Crewe Alex. | L | 1-3 | 1-1 | 500 | Yates | " | " | H.Hollis | " | K.Hollis | " | J.Park | " | " | " | J.McIntosh |

## FOOTBALL LEAGUE WAR CUP

| | Date | Opposition | | FT | HT | Att. | Goalscorers | | | | | | | | | | | |
|---|---|---|---|---|---|---|---|---|---|---|---|---|---|---|---|---|---|---|
| 1R1L | Jan 13 | BURNLEY | L | 1-3 | 1-2 | 2000 | Yates | W.Shortt | H.Hollis | V.Brown | H.Howarth | K.Hollis | R.Butcher | W.Horsman | T.Astbury | R.Yates | R.Sanders | A.Williams |
| 1R2L | Apr 13 | Burnley | L | 0-3 | 0-2 | 2458 | | " | " | K.Hollis | " | T.Walters | D.Cole | " | " | A.Williams | W.Pendergast | G.Warburton |

## WELSH CUP

| | Date | Opposition | | FT | HT | Att. | Goalscorers | | | | | | | | | | | |
|---|---|---|---|---|---|---|---|---|---|---|---|---|---|---|---|---|---|---|
| 4R | Apr 20 | SHREWSBURY T. | W | 4-2 | 3-1 | 1000 | og, Yates, Sanders, Astbury | J.Breeze | V.Brown | E.Common | H.Howarth | T.Walters | R.Butcher | W.Horsman | A.Williams | R.Yates | T.Astbury | R.Sanders |
| 6R | 27 | WELLINGTON | L | 1-3 | 1-0 | | Howarth(pen) | W.Shortt | H.Hollis | V.Brown | " | " | " | " | T.Astbury | " | J.McIntosh | " |

Chester were awarded a bye in the 5th round

## FRIENDLIES

| | Date | Opposition | | FT | HT | Att. | Goalscorers |
|---|---|---|---|---|---|---|---|
| 1 | Aug 19 | Wrexham * | W | 3-2 | 1-0 | 4764 | Law(2), Warburton |
| 2 | Sep 16 | LIVERPOOL | L | 0-5 | 0-1 | 5659 | |
| 3 | 23 | Wrexham | W | 2-0 | 1-0 | | Astbury, Marsh |
| 4 | 30 | WREXHAM | W | 3-2 | 2-1 | | Horsman, Astbury, Marsh |
| 5 | Oct 7 | WEST BROMWICH A. | L | 0-2 | 0-1 | 3313 | |
| 6 | Dec 16 | BURY | L | 3-4 | 3-0 | 1500 | Howarth(pen), Sanders, Yates |
| 7 | 25 | BIRMINGHAM | D | 1-1 | 1-1 | | Yates |
| 8 | 26 | Tranmere Rovers | L | 3-6 | 0-5 | 2000 | og, Brown, Astbury |
| 9 | Mar 22 | BLACKBURN R. | D | 0-0 | 0-0 | 3115 | |
| 10 | Apr 10 | ARMY XI # | L | 0-3 | 0-2 | 6000 | |

* Jubilee fund match

# Cheshire Regiments comfort fund

**First War Season (1939-40) notes:**

The Football League programme for the 1939/40 season was abandoned after three matches (at which time Chester were in 4th position out of 22 teams). In October a normal format League competition was organised on a regional basis, Chester finishing 9th out of 12 teams.

# SEASON 1940-41

| | Date | Opposition | | FT | HT | Att. | Goalscorers | | | | | | | | | | | |
|---|---|---|---|---|---|---|---|---|---|---|---|---|---|---|---|---|---|---|
| 1 | Aug 31 | STOCKPORT C | W | 5-3 | 3-1 | 1400 | Yates(2),Pendergast,Howarth,McIntosh | W.Shortt | H.Hollis | V.Brown | H.Howarth | T.Walters | D.Cole | W.Horsman | T.Astbury | W.Yates | W.Pendergast | J.McIntosh |
| 2 | Sep 7 | Crewe Alex. | W | 3-0 | 2-0 | 1600 | Astbury, McIntosh, Yates | " | " | G.Vose | " | " | " | J.McIntosh | G.Bremner | " | T.Astbury | W.Tunnicliffe |
| 3 | 14 | Stockport County | L | 0-4 | 0-1 | 2000 | | " | " | " | " | " | " | W.Horsman | " | " | " | J.McIntosh |
| 4 | 21 | Everton | L | 3-4 | 3-1 | 3000 | Astbury, og, Bremner | " | " | E.Reay | " | " | " | T.Astbury | " | " | W.Pendergast | " |
| 5 | 28 | LIVERPOOL | L | 0-2 | 0-0 | 2500 | | " | " | " | " | " | " | " | " | " | " | " |
| 6 | Oct 5 | Liverpool | L | 1-9 | 1-2 | 5000 | Yates | " | V.Brown | D.McNeil | " | " | " | " | " | " | " | " |
| 7 | 12 | TRANMERE ROVERS | L | 4-5 | 2-3 | | Yates, Cole, Bremner(2) | E.Goodall | E.Reay | " | " | W.Coley | " | W.Jones | " | " | W.Cairns | " |
| 8 | 19 | EVERTON | W | 1-0 | 1-0 | | Astbury | W.Shortt | V.Brown | " | " | T.Walters | " | " | " | " | T.Astbury | " |
| 9 | 26 | CREWE ALEX. | D | 3-3 | 0-1 | | Bremner, Astbury(2) | " | " | " | " | " | " | J.McIntosh | T.Astbury | " | G.Bremner | R.Sanders |
| 10 | Nov 2 | Tranmere Rovers | W | 4-2 | 3-1 | 700 | Yates(2), Pendergast(2) | " | J.E.Jones | " | " | G.Vose | " | F.Roberts | " | " | W.Pendergast | J.McIntosh |
| 11 | 9 | CREWE ALEX. | W | 6-0 | 6-0 | | Roberts,Yates(2),Pendergast, * | " | " | " | " | D.Williams | " | " | " | " | " | " |
| 12 | 16 | Burnley | D | 0-0 | 0-0 | | | " | V.Brown | T.Manley | " | " | " | " | " | " | G.Bremner | " |
| 13 | 23 | New Brighton | L | 2-4 | 1-3 | 1100 | Roberts, Pendergast | " | J.E.Jones | " | " | T.Walters | " | " | G.Bremner | " | W.Pendergast | " |
| 14 | 30 | Oldham Athletic | D | 0-0 | 0-0 | 1745 | | " | V.Brown | D.McNeil | " | D.Williams | " | T.Astbury | " | " | " | T.Manley |
| 15 | Dec 7 | NEW BRIGHTON | W | 6-2 | 5-1 | 500 | Pendergast,Yates(3),Astbury,McIntosh | " | J.E.Jones | " | " | " | " | H.Pearson | T.Astbury | " | " | J.McIntosh |
| 16 | 14 | BURNLEY | L | 3-4 | 0-2 | 300 | Pendergast(2), Howarth | " | " | " | " | " | " | " | " | " | " | " |
| 17 | 25 | Wrexham | L | 1-2 | 1-2 | 1680 | Cole | W.Rigby | V.Brown | " | " | " | L.Jones | D.Cole | " | " | G.Bremner | W.Pendergast |
| 18 | 25 | WREXHAM | L | 1-3 | 0-2 | 1600 | Pendergast | " | D.Cole | " | J.Boswell | " | H.Howarth | W.Pendergast | " | " | L.Jones | G.Bremner |
| 19 | Jan 4 | SOUTHPORT | W | 6-1 | 2-1 | 500 | Bremner(2),Pearson,Yates(2),Pendergast | " | V.Brown | T.Walters | H.Howarth | " | D.Cole | G.Bremner | " | " | W.Pendergast | H.Pearson |
| 20 | 11 | Southport | W | 3-2 | 2-1 | 700 | Pendergast, Yates, Bremner | " | " | D.McNeil | " | " | " | " | " | " | " | " |
| 21 | Feb 1 | NEW BRIGHTON | W | 7-1 | 4-1 | 400 | White(2),Pendergast(2),Yates(3) | " | H.Hollis | W.Quinton | " | " | " | F.White | " | " | " | " |
| 22 | 8 | New Brighton | L | 0-2 | 0-0 | 750 | | " | K.Hollis | " | " | " | " | " | " | " | B.Davies | " |
| 23 | Mar 1 | Blackpool | L | 2-5 | 1-1 | 5000 | Redfern, og | " | T.Walters | J.Turnbull | " | " | " | G.Bremner | " | " | W.Redfern | F.White |
| 24 | 8 | BLACKPOOL | W | 4-3 | 2-2 | 2000 | Pendergast,Glaister(2),Yates | " | J.Turnbull | V.Brown | " | " | " | F.White | " | " | W.Pendergast | G.Glaister |
| 25 | 22 | Wrexham | L | 2-5 | 1-4 | 1123 | Pendergast(2) | " | K.Hollis | T.Walters | " | " | " | " | " | " | " | F.Roberts |
| 26 | Apr 5 | NEW BRIGHTON | W | 7-3 | 3-3 | 300 | Pendergast,Glaister(2),Yates,Roberts(3 | W.Shortt | H.Howarth | J.Turnbull | G.Bremner | " | " | F.Roberts | " | " | " | G.Glaister |
| 27 | 12 | WREXHAM | D | 1-1 | 0-0 | | Pendergast | " | " | " | " | " | " | " | " | " | " | " |
| 28 | 14 | Preston North End | L | 0-3 | 0-1 | 6085 | | W.Rigby | " | " | " | " | " | " | " | " | " | " |
| 29 | 19 | MANCHESTER UTD | D | 4-4 | 1-1 | 3500 | 4-6 aet; White,Astbury,Yates(2) | W.Shortt | J.Turnbull | T.Walters | " | " | H.Howarth | F.White | " | " | " | H.Pearson |
| 30 | 26 | Stoke City | W | 2-1 | 1-0 | 600 | Yates(2) | " | " | D.McNeil | D.Cole | " | " | F.Roberts | " | " | " | G.Bremner |
| 31 | May 3 | STOKE CITY | W | 1-0 | 0-0 | | Roberts | " | H.Hollis | " | " | " | " | " | " | " | " | E.Lanceley |
| 32 | 10 | BOLTON WANDS. | W | 8-0 | 4-0 | | Pendergast(3),og,Yates(4) | " | D.Cole | " | J.Mercer | " | " | " | " | " | " | " |
| 33 | 17 | Tranmere Rovers | D | 1-1 | 1-0 | | 4-1 aet;Cole(2p),Pendergast,Lanceley | " | D.McNeil | J.Turnbull | D.Cole | " | " | " | " | " | " | " |
| 34 | 24 | LIVERPOOL | L | 1-6 | 1-3 | 700 | Yates | " | J.Turnbull | D.McNeil | " | " | " | G.Bremner | " | " | " | " |
| 35 | 31 | Blackpool | L | 2-4 | 1-0 | 4000 | Glaister, Brigham | " | H.Brigham | A.Owen | " | " | " | " | " | " | " | " |

* Other goalscorers: McIntosh, Astbury

Matches 19 & 20 also counted for the Lancs Cup 1st Round (2 legs)
Matches 21 & 22 also counted for the Lancs Cup 2nd Round (2 legs)
Match 29 also counted for the League Cup
Match 33 also counted for the Cheshire Bowl Semi-Final, the score of 1-1 counted for the League, the extra time score of 4-1 counted for the Cheshire Bowl

## LEAGUE WAR CUP

| | Date | Opposition | | FT | HT | Att. | Goalscorers | | | | | | | | | | | |
|---|---|---|---|---|---|---|---|---|---|---|---|---|---|---|---|---|---|---|
| 1R1L | Feb 15 | TRANMERE R. | W | 2-0 | 1-0 | 1000 | Bremner, Young | W.Rigby | V.Brown | T.Walters | H.Howarth | D.Williams | D.Cole | G.Bremner | T.Astbury | W.Yates | W.Young | F.White |
| 1R2L | 22 | Tranmere Rovers | L | 2-9 | 1-1 | 1900 | White, Pendergast | " | " | J.Turnbull | " | " | " | " | " | " | W.Pendergast | " |

## FRIENDLIES

| | Date | Opposition | | FT | HT | Att. | Goalscorers |
|---|---|---|---|---|---|---|---|
| 1 | Sep 4 | CZECH ARMY XI | W | 6-3 | 2-0 | 1552 | McIntosh(2),Mercer(2),Yates,Walters |
| 2 | Dec 21 | RAF | L | 2-3 | 1-3 | | Astbury, Yates |

**Second War Season (1940-41) notes:**

Chester competed in the North section of the regionalised Football League for the 1940-41 season. Clubs played varying numbers of games and not versus every team in their League. The final position was based on a goal average basis rather than points won (Chester finished 18th out of 36).

A countrywide knock-out Cup competition was held, the 'League War Cup', with the 1st round matches on a two-legged basis.

# SEASON 1941-42

| | Date | Opposition | | FT | HT | Att. | Goalscorers | | | | | | | | | | | |
|---|---|---|---|---|---|---|---|---|---|---|---|---|---|---|---|---|---|---|
| 1 | Aug 30 | STOCKPORT C | W | 3-1 | 1-1 | 1500 | Pendergast, Yates, Swain | W.Shortt | P.Hastings | D.McNeil | D.Cole | D.Williams | H.Howarth | F.Roberts | T.Astbury | R.Yates | W.Pendergast | J.Swain |
| 2 | Sep 6 | Stockport County | W | 4-2 | 0-1 | 2500 | Yates(2), Roberts(2,1pen) | " | J.Turnbull | " | " | " | " | " | " | " | " | " |
| 3 | 13 | Everton | D | 1-1 | 1-1 | | Roberts | " | " | " | " | " | " | " | " | " | " | C.Leyfield |
| 4 | 20 | EVERTON | W | 2-0 | 0-0 | 3850 | Yates, Roberts(pen) | " | " | H.Bates | " | " | " | " | " | " | " | " |
| 5 | 27 | Stoke City | W | 5-2 | 2-1 | 3500 | Leyfield, Roberts, Yates(3) | " | " | D.McNeil | " | " | " | " | " | " | " | " |
| 6 | Oct 4 | STOKE CITY | L | 3-4 | 0-2 | | Yates, Glaister(2) | " | " | " | " | " | " | " | " | " | G.Glaister | " |
| 7 | 11 | MANCHESTER UTD | L | 0-7 | 0-2 | 3500 | | J.Breeze | " | " | " | " | " | " | C.Leyfield | " | W.Pendergast | G.Glaister |
| 8 | 18 | Manchester United | L | 1-8 | 0-2 | 2500 | og | W.Shortt | " | " | " | " | P.Hastings | W.Horsman | T.Astbury | " | J.Moore | " |
| 9 | 25 | Tranmere Rovers | L | 0-1 | 0-0 | 2000 | | " | H.Hollis | " | " | " | A.Griffiths | F.Roberts | " | " | W.Graham | J.Bazley |
| 10 | Nov 1 | TRANMERE ROVERS | W | 6-1 | 3-1 | | Roberts(2,1p),Yates(2),og,Glaister | " | J.Turnbull | " | H.Howarth | " | " | " | " | " | " | " |
| 11 | 8 | LIVERPOOL | L | 3-4 | 1-1 | 3000 | Roberts, McNeil, Yates | " | D.Cole | " | " | " | " | " | " | " | G.Glaister | " |
| 12 | 15 | Liverpool | L | 2-4 | 1-2 | 4000 | Astbury(2) | " | " | " | " | " | " | " | " | " | W.Pendergast | " |
| 13 | 22 | Wrexham | D | 1-1 | 0-1 | 2113 | Bazley | W.Rigby | " | " | " | " | " | " | " | " | " | " |
| 14 | 29 | WREXHAM | D | 2-2 | 1-1 | | Astubry, Roberts | " | " | " | " | " | " | " | " | " | " | " |
| 15 | Dec 6 | MANCHESTER CITY | L | 1-3 | 1-1 | 1200 | Yates | " | " | " | A.Griffiths | V.Brown | D.Williams | " | " | " | F.Marsh | " |
| 16 | 13 | Manchester City | L | 2-7 | 0-3 | 3000 | Currier(2) | " | " | " | H.Howarth | D.Williams | A.Griffiths | " | " | " | J.Currier | " |
| 17 | 20 | New Brighton | L | 3-4 | 3-0 | 1000 | Stubbs, Astbury, Yates | " | " | " | " | " | J.Spedding | " | " | " | G.Jackson | E.Stubbs |
| 18 | 25 | NEW BRIGHTON | W | 6-1 | 4-0 | 3000 | Yates(5), Sharp | " | G.Jackson | " | " | " | D.Cole | E.Payne | " | " | N.Sharp | " |
| 19 | 27 | Wolverhampton W. | L | 1-2 | 1-2 | 6500 | Yates | " | " | " | A.Griffiths | " | " | " | " | " | " | " |
| 20 | Jan 3 | WOLVERHAMPTON W. | L | 1-3 | 0-2 | | Howarth | " | W.Gregg | " | H.Howarth | " | " | " | " | " | " | F.Marsh |
| 21 | 10 | Bolton Wanderers | L | 0-1 | 0-1 | | | " | G.Jackson | " | " | T.Walters | " | J.Bazley | " | " | J.Shepherd | E.Stubbs |
| 22 | 17 | BOLTON WANDS. | W | 3-1 | 0-0 | | Chambers, Yates(2) | " | H.Hollis | " | " | " | " | J.Veacock | J.Chambers | " | T.Astbury | G.O'Neill |
| 23 | 31 | WALSALL | W | 4-3 | 1-3 | 1000 | Yates(3), Lucas | " | G.Jackson | " | " | D.Williams | " | J.Bazley | W.Lucas | " | " | " |
| 24 | Feb 7 | Preston North End | L | 0-6 | 0-2 | | | " | " | " | " | T.Walters | " | " | T.Astbury | " | N.Sharp | G.Glaister |
| 25 | 14 | PRESTON N.E. | D | 2-2 | 1-0 | | Astbury, Fisher | W.Shortt | " | " | " | " | " | J.Veacock | " | " | L.Fisher | G.O'Neill |
| 26 | 21 | New Brighton | L | 1-2 | 0-0 | 1000 | Yates | W.Rigby | H.Bates | " | J.Alderson | D.Williams | H.Howarth | " | " | " | G.O'Neill | J.McIntosh |
| 27 | 28 | NEW BRIGHTON | W | 5-0 | 3-0 | 2500 | Yates(2), Bazley(2), Roberts | " | " | " | H.Howarth | " | E.Tagg | R.Birkett | " | " | F.Roberts | J.Bazley |
| 28 | Mar 14 | Walsall | W | 2-0 | 0-0 | 1059 | Bryant, Yates | " | W.Gregg | " | " | T.Walters | G.Wharton | W.Bryant | " | " | E.Tagg | " |
| 29 | 21 | LIVERPOOL | L | 1-3 | 1-1 | 3000 | Redfern | " | G.Jackson | " | " | T.Chadwick | E.Tagg | J.Bazley | " | " | W.Redfern | J.McIntosh |
| 30 | 28 | Tranmere Rovers | D | 1-1 | 1-1 | 1000 | McIntosh | " | " | H.Bates | " | " | R.Vasey | " | " | J.McIntosh | L.Armeson | R.Sanders |
| 31 | Apr 4 | Wolverhampton W. | L | 1-3 | 1-1 | 6310 | Yates | " | A.Hickman | D.McNeil | " | T.Walters | L.Armeson | " | " | R.Yates | W.Redfern | S.Polk |
| 32 | 6 | WOLVERHAMPTON W. | L | 0-1 | 0-1 | 4500 | | " | D.Cole | " | " | " | " | R.Birkett | " | " | " | J.McIntosh |
| 33 | 11 | Oldham Athletic | W | 3-2 | 2-1 | 2625 | Yates, Lanceley(2) | " | H.Bates | " | " | D.Williams | D.Cole | J.Bazley | " | " | S.Polk | E.Lanceley |
| 34 | 25 | STOKE CITY | L | 2-4 | 1-4 | | Astbury, Iddon | " | " | " | " | A.Griffiths | L.Armeson | R.Yates | H.Iddon | R.Guest | T.Astbury | S.Polk |
| 35 | May 2 | Stoke City | D | 2-2 | 2-0 | | Piercey, Yates | W.Shortt | " | " | " | D.Williams | D.Cole | E.Payne | T.Astbury | R.Yates | H.Iddon | R.Piercey |
| 36 | 9 | Liverpool | L | 0-3 | 0-2 | 5000 | | " | " | " | " | " | " | F.Roberts | " | J.McIntosh | " | J.Bazley |
| 37 | 16 | WREXHAM | L | 1-2 | 0-0 | | Astbury | " | " | " | " | T.Walters | " | H.Brooks | " | G.Jackson | " | E.Lanceley |
| 38 | 25 | Wrexham | W | 4-0 | 1-0 | 1059 | McIntosh(2), Brooks, Yates | " | G.Jackson | " | " | D.Williams | L.Armeson | " | " | R.Yates | N.Sharp | J.McIntosh |

**Matches 1 to 18**
War League (North)
Match 2 also counted for the Cheshire Bowl Final

**Matches 19 to 38**
War League Championship
Matches 19 to 28 also counted for the League Cup Qualifying competition
Matches 29 and 36 also counted for the Lancs Cup 1st Round (2 legs)
Matches 31 and 32 also counted for the League Cup 1st Round (2 legs)

## FRIENDLIES

| | | | | | | | |
|---|---|---|---|---|---|---|---|
| 1 | Apr 18 | BIRMINGHAM | D | 3-3 | 1-0 | | Roberts(3) |

### Third War Season (1941-42) notes:

The War League North competition was run on the same basis as the previous season, Chester finishing 24th out of 38 clubs. The War League Championship was run in a similar manner, but was nationwide. Of 51 clubs, Chester finished 21st. A qualifying competition for the (nationwide) War League Cup was also run on similar lines, with Chester finishing 30th out of 51. As one of the top 32 clubs they progressed to the competition proper.

# SEASON 1942-43

| | Date | Opposition | | FT | HT | Att. | Goalscorers | | | | | | | | | | | |
|---|---|---|---|---|---|---|---|---|---|---|---|---|---|---|---|---|---|---|
| 1 | Aug 29 | OLDHAM ATHLETIC | W | 5-1 | 2-0 | 2000 | Yates(3), Astbury, Lucas | W.Shortt | H.Bates | D.McNeil | G.Bird | T.Walters | D.Cole | J.McItosh | T.Astbury | R.Yates | N.Sharp | W.Lucas |
| 2 | Sep 5 | Oldham Athletic | W | 3-2 | 1-1 | 521 | Rawcliffe(2), Veacock | " | " | " | " | D.Williams | " | J.Veacock | H.Iddon | F.Rawcliffe | " | S.Ottewell |
| 3 | 12 | Manchester United | W | 2-0 | 2-0 | 3000 | Sharp, Veacock | " | " | " | R.Dutton | T.Walters | " | " | " | A.Keeley | " | J.McIntosh |
| 4 | 19 | MANCHESTER UTD | D | 2-2 | 1-0 | 4000 | Veacock, Yates | " | " | " | " | " | " | " | T.Astbury | R.Yates | " | " |
| 5 | 26 | HALIFAX TOWN | W | 4-1 | 2-0 | | Sharp, Thow(2), McIntosh | " | " | " | J.Mercer | " | " | " | " | J.McIntosh | " | L.Thow |
| 6 | Oct 3 | Halifax Town | L | 1-3 | 0-0 | | McIntosh | " | " | " | R.Dutton | " | " | " | H.Iddon | " | D.Williams | " |
| 7 | 10 | Tranmere Rovers | D | 2-2 | 0-1 | 2000 | McNeil(pen), McIntosh | " | " | " | " | " | " | " | " | F.Rawcliffe | N.Sharp | J.McIntosh |
| 8 | 17 | TRANMERE R. | W | 3-2 | 1-2 | | Glaister, Astbury, McIntosh | " | " | " | " | D.Williams | G.Booth | " | T.Astbury | J.McIntosh | " | G.Glaister |
| 9 | 24 | WREXHAM | W | 7-2 | 4-1 | | McIntosh(3),og,McNeil(pen), * | " | " | " | " | " | " | " | H.Iddon | " | G.Glaister | W.Hallard |
| 10 | 31 | Wrexham | L | 2-3 | 0-2 | 3729 | McIntosh, Hallard | " | " | " | " | " | J.Mercer | " | T.Astbury | " | " | " |
| 11 | Nov 7 | Liverpool | L | 2-4 | 2-1 | 11047 | Harris, McIntosh | J.Fairbrother | " | " | " | " | G.Booth | " | H.Iddon | " | F.Harris | " |
| 12 | 14 | LIVERPOOL | L | 1-5 | 1-2 | 5000 | Yates | W.Shortt | " | " | " | " | " | " | T.Astbury | R.Yates | H.Iddon | J.McIntosh |
| 13 | 21 | Manchester City | L | 2-4 | 1-2 | 3000 | McIntosh, Veacock | " | " | " | " | " | " | " | " | " | F.Harris | " |
| 14 | 28 | MANCHESTER CITY | D | 1-1 | 0-0 | 2500 | Compton | " | L.Compton | " | " | " | " | J.Kelly | " | J.McIntosh | H.Iddon | W.Hallard |
| 15 | Dec 5 | Everton | L | 1-3 | 0-2 | 5000 | Astbury | J.Fairbrother | " | " | " | " | " | J.Veacock | " | " | N.Sharp | L.Thow |
| 16 | 12 | EVERTON | L | 2-3 | 2-1 | | McIntosh, Roberts | W.Shortt | H.Bates | " | " | " | " | F.Roberts | " | R.Yates | J.McIntosh | " |
| 17 | 19 | STOCKPORT C | D | 1-1 | 0-1 | 500 | McIntosh | " | " | " | " | " | " | J.Veacock | H.Iddon | F.Roberts | " | M.McPeake |
| 18 | 25 | Stockport County | W | 2-1 | 0-0 | 4000 | Astbury, Kelly | " | G.Bird | " | J.Boswell | R.Clarke | " | " | T.Astbury | J.Kelly | G.O'Neill | " |
| 19 | 26 | Manchester United | L | 0-3 | 0-1 | 10449 | | " | " | " | R.Dutton | D.Williams | " | " | " | J.McIntosh | N.Sharp | " |
| 20 | Jan 2 | MANCHESTER UTD | W | 4-1 | 1-1 | 1500 | Iddon, McIntosh(2), Compton | " | W.Hughes | " | G.Bird | " | " | F.Roberts | H.Iddon | L.Compton | " | J.McIntosh |
| 21 | 9 | CREWE ALEX. | D | 0-0 | 0-0 | | | " | H.Bates | " | R.Dutton | " | G.Bird | " | " | " | T.Astbury | " |
| 22 | 16 | Crewe Alex. | D | 1-1 | 0-1 | 3452 | Veacock | " | L.Compton | " | " | " | W.Hughes | J.Veacock | T.Astbury | J.Kelly | F.Harris | G.Bird |
| 23 | 23 | Tranmere Rovers | W | 6-1 | 1-0 | 2500 | Kelly,Sharp(2),McIntosh(2),og | " | W.Hughes | " | " | " | G.Booth | F.Roberts | " | " | N.Sharp | J.McIntosh |
| 24 | 30 | TRANMERE R. | W | 1-0 | 0-0 | 2300 | Yates | " | L.Compton | " | " | " | W.Hughes | " | " | R.Yates | " | " |
| 25 | Feb 6 | Everton | W | 5-4 | 1-2 | 8000 | Kelly, Compton(3), Astbury | " | W.Hughes | " | " | " | G.Booth | " | " | L.Compton | J.Kelly | " |
| 26 | 13 | EVERTON | L | 0-1 | 0-1 | | | " | " | " | R.Clarke | " | " | " | " | J.Kelly | N.Sharp | " |
| 27 | 20 | WREXHAM | W | 3-0 | 2-0 | | McIntosh, Sharp, Welsh | W.Weight | " | " | " | " | F.Harris | G.Booth | " | D.Walsh | " | " |
| 28 | 27 | Wrexham | L | 2-3 | 2-1 | | Booth, Clarke | W.Shortt | J.Jones | " | R.Dutton | " | " | H.Iddon | " | R.Clarke | " | G.Booth |
| 29 | Mar 6 | STOKE CITY | L | 2-3 | 0-2 | 5634 | Harris, Compton | J.Fairbrother | D.McNeil | W.Hughes | F.Harris | " | D.Welsh | G.Collins | " | L.Compton | " | J.McIntosh |
| 30 | 13 | Stoke City | L | 2-5 | 1-3 | | Bremner, Compton | W.Shortt | W.Hughes | D.McNeil | R.Clarke | " | G.Booth | G.Bremner | H.Iddon | " | " | " |
| 31 | 20 | CREWE ALEX. | L | 1-3 | 0-2 | | McIntosh | J.Atherton | H.Hollis | " | R.Dutton | " | R.Clarke | D.Lacey | T.Astbury | J.McIntosh | D.Welsh | G.Booth |
| 32 | 27 | Crewe Alex. | D | 3-3 | 0-0 | 3200 | Sharp(2), Hughes(pen) | J.Brookbank | " | " | W.Hughes | " | " | J.Payne | G.Bremner | R.Yates | N.Sharp | J.McIntosh |
| 33 | Apr 3 | Liverpool | L | 1-4 | 0-1 | 10769 | Taylor | R.Brown | " | W.Hughes | R.Dutton | " | " | T.Taylor | T.Astbury | D.McNeil | " | " |
| 34 | 10 | LIVERPOOL | L | 2-5 | 2-3 | 4000 | Payne, J.Turner | " | " | D.McNeil | " | " | " | S.Jones | H.Iddon | J.Turner | " | J.Payne |
| 35 | 17 | Bolton Wanderers | L | 1-3 | 1-1 | | J.Turner | J.Brookbank | H.Riddihough | H.Hollis | " | " | G.Booth | D.Lacey | " | " | F.Harris | F.Wilkie |
| 36 | 24 | WREXHAM | W | 3-2 | 2-0 | | Lacey, Yates(2) | " | H.Hollis | D.McNeil | " | " | F.Harris | " | T.Astbury | R.Yates | N.Sharp | P.Turner |
| 37 | 26 | Wrexham | L | 1-3 | 1-3 | 3521 | McNeil(pen) | " | J.Kirby | " | " | " | R.Clarke | " | B.Jones | " | T.Astbury | G.Booth |
| 38 | May 1 | Southport | L | 2-4 | 2-2 | 1000 | Sharp(2) | " | G.Bird | " | " | " | W.Hughes | " | S.Thorpe | J.Turner | N.Sharp | H.Iddon |

* Other goalscorers: Veacock, Hallard

**Matches 1 to 18**
League North

**Matches 19 to 38**
League North (Second) Championship
Matches 19 to 28 also counted for the League North Cup Qualifying competition
Matches 29 and 30 also counted for the League Cup 1st round (2 legs)
Matches 33 and 34 also counted for the Lancashire Cup 1st round (2 legs)

## FRIENDLIES

| | Date | Opposition | | FT | HT | Att. | Goalscorers |
|---|---|---|---|---|---|---|---|
| 1 | May 8 | Army XI * | W | 11-4 | 5-2 | 500 | Bremner(2), Lawton(5), # |
| 2 | 15 | WESTERN COMMAND | L | 1-3 | 0-2 | | McIntosh |

* Played at Buckley
# Other goalscorers: Astbury(2), Ashcroft(2)

### Fourth War Season (1942-43) notes:

Competitions similar to previous season, Chester finishing 23rd out of 48 in the (first) League North and 36th out of 54 in the League North (second) Championship. In the League North Cup qualifying competition, Chester finished 15th out of 54 and thus qualified for the competition proper.

# SEASON 1943-44

| | Date | Opposition | | FT | HT | Att. | Goalscorers | | | | | | | | | | | |
|---|---|---|---|---|---|---|---|---|---|---|---|---|---|---|---|---|---|---|
| 1 | Aug 28 | Wrexham | L | 4-8 | 2-3 | 4197 | Newsome(2), Astbury, Moore | E.Adams | J.Hartley | D.McNeil | R.Dutton | E.Kirby | R.Clarke | R.Newsome | T.Astbury | D.Spendlove | N.Moore | T.Butler |
| 2 | Sep 4 | WREXHAM | D | 3-3 | 2-2 | 2455 | Spendlove(2), Harris | G.Scales | H.Bates | " | " | W.Hughes | D.Cole | " | " | " | F.Harris | G.O'Neill |
| 3 | 11 | Oldham Athletic | W | 3-0 | 0-0 | 2587 | Butler, Moore, Loxham | J.Brookbank | " | " | D.Cole | " | F.Harris | T.Butler | " | W.Loxham | N.Moore | " |
| 4 | 18 | OLDHAM ATHLETIC | W | 6-1 | 2-0 | 2000 | Harris(2), Yates(2), O'Neill(2) | " | " | " | " | " | " | " | " | R.Yates | " | " |
| 5 | 25 | Halifax Town | W | 4-1 | 1-0 | | Piercey, Yates(2), Moore | " | " | " | " | W.Ithell | E.Tagg | R.Newsome | " | " | " | R.Piercey |
| 6 | Oct 2 | HALIFAX TOWN | W | 3-1 | 1-0 | | Loxham(2), Browne | " | " | " | R.Dutton | W.Hughes | " | " | " | W.Loxham | " | J.Browne |
| 7 | 9 | Manchester United | L | 1-3 | 0-3 | 6058 | Leigh | G.Scales | E.Tagg | " | " | " | D.Cole | T.Butler | " | " | " | J.Leigh |
| 8 | 16 | MANCHESTER UTD | W | 5-4 | 3-1 | 4000 | Davies,Loxham(2),Mann,Moore | " | H.Bates | " | E.Tagg | M.Gillies | W.Hughes | A.Mann | N.Moore | " | T.Astbury | T.Davies |
| 9 | 23 | TRANMERE R | W | 3-2 | 2-2 | | Loxham(2), Matthews | " | " | " | R.Clarke | " | " | R.Slater | T.Astbury | " | E.Tagg | W.Matthews |
| 10 | 30 | Tranmere Rovers | L | 1-3 | 0-2 | | Astbury | " | " | " | D.Cole | " | " | E.Bryan | " | " | " | H.Smith |
| 11 | Nov 6 | LIVERPOOL | W | 3-1 | 2-1 | 2500 | Newsome(2), Loxham | " | J.Wheatman | " | " | W.Hughes | E.Tagg | F.Roberts | R. Newsome | " | T.Astbury | G.Makin |
| 12 | 13 | Liverpool | L | 0-9 | 0-4 | 9000 | | " | H.Bates | " | J.Wheatman | " | G.Booth | D.Miller | J.Essex | " | " | " |
| 13 | 20 | MANCHESTER CITY | L | 1-2 | 0-1 | 3500 | Roberts | " | " | " | D.Cole | " | E.Tagg | F.Roberts | T.Astbury | " | H.Hewitt | L.Jones |
| 14 | 27 | Manchester City | L | 0-3 | 0-2 | 3000 | | " | R.Walton | " | " | H.Bates | " | F.Roberts | " | " | G.Booth | E.Lanceley |
| 15 | Dec 4 | EVERTON | W | 1-0 | 1-0 | | Veacock | " | " | " | " | W.Hughes | " | J.Veacock | W.Loxham | E.Bryan | T.Astbury | G.O'Neill |
| 16 | 11 | Everton | W | 1-0 | 0-0 | | Harris | " | " | " | " | " | " | R.Newsome | T.Astbury | W.Loxham | F.Harris | F.Roberts |
| 17 | 18 | Stockport County | L | 0-1 | 0-1 | 1200 | | " | " | H.Bates | R.Clarke | " | " | R.Slater | R.Newsome | " | T.Astbury | G.Booth |
| 18 | 25 | STOCKPORT C | D | 1-1 | 0-0 | 4000 | Veacock | J.Brookban | H.Bates | D.McNeil | R.Dutton | " | " | J.Veacock | W.Loxham | E.Bryan | " | G.O'Neill |
| 19 | 27 | EVERTON | L | 3-5 | 2-3 | 9000 | O'Neill(2), Astbury | G.Scales | " | " | T.Tilston | " | " | " | R.Newsome | W.Loxham | " | " |
| 20 | Jan 1 | Everton | L | 0-7 | 0-2 | | | " | R.Walton | " | R.Brown | H.Bates | " | J.Hancocks | " | " | " | F.Dwyer |
| 21 | 8 | Wrexham | L | 0-3 | 0-1 | 6414 | | " | R.Coupland | " | F.Childs | M.McDonnell | " | R.Newsome | N.Moore | " | " | C.Leyfield |
| 22 | 15 | WREXHAM | L | 1-3 | 0-3 | 3436 | Moore | " | W.Hughes | " | D.Cole | " | " | " | " | J.Veacock | " | G.O'Neill |
| 23 | 22 | Crewe Alex. | D | 4-4 | 0-2 | 3570 | Hughes(3), McNeil(pen) | " | H.Bates | " | R.Dutton | F.Pincott | " | W.Loxham | J.Boswell | W.Hughes | " | T.Davies |
| 24 | 29 | CREWE ALEX. | W | 6-1 | 3-0 | | Loxham(2),Hughes(3),McNeil(p) | " | E.Tagg | " | N.Moore | " | R.Brown | F.Roberts | W.Loxham | " | " | M.Hulligan |
| 25 | Feb 5 | TRANMERE R. | W | 6-2 | 3-0 | | Loxham(2),Astbury(2),Newsome,Hughes | " | " | " | " | " | H.Cothliff | R.Newsome | " | " | " | R.Piercey |
| 26 | 12 | Tranmere Rovers | W | 3-2 | 2-0 | | Hughes(3) | " | R.Walton | " | H.Cothliff | " | E.Tagg | H.Jones | " | " | " | J.Brinton |
| 27 | 19 | Liverpool | L | 2-4 | 1-1 | 13355 | Yates, Hughes | " | E.Tagg | " | N.Moore | D.Williams | H.Cothliff | W.Loxham | R.Yates | " | " | T.Davies |
| 28 | 26 | LIVERPOOL | W | 6-0 | 0-0 | 6000 | Brinton,Moore(3),Loxham,Hughes | " | " | " | D.Williams | F.Pincott | " | " | N.Moore | " | " | J.Brinton |
| 29 | Mar 4 | Crewe Alex. | W | 9-5 | 4-3 | 2536 | Brinton(3),Loxham,Newsome(3)* | " | " | " | N.Moore | " | R.Clarke | R.Newsome | W.Loxham | " | " | " |
| 30 | 11 | CREWE ALEX. | W | 4-1 | 2-1 | | Moore, Hughes(2), Brinton | J.Atherton | " | " | P.Molloy | " | " | W.Loxham | N.Moore | " | J.Leyfield | " |
| 31 | 18 | Everton | L | 2-5 | 1-3 | 11139 | Hughes, Loxham | G.Scales | " | " | N.Moore | " | " | F.Roberts | W.Loxham | " | T.Astbury | " |
| 32 | 25 | EVERTON | L | 2-9 | 2-2 | | Astbury, Loxham | " | " | " | D.Williams | " | " | " | N.Moore | W.Loxham | " | " |
| 33 | Apr 8 | Wrexham | L | 0-5 | 0-2 | 6600 | | W.Rigby | " | " | A.Housam | " | " | R.Dutton | " | A.Black | " | " |
| 34 | 10 | WREXHAM | D | 2-2 | 0-1 | 5200 | McNeil(pen), Moore | J.Brookban | J.Mills | " | R.Clarke | W.Hughes | N.Moore | " | T.Astbury | W.Loxham | A.Black | J.Leigh |
| 35 | 15 | WOLVERHAMPTON W. | L | 1-3 | 0-2 | | Black | " | " | " | " | F.Pincott | " | W.Loxham | " | W.Hughes | " | " |
| 36 | 22 | Wolverhampton W. | W | 4-0 | 2-0 | 8000 | Black, Lee(2), Loxham | " | W.Corkhill | " | A.Housam | W.Hughes | " | R.Newsome | F.Harris | W.Loxham | " | G.Lee |
| 37 | 29 | Southport | W | 4-3 | 1-1 | 1500 | Loxham, Black, Moore, Astbury | G.Scales | " | " | " | " | " | " | T.Astbury | " | " | " |
| 38 | May 6 | STOCKPORT C | W | 6-1 | 3-1 | 800 | Astbury,Newsome(2),Loxham(2),Black | " | E.Tagg | " | " | N.Moore | F.Harris | " | " | " | " | " |

* Other goalscorers: og, Hughes

**Matches 1 to 18**
League North

**Matches 19 to 38**
League North (Second) Championship
Matches 19 to 28 also counted for the League North Cup Qualifying competition
Matches 29 and 30 also counted for the Cheshire Bowl Semi-Final (2 legs)
Matches 31 and 32 also counted for the Lancashire Cup 1st Round (2 legs)
Match 38 also counted for the Cheshire Bowl Final

## FRIENDLIES

| | | | | | | | |
|---|---|---|---|---|---|---|---|
| 1 | Apr 1 | Preston North End | W | 3-2 | 3-0 | | og, Clarke, Astbury |

### Fifth War Season (1943-44) notes:

Competitions similar to previous season, Chester finishing 20th out of 50 in the (first) League North and 27th out of 56 in the League North (second) Championship. In the League North Cup qualifying competition, Chester finished 35th out of 56 and failed to qualify for the competition proper.

# SEASON 1944-45

| | Date | Opposition | | FT | HT | Att. | Goalscorers | | | | | | | | | | | |
|---|---|---|---|---|---|---|---|---|---|---|---|---|---|---|---|---|---|---|
| 1 | Aug 26 | Crewe Alex. | W | 4-2 | 0-1 | 5400 | Lee, Black, Astbury(2) | W.Scales | W.Corkhill | D.McNeil | A.Housam | W.Hughes | F.Harris | R.Newsome | T.Astbury | R.Yates | A.Black | G.Lee |
| 2 | Sep 2 | CREWE ALEX. | W | 4-0 | 2-0 | | Black,Astbury,Leyfield,Newsome | " | " | " | " | G.Lunn | " | " | " | " | " | J.Leyfield |
| 3 | 9 | WREXHAM | W | 3-1 | 1-1 | 6500 | Black(2), Rhodes | " | " | " | " | W.Hughes | " | " | " | A.Rhodes | " | H.Tilling |
| 4 | 16 | Wrexham | D | 1-1 | 0-0 | 8430 | Neary | " | G.Lunn | " | W.Corkhill | D.Williams | " | " | " | F.Neary | " | " |
| 5 | 23 | Everton | L | 2-6 | 1-3 | 11100 | Black, Astbury | " | W.Corkhill | " | A.Housam | W.Hughes | " | " | " | " | " | " |
| 6 | 30 | EVERTON | L | 2-8 | 0-2 | | Astbury(2) | " | G.Lunn | " | " | F.Pincott | W.Corkhill | " | " | E.Webb | F.Harris | J.Brinton |
| 7 | Oct 7 | MANCHESTER UTD | W | 2-0 | 2-0 | 5000 | Hughes(2) | J.Brookbank | W.Corkhill | " | " | " | F.Harris | G.Warburton | " | W.Hughes | A.Black | H.Tilling |
| 8 | 14 | Manchester United | L | 0-1 | 0-0 | 3000 | | W.Scales | J.Dyer | " | R.Brown | G.Lunn | D.Edwards | A.Rhodes | " | E.Webb | T.Butler | J.Brinton |
| 9 | 21 | Bury | W | 4-2 | 1-2 | | Yates, Astbury, McNeil(2) | " | " | W.Hughes | R.Dutton | F.Pincott | J.Mills | F.Neary | " | R.Yates | F.Preskett | D.McNeil |
| 10 | 28 | BURY | D | 1-1 | 1-0 | | Astbury | " | " | D.McNeil | " | " | D.Williams | " | " | W.Hughes | F.Bett | C.McCormack |
| 11 | Nov 4 | STOCKPORT C | W | 5-2 | 1-2 | 3000 | Black(2), Neary, Astbury(2) | " | " | " | W.Corkhill | " | A.Housam | R.Newsome | " | F.Neary | A.Black | J.Campbell |
| 12 | 11 | Stockport County | L | 2-4 | 2-1 | 3000 | Preskett, Astbury | " | C.Tucker | " | R.Dutton | " | C.McCormack | T.Burden | " | N.Gorner | F.Preskett | " |
| 13 | 18 | TRANMERE R. | D | 2-2 | 0-1 | | Black(2) | " | W.Corkhill | " | A.Housam | W.Hughes | F.Harris | F.Neary | " | " | A.Black | T.Burden |
| 14 | 25 | Tranmere Rovers | W | 3-2 | 1-0 | | Burden(2), Neary | " | J.Dyer | C.Tucker | R.Dutton | F.Pincott | D.McNeil | " | " | T.Burden | F.Bett | G.Warburton |
| 15 | Dec 2 | Liverpool | L | 0-6 | 0-3 | 13609 | | " | " | W.Hughes | " | " | C.Tucker | A.Derrick | " | " | A.Black | " |
| 16 | 9 | LIVERPOOL | W | 3-2 | 1-2 | 3500 | Newsome, Black, Burden | R.King | " | C.Tucker | W.Corkhill | " | F.Harris | T.Burden | " | R.Newsome | " | D.McNeil |
| 17 | 16 | MANCHESTER CITY | W | 7-1 | 3-1 | 4500 | Black(2), Astbury(2), * | " | " | D.McNeil | R.Dutton | " | C.Tucker | A.Derrick | " | M.Armstrong | " | R.Hamilton |
| 18 | 23 | Manchester City | L | 0-6 | 0-1 | 14000 | | J.Brookbank | " | C.Tucker | " | " | D.Williams | F.Neary | M.Armstrong | R.Yates | T.Astbury | " |
| 19 | 25 | Wrexham | L | 2-4 | 1-0 | 8665 | Astbury, Hamilton | " | " | D.McNeil | C.Tucker | D.Williams | F.Harris | T.Burden | T.Astbury | " | R.Newsome | " |
| 20 | 30 | WREXHAM | L | 2-5 | 0-2 | 6497 | Yates, Neary | " | H.Hollis | " | " | " | D.Edwards | F.Neary | " | " | " | G.Warburton |
| 21 | Jan 6 | PORT VALE | L | 2-3 | 2-3 | | Hamilton, Astbury | " | " | H.Pitts | R.Dutton | R.Brown | C.Tucker | A.Derrick | " | F.Neary | G.Warburton | R.Hamilton |
| 22 | 13 | Port Vale | W | 2-0 | 0-0 | 5468 | Astbury, Black | R.King | W.Corkhill | D.McNeil | D.Kirby | F.Pincott | F.Harris | T.Burden | " | M.Armstrong | A.Black | " |
| 23 | 20 | Wolverhampton W. | L | 1-6 | 1-3 | 6000 | Armstrong | " | J.Dyer | " | W.Corkhill | " | D.Kirby | " | " | " | " | " |
| 24 | Feb 3 | STOKE CITY | L | 2-3 | 2-1 | | Armstrong(2) | " | " | " | " | R.Suart | F.Harris | K.Bainbridge | " | " | F.Bett | R.Newsome |
| 25 | 10 | Stoke City | L | 0-7 | 0-3 | 11000 | | " | C.Tucker | " | R.Dutton | F.Pincott | D.Williams | F.Neary | " | " | " | T.Howshall |
| 26 | 17 | CREWE ALEX. | D | 3-3 | 2-1 | | Armstrong(2), Piercey | " | T.Lewis | R.Suart | R.Brown | " | F.Harris | " | " | M.Armstrong | A.Black | R.Piercey |
| 27 | 24 | Crewe Alex. | L | 0-4 | 0-2 | 5360 | | N.Tapken | R.Suart | D.McNeil | W.Corkhill | " | A.Reeve | A.Rhodes | " | " | K.Bainbridge | " |
| 28 | Mar 3 | Everton | L | 1-4 | 0-2 | | Burden | R.King | T.Lewis | H.Hollis | T.Astbury | " | H.Cothliff | T.Burden | E.Naylor | R.Yates | A.Black | F.Bett |
| 29 | 10 | EVERTON + | W | 6-3 | 2-2 | | Hamilton, Astbury, Yates(2), # | " | " | D.McNeil | W.Corkhill | " | D.Kirby | K.Bainbridge | T.Astbury | " | K.Ellis | R.Hamilton |
| 30 | 17 | WOLVERHAMPTON W | L | 0-4 | 0-1 | | | " | J.Dyer | " | " | D.Williams | R.Brown | P.Turner | " | " | " | R.Piercey |
| 31 | 24 | Preston North End | L | 2-3 | 1-2 | | Kirby, Dewar | J.Brookbank | W.Corkhill | " | R.Brown | F.Pincott | D.Kirby | A.Derrick | R.Newsom | " | A.Black | J.Dewar |
| 32 | 31 | PRESTON N.E. | W | 4-1 | 1-1 | | Black(3), Bainbridge | " | " | " | " | " | " | K.Bainbridge | T.Astbury | " | " | R.Hamilton |
| 33 | Apr 2 | ROCHDALE | W | 3-0 | 0-0 | | Astbury, Yates, McNeil(pen) | " | J.Dyer | " | D.Kirby | J.Mills | D.Edwards | P.Turner | E.Naylor | " | T.Astbury | J.Dewar |
| 34 | 7 | Southport | W | 2-1 | 2-0 | 1500 | Burden, Black | " | J.Mills | " | " | F.Pincott | " | T.Burden | T.Astbury | " | A.Black | " |
| 35 | 14 | SOUTHPORT | W | 5-3 | 3-1 | | Yates(4), Burden | " | E.Bryan | " | R.Brown | D.Kirby | J.Wheatley | " | " | " | K.Ellis | R.Hamilton |
| 36 | 21 | Wrexham | D | 2-2 | 1-0 | 4950 | Yates(2) | " | J.Dyer | " | T.Astbury | F.Harris | D.Kirby | F.Neary | T.Burden | " | R.Newsome | C.Sargeant |
| 37 | 28 | WREXHAM | W | 2-1 | 1-0 | | Sargeant, Yates | W.Shortt | " | " | " | B.Radcliffe | " | R.Hamilton | J.McCormick | " | A.Black | " |
| 38 | May 5 | Rochdale | L | 1-2 | 0-0 | | Yates | W.Scales | " | " | R.Dutton | D.Williams | " | K.Bainbridge | T.Burden | " | F.Bett | R.Piercey |
| 39 | 19 | Crewe Alex. | W | 3-0 | 1-0 | | Turner, Hanson(2) | W.Shortt | E.Bryan | " | " | J.Mills | " | P.Turner | T.Astbury | " | A.Hanson | F.Bett |
| 40 | 26 | CREWE ALEX. | W | 4-2 | 1-2 | | Yates(3), Burden | W.Scales | " | " | D.Kirby | " | D.Skinner | K.Bainbridge | T.Burden | " | A.Black | A.Hanson |

* Other goalscorers: Armstrong(2), Derrick

# Other goalscorer: Bainbridge(2)

+ 6-4 after extra time

**Matches 1 to 18**
League North

**Matches 19 to 40**
League North Second Championship
Matches 19 to 27 and Match 30 also counted for the League North Cup Qualifying Competition
Matches 28 and 29 also counted for the Lancashire Cup 1st Round (2 legs). In the second leg, the score of 6-3 counted for the League, the extra time score of 6-4 counted for the Lancs Cup
Matches 39 and 40 also counted for the Cheshire Bowl Final (2 legs)

## Sixth War Season (1944-45) notes:

Competitions similar to previous season, Chester finishing 19th out of 54 in the (first) League North and 38th out of 60 in the League North (second) Championship. In the League North Cup qualifying competition, Chester finished 59th out of 60 and failed to qualify for the competition proper.

# SEASON 1945-46

## THIRD DIVISION NORTH (WEST REGION)

| | Date | Opposition | | FT | HT | Att. | Goalscorers | 1 | 2 | 3 | 4 | 5 | 6 | 7 | 8 | 9 | 10 | 11 |
|---|---|---|---|---|---|---|---|---|---|---|---|---|---|---|---|---|---|---|
| 1 | Aug 25 | Southport | W | 5-3 | 3-2 | 3176 | Bainbridge(3), Yates, Black | W.Shortt | W.Corkhill | D.McNeil | T.Burden | J.Mills | D.Skinner | K.Bainbridge | T.Astbury | R.Yates | A.Black | J.Dewar |
| 2 | Sep 1 | SOUTHPORT | W | 5-3 | 4-2 | 3907 | Yates(3), Black, Astbury | J.Brookbank | " | " | " | D.Williams | " | " | " | " | " | " |
| 3 | 8 | TRANMERE R. | W | 5-1 | 1-0 | 5213 | Black(4), Burden | " | " | E.Bryan | " | " | " | " | " | " | " | R.Hamilton |
| 4 | 15 | Tranmere Rovers | L | 0-3 | 0-1 | 5272 | | " | J.Dyer | D.McNeil | W.Corkhill | J.Mills | " | K.Ellis | " | " | W.Mills | J.Dewar |
| 5 | 22 | BARROW | W | 3-1 | 0-1 | 3909 | Astbury, Yates, Dewar | W.Shortt | W.Corkhill | J.Dyer | D.Cole | " | " | R.Hamilton | T.Burden | " | T.Astbury | " |
| 6 | 29 | Barrow | W | 3-1 | 1-0 | 6500 | Hamilton | J.Brookbank | J.Dyer | D.McNeil | T.Burden | " | " | " | F.Bett | " | " | G.Warburton |
| 7 | Oct 6 | Crewe Alex. | L | 0-2 | 0-2 | 5695 | | W.Shortt | " | " | R.Dutton | " | " | " | W.Bennett | " | " | " |
| 8 | 13 | CREWE ALEX. | D | 0-0 | 0-0 | 5795 | | J.Brookbank | " | " | T.Burden | " | W.Corkhill | " | T.Astbury | " | A.Black | I.Ferguson |
| 9 | 20 | Rochdale | L | 1-3 | 0-1 | 6693 | Yates | D.Whitelaw | " | " | W.Corkhill | " | D.Skinner | " | T.Burden | " | F.Bett | R.Piercy |
| 10 | 27 | ROCHDALE | D | 3-3 | 2-2 | 4180 | Yates(3) | R.Barwick | D.Cole | " | T.Burden | " | F.Marsh | " | F.Bett | " | T.Astbury | " |
| 11 | Nov 3 | Accrington Stanley | L | 2-5 | 1-3 | 5023 | Yates, Bett | W.Shortt | E.Bryan | " | " | " | D.Cole | K.Bainbridge | " | " | " | F.Marsh |
| 12 | 10 | ACCRINGTON S. | D | 3-3 | 3-0 | 4342 | Yates(2,1pen), Astbury | " | " | " | F.Marsh | " | D.Skinner | F.Bett | T.Burden | " | " | K.Bainbridge |
| 13 | Dec 1 | WREXHAM | W | 4-1 | 0-1 | 6975 | Astbury,Bainbridge,Hamilton,Yates | G.Scales | P.Stubbs | " | " | G.Lunn | D.Cole | R.Hamilton | T.Astbury | " | W.Pendergast | " |
| 14 | 22 | OLDHAM ATHLETIC | D | 2-2 | 1-0 | 2031 | Bett, Black(pen) | " | " | " | " | D.Cole | R.Butcher | F.Bett | " | N.Woof | A.Black | R.Hamilton |
| 15 | 24 | Wrexham | L | 0-2 | 0-2 | 7489 | | W.Shortt | " | " | " | E.Lee | " | " | " | C.McCormack | " | " |
| 16 | 25 | STOCKPORT C. | W | 4-2 | 2-0 | 1759 | Black(3), Yates | " | " | " | R.Dutton | G.Lunn | E.Lee | P.Turner | A.Black | R.Yates | T.Astbury | " |
| 17 | 26 | Stockport County | D | 1-1 | 1-1 | 8237 | Hamilton | " | " | R.Campbell | F.Marsh | E.Lee | D.Cole | " | T.Tilston | J.Bleaze | " | " |
| 18 | 29 | Oldham Athletic | W | 3-2 | 2-0 | 5095 | Yates(2), Black | G.Scales | " | D.McNeil | " | " | " | " | A.Black | R.Yates | F.Bett | " |

## F.A. CUP

| | Date | Opposition | | FT | HT | Att. | Goalscorers | 1 | 2 | 3 | 4 | 5 | 6 | 7 | 8 | 9 | 10 | 11 |
|---|---|---|---|---|---|---|---|---|---|---|---|---|---|---|---|---|---|---|
| 3R1 | Jan 5 | LIVERPOOL | L | 0-2 | 0-1 | 12200 | | W.Shortt | P.Stubbs | D.McNeil | F.Marsh | E.Lee | G.Cole | P.Turner | T.Burden | R.Yates | T.Astbury | R.Hamilton |
| 3R2 | 9 | Liverpool | L | 1-2 | 0-2 | 11000 | Astbury | " | " | " | " | " | " | " | " | " | " | " |

## THIRD DIVISION (NORTH) CUP QUALIFYING COMPETITION

| | Date | Opposition | | FT | HT | Att. | Goalscorers | 1 | 2 | 3 | 4 | 5 | 6 | 7 | 8 | 9 | 10 | 11 |
|---|---|---|---|---|---|---|---|---|---|---|---|---|---|---|---|---|---|---|
| 1 | Dec 8 | Stockport County | L | 0-2 | 0-0 | 2566 | | G.Scales | P.Stubbs | D.McNeil | F.Marsh | G.Lunn | R.Dutton | R.Hamilton | T.Astbury | W.Pendergast | A.Black | K.Bainbridge |
| 2 | Jan 12 | STOCKPORT C. | L | 1-2 | 1-1 | 3538 | Bainbridge | " | " | " | D.Cole | J.Mills | R.Butcher | " | F.Bett | F.Marsh | T.Astbury | " |
| 3 | 19 | ROCHDALE | W | 2-0 | 2-0 | 2484 | Hamilton(2) | W.Shortt | " | " | F.Marsh | T.Walters | D.Cole | P.Turner | D.Williams | E.Lee | " | R.Hamilton |
| 4 | 26 | Rochdale | L | 1-6 | 1-4 | 2397 | Turner | " | " | " | " | " | " | " | " | R.Yates | " | " |
| 5 | Feb 2 | CREWE ALEX. | W | 8-3 | 4-2 | 2610 | Leahy(3),Bett(2),Lee,Astbury,Hamilton | G.Scales | " | J.James | " | " | " | F.Bett | T.Leahy | E.Lee | " | " |
| 6 | 9 | Crewe Alex. | D | 5-5 | 2-2 | 3091 | Bett(4), Astbury | " | " | D.McNeil | " | " | T.Burden | P.Turner | " | F.Bett | " | K.Bainbridge |
| 7 | 16 | WREXHAM | W | 4-2 | 2-1 | 6317 | Burden(3), Hamilton | " | " | " | " | " | E.Lee | F.Bett | " | T.Burden | " | R.Hamilton |
| 8 | 23 | Wrexham | L | 0-2 | 0-2 | 7274 | | " | " | " | " | " | " | " | " | " | " | " |
| 9 | Mar 2 | ACCRINGTON S. | W | 4-1 | 1-1 | 3583 | Hamilton(2), Bett(2) | " | " | " | " | " | R.Butcher | P.Turner | F.Bett | " | " | " |
| 10 | 9 | Accrington Stanley | L | 1-2 | 1-2 | 4389 | Hamilton | " | " | " | " | " | " | " | T.Leahy | " | J.Long | " |

## THIRD DIVISION (NORTH) CUP

| | Date | Opposition | | FT | HT | Att. | Goalscorers | 1 | 2 | 3 | 4 | 5 | 6 | 7 | 8 | 9 | 10 | 11 |
|---|---|---|---|---|---|---|---|---|---|---|---|---|---|---|---|---|---|---|
| 1R1L | Mar 23 | BRADFORD CITY | W | 3-0 | 0-0 | 4547 | Astbury, Leahy, og | G.Scales | P.Stubbs | D.McNeil | F.Marsh | T.Walters | E.Lee | F.Bett | T.Leahy | T.Burden | T.Astbury | R.Hamilton |
| 1R2L | 30 | Bradford City | D | 2-2 | 1-1 | 10979 | Burden(2) | " | " | " | " | " | " | " | " | " | " | " |
| 2R1L | Apr 6 | YORK CITY | W | 4-0 | 3-0 | 6000 | Leahy(2), Bett(pen), Burden | " | J.James | " | " | " | " | " | " | " | " | " |
| 2R2L | 13 | York City | L | 0-1 | 0-1 | 5225 | | " | " | " | " | " | " | " | " | " | " | " |
| SF | 19 | SOUTHPORT | W | 3-0 | 2-0 | 9666 | Burden(2), Hamilton | " | P.Stubbs | " | " | " | " | " | " | " | " | " |
| SF | 22 | Southport | W | 4-2 | 0-2 | 7110 | Leahy, Burden(3) | " | J.James | " | " | " | " | D.Isherwood | " | " | " | " |
| F | 27 | Rotherham United | D | 2-2 | 1-1 | 10500 | Bett, Hamilton | " | " | " | " | " | " | F.Bett | " | " | " | " |
| F | May 4 | ROTHERHAM U. | L | 2-3 | 0-1 | 12680 | Leahy, Bett | " | " | " | " | " | " | " | " | " | " | " |

## FRIENDLIES

| | Date | Opposition | | FT | HT | Att. | Goalscorers |
|---|---|---|---|---|---|---|---|
| 1 | Nov 17 | Coventry City | W | 5-1 | 3-0 | 3044 | Hamilton(3),Bainbridge,Astbury |
| 2 | 24 | COVENTRY CITY | W | 3-2 | 2-1 | | Black, Yates, Hamilton |
| 3 | Dec 15 | Bradford City | D | 2-2 | 1-2 | 2647 | Astbury, Woof |

**Seventh War Season (1945/46) notes:**

Competitions ran more to normal peacetime format. In the Third Division North (West Region), Chester finished 4th out of 10. In the Third Division North Cup qualifying competition they finished 7th of 10 and qualified for the competition proper.

# SEASON 1946-47

## FOOTBALL LEAGUE DIVISION 3 (NORTH)

| | Date | Opposition | | FT | HT | Att. | Goalscorers | Rigby W. | Summerbee G. | McNeil D. | Marsh F. | Lee E. | Williams D. | Arthur J. | Burden T. | Yates R. | Astbury T. | Hamilton R. | Scales G. | Higgins C. | Butcher R. | Walters T. | Mills J. | Griffiths I. | Selby D. | Cole D. | Isherwood D. | Ellis K. | Leonard S. | Lacey D. | Turner P. | MacLaren J. | Brown J. | Dutton R. | Skinner D. | Davies M. |
|---|---|---|---|---|---|---|---|---|---|---|---|---|---|---|---|---|---|---|---|---|---|---|---|---|---|---|---|---|---|---|---|---|---|---|---|---|
| 1 | Aug 31 | York City | D | 4-4 | 1-3 | 7016 | Burden (2), Gledhill (og), Hamilton | 1 | 2 | 3 | 4 | 5 | 6 | 7 | 8 | 9 | 10 | 11 | | | | | | | | | | | | | | | | | | |
| 2 | Sep 4 | DONCASTER ROVERS | L | 1-3 | 0-1 | 4637 | Burden | | 2 | | 4 | 5 | 6 | 7 | 8 | 9 | 10 | 11 | 1 | 3 | | | | | | | | | | | | | | | | |
| 3 | 7 | TRANMERE ROVERS | W | 4-1 | 1-1 | 8100 | Lee, Arthur, Yates (2) | | 2 | | | 6 | | 7 | 8 | 9 | 10 | 11 | 1 | 3 | 4 | 5 | | | | | | | | | | | | | | |
| 4 | 10 | Southport | W | 4-2 | 1-1 | 4889 | Burden, Astbury, Yates (2) | | 2 | 3 | | 6 | | 7 | 8 | 9 | 10 | 11 | 1 | | 4 | 5 | | | | | | | | | | | | | | |
| 5 | 14 | Darlington | D | 3-3 | 1-2 | 8189 | Yates, Hamilton, Astbury | | 2 | 3 | 4 | 6 | | 7 | 8 | 9 | 10 | 11 | 1 | | | 5 | | | | | | | | | | | | | | |
| 6 | 18 | WREXHAM | W | 2-0 | 0-0 | 11866 | Burden, Yates | | 2 | 3 | 4 | 6 | | 7 | 8 | 9 | 10 | 11 | 1 | | | 5 | | | | | | | | | | | | | | |
| 7 | 21 | HULL CITY | W | 5-1 | 4-0 | 7766 | Arthur, Hamilton, Burden (3) | | 2 | 3 | 4 | 6 | | 7 | 8 | 9 | 10 | 11 | 1 | | | 5 | | | | | | | | | | | | | | |
| 8 | 25 | SOUTHPORT | W | 2-1 | 0-1 | 5800 | Astbury, Yates | | | 3 | 4 | 6 | | 7 | 8 | 9 | 10 | 11 | 1 | | | 5 | 2 | | | | | | | | | | | | | |
| 9 | 28 | Gateshead | W | 4-3 | 1-1 | 4842 | Burden (2), Astbury, Yates | | | 3 | 4 | 6 | | 7 | 8 | 9 | 10 | 11 | 1 | | | 5 | 2 | | | | | | | | | | | | | |
| 10 | Oct 5 | HARTLEPOOLS UNITED | W | 2-1 | 1-0 | 8323 | Astbury, Yates | | 2 | 3 | 4 | 6 | | 7 | 8 | 9 | 10 | 11 | 1 | | | 5 | | | | | | | | | | | | | | |
| 11 | 12 | Crewe Alex. | W | 2-0 | 0-0 | 10923 | Yates, Burden | | | 3 | 4 | 6 | | 7 | 8 | 9 | 10 | 11 | 1 | | | 5 | 2 | | | | | | | | | | | | | |
| 12 | 26 | Stockport County | W | 3-0 | 2-0 | 11738 | Yates, Hamilton, Astbury | | | 3 | 4 | 6 | | 7 | 8 | 9 | 10 | 11 | 1 | | 2 | 5 | | | | | | | | | | | | | | |
| 13 | Nov 2 | OLDHAM ATHLETIC | W | 2-0 | 2-0 | 10256 | Yates, Burden | | | 3 | 4 | 6 | | 7 | 8 | 9 | 10 | 11 | 1 | | 2 | 5 | | | | | | | | | | | | | | |
| 14 | 9 | Bradford City | D | 0-0 | 0-0 | 16775 | | | | 3 | 4 | 6 | | 7 | 8 | 9 | 10 | 11 | 1 | | 2 | 5 | | | | | | | | | | | | | | |
| 15 | 16 | BARROW | W | 3-0 | 2-0 | 7877 | Yates (2), Burden | | | 3 | 4 | 6 | | 7 | 8 | 9 | 10 | 11 | 1 | | 2 | 5 | | | | | | | | | | | | | | |
| 16 | 23 | Accrington Stanley | W | 4-1 | 3-1 | 3583 | Arthur, Hamilton, Yates, Astbury | | | 3 | 4 | 6 | | 7 | 8 | 9 | 10 | 11 | 1 | | 2 | 5 | | | | | | | | | | | | | | |
| 17 | Dec 7 | Halifax Town | W | 2-1 | 0-0 | 3830 | Burden, Yates | | | 3 | 4 | 6 | | 7 | 8 | 9 | 10 | 11 | 1 | | 2 | 5 | | | | | | | | | | | | | | |
| 18 | 14 | NEW BRIGHTON | W | 2-1 | 2-1 | 5942 | Yates (2) | | | 3 | 4 | 6 | | 7 | 8 | 9 | 10 | 11 | 1 | | 2 | 5 | | | | | | | | | | | | | | |
| 19 | 21 | Rochdale | L | 1-2 | 1-1 | 7738 | Yates | | | 3 | 4 | 6 | | 7 | 8 | 9 | 10 | | 1 | | 2 | 5 | | 11 | | | | | | | | | | | | |
| 20 | 25 | ROTHERHAM UNITED | D | 2-2 | 1-1 | 9096 | Lee, Hamilton | | | 3 | 4 | 6 | | 7 | 8 | 9 | 10 | 11 | 1 | | 2 | 5 | | | | | | | | | | | | | | |
| 21 | 26 | Rotherham United | L | 1-3 | 0-2 | 18000 | Burden | | | 3 | 4 | 6 | | | 8 | 9 | 10 | 7 | 1 | | 2 | 5 | | | 11 | | | | | | | | | | | |
| 22 | 28 | YORK CITY | W | 6-0 | 2-0 | 7358 | Yates (3), Astbury (2), Selby | | | 3 | 4 | 6 | | | 8 | 9 | 10 | 7 | 1 | | 2 | 5 | | | 11 | | | | | | | | | | | |
| 23 | Jan 4 | Tranmere Rovers | L | 2-3 | 1-1 | 11787 | Yates, Burden | | 2 | 3 | 4 | | | | 8 | 9 | 10 | 7 | 1 | | | 5 | | | 11 | 6 | | | | | | | | | | |
| 24 | 18 | DARLINGTON | D | 1-1 | 0-0 | 8266 | Astbury | | | 3 | 4 | 6 | | | 8 | 9 | 10 | 7 | 1 | | 2 | 5 | | | 11 | | | | | | | | | | | |
| 25 | Feb 1 | GATESHEAD | L | 0-1 | 0-0 | 5454 | | | | 3 | 4 | 6 | | 7 | 8 | 9 | 10 | 11 | 1 | | 2 | 5 | | | | | | | | | | | | | | |
| 26 | 8 | Hartlepools United | L | 1-5 | 0-3 | 4462 | Yates | | | 3 | 4 | 6 | | | 8 | 9 | 10 | | 1 | | 2 | 5 | | | 11 | | 7 | | | | | | | | | |
| 27 | 15 | CREWE ALEX. | W | 2-0 | 1-0 | 3953 | Astbury, Yates | | | 3 | 4 | 10 | | | 7 | 9 | 8 | | 1 | | 2 | 5 | | | | 6 | 11 | | | | | | | | | |
| 28 | Mar 6 | Hull City | L | 0-1 | 0-1 | 10367 | | | | 3 | 4 | 10 | | 7 | 6 | 9 | 8 | | 1 | | | 5 | | | | 2 | 11 | | | | | | | | | |
| 29 | 22 | Barrow | L | 0-1 | 0-0 | 5509 | | | | 3 | 4 | 6 | | 7 | 8 | 9 | 10 | 11 | 1 | | | 5 | | | | 2 | | | | | | | | | | |
| 30 | 29 | ACCRINGTON STANLEY | W | 3-1 | 1-1 | 3287 | Burden (2), Hamilton | | | 3 | 4 | | | 7 | 9 | | 10 | 11 | 1 | | 6 | 5 | | | | 2 | | 8 | | | | | | | | |
| 31 | Apr 4 | LINCOLN CITY | W | 3-0 | 0-0 | 6921 | Lee, Burden (2) | | | | 4 | 10 | | | 9 | | 8 | 11 | 1 | 3 | 6 | 5 | | | | 2 | | | 7 | | | | | | | |
| 32 | 5 | Carlisle United | L | 2-3 | 0-2 | 6810 | Lee, Burden | | | | 4 | 10 | | | 9 | 7 | 8 | 11 | 1 | 3 | 6 | 5 | | | | 2 | | | | | | | | | | |
| 33 | 7 | Lincoln City | D | 2-2 | 1-1 | 8785 | Yates, Burden | | | | 4 | 6 | | | 8 | 9 | 10 | 11 | 1 | | 3 | 5 | | | | 2 | | | | 7 | | | | | | |
| 34 | 12 | HALIFAX TOWN | W | 2-0 | 0-0 | 4627 | Burden (2) | | | 3 | | 6 | | | 8 | 9 | 10 | 11 | 1 | | 2 | 5 | | | | 4 | | | | | 7 | | | | | |
| 35 | 19 | New Brighton | W | 3-0 | 2-0 | 7006 | Hamilton, Yates (2) | | | | 4 | 6 | | | 8 | 9 | 10 | 11 | 1 | 3 | 2 | 5 | | | | | | | | | 7 | | | | | |
| 36 | 26 | ROCHDALE | W | 1-0 | 1-0 | 4278 | Yates | | | | 4 | 6 | | | 8 | 9 | 10 | 11 | 1 | 3 | 2 | 5 | | | | | | | | | 7 | | | | | |
| 37 | May 3 | Doncaster Rovers | L | 0-3 | 0-1 | 17015 | | | | | 4 | 6 | | | 8 | 9 | 10 | 11 | 1 | 3 | 2 | 5 | | | | | | | | | 7 | | | | | |
| 38 | 10 | BRADFORD CITY | W | 3-0 | 1-0 | 3376 | Burden, Yates (pen), Astbury | | | | 4 | | | | 8 | 9 | 10 | 11 | | 3 | 2 | 5 | | | | 6 | | | | | 7 | 1 | | | | |
| 39 | 17 | Oldham Athletic | L | 0-1 | 0-0 | 7378 | | | | | 4 | | | | 8 | 9 | 10 | 11 | 1 | 3 | 2 | 5 | | | | 6 | | | | | 7 | | | | | |
| 40 | 24 | STOCKPORT COUNTY | W | 3-0 | 2-0 | 4563 | Brown, Burden, Yates | | | | 4 | 6 | | | 8 | 9 | 10 | | 1 | 3 | 2 | 5 | | | | | | | | | 7 | | 11 | | | |
| 41 | 26 | Wrexham | W | 4-0 | 1-0 | 18746 | Yates (3), Burden | | | | | 6 | | | 8 | 9 | 10 | 11 | 1 | 3 | 2 | 5 | | | | 4 | | | | | 7 | | | | | |
| 42 | 31 | CARLISLE UNITED | W | 4-0 | 0-0 | 4037 | Yates (2,1 pen), Lee, Burden | | | 3 | 4 | 10 | | | 8 | 9 | | 7 | 1 | | 2 | 5 | | | | 6 | | | | | | | 11 | | | |
| | | | | | | | Apps. | 1 | 9 | 30 | 38 | 38 | 2 | 24 | 42 | 40 | 41 | 37 | 40 | 11 | 30 | 40 | 3 | 1 | 5 | 13 | 3 | 1 | 1 | 1 | 8 | 1 | 2 | | | |
| | | | | | | | Goals | | | | | 5 | | 3 | 28 | 36 | 12 | 8 | | | | | | | 1 | | | | | | | | 1 | | | |

Own Goals 1

## F.A. CUP

| | Date | Opposition | | FT | HT | Att. | Goalscorers | Rigby W. | Summerbee G. | McNeil D. | Marsh F. | Lee E. | Williams D. | Arthur J. | Burden T. | Yates R. | Astbury T. | Hamilton R. | Scales G. | Higgins C. | Butcher R. | Walters T. | Mills J. | Griffiths I. | Selby D. | Cole D. | Isherwood D. | Ellis K. | Leonard S. | Lacey D. | Turner P. | MacLaren J. | Brown J. | Dutton R. | Skinner D. | Davies M. |
|---|---|---|---|---|---|---|---|---|---|---|---|---|---|---|---|---|---|---|---|---|---|---|---|---|---|---|---|---|---|---|---|---|---|---|---|---|
| 3R | Jan 11 | PLYMOUTH ARGYLE | W | 2-0 | 1-0 | 18000 | Astbury, Burden | | | 3 | 4 | 6 | | | 8 | 9 | 10 | 7 | 1 | | 2 | 5 | | | 11 | | | | | | | | | | | |
| 4R | 25 | STOKE CITY | D | 0-0 | 0-0 | 18706 | | | | 3 | 4 | 6 | | 7 | 8 | 9 | 10 | 11 | 1 | | 2 | 5 | | | | | | | | | | | | | | |
| 4Rr | 29 | Stoke City | L | 2-3 | 0-1 | 22683 | Hamilton, Yates | | | 3 | 4 | 6 | | 7 | 8 | 9 | 10 | 11 | 1 | | 2 | 5 | | | | | | | | | | | | | | |

## WELSH CUP

| | Date | Opposition | | FT | HT | Att. | Goalscorers | Rigby W. | Summerbee G. | McNeil D. | Marsh F. | Lee E. | Williams D. | Arthur J. | Burden T. | Yates R. | Astbury T. | Hamilton R. | Scales G. | Higgins C. | Butcher R. | Walters T. | Mills J. | Griffiths I. | Selby D. | Cole D. | Isherwood D. | Ellis K. | Leonard S. | Lacey D. | Turner P. | MacLaren J. | Brown J. | Dutton R. | Skinner D. | Davies M. |
|---|---|---|---|---|---|---|---|---|---|---|---|---|---|---|---|---|---|---|---|---|---|---|---|---|---|---|---|---|---|---|---|---|---|---|---|---|
| 5R | Jan 15 | Bangor City | W | 5-3 | 2-0 | | Yates (3), Isherwood, Davies | | 2 | | | | 10 | | | 9 | | | | 3 | | | 5 | | | | 8 | | | 7 | | 1 | | 4 | 6 | 11 |
| 6R | Feb 13 | Swansea Town | W | 3-1 | 0-1 | 10000 | Yates, Astbury (2) | | | 3 | 8 | 6 | | 7 | | 9 | 10 | | 1 | | 2 | 5 | | | | 4 | 11 | | | | | | | | | |
| SF | May 14 | Newport County * | W | 3-2 | 2-0 | 7000 | Burden, Yates, Astbury | | | | 4 | | | | 8 | 9 | 10 | 11 | | 3 | 2 | 5 | | | | 6 | | | | | 7 | 1 | | | | |
| F | Jun 5 | Merthyr Tydfil @ | D | 0-0 | 0-0 | 27000 | | | | 3 | 4 | 6 | | | 8 | 9 | 10 | 11 | 1 | | 2 | 5 | | | | | | | | | 7 | | | | | |
| Fr | 12 | Merthyr Tydfil * | W | 5-1 | 2-1 | 11190 | Burden(2), Astbury, Yates, Turner | | | 3 | 4 | 6 | | | 8 | 9 | 10 | 11 | 1 | | 2 | 5 | | | | | | | | | 7 | | | | | |

* Played at Wrexham

@ Played at Cardiff

## FRIENDLIES

| | Date | Opposition | | FT | HT | Att. | Goalscorers |
|---|---|---|---|---|---|---|---|
| 1 | Nov 30 | Cardiff City | D | 2-2 | 2-2 | 14000 | Yates, Marsh |
| 2 | Jun 14 | NFS STARS * | L | 1-2 | 0-1 | | Yates |

* In aid of NFS Benevolent Fund

Final League Table

| | | Pl. | Home W | D | L | F | A | Away W | D | L | F | A | F. | A. | Pts |
|---|---|---|---|---|---|---|---|---|---|---|---|---|---|---|---|
| 1 | Doncaster Rovers | 42 | 15 | 5 | 1 | 67 | 16 | 18 | 1 | 2 | 56 | 24 | 123 | 40 | 72 |
| 2 | Rotherham United | 42 | 20 | 1 | 0 | 81 | 19 | 9 | 5 | 7 | 33 | 34 | 114 | 53 | 64 |
| ***3*** | ***Chester*** | ***42*** | ***17*** | ***2*** | ***2*** | ***53*** | ***13*** | ***8*** | ***4*** | ***9*** | ***42*** | ***38*** | ***95*** | ***51*** | ***56*** |
| 4 | Stockport County | 42 | 17 | 0 | 4 | 50 | 19 | 7 | 2 | 12 | 28 | 34 | 78 | 53 | 50 |
| 5 | Bradford City | 42 | 12 | 5 | 4 | 40 | 20 | 8 | 5 | 8 | 22 | 27 | 62 | 47 | 50 |
| 6 | Rochdale | 42 | 9 | 5 | 7 | 39 | 25 | 10 | 5 | 6 | 41 | 39 | 80 | 64 | 48 |
| 7 | Wrexham | 42 | 13 | 5 | 3 | 43 | 21 | 4 | 7 | 10 | 22 | 30 | 65 | 51 | 46 |
| 8 | Crewe Alexandra | 42 | 12 | 4 | 5 | 39 | 26 | 5 | 5 | 11 | 31 | 48 | 70 | 74 | 43 |
| 9 | Barrow | 42 | 10 | 2 | 9 | 28 | 24 | 7 | 5 | 9 | 26 | 38 | 54 | 62 | 41 |
| 10 | Tranmere Rovers | 42 | 11 | 5 | 5 | 43 | 33 | 6 | 2 | 13 | 23 | 44 | 66 | 77 | 41 |
| 11 | Hull City | 42 | 9 | 5 | 7 | 25 | 19 | 7 | 3 | 11 | 24 | 34 | 49 | 53 | 40 |
| 12 | Lincoln City | 42 | 12 | 3 | 6 | 52 | 32 | 5 | 2 | 14 | 34 | 55 | 86 | 87 | 39 |
| 13 | Hartlepools United | 42 | 10 | 5 | 6 | 36 | 26 | 5 | 4 | 12 | 28 | 47 | 64 | 73 | 39 |
| 14 | Gateshead | 42 | 10 | 3 | 8 | 39 | 33 | 6 | 3 | 12 | 23 | 39 | 62 | 72 | 38 |
| 15 | York City | 42 | 6 | 4 | 11 | 35 | 42 | 8 | 5 | 8 | 32 | 39 | 67 | 81 | 37 |
| 16 | Carlisle United | 42 | 10 | 5 | 6 | 45 | 38 | 4 | 4 | 13 | 25 | 55 | 70 | 93 | 37 |
| 17 | Darlington | 42 | 12 | 4 | 5 | 48 | 26 | 3 | 2 | 16 | 20 | 54 | 68 | 80 | 36 |
| 18 | New Brighton | 42 | 11 | 3 | 7 | 37 | 30 | 3 | 5 | 13 | 20 | 47 | 57 | 77 | 36 |
| 19 | Oldham Athletic | 42 | 6 | 5 | 10 | 29 | 31 | 6 | 3 | 12 | 26 | 49 | 55 | 80 | 32 |
| 20 | Accrington Stanley | 42 | 8 | 3 | 10 | 37 | 38 | 6 | 1 | 14 | 19 | 54 | 56 | 92 | 32 |
| 21 | Southport | 42 | 6 | 5 | 10 | 35 | 41 | 1 | 6 | 14 | 18 | 44 | 53 | 85 | 25 |
| 22 | Halifax Town | 42 | 6 | 3 | 12 | 28 | 36 | 2 | 3 | 16 | 15 | 56 | 43 | 92 | 22 |

**1946/47 Season**
(Back) Summerbee, Arthur, Rigby, Yates, Walters.
(Front) Marsh, Isherwood, Mills, Lee, Williams, Lacey

**1947/48 Season**
McLaren, Butcher, Hamilton, Tilston, Best, Walters, Astbury, Mills, Yates, Unknown, Willcox.

# *SEASON 1947-48*

## FOOTBALL LEAGUE DIVISION 3 (NORTH)

| | Date | Opposition | | FT | HT | Att. | Goalscorers | Scales G. | Butcher R. | McNeil D. | Marsh F. | Walters T. | Lee E. | Turner P. | Burden T. | Yates R. | Best T. | Hamilton R. | Astbury T. | Brown J. | Colville H. | Cole D. | Kirkpatrick R. | MacLaren J. | Coffin G. | Willcox F. | Williamson G. | Westwood R. | Davies J. |
|---|---|---|---|---|---|---|---|---|---|---|---|---|---|---|---|---|---|---|---|---|---|---|---|---|---|---|---|---|---|
| 1 | Aug 23 | OLDHAM ATHLETIC | W | 2-1 | 1-0 | 8505 | Yates, Best | 1 | 2 | 3 | 4 | 5 | 6 | 7 | 8 | 9 | 10 | 11 | | | | | | | | | | | |
| 2 | 28 | Barrow | L | 0-1 | 0-1 | 10293 | | 1 | 2 | 3 | 4 | 5 | 6 | | 8 | 9 | | 7 | 10 | 11 | | | | | | | | | |
| 3 | 30 | Tranmere Rovers | W | 3-2 | 1-2 | 11950 | Colville, Burden, Astbury | 1 | 2 | 3 | 4 | 5 | 6 | | 8 | 9 | 7 | | 10 | | 11 | | | | | | | | |
| 4 | Sep 3 | BARROW | D | 0-0 | 0-0 | 7751 | | 1 | 2 | 3 | 4 | 5 | | | 8 | 9 | 7 | | 10 | | 11 | 6 | | | | | | | |
| 5 | 6 | DARLINGTON | D | 1-1 | 0-0 | 7948 | Astbury | 1 | 2 | 3 | 4 | 5 | | | 8 | 9 | 7 | | 10 | | 11 | | 6 | | | | | | |
| 6 | 10 | CREWE ALEX. | W | 4-2 | 1-1 | 8300 | Best, Marsh (pen), Turner, Burden | | 2 | 3 | 4 | 5 | 6 | 7 | 9 | | 8 | | 10 | 11 | | | | 1 | | | | | |
| 7 | 13 | Gateshead | L | 1-2 | 0-1 | 5987 | Burden | | 2 | 3 | 4 | 5 | | 7 | 9 | | 8 | | 10 | 11 | | | 6 | 1 | | | | | |
| 8 | 17 | Crewe Alex. | L | 0-1 | 0-1 | 9124 | | | 2 | 3 | 4 | 5 | | | 8 | 9 | 7 | 11 | 10 | | | 6 | | 1 | | | | | |
| 9 | 20 | HARTLEPOOLS UNITED | W | 2-0 | 1-0 | 7146 | Turner, Hamilton | | 2 | 3 | 4 | 5 | | 7 | 8 | 9 | | 11 | 10 | | | 6 | | 1 | | | | | |
| 10 | 27 | Rotherham United | L | 1-2 | 0-2 | 14262 | Turner | | 2 | 3 | 4 | 5 | | 7 | | 9 | | 11 | 10 | 8 | | 6 | | 1 | | | | | |
| 11 | Oct 4 | CARLISLE UNITED | W | 4-1 | 0-1 | 7910 | Coffin, Astbury (2), Burden | | 2 | 3 | 4 | 5 | | 7 | 8 | | | 11 | 10 | | | 6 | | 1 | 9 | | | | |
| 12 | 11 | Wrexham | L | 1-2 | 0-1 | 21131 | Marsh (pen) | | 2 | 3 | 4 | 5 | | 7 | 8 | | | 11 | 10 | | | 6 | | 1 | 9 | | | | |
| 13 | 18 | HALIFAX TOWN | D | 0-0 | 0-0 | 6402 | | | 2 | 3 | 4 | 5 | | 7 | 8 | 9 | | 11 | 10 | | | 6 | | 1 | | | | | |
| 14 | 25 | Rochdale | D | 2-2 | 1-1 | 9582 | Turner, Best | | 6 | 3 | 4 | 5 | | 7 | 9 | | 8 | | 10 | 11 | | | | 1 | | 2 | | | |
| 15 | Nov 1 | NEW BRIGHTON | W | 4-2 | 4-1 | 7733 | Astbury (2), Burden (2) | 1 | 6 | 3 | 4 | 5 | | 7 | 9 | | 8 | | 10 | 11 | | | | | | 2 | | | |
| 16 | 8 | Southport | L | 0-3 | 0-2 | 8702 | | 1 | 6 | 3 | 4 | 5 | | 7 | 9 | | 10 | | 8 | 11 | | | | | | 2 | | | |
| 17 | 15 | LINCOLN CITY | D | 1-1 | 0-0 | 7849 | Best | | 6 | 3 | | | | 7 | 4 | 9 | 10 | 11 | 8 | | | | | 1 | | 2 | 5 | | |
| 18 | 22 | Accrington Stanley | L | 0-1 | 0-0 | 3660 | | | 6 | 3 | | | 8 | | 4 | 9 | 10 | 7 | | 11 | | | | 1 | | 2 | 5 | | |
| 19 | Dec 6 | Stockport County | L | 1-4 | 0-3 | 9630 | Monks (og) | | 6 | 3 | 4 | | | | 8 | 9 | 10 | 7 | | 11 | | | | 1 | | 2 | 5 | | |
| 20 | 20 | Oldham Athletic | L | 1-3 | 0-0 | 11807 | Williamson (pen) | | 2 | 3 | | 5 | 6 | | 8 | | | 7 | 10 | | 11 | | | 1 | 9 | | 4 | | |
| 21 | 26 | York City | L | 0-2 | 0-2 | 10435 | | | 6 | 3 | | 5 | 10 | | 9 | | | 7 | 8 | | | | 11 | 1 | | 2 | 4 | | |
| 22 | 27 | YORK CITY | L | 2-3 | 2-3 | 8754 | Westwood, Astbury | | 6 | 3 | | 5 | | | 9 | | 7 | 11 | 8 | | | | | 1 | | 2 | 4 | 10 | |
| 23 | Jan 3 | TRANMERE ROVERS | W | 4-0 | 3-0 | 8721 | Astbury, Brown, Burden (2) | 1 | 6 | 3 | | | 5 | | 9 | | 10 | 7 | 8 | 11 | | | | | | 2 | 4 | | |
| 24 | 17 | Darlington | D | 1-1 | 1-1 | 6816 | Westwood | 1 | 6 | 3 | 4 | | | | 9 | | | 7 | 8 | 11 | | | | | | 2 | 5 | 10 | |
| 25 | 31 | GATESHEAD | L | 2-3 | 0-3 | 6721 | Turner, Burden | 1 | 6 | 3 | 4 | | | 7 | 9 | | | 11 | 8 | | | | | | | 2 | 5 | 10 | |
| 26 | Feb 7 | Hartlepools United | L | 1-2 | 0-1 | 6353 | Astbury | 1 | 6 | 3 | 4 | | | 7 | 9 | | | 11 | 8 | | | | | | | 2 | 5 | 10 | |
| 27 | 14 | ROTHERHAM UNITED | L | 2-3 | 2-1 | 9994 | Astbury, Butcher | 1 | 6 | 3 | | | | 7 | 4 | | 9 | 11 | 8 | | | | | | | 2 | 5 | 10 | |
| 28 | 21 | Carlisle United | L | 0-2 | 0-1 | 11720 | | | 2 | 3 | 6 | | | | 4 | | 9 | 7 | 8 | | | | 11 | 1 | | | 5 | 10 | |
| 29 | 28 | WREXHAM | W | 4-1 | 1-0 | 16160 | Best, Westwood, Williamson (2) | 1 | 2 | 3 | 6 | 5 | | | 8 | | 9 | 7 | | | | | 11 | | | | 4 | 10 | |
| 30 | Mar 6 | Halifax Town | D | 1-1 | 1-0 | 7256 | Kirkpatrick | 1 | 2 | 3 | 6 | 5 | | | 8 | | 9 | 7 | | | | | 11 | | | | 4 | 10 | |
| 31 | 13 | ROCHDALE | W | 2-1 | 1-0 | 6427 | Westwood, Kirkpatrick | 1 | 2 | 3 | 6 | 5 | | | 8 | | 9 | 7 | | | | | 11 | | | | 4 | 10 | |
| 32 | 17 | HULL CITY | W | 4-1 | 1-0 | 6087 | Best, Burden (2), Kirkpatrick | 1 | 2 | 3 | | 5 | 6 | | 8 | | 9 | 7 | 10 | | | | 11 | | | | 4 | | |
| 33 | 20 | New Brighton | W | 1-0 | 1-0 | 4806 | Best | 1 | 2 | 3 | 6 | 5 | | | 8 | | 9 | 7 | 10 | | | | 11 | | | | 4 | | |
| 34 | 26 | MANSFIELD TOWN | L | 1-2 | 1-1 | 11209 | Best | 1 | 2 | 3 | | 5 | 6 | | 8 | | 9 | 7 | | | | | 11 | | | | 4 | 10 | |
| 35 | 27 | SOUTHPORT | D | 0-0 | 0-0 | 7366 | | 1 | 2 | 3 | 6 | 5 | 10 | | 8 | | 9 | | 7 | 11 | | | | | | | 4 | | |
| 36 | 29 | Mansfield Town | L | 1-2 | 0-0 | 12770 | Burden | 1 | 2 | 3 | 4 | 5 | 6 | | 9 | | | 7 | 10 | 11 | | | | | | | | 8 | |
| 37 | Apr 3 | Lincoln City | L | 2-4 | 1-2 | 13066 | Hamilton, Westwood | | 2 | 3 | 4 | 5 | 6 | | 7 | | 9 | 11 | 10 | | | | | 1 | | | | 8 | |
| 38 | 10 | ACCRINGTON STANLEY | W | 1-0 | 0-0 | 5811 | Best | | 2 | 3 | | 5 | 6 | 7 | 8 | | 9 | 11 | | | | | | 1 | | | 4 | 10 | |
| 39 | 17 | Hull City | L | 1-2 | 1-1 | 24138 | Turner | | 2 | | 6 | 5 | | 7 | 8 | | 9 | 11 | | | | | | 1 | | 3 | 4 | 10 | |
| 40 | 21 | BRADFORD CITY | W | 2-1 | 1-1 | 4604 | Westwood (2) | | 2 | | 6 | 5 | | 7 | | | 9 | | 8 | | | | | 1 | | 3 | 4 | 10 | 11 |
| 41 | 24 | STOCKPORT COUNTY | D | 2-2 | 1-0 | 3881 | Davies, Westwood | | 2 | | | 5 | 6 | 7 | 4 | | 9 | | 8 | | | | | 1 | | 3 | | 10 | 11 |
| 42 | May 1 | Bradford City | L | 2-3 | 2-2 | 3774 | Best, Astbury | | 2 | 3 | 6 | 5 | | | 8 | | 9 | 7 | 10 | | | | | 1 | | | 4 | | 11 |
| | | | | | | | Apps. | 20 | 42 | 39 | 31 | 33 | 15 | 19 | 40 | 12 | 30 | 31 | 33 | 13 | 4 | 7 | 10 | 22 | 3 | 16 | 23 | 16 | 3 |
| | | | | | | | Goals | | 1 | | 2 | | | 6 | 12 | 1 | 10 | 2 | 11 | 1 | 1 | | 3 | | 1 | | 3 | 8 | 1 |

Own Goals 1

## F.A. CUP

| | Date | Opposition | | FT | HT | Att. | Goalscorers | Scales G. | Butcher R. | McNeil D. | Marsh F. | Walters T. | Lee E. | Turner P. | Burden T. | Yates R. | Best T. | Hamilton R. | Astbury T. | Brown J. | Colville H. | Cole D. | Kirkpatrick R. | MacLaren J. | Coffin G. | Willcox F. | Williamson G. | Westwood R. | Davies J. |
|---|---|---|---|---|---|---|---|---|---|---|---|---|---|---|---|---|---|---|---|---|---|---|---|---|---|---|---|---|---|
| 1R | Nov 29 | BISHOP AUCKLAND | W | 3-1 | 2-1 | 8300 | Yates (2), Burden | | 4 | 3 | | | 6 | | 8 | 9 | 10 | 7 | | | 11 | | | 1 | | 2 | 5 | | |
| 2R | Dec 13 | Tranmere Rovers | W | 1-0 | 0-0 | 14132 | Burden | | 2 | 3 | | 5 | 6 | | 8 | | | 7 | 10 | | 11 | | | 1 | 9 | | 4 | | |
| 3R | Jan 10 | Crystal Palace | W | 1-0 | 1-0 | 22084 | Burden | 1 | 6 | 3 | | | 5 | | 9 | | | 7 | 8 | 11 | | | | | | 2 | 4 | 10 | |
| 4R | 24 | Blackpool | L | 0-4 | 0-2 | 26414 | | 1 | 6 | 3 | | | 5 | | 9 | | | 7 | 8 | 11 | | | | | | 2 | 4 | 10 | |

## WELSH CUP

| | Date | Opposition | | FT | HT | Att. | Goalscorers | Scales G. | Butcher R. | McNeil D. | Marsh F. | Walters T. | Lee E. | Turner P. | Burden T. | Yates R. | Best T. | Hamilton R. | Astbury T. | Brown J. | Colville H. | Cole D. | Kirkpatrick R. | MacLaren J. | Coffin G. | Willcox F. | Williamson G. | Westwood R. | Davies J. |
|---|---|---|---|---|---|---|---|---|---|---|---|---|---|---|---|---|---|---|---|---|---|---|---|---|---|---|---|---|---|
| 5R | Jan 14 | South Liverpool | L | 1-2 | 1-1 | | Brown | | | | 4 | 5 | | | | | 10 | 7 | 8 | 11 | | 2 | 6 | 1 | 9 | 3 | | | |

## FRIENDLIES

| | Date | Opposition | | FT | HT | Att. |
|---|---|---|---|---|---|---|
| 1 | Apr 14 | MANCHESTER CITY * | L | 0-1 | 0-1 | 8330 |

* Trevor Walters Benefit

Final League Table

| | | Pl. | Home W | D | L | F | A | Away W | D | L | F | A | F. | A. | Pts |
|---|---|---|---|---|---|---|---|---|---|---|---|---|---|---|---|
| 1 | Lincoln City | 42 | 14 | 3 | 4 | 47 | 18 | 12 | 5 | 4 | 34 | 22 | 81 | 40 | 60 |
| 2 | Rotherham United | 42 | 15 | 4 | 2 | 56 | 18 | 10 | 5 | 6 | 39 | 31 | 95 | 49 | 59 |
| 3 | Wrexham | 42 | 14 | 3 | 4 | 49 | 23 | 7 | 5 | 9 | 25 | 31 | 74 | 54 | 50 |
| 4 | Gateshead | 42 | 11 | 5 | 5 | 48 | 28 | 8 | 6 | 7 | 27 | 29 | 75 | 57 | 49 |
| 5 | Hull City | 42 | 12 | 5 | 4 | 38 | 21 | 6 | 6 | 9 | 21 | 27 | 59 | 48 | 47 |
| 6 | Accrington Stanley | 42 | 13 | 1 | 7 | 36 | 24 | 7 | 5 | 9 | 26 | 35 | 62 | 59 | 46 |
| 7 | Barrow | 42 | 9 | 4 | 8 | 24 | 19 | 7 | 9 | 5 | 25 | 21 | 49 | 40 | 45 |
| 8 | Mansfield Town | 42 | 11 | 4 | 6 | 37 | 24 | 6 | 7 | 8 | 20 | 27 | 57 | 51 | 45 |
| 9 | Carlisle United | 42 | 10 | 4 | 7 | 50 | 35 | 8 | 3 | 10 | 38 | 42 | 88 | 77 | 43 |
| 10 | Crewe Alexandra | 42 | 12 | 4 | 5 | 41 | 24 | 6 | 3 | 12 | 20 | 39 | 61 | 63 | 43 |
| 11 | Oldham Athletic | 42 | 6 | 10 | 5 | 25 | 25 | 8 | 3 | 10 | 38 | 39 | 63 | 64 | 41 |
| 12 | Rochdale | 42 | 12 | 4 | 5 | 32 | 23 | 3 | 7 | 11 | 16 | 49 | 48 | 72 | 41 |
| 13 | York City | 42 | 8 | 7 | 6 | 38 | 25 | 5 | 7 | 9 | 27 | 35 | 65 | 60 | 40 |
| 14 | Bradford City | 42 | 10 | 4 | 7 | 38 | 27 | 5 | 6 | 10 | 27 | 39 | 65 | 66 | 40 |
| 15 | Southport | 42 | 10 | 4 | 7 | 34 | 27 | 4 | 7 | 10 | 26 | 36 | 60 | 63 | 39 |
| 16 | Darlington | 42 | 7 | 8 | 6 | 30 | 31 | 6 | 5 | 10 | 24 | 39 | 54 | 70 | 39 |
| 17 | Stockport County | 42 | 9 | 6 | 6 | 42 | 28 | 4 | 6 | 11 | 21 | 39 | 63 | 67 | 38 |
| 18 | Tranmere Rovers | 42 | 10 | 1 | 10 | 30 | 28 | 6 | 3 | 12 | 24 | 44 | 54 | 72 | 36 |
| 19 | Hartlepools United | 42 | 10 | 6 | 5 | 34 | 23 | 4 | 2 | 15 | 17 | 50 | 51 | 73 | 36 |
| ***20*** | ***Chester*** | ***42*** | ***11*** | ***6*** | ***4*** | ***44*** | ***25*** | ***2*** | ***3*** | ***16*** | ***20*** | ***42*** | ***64*** | ***67*** | ***35*** |
| 21 | Halifax Town | 42 | 4 | 10 | 7 | 25 | 27 | 3 | 3 | 15 | 18 | 49 | 43 | 76 | 27 |
| 22 | New Brighton | 42 | 5 | 6 | 10 | 20 | 28 | 3 | 3 | 15 | 18 | 53 | 38 | 81 | 25 |

# SEASON 1948-49

## FOOTBALL LEAGUE DIVISION 3 (NORTH)

| | Date | Opposition | | FT | HT | Att. | Goalscorers |
|---|---|---|---|---|---|---|---|
| 1 | Aug 21 | Carlisle United | L | 1-2 | 1-1 | 11941 | Seed (og) |
| 2 | 25 | STOCKPORT COUNTY | W | 2-0 | 1-0 | 7644 | Foulkes, Best |
| 3 | 28 | GATESHEAD | D | 1-1 | 1-0 | 8734 | Foulds |
| 4 | Sep 1 | Stockport County | D | 1-1 | 0-0 | 11707 | Best |
| 5 | 4 | Hartlepools United | L | 1-2 | 0-1 | 9181 | Best |
| 6 | 8 | YORK CITY | W | 4-1 | 3-0 | 6818 | Astbury (2), Davies, Foulds |
| 7 | 11 | DARLINGTON | L | 1-2 | 1-1 | 8880 | Foulds |
| 8 | 13 | York City | L | 0-2 | 0-1 | 9511 | |
| 9 | 18 | Rochdale | L | 1-3 | 1-1 | 11965 | Best |
| 10 | 25 | NEW BRIGHTON | W | 2-0 | 2-0 | 8546 | Coffin (2) |
| 11 | Oct 2 | Mansfield Town | L | 0-1 | 0-0 | 12459 | |
| 12 | 9 | TRANMERE ROVERS | D | 2-2 | 1-1 | 8295 | Astbury, Westwood |
| 13 | 16 | Oldham Athletic | L | 1-2 | 0-1 | 15440 | Foulds |
| 14 | 23 | ACCRINGTON STANLEY | W | 3-0 | 1-0 | 7558 | Burgess (2), Harrigan |
| 15 | 30 | Rotherham United | L | 1-2 | 0-0 | 15080 | Harrigan |
| 16 | Nov 6 | HULL CITY | L | 0-2 | 0-1 | 13509 | |
| 17 | 13 | Doncaster Rovers | D | 0-0 | 0-0 | 10658 | |
| 18 | 20 | BRADFORD CITY | W | 3-0 | 2-0 | 5954 | Burgess, Harrigan, Foulds |
| 19 | Dec 4 | WREXHAM | W | 2-0 | 0-0 | 11909 | Burgess (2) |
| 20 | 18 | CARLISLE UNITED | W | 2-1 | 1-1 | 4628 | Burgess (2,1 pen) |
| 21 | 25 | Crewe Alex. | L | 0-1 | 0-0 | 8587 | |
| 22 | 27 | CREWE ALEX. | D | 1-1 | 0-1 | 7380 | Lee |
| 23 | Jan 1 | Gateshead | L | 1-2 | 1-1 | 8720 | Burgess |
| 24 | 8 | Wrexham | L | 0-1 | 0-0 | 11947 | |
| 25 | 15 | HARTLEPOOLS UNITED | D | 0-0 | 0-0 | 3215 | |
| 26 | 22 | Darlington | D | 3-3 | 1-1 | 7505 | Davies, Foulds, Westwood |
| 27 | 29 | Halifax Town | W | 2-1 | 0-0 | 9160 | Westwood, Foulds |
| 28 | Feb 5 | ROCHDALE | W | 2-1 | 0-1 | 5570 | Foulds (2) |
| 29 | 12 | Barrow | D | 1-1 | 0-0 | 5887 | Burgess |
| 30 | 19 | New Brighton | D | 1-1 | 0-1 | 8672 | Foulds |
| 31 | 26 | MANSFIELD TOWN | D | 1-1 | 0-1 | 5250 | Foulds |
| 32 | Mar 12 | OLDHAM ATHLETIC | D | 2-2 | 1-2 | 6642 | Foulds, Westwood |
| 33 | 19 | Accrington Stanley | L | 1-3 | 0-2 | 4767 | McNeil (pen) |
| 34 | 26 | ROTHERHAM UNITED | D | 1-1 | 0-1 | 6431 | Burgess |
| 35 | Apr 2 | Hull City | L | 2-3 | 1-1 | 36167 | Davies, Burgess |
| 36 | 9 | DONCASTER ROVERS | L | 1-2 | 0-1 | 6220 | Foulds |
| 37 | 15 | SOUTHPORT | W | 2-0 | 0-0 | 7237 | Forsyth, Burgess |
| 38 | 16 | Bradford City | L | 2-3 | 1-1 | 12220 | Davies, Foulds |
| 39 | 18 | Southport | L | 1-2 | 1-1 | 8706 | Davies |
| 40 | 23 | HALIFAX TOWN | L | 0-1 | 0-0 | 3858 | |
| 41 | May 2 | Tranmere Rovers | D | 1-1 | 0-0 | 6420 | Williamson |
| 42 | 4 | BARROW | W | 4-1 | 1-1 | 1858 | Westwood, Burgess(2), Harrigan |

| | MacLaren J. | Butcher R. | McNeil D. | Williamson G. | Lee E. | Mansley C. | Foulkes W. | Astbury T | Best T. | Westwood R. | Forsyth J. | Foulds A. | Davies J. | Hounslea W. | Greenwood P. | Scales G. | Coffin G. | Beaumont A. | Walters T. | Harrigan D. | Burgess A. | Elliott E. | Mackie T. | Kirkpatrick R. | Bryan E. | Booth G. | Tilston T. |
|---|---|---|---|---|---|---|---|---|---|---|---|---|---|---|---|---|---|---|---|---|---|---|---|---|---|---|---|
| 1 | 1 | 2 | 3 | 4 | 5 | 6 | 7 | 8 | 9 | 10 | 11 | | | | | | | | | | | | | | | | |
| 2 | 1 | 2 | 3 | 4 | 5 | 6 | 7 | 8 | 9 | | 11 | 10 | | | | | | | | | | | | | | | |
| 3 | 1 | 2 | 3 | 4 | 5 | 6 | 7 | 8 | 9 | | 11 | 10 | | | | | | | | | | | | | | | |
| 4 | 1 | 2 | 3 | 4 | 5 | 6 | 7 | 8 | 9 | | 11 | 10 | | | | | | | | | | | | | | | |
| 5 | 1 | 2 | 3 | 4 | 5 | 6 | 7 | 8 | 9 | | 11 | 10 | | | | | | | | | | | | | | | |
| 6 | 1 | 2 | 3 | 4 | 5 | 6 | 7 | 8 | 9 | | | 10 | 11 | | | | | | | | | | | | | | |
| 7 | 1 | | 3 | 4 | 5 | 6 | 7 | 8 | | | | 10 | 11 | 2 | 9 | | | | | | | | | | | | |
| 8 | | 2 | 3 | 4 | 5 | 6 | 7 | | 9 | | | 10 | 11 | | | 1 | 8 | | | | | | | | | | |
| 9 | | 2 | 3 | 4 | 5 | 6 | 7 | 8 | 9 | 10 | | | 11 | | | 1 | | | | | | | | | | | |
| 10 | | 2 | 3 | | 5 | 6 | 7 | 8 | | 10 | 11 | | | | | 1 | 9 | 4 | | | | | | | | | |
| 11 | | 2 | 3 | | | 6 | 7 | 8 | 9 | 10 | 11 | | | | | 1 | | 4 | 5 | | | | | | | | |
| 12 | | 2 | 3 | | 5 | 6 | 7 | 4 | 9 | 10 | 11 | | | | | 1 | 8 | | | | | | | | | | |
| 13 | | 2 | 3 | | 5 | 6 | 7 | 4 | | | 11 | 8 | | | | 1 | | | | 9 | 10 | | | | | | |
| 14 | | 2 | 3 | | 5 | | 7 | 6 | | | 11 | 10 | | | | | | 4 | | 9 | 8 | 1 | | | | | |
| 15 | | 2 | 3 | 6 | 5 | | 7 | 4 | | 11 | | 10 | | | | | | | | 9 | 8 | 1 | | | | | |
| 16 | | 2 | 3 | 6 | 5 | | 7 | 4 | | 10 | | | 11 | | | 1 | | | | 9 | 8 | | | | | | |
| 17 | | 2 | | 6 | 5 | | 7 | 4 | | | 11 | 10 | | | | 1 | | | | 9 | 8 | | 3 | | | | |
| 18 | | 2 | | 6 | 5 | | 7 | 4 | | | 11 | 10 | | | | 1 | | | | 9 | 8 | | 3 | | | | |
| 19 | | 2 | | 6 | 5 | | 7 | 4 | | | 11 | 10 | | | | | | | | 9 | 8 | 1 | 3 | | | | |
| 20 | | 2 | | 6 | 5 | | 7 | 4 | | | 11 | 10 | | | | | | | | 9 | 8 | 1 | 3 | | | | |
| 21 | | 2 | | 6 | 5 | | 7 | 4 | | | 11 | 10 | | | | | | | | 9 | 8 | 1 | 3 | | | | |
| 22 | | 2 | | 3 | 5 | 6 | | 4 | | | 11 | 10 | | | 9 | | | | | 7 | 8 | 1 | | | | | |
| 23 | | 2 | 3 | 5 | | 6 | | 4 | | | 11 | 10 | 7 | | | | | | | 9 | 8 | 1 | | | | | |
| 24 | | 2 | | 3 | 5 | 6 | | 4 | | 10 | | | 7 | | | | | | | 9 | 8 | 1 | | 11 | | | |
| 25 | | 2 | 3 | 6 | 5 | | 7 | 4 | | | 11 | 10 | | | | 1 | | | | 9 | 8 | | | | | | |
| 26 | | | 3 | 5 | | | | 4 | | 10 | 11 | 9 | 7 | | | 1 | | | | | 8 | | | | 2 | 6 | |
| 27 | | 2 | 3 | 5 | | | | 4 | | 10 | 11 | 9 | 7 | | | 1 | | | | | 8 | | | | | 6 | |
| 28 | | 2 | 3 | 5 | | | | 4 | | 10 | 11 | 9 | 7 | | | 1 | | | | | 8 | | | | | 6 | |
| 29 | | 2 | 3 | 5 | | | | 4 | | | 11 | 10 | 7 | | | 1 | | | | 9 | 8 | | | | | 6 | |
| 30 | | 2 | 3 | 5 | | | | 4 | | | 11 | 10 | 7 | | | 1 | | | | 9 | 8 | | | | | 6 | |
| 31 | | 2 | 3 | 5 | 6 | | | 4 | | 10 | 11 | 9 | 7 | | | 1 | | | | | 8 | | | | | | |
| 32 | | 2 | 3 | 5 | | | 11 | 4 | | 10 | | 9 | 7 | | | 1 | | | | | 8 | | | | | 6 | |
| 33 | | 2 | 3 | 5 | | | 11 | 4 | | 10 | | 9 | 7 | | | | | | | | 8 | 1 | | | | 6 | |
| 34 | | 2 | 3 | 6 | 5 | | | 4 | | 10 | 11 | 9 | 7 | | | | | | | | 8 | 1 | | | | | |
| 35 | | 2 | 3 | | 5 | | | 6 | | 10 | 11 | 9 | 7 | | | | | 4 | | | 8 | 1 | | | | | |
| 36 | | 2 | 3 | | 5 | | | 6 | | 10 | 11 | 9 | 7 | | | | | 4 | | | 8 | 1 | | | | | |
| 37 | | 2 | 3 | 5 | | 6 | | 4 | | 10 | 11 | 9 | 7 | | | 1 | | | | | 8 | | | | | | |
| 38 | | 2 | 3 | 5 | | 6 | | 4 | | | 11 | 10 | 7 | | | 1 | | | | 9 | 8 | | | | | | |
| 39 | | 2 | 3 | 4 | 5 | 6 | | 8 | | 10 | 11 | | 7 | | | | | | | 9 | | 1 | | | | | |
| 40 | | 2 | 3 | 4 | 5 | 6 | | | | 10 | 11 | | 7 | | | | | | | 9 | 8 | 1 | | | | | |
| 41 | | 2 | 3 | 5 | | 6 | | 4 | | 10 | 11 | | 7 | | | 1 | | | | 9 | 8 | | | | | | |
| 42 | | 2 | 3 | 5 | | 6 | 7 | 4 | | 10 | | | | | | 1 | | | | 9 | 8 | | | | | 11 | |
| Apps. | 7 | 40 | 35 | 35 | 29 | 22 | 25 | 40 | 10 | 22 | 32 | 31 | 23 | 1 | 2 | 21 | 3 | 5 | 1 | 20 | 29 | 14 | 5 | 1 | 1 | 8 | |
| Goals | | | 1 | 1 | 1 | | 1 | 3 | 4 | 5 | 1 | 14 | 5 | | | | 2 | | | 4 | 14 | | | | | | |

Own goals 1

## F.A. CUP

| | Date | Opposition | | FT | HT | Att. | Goalscorers |
|---|---|---|---|---|---|---|---|
| 1R | Nov 27 | Hartlepools United | W | 3-1 | 1-0 | 8563 | Williamson, Harrigan, Forsyth |
| 2R | Dec 11 | Aldershot | L | 0-1 | 0-1 | 10000 | |

| | MacLaren J. | Butcher R. | McNeil D. | Williamson G. | Lee E. | Mansley C. | Foulkes W. | Astbury T | Best T. | Westwood R. | Forsyth J. | Foulds A. | Davies J. | Hounslea W. | Greenwood P. | Scales G. | Coffin G. | Beaumont A. | Walters T. | Harrigan D. | Burgess A. | Elliott E. | Mackie T. | Kirkpatrick R. | Bryan E. | Booth G. | Tilston T. |
|---|---|---|---|---|---|---|---|---|---|---|---|---|---|---|---|---|---|---|---|---|---|---|---|---|---|---|---|
| 1R | | 2 | | 6 | 5 | | 7 | 4 | | | 11 | 10 | | | | | | | | 9 | 8 | 1 | 3 | | | | |
| 2R | | 2 | | 6 | 5 | | 7 | 4 | | | 11 | 10 | | | | | | | | 9 | 8 | 1 | 3 | | | | |

## WELSH CUP

| | Date | Opposition | | FT | HT | Att. | Goalscorers |
|---|---|---|---|---|---|---|---|
| 5R | Jan 12 | WREXHAM | L | 0-6 | 0-3 | 3790 | |

| | MacLaren J. | Butcher R. | McNeil D. | Williamson G. | Lee E. | Mansley C. | Foulkes W. | Astbury T | Best T. | Westwood R. | Forsyth J. | Foulds A. | Davies J. | Hounslea W. | Greenwood P. | Scales G. | Coffin G. | Beaumont A. | Walters T. | Harrigan D. | Burgess A. | Elliott E. | Mackie T. | Kirkpatrick R. | Bryan E. | Booth G. | Tilston T. |
|---|---|---|---|---|---|---|---|---|---|---|---|---|---|---|---|---|---|---|---|---|---|---|---|---|---|---|---|
| 5R | | 2 | | 5 | 3 | 6 | 7 | 4 | | | | | 8 | | | | | | | 11 | 9 | 1 | | | | | 10 |

## FRIENDLIES

| | Date | Opposition | | FT | HT | Att. | Goalscorers |
|---|---|---|---|---|---|---|---|
| 1 | Apr 6 | BOLTON WANDERERS * | L | 2-3 | 2-2 | 4939 | Foulds, Westwood |

* Tommy Astbury Benefit

### Final League Table

| | | Pl. | Home W | D | L | F | A | Away W | D | L | F | A | F. | A. | Pts |
|---|---|---|---|---|---|---|---|---|---|---|---|---|---|---|---|
| 1 | Hull City | 42 | 17 | 1 | 3 | 65 | 14 | 10 | 10 | 1 | 28 | 14 | 93 | 28 | 65 |
| 2 | Rotherham United | 42 | 16 | 4 | 1 | 47 | 17 | 12 | 2 | 7 | 43 | 29 | 90 | 46 | 62 |
| 3 | Doncaster Rovers | 42 | 10 | 8 | 3 | 26 | 12 | 10 | 2 | 9 | 27 | 28 | 53 | 40 | 50 |
| 4 | Darlington | 42 | 10 | 3 | 8 | 42 | 36 | 10 | 3 | 8 | 41 | 38 | 83 | 74 | 46 |
| 5 | Gateshead | 42 | 10 | 6 | 5 | 41 | 28 | 6 | 7 | 8 | 28 | 30 | 69 | 58 | 45 |
| 6 | Oldham Athletic | 42 | 12 | 4 | 5 | 49 | 28 | 6 | 5 | 10 | 26 | 39 | 75 | 67 | 45 |
| 7 | Rochdale | 42 | 14 | 3 | 4 | 37 | 16 | 4 | 6 | 11 | 18 | 37 | 55 | 53 | 45 |
| 8 | Stockport County | 42 | 13 | 5 | 3 | 44 | 16 | 3 | 6 | 12 | 17 | 40 | 61 | 56 | 43 |
| 9 | Wrexham | 42 | 12 | 6 | 3 | 35 | 22 | 5 | 3 | 13 | 21 | 40 | 56 | 62 | 43 |
| 10 | Mansfield Town | 42 | 13 | 6 | 2 | 39 | 15 | 1 | 8 | 12 | 13 | 33 | 52 | 48 | 42 |
| 11 | Tranmere Rovers | 42 | 8 | 9 | 4 | 23 | 19 | 5 | 6 | 10 | 23 | 38 | 46 | 57 | 41 |
| 12 | Crewe Alexandra | 42 | 13 | 4 | 4 | 31 | 18 | 3 | 5 | 13 | 21 | 56 | 52 | 74 | 41 |
| 13 | Barrow | 42 | 10 | 8 | 3 | 27 | 13 | 4 | 4 | 13 | 14 | 35 | 41 | 48 | 40 |
| 14 | York City | 42 | 11 | 3 | 7 | 49 | 28 | 4 | 6 | 11 | 25 | 46 | 74 | 74 | 39 |
| 15 | Carlisle United | 42 | 12 | 7 | 2 | 46 | 32 | 2 | 4 | 15 | 14 | 45 | 60 | 77 | 39 |
| 16 | Hartlepools United | 42 | 10 | 5 | 6 | 34 | 25 | 4 | 5 | 12 | 11 | 33 | 45 | 58 | 38 |
| 17 | New Brighton | 42 | 10 | 4 | 7 | 25 | 19 | 4 | 4 | 13 | 21 | 39 | 46 | 58 | 36 |
| ***18*** | ***Chester*** | ***42*** | ***10*** | ***7*** | ***4*** | ***36*** | ***19*** | ***1*** | ***6*** | ***14*** | ***21*** | ***37*** | ***57*** | ***56*** | ***35*** |
| 19 | Halifax Town | 42 | 8 | 4 | 9 | 26 | 27 | 4 | 7 | 10 | 19 | 35 | 45 | 62 | 35 |
| 20 | Accrington Stanley | 42 | 11 | 4 | 6 | 39 | 23 | 1 | 6 | 14 | 16 | 41 | 55 | 64 | 34 |
| 21 | Southport | 42 | 6 | 5 | 10 | 24 | 29 | 5 | 4 | 12 | 21 | 35 | 45 | 64 | 31 |
| 22 | Bradford City | 42 | 7 | 6 | 8 | 29 | 31 | 3 | 3 | 15 | 19 | 46 | 48 | 77 | 29 |

**1949/50 Season:** (Back) Davies, Butcher, Jackson, Elliott, Kirkpatrick, Coffin, Hindle. (Front) Burgess, Astbury, Molyneux, Foulkes.

**1950/51Season:** (Back) Morement, Greenwood, Astbury, Threadgold, Lee, Tilston, Hindle. (Front ) Foulkes, Hankinson, Burgess, Devonshire

# SEASON 1949-50

## FOOTBALL LEAGUE DIVISION 3 (NORTH)

| | Date | Opposition | | FT | HT | Att. | Goalscorers |
|---|---|---|---|---|---|---|---|
| 1 | Aug 20 | STOCKPORT COUNTY | L | 0-4 | 0-1 | 10026 | |
| 2 | 22 | Southport | D | 1-1 | 0-1 | 9133 | Jackson (pen) |
| 3 | 27 | Doncaster Rovers | L | 0-2 | 0-0 | 16945 | |
| 4 | 31 | SOUTHPORT | W | 4-1 | 1-0 | 5548 | Jackson (2), Jones, Burgess |
| 5 | Sep 3 | GATESHEAD | L | 0-3 | 0-1 | 7695 | |
| 6 | 5 | Rochdale | W | 1-0 | 0-0 | 7543 | Tilston |
| 7 | 10 | Hartlepools United | L | 1-5 | 1-2 | 9341 | Coffin |
| 8 | 14 | ROCHDALE | L | 0-2 | 0-1 | 5165 | |
| 9 | 17 | Darlington | L | 1-2 | 0-2 | 8577 | Coffin |
| 10 | 19 | Rotherham United | L | 2-3 | 0-1 | 8421 | Burgess (2) |
| 11 | 24 | New Brighton | D | 3-3 | 1-3 | 6417 | Jackson (2 ,1 pen), Burgess |
| 12 | Oct 1 | HALIFAX TOWN | W | 5-1 | 2-0 | 5451 | Burgess (4), Davies |
| 13 | 8 | WREXHAM | W | 2-1 | 0-0 | 14034 | Burgess, Jackson |
| 14 | 15 | Oldham Athletic | W | 2-0 | 1-0 | 16487 | Coffin, Burgess |
| 15 | 22 | YORK CITY | L | 2-3 | 0-2 | 6370 | Burgess, Astbury |
| 16 | 29 | Tranmere Rovers | L | 1-2 | 0-1 | 13020 | Jackson |
| 17 | Nov 5 | CREWE ALEX. | L | 0-1 | 0-0 | 10684 | |
| 18 | 12 | Barrow | L | 1-3 | 1-1 | 3482 | Kirkpatrick |
| 19 | 19 | LINCOLN CITY | W | 3-1 | 1-0 | 5312 | Davies, Burgess, Jackson (pen) |
| 20 | Dec 3 | CARLISLE UNITED | L | 2-4 | 1-2 | 4494 | Pearson, Davies |
| 21 | 17 | Stockport County | L | 0-3 | 0-2 | 8413 | |
| 22 | 24 | DONCASTER ROVERS | W | 3-1 | 1-1 | 6763 | Foulkes (2), Pearson |
| 23 | 26 | BRADFORD CITY | W | 4-1 | 1-0 | 8717 | Foulkes, Astbury (2), Pearson |
| 24 | 27 | Bradford City | L | 0-1 | 0-1 | 21246 | |
| 25 | 31 | Gateshead | L | 0-4 | 0-2 | 6542 | |
| 26 | Jan 14 | HARTLEPOOLS UNITED | W | 3-0 | 0-0 | 5138 | Foulkes, Astbury, Jackson (pen) |
| 27 | 21 | DARLINGTON | D | 4-4 | 3-0 | 5004 | Davison(og),Kirkpatrick,Jackson(pen),Burgess |
| 28 | Feb 4 | NEW BRIGHTON | W | 2-0 | 1-0 | 5953 | Burgess, Coffin |
| 29 | 11 | Mansfield Town | W | 2-0 | 1-0 | 9630 | Kirkpatrick, Coffin |
| 30 | 18 | Halifax Town | L | 1-2 | 1-0 | 6009 | Burgess |
| 31 | 25 | Lincoln City | L | 0-2 | 0-0 | 8634 | |
| 32 | Mar 4 | ROTHERHAM UNITED | W | 4-2 | 4-0 | 6533 | Kirkpatrick, Burgess (2), Coffin |
| 33 | 11 | York City | W | 3-2 | 2-0 | 5986 | Astbury, Burgess (2) |
| 34 | 18 | TRANMERE ROVERS | D | 0-0 | 0-0 | 6528 | |
| 35 | 25 | Crewe Alex. | W | 2-1 | 0-1 | 8399 | Burgess (2) |
| 36 | Apr 1 | BARROW | W | 1-0 | 0-0 | 5004 | Burgess |
| 37 | 7 | ACCRINGTON STANLEY | W | 1-0 | 1-0 | 8388 | Coffin |
| 38 | 8 | Wrexham | D | 1-1 | 0-0 | 8932 | Coffin |
| 39 | 10 | Accrington Stanley | L | 0-4 | 0-3 | 4611 | |
| 40 | 15 | OLDHAM ATHLETIC | D | 1-1 | 0-0 | 5578 | Kirkpatrick (pen) |
| 41 | 22 | Carlisle United | L | 1-5 | 1-2 | 9559 | Burgess |
| 42 | 29 | MANSFIELD TOWN | W | 6-3 | 3-2 | 2215 | Kirkpatrick, Coffin, Tilston (3), Burgess |

| | Elliott E. | Sibley E. | McNeil D. | Astbury T. | Lee E. | Butcher R. | Davies J. | Burgess A. | Jackson H. | Tilston T. | Pearson W. | Hindle F. | Jones E. | Williamson G. | Foulkes W. | Kirkpatrick R. | Coffin G. | Molyneux J. | Greenwood P. | Cole J. | Booth G. | Threadgold H. | Lawton W. | Richardson H. |
|---|---|---|---|---|---|---|---|---|---|---|---|---|---|---|---|---|---|---|---|---|---|---|---|---|
| 1 | 1 | 2 | 3 | 4 | 5 | 6 | 7 | 8 | 9 | 10 | 11 | | | | | | | | | | | | | |
| 2 | 1 | 2 | 3 | 4 | 5 | 6 | 7 | 8 | 9 | 10 | 11 | | | | | | | | | | | | | |
| 3 | 1 | 2 | | 4 | 5 | 6 | 7 | 8 | 9 | 10 | 11 | 3 | | | | | | | | | | | | |
| 4 | 1 | 2 | | 4 | 5 | 6 | 7 | 8 | 9 | | 11 | 3 | 10 | | | | | | | | | | | |
| 5 | 1 | 2 | | | 5 | 6 | 11 | 8 | 9 | | | 3 | 10 | 4 | 7 | | | | | | | | | |
| 6 | 1 | 2 | | 8 | 5 | 4 | 7 | | 9 | 10 | | 3 | | | 11 | 6 | | | | | | | | |
| 7 | 1 | 2 | | 8 | 5 | 4 | 11 | | | 10 | | 3 | | | 7 | 6 | 9 | | | | | | | |
| 8 | 1 | | | 8 | | 4 | 11 | | 9 | | | 3 | | 5 | 7 | 6 | | 2 | 10 | | | | | |
| 9 | 1 | | | 4 | | | 11 | 10 | 9 | | | 3 | | 5 | 7 | 6 | 8 | 2 | | | | | | |
| 10 | 1 | | | 4 | | 2 | 11 | 10 | 9 | | | 3 | | 5 | 7 | 6 | 8 | | | | | | | |
| 11 | 1 | | | 4 | | | 11 | 10 | 9 | | | 3 | | 5 | 7 | 6 | 8 | 2 | | | | | | |
| 12 | 1 | | | 4 | 5 | | 11 | 10 | 9 | | | 3 | | | 7 | 6 | 8 | 2 | | | | | | |
| 13 | 1 | | | 4 | | 3 | 11 | 10 | 9 | | | 5 | | | 7 | 6 | 8 | 2 | | | | | | |
| 14 | 1 | | | 4 | | 3 | 11 | 10 | 9 | | | 5 | | | 7 | 6 | 8 | 2 | | | | | | |
| 15 | 1 | | | 4 | | 3 | 11 | 10 | 9 | | | 5 | | | 7 | 6 | 8 | 2 | | | | | | |
| 16 | 1 | | | 4 | 5 | 2 | 11 | 10 | 9 | | | 3 | | | 7 | 6 | 8 | | | | | | | |
| 17 | 1 | | | 4 | 5 | | 11 | 10 | 9 | | | 3 | | | 7 | 6 | 8 | 2 | | | | | | |
| 18 | 1 | | | 4 | 5 | | 8 | 10 | | 9 | 11 | 3 | | | 7 | 6 | | 2 | | | | | | |
| 19 | 1 | | 3 | 4 | | | 8 | 10 | 9 | | 11 | 5 | | | 7 | 6 | | 2 | | | | | | |
| 20 | 1 | | | 4 | | 3 | 8 | 10 | 9 | | 11 | 5 | | | 7 | 6 | | 2 | | | | | | |
| 21 | 1 | | 3 | 4 | 6 | | | | 10 | | 11 | 5 | | | 7 | | 9 | 2 | 8 | | | | | |
| 22 | 1 | | | 10 | 5 | | 8 | | | | 11 | 3 | | 4 | 7 | 6 | 9 | 2 | | | | | | |
| 23 | 1 | | | 10 | 5 | | 8 | | | | 11 | 3 | | 4 | 7 | 6 | 9 | 2 | | | | | | |
| 24 | 1 | | | 10 | 5 | | 8 | | | | 11 | 3 | | 4 | 7 | 6 | 9 | 2 | | | | | | |
| 25 | 1 | | | 10 | 5 | | | | | | 11 | 3 | 8 | 4 | 7 | 6 | 9 | 2 | | | | | | |
| 26 | 1 | | | 10 | 5 | | | 8 | 9 | | | 3 | | 4 | 7 | 11 | | 2 | 6 | | | | | |
| 27 | 1 | | | 10 | 5 | | | 8 | 9 | | | 3 | | 4 | 7 | 11 | | 2 | 6 | | | | | |
| 28 | 1 | | | 10 | 5 | 4 | | 8 | | | | 3 | | | 7 | 11 | 9 | 2 | 6 | | | | | |
| 29 | 1 | | | 10 | 5 | 4 | | 8 | | | | 3 | | | 7 | 11 | 9 | 2 | 6 | | | | | |
| 30 | 1 | | | 10 | 5 | 4 | | 8 | | | | 3 | | | 7 | 11 | 9 | 2 | 6 | | | | | |
| 31 | 1 | | | 10 | 5 | 4 | | 8 | | | | 3 | | | 7 | 11 | 9 | 2 | 6 | | | | | |
| 32 | 1 | | | 10 | 5 | 4 | | 8 | | | | 3 | | | 7 | 11 | 9 | 2 | 6 | | | | | |
| 33 | 1 | | | 10 | 5 | | | 8 | | | | 3 | | 4 | 7 | 11 | 9 | 2 | 6 | | | | | |
| 34 | 1 | | | 10 | 5 | | | 8 | | | | 3 | | 4 | 7 | 11 | 9 | 2 | 6 | | | | | |
| 35 | 1 | | | 10 | 5 | | | 8 | | | | 3 | | 4 | 7 | 11 | 9 | 2 | 6 | | | | | |
| 36 | 1 | | | 10 | 5 | | | 8 | | | | 3 | | 4 | 7 | 11 | 9 | 2 | 6 | | | | | |
| 37 | 1 | | | 10 | 5 | | | 8 | | 4 | | 3 | | | 7 | 11 | 9 | 2 | 6 | | | | | |
| 38 | 1 | | | 10 | 5 | | | 8 | | 4 | | 3 | | | 7 | 11 | 9 | 2 | 6 | | | | | |
| 39 | 1 | | | 10 | 5 | 4 | | 8 | | | | 3 | | | 7 | 11 | 9 | 2 | 6 | | | | | |
| 40 | 1 | | | 10 | 5 | | | 8 | | | | 3 | | 4 | 7 | 11 | 9 | 2 | 6 | | | | | |
| 41 | 1 | | | 10 | 5 | | | 9 | | 4 | | 3 | 8 | | 7 | 11 | | | 6 | 2 | | | | |
| 42 | 1 | | | | 5 | | | 8 | | 10 | | 3 | 7 | 4 | | 11 | 9 | 2 | 6 | | | | | |
| Apps. | 42 | 7 | 4 | 40 | 33 | 20 | 23 | 34 | 21 | 10 | 12 | 40 | 5 | 17 | 37 | 36 | 29 | 32 | 19 | 1 | | | | |
| Goals | | | | 5 | | | 3 | 24 | 10 | 4 | 3 | | 1 | | 4 | 6 | 9 | | | | | | | |

Own goals 1

## F.A. CUP

| | Date | Opposition | | FT | HT | Att. | Goalscorers |
|---|---|---|---|---|---|---|---|
| 1R | Nov 26 | GOOLE TOWN | W | 4-1 | 1-0 | 6774 | Jackson (3), Burgess |
| 2R | Dec 10 | Exeter City | L | 0-2 | 0-1 | 11025 | |

| | Elliott E. | Sibley E. | McNeil D. | Astbury T. | Lee E. | Butcher R. | Davies J. | Burgess A. | Jackson H. | Tilston T. | Pearson W. | Hindle F. | Jones E. | Williamson G. | Foulkes W. | Kirkpatrick R. | Coffin G. | Molyneux J. | Greenwood P. | Cole J. | Booth G. | Threadgold H. | Lawton W. | Richardson H. |
|---|---|---|---|---|---|---|---|---|---|---|---|---|---|---|---|---|---|---|---|---|---|---|---|---|
| 1R | 1 | | 3 | 4 | | | 8 | 10 | 9 | | | 5 | | | 7 | 6 | | 2 | | | 11 | | | |
| 2R | 1 | | 3 | 4 | 6 | | 8 | 10 | 9 | | 11 | 5 | | | 7 | | | 2 | | | | | | |

## WELSH CUP

| | Date | Opposition | | FT | HT | Att. | Goalscorers |
|---|---|---|---|---|---|---|---|
| 5R | Jan 11 | South Liverpool | D | 0-0 | 0-0 | 1200 | |
| 5Rr | 25 | SOUTH LIVERPOOL * | D | 2-2 | 1-1 | | Jackson, Pearson |
| 5R2r | Feb 15 | SOUTH LIVERPOOL | W | 2-0 | 1-0 | 2000 | Greenwood, Burgess (pen) |
| 7R | Mar 1 | BARRY TOWN | W | 3-2 | 1-0 | | Coffin (2), Burgess |
| SF | 29 | Wrexham | D | 0-0 | 0-0 | 7041 | |
| SFr | Apr 17 | WREXHAM | L | 1-5 | 0-4 | | Williamson |

| | Elliott E. | Sibley E. | McNeil D. | Astbury T. | Lee E. | Butcher R. | Davies J. | Burgess A. | Jackson H. | Tilston T. | Pearson W. | Hindle F. | Jones E. | Williamson G. | Foulkes W. | Kirkpatrick R. | Coffin G. | Molyneux J. | Greenwood P. | Cole J. | Booth G. | Threadgold H. | Lawton W. | Richardson H. |
|---|---|---|---|---|---|---|---|---|---|---|---|---|---|---|---|---|---|---|---|---|---|---|---|---|
| 5R | | | | 10 | 5 | | | 8 | | 9 | 11 | 3 | | 4 | 7 | | | 2 | 6 | | | 1 | | |
| 5Rr | | | | 10 | 5 | 4 | | 8 | 9 | | 11 | 3 | | | 7 | | | 2 | 6 | | | 1 | | |
| 5R2r | 1 | | | 10 | 5 | | | 8 | | | 11 | 3 | | | 7 | | 9 | 2 | 6 | | | | 4 | |
| 7R | 1 | | | 10 | 5 | 4 | | 8 | | | | 3 | | | 7 | | 9 | 2 | 6 | | | | | 11 |
| SF | 1 | | | 10 | 5 | | | 8 | | | | 3 | 11 | 4 | 7 | | 9 | 2 | 6 | | | | | |
| SFr | 1 | | | 10 | 5 | | | 8 | | | | 3 | | 4 | 7 | 11 | 9 | 2 | 6 | | | | | |

* Extra time played following score of 2-2 after 90 minutes

Chester were awarded a bye in the 6th round

## FRIENDLIES

| | Date | Opposition | | FT | HT | Att. | Goalscorers |
|---|---|---|---|---|---|---|---|
| 1 | Jan 7 | Wrexham | W | 1-0 | 0-0 | 5000 | Astbury |
| 2 | 28 | STOKE CITY | L | 3-5 | 2-3 | 4592 | Burgess (2), Kirkpatrick |
| 3 | May 3 | BLACKPOOL * | L | 1-4 | 0-2 | 5332 | Burgess |

* Reg Butcher Benefit

Final League Table

| | | Pl. | Home W | Home D | Home L | Home F | Home A | Away W | Away D | Away L | Away F | Away A | F. | A. | Pts |
|---|---|---|---|---|---|---|---|---|---|---|---|---|---|---|---|
| 1 | Doncaster Rovers | 42 | 9 | 9 | 3 | 30 | 15 | 10 | 8 | 3 | 36 | 23 | 66 | 38 | 55 |
| 2 | Gateshead | 42 | 13 | 5 | 3 | 51 | 23 | 10 | 2 | 9 | 36 | 31 | 87 | 54 | 53 |
| 3 | Rochdale | 42 | 15 | 3 | 3 | 42 | 13 | 6 | 6 | 9 | 26 | 28 | 68 | 41 | 51 |
| 4 | Lincoln City | 42 | 14 | 5 | 2 | 35 | 9 | 7 | 4 | 10 | 25 | 30 | 60 | 39 | 51 |
| 5 | Tranmere Rovers | 42 | 15 | 3 | 3 | 35 | 21 | 4 | 8 | 9 | 16 | 27 | 51 | 48 | 49 |
| 6 | Rotherham United | 42 | 10 | 6 | 5 | 46 | 28 | 9 | 4 | 8 | 34 | 31 | 80 | 59 | 48 |
| 7 | Crewe Alexandra | 42 | 10 | 6 | 5 | 38 | 27 | 7 | 8 | 6 | 30 | 28 | 68 | 55 | 48 |
| 8 | Mansfield Town | 42 | 12 | 4 | 5 | 37 | 20 | 6 | 8 | 7 | 29 | 34 | 66 | 54 | 48 |
| 9 | Carlisle United | 42 | 12 | 6 | 3 | 39 | 20 | 4 | 9 | 8 | 29 | 31 | 68 | 51 | 47 |
| 10 | Stockport County | 42 | 14 | 2 | 5 | 33 | 21 | 5 | 6 | 11 | 22 | 31 | 55 | 52 | 45 |
| 11 | Oldham Athletic | 42 | 10 | 4 | 7 | 32 | 31 | 6 | 7 | 8 | 26 | 32 | 58 | 63 | 43 |
| ***12*** | ***Chester*** | ***42*** | ***12*** | ***3*** | ***6*** | ***47*** | ***33*** | ***5*** | ***3*** | ***13*** | ***23*** | ***46*** | ***70*** | ***79*** | ***40*** |
| 13 | Accrington Stanley | 42 | 12 | 5 | 4 | 41 | 21 | 4 | 2 | 15 | 16 | 41 | 57 | 62 | 39 |
| 14 | New Brighton | 42 | 10 | 5 | 6 | 27 | 25 | 4 | 5 | 12 | 18 | 38 | 45 | 63 | 38 |
| 15 | Barrow | 42 | 9 | 6 | 6 | 27 | 20 | 5 | 3 | 13 | 20 | 33 | 47 | 53 | 37 |
| 16 | Southport | 42 | 7 | 10 | 4 | 29 | 26 | 5 | 3 | 13 | 22 | 45 | 51 | 71 | 37 |
| 17 | Darlington | 42 | 9 | 8 | 4 | 35 | 27 | 2 | 5 | 14 | 21 | 42 | 56 | 69 | 35 |
| 18 | Hartlepools United | 42 | 10 | 3 | 8 | 37 | 35 | 4 | 2 | 15 | 15 | 44 | 52 | 79 | 33 |
| 19 | Bradford City | 42 | 11 | 1 | 9 | 38 | 32 | 1 | 7 | 13 | 23 | 44 | 61 | 76 | 32 |
| 20 | Wrexham | 42 | 8 | 7 | 6 | 24 | 17 | 2 | 5 | 14 | 15 | 37 | 39 | 54 | 32 |
| 21 | Halifax Town | 42 | 9 | 5 | 7 | 35 | 31 | 3 | 3 | 15 | 23 | 54 | 58 | 85 | 32 |
| 22 | York City | 42 | 6 | 7 | 8 | 29 | 33 | 3 | 6 | 12 | 23 | 37 | 52 | 70 | 31 |

# SEASON 1950-51

## FOOTBALL LEAGUE DIVISION 3 (NORTH)

| | Date | Opposition | | FT | HT | Att. | Goalscorers | Elliott E. | Molyneux J. | Hindle F. | Astbury T. | Lee E. | Kirkpatrick R. | Foulkes W. | Burgess A. | Morement R. | Hankinson J. | Devonshire L. | Threadgold H. | Greenwood P. | Jones E. | Coffin G. | Tilston T. | McNeil D. | Whitlock P. | Hilton J. |
|---|---|---|---|---|---|---|---|---|---|---|---|---|---|---|---|---|---|---|---|---|---|---|---|---|---|---|
| 1 | Aug 19 | Lincoln City | L | 1-2 | 1-0 | 10793 | Foulkes | 1 | 2 | 3 | 4 | 5 | 6 | 7 | 8 | 9 | 10 | 11 | | | | | | | | |
| 2 | 23 | OLDHAM ATHLETIC | W | 3-1 | 2-1 | 6720 | Devonshire, Foulkes, Kirkpatrick (pen) | 1 | 2 | 3 | 4 | 5 | 6 | 7 | 10 | 9 | 8 | 11 | | | | | | | | |
| 3 | 26 | DARLINGTON | W | 3-1 | 1-0 | 7510 | Morement (2), Burgess | | 2 | 3 | 4 | 5 | 6 | 7 | 10 | 9 | 8 | 11 | 1 | | | | | | | |
| 4 | 29 | Oldham Athletic | L | 0-1 | 0-1 | 11694 | | | 2 | 3 | 4 | 5 | 6 | 7 | 10 | 9 | 8 | 11 | 1 | | | | | | | |
| 5 | Sep 2 | Stockport County | W | 3-0 | 1-0 | 10834 | Foulkes, Burgess (2) | | 2 | 3 | 4 | 5 | 10 | 7 | 8 | 9 | | 11 | 1 | 6 | | | | | | |
| 6 | 6 | WREXHAM | D | 0-0 | 0-0 | 11280 | | | 2 | 3 | 4 | 5 | 10 | 7 | 8 | 9 | | 11 | 1 | 6 | | | | | | |
| 7 | 9 | HALIFAX TOWN | W | 2-1 | 1-0 | 7720 | Burgess, Morement | | 2 | 3 | 4 | 5 | 10 | 7 | 8 | 9 | | 11 | 1 | 6 | | | | | | |
| 8 | 13 | Wrexham | L | 0-2 | 0-2 | 16710 | | | 2 | 3 | 4 | 5 | 10 | 7 | 8 | 9 | | 11 | 1 | 6 | | | | | | |
| 9 | 16 | Hartlepools United | W | 2-1 | 1-1 | 8773 | Kirkpatrick (2) | | 2 | 3 | 4 | 5 | 10 | 7 | 8 | 9 | | 11 | 1 | 6 | | | | | | |
| 10 | 23 | GATESHEAD | D | 2-2 | 1-2 | 10363 | Morement, Burgess | | 2 | 3 | | 5 | 6 | 7 | 10 | 9 | 8 | 11 | 1 | 4 | | | | | | |
| 11 | 30 | Crewe Alex. | L | 0-3 | 0-0 | 10178 | | 1 | 2 | 3 | 4 | 5 | 10 | 7 | 8 | 9 | | 11 | | 6 | | | | | | |
| 12 | Oct 7 | CARLISLE UNITED | D | 1-1 | 0-0 | 7671 | Burgess | | 2 | 3 | 10 | 5 | 6 | 7 | 8 | 9 | | 11 | 1 | 4 | | | | | | |
| 13 | 14 | York City | D | 2-2 | 2-1 | 8852 | Devonshire, Astbury | | 2 | 3 | 10 | 5 | 6 | 7 | 8 | 9 | | 11 | 1 | 4 | | | | | | |
| 14 | 21 | SOUTHPORT | L | 0-2 | 0-2 | 7114 | | | 2 | 3 | 10 | 5 | 6 | | 8 | 9 | | 11 | 1 | 4 | 7 | | | | | |
| 15 | 28 | Accrington Stanley | W | 2-1 | 0-1 | 5744 | Burgess (2) | | 2 | 3 | 4 | 5 | | 7 | 10 | | 8 | 11 | 1 | 6 | | 9 | | | | |
| 16 | Nov 4 | BRADFORD P.A. | W | 2-0 | 2-0 | 7362 | Astbury, Coffin | | 2 | 3 | 4 | 5 | | 7 | 10 | | 8 | 11 | 1 | 6 | | 9 | | | | |
| 17 | 11 | Tranmere Rovers | L | 1-3 | 1-2 | 14343 | Devonshire | | 2 | 3 | 4 | 5 | | 7 | 10 | | 8 | 11 | 1 | 6 | | | 9 | | | |
| 18 | 18 | BARROW | L | 1-2 | 0-0 | 5200 | Morement | | 2 | 3 | 4 | 5 | | 7 | | 10 | | 11 | 1 | 6 | | 8 | 9 | | | |
| 19 | Dec 2 | MANSFIELD TOWN | L | 0-1 | 0-1 | 3963 | | | 2 | 3 | 8 | 5 | | 7 | | 4 | | 11 | 1 | 6 | | 9 | 10 | | | |
| 20 | 9 | Scunthorpe United | L | 0-2 | 0-1 | 7989 | | | 2 | 3 | 8 | 5 | | 7 | | 4 | | 11 | 1 | 6 | | 9 | 10 | | | |
| 21 | 23 | Darlington | D | 0-0 | 0-0 | 3570 | | | 2 | 3 | 10 | 5 | 6 | 7 | 8 | 4 | | 11 | 1 | | | | 9 | | | |
| 22 | 25 | SHREWSBURY TOWN | W | 3-1 | 1-0 | 5544 | Foulkes, Tilston (2) | | 2 | 3 | 10 | 5 | 6 | 7 | 8 | 4 | | 11 | 1 | | | | 9 | | | |
| 23 | 26 | Shrewsbury Town | L | 0-1 | 0-1 | 10857 | | | 2 | 3 | 10 | 5 | 6 | 7 | 8 | 4 | | 11 | 1 | | | | 9 | | | |
| 24 | Jan 13 | Halifax Town | L | 1-3 | 0-2 | 5421 | Hankinson | | 2 | 3 | | 5 | 6 | 7 | 10 | 4 | 8 | 11 | 1 | | | | 9 | | | |
| 25 | 16 | Rochdale | W | 3-2 | 1-1 | 1435 | Burgess (2), Devonshire | | 2 | 5 | 6 | | | 7 | 10 | 4 | 8 | 11 | 1 | | | | 9 | 3 | | |
| 26 | 20 | HARTLEPOOLS UNITED | W | 2-1 | 1-0 | 4809 | Tilston, Burgess | | 2 | 5 | 6 | | | 7 | 10 | 4 | 8 | 11 | 1 | | | | 9 | 3 | | |
| 27 | 27 | ROCHDALE | L | 1-3 | 1-2 | 4534 | Astbury | | 2 | 5 | 6 | | | 7 | 10 | 4 | 8 | 11 | 1 | | | | 9 | 3 | | |
| 28 | Feb 3 | Gateshead | L | 1-2 | 0-1 | 4804 | Coffin | | 2 | 3 | 6 | 5 | 10 | | 8 | 4 | 7 | 11 | 1 | | | 9 | | | | |
| 29 | 10 | Bradford City | W | 1-0 | 1-0 | 9444 | Coffin | | 2 | 3 | 4 | | 10 | | 8 | 5 | 7 | 11 | 1 | 6 | | 9 | | | | |
| 30 | 17 | CREWE ALEX. | D | 1-1 | 0-1 | 6178 | Coffin | | 2 | 3 | 6 | 5 | 10 | 7 | 8 | 4 | | 11 | 1 | | | 9 | | | | |
| 31 | 24 | Carlisle United | L | 1-2 | 0-1 | 11012 | Burgess | | 2 | 3 | 6 | 5 | 10 | 7 | 8 | 4 | | 11 | 1 | | | 9 | | | | |
| 32 | Mar 3 | YORK CITY | W | 3-1 | 2-1 | 4828 | Coffin (2), Burgess | | 2 | 3 | 4 | 5 | 10 | 7 | 8 | | | 11 | 1 | 6 | | 9 | | | | |
| 33 | 10 | Southport | W | 1-0 | 0-0 | 3997 | Burgess | | 2 | 3 | 4 | 5 | 10 | 7 | 8 | | | 11 | 1 | 6 | | 9 | | | | |
| 34 | 17 | ACCRINGTON STANLEY | D | 2-2 | 1-2 | 3400 | Burgess, Foulkes | | | 3 | 4 | 5 | 10 | 7 | 8 | 2 | | 11 | 1 | 6 | | 9 | | | | |
| 35 | 24 | Bradford P.A. | L | 0-2 | 0-1 | 11679 | | | | 3 | 4 | 5 | 10 | 7 | 8 | 2 | | 11 | 1 | 6 | | 9 | | | | |
| 36 | 31 | TRANMERE ROVERS | L | 1-3 | 1-1 | 5730 | Kirkpatrick | | 2 | 3 | 4 | 5 | 10 | 7 | 8 | | | 11 | 1 | 6 | | 9 | | | | |
| 37 | Apr 4 | STOCKPORT COUNTY | W | 3-0 | 2-0 | 2896 | Morement (3, 1pen) | | 2 | 3 | 4 | 5 | 10 | 7 | | 9 | | 11 | 1 | 6 | | 8 | | | | |
| 38 | 7 | Barrow | L | 0-2 | 0-2 | 4289 | | | 2 | 3 | 4 | 5 | 10 | 7 | | | | 11 | 1 | 6 | | 8 | 9 | | | |
| 39 | 11 | LINCOLN CITY | W | 2-1 | 1-0 | 4730 | Kirkpatrick, Morement (pen) | | 2 | 3 | 4 | 5 | 11 | 7 | 10 | 9 | | | 1 | 6 | | 8 | | | | |
| 40 | 14 | ROTHERHAM UNITED | L | 1-2 | 0-0 | 7760 | Burgess | | 2 | 3 | 4 | 5 | 11 | 7 | 10 | 9 | | | 1 | 6 | | 8 | | | | |
| 41 | 16 | Rotherham United | D | 0-0 | 0-0 | 18481 | | | 2 | 3 | 4 | 5 | | 7 | 10 | 9 | | 11 | 1 | 6 | | | | | 8 | |
| 42 | 21 | Mansfield Town | L | 1-2 | 1-2 | 10239 | Burgess | | 2 | | 4 | 5 | 6 | 7 | 10 | 9 | | 11 | 1 | 3 | | | | | 8 | |
| 43 | 25 | NEW BRIGHTON | W | 3-1 | 0-0 | 3535 | Kirkpatrick, Burgess, Morement | | 2 | | 4 | 5 | 6 | 7 | 8 | 9 | | 11 | 1 | 3 | | | | | | 10 |
| 44 | 28 | SCUNTHORPE UNITED | W | 4-1 | 0-1 | 3778 | Burgess (3), Morement (pen) | | 2 | | 4 | 5 | 6 | 7 | 8 | 9 | | 11 | 1 | | | | | 3 | | 10 |
| 45 | May 2 | New Brighton | L | 0-1 | 0-1 | 2421 | | | 2 | | 4 | 5 | | 7 | 10 | 9 | 8 | 11 | 1 | | | | | 3 | 6 | |
| 46 | 5 | BRADFORD CITY | D | 2-2 | 2-0 | 4247 | Burgess, Hilton | | 2 | | 4 | 5 | 6 | 7 | 8 | 9 | | 11 | 1 | | | | | 3 | | 10 |
| | | | | | | | Apps. | 3 | 44 | 41 | 44 | 42 | 35 | 43 | 41 | 39 | 15 | 44 | 43 | 29 | 1 | 18 | 12 | 6 | 3 | 3 |
| | | | | | | | Goals | | | | 3 | | 6 | 5 | 22 | 11 | 1 | 4 | | | | 8 | 3 | | | 1 |

## F.A. CUP

| | Date | Opposition | | FT | HT | Att. | Goalscorers | Elliott E. | Molyneux J. | Hindle F. | Astbury T. | Lee E. | Kirkpatrick R. | Foulkes W. | Burgess A. | Morement R. | Hankinson J. | Devonshire L. | Threadgold H. | Greenwood P. | Jones E. | Coffin G. | Tilston T. | McNeil D. | Whitlock P. | Hilton J. |
|---|---|---|---|---|---|---|---|---|---|---|---|---|---|---|---|---|---|---|---|---|---|---|---|---|---|---|
| 1R | Nov 25 | BRADFORD P.A. | L | 1-2 | 1-1 | 8255 | Coffin | | 2 | 3 | 4 | 5 | | 7 | 10 | | 8 | 11 | 1 | 6 | | 9 | | | | |

## WELSH CUP

| | Date | Opposition | | FT | HT | Att. | Goalscorers | Elliott E. | Molyneux J. | Hindle F. | Astbury T. | Lee E. | Kirkpatrick R. | Foulkes W. | Burgess A. | Morement R. | Hankinson J. | Devonshire L. | Threadgold H. | Greenwood P. | Jones E. | Coffin G. | Tilston T. | McNeil D. | Whitlock P. | Hilton J. |
|---|---|---|---|---|---|---|---|---|---|---|---|---|---|---|---|---|---|---|---|---|---|---|---|---|---|---|
| 5R | Jan 6 | RHYL | W | 2-1 | 0-1 | 4000 | Burgess (2) | | 2 | 3 | 10 | 5 | 6 | 7 | 8 | 4 | | 11 | 1 | | | | 9 | | | |
| 6R | Mar 1 | Merthyr Tydfil | L | 2-5 | 1-1 | 12000 | Devonshire, Burgess | | 2 | 3 | 6 | 5 | | 7 | 8 | 4 | | 11 | 1 | 10 | | 9 | | | | |

## FRIENDLIES

| | Date | Opposition | | FT | HT | Att. | Goalscorers |
|---|---|---|---|---|---|---|---|
| 1 | Apr 30 | EVERTON X1 * | W | 5-3 | 2-2 | 2000 | Foulkes,Morement, Devonshire(2), Burgess |
| 2 | May 12 | SHELBOURNE @ | W | 4-0 | | 2000 | Burgess (2), Kirkpatrick, Hilton |
| 3 | 14 | DUNDALK @ | W | 4-0 | 2-0 | | Tilston (3), Hilton |

* Dave McNeil Benefit

@ Festival of Britain

### Final League Table

| | | Pl. | Home W | D | L | F | A | Away W | D | L | F | A | F. | A. | Pts |
|---|---|---|---|---|---|---|---|---|---|---|---|---|---|---|---|
| 1 | Rotherham United | 46 | 16 | 3 | 4 | 55 | 16 | 15 | 6 | 2 | 48 | 25 | 103 | 41 | 71 |
| 2 | Mansfield Town | 46 | 17 | 6 | 0 | 54 | 19 | 9 | 6 | 8 | 24 | 29 | 78 | 48 | 64 |
| 3 | Carlisle United | 46 | 18 | 4 | 1 | 44 | 17 | 7 | 8 | 8 | 35 | 33 | 79 | 50 | 62 |
| 4 | Tranmere Rovers | 46 | 15 | 5 | 3 | 51 | 26 | 9 | 6 | 8 | 32 | 36 | 83 | 62 | 59 |
| 5 | Lincoln City | 46 | 18 | 1 | 4 | 62 | 23 | 7 | 7 | 9 | 27 | 35 | 89 | 58 | 58 |
| 6 | Bradford Park Ave. | 46 | 15 | 3 | 5 | 46 | 23 | 8 | 5 | 10 | 44 | 49 | 90 | 72 | 54 |
| 7 | Bradford City | 46 | 13 | 4 | 6 | 55 | 30 | 8 | 6 | 9 | 35 | 33 | 90 | 63 | 52 |
| 8 | Gateshead | 46 | 17 | 1 | 5 | 60 | 21 | 4 | 7 | 12 | 24 | 41 | 84 | 62 | 50 |
| 9 | Crewe Alexandra | 46 | 11 | 5 | 7 | 38 | 26 | 8 | 5 | 10 | 23 | 34 | 61 | 60 | 48 |
| 10 | Stockport County | 46 | 15 | 3 | 5 | 45 | 26 | 5 | 5 | 13 | 18 | 37 | 63 | 63 | 48 |
| 11 | Rochdale | 46 | 11 | 6 | 6 | 38 | 18 | 6 | 5 | 12 | 31 | 44 | 69 | 62 | 45 |
| 12 | Scunthorpe United | 46 | 10 | 12 | 1 | 32 | 9 | 3 | 6 | 14 | 26 | 48 | 58 | 57 | 44 |
| ***13*** | ***Chester*** | ***46*** | ***11*** | ***6*** | ***6*** | ***42*** | ***30*** | ***6*** | ***3*** | ***14*** | ***20*** | ***34*** | ***62*** | ***64*** | ***43*** |
| 14 | Wrexham | 46 | 12 | 6 | 5 | 37 | 28 | 3 | 6 | 14 | 18 | 43 | 55 | 71 | 42 |
| 15 | Oldham Athletic | 46 | 10 | 5 | 8 | 47 | 36 | 6 | 3 | 14 | 26 | 37 | 73 | 73 | 40 |
| 16 | Hartlepools United | 46 | 14 | 5 | 4 | 55 | 26 | 2 | 2 | 19 | 9 | 40 | 64 | 66 | 39 |
| 17 | York City | 46 | 7 | 12 | 4 | 37 | 24 | 5 | 3 | 15 | 29 | 53 | 66 | 77 | 39 |
| 18 | Darlington | 46 | 10 | 8 | 5 | 35 | 29 | 3 | 5 | 15 | 24 | 48 | 59 | 77 | 39 |
| 19 | Barrow | 46 | 12 | 3 | 8 | 38 | 27 | 4 | 3 | 16 | 13 | 49 | 51 | 76 | 38 |
| 20 | Shrewsbury Town | 46 | 11 | 3 | 9 | 28 | 30 | 4 | 4 | 15 | 15 | 44 | 43 | 74 | 37 |
| 21 | Southport | 46 | 9 | 4 | 10 | 29 | 25 | 4 | 6 | 13 | 27 | 47 | 56 | 72 | 36 |
| 22 | Halifax Town | 46 | 11 | 6 | 6 | 36 | 24 | 0 | 6 | 17 | 14 | 45 | 50 | 69 | 34 |
| 23 | Accrington Stanley | 46 | 10 | 4 | 9 | 28 | 29 | 1 | 6 | 16 | 14 | 72 | 42 | 101 | 32 |
| 24 | New Brighton | 46 | 7 | 6 | 10 | 22 | 32 | 4 | 2 | 17 | 18 | 58 | 40 | 90 | 30 |

# *SEASON 1951-52*

## FOOTBALL LEAGUE DIVISION 3 (NORTH)

|  | Date | Opposition |  | FT | HT | Att. | Goalscorers | Threadgold H. | Molyneux J. | Gill R. | Morement R. | Lee E. | Astbury T. | Foulkes W. | Burgess A. | Jones W. | Hilton J. | Kirkpatrick R. | Port B. | Fletcher J. | Davies J. | Coffin G. | Feeney J. | Windle W. | Greenwood P. | Whitlock P. | Yates J. | Morris S. | Smyth G. | Travis D. | Richardson F. | Stiffle N. | Hughes R. | Spink A. | Williams R. |
|---|---|---|---|---|---|---|---|---|---|---|---|---|---|---|---|---|---|---|---|---|---|---|---|---|---|---|---|---|---|---|---|---|---|---|---|
| 1 | Aug 18 | WREXHAM | W | 2-1 | 2-0 | 14244 | Gill, Burgess | 1 | 2 | 3 | 4 | 5 | 6 | 7 | 8 | 9 | 10 | 11 |  |  |  |  |  |  |  |  |  |  |  |  |  |  |  |  |  |
| 2 | 22 | SCUNTHORPE UNITED | W | 3-1 | 2-1 | 7045 | Burgess (2), Hilton |  | 2 | 3 | 4 | 5 | 6 | 7 | 8 |  | 10 |  | 1 | 9 | 11 |  |  |  |  |  |  |  |  |  |  |  |  |  |  |
| 3 | 25 | York City | L | 2-4 | 1-2 | 8095 | Hilton, Simpson (og) |  | 2 | 3 | 4 | 5 | 6 | 7 | 10 | 9 | 8 |  | 1 |  | 11 |  |  |  |  |  |  |  |  |  |  |  |  |  |  |
| 4 | 30 | Scunthorpe United | D | 2-2 | 2-2 | 6042 | Fletcher, Davies | 1 | 2 | 3 | 4 | 5 | 6 | 7 | 10 | 8 |  |  |  | 9 | 11 |  |  |  |  |  |  |  |  |  |  |  |  |  |  |
| 5 | Sep 1 | BRADFORD CITY | W | 1-0 | 0-0 | 7528 | Burgess | 1 | 2 | 3 | 4 | 5 | 6 | 7 | 10 | 8 |  |  |  | 9 | 11 |  |  |  |  |  |  |  |  |  |  |  |  |  |  |
| 6 | 5 | TRANMERE ROVERS | W | 4-1 | 2-1 | 8052 | Foulkes (3), Fletcher | 1 | 2 | 3 | 4 | 5 | 6 | 7 | 10 | 8 |  | 11 |  | 9 |  |  |  |  |  |  |  |  |  |  |  |  |  |  |  |
| 7 | 8 | Hartlepools United | L | 1-2 | 1-0 | 11053 | Foulkes | 1 | 2 | 3 | 4 | 5 | 6 | 7 | 10 |  |  | 11 |  |  | 8 | 9 |  |  |  |  |  |  |  |  |  |  |  |  |  |
| 8 | 11 | Tranmere Rovers | L | 1-3 | 0-2 | 11344 | Hilton | 1 | 2 | 3 | 4 | 5 | 6 | 7 |  | 8 | 10 | 11 |  | 9 |  |  |  |  |  |  |  |  |  |  |  |  |  |  |  |
| 9 | 15 | OLDHAM ATHLETIC | L | 1-2 | 0-0 | 10234 | Fletcher | 1 | 2 | 3 | 4 | 5 |  | 7 |  | 8 | 10 | 6 |  | 9 | 11 |  |  |  |  |  |  |  |  |  |  |  |  |  |  |
| 10 | 22 | Darlington | D | 1-1 | 1-0 | 5306 | Fletcher | 1 | 2 | 3 | 4 | 5 | 6 | 7 |  | 8 |  | 10 |  | 9 |  |  | 11 |  |  |  |  |  |  |  |  |  |  |  |  |
| 11 | 26 | Wrexham | L | 2-3 | 2-3 | 12213 | Fletcher, Kirkpatrick | 1 | 2 | 3 | 4 | 5 | 6 | 7 |  | 8 | 10 | 11 |  | 9 |  |  |  |  |  |  |  |  |  |  |  |  |  |  |  |
| 12 | 29 | GATESHEAD | L | 0-3 | 0-0 | 8072 |  | 1 | 2 | 3 | 4 | 5 | 6 | 7 |  | 8 | 10 | 11 |  | 9 |  |  |  |  |  |  |  |  |  |  |  |  |  |  |  |
| 13 | Oct 6 | Bradford P. A. | L | 0-3 | 0-0 | 11795 |  |  | 2 | 3 | 4 | 5 | 6 | 7 |  | 8 |  |  | 1 | 9 |  |  | 10 | 11 |  |  |  |  |  |  |  |  |  |  |  |
| 14 | 13 | HALIFAX TOWN | W | 5-1 | 2-0 | 4569 | Kirkpatrick (2), Morement (2), Jones |  | 2 | 3 | 8 | 5 | 4 |  |  | 9 |  | 10 | 1 |  |  |  |  | 11 | 6 | 7 |  |  |  |  |  |  |  |  |  |
| 15 | 20 | Mansfield Town | L | 1-3 | 0-2 | 9550 | Windle |  | 2 | 3 | 8 | 5 | 4 |  |  | 9 |  | 10 | 1 |  |  |  |  | 11 | 6 |  | 7 |  |  |  |  |  |  |  |  |
| 16 | 27 | ROCHDALE | W | 4-0 | 2-0 | 4628 | Astbury, Fletcher, Kirkpatrick (2) | 1 | 2 | 3 | 6 | 5 | 4 |  |  | 9 |  | 10 |  | 7 |  | 8 |  | 11 |  |  |  |  |  |  |  |  |  |  |  |
| 17 | Nov 3 | Accrington Stanley | L | 2-4 | 1-0 | 5712 | Coffin, Jones | 1 | 2 | 3 | 6 | 5 | 4 |  |  | 9 |  | 10 |  | 7 |  | 8 |  | 11 |  |  |  |  |  |  |  |  |  |  |  |
| 18 | 10 | CARLISLE UNITED | W | 4-2 | 2-0 | 6082 | Fletcher, Coffin, Jones, Twentyman (og) | 1 | 2 | 3 | 6 | 5 | 4 |  |  | 9 |  | 10 |  | 7 |  | 8 |  | 11 |  |  |  |  |  |  |  |  |  |  |  |
| 19 | 17 | Stockport County | D | 0-0 | 0-0 | 11822 |  | 1 | 2 | 3 | 6 | 5 | 4 |  |  | 9 |  | 10 |  | 7 |  | 8 |  | 11 |  |  |  |  |  |  |  |  |  |  |  |
| 20 | Dec 1 | Barrow | L | 0-1 | 0-1 | 6143 |  | 1 | 2 | 3 | 4 | 5 |  |  |  | 9 |  | 10 |  | 7 |  | 8 |  | 11 | 6 |  |  |  |  |  |  |  |  |  |  |
| 21 | 8 | GRIMSBY TOWN | L | 0-3 | 0-2 | 4955 |  | 1 | 2 | 3 | 4 | 5 | 8 |  |  | 9 |  | 10 |  | 7 |  |  |  | 11 | 6 |  |  |  |  |  |  |  |  |  |  |
| 22 | 22 | YORK CITY | L | 0-1 | 0-0 | 2998 |  | 1 | 2 | 3 | 10 | 5 | 4 |  |  | 9 |  |  |  | 7 |  | 8 |  | 11 | 6 |  |  |  |  |  |  |  |  |  |  |
| 23 | 25 | Chesterfield | L | 0-2 | 0-1 | 10032 |  | 1 | 2 | 3 | 6 | 5 | 4 |  |  |  |  |  |  | 7 |  | 9 | 8 | 11 |  | 10 |  |  |  |  |  |  |  |  |  |
| 24 | 26 | CHESTERFIELD | W | 3-0 | 2-0 | 7262 | Coffin (2), Fletcher (pen) | 1 | 2 | 3 | 6 | 5 | 4 |  |  |  |  |  |  | 7 |  | 9 | 8 | 11 |  | 10 |  |  |  |  |  |  |  |  |  |
| 25 | 29 | Bradford City | L | 0-1 | 0-0 | 10992 |  | 1 | 2 | 3 | 6 | 5 | 4 |  |  |  |  |  |  | 7 |  | 9 | 8 | 11 |  | 10 |  |  |  |  |  |  |  |  |  |
| 26 | Jan 5 | HARTLEPOOLS UNITED | D | 3-3 | 2-2 | 4902 | Greenwood, Fletcher (pen), Windle | 1 | 2 |  | 3 | 5 | 6 |  |  | 7 | 10 |  |  | 9 |  |  |  | 11 | 8 |  |  | 4 |  |  |  |  |  |  |  |
| 27 | 19 | Oldham Athletic | L | 2-11 | 2-6 | 13458 | Morement (pen), Jones | 1 | 2 |  | 3 | 5 | 6 |  |  | 7 |  |  |  |  |  | 9 |  | 11 | 10 | 8 |  | 4 |  |  |  |  |  |  |  |
| 28 | 23 | Lincoln City | L | 1-4 | 1-1 | 7682 | Greenwood |  | 2 |  | 3 |  | 6 |  |  | 9 |  |  | 1 |  |  | 5 |  | 11 | 10 | 8 |  | 4 | 7 |  |  |  |  |  |  |
| 29 | Feb 2 | LINCOLN CITY | L | 0-1 | 0-1 | 5537 |  | 1 | 2 |  | 3 | 5 | 6 |  |  | 7 |  |  |  |  |  | 9 |  | 11 | 10 | 8 |  | 4 |  |  |  |  |  |  |  |
| 30 | 9 | Gateshead | L | 0-1 | 0-1 | 5416 |  | 1 | 2 | 3 | 9 | 5 | 6 |  |  | 7 |  |  |  |  |  |  |  | 11 | 10 | 8 |  | 4 |  |  |  |  |  |  |  |
| 31 | 16 | BRADFORD P. A. | W | 4-2 | 2-2 | 5691 | Kirkpatrick (2), Travis, Windle | 1 | 2 | 3 | 8 | 5 | 6 |  |  |  |  | 10 |  |  |  |  |  | 11 |  |  |  | 4 | 7 | 9 |  |  |  |  |  |
| 32 | 23 | SOUTHPORT | W | 2-1 | 1-0 | 6600 | Travis (2) | 1 |  | 2 | 3 | 5 | 6 |  |  |  |  | 10 |  | 7 |  |  |  | 11 |  |  |  | 4 |  | 9 | 8 |  |  |  |  |
| 33 | Mar 1 | Halifax Town | L | 1-4 | 0-3 | 6922 | Windle | 1 |  | 2 | 3 | 5 | 6 |  |  |  |  | 10 |  | 7 |  |  |  | 11 |  |  |  | 4 |  | 9 | 8 |  |  |  |  |
| 34 | 8 | MANSFIELD TOWN | L | 1-5 | 1-1 | 5133 | Travis | 1 |  | 3 | 2 | 5 | 6 |  |  |  |  |  |  |  |  |  |  | 11 |  | 10 |  | 4 |  | 9 | 8 | 7 |  |  |  |
| 35 | 15 | Rochdale | W | 5-0 | 2-0 | 4561 | Travis (2), Stiffle, Astbury, Kirkpatrick | 1 |  | 3 | 4 |  | 6 |  |  |  |  | 10 |  |  |  | 5 |  | 11 |  |  |  |  |  | 9 | 8 | 7 | 2 |  |  |
| 36 | 22 | ACCRINGTON STANLEY | W | 3-1 | 1-0 | 4533 | Stiffle, Travis, Windle | 1 | 2 | 3 | 4 |  | 6 |  |  |  |  | 10 |  |  |  | 5 |  | 11 |  | 8 |  |  |  | 9 |  | 7 |  |  |  |
| 37 | 29 | Carlisle United | D | 0-0 | 0-0 | 4351 |  | 1 |  | 3 |  |  | 6 |  |  |  |  | 10 |  |  |  | 5 |  | 11 | 8 |  |  | 4 |  | 9 |  | 7 | 2 |  |  |
| 38 | Apr 2 | DARLINGTON | W | 2-0 | 1-0 | 2590 | Greenwood, Travis | 1 |  | 3 |  |  | 6 |  |  |  |  |  |  |  |  | 5 |  | 11 | 8 | 10 |  | 4 |  | 9 |  | 7 | 2 |  |  |
| 39 | 5 | STOCKPORT COUNTY | D | 0-0 | 0-0 | 5606 |  | 1 | 2 | 3 | 4 |  | 6 |  |  |  |  | 10 |  |  |  | 5 |  | 11 |  | 8 |  |  |  | 9 |  | 7 |  |  |  |
| 40 | 11 | Crewe Alex. | W | 2-1 | 2-0 | 8886 | Richardson, Kirkpatrick | 1 | 2 | 3 | 4 |  | 6 |  |  |  |  | 10 |  |  |  | 5 |  | 11 |  |  |  |  |  | 8 | 9 | 7 |  |  |  |
| 41 | 12 | Workington | D | 2-2 | 1-1 | 5584 | Coffin, Astbury | 1 |  | 3 | 4 |  | 6 |  |  | 7 |  | 8 |  |  |  | 5 |  | 11 |  |  |  |  |  | 10 | 9 |  | 2 |  |  |
| 42 | 14 | CREWE ALEX. | W | 2-0 | 2-0 | 7013 | Spink, Kirkpatrick | 1 | 2 | 3 | 4 |  | 6 |  |  | 7 |  | 10 |  |  |  | 5 |  | 11 |  |  |  |  |  | 8 |  |  |  | 9 |  |
| 43 | 19 | BARROW | D | 0-0 | 0-0 | 4767 |  | 1 | 2 | 3 | 4 |  |  |  |  | 7 | 6 | 10 |  |  |  | 5 |  | 11 |  |  |  |  |  | 8 |  |  |  | 9 |  |
| 44 | 23 | WORKINGTON | D | 2-2 | 0-2 | 3317 | Richardson, Windle | 1 |  | 3 | 4 |  | 6 |  |  | 10 |  |  |  |  |  | 5 |  | 11 |  |  |  |  |  |  | 8 |  | 2 | 9 | 7 |
| 45 | 26 | Grimsby Town | L | 1-2 | 1-1 | 12434 | Travis | 1 |  | 3 | 2 |  | 6 |  |  |  |  |  |  |  |  | 5 |  | 11 |  | 10 |  | 4 |  | 9 |  |  | 7 | 8 |  |
| 46 | May 3 | Southport | L | 0-1 | 0-0 | 2316 |  | 1 |  | 3 | 2 |  | 6 |  |  |  | 10 |  |  |  |  | 5 |  | 11 |  |  | 7 | 4 |  | 9 |  |  |  | 8 |  |
|  |  |  |  |  |  |  | Apps. | 40 | 36 | 42 | 44 | 33 | 43 | 13 | 7 | 29 | 10 | 27 | 6 | 23 | 6 | 25 | 5 | 34 | 12 | 13 | 2 | 13 | 2 | 15 | 7 | 7 | 6 | 5 | 1 |
|  |  |  |  |  |  |  | Goals |  |  | 1 | 3 |  | 3 | 4 | 4 | 4 | 3 | 10 |  | 9 | 1 | 5 |  | 6 | 3 |  |  |  |  | 9 | 2 | 2 |  | 1 |  |

Own goals 2

## F.A. CUP

|  | Date | Opposition |  | FT | HT | Att. | Goalscorers | Threadgold H. | Molyneux J. | Gill R. | Morement R. | Lee E. | Astbury T. | Foulkes W. | Burgess A. | Jones W. | Hilton J. | Kirkpatrick R. | Port B. | Fletcher J. | Davies J. | Coffin G. | Feeney J. | Windle W. | Greenwood P. | Whitlock P. | Yates J. | Morris S. | Smyth G. | Travis D. | Richardson F. | Stiffle N. | Hughes R. | Spink A. | Williams R. |
|---|---|---|---|---|---|---|---|---|---|---|---|---|---|---|---|---|---|---|---|---|---|---|---|---|---|---|---|---|---|---|---|---|---|---|---|
| 1R | Nov 24 | Accrington Stanley | W | 2-1 | 0-1 | 8312 | Fletcher, Kirkpatrick | 1 | 2 | 3 | 4 | 5 |  |  |  | 9 |  | 10 |  | 7 |  | 8 |  | 11 | 6 |  |  |  |  |  |  |  |  |  |  |
| 2R | Dec 15 | LEYTON | W | 5-2 | 3-1 | 6453 | Astbury,Jones,Morement,Dixon(og),Pullinger(og) | 1 | 2 | 3 | 10 | 5 | 4 |  |  | 7 | 8 |  |  | 9 |  |  |  | 11 | 6 |  |  |  |  |  |  |  |  |  |  |
| 3R | Jan 12 | Chelsea | D | 2-2 | 1-0 | 42954 | Coffin, Greenwood | 1 | 2 |  | 3 | 5 | 6 |  |  |  |  |  |  | 7 |  | 9 |  | 11 | 10 | 8 |  | 4 |  |  |  |  |  |  |  |
| 3Rr | 16 | CHELSEA * | L | 2-3 | 0-1 | 20378 | Willemse (og), Coffin | 1 | 2 |  | 3 | 5 | 6 |  |  |  |  |  |  | 7 |  | 9 |  | 11 | 10 | 8 |  | 4 |  |  |  |  |  |  |  |

* Extra time played following score of 1-1 after 90 minutes

## WELSH CUP

|  | Date | Opposition |  | FT | HT | Att. | Goalscorers | Threadgold H. | Molyneux J. | Gill R. | Morement R. | Lee E. | Astbury T. | Foulkes W. | Burgess A. | Jones W. | Hilton J. | Kirkpatrick R. | Port B. | Fletcher J. | Davies J. | Coffin G. | Feeney J. | Windle W. | Greenwood P. | Whitlock P. | Yates J. | Morris S. | Smyth G. | Travis D. | Richardson F. | Stiffle N. | Hughes R. | Spink A. | Williams R. |
|---|---|---|---|---|---|---|---|---|---|---|---|---|---|---|---|---|---|---|---|---|---|---|---|---|---|---|---|---|---|---|---|---|---|---|---|
| 5R | Jan 2 | BANGOR CITY | W | 3-1 | 3-1 | 1500 | Fletcher (2), R Evans (og) | 1 | 2 | 3 | 6 | 5 |  |  |  | 8 |  |  |  | 9 |  |  |  | 11 | 10 |  |  | 4 |  |  |  | 7 |  |  |  |
| 6R | Feb 6 | Wrexham | D | 0-0 | 0-0 | 7434 |  | 1 | 2 | 3 | 6 | 5 |  |  |  | 9 |  |  |  |  |  |  |  | 11 | 10 | 8 |  | 4 |  |  |  | 7 |  |  |  |
| 6Rr | 20 | WREXHAM | L | 0-2 | 0-2 | 4178 |  | 1 | 2 | 3 | 8 | 5 | 6 |  |  | 9 |  |  |  |  |  |  |  | 11 | 10 |  |  | 4 |  |  |  | 7 |  |  |  |

## FRIENDLIES

|  | Date | Opposition |  | FT | HT | Goalscorers |
|---|---|---|---|---|---|---|
| 1 | Apr 30 | LIVERPOOL X1 * | W | 3-1 | 1-0 | Spink (3) |
| 2 | May 7 | STIRLING ALBION @ | W | 4-3 | 1-2 | Travis (2), Jones (2) |

* Eric Lee Benefit

@ YMCA Benefit

Final League Table

|  |  | Pl. | Home |  |  |  |  | Away |  |  |  |  | F. | A. | Pts |
|---|---|---|---|---|---|---|---|---|---|---|---|---|---|---|---|
|  |  |  | W | D | L | F | A | W | D | L | F | A |  |  |  |
| 1 | Lincoln City | 46 | 19 | 2 | 2 | 80 | 23 | 11 | 7 | 5 | 41 | 29 | 121 | 52 | 69 |
| 2 | Grimsby Town | 46 | 19 | 2 | 2 | 59 | 14 | 10 | 6 | 7 | 37 | 31 | 96 | 45 | 66 |
| 3 | Stockport County | 46 | 12 | 9 | 2 | 47 | 17 | 11 | 4 | 8 | 27 | 23 | 74 | 40 | 59 |
| 4 | Oldham Athletic | 46 | 19 | 2 | 2 | 65 | 22 | 5 | 7 | 11 | 25 | 39 | 90 | 61 | 57 |
| 5 | Gateshead | 46 | 14 | 7 | 2 | 41 | 17 | 7 | 4 | 12 | 25 | 32 | 66 | 49 | 53 |
| 6 | Mansfield Town | 46 | 17 | 3 | 3 | 50 | 23 | 5 | 5 | 13 | 23 | 37 | 73 | 60 | 52 |
| 7 | Carlisle United | 46 | 10 | 7 | 6 | 31 | 24 | 9 | 6 | 8 | 31 | 33 | 62 | 57 | 51 |
| 8 | Bradford Park Ave. | 46 | 13 | 6 | 4 | 51 | 28 | 6 | 6 | 11 | 23 | 36 | 74 | 64 | 50 |
| 9 | Hartlepools United | 46 | 17 | 3 | 3 | 47 | 19 | 4 | 5 | 14 | 24 | 46 | 71 | 65 | 50 |
| 10 | York City | 46 | 16 | 4 | 3 | 53 | 19 | 2 | 9 | 12 | 20 | 33 | 73 | 52 | 49 |
| 11 | Tranmere Rovers | 46 | 17 | 2 | 4 | 59 | 29 | 4 | 4 | 15 | 17 | 42 | 76 | 71 | 48 |
| 12 | Barrow | 46 | 13 | 5 | 5 | 33 | 19 | 4 | 7 | 12 | 24 | 42 | 57 | 61 | 46 |
| 13 | Chesterfield | 46 | 15 | 7 | 1 | 47 | 16 | 2 | 4 | 17 | 18 | 50 | 65 | 66 | 45 |
| 14 | Scunthorpe United | 46 | 10 | 11 | 2 | 30 | 23 | 4 | 5 | 14 | 20 | 51 | 50 | 74 | 44 |
| 15 | Bradford City | 46 | 12 | 5 | 6 | 40 | 32 | 4 | 5 | 14 | 21 | 36 | 61 | 68 | 42 |
| 16 | Crewe Alexandra | 46 | 12 | 6 | 5 | 42 | 28 | 5 | 2 | 16 | 21 | 54 | 63 | 82 | 42 |
| 17 | Southport | 46 | 12 | 6 | 5 | 36 | 22 | 3 | 5 | 15 | 17 | 49 | 53 | 71 | 41 |
| 18 | Wrexham | 46 | 14 | 5 | 4 | 41 | 22 | 1 | 4 | 18 | 22 | 51 | 63 | 73 | 39 |
| ***19*** | ***Chester*** | ***46*** | ***13*** | ***4*** | ***6*** | ***46*** | ***30*** | ***2*** | ***5*** | ***16*** | ***26*** | ***55*** | ***72*** | ***85*** | ***39*** |
| 20 | Halifax Town | 46 | 11 | 4 | 8 | 31 | 23 | 3 | 3 | 17 | 30 | 74 | 61 | 97 | 35 |
| 21 | Rochdale | 46 | 10 | 5 | 8 | 32 | 34 | 1 | 8 | 14 | 15 | 45 | 47 | 79 | 35 |
| 22 | Accrington Stanley | 46 | 6 | 8 | 9 | 30 | 34 | 4 | 4 | 15 | 31 | 58 | 61 | 92 | 32 |
| 23 | Darlington | 46 | 10 | 5 | 8 | 39 | 34 | 1 | 4 | 18 | 25 | 69 | 64 | 103 | 31 |
| 24 | Workington | 46 | 8 | 4 | 11 | 33 | 34 | 3 | 3 | 17 | 17 | 57 | 50 | 91 | 29 |

**1951/52 Season:** (Back) Hill (Referee), Snowdon, Lee, Bryan, Collins (Trainer), Threadgold, Dutton (Groundsman), Molyneux, Kirkpatrick, Hall (Trainer), Coffin, Gill, Cleeton, Morement, Hughes, Davies, Burgess, Port, Brown (Manager) (Front) Peters (Secretary), Jones, Astbury, Foulkes, Comley, Smyth, Fletcher, Whitlock, Massey

**1952/53 Season:** (Back) Morris, Dickens, Morement, Port, Gill, Coffin (Front) Tomlinson, Richardson, Travis, Deakin, Windle

# SEASON 1952-53

## FOOTBALL LEAGUE DIVISION 3 (NORTH)

| | Date | Opposition | | FT | HT | Att. | Goalscorers | Port B. | Morement R. | Gill R. | Morris S. | Coffin G. | Dickens L. | Tomlinson F. | Richardson F. | Travis D. | Deakin W. | Windle W. | Wright R. | Molyneux J. | Astbury T. | Costello M. | Bullock N. | Sutcliffe F. | Hughes R. | Pilkington G. | Lee E. | Hilton J. | Whitlock P. | Spink A. | Kirkpatrick R. | Smith H. |
|---|---|---|---|---|---|---|---|---|---|---|---|---|---|---|---|---|---|---|---|---|---|---|---|---|---|---|---|---|---|---|---|---|
| 1 | Aug 23 | Stockport County | L | 1-4 | 1-2 | 10467 | Travis | 1 | 2 | 3 | 4 | 5 | 6 | 7 | 8 | 9 | 10 | 11 | | | | | | | | | | | | | | |
| 2 | 25 | YORK CITY | D | 1-1 | 1-1 | 6530 | Richardson | 1 | 2 | 3 | 4 | 5 | 6 | 7 | 8 | 9 | 10 | 11 | | | | | | | | | | | | | | |
| 3 | 30 | BRADFORD CITY | W | 2-0 | 2-0 | 6365 | Deakin, Bullock | | 4 | 3 | | 5 | | | 9 | | 8 | | 1 | 2 | 6 | 7 | 10 | 11 | | | | | | | | |
| 4 | Sep 1 | York City | D | 0-0 | 0-0 | 8759 | | | 4 | 3 | | 5 | | | 9 | 10 | 8 | | 1 | | 6 | 7 | | 11 | 2 | | | | | | | |
| 5 | 6 | Rochdale | L | 1-3 | 1-3 | 6557 | Richardson | | 4 | 3 | | 5 | | | 9 | | 8 | | 1 | 2 | 6 | 7 | 10 | 11 | | | | | | | | |
| 6 | 11 | Scunthorpe United | D | 1-1 | 0-0 | 6695 | Travis | | 4 | 3 | | 5 | | | 9 | 8 | 7 | 11 | 1 | | 6 | | 10 | | 2 | | | | | | | |
| 7 | 13 | DARLINGTON | W | 6-3 | 2-2 | 5519 | Bullock(2),Costello,Travis,Windle,Richardson | | 4 | 3 | | 5 | | | 9 | 8 | | 11 | 1 | | 6 | 7 | 10 | | | 2 | | | | | | |
| 8 | 17 | SCUNTHORPE UNITED | D | 1-1 | 1-1 | 5004 | Costello | | 4 | 3 | | 5 | | | 9 | 8 | | 11 | 1 | | 6 | 7 | 10 | | | 2 | | | | | | |
| 9 | 20 | Gateshead | L | 1-4 | 0-2 | 6186 | Windle | | 4 | 3 | | | | | 9 | 8 | | 11 | 1 | | 6 | 7 | | | | 2 | 5 | 10 | | | | |
| 10 | 24 | OLDHAM ATHLETIC | L | 0-1 | 0-1 | 5678 | | | 2 | 3 | 4 | | | | 9 | 8 | | 11 | 1 | | | 7 | 10 | | | | 5 | | 6 | | | |
| 11 | 27 | HARTLEPOOLS UNITED | L | 0-1 | 0-0 | 4110 | | | 2 | 3 | 4 | | | | 9 | 8 | | 11 | 1 | | | 7 | 10 | | | | 5 | | 6 | | | |
| 12 | 29 | Crewe Alex. | L | 1-4 | 1-3 | 5698 | Bullock | | 2 | 3 | | | | | 9 | | | 11 | 1 | | | 7 | 10 | | | 4 | 5 | 6 | | 8 | | |
| 13 | Oct 4 | Carlisle United | D | 1-1 | 1-0 | 9421 | Bullock | | 6 | 3 | | 5 | | | 9 | | 7 | 11 | 1 | | | | 10 | | 4 | 8 | 2 | | | | | |
| 14 | 11 | TRANMERE ROVERS | W | 3-2 | 1-0 | 9045 | Bullock, Travis, Deakin | | 6 | 3 | | 5 | | | 9 | 8 | 7 | 11 | 1 | | | | 10 | | 4 | | 2 | | | | | |
| 15 | 18 | Chesterfield | L | 1-2 | 1-1 | 8675 | Richardson | | 6 | 3 | | 5 | | | 9 | 8 | 7 | 11 | 1 | | | | 10 | | 4 | | 2 | | | | | |
| 16 | 25 | WORKINGTON | D | 1-1 | 0-1 | 5009 | Travis | | 6 | 3 | | 5 | | | 9 | 8 | 7 | | 1 | | | | 10 | 11 | 4 | | 2 | | | | | |
| 17 | Nov 1 | Accrington Stanley | D | 1-1 | 1-1 | 5903 | Bullock | | | 3 | | 5 | | | | 8 | 7 | 11 | 1 | | | | 10 | | 4 | | 2 | 6 | | 9 | | |
| 18 | 8 | HALIFAX TOWN | W | 2-1 | 0-0 | 5235 | Deakin, Travis | | | 3 | | | | | | 8 | 7 | 11 | 1 | | | | 10 | | 4 | 2 | 5 | 6 | | 9 | | |
| 19 | 15 | Mansfield Town | D | 2-2 | 0-1 | 6390 | Hilton, Coffin | | | 3 | | 8 | | | | 10 | 7 | 11 | 1 | | | | | | 4 | 2 | 5 | 6 | | 9 | | |
| 20 | 29 | Bradford P. A. | L | 0-1 | 0-0 | 8145 | | | 4 | 3 | | | | | | 9 | | 11 | 1 | | | | 8 | | 7 | 2 | 5 | 6 | | | 10 | |
| 21 | Dec 6 | ROCHDALE | W | 3-0 | 2-0 | 3324 | Bullock, Travis, Kirkpatrick | | 4 | 3 | | | 2 | | | 9 | | 11 | 1 | | | | 8 | | 7 | | 5 | 6 | | | 10 | |
| 22 | 13 | Barrow | L | 0-3 | 0-2 | 3744 | | | 4 | 3 | | | 2 | 7 | | 9 | | 11 | 1 | | | | 10 | | 8 | | 5 | 6 | | | | |
| 23 | 20 | STOCKPORT COUNTY | W | 4-0 | 0-0 | 3144 | Morement, Travis, Bullock, Windle | | 8 | 3 | | | | 7 | | 9 | | 11 | 1 | 2 | 4 | | 10 | | | | 5 | 6 | | | | |
| 24 | 26 | Southport | L | 0-2 | 0-1 | 6000 | | | 9 | 3 | | | | | | 8 | | 11 | 1 | 2 | 4 | | 10 | | 7 | | 5 | 6 | | | | |
| 25 | Jan 3 | Bradford City | D | 2-2 | 0-1 | 9172 | Travis, Windle | | 8 | 3 | | 5 | | 7 | | 9 | | 11 | 1 | | 4 | | 10 | | | 2 | | 6 | | | | |
| 26 | 13 | Grimsby Town | L | 4-5 | 2-3 | 6204 | Spink (2), Morement (pen), Windle | | 8 | 3 | | 5 | | 7 | | 10 | | 11 | 1 | | 4 | | | | | 2 | | 6 | | 9 | | |
| 27 | 24 | Darlington | L | 2-3 | 1-1 | 4243 | Hilton, Travis | | 8 | 3 | | 5 | | 7 | | 9 | | 11 | 1 | | 4 | | 10 | | | 2 | | 6 | | | | |
| 28 | 31 | GRIMSBY TOWN | L | 0-2 | 0-0 | 4005 | | | 8 | 3 | | 5 | | 7 | | 10 | | 11 | 1 | | 4 | | | | | | 2 | 6 | | 9 | | |
| 29 | Feb 7 | GATESHEAD | W | 2-0 | 0-0 | 5075 | Travis (2) | | | 3 | | | | 7 | | 9 | | 11 | 1 | | 4 | | 8 | 10 | | 2 | 5 | 6 | | | | |
| 30 | 14 | Hartlepools United | D | 2-2 | 2-2 | 6499 | Travis, Windle | | | 3 | | | | 7 | | 9 | | 11 | 1 | | 4 | | 8 | 10 | | 2 | 5 | 6 | | | | |
| 31 | 21 | CARLISLE UNITED | L | 1-2 | 0-2 | 5987 | Travis | | | 3 | | | | 7 | | 9 | | 11 | 1 | | 4 | | 8 | 10 | | 2 | 5 | 6 | | | | |
| 32 | 28 | Tranmere Rovers | L | 0-4 | 0-2 | 8633 | | | 7 | 3 | | 8 | | | | 9 | | 11 | 1 | | 4 | | | 10 | | 2 | 5 | 6 | | | | |
| 33 | Mar 7 | CHESTERFIELD | W | 2-0 | 1-0 | 3794 | Deakin, Astbury | | 8 | 3 | | | | | | 9 | 7 | 11 | 1 | | 4 | | | 10 | 2 | | 5 | 6 | | | | |
| 34 | 14 | Workington | W | 2-1 | 0-1 | 8466 | Travis (2) | | 8 | 3 | | | | | | 9 | 7 | 11 | 1 | | 4 | | | 10 | 2 | | 5 | 6 | | | | |
| 35 | 21 | ACCRINGTON STANLEY | W | 2-0 | 0-0 | 3818 | Deakin, Travis | | 8 | 3 | | | | | | 9 | 7 | 11 | 1 | | 4 | | | 10 | 2 | | 5 | 6 | | | | |
| 36 | 25 | SOUTHPORT | D | 0-0 | 0-0 | 2744 | | | 8 | 3 | | | | | | 9 | 7 | 11 | 1 | | 4 | | | 10 | 2 | | 5 | 6 | | | | |
| 37 | 28 | Halifax Town | L | 1-3 | 0-0 | 3296 | Travis | | 8 | 3 | | | | | | 9 | 7 | 11 | 1 | | 4 | | | 10 | 2 | | 5 | 6 | | | | |
| 38 | Apr 3 | Port Vale | D | 1-1 | 0-0 | 19413 | Sutcliffe | | | 3 | | 8 | | | | | 7 | 11 | 1 | | | | | 10 | 2 | 4 | 5 | 6 | | 9 | | |
| 39 | 4 | MANSFIELD TOWN | D | 2-2 | 1-1 | 5082 | Morement (2) | | 8 | 3 | | | | | | 9 | 7 | 11 | 1 | | 4 | | | 10 | 2 | | 5 | 6 | | | | |
| 40 | 6 | PORT VALE | D | 2-2 | 0-2 | 10553 | Morement, Travis | | 10 | 3 | | 8 | | | | 9 | 7 | | 1 | 2 | 6 | | | 11 | 4 | | 5 | | | | | |
| 41 | 11 | Oldham Athletic | L | 1-2 | 1-0 | 19058 | Travis | | 8 | 3 | | | | | | 9 | 7 | 11 | 1 | | 4 | | | 10 | 2 | | 5 | 6 | | | | |
| 42 | 15 | WREXHAM | L | 1-2 | 0-1 | 11371 | Sutcliffe | | 8 | 3 | | | | | | 9 | 7 | | 1 | | 4 | | | 11 | 2 | | 5 | 6 | | 10 | | |
| 43 | 18 | BRADFORD P. A. | L | 0-3 | 0-1 | 4441 | | | 10 | 3 | | 8 | | | | 9 | 7 | | 1 | | 4 | | | 11 | 2 | | 5 | 6 | | | | |
| 44 | 22 | CREWE ALEX. | D | 2-2 | 1-1 | 3468 | Travis (2) | | 8 | 3 | | | 2 | | | 9 | 7 | 11 | 1 | | 6 | | | 10 | 4 | | 5 | | | | | |
| 45 | 25 | Wrexham | L | 0-7 | 0-3 | 11082 | | | 8 | 3 | | 5 | 2 | | | 9 | 7 | | 1 | | 6 | | | 10 | 4 | | | | 11 | | | |
| 46 | 29 | BARROW | W | 2-1 | 1-0 | 1941 | Travis (2) | 1 | | 3 | | | 2 | | | 9 | 7 | 11 | | | 8 | | | | 4 | | 5 | | 6 | | | 10 |
| | | | | | | | Apps. | 3 | 38 | 46 | 4 | 23 | 7 | 11 | 16 | 41 | 27 | 38 | 43 | 5 | 30 | 9 | 24 | 21 | 27 | 16 | 34 | 28 | 4 | 8 | 2 | 1 |
| | | | | | | | Goals | | 5 | | | 1 | | | 4 | 24 | 5 | 6 | | | 1 | 2 | 9 | 2 | | | | 2 | | 2 | 1 | |

## F.A. CUP

| | Date | Opposition | | FT | HT | Att. | Goalscorers | Port B. | Morement R. | Gill R. | Morris S. | Coffin G. | Dickens L. | Tomlinson F. | Richardson F. | Travis D. | Deakin W. | Windle W. | Wright R. | Molyneux J. | Astbury T. | Costello M. | Bullock N. | Sutcliffe F. | Hughes R. | Pilkington G. | Lee E. | Hilton J. | Whitlock P. | Spink A. | Kirkpatrick R. | Smith H. |
|---|---|---|---|---|---|---|---|---|---|---|---|---|---|---|---|---|---|---|---|---|---|---|---|---|---|---|---|---|---|---|---|---|
| 1R | Nov 22 | HARTLEPOOLS UNITED | L | 0-1 | 0-1 | 6773 | | | | 3 | | 8 | | | | 10 | 7 | 11 | 1 | | | | | | 4 | 2 | 5 | 6 | | 9 | | |

## WELSH CUP

| | Date | Opposition | | FT | HT | Att. | Goalscorers | Port B. | Morement R. | Gill R. | Morris S. | Coffin G. | Dickens L. | Tomlinson F. | Richardson F. | Travis D. | Deakin W. | Windle W. | Wright R. | Molyneux J. | Astbury T. | Costello M. | Bullock N. | Sutcliffe F. | Hughes R. | Pilkington G. | Lee E. | Hilton J. | Whitlock P. | Spink A. | Kirkpatrick R. | Smith H. |
|---|---|---|---|---|---|---|---|---|---|---|---|---|---|---|---|---|---|---|---|---|---|---|---|---|---|---|---|---|---|---|---|---|
| 5R | Dec 31 | Wrexham | W | 4-3 | 1-2 | 5044 | Tomlinson (2), Morement, Windle | | 8 | 3 | | 5 | | 7 | | 9 | | 11 | 1 | | 4 | | 10 | | | 2 | | 6 | | | | |
| 6R | Feb 4 | PWLLHELI & DISTRICT | W | 2-0 | 1-0 | 1600 | Bullock, Sutcliffe | | | 3 | | | | 7 | | 9 | | 11 | 1 | | 4 | | 8 | 10 | | 2 | 5 | 6 | | | | |
| 7R | 18 | LOVELLS ATHLETIC | W | 5-0 | 4-0 | 1700 | Astbury, Bullock, Travis (3) | | | 3 | | | | 7 | | 9 | | 11 | 1 | | 4 | | 8 | 10 | | 2 | 5 | 6 | | | | |
| SF | Apr 1 | Connahs Quay Nomads * | W | 5-0 | 3-0 | 5218 | Morement(2,1 pen),Deakin,Hilton,Travis | | 8 | 3 | | | | | | 9 | 7 | 11 | 1 | | 4 | | | 10 | 2 | | 5 | 6 | | | | |
| F | 27 | Rhyl @ | L | 1-2 | 1-2 | 8539 | Travis | 1 | 8 | 3 | | | | | | 9 | 7 | 11 | | 2 | 4 | | | 10 | 6 | | 5 | | | | | |

* Played at Wrexham

@ Played at Bangor City

### Final League Table

| | | Pl. | Home W | Home D | Home L | Home F | Home A | Away W | Away D | Away L | Away F | Away A | F. | A. | Pts |
|---|---|---|---|---|---|---|---|---|---|---|---|---|---|---|---|
| 1 | Oldham Athletic | 46 | 15 | 4 | 4 | 48 | 21 | 7 | 11 | 5 | 29 | 24 | 77 | 45 | 59 |
| 2 | Port Vale | 46 | 13 | 9 | 1 | 41 | 10 | 7 | 9 | 7 | 26 | 25 | 67 | 35 | 58 |
| 3 | Wrexham | 46 | 18 | 3 | 2 | 59 | 24 | 6 | 5 | 12 | 27 | 42 | 86 | 66 | 56 |
| 4 | York City | 46 | 14 | 5 | 4 | 35 | 16 | 6 | 8 | 9 | 25 | 29 | 60 | 45 | 53 |
| 5 | Grimsby Town | 46 | 15 | 5 | 3 | 47 | 19 | 6 | 5 | 12 | 28 | 40 | 75 | 59 | 52 |
| 6 | Southport | 46 | 16 | 4 | 3 | 42 | 18 | 4 | 7 | 12 | 21 | 42 | 63 | 60 | 51 |
| 7 | Bradford Park Ave. | 46 | 10 | 8 | 5 | 37 | 23 | 9 | 4 | 10 | 38 | 38 | 75 | 61 | 50 |
| 8 | Gateshead | 46 | 13 | 6 | 4 | 51 | 24 | 4 | 9 | 10 | 25 | 36 | 76 | 60 | 49 |
| 9 | Carlisle United | 46 | 13 | 7 | 3 | 57 | 24 | 5 | 6 | 12 | 25 | 44 | 82 | 68 | 49 |
| 10 | Crewe Alexandra | 46 | 13 | 5 | 5 | 46 | 28 | 7 | 3 | 13 | 24 | 40 | 70 | 68 | 48 |
| 11 | Stockport County | 46 | 13 | 8 | 2 | 61 | 26 | 4 | 5 | 14 | 21 | 43 | 82 | 69 | 47 |
| 12 | Tranmere Rovers | 46 | 16 | 4 | 3 | 45 | 16 | 5 | 1 | 17 | 20 | 47 | 65 | 63 | 47 |
| 13 | Chesterfield | 46 | 13 | 6 | 4 | 40 | 23 | 5 | 5 | 13 | 25 | 40 | 65 | 63 | 47 |
| 14 | Halifax Town | 46 | 13 | 5 | 5 | 47 | 31 | 3 | 10 | 10 | 21 | 37 | 68 | 68 | 47 |
| 15 | Scunthorpe United | 46 | 10 | 6 | 7 | 38 | 21 | 6 | 8 | 9 | 24 | 35 | 62 | 56 | 46 |
| 16 | Bradford City | 46 | 14 | 7 | 2 | 54 | 29 | 0 | 11 | 12 | 21 | 51 | 75 | 80 | 46 |
| 17 | Hartlepools United | 46 | 14 | 6 | 3 | 39 | 16 | 2 | 8 | 13 | 18 | 45 | 57 | 61 | 46 |
| 18 | Mansfield Town | 46 | 11 | 9 | 3 | 34 | 25 | 5 | 5 | 13 | 21 | 37 | 55 | 62 | 46 |
| 19 | Barrow | 46 | 15 | 6 | 2 | 48 | 20 | 1 | 6 | 16 | 18 | 51 | 66 | 71 | 44 |
| ***20*** | ***Chester*** | ***46*** | ***10*** | ***7*** | ***6*** | ***39*** | ***27*** | ***1*** | ***8*** | ***14*** | ***25*** | ***58*** | ***64*** | ***85*** | ***37*** |
| 21 | Darlington | 46 | 13 | 4 | 6 | 33 | 27 | 1 | 2 | 20 | 25 | 69 | 58 | 96 | 34 |
| 22 | Rochdale | 46 | 12 | 5 | 6 | 41 | 27 | 2 | 0 | 21 | 21 | 56 | 62 | 83 | 33 |
| 23 | Workington | 46 | 9 | 5 | 9 | 40 | 33 | 2 | 5 | 16 | 15 | 58 | 55 | 91 | 32 |
| 24 | Accrington Stanley | 46 | 7 | 9 | 7 | 25 | 29 | 1 | 2 | 20 | 14 | 60 | 39 | 89 | 27 |

# SEASON 1953-54

## FOOTBALL LEAGUE DIVISION 3 (NORTH)

| | Date | Opposition | | FT | HT | Att. | Goalscorers | Jones R. | Hughes R. | Gill R. | Astbury T. | Lee E. | Hilton J. | Thomas J. | Williams R. | Travis D. | Sutcliffe F. | Windle W. | Molyneux J. | Whitlock P. | Fletcher K. | Pye W. | Coffin G. | Rolfe J. | Smith H. | Morris S. | Morrey B. | Basford J. | Bullock N. | Betteridge R. | Brandon K. |
|---|---|---|---|---|---|---|---|---|---|---|---|---|---|---|---|---|---|---|---|---|---|---|---|---|---|---|---|---|---|---|---|
| 1 | Aug 22 | HARTLEPOOLS UNITED | D | 1-1 | 0-1 | 6695 | Windle | 1 | 2 | 3 | 4 | 5 | 6 | 7 | 8 | 9 | 10 | 11 | | | | | | | | | | | | | |
| 2 | 26 | BARNSLEY | D | 1-1 | 0-0 | 7117 | Windle | 1 | | 3 | 4 | 5 | | 7 | 8 | 9 | 10 | 11 | 2 | 6 | | | | | | | | | | | |
| 3 | 29 | Gateshead | L | 1-2 | 1-0 | 8013 | Travis | 1 | 4 | 3 | | 5 | 10 | 7 | 8 | 9 | | 11 | | 6 | 2 | | | | | | | | | | |
| 4 | Sep 2 | Barnsley | L | 0-3 | 0-2 | 9969 | | 1 | 4 | 3 | | 5 | 10 | 7 | | 9 | | 11 | | 6 | 2 | 8 | | | | | | | | | |
| 5 | 5 | WORKINGTON | W | 3-0 | 0-0 | 5790 | Coffin (2 pens), Pye | 1 | 2 | 3 | | 5 | 10 | | | 9 | | 11 | | 6 | | 8 | 4 | 7 | | | | | | | |
| 6 | 9 | Darlington | L | 0-1 | 0-0 | 4875 | | 1 | 2 | 3 | | 5 | 8 | | | 10 | 6 | 11 | | 4 | | | 9 | 7 | | | | | | | |
| 7 | 12 | Scunthorpe United | L | 0-1 | 0-0 | 10234 | | 1 | 2 | 3 | | 5 | 4 | 7 | | 10 | 6 | 11 | | | | | 9 | | 8 | | | | | | |
| 8 | 16 | DARLINGTON | D | 2-2 | 0-1 | 3999 | Thomas, Travis | 1 | 2 | 3 | | 5 | 4 | 7 | | 10 | 6 | 11 | | | | 8 | 9 | | | | | | | | |
| 9 | 19 | YORK CITY | W | 3-1 | 0-0 | 5571 | Travis, Smith, Windle | 1 | 2 | 3 | | 5 | 4 | 7 | | 9 | 6 | 11 | | | | | 8 | | 10 | | | | | | |
| 10 | 23 | BRADFORD P. A. | L | 2-3 | 1-2 | 4906 | Coffin (2, 1 pen) | 1 | 2 | 3 | | 5 | 4 | 7 | | 9 | 6 | 11 | | | | | 8 | | 10 | | | | | | |
| 11 | 26 | Southport | W | 1-0 | 1-0 | 5770 | Pye | 1 | 2 | 3 | | 5 | | 7 | | 9 | 6 | 11 | | | | 8 | 10 | | | 4 | | | | | |
| 12 | 30 | Bradford P. A. | L | 0-5 | 0-2 | 5333 | | 1 | 2 | 3 | | 5 | | 7 | | 9 | 6 | 11 | | 8 | | | 10 | | | 4 | | | | | |
| 13 | Oct 3 | WREXHAM | W | 2-1 | 0-1 | 14627 | Thomas, Travis | 1 | 2 | 3 | | 5 | | 7 | | 9 | 10 | 11 | | 6 | | | 8 | | | 4 | | | | | |
| 14 | 10 | Barrow | L | 1-2 | 0-2 | 6258 | Thomas | 1 | 2 | 3 | | 5 | | 7 | | 9 | 10 | 11 | | 6 | | | 8 | | | 4 | | | | | |
| 15 | 17 | BRADFORD CITY | W | 3-0 | 1-0 | 6150 | Thomas, Coffin (pen), Travis | 1 | 2 | 3 | | 5 | | 7 | | 9 | 10 | 11 | | 6 | | | 8 | | | 4 | | | | | |
| 16 | 24 | Chesterfield | L | 0-4 | 0-1 | 8229 | | 1 | 2 | 3 | | 5 | | 7 | | 9 | 11 | | | 6 | | 8 | 10 | | | 4 | | | | | |
| 17 | 31 | TRANMERE ROVERS | L | 1-2 | 0-1 | 6824 | Hilton | 1 | 2 | 3 | | 5 | 10 | 7 | | 9 | 11 | | | 6 | | | 8 | | | 4 | | | | | |
| 18 | Nov 7 | Halifax Town | D | 1-1 | 0-1 | 3297 | Windle | 1 | 2 | 3 | 4 | 5 | 8 | 7 | | 10 | | 11 | 9 | 6 | | | | | | | | | | | |
| 19 | 14 | CARLISLE UNITED | L | 0-1 | 0-0 | 5104 | | 1 | 2 | 3 | 4 | 5 | 8 | 7 | | 9 | 10 | 11 | | 6 | | | | | | | | | | | |
| 20 | 28 | GRIMSBY TOWN | D | 1-1 | 1-0 | 5327 | Molyneux | 1 | 2 | 3 | 4 | 5 | | 7 | | 10 | 8 | 11 | 9 | 6 | | | | | | | | | | | |
| 21 | Dec 5 | Stockport County | L | 0-5 | 0-3 | 8252 | | 1 | 2 | 3 | 4 | 5 | | 7 | | 9 | 8 | 11 | | 6 | | | | | 10 | | | | | | |
| 22 | 12 | ROCHDALE | W | 2-0 | 0-0 | 3578 | Thomas, Travis | 1 | 2 | 3 | 4 | 5 | | 7 | | 9 | 8 | 11 | | 6 | | | | | 10 | | | | | | |
| 23 | 19 | Hartlepools United | L | 0-2 | 0-1 | 5481 | | 1 | | 3 | 8 | 5 | | 7 | | 10 | 6 | | | 4 | 2 | | | 9 | | | 11 | | | | |
| 24 | 25 | Port Vale | L | 0-1 | 0-0 | 15322 | | 1 | 4 | 3 | | 5 | | | | 10 | | 11 | 2 | 6 | | | 8 | 9 | | | 7 | | | | |
| 25 | 26 | PORT VALE | L | 0-1 | 0-0 | 10979 | | 1 | 4 | 3 | | 5 | | | | 10 | | 11 | 2 | 6 | | | 8 | 9 | | | 7 | | | | |
| 26 | 28 | Rochdale | L | 0-4 | 0-2 | 7226 | | 1 | 4 | 3 | 6 | 5 | | 7 | | 10 | | 11 | 2 | | | | | 9 | | | 8 | | | | |
| 27 | Jan 2 | GATESHEAD | W | 5-0 | 2-0 | 4197 | Travis (3), Rolfe, Morrey | 1 | 4 | 3 | | 5 | | | | 10 | 6 | 11 | | | 2 | | | 9 | 8 | | 7 | | | | |
| 28 | 9 | Mansfield Town | L | 1-2 | 1-1 | 6572 | Morrey | 1 | 4 | 3 | | 5 | | | | 10 | 6 | 11 | | | 2 | | | 9 | 8 | | 7 | | | | |
| 29 | 16 | Workington | L | 0-2 | 0-1 | 7212 | | 1 | | 4 | | 5 | | | | 10 | 6 | 11 | 2 | | 3 | | | 9 | 8 | | 7 | | | | |
| 30 | 23 | SCUNTHORPE UNITED | D | 0-0 | 0-0 | 5180 | | 1 | | 3 | | 5 | | | | | 6 | 11 | | | 2 | | | 9 | 8 | 4 | 7 | 10 | | | |
| 31 | Feb 6 | York City | L | 1-2 | 0-1 | 3960 | Morrey (pen) | 1 | | 3 | | 5 | | 7 | | 9 | | | | 6 | 2 | | 8 | | | 4 | 11 | 10 | | | |
| 32 | 13 | SOUTHPORT | W | 1-0 | 0-0 | 4802 | Morrey | 1 | | 3 | | 5 | | 7 | | 9 | | | | 6 | 2 | | 8 | | 10 | 4 | 11 | | | | |
| 33 | 20 | Wrexham | L | 1-2 | 0-1 | 10225 | Basford | 1 | | 3 | | 5 | | 7 | | | | | 9 | 6 | 2 | | | | | 4 | 11 | 8 | 10 | | |
| 34 | 27 | BARROW | D | 1-1 | 1-0 | 3023 | Hilton | 1 | 4 | 3 | | 5 | 9 | 7 | | 10 | 6 | | 2 | | | | | | | | 11 | 8 | | | |
| 35 | Mar 6 | Bradford City | L | 0-1 | 0-1 | 10971 | | 1 | 4 | 3 | | 5 | 9 | 7 | | 10 | 6 | | 2 | | | | | | | | 11 | | | 8 | |
| 36 | 13 | CHESTERFIELD | D | 2-2 | 1-0 | 4404 | Hilton, Lee | 1 | 4 | 3 | | 5 | 9 | 7 | | 10 | 6 | | 2 | | | | | | | | 11 | | | 8 | |
| 37 | 20 | Tranmere Rovers | L | 1-2 | 0-0 | 6773 | Coffin | 1 | 4 | 3 | | 5 | 9 | 7 | | 10 | 6 | | 2 | | | | 8 | | | | 11 | | | | |
| 38 | 24 | MANSFIELD TOWN | L | 0-2 | 0-0 | 1667 | | 1 | 4 | 3 | | 5 | 9 | | | 10 | 6 | 11 | 2 | | | | 8 | | | | 7 | | | | |
| 39 | 27 | HALIFAX TOWN | W | 3-1 | 1-0 | 3207 | Morrey, Travis, Windle | 1 | 4 | 3 | 6 | 5 | | | | 10 | | 11 | | | 2 | | | | | | 7 | 9 | | 8 | |
| 40 | Apr 3 | Carlisle United | D | 1-1 | 1-1 | 2329 | Travis | 1 | 4 | 3 | 6 | 5 | | | | 10 | | 11 | | | 2 | | | 7 | | | | 9 | | 8 | |
| 41 | 10 | ACCRINGTON STANLEY | W | 3-0 | 2-0 | 4031 | Rolfe (2), Windle | 1 | 4 | 3 | 6 | 5 | 10 | | | | | 11 | | | 2 | | | 7 | | | | 9 | | 8 | |
| 42 | 16 | Crewe Alex. | L | 0-1 | 0-1 | 6287 | | 1 | 4 | 3 | 6 | 5 | | | | 10 | | 11 | | | 2 | | | 7 | | | | 9 | | 8 | |
| 43 | 17 | Grimsby Town | D | 0-0 | 0-0 | 7330 | | 1 | 4 | 3 | 6 | 5 | | | | 10 | | 11 | | | 2 | | | 7 | | | | 9 | | 8 | |
| 44 | 19 | CREWE ALEX. | W | 2-0 | 1-0 | 5846 | Betteridge, Travis | 1 | 4 | 3 | 6 | 5 | | | | 10 | | 11 | | | 2 | | | 7 | | | | 9 | | 8 | |
| 45 | 24 | STOCKPORT COUNTY | L | 1-2 | 1-1 | 3545 | Coffin | 1 | 4 | 3 | 6 | 5 | 8 | | | 10 | | | 2 | | | | 9 | 7 | | | | | | | 11 |
| 46 | 28 | Accrington Stanley | L | 0-1 | 0-1 | 4687 | | 1 | 4 | 3 | | 5 | 8 | | | 10 | | 11 | 2 | 6 | | | 9 | 7 | | | | | | | |
| | | | | | | | Apps. | 46 | 39 | 46 | 16 | 46 | 20 | 29 | 3 | 43 | 28 | 35 | 15 | 23 | 16 | 5 | 21 | 17 | 10 | 11 | 17 | 10 | 1 | 8 | 1 |
| | | | | | | | Goals | | | | | 1 | 3 | 5 | | 12 | | 6 | 1 | | | 2 | 7 | 3 | 1 | | 5 | 1 | | 1 | |

## F.A. CUP

| | Date | Opposition | | FT | HT | Att. | Goalscorers | Jones R. | Hughes R. | Gill R. | Astbury T. | Lee E. | Hilton J. | Thomas J. | Williams R. | Travis D. | Sutcliffe F. | Windle W. | Molyneux J. | Whitlock P. | Fletcher K. | Pye W. | Coffin G. | Rolfe J. | Smith H. | Morris S. | Morrey B. | Basford J. | Bullock N. | Betteridge R. | Brandon K. |
|---|---|---|---|---|---|---|---|---|---|---|---|---|---|---|---|---|---|---|---|---|---|---|---|---|---|---|---|---|---|---|---|
| 1R | Nov 21 | Stockport County | L | 2-4 | 1-3 | 12363 | Molyneux, Windle | 1 | 2 | 3 | 4 | 5 | 8 | 7 | | 10 | | 11 | 9 | 6 | | | | | | | | | | | |

## WELSH CUP

| | Date | Opposition | | FT | HT | Att. | Goalscorers | Jones R. | Hughes R. | Gill R. | Astbury T. | Lee E. | Hilton J. | Thomas J. | Williams R. | Travis D. | Sutcliffe F. | Windle W. | Molyneux J. | Whitlock P. | Fletcher K. | Pye W. | Coffin G. | Rolfe J. | Smith H. | Morris S. | Morrey B. | Basford J. | Bullock N. | Betteridge R. | Brandon K. |
|---|---|---|---|---|---|---|---|---|---|---|---|---|---|---|---|---|---|---|---|---|---|---|---|---|---|---|---|---|---|---|---|
| 5R | Jan 13 | BRYMBO STEELWORKS | W | 6-1 | 1-1 | 766 | Rolfe, Morrey(pen), Morris, Smith, Fletcher, Travis | 1 | 4 | 3 | | | | | | 10 | 6 | 11 | | | 2 | | | 9 | 8 | 5 | 7 | | | | |
| 6R | Mar 3 | WREXHAM | W | 1-0 | 0-0 | 2133 | Travis | 1 | 4 | 3 | | 5 | 9 | 7 | | 10 | 6 | | 2 | | | | | | | | 11 | 8 | | | |
| SF | 17 | Newport County * | D | 2-2 | 1-2 | 7920 | Travis (2) | 1 | 4 | 3 | | 5 | 9 | 7 | | 10 | 6 | | 2 | | | | 8 | | | | 11 | | | | |
| SFr | Apr 5 | Newport County @ | W | 2-0 | 1-0 | 3000 | Basford, Hilton | 1 | 4 | 3 | 6 | 5 | 8 | | | | 10 | 11 | | | 2 | | | 7 | | | | 9 | | | |
| F | 21 | Flint Town United @ | L | 0-2 | 0-0 | 15584 | | 1 | 4 | 3 | 6 | 5 | | | | 10 | | 11 | | | 2 | | | 7 | | | | 9 | | 8 | |

* Played at Cardiff City
@ Played at Wrexham

Final League Table

| | | Pl. | Home W | Home D | Home L | Home F | Home A | Away W | Away D | Away L | Away F | Away A | F. | A. | Pts |
|---|---|---|---|---|---|---|---|---|---|---|---|---|---|---|---|
| 1 | Port Vale | 46 | 16 | 7 | 0 | 48 | 5 | 10 | 10 | 3 | 26 | 16 | 74 | 21 | 69 |
| 2 | Barnsley | 46 | 16 | 3 | 4 | 54 | 24 | 8 | 7 | 8 | 23 | 33 | 77 | 57 | 58 |
| 3 | Scunthorpe United | 46 | 14 | 7 | 2 | 49 | 24 | 7 | 8 | 8 | 28 | 32 | 77 | 56 | 57 |
| 4 | Gateshead | 46 | 15 | 4 | 4 | 49 | 22 | 6 | 9 | 8 | 25 | 33 | 74 | 55 | 55 |
| 5 | Bradford City | 46 | 15 | 6 | 2 | 40 | 14 | 7 | 3 | 13 | 20 | 41 | 60 | 55 | 53 |
| 6 | Chesterfield | 46 | 13 | 6 | 4 | 41 | 19 | 6 | 8 | 9 | 35 | 45 | 76 | 64 | 52 |
| 7 | Mansfield Town | 46 | 15 | 5 | 3 | 59 | 22 | 5 | 6 | 12 | 29 | 45 | 88 | 67 | 51 |
| 8 | Wrexham | 46 | 16 | 4 | 3 | 59 | 19 | 5 | 5 | 13 | 22 | 49 | 81 | 68 | 51 |
| 9 | Bradford Park Ave. | 46 | 13 | 6 | 4 | 57 | 31 | 5 | 8 | 10 | 20 | 37 | 77 | 68 | 50 |
| 10 | Stockport County | 46 | 14 | 6 | 3 | 57 | 20 | 4 | 5 | 14 | 20 | 47 | 77 | 67 | 47 |
| 11 | Southport | 46 | 12 | 5 | 6 | 41 | 26 | 5 | 7 | 11 | 22 | 34 | 63 | 60 | 46 |
| 12 | Barrow | 46 | 12 | 7 | 4 | 46 | 26 | 4 | 5 | 14 | 26 | 45 | 72 | 71 | 44 |
| 13 | Carlisle United | 46 | 10 | 8 | 5 | 53 | 27 | 4 | 7 | 12 | 30 | 44 | 83 | 71 | 43 |
| 14 | Tranmere Rovers | 46 | 11 | 4 | 8 | 40 | 34 | 7 | 3 | 13 | 19 | 36 | 59 | 70 | 43 |
| 15 | Accrington Stanley | 46 | 12 | 7 | 4 | 41 | 22 | 4 | 3 | 16 | 25 | 52 | 66 | 74 | 42 |
| 16 | Crewe Alexandra | 46 | 9 | 8 | 6 | 30 | 26 | 5 | 5 | 13 | 19 | 41 | 49 | 67 | 41 |
| 17 | Grimsby Town | 46 | 14 | 5 | 4 | 31 | 15 | 2 | 4 | 17 | 20 | 62 | 51 | 77 | 41 |
| 18 | Hartlepools United | 46 | 10 | 8 | 5 | 40 | 21 | 3 | 6 | 14 | 19 | 44 | 59 | 65 | 40 |
| 19 | Rochdale | 46 | 12 | 5 | 6 | 40 | 20 | 3 | 5 | 15 | 19 | 57 | 59 | 77 | 40 |
| 20 | Workington | 46 | 10 | 9 | 4 | 36 | 22 | 3 | 5 | 15 | 23 | 58 | 59 | 80 | 40 |
| 21 | Darlington | 46 | 11 | 3 | 9 | 31 | 27 | 1 | 11 | 11 | 19 | 44 | 50 | 71 | 38 |
| 22 | York City | 46 | 8 | 7 | 8 | 39 | 32 | 4 | 6 | 13 | 25 | 54 | 64 | 86 | 37 |
| 23 | Halifax Town | 46 | 9 | 6 | 8 | 26 | 21 | 3 | 4 | 16 | 18 | 52 | 44 | 73 | 34 |
| ***24*** | ***Chester*** | ***46*** | ***10*** | ***7*** | ***6*** | ***39*** | ***22*** | ***1*** | ***3*** | ***19*** | ***9*** | ***45*** | ***48*** | ***67*** | ***32*** |

**1953/54 Season:**
(Back) Thomas, Molyneux, Jones, Lee, Hughes, Travis.
(Front) Morrey, Rolfe, Gill, Windle, Astbury.

**1954/55 Season**:
(Back) Collins (Trainer), Molyneux, H Wright, Law, Fletcher, Jones, R Wright, Brandon, Gill, Whitlock, Lee, Page (Manager)..
(Front) Bullock, Rolfe, Smith, Hughes, Morris, Morrey, Windle..

# SEASON 1954-55

## FOOTBALL LEAGUE DIVISION 3 (NORTH)

| | Date | Opposition | | FT | HT | Att. | Goalscorers | Jones R. | Molyneux J. | Fletcher K. | Morris S. | Lee E. | Astbury T. | Hughes R. | Halstead R. | Gill R. | Wright H. | Windle W. | Bullock N. | Coffin G. | Rolfe J. | Wright R. | Smith H. | Morrey B. | Brandon K. | Hillier J. | Whitlock P. | Sutcliffe F. | Pye W. | Blears B. | Mayers A. |
|---|---|---|---|---|---|---|---|---|---|---|---|---|---|---|---|---|---|---|---|---|---|---|---|---|---|---|---|---|---|---|---|
| 1 | Aug 21 | Tranmere Rovers | D | 1-1 | 1-0 | 10244 | Hughes | 1 | 2 | 3 | 4 | 5 | 6 | 7 | 8 | 9 | 10 | 11 | | | | | | | | | | | | | |
| 2 | 25 | WREXHAM | W | 1-0 | 1-0 | 12044 | Capper (og) | 1 | 2 | 3 | 4 | 5 | 6 | 7 | 8 | 9 | 10 | 11 | | | | | | | | | | | | | |
| 3 | 28 | STOCKPORT COUNTY | W | 1-0 | 1-0 | 7431 | H Wright | 1 | 2 | 3 | 4 | 5 | | 7 | 8 | 9 | 10 | 11 | 6 | | | | | | | | | | | | |
| 4 | Sep 1 | Wrexham | L | 1-2 | 0-2 | 15495 | Halstead | 1 | 2 | 3 | 4 | 5 | | 7 | 8 | | 10 | 11 | 6 | 9 | | | | | | | | | | | |
| 5 | 4 | Hartlepools United | L | 1-3 | 1-1 | 7909 | Windle | 1 | 2 | 3 | | 5 | 4 | 7 | 8 | 9 | 10 | 11 | 6 | | | | | | | | | | | | |
| 6 | 8 | Grimsby Town | L | 1-3 | 1-2 | 10128 | Halstead | 1 | 2 | 3 | | | 4 | 7 | 8 | 9 | 10 | 11 | 6 | 5 | | | | | | | | | | | |
| 7 | 11 | GATESHEAD | L | 1-2 | 0-0 | 5801 | Gill | 1 | 2 | 3 | | | 4 | 7 | 8 | 9 | 10 | 11 | 6 | 5 | | | | | | | | | | | |
| 8 | 15 | GRIMSBY TOWN | W | 1-0 | 1-0 | 5133 | Hughes | 1 | 2 | | | | 4 | 9 | 8 | 3 | 10 | 11 | 6 | 5 | 7 | | | | | | | | | | |
| 9 | 18 | Darlington | L | 1-4 | 1-4 | 10446 | H Wright | | 2 | | | | 4 | 9 | 8 | 3 | 10 | 11 | 6 | 5 | 7 | 1 | | | | | | | | | |
| 10 | 21 | Carlisle United | W | 2-1 | 2-1 | 5607 | Hughes (2) | | 2 | | | 5 | | 9 | 8 | 3 | 10 | 11 | 6 | | 7 | 1 | 4 | | | | | | | | |
| 11 | 25 | CHESTERFIELD | W | 1-0 | 0-0 | 6735 | Halstead | 1 | 2 | | | 5 | | 9 | 8 | 3 | 10 | | 6 | | 7 | | 4 | 11 | | | | | | | |
| 12 | 29 | CARLISLE UNITED | L | 1-2 | 0-0 | 5354 | Hughes | | 2 | | | 5 | | 9 | 8 | 3 | 10 | | 6 | | 7 | 1 | 4 | 11 | | | | | | | |
| 13 | Oct 2 | Crewe Alex. | W | 3-1 | 1-0 | 7159 | Hughes (3) | | 2 | | | 5 | | 9 | 8 | 3 | 10 | | 6 | | 7 | 1 | 4 | | 11 | | | | | | |
| 14 | 9 | ACCRINGTON STANLEY | D | 1-1 | 0-0 | 8670 | Brandon | | 2 | | | 5 | | 9 | 8 | 3 | 10 | | 6 | | 7 | 1 | 4 | | 11 | | | | | | |
| 15 | 16 | Mansfield Town | L | 1-2 | 0-2 | 9464 | H Wright | | 2 | | | 5 | | 9 | 8 | 3 | 10 | | 6 | | 7 | 1 | 4 | | 11 | | | | | | |
| 16 | 23 | WORKINGTON | L | 0-2 | 0-2 | 6170 | | | 2 | | | 5 | | 9 | 8 | 3 | 10 | | 6 | | 7 | 1 | 4 | | 11 | | | | | | |
| 17 | 30 | Barrow | L | 0-2 | 0-2 | 4620 | | | 2 | | | 5 | 4 | 9 | | 3 | 10 | | 6 | 8 | 7 | 1 | | | 11 | | | | | | |
| 18 | Nov 13 | York City | L | 0-5 | 0-3 | 6824 | | | 2 | | | 5 | | 9 | 8 | 3 | 10 | | | | 7 | | | | 11 | 1 | 4 | 6 | | | |
| 19 | 27 | Oldham Athletic | L | 1-2 | 1-2 | 7593 | Halstead | | 2 | | 4 | 5 | 6 | 9 | 8 | 3 | 10 | 11 | | | | | | 7 | | 1 | | | | | |
| 20 | Dec 4 | BRADFORD CITY | W | 1-0 | 1-0 | 3285 | Windle | | 2 | | 4 | 5 | 6 | 9 | 8 | 3 | 10 | 11 | | | | | | 7 | | 1 | | | | | |
| 21 | 11 | HALIFAX TOWN | L | 1-3 | 0-0 | 3712 | H Wright | | 2 | | 4 | 5 | 6 | 9 | 8 | 3 | 10 | 11 | | | | | | 7 | | 1 | | | | | |
| 22 | 18 | TRANMERE ROVERS | L | 0-1 | 0-0 | 3532 | | 1 | 2 | | 4 | 5 | 10 | 9 | 8 | 3 | | 11 | 6 | | | | | 7 | | | | | | | |
| 23 | 25 | BRADFORD P. A. | W | 2-0 | 1-0 | 3203 | Bullock (2) | 1 | 2 | | 4 | 5 | 6 | 8 | | 3 | | 11 | 10 | 9 | 7 | | | | | | | | | | |
| 24 | 27 | Bradford P. A. | L | 0-3 | 0-1 | 8454 | | 1 | 2 | | 4 | 5 | 6 | 8 | | 3 | | 11 | 10 | 9 | 7 | | | | | | | | | | |
| 25 | Jan 1 | Stockport County | L | 0-3 | 0-2 | 8497 | | 1 | 2 | | 4 | 5 | 6 | 8 | | 3 | | 11 | 10 | 9 | 7 | | | | | | | | | | |
| 26 | 8 | SCUNTHORPE UNITED | L | 2-4 | 0-1 | 4083 | Pye, Rolfe | | 9 | 2 | 4 | 5 | | | | 3 | | 11 | 10 | | 7 | 1 | | | | | 6 | | 8 | | |
| 27 | 15 | HARTLEPOOLS UNITED | W | 1-0 | 0-0 | 1723 | Pye | | 2 | | | 5 | | 4 | | 3 | | | | 9 | 7 | | 10 | | 11 | 1 | 6 | | 8 | | |
| 28 | 29 | Scunthorpe United | D | 1-1 | 1-0 | 8328 | Smith | 1 | 2 | | | 5 | | 4 | | 3 | | | | 9 | 7 | | 10 | | 11 | | 6 | | 8 | | |
| 29 | Feb 5 | DARLINGTON | L | 0-2 | 0-0 | 4419 | | 1 | 2 | | | 5 | | 4 | | 3 | | | 10 | 9 | 7 | | | | 11 | | 6 | | 8 | | |
| 30 | 12 | Chesterfield | L | 3-5 | 1-1 | 4674 | Pye, Coffin (2) | 1 | 2 | | | 5 | | 4 | | 3 | | | 10 | 9 | 7 | | | | 11 | | 6 | | 8 | | |
| 31 | 19 | CREWE ALEX. | W | 3-1 | 0-1 | 3526 | Pye, Coffin, Hughes | 1 | 2 | | | 5 | | 4 | | 3 | | | | 9 | 7 | | 10 | | 11 | | 6 | | 8 | | |
| 32 | 26 | Accrington Stanley | L | 0-3 | 0-0 | 7999 | | 1 | 2 | | 4 | 5 | | | | 3 | | | | 9 | 7 | | 10 | | 11 | | 6 | | 8 | | |
| 33 | Mar 5 | MANSFIELD TOWN | W | 1-0 | 0-0 | 4864 | Pye | 1 | 2 | | 4 | 5 | | | | 3 | | | | 9 | 7 | | 10 | | 11 | | 6 | | 8 | | |
| 34 | 12 | Workington | D | 1-1 | 1-0 | 6753 | Brandon | 1 | 2 | | 4 | 5 | | | | 3 | | | | 9 | 7 | | 10 | | 11 | | 6 | | 8 | | |
| 35 | 19 | BARROW | W | 3-1 | 1-0 | 4371 | Pye, Coffin, Brandon | 1 | 2 | | 4 | 5 | | 7 | | 3 | | | | 9 | | | 10 | | 11 | | 6 | | 8 | | |
| 36 | 26 | Southport | D | 1-1 | 1-1 | 1317 | Pye | 1 | 2 | | | 5 | | 4 | | 3 | | | | 9 | 7 | | 10 | | 11 | | 6 | | 8 | | |
| 37 | 30 | Gateshead | D | 0-0 | 0-0 | 887 | | 1 | 2 | | | 5 | | 4 | | 3 | | | | 9 | 7 | | 10 | | 11 | | 6 | | 8 | | |
| 38 | Apr 2 | YORK CITY | L | 1-2 | 1-1 | 6456 | Pye | 1 | 2 | | | 5 | | 4 | | 3 | | | | 9 | 7 | | 10 | | 11 | | 6 | | 8 | | |
| 39 | 8 | ROCHDALE | L | 1-2 | 0-1 | 7293 | Smith | 1 | 2 | | | 5 | | 4 | | 3 | | | | 9 | 7 | | 10 | | 11 | | 6 | | 8 | | |
| 40 | 9 | Halifax Town | L | 1-3 | 0-2 | 6980 | Gill | 1 | 2 | | | 5 | | 4 | | 3 | | | | 9 | 7 | | | 10 | 11 | | 6 | | 8 | | |
| 41 | 11 | Rochdale | L | 0-2 | 0-1 | 6466 | | 1 | 2 | | 5 | | 6 | 4 | | 3 | | | | 9 | 7 | | | 10 | 11 | | | | 8 | | |
| 42 | 16 | OLDHAM ATHLETIC | D | 0-0 | 0-0 | 5057 | | 1 | 2 | | 5 | | | 4 | | 3 | | | | 9 | 7 | | | 10 | 11 | | 6 | | 8 | | |
| 43 | 20 | SOUTHPORT | D | 0-0 | 0-0 | 4544 | | 1 | 2 | | 5 | | | 4 | | 3 | | | | 9 | 7 | | | 10 | 11 | | 6 | | 8 | | |
| 44 | 23 | Bradford City | D | 0-0 | 0-0 | 6798 | | 1 | 2 | | 5 | | | 4 | | 3 | | 11 | | 9 | 7 | | 8 | 10 | | | 6 | | | | |
| 45 | 30 | BARNSLEY | L | 0-2 | 0-1 | 6566 | | 1 | 2 | | 5 | | | 4 | | 3 | | 11 | | 9 | 7 | | 8 | 10 | | | 6 | | | | |
| 46 | May 4 | Barnsley | L | 2-4 | 1-2 | 10044 | Brandon, Morrey | | 2 | | 5 | 9 | | 4 | | 3 | | | | 8 | | | | 7 | 11 | 1 | 6 | | | 10 | |
| | | | | | | | Apps. | 31 | 46 | 8 | 22 | 37 | 16 | 42 | 21 | 45 | 21 | 20 | 22 | 29 | 33 | 9 | 20 | 13 | 24 | 6 | 21 | 1 | 18 | 1 | |
| | | | | | | | Goals | | | | | | | 9 | 4 | 2 | 4 | 2 | 2 | 4 | 1 | | 2 | 1 | 4 | | | | 8 | | |

Own goals 1

## F.A. CUP

| | Date | Opposition | | FT | HT | Att. | Goalscorers | Jones R. | Molyneux J. | Fletcher K. | Morris S. | Lee E. | Astbury T. | Hughes R. | Halstead R. | Gill R. | Wright H. | Windle W. | Bullock N. | Coffin G. | Rolfe J. | Wright R. | Smith H. | Morrey B. | Brandon K. | Hillier J. | Whitlock P. | Sutcliffe F. | Pye W. | Blears B. | Mayers A. |
|---|---|---|---|---|---|---|---|---|---|---|---|---|---|---|---|---|---|---|---|---|---|---|---|---|---|---|---|---|---|---|---|
| 1R | Nov 20 | Gateshead | L | 0-6 | 0-3 | 8643 | | | 2 | | 5 | 9 | | 8 | | 3 | | | 10 | | 7 | 1 | | | 11 | | 4 | 6 | | | |

## WELSH CUP

| | Date | Opposition | | FT | HT | Att. | Goalscorers | Jones R. | Molyneux J. | Fletcher K. | Morris S. | Lee E. | Astbury T. | Hughes R. | Halstead R. | Gill R. | Wright H. | Windle W. | Bullock N. | Coffin G. | Rolfe J. | Wright R. | Smith H. | Morrey B. | Brandon K. | Hillier J. | Whitlock P. | Sutcliffe F. | Pye W. | Blears B. | Mayers A. |
|---|---|---|---|---|---|---|---|---|---|---|---|---|---|---|---|---|---|---|---|---|---|---|---|---|---|---|---|---|---|---|---|
| 5R | Jan 13 | Caernarvon Town | D | 1-1 | 0-0 | | Gill | | 9 | 2 | 5 | | | 4 | | 3 | | | | | 7 | 1 | 10 | | 11 | | 6 | | 8 | | |
| 5Rr | 26 | CAERNARVON TOWN | W | 9-1 | 5-1 | 1356 | Rolfe(2),Pye(2),Hughes,Coffin,Smith,Brandon(2) | | 2 | | | 5 | | 4 | | 3 | | | | 9 | 7 | | 10 | | 11 | 1 | 6 | | 8 | | |
| 6R | Feb 23 | FLINT TOWN UNITED | W | 3-0 | 3-0 | 3900 | Pye, Smith (2) | | 2 | | | 5 | | 4 | | 3 | | | | 9 | 7 | | 10 | | 11 | 1 | 6 | | 8 | | |
| SF | Apr 13 | Cardiff City * | W | 2-0 | 0-0 | 7951 | Coffin (2, 1 pen) | 1 | 2 | | 5 | | | 4 | | 3 | | | | 9 | 7 | | | 10 | 11 | | 6 | | 8 | | |
| F | May 11 | Barry Town * | D | 1-1 | 1-0 | 6766 | Brandon | 1 | 2 | | 5 | | | 4 | | 3 | | | | 9 | | | | 10 | 11 | | 6 | | 8 | | 7 |
| Fr | 14 | Barry Town @ | L | 3-4 | 1-3 | 8450 | Pye, Molyneux, Brandon | 1 | 9 | 2 | 4 | 5 | | | | 3 | | | | | | | 10 | 7 | 11 | | 6 | | 8 | | |

* Played at Wrexham

@ Played at Cardiff City

### Final League Table

| | | Pl. | Home W | Home D | Home L | Home F | Home A | Away W | Away D | Away L | Away F | Away A | F. | A. | Pts |
|---|---|---|---|---|---|---|---|---|---|---|---|---|---|---|---|
| 1 | Barnsley | 46 | 18 | 3 | 2 | 51 | 17 | 12 | 2 | 9 | 35 | 29 | 86 | 46 | 65 |
| 2 | Accrington Stanley | 46 | 18 | 2 | 3 | 65 | 32 | 7 | 9 | 7 | 31 | 35 | 96 | 67 | 61 |
| 3 | Scunthorpe United | 46 | 14 | 6 | 3 | 45 | 18 | 9 | 6 | 8 | 36 | 35 | 81 | 53 | 58 |
| 4 | York City | 46 | 13 | 5 | 5 | 43 | 27 | 11 | 5 | 7 | 49 | 36 | 92 | 63 | 58 |
| 5 | Hartlepools United | 46 | 16 | 3 | 4 | 39 | 20 | 9 | 2 | 12 | 25 | 29 | 64 | 49 | 55 |
| 6 | Chesterfield | 46 | 17 | 1 | 5 | 54 | 33 | 7 | 5 | 11 | 27 | 37 | 81 | 70 | 54 |
| 7 | Gateshead | 46 | 11 | 7 | 5 | 38 | 26 | 9 | 5 | 9 | 27 | 43 | 65 | 69 | 52 |
| 8 | Workington | 46 | 11 | 7 | 5 | 39 | 23 | 7 | 7 | 9 | 29 | 32 | 68 | 55 | 50 |
| 9 | Stockport County | 46 | 13 | 4 | 6 | 50 | 27 | 5 | 8 | 10 | 34 | 43 | 84 | 70 | 48 |
| 10 | Oldham Athletic | 46 | 14 | 5 | 4 | 47 | 22 | 5 | 5 | 13 | 27 | 46 | 74 | 68 | 48 |
| 11 | Southport | 46 | 10 | 9 | 4 | 28 | 18 | 6 | 7 | 10 | 19 | 26 | 47 | 44 | 48 |
| 12 | Rochdale | 46 | 13 | 7 | 3 | 39 | 20 | 4 | 7 | 12 | 30 | 46 | 69 | 66 | 48 |
| 13 | Mansfield Town | 46 | 14 | 4 | 5 | 40 | 28 | 4 | 5 | 14 | 25 | 43 | 65 | 71 | 45 |
| 14 | Halifax Town | 46 | 9 | 9 | 5 | 41 | 27 | 6 | 4 | 13 | 22 | 40 | 63 | 67 | 43 |
| 15 | Darlington | 46 | 10 | 7 | 6 | 41 | 28 | 4 | 7 | 12 | 21 | 45 | 62 | 73 | 42 |
| 16 | Bradford Park Ave. | 46 | 11 | 7 | 5 | 29 | 21 | 4 | 4 | 15 | 27 | 49 | 56 | 70 | 41 |
| 17 | Barrow | 46 | 12 | 4 | 7 | 39 | 34 | 5 | 2 | 16 | 31 | 55 | 70 | 89 | 40 |
| 18 | Wrexham | 46 | 9 | 6 | 8 | 40 | 35 | 4 | 6 | 13 | 25 | 42 | 65 | 77 | 38 |
| 19 | Tranmere Rovers | 46 | 9 | 6 | 8 | 37 | 30 | 4 | 5 | 14 | 18 | 40 | 55 | 70 | 37 |
| 20 | Carlisle United | 46 | 12 | 1 | 10 | 53 | 39 | 3 | 5 | 15 | 25 | 50 | 78 | 89 | 36 |
| 21 | Bradford City | 46 | 9 | 5 | 9 | 30 | 26 | 4 | 5 | 14 | 17 | 29 | 47 | 55 | 36 |
| 22 | Crewe Alexandra | 46 | 8 | 10 | 5 | 45 | 35 | 2 | 4 | 17 | 23 | 56 | 68 | 91 | 34 |
| 23 | Grimsby Town | 46 | 10 | 4 | 9 | 28 | 32 | 3 | 4 | 16 | 19 | 46 | 47 | 78 | 34 |
| ***24*** | ***Chester*** | ***46*** | ***10*** | ***3*** | ***10*** | ***23*** | ***25*** | ***2*** | ***6*** | ***15*** | ***21*** | ***52*** | ***44*** | ***77*** | ***33*** |

# SEASON 1955-56

## FOOTBALL LEAGUE DIVISION 3 (NORTH)

| | Date | Opposition | | FT | HT | Att. | Goalscorers |
|---|---|---|---|---|---|---|---|
| 1 | Aug 20 | TRANMERE ROVERS | D | 0-0 | 0-0 | 9784 | |
| 2 | 23 | Grimsby Town | L | 1-6 | 0-4 | 10873 | Lee (pen) |
| 3 | 27 | Southport | L | 0-1 | 0-0 | 4109 | |
| 4 | 31 | GRIMSBY TOWN | W | 2-0 | 1-0 | 6193 | Bullock, Haines |
| 5 | Sep 3 | GATESHEAD | W | 3-0 | 1-0 | 7900 | Allman (2), Collins |
| 6 | 7 | BRADFORD P. A. | D | 0-0 | 0-0 | 8801 | |
| 7 | 10 | Darlington | W | 1-0 | 0-0 | 8714 | Wayman |
| 8 | 12 | Bradford P. A. | D | 1-1 | 1-1 | 4081 | Allman |
| 9 | 17 | ACCRINGTON STANLEY | D | 1-1 | 1-1 | 10994 | Collins |
| 10 | 21 | Rochdale | L | 2-4 | 0-2 | 2936 | Jolley, Lee |
| 11 | 24 | Barrow | W | 2-1 | 0-1 | 6313 | Collins (2) |
| 12 | 28 | CARLISLE UNITED | D | 3-3 | 2-2 | 7916 | Collins (2), Allman |
| 13 | Oct 1 | WREXHAM | W | 2-1 | 0-1 | 15202 | Haines (2) |
| 14 | 8 | Bradford City | D | 1-1 | 1-0 | 12122 | Allman |
| 15 | 15 | MANSFIELD TOWN | W | 4-3 | 1-2 | 7709 | Collins (2), Allman, Haines |
| 16 | 22 | Oldham Athletic | L | 1-4 | 1-3 | 8240 | Allman |
| 17 | 29 | WORKINGTON | W | 1-0 | 0-0 | 7167 | Collins |
| 18 | Nov 5 | York City | L | 0-3 | 0-1 | 8176 | |
| 19 | 12 | DERBY COUNTY | L | 2-5 | 1-5 | 10182 | Collins, Allman |
| 20 | 26 | HARTLEPOOLS UNITED | L | 0-1 | 0-0 | 5876 | |
| 21 | Dec 3 | Stockport County | L | 1-2 | 1-1 | 5737 | Brandon |
| 22 | 17 | Tranmere Rovers | L | 0-4 | 0-1 | 4889 | |
| 23 | 24 | SOUTHPORT | L | 1-3 | 0-1 | 3531 | Haines |
| 24 | 26 | Chesterfield | L | 1-2 | 0-1 | 5815 | Hackett |
| 25 | 27 | CHESTERFIELD | W | 2-1 | 0-1 | 4331 | Hackett, Bullock |
| 26 | 31 | Gateshead | D | 1-1 | 1-1 | 3007 | Wayman |
| 27 | Jan 14 | DARLINGTON | W | 2-1 | 2-0 | 4509 | Bullock, Pye |
| 28 | 21 | Accrington Stanley | L | 0-4 | 0-1 | 6862 | |
| 29 | Feb 4 | BARROW | W | 1-0 | 0-0 | 3221 | Allman |
| 30 | 11 | Wrexham | D | 0-0 | 0-0 | 6673 | |
| 31 | 18 | BRADFORD CITY | D | 1-1 | 0-1 | 3829 | Hackett |
| 32 | 25 | Mansfield Town | L | 0-3 | 0-1 | 7693 | |
| 33 | Mar 3 | OLDHAM ATHLETIC | W | 3-2 | 1-1 | 4935 | Hackett, Haines, Whitlock |
| 34 | 10 | Workington | D | 0-0 | 0-0 | 5926 | |
| 35 | 17 | CREWE ALEX. | D | 0-0 | 0-0 | 6863 | |
| 36 | 24 | Derby County | L | 1-3 | 0-1 | 16378 | Bullock |
| 37 | 30 | HALIFAX TOWN | W | 1-0 | 0-0 | 5881 | Haines |
| 38 | 31 | YORK CITY | D | 2-2 | 2-0 | 6016 | Brandon, Collins |
| 39 | Apr 2 | Halifax Town | W | 1-0 | 0-0 | 4445 | Brandon |
| 40 | 7 | Hartlepools United | L | 1-3 | 0-0 | 6646 | Lee (pen) |
| 41 | 11 | Crewe Alex. | D | 0-0 | 0-0 | 3076 | |
| 42 | 14 | STOCKPORT COUNTY | L | 1-4 | 0-2 | 4425 | Allman |
| 43 | 21 | Scunthorpe United | L | 1-2 | 1-0 | 4452 | Allman |
| 44 | 24 | Carlisle United | L | 1-4 | 0-3 | 3872 | Haines |
| 45 | 28 | ROCHDALE | D | 0-0 | 0-0 | 4213 | |
| 46 | May 2 | SCUNTHORPE UNITED | L | 3-5 | 1-1 | 3253 | Jolley (2), Allman |

| | Jones R. | Hughes R. | Gill R. | Morris S. | Lee E. | Whitlock P. | Pye W. | Collins J. | Jolley C. | Haines J. | Brandon K. | Bullock N. | Smith H. | Wayman F. | Allman G. | Hackett B. | Griffiths K. | Fletcher K. | Griffiths R. | Roberts T. | Devine J. | Fields M. | Mayers A. | Blears B. | Tomley F. |
|---|---|---|---|---|---|---|---|---|---|---|---|---|---|---|---|---|---|---|---|---|---|---|---|---|---|
| 1 | 1 | 2 | 3 | 4 | 5 | 6 | 7 | 8 | 9 | 10 | 11 | | | | | | | | | | | | | | |
| 2 | 1 | 2 | 3 | 4 | 5 | | 7 | 8 | 9 | 10 | 11 | 6 | | | | | | | | | | | | | |
| 3 | 1 | 2 | 3 | | 5 | 6 | | 8 | 9 | 10 | | 11 | 4 | 7 | | | | | | | | | | | |
| 4 | 1 | 2 | 3 | | 5 | 6 | | 8 | | 10 | | 11 | 4 | 7 | 9 | | | | | | | | | | |
| 5 | 1 | 2 | 3 | | 5 | 6 | | 8 | | 10 | | 11 | 4 | 7 | 9 | | | | | | | | | | |
| 6 | 1 | 2 | 3 | | 5 | 6 | | 8 | | 10 | | 11 | 4 | 7 | 9 | | | | | | | | | | |
| 7 | 1 | 2 | 3 | | 5 | 6 | | 8 | | 10 | | 11 | 4 | 7 | 9 | | | | | | | | | | |
| 8 | 1 | 2 | 3 | | 5 | 6 | | 8 | | 10 | | 11 | 4 | 7 | 9 | | | | | | | | | | |
| 9 | 1 | 2 | 3 | | 5 | 6 | | 8 | | 10 | | 11 | 4 | | 9 | 7 | | | | | | | | | |
| 10 | 1 | 2 | 3 | | 5 | 6 | | 8 | 9 | 10 | | 11 | 4 | | | 7 | | | | | | | | | |
| 11 | 1 | 2 | 3 | | 5 | 6 | | 8 | | 10 | | 11 | 4 | 7 | 9 | | | | | | | | | | |
| 12 | | 2 | 3 | | 5 | 6 | | 8 | | 10 | | 11 | 4 | | 9 | 7 | 1 | | | | | | | | |
| 13 | 1 | 2 | 3 | | 5 | 6 | | 8 | | 10 | | 11 | 4 | 7 | 9 | | | | | | | | | | |
| 14 | 1 | 2 | 3 | | 5 | 6 | | 8 | | 10 | | 11 | 4 | 7 | 9 | | | | | | | | | | |
| 15 | 1 | 2 | 3 | | 5 | 6 | | 8 | | 10 | | 11 | 4 | 7 | 9 | | | | | | | | | | |
| 16 | 1 | 2 | 3 | | 5 | 6 | | 8 | | 10 | | 11 | 4 | 7 | 9 | | | | | | | | | | |
| 17 | | 2 | 3 | | 5 | 6 | | 8 | | 10 | | 11 | 4 | 7 | 9 | | 1 | | | | | | | | |
| 18 | | 2 | 3 | | 5 | 6 | | 8 | | 10 | | 11 | 4 | 7 | 9 | | 1 | | | | | | | | |
| 19 | | 2 | 3 | | 5 | 6 | | 8 | | 10 | 11 | | 4 | 7 | 9 | | 1 | | | | | | | | |
| 20 | 1 | | 3 | 4 | 5 | 6 | | 8 | | 10 | 11 | | | 7 | 9 | | | 2 | | | | | | | |
| 21 | 1 | 2 | 3 | | 5 | 6 | | 8 | | | 11 | | 4 | 10 | 9 | 7 | | | | | | | | | |
| 22 | 1 | 2 | 3 | | 5 | | | 8 | | 10 | 6 | 11 | 4 | 7 | 9 | | | | | | | | | | |
| 23 | 1 | 2 | 3 | 4 | 5 | 6 | | 8 | | 10 | | 11 | | 7 | 9 | | | | | | | | | | |
| 24 | | 2 | 3 | | 5 | | 8 | 4 | | 10 | | 11 | | 7 | | 9 | 1 | | 6 | | | | | | |
| 25 | | 2 | 3 | | 5 | | | 4 | | 10 | | 11 | | 7 | 8 | 9 | 1 | | 6 | | | | | | |
| 26 | 1 | 2 | 3 | | 5 | | | 4 | | 10 | | 11 | | 7 | 8 | 9 | | | 6 | | | | | | |
| 27 | 1 | 2 | 3 | 4 | 5 | | 10 | | | | | 11 | | 7 | 8 | 9 | | | 6 | | | | | | |
| 28 | 1 | 2 | 3 | 4 | 5 | | 10 | | | 8 | | 11 | | 7 | | 9 | | | 6 | | | | | | |
| 29 | 1 | 2 | 3 | | 5 | 6 | | 4 | | 10 | | 11 | | 7 | 8 | 9 | | | | | | | | | |
| 30 | 1 | 2 | 3 | | 5 | 6 | | 4 | | 10 | | 11 | | 7 | 8 | 9 | | | | | | | | | |
| 31 | 1 | 2 | 3 | | 5 | 6 | | 4 | | 10 | | 11 | | 7 | 8 | 9 | | | | | | | | | |
| 32 | 1 | 2 | 3 | | 5 | 6 | | 4 | | | | 11 | 10 | 7 | 8 | 9 | | | | | | | | | |
| 33 | 1 | 4 | 3 | | 5 | 6 | | 8 | | 10 | | 11 | | | 7 | 9 | | | | 2 | | | | | |
| 34 | 1 | 4 | 3 | | 5 | 6 | | 8 | | 10 | | 11 | | | 7 | 9 | | | | 2 | | | | | |
| 35 | 1 | 4 | 3 | | 5 | 6 | | 8 | | 10 | | 11 | | | 7 | 9 | | | | 2 | | | | | |
| 36 | 1 | 4 | 3 | | 5 | 6 | | 8 | | 10 | | 11 | | | 7 | 9 | | | | 2 | | | | | |
| 37 | 1 | 4 | 3 | | 5 | 6 | | 8 | 9 | 10 | | 11 | | | | | | 2 | | | 7 | | | | |
| 38 | 1 | 4 | 3 | | 5 | 6 | | 8 | 9 | 10 | 11 | | | | 7 | | | 2 | | | | | | | |
| 39 | 1 | 4 | 3 | | | 5 | | 8 | | 10 | 11 | | 6 | | 7 | | | 2 | | | | 9 | | | |
| 40 | 1 | | 3 | | 5 | 6 | | 8 | | 10 | 11 | | 4 | 9 | 7 | | | 2 | | | | | | | |
| 41 | 1 | 4 | 3 | | 5 | 6 | | 8 | | 10 | 11 | | | 7 | 9 | | | 2 | | | | | | | |
| 42 | 1 | 4 | 3 | | 5 | 6 | | 8 | | 10 | 11 | | | 7 | 9 | | | 2 | | | | | | | |
| 43 | 1 | | 3 | | 5 | | | 4 | | | 11 | | 8 | | 9 | | | 2 | 6 | | | 10 | 7 | | |
| 44 | 1 | 7 | 3 | | 5 | 6 | | 4 | | 10 | 11 | | 8 | | 9 | | | 2 | | | | | | | |
| 45 | 1 | 7 | 3 | | 5 | 6 | | 4 | | 8 | 11 | | | | 9 | | | 2 | | | | 10 | | | |
| 46 | 1 | 2 | | | | 6 | | | 9 | | | 11 | 8 | | 7 | | | | | 3 | | 10 | | 4 | 5 |
| Apps. | 40 | 43 | 45 | 6 | 44 | 38 | 5 | 43 | 7 | 41 | 14 | 34 | 25 | 30 | 39 | 17 | 6 | 10 | 6 | 5 | 1 | 4 | 1 | 1 | 1 |
| Goals | | | | | 3 | 1 | 1 | 11 | 3 | 8 | 3 | 4 | | 2 | 12 | 4 | | | | | | | | | |

## F.A. CUP

| | Date | Opposition | | FT | HT | Att. | Goalscorers |
|---|---|---|---|---|---|---|---|
| 1R | Nov 19 | Chesterfield | L | 0-1 | 0-0 | 9801 | |

| | Jones R. | Hughes R. | Gill R. | Morris S. | Lee E. | Whitlock P. | Pye W. | Collins J. | Jolley C. | Haines J. | Brandon K. | Bullock N. | Smith H. | Wayman F. | Allman G. | Hackett B. | Griffiths K. | Fletcher K. | Griffiths R. | Roberts T. | Devine J. | Fields M. | Mayers A. | Blears B. | Tomley F. |
|---|---|---|---|---|---|---|---|---|---|---|---|---|---|---|---|---|---|---|---|---|---|---|---|---|---|
| 1R | 1 | | 3 | 4 | 5 | 6 | | 8 | | 10 | 11 | | | 7 | 9 | | | 2 | | | | | | | |

## WELSH CUP

| | Date | Opposition | | FT | HT | Att. | Goalscorers |
|---|---|---|---|---|---|---|---|
| 5R | Jan 26 | Rhyl | W | 2-0 | 1-0 | | Hackett (2) |
| 6R | Mar 1 | Swansea Town | L | 0-1 | 0-0 | | |

| | Jones R. | Hughes R. | Gill R. | Morris S. | Lee E. | Whitlock P. | Pye W. | Collins J. | Jolley C. | Haines J. | Brandon K. | Bullock N. | Smith H. | Wayman F. | Allman G. | Hackett B. | Griffiths K. | Fletcher K. | Griffiths R. | Roberts T. | Devine J. | Fields M. | Mayers A. | Blears B. | Tomley F. |
|---|---|---|---|---|---|---|---|---|---|---|---|---|---|---|---|---|---|---|---|---|---|---|---|---|---|
| 5R | 1 | 2 | 3 | 4 | 5 | 6 | | | | 10 | | 11 | | 7 | 8 | 9 | | | | | | | | | |
| 6R | 1 | 2 | 3 | | 5 | 6 | | 4 | | 10 | | 11 | | 7 | 8 | 9 | | | | | | | | | |

## FRIENDLIES

| | Date | Opposition | | FT | HT | Att. | Goalscorers |
|---|---|---|---|---|---|---|---|
| 1 | Dec 10 | WREXHAM | L | 2-3 | 2-3 | 1650 | Allman, Lee (pen) |
| 2 | Jan 28 | HUDDERSFIELD TOWN | L | 1-6 | 1-2 | 5604 | Bullock |
| 3 | Apr 18 | SERVICES X1 * | W | 4-1 | 2-0 | | Gill, Bullock, Mitten, Smith |
| 4 | 30 | TRAUTMANNS X1 @ | D | 6-6 | 2-3 | 3796 | Lee (2), Smith (2), Whitlock, Hackett |

* Monty Wright Benefit

@ Geoff Coffin / Ray Gill Testimonial

### Final League Table

| | | Pl. | Home W | Home D | Home L | Home F | Home A | Away W | Away D | Away L | Away F | Away A | F. | A. | Pts |
|---|---|---|---|---|---|---|---|---|---|---|---|---|---|---|---|
| 1 | Grimsby Town | 46 | 20 | 1 | 2 | 54 | 10 | 11 | 5 | 7 | 22 | 19 | 76 | 29 | 68 |
| 2 | Derby County | 46 | 18 | 4 | 1 | 67 | 23 | 10 | 3 | 10 | 43 | 32 | 110 | 55 | 63 |
| 3 | Accrington Stanley | 46 | 17 | 4 | 2 | 61 | 19 | 8 | 5 | 10 | 31 | 38 | 92 | 57 | 59 |
| 4 | Hartlepools United | 46 | 18 | 2 | 3 | 47 | 15 | 8 | 3 | 12 | 34 | 45 | 81 | 60 | 57 |
| 5 | Southport | 46 | 12 | 9 | 2 | 39 | 18 | 11 | 2 | 10 | 27 | 35 | 66 | 53 | 57 |
| 6 | Chesterfield | 46 | 18 | 1 | 4 | 61 | 21 | 7 | 3 | 13 | 33 | 45 | 94 | 66 | 54 |
| 7 | Stockport County | 46 | 16 | 4 | 3 | 65 | 22 | 5 | 5 | 13 | 25 | 39 | 90 | 61 | 51 |
| 8 | Bradford City | 46 | 16 | 5 | 2 | 57 | 25 | 2 | 8 | 13 | 21 | 39 | 78 | 64 | 49 |
| 9 | Scunthorpe United | 46 | 12 | 4 | 7 | 40 | 26 | 8 | 4 | 11 | 35 | 37 | 75 | 63 | 48 |
| 10 | Workington | 46 | 13 | 4 | 6 | 47 | 20 | 6 | 5 | 12 | 28 | 43 | 75 | 63 | 47 |
| 11 | York City | 46 | 12 | 4 | 7 | 44 | 24 | 7 | 5 | 11 | 41 | 48 | 85 | 72 | 47 |
| 12 | Rochdale | 46 | 13 | 5 | 5 | 46 | 39 | 4 | 8 | 11 | 20 | 45 | 66 | 84 | 47 |
| 13 | Gateshead | 46 | 15 | 4 | 4 | 56 | 32 | 2 | 7 | 14 | 21 | 52 | 77 | 84 | 45 |
| 14 | Wrexham | 46 | 11 | 5 | 7 | 37 | 28 | 5 | 5 | 13 | 29 | 45 | 66 | 73 | 42 |
| 15 | Darlington | 46 | 11 | 6 | 6 | 41 | 28 | 5 | 3 | 15 | 19 | 45 | 60 | 73 | 41 |
| 16 | Tranmere Rovers | 46 | 11 | 4 | 8 | 33 | 25 | 5 | 5 | 13 | 26 | 59 | 59 | 84 | 41 |
| ***17*** | ***Chester*** | ***46*** | ***10*** | ***8*** | ***5*** | ***35*** | ***33*** | ***3*** | ***6*** | ***14*** | ***17*** | ***49*** | ***52*** | ***82*** | ***40*** |
| 18 | Mansfield Town | 46 | 13 | 6 | 4 | 59 | 21 | 1 | 5 | 17 | 25 | 60 | 84 | 81 | 39 |
| 19 | Halifax Town | 46 | 10 | 6 | 7 | 40 | 27 | 4 | 5 | 14 | 26 | 49 | 66 | 76 | 39 |
| 20 | Oldham Athletic | 46 | 7 | 12 | 4 | 48 | 36 | 3 | 6 | 14 | 28 | 50 | 76 | 86 | 38 |
| 21 | Carlisle United | 46 | 11 | 3 | 9 | 45 | 36 | 4 | 5 | 14 | 26 | 59 | 71 | 95 | 38 |
| 22 | Barrow | 46 | 11 | 6 | 6 | 44 | 25 | 1 | 3 | 19 | 17 | 58 | 61 | 83 | 33 |
| 23 | Bradford Park Ave. | 46 | 13 | 4 | 6 | 47 | 38 | 0 | 3 | 20 | 14 | 84 | 61 | 122 | 33 |
| 24 | Crewe Alexandra | 46 | 9 | 4 | 10 | 32 | 35 | 0 | 6 | 17 | 18 | 70 | 50 | 105 | 28 |

**1955/56 Season:**
(Back) Hughes, Morris, Jones, Gill, Whitlock, Lee. (Front) Pye, Collins, Jolley, Haines, Brandon.

**1956/57 Season:**
(Back) Davies, Harris (Player-Manager), Lee, Jones, Gill, Whitlock, Lang. (Front) Mulholland, Foulkes, Hansell, Allman, Collins, Bullock, Hughes.

# SEASON 1956-57

## FOOTBALL LEAGUE DIVISION 3 (NORTH)

| | Date | Opposition | | FT | HT | Att. | Goalscorers | Jones R. | Harris J. | Gill R. | Davies G. | Lee E. | Whitlock P. | Foulkes W. | Hansell R. | Allman G. | Collins J. | Bullock N. | Hackett B. | Haines J. | Mulholland J. | Fields M. | Lang G. | Hughes R. | Williams R. | Morris S. | Griffiths R. | Smith H. | Owen L. | Turner P. | Jepson B. |
|---|---|---|---|---|---|---|---|---|---|---|---|---|---|---|---|---|---|---|---|---|---|---|---|---|---|---|---|---|---|---|---|
| 1 | Aug 18 | Wrexham | D | 2-2 | 1-1 | 13506 | Bullock, Allman | 1 | 2 | 3 | 4 | 5 | 6 | 7 | 8 | 9 | 10 | 11 | | | | | | | | | | | | | |
| 2 | 22 | DERBY COUNTY | D | 2-2 | 2-0 | 12192 | Foulkes (2) | 1 | 2 | 3 | 4 | 5 | 6 | 7 | 8 | 9 | 10 | 11 | | | | | | | | | | | | | |
| 3 | 25 | HARTLEPOOLS UNITED | L | 0-1 | 0-1 | 8374 | | 1 | 2 | 3 | 4 | 5 | 6 | 7 | 8 | 9 | 10 | 11 | | | | | | | | | | | | | |
| 4 | 29 | Derby County | L | 0-3 | 0-2 | 20037 | | 1 | 2 | 3 | 4 | 5 | 6 | | 8 | 7 | | 11 | 9 | 10 | | | | | | | | | | | |
| 5 | Sep 1 | Bradford City | L | 0-1 | 0-1 | 14244 | | 1 | 2 | 3 | 4 | 5 | 6 | 7 | 8 | | | 11 | 9 | 10 | | | | | | | | | | | |
| 6 | 5 | Chesterfield | L | 0-3 | 0-0 | 7901 | | 1 | 2 | 3 | 4 | 5 | 6 | 7 | | | 10 | 11 | 9 | 8 | | | | | | | | | | | |
| 7 | 8 | STOCKPORT COUNTY | L | 1-4 | 0-1 | 9948 | Whitlock | 1 | 2 | 3 | | 5 | 6 | 7 | | | 10 | | | 8 | 4 | 9 | 11 | | | | | | | | |
| 8 | 12 | CHESTERFIELD | L | 3-4 | 0-1 | 5404 | Harris, Hansell, Fields | 1 | 2 | 3 | | 5 | 6 | 8 | 10 | | | | | | | 9 | 11 | 4 | 7 | | | | | | |
| 9 | 15 | Carlisle United | L | 0-3 | 0-0 | 6306 | | 1 | 2 | 3 | | | 6 | 8 | 10 | | | | | | | 9 | 11 | 4 | 7 | 5 | | | | | |
| 10 | 17 | York City | W | 1-0 | 1-0 | 9234 | Foulkes (pen) | 1 | 2 | 3 | | | 6 | 8 | 10 | | | 11 | | | | 9 | | 4 | 7 | 5 | | | | | |
| 11 | 22 | ACCRINGTON STANLEY | L | 0-2 | 0-1 | 8850 | | 1 | 2 | | | | 6 | 8 | 10 | | | 11 | | | | 9 | | 4 | 7 | 5 | 3 | | | | |
| 12 | 26 | YORK CITY | L | 3-4 | 2-3 | 4258 | Bullock, Williams, Hansell | 1 | 2 | | | | | 8 | 10 | 9 | | 11 | | | | | | 4 | 7 | 5 | 3 | 6 | | | |
| 13 | 29 | Tranmere Rovers | L | 1-3 | 1-3 | 6982 | Hansell | 1 | | | | | | 8 | 10 | 9 | | 11 | | | | | | 2 | 7 | 5 | 6 | 4 | 3 | | |
| 14 | Oct 6 | CREWE ALEX. | W | 4-1 | 1-1 | 6653 | Foulkes (2), Hansell, Bullock | 1 | 2 | 3 | | | | 8 | 10 | | | 11 | | | 9 | | | 3 | 7 | 5 | 6 | | | | |
| 15 | 13 | Scunthorpe United | L | 0-3 | 0-2 | 6377 | | 1 | 2 | 3 | | | | 8 | 10 | | | 11 | | | 9 | | | 3 | 7 | 5 | 6 | | | | |
| 16 | 20 | BRADFORD P. A. | W | 2-0 | 1-0 | 5385 | Foulkes, Hansell | 1 | 2 | 3 | | | | 8 | 10 | | | 11 | | | 9 | | | 3 | 7 | 5 | 6 | | | | |
| 17 | 27 | Halifax Town | L | 1-2 | 0-1 | 4982 | Mulholland | 1 | 2 | 3 | | | | 8 | 10 | | | 11 | | | 9 | | | 3 | 7 | 5 | 6 | | | | |
| 18 | Nov 3 | WORKINGTON | W | 1-0 | 1-0 | 6654 | Hansell | 1 | 2 | 3 | | | 6 | 7 | 10 | | | 11 | | | 9 | | | 4 | | 5 | | | | 8 | |
| 19 | 10 | Hull City | L | 0-2 | 0-0 | 8571 | | 1 | 2 | 3 | | | 6 | 7 | 10 | 9 | | 11 | | | | | | 4 | | 5 | | | | 8 | |
| 20 | 24 | Darlington | L | 1-5 | 0-3 | 4097 | Davies (pen) | 1 | | 3 | 4 | | | 7 | | | | 11 | | 10 | | 9 | | 2 | | 5 | 6 | | | 8 | |
| 21 | Dec 1 | ROCHDALE | D | 2-2 | 1-1 | 5492 | Davies (pen), Hansell | 1 | | 3 | 4 | | | 7 | 10 | | | 11 | | | 9 | | | 2 | | 5 | 6 | | | 8 | |
| 22 | 15 | WREXHAM | D | 0-0 | 0-0 | 10066 | | 1 | | 3 | 4 | | 6 | 7 | 10 | | | 11 | 9 | | | | | 2 | | 5 | | | | 8 | |
| 23 | 22 | Hartlepools United | D | 2-2 | 1-0 | 6515 | Bullock (2) | 1 | | 3 | 4 | | 6 | 7 | 10 | 9 | | 11 | | | | | | 2 | | 5 | | | | 8 | |
| 24 | 25 | Oldham Athletic | D | 0-0 | 0-0 | 7524 | | 1 | | 3 | 4 | | 6 | 7 | 10 | 9 | | 11 | | | | | | 2 | | 5 | | | | 8 | |
| 25 | 29 | BRADFORD CITY | L | 1-2 | 0-1 | 7330 | Foulkes | 1 | | 3 | 4 | | 6 | 7 | 10 | 9 | | 11 | | | | | | 2 | | 5 | | | | 8 | |
| 26 | Jan 5 | Mansfield Town | D | 1-1 | 1-0 | 5999 | Hansell | 1 | | 3 | 4 | | 6 | 7 | 10 | | | 11 | | | | | | 2 | | 5 | | 8 | | 9 | |
| 27 | 12 | Stockport County | L | 1-2 | 0-0 | 8958 | Hansell | 1 | 3 | | 4 | | 6 | 7 | 10 | | | 11 | | | | | | 2 | | 5 | | 8 | | 9 | |
| 28 | 19 | CARLISLE UNITED | L | 1-2 | 0-0 | 6533 | Turner | 1 | | 3 | 4 | | 6 | 7 | 10 | | | 11 | | | | | | 2 | | 5 | | | | 8 | 9 |
| 29 | 26 | MANSFIELD TOWN | W | 6-2 | 1-1 | 5681 | Jepson (3), Turner (2), Foulkes | 1 | | 3 | 4 | | 6 | 7 | 10 | | | 11 | | | | | | 2 | | 5 | | | | 8 | 9 |
| 30 | Feb 2 | Accrington Stanley | L | 0-4 | 0-2 | 6661 | | 1 | | 3 | 4 | | 6 | 7 | 10 | | | 11 | | | | | | 2 | | 5 | | | | 8 | 9 |
| 31 | 9 | TRANMERE ROVERS | D | 1-1 | 0-0 | 7625 | Davies (pen) | 1 | | 3 | 4 | | 6 | 7 | 10 | | | 11 | | | | | | 2 | | 5 | | | | 8 | 9 |
| 32 | 16 | Crewe Alex. | D | 0-0 | 0-0 | 6536 | | 1 | 2 | 3 | 6 | | | 7 | 8 | | | 11 | | | | 10 | | 4 | | 5 | | | | | 9 |
| 33 | 23 | SCUNTHORPE UNITED | D | 2-2 | 1-1 | 2691 | Jepson (2) | 1 | 2 | 3 | 6 | | | | 8 | | | 11 | | | | 10 | | 4 | | 5 | | 7 | | | 9 |
| 34 | Mar 2 | Bradford P. A. | L | 1-3 | 0-2 | 7547 | Smith | 1 | 2 | 3 | 6 | | | | 8 | | | 11 | | | | 10 | | 4 | | 5 | | 7 | | | 9 |
| 35 | 9 | HALIFAX TOWN | D | 1-1 | 0-0 | 5098 | Jepson | 1 | 2 | 3 | 6 | | | | | | | 11 | | | 10 | | | 4 | | 5 | | 7 | | 8 | 9 |
| 36 | 16 | Workington | W | 1-0 | 0-0 | 10414 | Jepson | 1 | 2 | 3 | 6 | | | 7 | 10 | | | 11 | | | | | | 4 | | 5 | | | | 8 | 9 |
| 37 | 23 | HULL CITY | D | 1-1 | 1-0 | 6272 | Jepson | 1 | 2 | 3 | 6 | | | 7 | 8 | | | 11 | | | | 10 | | 4 | | 5 | | | | | 9 |
| 38 | 30 | Barrow | L | 0-3 | 0-1 | 4069 | | 1 | 2 | 3 | 6 | | | 7 | 8 | | | 11 | | | | 10 | | 4 | | 5 | | | | | 9 |
| 39 | Apr 6 | DARLINGTON | L | 0-3 | 0-1 | 4786 | | 1 | 2 | 3 | 6 | | | 7 | 8 | | | 11 | | | | 10 | | 4 | | 5 | | | | | 9 |
| 40 | 10 | OLDHAM ATHLETIC | W | 1-0 | 0-0 | 3416 | Smith | 1 | | 3 | 6 | | 4 | 8 | | | | 11 | | | | | | 2 | 7 | 5 | | 10 | | | 9 |
| 41 | 13 | Rochdale | L | 1-2 | 1-1 | 4501 | Jepson | 1 | | 3 | 6 | | 4 | 8 | | | | 11 | | | | | | 2 | 7 | 5 | | 10 | | | 9 |
| 42 | 19 | Southport | D | 1-1 | 0-0 | 5216 | Bullock | 1 | | 3 | 6 | | 4 | 8 | | | | 11 | | | | | | 2 | 7 | 5 | | 10 | | | 9 |
| 43 | 20 | GATESHEAD | W | 4-1 | 1-0 | 5545 | Oldham (og), Foulkes (2), Davies | 1 | | 3 | 6 | 5 | 4 | 8 | | | | 11 | | | | | | 2 | 7 | | | 10 | | | 9 |
| 44 | 22 | SOUTHPORT | W | 2-0 | 0-0 | 6749 | Jepson, Foulkes | 1 | | 3 | 6 | 5 | 4 | 8 | | | | 11 | | | | | | 2 | 7 | | | 10 | | | 9 |
| 45 | 27 | Gateshead | L | 1-4 | 1-1 | 2599 | Smith | 1 | | 3 | 6 | 5 | 4 | 8 | | | | 11 | | | | | | 2 | 7 | | | 10 | | | 9 |
| 46 | 29 | BARROW | W | 2-0 | 1-0 | 3849 | Williams, Bullock | 1 | | 3 | 6 | 5 | 4 | 8 | 10 | | | 11 | | | | 9 | | 2 | 7 | | | | | | |
| | | | | | | | Apps. | 46 | 27 | 42 | 33 | 12 | 30 | 42 | 36 | 10 | 5 | 43 | 4 | 5 | 8 | 13 | 3 | 39 | 17 | 34 | 9 | 13 | 1 | 16 | 18 |
| | | | | | | | Goals | | 1 | | 4 | | 1 | 11 | 9 | 1 | | 7 | | | 1 | 1 | | | 2 | | | 3 | | 3 | 10 |

Own goals 1

## F.A. CUP

| | Date | Opposition | | FT | HT | Att. | Goalscorers | Jones R. | Harris J. | Gill R. | Davies G. | Lee E. | Whitlock P. | Foulkes W. | Hansell R. | Allman G. | Collins J. | Bullock N. | Hackett B. | Haines J. | Mulholland J. | Fields M. | Lang G. | Hughes R. | Williams R. | Morris S. | Griffiths R. | Smith H. | Owen L. | Turner P. | Jepson B. |
|---|---|---|---|---|---|---|---|---|---|---|---|---|---|---|---|---|---|---|---|---|---|---|---|---|---|---|---|---|---|---|---|
| 1R | Nov 17 | BARROW | D | 0-0 | 0-0 | 8311 | | 1 | 2 | 3 | | | 6 | 7 | | 9 | | 11 | | 10 | | | | 4 | | 5 | | | | 8 | |
| 1Rr | 22 | Barrow | L | 1-3 | 1-0 | 4052 | Turner | 1 | 2 | 3 | | | 6 | 7 | 10 | | | 11 | | 9 | | | | 4 | | 5 | | | | 8 | |

## WELSH CUP

| | Date | Opposition | | FT | HT | Att. | Goalscorers | Jones R. | Harris J. | Gill R. | Davies G. | Lee E. | Whitlock P. | Foulkes W. | Hansell R. | Allman G. | Collins J. | Bullock N. | Hackett B. | Haines J. | Mulholland J. | Fields M. | Lang G. | Hughes R. | Williams R. | Morris S. | Griffiths R. | Smith H. | Owen L. | Turner P. | Jepson B. |
|---|---|---|---|---|---|---|---|---|---|---|---|---|---|---|---|---|---|---|---|---|---|---|---|---|---|---|---|---|---|---|---|
| 5R | Jan 31 | Oswestry Town | W | 3-0 | 1-0 | 1095 | Bullock (2), Smith | 1 | | 3 | 4 | | 6 | 7 | 10 | | | 11 | | | | 9 | | 2 | | 5 | | 8 | | | |
| 6R | Feb 27 | Cardiff City | W | 2-0 | 1-0 | 5000 | Davies, Jepson | 1 | | 3 | 6 | | | | 8 | | | 11 | | | 10 | | | 2 | 4 | 5 | | 7 | | | 9 |
| SF | Mar 20 | Wrexham * | L | 0-2 | 0-1 | | | 1 | | 3 | 6 | | | 7 | 10 | | | 11 | | | | | | 2 | 4 | 5 | | | | 8 | 9 |

* Played at Rhyl

## FRIENDLIES

| | Date | Opposition | | FT | HT | Att. | Goalscorers |
|---|---|---|---|---|---|---|---|
| 1 | May 2 | EVERTON RES. * | W | 4-2 | 3-0 | 2500 | Williams, Foulkes (2), Fields |

* Ron Hughes \ Sam Morris \ Phil Whitlock Testimonial

Final League Table

| | | Pl. | Home W | D | L | F | A | Away W | D | L | F | A | F. | A. | Pts |
|---|---|---|---|---|---|---|---|---|---|---|---|---|---|---|---|
| 1 | Derby County | 46 | 18 | 3 | 2 | 69 | 18 | 8 | 8 | 7 | 42 | 35 | 111 | 53 | 63 |
| 2 | Hartlepools United | 46 | 18 | 4 | 1 | 56 | 21 | 7 | 5 | 11 | 34 | 42 | 90 | 63 | 59 |
| 3 | Accrington Stanley | 46 | 15 | 4 | 4 | 54 | 22 | 10 | 4 | 9 | 41 | 42 | 95 | 64 | 58 |
| 4 | Workington | 46 | 16 | 4 | 3 | 60 | 25 | 8 | 6 | 9 | 33 | 38 | 93 | 63 | 58 |
| 5 | Stockport County | 46 | 16 | 3 | 4 | 51 | 26 | 7 | 5 | 11 | 40 | 49 | 91 | 75 | 54 |
| 6 | Chesterfield | 46 | 17 | 5 | 1 | 60 | 22 | 5 | 4 | 14 | 36 | 57 | 96 | 79 | 53 |
| 7 | York City | 46 | 14 | 4 | 5 | 43 | 21 | 7 | 6 | 10 | 32 | 40 | 75 | 61 | 52 |
| 8 | Hull City | 46 | 14 | 6 | 3 | 45 | 24 | 7 | 4 | 12 | 39 | 45 | 84 | 69 | 52 |
| 9 | Bradford City | 46 | 14 | 3 | 6 | 47 | 31 | 8 | 5 | 10 | 31 | 37 | 78 | 68 | 52 |
| 10 | Barrow | 46 | 16 | 2 | 5 | 51 | 22 | 5 | 7 | 11 | 25 | 40 | 76 | 62 | 51 |
| 11 | Halifax Town | 46 | 16 | 2 | 5 | 40 | 24 | 5 | 5 | 13 | 25 | 46 | 65 | 70 | 49 |
| 12 | Wrexham | 46 | 12 | 7 | 4 | 63 | 33 | 7 | 3 | 13 | 34 | 41 | 97 | 74 | 48 |
| 13 | Rochdale | 46 | 14 | 6 | 3 | 38 | 19 | 4 | 6 | 13 | 27 | 46 | 65 | 65 | 48 |
| 14 | Scunthorpe United | 46 | 0 | 5 | 9 | 44 | 30 | 6 | 10 | 7 | 27 | 33 | 71 | 69 | 45 |
| 15 | Carlisle United | 46 | 9 | 9 | 5 | 44 | 36 | 7 | 4 | 12 | 32 | 49 | 76 | 85 | 45 |
| 16 | Mansfield Town | 46 | 13 | 3 | 7 | 58 | 38 | 4 | 7 | 12 | 33 | 52 | 91 | 90 | 44 |
| 17 | Gateshead | 46 | 9 | 6 | 8 | 42 | 40 | 8 | 4 | 11 | 30 | 50 | 72 | 90 | 44 |
| 18 | Darlington | 46 | 11 | 5 | 7 | 47 | 36 | 6 | 3 | 14 | 35 | 59 | 82 | 95 | 42 |
| 19 | Oldham Athletic | 46 | 9 | 7 | 7 | 35 | 31 | 3 | 8 | 12 | 31 | 43 | 66 | 74 | 39 |
| 20 | Bradford Park Ave. | 46 | 11 | 2 | 10 | 41 | 40 | 5 | 1 | 17 | 25 | 53 | 66 | 93 | 35 |
| ***21*** | ***Chester*** | ***46*** | ***8*** | ***7*** | ***8*** | ***40*** | ***35*** | ***2*** | ***6*** | ***15*** | ***15*** | ***49*** | ***55*** | ***84*** | ***33*** |
| 22 | Southport | 46 | 7 | 8 | 8 | 31 | 34 | 3 | 4 | 16 | 21 | 60 | 52 | 94 | 32 |
| 23 | Tranmere Rovers | 46 | 5 | 9 | 9 | 33 | 38 | 2 | 4 | 17 | 18 | 53 | 51 | 91 | 27 |
| 24 | Crewe Alexandra | 46 | 5 | 7 | 11 | 31 | 46 | 1 | 2 | 20 | 12 | 64 | 43 | 110 | 21 |

# SEASON 1957-58

## FOOTBALL LEAGUE DIVISION 3 (NORTH)

| | Date | Opposition | | FT | HT | Att. | Goalscorers |
|---|---|---|---|---|---|---|---|
| 1 | Aug 24 | TRANMERE ROVERS | L | 1-3 | 1-1 | 11572 | R Williams |
| 2 | 28 | CREWE ALEX. | W | 3-2 | 3-1 | 7736 | Jepson (2), Gordon Davies |
| 3 | 31 | Hartlepools United | L | 1-2 | 0-1 | 11629 | Mason |
| 4 | Sep 2 | Crewe Alex. | W | 3-0 | 1-0 | 8323 | Jepson (2), Mason |
| 5 | 7 | BRADFORD P. A. | L | 1-2 | 0-0 | 8353 | Jepson (pen) |
| 6 | 11 | Wrexham | L | 0-1 | 0-1 | 11754 | |
| 7 | 14 | Carlisle United | L | 2-3 | 1-2 | 8764 | Foulkes, Smith |
| 8 | 18 | WREXHAM | L | 0-1 | 0-0 | 12554 | |
| 9 | 21 | SOUTHPORT | D | 1-1 | 0-0 | 6454 | Bullock |
| 10 | 28 | York City | W | 2-1 | 2-0 | 7103 | A Williams, Hughes |
| 11 | 30 | Accrington Stanley | W | 2-1 | 2-0 | 7404 | Gordon Davies (2) |
| 12 | Oct 5 | BARROW | D | 2-2 | 0-2 | 7142 | Hughes, Saunders |
| 13 | 12 | DARLINGTON | L | 0-1 | 0-1 | 6852 | |
| 14 | 19 | Halifax Town | L | 1-2 | 1-1 | 5042 | Bullock |
| 15 | 26 | STOCKPORT COUNTY | W | 3-0 | 2-0 | 7518 | Bullock, Jepson, Gordon Davies |
| 16 | Nov 2 | Hull City | L | 0-3 | 0-2 | 11732 | |
| 17 | 9 | BRADFORD CITY | D | 0-0 | 0-0 | 6453 | |
| 18 | 23 | MANSFIELD TOWN | L | 1-2 | 1-1 | 7096 | Foulkes |
| 19 | 30 | Gateshead | L | 2-3 | 0-2 | 3844 | Pearson, Gordon Davies |
| 20 | Dec 14 | SCUNTHORPE UNITED | L | 1-2 | 1-2 | 4604 | Bullock |
| 21 | 21 | Tranmere Rovers | D | 2-2 | 1-1 | 9794 | Jepson (2) |
| 22 | 25 | Bury | W | 2-1 | 1-1 | 11031 | Jepson, Bullock |
| 23 | 26 | BURY | D | 0-0 | 0-0 | 9771 | |
| 24 | 28 | HARTLEPOOLS UNITED | W | 2-1 | 0-1 | 7725 | Saunders (2) |
| 25 | Jan 4 | OLDHAM ATHLETIC | D | 0-0 | 0-0 | 6159 | |
| 26 | 11 | Bradford P. A. | L | 0-3 | 0-1 | 7341 | |
| 27 | 18 | CARLISLE UNITED | D | 0-0 | 0-0 | 4949 | |
| 28 | 25 | Workington | L | 3-5 | 2-3 | 3813 | Jepson, Mason, Evans |
| 29 | Feb 1 | Southport | W | 4-2 | 1-0 | 3693 | Jepson, Ireland, Pearson, Richards |
| 30 | 8 | YORK CITY | W | 9-2 | 4-0 | 5217 | Jepson(5), Evans, Brown(og), Richards, Ireland |
| 31 | 15 | Barrow | L | 1-4 | 1-3 | 4271 | Pearson |
| 32 | 22 | Mansfield Town | L | 1-3 | 0-0 | 7603 | Mellor (og) |
| 33 | Mar 1 | HALIFAX TOWN | D | 1-1 | 1-1 | 6304 | Ireland |
| 34 | 8 | Stockport County | D | 2-2 | 0-0 | 7629 | Ireland, Richards |
| 35 | 15 | HULL CITY | D | 1-1 | 0-0 | 5721 | Hughes (pen) |
| 36 | 22 | Darlington | W | 3-2 | 1-1 | 4376 | Jepson (2), Richards |
| 37 | 29 | WORKINGTON | W | 4-3 | 2-0 | 4905 | Jepson (2), Richards, Pearson |
| 38 | Apr 4 | Chesterfield | L | 1-2 | 0-0 | 9156 | Pearson |
| 39 | 5 | Rochdale | D | 1-1 | 1-0 | 3273 | Whitlock |
| 40 | 7 | CHESTERFIELD | D | 0-0 | 0-0 | 6360 | |
| 41 | 12 | GATESHEAD | D | 1-1 | 0-0 | 4752 | Pearson |
| 42 | 16 | ROCHDALE | W | 2-0 | 1-0 | 3449 | Hughes (pen), Mason |
| 43 | 19 | Bradford City | L | 0-5 | 0-3 | 9232 | |
| 44 | 22 | Oldham Athletic | L | 1-5 | 1-2 | 8396 | Jepson |
| 45 | 26 | Scunthorpe United | L | 1-2 | 1-1 | 10403 | Pearson |
| 46 | 30 | ACCRINGTON STANLEY | W | 5-1 | 2-0 | 3373 | Jepson (2), Richards, Bullock, Pearson |

| | Jones R. | Hughes R. | Souter W. | Davies Geo. | Saunders J. | Anderson J. | Williams R. | Foulkes W. | Jepson B. | Davies Gor. | Mason J. | Griffiths K. | Williams A. | Fields M. | Smith H. | Ireland J. | Bullock N. | Whitlock P. | Gill R. | Pearson S. | Evans R. | Handscombe M. | Richards G. | Biggins B. | Croft A. |
|---|---|---|---|---|---|---|---|---|---|---|---|---|---|---|---|---|---|---|---|---|---|---|---|---|---|
| 1 | 1 | 2 | 3 | 4 | 5 | 6 | 7 | 8 | 9 | 10 | 11 | | | | | | | | | | | | | | |
| 2 | | 2 | 3 | 4 | 5 | 6 | 7 | 8 | 9 | 10 | 11 | 1 | | | | | | | | | | | | | |
| 3 | | 2 | 3 | | 5 | 6 | 7 | 8 | 9 | 10 | 11 | 1 | 4 | | | | | | | | | | | | |
| 4 | | 2 | 3 | | 5 | 6 | 7 | 8 | 9 | | 11 | 1 | 4 | 10 | | | | | | | | | | | |
| 5 | | 2 | 3 | | 5 | 6 | 7 | 8 | 9 | | 11 | 1 | 4 | 10 | | | | | | | | | | | |
| 6 | | 2 | 3 | | 5 | 6 | 7 | 8 | 9 | 10 | 11 | 1 | 4 | | | | | | | | | | | | |
| 7 | | 2 | 3 | | 5 | 6 | | 7 | 9 | 10 | 11 | 1 | 4 | | 8 | | | | | | | | | | |
| 8 | | 2 | 3 | | 5 | 6 | | 7 | 9 | 10 | 11 | 1 | 4 | | 8 | | | | | | | | | | |
| 9 | | 2 | 3 | | 5 | 6 | | 7 | 9 | 10 | | 1 | 4 | | | 8 | 11 | | | | | | | | |
| 10 | | 2 | 3 | | 5 | 6 | | 7 | 9 | 10 | | 1 | 8 | | | | 11 | 4 | | | | | | | |
| 11 | | 2 | 3 | | 5 | 6 | | 7 | | 10 | | 1 | 9 | | 8 | | 11 | 4 | | | | | | | |
| 12 | | 2 | 3 | | 5 | 6 | | 7 | 9 | 10 | | 1 | 8 | | | | 11 | 4 | | | | | | | |
| 13 | | 2 | | | 5 | 6 | | 7 | 9 | 10 | | 1 | 8 | | | | 11 | 4 | 3 | | | | | | |
| 14 | | 2 | | | 5 | 6 | | 7 | 9 | | 8 | 1 | 4 | 10 | | | 11 | | 3 | | | | | | |
| 15 | | 2 | | | 5 | 6 | 7 | | 9 | 10 | 8 | 1 | 4 | | | | 11 | | 3 | | | | | | |
| 16 | | 2 | | | 5 | 6 | | 7 | 9 | 10 | 8 | 1 | 4 | | | | 11 | | 3 | | | | | | |
| 17 | | 2 | | | 5 | 6 | | 7 | 9 | 10 | 8 | 1 | 4 | | | | 11 | | 3 | | | | | | |
| 18 | | 2 | 3 | | 5 | 6 | | 7 | 9 | | 8 | 1 | 4 | | | | 11 | | | 10 | | | | | |
| 19 | 1 | 2 | 3 | | 5 | 6 | | 7 | | 8 | 11 | | 4 | 9 | | | | | | 10 | | | | | |
| 20 | | 2 | | | 5 | 6 | | 7 | 9 | 8 | 10 | 1 | 4 | | | | 11 | | 3 | | | | | | |
| 21 | | 2 | | | 5 | 6 | | 8 | 9 | | | 1 | 4 | | | | 11 | | 3 | 10 | 7 | | | | |
| 22 | | 2 | | | 5 | 6 | | 8 | 9 | | | 1 | 4 | | | | 11 | | 3 | 10 | 7 | | | | |
| 23 | | 2 | | | 5 | 6 | | 8 | 9 | | | 1 | 4 | | | | 11 | | 3 | 10 | 7 | | | | |
| 24 | 1 | 2 | 3 | | 5 | 6 | | 8 | 9 | | | | 4 | | 10 | | 11 | | | | 7 | | | | |
| 25 | | 2 | | | 5 | 6 | | 8 | | | | 1 | 4 | 9 | | | 11 | | 3 | 10 | 7 | | | | |
| 26 | | 2 | | | 5 | 6 | | | 9 | 10 | 11 | 1 | 4 | | | 8 | | | 3 | | 7 | | | | |
| 27 | | 2 | | | 5 | 6 | | 8 | 9 | | 11 | 1 | 4 | | | | | | 3 | 10 | 7 | | | | |
| 28 | | 2 | | | 5 | 6 | | | 9 | | 11 | 1 | 4 | | | | 10 | 8 | 3 | | 7 | | | | |
| 29 | | 2 | | | | 6 | | | 9 | | | 1 | 4 | | | 8 | | | 3 | 10 | 7 | 5 | 11 | | |
| 30 | | 2 | | | | 6 | | | 9 | | | 1 | 4 | | | 8 | | | 3 | 10 | 7 | 5 | 11 | | |
| 31 | | 2 | | | | 6 | | | 9 | | | 1 | 4 | | | 8 | | | 3 | 10 | 7 | 5 | 11 | | |
| 32 | | 2 | | | | 6 | | | 9 | | | 1 | 4 | | | 8 | | | 3 | 10 | 7 | 5 | 11 | | |
| 33 | | 2 | | | 5 | 6 | | | 9 | | | 1 | 4 | | | 8 | | | 3 | 10 | 7 | | 11 | | |
| 34 | | 2 | | | 5 | 6 | | | 9 | | | 1 | 4 | | | 8 | | | 3 | 10 | 7 | | 11 | | |
| 35 | | 2 | | | 5 | 6 | | | 9 | | | 1 | 4 | | | 8 | 11 | | 3 | 10 | 7 | | | | |
| 36 | | 2 | | | 5 | 6 | | 7 | 9 | | 4 | 1 | | | | 8 | | | 3 | 10 | | | 11 | | |
| 37 | | 2 | | | 5 | 6 | | 7 | 9 | | 4 | 1 | | | | 8 | | | 3 | 10 | | | 11 | | |
| 38 | | 2 | | | 5 | 6 | | 7 | 9 | | 4 | 1 | | | | 8 | | | 3 | 10 | | | 11 | | |
| 39 | | 2 | | | 5 | | | 7 | | 9 | 6 | 1 | | | | 8 | | 4 | 3 | 10 | | | 11 | | |
| 40 | | 2 | | | 5 | 6 | | 7 | 9 | | 4 | 1 | | | | 8 | | | 3 | 10 | | | 11 | | |
| 41 | | 2 | | | 5 | | | 7 | 9 | | 6 | 1 | | | | 8 | | 4 | 3 | 10 | | | 11 | | |
| 42 | | 2 | | | 5 | 6 | | 7 | 9 | 8 | 4 | | | | | | | | 3 | 10 | | | 11 | 1 | |
| 43 | | 2 | | | 5 | 6 | | 7 | 9 | 8 | 4 | 1 | | | | | | | 3 | 10 | | | 11 | | |
| 44 | | 2 | | | 5 | 6 | | 7 | 9 | 8 | 4 | 1 | | | | | | | 3 | 10 | | | 11 | | |
| 45 | | 2 | 3 | | 5 | | | 7 | 9 | 8 | 6 | 1 | | | | | | 4 | | 10 | | | 11 | | |
| 46 | | 2 | | | 5 | | | 7 | 9 | | 6 | | | | | | 8 | 4 | 3 | 10 | | | 11 | 1 | |
| Apps. | 3 | 46 | 16 | 2 | 42 | 42 | 7 | 36 | 42 | 22 | 29 | 41 | 33 | 5 | 4 | 15 | 19 | 9 | 30 | 25 | 15 | 4 | 17 | 2 | |
| Goals | | 4 | | | 3 | | 1 | 2 | 23 | 5 | 4 | | 1 | | 1 | 4 | 6 | 1 | | 8 | 2 | | 6 | | |

Own goals 2

## F.A. CUP

| | Date | Opposition | | FT | HT | Att. | Goalscorers |
|---|---|---|---|---|---|---|---|
| 1R | Nov 16 | GATESHEAD | W | 4-3 | 2-2 | 7539 | Pearson, Foulkes, Jepson, Mason |
| 2R | Dec 7 | BRADFORD CITY | D | 3-3 | 3-1 | 8435 | Jepson (3) |
| 2Rr | 11 | Bradford City | L | 1-3 | 0-3 | 5281 | Jepson |

| | Jones R. | Hughes R. | Souter W. | Davies Geo. | Saunders J. | Anderson J. | Williams R. | Foulkes W. | Jepson B. | Davies Gor. | Mason J. | Griffiths K. | Williams A. | Fields M. | Smith H. | Ireland J. | Bullock N. | Whitlock P. | Gill R. | Pearson S. | Evans R. | Handscombe M. | Richards G. | Biggins B. | Croft A. |
|---|---|---|---|---|---|---|---|---|---|---|---|---|---|---|---|---|---|---|---|---|---|---|---|---|---|
| 1R | | 2 | | | 5 | 6 | | 7 | 9 | | 8 | 1 | 4 | | | | 11 | | 3 | 10 | | | | | |
| 2R | 1 | 2 | 3 | | 5 | 6 | | 7 | 9 | 8 | | | | | | | 11 | 4 | | 10 | | | | | |
| 2Rr | | 2 | | | 5 | 6 | | 7 | 9 | 8 | 10 | 1 | 4 | | | | 11 | | 3 | | | | | | |

## WELSH CUP

| | Date | Opposition | | FT | HT | Att. | Goalscorers |
|---|---|---|---|---|---|---|---|
| 5R | Jan 30 | Oswestry Town | W | 3-1 | 3-0 | | Ireland, Tomley (og), Smith |
| 6R | Mar 5 | SWANSEA TOWN | W | 2-0 | 1-0 | 1872 | Bullock, Hughes |
| SF | 19 | Hereford United * | D | 1-1 | 1-1 | 2538 | Jepson |
| SFr | 24 | Hereford United @ | W | 2-0 | 0-0 | 877 | Jepson, Ireland |
| F | May 7 | WREXHAM | D | 1-1 | 1-1 | 7742 | Hughes (pen) |
| Fr | 10 | Wrexham | L | 1-2 | 0-2 | 7542 | Evans |

| | Jones R. | Hughes R. | Souter W. | Davies Geo. | Saunders J. | Anderson J. | Williams R. | Foulkes W. | Jepson B. | Davies Gor. | Mason J. | Griffiths K. | Williams A. | Fields M. | Smith H. | Ireland J. | Bullock N. | Whitlock P. | Gill R. | Pearson S. | Evans R. | Handscombe M. | Richards G. | Biggins B. | Croft A. |
|---|---|---|---|---|---|---|---|---|---|---|---|---|---|---|---|---|---|---|---|---|---|---|---|---|---|
| 5R | | 2 | 3 | | | 6 | | | 9 | | | 1 | 4 | | 10 | 8 | 11 | | | | 7 | 5 | | | |
| 6R | | 2 | 3 | | 5 | 6 | | | 9 | | | 1 | 4 | | | 8 | 11 | | | 10 | 7 | | | | |
| SF | | 2 | | | 5 | 6 | | | 9 | | | 1 | 4 | | | 8 | 11 | | 3 | 10 | 7 | | | | |
| SFr | | 2 | 3 | | 5 | 6 | | | 9 | | 4 | 1 | | | | 8 | 11 | | | 10 | 7 | | | | |
| F | | 2 | | | 5 | | | 7 | 9 | 11 | 6 | | | | | | 8 | 4 | 3 | 10 | | | | 1 | |
| Fr | | 2 | | | 5 | 6 | | | 9 | | | | | | | | 8 | 4 | 3 | 10 | 7 | | | 1 | 11 |

* Played at Wrexham @ Played at Shrewsbury Town

## FRIENDLIES

| | Date | Opposition | | FT | HT | Att. | Goalscorers |
|---|---|---|---|---|---|---|---|
| 1 | May 1 | ALL STAR X1 * | L | 4-5 | 0-3 | 2231 | Croft, Bullock, Davies, Foulkes |

* Norman Bullock \ Harry Smith Testimonial

### Final League Table

| | | Pl. | Home W | D | L | F | A | Away W | D | L | F | A | F. | A. | Pts |
|---|---|---|---|---|---|---|---|---|---|---|---|---|---|---|---|
| 1 | Scunthorpe United | 46 | 16 | 5 | 2 | 46 | 19 | 13 | 3 | 7 | 42 | 31 | 88 | 50 | 66 |
| 2 | Accrington Stanley | 46 | 16 | 4 | 3 | 53 | 28 | 9 | 5 | 9 | 30 | 33 | 83 | 61 | 59 |
| 3 | Bradford City | 46 | 13 | 7 | 3 | 42 | 19 | 8 | 8 | 7 | 31 | 30 | 73 | 49 | 57 |
| 4 | Bury | 46 | 17 | 4 | 2 | 61 | 18 | 6 | 6 | 11 | 33 | 44 | 94 | 62 | 56 |
| 5 | Hull City | 46 | 15 | 6 | 2 | 49 | 20 | 4 | 9 | 10 | 29 | 47 | 78 | 67 | 53 |
| 6 | Mansfield Town | 46 | 16 | 3 | 4 | 68 | 42 | 6 | 5 | 12 | 32 | 50 | 100 | 92 | 52 |
| 7 | Halifax Town | 46 | 15 | 5 | 3 | 52 | 20 | 5 | 6 | 12 | 31 | 49 | 83 | 69 | 51 |
| 8 | Chesterfield | 46 | 12 | 8 | 3 | 39 | 28 | 6 | 7 | 10 | 32 | 41 | 71 | 69 | 51 |
| 9 | Stockport County | 46 | 15 | 4 | 4 | 54 | 28 | 3 | 7 | 13 | 20 | 39 | 74 | 67 | 47 |
| 10 | Rochdale | 46 | 14 | 4 | 5 | 50 | 25 | 5 | 4 | 14 | 29 | 42 | 79 | 67 | 46 |
| 11 | Tranmere Rovers | 46 | 12 | 6 | 5 | 51 | 32 | 6 | 4 | 13 | 31 | 44 | 82 | 76 | 46 |
| 12 | Wrexham | 46 | 13 | 8 | 2 | 39 | 18 | 4 | 4 | 15 | 22 | 45 | 61 | 63 | 46 |
| 13 | York City | 46 | 11 | 8 | 4 | 40 | 26 | 6 | 4 | 13 | 28 | 50 | 68 | 76 | 46 |
| 14 | Gateshead | 46 | 12 | 5 | 6 | 41 | 27 | 3 | 10 | 10 | 27 | 49 | 68 | 76 | 45 |
| 15 | Oldham Athletic | 46 | 11 | 7 | 5 | 44 | 32 | 3 | 10 | 10 | 28 | 52 | 72 | 84 | 45 |
| 16 | Carlisle United | 46 | 13 | 3 | 7 | 56 | 35 | 6 | 3 | 14 | 24 | 43 | 80 | 78 | 44 |
| 17 | Hartlepools United | 46 | 11 | 6 | 6 | 45 | 26 | 5 | 6 | 12 | 28 | 50 | 73 | 76 | 44 |
| 18 | Barrow | 46 | 9 | 7 | 7 | 36 | 32 | 4 | 8 | 11 | 30 | 42 | 66 | 74 | 41 |
| 19 | Workington | 46 | 11 | 6 | 6 | 46 | 33 | 3 | 7 | 13 | 26 | 48 | 72 | 81 | 41 |
| 20 | Darlington | 46 | 15 | 3 | 5 | 53 | 25 | 2 | 4 | 17 | 25 | 64 | 78 | 89 | 41 |
| ***21*** | ***Chester*** | ***46*** | ***7*** | ***10*** | ***6*** | ***38*** | ***26*** | ***6*** | ***3*** | ***14*** | ***35*** | ***55*** | ***73*** | ***81*** | ***39*** |
| 22 | Bradford Park Ave. | 46 | 8 | 6 | 9 | 41 | 41 | 5 | 5 | 13 | 27 | 54 | 68 | 95 | 37 |
| 23 | Southport | 46 | 8 | 3 | 12 | 29 | 40 | 3 | 3 | 17 | 23 | 48 | 52 | 88 | 28 |
| 24 | Crewe Alexandra | 46 | 6 | 5 | 12 | 29 | 41 | 2 | 2 | 19 | 18 | 52 | 47 | 93 | 23 |

**1957/58 Season:** (Back) Hughes, Whitlock, Saunders, Biggins, Mason, Gill.(Front) Foulkes, Bullock, Jepson, Pearson, Davies.

**1958/59 Season:** (Back) Hunt, Souter, Howells, Saunders, Gill, Mason. (Front) Foulkes, Webster, Bullock, Pearson, Richards.

# SEASON 1958-59

## FOOTBALL LEAGUE DIVISION 4

| | Date | Opposition | | FT | HT | Att. | Goalscorers |
|---|---|---|---|---|---|---|---|
| 1 | Aug 23 | TORQUAY UNITED | L | 0-2 | 0-0 | 9070 | |
| 2 | 27 | Crystal Palace | D | 3-3 | 2-1 | 18170 | Pearson, Mason, Foulkes |
| 3 | 30 | Crewe Alex. | W | 4-2 | 3-1 | 8657 | Jepson (3), Richards |
| 4 | Sep 3 | CRYSTAL PALACE | W | 3-2 | 2-1 | 7993 | Mason, Pearson, Webster |
| 5 | 6 | NORTHAMPTON TOWN | L | 2-3 | 2-2 | 9723 | Bullock (2) |
| 6 | 11 | Walsall | D | 2-2 | 2-1 | 11791 | Richards, Croft |
| 7 | 13 | Workington | L | 0-1 | 0-1 | 5717 | |
| 8 | 17 | WALSALL | W | 2-0 | 2-0 | 7800 | Webster (pen), Haddington (og) |
| 9 | 20 | YORK CITY | D | 2-2 | 1-0 | 8536 | Mason, Richards |
| 10 | 27 | Bradford P. A. | L | 0-3 | 0-2 | 7274 | |
| 11 | Oct 1 | WATFORD | W | 2-1 | 1-0 | 4579 | Webster (2, 1 pen) |
| 12 | 4 | PORT VALE | L | 1-2 | 0-1 | 8197 | Webster |
| 13 | 8 | HARTLEPOOLS UNITED | D | 1-1 | 1-0 | 3220 | Bullock |
| 14 | 11 | ALDERSHOT | D | 2-2 | 1-1 | 6655 | Bullock, Pearson |
| 15 | 14 | Watford | L | 2-4 | 0-2 | 7046 | Pearson, Bullock |
| 16 | 18 | Gateshead | W | 1-0 | 1-0 | 3963 | Jepson |
| 17 | 25 | OLDHAM ATHLETIC | W | 5-2 | 4-0 | 7097 | Richards (2), Bullock (2), Hughes (pen) |
| 18 | Nov 1 | Barrow | W | 2-1 | 2-1 | 4333 | Hughes (pen), Jepson |
| 19 | 8 | CARLISLE UNITED | W | 2-1 | 2-1 | 7351 | Richards, Foulkes |
| 20 | 22 | EXETER CITY | W | 4-2 | 3-2 | 8040 | Richards, Bullock, Webster (2) |
| 21 | 29 | Coventry City | L | 1-5 | 0-3 | 15814 | Pearson |
| 22 | Dec 13 | Darlington | D | 0-0 | 0-0 | 4995 | |
| 23 | 20 | Torquay United | L | 0-4 | 0-2 | 4013 | |
| 24 | 25 | Millwall | W | 1-0 | 1-0 | 9260 | Richards |
| 25 | 27 | MILLWALL | D | 0-0 | 0-0 | 9273 | |
| 26 | Jan 1 | Hartlepools United | W | 3-1 | 2-0 | 3952 | Pearson, Bullock, Foulkes |
| 27 | 17 | Gillingham | D | 3-3 | 1-1 | 5331 | B Griffiths, Bullock (2) |
| 28 | 24 | SHREWSBURY TOWN | L | 3-5 | 2-0 | 8170 | Jepson, Bullock, Richards |
| 29 | 31 | WORKINGTON | L | 1-2 | 0-1 | 6499 | Foulkes |
| 30 | Feb 7 | York City | D | 1-1 | 0-0 | 5414 | Jepson |
| 31 | 14 | BRADFORD P. A. | W | 2-0 | 0-0 | 6089 | Webster, Davis |
| 32 | 21 | Port Vale | L | 0-4 | 0-2 | 8851 | |
| 33 | 28 | Aldershot | L | 0-1 | 0-0 | 4518 | |
| 34 | Mar 7 | GATESHEAD | L | 0-1 | 0-1 | 4881 | |
| 35 | 14 | Oldham Athletic | W | 5-3 | 4-2 | 5226 | Foulkes (2), Davis, Pearson, Hunt |
| 36 | 21 | BARROW | W | 2-0 | 1-0 | 4791 | Davis (2) |
| 37 | 27 | Southport | D | 1-1 | 0-0 | 4384 | Jepson |
| 38 | 28 | Carlisle United | L | 3-4 | 2-1 | 4522 | Souter, Davis, Bradley (og) |
| 39 | 30 | SOUTHPORT | W | 2-1 | 1-0 | 5636 | Jepson, Davis |
| 40 | Apr 4 | GILLINGHAM | L | 1-2 | 0-0 | 5513 | Davis |
| 41 | 11 | Exeter City | D | 1-1 | 0-0 | 6464 | Pearson |
| 42 | 13 | Northampton Town | L | 0-4 | 0-3 | 3865 | |
| 43 | 18 | COVENTRY CITY | D | 1-1 | 1-0 | 5920 | Farmer (og) |
| 44 | 22 | CREWE ALEX. | L | 0-1 | 0-0 | 9565 | |
| 45 | 25 | Shrewsbury Town | L | 0-3 | 0-0 | 7260 | |
| 46 | 29 | DARLINGTON | W | 1-0 | 1-0 | 3314 | Webster |

| | Biggins B. | Hughes R. | Souter W. | Hunt R. | Saunders J. | Mason J. | Foulkes W. | Webster H. | Jepson B. | Pearson S. | Richards G. | Griffiths K. | Gill R. | Bullock N. | Owen D. | Croft A. | Howells R. | Spruce G. | Anderson J. | Williams R. | Evans R. | Griffiths B. | Ashfield G. | Davis E. | Whitlock P. | Ireland J. |
|---|---|---|---|---|---|---|---|---|---|---|---|---|---|---|---|---|---|---|---|---|---|---|---|---|---|---|
| 1 | 1 | 2 | 3 | 4 | 5 | 6 | 7 | 8 | 9 | 10 | 11 | | | | | | | | | | | | | | | |
| 2 | 1 | 2 | 3 | 4 | 5 | 6 | 7 | 8 | 9 | 10 | 11 | | | | | | | | | | | | | | | |
| 3 | | 2 | 3 | 4 | 5 | 6 | 7 | 8 | 9 | 10 | 11 | 1 | | | | | | | | | | | | | | |
| 4 | | 2 | 3 | 4 | 5 | 6 | 7 | 8 | 9 | 10 | 11 | 1 | | | | | | | | | | | | | | |
| 5 | | | 3 | 4 | 5 | 6 | 7 | 8 | 9 | | 11 | 1 | 2 | 10 | | | | | | | | | | | | |
| 6 | | | 3 | 4 | 5 | 6 | | 8 | 9 | | 11 | | 2 | 10 | 1 | 7 | | | | | | | | | | |
| 7 | | | 3 | 4 | 5 | 6 | | 8 | 9 | | 11 | | 2 | 10 | | 7 | 1 | | | | | | | | | |
| 8 | | | 3 | 4 | 5 | 6 | 7 | 8 | 9 | | 11 | | 2 | 10 | | | 1 | | | | | | | | | |
| 9 | | | 3 | 4 | | 6 | 7 | 8 | 9 | | 11 | | 2 | 10 | | | 1 | 5 | | | | | | | | |
| 10 | | | 3 | 4 | 5 | 6 | 7 | 8 | | 10 | 11 | | 2 | 9 | | | 1 | | | | | | | | | |
| 11 | | | 2 | 4 | 5 | 6 | 7 | 8 | | 10 | 11 | | 3 | 9 | | | 1 | | | | | | | | | |
| 12 | | | 2 | | 5 | 6 | 7 | 8 | | 10 | 11 | | 3 | 9 | | | 1 | | 4 | | | | | | | |
| 13 | | | | | 5 | 6 | 7 | 9 | | 10 | | | 3 | 8 | | 11 | 1 | | 4 | 2 | | | | | | |
| 14 | | | | | 5 | 6 | 7 | 9 | | 10 | 11 | | 3 | 8 | | | 1 | | 4 | 2 | | | | | | |
| 15 | | 2 | | 4 | 5 | 6 | 7 | 9 | | 10 | 11 | | | 8 | | | 1 | | | 3 | | | | | | |
| 16 | | 2 | 3 | 4 | 5 | 6 | 7 | | 9 | 10 | 11 | | | 8 | | | 1 | | | | | | | | | |
| 17 | | 2 | 3 | 4 | 5 | 6 | 7 | | 9 | 10 | 11 | | | 8 | | | 1 | | | | | | | | | |
| 18 | | 2 | 3 | 4 | 5 | 6 | | | 9 | 10 | 11 | | | 8 | | | 1 | | | | 7 | | | | | |
| 19 | | 2 | 3 | 4 | 5 | 6 | 7 | | 9 | 10 | 11 | | | 8 | | | 1 | | | | | | | | | |
| 20 | | 2 | 3 | 4 | 5 | 6 | 7 | 9 | | 10 | 11 | | | 8 | | | 1 | | | | | | | | | |
| 21 | | 2 | 3 | 4 | 5 | 6 | 7 | | | 9 | 10 | | | 8 | | | 1 | | | 11 | | | | | | |
| 22 | | 2 | 3 | 4 | | 6 | 7 | 9 | | 10 | 11 | | | 8 | | | 1 | 5 | | | | | | | | |
| 23 | | 2 | 3 | 4 | | 6 | 7 | 9 | | 10 | 11 | | | 8 | | | 1 | 5 | | | | | | | | |
| 24 | | 2 | 3 | 4 | | 6 | 7 | 9 | | 10 | 11 | | | 8 | | | 1 | 5 | | | | | | | | |
| 25 | | 2 | 3 | 4 | | 6 | 7 | 9 | | 10 | 11 | 1 | | 8 | | | | 5 | | | | | | | | |
| 26 | | | 3 | 4 | | 6 | 7 | | 9 | 10 | 11 | 1 | 2 | 8 | | | | 5 | | | | | | | | |
| 27 | | | 3 | 4 | 5 | 6 | 7 | | 9 | 10 | | 1 | 2 | 8 | | | | | | | | 11 | | | | |
| 28 | | | 3 | 4 | 5 | 6 | 7 | | 9 | 10 | 11 | 1 | 2 | 8 | | | | | | | | | | | | |
| 29 | | 2 | 3 | 4 | | 6 | 7 | | 9 | 10 | | | | 8 | | | 1 | 5 | | | | 11 | | | | |
| 30 | | | | | | 6 | 7 | 10 | 9 | | 11 | | 3 | 8 | | | 1 | 5 | | 4 | | | 2 | | | |
| 31 | | | | 4 | | | 7 | 10 | | | 11 | | 3 | 8 | | | 1 | 5 | 6 | | | | 2 | 9 | | |
| 32 | | | | 4 | | | 7 | 10 | | | 11 | | 3 | 8 | | | 1 | 5 | 6 | | | | 2 | 9 | | |
| 33 | | | | 4 | | | 7 | 10 | 9 | | 11 | | 3 | 8 | | | 1 | 5 | 6 | | | | 2 | | | |
| 34 | | | | 4 | | | 7 | 10 | | | 11 | | 3 | 8 | | | 1 | 5 | 6 | | | | 2 | 9 | | |
| 35 | | 2 | | 4 | | 6 | 7 | | 8 | 10 | 11 | | 3 | | | | 1 | 5 | | | | | | 9 | | |
| 36 | | 2 | | 4 | 5 | 6 | 7 | | 8 | 10 | 11 | | 3 | | | | 1 | | | | | | | 9 | | |
| 37 | | 2 | | 4 | 5 | 6 | 7 | | 8 | 10 | 11 | | 3 | | | | 1 | | | | | | | 9 | | |
| 38 | | 2 | 3 | 4 | 5 | 6 | 7 | | 8 | | 11 | | | 10 | | | 1 | | | | | | | 9 | | |
| 39 | | 2 | | 4 | | | 7 | | 8 | 10 | 11 | | 3 | | | | 1 | 5 | 6 | | | | | 9 | | |
| 40 | | 2 | | 4 | | | 7 | | 8 | 10 | 11 | | 3 | | | | 1 | 5 | 6 | | | | | 9 | | |
| 41 | | 2 | 4 | | | | | | | 10 | 11 | | 3 | 8 | | | 1 | 5 | 6 | 7 | | | | 9 | | |
| 42 | | 2 | 4 | | | 6 | | | | | 11 | | 3 | 10 | | | 1 | 5 | | 7 | | | | 9 | 8 | |
| 43 | | 2 | 4 | | | | | | 8 | 10 | | | 3 | 11 | | | 1 | 5 | 6 | 7 | | | | 9 | | |
| 44 | 1 | 2 | 4 | | | | 7 | | | 10 | 11 | | 3 | | | | | 5 | 6 | | | | | 9 | | 8 |
| 45 | | 2 | 4 | | | | 7 | | 8 | | | | 3 | 11 | | | 1 | 5 | 6 | | | | | 9 | | 10 |
| 46 | | 2 | 4 | | | | 7 | 10 | 9 | | | | 3 | | | | 1 | 5 | 6 | | | | | 11 | | 8 |
| Apps. | 3 | 28 | 33 | 36 | 25 | 35 | 40 | 26 | 28 | 32 | 40 | 7 | 29 | 35 | 1 | 3 | 35 | 21 | 14 | 8 | 1 | 2 | 5 | 15 | 1 | 3 |
| Goals | | 2 | 1 | 1 | | 3 | 6 | 9 | 9 | 8 | 9 | | | 12 | | 1 | | | | | | 1 | | 7 | | |

Own goals 3

## F.A. CUP

| | Date | Opposition | | FT | HT | Att. | Goalscorers |
|---|---|---|---|---|---|---|---|
| 1R | Nov 15 | BOSTON UNITED | W | 3-2 | 2-1 | 8495 | Bullock, Hughes (pen), Pearson |
| 2R | Dec 6 | BURY | D | 1-1 | 0-0 | 11606 | Webster |
| 2Rr | 9 | Bury | L | 1-2 | 1-2 | 15167 | Hunt |

| | Biggins B. | Hughes R. | Souter W. | Hunt R. | Saunders J. | Mason J. | Foulkes W. | Webster H. | Jepson B. | Pearson S. | Richards G. | Griffiths K. | Gill R. | Bullock N. | Owen D. | Croft A. | Howells R. | Spruce G. | Anderson J. | Williams R. | Evans R. | Griffiths B. | Ashfield G. | Davis E. | Whitlock P. | Ireland J. |
|---|---|---|---|---|---|---|---|---|---|---|---|---|---|---|---|---|---|---|---|---|---|---|---|---|---|---|
| 1R | | 2 | 3 | 4 | 5 | 6 | 7 | | | 10 | 11 | | | 8 | | | 1 | | | 9 | | | | | | |
| 2R | | 2 | 3 | 4 | | 6 | 7 | 9 | | 10 | 11 | | | 8 | | | 1 | 5 | | | | | | | | |
| 2Rr | | 2 | 3 | 4 | | 6 | 7 | 9 | | 10 | 11 | | | 8 | | | 1 | 5 | | | | | | | | |

## WELSH CUP

| | Date | Opposition | | FT | HT | Att. | Goalscorers |
|---|---|---|---|---|---|---|---|
| 5R | Jan 21 | RHYL | L | 1-4 | 0-2 | 1340 | B Griffiths |

| | Biggins B. | Hughes R. | Souter W. | Hunt R. | Saunders J. | Mason J. | Foulkes W. | Webster H. | Jepson B. | Pearson S. | Richards G. | Griffiths K. | Gill R. | Bullock N. | Owen D. | Croft A. | Howells R. | Spruce G. | Anderson J. | Williams R. | Evans R. | Griffiths B. | Ashfield G. | Davis E. | Whitlock P. | Ireland J. |
|---|---|---|---|---|---|---|---|---|---|---|---|---|---|---|---|---|---|---|---|---|---|---|---|---|---|---|
| 5R | | 2 | 3 | | | | | | 9 | | | 1 | | 8 | | 7 | | 5 | 6 | | | 11 | | | 4 | 10 |

### Final League Table

| | | Pl. | Home | | | | | Away | | | | | F. | A. | Pts |
|---|---|---|---|---|---|---|---|---|---|---|---|---|---|---|---|
| | | | W | D | L | F | A | W | D | L | F | A | | | |
| 1 | Port Vale | 46 | 14 | 6 | 3 | 62 | 30 | 12 | 6 | 5 | 48 | 28 | 110 | 58 | 64 |
| 2 | Coventry City | 46 | 18 | 4 | 1 | 50 | 11 | 6 | 8 | 9 | 34 | 36 | 84 | 47 | 60 |
| 3 | York City | 46 | 12 | 10 | 1 | 37 | 17 | 9 | 8 | 6 | 36 | 35 | 73 | 52 | 60 |
| 4 | Shrewsbury Town | 46 | 15 | 5 | 3 | 59 | 24 | 9 | 5 | 9 | 42 | 39 | 101 | 63 | 58 |
| 5 | Exeter City | 46 | 16 | 4 | 3 | 55 | 24 | 7 | 7 | 9 | 32 | 37 | 87 | 61 | 57 |
| 6 | Walsall | 46 | 13 | 5 | 5 | 56 | 25 | 8 | 5 | 10 | 39 | 39 | 95 | 64 | 52 |
| 7 | Crystal Palace | 46 | 12 | 8 | 3 | 54 | 27 | 8 | 4 | 11 | 36 | 44 | 90 | 71 | 52 |
| 8 | Northampton Town | 46 | 14 | 5 | 4 | 48 | 25 | 7 | 4 | 12 | 37 | 53 | 85 | 78 | 51 |
| 9 | Millwall | 46 | 13 | 6 | 4 | 46 | 23 | 7 | 4 | 12 | 30 | 46 | 76 | 69 | 50 |
| 10 | Carlisle United | 46 | 11 | 6 | 6 | 37 | 30 | 8 | 6 | 9 | 25 | 35 | 62 | 65 | 50 |
| 11 | Gillingham | 46 | 14 | 6 | 3 | 53 | 27 | 6 | 3 | 14 | 29 | 50 | 82 | 77 | 49 |
| 12 | Torquay United | 46 | 11 | 5 | 7 | 45 | 32 | 5 | 7 | 11 | 33 | 45 | 78 | 77 | 44 |
| ***13*** | ***Chester*** | ***46*** | ***10*** | ***5*** | ***8*** | ***39*** | ***33*** | ***6*** | ***7*** | ***10*** | ***33*** | ***51*** | ***72*** | ***84*** | ***44*** |
| 14 | Bradford Park Ave. | 46 | 15 | 1 | 7 | 51 | 29 | 3 | 6 | 14 | 24 | 48 | 75 | 77 | 43 |
| 15 | Watford | 46 | 10 | 6 | 7 | 46 | 36 | 6 | 4 | 13 | 35 | 43 | 81 | 79 | 42 |
| 16 | Darlington | 46 | 7 | 8 | 8 | 37 | 36 | 6 | 8 | 9 | 29 | 32 | 66 | 68 | 42 |
| 17 | Workington | 46 | 9 | 10 | 4 | 40 | 32 | 3 | 7 | 13 | 23 | 46 | 63 | 78 | 41 |
| 18 | Crewe Alexandra | 46 | 11 | 5 | 7 | 52 | 32 | 4 | 5 | 14 | 18 | 50 | 70 | 82 | 40 |
| 19 | Hartlepools United | 46 | 11 | 4 | 8 | 50 | 41 | 4 | 6 | 13 | 24 | 47 | 74 | 88 | 40 |
| 20 | Gateshead | 46 | 11 | 3 | 9 | 33 | 30 | 5 | 5 | 13 | 23 | 55 | 56 | 85 | 40 |
| 21 | Oldham Athletic | 46 | 15 | 0 | 8 | 39 | 29 | 1 | 4 | 18 | 20 | 55 | 59 | 84 | 36 |
| 22 | Aldershot | 46 | 8 | 4 | 11 | 37 | 45 | 6 | 3 | 14 | 26 | 52 | 63 | 97 | 35 |
| 23 | Barrow | 46 | 6 | 6 | 11 | 34 | 45 | 3 | 4 | 16 | 17 | 59 | 51 | 104 | 28 |
| 24 | Southport | 46 | 7 | 8 | 8 | 26 | 25 | 0 | 4 | 19 | 15 | 61 | 41 | 86 | 26 |

# SEASON 1959-60

## FOOTBALL LEAGUE DIVISION 4

| | Date | Opposition | | FT | HT | Att. | Goalscorers | Howells R. | Hughes R. | Gill R. | Anderson J. | Spruce G. | Clempson F. | Foulkes W. | Webster H. | Davis E. | Pimlott J. | Bullock N. | Griffiths R. | Souter W. | Hunt R. | Walton J. | Richards G. | Capper J. | Croft A. | Cooper J. | Evans R. | Kelly W. | Ireland J. | Williams R. | Jepson B. | Citron G. | Jones C. | Davies R. | Stopford L. | Owen D. |
|---|---|---|---|---|---|---|---|---|---|---|---|---|---|---|---|---|---|---|---|---|---|---|---|---|---|---|---|---|---|---|---|---|---|---|---|---|
| 1 | Aug 22 | Notts County | L | 1-2 | 1-0 | 9652 | Davis | 1 | 2 | 3 | 4 | 5 | 6 | 7 | 8 | 9 | 10 | 11 | | | | | | | | | | | | | | | | | | |
| 2 | 26 | CARLISLE UNITED | L | 0-1 | 0-1 | 7800 | | 1 | 2 | | 4 | 5 | 6 | 7 | 8 | 9 | 10 | 11 | 3 | | | | | | | | | | | | | | | | | |
| 3 | 29 | WALSALL | L | 1-3 | 1-0 | 7506 | Davis | 1 | | | | 5 | 6 | 7 | | 9 | | 10 | 3 | 2 | 4 | 8 | 11 | | | | | | | | | | | | | |
| 4 | Sep 1 | Carlisle United | L | 1-2 | 0-2 | 9344 | Davis | 1 | 2 | | | | 6 | 7 | 8 | 9 | | 10 | 3 | | 4 | | | 5 | 11 | | | | | | | | | | | |
| 5 | 5 | Hartlepools United | W | 3-2 | 1-2 | 5112 | Clempson (2), Webster | 1 | 2 | 3 | | | 6 | 7 | 8 | 9 | | 10 | | | 4 | | | 5 | 11 | | | | | | | | | | | |
| 6 | 7 | EXETER CITY | W | 1-0 | 1-0 | 6482 | Bullock | 1 | 2 | 3 | | | 6 | | 8 | 9 | | 10 | | | 4 | | | 5 | 11 | 7 | | | | | | | | | | |
| 7 | 12 | CREWE ALEX. | D | 0-0 | 0-0 | 9294 | | 1 | 2 | 3 | | | 6 | | 8 | 9 | | | | | 4 | | | 5 | 11 | 7 | 10 | | | | | | | | | |
| 8 | 17 | Exeter City | L | 0-2 | 0-1 | 7546 | | 1 | 2 | 3 | | | 6 | 11 | | 9 | 10 | | | | 4 | | | 5 | | 7 | 8 | | | | | | | | | |
| 9 | 19 | Gillingham | L | 1-3 | 1-0 | 7551 | Pimlott | 1 | 2 | 3 | | | 6 | 7 | | 9 | 10 | | | | 4 | | 11 | 5 | | | 8 | | | | | | | | | |
| 10 | 23 | OLDHAM ATHLETIC | D | 0-0 | 0-0 | 4059 | | 1 | 2 | 3 | 8 | | 6 | 7 | | 9 | 10 | | | | 4 | | | 5 | | 11 | | | | | | | | | | |
| 11 | 26 | Crystal Palace | W | 4-3 | 2-3 | 18312 | Cooper, Kelly (2), Webster | 1 | 2 | 3 | | 5 | 6 | 7 | 8 | | | 10 | | | 4 | | | | | 11 | | 9 | | | | | | | | |
| 12 | 29 | Oldham Athletic | D | 0-0 | 0-0 | 2970 | | 1 | 2 | 3 | | 5 | 6 | 7 | | | | 10 | | | 4 | | | | | 11 | | 9 | 8 | | | | | | | |
| 13 | Oct 3 | BRADFORD P. A. | D | 1-1 | 1-0 | 6806 | Kelly | 1 | 2 | 3 | | 5 | | 7 | 8 | | | 10 | | | 4 | | | | | 11 | | 9 | | 6 | | | | | | |
| 14 | 5 | Stockport County | L | 0-3 | 0-1 | 7530 | | 1 | 2 | 3 | | | 6 | 7 | | | | | | | 4 | | | 5 | | 11 | | 9 | 10 | | 8 | | | | | |
| 15 | 10 | ALDERSHOT | W | 5-1 | 3-0 | 5958 | Pimlott (2), Foulkes, Kelly, Hunt | 1 | 2 | 3 | | 5 | 6 | 8 | | | 10 | | | | 4 | | 11 | | | 7 | | 9 | | | | | | | | |
| 16 | 14 | STOCKPORT COUNTY | L | 1-2 | 1-0 | 3560 | Kelly | 1 | 2 | 3 | | 5 | 6 | 8 | | | 10 | | | | 4 | | 11 | | | 7 | | 9 | | | | | | | | |
| 17 | 17 | Darlington | D | 0-0 | 0-0 | 4717 | | 1 | 2 | 3 | | 5 | 6 | 8 | | | 10 | | | | 4 | | 11 | | | 7 | | 9 | | | | | | | | |
| 18 | 24 | GATESHEAD | W | 4-2 | 1-1 | 4790 | Clempson, Redhead (og), Kelly, Foulkes | 1 | 2 | 3 | | 5 | 6 | 8 | | | 10 | | | | 4 | | 11 | | | 7 | | 9 | | | | | | | | |
| 19 | 31 | Rochdale | D | 0-0 | 0-0 | 5643 | | 1 | 2 | 3 | | 5 | 6 | 8 | | | 10 | | | | 4 | | 11 | | | 7 | | 9 | | | | | | | | |
| 20 | Nov 7 | WORKINGTON | W | 3-1 | 1-0 | 5019 | Evans, Pimlott (2) | 1 | 2 | 3 | | 5 | 6 | 8 | | 9 | 10 | | | | 4 | | 11 | | | | 7 | | | | | | | | | |
| 21 | 21 | NORTHAMPTON TOWN | D | 1-1 | 1-0 | 7283 | Pimlott | 1 | 2 | 3 | | 5 | 6 | 8 | | | 10 | | | | 4 | | 11 | | | 7 | | 9 | | | | | | | | |
| 22 | 28 | Torquay United | W | 2-1 | 1-1 | 6034 | Cooper, Davis | 1 | 2 | 3 | | 5 | 6 | | | 8 | 10 | | | | 4 | | 11 | | | 7 | | 9 | | | | | | | | |
| 23 | Dec 12 | Southport | L | 1-3 | 0-1 | 2927 | Cooper | 1 | 2 | 3 | | 5 | 6 | 8 | | | 10 | | | | 4 | | 11 | | | 7 | | 9 | | | | | | | | |
| 24 | 19 | NOTTS COUNTY | W | 2-1 | 2-1 | 4209 | Cooper, Hughes (pen) | 1 | 2 | 3 | | 5 | 6 | 8 | | 10 | | | | | 4 | | | | | 7 | | 9 | | | | 11 | | | | |
| 25 | 26 | Barrow | L | 0-3 | 0-2 | 6338 | | 1 | 2 | 3 | | 5 | 6 | 8 | | 10 | | | | | 4 | | | | | 7 | | 9 | | | | 11 | | | | |
| 26 | 28 | BARROW | W | 3-2 | 1-1 | 4532 | Ireland, Richards, McNab (og) | 1 | 2 | 3 | | 5 | 6 | 8 | | | | | | | 4 | | 11 | | | | 7 | 9 | 10 | | | | | | | |
| 27 | Jan 2 | Walsall | L | 1-2 | 1-2 | 9751 | Ireland | 1 | 2 | 3 | 6 | 5 | | 8 | | | | | | | 4 | | 11 | | | | 7 | 9 | 10 | | | | | | | |
| 28 | 16 | HARTLEPOOLS UNITED | D | 1-1 | 0-1 | 4653 | Pimlott | 1 | 2 | 3 | 6 | 5 | | 7 | | | 10 | | | | 4 | | | | 11 | | | 9 | 8 | | | | | | | |
| 29 | 23 | Crewe Alex. | L | 1-2 | 1-0 | 12220 | Cooper | 1 | 2 | 3 | | 5 | 6 | 7 | | | 10 | | | | 4 | | | | | 11 | | 9 | 8 | | | | | | | |
| 30 | 30 | MILLWALL | W | 2-1 | 1-1 | 4323 | Foulkes, Ireland | 1 | 2 | 3 | | 5 | 6 | 7 | | | 10 | | | | 4 | | | | | 11 | | 9 | 8 | | | | | | | |
| 31 | Feb 6 | GILLINGHAM | W | 4-2 | 1-1 | 5022 | Ireland, Kelly (2), Cooper | 1 | 2 | 3 | | 5 | 6 | 7 | | | 10 | | | | 4 | | | | | 11 | | 9 | 8 | | | | | | | |
| 32 | 13 | CRYSTAL PALACE | L | 0-1 | 0-1 | 5132 | | 1 | 2 | 3 | | 5 | 6 | 7 | | | 10 | | | | 4 | | | | | 11 | | 9 | 8 | | | | | | | |
| 33 | 20 | Bradford P. A. | D | 1-1 | 1-0 | 5167 | Kelly | 1 | 2 | 3 | | 5 | 6 | 7 | | | 10 | | | | 4 | | | | | 11 | | 9 | 8 | | | | | | | |
| 34 | 27 | Aldershot | L | 2-3 | 2-2 | 5145 | Foulkes, Pimlott | 1 | 2 | 3 | | 5 | 6 | 7 | | | 10 | | | | 4 | | | | | 11 | | 9 | 8 | | | | | | | |
| 35 | Mar 5 | DARLINGTON | D | 1-1 | 1-0 | 4579 | Pimlott | 1 | 2 | 3 | | 5 | 6 | 7 | | | 10 | | | | 4 | | | | | 11 | | 9 | 8 | | | | | | | |
| 36 | 8 | Doncaster Rovers | L | 0-2 | 0-2 | 4909 | | 1 | 2 | 3 | | | | 7 | | | 10 | | | | 6 | | | 5 | | 11 | | 9 | 8 | | | | 4 | | | |
| 37 | 12 | Gateshead | W | 1-0 | 0-0 | 1735 | Kelly | 1 | | 3 | | 5 | 6 | 7 | | 9 | 10 | | | 2 | 4 | | | | | 11 | | 8 | | | | | | | | |
| 38 | 19 | ROCHDALE | W | 2-1 | 1-1 | 3965 | Pimlott (2) | 1 | 2 | 3 | | 5 | 6 | | | 9 | 10 | | | | 4 | | | | 11 | 7 | | 8 | | | | | | | | |
| 39 | 26 | Workington | L | 0-5 | 0-1 | 2344 | | 1 | 2 | 3 | 4 | | 6 | | | | 10 | | | | | | | 5 | 11 | 7 | | 8 | | | | | | 9 | | |
| 40 | Apr 2 | DONCASTER ROVERS | W | 2-0 | 1-0 | 3862 | Davies, Kilkenny (og) | 1 | 2 | 3 | | 5 | 6 | | | | 10 | | | | 4 | | | | 11 | 7 | | 8 | | | | | | 9 | | |
| 41 | 9 | Northampton Town | L | 0-1 | 0-0 | 7037 | | 1 | 2 | 3 | | 5 | 6 | 7 | | | 10 | | | | 4 | | | | 11 | | | | | | | | | 9 | 8 | |
| 42 | 15 | Watford | L | 2-4 | 2-2 | 13948 | Kelly, Clempson | 1 | 2 | 3 | | 5 | 6 | | | | | | | | 4 | | | | 11 | | 7 | 8 | 10 | | | | | 9 | | |
| 43 | 16 | TORQUAY UNITED | D | 1-1 | 1-0 | 5928 | Hughes (pen) | 1 | 2 | 3 | | 5 | 6 | | | | 10 | | | | 4 | | | | 11 | 7 | | | | | | | | 9 | 8 | |
| 44 | 18 | WATFORD | L | 0-1 | 0-1 | 5962 | | 1 | 2 | 3 | | 5 | 6 | | | | 10 | | | | 4 | | | | 11 | 7 | | | | | | | | 9 | 8 | |
| 45 | 23 | Millwall | L | 1-7 | 0-1 | 9246 | Brand (og) | 1 | 2 | 3 | | 5 | 6 | | | | 10 | | | | | | | | 11 | 7 | | 8 | | | | | 4 | 9 | | |
| 46 | 30 | SOUTHPORT | D | 2-2 | 1-2 | 3956 | Kelly, Stopford | | 2 | 3 | | | 6 | | | | | | | | | | | 5 | 11 | 7 | | 8 | | | | | 4 | 9 | 10 | 1 |
| | | | | | | | Apps. | 45 | 44 | 43 | 6 | 35 | 42 | 35 | 8 | 16 | 31 | 9 | 3 | 2 | 41 | 1 | 13 | 11 | 14 | 34 | 7 | 32 | 14 | 1 | 1 | 2 | 3 | 8 | 4 | 1 |
| | | | | | | | Goals | | 2 | | | | 4 | 4 | 2 | 4 | 11 | 1 | | | 1 | | 1 | | | 6 | 1 | 12 | 4 | | | | | 1 | 1 | |

Own goals 4

## F.A. CUP

| | Date | Opposition | | FT | HT | Att. | Goalscorers | Howells R. | Hughes R. | Gill R. | Anderson J. | Spruce G. | Clempson F. | Foulkes W. | Webster H. | Davis E. | Pimlott J. | Bullock N. | Griffiths R. | Souter W. | Hunt R. | Walton J. | Richards G. | Capper J. | Croft A. | Cooper J. | Evans R. | Kelly W. | Ireland J. | Williams R. | Jepson B. | Citron G. | Jones C. | Davies R. | Stopford L. | Owen D. |
|---|---|---|---|---|---|---|---|---|---|---|---|---|---|---|---|---|---|---|---|---|---|---|---|---|---|---|---|---|---|---|---|---|---|---|---|---|
| 1R | Nov 14 | Tranmere Rovers | W | 1-0 | 0-0 | 14205 | Kelly | 1 | 2 | 3 | | 5 | 6 | 8 | | | 10 | | | | 4 | | 11 | | | 7 | | 9 | | | | | | | | |
| 2R | Dec 5 | Mansfield Town | L | 0-2 | 0-1 | 11509 | | 1 | 2 | 3 | | 5 | 6 | | | 8 | 10 | | | | 4 | | 11 | | | 7 | | 9 | | | | | | | | |

## WELSH CUP

| | Date | Opposition | | FT | HT | Att. | Goalscorers | Howells R. | Hughes R. | Gill R. | Anderson J. | Spruce G. | Clempson F. | Foulkes W. | Webster H. | Davis E. | Pimlott J. | Bullock N. | Griffiths R. | Souter W. | Hunt R. | Walton J. | Richards G. | Capper J. | Croft A. | Cooper J. | Evans R. | Kelly W. | Ireland J. | Williams R. | Jepson B. | Citron G. | Jones C. | Davies R. | Stopford L. | Owen D. |
|---|---|---|---|---|---|---|---|---|---|---|---|---|---|---|---|---|---|---|---|---|---|---|---|---|---|---|---|---|---|---|---|---|---|---|---|---|
| 5R | Feb 3 | HOLYWELL TOWN | L | 0-2 | 0-2 | 822 | | | 2 | 3 | | | 6 | 7 | | | | | | | 4 | | | | | | 8 | 9 | | | | 10 | | | | |

Other players - Biggins B. 5R/1, Ashfield G. 5R/5, Wainwright A. 5R/11

**Final League Table**

| | | Pl. | Home W | D | L | F | A | Away W | D | L | F | A | F. | A. | Pts |
|---|---|---|---|---|---|---|---|---|---|---|---|---|---|---|---|
| 1 | Walsall | 46 | 14 | 5 | 4 | 57 | 33 | 14 | 4 | 5 | 45 | 27 | 102 | 60 | 65 |
| 2 | Notts County | 46 | 19 | 1 | 3 | 66 | 27 | 7 | 7 | 9 | 41 | 42 | 107 | 69 | 60 |
| 3 | Torquay United | 46 | 17 | 3 | 3 | 56 | 27 | 9 | 5 | 9 | 28 | 31 | 84 | 58 | 60 |
| 4 | Watford | 46 | 17 | 2 | 4 | 62 | 28 | 7 | 7 | 9 | 30 | 39 | 92 | 67 | 57 |
| 5 | Millwall | 46 | 12 | 8 | 3 | 54 | 28 | 6 | 9 | 8 | 30 | 33 | 84 | 61 | 53 |
| 6 | Northampton Town | 46 | 13 | 6 | 4 | 50 | 22 | 9 | 3 | 11 | 35 | 41 | 85 | 63 | 53 |
| 7 | Gillingham | 46 | 17 | 4 | 2 | 47 | 21 | 4 | 6 | 13 | 27 | 48 | 74 | 69 | 52 |
| 8 | Crystal Palace | 46 | 12 | 6 | 5 | 61 | 27 | 7 | 6 | 10 | 23 | 37 | 84 | 64 | 50 |
| 9 | Exeter City | 46 | 13 | 7 | 3 | 50 | 30 | 6 | 4 | 13 | 30 | 40 | 80 | 70 | 49 |
| 10 | Stockport County | 46 | 15 | 6 | 2 | 35 | 10 | 4 | 5 | 14 | 23 | 44 | 58 | 54 | 49 |
| 11 | Bradford Park Ave. | 46 | 12 | 10 | 1 | 48 | 25 | 5 | 5 | 13 | 22 | 43 | 70 | 68 | 49 |
| 12 | Rochdale | 46 | 15 | 4 | 4 | 46 | 19 | 3 | 6 | 14 | 19 | 41 | 65 | 60 | 46 |
| 13 | Aldershot | 46 | 14 | 5 | 4 | 50 | 22 | 4 | 4 | 15 | 27 | 52 | 77 | 74 | 45 |
| 14 | Crewe Alexandra | 46 | 14 | 3 | 6 | 51 | 31 | 4 | 6 | 13 | 28 | 57 | 79 | 88 | 45 |
| 15 | Darlington | 46 | 11 | 6 | 6 | 40 | 30 | 6 | 3 | 14 | 23 | 43 | 63 | 73 | 43 |
| 16 | Workington | 46 | 10 | 0 | 5 | 41 | 20 | 4 | 6 | 13 | 27 | 40 | 68 | 60 | 42 |
| 17 | Doncaster Rovers | 46 | 13 | 3 | 7 | 40 | 23 | 3 | 7 | 13 | 29 | 53 | 69 | 76 | 42 |
| 18 | Barrow | 46 | 11 | 8 | 4 | 52 | 29 | 4 | 3 | 16 | 25 | 58 | 77 | 87 | 41 |
| 19 | Carlisle United | 46 | 9 | 6 | 8 | 28 | 28 | 6 | 5 | 12 | 23 | 38 | 51 | 66 | 41 |
| ***20*** | ***Chester*** | ***46*** | ***10*** | ***8*** | ***5*** | ***37*** | ***26*** | ***4*** | ***4*** | ***15*** | ***22*** | ***51*** | ***59*** | ***77*** | ***40*** |
| 21 | Southport | 46 | 9 | 7 | 7 | 30 | 32 | 1 | 7 | 15 | 18 | 60 | 48 | 92 | 34 |
| 22 | Gateshead | 46 | 12 | 3 | 8 | 37 | 27 | 0 | 6 | 17 | 21 | 59 | 58 | 86 | 33 |
| 23 | Oldham Athletic | 46 | 5 | 7 | 11 | 20 | 30 | 3 | 5 | 15 | 21 | 53 | 41 | 83 | 28 |
| 24 | Hartlepools United | 46 | 9 | 2 | 12 | 40 | 41 | 1 | 5 | 17 | 19 | 68 | 59 | 109 | 27 |

**1959/60 Season:** (Back) Pearson (Manager), Hughes, Webster, Howells, Spruce, Griffiths, Bullock.
(Front) Foulkes, Anderson, Clempson, Davis, Pimlott.

**1960/61 Season:** (Back) Barrett, Jones, Gill, Brown, Hughes, Anderson. (Front) Pimlott, Clempson, Davies, Croft, Cooper.

# SEASON 1960-61

## FOOTBALL LEAGUE DIVISION 4

| | Date | Opposition | | FT | HT | Att. | Goalscorers |
|---|---|---|---|---|---|---|---|
| 1 | Aug 20 | GILLINGHAM | D | 2-2 | 0-1 | 7097 | Davies, Kelly |
| 2 | 22 | Bradford P.A. | L | 0-1 | 0-1 | 8244 | |
| 3 | 27 | Barrow | L | 0-3 | 0-1 | 4884 | |
| 4 | 31 | BRADFORD P.A. | W | 3-1 | 2-0 | 5246 | Kelly (2), Cooper |
| 5 | Sep 3 | MILLWALL | L | 1-4 | 1-2 | 5922 | Croft |
| 6 | 7 | Aldershot | L | 2-3 | 1-1 | 7830 | Kelly (2) |
| 7 | 10 | Accrington Stanley | L | 0-2 | 0-0 | 3597 | |
| 8 | 14 | ALDERSHOT | W | 2-0 | 1-0 | 3808 | Anderson, Davies |
| 9 | 17 | YORK CITY | W | 2-1 | 2-0 | 5567 | Anderson, Davies |
| 10 | 19 | Northampton Town | L | 2-3 | 0-2 | 9320 | Davies (2) |
| 11 | 24 | Crewe Alex. | L | 2-5 | 1-3 | 7367 | Hughes (pen), Davies |
| 12 | Oct 1 | WREXHAM | W | 1-0 | 0-0 | 9750 | Kelly |
| 13 | 5 | Workington | L | 0-1 | 0-0 | 2684 | |
| 14 | 8 | Rochdale | L | 0-2 | 0-1 | 3826 | |
| 15 | 15 | MANSFIELD TOWN | D | 3-3 | 2-2 | 5553 | Davies (2), Pritchard |
| 16 | 22 | Stockport County | D | 1-1 | 0-0 | 6770 | Barrett |
| 17 | 29 | EXETER CITY | D | 4-4 | 2-0 | 5173 | Cooper, Barrett, Davies (2) |
| 18 | Nov 12 | SOUTHPORT | W | 1-0 | 0-0 | 4332 | Hughes (pen) |
| 19 | 19 | Darlington | L | 1-5 | 1-2 | 5521 | Cooper |
| 20 | 26 | WORKINGTON | D | 2-2 | 1-1 | 3551 | Cooper, Davies |
| 21 | Dec 3 | Doncaster Rovers | L | 1-2 | 0-1 | 2584 | Davies |
| 22 | 10 | HARTLEPOOLS UNITED | L | 1-2 | 0-0 | 2644 | Davies |
| 23 | 17 | Gillingham | L | 0-3 | 0-2 | 4902 | |
| 24 | 26 | OLDHAM ATHLETIC | W | 3-1 | 1-1 | 6035 | Kelly, Clempson (2) |
| 25 | 27 | Oldham Athletic | L | 1-4 | 1-3 | 19315 | Kelly |
| 26 | 31 | BARROW | D | 0-0 | 0-0 | 3557 | |
| 27 | Jan 7 | CRYSTAL PALACE | W | 3-0 | 1-0 | 4243 | Davies, Clempson, Cooper |
| 28 | 14 | Millwall | L | 1-5 | 0-1 | 7947 | Kelly |
| 29 | 21 | ACCRINGTON STANLEY | L | 2-3 | 2-1 | 3878 | Davies, Cooper |
| 30 | 28 | Crystal Palace | L | 1-5 | 1-3 | 14150 | Davies |
| 31 | Feb 4 | York City | L | 0-2 | 0-2 | 4867 | |
| 32 | 11 | CREWE ALEX. | D | 0-0 | 0-0 | 7521 | |
| 33 | 18 | Wrexham | W | 2-1 | 1-1 | 9653 | Davies (2) |
| 34 | 25 | ROCHDALE | W | 3-1 | 1-1 | 3877 | Clempson, Hughes (pen), Cooper |
| 35 | Mar 4 | Mansfield Town | L | 1-3 | 1-2 | 4563 | Davies |
| 36 | 8 | NORTHAMPTON TOWN | L | 0-2 | 0-0 | 5455 | |
| 37 | 11 | STOCKPORT COUNTY | D | 0-0 | 0-0 | 3942 | |
| 38 | 13 | Peterborough United | L | 0-6 | 0-4 | 13180 | |
| 39 | 18 | Exeter City | L | 1-4 | 0-2 | 3642 | Edwards |
| 40 | 25 | PETERBOROUGH UNITED | L | 1-2 | 1-0 | 5473 | Davies |
| 41 | 31 | Carlisle United | L | 1-3 | 0-0 | 4381 | Croft |
| 42 | Apr 1 | Southport | W | 2-1 | 0-0 | 3295 | Kelly, Pritchard |
| 43 | 3 | CARLISLE UNITED | W | 3-2 | 2-2 | 3908 | Pritchard, Kelly (2) |
| 44 | 8 | DARLINGTON | L | 0-3 | 0-1 | 3515 | |
| 45 | 22 | DONCASTER ROVERS | L | 1-2 | 0-1 | 2466 | Davies |
| 46 | 29 | Hartlepools United | D | 4-4 | 1-2 | 4381 | Hughes (pen), Davies (2), Cooper |

| | Brown W. | Hughes R. | Gill R. | Jones H. | Barrett T. | Hunt R. | Foulkes W. | Kelly W. | Davies R. | Anderson J. | Croft A. | Morris E. | Watson J. | Stopford L. | Cooper J. | Capper J. | Clempson F. | Pimlott J. | Spruce G. | Pritchard A. | Owen D. | Raybould E. | Richards G. | Hennin D. | Edwards M. | Field A. | Ireland J. |
|---|---|---|---|---|---|---|---|---|---|---|---|---|---|---|---|---|---|---|---|---|---|---|---|---|---|---|---|
|1|1|2|3|4|5|6|7|8|9|10|11|||||||||||||||||
|2|1|||4|5|6|7|10|9|||2|3|8|11|||||||||||||
|3|1|2|3|4|6||8|10|9||11||||7|5||||||||||||
|4|1|2|3|4|5||10|9||8|11||||7||6|||||||||||
|5|1|2|3|4|5||10|9||8|11||||7||6|||||||||||
|6|1|2|3|4|5||10|9||8|11||||7||6|||||||||||
|7|1|2|3|4|5||8|10|9||11||||7||6|||||||||||
|8|1|2|3|4|5||||9|8|11||||7||6|10||||||||||
|9|1|2|3|4|5||||9|8|11||||7||6|10||||||||||
|10|1|2|3|4|5|||9|10|8|11||||7||6|||||||||||
|11|1|2|3|4|5||||9|8|11||||7||6|10||||||||||
|12|1|2|3||6||7|10|9|8|||||11|5|||4|||||||||
|13|1|2|||6||7|10|9|8|||3||11|5|||4|||||||||
|14|1|2|||6|4|7|10|9|8|||3||11|5||||||||||||
|15|1|2|||8|4|||9||7||3||11|5|6|||10||||||||
|16|1|2|||8|6|||9||7||3||11|5|||4|10||||||||
|17||2|||8|6|7||9||||3||11|5|||4|10|1|||||||
|18||2|3|4|6||7||9|8|||||11|5||10|||1|||||||
|19||2|3|4|6||7||9|8|||||11|5||10|||1|||||||
|20|1|2||4|6||8||9||7||3||11|5||||10||||||||
|21||2||4|6||7||9||11||3||8|5||||10|1|||||||
|22||2||4|||7||9||11||3||8|5|6|||10|1|||||||
|23|1|2|||4||7|9|8||11||3||10|5|6|||||||||||
|24|1|2|||4|||9|8||11||3||7|5|10|||||6||||||
|25|1||2||4|||9|8||11||3||7|5||10||||6||||||
|26|1|2|||4|||9|8||11||3||7|5|10|||||6||||||
|27|1|2|||4|||9|8||11||3||7|5|10|||||6||||||
|28|1|2|||6|||9|8||11||3||7|5|10|||||4||||||
|29|1|2|||6|||9|8||11||3||7|5|10|||||4||||||
|30|1|2|||6||7|9|8||||3|||5|10|||||4|11|||||
|31|1|2|||6||7|9|8|10|||3|||5||||||4|11|||||
|32|1|2|||6|4|||9|8|11||3||7|5|10|||||||||||
|33|1|2|||6||||9||11||3||7|5|8|||||||4|10|||
|34|1|2|||||8||9||7||3||11|5|10|||||||4|6|||
|35|1|2|||5||8||9||7||3||11||10|||||||4|6|||
|36|1|2|||5||10||8||7||3||11||||||||||4|6|9||
|37|1|2|3||5||7||9||||||||6|8|||||11|4|10|||
|38|1|2|||||10|8|||7||3||||4||||||11|5|6|9||
|39|1|2|3||5||||9||7||||11||10|8||||||4|6|||
|40|1|2|3||6||||9||7||||8|5||11||||||4|10|||
|41|1|2|3||||||9||7||||8|5|6|11||||||4|10|||
|42|1|2||3||||9|||7||||11||||5|8||||6|10||4|
|43|1|2||3||||9|||7||||11||||5|8||||6|10||4|
|44|1|2||3||||9|||7||||11||||5|8||||6|10||4|
|45|1|2|3||5||7||9|8|11|||||||||10||||4|6|||
|46|1|2|3||5||||9|8|11||||7|||||10||||4|6|||
|Apps.|41|44|20|19|39|7|25|24|39|17|36|1|24|1|40|26|25|10|7|11|5|8|4|14|14|2|3|
|Goals||4|||2|||12|23|2|2||||8||4|||3|||||1|||

## F.A. CUP

| | Date | Opposition | | FT | HT | Att. | Goalscorers |
|---|---|---|---|---|---|---|---|
| 1R | Nov 5 | CARLISLE UNITED | L | 0-1 | 0-1 | 5899 | |

| | Brown W. | Hughes R. | Gill R. | Jones H. | Barrett T. | Hunt R. | Foulkes W. | Kelly W. | Davies R. | Anderson J. | Croft A. | Morris E. | Watson J. | Stopford L. | Cooper J. | Capper J. | Clempson F. | Pimlott J. | Spruce G. | Pritchard A. | Owen D. | Raybould E. | Richards G. | Hennin D. | Edwards M. | Field A. | Ireland J. |
|---|---|---|---|---|---|---|---|---|---|---|---|---|---|---|---|---|---|---|---|---|---|---|---|---|---|---|---|
|1R||2|3||10|4|7|8|9||||||11|5|6||||1|||||||

## LEAGUE CUP

| | Date | Opposition | | FT | HT | Att. | Goalscorers |
|---|---|---|---|---|---|---|---|
| 1R | Oct 12 | LEYTON ORIENT | D | 2-2 | 0-2 | 9074 | Davies, Cooper |
| 1Rr | 17 | Leyton Orient | L | 0-1 | 0-0 | 5002 | |

| | Brown W. | Hughes R. | Gill R. | Jones H. | Barrett T. | Hunt R. | Foulkes W. | Kelly W. | Davies R. | Anderson J. | Croft A. | Morris E. | Watson J. | Stopford L. | Cooper J. | Capper J. | Clempson F. | Pimlott J. | Spruce G. | Pritchard A. | Owen D. | Raybould E. | Richards G. | Hennin D. | Edwards M. | Field A. | Ireland J. |
|---|---|---|---|---|---|---|---|---|---|---|---|---|---|---|---|---|---|---|---|---|---|---|---|---|---|---|---|
|1R|1|2|||8|4|||9||7||3||11|5|6|||10||||||||
|1Rr|1|2|||8|6|||9|10|7||3||11|5|||4|||||||||

## WELSH CUP

| | Date | Opposition | | FT | HT | Att. | Goalscorers |
|---|---|---|---|---|---|---|---|
| 5R | Feb 1 | PORTMADOC | W | 2-1 | 2-0 | 1709 | Kelly, Clempson |
| 6R | 22 | Bangor City | L | 1-3 | 0-1 | 2500 | Hughes (pen) |

| | Brown W. | Hughes R. | Gill R. | Jones H. | Barrett T. | Hunt R. | Foulkes W. | Kelly W. | Davies R. | Anderson J. | Croft A. | Morris E. | Watson J. | Stopford L. | Cooper J. | Capper J. | Clempson F. | Pimlott J. | Spruce G. | Pritchard A. | Owen D. | Raybould E. | Richards G. | Hennin D. | Edwards M. | Field A. | Ireland J. |
|---|---|---|---|---|---|---|---|---|---|---|---|---|---|---|---|---|---|---|---|---|---|---|---|---|---|---|---|
|5R|1|2|||4||7|9|8|10|||3|||5|6||||||11|||||
|6R|1|2|||6|4|7||9|8|11||3||||10||5|||||||||

## FRIENDLIES

| | Date | Opposition | | FT | HT | Att. | Goalscorers |
|---|---|---|---|---|---|---|---|
| 1 | Mar 1 | MANCHESTER UNITED | L | 0-6 | 0-1 | 8673 | |
| 2 | Apr 14 | THIRD LANARK | W | 2-0 | 2-0 | 3621 | Davies, Pritchard |
| 3 | 26 | ALL STAR XI * | L | 4-5 | 1-1 | 3188 | Foulkes, Kelly, Anderson, Clempson |

* Ron Hughes Testimonial

### Final League Table

| | | Pl. | Home W | D | L | F | A | Away W | D | L | F | A | F. | A. | Pts |
|---|---|---|---|---|---|---|---|---|---|---|---|---|---|---|---|
| 1 | Peterborough Utd. | 46 | 18 | 3 | 2 | 85 | 30 | 10 | 7 | 6 | 49 | 35 | 134 | 65 | 66 |
| 2 | Crystal Palace | 46 | 16 | 4 | 3 | 64 | 28 | 13 | 2 | 8 | 46 | 41 | 110 | 69 | 64 |
| 3 | Northampton Town | 46 | 16 | 4 | 3 | 53 | 25 | 9 | 6 | 8 | 37 | 37 | 90 | 62 | 60 |
| 4 | Bradford Park Ave. | 46 | 16 | 5 | 2 | 49 | 22 | 10 | 3 | 10 | 35 | 52 | 84 | 74 | 60 |
| 5 | York City | 46 | 17 | 3 | 3 | 50 | 14 | 4 | 6 | 13 | 30 | 46 | 80 | 60 | 51 |
| 6 | Millwall | 46 | 13 | 3 | 7 | 56 | 33 | 8 | 5 | 10 | 41 | 53 | 97 | 86 | 50 |
| 7 | Darlington | 46 | 11 | 7 | 5 | 41 | 24 | 7 | 6 | 10 | 37 | 46 | 78 | 70 | 49 |
| 8 | Workington | 46 | 14 | 3 | 6 | 38 | 28 | 7 | 4 | 12 | 36 | 48 | 74 | 76 | 49 |
| 9 | Crewe Alexandra | 46 | 11 | 4 | 8 | 40 | 29 | 9 | 5 | 9 | 21 | 38 | 61 | 67 | 49 |
| 10 | Aldershot | 46 | 16 | 4 | 3 | 55 | 19 | 2 | 5 | 16 | 24 | 50 | 79 | 69 | 45 |
| 11 | Doncaster Rovers | 46 | 15 | 0 | 8 | 52 | 33 | 4 | 7 | 12 | 24 | 45 | 76 | 78 | 45 |
| 12 | Oldham Athletic | 46 | 13 | 4 | 6 | 57 | 38 | 6 | 3 | 14 | 22 | 50 | 79 | 88 | 45 |
| 13 | Stockport County | 46 | 14 | 4 | 5 | 31 | 21 | 4 | 5 | 14 | 26 | 45 | 57 | 66 | 45 |
| 14 | Southport | 46 | 12 | 6 | 5 | 47 | 27 | 7 | 0 | 10 | 22 | 40 | 00 | 07 | 44 |
| 15 | Gillingham | 46 | 9 | 7 | 7 | 45 | 34 | 6 | 6 | 11 | 19 | 32 | 64 | 66 | 43 |
| 16 | Wrexham | 46 | 12 | 4 | 7 | 38 | 22 | 5 | 4 | 14 | 24 | 34 | 62 | 56 | 42 |
| 17 | Rochdale | 46 | 13 | 7 | 3 | 43 | 19 | 4 | 1 | 18 | 17 | 47 | 60 | 66 | 42 |
| 18 | Accrington Stanley | 46 | 12 | 4 | 7 | 44 | 32 | 4 | 4 | 15 | 30 | 56 | 74 | 88 | 40 |
| 19 | Carlisle United | 46 | 10 | 7 | 6 | 43 | 37 | 3 | 6 | 14 | 18 | 42 | 61 | 79 | 39 |
| 20 | Mansfield Town | 46 | 10 | 3 | 10 | 39 | 34 | 6 | 3 | 14 | 32 | 44 | 71 | 78 | 38 |
| 21 | Exeter City | 46 | 12 | 3 | 8 | 39 | 32 | 2 | 7 | 14 | 27 | 62 | 66 | 94 | 38 |
| 22 | Barrow | 46 | 10 | 6 | 7 | 33 | 28 | 3 | 5 | 15 | 19 | 51 | 52 | 79 | 37 |
| 23 | Hartlepools United | 46 | 10 | 4 | 9 | 46 | 40 | 2 | 4 | 17 | 25 | 63 | 71 | 103 | 32 |
| ***24*** | ***Chester*** | ***46*** | ***9*** | ***7*** | ***7*** | ***38*** | ***35*** | ***2*** | ***2*** | ***19*** | ***23*** | ***69*** | ***61*** | ***104*** | ***31*** |

# SEASON 1961-62

## FOOTBALL LEAGUE DIVISION 4

| | Date | Opposition | | FT | HT | Att. | Goalscorers |
|---|---|---|---|---|---|---|---|
| 1 | Aug 19 | OLDHAM ATHLETIC | W | 1-0 | 0-0 | 9248 | Edwards |
| 2 | 23 | BRADFORD CITY | L | 1-2 | 0-1 | 8692 | Jones |
| 3 | 26 | Accrington Stanley * | W | 1-0 | 1-0 | 4106 | Jones |
| 4 | 30 | Bradford City | L | 0-2 | 0-0 | 7877 | |
| 5 | Sep 2 | DARLINGTON | D | 2-2 | 1-1 | 6423 | White, Jones |
| 6 | 6 | CARLISLE UNITED | D | 1-1 | 0-1 | 6974 | Thompson (og) |
| 7 | 9 | Hartlepools United | W | 3-1 | 1-1 | 4838 | Cooper (2), Morris |
| 8 | 16 | SOUTHPORT | W | 2-0 | 1-0 | 6357 | Hennin, Davies |
| 9 | 19 | Doncaster Rovers | L | 0-2 | 0-0 | 6779 | |
| 10 | 23 | Tranmere Rovers | L | 1-4 | 0-2 | 9182 | Edwards |
| 11 | 27 | DONCASTER ROVERS | L | 2-3 | 2-2 | 6671 | Davies, Jones |
| 12 | 30 | WREXHAM | D | 1-1 | 0-0 | 14462 | Davies |
| 13 | Oct 2 | Colchester United | L | 2-5 | 0-1 | 7148 | Pritchard, Morris |
| 14 | 7 | Workington | L | 1-4 | 0-1 | 3145 | Davies |
| 15 | 11 | COLCHESTER UNITED | D | 2-2 | 1-1 | 7186 | Clarke, Davies |
| 16 | 14 | YORK CITY | D | 1-1 | 1-1 | 6399 | Bellett |
| 17 | 21 | Chesterfield | L | 1-4 | 0-2 | 4436 | Powell (og) |
| 18 | 28 | GILLINGHAM | D | 1-1 | 1-0 | 4439 | Pritchard |
| 19 | Nov 11 | MANSFIELD TOWN | L | 0-1 | 0-0 | 4186 | |
| 20 | 18 | Barrow | L | 2-3 | 1-0 | 4228 | White (2) |
| 21 | Dec 2 | Crewe Alex. | D | 1-1 | 0-1 | 5092 | Hennin |
| 22 | 9 | EXETER CITY | D | 1-1 | 1-0 | 3192 | Morris |
| 23 | 16 | Oldham Athletic | L | 1-4 | 0-3 | 9144 | Hennin |
| 24 | 23 | ACCRINGTON STANLEY * | D | 0-0 | 0-0 | 2153 | |
| 25 | 26 | ALDERSHOT | L | 2-3 | 1-2 | 2775 | Davies (2) |
| 26 | Jan 6 | Millwall | L | 0-2 | 0-2 | 10352 | |
| 27 | 13 | Darlington | L | 0-2 | 0-1 | 3741 | |
| 28 | 20 | HARTLEPOOLS UNITED | D | 4-4 | 2-2 | 2602 | Edwards (2), Clarke, Fitzgerald |
| 29 | 27 | ROCHDALE | L | 2-3 | 0-2 | 4082 | Davies, Aspden (og) |
| 30 | Feb 3 | Southport | L | 0-1 | 0-1 | 4018 | |
| 31 | 9 | TRANMERE ROVERS | D | 1-1 | 1-0 | 7371 | Jones |
| 32 | 17 | Wrexham | D | 0-0 | 0-0 | 14220 | |
| 33 | 24 | WORKINGTON | L | 1-3 | 0-1 | 4011 | Jones |
| 34 | Mar 3 | York City | L | 1-5 | 0-2 | 4600 | Davies |
| 35 | 10 | CHESTERFIELD | W | 4-1 | 2-0 | 4176 | Fitzgerald, Clarke(og), Hewitt, Davies |
| 36 | 17 | Gillingham | D | 0-0 | 0-0 | 5187 | |
| 37 | 24 | MILLWALL | L | 2-4 | 1-1 | 4970 | Fitzgerald, Hewitt |
| 38 | 30 | Mansfield Town | L | 0-3 | 0-1 | 5168 | |
| 39 | Apr 4 | Aldershot | L | 2-6 | 1-1 | 3833 | Davies, Hewitt |
| 40 | 7 | BARROW | L | 2-3 | 0-2 | 2927 | Davies, Cooper |
| 41 | 14 | Rochdale | L | 2-3 | 2-0 | 3061 | Hennin, Myerscough |
| 42 | 20 | Stockport County | W | 1-0 | 1-0 | 4388 | Fitzgerald |
| 43 | 21 | CREWE ALEX. | W | 1-0 | 1-0 | 3890 | Myerscough |
| 44 | 23 | STOCKPORT COUNTY | W | 2-0 | 1-0 | 5105 | Myerscough, Davies |
| 45 | 28 | Exeter City | L | 0-5 | 0-2 | 3219 | |
| 46 | May 1 | Carlisle United | L | 0-2 | 0-1 | 12660 | |

| | Hardie J. | Hughes R. | Donaldson F. | Hennin D. | Kennedy J. | Edwards M. | Morris F. | White W. | Davies R. | Fitzgerald P. | Jones M. | Pritchard A. | Ireland J. | Cooper J. | Barton R. | Bellett W. | Clarke R. | Raybould E. | Cartlidge D. | Gill R. | Evans J. | Stopford L. | Myerscough W. | Hewitt R. | Watson J. |
|---|---|---|---|---|---|---|---|---|---|---|---|---|---|---|---|---|---|---|---|---|---|---|---|---|---|
| 1 | 1 | 2 | 3 | 4 | 5 | 6 | 7 | 8 | 9 | 10 | 11 | | | | | | | | | | | | | | |
| 2 | 1 | 2 | 3 | 4 | 5 | 6 | 7 | 8 | 9 | 10 | 11 | | | | | | | | | | | | | | |
| 3 | 1 | 2 | 3 | 4 | 5 | 6 | 7 | | 9 | 8 | 11 | 10 | | | | | | | | | | | | | |
| 4 | 1 | 2 | 3 | 6 | 5 | | 7 | | 9 | 8 | 11 | 10 | 4 | | | | | | | | | | | | |
| 5 | 1 | 2 | 3 | 4 | 5 | 6 | 7 | 8 | 9 | 10 | 11 | | | | | | | | | | | | | | |
| 6 | 1 | 2 | 3 | 4 | 5 | 6 | 9 | | 8 | 10 | 11 | | | 7 | | | | | | | | | | | |
| 7 | 1 | 2 | 3 | 4 | 5 | 6 | 9 | | 8 | 10 | 11 | | | 7 | | | | | | | | | | | |
| 8 | 1 | 2 | 3 | 4 | 5 | 6 | 9 | | 8 | 10 | 11 | | | 7 | | | | | | | | | | | |
| 9 | 1 | 2 | 3 | 4 | 5 | 6 | 9 | | 8 | 10 | 11 | | | 7 | | | | | | | | | | | |
| 10 | 1 | 2 | 3 | 4 | 5 | 6 | 9 | | 8 | 10 | 11 | | | 7 | | | | | | | | | | | |
| 11 | | 2 | 3 | 4 | 5 | 6 | 8 | | 10 | 9 | 11 | | | 7 | 1 | | | | | | | | | | |
| 12 | 1 | 2 | 3 | 4 | 5 | 6 | | 10 | 8 | 9 | 11 | | | 7 | | | | | | | | | | | |
| 13 | 1 | 2 | | 4 | 5 | 6 | 7 | 8 | 9 | | 11 | 10 | | | | 3 | | | | | | | | | |
| 14 | 1 | 2 | 3 | 4 | 5 | 6 | 7 | 8 | 9 | | 11 | 10 | | | | | | | | | | | | | |
| 15 | 1 | 2 | 3 | 4 | 5 | 6 | | | 9 | 11 | | | | 7 | | 8 | 10 | | | | | | | | |
| 16 | 1 | 2 | 3 | 4 | 5 | 6 | | | 9 | 11 | | | | 7 | | 8 | 10 | | | | | | | | |
| 17 | 1 | 2 | 3 | 4 | 5 | 6 | | | 9 | 8 | 11 | | | 7 | | | 10 | | | | | | | | |
| 18 | 1 | 2 | | 4 | 5 | | 7 | | 9 | | 11 | 8 | | | | 3 | 10 | 6 | | | | | | | |
| 19 | 1 | 2 | 3 | 4 | 5 | | 9 | | | 7 | 11 | | | | | | 10 | 6 | 8 | | | | | | |
| 20 | 1 | 2 | 3 | 4 | 5 | | | 10 | 9 | 7 | 11 | | | | | | | | 8 | 6 | | | | | |
| 21 | 1 | 2 | 3 | 4 | | 6 | 9 | 10 | | 7 | 11 | | | | | | | | 8 | 5 | | | | | |
| 22 | 1 | 2 | 3 | 4 | 5 | 6 | 9 | 10 | | | 11 | | | 7 | | | | | 8 | | | | | | |
| 23 | 1 | 2 | 3 | 4 | 5 | | 9 | 10 | | | 11 | | | 7 | | 6 | | | 8 | | | | | | |
| 24 | 1 | 2 | | 4 | 5 | 10 | | 8 | 9 | 7 | 11 | | | | | 6 | | | | 3 | | | | | |
| 25 | 1 | 2 | | 4 | | 10 | | | 9 | 7 | 11 | | | | | 6 | 8 | | | 5 | 3 | | | | |
| 26 | 1 | 2 | | 4 | 5 | | | | 9 | 7 | 11 | | | 8 | | 6 | 10 | | | 3 | | | | | |
| 27 | 1 | 2 | | 4 | 5 | | | 8 | 9 | 7 | 11 | | | | | 6 | 10 | | | 3 | | | | | |
| 28 | 1 | 2 | | 4 | 5 | 6 | 7 | | 9 | 8 | 11 | | | | | | 10 | | | 3 | | | | | |
| 29 | 1 | 2 | 3 | | 5 | 6 | 7 | | 9 | 8 | 11 | | 4 | | | | 10 | | | | | | | | |
| 30 | 1 | 2 | | 4 | 5 | 6 | 7 | | 9 | 8 | 11 | | | | | | 10 | | | 3 | | | | | |
| 31 | 1 | 2 | | 4 | | 6 | | | 9 | 8 | 11 | 10 | | 7 | | 3 | | | | 5 | | | | | |
| 32 | 1 | 2 | | 4 | | 6 | | 10 | 9 | 8 | 11 | | | 7 | | 3 | | | | 5 | | | | | |
| 33 | 1 | 2 | | 4 | | 6 | | 10 | 9 | 8 | 11 | | | | | 3 | | | | 5 | | 7 | | | |
| 34 | 1 | 2 | | 4 | | 6 | | | 9 | 7 | 11 | | | | | 3 | | | | 5 | | | 8 | 10 | |
| 35 | 1 | | | 4 | 5 | | | | 9 | 7 | 11 | | | | | | | | 6 | 2 | 3 | | 8 | 10 | |
| 36 | 1 | 2 | | 4 | 5 | | | | 9 | 7 | 11 | | | | | | | | 6 | | 3 | | 8 | 10 | |
| 37 | 1 | 2 | | 6 | 5 | | 7 | | | 9 | 11 | | 4 | | | | | | | | 3 | | 8 | 10 | |
| 38 | 1 | 2 | | 4 | | 6 | 7 | | | 9 | 11 | | | | | | | | | 5 | 3 | | 8 | 10 | |
| 39 | 1 | 2 | | 4 | | | | | 9 | 11 | | | | 7 | | | | | 6 | 5 | 3 | | 8 | 10 | |
| 40 | 1 | | | | 5 | | 4 | | 9 | 11 | | | | 7 | | | | | 6 | 3 | 2 | | 8 | 10 | |
| 41 | 1 | | | 4 | | | 7 | | 9 | | 11 | | | | | | | | 6 | 2 | 3 | | 8 | 10 | 5 |
| 42 | 1 | 2 | | 4 | 5 | | 7 | | 9 | 11 | | | | | | | | | 6 | | 3 | | 8 | 10 | |
| 43 | 1 | 2 | | 4 | 5 | 6 | 7 | | 9 | 11 | | | | | | | | | | | 3 | | 8 | 10 | |
| 44 | 1 | 2 | | 4 | 5 | 6 | 7 | | 9 | 11 | | | | | | | | | | | 3 | | 8 | 10 | |
| 45 | 1 | 2 | | | 5 | 6 | 7 | | 9 | 11 | | | 4 | | | | | | | 3 | | | 8 | 10 | |
| 46 | 1 | 2 | | | 5 | | 7 | | 9 | 11 | | | 4 | | | | | | 6 | 3 | | | 8 | 10 | |
| Apps. | 43 | 41 | 21 | 40 | 35 | 29 | 29 | 13 | 38 | 38 | 35 | 5 | 5 | 17 | 1 | 12 | 11 | 2 | 12 | 18 | 11 | 1 | 13 | 13 | 1 |
| Goals | | | | 4 | | 4 | 3 | 3 | 13 | 4 | 5 | 2 | | 3 | | 1 | 2 | | | | | | 3 | 3 | |

Own goals 4

Accrington Stanley resigned from league, record expunged

## F.A. CUP

| | Date | Opposition | | FT | HT | Att. | Goalscorers | Hardie J. | Hughes R. | Donaldson F. | Hennin D. | Kennedy J. | Edwards M. | Morris F. | White W. | Davies R. | Fitzgerald P. | Jones M. | Pritchard A. | Ireland J. | Cooper J. | Barton R. | Bellett W. | Clarke R. | Raybould E. | Cartlidge D. | Gill R. | Evans J. | Stopford L. | Myerscough W. | Hewitt R. | Watson J. |
|---|---|---|---|---|---|---|---|---|---|---|---|---|---|---|---|---|---|---|---|---|---|---|---|---|---|---|---|---|---|---|---|---|
| 1R | Nov 4 | ASHINGTON | W | 4-1 | 1-0 | 4361 | Davies (2), Morris, Jones | 1 | 2 | 3 | 4 | | | 8 | | 9 | 7 | 11 | | | | | | 10 | 6 | | 5 | | | | | |
| 2R | 25 | MORECAMBE | L | 0-1 | 0-1 | 7982 | | 1 | 2 | 3 | 6 | | | 4 | 8 | 9 | 7 | 11 | | | | | | | | 10 | 5 | | | | | |

## LEAGUE CUP

| | Date | Opposition | | FT | HT | Att. | Goalscorers | Hardie J. | Hughes R. | Donaldson F. | Hennin D. | Kennedy J. | Edwards M. | Morris F. | White W. | Davies R. | Fitzgerald P. | Jones M. | Pritchard A. | Ireland J. | Cooper J. | Barton R. | Bellett W. | Clarke R. | Raybould E. | Cartlidge D. | Gill R. | Evans J. | Stopford L. | Myerscough W. | Hewitt R. | Watson J. |
|---|---|---|---|---|---|---|---|---|---|---|---|---|---|---|---|---|---|---|---|---|---|---|---|---|---|---|---|---|---|---|---|---|
| 1R | Sep 13 | Reading | L | 2-4 | 1-1 | 7786 | Cooper, Jones | 1 | 2 | 3 | 4 | 5 | 6 | 9 | | 8 | 10 | 11 | | | 7 | | | | | | | | | | | |

## WELSH CUP

| | Date | Opposition | | FT | HT | Att. | Goalscorers | Hardie J. | Hughes R. | Donaldson F. | Hennin D. | Kennedy J. | Edwards M. | Morris F. | White W. | Davies R. | Fitzgerald P. | Jones M. | Pritchard A. | Ireland J. | Cooper J. | Barton R. | Bellett W. | Clarke R. | Raybould E. | Cartlidge D. | Gill R. | Evans J. | Stopford L. | Myerscough W. | Hewitt R. | Watson J. |
|---|---|---|---|---|---|---|---|---|---|---|---|---|---|---|---|---|---|---|---|---|---|---|---|---|---|---|---|---|---|---|---|---|
| 5R | Jan 31 | HOLYHEAD TOWN | L | 1-2 | 0-1 | 1967 | Fitzgerald | 1 | 2 | 3 | | 5 | 6 | 7 | | 9 | 8 | 11 | | | | | 4 | 10 | | | | | | | | |

## FRIENDLIES

| | Date | Opposition | | FT | HT | Att. | Goalscorers |
|---|---|---|---|---|---|---|---|
| 1 | Dec 5 | STIRLING ALBION | W | 1-0 | 0-0 | 841 | Cartlidge |
| 2 | Apr 11 | HAMBORN | W | 4-1 | 1-0 | 2318 | Davies (2), Hewitt, Myerscough |
| 3 | 25 | SELECT XI * | W | 4-2 | 0-0 | 2831 | Myerscough (2), Morris (2, 1 pen) |

* Ray Gill Testimonial

### Final League Table

| | | Pl. | Home W | D | L | F | A | Away W | D | L | F | A | F. | A. | Pts |
|---|---|---|---|---|---|---|---|---|---|---|---|---|---|---|---|
| 1 | Millwall | 44 | 16 | 3 | 3 | 47 | 18 | 7 | 7 | 8 | 40 | 44 | 87 | 62 | 56 |
| 2 | Colchester United | 44 | 17 | 4 | 1 | 78 | 24 | 6 | 5 | 11 | 26 | 47 | 104 | 71 | 55 |
| 3 | Wrexham | 44 | 12 | 6 | 4 | 56 | 23 | 10 | 3 | 9 | 40 | 33 | 96 | 56 | 53 |
| 4 | Carlisle United | 44 | 15 | 3 | 4 | 35 | 22 | 7 | 5 | 10 | 29 | 41 | 64 | 63 | 52 |
| 5 | Bradford City | 44 | 14 | 5 | 3 | 58 | 32 | 7 | 4 | 11 | 36 | 54 | 94 | 86 | 51 |
| 6 | York City | 44 | 17 | 2 | 3 | 62 | 19 | 3 | 8 | 11 | 22 | 34 | 84 | 53 | 50 |
| 7 | Aldershot | 44 | 16 | 4 | 2 | 56 | 20 | 6 | 1 | 15 | 25 | 40 | 81 | 60 | 49 |
| 8 | Workington | 44 | 12 | 6 | 4 | 40 | 23 | 7 | 5 | 10 | 29 | 47 | 69 | 70 | 49 |
| 9 | Barrow | 44 | 12 | 7 | 3 | 49 | 20 | 5 | 7 | 10 | 25 | 38 | 74 | 58 | 48 |
| 10 | Crewe Alexandra | 44 | 16 | 3 | 3 | 53 | 24 | 4 | 3 | 15 | 26 | 46 | 79 | 70 | 46 |
| 11 | Oldham Athletic | 44 | 12 | 7 | 3 | 47 | 26 | 5 | 5 | 12 | 30 | 44 | 77 | 70 | 46 |
| 12 | Rochdale | 44 | 14 | 3 | 5 | 47 | 28 | 5 | 4 | 13 | 24 | 43 | 71 | 71 | 45 |
| 13 | Darlington | 44 | 13 | 5 | 4 | 37 | 24 | 5 | 4 | 13 | 24 | 49 | 61 | 73 | 45 |
| 14 | Mansfield Town | 44 | 14 | 3 | 5 | 51 | 19 | 5 | 3 | 14 | 26 | 47 | 77 | 66 | 44 |
| 15 | Tranmere Rovers | 44 | 15 | 2 | 5 | 53 | 37 | 5 | 2 | 15 | 17 | 44 | 70 | 81 | 44 |
| 16 | Stockport County | 44 | 13 | 3 | 6 | 42 | 27 | 4 | 6 | 12 | 28 | 42 | 70 | 69 | 43 |
| 17 | Southport | 44 | 13 | 5 | 4 | 36 | 25 | 4 | 4 | 14 | 25 | 46 | 61 | 71 | 43 |
| 18 | Exeter City | 44 | 11 | 5 | 6 | 43 | 32 | 2 | 6 | 14 | 19 | 45 | 62 | 77 | 37 |
| 19 | Chesterfield | 44 | 11 | 3 | 8 | 43 | 38 | 3 | 6 | 13 | 27 | 49 | 70 | 87 | 37 |
| 20 | Gillingham | 44 | 10 | 6 | 6 | 48 | 30 | 3 | 5 | 14 | 25 | 64 | 73 | 94 | 37 |
| 21 | Doncaster Rovers | 44 | 8 | 5 | 9 | 34 | 29 | 3 | 2 | 17 | 26 | 56 | 60 | 85 | 29 |
| 22 | Hartlepools United | 44 | 6 | 5 | 11 | 27 | 35 | 2 | 6 | 14 | 25 | 66 | 52 | 101 | 27 |
| ***23*** | ***Chester*** | ***44*** | ***5*** | ***9*** | ***8*** | ***36*** | ***37*** | ***2*** | ***3*** | ***17*** | ***18*** | ***59*** | ***54*** | ***96*** | ***26*** |

1961/62 Season

**1962/63 Season:** (Back) Jones, Clarke, Myerscough, Hewitt, Griffiths, Gregson, Fleming..
(Middle) Gardner, Collins, Wilson, Morris, Appleby, Butler, Hardie, Cartlidge, Davies, Fitzgerald, Moore, Lambton .
(Front) Peters, Dawson, Rowley, Cheshire, Rowlands, Auckland, Horne, Hall, Randles..

# SEASON 1962-63

## FOOTBALL LEAGUE DIVISION 4

| | Date | Opposition | | FT | HT | Att. | Goalscorers | Barton R. | Molyneux J. | Fleming B. | Wilson R. | Butler J. | Corbishley C. | Gregson J. | Myerscough W. | Hughes J. | Hewitt R. | Fitzgerald P. | Jones M. | Hardie J. | Davies R. | Clarke R. | Johnson A. | Cartlidge D. | Griffiths R. | Molyneux G. | Read D. | Evans J. | McGill J. | Pritchard A. | Keating D. | Jones R. | Wright B. | McGowan G. | Starkey M. | Morris E. | Appleby J. |
|---|---|---|---|---|---|---|---|---|---|---|---|---|---|---|---|---|---|---|---|---|---|---|---|---|---|---|---|---|---|---|---|---|---|---|---|---|---|
| 1 | Aug 18 | Gillingham | L | 1-2 | 0-2 | 6911 | Gregson | 1 | 2 | 3 | 4 | 5 | 6 | 7 | 8 | 9 | 10 | 11 | | | | | | | | | | | | | | | | | | | |
| 2 | 20 | Darlington | L | 1-2 | 1-2 | 5870 | Gregson | 1 | 2 | 3 | 4 | 5 | 6 | 7 | 8 | 9 | | 10 | 11 | | | | | | | | | | | | | | | | | | |
| 3 | 25 | STOCKPORT COUNTY | L | 0-1 | 0-0 | 6718 | | | 2 | 3 | 4 | 5 | 6 | 7 | 8 | | | 10 | 11 | 1 | 9 | | | | | | | | | | | | | | | | |
| 4 | 29 | DARLINGTON | L | 1-2 | 1-0 | 6249 | Myerscough | | 2 | 3 | 4 | 5 | 6 | 7 | 8 | | | 9 | 11 | 1 | | 10 | | | | | | | | | | | | | | | |
| 5 | Sep 1 | Doncaster Rovers | W | 2-1 | 1-0 | 6506 | Myerscough, Fitzgerald | | 2 | 3 | 4 | 5 | 6 | 7 | 8 | | | 9 | 11 | 1 | | 10 | | | | | | | | | | | | | | | |
| 6 | 8 | MANSFIELD TOWN | L | 0-2 | 0-0 | 7775 | | | 2 | 3 | 4 | 5 | 6 | 7 | 8 | | | 9 | 11 | 1 | | 10 | | | | | | | | | | | | | | | |
| 7 | 12 | YORK CITY | D | 0-0 | 0-0 | 5277 | | | 2 | 3 | 4 | 5 | 6 | 7 | | | 8 | 9 | | | | 11 | 1 | 10 | | | | | | | | | | | | | |
| 8 | 15 | Workington | L | 0-3 | 0-3 | 4130 | | | 2 | 3 | 4 | 5 | 6 | 7 | | | 8 | 11 | | | 9 | 10 | 1 | | | | | | | | | | | | | | |
| 9 | 19 | CREWE ALEX. | L | 1-2 | 0-1 | 9614 | Fitzgerald | | 2 | 3 | | 5 | 6 | 7 | | | 8 | 9 | | 1 | 10 | 11 | | | 4 | | | | | | | | | | | | |
| 10 | 22 | EXETER CITY | W | 3-1 | 1-0 | 5227 | Davies (2), Fitzgerald | | 2 | 3 | 4 | 5 | 6 | 11 | | | | 9 | | | 8 | 10 | 1 | | | 7 | | | | | | | | | | | |
| 11 | 29 | Chesterfield | D | 1-1 | 1-1 | 7652 | Fitzgerald | | 2 | 3 | 4 | 5 | 6 | 7 | | | | 9 | 11 | 1 | 8 | 10 | | | | | | | | | | | | | | | |
| 12 | Oct 3 | SOUTHPORT | W | 6-1 | 2-0 | 7938 | Jones, Davies (4), Clarke | | 2 | 3 | 4 | 5 | 6 | 7 | | | | 9 | 11 | 1 | 8 | 10 | | | | | | | | | | | | | | | |
| 13 | 6 | Aldershot | D | 2-2 | 1-0 | 5086 | Clarke, Corbishley | | 2 | 3 | 4 | 5 | 6 | 7 | | | | 9 | 11 | 1 | 8 | 10 | | | | | | | | | | | | | | | |
| 14 | 8 | Southport | L | 1-4 | 0-2 | 4415 | Gregson | | 2 | 3 | 4 | 5 | 6 | 7 | | | | 9 | 11 | 1 | 8 | 10 | | | | | | | | | | | | | | | |
| 15 | 13 | NEWPORT COUNTY | D | 2-2 | 2-1 | 8034 | Read, Davies | | 2 | 3 | 4 | 5 | 6 | 7 | | | | 9 | 11 | 1 | 8 | | | | | | 10 | | | | | | | | | | |
| 16 | 20 | Oxford United | L | 0-3 | 0-2 | 7615 | | | 2 | 3 | 4 | 5 | | | 8 | | | 9 | 11 | 1 | | 10 | | | | | 7 | 6 | | | | | | | | | |
| 17 | 27 | BRADFORD CITY | W | 2-0 | 1-0 | 5326 | Pritchard, Fitzgerald | | 2 | 3 | | 5 | 6 | 7 | 8 | | | 9 | | 1 | | | | | | | | | 4 | 10 | 11 | | | | | | |
| 18 | Nov 10 | TORQUAY UNITED | W | 3-1 | 1-0 | 4575 | Fitzgerald, Hewitt, Allen (og) | | 2 | 3 | | 5 | 6 | 7 | | | 10 | 9 | 11 | 1 | | | | | | | 8 | | 4 | | | | | | | | |
| 19 | 12 | York City | D | 0-0 | 0-0 | 3645 | | | 2 | 3 | | 5 | 6 | 7 | 10 | | | 9 | 11 | 1 | | | | | | | 8 | | 4 | | | | | | | | |
| 20 | 17 | Lincoln City | W | 3-1 | 2-0 | 5125 | Corbishley, Myerscough (2) | | 2 | 3 | | 5 | 9 | 7 | 8 | | | | 11 | 1 | | 10 | | 6 | | | | | 4 | | | | | | | | |
| 21 | Dec 1 | Barrow | L | 3-4 | 2-1 | 3291 | Clarke, Gregson, Jones | | 2 | 3 | | 5 | 6 | 7 | 8 | | | 9 | 11 | 1 | | 10 | | | | | | | 4 | | | | | | | | |
| 22 | 7 | HARTLEPOOLS UNITED | W | 1-0 | 1-0 | 4441 | Hewitt | | | 3 | | 5 | 6 | 7 | 8 | | 10 | 9 | 11 | 1 | | | | | | | | | 4 | | | 2 | | | | | |
| 23 | 15 | GILLINGHAM | W | 1-0 | 1-0 | 3663 | Gregson | | | 3 | | 5 | | 7 | 9 | | | 11 | | 1 | | 10 | | | | | 8 | | 4 | | | 2 | 6 | | | | |
| 24 | 26 | Brentford | L | 1-2 | 0-0 | 9724 | Myerscough | | | 3 | | 5 | | 7 | 9 | | | 11 | | 1 | | 10 | | 6 | | | 8 | | 4 | | | 2 | | | | | |
| 25 | Feb 23 | ALDERSHOT | L | 0-2 | 0-1 | 4244 | | | 2 | 3 | | 5 | | 7 | 9 | | 6 | | 11 | 1 | | 10 | | | | | 8 | | 4 | | | | | | | | |
| 26 | Mar 4 | Newport County | W | 1-0 | 0-0 | 3700 | Jones | | 2 | 3 | | 5 | | 7 | 8 | | 10 | 9 | 11 | 1 | | | | 6 | | | | | 4 | | | | | | | | |
| 27 | 9 | OXFORD UNITED | W | 2-1 | 0-1 | 3772 | Hewitt, Jones | | 2 | 3 | | 5 | | 7 | | | 10 | 9 | 11 | 1 | | | | 6 | | | 8 | | 4 | | | | | | | | |
| 28 | 13 | OLDHAM ATHLETIC | W | 1-0 | 0-0 | 6420 | Jones | | 2 | 3 | | 5 | | 7 | | | 10 | 9 | 11 | 1 | | | | 6 | | | 8 | | 4 | | | | | | | | |
| 29 | 16 | Bradford City | L | 0-2 | 0-0 | 3539 | | | 2 | 3 | | 5 | | 7 | 10 | | | 9 | 11 | 1 | | | | 6 | | | 8 | | 4 | | | | | | | | |
| 30 | 18 | Stockport County | L | 0-1 | 0-1 | 3154 | | | 2 | 3 | | 5 | | 7 | | | | 9 | 11 | 1 | | 10 | | 6 | | | 8 | | 4 | | | | | | | | |
| 31 | 23 | TRANMERE ROVERS | D | 0-0 | 0-0 | 7921 | | | 2 | 3 | | 5 | | 7 | 6 | | | 9 | 11 | 1 | | 10 | | | | | 8 | | 4 | | | | | | | | |
| 32 | 30 | Oldham Athletic | L | 0-2 | 0-2 | 8434 | | | 2 | 3 | | 5 | | 7 | 10 | | | | 11 | 1 | | | | | 6 | | 8 | | 4 | | | | | 9 | | | |
| 33 | Apr 3 | BRENTFORD | L | 1-2 | 1-0 | 5919 | McGowan | | 2 | 3 | | 5 | | 7 | 6 | | | 10 | 11 | 1 | | | | | | | 8 | | 4 | | | | | 9 | | | |
| 34 | 6 | LINCOLN CITY | W | 3-2 | 2-0 | 4125 | Myerscough (2, 1 pen), Read | | 2 | 3 | | 5 | 6 | | 8 | | | | 11 | 1 | | | | | | | 7 | | 4 | | | | | 9 | 10 | | |
| 35 | 13 | Torquay United | L | 0-1 | 0-0 | 4911 | | | 2 | 3 | | 5 | 6 | | 8 | | | | 11 | 1 | | | | | | | 7 | | 4 | | | | | 9 | 10 | | |
| 36 | 15 | ROCHDALE | W | 1-0 | 0-0 | 4979 | Fitzgerald (pen) | | 2 | 3 | | 5 | 6 | | | | | 11 | | 1 | | | | | | | 7 | | 4 | | | | | 9 | 10 | 8 | |
| 37 | 16 | Rochdale | D | 0-0 | 0-0 | 2926 | | | 2 | 3 | | 5 | 6 | | | | | 11 | | 1 | | | | | | | 7 | | 4 | | | | | 9 | 10 | 8 | |
| 38 | 19 | BARROW | W | 1-0 | 0-0 | 4924 | McGowan | | 2 | 3 | | 5 | 6 | | | | | 11 | | 1 | | | | | | | 7 | | 4 | | | | | 9 | 10 | 8 | |
| 39 | 22 | Crewe Alex. | L | 0-3 | 0-1 | 8236 | | | 2 | 3 | | 5 | 6 | | | | 8 | 11 | | 1 | | | | | | | 7 | | 4 | | | | | 9 | 10 | | |
| 40 | 27 | Hartlepools United | W | 3-0 | 3-0 | 2728 | McGowan, Morris (2) | | 2 | 3 | | 5 | 6 | | | | 4 | 11 | | 1 | | | | | | | 7 | | | | | | | 9 | 10 | 8 | |
| 41 | May 4 | Exeter City | L | 1-2 | 0-2 | 3927 | Corbishley | | 2 | 3 | | 5 | 6 | | | | 4 | 11 | | 1 | | | | | | | 7 | | | | | | | 9 | 10 | 8 | |
| 42 | 8 | WORKINGTON | D | 1-1 | 1-0 | 3473 | Starkey | | 2 | 3 | | 5 | 6 | | | | 4 | 11 | | 1 | | | | | | | 7 | | | | | | | 9 | 10 | 8 | |
| 43 | 11 | DONCASTER ROVERS | D | 1-1 | 0-0 | 2935 | Fitzgerald | | 2 | 3 | | 5 | 6 | | | | 8 | 11 | | 1 | | | | | | | 7 | | 4 | | | | | 9 | 10 | | |
| 44 | 13 | Tranmere Rovers | L | 0-3 | 0-3 | 5537 | | | 2 | 3 | | 5 | 6 | | | | | 11 | | 1 | | | | | | | 7 | | 4 | | | | | 9 | 10 | 8 | |
| 45 | 18 | Mansfield Town | L | 0-4 | 0-2 | 7415 | | | 2 | 3 | | | 6 | | 4 | | | 7 | 11 | 1 | | | | | | | | | | | | | | 9 | 10 | 8 | 5 |
| 46 | 22 | CHESTERFIELD | L | 0-2 | 0-1 | 3920 | | | 2 | 3 | | 5 | 6 | | | | 4 | 11 | | 1 | | | | | | | 7 | | | | | | | 9 | 10 | 8 | |
| | | | | | | | Apps. | 2 | 43 | 46 | 15 | 45 | 34 | 32 | 23 | 2 | 16 | 41 | 28 | 41 | 9 | 19 | 3 | 8 | 2 | 1 | 26 | 1 | 25 | 1 | 1 | 3 | 1 | 15 | 13 | 9 | 1 |
| | | | | | | | Goals | | | | | | 3 | 5 | 7 | | 3 | 8 | 5 | | 7 | 3 | | | | | 2 | | | 1 | | | | 3 | 1 | 2 | |

Own goals 1

## F.A. CUP

| | Date | Opposition | | FT | HT | Att. | Goalscorers | Barton R. | Molyneux J. | Fleming B. | Wilson R. | Butler J. | Corbishley C. | Gregson J. | Myerscough W. | Hughes J. | Hewitt R. | Fitzgerald P. | Jones M. | Hardie J. | Davies R. | Clarke R. | Johnson A. | Cartlidge D. | Griffiths R. | Molyneux G. | Read D. | Evans J. | McGill J. | Pritchard A. | Keating D. | Jones R. | Wright B. | McGowan G. | Starkey M. | Morris E. | Appleby J. |
|---|---|---|---|---|---|---|---|---|---|---|---|---|---|---|---|---|---|---|---|---|---|---|---|---|---|---|---|---|---|---|---|---|---|---|---|---|---|
| 1R | Nov 3 | TRANMERE ROVERS | L | 0-2 | 0-2 | 11448 | | | 2 | 3 | | 5 | 6 | 7 | 10 | | | 9 | | 1 | | | | 4 | | | 8 | | | | 11 | | | | | | |

## LEAGUE CUP

| | Date | Opposition | | FT | HT | Att. | Goalscorers | Barton R. | Molyneux J. | Fleming B. | Wilson R. | Butler J. | Corbishley C. | Gregson J. | Myerscough W. | Hughes J. | Hewitt R. | Fitzgerald P. | Jones M. | Hardie J. | Davies R. | Clarke R. | Johnson A. | Cartlidge D. | Griffiths R. | Molyneux G. | Read D. | Evans J. | McGill J. | Pritchard A. | Keating D. | Jones R. | Wright B. | McGowan G. | Starkey M. | Morris E. | Appleby J. |
|---|---|---|---|---|---|---|---|---|---|---|---|---|---|---|---|---|---|---|---|---|---|---|---|---|---|---|---|---|---|---|---|---|---|---|---|---|---|
| 1R | Sep 5 | STOCKPORT COUNTY | W | 2-0 | 1-0 | 5124 | Clarke, Fitzgerald | | 2 | 3 | 4 | 5 | 6 | 7 | 8 | | | 9 | 11 | 1 | | 10 | | | | | | | | | | | | | | | |
| 2R | Sep 26 | MANSFIELD TOWN | D | 2-2 | 1-1 | 6159 | Davies (2) | | 2 | 3 | 4 | 5 | 6 | 11 | | | | 9 | | | 8 | 10 | 1 | | | 7 | | | | | | | | | | | |
| 2Rr | Oct 10 | Mansfield Town | W | 1-0 | 1-0 | 8298 | Davies | | 2 | 3 | | 5 | | 7 | 4 | | 10 | 9 | 11 | 1 | 8 | | | 6 | | | | | | | | | | | | | |
| 3R | 15 | Leyton Orient | L | 2-9 | 0-3 | 7428 | Myerscough (2) | | 2 | 3 | 4 | 5 | 6 | 7 | 8 | | | 9 | 11 | 1 | | 10 | | | | | | | | | | | | | | | |

## WELSH CUP

| | Date | Opposition | | FT | HT | Att. | Goalscorers | Barton R. | Molyneux J. | Fleming B. | Wilson R. | Butler J. | Corbishley C. | Gregson J. | Myerscough W. | Hughes J. | Hewitt R. | Fitzgerald P. | Jones M. | Hardie J. | Davies R. | Clarke R. | Johnson A. | Cartlidge D. | Griffiths R. | Molyneux G. | Read D. | Evans J. | McGill J. | Pritchard A. | Keating D. | Jones R. | Wright B. | McGowan G. | Starkey M. | Morris E. | Appleby J. |
|---|---|---|---|---|---|---|---|---|---|---|---|---|---|---|---|---|---|---|---|---|---|---|---|---|---|---|---|---|---|---|---|---|---|---|---|---|---|
| 5R | Feb 18 | Wrexham | L | 0-1 | 0-1 | 5020 | | | 2 | 3 | | 5 | | 7 | 9 | | 6 | | 11 | 1 | | 10 | | | | | 8 | | 4 | | | | | | | | |

## FRIENDLIES

| | Date | Opposition | | FT | HT | Att. | Goalscorers |
|---|---|---|---|---|---|---|---|
| 1 | Aug 8 | New Brighton | W | 3-1 | 1-1 | | Davies, Myerscough (2) |
| 2 | 15 | NEW BRIGHTON | W | 3-1 | 1-1 | 2343 | Hewitt,Davies,Corbishley(pen) |
| 3 | Feb 27 | CREWE ALEX. | L | 0-2 | 0-1 | 719 | |

Final League Table

| | | Pl. | Home W | D | L | F | A | Away W | D | L | F | A | F. | A. | Pts |
|---|---|---|---|---|---|---|---|---|---|---|---|---|---|---|---|
| 1 | Brentford | 46 | 18 | 2 | 3 | 59 | 31 | 9 | 6 | 8 | 39 | 33 | 98 | 64 | 62 |
| 2 | Oldham Athletic | 46 | 18 | 4 | 1 | 65 | 23 | 6 | 7 | 10 | 30 | 37 | 95 | 60 | 59 |
| 3 | Crewe Alexandra | 46 | 15 | 4 | 4 | 50 | 21 | 9 | 7 | 7 | 36 | 37 | 86 | 58 | 59 |
| 4 | Mansfield Town | 46 | 16 | 4 | 3 | 61 | 20 | 8 | 5 | 10 | 47 | 49 | 108 | 69 | 57 |
| 5 | Gillingham | 46 | 17 | 3 | 3 | 49 | 23 | 5 | 10 | 8 | 22 | 26 | 71 | 49 | 57 |
| 6 | Torquay United | 46 | 14 | 8 | 1 | 45 | 20 | 6 | 8 | 9 | 30 | 36 | 75 | 56 | 56 |
| 7 | Rochdale | 46 | 16 | 6 | 1 | 48 | 21 | 4 | 5 | 14 | 19 | 38 | 67 | 59 | 51 |
| 8 | Tranmere Rovers | 46 | 15 | 3 | 5 | 57 | 25 | 5 | 7 | 11 | 24 | 42 | 81 | 67 | 50 |
| 9 | Barrow | 46 | 14 | 7 | 2 | 52 | 26 | 5 | 5 | 13 | 30 | 54 | 82 | 80 | 50 |
| 10 | Workington | 46 | 13 | 4 | 6 | 42 | 20 | 4 | 9 | 10 | 34 | 48 | 76 | 68 | 47 |
| 11 | Aldershot | 46 | 9 | 9 | 5 | 42 | 32 | 6 | 8 | 9 | 31 | 37 | 73 | 69 | 47 |
| 12 | Darlington | 46 | 13 | 3 | 7 | 44 | 33 | 6 | 3 | 14 | 28 | 54 | 72 | 87 | 44 |
| 13 | Southport | 46 | 11 | 9 | 3 | 47 | 35 | 4 | 5 | 14 | 25 | 71 | 72 | 106 | 44 |
| 14 | York City | 46 | 12 | 6 | 5 | 42 | 25 | 4 | 5 | 14 | 25 | 37 | 67 | 62 | 43 |
| 15 | Chesterfield | 46 | 7 | 10 | 6 | 43 | 29 | 6 | 6 | 11 | 27 | 35 | 70 | 64 | 42 |
| 16 | Doncaster Rovers | 46 | 9 | 10 | 4 | 36 | 26 | 5 | 4 | 14 | 28 | 51 | 64 | 77 | 42 |
| 17 | Exeter City | 46 | 9 | 6 | 8 | 27 | 32 | 7 | 4 | 12 | 30 | 45 | 57 | 77 | 42 |
| 18 | Oxford United | 46 | 10 | 10 | 3 | 44 | 27 | 3 | 5 | 15 | 26 | 44 | 70 | 71 | 41 |
| 19 | Stockport County | 46 | 9 | 7 | 7 | 34 | 29 | 6 | 4 | 13 | 22 | 41 | 56 | 70 | 41 |
| 20 | Newport County | 46 | 11 | 6 | 6 | 44 | 29 | 3 | 5 | 15 | 32 | 61 | 76 | 90 | 39 |
| ***21*** | ***Chester*** | ***46*** | ***11*** | ***5*** | ***7*** | ***31*** | ***23*** | ***4*** | ***4*** | ***15*** | ***20*** | ***43*** | ***51*** | ***66*** | ***39*** |
| 22 | Lincoln City | 46 | 11 | 1 | 11 | 48 | 46 | 2 | 8 | 13 | 20 | 43 | 68 | 89 | 35 |
| 23 | Bradford City | 46 | 8 | 5 | 10 | 37 | 40 | 3 | 5 | 15 | 27 | 53 | 64 | 93 | 32 |
| 24 | Hartlepools United | 46 | 5 | 7 | 11 | 33 | 39 | 2 | 4 | 17 | 23 | 65 | 56 | 104 | 25 |

# SEASON 1963-64

## FOOTBALL LEAGUE DIVISION 4

| | Date | Opposition | | FT | HT | Att. | Goalscorers |
|---|---|---|---|---|---|---|---|
| 1 | Aug 24 | OXFORD UNITED | L | 0-2 | 0-1 | 6008 | |
| 2 | 28 | BARROW | W | 2-0 | 1-0 | 5454 | Arrowsmith (og), Corbishley |
| 3 | 31 | Workington | D | 1-1 | 0-0 | 2902 | Read |
| 4 | Sep 7 | NEWPORT COUNTY | W | 3-0 | 0-0 | 5362 | Corbishley, Bades, Talbot |
| 5 | 9 | Barrow | D | 2-2 | 0-0 | 3441 | Talbot (2) |
| 6 | 14 | Stockport County | L | 0-1 | 0-1 | 6134 | |
| 7 | 21 | BRADFORD P. A. | W | 1-0 | 0-0 | 5569 | Corbishley |
| 8 | 28 | Chesterfield | L | 0-1 | 0-0 | 6143 | |
| 9 | Oct 2 | ROCHDALE | W | 2-0 | 1-0 | 5220 | Lee, Humes |
| 10 | 5 | DONCASTER ROVERS | D | 1-1 | 0-0 | 6214 | Lee |
| 11 | 7 | Darlington | L | 0-1 | 0-0 | 3062 | |
| 12 | 12 | EXETER CITY | W | 2-0 | 1-0 | 6966 | Talbot, Lee |
| 13 | 16 | DARLINGTON | L | 0-1 | 0-0 | 8103 | |
| 14 | 19 | Southport | W | 2-0 | 1-0 | 3690 | Morris, Corbishley |
| 15 | 23 | BRIGHTON & HOVE A. | D | 0-0 | 0-0 | 8398 | |
| 16 | 26 | GILLINGHAM | W | 1-0 | 1-0 | 8395 | Humes |
| 17 | 29 | Brighton & Hove A. | D | 0-0 | 0-0 | 11999 | |
| 18 | Nov 2 | Lincoln City | L | 2-3 | 2-1 | 5523 | Morris (2) |
| 19 | 9 | BRADFORD CITY | W | 3-0 | 1-0 | 7835 | Morris, Corbishley (pen), Lee |
| 20 | 23 | CARLISLE UNITED | W | 4-2 | 3-0 | 8223 | Talbot (4) |
| 21 | 30 | Torquay United | L | 0-5 | 0-0 | 4075 | |
| 22 | Dec 14 | Oxford United | L | 1-2 | 1-0 | 5283 | Lee |
| 23 | 21 | WORKINGTON | W | 2-1 | 0-0 | 4370 | Lee (2) |
| 24 | 26 | Hartlepools United | L | 0-2 | 0-0 | 5531 | |
| 25 | 28 | HARTLEPOOLS UNITED | W | 2-1 | 2-0 | 6317 | Read, Talbot |
| 26 | Jan 1 | Tranmere Rovers | D | 3-3 | 1-1 | 8504 | Talbot, Corbishley (pen), Morris |
| 27 | 11 | Newport County | W | 1-0 | 1-0 | 3983 | Metcalf |
| 28 | 18 | STOCKPORT COUNTY | W | 2-1 | 0-0 | 5403 | Morris (2) |
| 29 | 25 | HALIFAX TOWN | W | 5-2 | 2-1 | 6253 | Corbishley (pen),Talbot,Read,Metcalf(2) |
| 30 | Feb 1 | Bradford P. A. | L | 0-4 | 0-1 | 6071 | |
| 31 | 8 | CHESTERFIELD | W | 4-2 | 1-0 | 6272 | Talbot (2), Morris, Metcalf |
| 32 | 15 | Doncaster Rovers | L | 2-3 | 2-2 | 6554 | Metcalf, Talbot |
| 33 | 22 | Exeter City | L | 0-3 | 0-0 | 6579 | |
| 34 | 29 | SOUTHPORT | W | 5-0 | 3-0 | 6187 | Metcalf, Talbot (3), Bennion |
| 35 | Mar 4 | Rochdale | L | 0-1 | 0-0 | 2322 | |
| 36 | 7 | Gillingham | L | 1-2 | 1-2 | 5274 | Talbot |
| 37 | 9 | Aldershot | L | 1-2 | 0-1 | 2951 | Read |
| 38 | 13 | LINCOLN CITY | W | 3-1 | 2-1 | 5077 | Talbot (2), Bennion |
| 39 | 21 | Bradford City | D | 1-1 | 0-0 | 4405 | Bennion |
| 40 | 27 | York City | L | 0-1 | 0-0 | 4437 | |
| 41 | 28 | TRANMERE ROVERS | L | 0-2 | 0-2 | 7408 | |
| 42 | 30 | YORK CITY | D | 1-1 | 1-1 | 4326 | Metcalf |
| 43 | Apr 4 | Carlisle United | L | 1-3 | 1-2 | 6940 | Talbot |
| 44 | 11 | TORQUAY UNITED | W | 2-1 | 2-1 | 4727 | Talbot, Metcalf |
| 45 | 18 | Halifax Town | L | 0-1 | 0-1 | 3227 | |
| 46 | 25 | ALDERSHOT | W | 2-0 | 1-0 | 4105 | Talbot, Humes |

| | Adams F. | Molyneux J. | Fleming B. | Currie J. | Butler J. | Evans G. | Read D. | Hauser P. | McGowan G. | Fitzgerald P. | Humes J. | McGill J. | Corbishley C. | Bennion S. | Talbot G. | Bades B. | Starkey M. | Pritchard A. | Evans J. | Lee G. | Reeves D. | Jones R. | Haddock A. | Morris E. | Wheaton G. | Metcalf M. | Barton R. |
|---|---|---|---|---|---|---|---|---|---|---|---|---|---|---|---|---|---|---|---|---|---|---|---|---|---|---|---|
| 1 | 1 | 2 | 3 | 4 | 5 | 6 | 7 | 8 | 9 | 10 | 11 | | | | | | | | | | | | | | | | |
| 2 | 1 | 2 | 3 | | 5 | 10 | 7 | 8 | 9 | | | 4 | 6 | 11 | | | | | | | | | | | | | |
| 3 | 1 | 2 | 3 | | 5 | 10 | 7 | 8 | 9 | | | 4 | 6 | 11 | | | | | | | | | | | | | |
| 4 | 1 | 2 | 3 | | 5 | | 7 | 9 | | | | 4 | 6 | 8 | 10 | 11 | | | | | | | | | | | |
| 5 | 1 | 2 | 3 | | 5 | 10 | 7 | 6 | | | | 4 | | 8 | 9 | 11 | | | | | | | | | | | |
| 6 | 1 | 2 | 3 | | 5 | 6 | 7 | | | | | 4 | | 8 | 9 | 11 | 10 | | | | | | | | | | |
| 7 | 1 | 2 | 3 | | 5 | 10 | 7 | 9 | | | | 4 | 6 | | | 11 | | 8 | | | | | | | | | |
| 8 | 1 | 2 | | | 5 | 6 | 7 | | | | | 4 | 10 | | 9 | | | 8 | 3 | 11 | | | | | | | |
| 9 | | | | | 5 | 6 | | 4 | | | 8 | | 9 | 10 | | | | | 3 | 11 | 1 | 2 | 7 | | | | |
| 10 | | | | | 5 | 6 | | 4 | | | 8 | | 9 | 10 | | | | | 3 | 11 | 1 | 2 | 7 | | | | |
| 11 | | | | | 5 | 6 | | 4 | | | 8 | | 9 | 10 | | | | | 3 | 11 | 1 | 2 | 7 | | | | |
| 12 | | 2 | | | 5 | 6 | | 4 | | | 8 | | | | 9 | 10 | | | 3 | 11 | 1 | | 7 | | | | |
| 13 | | 2 | | 10 | 5 | 6 | | 4 | | | 8 | | | | 9 | | | | 3 | 11 | 1 | | 7 | | | | |
| 14 | | 2 | | | 5 | 6 | | 4 | | | 8 | | 10 | | | | | | 3 | 11 | 1 | | 7 | 9 | | | |
| 15 | | 2 | | | 5 | | | 4 | | | 8 | | 6 | | | 10 | | | 3 | 11 | 1 | | 7 | 9 | | | |
| 16 | | 2 | | | 5 | | | 4 | | | 8 | | 6 | | | 10 | | | 3 | 11 | 1 | | 7 | 9 | | | |
| 17 | | 2 | | | 5 | | | 4 | | | 8 | | 6 | | | 10 | | | 3 | 11 | 1 | | 7 | 9 | | | |
| 18 | | 2 | | | | | | 4 | | | 8 | | 6 | | | 10 | | | 3 | 11 | 1 | | 7 | 9 | 5 | | |
| 19 | | 2 | | | 5 | | | 4 | | | | | 6 | | 9 | 10 | | | 3 | 11 | 1 | | 7 | 8 | | | |
| 20 | | 2 | | | 5 | | | 4 | | | 8 | | 6 | | 9 | 7 | | | 3 | 11 | 1 | | | 10 | | | |
| 21 | | 2 | 3 | | 5 | | | 4 | | | 8 | | 6 | | 9 | 7 | | | | 11 | 1 | | | 10 | | | |
| 22 | | 2 | | | 5 | | 10 | | | | 8 | | 6 | | 9 | 7 | | | 3 | 11 | 1 | 4 | | | | | |
| 23 | | 2 | 4 | | 5 | | 7 | | | | 8 | | 6 | | 9 | | | | 3 | 11 | 1 | | | | | 10 | |
| 24 | | 3 | 4 | | 5 | | 8 | | | | | | 6 | | | 7 | | | 2 | 11 | 1 | | | 9 | | 10 | |
| 25 | | 2 | 4 | | 5 | | 7 | | | | | | 6 | | 9 | | | | 3 | 11 | 1 | | | 10 | | 8 | |
| 26 | | 2 | 4 | | 5 | | 7 | | | | | | 6 | | 9 | | | | 3 | 11 | 1 | | | 10 | | 8 | |
| 27 | | | 4 | | 5 | | 7 | | | | | | 6 | | 9 | | 3 | | | 11 | 1 | 2 | | 10 | | 8 | |
| 28 | | | 4 | | 5 | | 7 | | | | | | 6 | | 9 | | 3 | | 2 | 11 | 1 | | | 10 | | 8 | |
| 29 | | | 4 | | 5 | | 7 | | | | | | 6 | | 9 | | 3 | | 2 | 11 | 1 | | | 10 | | 8 | |
| 30 | | | 4 | | 5 | | 7 | | | | | | 6 | | 9 | | 3 | | 2 | 11 | 1 | | | 10 | | 8 | |
| 31 | | | 4 | | 5 | | 7 | | | | | | 6 | | 9 | | 3 | | 2 | 11 | 1 | | | 10 | | 8 | |
| 32 | | | 4 | | 5 | | 7 | | | | | | 6 | | 9 | | 3 | | 2 | 11 | 1 | | | 10 | | 8 | |
| 33 | | | | | 5 | 4 | 7 | | | | 11 | | 6 | | 9 | | 3 | | 2 | | | | | 10 | | 8 | 1 |
| 34 | | | | | 5 | 4 | 7 | | | | | | 6 | 11 | 9 | | 3 | | 2 | | | | | 10 | | 8 | 1 |
| 35 | | | | | 5 | 4 | 7 | | | | | | 6 | 11 | 9 | | 3 | | 2 | | | | | 10 | | 8 | 1 |
| 36 | | | | | 5 | 4 | 7 | | | | 8 | | 6 | 11 | 9 | | 3 | | 2 | | | | | | | 10 | 1 |
| 37 | | | | | 5 | 4 | 7 | | | | | | 6 | 10 | 9 | 11 | 3 | | | | | 2 | | | | 8 | 1 |
| 38 | | | | | 5 | 4 | 7 | | | | | | 6 | 11 | 9 | | 3 | | | | | 2 | | 10 | | 8 | 1 |
| 39 | | | | | 5 | 4 | 7 | | | | 10 | | 6 | 11 | 9 | | 3 | | | | 1 | 2 | | | | 8 | |
| 40 | | | | | 5 | 4 | 7 | | | | 10 | | 6 | 11 | | | 3 | | | | 1 | 2 | | 9 | | 8 | |
| 41 | | | | | 5 | 4 | 7 | | | | | | 6 | 11 | 9 | | 3 | | | | 1 | 2 | | 10 | | 8 | |
| 42 | | | | | 5 | 4 | 7 | | | | | | 6 | | 9 | | 3 | | | 11 | 1 | 2 | | 10 | | 8 | |
| 43 | | | | | 5 | 4 | 7 | | | | | | 6 | 10 | 9 | | 3 | | | 11 | 1 | 2 | | | | 8 | |
| 44 | | | | | 5 | 2 | 7 | 4 | | | 10 | | 6 | 11 | 9 | | 3 | | | | 1 | | | | | 8 | |
| 45 | | | | | 5 | | 7 | 4 | | | 10 | | 6 | 11 | 9 | | 3 | | | | 1 | 2 | | | | 8 | |
| 46 | | | | | 5 | | | 4 | | | 10 | | 6 | 11 | 9 | | 3 | | | | 1 | 2 | 7 | | | 8 | |
| Apps. | 8 | 23 | 18 | 2 | 45 | 25 | 32 | 22 | 3 | 1 | 22 | 7 | 41 | 20 | 32 | 15 | 21 | 2 | 27 | 27 | 32 | 14 | 12 | 24 | 1 | 24 | 6 |
| Goals | | | | | | | 4 | | | | 3 | | 7 | 3 | 23 | 1 | | | | 7 | | | | 8 | | 8 | |

Own goals 1

## F.A. CUP

| | Date | Opposition | | FT | HT | Att. | Goalscorers |
|---|---|---|---|---|---|---|---|
| 1R | Nov 16 | BLYTH SPARTANS | W | 3-2 | 2-0 | 9366 | Lee (2), Morris |
| 2R | Dec 7 | BARROW | L | 0-2 | 0-1 | 8737 | |

| | Adams F. | Molyneux J. | Fleming B. | Currie J. | Butler J. | Evans G. | Read D. | Hauser P. | McGowan G. | Fitzgerald P. | Humes J. | McGill J. | Corbishley C. | Bennion S. | Talbot G. | Bades B. | Starkey M. | Pritchard A. | Evans J. | Lee G. | Reeves D. | Jones R. | Haddock A. | Morris E. | Wheaton G. | Metcalf M. | Barton R. |
|---|---|---|---|---|---|---|---|---|---|---|---|---|---|---|---|---|---|---|---|---|---|---|---|---|---|---|---|
| 1R | | 2 | | | 5 | | | 4 | | | | | 6 | | 9 | 10 | | | 3 | 11 | 1 | | 7 | 8 | | | |
| 2R | | 2 | | | 5 | | | 4 | | | 8 | | 6 | | 9 | 7 | | | 3 | 11 | 1 | | | 10 | | | |

## LEAGUE CUP

| | Date | Opposition | | FT | HT | Att. | Goalscorers |
|---|---|---|---|---|---|---|---|
| 1R | Sep 4 | Rochdale | D | 1-1 | 0-0 | 2919 | Corbishley (pen) |
| 1Rr | 18 | ROCHDALE | L | 2-5 | 0-0 | 5073 | Pritchard, Humes |

| | Adams F. | Molyneux J. | Fleming B. | Currie J. | Butler J. | Evans G. | Read D. | Hauser P. | McGowan G. | Fitzgerald P. | Humes J. | McGill J. | Corbishley C. | Bennion S. | Talbot G. | Bades B. | Starkey M. | Pritchard A. | Evans J. | Lee G. | Reeves D. | Jones R. | Haddock A. | Morris E. | Wheaton G. | Metcalf M. | Barton R. |
|---|---|---|---|---|---|---|---|---|---|---|---|---|---|---|---|---|---|---|---|---|---|---|---|---|---|---|---|
| 1R | 1 | 2 | 3 | | 5 | 10 | 7 | 8 | 9 | | | 4 | 6 | 11 | | | | | | | | | | | | | |
| 1Rr | 1 | 2 | 3 | | 5 | 9 | 10 | 6 | | | 11 | 4 | | | | | | 8 | | | | | 7 | | | | |

## WELSH CUP

| | Date | Opposition | | FT | HT | Att. | Goalscorers |
|---|---|---|---|---|---|---|---|
| 5R | Jan 29 | BOROUGH UNITED | W | 5-1 | 3-1 | 7369 | Morris (3), Talbot, Lee |
| 6R | Feb 19 | Cardiff City | L | 1-3 | 1-1 | 3281 | Talbot |

| | Adams F. | Molyneux J. | Fleming B. | Currie J. | Butler J. | Evans G. | Read D. | Hauser P. | McGowan G. | Fitzgerald P. | Humes J. | McGill J. | Corbishley C. | Bennion S. | Talbot G. | Bades B. | Starkey M. | Pritchard A. | Evans J. | Lee G. | Reeves D. | Jones R. | Haddock A. | Morris E. | Wheaton G. | Metcalf M. | Barton R. |
|---|---|---|---|---|---|---|---|---|---|---|---|---|---|---|---|---|---|---|---|---|---|---|---|---|---|---|---|
| 5R | | | 4 | | 5 | | 7 | | | | | | 6 | | 9 | | 3 | | 2 | 11 | 1 | | | 10 | | 8 | |
| 6R | | | | | 5 | 4 | 7 | | | | 11 | | 6 | | 9 | | 3 | | 2 | | 1 | | | 10 | | 8 | |

## FRIENDLIES

| | Date | Opposition | | FT | HT | Att. | Goalscorers |
|---|---|---|---|---|---|---|---|
| 1 | Aug 17 | SHEFFIELD UNITED RES. | L | 0-4 | 0-1 | 2601 | |
| 2 | Jan 3 | CREWE ALEX. | W | 2-0 | 1-0 | 1876 | Lee, Metcalf |
| 3 | Apr 29 | WREXHAM * | D | 3-3 | 1-2 | 3400 | Talbot (2), Metcalf (pen) |

* W. P. Peters Testimonial

Final League Table

| | | Pl. | Home W | D | L | F | A | Away W | D | L | F | A | F. | A. | Pts |
|---|---|---|---|---|---|---|---|---|---|---|---|---|---|---|---|
| 1 | Gillingham | 46 | 16 | 7 | 0 | 37 | 10 | 7 | 7 | 9 | 22 | 20 | 59 | 30 | 60 |
| 2 | Carlisle United | 46 | 17 | 3 | 3 | 70 | 20 | 8 | 7 | 8 | 43 | 38 | 113 | 58 | 60 |
| 3 | Workington | 46 | 15 | 6 | 2 | 46 | 19 | 9 | 5 | 9 | 30 | 33 | 76 | 52 | 59 |
| 4 | Exeter City | 46 | 12 | 9 | 2 | 39 | 14 | 8 | 9 | 6 | 23 | 23 | 62 | 37 | 58 |
| 5 | Bradford City | 46 | 15 | 3 | 5 | 45 | 24 | 10 | 3 | 10 | 31 | 38 | 76 | 62 | 56 |
| 6 | Torquay United | 46 | 16 | 6 | 1 | 60 | 20 | 4 | 5 | 14 | 20 | 34 | 80 | 54 | 51 |
| 7 | Tranmere Rovers | 46 | 12 | 4 | 7 | 46 | 30 | 8 | 7 | 8 | 39 | 43 | 85 | 73 | 51 |
| 8 | Brighton & Hove A. | 46 | 13 | 3 | 7 | 45 | 22 | 6 | 9 | 8 | 26 | 30 | 71 | 52 | 50 |
| 9 | Aldershot | 46 | 15 | 3 | 5 | 58 | 28 | 4 | 7 | 12 | 25 | 50 | 83 | 78 | 48 |
| 10 | Halifax Town | 46 | 14 | 4 | 5 | 47 | 28 | 3 | 10 | 10 | 30 | 49 | 77 | 77 | 48 |
| 11 | Lincoln City | 46 | 15 | 2 | 6 | 49 | 31 | 4 | 7 | 12 | 18 | 44 | 67 | 75 | 47 |
| ***12*** | ***Chester*** | ***46*** | ***17*** | ***3*** | ***3*** | ***47*** | ***18*** | ***2*** | ***5*** | ***16*** | ***18*** | ***42*** | ***65*** | ***60*** | ***46*** |
| 13 | Bradford Park Ave. | 46 | 13 | 5 | 5 | 50 | 34 | 5 | 4 | 14 | 25 | 47 | 75 | 81 | 45 |
| 14 | Doncaster Rovers | 46 | 11 | 8 | 4 | 46 | 23 | 4 | 4 | 15 | 24 | 52 | 70 | 75 | 42 |
| 15 | Newport County | 46 | 12 | 3 | 8 | 35 | 24 | 5 | 5 | 13 | 29 | 49 | 64 | 73 | 42 |
| 16 | Chesterfield | 46 | 8 | 9 | 6 | 29 | 27 | 7 | 3 | 13 | 28 | 44 | 57 | 71 | 42 |
| 17 | Stockport County | 46 | 12 | 7 | 4 | 32 | 19 | 3 | 5 | 15 | 18 | 49 | 50 | 68 | 42 |
| 18 | Oxford United | 46 | 10 | 7 | 6 | 37 | 27 | 4 | 6 | 13 | 22 | 36 | 59 | 63 | 41 |
| 19 | Darlington | 46 | 8 | 9 | 6 | 40 | 37 | 6 | 3 | 14 | 26 | 56 | 66 | 93 | 40 |
| 20 | Rochdale | 46 | 9 | 8 | 6 | 36 | 24 | 3 | 7 | 13 | 20 | 35 | 56 | 59 | 39 |
| 21 | Southport | 46 | 12 | 6 | 5 | 42 | 29 | 3 | 3 | 17 | 21 | 59 | 63 | 88 | 39 |
| 22 | York City | 46 | 9 | 3 | 11 | 29 | 26 | 5 | 4 | 14 | 23 | 40 | 52 | 66 | 35 |
| 23 | Hartlepools United | 46 | 8 | 7 | 8 | 30 | 36 | 4 | 2 | 17 | 24 | 57 | 54 | 93 | 33 |
| 24 | Barrow | 46 | 4 | 10 | 9 | 30 | 36 | 2 | 8 | 13 | 21 | 57 | 51 | 93 | 30 |

**1963/64 Season:** (Back) McGill, Fitzgerald, Fleming, Read, Currie.
(Middle) Randles (Assistant Secretary), Morris, Corbishley, Adams, Barton, Jones. Wheaton, Humes, Hauser (Player-Manager), Gardner (Trainer).
(Front) Peters (Sec.), Bennion, Pritchard, Evans, Butler, McGowan, Starkey, Rowlands (Chair.), Hall (Dir.).

**1964/65 Season:**
(Back) Humes, Morris, Reeves, Butler, Jones, Durie. (Front) Talbot, Metcalf, Hauser (Player-Manager), Ryden, Starkey.

# *SEASON 1964-65*

## FOOTBALL LEAGUE DIVISION 4

| | Date | Opposition | | FT | HT | Att. | Goalscorers | Reeves D. | Molyneux J. | Starkey M. | Hauser P. | Butler J. | Corbishley C. | Humes J. | Metcalf M. | Talbot G. | Ryden H. | Lee G. | Jones B. | Evans G. | Morris E. | Jones R. | Harvey B. | Evans J. | Wildler F. | Harley L. | Durie D. | Read D. | Barton R. | Berry D. | Bennion S. |
|---|---|---|---|---|---|---|---|---|---|---|---|---|---|---|---|---|---|---|---|---|---|---|---|---|---|---|---|---|---|---|---|
| 1 | Aug 22 | Aldershot | L | 1-3 | 0-3 | 6151 | Metcalf | 1 | 2 | 3 | 4 | 5 | 6 | 7 | 8 | 9 | 10 | 11 | | | | | | | | | | | | | |
| 2 | 25 | Bradford City | W | 3-1 | 0-0 | 6202 | Talbot (2), Morris | 1 | | 3 | 4 | 5 | | 7 | 8 | 9 | 10 | | 2 | 6 | 11 | | | | | | | | | | |
| 3 | 29 | TORQUAY UNITED | L | 0-1 | 0-1 | 6830 | | 1 | | 3 | 4 | 5 | | 7 | 8 | 9 | 10 | | 2 | 6 | 11 | | | | | | | | | | |
| 4 | Sep 4 | Stockport County | W | 5-4 | 2-0 | 4367 | Talbot (3), Morris, Metcalf (pen) | 1 | | 3 | | 5 | | 7 | 8 | 9 | 10 | | | 6 | 11 | 2 | 4 | | | | | | | | |
| 5 | 7 | Millwall | L | 0-1 | 0-1 | 9198 | | 1 | | 6 | 4 | 5 | | 7 | 8 | 9 | 10 | | | | 11 | 2 | | 3 | | | | | | | |
| 6 | 12 | YORK CITY | W | 4-1 | 2-0 | 6095 | Talbot (2), Ryden, Morris | 1 | | 3 | 4 | 5 | 6 | 7 | 8 | 9 | 10 | | | | 11 | 2 | | | | | | | | | |
| 7 | 16 | MILLWALL | W | 3-1 | 2-0 | 7005 | Metcalf (2), Morris | 1 | | 3 | 4 | 5 | 6 | 7 | 8 | 9 | | | | | 11 | 2 | | | 10 | | | | | | |
| 8 | 19 | Lincoln City | D | 2-2 | 0-2 | 3897 | Humes (2) | 1 | | 3 | 4 | 5 | 6 | 7 | 8 | 9 | 10 | | | | 11 | 2 | | | | | | | | | |
| 9 | 26 | BRIGHTON & HOVE A. | W | 3-1 | 1-0 | 9068 | Ryden (2), Metcalf | 1 | | 3 | 4 | 5 | 6 | | 8 | 9 | 10 | | | | 11 | 2 | | | | 7 | | | | | |
| 10 | 28 | Hartlepools United | D | 1-1 | 1-0 | 8822 | Metcalf | 1 | | 3 | 4 | 5 | | | 8 | 9 | 10 | | | | 11 | 2 | | | | 7 | 6 | | | | |
| 11 | Oct 3 | Oxford United | L | 2-3 | 1-1 | 8758 | Morris (2) | 1 | | 3 | 4 | 5 | | 7 | 8 | 9 | 10 | | | | 11 | 2 | | | | | 6 | | | | |
| 12 | 7 | HARTLEPOOLS UNITED | W | 4-0 | 0-0 | 7796 | Humes, Ryden (2), Talbot | 1 | | 3 | 4 | 5 | | 8 | | 9 | 10 | | | | 11 | 2 | | | | | 6 | 7 | | | |
| 13 | 10 | SOUTHPORT | W | 3-1 | 1-1 | 7228 | Hauser, Talbot (2) | 1 | | 3 | 4 | 5 | | 8 | | 9 | 10 | | | | 11 | 2 | | | | | 6 | 7 | | | |
| 14 | 14 | Rochdale | L | 1-2 | 1-2 | 4845 | Humes | 1 | | 3 | 4 | 5 | | 8 | | 9 | 10 | | | | 11 | 2 | | | | | 6 | 7 | | | |
| 15 | 17 | Wrexham | L | 2-4 | 0-1 | 14690 | Metcalf (pen), Talbot | 1 | | 3 | 4 | 5 | | 7 | 8 | 9 | 10 | | | | 11 | 2 | | | | | 6 | | | | |
| 16 | 24 | TRANMERE ROVERS | W | 3-2 | 0-1 | 12076 | Talbot, Metcalf, Humes | 1 | | 3 | 4 | 5 | | 7 | 8 | 9 | 10 | | | | | 2 | | | | | 6 | 11 | | | |
| 17 | 31 | Darlington | L | 0-2 | 0-0 | 4229 | | 1 | | 3 | 4 | 5 | | 7 | 8 | 9 | 10 | | | | 11 | 2 | | | | | 6 | | | | |
| 18 | Nov 7 | CREWE ALEX. | D | 2-2 | 1-1 | 6922 | Durie, Metcalf | 1 | | 3 | 4 | 5 | 6 | 7 | 8 | 9 | | | | | 11 | 2 | | | | | 10 | | | | |
| 19 | 21 | HALIFAX TOWN | W | 1-0 | 1-0 | 6028 | Talbot | 1 | | 3 | 4 | 5 | | 7 | 8 | 9 | 10 | | | | 11 | 2 | | | | | 6 | | | | |
| 20 | 28 | Notts County | D | 1-1 | 1-1 | 5878 | Ryden | 1 | | 3 | 4 | 5 | | 7 | 8 | 9 | 10 | | | | 11 | 2 | | | | | 6 | | | | |
| 21 | Dec 12 | ALDERSHOT | W | 6-2 | 3-1 | 5152 | Talbot, Metcalf (2), Morris (3) | 1 | | 3 | 4 | 5 | | 7 | 8 | 9 | 10 | | | | 11 | 2 | | | | | 6 | | | | |
| 22 | 19 | Torquay United | L | 2-3 | 2-1 | 3627 | Ryden (2) | 1 | | 3 | 4 | 5 | | 7 | 8 | 9 | 10 | | | | 11 | 2 | | | | | 6 | | | | |
| 23 | 26 | BRADFORD P. A. | W | 3-0 | 2-0 | 10057 | Humes, Ryden, Metcalf (pen) | 1 | | 3 | 4 | 5 | | 7 | 8 | 9 | 10 | | | | 11 | 2 | | | | | 6 | | | | |
| 24 | 28 | Bradford P. A. | L | 1-3 | 0-2 | 9968 | Morris | 1 | | 3 | 4 | 5 | | 7 | 8 | 9 | 10 | | | | 11 | 2 | | | | | 6 | | | | |
| 25 | Jan 2 | STOCKPORT COUNTY | W | 4-0 | 2-0 | 7606 | Metcalf (2), Ryden (2) | 1 | | 3 | 4 | 5 | | 7 | 8 | 9 | 10 | | | | 11 | 2 | | | | | 6 | | | | |
| 26 | 16 | York City | L | 2-3 | 2-1 | 5118 | Humes (2) | 1 | | 3 | 4 | 5 | | 7 | 8 | 9 | 10 | | | | 11 | 2 | | | | | 6 | | | | |
| 27 | 23 | LINCOLN CITY | W | 5-1 | 2-0 | 7432 | Ryden, Talbot (2), Metcalf (2) | 1 | | 3 | 4 | 5 | | 7 | 8 | 9 | 10 | | | | 11 | 2 | | | | | 6 | | | | |
| 28 | 30 | Newport County | W | 1-0 | 0-0 | 3219 | Metcalf | 1 | | 3 | 4 | 5 | | 7 | 8 | 9 | 10 | | | | 11 | 2 | | | | | 6 | | | | |
| 29 | Feb 6 | Brighton & Hove A. | D | 4-4 | 2-2 | 16434 | Morris, Talbot (2), Metcalf | 1 | | 3 | 4 | 5 | | 7 | 8 | 9 | 10 | | | | 11 | 2 | | | | | 6 | | | | |
| 30 | 10 | BRADFORD CITY | W | 3-1 | 1-1 | 7759 | Morris (2), Talbot | 1 | | 3 | 4 | 5 | | 7 | 8 | 9 | 10 | | | | 11 | 2 | | | | | 6 | | | | |
| 31 | 13 | OXFORD UNITED | W | 2-1 | 1-1 | 7988 | Humes, Metcalf | 1 | | 3 | 4 | 5 | | 7 | 8 | 9 | 10 | | | | 11 | 2 | | | | | 6 | | | | |
| 32 | 20 | Southport | D | 2-2 | 0-1 | 3439 | Humes, Metcalf | 1 | | 3 | 4 | 5 | | 7 | 8 | 9 | 10 | | | | 11 | 2 | | | | | 6 | | | | |
| 33 | 24 | CHESTERFIELD | W | 4-0 | 2-0 | 7401 | Talbot, Metcalf, Morris, Humes | | | 3 | 4 | 5 | | 7 | 8 | 9 | 10 | | | | 11 | 2 | | | | | 6 | | 1 | | |
| 34 | 27 | WREXHAM | W | 6-1 | 4-1 | 14782 | Metcalf, Morris, Humes (3), Talbot | | | 3 | 4 | 5 | | 7 | 8 | 9 | 10 | | | | 11 | 2 | | | | | 6 | | 1 | | |
| 35 | Mar 10 | ROCHDALE | L | 0-1 | 0-0 | 8550 | | | | 3 | 4 | 5 | 9 | 7 | 8 | | 10 | | | | 11 | 2 | | | | | 6 | | 1 | | |
| 36 | 13 | DARLINGTON | L | 4-5 | 2-2 | 6455 | Morris (2), Corbishley, Metcalf (pen) | | | 3 | 4 | 5 | 9 | 7 | 8 | | 10 | | | | 11 | 2 | | | | | 6 | | 1 | | |
| 37 | 20 | Crewe Alex. | L | 1-5 | 0-1 | 5641 | Morris | | | 3 | 4 | 5 | | 7 | 8 | 9 | 10 | | | | 11 | 2 | | | | | 6 | | 1 | | |
| 38 | 26 | NEWPORT COUNTY | W | 4-3 | 1-2 | 5843 | Metcalf (3, 1 pen), Morris | 1 | | 3 | 4 | 5 | | 7 | 8 | 9 | 10 | | | | 11 | 2 | | | | | 6 | | | | |
| 39 | 29 | Tranmere Rovers | L | 1-4 | 0-1 | 15484 | Ryden | 1 | | 3 | 4 | 5 | | 7 | 8 | 9 | 10 | | | | 11 | 2 | | | | | 6 | | | | |
| 40 | Apr 3 | Halifax Town | W | 4-3 | 0-1 | 1945 | Ryden (2), Morris, Humes | 1 | | 3 | | 5 | | 7 | 8 | 9 | 10 | | | 4 | 11 | 2 | | | | | 6 | | | | |
| 41 | 6 | Doncaster Rovers | W | 4-1 | 1-0 | 8007 | Talbot, Morris (2), Ryden | 1 | | 3 | | 5 | | 7 | 8 | 9 | 10 | | | 4 | 11 | 2 | | | | | 6 | | | | |
| 42 | 10 | NOTTS COUNTY | W | 4-1 | 2-1 | 5684 | Talbot (2), Metcalf (pen), Ryden | 1 | | 3 | | 5 | | 7 | 8 | 9 | 10 | | | 4 | 11 | 2 | | | | | 6 | | | | |
| 43 | 16 | Barrow | L | 1-2 | 1-0 | 3816 | Morris | 1 | | 3 | | 5 | | 7 | 8 | 9 | 10 | | | 4 | 11 | 2 | | | | | 6 | | | | |
| 44 | 17 | Chesterfield | W | 3-1 | 1-0 | 5971 | Humes, Morris, Talbot | 1 | | 3 | 6 | 5 | | 7 | 8 | 9 | 10 | | | 4 | 11 | 2 | | | | | | | | | |
| 45 | 19 | BARROW | W | 4-1 | 2-1 | 6006 | Humes, Ryden, Talbot (2) | 1 | | 3 | | 5 | | 7 | 8 | 9 | 10 | | | 4 | 11 | 2 | | | | | 6 | | | | |
| 46 | 24 | DONCASTER ROVERS | W | 3-0 | 1-0 | 6405 | Ryden (2), Talbot | 1 | | 3 | | 5 | | 7 | 8 | 9 | 10 | | | 4 | 11 | 2 | | | | | 6 | | | | |
| | | | | | | | Apps. | 41 | 1 | 46 | 39 | 46 | 8 | 44 | 43 | 44 | 44 | 1 | 2 | 10 | 44 | 43 | 1 | 1 | 1 | 2 | 36 | 4 | 5 | | |
| | | | | | | | Goals | | | | 1 | | 1 | 17 | 27 | 28 | 20 | | | | 24 | | | | | | 1 | | | | |

## F.A. CUP

| | Date | Opposition | | FT | HT | Att. | Goalscorers | Reeves D. | Molyneux J. | Starkey M. | Hauser P. | Butler J. | Corbishley C. | Humes J. | Metcalf M. | Talbot G. | Ryden H. | Lee G. | Jones B. | Evans G. | Morris E. | Jones R. | Harvey B. | Evans J. | Wildler F. | Harley L. | Durie D. | Read D. | Barton R. | Berry D. | Bennion S. |
|---|---|---|---|---|---|---|---|---|---|---|---|---|---|---|---|---|---|---|---|---|---|---|---|---|---|---|---|---|---|---|---|
| 1R | Nov 14 | CREWE ALEX. | W | 5-0 | 1-0 | 9436 | Metcalf (2, 1 pen), Talbot (3) | 1 | | 3 | 4 | 5 | | 7 | 8 | 9 | 10 | | | | 11 | 2 | | | | | 6 | | | | |
| 2R | Dec 5 | Barnsley | W | 5-2 | 1-2 | 6674 | Metcalf (3), Humes, Morris | 1 | | 3 | 4 | 5 | | 7 | 8 | 9 | 10 | | | | 11 | 2 | | | | | 6 | | | | |
| 3R | Jan 9 | Manchester United | L | 1-2 | 1-0 | 45660 | Humes | 1 | | 3 | 4 | 5 | | 7 | 8 | 9 | 10 | | | | 11 | 2 | | | | | 6 | | | | |

## LEAGUE CUP

| | Date | Opposition | | FT | HT | Att. | Goalscorers | Reeves D. | Molyneux J. | Starkey M. | Hauser P. | Butler J. | Corbishley C. | Humes J. | Metcalf M. | Talbot G. | Ryden H. | Lee G. | Jones B. | Evans G. | Morris E. | Jones R. | Harvey B. | Evans J. | Wildler F. | Harley L. | Durie D. | Read D. | Barton R. | Berry D. | Bennion S. |
|---|---|---|---|---|---|---|---|---|---|---|---|---|---|---|---|---|---|---|---|---|---|---|---|---|---|---|---|---|---|---|---|
| 1R | Sep 2 | WREXHAM | W | 3-0 | 1-0 | 10331 | Metcalf (2), Talbot | 1 | | 3 | 4 | 5 | | 7 | 8 | 9 | 10 | | | 6 | 11 | 2 | | | | | | | | | |
| 2R | 23 | DERBY COUNTY | W | 5-4 | 3-3 | 9874 | Metcalf (2, 1 pen), Morris, Talbot (2) | 1 | | 3 | 4 | 5 | 6 | 7 | 8 | 9 | 10 | | | | 11 | 2 | | | | | | | | | |
| 3R | Oct 21 | Norwich City | L | 3-5 | 2-2 | 9345 | Metcalf, Talbot, Humes | 1 | | 3 | 4 | 5 | | 7 | 8 | 9 | 10 | | | | | 2 | | | | | 6 | 11 | | | |

## WELSH CUP

| | Date | Opposition | | FT | HT | Att. | Goalscorers | Reeves D. | Molyneux J. | Starkey M. | Hauser P. | Butler J. | Corbishley C. | Humes J. | Metcalf M. | Talbot G. | Ryden H. | Lee G. | Jones B. | Evans G. | Morris E. | Jones R. | Harvey B. | Evans J. | Wildler F. | Harley L. | Durie D. | Read D. | Barton R. | Berry D. | Bennion S. |
|---|---|---|---|---|---|---|---|---|---|---|---|---|---|---|---|---|---|---|---|---|---|---|---|---|---|---|---|---|---|---|---|
| 5R | Jan 20 | BANGOR CITY | D | 1-1 | 1-0 | 4321 | Metcalf | 1 | | 3 | 4 | 5 | | 7 | 8 | 9 | 10 | | | | 11 | 2 | | | | | 6 | | | | |
| 5Rr | 27 | Bangor City | W | 4-0 | 2-0 | 3542 | Ryden (2), Talbot, Humes | 1 | | 3 | 4 | 5 | | 7 | 8 | 9 | 10 | | | | 11 | 2 | | | | | 6 | | | | |
| 6R | Feb 17 | BOROUGH UNITED | D | 0-0 | 0-0 | 6934 | | 1 | | 3 | 4 | 5 | | 7 | 8 | 9 | 10 | | | | 11 | 2 | | | | | 6 | | | | |
| 6Rr | Mar 9 | Borough United * | D | 2-2 | 2-2 | | Humes, Owen (og) | | | 3 | 4 | 5 | | 9 | 8 | | 10 | | | | 11 | 2 | | | | 7 | 6 | | 1 | | |
| 6R2r | 16 | BOROUGH UNITED | W | 3-0 | 1-0 | 7175 | Talbot, Morris (2) | | | 3 | 4 | 5 | | 7 | 8 | 9 | 10 | | | | 11 | 2 | | | | | 6 | | 1 | | |
| SF | 30 | Wrexham | L | 0-3 | 0-1 | 12341 | | 1 | | 3 | 4 | 5 | | 7 | 8 | | | | | 6 | 11 | 2 | | | | | | | | 9 | 10 |

* Extra time played following score of 2-2 after 90 minutes

## FRIENDLIES

| | Date | Opposition | | FT | HT | | Goalscorers |
|---|---|---|---|---|---|---|---|
| 1 | Aug 11 | New Brighton | W | 4-3 | 2-2 | | Talbot, Bennion, Metcalf, Parkes (og) |
| 2 | Apr 30 | Chelmsford City | W | 2-0 | 0-0 | | Talbot (2) |

# FINAL LEAGUE TABLES: 1964/65 - 1971/72

Final League Table 1964/65 Division 4

| | | Pl. | Home W | Home D | Home L | Home F | Home A | Away W | Away D | Away L | Away F | Away A | F. | A. | Pts |
|---|---|---|---|---|---|---|---|---|---|---|---|---|---|---|---|
| 1 | Brighton & Hove A. | 46 | 18 | 5 | 0 | 68 | 20 | 8 | 6 | 9 | 34 | 37 | 102 | 57 | 63 |
| 2 | Millwall | 46 | 13 | 10 | 0 | 45 | 15 | 10 | 6 | 7 | 33 | 30 | 78 | 45 | 62 |
| 3 | York City | 46 | 20 | 1 | 2 | 63 | 21 | 8 | 5 | 10 | 28 | 35 | 91 | 56 | 62 |
| 4 | Oxford United | 46 | 18 | 4 | 1 | 54 | 13 | 5 | 11 | 7 | 33 | 31 | 87 | 44 | 61 |
| 5 | Tranmere Rovers | 46 | 20 | 2 | 1 | 72 | 20 | 7 | 4 | 12 | 27 | 36 | 99 | 56 | 60 |
| 6 | Rochdale | 46 | 15 | 4 | 4 | 46 | 22 | 7 | 10 | 6 | 28 | 31 | 74 | 53 | 58 |
| 7 | Bradford Park Ave. | 46 | 14 | 8 | 1 | 52 | 22 | 6 | 9 | 8 | 34 | 40 | 86 | 62 | 57 |
| ***8*** | ***Chester*** | ***46*** | ***19*** | ***1*** | ***3*** | ***75*** | ***26*** | ***6*** | ***5*** | ***12*** | ***44*** | ***55*** | ***119*** | ***81*** | ***56*** |
| 9 | Doncaster Rovers | 46 | 13 | 6 | 4 | 46 | 25 | 7 | 5 | 11 | 38 | 47 | 84 | 72 | 51 |
| 10 | Crewe Alexandra | 46 | 11 | 8 | 4 | 55 | 34 | 7 | 5 | 11 | 35 | 47 | 90 | 81 | 49 |
| 11 | Torquay United | 46 | 11 | 5 | 7 | 41 | 33 | 10 | 2 | 11 | 29 | 37 | 70 | 70 | 49 |
| 12 | Chesterfield | 46 | 13 | 5 | 5 | 36 | 22 | 7 | 3 | 13 | 22 | 48 | 58 | 70 | 48 |
| 13 | Notts County | 46 | 12 | 7 | 4 | 43 | 23 | 3 | 7 | 13 | 18 | 50 | 61 | 73 | 44 |
| 14 | Wrexham | 46 | 12 | 5 | 6 | 59 | 37 | 5 | 4 | 14 | 25 | 55 | 84 | 92 | 43 |
| 15 | Hartlepools United | 46 | 11 | 10 | 2 | 44 | 28 | 4 | 3 | 16 | 17 | 57 | 61 | 85 | 43 |
| 16 | Newport County | 46 | 14 | 5 | 4 | 54 | 26 | 3 | 3 | 17 | 31 | 55 | 85 | 81 | 42 |
| 17 | Darlington | 46 | 14 | 2 | 7 | 52 | 30 | 4 | 4 | 15 | 32 | 57 | 84 | 87 | 42 |
| 18 | Aldershot | 46 | 14 | 3 | 6 | 46 | 25 | 1 | 4 | 18 | 18 | 59 | 64 | 84 | 37 |
| 19 | Bradford City | 46 | 9 | 2 | 12 | 37 | 36 | 3 | 6 | 14 | 33 | 52 | 70 | 88 | 32 |
| 20 | Southport | 46 | 5 | 9 | 9 | 35 | 45 | 3 | 7 | 13 | 23 | 44 | 58 | 89 | 32 |
| 21 | Barrow | 46 | 9 | 4 | 10 | 30 | 38 | 3 | 2 | 18 | 29 | 67 | 59 | 105 | 30 |
| 22 | Lincoln City | 46 | 8 | 4 | 11 | 35 | 33 | 3 | 2 | 18 | 23 | 66 | 58 | 99 | 28 |
| 23 | Halifax Town | 46 | 9 | 4 | 10 | 37 | 37 | 2 | 2 | 19 | 17 | 66 | 54 | 103 | 28 |
| 24 | Stockport County | 46 | 8 | 4 | 11 | 30 | 34 | 2 | 3 | 18 | 14 | 53 | 44 | 87 | 27 |

Final League Table 1965/66 Division 4

| | | Pl. | Home W | Home D | Home L | Home F | Home A | Away W | Away D | Away L | Away F | Away A | F. | A. | Pts |
|---|---|---|---|---|---|---|---|---|---|---|---|---|---|---|---|
| 1 | Doncaster Rovers | 46 | 15 | 6 | 2 | 49 | 21 | 9 | 5 | 9 | 36 | 33 | 85 | 54 | 59 |
| 2 | Darlington | 46 | 16 | 3 | 4 | 41 | 17 | 9 | 6 | 8 | 31 | 36 | 72 | 53 | 59 |
| 3 | Torquay United | 46 | 17 | 2 | 4 | 43 | 20 | 7 | 8 | 8 | 29 | 29 | 72 | 49 | 58 |
| 4 | Colchester United | 46 | 13 | 7 | 3 | 45 | 21 | 10 | 3 | 10 | 25 | 26 | 70 | 47 | 56 |
| 5 | Tranmere Rovers | 46 | 15 | 1 | 7 | 56 | 32 | 9 | 7 | 7 | 37 | 34 | 93 | 66 | 56 |
| 6 | Luton Town | 46 | 19 | 2 | 2 | 65 | 27 | 5 | 6 | 12 | 25 | 43 | 90 | 70 | 56 |
| ***7*** | ***Chester*** | ***46*** | ***15*** | ***5*** | ***3*** | ***52*** | ***27*** | ***5*** | ***7*** | ***11*** | ***27*** | ***43*** | ***79*** | ***70*** | ***52*** |
| 8 | Notts County | 46 | 9 | 8 | 6 | 32 | 25 | 10 | 4 | 9 | 29 | 28 | 61 | 53 | 50 |
| 9 | Newport County | 46 | 14 | 6 | 3 | 46 | 24 | 4 | 6 | 13 | 29 | 51 | 75 | 75 | 48 |
| 10 | Southport | 46 | 15 | 6 | 2 | 47 | 20 | 3 | 6 | 14 | 21 | 49 | 68 | 69 | 48 |
| 11 | Bradford Park Ave. | 46 | 14 | 2 | 7 | 59 | 31 | 7 | 3 | 13 | 43 | 61 | 102 | 92 | 47 |
| 12 | Barrow | 46 | 12 | 8 | 3 | 48 | 31 | 4 | 7 | 12 | 24 | 45 | 72 | 76 | 47 |
| 13 | Stockport County | 46 | 12 | 4 | 7 | 42 | 29 | 6 | 2 | 15 | 29 | 41 | 71 | 70 | 42 |
| 14 | Crewe Alexandra | 46 | 12 | 4 | 7 | 42 | 23 | 4 | 5 | 14 | 19 | 40 | 61 | 63 | 41 |
| 15 | Halifax Town | 46 | 11 | 6 | 6 | 46 | 31 | 4 | 5 | 14 | 21 | 44 | 67 | 75 | 41 |
| 16 | Barnsley | 46 | 11 | 6 | 6 | 43 | 24 | 4 | 4 | 15 | 31 | 54 | 74 | 78 | 40 |
| 17 | Aldershot | 46 | 12 | 6 | 5 | 47 | 27 | 3 | 4 | 16 | 28 | 57 | 75 | 84 | 40 |
| 18 | Hartlepools United | 46 | 13 | 4 | 6 | 44 | 22 | 3 | 4 | 16 | 19 | 53 | 63 | 75 | 40 |
| 19 | Port Vale | 46 | 12 | 7 | 4 | 38 | 18 | 3 | 2 | 18 | 10 | 41 | 48 | 59 | 39 |
| 20 | Chesterfield | 46 | 8 | 9 | 6 | 37 | 35 | 5 | 4 | 14 | 25 | 43 | 62 | 78 | 39 |
| 21 | Rochdale | 46 | 12 | 1 | 10 | 46 | 27 | 4 | 4 | 15 | 25 | 60 | 71 | 87 | 37 |
| 22 | Lincoln City | 46 | 9 | 7 | 7 | 37 | 29 | 4 | 4 | 15 | 20 | 53 | 57 | 82 | 37 |
| 23 | Bradford City | 46 | 10 | 5 | 8 | 37 | 34 | 2 | 8 | 13 | 26 | 60 | 63 | 94 | 37 |
| 24 | Wrexham | 46 | 10 | 4 | 9 | 43 | 43 | 3 | 5 | 15 | 29 | 61 | 72 | 104 | 35 |

Final League Table 1966/67 Division 4

| | | Pl. | Home W | Home D | Home L | Home F | Home A | Away W | Away D | Away L | Away F | Away A | F. | A. | Pts |
|---|---|---|---|---|---|---|---|---|---|---|---|---|---|---|---|
| 1 | Stockport County | 46 | 16 | 5 | 2 | 41 | 18 | 10 | 7 | 6 | 28 | 24 | 69 | 42 | 64 |
| 2 | Southport | 46 | 19 | 2 | 2 | 47 | 15 | 4 | 11 | 8 | 22 | 27 | 69 | 42 | 59 |
| 3 | Barrow | 46 | 12 | 8 | 3 | 35 | 18 | 12 | 3 | 8 | 41 | 36 | 76 | 54 | 59 |
| 4 | Tranmere Rovers | 46 | 14 | 6 | 3 | 42 | 20 | 8 | 8 | 7 | 24 | 23 | 66 | 43 | 58 |
| 5 | Crewe Alexandra | 46 | 14 | 5 | 4 | 42 | 26 | 7 | 7 | 9 | 28 | 29 | 70 | 55 | 54 |
| 6 | Southend United | 46 | 15 | 5 | 3 | 44 | 12 | 7 | 4 | 12 | 26 | 37 | 70 | 49 | 53 |
| 7 | Wrexham | 46 | 11 | 12 | 0 | 46 | 20 | 5 | 8 | 10 | 30 | 42 | 76 | 62 | 52 |
| 8 | Hartlepools United | 46 | 15 | 3 | 5 | 44 | 29 | 7 | 4 | 12 | 22 | 35 | 66 | 64 | 51 |
| 9 | Brentford | 46 | 13 | 7 | 3 | 36 | 19 | 5 | 6 | 12 | 22 | 37 | 58 | 56 | 49 |
| 10 | Aldershot | 46 | 14 | 4 | 5 | 48 | 19 | 4 | 8 | 11 | 24 | 38 | 72 | 57 | 48 |
| 11 | Bradford City | 46 | 13 | 4 | 6 | 48 | 31 | 6 | 6 | 11 | 26 | 31 | 74 | 62 | 48 |
| 12 | Halifax Town | 46 | 10 | 11 | 2 | 37 | 27 | 5 | 3 | 15 | 22 | 41 | 59 | 68 | 44 |
| 13 | Port Vale | 46 | 9 | 7 | 7 | 33 | 27 | 5 | 8 | 10 | 22 | 31 | 55 | 58 | 43 |
| 14 | Exeter City | 46 | 11 | 6 | 6 | 30 | 24 | 3 | 9 | 11 | 20 | 36 | 50 | 60 | 43 |
| 15 | Chesterfield | 46 | 13 | 6 | 4 | 33 | 16 | 4 | 2 | 17 | 27 | 47 | 60 | 63 | 42 |
| 16 | Barnsley | 46 | 8 | 7 | 8 | 30 | 28 | 5 | 8 | 10 | 30 | 36 | 60 | 64 | 41 |
| 17 | Luton Town | 46 | 15 | 5 | 3 | 47 | 23 | 1 | 4 | 18 | 12 | 50 | 59 | 73 | 41 |
| 18 | Newport County | 46 | 9 | 9 | 5 | 35 | 23 | 3 | 7 | 13 | 21 | 40 | 56 | 63 | 40 |
| ***19*** | ***Chester*** | ***46*** | ***8*** | ***5*** | ***10*** | ***24*** | ***32*** | ***7*** | ***5*** | ***11*** | ***30*** | ***46*** | ***54*** | ***78*** | ***40*** |
| 20 | Notts County | 46 | 10 | 7 | 6 | 31 | 25 | 3 | 4 | 16 | 22 | 47 | 53 | 72 | 37 |
| 21 | Rochdale | 46 | 10 | 4 | 9 | 30 | 27 | 3 | 7 | 13 | 23 | 48 | 53 | 75 | 37 |
| 22 | York City | 46 | 11 | 5 | 7 | 45 | 31 | 1 | 6 | 16 | 20 | 48 | 65 | 79 | 35 |
| 23 | Bradford Park Ave. | 46 | 7 | 6 | 10 | 30 | 34 | 4 | 7 | 12 | 22 | 45 | 52 | 79 | 35 |
| 24 | Lincoln City | 46 | 7 | 8 | 8 | 39 | 39 | 2 | 5 | 16 | 19 | 43 | 58 | 82 | 31 |

Final League Table 1967/68 Division 4

| | | Pl. | Home W | Home D | Home L | Home F | Home A | Away W | Away D | Away L | Away F | Away A | F. | A. | Pts |
|---|---|---|---|---|---|---|---|---|---|---|---|---|---|---|---|
| 1 | Luton Town | 46 | 19 | 3 | 1 | 55 | 16 | 8 | 9 | 6 | 32 | 28 | 87 | 44 | 66 |
| 2 | Barnsley | 46 | 17 | 6 | 0 | 43 | 14 | 7 | 7 | 9 | 25 | 32 | 68 | 46 | 61 |
| 3 | Hartlepools United | 46 | 15 | 7 | 1 | 34 | 12 | 10 | 3 | 10 | 26 | 34 | 60 | 46 | 60 |
| 4 | Crewe Alexandra | 46 | 13 | 10 | 0 | 44 | 18 | 7 | 8 | 8 | 30 | 31 | 74 | 49 | 58 |
| 5 | Bradford City | 46 | 14 | 5 | 4 | 41 | 22 | 9 | 6 | 8 | 31 | 29 | 72 | 51 | 57 |
| 6 | Southend United | 46 | 12 | 8 | 3 | 45 | 21 | 8 | 6 | 9 | 32 | 37 | 77 | 58 | 54 |
| 7 | Chesterfield | 46 | 15 | 4 | 4 | 47 | 20 | 6 | 7 | 10 | 24 | 30 | 71 | 50 | 53 |
| 8 | Wrexham | 46 | 17 | 3 | 3 | 47 | 12 | 3 | 10 | 10 | 25 | 41 | 72 | 53 | 53 |
| 9 | Aldershot | 46 | 10 | 11 | 2 | 36 | 19 | 8 | 6 | 9 | 34 | 36 | 70 | 55 | 53 |
| 10 | Doncaster Rovers | 46 | 12 | 8 | 3 | 36 | 16 | 6 | 7 | 10 | 30 | 40 | 66 | 56 | 51 |
| 11 | Halifax Town | 46 | 10 | 6 | 7 | 34 | 24 | 5 | 10 | 8 | 18 | 25 | 52 | 49 | 46 |
| 12 | Newport County | 46 | 11 | 7 | 5 | 32 | 22 | 5 | 6 | 12 | 26 | 41 | 58 | 63 | 45 |
| 13 | Lincoln City | 46 | 11 | 3 | 9 | 41 | 31 | 6 | 6 | 11 | 30 | 37 | 71 | 68 | 43 |
| 14 | Brentford | 46 | 13 | 4 | 6 | 41 | 24 | 5 | 3 | 15 | 20 | 40 | 61 | 64 | 43 |
| 15 | Swansea Town | 46 | 11 | 8 | 4 | 38 | 25 | 5 | 2 | 16 | 25 | 52 | 63 | 77 | 42 |
| 16 | Darlington | 46 | 6 | 11 | 6 | 31 | 27 | 6 | 6 | 11 | 16 | 26 | 47 | 53 | 41 |
| 17 | Notts County | 46 | 10 | 7 | 6 | 27 | 27 | 5 | 4 | 14 | 26 | 52 | 53 | 79 | 41 |
| 18 | Port Vale | 46 | 10 | 5 | 8 | 41 | 31 | 2 | 10 | 11 | 20 | 41 | 61 | 72 | 39 |
| 19 | Rochdale | 46 | 9 | 8 | 6 | 35 | 32 | 3 | 6 | 14 | 16 | 40 | 51 | 72 | 38 |
| 20 | Exeter City | 46 | 9 | 7 | 7 | 30 | 30 | 2 | 9 | 12 | 15 | 35 | 45 | 65 | 38 |
| 21 | York City | 46 | 9 | 6 | 8 | 44 | 30 | 2 | 8 | 13 | 21 | 38 | 65 | 68 | 36 |
| ***22*** | ***Chester*** | ***46*** | ***6*** | ***6*** | ***11*** | ***35*** | ***38*** | ***3*** | ***8*** | ***12*** | ***22*** | 40 | 57 | 78 | 32 |
| 23 | Workington | 46 | 8 | 8 | 7 | 35 | 29 | 2 | 3 | 18 | 19 | 58 | 54 | 87 | 31 |
| 24 | Bradford Park Ave. | 46 | 3 | 7 | 13 | 18 | 35 | 1 | 8 | 14 | 12 | 47 | 30 | 82 | 23 |

Final League Table 1968/69 Division 4

| | | Pl. | Home W | Home D | Home L | Home F | Home A | Away W | Away D | Away L | Away F | Away A | F. | A. | Pts |
|---|---|---|---|---|---|---|---|---|---|---|---|---|---|---|---|
| 1 | Doncaster Rovers | 46 | 13 | 8 | 2 | 42 | 16 | 8 | 9 | 6 | 23 | 22 | 65 | 38 | 59 |
| 2 | Halifax Town | 46 | 15 | 5 | 3 | 36 | 18 | 5 | 12 | 6 | 17 | 19 | 53 | 37 | 57 |
| 3 | Rochdale | 46 | 14 | 7 | 2 | 47 | 11 | 4 | 13 | 6 | 21 | 24 | 68 | 35 | 56 |
| 4 | Bradford City | 46 | 11 | 10 | 2 | 36 | 18 | 7 | 10 | 6 | 29 | 28 | 65 | 46 | 56 |
| 5 | Darlington | 46 | 11 | 6 | 6 | 40 | 26 | 6 | 12 | 5 | 22 | 19 | 62 | 45 | 52 |
| 6 | Colchester United | 46 | 12 | 8 | 3 | 31 | 17 | 8 | 4 | 11 | 26 | 36 | 57 | 53 | 52 |
| 7 | Southend United | 46 | 15 | 3 | 5 | 51 | 21 | 4 | 10 | 9 | 27 | 40 | 78 | 61 | 51 |
| 8 | Lincoln City | 46 | 13 | 6 | 4 | 38 | 19 | 4 | 11 | 8 | 16 | 33 | 54 | 52 | 51 |
| 9 | Wrexham | 46 | 13 | 7 | 3 | 41 | 22 | 5 | 7 | 11 | 20 | 30 | 61 | 52 | 50 |
| 10 | Swansea Town | 46 | 11 | 8 | 4 | 35 | 20 | 8 | 3 | 12 | 23 | 34 | 58 | 54 | 49 |
| 11 | Brentford | 46 | 12 | 7 | 4 | 40 | 24 | 6 | 5 | 12 | 24 | 41 | 64 | 65 | 48 |
| 12 | Workington | 46 | 8 | 11 | 4 | 24 | 17 | 7 | 6 | 10 | 16 | 26 | 40 | 43 | 47 |
| 13 | Port Vale | 46 | 12 | 8 | 3 | 33 | 15 | 4 | 6 | 13 | 13 | 31 | 46 | 46 | 46 |
| ***14*** | ***Chester*** | ***46*** | ***12*** | ***4*** | ***7*** | ***43*** | ***24*** | ***4*** | ***9*** | ***10*** | ***33*** | ***42*** | ***76*** | ***66*** | ***45*** |
| 15 | Aldershot | 46 | 13 | 3 | 7 | 42 | 23 | 6 | 4 | 13 | 24 | 43 | 66 | 66 | 45 |
| 16 | Scunthorpe United | 46 | 10 | 5 | 8 | 28 | 22 | 8 | 3 | 12 | 33 | 38 | 61 | 60 | 44 |
| 17 | Exeter City | 46 | 11 | 8 | 4 | 45 | 24 | 5 | 3 | 15 | 21 | 41 | 66 | 65 | 43 |
| 18 | Peterborough Utd. | 46 | 8 | 9 | 6 | 32 | 23 | 5 | 7 | 11 | 28 | 34 | 60 | 57 | 42 |
| 19 | Notts County | 46 | 10 | 8 | 5 | 33 | 22 | 2 | 10 | 11 | 15 | 35 | 48 | 57 | 42 |
| 20 | Chesterfield | 46 | 7 | 7 | 9 | 24 | 22 | 6 | 8 | 9 | 19 | 28 | 43 | 50 | 41 |
| 21 | York City | 46 | 12 | 8 | 3 | 36 | 25 | 2 | 3 | 18 | 17 | 50 | 53 | 75 | 39 |
| 22 | Newport County | 46 | 9 | 9 | 5 | 31 | 26 | 2 | 5 | 16 | 18 | 48 | 49 | 74 | 36 |
| 23 | Grimsby Town | 46 | 5 | 7 | 11 | 25 | 31 | 4 | 8 | 11 | 22 | 38 | 47 | 69 | 33 |
| 24 | Bradford Park Ave. | 46 | 5 | 8 | 10 | 19 | 34 | 0 | 2 | 21 | 13 | 72 | 32 | 106 | 20 |

Final League Table 1969/70 Division 4

| | | Pl. | Home W | Home D | Home L | Home F | Home A | Away W | Away D | Away L | Away F | Away A | F. | A. | Pts |
|---|---|---|---|---|---|---|---|---|---|---|---|---|---|---|---|
| 1 | Chesterfield | 46 | 19 | 1 | 3 | 55 | 12 | 8 | 9 | 6 | 22 | 20 | 77 | 32 | 64 |
| 2 | Wrexham | 46 | 17 | 6 | 0 | 56 | 16 | 9 | 3 | 11 | 28 | 33 | 84 | 49 | 61 |
| 3 | Swansea Town | 46 | 14 | 8 | 1 | 43 | 14 | 7 | 10 | 6 | 23 | 31 | 66 | 45 | 60 |
| 4 | Port Vale | 46 | 13 | 9 | 1 | 39 | 10 | 7 | 10 | 6 | 22 | 23 | 61 | 33 | 59 |
| 5 | Brentford | 46 | 14 | 8 | 1 | 36 | 11 | 6 | 8 | 9 | 22 | 28 | 58 | 39 | 56 |
| 6 | Aldershot | 46 | 16 | 5 | 2 | 52 | 22 | 4 | 8 | 11 | 26 | 43 | 78 | 65 | 53 |
| 7 | Notts County | 46 | 14 | 4 | 5 | 44 | 21 | 8 | 4 | 11 | 29 | 41 | 73 | 62 | 52 |
| 8 | Lincoln City | 46 | 11 | 8 | 4 | 38 | 20 | 6 | 8 | 9 | 28 | 32 | 66 | 52 | 50 |
| 9 | Peterborough Utd. | 46 | 13 | 8 | 2 | 51 | 21 | 4 | 6 | 13 | 26 | 48 | 77 | 69 | 48 |
| 10 | Colchester United | 46 | 14 | 5 | 4 | 38 | 22 | 3 | 9 | 11 | 26 | 41 | 64 | 63 | 48 |
| ***11*** | ***Chester*** | ***46*** | ***14*** | ***3*** | ***6*** | ***39*** | ***23*** | ***7*** | ***3*** | ***13*** | ***19*** | ***43*** | ***58*** | ***66*** | ***48*** |
| 12 | Scunthorpe United | 46 | 11 | 6 | 6 | 34 | 23 | 7 | 4 | 12 | 33 | 42 | 67 | 65 | 46 |
| 13 | York City | 46 | 14 | 7 | 2 | 38 | 16 | 2 | 7 | 14 | 17 | 46 | 55 | 62 | 46 |
| 14 | Northampton Town | 46 | 11 | 7 | 5 | 41 | 19 | 5 | 5 | 13 | 23 | 36 | 64 | 55 | 44 |
| 15 | Crewe Alexandra | 46 | 12 | 6 | 5 | 37 | 18 | 4 | 6 | 13 | 14 | 33 | 51 | 51 | 44 |
| 16 | Grimsby Town | 46 | 9 | 9 | 5 | 33 | 24 | 5 | 6 | 12 | 21 | 34 | 54 | 58 | 43 |
| 17 | Southend United | 46 | 12 | 8 | 3 | 40 | 28 | 3 | 2 | 18 | 19 | 57 | 59 | 85 | 40 |
| 18 | Exeter City | 46 | 13 | 5 | 5 | 48 | 20 | 1 | 6 | 16 | 9 | 39 | 57 | 59 | 39 |
| 19 | Oldham Athletic | 46 | 11 | 4 | 8 | 45 | 28 | 2 | 9 | 12 | 15 | 37 | 60 | 65 | 39 |
| 20 | Workington | 46 | 9 | 9 | 5 | 31 | 21 | 3 | 5 | 15 | 15 | 43 | 46 | 64 | 38 |
| 21 | Newport County | 46 | 12 | 3 | 8 | 39 | 24 | 1 | 8 | 14 | 14 | 50 | 53 | 74 | 37 |
| 22 | Darlington | 46 | 8 | 7 | 8 | 31 | 27 | 5 | 3 | 15 | 22 | 46 | 53 | 73 | 36 |
| 23 | Hartlepool | 46 | 7 | 7 | 9 | 31 | 30 | 3 | 3 | 17 | 11 | 52 | 42 | 82 | 30 |
| 24 | Bradford Park Ave. | 46 | 6 | 5 | 12 | 23 | 32 | 0 | 6 | 17 | 18 | 64 | 41 | 96 | 23 |

Final League Table 1970/71 Division 4

| | | Pl. | Home W | Home D | Home L | Home F | Home A | Away W | Away D | Away L | Away F | Away A | F. | A. | Pts |
|---|---|---|---|---|---|---|---|---|---|---|---|---|---|---|---|
| 1 | Notts County | 46 | 19 | 4 | 0 | 59 | 12 | 11 | 5 | 7 | 30 | 24 | 89 | 36 | 69 |
| 2 | Bournemouth | 46 | 16 | 5 | 2 | 51 | 15 | 8 | 7 | 8 | 30 | 31 | 81 | 46 | 60 |
| 3 | Oldham Athletic | 46 | 14 | 6 | 3 | 57 | 29 | 10 | 5 | 8 | 31 | 34 | 88 | 63 | 59 |
| 4 | York City | 46 | 16 | 6 | 1 | 45 | 14 | 7 | 4 | 12 | 33 | 40 | 78 | 54 | 56 |
| ***5*** | ***Chester*** | ***46*** | ***17*** | ***2*** | ***4*** | ***42*** | ***18*** | ***7*** | ***5*** | ***11*** | ***27*** | ***37*** | ***69*** | ***55*** | ***55*** |
| 6 | Colchester United | 46 | 14 | 6 | 3 | 44 | 19 | 7 | 6 | 10 | 26 | 35 | 70 | 54 | 54 |
| 7 | Northampton Town | 46 | 15 | 4 | 4 | 39 | 24 | 4 | 9 | 10 | 24 | 35 | 63 | 59 | 51 |
| 8 | Southport | 46 | 15 | 2 | 6 | 42 | 24 | 6 | 4 | 13 | 21 | 33 | 63 | 57 | 48 |
| 9 | Exeter City | 46 | 12 | 7 | 4 | 40 | 23 | 5 | 7 | 11 | 27 | 45 | 67 | 68 | 48 |
| 10 | Workington | 46 | 13 | 7 | 3 | 28 | 13 | 5 | 5 | 13 | 20 | 36 | 48 | 49 | 48 |
| 11 | Stockport County | 46 | 12 | 8 | 3 | 28 | 17 | 4 | 6 | 13 | 21 | 48 | 49 | 65 | 46 |
| 12 | Darlington | 46 | 15 | 3 | 5 | 42 | 22 | 2 | 8 | 13 | 16 | 35 | 58 | 57 | 45 |
| 13 | Aldershot | 46 | 8 | 10 | 5 | 32 | 23 | 6 | 7 | 10 | 34 | 48 | 66 | 71 | 45 |
| 14 | Brentford | 46 | 13 | 3 | 7 | 45 | 27 | 5 | 5 | 13 | 21 | 35 | 66 | 62 | 44 |
| 15 | Crewe Alexandra | 46 | 13 | 1 | 9 | 49 | 35 | 5 | 7 | 11 | 26 | 41 | 75 | 76 | 44 |
| 16 | Peterborough Utd. | 46 | 14 | 3 | 6 | 46 | 23 | 4 | 4 | 15 | 24 | 48 | 70 | 71 | 43 |
| 17 | Scunthorpe United | 46 | 9 | 7 | 7 | 36 | 23 | 6 | 6 | 11 | 20 | 38 | 56 | 61 | 43 |
| 18 | Southend United | 46 | 8 | 11 | 4 | 32 | 24 | 6 | 4 | 13 | 21 | 42 | 53 | 66 | 43 |
| 19 | Grimsby Town | 46 | 13 | 4 | 6 | 37 | 26 | 5 | 3 | 15 | 20 | 45 | 57 | 71 | 43 |
| 20 | Cambridge United | 46 | 9 | 9 | 5 | 31 | 27 | 6 | 4 | 13 | 20 | 39 | 51 | 66 | 43 |
| 21 | Lincoln City | 46 | 11 | 4 | 8 | 45 | 33 | 2 | 9 | 12 | 25 | 38 | 70 | 71 | 39 |
| 22 | Newport County | 46 | 8 | 3 | 12 | 32 | 36 | 2 | 5 | 16 | 23 | 49 | 55 | 85 | 28 |
| 23 | Hartlepool | 46 | 6 | 10 | 7 | 28 | 27 | 2 | 2 | 19 | 6 | 47 | 34 | 74 | 28 |
| 24 | Barrow | 46 | 5 | 5 | 13 | 25 | 38 | 2 | 3 | 18 | 26 | 52 | 51 | 90 | 22 |

Final League Table 1971/72 Division 4

| | | Pl. | Home W | Home D | Home L | Home F | Home A | Away W | Away D | Away L | Away F | Away A | F. | A. | Pts |
|---|---|---|---|---|---|---|---|---|---|---|---|---|---|---|---|
| 1 | Grimsby Town | 46 | 18 | 3 | 2 | 61 | 26 | 10 | 4 | 9 | 27 | 30 | 88 | 56 | 63 |
| 2 | Southend United | 46 | 18 | 2 | 3 | 56 | 26 | 6 | 10 | 7 | 25 | 29 | 81 | 55 | 60 |
| 3 | Brentford | 46 | 16 | 2 | 5 | 52 | 21 | 8 | 9 | 6 | 24 | 23 | 76 | 44 | 59 |
| 4 | Scunthorpe United | 46 | 13 | 8 | 2 | 34 | 15 | 9 | 5 | 9 | 22 | 22 | 56 | 37 | 57 |
| 5 | Lincoln City | 46 | 17 | 5 | 1 | 46 | 15 | 4 | 9 | 10 | 31 | 44 | 77 | 59 | 56 |
| 6 | Workington | 46 | 12 | 9 | 2 | 34 | 7 | 4 | 10 | 9 | 16 | 27 | 50 | 34 | 51 |
| 7 | Southport | 46 | 15 | 5 | 3 | 48 | 21 | 3 | 9 | 11 | 18 | 25 | 66 | 46 | 50 |
| 8 | Peterborough Utd. | 46 | 14 | 6 | 3 | 51 | 24 | 3 | 10 | 10 | 31 | 40 | 82 | 64 | 50 |
| 9 | Bury | 46 | 16 | 4 | 3 | 55 | 22 | 3 | 8 | 12 | 18 | 37 | 73 | 59 | 50 |
| 10 | Cambridge United | 46 | 11 | 8 | 4 | 38 | 22 | 6 | 6 | 11 | 24 | 38 | 62 | 60 | 48 |
| 11 | Colchester United | 46 | 13 | 6 | 4 | 38 | 23 | 6 | 4 | 13 | 32 | 46 | 70 | 69 | 48 |
| 12 | Doncaster Rovers | 46 | 11 | 8 | 4 | 35 | 24 | 5 | 6 | 12 | 21 | 39 | 56 | 63 | 46 |
| 13 | Gillingham | 46 | 11 | 5 | 7 | 33 | 24 | 5 | 8 | 10 | 28 | 43 | 61 | 67 | 45 |
| 14 | Newport County | 46 | 13 | 5 | 5 | 34 | 20 | 5 | 3 | 15 | 26 | 52 | 60 | 72 | 44 |
| 15 | Exeter City | 46 | 11 | 5 | 7 | 40 | 30 | 5 | 6 | 12 | 21 | 38 | 61 | 68 | 43 |
| 16 | Reading | 46 | 14 | 3 | 6 | 37 | 26 | 3 | 5 | 15 | 19 | 50 | 56 | 76 | 42 |
| 17 | Aldershot | 46 | 5 | 13 | 5 | 27 | 20 | 4 | 9 | 10 | 21 | 34 | 48 | 54 | 40 |
| 18 | Hartlepool | 46 | 14 | 2 | 7 | 39 | 25 | 3 | 4 | 16 | 19 | 44 | 58 | 69 | 40 |
| 19 | Darlington | 46 | 9 | 9 | 5 | 37 | 24 | 5 | 2 | 16 | 27 | 58 | 64 | 82 | 39 |
| ***20*** | ***Chester*** | ***46*** | ***10*** | ***11*** | ***2*** | ***34*** | ***16*** | ***0*** | ***7*** | ***16*** | ***13*** | ***40*** | ***47*** | ***56*** | ***38*** |
| 21 | Northampton Town | 46 | 8 | 9 | 6 | 43 | 27 | 4 | 4 | 15 | 23 | 52 | 66 | 79 | 37 |
| 22 | Barrow | 46 | 8 | 8 | 7 | 23 | 26 | 5 | 3 | 15 | 17 | 45 | 40 | 71 | 37 |
| 23 | Stockport County | 46 | 7 | 10 | 6 | 33 | 32 | 2 | 4 | 17 | 22 | 55 | 55 | 87 | 32 |
| 24 | Crewe Alexandra | 46 | 9 | 4 | 10 | 27 | 25 | 1 | 5 | 17 | 16 | 44 | 43 | 69 | 29 |

# *SEASON 1965-66*

## FOOTBALL LEAGUE DIVISION 4

| No. | Date | Opposition | | FT | HT | Att. | Goalscorers | Reeves D. | Jones R. | Starkey M. | Hauser P. | Butler J. | Durie D. | Humes J. | Metcalf M. | Talbot G. | Ryden H. | Harley L. | Singleton T. | Jones L. | Morris E. | Evans G. | Jones B. | Chadwick G. | Read D. | Willder F. | Howard R. | Holland R. | Edwards K. |
|---|---|---|---|---|---|---|---|---|---|---|---|---|---|---|---|---|---|---|---|---|---|---|---|---|---|---|---|---|---|
| 1 | Aug 21 | STOCKPORT COUNTY | W | 1-0 | 0-0 | 9973 | Humes | 1 | 2 | 3* | 4 | 5 | 6 | 7 | 8 | 9 | 10 | 11 | 12 | | | | | | | | | | |
| 2 | 23 | Tranmere Rovers | L | 0-1 | 0-0 | 13206 | | 1 | 2 | | 4 | 5 | 6 | 7 | 8 | 9 | 10 | 11 | 3 | | | | | | | | | | |
| 3 | 28 | Darlington | W | 1-0 | 0-0 | 4144 | Humes | 1 | 2 | | 4 | 5 | 6 | 7 | 8 | 9 | 10 | | 3 | 11 | | | | | | | | | |
| 4 | Sep 4 | LINCOLN CITY | W | 4-2 | 1-1 | 6742 | Ryden, Metcalf, Talbot, Hauser | 1 | 2 | | 4 | 5 | 6 | 7 | 8 | 9 | 10 | | 3 | | 11 | | | | | | | | |
| 5 | 11 | Notts County | D | 3-3 | 2-2 | 4916 | Humes, Talbot, Metcalf | 1 | 2 | | | 5 | 6 | 7 | 8 | 9 | 10 | | 3 | | 11 | 4 | | | | | | | |
| 6 | 15 | TRANMERE ROVERS | W | 3-1 | 2-0 | 12859 | Ryden, Morris, Metcalf (pen) | 1 | 2 | | 4 | 5 | 6 | 7 | 8 | | 9 | | | 10 | 11 | | 3 | | | | | | |
| 7 | 18 | WREXHAM | W | 4-2 | 2-1 | 13004 | Morris (2), Ryden, L Jones | 1 | 2 | | 4 | 5 | 6 | 7 | 8 | | 9 | | | 10 | 11 | | 3 | | | | | | |
| 8 | 25 | HALIFAX TOWN | W | 1-0 | 1-0 | 6907 | Humes | 1 | 2 | | 4 | 5 | 6 | 7 | 8 | | 9 | | | 10 | 11 | | 3 | | | | | | |
| 9 | Oct 2 | Port Vale | L | 2-5 | 1-4 | 8108 | Morris (2) | 1 | 2 | | 4 | 5 | 6 | 7 | 8 | | 9* | | | 10 | 11 | | 3 | 12 | | | | | |
| 10 | 6 | BARNSLEY | D | 3-3 | 0-2 | 8412 | Talbot, Morris, Metcalf | 1 | 2 | 3 | 4 | 5 | 6 | | 8 | 9 | | 7 | | 10 | 11 | | | | | | | | |
| 11 | 9 | Aldershot | D | 2-2 | 1-2 | 4817 | L Jones, Durie | 1 | 2 | | 4 | 5 | 6 | 7 | 8 | 9 | | | | 10 | 11 | | 3 | | | | | | |
| 12 | 16 | NEWPORT COUNTY | W | 6-1 | 5-1 | 8027 | Metcalf, Morris (2), L Jones (2), Ryden | 1 | 2 | | 4 | 5 | 6 | 7 | 8 | | 9 | | | 10 | 11 | | 3 | | | | | | |
| 13 | 23 | Torquay United | L | 0-1 | 0-0 | 6470 | | 1 | 2 | | 4 | 5 | 6 | 7 | 8 | | 9 | | | 10 | 11 | | 3 | | | | | | |
| 14 | 27 | CREWE ALEX. | W | 3-0 | 1-0 | 10176 | Ryden (2), L Jones | 1 | 2 | | 4 | 5 | 6 | 7 | 8 | | 9 | | | 10 | 11 | | 3 | | | | | | |
| 15 | 30 | CHESTERFIELD | W | 3-0 | 2-0 | 8863 | L Jones, Morris, Metcalf (pen) | 1 | 2 | | | 5 | 6 | 7 | 8 | | 9 | | | 10 | 11 | 4 | 3 | | | | | | |
| 16 | Nov 5 | Rochdale | L | 0-3 | 0-0 | 3122 | | 1 | 2 | | | 5 | 6 | 9 | 7 | | 10 | | | 8 | 11 | 4 | 3 | | | | | | |
| 17 | 20 | Barrow | L | 1-4 | 0-0 | 4295 | Ryden | 1 | 2 | | 4 | 5 | 6 | 7 | 8 | | 9 | | | 10 | 11 | | 3 | | | | | | |
| 18 | 23 | Barnsley | W | 2-0 | 0-0 | 2959 | Morris, Ryden | 1 | 2 | | 4 | 5 | 6 | 7 | 8 | | 9 | | | 10 | 11 | | 3 | | | | | | |
| 19 | 27 | HARTLEPOOLS UNITED | W | 2-0 | 1-0 | 6547 | L Jones, Morris | 1 | 2 | | 4 | 5 | 6 | 7 | 8 | | 9 | | | 10 | 11 | | 3 | | | | | | |
| 20 | Dec 11 | SOUTHPORT | W | 1-0 | 0-0 | 7501 | Morris | 1 | 2 | | 4 | 5 | 6 | 7 | 8 | | 9 | | | 10 | 11 | | 3 | | | | | | |
| 21 | 27 | Colchester United | D | 1-1 | 0-1 | 7849 | Morris | 1 | 2 | | 4 | 5 | 6 | 7 | 8 | | 9 | | | 10 | 11 | | 3 | | | | | | |
| 22 | 28 | COLCHESTER UNITED | W | 2-1 | 1-0 | 8361 | Morris, L Jones | 1 | 2 | | 4 | 5 | 6 | 7 | 8 | | 9 | | | 10 | 11 | | 3* | | 12 | | | | |
| 23 | Jan 1 | ALDERSHOT | W | 3-2 | 2-1 | 8535 | Ryden (2), Metcalf | 1 | 2 | | 4 | 5 | 6 | 7 | 8 | | 9 | | | 10 | 11 | | 3* | | 12 | | | | |
| 24 | 8 | Luton Town | L | 2-5 | 1-2 | 6670 | Morris, Metcalf | 1 | | | 3 | 5 | | 7 | 8 | 12 | 9 | | 2 | 10 | 11 | 6 | | 4* | | | | | |
| 25 | 15 | TORQUAY UNITED | D | 1-1 | 0-0 | 9302 | Morris | 1 | | | 4 | 5 | 6 | 7 | 8 | | 9 | | 2 | 10 | 11 | 3 | | | | | | | |
| 26 | 28 | Stockport County | W | 1-0 | 1-0 | 8138 | Morris | 1 | | 3 | 4 | 5 | | | 8 | 9 | 7 | | 2 | 10 | 11 | 6 | | | | | | | |
| 27 | Feb 5 | DARLINGTON | W | 3-2 | 1-1 | 9494 | Talbot, Hauser, Morris | 1 | | 3 | 4 | 5 | | | 8 | 9* | 7 | | 2 | 10 | 11 | 6 | | | | 12 | | | |
| 28 | 12 | BRADFORD CITY | W | 4-0 | 2-0 | 8038 | Metcalf, Morris, L Jones (2) | 1 | | 3 | 4 | 5 | | 7 | 8 | | 9 | | 2 | 10 | 11 | 6 | | | | | | | |
| 29 | 19 | Lincoln City | D | 2-2 | 1-1 | 3111 | Humes, Metcalf | 1 | | 3 | 4 | 5 | | 7 | 8 | | 9 | | 2 | 10 | 11 | 6 | | | | | | | |
| 30 | 26 | NOTTS COUNTY | D | 1-1 | 0-1 | 8704 | Ryden | 1 | | 3 | 4 | 5 | | 7 | 8 | | 9 | | 2 | 10 | 11 | 6 | | | | | | | |
| 31 | Mar 5 | Bradford City | W | 2-1 | 2-0 | 5596 | Morris (2) | 1 | | 3 | 4 | 5 | | 7 | 8 | | 9 | | 2 | 10 | 11 | 6 | | | | | | | |
| 32 | 12 | Wrexham | L | 1-2 | 1-1 | 17178 | L Jones | 1 | | 3 | 4 | 5 | 6 | 7 | 8 | | 9 | | 2 | 10 | 11 | | | | | | | | |
| 33 | 18 | Halifax Town | L | 0-2 | 0-1 | 5117 | | 1 | | 3 | 4 | 5 | | 7 | 8 | | 9 | | 2 | 10 | 11 | 6 | | | | | | | |
| 34 | 26 | PORT VALE | W | 2-0 | 1-0 | 6520 | Metcalf, L Jones | 1 | | 3 | 4 | 5 | 11 | | 8 | | 7 | | 2 | 10 | 9 | 6 | | | | | | | |
| 35 | 28 | Chesterfield | D | 2-2 | 2-0 | 2844 | Morris, Humes | 1 | | 3 | | 5 | 6 | 11 | 8 | | 7 | | 2 | 10 | 9 | 4 | | | | | | | |
| 36 | Apr 2 | ROCHDALE | L | 1-2 | 0-2 | 6261 | Metcalf | 1 | | 3 | 12 | 5 | 6 | 7 | 8 | | 9 | | 2 | 10* | 11 | 4 | | | | | | | |
| 37 | 8 | BRADFORD P. A. | L | 2-4 | 2-2 | 9526 | Ryden, Morris | | | 3 | 4 | 5 | | | 8 | | 10 | 7 | 9 | | 11 | 6 | | | | | 1 | 2 | |
| 38 | 9 | Doncaster Rovers | D | 1-1 | 1-0 | 11443 | Morris | 1 | | 3 | 4 | 5 | 11* | | 8 | | 10 | 7 | 2 | | 9 | 6 | | | | | | 12 | |
| 39 | 12 | Bradford P. A. | W | 1-0 | 0-0 | 7030 | Harley | 1 | | 3 | 4 | 5 | | | 8 | 9* | 12 | 7 | 2 | | 10 | 6 | | 11 | | | | | |
| 40 | 16 | BARROW | D | 0-0 | 0-0 | 7165 | | 1 | | 3 | 4 | 5 | | 11 | 8 | | 10 | 7 | 2 | | 9 | 6 | | | | | | | |
| 41 | 23 | Hartlepools United | L | 0-2 | 0-1 | 4138 | | 1 | | 3 | 4* | 5 | | | 8 | | 9 | 7 | 2 | 10 | 11 | 6 | | | 12 | | | | |
| 42 | 30 | DONCASTER ROVERS | L | 1-4 | 0-0 | 9831 | Metcalf | 1 | | 3 | | 5 | | 9 | 8 | | 10 | 7 | 2 | | 11 | 6 | | 4 | | | | | |
| 43 | May 7 | Southport | L | 0-2 | 0-2 | 4694 | | 1 | | 3 | 4 | 5 | 6 | | 8 | | 9 | 7 | 2 | 10 | 11 | | | | | | | | |
| 44 | 18 | Crewe Alex. | D | 1-1 | 0-1 | 3947 | Ryden | 1 | | 3 | | 5 | 12 | 7 | 8 | | 9 | | 2 | 10 | 11 | 6* | | 4 | | | | | |
| 45 | 23 | Newport County | L | 2-3 | 0-0 | 1636 | Metcalf, L Jones | 1 | | 3 | | 5 | 6 | 7 | 8 | | | | 2 | 10 | 11 | | | 4 | | | | | 9 |
| 46 | 28 | LUTON TOWN | D | 1-1 | 0-1 | 4740 | Humes | 1 | | 3* | 12 | 5 | 6 | 7 | 8 | | 9 | | 2 | 10 | 11 | | | 4 | | | | | |
| | | | | | | | Apps. | 45 | 23 | 23 | 37 | 46 | 32 | 37 | 46 | 10 | 42 | 10 | 27 | 37 | 43 | 22 | 17 | 6 | | | 1 | 1 | 1 |
| | | | | | | | Subs. | | | | 2 | | 1 | | | 1 | 1 | | 1 | | | | | 1 | 3 | 1 | | 1 | |
| | | | | | | | Goals | | | | 2 | | 1 | 7 | 14 | 4 | 13 | 1 | | 13 | 24 | | | | | | | | |

## F.A. CUP

| Rd | Date | Opposition | | FT | HT | Att. | Goalscorers | Reeves D. | Jones R. | Starkey M. | Hauser P. | Butler J. | Durie D. | Humes J. | Metcalf M. | Talbot G. | Ryden H. | Harley L. | Singleton T. | Jones L. | Morris E. | Evans G. | Jones B. | Chadwick G. | Read D. | Willder F. | Howard R. | Holland R. | Edwards K. |
|---|---|---|---|---|---|---|---|---|---|---|---|---|---|---|---|---|---|---|---|---|---|---|---|---|---|---|---|---|---|
| 1R | Nov 13 | Chesterfield | W | 2-0 | 2-0 | 11690 | Metcalf, Humes | 1 | 2 | | 4 | 5 | 6 | 7 | 8 | | 9 | | | 10 | 11 | | 3 | | | | | | |
| 2R | Dec 4 | WIGAN ATHLETIC | W | 2-1 | 0-0 | 16283 | Humes, Morris | 1 | 2 | | 4 | 5 | 6 | 7 | 8 | | 9 | | | 10 | 11 | | 3 | | | | | | |
| 3R | Jan 22 | NEWCASTLE UNITED | L | 1-3 | 1-1 | 18251 | Morris | 1 | | | 4 | 5 | 6 | 7 | 8 | | 9 | | 2 | 10 | 11 | 3 | | | | | | | |

## LEAGUE CUP

| Rd | Date | Opposition | | FT | HT | Att. | Goalscorers | Reeves D. | Jones R. | Starkey M. | Hauser P. | Butler J. | Durie D. | Humes J. | Metcalf M. | Talbot G. | Ryden H. | Harley L. | Singleton T. | Jones L. | Morris E. | Evans G. | Jones B. | Chadwick G. | Read D. | Willder F. | Howard R. | Holland R. | Edwards K. |
|---|---|---|---|---|---|---|---|---|---|---|---|---|---|---|---|---|---|---|---|---|---|---|---|---|---|---|---|---|---|
| 1R | Sep 1 | Wrexham | L | 2-5 | 1-3 | 9996 | Metcalf (2) | 1 | 2 | | 4 | 5 | 6 | 7 | 8 | 9 | 10 | | 3 | 11 | | | | | | | | | |

## WELSH CUP

| Rd | Date | Opposition | | FT | HT | Att. | Goalscorers | Reeves D. | Jones R. | Starkey M. | Hauser P. | Butler J. | Durie D. | Humes J. | Metcalf M. | Talbot G. | Ryden H. | Harley L. | Singleton T. | Jones L. | Morris E. | Evans G. | Jones B. | Chadwick G. | Read D. | Willder F. | Howard R. | Holland R. | Edwards K. |
|---|---|---|---|---|---|---|---|---|---|---|---|---|---|---|---|---|---|---|---|---|---|---|---|---|---|---|---|---|---|
| 5R | Jan 5 | WREXHAM | W | 4-1 | 2-1 | 7213 | G Evans, Humes, Ryden, Talbot | 1 | | | 3 | | | 7 | 4 | 9 | 8 | | 5 | 10 | 11 | 6 | | 2 | | | | | |
| 6R | Feb 7 | Newport County | D | 2-2 | 0-1 | 1776 | Willder, Morris | 1 | | 3 | | 5 | | 7 | 4 | | 9 | | 2 | 10 | 11 | 6 | | | | 8 | | | |
| 6Rr | Feb 16 | NEWPORT COUNTY | W | 2-0 | 0-0 | 5296 | Ryden, Humes | 1 | | 3 | 4 | 5 | | 7 | 8 | | 9 | | 2 | 10 | 11 | 6 | | | | | | | |
| SF | Mar 23 | Bangor City | W | 3-0 | 3-0 | 5000 | Metcalf, L Jones (2) | | | 3 | 4 | 5 | 11 | | 8 | | 7 | | 2 | 10 | 9 | 6 | | | | | 1 | | |
| F1 | Apr 18 | Swansea Town | L | 0-3 | 0-1 | 9614 | | 1 | | 3 | 4 | 5 | | | 8 | | 10 | 7 | 2 | | 9 | 6 | | | | | | 11 | |
| F2 | Apr 25 | SWANSEA TOWN | W | 1-0 | 1-0 | 6346 | Morris | 1 | | 3 | | 5 | | 11 | 8 | | 10 | 7 | 2 | | 9 | 6 | | 4 | | | | | |
| FR | May 2 | SWANSEA TOWN | L | 1-2 | 0-0 | 6276 | L Jones | 1 | | 3 | 4 | 5 | 6 | | 8 | | 9 | 7 | 2 | 10 | 11 | | | | | | | | |

## FRIENDLIES

| No. | Date | Opposition | | FT | HT | Att. | Goalscorers |
|---|---|---|---|---|---|---|---|
| 1 | Aug 7 | Colwyn Bay | W | 2-1 | 0-1 | | K. Jones, Metcalf |
| 2 | 11 | Leeds United | L | 1-5 | 1-1 | 9000 | Morris |
| 3 | 16 | New Brighton | L | 0-1 | 0-0 | | |
| 4 | Nov 3 | Wrexham * | L | 2-3 | 1-1 | 4194 | Metcalf, Harley |

* Aly McGowan Testimonial

**1965/66 Season:** (Back) Cucchiero, Chadwick, B Jones, Lee, L Jones, Ryden, Read.
(Standing) Hauser(Player-Manager),Durie,Singleton,R.Jones,Reeves,Berry,Morris,Butler, Gardner(Trainer).
(Sitting) (Directors) Hall, Dawson, Horne, Rowlands (Chairman), Cheshire, Jones, Rowley, Milton.
(Front) Harley, Harvey, Talbot, Starkey, Willder, Metcalf, Owen.

**1966/67 Season:** (Back) Hauser (Player-Manager), B Jones, R Jones, Berry, Reeves, Durie,
L Jones, Harley, Holland, Butler, Talbot, Read, Harvey.
(Front) Ryden, Sealey, Bennett, Humes, Metcalf, Morris, Chadwick, Singleton.

# SEASON 1966-67

## FOOTBALL LEAGUE DIVISION 4

| | Date | Opposition | | FT | HT | Att. | Goalscorers | Reeves D. | Singleton T. | Evans G. | Hauser P. | Butler J. | Bennett J. | Ryden H. | Metcalf M. | Talbot G. | Jones L. | Morris E. | Holland R. | Sealey J. | Hignett A. | Harley L. | Humes J. | Durie D. | Chadwick G. | Starkey M. | Jones R. | Coates J. | Read D. | Carling T. | Jones B. | Seaton G. | Edwards K. | Berry D. |
|---|---|---|---|---|---|---|---|---|---|---|---|---|---|---|---|---|---|---|---|---|---|---|---|---|---|---|---|---|---|---|---|---|---|---|
| 1 | Aug 20 | Tranmere Rovers | D | 0-0 | 0-0 | 6756 | | 1 | 2 | 3 | 4 | 5 | 6 | 7 | 8 | 9 | 10 | 11 | | | | | | | | | | | | | | | | |
| 2 | 27 | BRADFORD P. A. | L | 0-3 | 0-2 | 6392 | | 1 | 2 | 3 | 4 | | 6 | 10 | 8 | 9 | | 11 | 5 | 7 | | | | | | | | | | | | | | |
| 3 | Sep 3 | Port Vale | D | 1-1 | 0-1 | 6853 | Miles (og) | 1 | 2 | 3 | | | 6 | 10 | 4 | 9 | 8 | 11 | 5 | 7 | | | | | | | | | | | | | | |
| 4 | 7 | SOUTHEND UNITED | D | 1-1 | 0-0 | 6132 | L Jones | 1 | 2 | 3 | | | 6 | | 4 | 9 | 10 | 11 | 5 | 7 | | 8 | | | | | | | | | | | | |
| 5 | 10 | CREWE ALEX. | L | 0-3 | 0-2 | 7143 | | 1 | 2* | | | 12 | 6 | 8 | 4 | 9 | 10 | | 5 | | 3 | 7 | 11 | | | | | | | | | | | |
| 6 | 16 | Barrow | D | 1-1 | 1-0 | 5199 | Metcalf | 1 | 2 | 6 | 4 | 5 | | | 8 | 9 | 10 | 11 | | | 3 | 7 | | | | | | | | | | | | |
| 7 | 24 | YORK CITY | W | 3-1 | 1-1 | 5315 | Harley, Singleton, Durie | 1 | 2 | 6 | 4 | 5 | | | 8 | 9 | 10* | | | | 3 | 7 | 11 | 12 | | | | | | | | | | |
| 8 | 26 | Southend United | L | 1-5 | 0-4 | 8945 | L Jones | 1 | 2 | 6 | 4 | 5 | | | 8 | 9 | 10 | | | | 3 | 7 | 11 | | | | | | | | | | | |
| 9 | Oct 1 | Lincoln City | W | 3-2 | 1-1 | 2818 | L Jones, Harley, Metcalf | 1 | 2 | 6 | | 5 | | | 9 | | 8 | | | | 3 | 7 | 11 | 10 | 4 | | | | | | | | | |
| 10 | 8 | WREXHAM | L | 1-3 | 0-1 | 12205 | Stacey (og) | 1 | 2 | 6 | | 5 | | | 9 | | 8 | 11 | | | 3 | 7 | | 10 | 4 | | | | | | | | | |
| 11 | 15 | Aldershot | L | 0-3 | 0-2 | 4510 | | 1 | 2 | 3 | 4 | 5 | | 10 | 9 | | 8 | | | | | 7 | 11 | 6 | | | | | | | | | | |
| 12 | 19 | ROCHDALE | W | 3-2 | 0-0 | 4316 | Metcalf, Talbot (2) | 1 | 2 | | 4 | 5 | | 7 | 8 | 9 | 10 | | | | | | 11 | 6 | | 3 | | | | | | | | |
| 13 | 22 | LUTON TOWN | D | 0-0 | 0-0 | 5751 | | 1 | 2 | | 4 | 5 | | 7 | 8 | 9 | | | | | | 10 | 11 | 6 | | 3 | | | | | | | | |
| 14 | 29 | Barnsley | W | 2-1 | 1-0 | 4474 | Talbot, Humes | 1 | 4 | | | 5 | 6 | 10 | 8 | 9 | | 11 | | | | | 7 | | | 3 | 2 | | | | | | | |
| 15 | Nov 5 | NEWPORT COUNTY | W | 4-2 | 4-2 | 5257 | Ryden, Morris, Metcalf (2) | 1 | 4 | | | 5 | 6 | 10 | 8 | 9 | | 11 | | | | | 7 | | | 3 | 2 | | | | | | | |
| 16 | 12 | Brentford | L | 0-4 | 0-1 | 6606 | | | 4 | | | 5 | 6 | 10 | 8 | 9 | | 11 | | | | | 7 | | | 3 | 2 | 1 | | | | | | |
| 17 | 19 | HALIFAX TOWN | L | 0-2 | 0-2 | 5265 | | 1 | 4 | | | 5 | 6 | 10 | 8 | 9* | | 11 | | | | | 7 | | | 3 | 2 | | 12 | | | | | |
| 18 | Dec 3 | EXETER CITY | L | 0-2 | 0-2 | 3086 | | 1 | 2 | 3 | | 5 | 6 | 9 | 8 | | 10 | 11 | | | | | 7 | | 4 | | | | | | | | | |
| 19 | 10 | Bradford City | W | 3-2 | 1-2 | 4293 | Ryden, L Jones (2) | | | | 4* | 5 | 12 | 9 | 8 | | 10 | | | | | | | 11 | | | 2 | | 7 | 1 | 3 | 6 | | |
| 20 | 17 | TRANMERE ROVERS | L | 0-1 | 0-0 | 6041 | | | | | | 5 | 6 | 9 | 8 | | 10 | | | | | | | 11 | | | 2 | | 7 | 1 | 3 | 4 | | |
| 21 | 23 | Stockport County | D | 1-1 | 0-1 | 8855 | Metcalf | | | | | 5 | 6 | 9 | 8 | | | 11 | | | | 12 | | 10 | | | 2 | | 7* | 1 | 3 | 4 | | |
| 22 | 26 | STOCKPORT COUNTY | D | 1-1 | 0-1 | 8825 | Talbot | | | | | 5 | 6 | 7 | 8 | 9 | | 11 | | | | | | 10 | | | 2 | | | 1 | 3 | 4 | | |
| 23 | 31 | Bradford P. A. | W | 3-2 | 2-2 | 3966 | Durie, Ryden, Talbot | | | | | 5 | 6 | 7 | 8 | 9 | | 11 | | | | | | 10 | | | 2 | | | 1 | 3 | 4 | | |
| 24 | Jan 14 | Crewe Alex. | L | 1-3 | 1-1 | 7200 | L Jones | | | | | 5 | 6 | 7 | 8 | 9 | 10 | | | | | | | 11 | | | 2 | | | 1 | 3 | 4 | | |
| 25 | 21 | BARROW | D | 1-1 | 0-0 | 5143 | Ryden | | 5 | | | | 6 | 7 | 8 | 9 | 10 | | | | | | | 11 | | | 2 | | | 1 | 3 | 4 | | |
| 26 | 28 | PORT VALE | L | 1-3 | 1-0 | 5586 | Talbot | | 5 | | 12 | | 6 | 7 | 8 | 9 | 10 | | | | | | | 11 | | | 2 | | | 1 | 3 | 4* | | |
| 27 | 30 | Hartlepools United | L | 2-3 | 0-1 | 7988 | L Jones, Ryden | | 5 | 6 | 11 | | | 7 | 8 | 9 | 10 | | | | | | 2 | | | | | | | 1 | 3 | 4 | | |
| 28 | Feb 4 | York City | D | 1-1 | 0-0 | 3094 | Ryden | | 5 | 6 | | | | 7 | 8 | 9 | 10 | | | | | | | 11 | | | 2 | | | 1 | 3 | 4 | | |
| 29 | 11 | LINCOLN CITY | L | 0-1 | 0-1 | 4251 | | | 5 | | | 2 | 6 | 7 | 8 | 9 | 10 | | | | | | 11 | | | | | | | 1 | 3 | 4 | | |
| 30 | 18 | SOUTHPORT | W | 2-1 | 1-0 | 5240 | Humes, L Jones | | 5 | 6 | | 2 | 3 | 10 | 8 | 9 | 11 | | | | | | 7 | | | | | | | 1 | | 4 | | |
| 31 | 25 | Wrexham | L | 1-3 | 0-0 | 11751 | L Jones | 1 | 5 | 6 | | 2 | 3 | 10 | 8 | 9* | 11 | | | | | 12 | 7 | | 4 | | | | | | | | | |
| 32 | Mar 1 | Rochdale | W | 1-0 | 1-0 | 2140 | Ryden | 1 | 5 | 6 | | 12 | 3 | 10 | 8 | | 11 | | | | | | 7 | | 4 | | 2* | | | | | | 9 | |
| 33 | 4 | ALDERSHOT | D | 0-0 | 0-0 | 3893 | | 1 | 5 | 6 | | 2 | 3 | 10 | 8 | | 11 | | | | | | 7 | | | | | | | | | 4 | 9 | |
| 34 | 11 | Southport | L | 3-4 | 0-0 | 4736 | Humes (2), L Jones | 1 | 5 | 6 | | 2 | 3 | 10 | 8 | | 11 | | | | | | 9 | | | | | | 7 | | | 4 | | |
| 35 | 18 | Luton Town | L | 0-1 | 0-0 | 6982 | | | 5 | | | 2 | 3 | 10 | 6 | | 8 | 11* | | | | | 9 | | | | | | 7 | 1 | | 4 | | 12 |
| 36 | 24 | NOTTS COUNTY | L | 1-2 | 1-1 | 4292 | L Jones | | 5 | 6 | 12 | 2 | 3 | 9 | 8 | | 10 | | | | | 11 | | | | | | | 7 | 1 | | 4* | | |
| 37 | 25 | HARTLEPOOLS UNITED | W | 1-0 | 1-0 | 3126 | Metcalf | | 5 | | 7 | | 3 | 9 | 8 | | 10 | 11 | | | | | | 6 | | | 2 | | | 1 | | 4 | | |
| 38 | 28 | Notts County | L | 0-3 | 0-1 | 3398 | | | 5 | | 7 | | 3 | 9 | 8 | | 10 | 11 | | | | | | 6 | | | 2 | | | 1 | | 4 | | |
| 39 | Apr 3 | Newport County | W | 3-2 | 1-0 | 2592 | Seaton, Ryden (2) | | 5 | | 7 | | 3 | 9 | 8 | | 10 | 11 | | | | | | 6 | | | 2 | | | 1 | | 4 | | |
| 40 | 8 | BRENTFORD | L | 1-2 | 0-1 | 2683 | Metcalf (pen) | | 5 | | 7 | | 3 | 9 | 8 | | 10 | 11 | | | | | | 6 | | | 2 | | | 1 | | 4 | | |
| 41 | 12 | CHESTERFIELD | W | 2-1 | 0-0 | 2559 | Ryden, L Jones | | 5 | 6 | 7 | | 3 | 9 | 8 | | 10 | 11 | | | | | | | | | 2 | | | 1 | | 4 | | |
| 42 | 15 | Halifax Town | L | 1-2 | 1-2 | 3506 | Ryden | | 5 | 6 | 7 | | 3 | 9 | 8 | | 10 | 11 | | | | | | | | | 2 | | | 1 | | 4 | | |
| 43 | 22 | BARNSLEY | W | 1-0 | 0-0 | 2969 | Morris | | 5 | 6 | | | 3 | 9 | 8 | | 10 | 11 | | | | | 7 | | | | 2 | | | 1 | | 4 | | |
| 44 | 24 | Chesterfield | W | 2-0 | 1-0 | 2547 | Morris, L Jones | | 5 | 6 | 7 | | 3 | 9 | 8 | | 10 | 11 | | | | | | | | | 2 | | | 1 | | 4 | | |
| 45 | 29 | Exeter City | L | 0-2 | 0-1 | 3077 | | | 5 | 6 | 7 | | 3 | 9 | 8 | | 10 | 11 | | | | | | | | | 2 | | | 1 | | 4 | | |
| 46 | May 6 | BRADFORD CITY | W | 1-0 | 0-0 | 3109 | Seaton | | 5 | 6 | 7 | | 3 | 9 | 8 | | | 11* | | | | 12 | | 10 | | | 2 | | | 1 | | 4 | | |
| | | | | | | | Apps. | 21 | 40 | 25 | 19 | 27 | 35 | 40 | 46 | 24 | 36 | 25 | 4 | 3 | 6 | 10 | 21 | 19 | 5 | 6 | 24 | 1 | 6 | 24 | 11 | 26 | 2 | |
| | | | | | | | Subs. | | | | 2 | 2 | 1 | | | | | | | | | 3 | | 1 | | | | | 1 | | | | | 1 |
| | | | | | | | Goals | | 1 | | | | | 11 | 8 | 6 | 13 | 3 | | | | 2 | 4 | 2 | | | | | | | | 2 | | |

Own goals 2

## F.A. CUP

| | Date | Opposition | | FT | HT | Att. | Goalscorers | Reeves D. | Singleton T. | Evans G. | Hauser P. | Butler J. | Bennett J. | Ryden H. | Metcalf M. | Talbot G. | Jones L. | Morris E. | Holland R. | Sealey J. | Hignett A. | Harley L. | Humes J. | Durie D. | Chadwick G. | Starkey M. | Jones R. | Coates J. | Read D. | Carling T. | Jones B. | Seaton G. | Edwards K. | Berry D. |
|---|---|---|---|---|---|---|---|---|---|---|---|---|---|---|---|---|---|---|---|---|---|---|---|---|---|---|---|---|---|---|---|---|---|---|
| 1R | Nov 26 | MIDDLESBROUGH | L | 2-5 | 1-4 | 7607 | Metcalf, Morris | 1 | 2 | 3 | 4 | 5 | 6 | 10 | 8 | | 12 | 11 | | | | | 7 | | | | | | | | | | 9 | |

## LEAGUE CUP

| | Date | Opposition | | FT | HT | Att. | Goalscorers | Reeves D. | Singleton T. | Evans G. | Hauser P. | Butler J. | Bennett J. | Ryden H. | Metcalf M. | Talbot G. | Jones L. | Morris E. | Holland R. | Sealey J. | Hignett A. | Harley L. | Humes J. | Durie D. | Chadwick G. | Starkey M. | Jones R. | Coates J. | Read D. | Carling T. | Jones B. | Seaton G. | Edwards K. | Berry D. |
|---|---|---|---|---|---|---|---|---|---|---|---|---|---|---|---|---|---|---|---|---|---|---|---|---|---|---|---|---|---|---|---|---|---|---|
| 1R | Aug 24 | TRANMERE ROVERS | L | 2-5 | 0-2 | 6660 | Ryden, Talbot | 1 | 2 | 3 | 4 | 5 | 6 | 7 | 8 | 9 | 10 | 11 | | | | | | | | | | | | | | | | |

## WELSH CUP

| | Date | Opposition | | FT | HT | Att. | Goalscorers | Reeves D. | Singleton T. | Evans G. | Hauser P. | Butler J. | Bennett J. | Ryden H. | Metcalf M. | Talbot G. | Jones L. | Morris E. | Holland R. | Sealey J. | Hignett A. | Harley L. | Humes J. | Durie D. | Chadwick G. | Starkey M. | Jones R. | Coates J. | Read D. | Carling T. | Jones B. | Seaton G. | Edwards K. | Berry D. |
|---|---|---|---|---|---|---|---|---|---|---|---|---|---|---|---|---|---|---|---|---|---|---|---|---|---|---|---|---|---|---|---|---|---|---|
| 5R | Jan 4 | Borough United | W | 5-2 | 3-1 | | Morris (2), L Jones (2), Talbot | | | | | 5 | 4 | 7 | 8 | 9 | 10 | 11 | | | | | 12 | 6 | | | 2 | | | 1 | 3 | | | |
| 6R | Feb 16 | Pwllheli | W | 3-2 | 1-2 | | Humes (pen), Talbot (2) | | 5 | 6 | | 2 | 4 | 10 | 8 | 9 | 11 | | 3 | | | | 7 | | | | | | | 1 | | | | |
| SF | Mar 15 | WREXHAM | D | 0-0 | 0-0 | 9496 | | | 5 | 6 | | 2 | 3 | 10 | 4 | | 8 | 11 | | | | | 9 | | | | | | 7 | 1 | | | | |
| SFr | 20 | Wrexham | L | 2-4 | 1-0 | 11329 | Humes, Ryden | | 5 | 6 | | 2 | 3 | 10 | 4 | | 8 | | | | | 11 | 9 | | | | | | 7 | 1 | | | | |

## FRIENDLIES

| | Date | Opposition | | FT | HT | Att. | Goalscorers |
|---|---|---|---|---|---|---|---|
| 1 | Aug 9 | STOCKPORT COUNTY * | W | 2-1 | 1-1 | 2029 | Metcalf (pen), Morris |
| 2 | 12 | Stockport County * | L | 0-2 | 0-1 | | |

* Shield match

# SEASON 1967-68

## FOOTBALL LEAGUE DIVISION 4

| | Date | Opposition | | FT | HT | Att. | Goalscorers | Carling T. | Jones R. | Bennett J. | Seaton G. | Singleton T. | Sutton M. | Moir I. | Metcalf M. | Loyden E. | Ryden H. | Jones L. | Ashworth B. | Morris E. | Butler J. | Evans G. | McLaughlin A. | Hancox D. | Hughes A. | Rampling E. | Jones S. | Turner G. | Sealey J. | Mannion G. | Haddock A. | Robinson A. |
|---|---|---|---|---|---|---|---|---|---|---|---|---|---|---|---|---|---|---|---|---|---|---|---|---|---|---|---|---|---|---|---|---|
| 1 | Aug 19 | Notts County | W | 2-1 | 2-1 | 6599 | Loyden (2, 1 pen) | 1 | 2 | 3 | 4 | 5 | 6 | 7 | 8 | 9 | 10 | 11 | | | | | | | | | | | | | | |
| 2 | 26 | PORT VALE | D | 1-1 | 1-1 | 7932 | Loyden (pen) | 1 | 2 | 3 | 6* | 4 | 5 | 8 | 7 | 9 | 10 | 11 | 12 | | | | | | | | | | | | | |
| 3 | Sep 2 | Wrexham | L | 0-2 | 0-0 | 11740 | | 1 | 2 | 3 | | 5 | 6 | 7 | 10 | 9 | 8 | 11 | 4 | | | | | | | | | | | | | |
| 4 | 6 | CREWE ALEX. | L | 0-4 | 0-1 | 7087 | | 1 | | 3 | 4 | 5 | 6 | 7 | | 9 | 10 | 8 | 2 | 11 | | | | | | | | | | | | |
| 5 | 9 | Chesterfield | L | 1-3 | 0-2 | 8618 | L Jones | 1 | | 3 | 4 | 5 | 6 | 7 | | 9 | 10 | 8 | 2 | 11 | | | | | | | | | | | | |
| 6 | 16 | EXETER CITY | W | 3-1 | 1-1 | 4045 | Morris, Loyden (2, 1 pen) | 1 | | 3 | 4 | | 6 | 7 | 8 | 9 | | 10 | 2 | 11 | 5 | | | | | | | | | | | |
| 7 | 23 | Darlington | W | 2-0 | 2-0 | 4877 | Morris, Loyden | 1 | | 3 | 4 | | 6 | 7 | 8 | 9 | 10 | | 2 | 11 | 5 | | | | | | | | | | | |
| 8 | 27 | Crewe Alex. | L | 0-2 | 0-0 | 8846 | | 1 | | 3 | 4 | | 6 | 7 | 8 | 9 | 10 | | 2 | 11 | 5 | | | | | | | | | | | |
| 9 | 30 | ALDERSHOT | L | 2-5 | 1-1 | 5380 | Loyden, Morris | 1 | | 3 | 4* | | 6 | 7 | 8 | 9 | 10 | 12 | 2 | 11 | 5 | | | | | | | | | | | |
| 10 | Oct 7 | LUTON TOWN | L | 1-3 | 1-1 | 3967 | L Jones | 1 | | 3 | | | 6 | 7 | 4 | 9 | 10 | 8 | 2 | 11 | | 5 | | | | | | | | | | |
| 11 | 14 | Doncaster Rovers | D | 0-0 | 0-0 | 6002 | | 1 | | | 4 | | 5 | 7 | 2 | 9 | 10 | 8 | 6 | 12 | | 3 | 11* | | | | | | | | | |
| 12 | 21 | BRADFORD P. A. | D | 0-0 | 0-0 | 3717 | | 1 | | | 6 | | 5 | 7 | 2 | 9 | 10 | 8 | 4 | 12 | | 3 | 11* | | | | | | | | | |
| 13 | 25 | HALIFAX TOWN | W | 3-2 | 2-2 | 3419 | Metcalf, Hancox, Morris | 1 | | | | | 6 | 7 | 2 | | 10 | 8 | 4 | 11 | 5 | 3 | | 9 | | | | | | | | |
| 14 | 28 | Brentford | L | 1-3 | 1-1 | 6285 | Hancox | 1 | | | | | 5 | 7 | 2 | | 10 | 8 | 4 | 11 | 6 | 3 | | 9 | | | | | | | | |
| 15 | 31 | Halifax Town | D | 2-2 | 1-1 | 4105 | Morris (2) | 1 | | | 12 | | 6 | 7 | 2 | | 10 | 8 | 4 | 11 | 5 | 3 | | 9* | | | | | | | | |
| 16 | Nov 4 | ROCHDALE | L | 0-1 | 0-0 | 4068 | | 1 | | | | | 6 | 7 | 2 | 8 | | 10 | 4 | 11 | 5 | 3 | | 9 | | | | | | | | |
| 17 | 11 | York City | L | 1-4 | 1-2 | 5226 | Metcalf | 1 | 2 | | 10 | | 6 | 7 | 8 | | | 11 | 4 | | 5 | 3 | | 9 | | | | | | | | |
| 18 | 15 | WREXHAM | D | 1-1 | 1-1 | 10733 | Metcalf | 1 | 2 | | 6 | | 5 | 7 | 8 | | | | 4 | 11* | | 3 | 12 | 10 | 9 | | | | | | | |
| 19 | 18 | NEWPORT COUNTY | W | 2-1 | 2-0 | 3704 | Moir, Hancox | 1 | 2 | | 6 | | 5 | 7 | 8 | | | | 4 | 11 | | 3* | 12 | 10 | 9 | | | | | | | |
| 20 | 24 | Hartlepools United | D | 0-0 | 0-0 | 4638 | | 1 | 2 | | 6 | | 5 | 7 | 8 | | | | 4 | 11 | | 3 | | 10 | 9 | | | | | | | |
| 21 | Dec 2 | SWANSEA TOWN | L | 2-3 | 2-2 | 4028 | Hughes, Ashworth | 1 | 2 | | 6 | | 5 | 7 | 8 | | | 12 | 4 | | | 3 | | 10 | 9 | 11* | | | | | | |
| 22 | 16 | NOTTS COUNTY | L | 1-3 | 0-1 | 3576 | Hancox | | 2 | 3 | 6 | | 5 | 7 | 8 | 11* | | | 4 | | | | | 10 | 9 | 12 | 1 | | | | | |
| 23 | 23 | Port Vale | D | 4-4 | 1-2 | 3740 | Hughes, Loyden (2), L Jones | | 3 | | | 2 | 6 | 7 | 8 | 10 | | 11 | 4 | | 5 | | | | 9 | | 1 | | | | | |
| 24 | 26 | Lincoln City | L | 0-3 | 0-2 | 8740 | | | 2 | 3 | | 7 | 6 | 8 | | 10 | | 11 | 4 | | 5 | | | | 9 | | 1 | | | | | |
| 25 | 30 | LINCOLN CITY | W | 6-0 | 1-0 | 2876 | Loyden (4), Moir (2) | 1 | 2 | 3 | 6 | | 5 | 7 | 8 | 10 | | | 4 | | | | | 11 | 9 | | | | | | | |
| 26 | Jan 20 | Exeter City | L | 0-1 | 0-0 | 4336 | | 1 | 2 | 3 | | | 6 | | 8 | 10 | | | 4 | 11 | | | | 7 | 9* | | | 5 | 12 | | | |
| 27 | 27 | SOUTHEND UNITED | D | 0-0 | 0-0 | 4623 | | 1 | 2 | | | | 6 | | 8 | | | 10 | 4 | 11 | | 3 | | 9 | | | | 5 | | 7 | | |
| 28 | Feb 3 | DARLINGTON | L | 0-1 | 0-0 | 3353 | | 1 | 2 | 3 | | | 6 | | 8 | 10 | | 11 | 4* | 12 | | | | 9 | | | | 5 | | 7 | | |
| 29 | 10 | Aldershot | L | 1-2 | 0-0 | 4821 | Morris | 1 | 2 | 3 | | | 6 | | 8 | 9 | | 10 | 4 | 11 | | | | | | | | 5 | | 7 | | |
| 30 | 17 | WORKINGTON | L | 1-2 | 1-1 | 3026 | Metcalf | 1 | 2 | 3 | 12 | | 6 | | 8 | 9 | | 10 | 4 | | | | | 11* | | | | 5 | | 7 | | |
| 31 | 24 | Newport County | D | 1-1 | 0-0 | 4369 | Morris | 1 | 2 | 3 | | | 6 | | 8 | 9 | | 10 | 4 | 11 | | | | | | | | 5 | | 7 | | |
| 32 | Mar 2 | DONCASTER ROVERS | L | 2-3 | 2-3 | 2484 | Loyden, Metcalf | 1 | 2 | 3 | 6 | | 5 | | 8 | 9 | | 10 | 4 | | | 12 | | | | 11* | | | | 7 | | |
| 33 | 8 | Southend United | L | 1-5 | 0-2 | 9437 | Metcalf | 1 | 2 | 3 | | | 6 | | 10* | 9 | | 8 | 4 | 11 | | 12 | | | | | | 5 | | | 7 | |
| 34 | 16 | Bradford P. A. | W | 2-0 | 1-0 | 3050 | Loyden, Metcalf | 1 | 2 | | | 5 | 6 | | 11 | 10 | | 8 | 7 | | | 4 | | | | | | 3 | | | 9 | |
| 35 | 23 | BRENTFORD | W | 3-0 | 2-0 | 2861 | Ashworth, Haddock, Loyden | 1 | 2 | 12 | | 3 | 8 | | 11 | 9 | | 10 | 4* | | | 6 | | | | | | 5 | | | 7 | |
| 36 | 30 | Rochdale | D | 1-1 | 1-0 | 2212 | Loyden | 1 | 2 | | | 3 | 8 | | 11 | 9 | | 10 | 4 | | | 6 | | | | | | 5 | | | 7 | |
| 37 | Apr 3 | CHESTERFIELD | W | 3-0 | 1-0 | 3103 | Metcalf, Loyden, L Jones | 1 | 2 | | | 3 | 8 | | 11 | 9 | | 10 | 4 | | | 6 | | | | | | 5 | | | 7 | |
| 38 | 6 | YORK CITY | D | 1-1 | 0-0 | 4170 | L Jones | 1 | 2 | | 11 | 3 | 8 | | | 9 | | 10 | 4 | | | 6 | | | | | | 5 | | | 7 | |
| 39 | 13 | Luton Town | D | 0-0 | 0-0 | 13266 | | 1 | 2 | 12 | | 3 | 8 | | 11 | 9 | | 10 | 4 | | | 6 | | | | | | 5 | | | 7* | |
| 40 | 15 | Bradford City | D | 2-2 | 1-0 | 6443 | Loyden (2) | 1 | 2 | 3 | 12 | 5 | 8 | | 11 | 9 | | 10 | 4* | | | 6 | | | | | | | | | 7 | |
| 41 | 16 | BRADFORD CITY | L | 2-3 | 1-0 | 5003 | Loyden, L Jones | 1 | 2 | 3 | 4 | 5 | 8 | | 11 | 9 | | 10 | | | | 6 | | 12 | | | | | | | 7* | |
| 42 | 20 | HARTLEPOOLS UNITED | L | 0-2 | 0-1 | 3990 | | 1 | 2 | | | 3 | 8 | | 11 | 9 | | 10 | 4 | | | 6 | | | | | | 5 | | | 7 | |
| 43 | 23 | Barnsley | L | 1-2 | 1-1 | 14596 | Murphy (og) | 1 | 2 | | | 3 | 8 | | 11 | 9 | | 10 | 4 | | | 6 | | 7 | | | | 5 | | | | |
| 44 | 27 | Swansea Town | L | 0-1 | 0-0 | 3617 | | 1 | 2 | 4 | | 3 | 10 | | 11 | 9 | | 7 | | | | 6 | | 8 | | | | 5 | | | | |
| 45 | May 4 | BARNSLEY | D | 1-1 | 1-1 | 4402 | Loyden | 1 | 2 | 10 | | 3 | 4 | | 11 | 9 | | 7 | | | | 6 | | | | | | 5 | | | | 8 |
| 46 | 11 | Workington | L | 0-1 | 0-0 | 1008 | | 1 | 2 | 11* | | 3 | 8 | | 10 | 9 | | 7 | | | | 4 | | 12 | | | | 5 | | | | 6 |
| | | | | | | | Apps. | 43 | 33 | 25 | 20 | 20 | 46 | 25 | 42 | 37 | 14 | 36 | 40 | 19 | 11 | 26 | 2 | 17 | 9 | 2 | 3 | 18 | | 6 | 10 | 2 |
| | | | | | | | Subs. | | | 2 | 3 | | | | | | | 2 | 1 | 3 | | 2 | 2 | 2 | | 1 | | | 1 | | | |
| | | | | | | | Goals | | | | | | | 3 | 8 | 22 | | 6 | 2 | 8 | | | | 4 | 2 | | | | | | 1 | |

Own goals 1

## F.A. CUP

| | Date | Opposition | | FT | HT | Att. | Goalscorers | Carling T. | Jones R. | Bennett J. | Seaton G. | Singleton T. | Sutton M. | Moir I. | Metcalf M. | Loyden E. | Ryden H. | Jones L. | Ashworth B. | Morris E. | Butler J. | Evans G. | McLaughlin A. | Hancox D. | Hughes A. | Rampling E. | Jones S. | Turner G. | Sealey J. | Mannion G. | Haddock A. | Robinson A. |
|---|---|---|---|---|---|---|---|---|---|---|---|---|---|---|---|---|---|---|---|---|---|---|---|---|---|---|---|---|---|---|---|---|
| 1R | Dec 9 | Port Vale | W | 2-1 | 2-1 | 4171 | Metcalf, Hancox | | 2 | 12 | 6 | | 5 | 7 | 8 | 11 | | | 4 | | | 3* | | 10 | 9 | | 1 | | | | | |
| 2R | Jan 6 | CHESTERFIELD | L | 0-1 | 0-1 | 11320 | | 1 | 2 | 3 | 6 | | 5 | 7 | 8 | 10 | | | 4 | | | | | 11 | 9 | | | | | | | |

## LEAGUE CUP

| | Date | Opposition | | FT | HT | Att. | Goalscorers | Carling T. | Jones R. | Bennett J. | Seaton G. | Singleton T. | Sutton M. | Moir I. | Metcalf M. | Loyden E. | Ryden H. | Jones L. | Ashworth B. | Morris E. | Butler J. | Evans G. | McLaughlin A. | Hancox D. | Hughes A. | Rampling E. | Jones S. | Turner G. | Sealey J. | Mannion G. | Haddock A. | Robinson A. |
|---|---|---|---|---|---|---|---|---|---|---|---|---|---|---|---|---|---|---|---|---|---|---|---|---|---|---|---|---|---|---|---|---|
| 1R | Aug 22 | Port Vale | L | 0-3 | 0-2 | 5006 | | 1 | 2 | 3 | 4 | 5 | 6 | 7 | 8 | 9 | 10 | 11 | | | | | | | | | | | | | | |

## WELSH CUP

| | Date | Opposition | | FT | HT | Att. | Goalscorers | Carling T. | Jones R. | Bennett J. | Seaton G. | Singleton T. | Sutton M. | Moir I. | Metcalf M. | Loyden E. | Ryden H. | Jones L. | Ashworth B. | Morris E. | Butler J. | Evans G. | McLaughlin A. | Hancox D. | Hughes A. | Rampling E. | Jones S. | Turner G. | Sealey J. | Mannion G. | Haddock A. | Robinson A. |
|---|---|---|---|---|---|---|---|---|---|---|---|---|---|---|---|---|---|---|---|---|---|---|---|---|---|---|---|---|---|---|---|---|
| 5R | Jan 17 | BANGOR CITY | W | 2-1 | 1-0 | 3363 | Hughes, Loyden | 1 | 2 | 3 | | | 5 | | 8 | 10 | | | 4 | 11 | | 6 | | 7 | 9* | | | | 12 | | | |
| 6R | Feb 14 | Brymbo Steelworks | W | 8-0 | 4-0 | 3000 | Bennett(2),Ashworth,Metcalf,Loyden,Hancox,L Jones(2) | 1 | 2 | 3 | 12 | | 6 | | 8 | 9 | | 10 | 4 | | | | | 11* | | | | 5 | | 7 | | |
| SF | Mar 27 | CARDIFF CITY | L | 0-3 | 0-2 | 5844 | | 1 | 2 | | | 3 | 8 | | 11 | 9 | | 10 | 4 | | | 6 | | | | | | 5 | | | 7 | |

## FRIENDLIES

| | Date | Opposition | | FT | HT | Att. | Goalscorers |
|---|---|---|---|---|---|---|---|
| 1 | Aug 5 | SHREWSBURY TOWN | W | 3-2 | 1-0 | 3021 | Hancox, Ryden, Loyden |
| 2 | 11 | Shrewsbury Town | W | 2-1 | 1-1 | 1400 | L Jones, Ryden |
| 3 | 15 | SHEFFIELD UNITED | D | 2-2 | 1-2 | 4845 | Loyden, L Jones |
| 4 | May 13 | SHEFFIELD UNITED * | L | 2-3 | 1-2 | 2958 | Metcalf (2) |

* John Butler \ Elfed Morris Testimonial

**1967/68 Season:** (Back) Pritchard (Trainer), Seaton, L Jones, Metcalf, Sutton, Ryden, Hancox, Bennett, Sealey.
(Standing) Durie, Butler, R Jones, Singleton, Reeves, Carling, E Morris, Moir, Loyden.
(Sitting) Gandy (Secretary), Milton (Director), Horne (Director), Hauser (Player/Manager), Rowlands (Chairman), Auckland (Director), Walker (Asst. Sec.).

**1968/69 Season** (Back) Ashworth, R Jones, Carling, Mannion, Talbot
(Middle) Brodie, Edwards, Turner, Robinson, Blunt, Sear. .(Front) Sutton, L Jones, Metcalf, Bennett, Dearden.

# SEASON 1968-69

## FOOTBALL LEAGUE DIVISION 4

| | Date | Opposition | | FT | HT | Att. | Goalscorers | Carling T. | Jones R. | Sear C. | Ashworth B. | Turner G. | Brodie E. | Dearden W. | Metcalf M. | Talbot G. | Sutton M. | Jones L. | Bennett J. | Weston D. | Provan A. | Robinson A. | Evans G. | Cheetham R. | Draper D. | Cullerton M. | Millington G. | Edwards N. |
|---|---|---|---|---|---|---|---|---|---|---|---|---|---|---|---|---|---|---|---|---|---|---|---|---|---|---|---|---|
| 1 | Aug 10 | YORK CITY | W | 2-0 | 0-0 | 7104 | Sear, Dearden | 1 | 2 | 3 | 4 | 5 | 6 | 7 | 8 | 9 | 10 | 11 | | | | | | | | | | |
| 2 | 17 | Bradford City | L | 0-2 | 0-2 | 6065 | | 1 | 2 | | 4 | 5 | 6 | 7 | 8* | 9 | 10 | 11 | 3 | 12 | | | | | | | | |
| 3 | 24 | COLCHESTER UNITED | W | 5-1 | 2-1 | 5813 | L Jones (2), Dearden, Talbot, Sutton | 1 | 2 | 3 | 4 | 5 | 6 | 7 | 8 | 9 | 10 | 11 | | | | | | | | | | |
| 4 | 30 | Scunthorpe United | D | 2-2 | 0-1 | 5072 | Talbot, Brodie | 1 | 2 | 3 | 4 | 5 | 6 | 7 | 8 | 9 | 10* | | | 12 | 11 | | | | | | | |
| 5 | Sep 3 | DONCASTER ROVERS | W | 2-1 | 2-1 | 6564 | Ashworth, Provan | 1 | 2 | 3 | 4 | 5 | 6 | 7 | 8 | 9 | 10 | | | | 11 | | | | | | | |
| 6 | 6 | PORT VALE | W | 2-0 | 1-0 | 8144 | Metcalf, Talbot | 1 | 2 | 3 | 4 | 5 | 6 | 7 | 8 | 9 | 10 | | | | 11 | | | | | | | |
| 7 | 14 | Exeter City | D | 2-2 | 1-1 | 5121 | Talbot, Sutton | 1 | 2 | 3 | 4 | 5 | 6 | 7* | 8 | 9 | 10 | 11 | | | 12 | | | | | | | |
| 8 | 18 | BRENTFORD | D | 2-2 | 2-0 | 8638 | Talbot, Brodie | 1 | 2 | 3 | 4 | 5 | 6 | 7 | 8 | 9 | 10 | 11 | | | | | | | | | | |
| 9 | 21 | CHESTERFIELD | W | 2-0 | 2-0 | 6785 | Talbot, Ashworth | 1 | 2 | 3 | 4* | 5 | 6 | 7 | 8 | 9 | 10 | 11 | | | 12 | | | | | | | |
| 10 | 28 | Peterborough United | W | 2-1 | 1-0 | 6897 | Sutton, Brodie | 1 | 2 | 3 | 4 | 5 | 6 | 7 | 8 | 9 | 10 | 11 | | | | | | | | | | |
| 11 | Oct 5 | SWANSEA TOWN | W | 3-0 | 1-0 | 7417 | Dearden, Sutton, Talbot | 1 | 2 | 3 | 4 | 5 | 6 | 7 | 8 | 9 | 10 | 11 | | | | | | | | | | |
| 12 | 8 | Doncaster Rovers | L | 3-4 | 0-3 | 10171 | Dearden, Metcalf, Sutton | 1 | 2 | 3 | 4 | 5 | 6 | 7 | 8 | 9 | 10 | 11 | | | | | | | | | | |
| 13 | 12 | Bradford P. A. | D | 1-1 | 1-1 | 2969 | Talbot | 1 | 2 | 3 | 4 | 5 | 6 | 7 | 8 | 9 | 10 | 11* | | | 12 | | | | | | | |
| 14 | 19 | ALDERSHOT | W | 3-1 | 1-0 | 6750 | Talbot (2), Metcalf | 1 | 2* | 3 | 4 | 5 | 6 | 7 | 8 | 9 | 10 | 11 | | | | 12 | | | | | | |
| 15 | 26 | Grimsby Town | D | 0-0 | 0-0 | 2838 | | 1 | | 3 | 4 | 5 | 6 | 7 | 2 | | 9 | 10 | | 8 | 11 | | | | | | | |
| 16 | Nov 2 | SOUTHEND UNITED | L | 1-2 | 1-1 | 5508 | Ashworth | 1 | 2 | 3 | 4 | 5 | 7 | 8 | 9 | 10 | 11 | 6* | | | 12 | | | | | | | |
| 17 | 6 | WREXHAM | D | 1-1 | 0-1 | 13943 | Talbot | 1 | 2 | 3 | 4 | 5 | | 7 | 6 | 9 | 10 | 8 | | | 11 | | | | | | | |
| 18 | 9 | Notts County | L | 2-3 | 1-2 | 3089 | Talbot, Dearden | 1 | 2 | 3* | 4 | 5 | | 7 | 8 | 9 | 10 | | 12 | | 11 | | 6 | | | | | |
| 19 | 23 | Lincoln City | L | 0-2 | 0-1 | 6033 | | 1 | 2 | 5 | 4 | | | 7 | 6 | 9 | 10 | 8 | 3 | | 11 | | | | | | | |
| 20 | 30 | WORKINGTON | L | 0-2 | 0-1 | 5205 | | 1 | | 3 | 4 | 5 | 6* | 7 | 10 | 9 | 12 | 8 | 2 | | 11 | | | | | | | |
| 21 | Dec 14 | BRADFORD P. A. | W | 4-1 | 1-1 | 3182 | Provan, Dearden, Sutton, Ashworth (pen) | 1 | 2 | 3 | 4 | 5 | 10 | 7 | | 9 | 8 | | | | 11 | | | 6 | | | | |
| 22 | 21 | Aldershot | L | 0-4 | 0-2 | 5595 | | 1 | 2 | 3 | 4 | 5 | 10 | 7 | | 9 | 8 | | | | 11 | | | 6 | | | | |
| 23 | 26 | Swansea Town | W | 5-0 | 3-0 | 11879 | Dearden, Provan (2), Brodie, Talbot | 1 | 2 | 3 | 4 | 5 | 10 | 7 | | 9 | 8 | 12 | | | 11 | | | 6* | | | | |
| 24 | Jan 4 | DARLINGTON | L | 1-2 | 1-1 | 5902 | Sutton | 1 | 2 | 3 | 4 | 5 | 6 | 7 | | 9 | 8 | 10 | | | 11 | | | | | | | |
| 25 | 10 | Southend United | W | 2-1 | 2-0 | 11342 | Talbot, Birks (og) | 1 | 2 | | 4 | 5 | 6 | 7 | | 9 | 8 | 10 | 3 | | 11* | | 12 | | | | | |
| 26 | 18 | NOTTS COUNTY | W | 3-1 | 2-1 | 5033 | Ashworth (2), L Jones | 1 | 2 | | 4 | 5 | | 7 | | 9 | 6 | 8 | 3 | | 11 | | | | 10 | | | |
| 27 | 25 | Wrexham | D | 1-1 | 0-1 | 13955 | Bermingham (og) | 1 | | 2 | 4 | 5 | | 7 | | 9 | 6 | 8 | 3 | | 11 | | | | 10 | | | |
| 28 | Feb 1 | Halifax Town | D | 0-0 | 0-0 | 4181 | | 1 | | 2 | 4 | 5 | 10 | | | 9 | 6 | 7 | 3 | | 11 | | | | 8 | | | |
| 29 | 15 | Workington | D | 0-0 | 0-0 | 1843 | | 1 | | 3* | 4 | 5 | 12 | 8 | | 9 | 6 | 7 | | | 11 | | | 2 | 10 | | | |
| 30 | 22 | NEWPORT COUNTY | W | 4-0 | 2-0 | 4690 | Provan (2), Dearden, Draper | 1 | | 3 | | 4 | 6 | 7 | | 9 | 5 | 10 | | | 11 | | | 2 | 8 | | | |
| 31 | Mar 3 | Darlington | D | 2-2 | 2-1 | 5341 | Talbot (2) | 1 | | 3 | 4 | 5 | 6 | 7 | | 9 | 8 | | | | 11 | | | 2 | 10 | | | |
| 32 | 8 | BRADFORD CITY | D | 0-0 | 0-0 | 7219 | | 1 | | 3 | 4 | 5 | 6 | 7 | | 9 | 8 | | | | 11 | | | 2 | 10 | | | |
| 33 | 12 | HALIFAX TOWN | D | 2-2 | 1-0 | 4452 | Provan, Talbot | 1 | 2* | | 4 | 5 | 6 | 7 | | 9 | 8 | | | | 11 | | 12 | 3 | 10 | | | |
| 34 | 14 | Colchester United | D | 1-1 | 1-0 | 7312 | Draper | 1 | | 3 | 4 | 5 | 6 | 7 | | 9 | 8 | | | | | | | 2 | 10 | 11 | | |
| 35 | 17 | Newport County | W | 5-2 | 1-0 | 1636 | Talbot (3), Provan, Dearden | 1 | | 3 | 4 | 5 | 6 | 7 | | 9 | 8 | | | | 11 | | | 2 | 10 | | | |
| 36 | 22 | SCUNTHORPE UNITED | L | 0-2 | 0-1 | 5483 | | 1 | | 3 | 4 | 5 | 6 | 7 | | 9 | 8 | | | | 11 | | | 2 | 10 | | | |
| 37 | 26 | GRIMSBY TOWN | L | 0-1 | 0-0 | 4051 | | 1 | | 3 | 4 | 5 | 6 | 7 | | 9 | 8 | | | | 11 | | | 2 | 10 | | | |
| 38 | 29 | Port Vale | L | 1-2 | 0-1 | 4690 | Provan | 1 | 12 | 3 | 4 | 5 | 6* | 7 | | 9 | 8 | | | | 11 | | | 2 | 10 | | | |
| 39 | Apr 5 | PETERBOROUGH UNITED | L | 2-3 | 1-0 | 4182 | Talbot, Ashworth (pen) | 1 | | 3 | 4 | 5 | | 7 | | 9 | 6 | | | | 11 | | | 2 | 10 | 8 | | |
| 40 | 8 | ROCHDALE | W | 2-1 | 1-0 | 3820 | Provan, Dearden | 1 | 2 | | 4 | 5 | | 7 | | 9 | 8 | | 3 | | 11* | | | 6 | 10 | 12 | | |
| 41 | 12 | Chesterfield | L | 0-2 | 0-1 | 3554 | | 1 | 2 | | | 5 | | 7 | | 9 | 4 | | 3 | | 11 | | | 6 | 10 | 8 | | |
| 42 | 14 | Rochdale | L | 1-4 | 1-1 | 4884 | Talbot | 1 | 2 | | | 5 | | 7 | | 9 | 4 | | 3 | | 11 | | | 6 | 10 | 8 | | |
| 43 | 19 | EXETER CITY | L | 0-1 | 0-0 | 2958 | | 1 | 2 | | | 5 | | 7 | | 9 | 4 | | 3 | | 11 | | | 6 | 10 | 8 | | |
| 44 | 23 | LINCOLN CITY | W | 2-0 | 1-0 | 2488 | Provan, Draper | | | 3 | 4 | 5 | | 7 | | 9 | 8 | | | | 11 | | | 6 | 10 | | 1 | 2 |
| 45 | 28 | York City | L | 2-4 | 1-3 | 3397 | Dearden, Provan | 1 | | 5 | 4 | | | 7 | | | 8 | | 3* | | 11 | 10 | | 6 | 9 | 12 | | 2 |
| 46 | 30 | Brentford | L | 1-2 | 1-1 | 4090 | Nelmes (og) | 1 | | 3 | 4 | 5 | | 7 | | | 8 | | | | 11 | 10 | | 6 | 9 | | | 2 |
| | | | | | | | Apps. | 46 | 29 | 38 | 42 | 44 | 32 | 45 | 20 | 43 | 45 | 23 | 12 | 1 | 33 | 2 | 1 | 21 | 21 | 5 | 1 | 3 |
| | | | | | | | Subs. | | 1 | | | | 1 | | | | 1 | 1 | 1 | 2 | 4 | 1 | 2 | | | 2 | | |
| | | | | | | | Goals | | | 1 | 7 | | 4 | 11 | 3 | 22 | 7 | 3 | | | 12 | | | | 3 | | | |

Own goals 3

## F.A. CUP

| | Date | Opposition | | FT | HT | Att. | Goalscorers | Carling T. | Jones R. | Sear C. | Ashworth B. | Turner G. | Brodie E. | Dearden W. | Metcalf M. | Talbot G. | Sutton M. | Jones L. | Bennett J. | Weston D. | Provan A. | Robinson A. | Evans G. | Cheetham R. | Draper D. | Cullerton M. | Millington G. | Edwards N. |
|---|---|---|---|---|---|---|---|---|---|---|---|---|---|---|---|---|---|---|---|---|---|---|---|---|---|---|---|---|
| 1R | Nov 16 | Bradford City | W | 2-1 | 2-0 | 7404 | Dearden, Talbot | 1 | 2 | 5 | 4 | | | 7 | 6 | 9 | 10 | 8 | 3 | | 11 | | | | | | | |
| 2R | Dec 7 | LINCOLN CITY | D | 1-1 | 0-0 | 6065 | Dearden | 1 | 2 | 3 | 4 | 5 | 6 | 7 | 8 | 9 | 10 | | | | 11 | | | | | | | |
| 2Rr | Dec 11 | Lincoln City | L | 1-2 | 0-1 | 9703 | L Jones | 1 | 2 | 3 | 4 | 5 | 6 | 7 | 8 | 9 | | 10 | | | 11 | | | | | | | |

## LEAGUE CUP

| | Date | Opposition | | FT | HT | Att. | Goalscorers | Carling T. | Jones R. | Sear C. | Ashworth B. | Turner G. | Brodie E. | Dearden W. | Metcalf M. | Talbot G. | Sutton M. | Jones L. | Bennett J. | Weston D. | Provan A. | Robinson A. | Evans G. | Cheetham R. | Draper D. | Cullerton M. | Millington G. | Edwards N. |
|---|---|---|---|---|---|---|---|---|---|---|---|---|---|---|---|---|---|---|---|---|---|---|---|---|---|---|---|---|
| 1R | Aug 14 | TRANMERE ROVERS | D | 0-0 | 0-0 | 8146 | | 1 | 2 | | 4 | 5 | 6 | 7 | 8 | 9 | 10 | 11 | 3 | | | | | | | | | |
| 1Rr | 21 | Tranmere Rovers * | D | 2-2 | 1-2 | 11478 | Talbot, Cumbes (og) | 1 | 2 | 3* | 4 | 5 | 6 | 7 | 8 | 9 | 10 | 11 | 12 | | | | | | | | | |
| 1R2r | 26 | Tranmere Rovers @ | D | 1-1 | 0-1 | 13627 | Sutton | 1 | 2 | 3 | 4 | 5 | 6 | 7 | 8 | 9 | 10 | 11 | | | | | | | | | | |
| 1R3r | 28 | TRANMERE ROVERS | L | 1-2 | 0-2 | 13017 | Ashworth | 1 | 2 | 3 | 4 | 5 | 6 | 11 | 8 | 9 | 10 | | | 7 | | | | | | | | |

* Extra time played following score of 2-2 after 90 minutes

@ Extra time played following score of 1-1 after 90 minutes

## WELSH CUP

| | Date | Opposition | | FT | HT | Att. | Goalscorers | Carling T. | Jones R. | Sear C. | Ashworth B. | Turner G. | Brodie E. | Dearden W. | Metcalf M. | Talbot G. | Sutton M. | Jones L. | Bennett J. | Weston D. | Provan A. | Robinson A. | Evans G. | Cheetham R. | Draper D. | Cullerton M. | Millington G. | Edwards N. |
|---|---|---|---|---|---|---|---|---|---|---|---|---|---|---|---|---|---|---|---|---|---|---|---|---|---|---|---|---|
| 5R | Jan 16 | Rhyl | W | 3-0 | 1-0 | | Talbot (2), Dearden | 1 | 2 | | 4 | 5 | 6 | 7 | | 9 | 8 | 10 | 3 | | 11 | | | | | | | |
| 6R | Feb 12 | LOVELLS ATHLETIC | W | 5-1 | 3-0 | 2385 | L Jones, Talbot (3), Provan | 1 | | 2 | 4 | 5 | | | | 9 | 8 | 7 | 3* | | 11 | | 12 | 6 | 10 | | | |
| SF | Mar 19 | CARDIFF CITY | L | 0-2 | 0-2 | 8404 | | 1 | 12 | 3 | 4 | 5 | 6 | 7 | | 9 | 8 | | | | 11* | | | 2 | 10 | | | |

## FRIENDLIES

| | Date | Opposition | | FT | HT | Att. | Goalscorers |
|---|---|---|---|---|---|---|---|
| 1 | Jul 27 | MANCHESTER CITY | D | 4-4 | 1-1 | | L Jones, Sutton (3) |
| 2 | 31 | DUMBARTON | W | 4-1 | 3-1 | 3904 | Ashworth (pen), Sutton, Talbot, Weston |
| 3 | Aug 3 | Rhyl | W | 4-1 | 2-1 | | Brodie, Talbot, Blunt, Jones |

# SEASON 1969-70

## FOOTBALL LEAGUE DIVISION 4

| | Date | Opposition | | FT | HT | Att. | Goalscorers | Carling T. | Bradbury T. | Sear C. | Ashworth B. | Turner G. | Cheetham R. | Dearden W. | Sutton M. | Chapman R. | Brodie E. | Provan A. | Webber K. | Draper D. | Harley A. | Caughter A. | Edwards N. | Birks G. | Tarbuck A. | McMillan S. | Spence A. | Stacey S. | Lang G. |
|---|---|---|---|---|---|---|---|---|---|---|---|---|---|---|---|---|---|---|---|---|---|---|---|---|---|---|---|---|---|
| 1 | Aug 9 | Scunthorpe United | W | 3-2 | 1-1 | 3480 | Ashworth, Chapman (2) | 1 | 2 | 3 | 4 | 5 | 6 | 7* | 8 | 9 | 10 | 11 | 12 | | | | | | | | | | |
| 2 | 16 | SWANSEA TOWN | D | 2-2 | 2-1 | 5988 | Sutton, Chapman | 1 | 2 | 3 | 4 | 5 | 8 | 7 | 8 | 9 | 10* | 11 | 12 | | | | | | | | | | |
| 3 | 23 | Wrexham | L | 0-2 | 0-1 | 11959 | | 1 | 2 | | 4 | 5 | 6 | | 3 | 9 | 10 | 11 | 7 | 8 | | | | | | | | | |
| 4 | 27 | BRENTFORD | L | 1-2 | 0-1 | 4426 | Bradbury | 1 | 2 | 3 | 4 | | 6 | 7 | 8 | 9 | 5 | 11 | | 10 | | | | | | | | | |
| 5 | 30 | WORKINGTON | W | 3-0 | 1-0 | 3684 | Draper, Sutton, Harley | 1 | 2 | 3* | 5 | | 6 | 7 | 8 | | 4 | 11 | 12 | 9 | 10 | | | | | | | | |
| 6 | Sep 6 | Port Vale | L | 0-3 | 0-1 | 6874 | | 1 | 2 | 3 | 4 | 12 | 6 | 7 | 8 | | 5 | 11 | | 9 | 10* | | | | | | | | |
| 7 | 13 | NOTTS COUNTY | L | 0-1 | 0-0 | 3645 | | 1 | 4 | 3* | 8 | 2 | | 7 | 6 | 9 | 5 | 11 | 12 | 10 | | | | | | | | | |
| 8 | 16 | Grimsby Town | L | 1-4 | 0-2 | 4186 | Draper | 1 | 2 | | 4 | 5 | 8 | 7 | 6 | | 10 | 11 | | 9 | | 3 | | | | | | | |
| 9 | 20 | Lincoln City | L | 0-2 | 0-2 | 4482 | | 1 | 3 | | 4 | 5 | 8 | 7 | 10 | | 6 | 11 | | 9 | | | 2 | | | | | | |
| 10 | 27 | CREWE ALEX. | W | 2-1 | 2-0 | 3722 | Cheetham, Draper | 1 | 6 | 3 | 5 | | 8 | 7 | 4 | | 10 | 11 | | 9 | | | 2 | | | | | | |
| 11 | Oct 1 | BRADFORD P. A. | W | 1-0 | 0-0 | 3203 | Draper | 1 | 6 | 3 | 5 | | | 7 | 4 | 9 | 10 | 11 | | 8 | | | 2 | | | | | | |
| 12 | 4 | Darlington | W | 2-1 | 0-0 | 3348 | Draper, Dearden | 1 | 4 | 3* | 5 | 12 | 10 | 7 | 6 | 8 | | 11 | | 9 | | | 2 | | | | | | |
| 13 | 7 | Swansea Town | L | 1-2 | 1-2 | 6864 | Dearden | 1 | 6 | | 5 | 3 | 8 | 7 | 4 | 9 | | 11 | | 10 | | | 2 | | | | | | |
| 14 | 11 | HARTLEPOOL | W | 2-1 | 0-1 | 4175 | Ashworth, Goad (og) | 1 | 6 | | 5 | | 8 | 7 | 4 | 9 | | 11 | 10 | 12 | | | 2* | 3 | | | | | |
| 15 | 18 | CHESTERFIELD | L | 1-2 | 0-2 | 4436 | Draper | 1 | 6 | | 5 | | 2 | 7 | 4 | | | 11 | 9 | 10 | 8 | | | 3 | | | | | |
| 16 | 25 | Colchester United | W | 1-0 | 0-0 | 3754 | Bradbury | 1 | 6 | | 5 | | 2 | 7 | 4 | | | 11 | 9 | 10 | | | | 3 | 8 | | | | |
| 17 | Nov 1 | EXETER CITY | W | 2-0 | 2-0 | 4487 | Tarbuck (2) | 1 | 6 | | 5* | 12 | 2 | 7 | 4 | | | 11 | 9 | 10 | | | | 3 | 8 | | | | |
| 18 | 8 | Northampton Town | W | 1-0 | 0-0 | 5659 | Tarbuck | 1 | 6 | | | 5 | 2 | 7 | 4 | | | 11 | 9 | 10 | | | | 3 | 8 | | | | |
| 19 | 22 | Aldershot | L | 1-3 | 1-1 | 5385 | Provan | 1 | 6 | | 3 | 5 | 2 | 7 | 4 | | | 11 | 9 | 10 | | | | | 8 | | | | |
| 20 | 26 | SOUTHEND UNITED | W | 2-0 | 1-0 | 4501 | Provan, Dearden | 1 | 6 | | | 5 | 2 | 7 | 4 | | | 11 | 9 | 10 | | | | 3 | 8 | | | | |
| 21 | 29 | YORK CITY | W | 3-0 | 2-0 | 4201 | Tarbuck, Draper (2) | 1 | 6 | | | 5 | 2 | 7 | 4 | | | 11 | 9 | 10 | | | | 3 | 8 | | | | |
| 22 | Dec 13 | Notts County | L | 0-3 | 0-1 | 4231 | | 1 | 6 | | | 5 | 2 | 7 | 4 | | | 11 | 9 | 10 | | | 12 | 3 | 8* | | | | |
| 23 | 20 | PORT VALE | D | 1-1 | 0-1 | 5235 | Provan | 1 | 6 | | | 5 | 2 | 7 | 4 | | | 11 | 10 | 8 | | | | 3 | | 9 | | | |
| 24 | 26 | WREXHAM | W | 2-0 | 2-0 | 15024 | Dearden (2) | 1 | 6 | | | 5 | 2 | 7 | 4 | | | 11 | 9 | 10 | | | | 3 | | 8* | 12 | | |
| 25 | Jan 10 | LINCOLN CITY | L | 1-2 | 0-2 | 5768 | Provan | 1 | 6 | | | 5 | 2 | 7 | 4 | | | 11 | 9 | 10 | | | | | | 8 | | 3 | |
| 26 | 17 | Crewe Alex. | L | 0-3 | 0-2 | 4704 | | 1 | 6 | | | 5 | 2 | 7 | 4 | | | 11 | 9* | 10 | | | 3 | | | 12 | 8 | | |
| 27 | 19 | Bradford P. A. | W | 2-1 | 1-1 | 5997 | Spence, Dearden | 1 | 6 | 12 | | 5 | 3 | 7 | 4 | | | 11 | | 10 | | | 2* | | | 8 | 9 | | |
| 28 | 31 | DARLINGTON | L | 1-3 | 1-3 | 4290 | Spence | 1 | 6 | 3 | 12 | 5 | 2 | | 4 | | | 11 | 9 | 10 | | | | | | 8 | 7* | | |
| 29 | Feb 7 | Hartlepool | W | 2-1 | 0-0 | 2233 | Provan, Gill (og) | 1 | 6 | | 12 | 5 | 3* | 7 | 4 | | | 11 | 9 | 10 | | | 2 | | | 8 | | | |
| 30 | 14 | SCUNTHORPE UNITED | D | 1-1 | 1-1 | 3968 | Dearden | 1 | 3 | | 4 | 5 | | 7 | 6 | | | 11 | 9 | 10 | | | 2 | | | 8 | | | |
| 31 | 18 | Workington | D | 1-1 | 0-1 | 1474 | Webber | 1 | 3 | | 4 | 5 | 2 | 7 | 6 | | | 11 | 9 | 10 | | | | | | 8 | | | |
| 32 | 21 | NORTHAMPTON TOWN | W | 2-1 | 0-1 | 3782 | Draper, Clarke (og) | 1 | 3 | | 4 | 5 | 2 | 7 | 6 | | | 11 | 9 | 10 | | | | | | 8 | | | |
| 33 | 25 | NEWPORT COUNTY | W | 2-0 | 1-0 | 3664 | Turner, Webber | 1 | 3 | | 4 | 5 | 2 | 7 | 6 | | | 11 | 9 | 10 | | | | | | 8 | | | |
| 34 | 28 | Chesterfield | W | 1-0 | 0-0 | 13154 | Dearden | 1 | 3 | | 4 | 5 | 2 | 7 | 6* | | | 11 | 9 | 10 | | | | | | 8 | 12 | | |
| 35 | Mar 11 | OLDHAM ATHLETIC | W | 2-1 | 2-0 | 4522 | Dearden, Draper | 1 | 3 | | 4 | 5 | 2 | 7 | 6 | | | 11 | 9 | 10 | | | 12 | | | 8* | | | |
| 36 | 13 | York City | D | 0-0 | 0-0 | 3310 | | 1 | 3 | | 4 | 5 | 2 | 7 | 6 | | | 11 | 9 | 10 | | | | | 8 | | | | |
| 37 | 16 | Newport County | L | 1-3 | 1-1 | 2638 | Webber | 1 | 3 | | 4 | 5 | 2 | 7 | 6 | | | 11 | 9 | 10 | | | | | 8 | | | | |
| 38 | 21 | PETERBOROUGH UNITED | L | 2-3 | 2-1 | 4024 | Cheetham (pen), Dearden | 1 | 6 | | | 5 | 2 | 7 | 4 | | | 11 | | 8 | | | 12 | 3 | 10 | | 9* | | |
| 39 | 28 | Oldham Athletic | L | 0-5 | 0-2 | 4611 | | 1 | 9 | | 4 | 5 | 2 | 7 | 8 | | | 11 | | 10 | | | 3 | | 8 | | | | |
| 40 | 30 | Exeter City | L | 0-1 | 0-1 | 5717 | | 1 | 3 | | 4 | 5 | 2 | 7 | 6 | | | 11 | 9 | 10 | | | | | 8 | | | | |
| 41 | Apr 1 | COLCHESTER UNITED | W | 1-0 | 0-0 | 2580 | Tarbuck | 1 | 3 | | 4 | 5 | 2 | | 6 | | | 11 | 9 | 10 | | | | | 7 | 8 | | | |
| 42 | 4 | Brentford | L | 0-2 | 0-0 | 4748 | | 1 | 3 | | 4 | 5 | 2 | | 6 | | | 11 | 9 | 10 | | | 12 | | 7* | 8 | | | |
| 43 | 6 | Southend United | L | 2-4 | 1-0 | 5512 | Tarbuck, Dearden | 1 | 3 | | 4 | 6 | 2 | 7* | 5 | | | 11 | 9 | 10 | | | | | 8 | 12 | | | |
| 44 | 15 | GRIMSBY TOWN | W | 3-1 | 1-0 | 2186 | Provan, Webber, Ashworth | 1 | 3 | | 4 | 5 | 2 | 7 | 6 | | | 11 | 9 | 10 | | | | | | 8* | 12 | | |
| 45 | 18 | Peterborough United | D | 0-0 | 0-0 | 4763 | | 1 | | | 4 | 5 | 2 | | 6 | | | 11* | 9 | 10 | | 12 | 3 | | 8 | | 7 | | |
| 46 | 30 | ALDERSHOT | W | 2-1 | 0-1 | 1691 | Draper (2) | 1 | 8 | | 4 | 5 | 2 | | 6 | | | | 9 | 10 | | | 3* | | 7 | 11 | 12 | | |
| | | | | | | | Apps. | 46 | 45 | 10 | 34 | 36 | 43 | 40 | 46 | 9 | 11 | 45 | 31 | 43 | 3 | 1 | 13 | 11 | 17 | 16 | 5 | 1 | |
| | | | | | | | Subs. | | | 1 | 2 | 3 | | | | | | | 4 | 1 | | 1 | 4 | | | 2 | 4 | | |
| | | | | | | | Goals | | 2 | | 3 | 1 | 2 | 11 | 2 | 3 | | 6 | 4 | 12 | 1 | | | | 6 | | 2 | | |

Own goals 3

## F.A. CUP

| | Date | Opposition | | FT | HT | Att. | Goalscorers | Carling T. | Bradbury T. | Sear C. | Ashworth B. | Turner G. | Cheetham R. | Dearden W. | Sutton M. | Chapman R. | Brodie E. | Provan A. | Webber K. | Draper D. | Harley A. | Caughter A. | Edwards N. | Birks G. | Tarbuck A. | McMillan S. | Spence A. | Stacey S. | Lang G. |
|---|---|---|---|---|---|---|---|---|---|---|---|---|---|---|---|---|---|---|---|---|---|---|---|---|---|---|---|---|---|
| 1R | Nov 15 | Halifax Town | D | 3-3 | 2-1 | 5032 | Tarbuck (2), Dearden | 1 | 6 | | | 5 | 2 | 7 | 4 | | | 11 | 9 | 10 | | | | 3 | 8 | | | | |
| 1Rr | 19 | HALIFAX TOWN | W | 1-0 | 0-0 | 8352 | Provan | 1 | 6 | | | 5 | 2 | 7 | 4 | | | 11 | 9 | 10 | | | | 3 | 8 | | | | |
| 2R | Dec 6 | DONCASTER ROVERS | D | 1-1 | 0-1 | 7705 | Tarbuck | 1 | 6 | | | 5 | 2 | 7 | 4 | | | 11 | 9 | 10 | | | | 3 | 8 | | | | |
| 2Rr | 9 | Doncaster Rovers | W | 2-0 | 0-1 | 10822 | Webber, Dearden | 1 | 8 | | | | 2 | 7 | 4 | | | 11 | 9 | 10 | | | 5 | 3 | 8 | | | | |
| 3R | Jan 3 | BRISTOL CITY | W | 2-1 | 1-0 | 10030 | Webber, Dearden | 1 | 6 | | | 5 | 2 | 7 | 4 | | | 11 | 9 | 10 | | | 12 | 3* | | | 8 | | |
| 4R | 24 | Swindon Town | L | 2-4 | 1-2 | 21937 | Cheetham (pen), Lang | 1 | 6 | 3 | | 5 | 2 | | 4 | | | 11 | 9 | 10 | | | 12 | | | | 8* | | 7 |

## LEAGUE CUP

| | Date | Opposition | | FT | HT | Att. | Goalscorers | Carling T. | Bradbury T. | Sear C. | Ashworth B. | Turner G. | Cheetham R. | Dearden W. | Sutton M. | Chapman R. | Brodie E. | Provan A. | Webber K. | Draper D. | Harley A. | Caughter A. | Edwards N. | Birks G. | Tarbuck A. | McMillan S. | Spence A. | Stacey S. | Lang G. |
|---|---|---|---|---|---|---|---|---|---|---|---|---|---|---|---|---|---|---|---|---|---|---|---|---|---|---|---|---|---|
| 1R | Aug 13 | ASTON VILLA | L | 1-2 | 0-1 | 10510 | Dearden | 1 | 2 | 3 | 4 | 5 | 6 | 7 | 8* | 9 | 10 | 11 | 12 | | | | | | | | | | |

## WELSH CUP

| | Date | Opposition | | FT | HT | Att. | Goalscorers | Carling T. | Bradbury T. | Sear C. | Ashworth B. | Turner G. | Cheetham R. | Dearden W. | Sutton M. | Chapman R. | Brodie E. | Provan A. | Webber K. | Draper D. | Harley A. | Caughter A. | Edwards N. | Birks G. | Tarbuck A. | McMillan S. | Spence A. | Stacey S. | Lang G. |
|---|---|---|---|---|---|---|---|---|---|---|---|---|---|---|---|---|---|---|---|---|---|---|---|---|---|---|---|---|---|
| 5R | Jan 14 | Llandudno Borough * | W | 6-0 | 3-0 | 2464 | Edwards, Spence, Webber, Provan (3) | 1 | 6 | | | 5 | 2 | 7 | 4 | | | 11 | 9 | 10 | | | 3 | | | | 8 | | |
| 6R | Feb 11 | Llanelli | W | 3-1 | 1-0 | 1925 | Turner, Dearden, Webber | 1 | 3 | | 4 | 5 | | 7 | 6 | | | 11 | 9 | 10 | | | 2 | | | 8 | | | |
| SF | Mar 18 | Hereford United | D | 3-3 | 3-1 | 5125 | Dearden (2), Tarbuck | 1 | 9 | | 4 | 5 | 2 | 7 | | | | 11 | | 10 | | | 3 | | 8 | 6 | | | |
| SFr | 25 | HEREFORD UNITED | W | 3-0 | 1-0 | 3916 | Dearden, Draper (2) | 1 | 3 | | 4 | 5 | 2 | 7 | 6 | | | 11 | | 9 | | | | | 8 | 10 | | | |
| F1 | May 8 | CARDIFF CITY | L | 0-1 | 0-1 | 3087 | | 1 | 8 | | 4 | 5 | 2 | | 6 | | | | 9 | 10 | | | 3 | | 7 | 11 | | | |
| F2 | 15 | Cardiff City | L | 0-4 | 0-4 | 5567 | | 1 | 4 | | | 5 | 2 | | 6 | | | | 9 | 10 | | | 3 | | 8 | 11 | 7 | | |

* Played at Chester

## FRIENDLIES

| | Date | Opposition | | FT | HT | Att. | Goalscorers |
|---|---|---|---|---|---|---|---|
| 1 | Jul 28 | Kidderminster Harriers | W | 2-1 | 2-0 | | Chapman (2) |
| 2 | 30 | SHEFFIELD UNITED RES. | W | 4-0 | 0-0 | 2590 | Draper (3), Cheetham |
| 3 | Aug 2 | TRANMERE ROVERS | W | 2-1 | 1-1 | 2833 | Chapman (2) |
| 4 | 5 | EVERTON RES. | W | 4-2 | 2-0 | 2381 | Webber (2), Chapman, Provan |

**1969/70 Season:**
(Back) Brodie, Turner, Cheetham, Draper, Carling, Dearden, Chapman, Harley, Ashworth.
(Front) Bradbury, Sutton, Webber, Sear, Provan, Edwards, Caughter.

**1970/71 Season:**
(Back) Sear, Birks, Bradbury, Draper, Worrall, Pritchard (Trainer). (Middle) Pountney, Turner, Carling, Taylor, Edwards, Cheetham, Griffiths
(Front) Woodall, Tarbuck, Kennedy, Roberts (Manager), Groves, Webber

# SEASON 1970-71

## FOOTBALL LEAGUE DIVISION 4

| | Date | Opposition | | FT | HT | Att. | Goalscorers | Carling T. | Cheetham R. | Birks G. | Bradbury T. | Turner G. | Pountney D. | Woodall B. | Tarbuck A. | Webber K. | Draper D. | Groves A. | Edwards N. | Kennedy D. | Hawkins D. | McHale K. | Taylor J. | Loyden E. | Griffiths N. |
|---|---|---|---|---|---|---|---|---|---|---|---|---|---|---|---|---|---|---|---|---|---|---|---|---|---|
| 1 | Aug 15 | Brentford | W | 2-1 | 2-0 | 6480 | Woodall, Tarbuck | 1 | 2 | 3 | 4 | 5 | 6 | 7 | 8 | 9* | 10 | 11 | 12 | | | | | | |
| 2 | 22 | COLCHESTER UNITED | W | 2-1 | 2-1 | 5447 | Draper, Cheetham | 1 | 2 | 3* | 4 | 5 | 6 | 7 | 8 | 9 | 10 | 11 | 12 | | | | | | |
| 3 | 29 | Workington | L | 0-1 | 0-0 | 3907 | | 1 | 2 | 3 | 4 | 5 | 6 | 7 | 8 | 9 | 10 | 11 | | | | | | | |
| 4 | Sep 2 | LINCOLN CITY | W | 1-0 | 0-0 | 4709 | Tarbuck | 1 | 2 | 3 | 4 | 5 | 6 | 7 | 8 | 9 | 10 | 11 | | | | | | | |
| 5 | 12 | York City | D | 1-1 | 0-0 | 3021 | Webber | 1 | 2 | 3 | 4 | 5 | 6 | | 8 | 9 | 10 | 12 | | 7 | 11* | | | | |
| 6 | 19 | EXETER CITY | W | 3-1 | 1-0 | 4337 | Draper, Woodall, Hawkins | 1 | 2 | 3 | 4 | 5 | 6 | 7 | 8 | 12 | 10 | 11* | | | 9 | | | | |
| 7 | 23 | CAMBRIDGE UNITED | W | 2-1 | 1-1 | 5982 | Tarbuck, Draper | 1 | 2 | 3 | 4 | 5 | 6 | 7 | 8 | | 10 | 11 | | | 9 | | | | |
| 8 | 26 | Newport County | W | 1-0 | 0-0 | 1827 | Draper | 1 | 2 | 3 | 4 | 5 | 6 | 7 | 8 | | 10 | 11 | | | 9 | | | | |
| 9 | 30 | SOUTHPORT | W | 1-0 | 0-0 | 6749 | Tarbuck | 1 | 2 | | 4 | 5 | 6 | 7* | 8 | 12 | 10 | 11 | 3 | | 9 | | | | |
| 10 | Oct 3 | ALDERSHOT | L | 1-2 | 0-1 | 5069 | Cheetham (pen) | 1 | 2 | 3 | 4 | 5 | 6 | 7 | 8 | 12 | 10 | 11 | | | 9* | | | | |
| 11 | 7 | GRIMSBY TOWN | W | 5-0 | 3-0 | 4596 | Webber (2), Groves, Turner (2) | 1 | 2 | 3 | 4 | 5 | 6 | | 8 | 9 | 10 | 11 | | 7 | | | | | |
| 12 | 10 | Barrow | W | 4-1 | 2-1 | 2326 | Tarbuck (2), Groves, Kennedy | 1 | 2 | 3 | 4 | 5 | 6 | | 8 | 9 | 10 | 11 | | 7 | | | | | |
| 13 | 17 | BRENTFORD | L | 1-2 | 1-0 | 5834 | Tarbuck | 1 | 2 | 3 | 4 | 5 | 6 | | 8 | 9 | 10 | 11 | | 7 | | | | | |
| 14 | 20 | Northampton Town | L | 1-3 | 0-0 | 6232 | Webber | 1 | 2 | 3 | 4 | 5 | 6 | 7 | 8 | 9 | 10 | 11* | | | 12 | | | | |
| 15 | 24 | BOURNEMOUTH & B. A. | W | 4-2 | 3-0 | 5702 | Webber (2), Tarbuck, Draper | 1 | 2 | 3 | 4 | 5 | 6 | | 9 | 7 | 10 | 11 | | | | 8 | | | |
| 16 | 31 | Peterborough United | L | 0-1 | 0-0 | 5355 | | | 2 | 3 | 4 | 5 | 6 | 11 | 8 | 7 | 9 | | | | | 10 | 1 | | |
| 17 | Nov 7 | OLDHAM ATHLETIC | L | 0-1 | 0-0 | 7367 | | | 2 | 3 | 4 | 5 | 6 | | 8 | 7 | 10 | | | | | 11 | 1 | 9 | |
| 18 | 11 | Crewe Alex. | L | 3-6 | 1-2 | 5000 | Cheetham (pen), Loyden, Draper | 1 | 2 | 3 | | 5 | 4 | | 8 | 7 | 6 | 11 | | | | 10 | | 9 | |
| 19 | 14 | Scunthorpe United | W | 2-0 | 0-0 | 3099 | Loyden, Cheetham (pen) | 1 | 2 | 3 | 4 | 5 | 6 | | 8 | | 10 | 11 | | | | 7 | | 9 | |
| 20 | 28 | HARTLEPOOL | L | 0-1 | 0-1 | 4361 | | 1 | 2 | 3 | 4 | 5 | 6 | 12 | 9 | | 8* | 11 | | | | 7 | | 10 | |
| 21 | Dec 5 | Darlington | L | 1-5 | 0-0 | 3527 | McHale | 1 | 2 | 3 | 4 | 5 | 6 | | 8 | 7* | | 11 | | 12 | | 10 | | 9 | |
| 22 | 18 | Colchester United | W | 1-0 | 1-0 | 4342 | Draper | 1 | 2 | 3 | 4 | 5 | 6 | | 8 | | 10 | 11 | | | | 7 | | 9 | |
| 23 | 26 | STOCKPORT COUNTY | W | 3-0 | 2-0 | 5816 | Tarbuck, Loyden, Groves | 1 | 2 | 3 | 4 | 5 | 6 | | 8 | | 10 | 11 | | | | 7 | | 9 | |
| 24 | Jan 9 | Southport | L | 0-2 | 0-1 | 3180 | | 1 | 2 | 3 | 4 | 5 | | | 8 | 12 | 10 | 11* | 6 | | | 7 | | 9 | |
| 25 | 16 | NORTHAMPTON TOWN | D | 2-2 | 1-0 | 4032 | Tarbuck, Loyden | 1 | | 3 | 4 | 5 | 6 | | 10 | 7 | 8 | | 2 | | | 11 | | 9 | |
| 26 | 23 | NOTTS COUNTY | W | 2-1 | 1-0 | 5835 | Loyden, Tarbuck | 1 | | 3 | 4 | 5 | 6 | | 10 | 7 | 8 | | 2 | | | 11 | | 9 | |
| 27 | 30 | Hartlepool | W | 2-0 | 1-0 | 1191 | Green (og), Loyden | | | 3 | 4 | 5 | 6 | | 11 | 7 | 8 | | 2 | | | 10 | 1 | 9 | |
| 28 | Feb 6 | DARLINGTON | W | 2-1 | 1-1 | 4714 | Tarbuck, Loyden | | | 3 | 4 | 5 | 6 | | 10 | 7 | 8 | | 2 | | | 11 | 1 | 9 | |
| 29 | 13 | Notts County | L | 1-2 | 0-2 | 10545 | McHale | | | 3 | 4 | 5 | 6 | | 10 | 7 | 8 | | 2 | | | 11 | 1 | 9 | |
| 30 | 20 | CREWE ALEX. | W | 1-0 | 1-0 | 5585 | Tarbuck | 1 | | 3 | 4 | 5 | 6 | | 11 | 7 | 8 | | 2 | | | 10 | | 9 | |
| 31 | 22 | Southend United | D | 1-1 | 1-0 | 5550 | Loyden | 1 | | 3 | 4 | 5 | 6 | | 11 | 7 | 8 | | 2 | | | 10 | | 9 | |
| 32 | 27 | PETERBOROUGH UNITED | W | 2-0 | 2-0 | 4223 | Loyden (2) | 1 | | 3 | 4 | 5 | 6 | 12 | 11 | 7 | 8 | | 2 | | | 10 | | 9* | |
| 33 | Mar 6 | Bournemouth & B. A. | L | 1-3 | 0-2 | 8691 | Tarbuck | 1 | | 3 | 4 | 5 | 6 | | 11 | 7 | 8 | | 2 | 12 | | 10 | | 9* | |
| 34 | 8 | Cambridge United | D | 1-1 | 1-0 | 3576 | Tarbuck | 1 | | 3 | 4 | 5 | 6 | | 11 | 7 | 8 | | 2 | 9 | | 10 | | | |
| 35 | 13 | SCUNTHORPE UNITED | W | 2-0 | 1-0 | 3738 | Tarbuck (2) | 1 | 12 | 3 | 4 | 5 | 6 | | 11 | 7 | 8 | | 2* | 9 | | 10 | | | |
| 36 | 17 | SOUTHEND UNITED | W | 2-0 | 1-0 | 3870 | Loyden, Webber | 1 | | 3 | 4 | 5 | 6 | | 11 | 7 | 8 | | 2 | | | 10 | | 9 | |
| 37 | 20 | Oldham Athletic | D | 1-1 | 0-1 | 10117 | Webber | 1 | | 3 | 4 | 5 | 6 | | 11 | 7 | 8 | | 2 | 12 | | 10* | | 9 | |
| 38 | 27 | Grimsby Town | D | 2-2 | 1-1 | 2591 | Webber, Loyden | 1 | | 3 | 4 | 5 | 6 | | 11 | 7 | 8 | | 2 | | | 10 | | 9 | |
| 39 | Apr 3 | WORKINGTON | W | 1-0 | 0-0 | 3921 | Loyden | 1 | | 3 | 4 | 5 | 6 | | 11 | 7 | 8 | | 2 | | | 10 | | 9 | |
| 40 | 9 | Aldershot | L | 0-1 | 0-0 | 4923 | | 1 | | 3 | 4 | 5 | 6 | | 11 | 7 | 8 | | 2 | | | 10 | | 9 | |
| 41 | 10 | Stockport County | W | 1-0 | 0-0 | 2174 | Edwards | 1 | | 3 | 4 | 5 | 6 | | 11 | 7 | 8 | | 2 | | | 10 | | 9 | |
| 42 | 12 | YORK CITY | D | 1-1 | 0-0 | 7898 | Turner | 1 | | 3 | 4 | 5 | 6 | | 11 | 7 | 8 | | 2 | | | 10 | | 9 | |
| 43 | 17 | BARROW | W | 2-1 | 2-0 | 4440 | Tarbuck, Loyden | 1 | | 3 | 4 | 5 | 6 | | 11 | 7 | 8* | | 2 | 12 | | 10 | | 9 | |
| 44 | 24 | Exeter City | L | 1-3 | 0-1 | 4024 | Webber | 1 | | 3 | 4 | 5 | 6 | | 11 | 7 | 8 | | 2 | | | 10 | | 9 | |
| 45 | 28 | Lincoln City | L | 0-2 | 0-1 | 3086 | | 1 | | 3 | 4 | 5 | 6 | | 8 | 11 | 10 | | 2* | 12 | | 7 | | 9 | |
| 46 | May 1 | NEWPORT COUNTY | W | 2-1 | 1-0 | 2646 | Loyden, McHale | 1 | 2 | 11 | 4 | 5 | 6 | | 8 | | | | | 7 | | 10 | | 9 | 3 |
| | | | | | | | Apps. | 41 | 25 | 45 | 45 | 46 | 45 | 11 | 46 | 35 | 44 | 21 | 23 | 7 | 6 | 32 | 5 | 28 | 1 |
| | | | | | | | Subs. | | 1 | | | | | 2 | | 4 | | 1 | 2 | 5 | 1 | | | | |
| | | | | | | | Goals | | 4 | | | 3 | | 2 | 18 | 10 | 7 | 3 | 1 | 1 | 1 | 3 | | 15 | |

Own goals 1

## F.A. CUP

| | Date | Opposition | | FT | HT | Att. | Goalscorers | Carling T. | Cheetham R. | Birks G. | Bradbury T. | Turner G. | Pountney D. | Woodall B. | Tarbuck A. | Webber K. | Draper D. | Groves A. | Edwards N. | Kennedy D. | Hawkins D. | McHale K. | Taylor J. | Loyden E. | Griffiths N. |
|---|---|---|---|---|---|---|---|---|---|---|---|---|---|---|---|---|---|---|---|---|---|---|---|---|---|
| 1R | Nov 21 | Preston North End | D | 1-1 | 0-1 | 15023 | Tarbuck | 1 | 2 | 3* | 4 | 5 | 6 | | 8 | 12 | 10 | 11 | | | | 7 | | 9 | |
| 1Rr | 25 | PRESTON NORTH END | W | 1-0 | 0-0 | 11164 | Loyden | 1 | 2 | 3 | 4 | 5 | 6 | | 8 | 12 | 10 | 11* | | | | 7 | | 9 | |
| 2R | Dec 12 | CREWE ALEX. | W | 1-0 | 1-0 | 9353 | Turner | 1 | 2 | 3 | 4 | 5 | 6 | | 8 | | 10 | 11 | | | | 7 | | 9 | |
| 3R | Jan 2 | DERBY COUNTY | L | 1-2 | 0-1 | 15882 | Webber | 1 | 2 | 3 | 4 | 5 | 6 | | 8 | 12 | 10 | 11* | | | | 7 | | 9 | |

## LEAGUE CUP

| | Date | Opposition | | FT | HT | Att. | Goalscorers | Carling T. | Cheetham R. | Birks G. | Bradbury T. | Turner G. | Pountney D. | Woodall B. | Tarbuck A. | Webber K. | Draper D. | Groves A. | Edwards N. | Kennedy D. | Hawkins D. | McHale K. | Taylor J. | Loyden E. | Griffiths N. |
|---|---|---|---|---|---|---|---|---|---|---|---|---|---|---|---|---|---|---|---|---|---|---|---|---|---|
| 1R | Aug 19 | SHREWSBURY TOWN | W | 2-1 | 1-1 | 5847 | Cheetham, Pountney | 1 | 2 | 3 | 4 | 5 | 6 | 7 | 8 | 9 | 10 | 11 | | | | | | | |
| 2R | Sep 9 | Norwich City | D | 0-0 | 0-0 | 11081 | | 1 | 2 | 3 | 4 | 5 | 6 | 7* | 8 | 9 | 10 | 11 | | 12 | | | | | |
| 2Rr | 16 | NORWICH CITY | L | 1-2 | 1-2 | 7474 | Woodall | 1 | 2 | 3 | 4 | 5 | 6 | 7 | 8 | 9 | 10 | 11 | | | | | | | |

## WELSH CUP

| | Date | Opposition | | FT | HT | Att. | Goalscorers | Carling T. | Cheetham R. | Birks G. | Bradbury T. | Turner G. | Pountney D. | Woodall B. | Tarbuck A. | Webber K. | Draper D. | Groves A. | Edwards N. | Kennedy D. | Hawkins D. | McHale K. | Taylor J. | Loyden E. | Griffiths N. |
|---|---|---|---|---|---|---|---|---|---|---|---|---|---|---|---|---|---|---|---|---|---|---|---|---|---|
| 5R | Jan 27 | RHYL | D | 1-1 | 1-0 | 3136 | Draper | 1 | | 3 | 4 | 5 | 6 | 9 | | 7 | 8 | 11 | 2 | | | 10 | | | |
| 5Rr | Feb 4 | Rhyl | W | 2-0 | 0-0 | 1698 | Turner, Webber | | | 3 | 4 | 5 | 6 | | 11 | 7 | 8 | | 2 | | | 10 | 1 | 9 | |
| 6R | 17 | SWANSEA CITY | W | 2-1 | 1-0 | 2737 | Edwards, Webber | | | 3 | 4 | 5 | 6 | | 11 | 7 | 8 | | 2 | | | 10 | 1 | 9 | |
| SF | Mar 31 | Cardiff City | D | 0-0 | 0-0 | 5522 | | 1 | | 3 | 4 | 5 | 6 | | 11 | 7 | 10 | | 2 | 8 | | | | 9 | |
| SFr | Apr 19 | CARDIFF CITY | L | 1-2 | 1-0 | 7325 | Webber | 1 | | 3 | 4 | 5 | 6 | | 8 | 11 | 10 | | 2 | | | 7 | | 9 | |

## FRIENDLIES

| | Date | Opposition | | FT | HT | Att. | Goalscorers |
|---|---|---|---|---|---|---|---|
| 1 | Aug 1 | Telford United | D | 1-1 | 0-1 | | Birks |
| 2 | 3 | PARTICK THISTLE | W | 4-1 | 1-0 | 2283 | Tarbuck (2), Groves (2) |
| 3 | 8 | Bangor City | W | 2-0 | 1-0 | 1189 | Woodall, Groves |
| 4 | May 7 | WREXHAM * | W | 10-6 | | 1664 | Loyden(4),Carling(2),Kennedy,Birks(2),Tarbuck |

* Terry Carling Benefit

# SEASON 1971-72

## FOOTBALL LEAGUE DIVISION 4

| | Date | Opposition | | FT | HT | Att. | Goalscorers | Livsey G. | Edwards N. | Cheetham R. | Smith R. | Turner G. | Pountney D. | McHale K. | Tarbuck A. | Loyden E. | Draper D. | Moore A. | Purdie B. | Kennedy D. | Griffiths N. | Carter R. | Birks G. | Futcher G. | Morrissey P. | Sinclair R. | Tinnion B. | Taylor J. | Ashworth J. | Clapham G. | Bingham J. |
|---|---|---|---|---|---|---|---|---|---|---|---|---|---|---|---|---|---|---|---|---|---|---|---|---|---|---|---|---|---|---|---|
| 1 | Aug 14 | CAMBRIDGE UNITED | D | 1-1 | 1-0 | 4539 | Loyden | 1 | 2 | 3 | 4 | 5 | 6 | 7 | 8 | 9 | 10 | 11* | 12 | | | | | | | | | | | | |
| 2 | 21 | Reading | L | 0-1 | 0-1 | 4013 | | 1 | 2 | 3 | | 5 | 6 | 11 | 10 | 9 | 4 | 12 | 8* | 7 | | | | | | | | | | | |
| 3 | 28 | GILLINGHAM | W | 5-1 | 2-0 | 3303 | Purdie (4), Loyden | 1 | 2 | 3 | | 5 | 6 | | 11 | 10 | 8 | | 9 | 7 | 4 | | | | | | | | | | |
| 4 | Sep 1 | Aldershot | D | 0-0 | 0-0 | 4591 | | 1 | 2 | 4 | | 5 | 6 | | 8 | 9 | 10 | | 11 | 7 | 3 | | | | | | | | | | |
| 5 | 4 | Workington | D | 0-0 | 0-0 | 2276 | | 1 | 2 | 3 | | 5 | 6 | | 9 | 10 | 8 | | 11 | 7 | 4 | | | | | | | | | | |
| 6 | 11 | BARROW | D | 0-0 | 0-0 | 3965 | | 1 | 2 | 4 | | 5 | 6 | 12 | 9 | 10 | 8 | | 11* | 7 | 3 | | | | | | | | | | |
| 7 | 18 | Exeter City | D | 1-1 | 0-0 | 4040 | Moore | 1 | | 2 | | 5 | 6 | 11 | | 9 | 10 | 4 | 8 | 7 | 3 | | | | | | | | | | |
| 8 | 25 | BRENTFORD | D | 0-0 | 0-0 | 4088 | | 1 | | 2 | | 5 | 6 | 8 | | 9 | 4 | 10* | 11 | 7 | 3 | 12 | | | | | | | | | |
| 9 | 29 | NORTHAMPTON TOWN | W | 3-2 | 1-0 | 3454 | Purdie, Draper (2) | 1 | | 2* | 5 | 6 | 3 | 11 | | 7 | 10 | | 9 | | 4 | 8 | 12 | | | | | | | | |
| 10 | Oct 1 | Colchester United | L | 0-1 | 0-1 | 6048 | | 1 | 2 | | | 5 | 6 | | | 8 | 4 | 10* | 9 | | 11 | 7 | 3 | 12 | | | | | | | |
| 11 | 9 | SOUTHEND UNITED | D | 1-1 | 1-1 | 4092 | Draper | 1 | 2 | 4 | | 5 | 6 | 11 | | 8 | 10 | | | | | 7 | 3 | | 9 | | | | | | |
| 12 | 16 | Cambridge United | L | 0-2 | 0-2 | 3289 | | 1 | | 2 | | 5 | 6 | 10 | | 8 | 4 | | 11* | 7 | 12 | | 3 | | 9 | | | | | | |
| 13 | 18 | Southport | L | 3-4 | 0-3 | 3659 | Loyden (2), Purdie | 1 | | 2 | | 5 | 6 | | | 9 | 4 | 10 | 11 | 8 | | | 3 | | 7 | | | | | | |
| 14 | 23 | HARTLEPOOL | W | 4-0 | 1-0 | 3466 | Morrissey, Loyden, Cheetham (pen), Kennedy | 1 | 4* | 2 | | 5 | 6 | 12 | | 10 | 8 | | 11 | 7 | | | 3 | | 9 | | | | | | |
| 15 | 30 | Darlington | D | 1-1 | 0-0 | 2012 | Loyden | 1 | | 2 | | 5 | 6 | 11 | | 9 | 4 | | 10 | 8 | | | 3 | | 7 | | | | | | |
| 16 | Nov 6 | BURY | W | 2-0 | 2-0 | 3873 | Loyden, McHale | 1 | | 2 | | 6 | 5 | 11 | | 9 | 4 | | 10 | 8 | | | 3 | | 7 | | | | | | |
| 17 | 13 | Peterborough United | L | 0-2 | 0-1 | 4659 | | 1 | | 2 | | 5 | 6 | 11 | | 9 | 4 | | 10 | 8 | | | 3 | | 7 | | | | | | |
| 18 | 27 | DONCASTER ROVERS | D | 1-1 | 1-0 | 2716 | Loyden | 1 | | | | 5 | 6 | 10 | | 9 | 4 | | 12 | 8 | 3 | 11 | 2 | | 7* | | | | | | |
| 19 | Dec 4 | Crewe Alex. | L | 1-3 | 0-1 | 2671 | Loyden | 1 | | | | 5* | 6 | 8 | | 10 | 4 | | 12 | 7 | 3 | 11 | 2 | | 9 | | | | | | |
| 20 | 11 | Scunthorpe United | L | 0-2 | 0-1 | 3776 | | 1 | 2 | | | 5 | 6 | | | 9 | 4 | | 11 | 10 | 8* | 7 | 3 | 12 | | | | | | | |
| 21 | 18 | WORKINGTON | W | 2-1 | 1-1 | 2690 | Sinclair, Loyden | 1 | 2 | | | 5 | 6 | | | 9 | 4 | | 12 | 10* | | 11 | 3 | | | 7 | 8 | | | | |
| 22 | 27 | Newport County | L | 0-1 | 0-1 | 7664 | | 1 | 2 | | | 5 | 6 | 10 | | 9 | 8 | | 11 | | | | 3 | | | 4 | 7 | | | | |
| 23 | Jan 1 | EXETER CITY | L | 1-2 | 1-1 | 3610 | Sinclair | | 2 | 12 | | 5 | 6 | | | 9 | 8 | | | | 3 | 11 | | | | 7 | 10* | 1 | 4 | | |
| 24 | 8 | Gillingham | L | 0-1 | 0-1 | 5614 | | 1 | 2 | | | 5 | 6 | 11 | | 9 | 8 | | | 10 | 3 | | | | | 7 | | | 4 | | |
| 25 | 15 | STOCKPORT COUNTY | D | 0-0 | 0-0 | 2554 | | 1 | 2 | | | 4 | 6 | 11 | | 9 | 8 | | | 10 | 3 | | | | | 7 | | | 5 | | |
| 26 | 22 | Northampton Town | L | 2-4 | 0-2 | 3161 | Edwards, Pountney | 1 | 2 | 7 | | 4 | 6 | | | 9 | 8 | | 10 | 11* | 3 | | 12 | | | | | | 5 | | |
| 27 | 29 | SOUTHPORT | D | 1-1 | 0-0 | 2585 | Clapham | | 2 | | | 5 | 6 | | | 9 | 8 | | 12 | 7 | 3 | 10 | | | | | | 1 | 4 | 11* | |
| 28 | Feb 5 | Grimsby Town | L | 0-1 | 0-0 | 9431 | | 1 | 2 | | | 5 | 6 | | | 9 | 4 | 8 | 11 | 7 | 3 | 10 | | | | | | | | | |
| 29 | 12 | Hartlepool | L | 1-2 | 1-0 | 2718 | Edwards | 1 | 3 | 2 | | 5 | 6 | | | 9 | 8 | 4 | 12 | 7 | | 10 | | | | | | | | 11* | |
| 30 | 19 | DARLINGTON | W | 2-1 | 0-0 | 2053 | Draper, Purdie | 1 | 2 | 4 | | 5 | 6 | 10* | | | 8 | | 9 | 7 | | | 3 | 12 | | | | | | 11 | |
| 31 | 26 | Bury | L | 1-3 | 0-1 | 3212 | Clapham | 1 | 2 | 4 | | 5 | 6 | 10* | | | 8 | | | 7 | 3 | 12 | | 9 | | | | | | 11 | |
| 32 | Mar 4 | PETERBOROUGH UNITED | D | 1-1 | 1-0 | 1868 | Clapham | 1 | 2 | 4 | | 5 | 6 | 10 | | | 8 | 12 | | 7 | | | 3 | 9* | | | | | | 11 | |
| 33 | 10 | Southend United | L | 2-4 | 2-3 | 8197 | Kennedy (2) | 1 | 2 | 4 | | 5 | 6 | 8 | | | 9 | | | 7 | 3 | | | | | | | | | 10 | 11 |
| 34 | 13 | Stockport County | D | 0-0 | 0-0 | 2102 | | 1 | 2 | 4 | | 5 | 6 | 8 | | | 9 | | | 7 | 3 | | | | | | | | | 10 | 11 |
| 35 | 18 | READING | W | 2-0 | 2-0 | 2165 | Cheetham (pen), Bingham | 1 | 2 | 4 | | 5 | 6 | 8* | | | 9 | | | 7 | 3 | 12 | | | | | | | | 10 | 11 |
| 36 | 21 | LINCOLN CITY | W | 2-1 | 1-1 | 2372 | Kennedy, Griffiths | 1 | 2 | 4 | | 5 | 6 | | | 7* | 9 | | | 8 | 3 | 12 | | | | | | | | 10 | 11 |
| 37 | 25 | Barrow | L | 0-2 | 0-2 | 2105 | | 1 | 2* | 4 | | 5 | 6 | 12 | | | 8 | | | 7 | 3 | 11 | | | | | | | | 10 | 9 |
| 38 | 31 | Brentford | D | 1-1 | 1-1 | 18520 | Clapham | 1 | 2 | 4 | | 5 | 6 | 8 | | | 9 | 12 | | 7 | 3 | 11 | | | | | | | | 10* | |
| 39 | Apr 1 | NEWPORT COUNTY | W | 3-0 | 2-0 | 2563 | Sprague (og), Kennedy, Edwards | 1 | 2 | 4 | | 5 | 6 | 8* | | | 9 | 12 | | 7 | 3 | 10 | | | | | | | | | 11 |
| 40 | 3 | COLCHESTER UNITED | W | 2-1 | 1-0 | 3317 | Moore (2) | 1 | 2 | 4 | | 5 | 6 | | | | 9 | 10 | | 11 | 3 | 8* | | 12 | | | | | | | 7 |
| 41 | 8 | GRIMSBY TOWN | L | 1-2 | 0-0 | 2823 | Loyden | 1 | | 2 | | 5 | 6 | 8 | | 7 | 9 | 10 | | 4 | 3 | 11 | | | | | | | | | |
| 42 | 15 | Doncaster Rovers | D | 0-0 | 0-0 | 2370 | | 1 | 2 | 4 | | 5 | 6 | 8 | | | 9 | | | 7 | 3 | 11 | | | | | | | | 10 | |
| 43 | 19 | SCUNTHORPE UNITED | D | 0-0 | 0-0 | 2347 | | 1 | 2 | 4 | | 5 | 6 | 8 | | | 9 | | | 7 | 3 | 11 | | | | | | | | 10 | |
| 44 | 22 | CREWE ALEX. | D | 0-0 | 0-0 | 2608 | | 1 | 2 | 4 | | 5 | 6 | 8 | | 7 | 9 | | 11 | | 3 | | | | | | | | | 10 | |
| 45 | 26 | ALDERSHOT | D | 0-0 | 0-0 | 1979 | | 1 | 2 | | | 5 | 6 | 8 | | 7 | 9 | | 11 | 4 | 3 | | | | | | | | | 10 | |
| 46 | 29 | Lincoln City | L | 0-4 | 0-1 | 3033 | | 1 | 2 | | | 5 | 6 | 7* | | 9 | 8 | | 11 | 4 | 3 | 12 | | | | | | | | 10 | |
| | | | | | | | Apps. | 44 | 35 | 33 | 2 | 46 | 46 | 29 | 6 | 34 | 46 | 9 | 23 | 39 | 32 | 18 | 15 | 2 | 9 | 5 | 3 | 2 | 5 | 16 | 7 |
| | | | | | | | Subs. | | | 1 | | | | 3 | | | | 4 | 6 | | 1 | 5 | 2 | 4 | | | | | | | |
| | | | | | | | Goals | | 3 | 2 | | | 1 | 1 | | 11 | 4 | 3 | 7 | 5 | 1 | | | | 1 | 2 | | | | 4 | 1 |

Own goals 1

## F.A. CUP

| | Date | Opposition | | FT | HT | Att. | Goalscorers | Livsey G. | Edwards N. | Cheetham R. | Smith R. | Turner G. | Pountney D. | McHale K. | Tarbuck A. | Loyden E. | Draper D. | Moore A. | Purdie B. | Kennedy D. | Griffiths N. | Carter R. | Birks G. | Futcher G. | Morrissey P. | Sinclair R. | Tinnion B. | Taylor J. | Ashworth J. | Clapham G. | Bingham J. |
|---|---|---|---|---|---|---|---|---|---|---|---|---|---|---|---|---|---|---|---|---|---|---|---|---|---|---|---|---|---|---|---|
| 1R | Nov 20 | MANSFIELD TOWN | D | 1-1 | 1-1 | 3669 | McHale | 1 | | 2 | | 5 | 6 | 10 | | 9 | 4 | | 11 | 8 | | | 3 | | 7 | | | | | | |
| 1Rr | 22 | Mansfield Town | L | 3-4 | 1-2 | 5310 | Draper, Kennedy, Loyden | 1 | | | | 5 | 6 | 8 | | 9 | 4 | | | 7 | 3 | 11 | 2 | | 10 | | | | | | |

## LEAGUE CUP

| | Date | Opposition | | FT | HT | Att. | Goalscorers | Livsey G. | Edwards N. | Cheetham R. | Smith R. | Turner G. | Pountney D. | McHale K. | Tarbuck A. | Loyden E. | Draper D. | Moore A. | Purdie B. | Kennedy D. | Griffiths N. | Carter R. | Birks G. | Futcher G. | Morrissey P. | Sinclair R. | Tinnion B. | Taylor J. | Ashworth J. | Clapham G. | Bingham J. |
|---|---|---|---|---|---|---|---|---|---|---|---|---|---|---|---|---|---|---|---|---|---|---|---|---|---|---|---|---|---|---|---|
| 1R | Aug 18 | Tranmere Rovers | D | 1-1 | 0-0 | 4434 | Purdie | 1 | 2 | 3 | | 5 | 6 | 11 | 10 | 9 | 4 | | 8 | 7 | | | | | | | | | | | |
| 1Rr | 25 | TRANMERE ROVERS | L | 1-3 | 1-2 | 5117 | Tarbuck (pen) | 1 | 2 | 3 | | 5 | 6 | | 8 | 9 | 4 | | 11 | 7 | | | | 10 | | | | | | | |

## WELSH CUP

| | Date | Opposition | | FT | HT | Att. | Goalscorers | Livsey G. | Edwards N. | Cheetham R. | Smith R. | Turner G. | Pountney D. | McHale K. | Tarbuck A. | Loyden E. | Draper D. | Moore A. | Purdie B. | Kennedy D. | Griffiths N. | Carter R. | Birks G. | Futcher G. | Morrissey P. | Sinclair R. | Tinnion B. | Taylor J. | Ashworth J. | Clapham G. | Bingham J. |
|---|---|---|---|---|---|---|---|---|---|---|---|---|---|---|---|---|---|---|---|---|---|---|---|---|---|---|---|---|---|---|---|
| 5R | Jan 11 | Holyhead Town | D | 0-0 | 0-0 | | | 1 | 2 | 4 | | 5 | 6 | 7 | | 9 | 8 | | 12 | 11 | 3 | | | | | 10* | | | | | |
| 5Rr | 19 | HOLYHEAD TOWN | W | 7-2 | 3-0 | 1120 | Loyden (3, 1 pen), Draper, Purdie (2), Turner | 1 | 2 | 4 | | 5 | 6 | | | 9 | 8 | | 11 | 10 | 3 | 7* | | 12 | | | | | | | |
| 6R | Feb 7 | Rhyl | L | 1-2 | 1-0 | 2000 | Draper | 1 | 2 | | | 5 | 6 | | | | 8 | 11 | 9 | 7* | 3 | 10 | | 12 | | | | | 4 | | |

## FRIENDLIES

| | Date | Opposition | | FT | HT | Att. | Goalscorers |
|---|---|---|---|---|---|---|---|
| 1 | Jul 31 | Pwllheli | W | 4-2 | 2-2 | | Tarbuck (3), Futcher |
| 2 | Aug 6 | Shrewsbury Town | D | 1-1 | 0-0 | 1494 | Moore |
| 3 | 9 | Connah's Quay Nomads | W | 3-1 | 1-0 | | Futcher, Purdie, Draper |

**1971/72 Season:**
(Back) Pritchard (Trainer), Carter, G Futcher, Kennedy, Moore, Smith, Worrall, Relish, Sear (Coach).
(Middle) Purdie, Arthur, Pountney, Turchet, Turner, Taylor, Cheetham, Griffiths, Birks, Walker (Assistant Secretary).
(Front) Gandy (Secretary), Dutton (Director), McHale, Loyden, Roberts (Manager), Draper, Tarbuck, Rowlands (Chairman), Auckland. (Director)

**1972/73 Season:**
(Back) Wallace, Draper, Pountney, Turner, Taylor, Griffiths, Relish, Hollis.
(Front) G Futcher, Clapham, Carter, Kennedy, Purdie, Edwards, Owen.

# FINAL LEAGUE TABLES: 1972/73 - 1979/80

Final League Table 1972/73 Division

| | | Pl. | Home | | | | | Away | | | | | F. | A. | Pts |
|---|---|---|---|---|---|---|---|---|---|---|---|---|---|---|---|
| | | | W | D | L | F | A | W | D | L | F | A | | | |
| 1 | Southport | 46 | 17 | 4 | 2 | 40 | 19 | 9 | 6 | 8 | 31 | 29 | 71 | 48 | 62 |
| 2 | Hereford United | 46 | 18 | 4 | 1 | 39 | 12 | 5 | 8 | 10 | 17 | 26 | 56 | 38 | 58 |
| 3 | Cambridge United | 46 | 15 | 6 | 2 | 40 | 23 | 5 | 11 | 7 | 27 | 34 | 67 | 57 | 57 |
| 4 | Aldershot | 46 | 14 | 6 | 3 | 33 | 14 | 8 | 6 | 9 | 27 | 24 | 60 | 38 | 56 |
| 5 | Newport County | 46 | 14 | 6 | 3 | 37 | 18 | 8 | 6 | 9 | 27 | 26 | 64 | 44 | 56 |
| 6 | Mansfield Town | 46 | 15 | 7 | 1 | 52 | 17 | 5 | 7 | 11 | 26 | 34 | 78 | 51 | 54 |
| 7 | Reading | 46 | 14 | 7 | 2 | 33 | 7 | 3 | 11 | 9 | 18 | 31 | 51 | 38 | 52 |
| 8 | Exeter City | 46 | 13 | 8 | 2 | 40 | 18 | 5 | 6 | 12 | 17 | 33 | 57 | 51 | 50 |
| 9 | Gillingham | 46 | 15 | 4 | 4 | 44 | 20 | 4 | 7 | 12 | 19 | 38 | 63 | 58 | 49 |
| 10 | Lincoln City | 46 | 12 | 7 | 4 | 38 | 27 | 4 | 9 | 10 | 26 | 30 | 64 | 57 | 48 |
| 11 | Stockport County | 46 | 14 | 7 | 2 | 38 | 18 | 4 | 5 | 14 | 15 | 35 | 53 | 53 | 48 |
| 12 | Bury | 46 | 11 | 7 | 5 | 37 | 19 | 3 | 11 | 9 | 21 | 32 | 58 | 51 | 46 |
| 13 | Workington | 46 | 15 | 7 | 1 | 44 | 20 | 2 | 5 | 16 | 15 | 41 | 59 | 61 | 46 |
| 14 | Barnsley | 46 | 9 | 8 | 6 | 32 | 24 | 5 | 8 | 10 | 26 | 36 | 58 | 60 | 44 |
| ***15*** | ***Chester*** | ***46*** | ***11*** | ***6*** | ***6*** | ***40*** | ***19*** | ***3*** | ***9*** | ***11*** | ***21*** | ***33*** | ***61*** | ***52*** | ***43*** |
| 16 | Bradford City | 46 | 12 | 6 | 5 | 42 | 25 | 4 | 5 | 14 | 19 | 40 | 61 | 65 | 43 |
| 17 | Doncaster Rovers | 46 | 10 | 8 | 5 | 28 | 19 | 5 | 4 | 14 | 21 | 39 | 49 | 58 | 42 |
| 18 | Torquay United | 46 | 8 | 10 | 5 | 23 | 17 | 4 | 7 | 12 | 21 | 30 | 44 | 47 | 41 |
| 19 | Peterborough Utd. | 46 | 10 | 8 | 5 | 42 | 29 | 4 | 5 | 14 | 29 | 47 | 71 | 76 | 41 |
| 20 | Hartlepool | 46 | 8 | 10 | 5 | 17 | 15 | 4 | 7 | 12 | 17 | 34 | 34 | 49 | 41 |
| 21 | Crewe Alexandra | 46 | 7 | 8 | 8 | 18 | 23 | 2 | 10 | 11 | 20 | 38 | 38 | 61 | 36 |
| 22 | Colchester United | 46 | 8 | 8 | 7 | 36 | 28 | 2 | 3 | 18 | 12 | 48 | 48 | 76 | 31 |
| 23 | Northampton Town | 46 | 7 | 6 | 10 | 24 | 30 | 3 | 5 | 15 | 16 | 43 | 40 | 73 | 31 |
| 24 | Darlington | 46 | 5 | 9 | 9 | 28 | 41 | 2 | 6 | 15 | 14 | 44 | 42 | 85 | 29 |

Final League Table 1973/74 Division 4

| | | Pl. | Home | | | | | Away | | | | | F. | A. | Pts |
|---|---|---|---|---|---|---|---|---|---|---|---|---|---|---|---|
| | | | W | D | L | F | A | W | D | L | F | A | | | |
| 1 | Peterborough Utd. | 46 | 19 | 4 | 0 | 49 | 10 | 8 | 7 | 8 | 26 | 28 | 75 | 38 | 65 |
| 2 | Gillingham | 46 | 16 | 5 | 2 | 51 | 16 | 9 | 7 | 7 | 39 | 33 | 90 | 49 | 62 |
| 3 | Colchester United | 46 | 16 | 5 | 2 | 46 | 14 | 8 | 7 | 8 | 27 | 22 | 73 | 36 | 60 |
| 4 | Bury | 46 | 18 | 3 | 2 | 51 | 14 | 6 | 8 | 9 | 30 | 35 | 81 | 49 | 59 |
| 5 | Northampton Town | 46 | 14 | 7 | 2 | 39 | 14 | 6 | 6 | 11 | 24 | 34 | 63 | 48 | 53 |
| 6 | Reading | 46 | 11 | 9 | 3 | 37 | 13 | 5 | 10 | 8 | 21 | 24 | 58 | 37 | 51 |
| ***7*** | ***Chester*** | ***46*** | ***13*** | ***6*** | ***4*** | ***31*** | ***19*** | ***4*** | ***9*** | ***10*** | ***23*** | ***36*** | ***54*** | ***55*** | ***49*** |
| 8 | Bradford City | 46 | 14 | 7 | 2 | 45 | 20 | 3 | 7 | 13 | 13 | 32 | 58 | 52 | 48 |
| 9 | Newport County | 46 | 13 | 6 | 4 | 39 | 23 | 3 | 8 | 12 | 17 | 42 | 56 | 65 | 45 |
| 10 | Exeter City | 45 | 12 | 5 | 6 | 37 | 20 | 6 | 3 | 13 | 21 | 35 | 58 | 55 | 44 |
| 11 | Hartlepool | 46 | 11 | 4 | 8 | 29 | 16 | 5 | 8 | 10 | 19 | 31 | 48 | 47 | 44 |
| 12 | Lincoln City | 46 | 10 | 8 | 5 | 40 | 30 | 6 | 4 | 13 | 23 | 37 | 63 | 67 | 44 |
| 13 | Barnsley | 46 | 15 | 5 | 3 | 42 | 16 | 2 | 5 | 16 | 16 | 48 | 58 | 64 | 44 |
| 14 | Swansea City | 46 | 11 | 6 | 6 | 28 | 15 | 5 | 5 | 13 | 17 | 31 | 45 | 46 | 43 |
| 15 | Rotherham United | 46 | 10 | 9 | 4 | 33 | 22 | 5 | 4 | 14 | 23 | 36 | 56 | 58 | 43 |
| 16 | Torquay United | 46 | 11 | 7 | 5 | 37 | 23 | 2 | 10 | 11 | 15 | 34 | 52 | 57 | 43 |
| 17 | Mansfield Town | 46 | 13 | 8 | 2 | 47 | 24 | 0 | 9 | 14 | 15 | 45 | 62 | 69 | 43 |
| 18 | Scunthorpe United | 45 | 12 | 7 | 3 | 33 | 17 | 2 | 5 | 16 | 14 | 47 | 47 | 64 | 42 |
| 19 | Brentford | 46 | 9 | 7 | 7 | 31 | 20 | 3 | 9 | 11 | 17 | 30 | 48 | 50 | 40 |
| 20 | Darlington | 46 | 9 | 8 | 6 | 29 | 24 | 4 | 5 | 14 | 11 | 38 | 40 | 62 | 39 |
| 21 | Crewe Alexandra | 46 | 11 | 5 | 7 | 28 | 30 | 3 | 5 | 15 | 15 | 41 | 43 | 71 | 38 |
| 22 | Doncaster Rovers | 46 | 10 | 7 | 6 | 32 | 22 | 2 | 4 | 17 | 15 | 58 | 47 | 80 | 35 |
| 23 | Workington | 46 | 10 | 8 | 5 | 33 | 26 | 1 | 5 | 17 | 10 | 48 | 43 | 74 | 35 |
| 24 | Stockport County | 46 | 4 | 12 | 7 | 22 | 25 | 3 | 8 | 12 | 22 | 44 | 44 | 69 | 34 |

Final League Table 1974/75 Division 4

| | | Pl. | Home | | | | | Away | | | | | F. | A. | Pts |
|---|---|---|---|---|---|---|---|---|---|---|---|---|---|---|---|
| | | | W | D | L | F | A | W | D | L | F | A | | | |
| 1 | Mansfield Town | 46 | 17 | 6 | 0 | 55 | 15 | 11 | 6 | 6 | 35 | 25 | 90 | 40 | 68 |
| 2 | Shrewsbury Town | 46 | 16 | 3 | 4 | 46 | 18 | 10 | 7 | 6 | 34 | 25 | 80 | 43 | 62 |
| 3 | Rotherham United | 46 | 13 | 7 | 3 | 40 | 19 | 9 | 8 | 6 | 31 | 22 | 71 | 41 | 59 |
| ***4*** | ***Chester*** | ***46*** | ***17*** | ***5*** | ***1*** | ***48*** | ***9*** | ***6*** | ***6*** | ***11*** | ***16*** | ***29*** | ***64*** | ***38*** | ***57*** |
| 5 | Lincoln City | 46 | 14 | 8 | 1 | 47 | 14 | 7 | 7 | 9 | 32 | 34 | 79 | 48 | 57 |
| 6 | Cambridge United | 46 | 15 | 5 | 3 | 43 | 16 | 5 | 9 | 9 | 19 | 28 | 62 | 44 | 54 |
| 7 | Reading | 46 | 13 | 6 | 4 | 38 | 20 | 8 | 4 | 11 | 25 | 27 | 63 | 47 | 52 |
| 8 | Brentford | 40 | 15 | 0 | 2 | 30 | 14 | 3 | 7 | 13 | 15 | 31 | 53 | 45 | 49 |
| 9 | Exeter City | 46 | 14 | 3 | 6 | 33 | 24 | 5 | 8 | 10 | 27 | 39 | 60 | 63 | 49 |
| 10 | Bradford City | 46 | 10 | 5 | 8 | 32 | 21 | 7 | 8 | 8 | 24 | 30 | 56 | 51 | 47 |
| 11 | Southport | 46 | 13 | 7 | 3 | 36 | 19 | 2 | 10 | 11 | 20 | 37 | 56 | 56 | 47 |
| 12 | Newport County | 46 | 13 | 5 | 5 | 43 | 30 | 6 | 4 | 13 | 25 | 45 | 68 | 75 | 47 |
| 13 | Hartlepool | 46 | 13 | 6 | 4 | 40 | 24 | 3 | 5 | 15 | 12 | 38 | 52 | 62 | 43 |
| 14 | Torquay United | 46 | 10 | 7 | 6 | 30 | 25 | 4 | 7 | 12 | 16 | 36 | 46 | 61 | 42 |
| 15 | Barnsley | 46 | 10 | 7 | 6 | 34 | 24 | 5 | 4 | 14 | 28 | 41 | 62 | 65 | 41 |
| 16 | Northampton Town | 46 | 12 | 6 | 5 | 43 | 22 | 3 | 5 | 15 | 24 | 51 | 67 | 73 | 41 |
| 17 | Doncaster Rovers | 46 | 10 | 9 | 4 | 41 | 29 | 4 | 3 | 16 | 24 | 50 | 65 | 79 | 40 |
| 18 | Crewe Alexandra | 46 | 9 | 9 | 5 | 22 | 16 | 2 | 9 | 12 | 12 | 31 | 34 | 47 | 40 |
| 19 | Rochdale | 46 | 9 | 9 | 5 | 35 | 22 | 4 | 4 | 15 | 24 | 53 | 59 | 75 | 39 |
| 20 | Stockport County | 46 | 10 | 8 | 5 | 26 | 27 | 2 | 6 | 15 | 17 | 43 | 43 | 70 | 38 |
| 21 | Darlington | 46 | 11 | 4 | 8 | 38 | 27 | 2 | 6 | 15 | 16 | 40 | 54 | 67 | 36 |
| 22 | Swansea City | 46 | 9 | 4 | 10 | 25 | 31 | 6 | 2 | 15 | 21 | 42 | 46 | 73 | 36 |
| 23 | Workington | 46 | 7 | 5 | 11 | 23 | 29 | 3 | 6 | 14 | 13 | 37 | 36 | 66 | 31 |
| 24 | Scunthorpe United | 46 | 7 | 8 | 8 | 27 | 29 | 0 | 7 | 16 | 14 | 49 | 41 | 78 | 29 |

Final League Table 1975/76 Division 3

| | | Pl. | Home | | | | | Away | | | | | F. | A. | Pts |
|---|---|---|---|---|---|---|---|---|---|---|---|---|---|---|---|
| | | | W | D | L | F | A | W | D | L | F | A | | | |
| 1 | Hereford United | 46 | 14 | 6 | 3 | 45 | 24 | 12 | 5 | 6 | 41 | 31 | 86 | 55 | 63 |
| 2 | Cardiff City | 46 | 14 | 7 | 2 | 38 | 13 | 8 | 6 | 9 | 31 | 35 | 69 | 48 | 57 |
| 3 | Millwall | 46 | 16 | 6 | 1 | 35 | 14 | 4 | 10 | 9 | 19 | 29 | 54 | 43 | 56 |
| 4 | Brighton & Hove A. | 46 | 18 | 3 | 2 | 58 | 15 | 4 | 6 | 13 | 20 | 38 | 78 | 53 | 53 |
| 5 | Crystal Palace | 46 | 7 | 12 | 4 | 30 | 20 | 11 | 5 | 7 | 31 | 26 | 61 | 46 | 53 |
| 6 | Wrexham | 46 | 13 | 6 | 4 | 38 | 21 | 7 | 6 | 10 | 28 | 34 | 66 | 55 | 52 |
| 7 | Walsall | 46 | 11 | 8 | 4 | 43 | 22 | 7 | 6 | 10 | 31 | 39 | 74 | 61 | 50 |
| 8 | Preston North End | 46 | 15 | 4 | 4 | 45 | 23 | 4 | 6 | 13 | 17 | 34 | 62 | 57 | 48 |
| 9 | Shrewsbury Town | 46 | 14 | 2 | 7 | 36 | 25 | 5 | 8 | 10 | 25 | 34 | 61 | 59 | 48 |
| 10 | Peterborough Utd. | 46 | 12 | 7 | 4 | 37 | 23 | 3 | 11 | 9 | 26 | 40 | 63 | 63 | 48 |
| 11 | Mansfield Town | 46 | 8 | 11 | 4 | 31 | 22 | 8 | 4 | 11 | 27 | 30 | 58 | 52 | 47 |
| 12 | Port Vale | 46 | 10 | 10 | 3 | 33 | 21 | 5 | 6 | 12 | 22 | 33 | 55 | 54 | 46 |
| 13 | Bury | 46 | 11 | 7 | 5 | 33 | 16 | 3 | 9 | 11 | 18 | 30 | 51 | 46 | 44 |
| 14 | Chesterfield | 46 | 11 | 5 | 7 | 45 | 30 | 6 | 4 | 13 | 24 | 39 | 69 | 69 | 43 |
| 15 | Gillingham | 46 | 10 | 8 | 5 | 38 | 27 | 2 | 11 | 10 | 20 | 41 | 58 | 68 | 43 |
| 16 | Rotherham United | 46 | 11 | 6 | 6 | 35 | 22 | 4 | 6 | 13 | 19 | 43 | 54 | 65 | 42 |
| ***17*** | ***Chester*** | ***46*** | ***13*** | ***7*** | ***3*** | ***34*** | ***19*** | ***2*** | ***5*** | ***16*** | ***9*** | ***43*** | ***43*** | ***62*** | ***42*** |
| 18 | Grimsby Town | 46 | 13 | 7 | 3 | 39 | 21 | 2 | 3 | 18 | 23 | 53 | 62 | 74 | 40 |
| 19 | Swindon Town | 46 | 11 | 4 | 8 | 42 | 31 | 5 | 4 | 14 | 20 | 44 | 62 | 75 | 40 |
| 20 | Sheffield Wed. | 46 | 12 | 6 | 5 | 34 | 25 | 0 | 10 | 13 | 14 | 34 | 48 | 59 | 40 |
| 21 | Aldershot | 46 | 10 | 8 | 5 | 34 | 26 | 3 | 5 | 15 | 25 | 49 | 59 | 75 | 39 |
| 22 | Colchester United | 46 | 9 | 6 | 8 | 25 | 27 | 3 | 8 | 12 | 16 | 38 | 41 | 65 | 38 |
| 23 | Southend United | 46 | 9 | 7 | 7 | 40 | 31 | 3 | 6 | 14 | 25 | 44 | 65 | 75 | 37 |
| 24 | Halifax Town | 46 | 6 | 5 | 12 | 22 | 32 | 5 | 8 | 10 | 19 | 29 | 41 | 61 | 35 |

Final League Table 1976/77 Division 3

| | | Pl. | Home | | | | | Away | | | | | F. | A. | Pts |
|---|---|---|---|---|---|---|---|---|---|---|---|---|---|---|---|
| | | | W | D | L | F | A | W | D | L | F | A | | | |
| 1 | Mansfield Town | 46 | 17 | 6 | 0 | 52 | 13 | 11 | 2 | 10 | 26 | 29 | 78 | 42 | 64 |
| 2 | Brighton & Hove A. | 46 | 19 | 3 | 1 | 63 | 14 | 6 | 8 | 9 | 20 | 26 | 83 | 40 | 61 |
| 3 | Crystal Palace | 46 | 17 | 5 | 1 | 46 | 15 | 6 | 8 | 9 | 22 | 25 | 68 | 40 | 59 |
| 4 | Rotherham United | 46 | 11 | 9 | 3 | 30 | 15 | 11 | 6 | 6 | 39 | 29 | 69 | 44 | 59 |
| 5 | Wrexham | 46 | 15 | 6 | 2 | 47 | 22 | 9 | 4 | 10 | 33 | 32 | 80 | 54 | 58 |
| 6 | Preston North End | 46 | 15 | 4 | 4 | 48 | 21 | 6 | 8 | 9 | 16 | 22 | 64 | 43 | 54 |
| 7 | Bury | 46 | 15 | 2 | 6 | 41 | 21 | 8 | 6 | 9 | 23 | 38 | 64 | 59 | 54 |
| 8 | Sheffield Wed. | 46 | 15 | 4 | 4 | 39 | 18 | 7 | 5 | 11 | 26 | 37 | 65 | 55 | 53 |
| 9 | Lincoln City | 46 | 12 | 9 | 2 | 50 | 30 | 7 | 5 | 11 | 27 | 40 | 77 | 70 | 52 |
| 10 | Shrewsbury Town | 46 | 13 | 7 | 3 | 40 | 21 | 5 | 4 | 14 | 25 | 38 | 65 | 59 | 47 |
| 11 | Swindon Town | 46 | 12 | 6 | 5 | 48 | 33 | 3 | 9 | 11 | 20 | 42 | 68 | 75 | 45 |
| 12 | Gillingham | 46 | 11 | 8 | 4 | 31 | 21 | 5 | 4 | 14 | 24 | 43 | 55 | 64 | 44 |
| ***13*** | ***Chester*** | ***46*** | ***14*** | ***3*** | ***6*** | ***28*** | ***20*** | ***4*** | ***5*** | ***14*** | ***20*** | ***38*** | ***48*** | ***58*** | ***44*** |
| 14 | Tranmere Rovers | 46 | 10 | 7 | 6 | 31 | 23 | 3 | 10 | 10 | 20 | 30 | 51 | 53 | 43 |
| 15 | Walsall | 46 | 8 | 7 | 8 | 39 | 32 | 5 | 8 | 10 | 18 | 33 | 57 | 65 | 41 |
| 16 | Peterborough Utd. | 46 | 11 | 4 | 8 | 33 | 28 | 2 | 11 | 10 | 22 | 37 | 55 | 65 | 41 |
| 17 | Oxford United | 46 | 9 | 8 | 6 | 34 | 29 | 3 | 7 | 13 | 21 | 36 | 55 | 65 | 39 |
| 18 | Chesterfield | 46 | 10 | 6 | 7 | 30 | 20 | 4 | 4 | 15 | 26 | 44 | 56 | 64 | 38 |
| 19 | Port Vale | 46 | 9 | 7 | 7 | 29 | 28 | 2 | 9 | 12 | 18 | 43 | 47 | 71 | 38 |
| 20 | Portsmouth | 46 | 8 | 9 | 6 | 28 | 26 | 3 | 5 | 15 | 25 | 44 | 53 | 70 | 36 |
| 21 | Reading | 46 | 10 | 5 | 8 | 29 | 24 | 3 | 4 | 16 | 20 | 49 | 49 | 73 | 35 |
| 22 | Northampton Town | 46 | 9 | 4 | 10 | 33 | 29 | 4 | 4 | 15 | 27 | 46 | 60 | 75 | 34 |
| 23 | Grimsby Town | 46 | 10 | 6 | 7 | 29 | 22 | 2 | 3 | 18 | 16 | 47 | 45 | 69 | 33 |
| 24 | York City | 46 | 7 | 8 | 8 | 25 | 34 | 3 | 4 | 16 | 25 | 55 | 50 | 89 | 32 |

Final League Table 1977/78 Division 3

| | | Pl. | Home | | | | | Away | | | | | F. | A. | Pts |
|---|---|---|---|---|---|---|---|---|---|---|---|---|---|---|---|
| | | | W | D | L | F | A | W | D | L | F | A | | | |
| 1 | Wrexham | 46 | 14 | 8 | 1 | 48 | 19 | 9 | 7 | 7 | 30 | 26 | 78 | 45 | 61 |
| 2 | Cambridge United | 46 | 19 | 3 | 1 | 49 | 11 | 4 | 9 | 10 | 23 | 40 | 72 | 51 | 58 |
| 3 | Preston North End | 46 | 16 | 5 | 2 | 48 | 19 | 4 | 11 | 8 | 15 | 19 | 63 | 38 | 56 |
| 4 | Peterborough Utd. | 46 | 15 | 7 | 1 | 32 | 11 | 5 | 9 | 9 | 15 | 22 | 47 | 33 | 56 |
| ***5*** | ***Chester*** | ***46*** | ***14*** | ***8*** | ***1*** | ***41*** | ***24*** | ***2*** | ***14*** | ***7*** | ***18*** | ***32*** | ***59*** | ***56*** | ***54*** |
| 6 | Walsall | 46 | 12 | 8 | 3 | 35 | 17 | 6 | 9 | 8 | 26 | 33 | 61 | 50 | 53 |
| 7 | Gillingham | 46 | 11 | 10 | 2 | 36 | 21 | 4 | 10 | 9 | 31 | 39 | 67 | 60 | 50 |
| 8 | Colchester United | 46 | 10 | 11 | 2 | 36 | 16 | 5 | 7 | 11 | 19 | 28 | 55 | 44 | 48 |
| 9 | Chesterfield | 46 | 14 | 6 | 3 | 40 | 16 | 3 | 8 | 12 | 18 | 33 | 58 | 49 | 48 |
| 10 | Swindon Town | 46 | 12 | 7 | 4 | 40 | 22 | 4 | 9 | 10 | 27 | 38 | 67 | 60 | 48 |
| 11 | Shrewsbury Town | 46 | 11 | 7 | 5 | 42 | 23 | 5 | 8 | 10 | 21 | 34 | 63 | 57 | 47 |
| 12 | Tranmere Rovers | 46 | 13 | 7 | 3 | 39 | 19 | 3 | 8 | 12 | 18 | 33 | 57 | 52 | 47 |
| 13 | Carlisle United | 46 | 10 | 9 | 4 | 32 | 26 | 4 | 10 | 9 | 27 | 33 | 59 | 59 | 47 |
| 14 | Sheffield Wed. | 46 | 13 | 7 | 3 | 28 | 14 | 2 | 9 | 12 | 22 | 38 | 50 | 52 | 46 |
| 15 | Bury | 46 | 7 | 13 | 3 | 34 | 22 | 6 | 6 | 11 | 28 | 34 | 62 | 56 | 45 |
| 16 | Lincoln City | 46 | 10 | 8 | 5 | 35 | 26 | 5 | 7 | 11 | 18 | 35 | 53 | 61 | 45 |
| 17 | Exeter City | 46 | 11 | 8 | 4 | 30 | 18 | 4 | 6 | 13 | 19 | 41 | 49 | 59 | 44 |
| 18 | Oxford United | 46 | 11 | 10 | 2 | 38 | 21 | 2 | 4 | 17 | 26 | 46 | 64 | 67 | 40 |
| 19 | Plymouth Argyle | 46 | 7 | 8 | 8 | 33 | 28 | 4 | 9 | 10 | 28 | 40 | 61 | 68 | 39 |
| 20 | Rotherham United | 46 | 11 | 5 | 7 | 26 | 19 | 2 | 8 | 13 | 25 | 49 | 51 | 68 | 39 |
| 21 | Port Vale | 46 | 7 | 11 | 5 | 28 | 23 | 1 | 9 | 13 | 18 | 44 | 46 | 67 | 36 |
| 22 | Bradford City | 46 | 11 | 6 | 6 | 40 | 29 | 1 | 4 | 18 | 16 | 57 | 56 | 86 | 34 |
| 23 | Hereford United | 46 | 9 | 9 | 5 | 28 | 22 | 0 | 5 | 18 | 6 | 38 | 34 | 60 | 32 |
| 24 | Portsmouth | 46 | 4 | 11 | 8 | 31 | 38 | 3 | 6 | 14 | 10 | 37 | 41 | 75 | 31 |

Final League Table 1978/79 Division 3

| | | Pl. | Home | | | | | Away | | | | | F. | A. | Pts |
|---|---|---|---|---|---|---|---|---|---|---|---|---|---|---|---|
| | | | W | D | L | F | A | W | D | L | F | A | | | |
| 1 | Shrewsbury Town | 46 | 14 | 9 | 0 | 36 | 11 | 7 | 10 | 6 | 25 | 30 | 61 | 41 | 61 |
| 2 | Watford | 46 | 15 | 5 | 3 | 47 | 22 | 9 | 7 | 7 | 36 | 30 | 83 | 52 | 60 |
| 3 | Swansea City | 46 | 16 | 6 | 1 | 57 | 32 | 8 | 6 | 9 | 26 | 29 | 83 | 61 | 60 |
| 4 | Gillingham | 46 | 15 | 7 | 1 | 39 | 15 | 6 | 10 | 7 | 26 | 27 | 65 | 42 | 59 |
| 5 | Swindon Town | 46 | 17 | 2 | 4 | 44 | 14 | 8 | 5 | 10 | 30 | 38 | 74 | 52 | 57 |
| 6 | Carlisle United | 46 | 11 | 10 | 2 | 31 | 13 | 4 | 12 | 7 | 22 | 29 | 53 | 42 | 52 |
| 7 | Colchester United | 46 | 13 | 9 | 1 | 35 | 19 | 4 | 8 | 11 | 25 | 36 | 60 | 55 | 51 |
| 8 | Hull City | 46 | 12 | 9 | 2 | 36 | 14 | 7 | 2 | 14 | 30 | 47 | 66 | 61 | 49 |
| 9 | Exeter City | 46 | 14 | 6 | 3 | 38 | 18 | 3 | 9 | 11 | 23 | 38 | 61 | 56 | 49 |
| 10 | Brentford | 46 | 14 | 4 | 5 | 35 | 19 | 5 | 5 | 13 | 18 | 30 | 53 | 49 | 47 |
| 11 | Oxford United | 46 | 10 | 8 | 5 | 27 | 20 | 4 | 10 | 9 | 17 | 30 | 44 | 50 | 46 |
| 12 | Blackpool | 46 | 12 | 5 | 6 | 38 | 19 | 6 | 4 | 13 | 23 | 40 | 61 | 59 | 45 |
| 13 | Southend United | 46 | 11 | 6 | 6 | 30 | 17 | 4 | 9 | 10 | 21 | 32 | 51 | 49 | 45 |
| 14 | Sheffield Wed. | 46 | 9 | 8 | 6 | 30 | 22 | 4 | 11 | 8 | 23 | 31 | 53 | 53 | 45 |
| 15 | Plymouth Argyle | 46 | 11 | 9 | 3 | 40 | 27 | 4 | 5 | 14 | 27 | 41 | 67 | 68 | 44 |
| ***16*** | ***Chester*** | ***46*** | ***11*** | ***9*** | ***3*** | ***42*** | ***21*** | ***3*** | ***7*** | ***13*** | ***15*** | ***40*** | ***57*** | ***61*** | ***44*** |
| 17 | Rotherham United | 46 | 13 | 3 | 7 | 30 | 23 | 4 | 7 | 12 | 19 | 32 | 49 | 55 | 44 |
| 18 | Mansfield Town | 46 | 7 | 11 | 5 | 30 | 24 | 5 | 8 | 10 | 21 | 28 | 51 | 52 | 43 |
| 19 | Bury | 46 | 6 | 11 | 6 | 35 | 32 | 5 | 9 | 9 | 24 | 33 | 59 | 65 | 42 |
| 20 | Chesterfield | 46 | 10 | 5 | 8 | 35 | 34 | 3 | 9 | 11 | 16 | 31 | 51 | 65 | 40 |
| 21 | Peterborough Utd. | 46 | 8 | 7 | 8 | 26 | 24 | 3 | 7 | 13 | 18 | 39 | 44 | 63 | 36 |
| 22 | Walsall | 46 | 7 | 6 | 10 | 34 | 32 | 3 | 6 | 14 | 22 | 39 | 56 | 71 | 32 |
| 23 | Tranmere Rovers | 46 | 4 | 12 | 7 | 26 | 31 | 2 | 4 | 17 | 19 | 47 | 45 | 78 | 28 |
| 24 | Lincoln City | 46 | 5 | 7 | 11 | 26 | 38 | 2 | 4 | 17 | 15 | 50 | 41 | 88 | 25 |

Final League Table 1979/80 Division 3

| | | Pl. | Home | | | | | Away | | | | | F. | A. | Pts |
|---|---|---|---|---|---|---|---|---|---|---|---|---|---|---|---|
| | | | W | D | L | F | A | W | D | L | F | A | | | |
| 1 | Grimsby Town | 46 | 18 | 2 | 3 | 46 | 16 | 8 | 8 | 7 | 27 | 26 | 73 | 42 | 62 |
| 2 | Blackburn Rovers | 46 | 13 | 5 | 5 | 34 | 17 | 12 | 4 | 7 | 24 | 19 | 58 | 36 | 59 |
| 3 | Sheffield Wed. | 46 | 12 | 6 | 5 | 44 | 20 | 9 | 10 | 4 | 37 | 27 | 81 | 47 | 58 |
| 4 | Chesterfield | 46 | 16 | 5 | 2 | 46 | 16 | 7 | 6 | 10 | 25 | 30 | 71 | 46 | 57 |
| 5 | Colchester United | 46 | 10 | 10 | 3 | 39 | 20 | 10 | 2 | 11 | 25 | 36 | 64 | 56 | 52 |
| 6 | Carlisle United | 46 | 13 | 6 | 4 | 45 | 26 | 5 | 6 | 12 | 21 | 30 | 66 | 56 | 48 |
| 7 | Reading | 46 | 14 | 6 | 3 | 43 | 19 | 2 | 10 | 11 | 23 | 46 | 66 | 65 | 48 |
| 8 | Exeter City | 46 | 14 | 5 | 4 | 38 | 22 | 5 | 5 | 13 | 22 | 46 | 60 | 68 | 48 |
| ***9*** | ***Chester*** | ***46*** | ***14*** | ***6*** | ***3*** | ***29*** | ***18*** | ***3*** | ***7*** | ***13*** | ***20*** | ***39*** | ***49*** | ***57*** | ***47*** |
| 10 | Swindon Town | 46 | 15 | 4 | 4 | 50 | 20 | 4 | 4 | 15 | 21 | 43 | 71 | 63 | 46 |
| 11 | Barnsley | 46 | 10 | 7 | 6 | 29 | 20 | 6 | 7 | 10 | 24 | 36 | 53 | 56 | 46 |
| 12 | Sheffield United | 46 | 13 | 5 | 5 | 35 | 21 | 5 | 5 | 13 | 25 | 45 | 60 | 66 | 46 |
| 13 | Rotherham United | 46 | 13 | 4 | 6 | 38 | 24 | 5 | 6 | 12 | 20 | 42 | 58 | 66 | 46 |
| 14 | Millwall | 46 | 14 | 6 | 3 | 49 | 23 | 2 | 7 | 14 | 16 | 36 | 65 | 59 | 45 |
| 15 | Plymouth Argyle | 46 | 13 | 7 | 3 | 39 | 17 | 3 | 5 | 15 | 20 | 38 | 59 | 55 | 44 |
| 16 | Gillingham | 46 | 8 | 9 | 6 | 26 | 18 | 6 | 5 | 12 | 23 | 33 | 49 | 51 | 42 |
| 17 | Oxford United | 46 | 10 | 4 | 9 | 34 | 24 | 4 | 9 | 10 | 23 | 38 | 57 | 62 | 41 |
| 18 | Blackpool | 46 | 10 | 7 | 6 | 39 | 34 | 5 | 4 | 14 | 23 | 40 | 62 | 74 | 41 |
| 19 | Brentford | 46 | 10 | 6 | 7 | 33 | 26 | 5 | 5 | 13 | 26 | 47 | 59 | 73 | 41 |
| 20 | Hull City | 46 | 11 | 7 | 5 | 29 | 21 | 1 | 9 | 13 | 22 | 48 | 51 | 69 | 40 |
| 21 | Bury | 46 | 10 | 4 | 9 | 30 | 23 | 6 | 3 | 14 | 15 | 36 | 45 | 59 | 39 |
| 22 | Southend United | 46 | 11 | 6 | 6 | 33 | 23 | 3 | 4 | 16 | 14 | 35 | 47 | 58 | 38 |
| 23 | Mansfield Town | 46 | 9 | 9 | 5 | 31 | 24 | 1 | 7 | 15 | 16 | 34 | 47 | 58 | 36 |
| 24 | Wimbledon | 46 | 6 | 8 | 9 | 34 | 38 | 4 | 6 | 13 | 18 | 43 | 52 | 81 | 34 |

# *SEASON 1972-73*

## FOOTBALL LEAGUE DIVISION 4

| | Date | Opposition | | FT | HT | Att. | Goalscorers | Eadie J. | Edwards N. | Relish J. | Wallace R. | Turner G. | Pountney D. | Owen T. | Purdie B. | Draper D. | Clapham G. | Hollis M. | Griffiths N. | Davies G. | Kennedy D. | Carter R. | Taylor J. | Futcher G. | Matthewson R. | James J. | Futcher P. | Potter G. |
|---|---|---|---|---|---|---|---|---|---|---|---|---|---|---|---|---|---|---|---|---|---|---|---|---|---|---|---|---|
| 1 | Aug 12 | BURY | W | 2-0 | 1-0 | 3444 | Draper, Purdie | 1 | 2 | 3 | 4 | 5 | 6 | 7 | 8 | 9 | 10 | 11 | | | | | | | | | | |
| 2 | 19 | Newport County | L | 2-3 | 0-1 | 3342 | Draper, Relish | 1 | 5 | 3 | 4 | | 6 | 7 | | 9 | 10 | 11 | 2 | 8* | 12 | | | | | | | |
| 3 | 26 | PETERBOROUGH UNITED | W | 8-2 | 2-1 | 3162 | Purdie,Wallace(2,1 pen),Draper,Owen,Hollis(3) | 1 | 2 | | 4 | 5 | 6 | 7 | 8 | 9 | 10 | 11 | 3 | | | | | | | | | |
| 4 | 30 | COLCHESTER UNITED | W | 4-0 | 3-0 | 4304 | Wallace (2 pens), Hollis, Owen | 1 | 2 | | 4 | 5 | 6 | 7 | 8* | 9 | 10 | 11 | 3 | 12 | | | | | | | | |
| 5 | Sep 1 | Northampton Town | L | 0-1 | 0-0 | 4766 | | 1 | 2 | | 4 | 5 | 6 | 7 | 8* | 9 | 10 | 11 | 3 | | 12 | | | | | | | |
| 6 | 9 | ALDERSHOT | D | 0-0 | 0-0 | 3846 | | 1 | | 2 | 4 | 5 | 6 | | 9 | | 10 | 11 | 3 | 12 | 7 | 8* | | | | | | |
| 7 | 16 | Darlington | D | 1-1 | 0-1 | 1401 | Owen | | 2 | 3 | 4 | 5 | 6 | 7 | 8 | | 12 | 11 | | | 10 | 9* | 1 | | | | | |
| 8 | 23 | CREWE ALEX. | W | 2-1 | 2-0 | 3834 | Wallace (pen), Purdie | | 2 | | 4 | 5 | 6 | 7 | 8 | | | 11 | 3 | 9 | 10 | | 1 | | | | | |
| 9 | 26 | SOUTHPORT | D | 0-0 | 0-0 | 4564 | | | 2 | | 4 | 5 | 6 | 7 | 8 | | 11 | | 3 | 9 | 10 | | 1 | | | | | |
| 10 | 30 | Barnsley | D | 0-0 | 0-0 | 2784 | | | 2 | | 4 | 5 | 6 | 8 | 9 | 10 | 11 | | 3 | | 7 | | 1 | | | | | |
| 11 | Oct 4 | Bradford City | W | 1-0 | 1-0 | 2283 | Hollis | | 2 | | 4 | 5 | 6 | 7 | 8 | 9 | | 11 | 3 | | 10 | | 1 | | | | | |
| 12 | 7 | Workington | L | 1-3 | 0-0 | 1379 | Draper | | 2 | | 4 | 5 | 6 | 7* | 8 | 9 | 12 | 11 | 3 | | 10 | | 1 | | | | | |
| 13 | 11 | HARTLEPOOL | W | 2-0 | 0-0 | 3254 | Wallace (pen), Purdie | | 2 | | 4 | 5 | 6 | 7 | 8 | 9 | | 11 | 3 | | 10 | | 1 | | | | | |
| 14 | 14 | LINCOLN CITY | W | 2-1 | 2-0 | 3616 | Hollis, Draper | | 2 | | 4 | 5 | 6 | 7 | 8* | 9 | 12 | 11 | 3 | | 10 | | 1 | | | | | |
| 15 | 21 | Mansfield Town | L | 1-4 | 1-1 | 5787 | Griffiths | | 2 | | 4 | 5 | 6 | 7 | | 9 | 12 | 11* | 3 | | 8 | 10 | 1 | | | | | |
| 16 | 24 | Doncaster Rovers | D | 0-0 | 0-0 | 2240 | | | 2 | | 4 | 5 | 6 | | | 8 | 10 | 11 | 3 | 9 | 7 | | 1 | | | | | |
| 17 | 28 | CAMBRIDGE UNITED | D | 1-1 | 1-1 | 3412 | Turner | | 2 | | 4 | 5 | 6 | 7 | 8 | 9 | 10* | 11 | 3 | 12 | | | 1 | | | | | |
| 18 | Nov 3 | Southport | L | 2-3 | 1-1 | 3662 | Draper, Purdie | | 2 | | 4 | 5 | 6 | 7 | 8 | 9 | | 11* | 3 | 12 | 10 | | 1 | | | | | |
| 19 | 11 | BRADFORD CITY | D | 1-1 | 0-1 | 2710 | Draper | | 2 | | 4 | 5 | 6 | 7 | 8 | 9 | | 11* | 3 | 12 | 10 | | 1 | | | | | |
| 20 | 25 | Torquay United | W | 2-1 | 0-1 | 2511 | Owen, Draper | | 2 | | 4 | 5 | 6 | 7 | 8 | 9 | | 11 | 3 | | 10 | | 1 | | | | | |
| 21 | Dec 1 | STOCKPORT COUNTY | W | 2-0 | 2-0 | 3196 | Kennedy, Draper | | 2 | | 4 | 5 | 6 | 7 | 8 | 9 | | 11 | 3 | | 10 | | 1 | | | | | |
| 22 | 9 | Gillingham | L | 0-1 | 0-1 | 3162 | | | 2 | | 4 | 5 | 6 | | 8 | 9 | | 11* | 3 | 12 | 7 | | 1 | 10 | | | | |
| 23 | 23 | EXETER CITY | L | 0-1 | 0-1 | 2560 | | | 2 | 3 | 4 | 5 | 6 | 7* | 8 | 9 | | 11 | | 12 | 10 | | 1 | | | | | |
| 24 | 26 | Crewe Alex. | D | 1-1 | 1-1 | 3204 | Davies | | 2 | 3 | 4 | 5 | 6 | | 8 | 10 | 11 | 12 | | 9 | 7* | | 1 | | | | | |
| 25 | 30 | NEWPORT COUNTY | L | 0-2 | 0-2 | 2844 | | | 2 | 3 | 4 | 5 | 6 | | 8 | 10 | 11* | 12 | | 9 | 7 | | 1 | | | | | |
| 26 | Jan 6 | Peterborough United | D | 2-2 | 0-1 | 3821 | Davies, Kennedy | | 2 | | | 5 | 6 | | | 9 | 10 | 11 | 3 | 8 | 7 | 4 | 1 | | | | | |
| 27 | 17 | Hereford United | L | 1-3 | 0-3 | 8795 | Clapham | | 2 | | 6 | | 5 | | 12 | 9 | 10 | 11* | 3 | 8 | 7 | 4 | 1 | | | | | |
| 28 | 27 | Aldershot | D | 1-1 | 0-0 | 3581 | Purdie | | 2 | | 4 | | 6 | 7* | 8 | 9 | 10 | 11 | 3 | 12 | | | 1 | | 5 | | | |
| 29 | Feb 3 | Hartlepool | D | 0-0 | 0-0 | 2826 | | | 2 | | 4 | | 6 | | 8 | 9 | 10 | 11 | 3 | 7 | | | 1 | | 5 | | | |
| 30 | 10 | DARLINGTON | W | 5-0 | 2-0 | 1873 | Davies, Griffiths, James, Hollis, Purdie | | 2 | | | | 6 | 7* | 10 | 4 | | 11 | 3 | 8 | | | 1 | 12 | 5 | 9 | | |
| 31 | 17 | Bury | D | 1-1 | 1-0 | 3461 | James | | 2 | | 6 | | | | 11 | 4 | 10 | 7 | 3 | 8 | | | 1 | | 5 | 9 | | |
| 32 | 20 | DONCASTER ROVERS | L | 1-2 | 0-0 | 2561 | Hollis | | 2 | | 6 | | | | 11* | 4 | 10 | 7 | 3 | 8 | 12 | | 1 | | 5 | 9 | | |
| 33 | 24 | HEREFORD UNITED | L | 0-1 | 0-1 | 4264 | | | | | 2 | | 6 | | | 4 | 10 | 11 | 3 | 8 | 7 | | 1 | | 5 | 9 | | |
| 34 | Mar 3 | WORKINGTON | L | 1-3 | 1-1 | 1611 | Walker (og) | | 2 | | 4 | | 6 | 7 | | | | 11 | 3 | 8 | 10 | | 1 | | 5 | 9 | | |
| 35 | 7 | READING | W | 2-0 | 2-0 | 1264 | Wallace (pen), James | | 2 | | 4 | | 5 | 11 | | 9 | | | 3 | | 10 | | 1 | 7 | 6 | 8 | | |
| 36 | 10 | Lincoln City | L | 0-1 | 0-1 | 3591 | | | 2 | | 4 | | 5 | 11 | | 9 | | | 3 | 12 | 10 | | 1 | 7* | 6 | 8 | | |
| 37 | 17 | MANSFIELD TOWN | D | 2-2 | 0-1 | 1964 | Draper (2) | | 2* | | 4 | | 5 | 7 | | 9 | | 11 | 3 | 12 | 10 | | 1 | | 6 | 8 | | |
| 38 | 24 | Cambridge United | L | 0-1 | 0-0 | 3935 | | | | | 4 | | 6 | 7 | | 8 | | 10 | 3 | | | 11 | 1 | | 5 | 9 | 2 | |
| 39 | 28 | NORTHAMPTON TOWN | W | 3-0 | 1-0 | 1336 | James, Draper (2) | | | | | | 6 | 7 | | 10 | | 11 | 3 | | 8 | 4 | 1 | | 5 | 9 | 2 | |
| 40 | 31 | TORQUAY UNITED | L | 1-2 | 0-0 | 1268 | Kennedy | | 2 | | | | 6 | 8 | 12 | 9 | | 11 | 3 | | 7 | 4 | 1 | | 5 | 10* | | |
| 41 | Apr 6 | Stockport County | L | 1-2 | 0-1 | 2638 | Wallace (pen) | | 2 | | 8 | | 6 | 7 | | 9 | 11 | | 3 | | 10 | 4 | 1 | | 5 | | | |
| 42 | 14 | GILLINGHAM | W | 1-0 | 0-0 | 1286 | Davies | | 2 | | 10 | | 6 | 7 | 8 | 9 | 11* | | 3 | 12 | | 4 | 1 | | 5 | | | |
| 43 | 20 | BARNSLEY | D | 0-0 | 0-0 | 2136 | | | 2 | | 10 | | 6 | 7 | 11 | 9* | | 12 | 3 | | | 4 | 1 | | 5 | 8 | | |
| 44 | 21 | Reading | L | 1-2 | 0-0 | 4478 | Wallace (pen) | | 2 | | 10 | | 6 | 7 | 8 | | | | 3 | | 11 | 4 | 1 | | 5 | 9 | | |
| 45 | 23 | Exeter City | D | 0-0 | 0-0 | 3863 | | | 2 | | 10 | | 6 | 7 | 12 | | | | 3 | 9 | 11* | 4 | 1 | | 5 | 8 | | |
| 46 | 27 | Colchester United | W | 3-2 | 3-0 | 2689 | James (2), Davies | | 2 | 3 | | | 6 | 7 | 11 | | | | | 9 | 10 | 4 | 1 | | 5 | 8 | | |
| | | | | | | | Apps. | 6 | 42 | 8 | 41 | 25 | 44 | 35 | 31 | 38 | 21 | 34 | 40 | 16 | 32 | 14 | 40 | 3 | 19 | 15 | 2 | |
| | | | | | | | Subs. | | | | | | | | 3 | | 4 | 3 | | 11 | 3 | | | 1 | | | | |
| | | | | | | | Goals | | | 1 | 9 | 1 | | 4 | 7 | 13 | 1 | 8 | 2 | 5 | 3 | | | | | 6 | | |

Own goals 1

## F.A. CUP

| | Date | Opposition | | FT | HT | Att. | Goalscorers | Eadie J. | Edwards N. | Relish J. | Wallace R. | Turner G. | Pountney D. | Owen T. | Purdie B. | Draper D. | Clapham G. | Hollis M. | Griffiths N. | Davies G. | Kennedy D. | Carter R. | Taylor J. | Futcher G. | Matthewson R. | James J. | Futcher P. | Potter G. |
|---|---|---|---|---|---|---|---|---|---|---|---|---|---|---|---|---|---|---|---|---|---|---|---|---|---|---|---|---|
| 1R | Nov 18 | Bolton Wanderers | D | 1-1 | 0-1 | 9620 | Hollis | | 2 | | 4 | 5 | 6 | 7 | 12 | 8 | | 11 | 3 | 9* | 10 | | 1 | | | | | |
| 1Rr | 22 | BOLTON WANDERERS | L | 0-1 | 0-1 | 7611 | | | 2 | | 4 | 5 | 6 | 7 | 8 | 9 | | 11 | 3 | | 10 | | 1 | | | | | |

## LEAGUE CUP

| | Date | Opposition | | FT | HT | Att. | Goalscorers | Eadie J. | Edwards N. | Relish J. | Wallace R. | Turner G. | Pountney D. | Owen T. | Purdie B. | Draper D. | Clapham G. | Hollis M. | Griffiths N. | Davies G. | Kennedy D. | Carter R. | Taylor J. | Futcher G. | Matthewson R. | James J. | Futcher P. | Potter G. |
|---|---|---|---|---|---|---|---|---|---|---|---|---|---|---|---|---|---|---|---|---|---|---|---|---|---|---|---|---|
| 1R | Aug 16 | SHREWSBURY TOWN | W | 4-3 | 0-2 | 3521 | Hollis, Wallace (pen), Draper (2) | 1 | 2 | 3 | 4 | 5 | 6 | 7 | 8 | 9 | 10 | 11 | | | | | | | | | | |
| 2R | Sep 5 | Southampton | D | 0-0 | 0-0 | 10236 | | 1 | | 2 | 4 | 5 | 6 | | 8 | 9 | | 11 | 3 | | 10 | 7 | | | | | | |
| 2Rr | 13 | SOUTHAMPTON * | D | 2-2 | 0-1 | 8308 | Hollis, Draper | | 2 | 3 | 4 | 5 | 6 | 7* | 8 | 9 | 12 | 11 | | | 10 | | 1 | | | | | |
| 2R2r | 20 | Southampton @ | L | 0-2 | 0-1 | 2417 | | | 2 | | 4 | 5 | 6 | 7 | 8 | | | 11 | 3 | 9 | 10 | | 1 | | | | | |

* Extra time played following score of 1-1 after 90 minutes

@ Played at West Bromwich Albion

## WELSH CUP

| | Date | Opposition | | FT | HT | Att. | Goalscorers | Eadie J. | Edwards N. | Relish J. | Wallace R. | Turner G. | Pountney D. | Owen T. | Purdie B. | Draper D. | Clapham G. | Hollis M. | Griffiths N. | Davies G. | Kennedy D. | Carter R. | Taylor J. | Futcher G. | Matthewson R. | James J. | Futcher P. | Potter G. |
|---|---|---|---|---|---|---|---|---|---|---|---|---|---|---|---|---|---|---|---|---|---|---|---|---|---|---|---|---|
| 4R | Jan 13 | WREXHAM | W | 1-0 | 1-0 | 3588 | Wallace (pen) | | 2 | | 6 | | 5 | | | 9 | 10 | 11 | 3 | 8 | 7 | 4 | 1 | | | | | |
| 5R | Feb 15 | Welshpool Town | D | 1-1 | 0-0 | | Davies | | 6 | 2 | | | | 7 | 8 | 4 | | 10 | 3 | 9 | 11 | | 1 | | 5 | | | |
| 5Rr | 28 | WELSHPOOL TOWN | W | 1-0 | 1-0 | 1755 | Draper | | 2 | | 4 | | 6 | 7 | | 9 | | 11 | 3 | 8 | 10 | | 1 | | 5 | | | |
| SF | Mar 21 | CARDIFF CITY | L | 0-1 | 0-0 | 2158 | | | | | 4 | | 6 | 7 | | 9 | | | 3 | | 10 | 11 | 1 | | 2 | 8 | | 5 |

## FRIENDLIES

| | Date | Opposition | | FT | HT | Att. | Goalscorers |
|---|---|---|---|---|---|---|---|
| 1 | Jul 31 | Kidderminster Harriers | W | 3-2 | | | Hollis, Owen, Wallace |
| 2 | Aug 5 | Walsall | D | 0-0 | 0-0 | 1188 | |

# SEASON 1973-74

## FOOTBALL LEAGUE DIVISION 4

| | Date | Opposition | | FT | HT | Att. | Goalscorers | Taylor J. | Mason S. | Relish J. | Horne S. | James J. | Grummett J. | Redfern J. | Davies G. | Draper D. | Kennedy D. | Whitehead N. | Edwards N. | Griffiths N. | Potter G. | Carter R. | Owen T. | Dunleavy C. | Seddon I. | Futcher P. | Futcher R. | Millington G. | Matthewson R. | Loska A. |
|---|---|---|---|---|---|---|---|---|---|---|---|---|---|---|---|---|---|---|---|---|---|---|---|---|---|---|---|---|---|---|
| 1 | Aug 25 | Swansea City | L | 0-2 | 0-0 | 2500 | | 1 | 2 | 3* | 4 | 5 | 6 | 7 | 8 | 9 | 10 | 11 | 12 | | | | | | | | | | | |
| 2 | 31 | HARTLEPOOL | W | 3-1 | 2-1 | 2193 | James (2), Whitehead | 1 | 2 | | 4 | 8 | 6 | 7 | | 9 | | 11 | | 3 | 5 | 10 | | | | | | | | |
| 3 | Sep 8 | Newport County | W | 2-0 | 1-0 | 3660 | James, Whitehead | 1 | 2 | | 4 | 8 | 6 | 7 | | 9 | | 11 | | 3 | 5 | 10 | | | | | | | | |
| 4 | 12 | WORKINGTON | W | 1-0 | 1-0 | 3071 | Draper | 1 | 2 | | 4 | 8 | 6 | 7* | 12 | 9 | | 11 | | 3 | 5 | 10 | | | | | | | | |
| 5 | 15 | EXETER CITY | L | 0-1 | 0-0 | 2884 | | 1 | 2 | | 4 | 8 | 6 | 7 | 12 | 9* | | 11 | | 3 | 5 | 10 | | | | | | | | |
| 6 | 17 | Mansfield Town | L | 0-3 | 0-1 | 3936 | | 1 | 2 | | 4 | 8 | 6 | 7 | | 9 | | 11 | | 3 | 5 | 10* | 12 | | | | | | | |
| 7 | 22 | Darlington | W | 2-1 | 1-0 | 1818 | James (2) | 1 | 2 | | 4 | 10 | 6 | | 8 | 9 | | 11 | | 3 | | | 7 | 5 | | | | | | |
| 8 | 29 | LINCOLN CITY | L | 2-3 | 1-3 | 2762 | Owen, Griffiths | 1 | 2 | | 4 | 10 | 6 | | 12 | 9 | | 11* | | 3 | | | 7 | 5 | 8 | | | | | |
| 9 | Oct 3 | MANSFIELD TOWN | D | 1-1 | 0-1 | 2547 | James | 1 | 2 | | 4 | 10 | 6 | 7 | | 9 | | 12 | | 3 | | | 11 | 5 | 8* | | | | | |
| 10 | 6 | Bury | L | 1-3 | 0-2 | 5519 | Griffiths | 1 | | | 4 | 10 | 6 | 7 | | 9 | | 11 | | 3 | | | 8* | 5 | 12 | 2 | | | | |
| 11 | 13 | DONCASTER ROVERS | W | 3-0 | 1-0 | 2006 | Redfern, Draper, James | 1 | | | 4 | 10 | 6 | 7 | | 9 | | 11 | 2 | 3 | | 8 | | 5 | | | | | | |
| 12 | 20 | GILLINGHAM | L | 2-4 | 1-1 | 2055 | Redfern, Seddon | 1 | 12 | | 4 | 9 | 6 | 7 | | | | 11 | 2* | 3 | | 10 | | 5 | 8 | | | | | |
| 13 | 24 | Workington | D | 1-1 | 1-1 | 862 | James | 1 | 2 | | 4 | 10 | | 11 | | 9 | | 7 | | 3 | | | | 5 | | 6 | 8 | | | |
| 14 | 27 | Bradford City | D | 1-1 | 1-0 | 3361 | Draper | 1 | 2 | | | 10 | 6 | 7 | | 9 | | 11 | | 3 | | | | 5 | | 4 | 8 | | | |
| 15 | Nov 3 | ROTHERHAM UNITED | W | 1-0 | 0-0 | 2385 | Mason | 1 | 2 | | 4 | 10 | | 7 | | 9 | | 11 | | 3 | | | | 5 | 12 | 6 | 8* | | | |
| 16 | 10 | Scunthorpe United | L | 1-2 | 0-1 | 2164 | James | 1 | 2 | | 4 | 11 | 12 | 7 | | 9 | | | | 3 | | | | 5 | 8 | 6 | 10* | | | |
| 17 | 14 | COLCHESTER UNITED | L | 0-4 | 0-2 | 1973 | | 1 | 2 | | 8* | 10 | 4 | 11 | | 9 | | | 12 | 3 | | | | 5 | 7 | 6 | | | | |
| 18 | 17 | Brentford | L | 0-3 | 0-2 | 5167 | | 1 | 3 | | 12 | 10 | 6* | 7 | | 9 | | 11 | 2 | | | | | 5 | 8 | 4 | | | | |
| 19 | Dec 8 | TORQUAY UNITED | D | 1-1 | 1-0 | 1550 | James | | 2 | | 4 | 10 | | 11 | | 9 | | 7 | 3 | | | 8* | | | | 6 | | 1 | 5 | 12 |
| 20 | 22 | Lincoln City | D | 2-2 | 0-1 | 3142 | Owen, Loska | | 2 | | | | | 8 | | 9 | | 7 | 3 | | | 4 | 10 | 5 | | | | 1 | 6 | 11 |
| 21 | 26 | CREWE ALEX. | W | 1-0 | 0-0 | 3339 | James | | 2 | | | 10 | | 8 | | 9 | | 7 | 3 | | | 4* | 11 | 5 | | | | 1 | 6 | 12 |
| 22 | 29 | NEWPORT COUNTY | W | 3-0 | 1-0 | 2621 | Owen (2), James | | 2 | | | 10 | | 8 | | 9 | | 7 | 3 | | | 4 | 11 | 5 | | | | 1 | 6 | |
| 23 | Jan 1 | Hartlepool | D | 0-0 | 0-0 | 3050 | | | 2 | | | 10 | | 8 | | 9 | | 7 | 3 | | | 4 | 11 | 5 | | | | 1 | 6 | |
| 24 | 12 | Exeter City | L | 1-2 | 1-2 | 5047 | Draper | | | 3 | | 10 | | 8 | | 9 | | 7 | 2 | | | 4* | 11 | 5 | 12 | | | 1 | 6 | |
| 25 | 19 | SWANSEA CITY | W | 1-0 | 1-0 | 2407 | James (pen) | | 2 | | | 10 | | 8 | | 9 | | 7 | 3 | | | 4* | 11 | 5 | 12 | | | 1 | 6 | |
| 26 | 27 | Barnsley | D | 1-1 | 0-0 | 8294 | Murphy (og) | | 2 | | | 10 | | 8 | | 9 | | 7 | 3 | | | 4 | 11* | 5 | 12 | | | 1 | 6 | |
| 27 | Feb 2 | Peterborough United | D | 0-0 | 0-0 | 7683 | | | 2 | | | 10* | | 8 | | 9 | | 7 | 3 | | | 4 | | 5 | 11 | | | 1 | 6 | 12 |
| 28 | 10 | DARLINGTON | W | 1-0 | 0-0 | 3172 | Owen | | 2 | | | | | 8 | | 9 | | 7 | 3 | | | 4 | 11 | 5 | 10 | | | 1 | 6* | 12 |
| 29 | 17 | Doncaster Rovers | W | 2-1 | 0-1 | 2478 | Seddon, Draper | | 2 | | | | | | | 9 | | 7 | 3 | | | 4 | 11 | 5 | 8 | 6 | | 1 | | 10 |
| 30 | 24 | BURY | D | 1-1 | 0-1 | 6075 | James | | 2 | | | 10 | | | | 9 | | 7* | 3 | | | 4 | 11 | 5 | 8 | 6 | | 1 | | 12 |
| 31 | Mar 3 | Crewe Alex. | L | 0-1 | 0-1 | 3251 | | | 3 | | | 10 | | | | 9 | | 7 | 2 | | | 4 | 11* | 5 | 8 | | | 1 | 6 | 12 |
| 32 | 10 | BRADFORD CITY | W | 1-0 | 1-0 | 2534 | Seddon | 1 | 2 | 12 | | 10 | | | | 9 | | 7 | 3 | | | 4 | | 5 | 8 | | | | 6* | 11 |
| 33 | 17 | Gillingham | L | 0-1 | 0-1 | 7541 | | 1 | | | | 10 | | 11 | | 9 | | 7 | 2 | | 5 | 4 | | 6 | 8 | | | | | 3 |
| 34 | 20 | PETERBOROUGH UNITED | W | 2-1 | 2-1 | 1678 | Redfern, Seddon | 1 | | | | 10 | | 11 | | 9 | | 7 | 2 | | 5 | 4* | 12 | 6 | 8 | | | | | 3 |
| 35 | 23 | SCUNTHORPE UNITED | W | 2-0 | 2-0 | 2038 | Owen, Mason | 1 | 4 | | | | | 11 | | 9 | | 7 | 2 | | 5 | | 10 | 6 | 8 | | | | | 3 |
| 36 | 26 | Northampton Town | D | 3-3 | 1-2 | 5969 | Tucker (og), Whitehead, Redfern | 1 | 4 | | | | | 11 | | 9 | | 7 | 2 | | 5 | | 10 | 6 | 8 | | | | | 3 |
| 37 | 30 | Rotherham United | L | 2-3 | 1-1 | 1945 | Owen, James | | 4 | | | 9 | | 10 | | | | 11* | 2 | | 5 | | 8 | 6 | 7 | | | 1 | 12 | 3 |
| 38 | Apr 3 | BARNSLEY | W | 3-1 | 2-1 | 2001 | James (2), Loska | | 4 | | | 10 | | 7 | | 9 | | | 2 | | | | 11 | 5 | 8 | 6 | | 1 | | 3 |
| 39 | 5 | Colchester United | D | 1-1 | 1-0 | 6371 | Owen | | 4 | | | 10 | | 7 | | 9 | | | 2 | | | 12 | 11 | 5* | 8 | 6 | | 1 | | 3 |
| 40 | 13 | BRENTFORD | D | 0-0 | 0-0 | 2643 | | | 8 | | | 10 | | 11 | | | | | 2 | | | 4 | 9 | | 7 | 6 | | 1 | 5 | 3 |
| 41 | 15 | Stockport County | W | 1-0 | 1-0 | 2111 | Mason | | 4 | | | 10 | | 7 | | 9 | | | 2 | | | | 11 | | 8 | 6 | | 1 | 5 | 3 |
| 42 | 16 | STOCKPORT COUNTY | W | 2-1 | 0-0 | 2438 | James (2) | | 4 | | | 10* | | 7 | | 9 | | 12 | 2 | | | | 11 | | 8 | 6 | | 1 | 5 | 3 |
| 43 | 20 | Torquay United | D | 2-2 | 1-0 | 2718 | James (2, 1 pen) | | 4* | | | 10 | | 7 | | 9 | | 12 | 2 | | | | 11 | 5 | 8 | 6 | | 1 | | 3 |
| 44 | 22 | Reading | L | 0-3 | 0-0 | 3121 | | | 4 | | | 10 | | 7* | | 9 | | 12 | 2 | | | | 11 | 5 | 8 | 6 | | 1 | | 3 |
| 45 | 27 | READING | D | 0-0 | 0-0 | 2076 | | | 4 | | | 10 | | 7* | | 9 | | 12 | 2 | | | | 11 | 5 | 8 | 6 | | 1 | | 3 |
| 46 | May 1 | NORTHAMPTON TOWN | D | 0-0 | 0-0 | 1800 | | | 4 | | | 10 | | | | 9 | | 7 | 2 | | | | 11 | 5 | 8 | | | 1 | 6 | 3 |
| | | | | | | | Apps. | 23 | 40 | 2 | 17 | 41 | 15 | 39 | 2 | 43 | 1 | 35 | 31 | 16 | 10 | 24 | 27 | 36 | 26 | 18 | 4 | 23 | 16 | 17 |
| | | | | | | | Subs. | | 1 | 1 | 1 | | 1 | | 3 | | | 5 | 2 | | | 1 | 2 | | 5 | | | | 1 | 6 |
| | | | | | | | Goals | | 3 | | | 21 | | 4 | | 5 | | 3 | | 2 | | | 8 | | 4 | | | | | 2 |

Own goals 2

## F.A. CUP

| | Date | Opposition | | FT | HT | Att. | Goalscorers | Taylor J. | Mason S. | Relish J. | Horne S. | James J. | Grummett J. | Redfern J. | Davies G. | Draper D. | Kennedy D. | Whitehead N. | Edwards N. | Griffiths N. | Potter G. | Carter R. | Owen T. | Dunleavy C. | Seddon I. | Futcher P. | Futcher R. | Millington G. | Matthewson R. | Loska A. |
|---|---|---|---|---|---|---|---|---|---|---|---|---|---|---|---|---|---|---|---|---|---|---|---|---|---|---|---|---|---|---|
| 1R | Nov 24 | TELFORD UNITED | W | 1-0 | 0-0 | 2729 | Grummett | | 2 | | 8 | 10 | 6 | 11 | | 9 | | 7 | 3 | | | | | 5 | | 4 | | 1 | | |
| 2R | Dec 15 | HUDDERSFIELD TOWN | W | 3-2 | 3-1 | 3298 | Owen, James, Draper | | 2 | | | 10 | | 8 | | 9 | | 7 | 3 | | | 4 | 11 | 5 | | | | 1 | 6 | |
| 3R | Jan 5 | Aston Villa | L | 1-3 | 1-1 | 16545 | James | | 2 | | | 10 | | 8 | | 9 | | 7 | 3 | | | 4 | 11* | 5 | 12 | | | 1 | 6 | |

## LEAGUE CUP

| | Date | Opposition | | FT | HT | Att. | Goalscorers | Taylor J. | Mason S. | Relish J. | Horne S. | James J. | Grummett J. | Redfern J. | Davies G. | Draper D. | Kennedy D. | Whitehead N. | Edwards N. | Griffiths N. | Potter G. | Carter R. | Owen T. | Dunleavy C. | Seddon I. | Futcher P. | Futcher R. | Millington G. | Matthewson R. | Loska A. |
|---|---|---|---|---|---|---|---|---|---|---|---|---|---|---|---|---|---|---|---|---|---|---|---|---|---|---|---|---|---|---|
| 1R | Aug 29 | WREXHAM | L | 0-2 | 0-1 | 4791 | | 1 | 2 | | 4 | 8 | 6 | 7 | | 9 | 10 | 11 | 5 | 3 | | | | | | | | | | |

## WELSH CUP

| | Date | Opposition | | FT | HT | Att. | Goalscorers | Taylor J. | Mason S. | Relish J. | Horne S. | James J. | Grummett J. | Redfern J. | Davies G. | Draper D. | Kennedy D. | Whitehead N. | Edwards N. | Griffiths N. | Potter G. | Carter R. | Owen T. | Dunleavy C. | Seddon I. | Futcher P. | Futcher R. | Millington G. | Matthewson R. | Loska A. |
|---|---|---|---|---|---|---|---|---|---|---|---|---|---|---|---|---|---|---|---|---|---|---|---|---|---|---|---|---|---|---|
| 4R | Jan 23 | BETHESDA ATHLETIC | W | 2-1 | 2-0 | 679 | James, Redfern | | 2 | 3 | | 10 | | 8 | | | | 7 | | | | | | 5 | 4 | 6 | 9 | 1 | | 11 |
| 5R | Feb 6 | Wrexham | L | 0-1 | 0-0 | 6904 | | | 4 | 3 | | | | 8* | | | | 7 | 2 | | | | | 5 | 10 | 12 | 9 | 1 | 6 | 11 |

## FRIENDLIES

| | Date | Opposition | | FT | HT | Att. | Goalscorers |
|---|---|---|---|---|---|---|---|
| 1 | Aug 11 | Shrewsbury Town | L | 0-2 | 0-2 | | |
| 2 | 13 | Colwyn Bay | W | 5-0 | 0-0 | | Unknown (5) |
| 3 | 15 | PORT VALE | L | 0-1 | 0-1 | 1148 | |
| 4 | 16 | Warley County Borough | W | 4-0 | | | Unknown (4) |

**1973/74 Season:** (Back) James, Taylor, Griffiths.
(Middle) Mason, Dunleavy, Grummett, Millington, Horne, Davies, Sear (Coach)
(Front) Carter, Whitehead, Owen, Roberts (Manager), Redfern, Draper, Seddon.

**1974/75 Season:**
(Back) Sear (Youth Team Coach), Storton, Edwards, Matthewson, Millington, Loska, Mason, Coxon, Green (Coach).
(Front) Whitehead, Seddon, Draper, Roberts (Manager), James, Lennard, Owen.

# *SEASON 1974-75*

## FOOTBALL LEAGUE DIVISION 4

| | Date | Opposition | | FT | HT | Att. | Goalscorers | Millington G. | Edwards N. | Loska A. | Storton T. | Matthewson R. | Mason S. | Whitehead N. | Seddon I. | Draper D. | James J. | Owen T. | Moore G. | Dunleavy C. | Lennard D. | Redfern J. | Potter G. | Pugh G. | Taylor J. | Raynor P. | Lunn P. | Rowlands C. | Morris A. |
|---|---|---|---|---|---|---|---|---|---|---|---|---|---|---|---|---|---|---|---|---|---|---|---|---|---|---|---|---|---|
| 1 | Aug 17 | Lincoln City | L | 1-2 | 1-0 | 2903 | Owen | 1 | 2 | 3 | 4 | 5 | 6 | 7 | 8 | 9 | 10 | 11 | | | | | | | | | | | |
| 2 | 24 | HARTLEPOOL | W | 3-0 | 1-0 | 2728 | Seddon, Draper, James | 1 | 2 | 3 | | 6 | | 7 | 8 | 9 | 10 | 11 | 4 | 5 | | | | | | | | | |
| 3 | 31 | Barnsley | W | 1-0 | 1-0 | 6006 | Edwards | 1 | 2 | 3 | 4 | 6 | | 7* | 8 | 9 | 10 | 11 | 12 | 5 | | | | | | | | | |
| 4 | Sep 3 | Cambridge United | L | 0-3 | 0-2 | 2763 | | 1 | 2 | 3 | 4 | 6 | 12 | 7 | 8* | 9 | 10 | | 11 | 5 | | | | | | | | | |
| 5 | 7 | BRENTFORD | W | 2-0 | 0-0 | 2469 | Draper, Owen | 1 | 2 | 3 | 4* | 6 | | 7 | 8 | 9 | 10 | 11 | 12 | 5 | | | | | | | | | |
| 6 | 14 | Bradford City | L | 0-2 | 0-2 | 3329 | | 1 | 2 | 3 | 4 | 6 | | 7 | 8 | 9 | 10* | 11 | 12 | 5 | | | | | | | | | |
| 7 | 17 | Shrewsbury Town | L | 0-2 | 0-1 | 3637 | | 1 | 2 | 3 | 4 | | 6 | 7 | 8 | 9 | 10 | | 11 | 5 | | | | | | | | | |
| 8 | 21 | TORQUAY UNITED | W | 3-0 | 1-0 | 2467 | James, Edwards, Seddon | 1 | 2 | 3 | 4 | 6 | 11 | 7 | 8 | 9 | 10 | | 12 | 5* | | | | | | | | | |
| 9 | 25 | READING | W | 2-0 | 2-0 | 6642 | James, Whitehead | 1 | 2 | 3 | 4 | 5 | 6 | 7 | 8 | 9* | 10 | | 12 | | 11 | | | | | | | | |
| 10 | 27 | Mansfield Town | D | 0-0 | 0-0 | 3182 | | 1 | 2 | 3 | 4 | 5 | 6 | 7 | 8 | | 10 | | 9 | | 11 | | | | | | | | |
| 11 | Oct 2 | DONCASTER ROVERS | W | 3-0 | 3-0 | 2748 | Loska, James, Draper | 1 | 2 | 3 | 4 | 5 | 6 | 7* | 8 | 9 | 10 | | 12 | | 11 | | | | | | | | |
| 12 | 5 | SCUNTHORPE UNITED | W | 1-0 | 1-0 | 2857 | James (pen) | 1 | 2 | 3 | 4 | 5 | 6 | | 8 | 9 | 10 | | 12 | | 11 | 7* | | | | | | | |
| 13 | 11 | Southport | L | 1-2 | 0-1 | 2179 | Lennard | 1 | 2 | 3 | 4 | 5 | 6 | | 8 | 9 | 10* | | 12 | | 11 | 7 | | | | | | | |
| 14 | 19 | CREWE ALEX. | W | 2-0 | 0-0 | 4063 | Lennard, Draper | 1 | 2 | 3 | 4 | 5 | 6 | | 8 | 9 | 10 | | | | 11 | 7 | | | | | | | |
| 15 | 23 | CAMBRIDGE UNITED | D | 1-1 | 1-1 | 3583 | Seddon | 1 | 2 | 3 | 4 | 5 | 6 | | 7 | 9 | 10* | 12 | | | 11 | 8 | | | | | | | |
| 16 | 26 | Exeter City | L | 0-1 | 0-0 | 3664 | | 1 | 2 | 3 | 4 | 5 | 6 | | 7 | 9 | 10 | 12 | | | 11 | 8* | | | | | | | |
| 17 | Nov 2 | ROCHDALE | W | 4-0 | 0-0 | 3100 | Edwards, Draper (3) | 1 | 2 | 3 | 4 | 5 | 6 | 7 | | 9 | 10* | 8 | 12 | | 11 | | | | | | | | |
| 18 | 5 | Doncaster Rovers | D | 1-1 | 0-0 | 1286 | James | 1 | 2 | 3 | 4 | 5 | 6 | 7 | | 9 | 10 | 8 | | | 11 | | | | | | | | |
| 19 | 9 | Northampton Town | L | 0-2 | 0-1 | 5240 | | 1 | 2 | 3 | 4 | 5 | 6 | 7 | | 9* | 10 | 8 | 12 | | 11 | | | | | | | | |
| 20 | 16 | SWANSEA CITY | W | 3-0 | 2-0 | 4641 | James (2), Draper | 1 | 2 | 3 | 4 | 5 | 6 | 7 | 8 | 9 | 10 | 12 | | | 11* | | | | | | | | |
| 21 | 30 | STOCKPORT COUNTY | W | 3-1 | 2-1 | 3289 | Edwards, Lennard, James | 1 | 2 | 3 | 4 | 5 | 6 | 7 | 8 | 9* | 10 | 12 | | | 11 | | | | | | | | |
| 22 | Dec 7 | Rotherham United | W | 2-1 | 1-0 | 4412 | James (2) | 1 | 2 | 3 | 4 | 5 | 6 | 7 | 8 | 9 | 10 | 12 | | | 11* | | | | | | | | |
| 23 | 21 | Workington | D | 0-0 | 0-0 | 1455 | | 1 | 2 | 3 | 4 | 5 | 6 | 7 | 8 | 9 | 10* | 12 | | | 11 | | | | | | | | |
| 24 | 26 | BRADFORD CITY | W | 1-0 | 0-0 | 8372 | Lennard | 1 | 2 | 3 | 4 | 5 | 6* | 7 | 8 | 9 | 10 | 12 | | | 11 | | | | | | | | |
| 25 | 28 | Darlington | D | 1-1 | 0-1 | 2690 | Lennard | 1 | 2 | 3 | 4 | 5 | | 7 | 6 | 9 | 10 | 8 | | | 11 | | | | | | | | |
| 26 | Jan 4 | SHREWSBURY TOWN | D | 1-1 | 0-1 | 8019 | Draper | 1 | 2 | 3 | 4 | | | 7 | 6 | 9 | 10 | 8 | | | 11 | | 5 | | | | | | |
| 27 | 11 | ROTHERHAM UNITED | L | 0-1 | 0-0 | 5835 | | 1 | 2 | 3 | 4 | 5 | | 7 | 8 | 9 | 10 | 6 | | | 11 | | | | | | | | |
| 28 | 17 | Stockport County | D | 1-1 | 1-0 | 2721 | Matthewson | 1 | 2 | 3 | 4 | 5 | 6 | | 8* | | 10 | 7 | 9 | | 11 | 12 | | | | | | | |
| 29 | 25 | Newport County | L | 0-3 | 0-0 | 4144 | | 1 | 2 | 3 | 4 | 5 | 6 | 7 | | | 10 | 9 | | | 11 | 8 | | | | | | | |
| 30 | Feb 1 | NORTHAMPTON TOWN | W | 4-1 | 2-0 | 5027 | Lennard, Owen (2), James (pen) | 1 | 2 | 3 | 4 | 5 | 6 | | | 9* | 10 | 12 | | | 11 | 8 | | 7 | | | | | |
| 31 | 8 | Rochdale | W | 1-0 | 0-0 | 2161 | Redfern | 1 | 2 | 3 | 4 | 5 | 6 | | | | 10 | 9 | | | 11 | 8 | | 7 | | | | | |
| 32 | 15 | NEWPORT COUNTY | W | 4-1 | 4-1 | 5427 | Owen (3), James | 1 | 2 | 3 | 4 | 5 | 6 | | | | 10 | 9 | | | 11 | 8 | | 7 | | | | | |
| 33 | 22 | Swansea City | W | 1-0 | 0-0 | 2174 | Moore | 1 | 2 | 3 | 4 | 5 | 6 | | | | 10* | 9 | 12 | | 11 | 7 | | 8 | | | | | |
| 34 | Mar 1 | BARNSLEY | W | 2-1 | 1-0 | 4976 | Edwards, Owen | 1 | 2 | 3 | 4 | 5 | 6 | 7* | | 12 | | 9 | 10 | | 11 | | | 8 | | | | | |
| 35 | 8 | Reading | L | 1-2 | 0-2 | 5759 | Moore | 1 | 2 | 3 | 4 | 5 | 6 | | | 9 | | 8 | 10 | | 11 | | | 7 | | | | | |
| 36 | 15 | MANSFIELD TOWN | D | 0-0 | 0-0 | 7518 | | 1 | 2 | 3 | 4 | 5 | 6 | | | 9 | | 8 | 10 | | 11 | 12 | | 7* | | | | | |
| 37 | 19 | LINCOLN CITY | W | 4-1 | 2-1 | 6765 | Storton, Moore (2), Edwards | 1 | 2 | 3 | 4 | 5 | 6 | | | 9 | | 7 | 10 | | 11* | 12 | | 8 | | | | | |
| 38 | 22 | Brentford | D | 1-1 | 1-0 | 5800 | Owen | 1 | 2 | 3 | 4 | 5 | 6* | | 7 | 9 | | 11 | 10 | | | 12 | | 8 | | | | | |
| 39 | 29 | WORKINGTON | D | 0-0 | 0-0 | 5761 | | 1 | 2 | 3 | 4 | 5 | | | 6* | 9 | 12 | 11 | 10 | | | 7 | | 8 | | | | | |
| 40 | 31 | Torquay United | L | 0-3 | 0-2 | 3713 | | 1 | 2 | 3 | 4 | 5 | 6 | | 12 | 9* | 10 | 11 | 7 | | | | | 8 | | | | | |
| 41 | Apr 5 | EXETER CITY | D | 1-1 | 0-1 | 3318 | Owen | 1 | 2* | 3 | 4 | 5 | 6 | | 12 | 9 | 10 | 11 | | | | 8 | | 7 | | | | | |
| 42 | 12 | Scunthorpe United | W | 3-1 | 1-0 | 1877 | Owen (2), Redfern | 1 | | 3 | 4 | 5 | 2 | | 6 | | 10 | 9 | | | 11 | 8 | | 7 | | | | | |
| 43 | 16 | DARLINGTON | W | 1-0 | 0-0 | 4652 | Loska | 1 | | 3 | 4 | 5 | 2 | | 6* | 12 | 10 | 9 | | | 11 | 7 | | 8 | | | | | |
| 44 | 19 | SOUTHPORT | W | 3-0 | 2-0 | 4804 | Storton, Owen (2) | 1 | | 3 | 4 | 5 | 2 | | 6 | | 10 | 9 | | | 11 | 8 | | 7 | | | | | |
| 45 | 21 | Hartlepool | L | 0-1 | 0-1 | 2047 | | 1 | | 3 | 4 | 5 | 2 | | 6* | 12 | 10 | 9 | | | 11 | 7 | | 8 | | | | | |
| 46 | 26 | Crewe Alex. | W | 1-0 | 0-0 | 5118 | Mason | 1 | 2 | 3 | 4 | 5 | 8* | | 12 | | 10 | 9 | | | 11 | 7 | | 6 | | | | | |
| | | | | | | | Apps. | 46 | 42 | 46 | 45 | 44 | 37 | 24 | 31 | 34 | 40 | 29 | 12 | 7 | 34 | 17 | 1 | 17 | | | | | |
| | | | | | | | Subs. | | | | | | 1 | | 3 | 3 | 1 | 8 | 11 | | | 4 | | | | | | | |
| | | | | | | | Goals | | 6 | 2 | 2 | 1 | 1 | 1 | 3 | 9 | 13 | 14 | 4 | | 6 | 2 | | | | | | | |

## F.A. CUP

| | Date | Opposition | | FT | HT | Att. | Goalscorers | Millington G. | Edwards N. | Loska A. | Storton T. | Matthewson R. | Mason S. | Whitehead N. | Seddon I. | Draper D. | James J. | Owen T. | Moore G. | Dunleavy C. | Lennard D. | Redfern J. | Potter G. | Pugh G. | Taylor J. | Raynor P. | Lunn P. | Rowlands C. | Morris A. |
|---|---|---|---|---|---|---|---|---|---|---|---|---|---|---|---|---|---|---|---|---|---|---|---|---|---|---|---|---|---|
| 1R | Nov 23 | Rotherham United | L | 0-1 | 0-1 | 5358 | | 1 | 2 | 3 | 4 | 5 | 6 | 7 | 8 | 9 | 10 | 12 | | | 11* | | | | | | | | |

## LEAGUE CUP

| | Date | Opposition | | FT | HT | Att. | Goalscorers | Millington G. | Edwards N. | Loska A. | Storton T. | Matthewson R. | Mason S. | Whitehead N. | Seddon I. | Draper D. | James J. | Owen T. | Moore G. | Dunleavy C. | Lennard D. | Redfern J. | Potter G. | Pugh G. | Taylor J. | Raynor P. | Lunn P. | Rowlands C. | Morris A. |
|---|---|---|---|---|---|---|---|---|---|---|---|---|---|---|---|---|---|---|---|---|---|---|---|---|---|---|---|---|---|
| 1R | Aug 21 | WALSALL | W | 2-1 | 0-1 | 3583 | Draper (2) | 1 | 2 | 3 | 4 | 5 | 6* | 7 | 8 | 9 | 10 | 11 | | 12 | | | | | | | | | |
| 2R | Sep 11 | BLACKPOOL | W | 3-1 | 3-1 | 5854 | Edwards, Owen, Whitehead | 1 | 2 | 3 | 4 | 6 | | 7 | 8 | 9 | 10* | 11 | 12 | 5 | | | | | | | | | |
| 3R | Oct 9 | PRESTON NORTH END | W | 1-0 | 1-0 | 11262 | Lennard | 1 | 2 | 3 | 4 | 5 | 6 | | 8 | 9 | 10 | | | | 11 | 7 | | | | | | | |
| 4R | Nov 13 | LEEDS UNITED | W | 3-0 | 1-0 | 19000 | James (2, 1 pen), Storton | 1 | 2 | 3 | 4 | 5 | 6 | 7 | 8 | 9 | 10 | | | | 11 | | | | | | | | |
| 5R | Dec 4 | Newcastle United | D | 0-0 | 0-0 | 29716 | | 1 | 2 | 3 | 4 | 5 | 6 | 7 | 8 | 9 | 10 | | | | 11 | | | | | | | | |
| 5Rr | 18 | NEWCASTLE UNITED | W | 1-0 | 0-0 | 19000 | James | 1 | 2 | 3 | 4 | 5 | 6 | 7 | 8* | 9 | 10 | 12 | | | 11 | | | | | | | | |
| SF1 | Jan 15 | ASTON VILLA | D | 2-2 | 1-1 | 19000 | Owen, Moore | 1 | 2 | 3 | 4 | 5 | | 7 | 8 | 9 | 10* | 6 | 12 | | 11 | | | | | | | | |
| SF2 | 22 | Aston Villa | L | 2-3 | 1-2 | 47632 | Mason, James | 1 | 2 | 3 | 4 | 5 | 6 | 7 | | | 10 | 11 | 9 | | 8 | | | | | | | | |

## WELSH CUP

| | Date | Opposition | | FT | HT | Att. | Goalscorers | Millington G. | Edwards N. | Loska A. | Storton T. | Matthewson R. | Mason S. | Whitehead N. | Seddon I. | Draper D. | James J. | Owen T. | Moore G. | Dunleavy C. | Lennard D. | Redfern J. | Potter G. | Pugh G. | Taylor J. | Raynor P. | Lunn P. | Rowlands C. | Morris A. |
|---|---|---|---|---|---|---|---|---|---|---|---|---|---|---|---|---|---|---|---|---|---|---|---|---|---|---|---|---|---|
| 4R | Jan 29 | OSWESTRY TOWN | L | 1-3 | 1-1 | 1728 | Lunn | | | | | | 6 | 7 | | | | 9 | | | 11 | 8 | 5 | | 1 | 2 | 3 | 4 | 10 |

## FRIENDLIES

| | Date | Opposition | | FT | HT | Att. | Goalscorers |
|---|---|---|---|---|---|---|---|
| 1 | Aug 3 | Runcorn | D | 1-1 | 0-0 | | James |
| 2 | 5 | Colwyn Bay | W | 5-0 | | | Edwards (2), Raynor, Owen, Draper |
| 3 | 10 | Walsall | L | 0-1 | 0-0 | 1212 | |

# SEASON 1975-76

## FOOTBALL LEAGUE DIVISION 3

| | Date | Opposition | | FT | HT | Att. | Goalscorers | Millington G. | Edwards N. | Loska A. | Matthewson R. | Dunleavy C. | Seddon I. | Whitehead N. | Pugh G. | Draper D. | James J. | Lennard D. | Storton T. | Mason S. | Daniels B. | Moore G. | Redfern J. | Owen T. | Craven M. | Crossley P. | Watling B. | Delgado R. | Dearden W. | Nickeas M. | Raynor P. |
|---|---|---|---|---|---|---|---|---|---|---|---|---|---|---|---|---|---|---|---|---|---|---|---|---|---|---|---|---|---|---|---|
| 1 | Aug 16 | Crystal Palace | L | 0-2 | 0-1 | 13009 | | 1 | 2 | 3 | 4 | 5 | 6 | 7 | 8 | 9 | 10 | 11 | | | | | | | | | | | | | |
| 2 | 23 | SOUTHEND UNITED | D | 1-1 | 1-0 | 4781 | Daniels | 1 | 2 | 3* | | 5 | 8 | 7 | | 9 | | 11 | 4 | 6 | 10 | 12 | | | | | | | | | |
| 3 | 30 | Mansfield Town | D | 1-1 | 0-0 | 6164 | Redfern | 1 | 3 | | | 5 | 6 | | 8 | | | 11 | 4 | 2 | | 9 | 7 | 10 | | | | | | | |
| 4 | Sep 6 | GRIMSBY TOWN | L | 1-2 | 0-1 | 4092 | Owen | 1 | 3 | | | 5 | 6 | | 8 | | | 11* | 4 | 2 | 12 | 9 | 7 | 10 | | | | | | | |
| 5 | 13 | Brighton & Hove A. | L | 0-6 | 0-2 | 7924 | | | 3 | | | 5 | 6 | | 12 | | | 10 | 4 | 2 | | 8 | 7* | 9 | 1 | 11 | | | | | |
| 6 | 20 | PETERBOROUGH UNITED | D | 1-1 | 1-0 | 4063 | Crossley | | 2 | 3 | | 5 | | | 8 | | | 12 | 4 | 6 | 10 | | 7 | 9 | | 11* | 1 | | | | |
| 7 | 24 | COLCHESTER UNITED | W | 1-0 | 1-0 | 3954 | Owen | | 2 | 3 | | 5 | | | 8 | | | 11 | 4 | 6 | 9 | | 7 | 10 | | | 1 | | | | |
| 8 | 27 | Halifax Town | L | 2-5 | 1-3 | 2240 | Owen, Whitehead | | 2 | 3 | | 5 | 12 | 7 | 8 | | | 11 | 4 | 6 | 10 | | | 9* | | | 1 | | | | |
| 9 | Oct 4 | HEREFORD UNITED | L | 0-1 | 0-0 | 4144 | | | 2 | 3 | 5 | | 12 | 7 | 10 | | | 11* | 4 | 6 | | 9 | 8 | | | | 1 | | | | |
| 10 | 11 | ALDERSHOT | W | 1-0 | 1-0 | 3375 | Storton | | 2 | 3 | 5 | | | | 8 | 9 | | 11 | 4 | 6 | 10 | | 7 | | | | 1 | | | | |
| 11 | 18 | Walsall | L | 0-1 | 0-0 | 4146 | | 1 | 2 | 3 | 5* | 12 | | | 8 | 9 | | 11 | 4 | 6 | 10 | | 7 | | | | | | | | |
| 12 | 21 | SHEFFIELD WEDNESDAY | W | 1-0 | 0-0 | 6248 | Owen | 1 | 2* | 3 | 5 | 12 | | | 8 | 9 | | 10 | 4 | 6 | | | 7 | 11 | | | | | | | |
| 13 | 25 | CARDIFF CITY | D | 1-1 | 1-1 | 5348 | Pugh | 1 | | 3 | 5 | 2 | 12 | | 10 | 8 | | 11 | 4 | 6 | | | 7* | 9 | | | | | | | |
| 14 | Nov 1 | Shrewsbury Town | L | 0-2 | 0-0 | 4567 | | 1 | 2 | 3 | | | | | 6 | 9 | | 11 | 4 | | | 8 | 7 | 10 | | | | 5 | | | |
| 15 | 4 | Rotherham United | W | 1-0 | 1-0 | 4282 | Lennard | 1 | 2 | 3 | | | | | 8 | 6 | | 10 | 4 | | | 9 | 7 | 11 | | | | 5 | | | |
| 16 | 8 | MILLWALL | W | 3-1 | 2-1 | 4811 | Redfern, Lennard, Owen | 1 | 2 | 3 | | | | | 6 | 9 | | 11 | 4 | | | 8 | 7 | 10 | | | | 5 | | | |
| 17 | 15 | Port Vale | W | 1-0 | 1-0 | 3908 | Lennard | 1 | 2 | 3 | | | | | 6 | 8 | | 11 | 4 | | | 9 | 7 | 10 | | | | 5 | | | |
| 18 | 29 | Chesterfield | D | 1-1 | 0-1 | 4338 | Storton | 1 | 2 | 3 | | | | | 8 | | | 10 | 4 | 6 | 11 | 9 | 7* | | | 12 | | 5 | | | |
| 19 | Dec 6 | GILLINGHAM | D | 2-2 | 1-0 | 4451 | Owen, Edwards | 1 | 2 | 3 | | | | | 6 | 8 | | 11 | 4 | | | 9* | 7 | 10 | | 12 | | 5 | | | |
| 20 | 20 | SWINDON TOWN | W | 2-1 | 0-0 | 3674 | Delgado, Storton | 1 | 2 | 3 | | | | | 6 | 8 | | 10 | 4 | | | | 7 | 9 | | 11 | | 5 | | | |
| 21 | 26 | Wrexham | D | 1-1 | 1-1 | 10486 | Lennard | 1 | 2 | 3 | | | | | 8 | 6 | | 10 | 4 | | | | 7 | 9 | | 11 | | 5 | | | |
| 22 | 27 | PRESTON NORTH END | W | 3-0 | 1-0 | 8137 | Pugh, McMahon (og), Owen | 1 | 2 | 3 | | | | | 6 | 8 | | 10 | 4 | | | | 7 | 9 | | 11 | | 5 | | | |
| 23 | Jan 10 | MANSFIELD TOWN | D | 1-1 | 1-1 | 4623 | Delgado | 1 | 2 | 3 | | | | | 8 | 6 | | 10 | 4 | | | | 7 | 9 | | 11 | | 5 | | | |
| 24 | 17 | Peterborough United | L | 0-3 | 0-1 | 8674 | | 1 | 2 | 3 | | | | | 8 | 6 | | 10 | 4 | | | | 7 | 9 | | 11 | | 5 | | | |
| 25 | 24 | BRIGHTON & HOVE A. | W | 3-0 | 0-0 | 5099 | Pugh, Redfern, Owen | 1 | 2 | 3 | | | | | 8 | 6 | | 10 | 4 | | | | 7 | 9 | | 11 | | 5 | | | |
| 26 | 31 | Sheffield Wednesday | L | 0-2 | 0-2 | 7558 | | 1 | 2 | 3 | | | | | 8 | 6 | | 10 | 4 | 12 | | | 7 | 9 | | 11* | | 5 | | | |
| 27 | Feb 7 | ROTHERHAM UNITED | W | 3-1 | 1-0 | 4573 | Redfern (pen), Lennard, Loska | 1 | | 3 | | | | 12 | 8 | 6* | | 10 | 4 | 2 | | | 7 | 9 | | 11 | | 5 | | | |
| 28 | 14 | Millwall | L | 0-1 | 0-0 | 4965 | | 1 | 12 | 3 | | | | | 8 | 6 | | 10 | 4 | 2 | | | 7 | 9 | | 11* | | 5 | | | |
| 29 | 21 | PORT VALE | W | 1-0 | 0-0 | 5707 | Redfern (pen) | 1 | 2 | 3 | | 5 | | | 8 | 6 | | | 4 | 10 | | | 7 | 9 | | | | | 11 | | |
| 30 | 24 | Colchester United | L | 0-1 | 0-0 | 3534 | | 1 | 2 | 3 | | 4 | | | 8 | 6 | | 10 | | | | | 7 | 9 | | | | 5 | 11 | | |
| 31 | 28 | Cardiff City | L | 0-2 | 0-0 | 10000 | | 1 | | 3 | | 5 | | | 8 | 6 | | 10* | | 2 | | 12 | 7 | 9 | | 11 | | 4 | | | |
| 32 | Mar 6 | SHREWSBURY TOWN | W | 1-0 | 1-0 | 5916 | Owen | 1 | | 3 | | 5 | | | 8 | 6 | | 11 | 4 | 2 | | 10 | 7* | 9 | | 12 | | | | | |
| 33 | 10 | Hereford United | L | 0-5 | 0-3 | 7103 | | 1 | | 3* | | 5 | | | 8 | 6 | | 11 | 10 | 2 | | 9 | | 7 | | 12 | | 4 | | | |
| 34 | 13 | Aldershot | D | 1-1 | 0-1 | 3831 | Edwards | 1 | 2 | | | | | | 8 | 6 | | | 4 | 3 | | 10 | 7 | 9 | | 11 | | 5 | | | |
| 35 | 16 | WALSALL | D | 1-1 | 0-1 | 4059 | Edwards | 1 | 2 | | | | | | 8 | 6 | | 12 | 4 | 3 | | 10* | 7 | 9 | | 11 | | 5 | | | |
| 36 | 20 | CHESTERFIELD | W | 2-1 | 1-0 | 4018 | Redfern (pen), Owen | 1 | 2 | 3 | | 5 | | | 8 | 6 | | 10 | 4 | | | | 7 | 9 | | 11 | | | | | |
| 37 | 27 | Gillingham | L | 0-2 | 0-1 | 4983 | | 1 | 2 | 3 | | 5 | | | 8 | 6 | | 10 | 4 | | 7* | | | 9 | | 11 | | 12 | | | |
| 38 | 30 | Swindon Town | L | 1-2 | 1-2 | 5117 | Owen | 1 | 2 | 3 | | 5 | | | 8 | | | | 4 | 6 | | 12 | 7 | 9 | | 11 | | 10* | | | |
| 39 | Apr 7 | HALIFAX TOWN | W | 2-1 | 0-1 | 3369 | Storton, Redfern | 1 | 2 | 3 | | 5 | | 7 | 8 | 6 | | | 4 | 10* | | | 11 | 9 | | | | 12 | | | |
| 40 | 10 | Grimsby Town | L | 0-2 | 0-2 | 4644 | | 1 | 2* | 3 | | 5 | | | 8 | 6 | | 11 | 4 | | | | 7 | 9 | | 12 | | 10 | | | |
| 41 | 16 | BURY | D | 0-0 | 0-0 | 5045 | | 1 | | 3 | | | | 12 | 8* | 6 | | 10 | | 2 | | 11 | | 9 | | 7 | | 5 | | 4 | |
| 42 | 17 | WREXHAM | L | 1-3 | 0-1 | 6553 | Draper | 1 | | 3 | 5 | | | 12 | 7* | 6 | | 10 | | 2 | | | | 9 | | 11 | | 8 | | 4 | |
| 43 | 19 | Preston North End | D | 0-0 | 0-0 | 6719 | | 1 | | | | 2 | | 7 | | 6 | | 10 | 4 | 3 | | 8 | | 9 | | 11 | | 5 | | | |
| 44 | 23 | Southend United | L | 0-2 | 0-1 | 3553 | | 1 | | | | 2 | | 7 | 12 | 6 | | 10 | | 3 | | 8 | | 9 | | 11* | | 5 | | 4 | |
| 45 | 27 | Bury | L | 0-1 | 0-0 | 3748 | | 1 | 3 | | | 2 | | | 8* | 10 | | 11 | 4 | 6 | | | 7 | 9 | | 12 | | 5 | | | |
| 46 | May 4 | CRYSTAL PALACE | W | 2-1 | 1-1 | 6702 | Crossley (2) | 1 | 3 | | | 2 | | | 8 | 10 | | | 4 | 6 | | | 7 | 9 | | 11 | | 5 | | | |
| | | | | | | | Apps. | 40 | 36 | 37 | 7 | 23 | 5 | 7 | 42 | 37 | 1 | 39 | 40 | 29 | 8 | 17 | 37 | 40 | 1 | 22 | 5 | 28 | 2 | 3 | |
| | | | | | | | Subs. | | 1 | | | 2 | 3 | 3 | 2 | | | 2 | | 1 | 1 | 3 | | | | 6 | | 2 | | | |
| | | | | | | | Goals | | 3 | 1 | | | | 1 | 3 | 1 | | 5 | 4 | | 1 | | 7 | 11 | | 3 | | 2 | | | |

Own goals 1

## F.A. CUP

| | Date | Opposition | | FT | HT | Att. | Goalscorers | Millington G. | Edwards N. | Loska A. | Matthewson R. | Dunleavy C. | Seddon I. | Whitehead N. | Pugh G. | Draper D. | James J. | Lennard D. | Storton T. | Mason S. | Daniels B. | Moore G. | Redfern J. | Owen T. | Craven M. | Crossley P. | Watling B. | Delgado R. | Dearden W. | Nickeas M. | Raynor P. |
|---|---|---|---|---|---|---|---|---|---|---|---|---|---|---|---|---|---|---|---|---|---|---|---|---|---|---|---|---|---|---|---|
| 1R | Nov 22 | Darlington | D | 0-0 | 0-0 | 2620 | | 1 | 2 | 3 | | | | | 8 | 6 | | 10 | 4 | | | 9 | 7 | 11 | | | | 5 | | | |
| 1Rr | 26 | DARLINGTON | W | 2-0 | 1-0 | 5238 | Moore, Redfern | 1 | 2 | 3 | | | | | 8 | | | 10 | 4 | 6 | | 9 | 7 | 11* | | 12 | | 5 | | | |
| 2R | Dec 13 | Shrewsbury Town | L | 1-3 | 1-2 | 6061 | Edwards | 1 | 2 | 3 | | | | | 8 | 9 | | 10 | 4 | 6 | | | 7* | 11 | | 12 | | 5 | | | |

## LEAGUE CUP

| | Date | Opposition | | FT | HT | Att. | Goalscorers | Millington G. | Edwards N. | Loska A. | Matthewson R. | Dunleavy C. | Seddon I. | Whitehead N. | Pugh G. | Draper D. | James J. | Lennard D. | Storton T. | Mason S. | Daniels B. | Moore G. | Redfern J. | Owen T. | Craven M. | Crossley P. | Watling B. | Delgado R. | Dearden W. | Nickeas M. | Raynor P. |
|---|---|---|---|---|---|---|---|---|---|---|---|---|---|---|---|---|---|---|---|---|---|---|---|---|---|---|---|---|---|---|---|
| 1R1 | Aug 20 | Wrexham | L | 0-3 | 0-1 | 8267 | | 1 | 2 | 3 | 4 | 5 | 6 | 7 | 8* | 9 | 10 | 11 | | | 12 | | | | | | | | | | |
| 1R2 | 27 | WREXHAM | D | 0-0 | 0-0 | 6346 | | 1 | 2 | | | 5 | 8 | | 6 | 9 | | 11 | 4 | 3 | 10* | | 7 | 12 | | | | | | | |

## WELSH CUP

| | Date | Opposition | | FT | HT | Att. | Goalscorers | Millington G. | Edwards N. | Loska A. | Matthewson R. | Dunleavy C. | Seddon I. | Whitehead N. | Pugh G. | Draper D. | James J. | Lennard D. | Storton T. | Mason S. | Daniels B. | Moore G. | Redfern J. | Owen T. | Craven M. | Crossley P. | Watling B. | Delgado R. | Dearden W. | Nickeas M. | Raynor P. |
|---|---|---|---|---|---|---|---|---|---|---|---|---|---|---|---|---|---|---|---|---|---|---|---|---|---|---|---|---|---|---|---|
| 4R | Jan 3 | KIDDERMINSTER H. | W | 8-1 | 3-1 | 1332 | Edwards,Loska,Daniels,Owen,Mason,Lennard(2),Crossley | 1 | 2 | 3 | | | | | 8* | 6 | | 10 | 4 | 12 | 7 | | | 9 | | 11 | | 5 | | | |
| 5R | Feb 16 | Wrexham | D | 0-0 | 0-0 | 3787 | | 1 | 3 | | | 5 | | 7 | 8 | 9 | | | 4 | 2 | | | | 10 | | 11 | | 6 | | | |
| 5Rr | 26 | WREXHAM | W | 2-1 | 1-1 | 4734 | Delgado, Owen | 1 | 2* | 3 | | 5 | | 8 | | | | 10 | | 6 | | 12 | 7 | 9 | | 11 | | 4 | | | |
| SF | Mar 23 | CARDIFF CITY | D | 0-0 | 0-0 | 3743 | | 1 | 2 | 3 | | 5 | | | 8 | 6 | | 10 | 4 | | 7 | | | 9 | | 11 | | | | | |
| SFr | Apr 1 | Cardiff City | L | 0-1 | 0-0 | 4207 | | 1 | | 3 | | 5 | | 7 | 8 | | | 10 | | | | 11 | | 9 | | | | 4 | | 6 | 2 |

## FRIENDLIES

| | Date | Opposition | | FT | HT | Att. | Goalscorers |
|---|---|---|---|---|---|---|---|
| 1 | Aug 2 | DUMBARTON | D | 1-1 | 1-0 | 1885 | Lennard |
| 2 | 6 | PLYMOUTH ARGYLE | L | 1-3 | 0-0 | 2311 | Seddon |
| 3 | 11 | Witton Albion | L | 1-2 | 1-1 | | Whitehead |

**1975/76 Season:**
(Back) Dunleavy, Loska, Mason, Lennard, Redfern. (Middle) Whitehead, Storton, Edwards, Millington, Moore, Pugh, Draper.
(Front) Owen, Seddon, Matthewson, Daniels, James.

**1976/77 Season:**
(Back) Thirkill, Craven, Millington, Raynor, Howat. (Middle) Williams, Nickeas, Delgado, Storton, Edwards, Dunleavy.
(Front) Oakes (Player-Manager), Crossley, Mason, Owen, Dearden, Loska, Draper.

# SEASON 1976-77

## FOOTBALL LEAGUE DIVISION 3

| | Date | Opposition | | FT | HT | Att. | Goalscorers | Craven M. | Edwards N. | Loska A. | Storton T. | Dunleavy C. | Oakes A. | Mason S. | Pugh G. | Owen T. | Dearden W. | Crossley P. | Delgado R. | Draper D. | Millington G. | Raynor P. | Williams P. | Redfern J. | Richardson P. | Howat I. | Nickeas M. | Walker J. | Edwards I. | Kearney M. | Burns D. | Jones B. |
|---|---|---|---|---|---|---|---|---|---|---|---|---|---|---|---|---|---|---|---|---|---|---|---|---|---|---|---|---|---|---|---|---|
| 1 | Aug 21 | Tranmere Rovers | W | 1-0 | 0-0 | 4904 | Philpotts (og) | 1 | 2 | 3 | 4 | 5 | 6 | 7 | 8 | 9 | 10* | 11 | 12 | | | | | | | | | | | | | |
| 2 | 24 | BRIGHTON & HOVE A. | L | 0-1 | 0-0 | 4573 | | 1 | 2 | 3 | 4 | 5 | 6 | 7* | 8 | 9 | 12 | 11 | | 10 | | | | | | | | | | | | |
| 3 | 28 | OXFORD UNITED | L | 1-3 | 0-1 | 3587 | Crossley (pen) | 1 | 2 | 3 | 4 | 5 | 6 | 7 | 8 | 12 | 10* | 11 | | 9 | | | | | | | | | | | | |
| 4 | Sep 4 | Crystal Palace | W | 2-1 | 0-1 | 12746 | Crossley, Mason | | 3 | 12 | 4 | 5 | 6 | 7 | | 10 | 9 | 11* | 8 | | 1 | 2 | | | | | | | | | | |
| 5 | 11 | PRESTON NORTH END | D | 0-0 | 0-0 | 4151 | | | 3 | | 4 | 5 | 6 | 7 | | 10 | | 11 | | 8 | 1 | 2 | 9 | | | | | | | | | |
| 6 | 18 | Bury | L | 0-2 | 0-1 | 4976 | | | 3 | | 4 | 5 | 6 | | 8 | 10 | | 11 | | 9 | 1 | 2 | | 7 | | | | | | | | |
| 7 | 25 | Rotherham United | D | 1-1 | 1-0 | 3913 | Redfern | | 2 | | 4 | 5 | 6 | | 8 | | | 11 | 10 | 9 | 1 | 3 | | 7 | | | | | | | | |
| 8 | Oct 2 | PETERBOROUGH UNITED | W | 2-1 | 1-0 | 3614 | Crossley (2, 1 pen) | | 2 | | 4 | 5* | 6 | | 8 | 12 | | 11 | 10 | 9 | 1 | 3 | | 7 | | | | | | | | |
| 9 | 5 | Sheffield Wednesday | L | 0-3 | 0-0 | 13209 | | | 2 | | 4 | | 6 | | 10 | 7 | | 11 | 5 | 9 | 1 | 3 | | | 8 | | | | | | | |
| 10 | 9 | Grimsby Town | D | 0-0 | 0-0 | 3910 | | | 2 | | 4 | | 6 | 7 | | 10 | 9 | 11 | 5 | | 1 | 3 | | | 8 | | | | | | | |
| 11 | 16 | MANSFIELD TOWN | W | 1-0 | 1-0 | 4033 | Mackenzie (og) | | 2 | | 4 | | 6 | 7 | | 10 | 9 | 11 | 5 | | 1 | 3 | | | 8* | 12 | | | | | | |
| 12 | 23 | York City | W | 2-0 | 1-0 | 2182 | Crossley (pen), Dearden | | 2 | | 4 | | 6 | 7 | | 10 | 9 | 11 | 5 | | 1 | 3 | | | 8 | | | | | | | |
| 13 | 30 | Reading | L | 0-2 | 0-1 | 5550 | | | 2 | | | | 6 | 7 | | 10 | 9 | 11 | 5 | | 1 | 3 | | | 8 | | 4 | | | | | |
| 14 | Nov 2 | Portsmouth | L | 1-2 | 0-1 | 8480 | Dearden | | 2 | | | | 6 | 10* | | 7 | 9 | 11 | 5 | | 1 | 3 | | | 8 | 12 | 4 | | | | | |
| 15 | 6 | WALSALL | W | 1-0 | 0-0 | 3899 | Redfern | | 2 | | 4 | | 6 | | | 10 | 9* | 11 | 5 | | 1 | | | 7 | 8 | 12 | | 3 | | | | |
| 16 | 10 | Chesterfield | L | 0-1 | 0-1 | 3500 | | | 2 | | 4 | | 6 | | | 9* | | 11 | 5 | | 1 | 3 | | 7 | 8 | 12 | | 10 | | | | |
| 17 | 27 | NORTHAMPTON TOWN | W | 2-1 | 1-0 | 3721 | Oakes, I Edwards | | 2 | | 4 | | 6 | | 8 | | 7* | 11 | 5 | | 1 | | | 12 | | 10 | | 3 | 9 | | | |
| 18 | Dec 18 | SWINDON TOWN | W | 2-1 | 0-1 | 3399 | Richardson, Howat | | 2 | | 4 | | 6 | | | | 7 | 11 | 5 | | 1 | | | | 8 | 10 | | 3 | 9 | | | |
| 19 | 27 | Wrexham | L | 2-4 | 1-2 | 10000 | I Edwards, Crossley (pen) | | 2 | | 4 | | 6 | | | | 7 | 11 | 5 | | 1 | | | | 8 | 10 | | 3 | 9 | | | |
| 20 | 28 | SHREWSBURY TOWN | L | 1-2 | 1-2 | 8155 | Crossley | | 2 | | 4 | | 6 | | | 12 | | 11 | 5 | | 1 | | | | 8 | 10* | 7 | 3 | 9 | | | |
| 21 | Jan 15 | Brighton & Hove A. | L | 0-3 | 0-1 | 16495 | | | 2 | | 4 | | 6 | | | | 7 | 11 | 5 | | 1 | | | | 8 | 10* | 12 | 3 | 9 | | | |
| 22 | 22 | TRANMERE ROVERS | W | 1-0 | 1-0 | 5695 | Griffiths (og) | | 2 | | 4 | | 6 | | | 12 | 7 | 11 | 5 | | 1 | | | | 8 | 10* | | 3 | 9 | | | |
| 23 | Feb 1 | READING | W | 3-1 | 0-1 | 3151 | Richardson, I Edwards, Crossley | | 2 | | 4 | | 6 | | | | 7 | 11 | 5 | | 1 | | | 12 | 8 | 10* | | 3 | 9 | | | |
| 24 | 5 | Oxford United | L | 0-2 | 0-1 | 4653 | | | 2 | | 4 | | 6 | | | 10 | 7 | 11 | 8 | | 1 | | | 12 | | | 5* | 3 | 9 | | | |
| 25 | 12 | CRYSTAL PALACE | W | 2-1 | 0-1 | 5442 | Owen, Crossley (pen) | | 2 | | 4 | | 6 | 8 | | 10 | 7 | 11 | 5 | | 1 | | | | | | | 3 | 9 | | | |
| 26 | 15 | SHEFFIELD WEDNESDAY | W | 1-0 | 0-0 | 5613 | Owen | | 2 | | 4 | | 6 | 8 | | 10 | 7 | 11 | 5 | | 1 | | | | | | | 3 | 9 | | | |
| 27 | 19 | Preston North End | W | 4-3 | 2-1 | 10101 | Crossley (2), Owen (2) | | 2 | | 4 | | 6 | 7 | | 10 | | 11 | 5 | | 1 | | | | 8 | | | 3 | 9 | | | |
| 28 | 22 | GILLINGHAM | W | 1-0 | 1-0 | 4048 | Crossley | | 2 | | 4 | | 6 | | | 10 | 7 | 11* | 5 | | 1 | | | 12 | 8 | | | 3 | 9 | | | |
| 29 | Mar 5 | ROTHERHAM UNITED | L | 1-3 | 1-1 | 6150 | I Edwards | | 2 | | 4 | | 6 | 12 | | 10 | 7 | 11 | 5 | | 1 | | | | 8 | | | 3 | 9* | | | |
| 30 | 8 | BURY | W | 1-0 | 1-0 | 3975 | Mason | | 2 | | 4 | | 6 | 8 | | 10 | 7 | 11 | 5 | | 1 | | | | | 9 | | 3 | | | | |
| 31 | 11 | Peterborough United | L | 2-3 | 2-2 | 4781 | Dearden, N Edwards | | 2 | | 4 | | 6 | 8 | | 10* | 7 | 11 | 5 | | 1 | | | | | 12 | | 3 | | 9 | | |
| 32 | 14 | Port Vale | L | 0-1 | 0-0 | 4451 | | | 2 | | 4 | | 6 | 8 | | 10 | | 11 | 5 | 7 | 1 | | | | | | | 3 | | 9 | | |
| 33 | 19 | GRIMSBY TOWN | W | 2-0 | 1-0 | 3246 | Dearden (2) | | 2 | | 4 | | 6 | | | | 7 | 11* | 5 | 12 | 1 | | | | 8 | 10 | | 3 | | 9 | | |
| 34 | 22 | Walsall | L | 0-1 | 0-0 | 4247 | | | 2 | | 4 | | 6 | | | 12 | 7 | | 5 | 11 | 1 | | | | 8* | 10 | | 3 | | 9 | | |
| 35 | 26 | Mansfield Town | D | 1-1 | 1-1 | 6976 | Dearden | | 2 | | 4 | | 6 | | | 10 | 7 | 11 | 5 | | 1 | | | | 8 | | | 3 | | 9 | | |
| 36 | 29 | Lincoln City | D | 3-3 | 1-0 | 5567 | Dearden, Kearney, N Edwards | | 2 | | 4 | | 6 | | | 10 | 7 | 11 | 5 | | 1 | | | | 8 | | | 3 | | 9 | | |
| 37 | Apr 2 | YORK CITY | W | 1-0 | 0-0 | 3045 | Delgado | | 2 | | 4 | | 6 | | | 10 | 7 | 11 | 5 | | 1 | | | | 8 | | | 3 | | 9 | | |
| 38 | 8 | WREXHAM | L | 1-2 | 1-2 | 11280 | Crossley (pen) | | 2 | | 4 | | 6 | | | | 7 | 11 | 5 | | 1 | | | | 8 | | | 3 | 10 | 9 | | |
| 39 | 9 | Shrewsbury Town | L | 0-2 | 0-0 | 3362 | | | 2 | | 4 | | 6 | | | | 7 | 11 | 5 | 12 | 1 | | | | 8 | | | 3 | 10* | 9 | | |
| 40 | 11 | PORTSMOUTH | D | 1-1 | 0-1 | 3309 | Crossley | | 2 | | 4 | | | | | 10 | 7 | 11 | 5 | 8 | 1 | | | | 6 | | | 3 | | 9 | | |
| 41 | 16 | Gillingham | L | 0-1 | 0-0 | 3963 | | | | | 4 | | 6 | | | 10 | 7 | 11 | 5 | | 1 | 2 | | | 8 | | | 3 | | 9 | | |
| 42 | 23 | CHESTERFIELD | L | 1-2 | 1-1 | 2637 | Walker | | | | 4 | | 6 | | | 10 | 7 | | 5 | | 1 | 2 | | | 8 | | | 3 | | 9 | 11 | |
| 43 | 29 | Northampton Town | D | 0-0 | 0-0 | 5105 | | | 12 | | 4 | | 6 | 10 | | | 7 | | 5 | | 1 | 2 | | | 8* | | | 3 | | 9 | 11 | |
| 44 | May 3 | LINCOLN CITY | W | 1-0 | 0-0 | 1836 | Burns | | 2 | | 4 | | 6 | 8 | | 7 | | | 5 | | 1 | 3 | | | | | | 10 | | 9 | 11 | |
| 45 | 7 | PORT VALE | D | 1-1 | 1-1 | 2814 | Delgado | | 2 | | 4 | | 6 | 8 | | 7 | | | 5 | | 1 | 3 | | | | | | 10 | 9 | | 11 | |
| 46 | 14 | Swindon Town | L | 1-2 | 1-1 | 4520 | I Edwards | | 2 | | 4 | | 6 | 8 | | | | | 5 | | 1 | | | | | | | 3 | 9 | 10 | 11 | 7 |
| | | | | | | | Apps. | 3 | 43 | 3 | 44 | 8 | 45 | 20 | 8 | 30 | 33 | 40 | 41 | 10 | 43 | 17 | 1 | 5 | 28 | 10 | 4 | 32 | 17 | 15 | 5 | 1 |
| | | | | | | | Subs. | | 1 | 1 | | | | 1 | | 5 | 1 | | 1 | 2 | | | | 4 | | 5 | 1 | | | | | |
| | | | | | | | Goals | | 2 | | | | 1 | 2 | | 4 | 7 | 14 | 2 | | | | | 2 | 2 | 1 | | 1 | 5 | 1 | 1 | |

Own goals 3

## F.A. CUP

| | Date | Opposition | | FT | HT | Att. | Goalscorers | Craven M. | Edwards N. | Loska A. | Storton T. | Dunleavy C. | Oakes A. | Mason S. | Pugh G. | Owen T. | Dearden W. | Crossley P. | Delgado R. | Draper D. | Millington G. | Raynor P. | Williams P. | Redfern J. | Richardson P. | Howat I. | Nickeas M. | Walker J. | Edwards I. | Kearney M. | Burns D. | Jones B. |
|---|---|---|---|---|---|---|---|---|---|---|---|---|---|---|---|---|---|---|---|---|---|---|---|---|---|---|---|---|---|---|---|---|
| 1R | Nov 20 | HARTLEPOOL | W | 1-0 | 1-0 | 3724 | N Edwards | | 2 | | 4 | | 6 | | | 9 | 10 | 11 | 5 | | 1 | | | 7 | 8* | 12 | | 3 | | | | |
| 2R | Dec 11 | Grimsby Town | W | 1-0 | 0-0 | 5729 | Howat | | | | 4 | | 6 | | | | 7 | 11 | 5 | | 1 | | | | 8 | 10 | 2 | 3 | 9 | | | |
| 3R | Jan 8 | Southend United | W | 4-0 | 1-0 | 10397 | Howat, I Edwards (3) | | 2 | | 4 | | 6 | | | | 7 | 11 | 5 | | 1 | | | | 8 | 10 | | 3 | 9 | | | |
| 4R | 29 | LUTON TOWN | W | 1-0 | 0-0 | 10608 | I Edwards | | 2 | | 4 | | 6 | | | | 7 | 11 | 5 | | 1 | | | | 8 | 10 | | 3 | 9 | | | |
| 5R | Feb 26 | Wolverhampton W. | L | 0-1 | 0-0 | 37803 | | | 2 | | 4 | | 6 | | | 10 | 7 | 11 | 5 | | 1 | | | | 8 | | | 3 | 9 | | | |

## LEAGUE CUP

| | Date | Opposition | | FT | HT | Att. | Goalscorers | Craven M. | Edwards N. | Loska A. | Storton T. | Dunleavy C. | Oakes A. | Mason S. | Pugh G. | Owen T. | Dearden W. | Crossley P. | Delgado R. | Draper D. | Millington G. | Raynor P. | Williams P. | Redfern J. | Richardson P. | Howat I. | Nickeas M. | Walker J. | Edwards I. | Kearney M. | Burns D. | Jones B. |
|---|---|---|---|---|---|---|---|---|---|---|---|---|---|---|---|---|---|---|---|---|---|---|---|---|---|---|---|---|---|---|---|---|
| 1R1 | Aug 14 | HEREFORD UNITED | W | 2-0 | 1-0 | 3866 | Crossley (pen), Draper | | 2 | 3 | 4 | 5 | 6 | 7 | 8 | 9 | | 11 | | 10 | 1 | | | | | | | | | | | |
| 1R2 | 18 | Hereford United | L | 3-4 | 2-2 | 5028 | Draper, Crossley, Paine (og) | | 2 | 3 | 4 | 5 | 6 | 7 | 8 | 9 | | 11 | | 10 | 1 | | | | | | | | | | | |
| 2R | 31 | SWANSEA CITY | L | 2-3 | 1-0 | 3326 | Dearden, Crossley | 1 | 2 | 3 | 4 | 5 | 6 | 12 | 8* | 9 | 7 | 11 | 10 | | | | | | | | | | | | | |

## WELSH CUP

| | Date | Opposition | | FT | HT | Att. | Goalscorers | Craven M. | Edwards N. | Loska A. | Storton T. | Dunleavy C. | Oakes A. | Mason S. | Pugh G. | Owen T. | Dearden W. | Crossley P. | Delgado R. | Draper D. | Millington G. | Raynor P. | Williams P. | Redfern J. | Richardson P. | Howat I. | Nickeas M. | Walker J. | Edwards I. | Kearney M. | Burns D. | Jones B. |
|---|---|---|---|---|---|---|---|---|---|---|---|---|---|---|---|---|---|---|---|---|---|---|---|---|---|---|---|---|---|---|---|---|
| 4R | Jan 18 | Shrewsbury Town | D | 3-3 | 2-1 | 1364 | Atkins (og), Owen, Crossley | | 2 | | 4 | | 6 | | | 10 | 7 | 11 | 5 | | 1 | | | | 8 | | | 3 | 9 | | | |
| 4Rr | 25 | SHREWSBURY TOWN | L | 1-2 | 1-0 | 1442 | Owen | 1 | 2 | | 4 | | | 7 | | 6 | | 11 | 5 | 8 | | | | | | 10 | | 3 | 9 | | | |

## DEBENHAMS CUP

| | Date | Opposition | | FT | HT | Att. | Goalscorers | Craven M. | Edwards N. | Loska A. | Storton T. | Dunleavy C. | Oakes A. | Mason S. | Pugh G. | Owen T. | Dearden W. | Crossley P. | Delgado R. | Draper D. | Millington G. | Raynor P. | Williams P. | Redfern J. | Richardson P. | Howat I. | Nickeas M. | Walker J. | Edwards I. | Kearney M. | Burns D. | Jones B. |
|---|---|---|---|---|---|---|---|---|---|---|---|---|---|---|---|---|---|---|---|---|---|---|---|---|---|---|---|---|---|---|---|---|
| F1 | May 16 | Port Vale | L | 0-2 | 0-0 | 3459 | | 1 | 2 | | 4 | | 6 | 8 | | | 7 | | 5 | | | | | | | | | 3 | 10 | 9 | 11 | |
| F2 | 24 | PORT VALE | W | 4-1 | 0-0 | 3939 | Mason, Burns, Griffiths (og), Howat | 1 | 2 | | 4 | | 6 | 8 | | | 7 | | 5 | | | | | | | 12 | | 3 | 10* | 9 | 11 | |

## FRIENDLIES

| | Date | Opposition | | FT | HT | Att. | Goalscorers |
|---|---|---|---|---|---|---|---|
| 1 | Jul 31 | Runcorn | L | 0-1 | 0-0 | 570 | |
| 2 | Aug 3 | BLACKBURN ROVERS | W | 1-0 | 1-0 | 1550 | Owen |
| 3 | 10 | Witton Albion | W | 1-0 | 0-0 | | Williams |

# SEASON 1977-78

## FOOTBALL LEAGUE DIVISION 3

| | Date | Opposition | | FT | HT | Att. | Goalscorers | Millington G. | Raynor P. | Walker J. | Delgado R. | Storton T. | Oakes A. | Mason S. | Edwards I. | Kearney M. | Jeffries D. | Burns D. | Jones B. | Howat I. | Crossley P. | Phillips R. | Lloyd B. | Livermore D. | Edwards N. | Nickeas M. | Mellor I. | Clutton N. |
|---|---|---|---|---|---|---|---|---|---|---|---|---|---|---|---|---|---|---|---|---|---|---|---|---|---|---|---|---|
| 1 | Aug 20 | HEREFORD UNITED | W | 4-1 | 2-1 | 3276 | Kearney (2, 1pen), I Edwards, Mason | 1 | 2 | 3 | 4 | 5 | 6 | 7 | 8 | 9 | 10 | 11 | | | | | | | | | | |
| 2 | 27 | Colchester United | L | 0-2 | 0-0 | 4169 | | 1* | 2 | 3 | 4 | 5 | 6 | 7 | 8 | 9 | 11 | 10 | 12 | | | | | | | | | |
| 3 | Sep 2 | CAMBRIDGE UNITED | D | 0-0 | 0-0 | 3794 | | 1 | 2 | 3 | 5 | 4 | 6 | 7* | 8 | 9 | 10 | 11 | | 12 | | | | | | | | |
| 4 | 10 | Bradford City | D | 2-2 | 0-2 | 3612 | Crossley, Kearney | 1 | 2 | 3 | 4 | 5 | 6 | 12 | 8 | 9 | 11 | | | | 7 | 10* | | | | | | |
| 5 | 14 | SHEFFIELD WEDNESDAY | W | 2-1 | 0-0 | 4520 | I Edwards, Crossley | 1 | 2 | 3 | 4 | 5 | 6 | | 10 | 9 | 8 | | | | 7 | 11 | | | | | | |
| 6 | 17 | GILLINGHAM | D | 2-2 | 0-2 | 3367 | Storton, Phillips | 1 | 2 | 3 | 4 | 5 | 6 | | 10 | 9 | 8* | 11 | | 12 | | 7 | | | | | | |
| 7 | 20 | Carlisle United | D | 0-0 | 0-0 | 4941 | | 1 | 2 | 3 | 5 | 4 | 6 | 7 | | 9 | 8 | | | 10 | | 11 | | | | | | |
| 8 | 24 | Oxford United | L | 1-4 | 0-1 | 4283 | Kearney | 1 | 2 | 3 | 4 | 5 | 6 | 7 | 10 | 9 | 11 | | | | | 8 | | | | | | |
| 9 | 28 | WREXHAM | D | 1-1 | 1-1 | 9514 | Delgado | 1 | 2 | 3 | 5 | 4 | 6 | | 10 | 9 | 8 | | | | 7 | 11 | | | | | | |
| 10 | 30 | Tranmere Rovers | L | 0-5 | 0-4 | 4352 | | 1 | 2 | 3 | 5 | 4 | 6 | | 10 | 9 | 8 | | | | 7 | 11 | | | | | | |
| 11 | Oct 4 | Portsmouth | D | 0-0 | 0-0 | 10465 | | | 2 | 3 | 5 | 4 | 6 | | 10 | 9 | 8 | | | | 7 | 11 | 1 | | | | | |
| 12 | 8 | PLYMOUTH ARGYLE | D | 1-1 | 0-0 | 3367 | Hall (og) | | 2 | 3 | 5 | 4 | 6* | 8 | 10 | 9 | 11 | 12 | | | 7 | | 1 | | | | | |
| 13 | 15 | Rotherham United | D | 1-1 | 1-0 | 4825 | Phillips | | 2 | 3 | 4 | 5 | 6 | | 10 | 9 | | | | | 7 | 11 | 1 | 8 | | | | |
| 14 | 22 | SWINDON TOWN | W | 1-0 | 0-0 | 3292 | Storton | | 2 | 3 | 4 | 5 | 6 | | 10 | 9 | | | | | 7 | 11 | 1 | 8 | | | | |
| 15 | 29 | Preston North End | L | 1-2 | 0-1 | 7550 | Delgado | | 2 | 3 | 4 | 5 | 6 | | 10 | 9 | | | | | 7 | 11 | 1 | 8 | | | | |
| 16 | Nov 5 | Lincoln City | L | 1-2 | 1-0 | 4270 | Phillips | | | 3 | 4 | 5 | 6 | | 10 | 9 | | | | | 7 | 11 | 1 | 8 | 2 | | | |
| 17 | 12 | PORT VALE | W | 2-1 | 1-1 | 3117 | I Edwards, Jeffries | | | 3 | 5 | 4 | | | 10 | 9 | 6 | | | | 7 | 11 | 1 | 8 | 2 | | | |
| 18 | 19 | Bury | D | 1-1 | 0-1 | 4020 | Delgado | | | 3 | 5 | 4 | 6 | | 10 | 9 | | | | | 7 | 11 | 1 | 8 | 2 | | | |
| 19 | Dec 3 | CHESTERFIELD | W | 2-1 | 0-1 | 2803 | Storton, Livermore | | | 3 | 5 | 4 | 6 | | 10 | 9 | | | | | 7 | 11 | 1 | 8 | 2 | | | |
| 20 | 10 | Peterborough United | D | 0-0 | 0-0 | 5844 | | | | 3 | 5 | 4 | 6 | | 10 | 9 | | | | | 7 | 11 | 1 | 8 | 2 | | | |
| 21 | 26 | SHREWSBURY TOWN | W | 1-0 | 0-0 | 5701 | Crossley | | | 3 | 5 | 4 | 6 | | 10 | 9 | | | | | 7 | 11 | 1 | 8 | | 2 | | |
| 22 | 27 | Walsall | L | 0-3 | 0-1 | 4990 | | | | 3 | 5 | 4 | 6 | | 10 | 9 | 8 | | | | 7 | 11 | 1 | | | 2 | | |
| 23 | 31 | LINCOLN CITY | D | 2-2 | 1-1 | 3322 | Storton, I Edwards | | | 3 | 5 | 4* | 6 | | 9 | 12 | | 10 | | | 7 | 11 | 1 | 8 | | 2 | | |
| 24 | Jan 2 | Exeter City | D | 1-1 | 1-0 | 6193 | Crossley | | | 3 | 5 | | 6 | | 9 | | | | 10 | | 7 | 11 | 1 | 8 | 2 | 4 | | |
| 25 | 14 | Hereford United | D | 2-2 | 1-1 | 4216 | I Edwards, Jones | | | 3 | 5 | | 6 | | 10 | | | | 9 | | 7 | 11 | 1 | 8 | 2 | 4 | | |
| 26 | 21 | COLCHESTER UNITED | W | 2-1 | 1-1 | 2855 | Crossley (pen), I Edwards | | 3 | | 4 | 5 | 6 | | 9 | | | | 10 | | 7 | 11 | 1 | 8 | 2 | | | |
| 27 | 28 | Cambridge United | D | 0-0 | 0-0 | 4542 | | | | 3 | 5 | 4 | 6 | | 9 | | 12 | | 7 | | 10 | 11* | 1 | 8 | 2 | | | |
| 28 | Feb 4 | BRADFORD CITY | W | 3-2 | 2-1 | 2957 | Livermore (2), Oakes | | | 3 | 5 | 4 | 6 | | 9 | | | | 7 | | 11 | 10 | 1 | 8 | 2 | | | |
| 29 | 21 | Gillingham | L | 0-1 | 0-0 | 7863 | | | 3 | | 5 | 4 | 6 | | 9 | | | | 7 | | 10 | 11 | 1 | 8 | 2 | | | |
| 30 | 25 | TRANMERE ROVERS | D | 0-0 | 0-0 | 5494 | | | 3 | | 5 | 4 | 6 | | 9 | | | | | | 10 | 7 | 1 | 8 | 2 | | 11 | |
| 31 | Mar 1 | CARLISLE UNITED | D | 2-2 | 1-0 | 2934 | Phillips, Crossley | | 2 | 3 | 5 | 4 | 6 | | | | | | 12 | | 7* | 11 | 1 | 8 | | | 10 | 9 |
| 32 | 4 | Plymouth Argyle | D | 2-2 | 1-1 | 5322 | Oakes, Mellor | | 2 | 3 | 5 | 4 | 6 | | | | 8 | | 7 | | 10 | 11 | 1 | | | | 9 | |
| 33 | 7 | Sheffield Wednesday | D | 1-1 | 1-1 | 10678 | Jones | | 2 | 3 | 5 | 4 | 6 | | 9 | | | | 7 | | | 11 | 1 | 8 | | | 10 | |
| 34 | 11 | ROTHERHAM UNITED | W | 2-1 | 1-1 | 3421 | Oakes, Crossley | | 2 | 3 | 5 | | 6 | | 9* | | | | 12 | | 7 | 11 | 1 | 8 | | 4 | 10 | |
| 35 | 17 | Swindon Town | D | 1-1 | 0-1 | 4275 | Phillips | | 2 | 3* | 5 | | 6 | | 9 | | | | 12 | | 7 | 11 | 1 | 8 | | 4 | 10 | |
| 36 | 24 | PRESTON NORTH END | L | 1-2 | 1-1 | 7864 | Crossley | | 3 | | 5 | | 6 | | | | | | | 9 | 7 | 11 | 1 | 8 | 2 | 4 | 10 | |
| 37 | 25 | Shrewsbury Town | D | 0-0 | 0-0 | 2592 | | | 3 | | 5 | 4 | 6 | | | | | | 7 | | 9 | 11 | 1 | 8 | | 2 | 10 | |
| 38 | 27 | WALSALL | D | 1-1 | 0-1 | 4671 | Crossley (pen) | | 3 | | 5 | 4 | | | 9 | | 12 | | 6* | | 7 | 11 | 1 | 8 | | 2 | 10 | |
| 39 | Apr 1 | EXETER CITY | W | 2-1 | 2-0 | 1996 | Mellor, Phillips | | 3 | | 7 | 5 | 6 | | | | 4 | | | 9 | | 11 | 1 | 8 | | 2 | 10 | |
| 40 | 3 | Wrexham | W | 2-1 | 2-0 | 19125 | Howat, Mellor | | 3 | | 9 | 4 | 6 | | | | 5 | | | 7 | | 11 | 1 | 8 | | 2 | 10 | |
| 41 | 8 | Port Vale | D | 0-0 | 0-0 | 3615 | | | 3 | | 9 | 4 | 6 | | | | 5 | | 12 | 7 | | 11* | 1 | 8 | | 2 | 10 | |
| 42 | 12 | OXFORD UNITED | W | 3-1 | 2-0 | 2351 | Howat (2), Livermore | | 3 | | | 4 | 6 | | | | 5 | | 7 | 9 | | 11 | 1 | 8 | | 2 | 10 | |
| 43 | 15 | BURY | W | 1-0 | 0-0 | 3377 | Nickeas | | 3 | | | 4 | 6 | | | | 5 | | 7 | 9 | | 11 | 1 | 8 | | 2 | 10 | |
| 44 | 22 | Chesterfield | W | 2-1 | 0-1 | 3753 | Oakes, Phillips | | 3 | | | 4 | 6 | | | | 5 | | 7 | 9 | | 11 | 1 | 8 | | 2 | 10 | |
| 45 | 26 | PORTSMOUTH | W | 2-0 | 2-0 | 2837 | Livermore (pen), Mellor | | 3 | | | 4 | 6 | | | | 5 | | 7 | 9 | | 11 | 1 | 8 | | 2 | 10 | |
| 46 | 29 | PETERBOROUGH UNITED | W | 4-3 | 1-1 | 4237 | Howat, Mellor, Oakes, Turner (og) | | 3 | | | 4 | 6 | | | | 5 | | 7 | 9 | | 11 | 1 | 8 | | 2 | 10 | |
| | | | | | | | Apps. | 10 | 34 | 32 | 41 | 41 | 44 | 6 | 33 | 22 | 23 | 5 | 15 | 10 | 31 | 42 | 36 | 32 | 13 | 18 | 17 | 1 |
| | | | | | | | Subs. | | | | | | | 1 | | 1 | 2 | 1 | 5 | 2 | | | | | | | | |
| | | | | | | | Goals | | | | 3 | 4 | 5 | 1 | 6 | 4 | 1 | | 2 | 4 | 9 | 7 | | 5 | | 1 | 5 | |

Own goals 2

## F.A. CUP

| | Date | Opposition | | FT | HT | Att. | Goalscorers | Millington G. | Raynor P. | Walker J. | Delgado R. | Storton T. | Oakes A. | Mason S. | Edwards I. | Kearney M. | Jeffries D. | Burns D. | Jones B. | Howat I. | Crossley P. | Phillips R. | Lloyd B. | Livermore D. | Edwards N. | Nickeas M. | Mellor I. | Clutton N. |
|---|---|---|---|---|---|---|---|---|---|---|---|---|---|---|---|---|---|---|---|---|---|---|---|---|---|---|---|---|
| 1R | Nov 26 | DARLINGTON | W | 4-1 | 1-0 | 3330 | Crossley (3), Kearney | | | 3 | 5 | 4 | 6 | | 10 | 9 | | | | | 7 | 11 | 1 | 8 | 2 | | | |
| 2R | Dec 17 | Carlisle United | L | 1-3 | 1-1 | 5577 | Crossley | | 12 | 3 | 5 | 4 | | | 10 | 9 | 6 | | | | 7 | 11* | 1 | 8 | 2 | | | |

## LEAGUE CUP

| | Date | Opposition | | FT | HT | Att. | Goalscorers | Millington G. | Raynor P. | Walker J. | Delgado R. | Storton T. | Oakes A. | Mason S. | Edwards I. | Kearney M. | Jeffries D. | Burns D. | Jones B. | Howat I. | Crossley P. | Phillips R. | Lloyd B. | Livermore D. | Edwards N. | Nickeas M. | Mellor I. | Clutton N. |
|---|---|---|---|---|---|---|---|---|---|---|---|---|---|---|---|---|---|---|---|---|---|---|---|---|---|---|---|---|
| 1R1 | Aug 13 | Burnley | L | 0-2 | 0-1 | 4736 | | 1 | | 3 | 8 | 5 | 6 | 4 | 9 | 7 | 11 | 10 | | | | | | | 2 | | | |
| 1R2 | 17 | BURNLEY | W | 1-0 | 1-0 | 4048 | Kearney | 1 | | 3 | 5 | 4 | 6 | 7 | 8 | 9 | 10 | 11 | | 12 | | | | | 2* | | | |

## WELSH CUP

| | Date | Opposition | | FT | HT | Att. | Goalscorers | Millington G. | Raynor P. | Walker J. | Delgado R. | Storton T. | Oakes A. | Mason S. | Edwards I. | Kearney M. | Jeffries D. | Burns D. | Jones B. | Howat I. | Crossley P. | Phillips R. | Lloyd B. | Livermore D. | Edwards N. | Nickeas M. | Mellor I. | Clutton N. |
|---|---|---|---|---|---|---|---|---|---|---|---|---|---|---|---|---|---|---|---|---|---|---|---|---|---|---|---|---|
| 4R | Jan 25 | WREXHAM | L | 0-2 | 0-0 | 6921 | | | 3 | | 5 | 4 | 6 | | 9 | | | | 8 | 10 | 7 | 11 | 1 | | 2 | | | |

## FRIENDLIES

| | Date | Opposition | | FT | HT | Att. | Goalscorers |
|---|---|---|---|---|---|---|---|
| 1 | Jul 25 | Porthmadog | W | 2-1 | | | I Edwards (2) |
| 2 | 27 | Bangor City | L | 0-1 | 0-0 | | |

**1977/78 Season:**
(Back) Oakes (Player-Manager), Jones, N Edwards, Storton, Millington, Howat, Walker, Raynor, Draper.
(Middle) Prichard (Trainer), Mason, Jeffries, Delgado, Kearney, I Edwards, Burns, Sear (Youth Team Manager). (Front) Rush, Gregory, Needham

**1978/79 Season:**
(Back) Mellor, Delgado, Lloyd, Oakes (Player-Manager), Millington, Storton, Nickeas, Jeffries.
(Front) Raynor, Burns, Livermore, Edwards, Jones, Howat, Phillips, Walker.

# *SEASON 1978-79*

## FOOTBALL LEAGUE DIVISION 3

| | Date | Opposition | | FT | HT | Att. | Goalscorers | Lloyd B. | Raynor P. | Walker J. | Storton T. | Jeffries D. | Oakes A. | Livermore D. | Mellor I. | Edwards I. | Delgado R. | Phillips R. | Jones B. | Nickeas M. | Millington G. | Howat I. | Sutcliffe P. | Burns D. | Felix G. | Henderson P. | Rush I. |
|---|---|---|---|---|---|---|---|---|---|---|---|---|---|---|---|---|---|---|---|---|---|---|---|---|---|---|---|
| 1 | Aug 19 | Southend United | W | 1-0 | 0-0 | 4223 | Edwards | 1 | 2 | 3 | 4 | 5 | 6 | 7 | 8 | 9 | 10 | 11 | | | | | | | | | |
| 2 | 23 | WALSALL | W | 2-1 | 1-1 | 4257 | Phillips, Mellor (pen) | 1 | 2 | 3 | 4 | 5 | 6 | 8 | 10 | 9 | 7 | 11 | | | | | | | | | |
| 3 | 26 | EXETER CITY | W | 3-0 | 1-0 | 3431 | Mellor (pen), Edwards (2) | 1 | 2 | 3 | 4 | 5 | 6 | 8 | 10 | 9 | 7 | 11 | | | | | | | | | |
| 4 | Sep 2 | Hull City | L | 0-3 | 0-2 | 5325 | | 1 | 2 | 3 | 4 | 5 | 6 | 8 | 10 | 9 | 7* | 11 | 12 | | | | | | | | |
| 5 | 8 | PETERBOROUGH UNITED | D | 1-1 | 0-0 | 4506 | Edwards | 1 | 2 | 3 | 4 | 5 | 6 | 8 | 10 | 9 | 7 | 11 | | | | | | | | | |
| 6 | 12 | Colchester United | L | 1-2 | 0-0 | 2311 | Phillips | 1 | 2 | 3 | 4 | 5 | 6 | 8 | 10 | 9 | 7 | 11 | | | | | | | | | |
| 7 | 16 | Gillingham | L | 0-1 | 0-0 | 4743 | | 1 | 3 | 11 | 4 | 5 | 6 | 8 | 10 | 9 | 7 | | | 2 | | | | | | | |
| 8 | 23 | SWANSEA CITY | W | 2-0 | 1-0 | 8583 | Mellor, Edwards | 1 | 3 | 11 | 4 | 5 | 6 | 8 | 10 | 9 | 7 | | | 2 | | | | | | | |
| 9 | 27 | SWINDON TOWN | W | 2-0 | 1-0 | 3311 | Delgado, Oakes | 1 | 2 | 3 | 4 | 5 | 6 | 8 | 10 | 9 | 7 | 11 | | | | | | | | | |
| 10 | 30 | Bury | D | 1-1 | 1-1 | 4056 | Edwards | 1 | 3 | 11 | 4 | 5 | 6 | 8 | 10 | 9 | 7 | | | 2 | | | | | | | |
| 11 | Oct 7 | WATFORD | W | 2-1 | 1-1 | 6468 | Edwards, Phillips | 1 | 3 | 11 | 4 | 5 | | 8 | 10 | 9 | 7 | 6 | | 2 | | | | | | | |
| 12 | 13 | Tranmere Rovers | L | 2-6 | 1-1 | 5587 | Edwards, Mellor | 1 | 3 | 11* | 4 | 5 | | 8 | 10 | 9 | 7 | 6 | 12 | 2 | | | | | | | |
| 13 | 18 | PLYMOUTH ARGYLE | D | 0-0 | 0-0 | 3921 | | | | 3 | 4 | | 6 | 8 | 10 | 9 | 5 | 11 | 7 | 2 | 1 | | | | | | |
| 14 | 21 | Oxford United | D | 0-0 | 0-0 | 3908 | | | 3 | | 4 | 5 | 6 | 8 | 10 | 9 | | 11 | 7 | 2 | 1 | | | | | | |
| 15 | 28 | BRENTFORD | W | 3-1 | 0-1 | 4301 | Edwards (3) | | 3 | | 4 | 5 | 6 | 8 | 10 | 9 | | 11 | 7 | 2 | 1 | | | | | | |
| 16 | Nov 4 | Chesterfield | L | 1-3 | 0-2 | 5015 | Raynor | | 3 | | 4 | 5 | 6 | 8 | 10 | 9 | | 11 | 7 | 2 | 1 | | | | | | |
| 17 | 11 | HULL CITY | W | 2-1 | 2-1 | 4249 | Edwards (2) | | 3 | | 4 | 5 | | 8 | 10 | 9 | 6 | 11 | 7 | 2 | 1 | | | | | | |
| 18 | 18 | Exeter City | W | 1-0 | 0-0 | 3985 | Mellor | 1 | 3 | | 4 | 5 | 6 | 8 | 10 | | | 11 | 7 | 2 | | 9 | | | | | |
| 19 | Dec 9 | Sheffield Wednesday | D | 0-0 | 0-0 | 8872 | | 1 | 3 | | 4 | 5 | 6 | 8 | 10 | | 7 | 11 | | 2 | | 9 | | | | | |
| 20 | 23 | Blackpool | L | 0-3 | 0-1 | 4106 | | 1 | 3 | 11 | 4 | 5 | | 8 | | | | 6 | 10 | 2 | | 9* | 7 | 12 | | | |
| 21 | 26 | CARLISLE UNITED | L | 1-2 | 1-1 | 4690 | Walker | 1 | 3 | 10 | 4 | 5 | | 8 | | | | 6 | 11 | 2 | | 9* | 7 | 12 | | | |
| 22 | Jan 13 | Peterborough United | L | 1-2 | 0-2 | 4445 | Edwards | 1 | | 3 | 4 | 5 | | 8 | | 9 | | 6 | | 2 | | | 7 | | 10 | 11 | |
| 23 | 17 | COLCHESTER UNITED | D | 2-2 | 1-1 | 2339 | Henderson, Phillips | 1 | | 3 | 4 | 5 | | 8 | | 9 | | 6 | | 2 | | | 7 | | 10 | 11 | |
| 24 | 30 | Shrewsbury Town | L | 0-1 | 0-0 | 6693 | | 1 | | 3 | 4 | 5 | 6 | 8 | | 9 | | 10 | | 2 | | | | | 7 | 11 | |
| 25 | Feb 3 | Swindon Town | L | 0-2 | 0-1 | 6036 | | 1 | 3 | | 4 | 5 | | 8 | | 9 | | 6 | 7 | 2 | | | | | 10 | 11 | |
| 26 | 10 | BURY | D | 1-1 | 1-0 | 3160 | Henderson | 1 | | 3 | 4 | 5 | 6 | 8 | 12 | 9 | | 11 | | 2 | | | 7* | | | 10 | |
| 27 | 21 | GILLINGHAM | D | 1-1 | 1-1 | 2421 | Jeffries | 1 | 2 | 3 | 4 | 5 | 6 | | | 9 | | 10 | | | | | 7 | | 8 | 11 | |
| 28 | 24 | TRANMERE ROVERS | D | 1-1 | 1-1 | 4375 | Raynor (pen) | 1 | 2 | 3 | 4 | 5 | 6 | | | 9 | | 11* | 12 | | | | 7 | | 8 | 10 | |
| 29 | 27 | Swansea City | D | 2-2 | 1-0 | 7983 | Henderson, Raynor (pen) | 1 | 2 | 3 | 4 | 5 | 6 | | | | | 10 | 7 | | | 9* | 12 | | 8 | 11 | |
| 30 | Mar 3 | OXFORD UNITED | W | 4-1 | 2-1 | 2476 | Oakes, Jones, Phillips, Edwards | 1 | 2 | 3 | 4* | 5 | 6 | | | 9 | | 10 | 7 | 12 | | | 8 | | | 11 | |
| 31 | 7 | LINCOLN CITY | W | 5-1 | 0-1 | 2585 | Henderson (3), Edwards, Phillips | 1 | 2 | 3 | 4 | 5 | 6 | | | 9 | | 10 | 8 | | | | 7 | | | 11 | |
| 32 | 10 | Brentford | L | 0-6 | 0-1 | 6420 | | 1 | 2 | 3 | 4 | 5 | 6 | | | 9 | | 10 | 8 | | | | 7 | | | 11 | |
| 33 | 14 | ROTHERHAM UNITED | L | 0-1 | 0-1 | 2473 | | 1 | 3 | 10 | 4 | 5 | 6 | 8 | | 9 | | | 7 | 2 | | | | | | 11 | |
| 34 | 21 | SOUTHEND UNITED | L | 0-1 | 0-0 | 2108 | | 1 | 3 | 10 | 4 | 5 | 6 | | | 9 | | | | 2 | | | 7 | | 8 | 11 | |
| 35 | 24 | Walsall | L | 1-2 | 1-0 | 2795 | Oakes | 1 | | 3 | 4 | 5 | 6 | 8 | | 9 | | 10 | 7 | 2 | | | | | | 11 | |
| 36 | 28 | CHESTERFIELD | W | 3-0 | 2-0 | 1804 | Jones, Livermore, Phillips | 1 | | 3 | 4 | 5 | 6 | 8 | | 9 | | 10 | 7 | 2 | | | | | | 11 | |
| 37 | 31 | MANSFIELD TOWN | D | 1-1 | 0-0 | 2205 | Edwards | 1 | 12 | 3* | 4 | 5 | 6 | 8 | | 9 | | 11 | 7 | 2 | | | | | | 10 | |
| 38 | Apr 7 | Lincoln City | D | 0-0 | 0-0 | 3489 | | 1 | | | 4 | 5 | 6 | 8 | | 9 | | 11 | 7 | 2 | | | | 3 | | 10 | |
| 39 | 13 | BLACKPOOL | W | 4-2 | 1-0 | 4439 | Oakes, Phillips (pen), Henderson, Edwards | 1 | | | 4 | 5 | 6 | 8 | | 9 | | 10 | 7 | 2 | | | 12 | 3* | | 11 | |
| 40 | 14 | Carlisle United | D | 1-1 | 0-1 | 5309 | Phillips | 1 | 3 | | 4 | 5 | 6 | 8 | 12 | 9 | | 11 | 7 | 2 | | | | | | 10* | |
| 41 | 16 | SHREWSBURY TOWN | D | 0-0 | 0-0 | 6249 | | 1 | 3 | | 4 | 5 | 6 | 8 | | 9 | | 10 | 7 | 2 | | | 12 | | | 11* | |
| 42 | 21 | Rotherham United | W | 1-0 | 1-0 | 2893 | Edwards | 1 | 2 | | 4 | | 6 | 8 | | 9 | | 11 | 7 | 3 | | | | 5 | | 10 | |
| 43 | 24 | Plymouth Argyle | D | 2-2 | 2-1 | 4686 | Raynor (pen), Edwards | 1 | 5 | | 4 | | 6 | 8 | | 9 | | 10 | 7 | 2 | | | | 3 | | 11 | |
| 44 | 28 | SHEFFIELD WEDNESDAY | D | 2-2 | 1-1 | 4200 | Mellor, Phillips | 1 | 2 | | 5 | | | 8 | 9 | | | 10 | 7 | 6 | | | | 3 | | 11 | 4 |
| 45 | May 2 | Watford | L | 0-1 | 0-1 | 12167 | | 1 | 5 | 12 | 4 | | 6 | 8 | 9 | | | 10* | 7 | 2 | | | | 3 | | 11 | |
| 46 | 5 | Mansfield Town | L | 0-2 | 0-0 | 4173 | | 1 | 5 | 11 | 4 | | 6 | 8 | | 9 | | | 7 | 2 | | | | 3 | | 10 | |
| | | | | | | | Apps. | 41 | 36 | 31 | 46 | 40 | 37 | 39 | 21 | 39 | 15 | 40 | 26 | 33 | 5 | 5 | 11 | 7 | 8 | 25 | 1 |
| | | | | | | | Subs. | | 1 | 1 | | | | | 2 | | | | 3 | 1 | | | 3 | 2 | | | |
| | | | | | | | Goals | | 4 | 1 | | 1 | 4 | 1 | 6 | 20 | 1 | 10 | 2 | | | | | | | 7 | |

## F.A. CUP

| | Date | Opposition | | FT | HT | Att. | Goalscorers | Lloyd B. | Raynor P. | Walker J. | Storton T. | Jeffries D. | Oakes A. | Livermore D. | Mellor I. | Edwards I. | Delgado R. | Phillips R. | Jones B. | Nickeas M. | Millington G. | Howat I. | Sutcliffe P. | Burns D. | Felix G. | Henderson P. | Rush I. |
|---|---|---|---|---|---|---|---|---|---|---|---|---|---|---|---|---|---|---|---|---|---|---|---|---|---|---|---|
| 1R | Nov 25 | RUNCORN | D | 1-1 | 0-0 | 5421 | Phillips | 1 | 3 | 12 | 4 | 5 | 6 | 8* | 10 | | | 11 | 7 | 2 | | 9 | | | | | |
| 1Rr | 28 | Runcorn | W | 5-0 | 4-0 | 4441 | Mellor (2), Jones, Phillips, Howat | 1 | 3 | | 4 | 5 | | 8 | 10 | | 6 | 11 | 7 | 2 | | 9 | | | | | |
| 2R | Dec 16 | Darlington | L | 1-2 | 0-0 | 2491 | Mellor | 1 | 3 | 12 | 4 | 5 | 6 | 8 | 10 | | 7* | 11 | | 2 | | 9 | | | | | |

## LEAGUE CUP

| | Date | Opposition | | FT | HT | Att. | Goalscorers | Lloyd B. | Raynor P. | Walker J. | Storton T. | Jeffries D. | Oakes A. | Livermore D. | Mellor I. | Edwards I. | Delgado R. | Phillips R. | Jones B. | Nickeas M. | Millington G. | Howat I. | Sutcliffe P. | Burns D. | Felix G. | Henderson P. | Rush I. |
|---|---|---|---|---|---|---|---|---|---|---|---|---|---|---|---|---|---|---|---|---|---|---|---|---|---|---|---|
| 1R1 | Aug 12 | Port Vale | W | 3-0 | 2-0 | 2805 | Edwards (2), Phillips | 1 | 2 | 3 | 4 | 5 | 6 | 7 | 10 | 9 | 8 | 11 | | | | | | | | | |
| 1R2 | 16 | PORT VALE | D | 1-1 | 1-1 | 3741 | Livermore (pen) | 1 | 2 | 3 | 4 | 5 | 6 | 8 | 10 | 9 | 7* | 11 | 12 | | | | | | | | |
| 2R | 30 | COVENTRY CITY | W | 2-1 | 1-0 | 8598 | Edwards, Mellor | 1 | 2 | 3 | 4 | 5 | 6 | 8 | 10 | 9 | 7 | 11 | | | | | | | | | |
| 3R | Oct 4 | NORWICH CITY | L | 0-2 | 0-0 | 8749 | | 1 | 3 | 11 | 4 | 5 | 6 | 8 | 10 | 9 | 7* | 12 | | 2 | | | | | | | |

## WELSH CUP

| | Date | Opposition | | FT | HT | Att. | Goalscorers | Lloyd B. | Raynor P. | Walker J. | Storton T. | Jeffries D. | Oakes A. | Livermore D. | Mellor I. | Edwards I. | Delgado R. | Phillips R. | Jones B. | Nickeas M. | Millington G. | Howat I. | Sutcliffe P. | Burns D. | Felix G. | Henderson P. | Rush I. |
|---|---|---|---|---|---|---|---|---|---|---|---|---|---|---|---|---|---|---|---|---|---|---|---|---|---|---|---|
| 4R | Jan 10 | BANGOR CITY | D | 0-0 | 0-0 | 1100 | | 1 | 3 | 10 | 4 | 5 | | 8 | | 9 | | 6 | 11 | 2 | | | 7 | | | | |
| 4Rr | 23 | Bangor City | W | 1-0 | 0-0 | | Edwards | 1 | | 3 | 4 | 5 | | 8 | | 9 | | 6 | 11 | 2 | | 10 | 7 | | | | |
| 5R | Feb 14 | OSWESTRY TOWN | W | 4-3 | 1-2 | 438 | Felix, Edwards, Phillips, Leggett (og) | 1 | 2 | 3 | 4 | | 6 | | | 9 | | 10 | | 5 | | | 7 | | 8 | 11 | |
| SF | Apr 4 | WREXHAM | L | 0-1 | 0-0 | 7275 | | 1 | | | 4 | 5 | 7 | 8 | 12 | 9 | | 10 | 6* | 2 | | | | 3 | | 11 | |

## FRIENDLIES

| | Date | Opposition | | FT | HT | Att. | Goalscorers |
|---|---|---|---|---|---|---|---|
| 1 | Aug 5 | York City | D | 1-1 | 1-0 | 1008 | Phillips |

# *SEASON 1979-80*

## FOOTBALL LEAGUE DIVISION 3

| | Date | Opposition | | FT | HT | Att. | Goalscorers | Lloyd B. | Raynor P. | Walker J. | Storton T. | Cottam J. | Oakes A. | Jeffries D. | Ruggiero J. | Edwards I. | Henderson P. | Phillips R. | Jones B. | Howat I. | Burns D. | Sutcliffe P. | Rush I. | Millington G. | Fear K. | Phillips T. | Lewis P. |
|---|---|---|---|---|---|---|---|---|---|---|---|---|---|---|---|---|---|---|---|---|---|---|---|---|---|---|---|
| 1 | Aug 18 | Wimbledon | W | 3-2 | 2-1 | 3549 | Ruggiero, Henderson, Edwards | 1 | 2 | 3 | 4 | 5 | 6 | 7 | 8 | 9 | 10 | 11 | | | | | | | | | |
| 2 | 22 | GRIMSBY TOWN | W | 3-1 | 1-1 | 3779 | Edwards (2), Raynor (pen) | 1 | 2 | 3 | 4 | 5 | 6 | 7* | 8 | 9 | 11 | 10 | 12 | | | | | | | | |
| 3 | 25 | SHEFFIELD UNITED | D | 1-1 | 0-1 | 6361 | Jones | 1 | 2 | 3 | 4* | 5 | 6 | 12 | 8 | 9 | | 11 | 7 | 10 | | | | | | | |
| 4 | Sep 1 | Bury | L | 0-2 | 0-1 | 3447 | | 1 | 2 | 3 | 4 | 5 | 6 | 8 | 12 | 9 | | 11 | 7 | 10* | | | | | | | |
| 5 | 8 | MILLWALL | D | 1-1 | 1-0 | 3473 | Storton | 1 | 2 | | 4 | 5 | | 6 | 8 | 9 | 11 | 10 | 12 | | 3* | 7 | | | | | |
| 6 | 15 | Gillingham | D | 2-2 | 1-1 | 7397 | Oakes, Rush | 1 | 2 | 3 | 4 | 5 | 6 | 8 | 12 | 9* | | 10 | | | | 7 | 11 | | | | |
| 7 | 18 | Swindon Town | L | 1-3 | 0-0 | 6102 | Henderson | 1 | 2 | 3 | 4 | 5 | 6* | 8 | 12 | 9 | 11 | 10 | | | | 7 | | | | | |
| 8 | 22 | READING | L | 0-2 | 0-0 | 3226 | | 1 | 2 | 3 | 4 | 5 | | 8 | 10 | 9 | | 6* | 12 | | | 7 | 11 | | | | |
| 9 | 29 | Carlisle United | D | 2-2 | 0-0 | 4324 | Jones, Raynor (pen) | | 2 | 3 | 4 | 5 | | | 8 | 9 | 10 | 6 | 11 | | | 7 | | 1 | | | |
| 10 | Oct 6 | PLYMOUTH ARGYLE | W | 1-0 | 1-0 | 2818 | Henderson | | 2 | 11 | 4 | 5 | 6 | | 8 | 9 | 10 | | 7 | | 3 | | | 1 | | | |
| 11 | 9 | Grimsby Town | W | 2-0 | 1-0 | 8007 | Oakes, Edwards | | | 3 | 4 | 5 | 6 | | | 9 | 11 | 10 | 8 | | 2 | 7* | 12 | 1 | | | |
| 12 | 13 | Exeter City | L | 0-1 | 0-0 | 3454 | | 1 | 2 | 11 | 4 | 5 | 6 | | | 9 | 10 | 12 | 7 | 8* | 3 | | | | | | |
| 13 | 20 | HULL CITY | W | 2-1 | 1-1 | 3209 | Sutcliffe, Jones | 1 | 2 | 3 | 4 | 5 | 6 | | | 9 | 11 | 10 | 8 | | | 7 | | | | | |
| 14 | 24 | BLACKBURN ROVERS | D | 0-0 | 0-0 | 3955 | | 1 | 2 | 3 | 4 | 5 | 6 | | | 9 | 11 | 10 | 8 | | | 7 | | | | | |
| 15 | 27 | Barnsley | D | 1-1 | 0-0 | 9879 | Edwards | 1 | 2 | 3 | 4 | 5 | 6 | | | 9 | 10 | 11 | | | | 7 | 8 | | | | |
| 16 | Nov 3 | WIMBLEDON | W | 3-1 | 0-1 | 2891 | Rush, Walker, Storton | | 2 | 3 | 4 | 5 | 6 | 8 | | | 11 | 10 | | | | 7 | 9 | 1 | | | |
| 17 | 7 | Blackburn Rovers | L | 0-2 | 0-0 | 5759 | | | 2 | 3 | 4 | 5 | 6 | 12 | | | 11 | 10 | 8 | | | 7* | 9 | 1 | | | |
| 18 | 10 | Oxford United | W | 1-0 | 0-0 | 4026 | Rush | | 2 | 3 | 4 | 5 | 6 | | | | 11 | 10 | 8 | | | 7 | 9 | 1 | | | |
| 19 | 17 | MANSFIELD TOWN | W | 1-0 | 0-0 | 2920 | R Phillips | | 2 | 3 | 4 | 5 | 6 | | | | 10 | 11 | 8 | | | 7 | 9 | 1 | | | |
| 20 | Dec 1 | SHEFFIELD WEDNESDAY | D | 2-2 | 1-1 | 6241 | Rush, R Phillips | | 2 | 3 | 4 | 5 | | 6 | | | 11 | 10 | 8 | | | 7 | 9 | 1 | | | |
| 21 | 7 | Southend United | L | 1-4 | 1-1 | 3885 | Rush | | 2 | 3 | 4 | 5 | 6 | | | | 11 | 10 | 8 | | | 7 | 9 | 1 | | | |
| 22 | 21 | ROTHERHAM UNITED | W | 3-1 | 0-1 | 2727 | Rush (2), Storton | | 2 | 3 | 4 | 5 | 6 | | | | 11 | 10 | 8 | | | 7 | 9 | 1 | | | |
| 23 | 26 | Brentford | D | 2-2 | 0-1 | 10140 | Sutcliffe, Jones | | 2 | 3 | 4 | 5 | 6 | | | | 11 | 10 | 8 | | | 7 | 9 | 1 | | | |
| 24 | 29 | BLACKPOOL | W | 1-0 | 0-0 | 4212 | Rush | | 2* | 3 | 4 | 5 | 6 | 12 | | | 11 | 10 | 8 | | | 7 | 9 | 1 | | | |
| 25 | Jan 8 | Colchester United | D | 1-1 | 0-0 | 3251 | R Phillips (pen) | | | 3 | 4 | 5 | 6 | 2 | 7 | | 11 | 10 | 8 | | | | 9 | 1 | | | |
| 26 | 12 | BURY | W | 1-0 | 0-0 | 4692 | Jones | | | 3 | 4 | 5 | 6 | 2 | 7* | | 11 | 10 | 8 | | 12 | | 9 | 1 | | | |
| 27 | 19 | Millwall | L | 1-3 | 1-3 | 5270 | Coleman (og) | | | 3 | 4 | 5 | 6 | 2 | | | 11 | 10 | 8* | | | 7 | 9 | 1 | 12 | | |
| 28 | Feb 9 | Reading | L | 1-2 | 0-2 | 5381 | Rush | | | 3 | 4 | 5 | 6 | 2 | | | | 10* | 8 | | 12 | 7 | 9 | 1 | 11 | | |
| 29 | 20 | CARLISLE UNITED | W | 1-0 | 0-0 | 3765 | Rush | | | 3 | 4 | 5 | 6 | 2 | | | 11 | 10 | 8 | | | 7 | 9 | 1 | | | |
| 30 | 26 | Sheffield United | D | 1-1 | 0-1 | 13738 | Rush | | 2 | 3 | | 5 | | 4 | | | 11 | 10 | 8 | | | 7 | 9 | 1 | 6 | | |
| 31 | Mar 1 | Hull City | L | 0-1 | 0-0 | 5771 | | | 2 | 3 | | 5 | 6 | 4 | | | 11 | 10 | 8 | | | 7 | 9 | 1 | | | |
| 32 | 8 | BARNSLEY | D | 0-0 | 0-0 | 5024 | | | | 3 | 4 | 5 | | 2 | | | 11 | 10 | 8 | | | 7 | 9 | 1 | 6 | | |
| 33 | 15 | Plymouth Argyle | L | 0-1 | 0-1 | 4095 | | | 2 | 3 | 4 | 5 | | 6 | | | 11 | 10 | 8* | | | 12 | 9 | 1 | | 7 | |
| 34 | 19 | SWINDON TOWN | W | 1-0 | 1-0 | 2611 | Raynor (pen) | | 2 | 3 | 4 | 6 | | 5 | | | 11 | 10 | 8 | | | | 9 | 1 | | 7 | |
| 35 | 22 | OXFORD UNITED | W | 1-0 | 1-0 | 3088 | Rush | | 2 | 3 | 4 | 5 | | 6 | | | 11 | 10 | 8 | | | | 9 | 1 | | 7 | |
| 36 | 26 | EXETER CITY | L | 1-3 | 1-1 | 2867 | R Phillips | 1 | 2 | 3 | 4 | 5 | | 6 | | | 12 | 11 | 8* | | | 7 | 9 | | | 10 | |
| 37 | 29 | Mansfield Town | L | 1-2 | 1-1 | 3097 | Jones | 1 | | 3 | 4 | 5 | | 2 | | | | 6 | 8 | | | 7 | 9 | | 10 | 11 | |
| 38 | Apr 1 | Rotherham United | L | 0-2 | 0-1 | 4631 | | 1 | | 3 | 4* | 5 | 6 | 2 | | | | 11 | 8 | | | 7 | 9 | | 12 | 10 | |
| 39 | 5 | BRENTFORD | D | 1-1 | 0-1 | 2751 | T Phillips | 1 | 2 | 3 | | 5 | 6 | 4 | | | 12 | 10* | 8 | | | 7 | 9 | | | 11 | |
| 40 | 7 | Chesterfield | L | 0-2 | 0-2 | 9100 | | 1 | 2 | 3 | | 5 | 6 | 4 | | | 12 | 11 | 8* | | | | 9 | | 7 | 10 | |
| 41 | 12 | COLCHESTER UNITED | W | 2-1 | 1-1 | 2282 | Rush (2) | | 2 | 3 | | 5 | 6* | 4 | | | 12 | 11 | | | | 7 | 9 | 1 | 8 | 10 | |
| 42 | 19 | Sheffield Wednesday | L | 0-3 | 0-1 | 19130 | | | 2 | 3 | 4 | | | 5 | | | 12 | 6 | 8 | | | 7 | 9 | 1 | 10 | 11* | |
| 43 | 23 | CHESTERFIELD | W | 1-0 | 1-0 | 3737 | Walker | | 2 | 3 | | 5 | 6 | 4 | | | 11 | 10 | | | | 7 | 9 | 1 | 8 | | |
| 44 | 26 | SOUTHEND UNITED | W | 2-1 | 1-0 | 2461 | Fear, Sutcliffe | | 2 | 3 | | 5 | 6 | 4 | | | 11 | 10 | | | | 7 | 9 | 1 | 8 | | |
| 45 | 30 | GILLINGHAM | L | 0-2 | 0-0 | 2027 | | | 2 | 3* | 4 | 5 | | 6 | | | 9 | 10 | | | 12 | 7 | | 1 | 8 | 11 | |
| 46 | May 3 | Blackpool | D | 0-0 | 0-0 | 5925 | | | 2 | | 4 | 5 | | 6 | | | 9 | 10 | | | 3 | 7 | | 1 | 8 | 11 | |
| | | | | | | | Apps. | 17 | 37 | 44 | 39 | 45 | 32 | 31 | 9 | 15 | 34 | 44 | 33 | 3 | 5 | 34 | 32 | 29 | 11 | 12 | |
| | | | | | | | Subs. | | | | | | | 3 | 3 | | 5 | 1 | 3 | | 3 | 1 | 1 | | 2 | | |
| | | | | | | | Goals | | 3 | 2 | 3 | | 2 | | 1 | 5 | 3 | 4 | 6 | | | 3 | 14 | | 1 | 1 | |

Own goals 1

## F.A. CUP

| | Date | Opposition | | FT | HT | Att. | Goalscorers | Lloyd B. | Raynor P. | Walker J. | Storton T. | Cottam J. | Oakes A. | Jeffries D. | Ruggiero J. | Edwards I. | Henderson P. | Phillips R. | Jones B. | Howat I. | Burns D. | Sutcliffe P. | Rush I. | Millington G. | Fear K. | Phillips T. | Lewis P. |
|---|---|---|---|---|---|---|---|---|---|---|---|---|---|---|---|---|---|---|---|---|---|---|---|---|---|---|---|
| 1R | Nov 24 | WORKINGTON | W | 5-1 | 3-1 | 2934 | Henderson (2), Sutcliffe, Rush (2) | | 2 | 3 | 4 | 5 | 6* | 12 | | | 10 | 11 | 8 | | | 7 | 9 | 1 | | | |
| 2R | Dec 18 | BARNSLEY | W | 1-0 | 0-0 | 4561 | Raynor (pen) | | 2 | 3 | 4 | 5 | 6 | | | | 10 | 11 | 8 | | | 7 | 9 | 1 | | | |
| 3R | Jan 5 | Newcastle United | W | 2-0 | 1-0 | 24548 | Henderson, Rush | | | 3 | 4 | 5 | 6 | 2 | | | 10 | 11 | 8 | | | 7 | 9 | 1 | | | |
| 4R | 26 | MILLWALL | W | 2-0 | 2-0 | 7966 | Storton, Rush | | | 3 | 4 | 5 | 6 | 2 | | | 11* | 10 | 8 | 12 | | 7 | 9 | 1 | | | |
| 5R | Feb 16 | Ipswich Town | L | 1-2 | 1-2 | 26353 | Jones | | | 3 | 4 | 5 | 6 | 2 | | | | 10 | 8 | 11 | | 7 | 9 | 1 | | | |

## LEAGUE CUP

| | Date | Opposition | | FT | HT | Att. | Goalscorers | Lloyd B. | Raynor P. | Walker J. | Storton T. | Cottam J. | Oakes A. | Jeffries D. | Ruggiero J. | Edwards I. | Henderson P. | Phillips R. | Jones B. | Howat I. | Burns D. | Sutcliffe P. | Rush I. | Millington G. | Fear K. | Phillips T. | Lewis P. |
|---|---|---|---|---|---|---|---|---|---|---|---|---|---|---|---|---|---|---|---|---|---|---|---|---|---|---|---|
| 1R1 | Aug 11 | WALSALL | W | 2-1 | 1-1 | 3872 | Henderson (2) | 1 | 2 | 3 | 4 | 5 | 6 | | 8 | 9 | 11 | 10 | | | | 7 | | | | | |
| 1R2 | 14 | Walsall | D | 0-0 | 0-0 | 3611 | | 1 | 2 | 3 | 4 | 5 | 6 | 7 | 8 | 9 | 11 | 10 | | | | | | | | | |
| 2R1 | 28 | Swindon Town | L | 0-1 | 0-1 | 6965 | | 1 | 2 | 3 | | 5 | 6 | 4 | 8 | 9 | 11* | 10 | 7 | 12 | | | | | | | |
| 2R2 | Sep 5 | SWINDON TOWN | D | 1-1 | 0-0 | 3930 | Sutcliffe | 1 | 2 | 3 | 4 | 5 | 6 | 8 | | 9 | 11 | 10 | | | | 7 | | | | | |

## WELSH CUP

| | Date | Opposition | | FT | HT | Att. | Goalscorers | Lloyd B. | Raynor P. | Walker J. | Storton T. | Cottam J. | Oakes A. | Jeffries D. | Ruggiero J. | Edwards I. | Henderson P. | Phillips R. | Jones B. | Howat I. | Burns D. | Sutcliffe P. | Rush I. | Millington G. | Fear K. | Phillips T. | Lewis P. |
|---|---|---|---|---|---|---|---|---|---|---|---|---|---|---|---|---|---|---|---|---|---|---|---|---|---|---|---|
| 4R | Jan 21 | BANGOR CITY | D | 1-1 | 1-1 | 923 | Phillips | | | 3 | 4 | 5 | 6 | | | | 11* | 10 | | 8 | 2 | 7 | 9 | 1 | | | 12 |
| 4Rr | Feb 5 | Bangor City | W | 2-0 | 1-0 | 1937 | Howat, Rush | | 8 | 3 | 4 | 5 | 6 | 2 | | | | 10 | | 7 | 11 | | 9 | 1 | | | |
| 5R | Mar 4 | Merthyr Tydfil | L | 0-1 | 0-0 | 1700 | | | 12 | 3 | 4 | 5 | 6 | 2 | | | | 10* | 8 | 9 | | | | 1 | 7 | | 11 |

## FRIENDLIES

| | Date | Opposition | | FT | HT | Att. | Goalscorers |
|---|---|---|---|---|---|---|---|
| 1 | Jul 21 | Bangor City | L | 0-2 | | | |

**1979/80 Season:**
(Back) Sear (Assistant Manager), Burns, Cottam, Howat, Millington, Storton, Raynor, Walker, Pritchard (Physio).
(Front) Sutcliffe, Henderson, Phillips, Oakes (Player-Manager), Rush, Jones, Jeffries.

**1980/81 Season:**
(Back) Jeffries, Cottam, Kearney, Walker, Millington, Lloyd, Zelem, Storton, Raynor, Anderson.
(Front) Jones, Howat, Fear, T Phillips, Oakes (Player-Manager), Ludlam, Sutcliffe, Birch, R Phillips, Burns.

# SEASON 1980-81

## FOOTBALL LEAGUE DIVISION 3

| | Date | Opposition | | FT | HT | Att. | Goalscorers | Millington G. | Jeffries D. | Walker J. | Storton T. | Cottam J. | Oakes A. | Burns D. | Kearney M. | Birch T. | Jones B. | Ludlam S. | Fear K. | Phillips R. | Raynor P. | Zelem P. | Sutcliffe P. | Phillips T. | Cooke T. | Gendall R. | Howat I. | Needham P. | Anderson J. |
|---|---|---|---|---|---|---|---|---|---|---|---|---|---|---|---|---|---|---|---|---|---|---|---|---|---|---|---|---|---|
| 1 | Aug 16 | OXFORD UNITED | L | 0-1 | 0-1 | 2203 | | 1 | 2 | 3 | 4 | 5 | 6 | 7* | 8 | 9 | 10 | 11 | 12 | | | | | | | | | | |
| 2 | 19 | Plymouth Argyle | L | 0-2 | 0-0 | 4823 | | 1 | 2 | 3 | 4 | 5* | 6 | 7 | 8 | 9 | 10 | 11 | | 12 | | | | | | | | | |
| 3 | 23 | CARLISLE UNITED | W | 1-0 | 0-0 | 2007 | Oakes | 1 | | 3 | 4 | | 6 | | 8 | | 10 | 11 | | | 2 | 5 | 7 | 9 | | | | | |
| 4 | 30 | Millwall | L | 0-1 | 0-0 | 3264 | | 1 | | 3 | 4 | 5 | 6 | | 8 | | 10 | 11 | | | 2 | | 7 | 9 | | | | | |
| 5 | Sep 6 | EXETER CITY | W | 1-0 | 0-0 | 1974 | Cooke | 1 | | 3 | 4 | 5 | 6 | | 8 | | 10 | 11* | | | 2 | | 7 | 9 | 12 | | | | |
| 6 | 13 | Charlton Athletic | L | 0-1 | 0-0 | 4422 | | 1 | | 3 | 4 | 5 | 6 | | 9 | 7 | 8 | 10 | | | 2 | | | 12 | 11* | | | | |
| 7 | 20 | BURNLEY | D | 0-0 | 0-0 | 3402 | | 1 | | 3 | 4 | 5 | | | 9 | 7 | 8 | 10 | | 6 | 2 | | | | 11* | 12 | | | |
| 8 | 27 | Colchester United | D | 1-1 | 0-0 | 2147 | Jones | 1 | | 3 | 4 | 5 | | | 9 | 7 | 10 | 11 | 6 | | 2 | | | | | | 8 | | |
| 9 | Oct 4 | Swindon Town | W | 2-1 | 0-0 | 5577 | Howat, Ludlam | 1 | | 3 | 4 | 5 | | | 9 | 7 | 10 | 11 | 6 | | 2 | | | | | | 8 | | |
| 10 | 8 | HULL CITY | W | 4-1 | 2-0 | 1964 | T Phillips (2), Ludlam, Howat | 1 | | 3 | 4 | 5 | | | | 7 | 8 | 11 | 6 | | 2 | | | 10 | | | 9 | | |
| 11 | 11 | READING | W | 1-0 | 0-0 | 2444 | T Phillips | 1 | | 3 | 4 | 5 | | | | 7 | 10 | 11 | 6 | | 2 | | | 8 | | | 9 | | |
| 12 | 18 | Brentford | W | 1-0 | 1-0 | 6600 | Howat | 1 | | 3 | 4 | 5 | | 12 | | 7 | 8 | 11 | 6* | | 2 | | | 10 | | | 9 | | |
| 13 | 21 | Rotherham United | D | 0-0 | 0-0 | 6635 | | 1 | | 3 | 4 | 5 | | | | 7 | 10 | 11 | | 6 | 2 | | | 8 | | | 9 | | |
| 14 | 25 | FULHAM | L | 0-1 | 0-0 | 3169 | | 1 | | 3 | 4 | 5 | | 12 | | 7 | 10 | 11 | 6 | | 2 | | | 8 | | | 9* | | |
| 15 | 29 | HUDDERSFIELD TOWN | L | 0-2 | 0-2 | 4331 | | 1 | | 3 | 4 | 5 | | 12 | | 7* | 10 | 11 | | | 2 | | | 8 | | 6 | 9 | | |
| 16 | Nov 1 | Barnsley | L | 0-2 | 0-1 | 9330 | | 1 | | 3 | 4 | 5 | | | | 7 | 10 | 11 | | | 2 | | | 8 | | 6 | 9 | | |
| 17 | 4 | Hull City | D | 0-0 | 0-0 | 3335 | | 1 | 6 | 3 | 4 | 5 | | 11 | | 9 | 10 | | | | 2 | | 7 | 8 | | | | | |
| 18 | 8 | SHEFFIELD UNITED | W | 3-2 | 0-0 | 4563 | Burns, T Phillips, Sutcliffe | 1 | 5 | 3 | 4 | | | 11 | | 9 | 10 | 6 | | | 2 | | 7 | 8 | | | | | |
| 19 | 12 | PLYMOUTH ARGYLE | W | 1-0 | 0-0 | 2247 | Ludlam | 1 | 4 | | | 5 | | 3 | | 9 | 10 | 6 | | | 2 | | 7 | 8 | | 11 | | | |
| 20 | 15 | Oxford United | L | 0-1 | 0-0 | 2526 | | 1 | 2 | | 4 | 5 | | 3 | | 9 | 10 | 6 | | | | | 7 | 8 | | 11* | | 12 | |
| 21 | 29 | Portsmouth | L | 0-2 | 0-1 | 10515 | | 1 | 2 | 3 | 4 | 5 | 6 | 11 | | 9 | 10 | | 7 | | | | | 8 | | | | | |
| 22 | Dec 3 | NEWPORT COUNTY | D | 1-1 | 0-1 | 1640 | Sutcliffe | 1 | 2 | 3 | 4 | 5* | 6 | 11 | | 9 | | 10 | 7 | | | | 12 | 8 | | | | | |
| 23 | 6 | WALSALL | W | 1-0 | 0-0 | 2215 | T Phillips | 1 | 5 | 3 | 4 | | 6 | | | 9 | | 10 | 2 | | | | 7 | 8 | | | 11 | | |
| 24 | 13 | Newport County | D | 1-1 | 1-1 | 4169 | Cottam | 1 | 2 | 3 | 4 | 5 | 6 | | | | | 10 | 9 | | | | 7 | 8 | | | 11 | | |
| 25 | 20 | GILLINGHAM | L | 1-2 | 1-1 | 1740 | Ludlam | 1 | 2 | 3 | 4 | 5 | 6 | | | | 12 | 10 | 9 | | | | 7 | 8 | | | 11* | | |
| 26 | 26 | Blackpool | W | 3-2 | 0-2 | 4878 | Fear, Ludlam, Cooke | 1 | 2 | 3 | 4 | 5 | 6 | | | | 10 | 11 | 9 | | | | 7 | 8* | 12 | | | | |
| 27 | 27 | CHESTERFIELD | W | 2-1 | 1-0 | 4222 | Cooke, Fear | 1 | 2 | 3 | 4 | 5 | 6 | | | | 8 | 11 | 9 | | | | 7 | | 10 | | | | |
| 28 | Jan 2 | Reading | L | 0-3 | 0-0 | 3804 | | 1 | 2 | 3 | 4 | 5 | 6 | | | | 8 | 11 | 9 | | | | 7 | | 10 | | | | |
| 29 | 10 | BRENTFORD | D | 0-0 | 0-0 | 2041 | | 1 | 2 | 3 | 4 | 5 | 6 | | | | 8 | 11* | 9 | | | | 7 | 12 | 10 | | | | |
| 30 | 17 | Walsall | L | 1-2 | 1-0 | 3483 | Jones | 1 | 2 | 3 | 4 | 5 | 6 | | | 9 | 8 | | 10 | | | | 7 | | 11 | | | | |
| 31 | 24 | MILLWALL | L | 0-1 | 0-1 | 2114 | | 1 | 5 | 3 | 4 | | 6 | 11 | | 9 | 8 | | 7 | | 2* | | | 12 | 10 | | | | |
| 32 | 31 | Carlisle United | L | 0-3 | 0-3 | 3282 | | 1 | 2 | 3 | 4 | 5 | | 6 | | 9 | 8 | | 7* | | | 12 | | 10 | 11 | | | | |
| 33 | Feb 7 | CHARLTON ATHLETIC | W | 4-0 | 3-0 | 2461 | T Phillips, Jones, Howat, Raynor (pen) | 1 | 6 | 3 | 4 | 5 | | 11 | | | 8 | | | | 2 | | 7 | 10 | | | 9 | | |
| 34 | 21 | COLCHESTER UNITED | D | 0-0 | 0-0 | 1778 | | 1 | 6 | 3* | 4 | 5 | | 11 | | | 8 | 12 | | | 2 | | 7 | 10 | | | 9 | | |
| 35 | 28 | Burnley | L | 0-1 | 0-0 | 4993 | | 1 | 2 | | 4 | 5 | | | | | 8 | 6 | 11 | | 3 | | 7 | 10* | | | 9 | 12 | |
| 36 | Mar 7 | SWINDON TOWN | W | 1-0 | 1-0 | 1810 | Rollings (og) | 1 | 2* | | 4 | 5 | 6 | | | | 8 | 11 | 9 | | 3 | 12 | 7 | 10 | | | | | |
| 37 | 17 | Fulham | W | 1-0 | 1-0 | 3387 | T Phillips | 1 | | | 4 | 5 | 6 | | | | 8 | 11 | 9 | | 3 | | 7 | 10 | | | | 2 | |
| 38 | 21 | ROTHERHAM UNITED | L | 0-1 | 0-1 | 3945 | | 1 | | | 4 | 5 | 6 | | | 12 | 8 | 11 | 9 | | 3 | | 7 | 10* | | | | 2 | |
| 39 | 28 | Huddersfield Town | D | 0-0 | 0-0 | 11117 | | 1 | | | 4 | 5 | 6 | | | 10 | 8 | 11 | 9 | | 3 | | 7 | | | | | 2 | |
| 40 | Apr 4 | BARNSLEY | D | 2-2 | 1-1 | 4680 | Ludlam (2) | 1 | | | 4 | 5 | 6 | | | 10 | 8 | 11 | 9 | | 3 | | 7 | | | | | 2 | |
| 41 | 7 | Sheffield United | L | 0-2 | 0-2 | 10027 | | 1 | | | 4 | 5 | 6 | | | 10 | 8 | 11 | 9 | | 3 | | 7 | | | | | 2 | |
| 42 | 17 | BLACKPOOL | W | 2-1 | 0-0 | 2804 | Cooke (2) | 1 | | | 4 | 5 | 6 | | | 10 | 8 | 11 | 9 | | 3 | | 7 | | 12 | | | 2* | |
| 43 | 18 | Chesterfield | L | 0-2 | 0-2 | 3850 | | 1 | | | 4 | 5 | 6 | 3 | | 9* | | 11 | 7 | | 2 | 12 | | 8 | 10 | | | | |
| 44 | 25 | Gillingham | L | 1-2 | 0-2 | 3228 | Oakes | 1 | | | 4 | 5 | 6 | 3 | | 10 | 8 | 11 | 9 | | 2 | | 7* | | 12 | | | | |
| 45 | 29 | Exeter City | D | 2-2 | 0-1 | 3056 | Jones, Howat | 1 | | | 4 | 5 | 6* | 3 | | 9 | 8 | 11 | 7 | | 2 | 12 | | | | | 10 | | |
| 46 | May 2 | PORTSMOUTH | L | 0-1 | 0-0 | 2153 | | 1 | | | | 5 | 6 | | | | 8 | 11 | 7 | | 3 | 4 | | | 10 | | 9 | 2 | |
| | | | | | | | Apps. | 46 | 22 | 32 | 44 | 42 | 28 | 15 | 9 | 30 | 41 | 39 | 30 | 2 | 32 | 2 | 26 | 28 | 10 | 4 | 17 | 7 | |
| | | | | | | | Subs. | | | | | | | 3 | | 1 | 1 | 1 | 1 | 1 | | 4 | 1 | 3 | 4 | 1 | | 2 | |
| | | | | | | | Goals | | | | | 1 | 2 | 1 | | | 4 | 7 | 2 | | 1 | | 2 | 7 | 5 | | 5 | | |

Own goals 1

## F.A. CUP

| | Date | Opposition | | FT | HT | Att. | Goalscorers | Millington G. | Jeffries D. | Walker J. | Storton T. | Cottam J. | Oakes A. | Burns D. | Kearney M. | Birch T. | Jones B. | Ludlam S. | Fear K. | Phillips R. | Raynor P. | Zelem P. | Sutcliffe P. | Phillips T. | Cooke T. | Gendall R. | Howat I. | Needham P. | Anderson J. |
|---|---|---|---|---|---|---|---|---|---|---|---|---|---|---|---|---|---|---|---|---|---|---|---|---|---|---|---|---|---|
| 1R | Nov 22 | BARNSLEY | L | 1-2 | 1-1 | 7135 | Birch | 1 | 2 | | 4 | 5 | | 11 | | 9 | 10 | 6 | | | 3 | | 7* | 8 | | | 12 | | |

## LEAGUE CUP

| | Date | Opposition | | FT | HT | Att. | Goalscorers | Millington G. | Jeffries D. | Walker J. | Storton T. | Cottam J. | Oakes A. | Burns D. | Kearney M. | Birch T. | Jones B. | Ludlam S. | Fear K. | Phillips R. | Raynor P. | Zelem P. | Sutcliffe P. | Phillips T. | Cooke T. | Gendall R. | Howat I. | Needham P. | Anderson J. |
|---|---|---|---|---|---|---|---|---|---|---|---|---|---|---|---|---|---|---|---|---|---|---|---|---|---|---|---|---|---|
| 1R1 | Aug 9 | STOCKPORT COUNTY | D | 1-1 | 0-0 | 2468 | Oakes | 1 | | 3 | 4 | 5 | 6 | | 8 | 9 | 10 | 11* | | 12 | 2 | | | | | | | | 7 |
| 1R2 | 11 | Stockport County * | L | 0-1 | 0-0 | 2720 | | 1 | 2 | 3 | 4 | 5 | 6 | | 8 | 9 | 7 | 11 | | 10 | | | | | | | | | |

* Extra time played following score of 0-0 after 90 minutes

## FRIENDLIES

| | Date | Opposition | | FT | HT | Att. | Goalscorers |
|---|---|---|---|---|---|---|---|
| 1 | Jul 19 | Caernarfon United | W | 6-1 | | | Kearney (2), T Phillips (2), Birch, Anderson |

# FINAL LEAGUE TABLES: 1980/81 - 1987/88

Final League Table 1980/81 Division 3

| | | Pl. | Home | | | | | Away | | | | | F. | A. | Pts |
|---|---|---|---|---|---|---|---|---|---|---|---|---|---|---|---|
| | | | W | D | L | F | A | W | D | L | F | A | | | |
| 1 | Rotherham United | 46 | 17 | 6 | 0 | 43 | 8 | 7 | 7 | 9 | 19 | 24 | 62 | 32 | 61 |
| 2 | Barnsley | 46 | 15 | 5 | 3 | 46 | 19 | 6 | 12 | 5 | 26 | 26 | 72 | 45 | 59 |
| 3 | Charlton Athletic | 46 | 14 | 6 | 3 | 36 | 17 | 11 | 3 | 9 | 27 | 27 | 63 | 44 | 59 |
| 4 | Huddersfield Town | 46 | 14 | 6 | 3 | 40 | 11 | 7 | 8 | 8 | 31 | 29 | 71 | 40 | 56 |
| 5 | Chesterfield | 46 | 17 | 4 | 2 | 42 | 16 | 6 | 6 | 11 | 30 | 32 | 72 | 48 | 56 |
| 6 | Portsmouth | 46 | 14 | 5 | 4 | 35 | 19 | 8 | 4 | 11 | 20 | 28 | 55 | 47 | 53 |
| 7 | Plymouth Argyle | 46 | 14 | 5 | 4 | 35 | 18 | 5 | 9 | 9 | 21 | 26 | 56 | 44 | 52 |
| 8 | Burnley | 46 | 13 | 5 | 5 | 37 | 21 | 5 | 9 | 9 | 23 | 27 | 60 | 48 | 50 |
| 9 | Brentford | 46 | 7 | 9 | 7 | 30 | 25 | 7 | 10 | 6 | 22 | 24 | 52 | 49 | 47 |
| 10 | Reading | 46 | 13 | 5 | 5 | 39 | 22 | 5 | 5 | 13 | 23 | 40 | 62 | 62 | 46 |
| 11 | Exeter City | 46 | 9 | 9 | 5 | 36 | 30 | 7 | 4 | 12 | 26 | 36 | 62 | 66 | 45 |
| 12 | Newport County | 46 | 11 | 6 | 6 | 38 | 22 | 4 | 7 | 12 | 26 | 39 | 64 | 61 | 43 |
| 13 | Fulham | 46 | 8 | 7 | 8 | 28 | 29 | 7 | 6 | 10 | 29 | 35 | 57 | 64 | 43 |
| 14 | Oxford United | 46 | 7 | 8 | 8 | 20 | 24 | 6 | 9 | 8 | 19 | 23 | 39 | 47 | 43 |
| 15 | Gillingham | 46 | 9 | 8 | 6 | 23 | 19 | 3 | 10 | 10 | 25 | 39 | 48 | 58 | 42 |
| 16 | Millwall | 46 | 10 | 9 | 4 | 30 | 21 | 4 | 5 | 14 | 13 | 39 | 43 | 60 | 42 |
| 17 | Swindon Town | 46 | 10 | 6 | 7 | 35 | 27 | 3 | 9 | 11 | 16 | 29 | 51 | 56 | 41 |
| ***18*** | ***Chester*** | ***46*** | ***11*** | ***5*** | ***7*** | ***25*** | ***17*** | ***4*** | ***6*** | ***13*** | ***13*** | ***31*** | ***38*** | ***48*** | ***41*** |
| 19 | Carlisle United | 46 | 8 | 9 | 6 | 32 | 29 | 6 | 4 | 13 | 24 | 41 | 56 | 70 | 41 |
| 20 | Walsall | 46 | 8 | 9 | 6 | 43 | 43 | 5 | 6 | 12 | 16 | 31 | 59 | 74 | 41 |
| 21 | Sheffield United | 46 | 12 | 6 | 5 | 38 | 20 | 2 | 6 | 15 | 27 | 43 | 65 | 63 | 40 |
| 22 | Colchester United | 46 | 12 | 7 | 4 | 35 | 22 | 2 | 4 | 17 | 10 | 43 | 45 | 65 | 39 |
| 23 | Blackpool | 46 | 5 | 9 | 9 | 19 | 28 | 4 | 5 | 14 | 26 | 47 | 45 | 75 | 32 |
| 24 | Hull City | 46 | 7 | 8 | 8 | 23 | 22 | 1 | 8 | 14 | 17 | 49 | 40 | 71 | 32 |

Final League Table 1981/82 Division 3

| | | Pl. | Home | | | | | Away | | | | | F. | A. | Pts |
|---|---|---|---|---|---|---|---|---|---|---|---|---|---|---|---|
| | | | W | D | L | F | A | W | D | L | F | A | | | |
| 1 | Burnley | 46 | 13 | 7 | 3 | 37 | 20 | 8 | 10 | 5 | 29 | 25 | 66 | 45 | 80 |
| 2 | Carlisle United | 46 | 17 | 4 | 2 | 44 | 21 | 6 | 7 | 10 | 21 | 29 | 65 | 50 | 80 |
| 3 | Fulham | 46 | 12 | 9 | 2 | 44 | 22 | 9 | 6 | 8 | 33 | 29 | 77 | 51 | 78 |
| 4 | Lincoln City | 46 | 13 | 7 | 3 | 40 | 16 | 8 | 7 | 8 | 26 | 24 | 66 | 40 | 77 |
| 5 | Oxford United | 46 | 10 | 8 | 5 | 28 | 18 | 9 | 6 | 8 | 35 | 31 | 63 | 49 | 71 |
| 6 | Gillingham | 46 | 14 | 5 | 4 | 44 | 26 | 6 | 6 | 11 | 20 | 30 | 64 | 56 | 71 |
| 7 | Southend United | 46 | 11 | 7 | 5 | 35 | 23 | 7 | 8 | 8 | 28 | 28 | 63 | 51 | 69 |
| 8 | Brentford | 46 | 8 | 6 | 9 | 28 | 22 | 11 | 5 | 7 | 28 | 25 | 56 | 47 | 68 |
| 9 | Millwall | 46 | 12 | 4 | 7 | 36 | 28 | 6 | 9 | 8 | 26 | 34 | 62 | 62 | 67 |
| 10 | Plymouth Argyle | 46 | 12 | 5 | 6 | 37 | 24 | 6 | 6 | 11 | 27 | 32 | 64 | 56 | 65 |
| 11 | Chesterfield | 46 | 12 | 4 | 7 | 33 | 27 | 6 | 6 | 11 | 24 | 31 | 57 | 58 | 64 |
| 12 | Reading | 46 | 11 | 6 | 6 | 43 | 35 | 6 | 5 | 12 | 24 | 40 | 67 | 75 | 62 |
| 13 | Portsmouth | 46 | 11 | 10 | 2 | 33 | 14 | 3 | 9 | 11 | 23 | 37 | 56 | 51 | 61 |
| 14 | Preston North End | 46 | 10 | 7 | 6 | 25 | 22 | 6 | 6 | 11 | 25 | 34 | 50 | 56 | 61 |
| 15 | Bristol Rovers | 46 | 12 | 4 | 7 | 35 | 28 | 6 | 5 | 12 | 23 | 37 | 58 | 65 | 61 |
| 16 | Newport County | 46 | 9 | 10 | 4 | 28 | 21 | 5 | 6 | 12 | 26 | 33 | 54 | 54 | 58 |
| 17 | Huddersfield Town | 46 | 10 | 5 | 8 | 38 | 25 | 5 | 7 | 11 | 26 | 34 | 64 | 59 | 57 |
| 18 | Exeter City | 46 | 14 | 4 | 5 | 46 | 33 | 2 | 5 | 16 | 25 | 51 | 71 | 84 | 57 |
| 19 | Doncaster Rovers | 46 | 9 | 9 | 5 | 31 | 24 | 4 | 8 | 11 | 24 | 44 | 55 | 68 | 56 |
| 20 | Walsall | 46 | 10 | 7 | 6 | 32 | 23 | 3 | 7 | 13 | 19 | 32 | 51 | 55 | 53 |
| 21 | Wimbledon | 46 | 10 | 6 | 7 | 33 | 27 | 4 | 5 | 14 | 28 | 48 | 61 | 75 | 53 |
| 22 | Swindon Town | 46 | 9 | 5 | 9 | 37 | 36 | 4 | 8 | 11 | 18 | 35 | 55 | 71 | 52 |
| 23 | Bristol City | 46 | 7 | 6 | 10 | 24 | 29 | 4 | 7 | 12 | 16 | 36 | 40 | 65 | 46 |
| ***24*** | ***Chester*** | ***46*** | ***2*** | ***10*** | ***11*** | ***16*** | ***30*** | ***5*** | ***1*** | ***17*** | ***20*** | ***48*** | ***36*** | ***78*** | ***32*** |

Final League Table 1982/83 Division 4

| | | Pl. | Home | | | | | Away | | | | | F. | A. | Pts |
|---|---|---|---|---|---|---|---|---|---|---|---|---|---|---|---|
| | | | W | D | L | F | A | W | D | L | F | A | | | |
| 1 | Wimbledon | 46 | 17 | 4 | 2 | 57 | 23 | 12 | 7 | 4 | 39 | 22 | 96 | 45 | 98 |
| 2 | Hull City | 46 | 14 | 8 | 1 | 48 | 14 | 11 | 7 | 5 | 27 | 20 | 75 | 34 | 90 |
| 3 | Port Vale | 46 | 15 | 4 | 4 | 37 | 16 | 11 | 6 | 6 | 30 | 18 | 67 | 34 | 88 |
| 4 | Scunthorpe United | 46 | 13 | 7 | 3 | 41 | 17 | 10 | 7 | 6 | 30 | 25 | 71 | 42 | 83 |
| 5 | Bury | 46 | 15 | 4 | 4 | 43 | 20 | 8 | 8 | 7 | 31 | 26 | 74 | 46 | 81 |
| 6 | Colchester United | 46 | 17 | 5 | 1 | 51 | 19 | 7 | 4 | 12 | 24 | 36 | 75 | 55 | 81 |
| 7 | York City | 46 | 18 | 4 | 1 | 59 | 19 | 4 | 9 | 10 | 29 | 39 | 88 | 58 | 79 |
| 8 | Swindon Town | 46 | 14 | 3 | 6 | 45 | 27 | 5 | 8 | 10 | 16 | 27 | 61 | 54 | 68 |
| 9 | Peterborough Utd. | 46 | 13 | 6 | 4 | 38 | 23 | 4 | 7 | 12 | 20 | 29 | 58 | 52 | 64 |
| 10 | Mansfield Town | 46 | 11 | 6 | 6 | 32 | 26 | 5 | 7 | 11 | 29 | 44 | 61 | 70 | 61 |
| 11 | Halifax Town | 46 | 9 | 8 | 6 | 31 | 23 | 7 | 4 | 12 | 28 | 43 | 59 | 66 | 60 |
| 12 | Torquay United | 46 | 12 | 3 | 8 | 38 | 30 | 5 | 4 | 14 | 18 | 35 | 56 | 65 | 58 |
| ***13*** | ***Chester*** | ***46*** | ***8*** | ***6*** | ***9*** | ***28*** | ***24*** | ***7*** | ***5*** | ***11*** | ***27*** | ***36*** | ***55*** | ***60*** | ***56*** |
| 14 | Bristol City | 46 | 10 | 8 | 5 | 32 | 25 | 3 | 9 | 11 | 27 | 45 | 59 | 70 | 56 |
| 15 | Northampton Town | 46 | 10 | 8 | 5 | 43 | 29 | 4 | 4 | 15 | 22 | 46 | 65 | 75 | 54 |
| 16 | Stockport County | 46 | 11 | 8 | 4 | 41 | 31 | 3 | 4 | 16 | 19 | 48 | 60 | 79 | 54 |
| 17 | Darlington | 46 | 8 | 5 | 10 | 27 | 30 | 5 | 8 | 10 | 34 | 41 | 61 | 71 | 52 |
| 18 | Aldershot | 46 | 11 | 5 | 7 | 40 | 35 | 1 | 10 | 12 | 21 | 47 | 61 | 82 | 51 |
| 19 | Tranmere Rovers | 46 | 8 | 8 | 7 | 30 | 29 | 5 | 3 | 15 | 19 | 42 | 49 | 71 | 50 |
| 20 | Rochdale | 46 | 11 | 8 | 4 | 38 | 25 | 0 | 8 | 15 | 17 | 48 | 55 | 73 | 49 |
| 21 | Blackpool | 46 | 10 | 8 | 5 | 32 | 23 | 3 | 4 | 16 | 23 | 51 | 55 | 74 | 49 |
| 22 | Hartlepool United | 46 | 11 | 5 | 7 | 30 | 24 | 2 | 4 | 17 | 16 | 52 | 46 | 76 | 48 |
| 23 | Crewe Alexandra | 46 | 9 | 5 | 9 | 35 | 32 | 2 | 3 | 18 | 18 | 39 | 53 | 71 | 41 |
| 24 | Hereford United | 46 | 8 | 6 | 9 | 19 | 23 | 3 | 2 | 18 | 23 | 56 | 42 | 79 | 41 |

Final League Table 1983/84 Division 4

| | | Pl. | Home | | | | | Away | | | | | F. | A. | Pts |
|---|---|---|---|---|---|---|---|---|---|---|---|---|---|---|---|
| | | | W | D | L | F | A | W | D | L | F | A | | | |
| 1 | York City | 46 | 18 | 4 | 1 | 58 | 16 | 13 | 4 | 6 | 38 | 23 | 96 | 39 | 101 |
| 2 | Doncaster Rovers | 46 | 15 | 6 | 2 | 46 | 22 | 9 | 7 | 7 | 36 | 32 | 82 | 54 | 85 |
| 3 | Reading | 46 | 17 | 6 | 0 | 51 | 14 | 5 | 10 | 8 | 33 | 42 | 84 | 56 | 82 |
| 4 | Bristol City | 46 | 18 | 3 | 2 | 51 | 17 | 6 | 7 | 10 | 19 | 27 | 70 | 44 | 82 |
| 5 | Aldershot | 46 | 14 | 6 | 3 | 49 | 29 | 8 | 3 | 12 | 27 | 40 | 76 | 69 | 75 |
| 6 | Blackpool | 46 | 15 | 4 | 4 | 47 | 19 | 6 | 5 | 12 | 23 | 33 | 70 | 52 | 72 |
| 7 | Peterborough Utd. | 46 | 15 | 5 | 3 | 52 | 16 | 3 | 9 | 11 | 20 | 32 | 72 | 48 | 68 |
| 8 | Colchester United | 46 | 14 | 7 | 2 | 45 | 14 | 3 | 9 | 11 | 24 | 39 | 69 | 53 | 67 |
| 9 | Torquay United | 46 | 13 | 7 | 3 | 32 | 18 | 5 | 6 | 12 | 27 | 46 | 59 | 64 | 67 |
| 10 | Tranmere Rovers | 46 | 11 | 5 | 7 | 33 | 26 | 6 | 10 | 7 | 20 | 27 | 53 | 53 | 66 |
| 11 | Hereford United | 46 | 11 | 6 | 6 | 31 | 21 | 5 | 9 | 9 | 23 | 32 | 54 | 53 | 63 |
| 12 | Stockport County | 46 | 12 | 5 | 6 | 34 | 25 | 5 | 6 | 12 | 26 | 39 | 60 | 64 | 62 |
| 13 | Chesterfield | 46 | 10 | 11 | 2 | 34 | 24 | 5 | 4 | 14 | 25 | 37 | 59 | 61 | 60 |
| 14 | Darlington | 46 | 13 | 4 | 6 | 31 | 19 | 4 | 4 | 15 | 18 | 31 | 49 | 50 | 59 |
| 15 | Bury | 46 | 9 | 7 | 7 | 34 | 32 | 6 | 7 | 10 | 27 | 32 | 61 | 64 | 59 |
| 16 | Crewe Alexandra | 46 | 10 | 8 | 5 | 35 | 27 | 6 | 3 | 14 | 21 | 40 | 56 | 67 | 59 |
| 17 | Swindon Town | 46 | 11 | 7 | 5 | 34 | 23 | 4 | 6 | 13 | 24 | 33 | 58 | 56 | 58 |
| 18 | Northampton Town | 46 | 10 | 8 | 5 | 32 | 32 | 3 | 6 | 14 | 21 | 46 | 53 | 78 | 53 |
| 19 | Mansfield Town | 46 | 9 | 7 | 7 | 44 | 27 | 4 | 6 | 13 | 22 | 43 | 66 | 70 | 52 |
| 20 | Wrexham | 46 | 7 | 6 | 10 | 34 | 33 | 4 | 9 | 10 | 25 | 41 | 59 | 74 | 48 |
| 21 | Halifax Town | 46 | 11 | 6 | 6 | 36 | 25 | 1 | 6 | 16 | 19 | 64 | 55 | 89 | 48 |
| 22 | Rochdale | 46 | 8 | 9 | 6 | 35 | 31 | 3 | 4 | 16 | 17 | 49 | 52 | 80 | 46 |
| 23 | Hartlepool United | 46 | 7 | 8 | 8 | 31 | 28 | 3 | 2 | 18 | 16 | 57 | 47 | 85 | 40 |
| ***24*** | ***Chester City*** | ***46*** | ***7*** | ***5*** | ***11*** | ***23*** | ***35*** | ***0*** | ***8*** | ***15*** | ***22*** | ***47*** | ***45*** | ***82*** | ***34*** |

Final League Table 1984/85 Division 4

| | | Pl. | Home | | | | | Away | | | | | F. | A. | Pts |
|---|---|---|---|---|---|---|---|---|---|---|---|---|---|---|---|
| | | | W | D | L | F | A | W | D | L | F | A | | | |
| 1 | Chesterfield | 46 | 16 | 6 | 1 | 40 | 13 | 10 | 7 | 6 | 24 | 22 | 64 | 35 | 91 |
| 2 | Blackpool | 46 | 15 | 7 | 1 | 42 | 15 | 9 | 7 | 7 | 31 | 24 | 73 | 39 | 86 |
| 3 | Darlington | 46 | 16 | 4 | 3 | 41 | 22 | 8 | 9 | 6 | 25 | 27 | 66 | 49 | 85 |
| 4 | Bury | 46 | 15 | 6 | 2 | 46 | 20 | 9 | 6 | 8 | 30 | 30 | 76 | 50 | 84 |
| 5 | Hereford United | 46 | 16 | 2 | 5 | 38 | 21 | 6 | 9 | 8 | 27 | 26 | 65 | 47 | 77 |
| 6 | Tranmere Rovers | 46 | 17 | 1 | 5 | 50 | 21 | 7 | 2 | 14 | 33 | 45 | 83 | 66 | 75 |
| 7 | Colchester United | 46 | 13 | 7 | 3 | 49 | 29 | 7 | 7 | 9 | 38 | 36 | 87 | 65 | 74 |
| 8 | Swindon Town | 46 | 16 | 4 | 3 | 42 | 21 | 5 | 5 | 13 | 20 | 37 | 62 | 58 | 72 |
| 9 | Scunthorpe United | 46 | 14 | 6 | 3 | 61 | 33 | 5 | 8 | 10 | 22 | 29 | 83 | 62 | 71 |
| 10 | Crewe Alexandra | 46 | 10 | 7 | 6 | 32 | 28 | 8 | 5 | 10 | 33 | 41 | 65 | 69 | 66 |
| 11 | Peterborough Utd. | 46 | 11 | 7 | 5 | 29 | 21 | 5 | 7 | 11 | 25 | 32 | 54 | 53 | 62 |
| 12 | Port Vale | 46 | 11 | 8 | 4 | 39 | 24 | 3 | 10 | 10 | 22 | 35 | 61 | 59 | 60 |
| 13 | Aldershot | 46 | 11 | 6 | 6 | 33 | 20 | 6 | 2 | 15 | 23 | 43 | 56 | 63 | 59 |
| 14 | Mansfield Town | 46 | 10 | 8 | 5 | 25 | 15 | 3 | 10 | 10 | 16 | 23 | 41 | 38 | 57 |
| 15 | Wrexham | 46 | 10 | 6 | 7 | 39 | 27 | 5 | 3 | 15 | 28 | 43 | 67 | 70 | 54 |
| ***16*** | ***Chester City*** | ***46*** | ***11*** | ***3*** | ***9*** | ***35*** | ***30*** | ***4*** | ***6*** | ***13*** | ***25*** | ***42*** | ***60*** | ***72*** | ***54*** |
| 17 | Rochdale | 46 | 8 | 7 | 8 | 33 | 30 | 5 | 7 | 11 | 22 | 39 | 55 | 69 | 53 |
| 18 | Exeter City | 46 | 9 | 7 | 7 | 30 | 27 | 4 | 7 | 12 | 27 | 52 | 57 | 79 | 53 |
| 19 | Hartlepool United | 46 | 10 | 6 | 7 | 34 | 29 | 4 | 4 | 15 | 20 | 38 | 54 | 67 | 52 |
| 20 | Southend United | 46 | 8 | 8 | 7 | 30 | 34 | 5 | 3 | 15 | 28 | 49 | 58 | 83 | 50 |
| 21 | Halifax Town | 46 | 9 | 3 | 11 | 26 | 32 | 6 | 2 | 15 | 16 | 37 | 42 | 69 | 50 |
| 22 | Stockport County | 46 | 11 | 5 | 7 | 40 | 26 | 2 | 3 | 18 | 18 | 53 | 58 | 79 | 47 |
| 23 | Northampton Town | 46 | 10 | 1 | 12 | 32 | 32 | 4 | 4 | 15 | 21 | 42 | 53 | 74 | 47 |
| 24 | Torquay United | 46 | 5 | 11 | 7 | 18 | 24 | 4 | 3 | 16 | 20 | 39 | 38 | 63 | 41 |

Final League Table 1985/86 Division 4

| | | Pl. | Home | | | | | Away | | | | | F. | A. | Pts |
|---|---|---|---|---|---|---|---|---|---|---|---|---|---|---|---|
| | | | W | D | L | F | A | W | D | L | F | A | | | |
| 1 | Swindon Town | 46 | 20 | 2 | 1 | 52 | 19 | 12 | 4 | 7 | 30 | 24 | 82 | 43 | 102 |
| ***2*** | ***Chester City*** | ***46*** | ***15*** | ***5*** | ***3*** | ***44*** | ***16*** | ***8*** | ***10*** | ***5*** | ***39*** | ***34*** | ***83*** | ***50*** | ***84*** |
| 3 | Mansfield Town | 46 | 13 | 8 | 2 | 43 | 17 | 10 | 4 | 9 | 31 | 30 | 74 | 47 | 81 |
| 4 | Port Vale | 46 | 13 | 9 | 1 | 42 | 11 | 8 | 7 | 8 | 25 | 26 | 67 | 37 | 79 |
| 5 | Orient | 46 | 11 | 6 | 6 | 39 | 21 | 9 | 6 | 8 | 40 | 43 | 79 | 64 | 72 |
| 6 | Colchester United | 46 | 12 | 6 | 5 | 51 | 22 | 7 | 7 | 9 | 37 | 41 | 88 | 63 | 70 |
| 7 | Hartlepool United | 46 | 15 | 6 | 2 | 41 | 20 | 5 | 4 | 14 | 27 | 47 | 68 | 67 | 70 |
| 8 | Northampton Town | 46 | 9 | 7 | 7 | 44 | 29 | 9 | 3 | 11 | 35 | 29 | 79 | 58 | 64 |
| 9 | Southend United | 46 | 13 | 4 | 6 | 43 | 27 | 5 | 6 | 12 | 26 | 40 | 69 | 67 | 64 |
| 10 | Hereford United | 46 | 15 | 6 | 2 | 55 | 30 | 3 | 4 | 16 | 19 | 43 | 74 | 73 | 64 |
| 11 | Stockport County | 46 | 9 | 9 | 5 | 35 | 28 | 8 | 4 | 11 | 28 | 43 | 63 | 71 | 64 |
| 12 | Crewe Alexandra | 46 | 10 | 6 | 7 | 35 | 26 | 8 | 3 | 12 | 19 | 35 | 54 | 61 | 63 |
| 13 | Wrexham | 46 | 11 | 5 | 7 | 34 | 24 | 6 | 4 | 13 | 34 | 56 | 68 | 80 | 60 |
| 14 | Burnley | 46 | 11 | 3 | 9 | 35 | 30 | 5 | 8 | 10 | 25 | 35 | 60 | 65 | 59 |
| 15 | Scunthorpe United | 46 | 11 | 7 | 5 | 33 | 23 | 4 | 7 | 12 | 17 | 32 | 50 | 55 | 59 |
| 16 | Aldershot | 46 | 12 | 5 | 6 | 45 | 25 | 5 | 2 | 16 | 21 | 49 | 66 | 74 | 58 |
| 17 | Peterborough Utd. | 46 | 9 | 11 | 3 | 31 | 19 | 4 | 6 | 13 | 21 | 45 | 52 | 64 | 56 |
| 18 | Rochdale | 46 | 12 | 7 | 4 | 41 | 29 | 2 | 6 | 15 | 16 | 48 | 57 | 77 | 55 |
| 19 | Tranmere Rovers | 46 | 9 | 1 | 13 | 46 | 41 | 6 | 8 | 9 | 28 | 32 | 74 | 73 | 54 |
| 20 | Halifax Town | 46 | 10 | 8 | 5 | 35 | 27 | 4 | 4 | 15 | 25 | 44 | 60 | 71 | 54 |
| 21 | Exeter City | 46 | 10 | 4 | 9 | 26 | 25 | 3 | 11 | 9 | 21 | 34 | 47 | 59 | 54 |
| 22 | Cambridge United | 46 | 12 | 2 | 9 | 45 | 38 | 3 | 7 | 13 | 20 | 42 | 65 | 80 | 54 |
| 23 | Preston North End | 46 | 7 | 4 | 12 | 32 | 41 | 4 | 6 | 13 | 22 | 48 | 54 | 89 | 43 |
| 24 | Torquay United | 46 | 8 | 5 | 10 | 29 | 32 | 1 | 5 | 17 | 14 | 56 | 43 | 88 | 37 |

Final League Table 1986/87 Division 3

| | | Pl. | Home | | | | | Away | | | | | F. | A. | Pts |
|---|---|---|---|---|---|---|---|---|---|---|---|---|---|---|---|
| | | | W | D | L | F | A | W | D | L | F | A | | | |
| 1 | Bournemouth | 46 | 19 | 3 | 1 | 44 | 14 | 10 | 7 | 6 | 32 | 26 | 76 | 40 | 97 |
| 2 | Middlesbrough | 46 | 16 | 5 | 2 | 38 | 11 | 12 | 5 | 6 | 29 | 19 | 67 | 30 | 94 |
| 3 | Swindon Town | 46 | 14 | 5 | 4 | 37 | 19 | 11 | 7 | 5 | 40 | 28 | 77 | 47 | 87 |
| 4 | Wigan Athletic | 46 | 15 | 5 | 3 | 47 | 26 | 10 | 5 | 8 | 36 | 34 | 83 | 60 | 85 |
| 5 | Gillingham | 46 | 16 | 5 | 2 | 42 | 14 | 7 | 4 | 12 | 23 | 34 | 65 | 48 | 78 |
| 6 | Bristol City | 46 | 14 | 6 | 3 | 42 | 15 | 7 | 8 | 8 | 21 | 21 | 63 | 36 | 77 |
| 7 | Notts County | 46 | 14 | 6 | 3 | 52 | 24 | 7 | 7 | 9 | 25 | 32 | 77 | 56 | 76 |
| 8 | Walsall | 46 | 16 | 4 | 3 | 50 | 27 | 6 | 5 | 12 | 30 | 40 | 80 | 67 | 75 |
| 9 | Blackpool | 46 | 11 | 7 | 5 | 35 | 20 | 5 | 9 | 9 | 39 | 39 | 74 | 59 | 64 |
| 10 | Mansfield Town | 46 | 9 | 9 | 5 | 30 | 23 | 6 | 7 | 10 | 22 | 32 | 52 | 55 | 61 |
| 11 | Brentford | 46 | 9 | 7 | 7 | 39 | 32 | 6 | 8 | 9 | 25 | 34 | 64 | 66 | 60 |
| 12 | Port Vale | 46 | 8 | 6 | 9 | 43 | 36 | 7 | 6 | 10 | 33 | 34 | 76 | 70 | 57 |
| 13 | Doncaster Rovers | 46 | 11 | 8 | 4 | 32 | 19 | 3 | 7 | 13 | 24 | 43 | 56 | 62 | 57 |
| 14 | Rotherham United | 46 | 10 | 6 | 7 | 29 | 23 | 5 | 6 | 12 | 19 | 34 | 48 | 57 | 57 |
| ***15*** | ***Chester City*** | ***46*** | ***7*** | ***9*** | ***7*** | ***32*** | ***28*** | ***6*** | ***8*** | ***9*** | ***29*** | ***31*** | ***61*** | ***59*** | ***56*** |
| 16 | Bury | 46 | 9 | 7 | 7 | 30 | 26 | 5 | 6 | 12 | 24 | 34 | 54 | 60 | 55 |
| 17 | Chesterfield | 46 | 11 | 5 | 7 | 36 | 33 | 2 | 10 | 11 | 20 | 36 | 56 | 69 | 54 |
| 18 | Fulham | 46 | 8 | 8 | 7 | 35 | 41 | 4 | 9 | 10 | 24 | 36 | 59 | 77 | 53 |
| 19 | Bristol Rovers | 46 | 7 | 8 | 8 | 26 | 29 | 6 | 4 | 13 | 23 | 46 | 49 | 75 | 51 |
| 20 | York City | 46 | 11 | 8 | 4 | 34 | 29 | 1 | 5 | 17 | 21 | 50 | 55 | 79 | 49 |
| 21 | Bolton Wanderers | 46 | 8 | 5 | 10 | 29 | 26 | 2 | 10 | 11 | 17 | 32 | 46 | 58 | 45 |
| 22 | Carlisle United | 46 | 7 | 5 | 11 | 26 | 35 | 3 | 3 | 17 | 13 | 43 | 39 | 78 | 38 |
| 23 | Darlington | 46 | 6 | 10 | 7 | 25 | 28 | 1 | 6 | 16 | 20 | 49 | 45 | 77 | 37 |
| 24 | Newport County | 46 | 4 | 9 | 10 | 26 | 34 | 4 | 4 | 15 | 23 | 52 | 49 | 86 | 37 |

Final League Table 1987/88 Division 3

| | | Pl. | Home | | | | | Away | | | | | F. | A. | Pts |
|---|---|---|---|---|---|---|---|---|---|---|---|---|---|---|---|
| | | | W | D | L | F | A | W | D | L | F | A | | | |
| 1 | Sunderland | 46 | 14 | 7 | 2 | 51 | 22 | 13 | 5 | 5 | 41 | 26 | 92 | 48 | 93 |
| 2 | Brighton & Hove A. | 46 | 15 | 7 | 1 | 37 | 16 | 8 | 8 | 7 | 32 | 31 | 69 | 47 | 84 |
| 3 | Walsall | 46 | 15 | 6 | 2 | 39 | 22 | 8 | 7 | 8 | 29 | 28 | 68 | 50 | 82 |
| 4 | Notts County | 46 | 14 | 4 | 5 | 53 | 24 | 9 | 8 | 6 | 29 | 25 | 82 | 49 | 81 |
| 5 | Bristol City | 46 | 14 | 6 | 3 | 51 | 30 | 7 | 6 | 10 | 26 | 32 | 77 | 62 | 75 |
| 6 | Northampton Town | 46 | 12 | 8 | 3 | 36 | 18 | 6 | 11 | 6 | 34 | 33 | 70 | 51 | 73 |
| 7 | Wigan Athletic | 46 | 11 | 8 | 4 | 36 | 23 | 9 | 4 | 10 | 34 | 38 | 70 | 61 | 72 |
| 8 | Bristol Rovers | 46 | 14 | 5 | 4 | 43 | 19 | 4 | 7 | 12 | 25 | 37 | 68 | 56 | 66 |
| 9 | Fulham | 46 | 10 | 5 | 8 | 36 | 24 | 9 | 4 | 10 | 33 | 36 | 69 | 60 | 66 |
| 10 | Blackpool | 46 | 13 | 4 | 6 | 45 | 27 | 4 | 10 | 9 | 26 | 35 | 71 | 62 | 65 |
| 11 | Port Vale | 46 | 12 | 8 | 3 | 36 | 19 | 6 | 3 | 14 | 22 | 37 | 58 | 56 | 65 |
| 12 | Brentford | 46 | 9 | 8 | 6 | 27 | 23 | 7 | 6 | 10 | 26 | 36 | 53 | 59 | 62 |
| 13 | Gillingham | 46 | 8 | 9 | 6 | 45 | 21 | 6 | 8 | 9 | 32 | 40 | 77 | 61 | 59 |
| 14 | Bury | 46 | 9 | 7 | 7 | 33 | 26 | 6 | 7 | 10 | 25 | 31 | 58 | 57 | 59 |
| ***15*** | ***Chester City*** | ***46*** | ***9*** | ***8*** | ***6*** | ***29*** | ***30*** | ***5*** | ***8*** | ***10*** | ***22*** | ***32*** | ***51*** | ***62*** | ***58*** |
| 16 | Preston North End | 46 | 10 | 6 | 7 | 30 | 23 | 5 | 7 | 11 | 18 | 36 | 48 | 59 | 58 |
| 17 | Southend United | 46 | 10 | 6 | 7 | 42 | 33 | 4 | 7 | 12 | 23 | 50 | 65 | 83 | 55 |
| 18 | Chesterfield | 46 | 10 | 5 | 8 | 25 | 28 | 5 | 5 | 13 | 16 | 42 | 41 | 70 | 55 |
| 19 | Mansfield Town | 46 | 10 | 6 | 7 | 25 | 21 | 4 | 6 | 13 | 23 | 38 | 48 | 59 | 54 |
| 20 | Aldershot | 46 | 12 | 3 | 8 | 45 | 32 | 3 | 5 | 15 | 19 | 42 | 64 | 74 | 53 |
| 21 | Rotherham United | 46 | 8 | 8 | 7 | 28 | 25 | 4 | 8 | 11 | 22 | 41 | 50 | 66 | 52 |
| 22 | Grimsby Town | 46 | 6 | 7 | 10 | 25 | 29 | 6 | 7 | 10 | 23 | 29 | 48 | 58 | 50 |
| 23 | York City | 46 | 4 | 7 | 12 | 27 | 45 | 4 | 2 | 17 | 21 | 46 | 48 | 91 | 33 |
| 24 | Doncaster Rovers | 46 | 6 | 5 | 12 | 25 | 36 | 2 | 4 | 17 | 15 | 48 | 40 | 84 | 33 |

# SEASON 1981-82

## FOOTBALL LEAGUE DIVISION 3

| | Date | Opposition | | FT | HT | Att. | Goalscorers | Millington G. | Needham P. | Raynor P. | Storton T. | Zelem P. | Oakes A. | Jones B. | Simpson G. | Ludlam S. | Phillips T. | Sutcliffe P. | Cottam J. | Howat I. | Cooke T. | Allen J. | Burns D. | Blackwell P. | Hornsby B. | Henderson P. | Harrington P. | Dean M. | Williams M. |
|---|---|---|---|---|---|---|---|---|---|---|---|---|---|---|---|---|---|---|---|---|---|---|---|---|---|---|---|---|---|
| 1 | Aug 29 | Bristol Rovers | D | 2-2 | 2-0 | 5554 | Zelem, Oakes | 1 | 2 | 3 | 4 | 5 | 6 | 7 | 8 | 9 | 10 | 11* | 12 | | | | | | | | | | |
| 2 | Sep 5 | SWINDON TOWN | D | 0-0 | 0-0 | 1798 | | 1 | 2 | 3 | 4 | 5 | 6 | 7 | 8 | 9 | 10* | 11 | | 12 | | | | | | | | | |
| 3 | 12 | Gillingham | W | 1-0 | 0-0 | 3990 | Simpson | 1 | 2 | 3 | 4 | | 6 | 7 | 8 | 9 | | 11 | 5 | 10 | | | | | | | | | |
| 4 | 19 | MILLWALL | D | 0-0 | 0-0 | 2052 | | 1 | 2 | 3 | 4 | 5 | 6 | 7 | 8 | 9 | | 11 | | | 10* | 12 | | | | | | | |
| 5 | 23 | WALSALL | D | 0-0 | 0-0 | 1978 | | 1 | 2 | 3 | 4 | 5 | 6 | 7 | 8 | 9 | | 11 | | | 10* | 12 | | | | | | | |
| 6 | 26 | Fulham | L | 0-2 | 0-2 | 3629 | | 1 | 2 | 3 | 4 | 5 | 6 | 7 | 8 | 9 | | 11 | 12 | | | 10* | | | | | | | |
| 7 | 29 | Huddersfield Town | W | 2-1 | 1-1 | 7747 | Simpson (2) | 1 | 2 | 3 | 4 | 5 | 6 | 7 | 8 | 9 | 10 | 11 | | | | | | | | | | | |
| 8 | Oct 10 | OXFORD UNITED | D | 2-2 | 1-1 | 2008 | Phillips, Sutcliffe | 1 | 2 | 3 | 4 | 5 | 6 | 7 | 8 | 9 | 10 | 11 | | | | | | | | | | | |
| 9 | 17 | Wimbledon | L | 0-1 | 0-1 | 1659 | | 1 | 2 | 3 | 4 | | 6 | 7* | 8 | 9 | 10 | 11 | 5 | | | | 12 | | | | | | |
| 10 | 21 | CHESTERFIELD | L | 0-2 | 0-0 | 2329 | | 1 | 2 | 3 | 4 | | 6 | 7 | 8 | 9 | 10 | 11* | 5 | | | | 12 | | | | | | |
| 11 | 24 | Plymouth Argyle | L | 1-5 | 1-2 | 2646 | Jones | 1 | 2 | 3 | 4 | | 6 | 7 | 8* | 9 | 10 | | 5 | 12 | | | 11 | | | | | | |
| 12 | 31 | READING | L | 2-3 | 2-2 | 1765 | Phillips, Needham | 1 | 6 | 3 | 4 | 5 | | 7 | | 9* | 10 | 11 | 2 | 8 | | 12 | | | | | | | |
| 13 | Nov 3 | Burnley | L | 0-1 | 0-0 | 3455 | | 1 | 2* | 3 | 4 | 6 | | | | 9 | 10 | 7 | 5 | 8 | | | 11 | 12 | | | | | |
| 14 | 7 | Preston North End | W | 1-0 | 1-0 | 5181 | Storton | 1 | | | 4 | 2 | 6 | | | 9 | 10 | 11 | 5 | | | 7 | 3 | | 8 | | | | |
| 15 | 14 | EXETER CITY | L | 0-2 | 0-0 | 2125 | | 1 | | | 4 | 2 | | 6 | 12 | 9 | 10 | 11 | 5 | | | 7* | 3 | | 8 | | | | |
| 16 | 28 | Brentford | L | 0-1 | 0-1 | 5200 | | 1 | | 2 | 4 | | | | 8 | 9 | 10 | 11 | 5 | | | | 3 | 6 | 7 | | | | |
| 17 | Dec 2 | DONCASTER ROVERS | D | 1-1 | 0-0 | 1555 | Cooke | 1 | | 2* | 4 | | | | 8 | 9 | 10 | 11 | 5 | | 12 | | 3 | 6 | 7 | | | | |
| 18 | 5 | SOUTHEND UNITED | D | 1-1 | 0-0 | 1388 | Cooke | 1 | 2 | | 4 | | | | 8 | 9 | 10 | 7 | 5 | | 11 | | 3 | 6 | | | | | |
| 19 | 26 | Newport County | W | 1-0 | 1-0 | 4908 | Ludlam | 1 | 2 | | 4 | | 6 | | 8 | 9 | | | 5 | | 11 | | 3 | 7 | | 10 | | | |
| 20 | Jan 19 | PORTSMOUTH | W | 3-2 | 1-1 | 1444 | Sutcliffe, Jones, Simpson | 1 | | 2 | 4 | | 6 | 8 | 9 | | | 7 | 5 | | | | 3 | 10 | | 11 | | | |
| 21 | 23 | BRISTOL ROVERS | D | 1-1 | 1-0 | 2040 | Simpson | 1 | | 2 | 4 | | 6 | 8 | 9* | | | 7 | 5 | | 12 | | 3 | 10 | | 11 | | | |
| 22 | 30 | Millwall | L | 1-2 | 1-1 | 3250 | Cooke | 1 | | 2 | 4 | | 6 | 8* | | | 10 | | 5 | | 11 | 12 | 3 | 7 | | 9 | | | |
| 23 | Feb 3 | Lincoln City | L | 0-3 | 0-0 | 2120 | | 1 | | 2 | 4 | 10 | 6 | | | | 8* | | 5 | | 11 | 12 | 3 | 7 | | 9 | | | |
| 24 | 6 | GILLINGHAM | D | 0-0 | 0-0 | 1543 | | 1 | | 2 | 4 | 5 | 6 | 8 | | | 12 | 7 | | | 11* | | 3 | 10 | | 9 | | | |
| 25 | 9 | Walsall | L | 1-2 | 1-2 | 3668 | Henderson | 1 | 2 | 3 | 4 | 5 | | 8 | 9 | | 12 | 7 | | | | | 6* | 10 | | 11 | | | |
| 26 | 13 | Doncaster Rovers | L | 3-4 | 1-2 | 4098 | Henderson, Simpson (2) | 1 | 2 | 3 | 4 | 5 | | 8 | 9 | | 12 | 7* | | | | | 6 | 10 | | 11 | | | |
| 27 | 20 | HUDDERSFIELD TOWN | W | 3-1 | 1-0 | 3120 | Henderson, Cooke, Simpson | | | 2 | 4 | 5 | 6 | 8 | 9 | | | | | | 7 | | 3 | 10 | | 11 | 1 | | |
| 28 | 27 | Oxford United | L | 1-3 | 0-1 | 5049 | Cooke | | | 2 | 4 | 5 | 6 | 8 | 9 | | | | | | 7 | | 3 | 10 | | 11 | 1 | | |
| 29 | Mar 9 | Chesterfield | W | 5-3 | 1-2 | 4291 | Simpson (2), Raynor (pen), Henderson (2) | | 10 | 3 | 4 | 5 | 6 | 8 | 9 | | | | 2 | | 7 | | | | | 11 | 1 | | |
| 30 | 13 | PLYMOUTH ARGYLE | L | 0-3 | 0-1 | 1988 | | | 10 | 3 | 4 | 5 | 6 | 8 | 9 | | 12 | | 2 | | 7* | | | | | 11 | 1 | | |
| 31 | 17 | BURNLEY | L | 0-1 | 0-1 | 3261 | | | 8 | 3 | 4 | 5 | 6 | | 9 | | | 7 | 2 | | | | 10 | | | 11 | 1 | | |
| 32 | 20 | Reading | L | 1-4 | 0-3 | 3093 | Simpson | | 2 | 3 | 4 | | 6 | | 9 | | | 7 | 5 | | | 12 | 10 | 8* | | 11 | 1 | | |
| 33 | 27 | PRESTON NORTH END | L | 0-1 | 0-0 | 2842 | | | | 2 | 4 | 5 | 6 | 8 | 9 | 10 | | 7 | | | | 12 | 3 | | | 11* | 1 | | |
| 34 | 31 | WIMBLEDON | D | 1-1 | 0-0 | 1359 | Simpson | 1 | | 2 | | 5 | | 8 | 9 | 10 | | 7 | 4 | | | | 3 | 6 | | 11 | | | |
| 35 | Apr 3 | Exeter City | L | 0-3 | 0-1 | 2498 | | | 6 | 2 | 4 | 5 | | | 9 | 8 | | 10 | | | | 7 | 3 | | | 11 | 1 | | |
| 36 | 10 | NEWPORT COUNTY | L | 0-2 | 0-0 | 1451 | | | 6 | 2 | 4 | 5 | | | 9 | 8 | | 10 | | | | 7 | 3 | | | 11 | 1 | | |
| 37 | 13 | Carlisle United | L | 0-3 | 0-1 | 5340 | | | 6 | 2 | 4 | 5 | | 8 | 9 | 10 | | | 12 | | | 7 | 3* | | | 11 | 1 | | |
| 38 | 17 | Southend United | L | 0-2 | 0-1 | 3427 | | 1 | 2 | 3 | | 5 | | 8 | 9* | 10 | | 12 | 4 | | | 7 | 6 | | | 11 | | | |
| 39 | 21 | BRISTOL CITY | D | 0-0 | 0-0 | 1034 | | 1 | | | 4 | 5 | | 8 | | 10 | | 7 | 2 | | | 9 | 3 | 6 | | 11 | | | |
| 40 | 24 | BRENTFORD | L | 1-2 | 0-1 | 1304 | Storton | 1 | | | 4 | 5 | | | 12 | 10 | | 8 | 2 | | | 9 | 3 | 6 | | 11* | | 7 | |
| 41 | 27 | Swindon Town | L | 0-3 | 0-1 | 3848 | | 1 | | 2 | 4 | | | 8 | 12 | 10 | | 7* | 5 | | | 9 | 3 | 6 | | 11 | | | |
| 42 | May 1 | Portsmouth | L | 0-2 | 0-0 | 6196 | | 1 | 3 | 2 | 4 | 5 | | 8 | 9 | 10 | | | 6 | | | 7 | 12 | | | 11* | | | |
| 43 | 5 | FULHAM | L | 0-2 | 0-1 | 1174 | | 1 | 3 | 2 | 4 | | | 8 | | 9 | | | 5 | | | 7 | 11 | 6 | | 10 | | | |
| 44 | 8 | LINCOLN CITY | L | 1-2 | 0-0 | 1176 | Jones | 1 | | 3 | 4 | | | 12 | | 10 | | 7* | 5 | | | 9 | | 6 | | 11 | | 2 | 8 |
| 45 | 15 | Bristol City | L | 0-1 | 0-1 | 3934 | | 1 | | 3 | | 4 | | 10 | 9 | 6 | | | 5 | | | 7 | | 12 | | 11 | | 2 | 8* |
| 46 | 19 | CARLISLE UNITED | L | 0-1 | 0-1 | 2535 | | 1 | | 3 | | 5 | | 10 | 12 | 6 | 7 | | 4 | | | 9 | | 8* | | 11 | | 2 | |
| | | | | | | | Apps. | 36 | 27 | 40 | 42 | 31 | 25 | 33 | 33 | 33 | 17 | 32 | 30 | 3 | 11 | 15 | 29 | 21 | 4 | 28 | 10 | 4 | 2 |
| | | | | | | | Subs. | | | | | | | 1 | 4 | | 4 | 1 | 3 | 2 | 2 | 7 | 3 | 2 | | | | | |
| | | | | | | | Goals | | 1 | 1 | 2 | 1 | 1 | 3 | 12 | 1 | 2 | 2 | | | 5 | | | | | 5 | | | |

## F.A. CUP

| | Date | Opposition | | FT | HT | Att. | Goalscorers | Millington G. | Needham P. | Raynor P. | Storton T. | Zelem P. | Oakes A. | Jones B. | Simpson G. | Ludlam S. | Phillips T. | Sutcliffe P. | Cottam J. | Howat I. | Cooke T. | Allen J. | Burns D. | Blackwell P. | Hornsby B. | Henderson P. | Harrington P. | Dean M. | Williams M. |
|---|---|---|---|---|---|---|---|---|---|---|---|---|---|---|---|---|---|---|---|---|---|---|---|---|---|---|---|---|---|
| 1R | Nov 21 | Penrith | L | 0-1 | 0-0 | 2700 | | 1 | 7* | 2 | 4 | 5 | | 6 | 8 | 9 | 10 | 11 | | 12 | | | 3 | | | | | | |

## LEAGUE CUP

| | Date | Opposition | | FT | HT | Att. | Goalscorers | Millington G. | Needham P. | Raynor P. | Storton T. | Zelem P. | Oakes A. | Jones B. | Simpson G. | Ludlam S. | Phillips T. | Sutcliffe P. | Cottam J. | Howat I. | Cooke T. | Allen J. | Burns D. | Blackwell P. | Hornsby B. | Henderson P. | Harrington P. | Dean M. | Williams M. |
|---|---|---|---|---|---|---|---|---|---|---|---|---|---|---|---|---|---|---|---|---|---|---|---|---|---|---|---|---|---|
| 1R1 | Sep 8 | PLYMOUTH ARGYLE | D | 1-1 | 1-1 | 1690 | Jones | 1 | 2 | 3 | 4 | | 6 | 7 | 8 | 9 | | 11 | 5 | 10 | | | | | | | | | |
| 1R2 | 15 | Plymouth Argyle | L | 0-1 | 0-1 | 2348 | | 1 | 2 | 3 | 4 | | 6 | 7 | 8 | 9 | | 11 | 5 | 10* | 12 | | | | | | | | |

## FOOTBALL LEAGUE GROUP CUP

| | Date | Opposition | | FT | HT | Att. | Goalscorers | Millington G. | Needham P. | Raynor P. | Storton T. | Zelem P. | Oakes A. | Jones B. | Simpson G. | Ludlam S. | Phillips T. | Sutcliffe P. | Cottam J. | Howat I. | Cooke T. | Allen J. | Burns D. | Blackwell P. | Hornsby B. | Henderson P. | Harrington P. | Dean M. | Williams M. |
|---|---|---|---|---|---|---|---|---|---|---|---|---|---|---|---|---|---|---|---|---|---|---|---|---|---|---|---|---|---|
| GM | Aug 15 | Bury | W | 2-1 | 2-0 | 1504 | Simpson, Jones | 1 | 3 | 2 | 4 | 5 | 6 | 7 | 8 | 9 | 10* | | | 12 | 11 | | | | | | | | |
| GM | 18 | Shrewsbury Town | L | 0-1 | 0-0 | 1567 | | 1 | 3 | 2 | 4 | 5 | 6 | 7 | 8 | 9 | 10* | | 12 | | 11 | | | | | | | | |
| GM | 22 | BOLTON WANDERERS | L | 1-2 | 0-1 | 1291 | Burns | 1 | 8 | 3 | 4 | 5 | 6 | 7 | | 9 | 10 | | 2 | | | | 11 | | | | | | |

**1981/82 Season:**
(Back) Burns, Raynor, Zelem, Harrington, Cottam, Millington, Storton, Needham, Ludlam.
(Front) Sutcliffe, Phillips, Jones, Oakes (Player-Manager), Simpson, Howat, Cooke.

**1982/83 Season:**
(Back) Ludlam, Edwards, Simpson, Storton, Harrington, Millington, Zelem, Blackwell, Allen, Dean.
(Front) Moffatt, Lane, Johnson, Bradley, Sear (Manager), Thomas, Sloan, Cooke, Needham.

# SEASON 1982-83

## FOOTBALL LEAGUE DIVISION 4

| | Date | Opposition | | FT | HT | Att. | Goalscorers | Millington G. | Bradley N. | Edwards N. | Zelem P. | Lane M. | Dean M. | Sloan T. | Johnson P. | Simpson G. | Cooke T. | Thomas J. | Storton T. | Ludlam S. | Allen J. | Wilson C. | Kinsey S. | Salmon M. | Needham P. | Blackwell P. | Williams M. | Moffatt G. | Bulmer P. | Workman I. | Harrington P. | Manns P. |
|---|---|---|---|---|---|---|---|---|---|---|---|---|---|---|---|---|---|---|---|---|---|---|---|---|---|---|---|---|---|---|---|---|
| 1 | Aug 28 | CREWE ALEX. | W | 1-0 | 1-0 | 3180 | Edwards | 1 | 2 | 3 | 4 | 5 | 6 | 7 | 8 | 9 | 10 | 11 | | | | | | | | | | | | | | |
| 2 | Sep 4 | Rochdale | W | 1-0 | 1-0 | 1489 | Thomas | 1 | 2 | | 5 | 3 | 12 | 7 | 10* | | 11 | 8 | 4 | 6 | 9 | | | | | | | | | | | |
| 3 | 7 | Northampton Town | D | 1-1 | 0-0 | 2171 | Thomas | 1 | 2 | | 5 | 3 | | 7 | 10 | | 11 | 8 | 4 | 6 | 9 | | | | | | | | | | | |
| 4 | 11 | TORQUAY UNITED | D | 0-0 | 0-0 | 2370 | | 1 | 2* | | 5 | 3 | | 7 | 10 | 12 | 8 | 11 | 4 | 6 | 9 | | | | | | | | | | | |
| 5 | 18 | Port Vale | L | 1-2 | 1-0 | 3303 | Sproson (og) | 1 | 2* | | 5 | 3 | | 7 | 10 | 9 | | 11 | 4 | 12 | | 6 | 8 | | | | | | | | | |
| 6 | 25 | HEREFORD UNITED | W | 5-0 | 2-0 | 1828 | Ludlam, Thomas(2, 1 pen), Simpson, Sloan | 1 | | 2 | 5 | 3* | | 7 | 8 | 9 | 12 | 10 | 4 | 6 | | 11 | | | | | | | | | | |
| 7 | 29 | BLACKPOOL | L | 1-2 | 1-1 | 2256 | Thomas | 1 | | 2 | 5 | 3* | | 7 | 8 | 9 | 12 | 10 | 4 | 6 | | 11 | | | | | | | | | | |
| 8 | Oct 1 | Halifax Town | D | 0-0 | 0-0 | 1925 | | 1 | | 2 | 5 | 3 | 6 | 7 | | | | 9 | 4 | 10 | | 11 | 8 | | | | | | | | | |
| 9 | 9 | Darlington | W | 2-0 | 1-0 | 1387 | Thomas, Kinsey | 1 | | 2 | 5 | 3 | 6 | 7 | | | | 9 | 4 | 10 | | 11 | 8 | | | | | | | | | |
| 10 | 16 | MANSFIELD TOWN | L | 1-3 | 0-1 | 1668 | Ludlam | 1 | | 2* | 5 | 3 | 6 | 7 | 8 | 9 | 11 | | 4 | 10 | 12 | | | | | | | | | | | |
| 11 | 20 | PETERBOROUGH UNITED | D | 1-1 | 1-0 | 1401 | Zelem | | 2 | | 5 | 3 | 6 | 7 | | 9 | 11 | 8 | 4 | 10 | | | | 1 | | | | | | | | |
| 12 | 30 | SWINDON TOWN | L | 0-1 | 0-0 | 1544 | | | 2 | | 5 | | 6 | 7 | | 9 | 11 | 10 | 4 | 8 | | | | 1 | 3 | | | | | | | |
| 13 | Nov 2 | Bristol City | D | 0-0 | 0-0 | 3942 | | | 2 | | 5 | | 6 | 7 | | | 11 | 9 | 4 | 10 | | | | 1 | 3 | 8 | | | | | | |
| 14 | 6 | BURY | L | 0-1 | 0-1 | 2023 | | | 2* | | 5 | | 6 | 7 | | 12 | 11 | 9 | 4 | 10 | | | | 1 | 3 | 8 | | | | | | |
| 15 | 9 | Colchester United | L | 0-1 | 0-0 | 2362 | | | | | 5 | | 2 | 7 | 8 | | 11 | 9 | 4 | 10 | | | | 1 | 3 | 6 | | | | | | |
| 16 | 13 | Aldershot | W | 2-1 | 2-1 | 1675 | Allen, Sloan | | | 2* | 5 | 3 | | 7 | 6 | 11 | | 9 | 4 | 10 | 8 | | | 1 | | | 12 | | | | | |
| 17 | 27 | Hull City | L | 0-2 | 0-0 | 5047 | | | 2 | | 5 | 3 | | 7 | | | 8 | 9 | 4 | | | 10 | | 1 | 11* | 6 | | 12 | | | | |
| 18 | Dec 4 | HARTLEPOOL UNITED | W | 2-1 | 2-1 | 1114 | Storton, Thomas | | 2 | | | 3 | | 7 | 6 | | 12 | 9 | 4 | 10 | 8* | 11 | | 1 | 5 | | | | | | | |
| 19 | 11 | BRISTOL CITY | W | 1-0 | 0-0 | 1163 | Cooper (og) | | 5 | | 12 | 3 | 2 | | 6 | | 8 | 9 | 4 | 10 | | 11 | | 1 | | | 7* | | | | | |
| 20 | 18 | YORK CITY | L | 0-1 | 0-1 | 1185 | | | 5 | | | 3 | 2 | 7 | 6 | | 8 | 9 | 4 | 10* | | 11 | | 1 | | | | | 12 | | | |
| 21 | 27 | Tranmere Rovers | W | 4-2 | 2-1 | 5245 | Lane (2), Thomas, Ludlam | | 5 | | | 8 | 2 | 7 | 6 | | | 9 | 4 | 10 | | 3 | | 1 | | 11 | | | | | | |
| 22 | 28 | STOCKPORT COUNTY | L | 0-2 | 0-0 | 2459 | | | 5 | | | 8 | 2 | 7 | 6 | | 12 | 9 | 4 | 10 | | 3 | | 1 | | 11* | | | | | | |
| 23 | Jan 1 | Scunthorpe United | L | 0-2 | 0-2 | 3639 | | | 5 | 6* | | 4 | 2 | 7 | | | | 9 | | 10 | | 3 | | 1 | 8 | | 12 | | 11 | | | |
| 24 | 3 | WIMBLEDON | L | 1-2 | 0-0 | 1549 | Thomas | | 5 | | | 8 | 2* | 7 | | | 12 | 9 | | 10 | | 3 | | 1 | 6 | | | 4 | 11 | | | |
| 25 | 8 | ROCHDALE | W | 5-2 | 1-1 | 1562 | Thomas (3), Zelem, Wilson (pen) | | 2* | | 5 | 3 | | 7 | 12 | 8 | 6 | 9 | 4 | 10 | | 11 | | 1 | | | | | | | | |
| 26 | 15 | Crewe Alex. | L | 2-3 | 0-2 | 2895 | Thomas, Cooke | | | | 5 | 3 | | 11 | | 10 | 8 | 9 | 4 | 7 | | 6 | | 1 | | | | | | 2 | | |
| 27 | 22 | PORT VALE | W | 1-0 | 0-0 | 4056 | Moss (og) | | 2 | | 5 | 3 | | 7 | | 8 | 12 | 9 | 4 | 10* | | 11 | | | | | | | | 6 | 1 | |
| 28 | 29 | Blackpool | D | 1-1 | 0-0 | 2054 | Ludlam | | 2 | | 4 | 3 | | 7 | 6 | 9* | | 10 | | 8 | | 11 | | | 5 | | | | 12 | | 1 | |
| 29 | Feb 5 | Hereford United | L | 2-5 | 1-3 | 1961 | Bulmer, Williams | | 5 | | | 4 | | 7 | 6 | | 10 | 8 | | 9 | 12 | 3 | | | | | 2 | | 11* | | 1 | |
| 30 | 12 | HALIFAX TOWN | W | 2-0 | 1-0 | 1907 | Zelem, Williams | | | | 5 | 3 | | 7 | | 8 | | 9 | | | | 11 | | | 2 | 4 | 6 | | | 10 | 1 | |
| 31 | 16 | Peterborough United | W | 1-0 | 1-0 | 1661 | Wilson | | 4 | | 5 | 3 | | 7 | | 8 | | 9 | | 6 | | 11 | | | 2 | 10 | | | | | 1 | |
| 32 | 19 | DARLINGTON | L | 2-3 | 2-2 | 1323 | Simpson, Thomas | | 4 | | 5 | 3 | | 7 | | 8 | | 9 | | | | 11 | | | 2 | 10 | 6 | | | | 1 | |
| 33 | 26 | Mansfield Town | L | 1-2 | 1-0 | 1803 | Thomas | | 4 | | | 3 | | 7 | | 8 | | 9 | | 11 | | | | | 2 | 10 | | 5 | 6 | | 1 | |
| 34 | Mar 5 | COLCHESTER UNITED | D | 1-1 | 0-0 | 1136 | Simpson | | 12 | | 5* | 3 | | 7 | | 8 | | 9 | 4 | | | | | | 2 | 6 | 10 | | 11 | | 1 | |
| 35 | 12 | Swindon Town | W | 3-2 | 1-1 | 3238 | Sloan, Thomas (2) | | | | 5 | 3 | | 7 | | 10 | | 9 | 4 | | | | | | 2 | 6 | 11 | | | | 1 | 8 |
| 36 | 19 | Bury | L | 2-3 | 1-1 | 2453 | Simpson (2) | | 2* | | 5 | 3 | | 7 | | 8 | | 9 | 4 | | 12 | | | | 11 | 6 | | | | | 1 | 10 |
| 37 | 26 | ALDERSHOT | D | 1-1 | 1-0 | 1197 | Manns | | | | 5 | 3 | | 7 | | 8 | | 9 | 4 | | | | | | 2 | 6 | 11 | | | | 1 | 10 |
| 38 | Apr 2 | Stockport County | D | 3-3 | 2-1 | 2008 | Thomas, Simpson, Manns | | | | 5* | 3 | 12 | | | 8 | | 9 | 4 | | 7 | | | | 2 | 6 | 11 | | | | 1 | 10 |
| 39 | 4 | TRANMERE ROVERS | D | 0-0 | 0-0 | 2897 | | | | | | 3 | 5 | 7* | | 8 | | 9 | 4 | | | | | | 2 | 6 | 11 | | 12 | | 1 | 10 |
| 40 | 9 | Hartlepool United | L | 0-1 | 0-0 | 1034 | | | | | | | 3 | 7 | 11 | 8 | | 9 | 4 | | | | | | 2 | 6 | 5* | | 12 | | 1 | 10 |
| 41 | 16 | NORTHAMPTON TOWN | W | 2-1 | 1-0 | 1121 | Allen, Manns | | 6 | | 5 | 3 | 2 | 7 | | | | 9 | 4 | | 8 | | | | | 11 | | | | | 1 | 10 |
| 42 | 23 | York City | L | 0-1 | 0-1 | 3264 | | | 6 | | 5 | 3 | 2 | 7 | | 9* | | | 4 | | 8 | | | | | 11 | | | 12 | | 1 | 10 |
| 43 | 30 | HULL CITY | D | 0-0 | 0-0 | 2281 | | | | | 5 | 3 | | 7 | | | | 9 | 4 | | 8 | | | | | 6 | | 2 | 11 | | 1 | 10 |
| 44 | May 2 | Wimbledon | L | 0-4 | 0-1 | 2576 | | | 12 | | 5 | 3* | | 7 | | | | 9 | 4 | | 8 | | | | | 6 | | 2 | 11 | | 1 | 10 |
| 45 | 7 | Torquay United | W | 1-0 | 0-0 | 1478 | Thomas | | 12 | | | 3 | | 7 | | | | 9 | 4 | | 8 | | | | 5 | 6 | | 2 | 11 | | 1* | 10 |
| 46 | 14 | SCUNTHORPE UNITED | L | 1-2 | 1-1 | 2560 | Thomas | 1 | 12 | | 5 | 3* | | 7 | | | | 9 | 4 | | 8 | | | | | 6 | | 2 | 11 | | | 10 |
| | | | | | | | Apps. | 11 | 27 | 8 | 34 | 41 | 19 | 44 | 18 | 24 | 16 | 44 | 37 | 28 | 12 | 21 | 3 | 16 | 21 | 23 | 10 | 6 | 9 | 3 | 19 | 12 |
| | | | | | | | Subs. | | 4 | | 1 | | 2 | | 1 | 2 | 6 | | | 1 | 3 | | | | | | 2 | 1 | 5 | | | |
| | | | | | | | Goals | | | 1 | 3 | 2 | | 3 | | 6 | 1 | 20 | 1 | 4 | 2 | 2 | 1 | | | | 2 | | 1 | | | 3 |

Own goals 3

## F.A. CUP

| | Date | Opposition | | FT | HT | Att. | Goalscorers | Millington G. | Bradley N. | Edwards N. | Zelem P. | Lane M. | Dean M. | Sloan T. | Johnson P. | Simpson G. | Cooke T. | Thomas J. | Storton T. | Ludlam S. | Allen J. | Wilson C. | Kinsey S. | Salmon M. | Needham P. | Blackwell P. | Williams M. | Moffatt G. | Bulmer P. | Workman I. | Harrington P. | Manns P. |
|---|---|---|---|---|---|---|---|---|---|---|---|---|---|---|---|---|---|---|---|---|---|---|---|---|---|---|---|---|---|---|---|---|
| 1R | Nov 20 | NORTHWICH VICS. | D | 1-1 | 0-1 | 4400 | Lane | | 2 | | 5 | 3 | | 7 | 6* | 9 | | 11 | 4 | 10 | 8 | | | 1 | | 12 | | | | | | |
| 1Rr | 22 | Northwich Vics. * | L | 1-3 | 0-0 | 4014 | Williams | | 2 | | 5 | 3 | | 7 | | | 8 | 9 | 4 | 10* | | | | 1 | 11 | 6 | 12 | | | | | |

* Extra time played following score of 1-1 after 90 minutes

## LEAGUE (MILK) CUP

| | Date | Opposition | | FT | HT | Att. | Goalscorers | Millington G. | Bradley N. | Edwards N. | Zelem P. | Lane M. | Dean M. | Sloan T. | Johnson P. | Simpson G. | Cooke T. | Thomas J. | Storton T. | Ludlam S. | Allen J. | Wilson C. | Kinsey S. | Salmon M. | Needham P. | Blackwell P. | Williams M. | Moffatt G. | Bulmer P. | Workman I. | Harrington P. | Manns P. |
|---|---|---|---|---|---|---|---|---|---|---|---|---|---|---|---|---|---|---|---|---|---|---|---|---|---|---|---|---|---|---|---|---|
| 1R1 | Sep 1 | BLACKPOOL | L | 1-2 | 1-0 | 2557 | Sloan | 1 | 3 | 2 | 4 | 5 | 6 | 7 | 8 | 9 | 10 | 11 | | | | | | | | | | | | | | |
| 1R2 | 14 | Blackpool | L | 1-5 | 0-2 | 3429 | Thomas | 1 | 2 | | 5 | 3 | | 7 | 10 | 9 | 11 | 8 | 4 | 6 | | | | | | | | | | | | |

## FOOTBALL LEAGUE TROPHY

| | Date | Opposition | | FT | HT | Att. | Goalscorers | Millington G. | Bradley N. | Edwards N. | Zelem P. | Lane M. | Dean M. | Sloan T. | Johnson P. | Simpson G. | Cooke T. | Thomas J. | Storton T. | Ludlam S. | Allen J. | Wilson C. | Kinsey S. | Salmon M. | Needham P. | Blackwell P. | Williams M. | Moffatt G. | Bulmer P. | Workman I. | Harrington P. | Manns P. |
|---|---|---|---|---|---|---|---|---|---|---|---|---|---|---|---|---|---|---|---|---|---|---|---|---|---|---|---|---|---|---|---|---|
| GM | Aug 14 | Chesterfield | D | 1-1 | 0-1 | 1149 | Sloan | 1 | 2 | | 5 | 3 | 6 | 7 | | 9* | 11 | | 4 | 10 | 8 | | | | | | | | | | | |
| GM | 18 | Tranmere Rovers | L | 1-2 | 0-1 | 1143 | Simpson | | 2 | 12 | 5 | 3 | 6" | 7 | 10 | 9 | | 11 | 4* | 13 | 8 | | | | | | | | | | 1 | |
| GM | 21 | SHREWSBURY TOWN | W | 5-0 | 2-0 | 1022 | Sloan, Thomas(2, 1 pen), McLaren(og), Edwards | 1 | 3 | 2 | 4 | 5 | 6 | 7 | 8 | 9 | 10 | 11 | | | | | | | | | | | | | | |
| QF | Jan 26 | NEWPORT COUNTY* | W | 0-0 | 0-0 | 999 | | | 2 | | 5 | 3 | | 7 | 12 | 8" | 13 | 9 | 4 | 10 | | 11 | | | | | | | | 6* | 1 | |
| SF | Feb 8 | LINCOLN CITY @ | L | 1-3 | 1-1 | 1058 | Thomas | | 4 | 2* | 5 | 3 | | 7 | | 8 | 12 | 9 | | | | 11 | | | | | 10 | | | 6 | 1 | |

* Extra time played following score of 0-0 after 90 minutes, Chester won 5-4 on penalties
@ Extra time played following score of 1-1 after 90 minutes

## FRIENDLIES

| | Date | Opposition | | FT | | Goalscorers |
|---|---|---|---|---|---|---|
| 1 | Aug 4 | Runcorn | L | 1-3 | | Blackwell |

# *SEASON 1983-84*

## FOOTBALL (CANON) LEAGUE DIV. 4

| | Date | Opposition | | FT | HT | Att. | Goalscorers | Harrington P. | Raynor P. | Lane M. | Brett D. | Zelem P. | Holden A. | Bulmer P. | Allen J. | Manns P. | Blackwell P. | Williams M. | Phillips T. | Elliott A. | Burke J. | Storton T. | Parker S. | Williams P. | Ryan J. | Wann D. | Sutcliffe P. | Camden C. | Evans D. | Hildersley R. | Sanderson P. | Dixon L. | Wharton A. | Wintersgill D. | Coy R. | O'Rourke W. | Donnelly P. |
|---|---|---|---|---|---|---|---|---|---|---|---|---|---|---|---|---|---|---|---|---|---|---|---|---|---|---|---|---|---|---|---|---|---|---|---|---|---|
| 1 | Aug 27 | NORTHAMPTON TOWN | D | 1-1 | 1-1 | 1680 | M Williams |1|2|3|4*|5|6|7|8|9|10|11|12|||||||||||||||||||
| 2 | Sep 3 | Swindon Town | L | 0-4 | 0-1 | 2891 | |1|2|3||5|6|7|8|9|11|||4|10||||||||||||||||||
| 3 | 7 | Hereford United | L | 1-2 | 1-1 | 3480 | Allen |1|2|3||5|6||8|7|10|12|9|4|11*||||||||||||||||||
| 4 | 10 | CREWE ALEX. | L | 0-1 | 0-0 | 2090 | |1||3||5|6|12|8|7|11|2|9|4|10*||||||||||||||||||
| 5 | 17 | York City | L | 1-4 | 1-3 | 3037 | Holden |1||3||5|10|12|8|7|11|2|9*|4||6||||||||||||||||
| 6 | 24 | READING | W | 2-1 | 1-1 | 1367 | Parker, Blackwell |1||3||5|6||8|7|10|4*||12||2|9|11||||||||||||||
| 7 | 28 | TORQUAY UNITED | L | 1-2 | 0-1 | 1356 | Elliott |1||3||5|6|12|8|7*|10|||4||2|9|11||||||||||||||
| 8 | Oct 1 | Colchester United | L | 0-1 | 0-0 | 1976 | |1||3||5|6|12|8||10*|2||4|||9|11|7|||||||||||||
| 9 | 8 | Darlington | L | 1-2 | 0-0 | 1117 | Gilbert (og) |1||3|4|5|6||8||10|2||9||||11|7|||||||||||||
| 10 | 19 | Hartlepool United | D | 1-1 | 0-0 | 1150 | Parker |1|||4*|5|6|11|9|7||2||||8|10|12|3|||||||||||||
| 11 | 22 | STOCKPORT COUNTY | L | 2-4 | 1-2 | 1495 | Storton, M Williams |1||3|||6|7*|12|8|10|2||4||5|9|11||||||||||||||
| 12 | 29 | Rochdale | D | 1-1 | 0-0 | 1481 | Parker |1||3||5|6||8|4*|10|7||12|||9||2|11|||||||||||||
| 13 | Nov 2 | HALIFAX TOWN | D | 1-1 | 0-0 | 1211 | Parker |1||3||8|6|9||7||2||4||5|10|||11|||||||||||||
| 14 | 5 | Chesterfield | D | 1-1 | 0-1 | 3513 | Parker |1||3||8|6|9|11|7*|4|2||12||5|10|||||||||||||||
| 15 | 9 | BLACKPOOL | L | 0-2 | 0-1 | 2286 | |1||3||8|6||11*|7|12|2||4||5|10||||9|||||||||||
| 16 | 12 | ALDERSHOT | L | 1-2 | 0-2 | 975 | Holden |1||3|4|5|6|11||10||2||||8||||12|7*|9||||||||||
| 17 | 26 | Doncaster Rovers | D | 0-0 | 0-0 | 2967 | |1||3|4|5|6||7|10||||||8|||||11|9|2||||||||
| 18 | Dec 3 | BURY | W | 2-1 | 0-0 | 1341 | Allen, Camden |1||3|4|5|6||7|10*||||12||8|||||11|9|2||||||||
| 19 | 17 | PETERBOROUGH UNITED | D | 1-1 | 1-0 | 1191 | Waddle (og) |1||3|4*|5|6||7||12||10|||8|||||11|9|2||||||||
| 20 | 26 | Wrexham | L | 0-2 | 0-1 | 5756 | |1||3|4|5|6||7||12||10|||8|||||11|9*|2||||||||
| 21 | 27 | MANSFIELD TOWN | L | 0-4 | 0-3 | 1431 | |1|||12|5|9||7||6|3|10|4*||8|||||11||2||||||||
| 22 | 31 | Bristol City | L | 2-4 | 1-0 | 7293 | Camden, Brett |1|||4|5|6||7||3|||10||8|||||11|9|2||||||||
| 23 | Jan 2 | TRANMERE ROVERS | D | 0-0 | 0-0 | 2672 | |1|||8|5|||11||3|4|||||||||7|9|2|6|10||||||
| 24 | 14 | Northampton Town | L | 1-2 | 1-1 | 2198 | Phillips |1|||7||6||11||3|5|8||||||||||10|2|4|9||||||
| 25 | 28 | Crewe Alex. | D | 1-1 | 1-1 | 3096 | Phillips |1||3||5|10||11||||9|||4|||||7||2|6|8||||||
| 26 | Feb 4 | COLCHESTER UNITED | L | 1-4 | 0-2 | 1179 | Blackwell |1||3||5|10||11||2|12|9*|||4|||||7|||6|8||||||
| 27 | 8 | SWINDON TOWN | L | 0-3 | 0-3 | 880 | |1||3||5*|10||11||9|7||12||4||||||||2|6|8||||||
| 28 | 11 | Reading | L | 0-1 | 0-0 | 3280 | |1||3|7|5|10|11*|12||2|||4|||||||||9||6|8||||||
| 29 | 14 | Halifax Town | D | 2-2 | 2-1 | 1500 | Elliott, Holden |1||3|7|5|9|2|11||10|||4|||||||||||6|8||||||
| 30 | 18 | ROCHDALE | W | 1-0 | 0-0 | 1423 | Zelem |1||3||5|4||9||11|||7|||||||||||6|8|2|10|||||
| 31 | 24 | Stockport County | L | 1-2 | 1-1 | 2006 | Holden |1||3|12|5|4||9||11|||7*|||||||||||6|8|2|10|||||
| 32 | Mar 3 | HARTLEPOOL UNITED | W | 4-1 | 3-1 | 1241 | Wharton,Holden,Zelem(pen),Sanderson |1||3|7|5|4||9||11|||12||||||||||||8|2|10|6*||||
| 33 | 7 | CHESTERFIELD | L | 0-2 | 0-1 | 1334 | |1|||4|5|7|12|9*||11||||||||||||||8|2|10|6|3|||
| 34 | 10 | Aldershot | L | 2-5 | 0-3 | 2879 | Dixon, Holden |1|||7||4|12|9||3|||6||||||||||||8*|2|10|11|5|||
| 35 | 17 | DARLINGTON | W | 2-1 | 1-0 | 981 | Zelem (2 pens) |||3|7|5|4||||11||||||||||||||8|2|10|6|9|1||
| 36 | 24 | Blackpool | D | 3-3 | 0-1 | 4746 | Zelem, Wharton, Sanderson |||3|7|4|11||||9|||12||||||||||||10|2|8|6*|5|1||
| 37 | Apr 7 | HEREFORD UNITED | L | 0-1 | 0-0 | 1346 | |||3|7*|5|4||9||11|||12||||||||||||8|2|10||6|1||
| 38 | 14 | Bury | L | 1-2 | 1-1 | 1414 | Holden ||||7*|5|4|12|9||11|||8||||||||||||10|2|3||6|1||
| 39 | 18 | YORK CITY | D | 1-1 | 1-1 | 1750 | Brett |1||3|7||6|2|9||11|5||4||||||||||||8|2|||10|||
| 40 | 21 | WREXHAM | W | 1-0 | 0-0 | 3486 | Sanderson |1||3|12|5|4||7||11|||6*||||||||||||8|2|10||9|||
| 41 | 24 | Mansfield Town | L | 1-3 | 1-0 | 2346 | Zelem |1||3|12|5|4||7||11|||6||||||||||||8*|2|10||9|||
| 42 | 28 | DONCASTER ROVERS | W | 1-0 | 1-0 | 1549 | Elliott |1||3||5|4||7||11|||6||||||||||||8|2|10||9|||
| 43 | May 2 | Torquay United | L | 0-1 | 0-1 | 967 | |||3|12|5|4||7||11|||6*||||||||||||8|2|10||9|1||
| 44 | 5 | Tranmere Rovers | D | 2-2 | 1-1 | 1592 | Blackwell, Allen |1||3|6|5|4||7||11||||||||||||||8|2|10||9|||
| 45 | 7 | BRISTOL CITY | L | 1-2 | 0-1 | 3900 | Zelem |1||3|11|5||12|7|||4||6||||||||||||8|2|10*||9|||
| 46 | 12 | Peterborough United | L | 0-1 | 0-0 | 1679 | |1||3|10|5|6|12|7||11*||||||||||||||8|2|||9||4|
| | | | | | | | Apps. |41|3|38|24|42|44|10|40|16|36|19|9|24|3|18|9|5|4|2|11|9|10|9|24|16|15|5|14|5|1|
| | | | | | | | Subs. ||||5|||9|2||3|2|1|8||||1||1|||||||||||
| | | | | | | | Goals ||||2|7|7||3||3|2|2|3||1|5|||||2|||3|1|2|||||

Own goals 2

## F.A. CUP

| | Date | Opposition | | FT | HT | Att. | Goalscorers | Harrington P. | Raynor P. | Lane M. | Brett D. | Zelem P. | Holden A. | Bulmer P. | Allen J. | Manns P. | Blackwell P. | Williams M. | Phillips T. | Elliott A. | Burke J. | Storton T. | Parker S. | Williams P. | Ryan J. | Wann D. | Sutcliffe P. | Camden C. | Evans D. | Hildersley R. | Sanderson P. | Dixon L. | Wharton A. | Wintersgill D. | Coy R. | O'Rourke W. | Donnelly P. |
|---|---|---|---|---|---|---|---|---|---|---|---|---|---|---|---|---|---|---|---|---|---|---|---|---|---|---|---|---|---|---|---|---|---|---|---|---|---|
| 1R | Nov 19 | CHESTERFIELD | L | 1-2 | 0-2 | 1774 | Holden |1||3|4|5|6|11*|7|10|8|2||12||||||||9||||||||||

## LEAGUE (MILK) CUP

| | Date | Opposition | | FT | HT | Att. | Goalscorers | Harrington P. | Raynor P. | Lane M. | Brett D. | Zelem P. | Holden A. | Bulmer P. | Allen J. | Manns P. | Blackwell P. | Williams M. | Phillips T. | Elliott A. | Burke J. | Storton T. | Parker S. | Williams P. | Ryan J. | Wann D. | Sutcliffe P. | Camden C. | Evans D. | Hildersley R. | Sanderson P. | Dixon L. | Wharton A. | Wintersgill D. | Coy R. | O'Rourke W. | Donnelly P. |
|---|---|---|---|---|---|---|---|---|---|---|---|---|---|---|---|---|---|---|---|---|---|---|---|---|---|---|---|---|---|---|---|---|---|---|---|---|---|
| 1R1 | Aug 30 | Bolton Wanderers | L | 0-3 | 0-2 | 2665 | |1|2|3||5|6|7|8|9|11|10||4||||||||||||||||||
| 1R2 | Sep 14 | BOLTON WANDERERS* | W | 3-0 | 1-0 | 1502 | Holden,Zelem(pen),Phillips |1||3||5|10|12|8|7|11|2|9|4||6*||||||||||||||||
| 2R1 | Oct 5 | Leeds United | W | 1-0 | 1-0 | 8106 | Elliott |1||3|12|5|6|7|8|||2|10*|4|||9|11||||||||||||||
| 2R2 | 26 | LEEDS UNITED | L | 1-4 | 0-1 | 8044 | Zelem |1||3||5|6|12|9|||7|8*|4||2|10|||11|||||||||||||

* Extra time played following score of 3-0 after 90 minutes. Chester won 2-0 on penalties

## ASSOCIATE MEMBERS CUP

| | Date | Opposition | | FT | HT | Att. | Goalscorers | Harrington P. | Raynor P. | Lane M. | Brett D. | Zelem P. | Holden A. | Bulmer P. | Allen J. | Manns P. | Blackwell P. | Williams M. | Phillips T. | Elliott A. | Burke J. | Storton T. | Parker S. | Williams P. | Ryan J. | Wann D. | Sutcliffe P. | Camden C. | Evans D. | Hildersley R. | Sanderson P. | Dixon L. | Wharton A. | Wintersgill D. | Coy R. | O'Rourke W. | Donnelly P. |
|---|---|---|---|---|---|---|---|---|---|---|---|---|---|---|---|---|---|---|---|---|---|---|---|---|---|---|---|---|---|---|---|---|---|---|---|---|---|
| 1R | Feb 22 | BLACKPOOL * | W | 2-1 | 1-1 | 1046 | Zelem (pen), Serella (og) |1||3|12|5|4||9||11|||7*|||||||||||6|8|2|10|||||
| 2R | Mar 12 | Tranmere Rovers | L | 1-4 | 0-1 | 2116 | Holden |||3|7|5|4||||11||||||||||||||8|2|10|6|9|||

* Extra time played following score of 1-1 after 90 minutes.
Other player - 2R/1 Burke D.

## FRIENDLIES

| | Date | Opposition | | FT | HT | Att. | Goalscorers |
|---|---|---|---|---|---|---|---|
| 1 | Aug 2 | Flint Town United | W | 3-0 | | | Thomas, Doyle, Brett |
| 2 | 4 | PORT VALE | L | 1-4 | 1-1 | 545 | Holden |
| 3 | 9 | Rhyl | W | 4-0 | 4-0 | | Thomas,Bulmer,Elliott,Zelem |
| 4 | 13 | MANCHESTER CITY X1 | W | 2-0 | 0-0 | 459 | Holden, Manns |
| 5 | 18 | MANCHESTER UNITED X1 | L | 0-1 | 0-0 | 798 | |

**1983/84 Season:**
(Back) Sear (Assistant Manager), Blackwell, Storton, Allen, Harrington, Connor, Holden, Evans, Zelem, Sainty (Manager).
(Front) Manns, Thomas, Bulmer, Elliott, Lane, Williams.

**1984/85 Season:**
(Back) Speight, Walker, Coy, Evans, Morris, Higgins, Holden, Sanderson, Zelem, Blackwell.
(Front) Hildersley, Wharton, Sayer, Lane, Harrington, Fox, Dixon, Bulmer, Brett.

# SEASON 1984-85

## FOOTBALL (CANON) LEAGUE DIVISION 4

| | Date | Opposition | | FT | HT | Att. | Goalscorers |
|---|---|---|---|---|---|---|---|
| 1 | Aug 25 | SCUNTHORPE UNITED | D | 1-1 | 1-1 | 2050 | Zelem |
| 2 | Sep 1 | Aldershot | W | 2-1 | 0-1 | 2203 | Sayer, Brown |
| 3 | 8 | BURY | L | 2-3 | 0-2 | 2030 | Brett, Brown |
| 4 | 14 | Southend United | D | 1-1 | 1-0 | 2034 | Brett |
| 5 | 19 | Hereford United | D | 0-0 | 0-0 | 3847 | |
| 6 | 22 | NORTHAMPTON TOWN | W | 1-0 | 1-0 | 1723 | Brown |
| 7 | 29 | Blackpool | L | 1-3 | 1-1 | 4566 | Brett |
| 8 | Oct 3 | TRANMERE ROVERS | L | 2-4 | 1-3 | 2727 | Sayer, Brett |
| 9 | 6 | HALIFAX TOWN | W | 2-0 | 0-0 | 1412 | Zelem (pen), Fox |
| 10 | 13 | Exeter City | D | 1-1 | 1-1 | 2347 | Sayer |
| 11 | 20 | COLCHESTER UNITED | L | 1-2 | 0-2 | 1400 | Fox |
| 12 | 23 | Crewe Alex. | L | 0-2 | 0-1 | 3287 | |
| 13 | 27 | CHESTERFIELD | D | 1-1 | 0-1 | 2201 | Holden |
| 14 | Nov 3 | Darlington | L | 1-2 | 0-2 | 2403 | Zelem |
| 15 | 7 | Mansfield Town | L | 0-2 | 0-0 | 1789 | |
| 16 | 10 | TORQUAY UNITED | L | 0-1 | 0-0 | 1320 | |
| 17 | 23 | Port Vale | D | 0-0 | 0-0 | 3391 | |
| 18 | Dec 11 | ROCHDALE | L | 0-1 | 0-0 | 1173 | |
| 19 | 14 | Stockport County | L | 1-5 | 1-4 | 1462 | Higgins |
| 20 | 22 | Hartlepool United | L | 1-2 | 1-0 | 1849 | Zelem (pen) |
| 21 | 26 | WREXHAM | W | 2-1 | 2-1 | 3968 | Holden, Walker (pen) |
| 22 | Jan 1 | Peterborough United | L | 1-3 | 1-1 | 3799 | Fox |
| 23 | 26 | SOUTHEND UNITED | W | 5-1 | 2-1 | 1410 | Rimmer (3), Holden, Coy |
| 24 | 30 | SWINDON TOWN | W | 2-0 | 1-0 | 1710 | O'Berg, Greenhough |
| 25 | Feb 2 | BLACKPOOL | D | 0-0 | 0-0 | 3307 | |
| 26 | 23 | DARLINGTON | W | 5-2 | 3-0 | 1879 | Greenhough, Rimmer, Evans, Holden, Fox |
| 27 | Mar 2 | Chesterfield | L | 1-3 | 1-1 | 3002 | Rimmer |
| 28 | 6 | CREWE ALEX. | L | 0-2 | 0-0 | 2536 | |
| 29 | 8 | Colchester United | D | 1-1 | 1-0 | 2224 | Rimmer |
| 30 | 12 | Scunthorpe United | L | 1-2 | 1-2 | 1875 | Walker |
| 31 | 16 | EXETER CITY | L | 1-3 | 0-1 | 1400 | Walker (pen) |
| 32 | 19 | Northampton Town | W | 2-0 | 1-0 | 942 | Rimmer, Greenhough |
| 33 | 22 | Halifax Town | W | 4-0 | 3-0 | 1014 | Greenhough, Speight, Bulmer, Sayer |
| 34 | 27 | ALDERSHOT | W | 2-0 | 2-0 | 1534 | Kitchen, Rimmer |
| 35 | 30 | MANSFIELD TOWN | L | 0-3 | 0-1 | 1535 | |
| 36 | Apr 5 | PETERBOROUGH UNITED | L | 1-3 | 1-1 | 2020 | Holden |
| 37 | 6 | Wrexham | L | 0-2 | 0-1 | 3487 | |
| 38 | 13 | Torquay United | L | 0-2 | 0-2 | 1186 | |
| 39 | 16 | Tranmere Rovers | L | 0-1 | 0-0 | 1381 | |
| 40 | 20 | PORT VALE | W | 2-0 | 2-0 | 1531 | Walker (2) |
| 41 | 23 | Bury | L | 1-4 | 0-0 | 2703 | Walker (pen) |
| 42 | 27 | Rochdale | W | 2-1 | 2-0 | 1358 | Sayer, Rimmer (pen) |
| 43 | May 1 | HEREFORD UNITED | W | 2-1 | 0-1 | 1301 | Rimmer (2, 1 pen) |
| 44 | 4 | STOCKPORT COUNTY | W | 2-1 | 1-1 | 1545 | Sayer, Rimmer |
| 45 | 6 | Swindon Town | D | 4-4 | 1-1 | 3796 | Rimmer, Walker (3) |
| 46 | 11 | HARTLEPOOL UNITED | W | 1-0 | 1-0 | 1574 | Rimmer (pen) |

| | Butcher J. | Dixon L. | Lane M. | Evans D. | Zelem P. | Coy R. | Fox S. | Walker N. | Higgins A. | Sayer P. | Speight M. | Hildersley R. | Brown O. | Brett D. | Wharton A. | Bulmer P. | Holden A. | Blackwell P. | Morris A. | O'Berg P. | Rimmer S. | Greenhough R. | Harrington P. | Blease R. | Kitchen P. | Kaye D. |
|---|---|---|---|---|---|---|---|---|---|---|---|---|---|---|---|---|---|---|---|---|---|---|---|---|---|---|
| 1 | 1 | 2 | 3 | 4 | 5 | 6 | 7 | 8 | 9* | 10 | 11 | 12 | | | | | | | | | | | | | | |
| 2 | 1 | 2 | 3 | 4* | 5 | 6 | 7 | 8 | 12 | 10 | 11 | | 9 | | | | | | | | | | | | | |
| 3 | 1 | 2 | 3 | | 5 | 6 | 7 | 8* | 4 | 10 | | | 9 | 11 | 12 | | | | | | | | | | | |
| 4 | 1 | 2 | | | 5 | 6 | 7 | 8 | 4 | 10 | | | 9 | 11 | | 3 | | | | | | | | | | |
| 5 | 1 | 2 | | | 5 | 6* | 7 | 8 | 4 | 10 | | | | 11 | 12 | 3 | 9 | | | | | | | | | |
| 6 | 1 | 2 | | | | | 7 | 8 | 5 | 10 | | | 9 | 11 | 6 | 3 | 4 | | | | | | | | | |
| 7 | 1 | 2* | | | | | 7 | 8 | 5 | 10 | 9 | | 12 | 11 | 6 | 3 | 4 | | | | | | | | | |
| 8 | 1 | 2 | | | 5 | | 7 | 8 | 9 | 10 | 6 | | | 11 | | 3 | 4 | | | | | | | | | |
| 9 | 1 | 2 | | | 5 | | 7 | 8 | 6 | 12 | 10* | | 9 | 11 | | 3 | 4 | | | | | | | | | |
| 10 | 1 | 2 | | | | | 7 | 8 | 6 | 4 | 10 | | 9 | 11* | 12 | 3 | | 5 | | | | | | | | |
| 11 | 1 | 2 | | | | | 7 | 8* | 5 | 10 | 6 | | 9 | | | 3 | 4 | 11 | 12 | | | | | | | |
| 12 | 1 | 2 | | | | | 7 | 8 | 5 | 10 | 6 | | 9* | 12 | | 3 | 4 | 11 | | | | | | | | |
| 13 | 1 | 2 | | | 5 | 6 | | 8 | | 10 | 7 | | 9 | 11 | | 3 | 4 | | | | | | | | | |
| 14 | 1 | 2 | | | 5 | 6 | | 8* | 9 | 10 | 7 | | | 11 | 12 | 3 | 4 | | | | | | | | | |
| 15 | 1 | 2 | | | 5 | 6 | 7 | 8 | | 10* | 9 | 12 | | | 11 | 3 | 4 | | | | | | | | | |
| 16 | 1 | 2 | | | 5 | 6 | 7 | | | 9* | 8 | 11 | | 12 | 10 | 3 | 4 | | | | | | | | | |
| 17 | 1 | 2 | 3 | | 5 | | 7 | 10 | 9 | | 8 | 6 | | 11 | | | 4 | | | | | | | | | |
| 18 | 1 | | 3 | | 5 | | 7 | 8 | 12 | 9 | 10* | 6 | | 11 | | 2 | 4 | | | | | | | | | |
| 19 | 1 | 2 | 3 | | 5 | | 7 | 8 | 10 | 9 | | 6* | | 11 | | 12 | 4 | | | | | | | | | |
| 20 | 1 | 2 | 3 | | 5* | | 7 | 8 | 9 | 10 | 6 | | | 12 | | 11 | 4 | | | | | | | | | |
| 21 | 1 | 2 | 3 | | | 5 | 7 | 8 | 9 | 10 | 6 | | | | | 11 | 4 | | | | | | | | | |
| 22 | 1 | 2* | 3 | | | 5 | 7 | 8 | 12 | 10 | 6 | | | | | 11 | 4 | | | 9 | | | | | | |
| 23 | 1 | 2 | 11 | | | 5 | | 8 | | | | | | 6 | | 3 | 4 | | | 10 | 7 | 9 | | | | |
| 24 | 1 | 2 | 6 | | | 5 | | 8 | | | | | | 11 | | 3 | 4 | | | 10 | 7 | 9 | | | | |
| 25 | 1 | 2 | 6 | | | 5 | 12 | 8 | | | | | | 11 | | 3 | 4 | | | 10* | 7 | 9 | | | | |
| 26 | | 6 | 3 | 2 | | 5 | 12 | 8 | | | | | | 11 | | | 4 | | | 10 | 7 | 9* | 1 | | | |
| 27 | | 6 | 3 | 2* | | 5 | 12 | 8 | | | | | | 11 | | | 4 | | | | 7 | 9 | 1 | 10 | | |
| 28 | | | 3 | 2 | | 5 | 12 | 8 | | | | | | 6 | | 11 | 4* | | | | 7 | 9 | 1 | 10 | | |
| 29 | | | 3 | | | 5 | | 8 | | | 4 | | | 6 | | 11 | | 2 | | | 7 | 9 | 1 | 10 | | |
| 30 | | 12 | 3 | | | 5 | | 8 | | | 4 | | | 6 | | 11 | | 2 | | | 7 | 9 | 1 | 10* | | |
| 31 | | 2 | | 12 | | 5 | | 8 | | 10 | | | | 6* | | 11 | 4 | 3 | | | 7 | 9 | 1 | | | |
| 32 | 1 | 2 | 6 | | | 5 | | 8 | | 10 | 11 | | | | | 3 | 4 | | | | 7 | 9 | | | | |
| 33 | 1 | 2 | 3 | | | 5 | | 8 | | 10 | 11* | | | | | 6 | 4 | | | | 7 | 9 | | | 12 | |
| 34 | 1 | | 3 | | | 5 | | 8 | | 6 | 11* | | | 12 | | | 4 | 2 | | | 7 | 9 | | | 10 | |
| 35 | 1 | | 3 | | | 5 | | 8 | | 6 | | | | 11 | | | 4 | 2 | | | 7 | 9 | | | 10 | |
| 36 | 1 | 2 | 3 | | | 5 | | 10 | | 8 | 6 | | | | | 11 | 4* | | | | 7 | 9 | | | 12 | |
| 37 | 1 | 2 | 3 | | | 5 | | | | 8* | 6 | | | | | 11 | 4 | 10 | | | 7 | 12 | | | 9 | |
| 38 | 1 | 2 | 3 | | | 5 | | 10 | | 8* | 6 | 12 | | | | 11 | 4 | | | | 7 | 9 | | | | |
| 39 | 1 | 2 | 3 | | | 5 | 7 | 10 | | | 6 | | | | | 11 | 4 | | | | 8 | 9 | | | | |
| 40 | | 2 | 3 | | | 5 | 7 | 10 | | 6 | | 12 | | | | 11* | 4 | | | | 8 | 9 | | | | 1 |
| 41 | | 2 | | | | 5 | 7 | 10 | | 6 | | 11* | | 12 | | 3 | 4 | | | | 8 | 9 | | | | 1 |
| 42 | | 2 | 3 | | | 5 | 7 | | | 10 | 6 | | | | | 11 | 4 | | | | 8 | 9 | | | | 1 |
| 43 | | 2 | 3 | | | 5 | 7 | | | 10 | 6 | | | | | 11 | 4 | | | | 8 | 9 | | | | 1 |
| 44 | | 2 | 3 | | | 5 | 7 | | | 10 | 6* | | | 12 | | 11 | 4 | | | | 8 | 9 | | | | 1 |
| 45 | | 2 | 3 | | | 5 | 7 | 10 | | 6 | 4 | | | 12 | | 11* | | | | | 8 | 9 | | | | 1 |
| 46 | | 2 | 3 | | | 5 | 7 | 10 | | 6 | | | | 12 | | 11 | 4 | | | | 8 | 9* | | | | 1 |
| Apps. | 33 | 40 | 31 | 5 | 15 | 35 | 28 | 41 | 16 | 35 | 30 | 5 | 9 | 23 | 4 | 37 | 38 | 9 | | 5 | 24 | 23 | 6 | 4 | 3 | 7 |
| Subs. | | 1 | | 1 | | | 4 | | 3 | 1 | | 4 | 1 | 8 | 4 | 1 | | | 1 | | | 1 | | | 2 | |
| Goals | | | | 1 | 4 | 1 | 4 | 9 | 1 | 6 | 1 | | 3 | 4 | | 1 | 5 | | | 1 | 14 | 4 | | | 1 | |

## F.A. CUP

| | Date | Opposition | | FT | HT | Att. | Goalscorers |
|---|---|---|---|---|---|---|---|
| 1R | Nov 17 | Darlington | L | 2-3 | 1-2 | 3726 | Fox, Holden |

| | Butcher J. | Dixon L. | Lane M. | Evans D. | Zelem P. | Coy R. | Fox S. | Walker N. | Higgins A. | Sayer P. | Speight M. | Hildersley R. | Brown O. | Brett D. | Wharton A. | Bulmer P. | Holden A. | Blackwell P. | Morris A. | O'Berg P. | Rimmer S. | Greenhough R. | Harrington P. | Blease R. | Kitchen P. | Kaye D. |
|---|---|---|---|---|---|---|---|---|---|---|---|---|---|---|---|---|---|---|---|---|---|---|---|---|---|---|
| 1R | 1 | 2 | 3 | | 5 | | 7 | 10 | 9 | 12 | 8* | 6 | | 11 | | | 4 | | | | | | | | | |

## LEAGUE (MILK) CUP

| | Date | Opposition | | FT | HT | Att. | Goalscorers |
|---|---|---|---|---|---|---|---|
| 1R1 | Aug 28 | Blackpool | L | 0-1 | 0-1 | 3318 | |
| 1R2 | Sep 5 | BLACKPOOL | L | 0-3 | 0-3 | 3001 | |

| | Butcher J. | Dixon L. | Lane M. | Evans D. | Zelem P. | Coy R. | Fox S. | Walker N. | Higgins A. | Sayer P. | Speight M. | Hildersley R. | Brown O. | Brett D. | Wharton A. | Bulmer P. | Holden A. | Blackwell P. | Morris A. | O'Berg P. | Rimmer S. | Greenhough R. | Harrington P. | Blease R. | Kitchen P. | Kaye D. |
|---|---|---|---|---|---|---|---|---|---|---|---|---|---|---|---|---|---|---|---|---|---|---|---|---|---|---|
| 1R1 | 1 | 2 | 3 | 4 | 5 | 6 | 7 | 8 | 9 | 10 | 11* | | | | | | | 12 | | | | | | | | |
| 1R2 | 1 | 2 | 3 | | 5 | 6 | 7 | 8 | 12 | 10 | 11 | | 9 | | | | 4* | | | | | | | | | |

## ASSOCIATE MEMBERS (FREIGHT ROVER) TROPHY

| | Date | Opposition | | FT | HT | Att. | Goalscorers |
|---|---|---|---|---|---|---|---|
| 1R1 | Feb 5 | Bury | D | 1-1 | 1-0 | 1814 | Holden |
| 1R2 | 20 | BURY | L | 1-2 | 1-0 | 1391 | Brett |

| | Butcher J. | Dixon L. | Lane M. | Evans D. | Zelem P. | Coy R. | Fox S. | Walker N. | Higgins A. | Sayer P. | Speight M. | Hildersley R. | Brown O. | Brett D. | Wharton A. | Bulmer P. | Holden A. | Blackwell P. | Morris A. | O'Berg P. | Rimmer S. | Greenhough R. | Harrington P. | Blease R. | Kitchen P. | Kaye D. |
|---|---|---|---|---|---|---|---|---|---|---|---|---|---|---|---|---|---|---|---|---|---|---|---|---|---|---|
| 1R1 | | 2 | 6* | | | 5 | 13 | 8 | | 12 | | | | 11 | | 3 | 4 | | | 10' | 7 | 9 | 1 | | | |
| 1R2 | | | 6 | 2 | | 5 | | 8 | | | | | | 11 | | 3 | 4 | | | 10 | 7 | 9 | 1 | | | |

## FRIENDLIES

| | Date | Opposition | | FT | HT | Att. | Goalscorers |
|---|---|---|---|---|---|---|---|
| 1 | Jul 30 | Parkway Clayton | W | 5-2 | | | Fox (2), Brett, Zelem, Dixon |
| 2 | Aug 6 | SHREWSBURY TOWN | L | 1-2 | 1-0 | | Fox |
| 3 | 8 | WIGAN ATHLETIC | L | 0-1 | 0-0 | | |
| 4 | 11 | BRISTOL ROVERS | D | 1-1 | 1-1 | | Williams (og) |
| 5 | 14 | Rhyl | D | 1-1 | 0-1 | | Wharton |
| 6 | 19 | MANCHESTER CITY | W | 2-1 | 1-1 | | Dixon, Higgins |
| 7 | Dec 7 | MANCHESTER UNITED RES. | D | 1-1 | 1-1 | 1739 | Fox |
| 8 | May 26 | WREXHAM * | L | 1-2 | 1-2 | 3772 | R Futcher |

* Bradford City Disaster Appeal

# SEASON 1985-86

## FOOTBALL (CANON) LEAGUE DIVISION 4

| | Date | Opposition | | FT | HT | Att. | Goalscorers | Butcher J. | Glenn D. | Lane M. | Holden A. | Gage W. | Coy R. | Speight M. | Graham M. | Rimmer S. | Fox S. | Brett D. | Harley L. | Kaye D. | Bennett G. | Houghton P. | Croft B. | Kelly J. | Greenhough R. | Murray D. | Cashley R. | Abel G. | Bramhall J. | Richardson I. | Butler B. | Wright W. | Sconce M. | Barrett E. | Johnson S. |
|---|---|---|---|---|---|---|---|---|---|---|---|---|---|---|---|---|---|---|---|---|---|---|---|---|---|---|---|---|---|---|---|---|---|---|---|
| 1 | Aug 17 | HALIFAX TOWN | D | 1-1 | 1-0 | 1750 | Rimmer | 1 | 2 | 3 | 4 | 5 | 6 | 7 | 8* | 9 | 10 | 11 | 12 | | | | | | | | | | | | | | | | |
| 2 | 24 | Peterborough United | L | 0-3 | 0-0 | 2667 | | | 2 | 3 | 4 | 5 | 7 | 6 | | 8 | | 11 | | 1 | 9 | 10* | 12 | | | | | | | | | | | | |
| 3 | 26 | HARTLEPOOL UNITED | D | 1-1 | 0-1 | 1429 | Rimmer (pen) | | 2 | 3 | 4 | 5 | 6 | 7 | | 9 | | | | 1 | 11 | 10 | | 8 | | | | | | | | | | | |
| 4 | 31 | Tranmere Rovers | W | 3-2 | 1-0 | 1703 | Holden, Burgess (og), Rimmer | | 2 | 3 | 4 | 5 | 6 | | | 9 | | | | 1 | 11 | 10 | | 7 | 8 | | | | | | | | | | |
| 5 | Sep 7 | HEREFORD UNITED | W | 1-0 | 1-0 | 1720 | Houghton | 1 | 2 | 3 | | 5 | 6 | | 8 | 9 | | | | | 11 | 10 | | 7 | 4 | | | | | | | | | | |
| 6 | 14 | Torquay United | W | 3-0 | 1-0 | 1111 | Houghton, Rimmer (2) | 1 | 2 | 3 | | 5 | 4 | 6 | 8 | 9 | | 12 | | | 11* | 10 | | 7 | | | | | | | | | | | |
| 7 | 21 | CREWE ALEX. | W | 4-0 | 1-0 | 2369 | Rimmer (pen), Gage, Bennett (2) | 1 | 2 | 3 | | 5 | 6 | | 8 | 9 | | | | | 11 | 10 | | 7 | 4 | | | | | | | | | | |
| 8 | 28 | Stockport County | D | 2-2 | 1-1 | 1801 | Bennett (2) | 1 | 2 | 3 | 4 | 5 | 6 | | 8 | 9 | | 10* | | | 11 | | | 7 | 12 | | | | | | | | | | |
| 9 | Oct 2 | MANSFIELD TOWN | W | 1-0 | 1-0 | 2127 | Rimmer (pen) | 1 | 2 | 3 | | 5 | 6 | | 8 | 9 | | 12 | | | 11 | 10* | | 7 | 4 | | | | | | | | | | |
| 10 | 5 | BURNLEY | W | 4-0 | 2-0 | 3005 | Rimmer, Graham, Kelly, Bennett | 1 | 2 | 3 | | 5 | 6 | | 8 | 9 | | 10 | | | 11 | | | 7 | 4 | | | | | | | | | | |
| 11 | 12 | Preston North End | W | 6-3 | 4-1 | 4073 | Rimmer(4,1 pen),Kelly,Greenhough | 1 | 2 | 3 | | 5 | 6 | 4 | 8 | 9 | | 10 | | | | | | 7 | 12 | 11* | | | | | | | | | |
| 12 | 19 | SWINDON TOWN | L | 0-1 | 0-1 | 3109 | | | 2 | 3 | 4 | 5 | 6 | 10 | 8* | 9 | | | | | 11 | | | 7 | | 12 | 1 | | | | | | | | |
| 13 | 22 | Northampton Town | D | 2-2 | 1-1 | 2323 | Graham, Murray | | 2 | 3 | | 5 | 6 | 4 | 8 | 9 | | | | | 10 | | | 7 | 12 | 11* | 1 | | | | | | | | |
| 14 | 26 | Wrexham | D | 1-1 | 1-0 | 3500 | Coy | | 2 | 3 | | 5 | 6 | 4 | 8 | 9 | | | | | 11 | 12 | | 7 | 10* | | 1 | | | | | | | | |
| 15 | Nov 2 | ALDERSHOT | W | 1-0 | 0-0 | 2180 | Rimmer (pen) | | | 3 | | 5 | 6 | 4 | 8 | 9 | | | | | 11 | 10 | | 7 | | 12 | 1 | 2* | | | | | | | |
| 16 | 6 | COLCHESTER UNITED | W | 4-0 | 1-0 | 2809 | Greenhough, Rimmer (2), Abel | | | 3 | | 5 | 6 | | 8 | 9 | | | | | 11 | 10 | | 7 | 4 | | 1 | 2 | | | | | | | |
| 17 | 9 | Exeter City | W | 3-1 | 2-1 | 1888 | Greenhough, Houghton (2) | | | 3 | | 5 | 6 | | 8 | 9 | | | | | 11 | 10 | | 7 | 4 | | 1 | 2 | | | | | | | |
| 18 | 23 | ORIENT | W | 3-0 | 1-0 | 2653 | Kelly (2), Rimmer | 1 | 2 | 3 | | | 6 | 4 | | 9* | | | | | 11 | 10 | | 7 | 12 | | | 8 | 5 | | | | | | |
| 19 | 29 | Southend United | D | 1-1 | 0-0 | 3525 | Houghton | 1 | 2 | 3 | | | 6 | | | | | | | | 11 | 10 | | 7 | 4 | | | 8 | 5 | 9 | | | | | |
| 20 | Dec 7 | Aldershot | D | 1-1 | 0-0 | 1528 | Richardson (pen) | 1 | 2 | 3 | | | 6 | | | | | | | | 11 | 10 | | 7 | 4 | | | 8 | 5 | 9 | | | | | |
| 21 | 14 | SCUNTHORPE UNITED | D | 1-1 | 1-1 | 2657 | Kelly | 1 | 2 | 3 | | | 6 | | 4 | | | | | | 11 | 10 | | 7 | | | | 8 | 5 | 9 | | | | | |
| 22 | 21 | PETERBOROUGH UNITED | W | 2-1 | 1-0 | 2331 | Holden, Bennett | 1 | 2 | 3 | 4 | | 6 | | 8 | | | | | | 11 | 10 | | 7 | | | | 5 | | 9 | | | | | |
| 23 | 26 | Cambridge United | L | 2-3 | 1-2 | 2395 | Richardson, Bennett | 1 | 2 | 3 | 4 | | 6 | | 8* | | | | | | 11 | 10 | | 7 | 12 | | | 5 | | 9 | | | | | |
| 24 | Jan 1 | PORT VALE | W | 4-1 | 2-1 | 5010 | Houghton(2),Richardson(pen),Bennett | 1 | 2 | 3 | 4 | | 6 | | 8 | | | | | | 11 | 10 | | 7 | | | | 5 | | 9 | | | | | |
| 25 | 8 | Hartlepool United | D | 1-1 | 1-0 | 3891 | Abel | 1 | 2 | 3 | 4 | | 6 | | 8 | | | | | | 11 | 10 | | 7 | | | | 5 | | 9 | | | | | |
| 26 | 11 | TRANMERE ROVERS | W | 1-0 | 0-0 | 3700 | Graham | 1 | 2 | 3 | | | 6 | | 12 | | | | | | 11 | 10 | | 7 | 4 | | | 5 | | 9* | 8 | | | | |
| 27 | 17 | Halifax Town | W | 2-1 | 1-0 | 1473 | Houghton (2) | 1 | 2 | 3 | | | 6 | | | | | | | | 11 | 10 | | 7 | 4 | | | 5 | | 9 | 8 | | | | |
| 28 | 25 | TORQUAY UNITED | W | 3-1 | 2-1 | 2808 | Richardson (2), Bennett | | 2 | 3 | | | 6 | | 8 | | | | | | 11 | 10 | | | 4 | | 1 | 5 | | 9 | 7 | | | | |
| 29 | Feb 1 | Hereford United | W | 2-0 | 1-0 | 3255 | Bennett (2, 1 pen) | | 2* | 3 | | | 6 | | 8 | | | | | | 11 | 10 | | 7 | 4 | | 1 | 5 | | 9 | 12 | | | | |
| 30 | 5 | NORTHAMPTON TOWN | L | 2-3 | 2-1 | 3304 | Richardson (pen), Chard (og) | | | 3 | | | 6 | | 8 | | | | | | 11* | 10 | | 7 | 4 | 12 | 1 | 5 | | 9 | 2 | | | | |
| 31 | 15 | ROCHDALE | D | 1-1 | 1-0 | 3232 | Richardson (pen) | 1 | | 3 | | | 6 | | 8 | | | | | | 11 | 10 | | 7 | 2 | | | 5 | | 9 | | 4 | | | |
| 32 | 22 | Crewe Alex. | D | 2-2 | 2-1 | 3271 | Kelly, Richardson (pen) | 1 | | 3 | | | 6 | | 8 | | | | | | 11 | 10 | | 7 | 2 | | | 5 | | 9 | | 4 | | | |
| 33 | Mar 1 | STOCKPORT COUNTY | L | 1-2 | 1-2 | 2919 | Richardson | 1 | | 3 | | | 6 | | 8 | | | | | | 11* | 10 | | 7 | | | | 5 | | 9 | 12 | 4 | 2 | | |
| 34 | 4 | Mansfield Town | D | 0-0 | 0-0 | 3957 | | 1 | | 3 | | | 6* | | 8 | | | | | | 11 | 10 | | 7 | | | | 5 | | 9 | 12 | 4 | | 2 | |
| 35 | 8 | Burnley | L | 0-1 | 0-0 | 3690 | | 1 | | 3 | | | | | 8 | | | | | | 11 | 10* | | 7 | | | | 5 | | 9 | 6 | 4 | 12 | 2 | |
| 36 | 15 | PRESTON NORTH END | W | 2-0 | 1-0 | 3062 | Wright, Kelly | 1 | | 3 | | | | | 8 | | | | | | 12 | | | 7 | 10 | 11* | | 5 | | 9 | 6 | 4 | | 2 | |
| 37 | 22 | WREXHAM | W | 2-1 | 1-1 | 4791 | Richardson, Bennett | 1 | | 3 | | | 6 | | 8 | | | | | | 12 | 10* | | 7 | 4 | | | 5 | | 9 | | | | 2 | 11 |
| 38 | 29 | Port Vale | D | 1-1 | 0-1 | 4490 | Greenhough | 1 | | 3 | | | 6 | | 8 | | | | | | 11 | 10 | | 7 | 4 | | | | | 9 | | | | 2 | 5 |
| 39 | 31 | CAMBRIDGE UNITED | D | 1-1 | 1-0 | 2893 | Houghton | 1 | | 3 | | | 6 | | 8 | | | | | | 11 | 10* | | 7 | 4 | | | | | 9 | 12 | | | 2 | 5 |
| 40 | Apr 4 | Colchester United | W | 3-2 | 2-0 | 2281 | Johnson, Glenn, Greenhough | 1 | 2 | | | | 6 | | 8 | | | | | | 11* | 12 | | 7 | 4 | | | | | 9 | 5 | | | 3 | 10 |
| 41 | 8 | Swindon Town | L | 2-4 | 2-1 | 12630 | Johnson (2, 1 pen) | 1 | 2 | | | | 6 | | 8 | | | | | | 11 | 10 | | 7 | 4 | | | | | | 5 | | | 3 | 9 |
| 42 | 12 | EXETER CITY | W | 2-1 | 1-0 | 2899 | Lane, Johnson (pen) | 1 | 2 | 3 | | | 6 | | 8 | | | | | | 12 | 11* | | 7 | 4 | | | | | 9 | | | | 5 | 10 |
| 43 | 19 | Orient | D | 0-0 | 0-0 | 2617 | | 1 | 2 | 3 | | | 6 | | 8 | | | | | | | 11 | | 7 | 4 | | | | | 9 | | | | 5 | 10 |
| 44 | 26 | SOUTHEND UNITED | W | 2-0 | 1-0 | 4453 | Bennett, Johnson (pen) | 1 | 2 | 3 | | | 6 | | | | | | | | 11 | | | 7 | 4 | | | | | 9 | 8 | | | 5 | 10 |
| 45 | 29 | Rochdale | W | 2-1 | 1-0 | 1963 | Kelly, Johnson | 1 | 2 | 3 | | | 6 | | 8 | | | | | | 11 | | | 7 | 4 | | | | | 9 | | | | 5 | 10 |
| 46 | May 3 | Scunthorpe United | L | 0-2 | 0-1 | 2256 | | 1 | 2* | 3 | | | 6 | | 8 | | | | | | 11 | 12 | | 7 | 4 | | | | | 9 | 5 | | | | 10 |
| | | | | | | | Apps. | 34 | 33 | 44 | 10 | 17 | 44 | 10 | 37 | 18 | 1 | 5 | | 3 | 40 | 34 | | 43 | 28 | 3 | 9 | 23 | 4 | 27 | 10 | 6 | 1 | 12 | 10 |
| | | | | | | | Subs. | | | | | | | | 1 | | | 2 | 1 | | 3 | 3 | 1 | | 5 | 3 | | | | | 4 | | 1 | | |
| | | | | | | | Goals | | 1 | 1 | 2 | 1 | 1 | | 3 | 16 | | | | | 13 | 10 | | 8 | 5 | 1 | | 2 | | 10 | | 1 | | | 6 |

Own goals 2

## F.A. CUP

| | Date | Opposition | | FT | HT | Att. | Goalscorers | Butcher J. | Glenn D. | Lane M. | Holden A. | Gage W. | Coy R. | Speight M. | Graham M. | Rimmer S. | Fox S. | Brett D. | Harley L. | Kaye D. | Bennett G. | Houghton P. | Croft B. | Kelly J. | Greenhough R. | Murray D. | Cashley R. | Abel G. | Bramhall J. | Richardson I. | Butler B. | Wright W. | Sconce M. | Barrett E. | Johnson S. |
|---|---|---|---|---|---|---|---|---|---|---|---|---|---|---|---|---|---|---|---|---|---|---|---|---|---|---|---|---|---|---|---|---|---|---|---|
| 1R | Nov 16 | Bury | L | 0-2 | 0-0 | 3424 | | 1 | 12 | 3 | | 5 | 6 | 4 | 8* | 9 | | | | | 11 | 10 | | 7 | 2 | | | | | | | | | | |

## LEAGUE (MILK) CUP

| | Date | Opposition | | FT | HT | Att. | Goalscorers | Butcher J. | Glenn D. | Lane M. | Holden A. | Gage W. | Coy R. | Speight M. | Graham M. | Rimmer S. | Fox S. | Brett D. | Harley L. | Kaye D. | Bennett G. | Houghton P. | Croft B. | Kelly J. | Greenhough R. | Murray D. | Cashley R. | Abel G. | Bramhall J. | Richardson I. | Butler B. | Wright W. | Sconce M. | Barrett E. | Johnson S. |
|---|---|---|---|---|---|---|---|---|---|---|---|---|---|---|---|---|---|---|---|---|---|---|---|---|---|---|---|---|---|---|---|---|---|---|---|
| 1R1 | Aug 28 | Tranmere Rovers | W | 3-1 | 2-1 | 2207 | Rimmer (3, 1 pen) | | 2 | 3 | 4 | 5 | 6 | | | 9 | | | | 1 | 10 | 11 | | 7 | 8 | | | | | | | | | | |
| 1R2 | Sep 4 | TRANMERE ROVERS | D | 0-0 | 0-0 | 2384 | | 1 | 2 | 3 | 4 | 5 | 6 | | 9 | 8 | | | | | 10 | 11 | | 7 | | | | | | | | | | | |
| 2R1 | 25 | COVENTRY CITY | L | 1-2 | 0-0 | 4863 | Rimmer (pen) | 1 | 2 | 3 | 4 | 5 | 6 | | 8 | 9 | | | | | 11 | 10 | | 7 | | | | | | | | | | | |
| 2R2 | Oct 9 | Coventry City | L | 2-7 | 2-4 | 5504 | Murray, Rimmer (pen) | 1 | 2 | 3 | | | 6 | 4 | 8 | 9 | | 11 | | | | | | 7 | 5 | 10 | | | | | | | | | |

## ASSOCIATE MEMBERS (FREIGHT ROVER) TROPHY

| | Date | Opposition | | FT | HT | Att. | Goalscorers | Butcher J. | Glenn D. | Lane M. | Holden A. | Gage W. | Coy R. | Speight M. | Graham M. | Rimmer S. | Fox S. | Brett D. | Harley L. | Kaye D. | Bennett G. | Houghton P. | Croft B. | Kelly J. | Greenhough R. | Murray D. | Cashley R. | Abel G. | Bramhall J. | Richardson I. | Butler B. | Wright W. | Sconce M. | Barrett E. | Johnson S. |
|---|---|---|---|---|---|---|---|---|---|---|---|---|---|---|---|---|---|---|---|---|---|---|---|---|---|---|---|---|---|---|---|---|---|---|---|
| GM | Jan 20 | Rochdale | L | 0-1 | 0-0 | 1164 | | 1* | | | | | 6 | | | | | 12 | | | 9 | | 11 | | 4 | 10 | | 5 | | | 8 | | 2 | | |
| GM | 22 | WIGAN ATHLETIC | L | 0-2 | 0-2 | 1375 | | | | 6 | | | | | | | | 7 | | | 11 | | 10 | | 4 | | 1 | 5 | | | 8 | | 2 | | |

Other players - Woodthorpe C. GM1/3, GM2/3, Palmer R. GM1/7', Bailey I. GM1/13, GM2/9

## FRIENDLIES

| | Date | Opposition | | FT | HT | Att. | Goalscorers |
|---|---|---|---|---|---|---|---|
| 1 | Jul 27 | Runcorn | W | 2-1 | 0-0 | | Kelly (2) |
| 2 | Aug 7 | WOLVERHAMPTON W. | W | 3-2 | 1-1 | 850 | Rimmer, Graham, Kelly |
| 3 | 9 | Altrincham | W | 3-0 | | | Houghton (2), Rimmer |

**1985/86 Season:**
(Back) Clarke (Trainer), Coy, Holden, Greenhough, Butcher, Evans, Houghton, Graham, Lane, Sear (Youth Team Coach).
(Front) Kelly, Glenn, Rimmer, McNally (Manager), Speight, Brett, Fox .

**1986/87 Season:**
(Back) Clarke (Trainer), Lane, Bennett, Greenhough, Stewart, Holden, Butcher, Butler, Abel, Houghton, Sear (Youth Team Coach).
(Front) Croft, Richardson, Glenn, Rimmer, McNally (Manager), Barrow (Assistant Manager), Graham, Kelly, Sconce.

# SEASON 1986-87

## FOOTBALL (TODAY) LEAGUE DIVISION 3

| | Date | Opposition | | FT | HT | Att. | Goalscorers | Stewart W. | Glenn D. | Lane M. | Holden A. | Abel G. | Butler B. | Kelly J. | Barrow G. | Bennett G. | Houghton P. | Graham M. | Croft B. | Greenhough R. | Woodthorpe C. | Richardson I. | Rimmer S. | Butcher J. | Lundon S. | Howard T. | Fazackerley D. | Sconce M. |
|---|---|---|---|---|---|---|---|---|---|---|---|---|---|---|---|---|---|---|---|---|---|---|---|---|---|---|---|---|
| 1 | Aug 23 | CARLISLE UNITED | D | 2-2 | 1-2 | 3425 | Holden (pen), Houghton | 1 | 2 | 3 | 4* | 5 | 6 | 7 | 8 | 9 | 10 | 11 | 12 | | | | | | | | | |
| 2 | 30 | Bury | D | 1-1 | 0-1 | 2985 | Kelly | 1 | | 4 | | 5 | 6 | 7 | 8 | 9* | 10 | 11 | | 2 | 3 | 12 | | | | | | |
| 3 | Sep 6 | FULHAM | D | 2-2 | 1-0 | 2568 | Greenhough, Bennett | 1 | | 5 | 4 | | 6 | 7 | 8 | 9 | 10 | 11 | 12 | 2 | 3* | | | | | | | |
| 4 | 13 | Swindon Town | D | 1-1 | 0-0 | 5669 | Barrow | 1 | | 5 | 4 | | 6 | 7 | 8 | 9 | 10 | 11 | 3* | 2 | | 12 | | | | | | |
| 5 | 16 | AFC Bournemouth | L | 0-2 | 0-0 | 3027 | | 1 | | 3 | 4 | 5 | 6 | 7 | 8 | 12 | 10* | 11 | | 2 | | 9 | | | | | | |
| 6 | 27 | Darlington | L | 0-1 | 0-1 | 1902 | | 1 | | 3 | | 5 | 6 | 7 | 8 | 4* | 10 | 11 | 12 | 2 | | 9 | | | | | | |
| 7 | Oct 1 | DONCASTER ROVERS | W | 1-0 | 1-0 | 2578 | Holden (pen) | 1 | | 3 | 4 | 5 | 6 | 7 | 8 | | 10 | 11 | | 2 | | 9* | 12 | | | | | |
| 8 | 4 | BRISTOL CITY | L | 0-3 | 0-1 | 2796 | | 1 | | 3 | 4 | 5 | 6 | 7 | 8 | | 10* | 11 | | 2 | | 9 | 12 | | | | | |
| 9 | 11 | Newport County | D | 2-2 | 2-1 | 2119 | Kelly (2) | 1 | | | 4 | 5 | 6 | 7 | 8 | | 10 | 11* | | 2 | 3 | 12 | 9 | | | | | |
| 10 | 15 | GILLINGHAM | D | 1-1 | 0-1 | 2169 | Greenhough | | | 4 | | 2 | 6 | 7 | 8 | | 10 | 11* | | 5 | 3 | 12 | 9 | 1 | | | | |
| 11 | 18 | MANSFIELD TOWN | D | 1-1 | 1-0 | 2377 | Rimmer (pen) | | | 4 | | 2 | 6 | 7 | 8 | 12 | 10 | 11 | | 5 | 3* | | 9 | 1 | | | | |
| 12 | 21 | York City | D | 1-1 | 1-0 | 3322 | Rimmer (pen) | | | 3 | 4 | 2 | 6 | 7 | 8 | 12 | 10* | 11 | | 5 | | | 9 | 1 | | | | |
| 13 | 25 | Bolton Wanderers | D | 1-1 | 0-1 | 4607 | Houghton | | | 4 | | 2 | 6 | 7 | 8 | 12 | 10 | 11 | | 5 | | | 9* | 1 | 3 | | | |
| 14 | Nov 1 | WALSALL | D | 0-0 | 0-0 | 2872 | | | | 4 | | 2 | | 7 | | 11 | 10 | 8 | 6 | 5 | | | 9 | 1 | 3 | | | |
| 15 | 4 | Rotherham United | L | 0-3 | 0-2 | 2439 | | | | 4 | | 2* | 6 | 7 | | 12 | 10 | 11 | 8 | 5 | 3 | | 9 | 1 | | | | |
| 16 | 8 | BRENTFORD | D | 1-1 | 0-1 | 2016 | Bennett (pen) | | | 4 | | 2 | 6 | 7 | | 12 | 10 | 11 | 8 | 5 | | | 9* | 1 | 3 | | | |
| 17 | 22 | BRISTOL ROVERS | W | 3-1 | 2-0 | 2026 | Bennett (2), Croft | 1 | | 4 | | 2 | 6 | 7 | 8 | 9 | | 11 | 10 | 5 | | | | | 3 | | | |
| 18 | 29 | Middlesbrough | W | 2-1 | 1-1 | 9464 | Greenhough, Abel | 1 | | 4 | | 2 | 6 | 7 | 8 | 9 | | 11 | 10* | 5 | | | 12 | | 3 | | | |
| 19 | Dec 14 | Port Vale | L | 1-2 | 0-0 | 3347 | Kelly | 1 | | 4 | | 2 | 6 | 7 | 8 | 9 | 10 | 11 | | 5 | | | | | 3 | | | |
| 20 | 19 | CHESTERFIELD | D | 1-1 | 0-0 | 1706 | Bennett | | | 4 | | 2 | 6 | | 8 | 9 | | 11 | | 5 | 10 | | 7 | 1 | 3 | | | |
| 21 | 26 | Wigan Athletic | D | 2-2 | 2-1 | 4187 | Bennett (2) | | | 4 | | 2 | 6 | | 8 | 9 | 10 | 11 | | 5 | | | 7 | 1 | 3 | | | |
| 22 | 27 | BLACKPOOL | L | 1-4 | 0-3 | 4002 | Barrow | | | 4 | | 2 | 6* | | 8 | 9 | 10 | 11 | 12 | 5 | 3 | | 7 | 1 | | | | |
| 23 | Jan 24 | Fulham | W | 5-0 | 0-0 | 3067 | Kelly (2), Graham, Barrow, Bennett | 1 | | | | 6 | | 7 | 8 | 9 | 12 | 11 | | 5 | 3 | | 10* | | | 2 | 4 | |
| 24 | Feb 7 | AFC BOURNEMOUTH | D | 2-2 | 1-1 | 2838 | Kelly, Bennett | 1 | | | | 5 | 6 | 7 | 8 | 9 | 10 | 11 | | | 3 | | 12 | | | 2* | 4 | |
| 25 | 14 | Gillingham | W | 2-1 | 2-1 | 4467 | Rimmer, Woodthorpe | 1 | | | | 5 | 6 | 7 | 8 | 9 | | 11 | | 2 | 3 | | 10 | | | | 4 | |
| 26 | 17 | NOTTS COUNTY | L | 1-2 | 0-1 | 2784 | Bennett | 1 | | | | 5 | 6 | 7 | 8 | 9 | | 11 | | 2 | 3 | | 10 | | | | 4 | |
| 27 | 21 | DARLINGTON | W | 6-0 | 5-0 | 2380 | Barrow (2), Graham, Bennett (2), Rimmer | 1 | | | | 5 | 6 | 7 | 8 | 9 | | 11 | | 2 | 3 | | 10 | | | | 4 | |
| 28 | 27 | Doncaster Rovers | D | 1-1 | 1-1 | 2176 | Woodthorpe | 1 | | | | 5 | 6 | 7 | 8 | 9 | | 11 | | 2 | 3 | | 10 | | | | 4 | |
| 29 | Mar 7 | BOLTON WANDERERS | D | 0-0 | 0-0 | 2764 | | 1 | | | | 5 | 6 | 7 | 8 | 9 | | 11 | | 2 | 3 | | 10 | | | | 4 | |
| 30 | 14 | Mansfield Town | W | 3-2 | 2-0 | 2742 | Rimmer, Kelly, Graham | 1 | | | | 5 | 6 | 7 | 8 | 9 | 4 | 11 | | 2 | 3 | | 10 | | | | | |
| 31 | 18 | YORK CITY | W | 2-1 | 0-1 | 2325 | Walwyn (og), Greenhough | 1 | | | | 5 | 6 | 7 | 8 | 9* | 12 | 11 | | 2 | 3 | | 10 | | | | 4 | |
| 32 | 21 | NEWPORT COUNTY | W | 2-0 | 0-0 | 2561 | Houghton, Rimmer | 1 | | | | 5 | 6 | 7* | 8 | | 10 | 11 | 12 | 2 | 3 | | 9 | | | | 4 | |
| 33 | 25 | BURY | L | 0-1 | 0-0 | 2729 | | 1 | | | | 5 | 6 | 7 | 8 | | 10* | 11 | 12 | 2 | 3 | | 9 | | | | 4 | |
| 34 | 28 | Bristol City | L | 0-1 | 0-0 | 8230 | | 1 | | | | 5 | 6* | 7 | 8 | | 10 | 11 | 12 | 2 | 3 | | 9 | | | | 4 | |
| 35 | Apr 1 | SWINDON TOWN | W | 2-0 | 1-0 | 2626 | Greenhough, Rimmer | 1 | | | | 5 | 6 | 7 | 8 | | 10 | 11 | | 2 | 3 | | 9 | | | | 4 | |
| 36 | 4 | Brentford | L | 1-3 | 1-1 | 3496 | Kelly | 1 | | | | 5 | 6 | 7 | 8 | | 10 | 11 | | 2 | 3 | | 9 | | | | 4 | |
| 37 | 11 | ROTHERHAM UNITED | W | 1-0 | 0-0 | 2174 | Greenhough | 1 | | | | | 6 | 7 | 8 | 9* | 5 | 11 | 12 | 2 | 3 | | 10 | | | | 4 | |
| 38 | 18 | Notts County | D | 1-1 | 0-0 | 4528 | Rimmer | | | | | 5 | 6 | | 8 | 9* | 7 | 11 | 12 | 2 | 3 | | 10 | 1 | | | 4 | |
| 39 | 20 | WIGAN ATHLETIC | L | 1-2 | 1-1 | 3813 | Rimmer | | | | | 5 | 6 | 7 | 8 | | 9 | | 11 | 2 | 3 | | 10 | 1 | | | 4 | |
| 40 | 22 | Walsall | L | 0-1 | 0-1 | 5117 | | | | | | 5 | 6 | 7 | 8 | | 9 | | 11 | 2 | 3 | | 10 | 1 | | | 4 | |
| 41 | 25 | Chesterfield | W | 1-0 | 1-0 | 1667 | Rimmer | | | | | 5 | 6 | 7 | 8 | | 9 | | 11 | 2 | | | 10 | 1 | 3 | | 4 | |
| 42 | 28 | Bristol Rovers | L | 2-3 | 2-1 | 2323 | Greenhough, Rimmer | | | | | 5 | 6 | 7 | 8 | | 9 | | 11 | 2 | | | 10 | 1 | 3 | | 4 | |
| 43 | May 2 | MIDDLESBROUGH | L | 1-2 | 1-1 | 3780 | Rimmer | | | | | 5 | 6 | 7 | 8 | 12 | 9* | 11 | | 2 | 3 | | 10 | 1 | | | 4 | |
| 44 | 4 | Blackpool | L | 0-1 | 0-0 | 2069 | | | | | | 5 | 6 | 7 | 8* | 9 | | 11 | 12 | 2 | 3 | | 10 | 1 | | | 4 | |
| 45 | 6 | Carlisle United | W | 2-0 | 1-0 | 1287 | Rimmer (pen), Bennett | 1 | | | | | 6 | 7 | | 9 | 8 | 11 | | 2 | 3 | | 10 | | 5 | | 4 | |
| 46 | 9 | PORT VALE | L | 1-2 | 1-1 | 3013 | Graham | 1 | | | | | 6 | 7* | | 9 | 8 | 11 | 12 | 2 | 3 | | 10 | | 5 | | 4 | |
| | | | | | | | Apps. | 29 | 1 | 21 | 8 | 41 | 44 | 42 | 41 | 26 | 35 | 42 | 10 | 44 | 30 | 4 | 34 | 17 | 12 | 2 | 23 | |
| | | | | | | | Subs. | | | | | | | | | 7 | 2 | | 11 | | | 4 | 4 | | | | | |
| | | | | | | | Goals | | | | 2 | 1 | | 9 | 5 | 13 | 3 | 4 | 1 | 7 | 2 | | 13 | | | | | |

Own goals 1

## F.A. CUP

| | Date | Opposition | | FT | HT | Att. | Goalscorers | Stewart W. | Glenn D. | Lane M. | Holden A. | Abel G. | Butler B. | Kelly J. | Barrow G. | Bennett G. | Houghton P. | Graham M. | Croft B. | Greenhough R. | Woodthorpe C. | Richardson I. | Rimmer S. | Butcher J. | Lundon S. | Howard T. | Fazackerley D. | Sconce M. |
|---|---|---|---|---|---|---|---|---|---|---|---|---|---|---|---|---|---|---|---|---|---|---|---|---|---|---|---|---|
| 1R | Nov 15 | ROTHERHAM UNITED | D | 1-1 | 0-0 | 2749 | Bennett (pen) | | | 4 | | 2 | 6 | 7 | 8 | 9 | 10' | 11 | 12 | 5 | | | 13 | 1 | 3* | | | |
| 1Rr | 18 | Rotherham United * | D | 1-1 | 0-0 | 2692 | Kelly | | | | | 2 | 4 | 7 | 8 | 9 | 10* | 11 | 12 | 5 | | | 6 | 1 | 3 | | | |
| 1R2r | 24 | ROTHERHAM UNITED | W | 1-0 | 0-0 | 3203 | Croft | 1 | | 4 | | 2 | 6 | 7 | 8 | 9 | | 11 | 10 | 5 | | | 12 | | 3* | | | |
| 2R | Dec 6 | DONCASTER ROVERS | W | 3-1 | 0-0 | 3821 | Bennett (pen), Graham, Houghton | 1 | | 4 | | 2 | 6 | 7 | 8 | 9 | 10 | 11 | | 5 | | | | | 3 | | | |
| 3R | Jan 10 | Wrexham | W | 2-1 | 0-1 | 9265 | Bennett (2) | 1 | | 4 | | 2 | 6 | 7 | | 9 | 3 | 11 | 12 | 5 | 13 | | 8* | | 10' | | | |
| 4R | 31 | SHEFFIELD WEDNESDAY | D | 1-1 | 1-0 | 8146 | Kelly | 1 | | | | 6 | 5 | 7 | 8 | 9 | 10 | 11 | | | 3 | | | | | 2 | 4 | |
| 4Rr | Feb 4 | Sheffield Wednesday | L | 1-3 | 1-2 | 20726 | Bennett | 1 | | | | 5 | 6 | 7 | 8 | 9 | 10 | 11 | | | 3 | | 12 | | | 2* | 4 | |

* Extra time played following score of 0-0 after 90 minutes

## LEAGUE (LITTLEWOODS) CUP

| | Date | Opposition | | FT | HT | Att. | Goalscorers | Stewart W. | Glenn D. | Lane M. | Holden A. | Abel G. | Butler B. | Kelly J. | Barrow G. | Bennett G. | Houghton P. | Graham M. | Croft B. | Greenhough R. | Woodthorpe C. | Richardson I. | Rimmer S. | Butcher J. | Lundon S. | Howard T. | Fazackerley D. | Sconce M. |
|---|---|---|---|---|---|---|---|---|---|---|---|---|---|---|---|---|---|---|---|---|---|---|---|---|---|---|---|---|
| 1R1 | Aug 27 | Derby County | W | 1-0 | 1-0 | 8531 | Houghton | 1 | 2 | 4 | | 5 | 6 | 7 | 8 | 9* | 10 | 11 | | | 3 | 12 | | | | | | |
| 1R2 | Sep 3 | DERBY COUNTY * | L | 1-2 | 0-0 | 4012 | Bennett | 1 | | 4 | | 5 | 6 | 7 | 8 | 12 | 10 | 11 | | 2 | 3 | 9* | | | | | | |

* Extra time played following score of 0-1 after 90 minutes. Derby won on away goals.

## ASSOCIATE MEMBERS (FREIGHT ROVER) TROPHY

| | Date | Opposition | | FT | HT | Att. | Goalscorers | Stewart W. | Glenn D. | Lane M. | Holden A. | Abel G. | Butler B. | Kelly J. | Barrow G. | Bennett G. | Houghton P. | Graham M. | Croft B. | Greenhough R. | Woodthorpe C. | Richardson I. | Rimmer S. | Butcher J. | Lundon S. | Howard T. | Fazackerley D. | Sconce M. |
|---|---|---|---|---|---|---|---|---|---|---|---|---|---|---|---|---|---|---|---|---|---|---|---|---|---|---|---|---|
| PR | Dec 2 | Crewe Alex. | W | 2-1 | 0-1 | 1271 | Kelly, Bennett | 1 | | 4 | | 2 | 6 | 7 | | 9 | 12 | 11 | 10* | 5 | | | 8 | | 3 | | | |
| PR | 16 | PRESTON NORTH END | D | 1-1 | 1-0 | 1125 | Bennett | | | 4 | | 2 | 6 | | 8* | 9 | 12 | 11 | | 5 | 10 | | 7 | 1 | 3 | | | |
| 1R | Jan 21 | LINCOLN CITY * | W | 1-1 | 0-0 | 1194 | Bennett | 1 | | | | 2 | 6* | 7 | | 9 | | 11 | 10 | 5 | 3 | | 8 | | | | 4 | 12 |
| QF | Feb 10 | Bolton Wanderers | W | 2-1 | 0-0 | 3900 | Bennett, Barrow | 1 | | | | 5 | 6 | 7 | 8 | 9 | 10* | 11 | | 2 | 3 | | 12 | | | | 4 | |
| SF | Mar 23 | Wrexham @ | W | 3-1 | 0-0 | 5662 | Barrow, Fazackerley (pen), Rimmer | 1 | | | | 5 | 6 | 7 | 8 | | 10* | 11 | 12 | 2 | 3 | | 9 | | | | 4 | |
| NF1 | Apr 8 | Mansfield Town | L | 0-2 | 0-1 | 7879 | | 1 | | | | 5 | 6 | 7 | 8 | 9' | 12 | 11 | 13 | 2* | 3 | | 10 | | | | 4 | |
| NF2 | 15 | MANSFIELD TOWN | W | 1-0 | 1-0 | 8187 | Woodthorpe | 1 | | | | 5 | 6 | 7 | 8 | 9 | | 11 | 12 | 2 | 3 | | 10 | | | | 4* | |

* Extra time played following score of 0-0 after 90 minutes. Chester won 5-4 on penalties. @ Extra time played following score of 1-1 after 90 minutes.

## FRIENDLIES

| | Date | Opposition | | FT | HT | Att. | Goalscorers |
|---|---|---|---|---|---|---|---|
| 1 | Jul 6 | BBB * | W | 1-0 | | | Croft |
| 2 | 8 | HB * | W | 4-1 | | | Barrow, Graham, Houghton, Holden (pen) |
| 3 | 10 | IF * | W | 2-0 | | | Graham (2) |
| 4 | Aug 2 | Caernarfon Town | W | 3-1 | | | Barrow, Holden, Croft |
| 5 | 5 | Witton Albion | D | 1-1 | 1-0 | | Abel |
| 6 | 9 | Kettering Town | D | 0-0 | 0-0 | | |
| 7 | 15 | OLDHAM ATHLETIC | D | 1-1 | 1-0 | 1036 | Bennett (pen) |

* Faroe Islands Tour

# SEASON 1987-88

## FOOTBALL (BARCLAYS) LEAGUE DIV. 3

| | Date | Opposition | | FT | HT | Att. | Goalscorers | Stewart W. | Greenhough R. | Woodthorpe C. | Fazackerley D. | Abel G. | Hetzke S. | Butler B. | Lundon S. | Rimmer S. | Houghton P. | Graham M. | Croft B. | Moore S. | Parry M. | Barrow G. | Bennett G. | Stowell M. | Maddy P. | Lightfoot C. | Hawtin C. | Banks J. | Painter R. | Astbury M. | Howlett G. | Glenn D. | Caldwell T. | Langley K. | Lowey J. | Newhouse A. |
|---|---|---|---|---|---|---|---|---|---|---|---|---|---|---|---|---|---|---|---|---|---|---|---|---|---|---|---|---|---|---|---|---|---|---|---|---|
| 1 | Aug 15 | NORTHAMPTON TOWN | L | 0-5 | 0-1 | 3458 | | 1 | 2 | 3 | 4 | 5 | 6 | 7" | 8* | 9 | 10 | 11 | 12 | 14 | | | | | | | | | | | | | | | | |
| 2 | 22 | Southend United | D | 2-2 | 1-1 | 2369 | Graham, Parry | 1 | | 3 | 4 | 2 | 6 | | 5 | 9 | | 11 | | | 7 | 8 | 10 | | | | | | | | | | | | | |
| 3 | 29 | YORK CITY | W | 1-0 | 0-0 | 2010 | Rimmer (pen) | 1 | 4 | 3 | | 2 | 6 | | | 9 | | 11 | 5 | | 7 | 8 | 10 | | | | | | | | | | | | | |
| 4 | 31 | Rotherham United | L | 2-5 | 0-1 | 2551 | Rimmer (pen), Graham | 1 | 2 | 3 | | 5 | 6 | | | 9 | | 11 | 4 | | 7 | 8 | 10 | | | | | | | | | | | | | |
| 5 | Sep 5 | ALDERSHOT | W | 4-1 | 1-0 | 1700 | Croft,Rimmer(2,1 pen),Bennett | | 4 | 3 | 5 | 2 | 6 | | | 9 | | 11 | 7 | | | 8 | 10 | 1 | | | | | | | | | | | | |
| 6 | 12 | Blackpool | W | 1-0 | 0-0 | 4035 | Rimmer | | 4 | 3 | 5 | 2 | 6 | | | 9 | | 11 | 7 | | | 8 | 10 | 1 | | | | | | | | | | | | |
| 7 | 16 | FULHAM | L | 1-2 | 1-1 | 2469 | Graham | 1 | 2 | 3 | 4 | 5 | | | | 9 | | 11 | 7 | | | 8 | 10 | | 6 | | | | | | | | | | | |
| 8 | 19 | GRIMSBY TOWN | W | 1-0 | 0-0 | 1897 | Rimmer | | 2 | 3 | 5 | 4 | | | | 9 | | 11 | 7 | | 14 | 8 | 10" | 1 | | 6* | 12 | | | | | | | | | |
| 9 | 26 | Sunderland | W | 2-0 | 0-0 | 12760 | Rimmer, Croft | | 6 | 3 | 4 | 5 | | | | 9 | | | 7 | | | 8 | 10 | 1 | 11 | | 2 | | | | | | | | | |
| 10 | 29 | Gillingham | W | 1-0 | 0-0 | 5193 | Rimmer | | 6 | 3 | 4 | 5 | | | | 9 | | | 7 | | | 8 | 10 | 1 | 11 | | 2 | | | | | | | | | |
| 11 | Oct 3 | NOTTS COUNTY | L | 1-2 | 1-0 | 3365 | Rimmer (pen) | | 6 | 3 | 4 | 5 | | | | 9 | | | 7 | | | 8 | 10 | 1 | 11 | | 2 | | | | | | | | | |
| 12 | 17 | Bristol Rovers | D | 2-2 | 1-2 | 3038 | Rimmer, Bennett | | 2 | 3 | | 5 | 4 | 6 | | 9 | | | 12 | | 7* | 8 | 10 | 1 | 11 | | | | | | | | | | | |
| 13 | 20 | Brentford | D | 1-1 | 0-0 | 4027 | Rimmer | | 2 | 3 | 4 | 5 | 6 | 7 | | 9 | | | 12 | | | 8 | 10 | 1 | 11* | | | | | | | | | | | |
| 14 | 24 | MANSFIELD TOWN | L | 0-2 | 0-0 | 2453 | | | 2* | 3 | 4 | 5 | 6 | 7 | | 9 | | | 12 | | | 8 | 10 | 1 | 11 | | | | | | | | | | | |
| 15 | 31 | Preston North End | D | 1-1 | 0-1 | 5657 | Rimmer (pen) | | 2 | 3 | 4 | 5 | 6 | | | 9 | | | 7 | | | 8 | 10 | 1 | 11 | | | | | | | | | | | |
| 16 | Nov 4 | PORT VALE | W | 1-0 | 0-0 | 2789 | Rimmer (pen) | | 10 | 3 | 4 | 5 | 6 | 2 | | 9 | | | 7 | | | 8 | | 1 | 11" | | | 14 | | | | | | | | |
| 17 | 7 | WALSALL | D | 1-1 | 0-0 | 3269 | Lightfoot | | 10* | 3 | 4 | | 6 | 7 | | 9 | | | 11 | | | 8 | 12 | 1 | | 5 | | 2 | | | | | | | | |
| 18 | 21 | Bristol City | D | 2-2 | 2-1 | 8103 | Rimmer (2, 1 pen) | | 2 | 3 | 4 | 5 | | | 6 | 9 | | | 11" | | | 8 | 10 | 1 | 7 | | | | 14 | | | | | | | |
| 19 | 28 | CHESTERFIELD | D | 1-1 | 1-0 | 1843 | Rimmer | | 2 | 3 | 4 | 5 | | | | 9 | 8 | | 11 | | | | 10 | 1 | 7 | 6 | | | | | | | | | | |
| 20 | Dec 5 | DONCASTER ROVERS | D | 1-1 | 1-0 | 1853 | Rimmer (pen) | | 2 | 3 | 4 | 5 | | | 6 | 9 | 8 | | 11* | | | | 10 | | 7 | | | | 12 | 1 | | | | | | |
| 21 | 12 | Brighton & Hove A. | L | 0-1 | 0-0 | 6738 | | | 2 | 3 | 4 | 5 | | | 6 | 9 | 8* | | 12 | | | | 10 | | 7 | | | | | 1 | 11 | | | | | |
| 22 | 18 | BURY | D | 4-4 | 1-0 | 1772 | Bennett, Rimmer (2), Howlett | | 2 | | 4 | 5 | | | 3 | 9 | 11 | | | | | 8 | 10 | | 7 | | | | | 1 | 6 | | | | | |
| 23 | 26 | SUNDERLAND | L | 1-2 | 0-2 | 6663 | Abel | | 2 | | 4 | 5 | | | 3 | 9 | 11 | | | | | 8 | 10 | | 7 | | | | | 1 | 6* | 12 | | | | |
| 24 | 28 | Wigan Athletic | L | 0-1 | 0-0 | 4394 | | | 2 | | 4 | 5 | | | 3 | 9 | 11* | | | | | 8 | 10 | | | 6 | | | | 1 | 7 | 12 | | | | |
| 25 | Jan 1 | York City | L | 0-2 | 0-1 | 2686 | | 1 | 11 | | 4 | 5 | | | 3 | 9 | | | 12 | | | 8 | 10 | | | 6* | | | | | 7 | 2 | | | | |
| 26 | 2 | BLACKPOOL | D | 1-1 | 0-1 | 3093 | Bennett | 1 | 10 | | 4 | 5 | | | 3 | | | | 11 | | | 8 | 9 | | | 6 | | | | | 7 | 2 | | | | |
| 27 | 9 | SOUTHEND UNITED | D | 1-1 | 0-1 | 2065 | Maddy | 1 | | | 4 | 5 | | | 3 | 9 | | | 11 | | | 8 | 12 | | 7 | 6* | | | | | | 2 | 10 | | | |
| 28 | 16 | Grimsby Town | L | 1-2 | 0-0 | 2594 | Rimmer | 1 | | 14 | 4 | 5 | | 6* | 3" | 9 | | 12 | 11 | | | 8 | | | 7 | | | | | | | 2 | 10 | | | |
| 29 | 30 | ROTHERHAM UNITED | W | 1-0 | 0-0 | 2059 | Barrow | 1 | | 3 | 4 | 5 | | | | 9 | | 11* | 12 | | | 8 | 6 | | | | | | | | | 2 | 10 | 7 | | |
| 30 | Feb 6 | Aldershot | L | 1-4 | 1-1 | 2578 | Barrow | 1 | | 3 | 4 | 5 | | | | 9 | | 11 | | | | 8 | 6 | | 12 | | | | | | | 2 | 10* | 7 | | |
| 31 | 13 | WIGAN ATHLETIC | W | 1-0 | 0-0 | 3088 | Rimmer (pen) | 1 | | 3 | 4 | 5 | 6 | | | 9 | | 11 | | | | 8 | 7 | | | | | | | | | 2 | | 10 | | |
| 32 | 20 | Northampton Town | L | 0-2 | 0-0 | 4285 | | 1 | | 3 | 4 | 5 | 6 | | | 9 | | 11 | | | | 8 | 7 | | | | | | | | | 2 | | 10 | | |
| 33 | 27 | Notts County | L | 0-1 | 0-0 | 5868 | | 1 | | 3 | 4 | 5 | | 6 | | 9 | | 11 | | | | 8 | 7 | | | | | | | | | 2 | | 10 | | |
| 34 | Mar 2 | GILLINGHAM | W | 3-1 | 0-0 | 1638 | Rimmer (3, 1 pen) | 1 | 12 | 3 | 4 | 5 | | 6" | | 9 | | 11 | 14 | | | 8* | 7 | | | | | | | | | 2 | | 10 | | |
| 35 | 5 | BRISTOL ROVERS | L | 0-3 | 0-2 | 2067 | | 1 | 12 | 3 | 4 | 5 | | 6 | | 9 | 14 | 11 | 8 | | | | 7* | | | | | | | | | 2" | | 10 | | |
| 36 | 11 | Doncaster Rovers | D | 2-2 | 1-1 | 1482 | Bennett (2, 1 pen) | 1 | 12 | 3 | 4 | 5* | | 7 | | | 11" | 8 | 14 | | | | 9 | | | 6 | | | | | | 2 | | 10 | | |
| 37 | 19 | PRESTON NORTH END | W | 1-0 | 1-0 | 3724 | Bennett | 1 | | 3 | 4 | 5 | | | 11 | | | 8 | 7 | | | | 9 | | | 6 | | | | | | 2 | | 10 | | |
| 38 | 26 | Mansfield Town | W | 2-1 | 1-1 | 2918 | Lundon, Bennett | 1 | | 3 | 4 | 5 | | | 7 | | | 11 | 10 | | | | 9 | | | 6 | | | | | | 2 | | | 8 | |
| 39 | Apr 2 | Walsall | L | 0-1 | 0-1 | 4978 | | 1 | | | 4 | 5 | | 12 | 7 | | | 11 | 10 | | | 8 | 9 | | | 6 | | | | | | 2* | | | 3 | |
| 40 | 4 | BRISTOL CITY | W | 1-0 | 1-0 | 2849 | Bennett | 1 | | | 4 | 5 | | 2 | 3 | | | 11 | 10 | | | 8 | 9 | | | 6 | | | | | | | | | 7 | |
| 41 | 9 | Port Vale | D | 1-1 | 1-1 | 4278 | Lundon | 1 | | | 4 | 5 | | 2 | 3 | | | 11 | 10 | | | 8 | 9 | | | 6 | | | | | | | | | 7 | |
| 42 | 15 | Fulham | L | 0-1 | 0-0 | 4131 | | 1 | | | 4 | 5 | | 2 | 3 | | 12 | 11 | 10* | | | 8 | 9 | | | 6 | | | | | | | | | 7 | |
| 43 | 23 | BRENTFORD | D | 1-1 | 0-0 | 1777 | Barrow | 1 | | | 4 | 10 | | 5 | 3 | | | 11* | 12 | | | 8 | 9 | | | 6 | | | | | | 2 | | | 7 | |
| 44 | 30 | Chesterfield | D | 0-0 | 0-0 | 2225 | | 1 | 6 | 11 | 4 | 5 | | | 3 | | 10* | | 12 | | | 8 | 9 | | | | | | | | | 2 | | | 7 | |
| 45 | May 2 | BRIGHTON & HOVE A. | D | 2-2 | 1-2 | 3345 | Abel, Barrow | 1 | 6 | 10 | 4 | 5 | | | 3 | | | 11 | | | | 8 | 9 | | | | | | | | | 2 | | | 7 | |
| 46 | 7 | Bury | W | 1-0 | 0-0 | 1942 | Bennett | 1 | 6 | 3 | 4 | 5 | | | 10 | | | | 11* | | | 8 | 9" | | | 12 | | | | | | 2 | | | 7 | 14 |
| | | | | | | | Apps. | 27 | 28 | 34 | 43 | 45 | 14 | 15 | 22 | 34 | 9 | 24 | 26 | | 4 | 38 | 41 | 14 | 17 | 15 | 3 | 1 | | 5 | 6 | 19 | 4 | 9 | 9 | |
| | | | | | | | Subs. | | 3 | 1 | | | | 1 | | | 2 | 1 | 11 | 1 | 1 | | 2 | | 1 | 1 | 1 | 1 | 2 | | | 2 | | | | 1 |
| | | | | | | | Goals | | | | | 2 | | | 2 | 24 | | 3 | 2 | | 1 | 4 | 10 | | 1 | 1 | | | | | 1 | | | | | |

## F.A. CUP

| | Date | Opposition | | FT | HT | Att. | Goalscorers | Stewart W. | Greenhough R. | Woodthorpe C. | Fazackerley D. | Abel G. | Hetzke S. | Butler B. | Lundon S. | Rimmer S. | Houghton P. | Graham M. | Croft B. | Moore S. | Parry M. | Barrow G. | Bennett G. | Stowell M. | Maddy P. | Lightfoot C. | Hawtin C. | Banks J. | Painter R. | Astbury M. | Howlett G. | Glenn D. | Caldwell T. | Langley K. | Lowey J. | Newhouse A. |
|---|---|---|---|---|---|---|---|---|---|---|---|---|---|---|---|---|---|---|---|---|---|---|---|---|---|---|---|---|---|---|---|---|---|---|---|---|
| 1R | Nov 14 | RUNCORN | L | 0-1 | 0-1 | 3533 | | 1 | 10 | 3 | 4 | 5 | | 7 | | 9 | | | 11 | | | 8 | 12 | | | 6 | | 2* | | | | | | | | |

## LEAGUE (LITTLEWOODS) CUP

| | Date | Opposition | | FT | HT | Att. | Goalscorers | Stewart W. | Greenhough R. | Woodthorpe C. | Fazackerley D. | Abel G. | Hetzke S. | Butler B. | Lundon S. | Rimmer S. | Houghton P. | Graham M. | Croft B. | Moore S. | Parry M. | Barrow G. | Bennett G. | Stowell M. | Maddy P. | Lightfoot C. | Hawtin C. | Banks J. | Painter R. | Astbury M. | Howlett G. | Glenn D. | Caldwell T. | Langley K. | Lowey J. | Newhouse A. |
|---|---|---|---|---|---|---|---|---|---|---|---|---|---|---|---|---|---|---|---|---|---|---|---|---|---|---|---|---|---|---|---|---|---|---|---|---|
| 1R1 | Aug 18 | Blackpool | L | 0-2 | 0-1 | 3114 | | 1 | | 3 | 4 | 5 | 6 | | 7 | 9 | 10* | 11 | 8 | 2 | | | | | | | 12 | | | | | | | | | |
| 1R2 | 26 | BLACKPOOL | W | 1-0 | 1-0 | 2143 | Rimmer | 1 | | 3 | 4 | 2 | 6 | | 5 | 9 | | 11 | | | 7 | 8 | 10 | | | | | | | | | | | | | |

## ASSOCIATE MEMBERS (FREIGHT ROVER) TROPHY

| | Date | Opposition | | FT | HT | Att. | Goalscorers | Stewart W. | Greenhough R. | Woodthorpe C. | Fazackerley D. | Abel G. | Hetzke S. | Butler B. | Lundon S. | Rimmer S. | Houghton P. | Graham M. | Croft B. | Moore S. | Parry M. | Barrow G. | Bennett G. | Stowell M. | Maddy P. | Lightfoot C. | Hawtin C. | Banks J. | Painter R. | Astbury M. | Howlett G. | Glenn D. | Caldwell T. | Langley K. | Lowey J. | Newhouse A. |
|---|---|---|---|---|---|---|---|---|---|---|---|---|---|---|---|---|---|---|---|---|---|---|---|---|---|---|---|---|---|---|---|---|---|---|---|---|
| PR | Oct 13 | Carlisle United | L | 1-2 | 0-1 | 1418 | Rimmer | | 2 | 3 | 4 | 5 | | 6 | | 9 | | | 7 | | | 8 | 10 | 1 | 11 | | | | | | | | | | | |
| PR | 28 | BLACKPOOL | W | 2-1 | 2-0 | 1226 | Rimmer, Bennett | | 2 | 3 | 4 | 5 | 6 | 7 | | 9 | | | 8 | | | | 10 | 1 | 11 | | | | | | | | | | | |
| 1R | Jan 19 | Burnley | L | 0-1 | 0-0 | 3436 | | 1 | 12 | 3 | 4 | 5 | | 6 | | 9 | | 10 | 11 | | | 8 | | | 7 | | | | | | | 2* | | | | |

## FRIENDLIES

| | Date | Opposition | | FT | HT | Att. | Goalscorers |
|---|---|---|---|---|---|---|---|
| 1 | Jul 26 | Cork City | W | 3-1 | 3-1 | | Maddy, Rimmer, Hetzke |
| 2 | 29 | Waterford United | W | 2-1 | | | Bennett (2) |
| 3 | Aug 4 | Tranmere Rovers | L | 0-2 | 0-1 | 1175 | |
| 4 | 7 | STOCKPORT COUNTY | L | 0-1 | 0-1 | | |

**1987/88 Season:**
(Back) Bennett, Abel, Greenhough, Stewart, Hetzke, Astbury, Butler, Houghton, Woodthorpe.
(Front) Lundon, Glenn, Rimmer, Barrow, McNally (Manager), Fazackerley, Maddy, Croft, Graham.

**1988/89 Season:**
(Back ) Walker (Physio), Abel, Butler, Benjamin, Lightfoot, Stewart, Johnson, Hinnigan, Bennett, Woodthorpe
(Front) Dale, Glenn, Barrow, McNally (Manager), Graham, Jakub, Lundon

# SEASON 1988-89

## FOOTBALL (BARCLAYS) LEAGUE DIVISION 3

| | Date | Opposition | | FT | HT | Att. | Goalscorers | Stewart W. | Glenn D. | Woodthorpe C. | Hinnigan J. | Abel G. | Lightfoot C. | Jakub J. | Butler B. | Benjamin I. | Johnson S. | Bennett G. | Dale C. | Newhouse A. | Barrow G. | Lundon S. | Kelly A. | Hawtin C. | Painter R. | Graham M. | Lane M. | O'Keefe E. | Wynne D. |
|---|---|---|---|---|---|---|---|---|---|---|---|---|---|---|---|---|---|---|---|---|---|---|---|---|---|---|---|---|---|
| 1 | Aug 27 | BLACKPOOL | D | 1-1 | 1-0 | 3496 | Johnson | 1 | 2 | 3 | 4 | 5 | 6 | 7 | 8 | 9* | 10 | 11" | 12 | 14 | | | | | | | | | |
| 2 | Sep 3 | Port Vale | W | 2-1 | 2-0 | 4213 | Woodthorpe, Johnson | 1 | 2 | 3 | 4 | 5 | 6 | 7 | | 9 | 10 | | | 11 | 8 | | | | | | | | |
| 3 | 10 | BRISTOL CITY | W | 2-0 | 0-0 | 2823 | Lightfoot, Dale | 1 | 2 | 3 | 4 | 5 | 6 | 7 | | 9 | 10 | | 14 | 11" | 8 | | | | | | | | |
| 4 | 17 | Sheffield United | L | 1-6 | 0-3 | 8675 | Lightfoot | 1 | 2 | 3 | 4 | 5 | 6* | 7 | | 9 | 10 | 12 | | 11 | 8 | | | | | | | | |
| 5 | 20 | Preston North End | D | 3-3 | 1-1 | 5415 | Dale (2), Johnson | 1 | 2 | 3 | 4* | 5 | | 7 | 6 | 12 | 10 | | 9 | | 8 | 11 | | | | | | | |
| 6 | 24 | HUDDERSFIELD TOWN | W | 3-0 | 2-0 | 3319 | Newhouse, Johnson (pen), Tucker (og) | 1 | 2* | 3 | | 5 | 6 | 7 | | 12 | 10 | | 9 | 11 | 8 | | 4 | | | | | | |
| 7 | Oct 1 | Reading | L | 1-3 | 0-2 | 4376 | Woodthorpe | 1 | 2 | 3 | | 5 | 6 | 7 | | 12 | 10 | | 9* | 11 | 8 | | 4 | | | | | | |
| 8 | 5 | BRENTFORD | W | 3-2 | 3-2 | 2004 | Jakub, Barrow, Dale | 1 | 2 | 3 | | 5 | 6 | 7 | | | 10 | 14 | 9 | 11" | 8 | | 4 | | | | | | |
| 9 | 9 | Notts County | D | 2-2 | 1-1 | 5772 | Benjamin, Barrow | 1 | 2 | 3 | 4 | 5 | 6 | 7 | | 9 | 10 | | | | 8 | | 11 | | | | | | |
| 10 | 15 | CARDIFF CITY | D | 0-0 | 0-0 | 2796 | | 1 | 2 | 3 | | 5 | 6 | 7 | | 9" | 10 | 14 | 11 | | 8 | | 4 | | | | | | |
| 11 | 22 | Bristol Rovers | L | 1-4 | 1-2 | 3811 | Benjamin | 1 | 2 | 3" | 4 | 5 | 6* | 7 | | 9 | 10 | 12 | 14 | | 8 | 11 | | | | | | | |
| 12 | 26 | MANSFIELD TOWN | D | 0-0 | 0-0 | 1805 | | 1 | 2 | 3 | | 5 | 6 | 7 | 4 | 9 | 10 | | 11 | | 8 | | | | | | | | |
| 13 | 29 | Aldershot | D | 1-1 | 1-1 | 1862 | Hawtin | 1 | | 3 | | 5 | 6 | 7 | 4 | 9 | 10 | 12 | 11* | | 8 | | | 2 | | | | | |
| 14 | Nov 5 | SWANSEA CITY | W | 3-1 | 2-0 | 2263 | Dale (2), Abel | 1 | 2 | 3 | 4 | 5" | 6 | 7 | 14 | 9 | 12 | 10 | 11 | | 8 | | | | | | | | |
| 15 | 8 | Bury | L | 1-2 | 0-1 | 2497 | Newhouse | 1 | | 3 | 4 | | 6 | 7 | 5 | 9 | 10" | | 11 | 12 | 8 | 14 | | 2 | | | | | |
| 16 | 12 | CHESTERFIELD | W | 3-1 | 1-1 | 2099 | Hewitt (og), Dale (2) | 1 | | 3 | 4 | 5 | 6 | 7 | 2 | 9* | 12 | | 11 | 10 | 8 | | | | | | | | |
| 17 | 26 | SOUTHEND UNITED | L | 2-4 | 1-1 | 2050 | Johnson (2) | 1 | | 3 | 4 | | 6 | 7 | 5 | 9 | 10 | | 11 | | 8 | | | 2 | | | | | |
| 18 | Dec 3 | Gillingham | W | 2-0 | 1-0 | 3329 | Dale, Johnson | 1 | | | 4 | 5 | 6 | 7 | 2 | 9 | 10 | | 11 | | 8 | 3" | | | | | | | 14 |
| 19 | 17 | Bolton Wanderers | W | 1-0 | 0-0 | 4318 | Dale | 1 | 2 | 3 | 4 | 5 | | 7 | 6 | 9 | 10 | | 11 | | 8 | | | | | | | | |
| 20 | 26 | WIGAN ATHLETIC | W | 1-0 | 0-0 | 3262 | Lightfoot | 1 | 2" | 3 | 4 | 5 | 14 | 7 | 6 | 9 | | | 11 | 10* | 8 | | | | | 12 | | | |
| 21 | 31 | NORTHAMPTON TOWN | W | 2-1 | 0-1 | 2733 | Dale, Abel | 1 | | 3 | 4 | 5 | 6 | 7 | 2 | 12 | 9 | | 11 | | | 8 | | | | 10* | | | |
| 22 | Jan 2 | Wolverhampton W. | L | 1-3 | 1-3 | 21901 | Johnson | 1 | | 3 | 4" | 5 | 6 | 7 | 2 | 10 | 9 | | 11 | 14 | | 8* | | | | 12 | | | |
| 23 | 7 | Fulham | L | 1-4 | 0-3 | 4196 | Lightfoot | 1 | | 3 | 4* | 5 | 6 | 7 | 2 | 9 | 12 | | 11 | | 8 | | | | | 10 | | | |
| 24 | 14 | PORT VALE | L | 1-2 | 1-0 | 4891 | Dale | 1 | | 3 | 4 | 5 | | 7 | 2 | | 9 | | 11 | | 8 | | | | | 10 | 6 | | |
| 25 | 21 | Bristol City | W | 1-0 | 0-0 | 9586 | Johnson | 1 | | 3 | 4 | 5 | 14 | 7 | 2" | | 9 | | 11 | 12 | 8 | | | | | 10* | 6 | | |
| 26 | Feb 4 | READING | W | 3-0 | 1-0 | 2354 | Dale (2), Hinnigan | 1 | | 3 | 4 | 5 | | 7 | 2 | | 9 | | 11 | 10* | 8 | | | | | 12 | 6 | | |
| 27 | 11 | Brentford | W | 1-0 | 1-0 | 5748 | Dale | 1 | | 3 | 4 | 5 | 12 | 7 | 2 | | 9 | | 11 | 10* | 8 | | | | | | 6 | | |
| 28 | 18 | NOTTS COUNTY | W | 1-0 | 0-0 | 3157 | Johnson | 1 | 12 | 3 | 4 | 5 | | 7 | 2 | | 9 | | 11 | 10* | 8 | | | | | | 6 | | |
| 29 | 28 | Mansfield Town | L | 0-2 | 0-1 | 2796 | | 1 | | 3 | 4 | 5 | | 7 | 2 | | 9 | | 11 | 10 | 8 | | | | | | 6 | | |
| 30 | Mar 4 | BRISTOL ROVERS | L | 0-2 | 0-0 | 3082 | | 1 | | 3 | 4* | 5 | | 7 | 2 | | 9 | | 11 | 12 | 8 | | | | | 10 | 6 | | |
| 31 | 11 | Swansea City | D | 1-1 | 1-1 | 4311 | Dale | 1 | | 3 | 4 | 5 | | 7 | 2 | | 9 | | 11 | | 8 | | | | | 10 | 6 | | |
| 32 | 15 | ALDERSHOT | D | 1-1 | 0-1 | 2038 | Dale | 1 | | 3 | 4* | 5 | | 7 | 2 | | 9 | | 11 | 12 | 8 | | | | | 10 | 6 | | |
| 33 | 18 | Blackpool | D | 1-1 | 0-0 | 2795 | O'Keefe | 1 | | 3 | | 5 | | 7 | 2 | | 9 | | 11 | | 8 | | | | | 10* | 6 | 12 | |
| 34 | 25 | WOLVERHAMPTON W. | D | 1-1 | 1-1 | 8236 | Abel | 1 | | 3 | 4" | 5 | 14 | 7 | 2 | | 9 | | 11 | | 8 | | | | | 12 | 6 | 10* | |
| 35 | 27 | Wigan Athletic | L | 0-3 | 0-1 | 3132 | | 1 | 2 | 3 | 4* | 5 | 12 | 7 | | | 9 | | | 11 | | | | | | 8 | 6 | 10" | 14 |
| 36 | Apr 1 | BOLTON WANDERERS | D | 0-0 | 0-0 | 3225 | | 1 | | 3 | 4 | | 5 | 7 | 2 | | | | 11 | 9* | | | | | 12 | 10 | 6 | 8 | |
| 37 | 5 | FULHAM | W | 7-0 | 2-0 | 2121 | Hinnigan,Woodthorpe,O'Keefe (pen),Graham,Dale(3) | 1 | | 3 | 4 | 9* | 5 | 7 | 2 | | | | 11 | | | | | | 12 | 10 | 6 | 8 | |
| 38 | 8 | Northampton Town | W | 2-0 | 0-0 | 2845 | Lightfoot, O'Keefe (pen) | 1 | | 3 | 4 | | 5 | 7 | 2 | | | | 11* | 12 | | | | | 9 | 10 | 6 | 8 | |
| 39 | 15 | Huddersfield Town | L | 1-3 | 0-1 | 6109 | Painter | 1 | | 3 | 4 | | 5 | 7 | 2" | | 9* | | | 12 | | | | | 11 | 10 | 6 | 8 | 14 |
| 40 | 19 | SHEFFIELD UNITED | L | 0-1 | 0-1 | 4282 | | 1 | | 3 | 4 | 8 | 5 | 7 | 2 | | 9* | | 11 | | | | | | | 10 | 6 | 12 | |
| 41 | 22 | PRESTON NORTH END | L | 0-1 | 0-0 | 4617 | | 1 | 2 | 3 | 4 | 9 | 5 | | | | | | 11 | 14 | 8 | | | | 7" | 10* | 6 | 12 | |
| 42 | 29 | Chesterfield | W | 2-1 | 0-0 | 3529 | Dale, Lightfoot | 1 | | 3 | 4* | 9 | 5 | | 2 | | | | 11 | | 8 | | | | 12 | 10 | 6 | 7 | |
| 43 | May 1 | BURY | W | 2-0 | 1-0 | 2110 | Barrow, Lightfoot | 1 | | 3 | | 4 | 5 | | 2 | | | | 11 | | 8 | | | | 9 | 10 | 6 | 7" | 14 |
| 44 | 5 | GILLINGHAM | W | 2-0 | 1-0 | 2106 | Dale, O'Keefe (pen) | 1 | | 3 | 12 | 4 | 5 | | 2 | | | | 11 | | 8* | | | | 9" | 10 | 6 | 7 | 14 |
| 45 | 9 | Cardiff City | L | 0-2 | 0-0 | 3002 | | 1 | | | 4* | 6 | 5 | 8 | 2 | | 9 | | 11 | 12 | | | | | | 10 | 3 | 7 | |
| 46 | 13 | Southend United | L | 0-1 | 0-0 | 4089 | | 1 | | 3 | 4 | | 5 | 8 | 2" | | 9* | | 11 | 12 | | | | | | 10 | 6 | 7 | 14 |
| | | | | | | | Apps. | 46 | 17 | 44 | 38 | 40 | 31 | 42 | 34 | 18 | 35 | 2 | 38 | 14 | 35 | 5 | 5 | 3 | 5 | 20 | 23 | 11 | |
| | | | | | | | Subs. | | 1 | | 1 | | 5 | | 1 | 4 | 3 | 5 | 3 | 11 | | 1 | | | 3 | 4 | | 3 | 6 |
| | | | | | | | Goals | | | 3 | 2 | 3 | 7 | 1 | | 2 | 10 | | 22 | 2 | 3 | | | 1 | 1 | 1 | | 4 | |

Own goals 2

## F.A. CUP

| | Date | Opposition | | FT | HT | Att. | Goalscorers | Stewart W. | Glenn D. | Woodthorpe C. | Hinnigan J. | Abel G. | Lightfoot C. | Jakub J. | Butler B. | Benjamin I. | Johnson S. | Bennett G. | Dale C. | Newhouse A. | Barrow G. | Lundon S. | Kelly A. | Hawtin C. | Painter R. | Graham M. | Lane M. | O'Keefe E. | Wynne D. |
|---|---|---|---|---|---|---|---|---|---|---|---|---|---|---|---|---|---|---|---|---|---|---|---|---|---|---|---|---|---|
| 1R | Nov 19 | Burnley | W | 2-0 | 0-0 | 8475 | Dale, Benjamin | 1 | | 3 | 4 | 5* | 6 | 7 | 2 | 9 | 10 | | 11 | | 8 | | | 12 | | | | | |
| 2R | Dec 10 | Huddersfield Town | L | 0-1 | 0-0 | 6295 | | 1 | 2 | 3 | 4 | 5 | | 7 | 6 | 9 | 10 | | 11 | | 8 | | | | | | | | |

## LEAGUE (LITTLEWOODS) CUP

| | Date | Opposition | | FT | HT | Att. | Goalscorers | Stewart W. | Glenn D. | Woodthorpe C. | Hinnigan J. | Abel G. | Lightfoot C. | Jakub J. | Butler B. | Benjamin I. | Johnson S. | Bennett G. | Dale C. | Newhouse A. | Barrow G. | Lundon S. | Kelly A. | Hawtin C. | Painter R. | Graham M. | Lane M. | O'Keefe E. | Wynne D. |
|---|---|---|---|---|---|---|---|---|---|---|---|---|---|---|---|---|---|---|---|---|---|---|---|---|---|---|---|---|---|
| 1R1 | Aug 30 | Bolton Wanderers | L | 0-1 | 0-1 | 3535 | | 1 | 2 | 3 | 4 | 5 | 6 | 7 | 8* | 9 | 10 | 11" | | 14 | | 12 | | | | | | | |
| 1R2 | Sep 7 | BOLTON WANDERERS | W | 3-1 | 2-0 | 3784 | Lightfoot, Winstanley (og), Barrow | 1 | 2 | 3 | 4 | 5 | 6 | 7 | | 9* | 10 | 12 | | 11 | 8 | | | | | | | | |
| 2R1 | 28 | Nottingham Forest | L | 0-6 | 0-3 | 11958 | | 1 | 2 | 3 | | 5 | 6 | 7 | | | 10 | 14 | 9" | 11 | 8 | | 4 | | | | | | |
| 2R2 | Oct 12 | NOTTINGHAM FOREST | L | 0-4 | 0-1 | 4747 | | 1 | 2 | 3 | 4" | 5 | 6 | 7 | | | 10 | 14 | 12 | 9* | 8 | | 11 | | | | | | |

## ASSOCIATE MEMBERS (SHERPA VAN) TROPHY

| | Date | Opposition | | FT | HT | Att. | Goalscorers | Stewart W. | Glenn D. | Woodthorpe C. | Hinnigan J. | Abel G. | Lightfoot C. | Jakub J. | Butler B. | Benjamin I. | Johnson S. | Bennett G. | Dale C. | Newhouse A. | Barrow G. | Lundon S. | Kelly A. | Hawtin C. | Painter R. | Graham M. | Lane M. | O'Keefe E. | Wynne D. |
|---|---|---|---|---|---|---|---|---|---|---|---|---|---|---|---|---|---|---|---|---|---|---|---|---|---|---|---|---|---|
| PR | Dec 13 | Sheffield United | D | 2-2 | 1-1 | 2981 | Benjamin, Dale | 1 | 2 | 3 | 4 | 5 | | 7 | 6 | 9" | 10 | | 11 | | 8 | | | | 14 | | | | |
| PR | 21 | WREXHAM | L | 1-2 | 0-1 | 3887 | Hinnigan | 1 | 2* | 3 | 4 | 5 | 12 | 7 | 6 | 9" | 10 | | 11 | 14 | 8 | | | | | | | | |

## FRIENDLIES

| | Date | Opposition | | FT | HT | Att. | Goalscorers |
|---|---|---|---|---|---|---|---|
| 1 | Aug 6 | CORK CITY | W | 5-0 | 2-0 | 504 | Lightfoot (pen), Bennett (2), Dale, Abel |
| 2 | 13 | Bangor City | D | 1-1 | 1-0 | | Benjamin |
| 3 | 19 | WATFORD | D | 0-0 | 0-0 | 1858 | |

# FINAL LEAGUE TABLES: 1988/89 - 1995/96

### Final League Table 1988/89 Division 3

| | | Pl. | Home | | | | | Away | | | | | F. | A. | Pts |
|---|---|---|---|---|---|---|---|---|---|---|---|---|---|---|---|
| | | | W | D | L | F | A | W | D | L | F | A | | | |
| 1 | Wolverhampton W. | 46 | 18 | 4 | 1 | 61 | 19 | 8 | 10 | 5 | 35 | 30 | 96 | 49 | 92 |
| 2 | Sheffield United | 46 | 16 | 3 | 4 | 57 | 21 | 9 | 6 | 8 | 36 | 33 | 93 | 54 | 84 |
| 3 | Port Vale | 46 | 15 | 3 | 5 | 46 | 21 | 9 | 9 | 5 | 32 | 27 | 78 | 48 | 84 |
| 4 | Fulham | 46 | 12 | 7 | 4 | 42 | 28 | 10 | 2 | 11 | 27 | 39 | 69 | 67 | 75 |
| 5 | Bristol Rovers | 46 | 9 | 11 | 3 | 34 | 21 | 10 | 6 | 7 | 33 | 30 | 67 | 51 | 74 |
| 6 | Preston North End | 46 | 14 | 7 | 2 | 56 | 31 | 5 | 8 | 10 | 23 | 29 | 79 | 60 | 72 |
| 7 | Brentford | 46 | 14 | 5 | 4 | 36 | 21 | 4 | 9 | 10 | 30 | 40 | 66 | 61 | 68 |
| **8** | **Chester City** | **46** | **12** | **6** | **5** | **38** | **18** | **7** | **5** | **11** | **26** | **43** | **64** | **61** | **68** |
| 9 | Notts County | 46 | 11 | 7 | 5 | 37 | 22 | 7 | 6 | 10 | 27 | 32 | 64 | 54 | 67 |
| 10 | Bolton Wanderers | 46 | 12 | 8 | 3 | 42 | 23 | 4 | 8 | 11 | 16 | 31 | 58 | 54 | 64 |
| 11 | Bristol City | 46 | 10 | 3 | 10 | 32 | 25 | 8 | 6 | 9 | 21 | 30 | 53 | 55 | 63 |
| 12 | Swansea City | 46 | 11 | 8 | 4 | 33 | 22 | 4 | 8 | 11 | 18 | 31 | 51 | 53 | 61 |
| 13 | Bury | 46 | 11 | 7 | 5 | 27 | 22 | 5 | 6 | 12 | 28 | 45 | 55 | 67 | 61 |
| 14 | Huddersfield Town | 46 | 10 | 8 | 5 | 35 | 25 | 7 | 1 | 15 | 28 | 48 | 63 | 73 | 60 |
| 15 | Mansfield Town | 46 | 10 | 8 | 5 | 32 | 22 | 4 | 9 | 10 | 16 | 30 | 48 | 52 | 59 |
| 16 | Cardiff City | 46 | 10 | 9 | 4 | 30 | 16 | 4 | 6 | 13 | 14 | 40 | 44 | 56 | 57 |
| 17 | Wigan Athletic | 46 | 9 | 5 | 9 | 28 | 22 | 5 | 9 | 9 | 27 | 31 | 55 | 53 | 56 |
| 18 | Reading | 46 | 10 | 6 | 7 | 37 | 29 | 5 | 5 | 13 | 31 | 43 | 68 | 72 | 56 |
| 19 | Blackpool | 46 | 10 | 6 | 7 | 36 | 29 | 4 | 7 | 12 | 20 | 30 | 56 | 59 | 55 |
| 20 | Northampton Town | 46 | 11 | 2 | 10 | 41 | 34 | 5 | 4 | 14 | 25 | 42 | 66 | 76 | 54 |
| 21 | Southend United | 46 | 10 | 9 | 4 | 33 | 26 | 3 | 6 | 14 | 23 | 49 | 56 | 75 | 54 |
| 22 | Chesterfield | 46 | 9 | 5 | 9 | 35 | 35 | 5 | 2 | 16 | 16 | 51 | 51 | 86 | 49 |
| 23 | Gillingham | 46 | 7 | 3 | 13 | 25 | 32 | 5 | 1 | 17 | 22 | 49 | 47 | 81 | 40 |
| 24 | Aldershot | 46 | 7 | 6 | 10 | 29 | 29 | 1 | 7 | 15 | 19 | 49 | 48 | 78 | 37 |

### Final League Table 1989/90 Division 3

| | | Pl. | Home | | | | | Away | | | | | F. | A. | Pts |
|---|---|---|---|---|---|---|---|---|---|---|---|---|---|---|---|
| | | | W | D | L | F | A | W | D | L | F | A | | | |
| 1 | Bristol Rovers | 46 | 15 | 8 | 0 | 43 | 14 | 11 | 7 | 5 | 28 | 21 | 71 | 35 | 93 |
| 2 | Bristol City | 46 | 15 | 5 | 3 | 40 | 16 | 12 | 5 | 6 | 36 | 24 | 76 | 40 | 91 |
| 3 | Notts County | 46 | 17 | 4 | 2 | 40 | 18 | 8 | 8 | 7 | 33 | 35 | 73 | 53 | 87 |
| 4 | Tranmere Rovers | 46 | 15 | 5 | 3 | 54 | 22 | 8 | 6 | 9 | 32 | 27 | 86 | 49 | 80 |
| 5 | Bury | 46 | 11 | 7 | 5 | 35 | 19 | 10 | 4 | 9 | 35 | 30 | 70 | 49 | 74 |
| 6 | Bolton Wanderers | 46 | 12 | 7 | 4 | 32 | 19 | 6 | 8 | 9 | 27 | 29 | 59 | 48 | 69 |
| 7 | Birmingham City | 46 | 10 | 7 | 6 | 33 | 19 | 8 | 5 | 10 | 27 | 40 | 60 | 59 | 66 |
| 8 | Huddersfield Town | 46 | 11 | 5 | 7 | 30 | 23 | 6 | 9 | 8 | 31 | 39 | 61 | 62 | 65 |
| 9 | Rotherham United | 46 | 12 | 6 | 5 | 48 | 28 | 5 | 7 | 11 | 23 | 34 | 71 | 62 | 64 |
| 10 | Reading | 46 | 10 | 9 | 4 | 33 | 21 | 5 | 10 | 8 | 24 | 32 | 57 | 53 | 64 |
| 11 | Shrewsbury Town | 46 | 10 | 9 | 4 | 38 | 24 | 6 | 6 | 11 | 21 | 30 | 59 | 54 | 63 |
| 12 | Crewe Alexandra | 46 | 10 | 8 | 5 | 32 | 24 | 5 | 9 | 9 | 24 | 29 | 56 | 53 | 62 |
| 13 | Brentford | 46 | 11 | 4 | 8 | 41 | 31 | 7 | 3 | 13 | 25 | 35 | 66 | 66 | 61 |
| 14 | Leyton Orient | 46 | 9 | 6 | 8 | 28 | 24 | 7 | 4 | 12 | 24 | 32 | 52 | 56 | 58 |
| 15 | Mansfield Town | 46 | 13 | 2 | 8 | 34 | 25 | 3 | 5 | 15 | 16 | 40 | 50 | 65 | 55 |
| **16** | **Chester City** | **46** | **11** | **7** | **5** | **30** | **23** | **2** | **8** | **13** | **13** | **32** | **43** | **55** | **54** |
| 17 | Swansea City | 46 | 10 | 6 | 7 | 25 | 27 | 4 | 6 | 13 | 20 | 36 | 45 | 63 | 54 |
| 18 | Wigan Athletic | 46 | 10 | 6 | 7 | 29 | 22 | 3 | 8 | 12 | 19 | 42 | 48 | 64 | 53 |
| 19 | Preston North End | 46 | 10 | 7 | 6 | 42 | 30 | 4 | 3 | 16 | 23 | 49 | 65 | 79 | 52 |
| 20 | Fulham | 46 | 8 | 8 | 7 | 33 | 27 | 4 | 7 | 12 | 22 | 39 | 55 | 66 | 51 |
| 21 | Cardiff City | 46 | 6 | 9 | 8 | 30 | 35 | 6 | 5 | 12 | 21 | 35 | 51 | 70 | 50 |
| 22 | Northampton Town | 46 | 7 | 7 | 9 | 27 | 31 | 4 | 7 | 12 | 24 | 37 | 51 | 68 | 47 |
| 23 | Blackpool | 46 | 8 | 6 | 9 | 29 | 33 | 2 | 10 | 11 | 20 | 40 | 49 | 73 | 46 |
| 24 | Walsall | 46 | 6 | 8 | 9 | 23 | 30 | 3 | 6 | 14 | 17 | 42 | 40 | 72 | 41 |

### Final League Table 1990/91 Division 3

| | | Pl. | Home | | | | | Away | | | | | F. | A. | Pts |
|---|---|---|---|---|---|---|---|---|---|---|---|---|---|---|---|
| | | | W | D | L | F | A | W | D | L | F | A | | | |
| 1 | Cambridge United | 46 | 14 | 5 | 4 | 42 | 22 | 11 | 6 | 6 | 33 | 23 | 75 | 45 | 86 |
| 2 | Southend United | 46 | 13 | 6 | 4 | 34 | 23 | 13 | 1 | 9 | 33 | 28 | 67 | 51 | 85 |
| 3 | Grimsby Town | 46 | 16 | 3 | 4 | 42 | 13 | 8 | 8 | 7 | 24 | 21 | 66 | 34 | 83 |
| 4 | Bolton Wanderers | 46 | 14 | 5 | 4 | 33 | 18 | 10 | 6 | 7 | 31 | 32 | 64 | 50 | 83 |
| 5 | Tranmere Rovers | 46 | 13 | 5 | 5 | 38 | 21 | 10 | 4 | 9 | 26 | 25 | 64 | 46 | 78 |
| 6 | Brentford | 46 | 12 | 4 | 7 | 30 | 22 | 9 | 9 | 5 | 29 | 25 | 59 | 47 | 76 |
| 7 | Bury | 46 | 13 | 6 | 4 | 39 | 26 | 7 | 7 | 9 | 28 | 30 | 67 | 56 | 73 |
| 8 | Bradford City | 46 | 13 | 3 | 7 | 36 | 22 | 7 | 7 | 9 | 26 | 32 | 62 | 54 | 70 |
| 9 | Bournemouth | 46 | 14 | 6 | 3 | 37 | 20 | 5 | 7 | 11 | 21 | 38 | 58 | 58 | 70 |
| 10 | Wigan Athletic | 46 | 14 | 3 | 6 | 40 | 20 | 6 | 6 | 11 | 31 | 34 | 71 | 54 | 69 |
| 11 | Huddersfield Town | 46 | 13 | 3 | 7 | 37 | 23 | 5 | 10 | 8 | 20 | 28 | 57 | 51 | 67 |
| 12 | Birmingham City | 46 | 8 | 9 | 6 | 21 | 21 | 8 | 8 | 7 | 24 | 28 | 45 | 49 | 65 |
| 13 | Leyton Orient | 46 | 15 | 2 | 6 | 35 | 19 | 3 | 8 | 12 | 20 | 39 | 55 | 58 | 64 |
| 14 | Stoke City | 46 | 9 | 7 | 7 | 36 | 29 | 7 | 5 | 11 | 19 | 30 | 55 | 59 | 60 |
| 15 | Reading | 46 | 11 | 5 | 7 | 34 | 28 | 6 | 3 | 14 | 19 | 38 | 53 | 66 | 59 |
| 16 | Exeter City | 46 | 12 | 6 | 5 | 35 | 16 | 4 | 3 | 16 | 23 | 36 | 58 | 52 | 57 |
| 17 | Preston North End | 46 | 11 | 5 | 7 | 33 | 29 | 4 | 6 | 13 | 21 | 38 | 54 | 67 | 56 |
| 18 | Shrewsbury Town | 46 | 8 | 7 | 8 | 29 | 22 | 6 | 3 | 14 | 32 | 46 | 61 | 68 | 52 |
| **19** | **Chester City** | **46** | **10** | **3** | **10** | **27** | **27** | **4** | **6** | **13** | **19** | **31** | **46** | **58** | **51** |
| 20 | Swansea City | 46 | 8 | 6 | 9 | 31 | 33 | 5 | 3 | 15 | 18 | 39 | 49 | 72 | 48 |
| 21 | Fulham | 46 | 8 | 8 | 7 | 27 | 22 | 2 | 8 | 13 | 14 | 34 | 41 | 56 | 46 |
| 22 | Crewe Alexandra | 46 | 6 | 9 | 8 | 35 | 35 | 5 | 2 | 16 | 27 | 45 | 62 | 80 | 44 |
| 23 | Rotherham United | 46 | 5 | 10 | 8 | 31 | 38 | 5 | 2 | 16 | 19 | 49 | 50 | 87 | 42 |
| 24 | Mansfield Town | 46 | 5 | 8 | 10 | 23 | 27 | 3 | 6 | 14 | 19 | 36 | 42 | 63 | 38 |

### Final League Table 1991/92 Division 3

| | | Pl. | Home | | | | | Away | | | | | F. | A. | Pts |
|---|---|---|---|---|---|---|---|---|---|---|---|---|---|---|---|
| | | | W | D | L | F | A | W | D | L | F | A | | | |
| 1 | Brentford | 46 | 17 | 2 | 4 | 55 | 29 | 8 | 5 | 10 | 26 | 26 | 81 | 55 | 82 |
| 2 | Birmingham City | 46 | 15 | 6 | 2 | 42 | 22 | 8 | 6 | 9 | 27 | 30 | 69 | 52 | 81 |
| 3 | Huddersfield Town | 46 | 15 | 4 | 4 | 36 | 15 | 7 | 8 | 8 | 23 | 23 | 59 | 38 | 78 |
| 4 | Stoke City | 46 | 14 | 5 | 4 | 45 | 24 | 7 | 9 | 7 | 24 | 25 | 69 | 49 | 77 |
| 5 | Stockport County | 46 | 15 | 5 | 3 | 47 | 19 | 7 | 5 | 11 | 28 | 32 | 75 | 51 | 76 |
| 6 | Peterborough Utd. | 46 | 13 | 7 | 3 | 38 | 20 | 7 | 7 | 9 | 27 | 38 | 65 | 58 | 74 |
| 7 | West Bromwich A. | 46 | 12 | 6 | 5 | 45 | 25 | 7 | 8 | 8 | 19 | 24 | 64 | 49 | 71 |
| 8 | Bournemouth | 46 | 13 | 4 | 6 | 33 | 18 | 7 | 7 | 9 | 19 | 30 | 52 | 48 | 71 |
| 9 | Fulham | 46 | 11 | 7 | 5 | 29 | 16 | 8 | 6 | 9 | 28 | 37 | 57 | 53 | 70 |
| 10 | Leyton Orient | 46 | 12 | 7 | 4 | 36 | 18 | 6 | 4 | 13 | 26 | 34 | 62 | 52 | 65 |
| 11 | Hartlepool United | 46 | 12 | 5 | 6 | 30 | 21 | 6 | 6 | 11 | 27 | 36 | 57 | 57 | 65 |
| 12 | Reading | 46 | 9 | 8 | 6 | 33 | 27 | 7 | 5 | 11 | 26 | 35 | 59 | 62 | 61 |
| 13 | Bolton Wanderers | 46 | 10 | 9 | 4 | 26 | 19 | 4 | 8 | 11 | 31 | 37 | 57 | 56 | 59 |
| 14 | Hull City | 46 | 9 | 4 | 10 | 28 | 23 | 7 | 7 | 9 | 26 | 31 | 54 | 54 | 59 |
| 15 | Wigan Athletic | 46 | 11 | 6 | 6 | 33 | 21 | 4 | 8 | 11 | 25 | 43 | 58 | 64 | 59 |
| 16 | Bradford City | 46 | 8 | 10 | 5 | 36 | 30 | 5 | 9 | 9 | 26 | 31 | 62 | 61 | 58 |
| 17 | Preston North End | 46 | 12 | 7 | 4 | 42 | 32 | 3 | 5 | 15 | 19 | 40 | 61 | 72 | 57 |
| **18** | **Chester City** | **46** | **10** | **6** | **7** | **34** | **29** | **4** | **8** | **11** | **22** | **30** | **56** | **59** | **56** |
| 19 | Swansea City | 46 | 10 | 9 | 4 | 35 | 24 | 4 | 5 | 14 | 20 | 41 | 55 | 65 | 56 |
| 20 | Exeter City | 46 | 11 | 7 | 5 | 34 | 25 | 3 | 4 | 16 | 23 | 55 | 57 | 80 | 53 |
| 21 | Bury | 46 | 8 | 7 | 8 | 31 | 31 | 5 | 5 | 13 | 24 | 43 | 55 | 74 | 51 |
| 22 | Shrewsbury Town | 46 | 7 | 7 | 9 | 30 | 31 | 5 | 4 | 14 | 23 | 37 | 53 | 68 | 47 |
| 23 | Torquay United | 46 | 13 | 3 | 7 | 29 | 19 | 0 | 5 | 18 | 13 | 49 | 42 | 68 | 47 |
| 24 | Darlington | 46 | 5 | 5 | 13 | 31 | 39 | 5 | 2 | 16 | 25 | 51 | 56 | 90 | 37 |

### Final League Table 1992/93 Division 2 (Divisions re-numbered)

| | | Pl. | Home | | | | | Away | | | | | F. | A. | Pts |
|---|---|---|---|---|---|---|---|---|---|---|---|---|---|---|---|
| | | | W | D | L | F | A | W | D | L | F | A | | | |
| 1 | Stoke City | 46 | 17 | 4 | 2 | 41 | 13 | 10 | 8 | 5 | 32 | 21 | 73 | 34 | 93 |
| 2 | Bolton Wanderers | 46 | 18 | 2 | 3 | 48 | 14 | 9 | 7 | 7 | 32 | 27 | 80 | 41 | 90 |
| 3 | Port Vale | 46 | 14 | 7 | 2 | 44 | 17 | 12 | 4 | 7 | 35 | 27 | 79 | 44 | 89 |
| 4 | West Bromwich A. | 46 | 17 | 3 | 3 | 56 | 22 | 8 | 7 | 8 | 32 | 32 | 88 | 54 | 85 |
| 5 | Swansea City | 46 | 12 | 7 | 4 | 38 | 17 | 8 | 6 | 9 | 27 | 30 | 65 | 47 | 73 |
| 6 | Stockport County | 46 | 11 | 11 | 1 | 47 | 18 | 8 | 4 | 11 | 34 | 39 | 81 | 57 | 72 |
| 7 | Leyton Orient | 46 | 16 | 4 | 3 | 49 | 20 | 5 | 5 | 13 | 20 | 33 | 69 | 53 | 72 |
| 8 | Reading | 46 | 14 | 4 | 5 | 44 | 20 | 4 | 11 | 8 | 22 | 31 | 66 | 51 | 69 |
| 9 | Brighton & Hove A. | 46 | 13 | 4 | 6 | 36 | 24 | 7 | 5 | 11 | 27 | 35 | 63 | 59 | 69 |
| 10 | Bradford City | 46 | 12 | 5 | 6 | 36 | 24 | 6 | 9 | 8 | 33 | 43 | 69 | 67 | 68 |
| 11 | Rotherham United | 46 | 9 | 7 | 7 | 30 | 27 | 8 | 7 | 8 | 30 | 33 | 60 | 60 | 65 |
| 12 | Fulham | 46 | 9 | 9 | 5 | 28 | 22 | 7 | 8 | 8 | 29 | 33 | 57 | 55 | 65 |
| 13 | Burnley | 46 | 11 | 8 | 4 | 38 | 21 | 4 | 8 | 11 | 19 | 38 | 57 | 59 | 61 |
| 14 | Plymouth Argyle | 46 | 11 | 6 | 6 | 38 | 28 | 5 | 6 | 12 | 21 | 36 | 59 | 64 | 60 |
| 15 | Huddersfield Town | 46 | 10 | 6 | 7 | 30 | 22 | 7 | 3 | 13 | 24 | 39 | 54 | 61 | 60 |
| 16 | Hartlepool United | 46 | 8 | 6 | 9 | 19 | 23 | 6 | 6 | 11 | 23 | 37 | 42 | 60 | 54 |
| 17 | Bournemouth | 46 | 7 | 10 | 6 | 28 | 24 | 5 | 7 | 11 | 17 | 28 | 45 | 52 | 53 |
| 18 | Blackpool | 46 | 9 | 9 | 5 | 40 | 30 | 3 | 6 | 14 | 23 | 45 | 63 | 75 | 51 |
| 19 | Exeter City | 46 | 5 | 8 | 10 | 26 | 30 | 6 | 9 | 8 | 28 | 39 | 54 | 69 | 50 |
| 20 | Hull City | 46 | 9 | 5 | 9 | 28 | 26 | 4 | 6 | 13 | 18 | 43 | 46 | 69 | 50 |
| 21 | Preston North End | 46 | 8 | 5 | 10 | 41 | 47 | 5 | 3 | 15 | 24 | 47 | 65 | 94 | 47 |
| 22 | Mansfield Town | 46 | 7 | 8 | 8 | 34 | 34 | 4 | 3 | 16 | 18 | 46 | 52 | 80 | 44 |
| 23 | Wigan Athletic | 46 | 6 | 6 | 11 | 26 | 34 | 4 | 5 | 14 | 17 | 38 | 43 | 72 | 41 |
| **24** | **Chester City** | **46** | **6** | **2** | **15** | **30** | **47** | **2** | **3** | **18** | **19** | **55** | **49** | **102** | **29** |

### Final League Table 1993/94 Division 3

| | | Pl. | Home | | | | | Away | | | | | F. | A. | Pts |
|---|---|---|---|---|---|---|---|---|---|---|---|---|---|---|---|
| | | | W | D | L | F | A | W | D | L | F | A | | | |
| 1 | Shrewsbury Town | 42 | 10 | 8 | 3 | 28 | 17 | 12 | 5 | 4 | 35 | 22 | 63 | 39 | 79 |
| **2** | **Chester City** | **42** | **13** | **5** | **3** | **35** | **18** | **8** | **6** | **7** | **34** | **28** | **69** | **46** | **74** |
| 3 | Crewe Alexandra | 42 | 12 | 4 | 5 | 45 | 30 | 9 | 6 | 6 | 35 | 31 | 80 | 61 | 73 |
| 4 | Wycombe Wands. | 42 | 11 | 6 | 4 | 34 | 21 | 8 | 7 | 6 | 33 | 32 | 67 | 53 | 70 |
| 5 | Preston North End | 42 | 13 | 5 | 3 | 46 | 23 | 5 | 8 | 8 | 33 | 37 | 79 | 60 | 67 |
| 6 | Torquay United | 42 | 8 | 10 | 3 | 30 | 24 | 9 | 6 | 6 | 34 | 32 | 64 | 56 | 67 |
| 7 | Carlisle United | 42 | 10 | 4 | 7 | 35 | 23 | 8 | 6 | 7 | 22 | 19 | 57 | 42 | 64 |
| 8 | Chesterfield | 42 | 8 | 8 | 5 | 32 | 22 | 8 | 6 | 7 | 23 | 26 | 55 | 48 | 62 |
| 9 | Rochdale | 42 | 10 | 5 | 6 | 38 | 22 | 6 | 7 | 8 | 25 | 29 | 63 | 51 | 60 |
| 10 | Walsall | 42 | 7 | 5 | 9 | 28 | 26 | 10 | 4 | 7 | 20 | 27 | 48 | 53 | 60 |
| 11 | Scunthorpe United | 42 | 9 | 7 | 5 | 40 | 26 | 6 | 7 | 8 | 24 | 30 | 64 | 56 | 59 |
| 12 | Mansfield Town | 42 | 9 | 3 | 9 | 28 | 30 | 6 | 7 | 8 | 25 | 32 | 53 | 62 | 55 |
| 13 | Bury | 42 | 9 | 6 | 6 | 33 | 22 | 5 | 5 | 11 | 22 | 34 | 55 | 56 | 53 |
| 14 | Scarborough | 42 | 8 | 4 | 9 | 29 | 28 | 7 | 4 | 10 | 26 | 33 | 55 | 61 | 53 |
| 15 | Doncaster Rovers | 42 | 8 | 6 | 7 | 24 | 26 | 6 | 4 | 11 | 20 | 31 | 44 | 57 | 52 |
| 16 | Gillingham | 42 | 8 | 8 | 5 | 27 | 23 | 4 | 7 | 10 | 17 | 28 | 44 | 51 | 51 |
| 17 | Colchester United | 42 | 8 | 4 | 9 | 31 | 33 | 5 | 6 | 10 | 25 | 38 | 56 | 71 | 49 |
| 18 | Lincoln City | 42 | 7 | 4 | 10 | 26 | 29 | 5 | 7 | 9 | 26 | 34 | 52 | 63 | 47 |
| 19 | Wigan Athletic | 42 | 6 | 7 | 8 | 33 | 33 | 5 | 5 | 11 | 18 | 37 | 51 | 70 | 45 |
| 20 | Hereford United | 42 | 6 | 4 | 11 | 34 | 33 | 6 | 2 | 13 | 26 | 46 | 60 | 79 | 42 |
| 21 | Darlington | 42 | 7 | 5 | 9 | 24 | 28 | 3 | 6 | 12 | 18 | 36 | 42 | 64 | 41 |
| 22 | Northampton Town | 42 | 6 | 7 | 8 | 25 | 23 | 3 | 4 | 14 | 19 | 43 | 44 | 66 | 38 |

### Final League Table 1994/95 Division 2

| | | Pl. | Home | | | | | Away | | | | | F. | A. | Pts |
|---|---|---|---|---|---|---|---|---|---|---|---|---|---|---|---|
| | | | W | D | L | F | A | W | D | L | F | A | | | |
| 1 | Birmingham City | 46 | 15 | 6 | 2 | 53 | 18 | 10 | 8 | 5 | 31 | 19 | 84 | 37 | 89 |
| 2 | Brentford | 46 | 14 | 4 | 5 | 44 | 15 | 11 | 6 | 6 | 37 | 24 | 81 | 39 | 85 |
| 3 | Crewe Alexandra | 46 | 14 | 3 | 6 | 46 | 33 | 11 | 5 | 7 | 34 | 35 | 80 | 68 | 83 |
| 4 | Bristol Rovers | 46 | 15 | 7 | 1 | 48 | 20 | 7 | 9 | 7 | 22 | 20 | 70 | 40 | 82 |
| 5 | Huddersfield Town | 46 | 14 | 5 | 4 | 45 | 21 | 8 | 10 | 5 | 34 | 28 | 79 | 49 | 81 |
| 6 | Wycombe Wands. | 46 | 13 | 7 | 3 | 36 | 19 | 8 | 8 | 7 | 24 | 27 | 60 | 46 | 78 |
| 7 | Oxford United | 46 | 13 | 6 | 4 | 30 | 18 | 8 | 6 | 9 | 36 | 34 | 66 | 52 | 75 |
| 8 | Hull City | 46 | 13 | 6 | 4 | 40 | 18 | 8 | 5 | 10 | 30 | 39 | 70 | 57 | 74 |
| 9 | York City | 46 | 13 | 4 | 6 | 37 | 21 | 8 | 5 | 10 | 30 | 30 | 67 | 51 | 72 |
| 10 | Swansea City | 46 | 10 | 8 | 5 | 23 | 13 | 9 | 6 | 8 | 34 | 32 | 57 | 45 | 71 |
| 11 | Stockport County | 46 | 12 | 3 | 8 | 40 | 29 | 7 | 5 | 11 | 23 | 31 | 63 | 60 | 65 |
| 12 | Blackpool | 46 | 11 | 4 | 8 | 40 | 36 | 7 | 6 | 10 | 24 | 34 | 64 | 70 | 64 |
| 13 | Wrexham | 46 | 10 | 7 | 6 | 38 | 27 | 6 | 8 | 9 | 27 | 37 | 65 | 64 | 63 |
| 14 | Bradford City | 46 | 8 | 6 | 9 | 29 | 32 | 8 | 6 | 9 | 28 | 32 | 57 | 64 | 60 |
| 15 | Peterborough Utd. | 46 | 7 | 11 | 5 | 26 | 29 | 7 | 7 | 9 | 28 | 40 | 54 | 69 | 60 |
| 16 | Brighton & Hove A. | 46 | 9 | 10 | 4 | 25 | 15 | 5 | 7 | 11 | 29 | 38 | 54 | 53 | 59 |
| 17 | Rotherham United | 46 | 12 | 6 | 5 | 36 | 26 | 2 | 8 | 13 | 21 | 35 | 57 | 61 | 56 |
| 18 | Shrewsbury Town | 46 | 9 | 9 | 5 | 34 | 27 | 4 | 5 | 14 | 20 | 35 | 54 | 62 | 53 |
| 19 | Bournemouth | 46 | 9 | 4 | 10 | 30 | 34 | 4 | 7 | 12 | 19 | 35 | 49 | 69 | 50 |
| 20 | Cambridge United | 46 | 8 | 9 | 6 | 33 | 28 | 3 | 6 | 14 | 19 | 41 | 52 | 69 | 48 |
| 21 | Plymouth Argyle | 46 | 7 | 6 | 10 | 22 | 36 | 5 | 4 | 14 | 23 | 47 | 45 | 83 | 46 |
| 22 | Cardiff City | 46 | 5 | 6 | 12 | 25 | 31 | 4 | 5 | 14 | 21 | 43 | 46 | 74 | 38 |
| **23** | **Chester City** | **46** | **5** | **6** | **12** | **23** | **42** | **1** | **5** | **17** | **14** | **42** | **37** | **84** | **29** |
| 24 | Leyton Orient | 46 | 6 | 6 | 11 | 21 | 29 | 0 | 2 | 21 | 9 | 46 | 30 | 75 | 26 |

### Final League Table 1995/96 Division 3

| | | Pl. | Home | | | | | Away | | | | | F. | A. | Pts |
|---|---|---|---|---|---|---|---|---|---|---|---|---|---|---|---|
| | | | W | D | L | F | A | W | D | L | F | A | | | |
| 1 | Preston North End | 46 | 11 | 8 | 4 | 44 | 22 | 12 | 9 | 2 | 34 | 16 | 78 | 38 | 86 |
| 2 | Gillingham | 46 | 16 | 6 | 1 | 33 | 6 | 6 | 11 | 6 | 16 | 14 | 49 | 20 | 83 |
| 3 | Bury | 46 | 11 | 6 | 6 | 33 | 21 | 11 | 7 | 5 | 33 | 27 | 66 | 48 | 79 |
| 4 | Plymouth Argyle | 46 | 14 | 5 | 4 | 41 | 20 | 8 | 7 | 8 | 27 | 29 | 68 | 49 | 78 |
| 5 | Darlington | 46 | 10 | 6 | 7 | 30 | 21 | 10 | 12 | 1 | 30 | 21 | 60 | 42 | 78 |
| 6 | Hereford United | 46 | 13 | 5 | 5 | 40 | 22 | 7 | 9 | 7 | 25 | 25 | 65 | 47 | 74 |
| 7 | Colchester United | 46 | 13 | 7 | 3 | 37 | 22 | 5 | 11 | 7 | 24 | 29 | 61 | 51 | 72 |
| **8** | **Chester City** | **46** | **11** | **9** | **3** | **45** | **22** | **7** | **7** | **9** | **27** | **31** | **72** | **53** | **70** |
| 9 | Barnet | 46 | 13 | 6 | 4 | 40 | 19 | 5 | 10 | 8 | 25 | 26 | 65 | 45 | 70 |
| 10 | Wigan Athletic | 46 | 15 | 3 | 5 | 36 | 21 | 5 | 7 | 11 | 26 | 35 | 62 | 56 | 70 |
| 11 | Northampton Town | 46 | 9 | 10 | 4 | 32 | 22 | 9 | 3 | 11 | 19 | 22 | 51 | 44 | 67 |
| 12 | Scunthorpe United | 46 | 8 | 8 | 7 | 36 | 30 | 7 | 7 | 9 | 31 | 31 | 67 | 61 | 60 |
| 13 | Doncaster Rovers | 46 | 11 | 6 | 6 | 25 | 19 | 5 | 5 | 13 | 24 | 41 | 49 | 60 | 59 |
| 14 | Exeter City | 46 | 9 | 9 | 5 | 25 | 22 | 4 | 9 | 10 | 21 | 31 | 46 | 53 | 57 |
| 15 | Rochdale | 46 | 7 | 8 | 8 | 32 | 33 | 7 | 5 | 11 | 25 | 28 | 57 | 61 | 55 |
| 16 | Cambridge United | 46 | 8 | 8 | 7 | 34 | 30 | 6 | 4 | 13 | 27 | 41 | 61 | 71 | 54 |
| 17 | Fulham | 46 | 10 | 9 | 4 | 39 | 26 | 2 | 8 | 13 | 18 | 37 | 57 | 63 | 52 |
| 18 | Lincoln City | 46 | 8 | 7 | 8 | 32 | 26 | 5 | 7 | 11 | 25 | 47 | 57 | 73 | 53 |
| 19 | Mansfield Town | 46 | 6 | 10 | 7 | 25 | 29 | 5 | 10 | 8 | 29 | 35 | 54 | 64 | 53 |
| 20 | Hartlepool United | 46 | 8 | 9 | 6 | 30 | 24 | 4 | 4 | 15 | 17 | 43 | 47 | 67 | 49 |
| 21 | Leyton Orient | 46 | 11 | 4 | 8 | 29 | 22 | 1 | 7 | 15 | 15 | 41 | 44 | 63 | 47 |
| 22 | Cardiff City | 46 | 8 | 6 | 9 | 24 | 22 | 3 | 6 | 14 | 17 | 42 | 41 | 64 | 45 |
| 23 | Scarborough | 46 | 5 | 11 | 7 | 22 | 28 | 3 | 5 | 15 | 17 | 41 | 39 | 69 | 40 |
| 24 | Torquay United | 46 | 4 | 9 | 10 | 17 | 36 | 1 | 5 | 17 | 13 | 48 | 30 | 84 | 29 |

# SEASON 1989-90

## FOOTBALL (BARCLAYS) LEAGUE DIV. 3

| | Date | Opposition | | FT | HT | Att. | Goalscorers | Stewart W. | Reeves A. | Woodthorpe C. | Lane M. | Abel G. | Hinnigan J. | Hamilton D. | Pugh D. | Newhouse A. | Dale C. | Croft B. | O'Keefe E. | Hayde M. | Butler B. | Painter R. | Lightfoot C. | Lundon S. | Wynne D. | Hulme K. | Barrow G. | Greer R. | Parsley N. | Senior K. | Danzey M. | Nassari D. | Bennett G. |
|---|---|---|---|---|---|---|---|---|---|---|---|---|---|---|---|---|---|---|---|---|---|---|---|---|---|---|---|---|---|---|---|---|---|
| 1 | Aug 19 | MANSFIELD TOWN | L | 0-2 | 0-1 | 2293 | |1|2|3|4|5|6"|7|8|9|10|11*|12|14||||||||||||||
| 2 | 26 | Brentford | D | 1-1 | 1-1 | 5153 | Dale |1|2|3|6|5|4||7|8|9||||10|11||||||||||||
| 3 | Sep 2 | CREWE ALEX. | W | 2-1 | 0-1 | 2170 | Newhouse, Abel |1|2|3|6|4|||8|9|10|14|||7|11"|5|||||||||||
| 4 | 9 | Swansea City | L | 1-2 | 0-2 | 2738 | Newhouse |1|2|3|6|4|12||8|9|10|11|||7||5*|||||||||||
| 5 | 15 | NOTTS COUNTY | D | 3-3 | 1-2 | 2383 | Newhouse (pen), Lightfoot, Croft |1|2|3|6|4|||8|9|10|11|||7||5|||||||||||
| 6 | 23 | Preston North End | L | 0-5 | 0-1 | 5230 | |1|2|3|6|4|||8|9|10|11|||7"||5*|12|14|||||||||
| 7 | 26 | Reading | D | 1-1 | 1-0 | 4296 | Lundon |1|2|3|6|5|4||8|9|10*|12|||7|||11||||||||||
| 8 | 30 | FULHAM | L | 0-2 | 0-1 | 2135 | |1|12|3|6|5*|4||8|9|10"|7|||2||14|11||||||||||
| 9 | Oct 7 | BURY | L | 1-4 | 0-2 | 2168 | Lundon |1|2"|3||5|4*||8|9||11|12||7||6|10|14|||||||||
| 10 | 13 | Cardiff City | D | 1-1 | 0-1 | 3675 | Newhouse |1|2|3||5|4||8|9||11|10"||7|14|6|||||||||||
| 11 | 17 | BIRMINGHAM CITY | W | 4-0 | 0-0 | 1882 | Croft, Pugh, Painter, Butler |1|2|3||5|4||8|9||11|||7|10|6|||||||||||
| 12 | 21 | Bolton Wanderers | L | 0-1 | 0-1 | 6496 | |1|2|3||5|4*||8|9"||11|||7|10|6|12|14|||||||||
| 13 | 28 | BRISTOL ROVERS | D | 0-0 | 0-0 | 2618 | |1|2*|3||5||4|8|||11|||7|10|6|12||9||||||||
| 14 | 31 | Leyton Orient | W | 3-0 | 2-0 | 3979 | Painter, Abel (pen), Butler |1|2|3||5||4|8|||11|||7|10|6|||9||||||||
| 15 | Nov 4 | HUDDERSFIELD TOWN | W | 2-1 | 1-0 | 2660 | Painter, Reeves |1|2|3|5|||4|8||14|11|||7|10|6|||9"||||||||
| 16 | 11 | Rotherham United | L | 0-5 | 0-2 | 5216 | |1|2*|3|5"|6||4|8||12|11|||7|10|14|||9||||||||
| 17 | 24 | WALSALL | D | 1-1 | 1-0 | 2507 | Abel (pen) |1|2"|3|6|5||4|||12|11|||7|10*||14|||8|9||||||
| 18 | Dec 2 | Shrewsbury Town | L | 0-2 | 0-2 | 2905 | |1||3|2|5||4*||10||11|||7||6|12|14||8|9"||||||
| 19 | 15 | Tranmere Rovers | D | 0-0 | 0-0 | 5594 | |1||3|6|5||4|11|9*||12|||7|10|||||8||2|||||
| 20 | 26 | WIGAN ATHLETIC | D | 0-0 | 0-0 | 3165 | |1||3|6|9||4|7|||11||||10|5|12|||8*||2|||||
| 21 | 30 | BLACKPOOL | W | 2-0 | 1-0 | 2404 | Barrow, Abel |1||3|6|9||4||||11|||7|10|5||||8||2|||||
| 22 | Jan 1 | Northampton Town | L | 0-1 | 0-0 | 3823 | |1||3|6|9||4|12|||11|||7|10*|5||||8||2|||||
| 23 | 6 | LEYTON ORIENT | W | 1-0 | 1-0 | 1722 | Painter |1||3|6|9||4*|12|||11|||7|10|5||||8||2|||||
| 24 | 12 | BRENTFORD | D | 1-1 | 0-0 | 2294 | Pugh |1||3|6|9|||7|12||11|||4|10*|5||||8||2|||||
| 25 | 20 | Mansfield Town | L | 0-1 | 0-0 | 2257 | |1|2|3|6||4|||9"|||||7|10*|5|11|14||8|||12||||
| 26 | 26 | SWANSEA CITY | W | 1-0 | 0-0 | 2150 | Dale |1|2|3|6|9|4||||10|11|||7||5||||8|||||||
| 27 | 30 | Bristol City | L | 0-1 | 0-0 | 8769 | |1|2|3|6|9|4|14||12|10*|11|||7"||5||||8|||||||
| 28 | Feb 3 | PRESTON NORTH END | W | 3-1 | 1-0 | 2499 | Woodthorpe, Butler, Croft |1|2|3|6|9||4||14|10"|11|||7||5||||8|||||||
| 29 | 10 | Notts County | D | 0-0 | 0-0 | 5077 | |1|2|3|6|9||4|12||10"|11|||7*|14|5||||8|||||||
| 30 | 13 | Crewe Alex. | D | 0-0 | 0-0 | 4260 | |1|2|3|6|9||4|||10|11|||7||5||||8|||||||
| 31 | 17 | SHREWSBURY TOWN | W | 1-0 | 1-0 | 2500 | Abel |1|2*|3|6|9||4|12||10"|11|||7|14|5||||8|||||||
| 32 | 24 | Walsall | D | 1-1 | 1-0 | 3315 | Butler |1|2|3|6||4||10||12|11|||7|9*|5||||8|||||||
| 33 | Mar 3 | BRISTOL CITY | L | 0-3 | 0-2 | 2496 | |1|2|3|6||4"||10*||9|11|||7|14|5||||8||||12|||
| 34 | 6 | Fulham | L | 0-1 | 0-0 | 3824 | |1||2|6|9||4|3||10"|11*|||7|12|5||||8||||14|||
| 35 | 9 | READING | D | 1-1 | 1-0 | 1978 | Dale |1||2|6|9||4|3||10*|11|||7|12|5||||8|||||||
| 36 | 17 | Bury | L | 0-1 | 0-0 | 2851 | |1|2|3|6||5|4*|10|||11|||7|9||8"|12|||||||14||
| 37 | 20 | CARDIFF CITY | W | 1-0 | 0-0 | 1866 | Dale |1|2|3|6|5*||12|10||9|11|||7||4||||8|||||||
| 38 | 24 | Birmingham City | D | 0-0 | 0-0 | 7584 | |1||3|6|5||4|10||9|11|||7||2||||8|||||||
| 39 | 31 | BOLTON WANDERERS | W | 2-0 | 2-0 | 2738 | Cowdrill (og), Dale |1||3|6|5|||10||9|11|||2|12|4||||8||||||7*|
| 40 | Apr 7 | Bristol Rovers | L | 1-2 | 1-2 | 6589 | Reeves |1|2|3|6|5|||||9|11|||7|12|4||||8||||||10*|
| 41 | 14 | NORTHAMPTON TOWN | L | 0-1 | 0-1 | 2234 | |1||3|2|5||4|||9|11|||7|8|6|||||||||10|
| 42 | 16 | Wigan Athletic | L | 0-1 | 0-0 | 2277 | |1||3|2|5||4|||9|11|||7|12|6||||8||||||10*|
| 43 | 20 | TRANMERE ROVERS | D | 2-2 | 2-0 | 4210 | Dale, Pugh |1||3||5||4|7||9|11|||2|12|6||||8||||||10*|
| 44 | 24 | Blackpool | W | 3-1 | 3-0 | 3724 | Gore (og), Dale (2) |1||3||5||4|7||9|11|||2|12|6||||8||||||10*|
| 45 | 28 | ROTHERHAM UNITED | W | 2-0 | 2-0 | 3827 | Bennett, Abel |1||3||5||4|7||9|11|||2|12|6||||8||||||10*|
| 46 | May 5 | Huddersfield Town | L | 1-4 | 0-2 | 3514 | Abel |1|14|3||5||4|7||9|11|||2*|12|6||||8||||||10"|
| | | | | | | | Apps. |46|28|46|36|41|14|26|31|15|27|41|1||44|19|38|5||4|28|2|6||||8|
| | | | | | | | Subs. ||2||||1|2|4|3|4|3|2|1||13|2|6|6|||||1|2|1||
| | | | | | | | Goals ||2|1||7|||3|4|8|3|||4|4|1|2|||1||||||1|

Own goals 2

## F.A. CUP

| | Date | Opposition | | FT | HT | Att. | Goalscorers | Stewart W. | Reeves A. | Woodthorpe C. | Lane M. | Abel G. | Hinnigan J. | Hamilton D. | Pugh D. | Newhouse A. | Dale C. | Croft B. | O'Keefe E. | Hayde M. | Butler B. | Painter R. | Lightfoot C. | Lundon S. | Wynne D. | Hulme K. | Barrow G. | Greer R. | Parsley N. | Senior K. | Danzey M. | Nassari D. | Bennett G. |
|---|---|---|---|---|---|---|---|---|---|---|---|---|---|---|---|---|---|---|---|---|---|---|---|---|---|---|---|---|---|---|---|---|---|
| 1R | Nov 18 | Macclesfield Town | D | 1-1 | 1-0 | 4200 | Painter |1|2|3|6|5||4|8||9|11|||7|10||||||||||||
| 1Rr | 21 | MACCLESFIELD TOWN | W | 3-2 | 2-1 | 4202 | Abel (pen), Butler, Croft |1||3|2|5||4|8"|12|9*|11|||7|10|6||||14|||||||
| 2R | Dec 9 | Blackpool | L | 0-3 | 0-2 | 4099 | |1||3|6|9||4|12"|14||11|||2|10|5*||||8|7||||||

## LEAGUE (LITTLEWOODS) CUP

| | Date | Opposition | | FT | HT | Att. | Goalscorers | Stewart W. | Reeves A. | Woodthorpe C. | Lane M. | Abel G. | Hinnigan J. | Hamilton D. | Pugh D. | Newhouse A. | Dale C. | Croft B. | O'Keefe E. | Hayde M. | Butler B. | Painter R. | Lightfoot C. | Lundon S. | Wynne D. | Hulme K. | Barrow G. | Greer R. | Parsley N. | Senior K. | Danzey M. | Nassari D. | Bennett G. |
|---|---|---|---|---|---|---|---|---|---|---|---|---|---|---|---|---|---|---|---|---|---|---|---|---|---|---|---|---|---|---|---|---|---|
| 1R1 | Aug 22 | Crewe Alex. | L | 0-4 | 0-2 | 3200 | |1||3|6|7|4|2|8|9*|10|11|||5|12||||||||||||
| 1R2 | 29 | CREWE ALEX. | L | 0-2 | 0-0 | 1758 | |1|2|3|6|4|||8|9|10||||7|11|5|||||||||||

## ASSOCIATE MEMBERS (LEYLAND DAF) TROPHY

| | Date | Opposition | | FT | HT | Att. | Goalscorers | Stewart W. | Reeves A. | Woodthorpe C. | Lane M. | Abel G. | Hinnigan J. | Hamilton D. | Pugh D. | Newhouse A. | Dale C. | Croft B. | O'Keefe E. | Hayde M. | Butler B. | Painter R. | Lightfoot C. | Lundon S. | Wynne D. | Hulme K. | Barrow G. | Greer R. | Parsley N. | Senior K. | Danzey M. | Nassari D. | Bennett G. |
|---|---|---|---|---|---|---|---|---|---|---|---|---|---|---|---|---|---|---|---|---|---|---|---|---|---|---|---|---|---|---|---|---|---|
| PR | Nov 7 | Tranmere Rovers | L | 0-1 | 0-1 | 10559 | |1|2|3|6|5||4|8|12|9*|11|||7|10||||||||||||
| PR | 28 | ROCHDALE | D | 0-0 | 0-0 | 1222 | |1||3|6|5||4||10*||11|||7||12|2|||8|9||||||
| PRr | Dec 20 | Rochdale | W | 2-1 | 2-1 | 787 | Lightfoot (2) |1||2|5|9||4|11*|||12|||7|10|6|3|||8|||||||
| 1R | Jan 16 | Blackpool | W | 1-0 | 1-0 | 1433 | Newhouse |1||2|6||4||10*|9||11|||7|12|5|3|||8|||||||
| NQF | Feb 6 | Tranmere Rovers | L | 0-3 | 0-0 | 4183 | |1|2|3|6|9"||4||14|10|11|||7*|12|5||||8|||||||

## FRIENDLIES

| | Date | Opposition | | FT | HT | Att. | Goalscorers |
|---|---|---|---|---|---|---|---|
| 1 | Jul 31 | Queens Park | W | 4-1 | | | Dale (2), Hamilton, Croft |
| 2 | Aug 5 | Macclesfield Town | W | 1-0 | 0-0 | | Dale |
| 3 | 9 | ASTON VILLA | L | 0-5 | 0-2 | 2832 | |
| 4 | 12 | BANGOR CITY | W | 3-2 | 2-1 | 712 | Croft, Pugh, Dale |

**1989/90 Season:**
(Back) Walker (Physio), Lane, Abel, Lightfoot, Pugh, Stewart, Butler, Reeves, Woodthorpe, Newhouse.
(Middle) Dale, Hamilton, Barrow, McNally (Manager), Hinnigan, O'Keefe, Croft.
(Front) Wynne, Painter, Lundon, Carroll.

**1990/91 Season:**
(Back) Bennett, Whelan, Lightfoot, Butler, Stewart, Abel, Reeves, Pugh, Ellis, Hinnigan (Physio).
(Front) Lane, Croft, Dale, Barrow (Assistant Manager), McNally (Manager), Crofts (Chairman), Lundon, Painter, Preece.

# *SEASON 1990-91*

## FOOTBALL (BARCLAYS) LEAGUE DIVISION 3

| | Date | Opposition | | FT | HT | Att. | Goalscorers | Stewart W. | Preece R. | Lundon S. | Butler B. | Abel G. | Lane M. | Pugh D. | Barrow G. | Bennett G. | Dale C. | Croft B. | Ellis N. | Lightfoot C. | Painter R. | Reeves A. | Morton N. | Barber F. | Withe C. | Whelan S. | Bertschin K. | Bishop E. | Brightwell D. |
|---|---|---|---|---|---|---|---|---|---|---|---|---|---|---|---|---|---|---|---|---|---|---|---|---|---|---|---|---|---|
| 1 | Aug 25 | Bury | L | 1-2 | 1-2 | 2628 | Pugh | 1 | 2 | 3 | 4 | 5 | 6 | 7• | 8 | 9 | 10 | 11 | 12 | | | | | | | | | | |
| 2 | Sep 1 | EXETER CITY | L | 1-2 | 0-1 | 1377 | Abel (pen) | 1 | 2 | 3• | | 5 | 6 | 7 | 8 | 12 | 10 | 11 | 9 | 4 | | | | | | | | | |
| 3 | 8 | Brentford | W | 1-0 | 0-0 | 4812 | Painter | 1 | 2 | | 4 | 5 | 6 | 3 | 8 | 7 | 10 | 11" | 9• | | 12 | 14 | | | | | | | |
| 4 | 15 | LEYTON ORIENT | W | 2-0 | 0-0 | 1716 | Bennett, Painter | 1 | 2 | | 4 | 5 | 6 | 3 | 8 | 7 | 10 | | 11 | | 9 | | | | | | | | |
| 5 | 18 | STOKE CITY | D | 1-1 | 0-1 | 3579 | Ellis | 1 | 2 | | 4 | 5 | 6 | 3 | 8 | 7 | 10 | | 11 | 14 | 9" | | | | | | | | |
| 6 | 21 | Cambridge United | D | 1-1 | 0-1 | 3687 | Butler | 1 | 2 | 14 | 4 | | 6 | 3 | 8 | 7 | 10 | | 11 | 5 | 9" | | | | | | | | |
| 7 | 29 | HUDDERSFIELD TOWN | L | 1-2 | 1-1 | 1540 | Charlton (og) | 1 | 2 | | 4 | 5 | 6 | 3 | 8" | 7 | 10 | 11 | 9• | 12 | | 14 | | | | | | | |
| 8 | Oct 3 | Bradford City | L | 1-2 | 0-0 | 5519 | Abel (pen) | 1 | 2 | | 4 | 5 | 6 | 3 | | 7 | 9 | 10 | 11 | 12 | 8• | | | | | | | | |
| 9 | 6 | Tranmere Rovers | W | 2-1 | 1-0 | 6642 | Pugh, Abel (pen) | 1 | 2 | 8• | 4 | 5 | 6 | 3 | | 7 | 10 | 11 | 9" | 12 | 14 | | | | | | | | |
| 10 | 13 | GRIMSBY TOWN | L | 1-2 | 0-2 | 1875 | Dale | 1 | 2 | 8• | 4 | | 6 | 3 | | 7 | 10 | 11 | | 5" | 12 | 14 | 9 | | | | | | |
| 11 | 20 | SHREWSBURY TOWN | W | 3-2 | 1-0 | 1431 | Bennett, Morton, Dale | | 2 | | 4 | 5 | 6 | | | 7 | 10 | 11 | 8• | | 12 | | 9 | 1 | 3 | | | | |
| 12 | 23 | Preston North End | D | 0-0 | 0-0 | 5465 | | | 2 | | 4 | 5 | 6 | | | 7 | 10 | 11 | 8• | | 12 | 14 | 9 | 1 | 3" | | | | |
| 13 | 27 | Crewe Alex. | W | 3-1 | 2-1 | 4262 | Morton (2), Pugh (pen) | | 2• | | 4 | 5 | 6 | 3 | | 7 | 10 | 11 | | | 8 | 12 | 9 | 1 | | | | | |
| 14 | Nov 3 | BOLTON WANDERERS | L | 0-2 | 0-0 | 2553 | | 1 | | | 4 | 5 | 6 | 3 | | 7 | 10 | 11 | 12 | | 8• | 2" | 9 | | | 14 | | | |
| 15 | 10 | BIRMINGHAM CITY | L | 0-1 | 0-0 | 2273 | | 1 | 2• | | 4 | 5 | 6 | 3 | | 7 | 10 | 11 | 12 | 8 | | | 9 | | | | | | |
| 16 | 24 | Swansea City | L | 0-1 | 0-0 | 3361 | | 1 | | | 4 | 5 | 6 | 3 | | 7 | 10• | 11 | 12 | | 8 | 2 | | | | | 9 | | |
| 17 | Dec 1 | AFC BOURNEMOUTH | D | 0-0 | 0-0 | 1103 | | 1 | | | 4 | 5 | 6 | 3 | | 7 | 10• | 12 | | | 8 | 2 | 11 | | | | 9 | | |
| 18 | 15 | Mansfield Town | L | 0-1 | 0-1 | 1919 | | 1 | | | 2 | 5 | 3 | | 8 | 12 | 7 | 11 | | 4 | 6 | | 10• | | | | 9 | | |
| 19 | 22 | SOUTHEND UNITED | W | 1-0 | 0-0 | 1523 | Dale | 1 | | | 2 | 5 | 3 | 12 | 8• | | 7 | 11 | | 4 | 6 | 14 | 10" | | | | 9 | | |
| 20 | 26 | Rotherham United | L | 1-2 | 0-0 | 3547 | Butler | 1 | | | 2 | 5 | | 3 | 8• | | 7 | 11 | 14 | 4 | 6 | | 10" | | | 12 | 9 | | |
| 21 | 29 | Fulham | L | 1-4 | 0-1 | 3084 | Dale | 1 | | | 2 | 5 | 3 | | 8 | 7 | 10 | 11 | | 4 | 12 | | | | | | 9• | 6 | |
| 22 | Jan 12 | Exeter City | D | 1-1 | 1-1 | 4008 | Bishop | 1 | | | 7 | 5 | 3 | | | 12 | 10 | | 11• | 4 | 8 | | 9 | | | 2 | | 6 | |
| 23 | 19 | BURY | W | 1-0 | 0-0 | 1421 | Barrow | 1 | | | 2 | 5 | 3 | 12 | 8 | | 10 | 11 | | 4 | 6 | | 9• | | | | | 7 | |
| 24 | 26 | Leyton Orient | L | 0-1 | 0-1 | 3437 | | 1 | | | 2 | 5 | 3 | 12 | 8 | | 10 | 11 | | 4 | 6 | | 9• | | | | | 7 | |
| 25 | Feb 2 | Stoke City | W | 3-2 | 1-0 | 11037 | Dale, Bishop (2) | 1 | | | 2 | 5 | | 6 | 8 | 12 | 10 | 11 | | 4 | 3 | | 9• | | | | | 7 | |
| 26 | 23 | Birmingham City | L | 0-1 | 0-0 | 6702 | | 1 | 2 | | 5" | | 14 | 6 | 8 | | 10 | 11• | | 4 | 3 | | 12 | | | | 9 | 7 | |
| 27 | 26 | WIGAN ATHLETIC | L | 1-2 | 0-1 | 914 | Bishop | 1 | 2 | | | | 5 | 6 | 8 | | 10 | 11 | | 4 | 3 | | 12 | | | | 9• | 7 | |
| 28 | Mar 2 | AFC Bournemouth | L | 0-1 | 0-0 | 4669 | | 1 | 2 | | | | 6 | | 8 | | 10• | 11 | | 4 | 3 | | 12 | | | 5 | 9 | 7 | |
| 29 | 5 | READING | W | 1-0 | 0-0 | 631 | Butler | 1 | 2 | | 14 | | 6 | | 8 | | 12 | 11" | | 4 | 3 | | 10 | | | 5 | 9• | 7 | |
| 30 | 9 | MANSFIELD TOWN | W | 1-0 | 1-0 | 1157 | Morton | 1 | 2 | | 11 | | 6 | 14 | 8 | | 10 | | | 4 | 3 | | 9 | | | 5" | | 7 | |
| 31 | 12 | BRADFORD CITY | W | 4-2 | 1-0 | 1303 | Morton, Dale (2), Lightfoot | 1 | 2 | | 11 | | 5 | 6 | 8 | | 10 | | | 4 | 3 | | 9 | | | | | 7 | |
| 32 | 16 | Huddersfield Town | D | 1-1 | 0-1 | 5337 | Lightfoot | 1 | 2 | | 11 | | 5 | 6" | | 14 | 10 | 12 | | 4 | 8• | | 9 | | | 3 | | 7 | |
| 33 | 20 | Grimsby Town | L | 0-2 | 0-1 | 6012 | | 1 | 2 | | 11 | | 5 | | | 7 | 10 | 8 | | 4 | 6 | | 9 | | | 3 | | | |
| 34 | 23 | TRANMERE ROVERS | L | 0-2 | 0-1 | 2705 | | 1 | 2 | | 11 | | 5 | | | 14 | 10 | 8• | | 4 | 6" | | 9 | | | 3 | 12 | 7 | |
| 35 | 25 | CAMBRIDGE UNITED | L | 0-2 | 0-1 | 1015 | | 1 | 2 | | 11 | | 5 | 3 | | 10 | 14 | | | 4 | 6" | | 9 | | | | | 7 | 8 |
| 36 | 30 | ROTHERHAM UNITED | L | 1-2 | 0-1 | 1079 | Butler | 1 | 2 | | 8 | | | 3 | | 11 | 10 | | 14 | 4 | 6" | | 9 | | | | | 7 | 5 |
| 37 | Apr 2 | Southend United | D | 1-1 | 1-0 | 6190 | Bishop | | 2 | | 8 | | | 3 | | 6 | | 12 | 11• | 4 | 14 | | 9 | 1 | | | 10 | 7 | 5" |
| 38 | 6 | FULHAM | W | 1-0 | 1-0 | 1047 | Morton | | 2 | | 8 | | | 3 | | 6• | 14 | 11 | | 4 | 12 | | 9 | 1 | | | 10" | 7 | 5 |
| 39 | 13 | Reading | D | 2-2 | 1-1 | 2707 | Painter, Bishop | | 2 | | 8 | 6" | | 3 | | | 10 | 14 | | 4 | 11 | | 9 | 1 | | | | 7 | 5 |
| 40 | 16 | Wigan Athletic | L | 0-2 | 0-2 | 2131 | | | 2 | | 8 | 6" | 12 | 3 | | | 10 | 14 | | 4 | 11 | | 9 | 1 | | | | 7 | 5• |
| 41 | 20 | Shrewsbury Town | L | 0-1 | 0-1 | 2952 | | | 2 | | 8 | 6 | 5 | 3 | | 14 | 10• | 12 | | 4 | 11 | | 9 | 1 | | | 7• | | |
| 42 | 23 | SWANSEA CITY | W | 2-1 | 1-1 | 852 | Bennett, Butler | 1 | 2 | | 7 | 5 | 6 | 3 | | 10• | | 11 | | 4 | 8 | | 9 | | | | 12 | | |
| 43 | 27 | PRESTON NORTH END | D | 1-1 | 1-0 | 1351 | Abel (pen) | 1 | 2 | | 7 | 5 | 6 | 3 | | | 10 | 11" | 14 | 4 | 8 | | 9• | | | | 12 | | |
| 44 | 30 | BRENTFORD | L | 1-2 | 0-2 | 1275 | Dale | 1 | 2 | | 7 | 5 | 6 | 3 | | | 10 | 11" | 14 | 4 | 8 | | | | | | 9 | | |
| 45 | May 4 | CREWE ALEX. | W | 3-1 | 3-0 | 3126 | Morton, Dale (2) | 1 | 2 | | 7 | | 6 | 3 | | | 10 | 14 | 11" | 4 | 8 | | 9• | | | 5 | 12 | | |
| 46 | 11 | Bolton Wanderers | L | 0-1 | 0-1 | 12826 | | 1 | 2• | | 7 | | 6 | 3 | | | 10 | 11 | | 4 | 8" | 14 | 9 | | | 5 | 12 | | |
| | | | | | | | Apps. | 38 | 35 | 4 | 42 | 29 | 38 | 33 | 20 | 23 | 41 | 31 | 13 | 33 | 34 | 3 | 31 | 8 | 2 | 9 | 14 | 19 | 6 |
| | | | | | | | Subs. | | | 1 | 1 | | 2 | 4 | | 7 | 3 | 7 | 8 | 4 | 8 | 7 | 3 | | | 2 | 5 | | |
| | | | | | | | Goals | | | | 5 | 4 | | 3 | 1 | 3 | 10 | | 1 | 2 | 3 | | 7 | | | | | 6 | |

Own goals 1

## F.A. CUP

| | Date | Opposition | | FT | HT | Att. | Goalscorers | Stewart W. | Preece R. | Lundon S. | Butler B. | Abel G. | Lane M. | Pugh D. | Barrow G. | Bennett G. | Dale C. | Croft B. | Ellis N. | Lightfoot C. | Painter R. | Reeves A. | Morton N. | Barber F. | Withe C. | Whelan S. | Bertschin K. | Bishop E. | Brightwell D. |
|---|---|---|---|---|---|---|---|---|---|---|---|---|---|---|---|---|---|---|---|---|---|---|---|---|---|---|---|---|---|
| 1R | Nov 17 | DONCASTER ROVERS | D | 2-2 | 1-0 | 1749 | Bennett, Dale | 1 | | | 4 | 5 | 3 | 8 | | 7 | 10 | 11" | 14 | 6 | 12 | 2 | 9• | | | | | | |
| 1Rr | 20 | Doncaster Rovers • | W | 2-1 | 0-0 | 3543 | Dale, Painter | 1 | | | 4 | 5 | 6 | 3 | | 7 | 10 | 11• | 9 | 12 | 8 | 2 | | | | | | | |
| 2R | Dec 12 | Leek Town | D | 1-1 | 1-0 | 3046 | Dale | 1 | | | 2 | 5 | 4 | 3" | 8 | | 7 | 11 | | 14 | 6 | | 10 | | | | 9 | | |
| 2Rr | 17 | LEEK TOWN | W | 4-0 | 2-0 | 2420 | Bertschin, Dale, Abel (pen), Painter | 1 | | | 2 | 5 | 3 | | 8 | 7• | 10 | 11 | | 4 | 6 | | 12 | | | | 9 | | |
| 3R | Jan 5 | AFC BOURNEMOUTH | L | 2-3 | 0-2 | 1833 | Croft (2) | 1 | | | 7 | 5 | 3 | | 8 | | 10 | 11 | | 4 | 6 | | | | | 2 | 9 | | |

• Extra time played following score of 1-1 after 90 minutes

## LEAGUE (RUMBELOWS) CUP

| | Date | Opposition | | FT | HT | Att. | Goalscorers | Stewart W. | Preece R. | Lundon S. | Butler B. | Abel G. | Lane M. | Pugh D. | Barrow G. | Bennett G. | Dale C. | Croft B. | Ellis N. | Lightfoot C. | Painter R. | Reeves A. | Morton N. | Barber F. | Withe C. | Whelan S. | Bertschin K. | Bishop E. | Brightwell D. |
|---|---|---|---|---|---|---|---|---|---|---|---|---|---|---|---|---|---|---|---|---|---|---|---|---|---|---|---|---|---|
| 1R1 | Aug 28 | Preston North End | L | 0-2 | 0-0 | 3503 | | 1 | 2 | 3 | | 5 | 6 | | 8 | 9 | 10 | 11 | 12 | 4 | 7• | | | | | | | | |
| 1R2 | Sep 4 | PRESTON NORTH END • | W | 5-1 | 2-0 | 1009 | Abel (pen), Croft (2), Ellis, Williams (og) | 1 | 2 | | 4 | 5• | 6 | 3 | 8 | 7 | 10 | 11 | 9" | 12 | 14 | | | | | | | | |
| 2R1 | 25 | ARSENAL | L | 0-1 | 0-0 | 4135 | | 1 | 2 | | 4 | 5 | 6 | 3 | 8 | 7 | 10 | 11• | 9 | 12 | | | | | | | | | |
| 2R2 | Oct 9 | Arsenal | L | 0-5 | 0-3 | 22902 | | 1 | 2 | | 4 | | 6 | 3 | 8• | 7 | 10 | 11 | 12 | 5 | | 14 | 9" | | | | | | |

• Extra time played following score of 3-1 after 90 minutes

## ASSOCIATE MEMBERS (LEYLAND DAF) CUP

| | Date | Opposition | | FT | HT | Att. | Goalscorers | Stewart W. | Preece R. | Lundon S. | Butler B. | Abel G. | Lane M. | Pugh D. | Barrow G. | Bennett G. | Dale C. | Croft B. | Ellis N. | Lightfoot C. | Painter R. | Reeves A. | Morton N. | Barber F. | Withe C. | Whelan S. | Bertschin K. | Bishop E. | Brightwell D. |
|---|---|---|---|---|---|---|---|---|---|---|---|---|---|---|---|---|---|---|---|---|---|---|---|---|---|---|---|---|---|
| GM | Nov 6 | Wigan Athletic | L | 0-4 | 0-3 | 1800 | | 1 | 2 | | 4 | 5 | 6 | 3 | | 7 | 10 | 11 | 8" | | 14 | | 9 | | | | | | |
| GM | 27 | BURY | W | 2-0 | 1-0 | 409 | Dale, Morton | 1 | | | 4 | 5 | 6 | 3 | | 7 | 10 | 11 | | | 8 | 2 | 9 | | | | | | |

## FRIENDLIES

| | Date | Opposition | | FT | HT | Goalscorers |
|---|---|---|---|---|---|---|
| 1 | Aug 4 | Berwick Rangers | D | 1-1 | 0-1 | Dale |
| 2 | 6 | East Fife | W | 3-1 | 0-0 | Ellis, Barrow, Dale |
| 3 | 8 | Meadowbank Thistle | D | 0-0 | 0-0 | |
| 4 | 14 | Bangor City | W | 2-0 | 1-0 | Lightfoot, Barrow |

# *SEASON 1991-92*

## FOOTBALL (BARCLAYS) LEAGUE DIVISION 2

| | Date | Opposition | | FT | HT | Att. | Goalscorers | Siddall B. | Whelan S. | Albiston A. | Butler B. | Abel G. | Lightfoot C. | Bishop E. | Barrow G. | Rimmer S. | Bennett G. | Pugh D. | McGuinness P. | Croft B. | Stewart W. | Morton N. | Preece R. | Allen A. | Comstive P. | Nolan D. |
|---|---|---|---|---|---|---|---|---|---|---|---|---|---|---|---|---|---|---|---|---|---|---|---|---|---|---|
| 1 | Aug 17 | FULHAM | W | 2-0 | 1-0 | 1444 | Lightfoot, Bennett | 1 | 2 | 3 | 4* | 5 | 6 | 7 | 8 | 9 | 10 | 11 | 12 | | | | | | | |
| 2 | 23 | Wigan Athletic | L | 1-2 | 1-0 | 2637 | Rimmer | 1 | 2 | 3 | 4 | 5 | 6 | 7 | 8 | 9 | 10 | 11" | | 14 | | | | | | |
| 3 | 31 | SWANSEA CITY | W | 2-0 | 0-0 | 1162 | Abel, Morton | | 2 | 3 | 4 | 5 | 6 | 7 | 8 | 9 | 10" | 11* | | 12 | 1 | 14 | | | | |
| 4 | Sep 4 | Huddersfield Town | L | 0-2 | 0-1 | 5321 | | | 2 | 3 | 4* | 5 | 6 | 7 | 8 | 9 | 12 | | 14 | 11 | 1 | 10" | | | | |
| 5 | 7 | AFC BOURNEMOUTH | L | 0-1 | 0-0 | 1117 | | | 2 | 3 | 4" | 5 | 6 | 7 | 8 | 9 | 12 | 14 | | 11 | 1 | 10* | | | | |
| 6 | 14 | Bradford City | D | 1-1 | 1-0 | 4843 | Bishop | | 2 | 3 | 4 | 5 | 6 | 7 | 8 | 9 | 10* | | | 11 | 1 | 12 | | | | |
| 7 | 17 | Birmingham City | L | 2-3 | 2-2 | 8154 | Bishop, Rimmer | | 2 | 3 | 4 | 5 | 6 | 7 | 8 | 9 | 10" | 14 | | 11 | 1 | | | | | |
| 8 | 21 | WEST BROMWICH A. | L | 1-2 | 1-1 | 3895 | Barrow | | | 3 | 4 | 5 | 6 | 7 | 8 | 9 | 10 | 2 | | 11 | 1 | | | | | |
| 9 | 28 | Torquay United | L | 2-3 | 1-2 | 2062 | Bishop, Rimmer | | | 3 | 8 | 5 | 6 | 7 | | 9* | 10 | 4 | 2 | | 1 | 11 | 12 | | | |
| 10 | Oct 5 | STOKE CITY | D | 0-0 | 0-0 | 4212 | | | 6 | 3 | 12 | 5* | | 7 | 8 | | 10 | 4 | 2 | 11 | 1 | 9 | | | | |
| 11 | 12 | Leyton Orient | L | 0-1 | 0-1 | 4049 | | | 2 | 3 | 6 | 5 | | 7 | | 9 | 10 | 4 | 8 | 11* | 1 | 12 | | | | |
| 12 | 18 | Stockport County | W | 4-0 | 1-0 | 4838 | Bennett (3), Rimmer | | 2 | 3 | | 5 | 6 | 7 | 8 | 9 | 10 | 4 | | 11 | 1 | | | | | |
| 13 | 26 | BOLTON WANDERERS | L | 0-1 | 0-0 | 1867 | | | 2" | 3 | 14 | 5 | 6 | 7 | 8 | 9 | 10* | 4 | | 11 | 1 | 12 | | | | |
| 14 | Nov 2 | PRESTON NORTH END | W | 3-2 | 1-0 | 1219 | Rimmer (2), Bishop | | 2 | 3 | 14 | 5 | 6 | 7 | 8 | 9 | 10* | 4" | | 11 | 1 | 12 | | | | |
| 15 | 5 | Peterborough United | L | 0-2 | 0-2 | 2810 | | | 2 | 3 | 4* | 5" | 6 | 7 | 8 | 9 | | | 14 | 11 | 1 | 10 | 12 | | | |
| 16 | 9 | Hull City | L | 0-1 | 0-1 | 4305 | | | 2 | 3 | | 5 | 6 | 7 | 8 | 9 | | | | 11 | 1 | 10" | 4 | 14 | | |
| 17 | 23 | READING | D | 2-2 | 1-1 | 1124 | Rimmer, Abel | 1 | 2 | 3 | 4 | 5 | 6 | 7 | 8 | 9 | 10* | | | 11 | | 12 | | | | |
| 18 | 30 | Exeter City | D | 0-0 | 0-0 | 3235 | | | 2 | 3 | 14 | 5 | 6 | 7 | 8 | 9 | 10" | | | 11* | 1 | 12 | | | 4 | |
| 19 | Dec 14 | SHREWSBURY TOWN | L | 1-4 | 1-1 | 1016 | Morton | | 2 | 3 | 12 | 5 | 6 | 7 | 8 | | 10 | | | 11* | 1 | 9 | | | 4 | |
| 20 | 26 | Swansea City | L | 0-3 | 0-2 | 4098 | | 1 | 2 | 3 | 11" | 5 | 6 | 7* | 8 | 9 | 10 | | | 14 | | | 12 | | 4 | |
| 21 | 28 | Fulham | D | 2-2 | 0-0 | 3708 | Abel (2,1 pen) | | 2 | 3 | | 5 | 6 | | 8 | 9 | 10 | | | 11* | 1 | 12 | 7 | | 4 | |
| 22 | Jan 1 | HUDDERSFIELD TOWN | D | 0-0 | 0-0 | 3504 | | | 2 | 3 | | 5 | 6 | | 8 | 9 | 10 | | | 14 | 1 | 7" | 11 | | 4 | |
| 23 | 4 | DARLINGTON | L | 2-5 | 2-2 | 1020 | Comstive, Tait (og) | | | 3* | 2 | 5 | 6 | | 8 | 9 | 10 | | 12 | 14 | 1 | 7" | 11 | | 4 | |
| 24 | 11 | Hartlepool United | L | 0-1 | 0-0 | 3088 | | | | | | 5 | 6 | | 8 | 9 | 11 | 3 | | 14 | 1 | 10" | 2 | | 4 | 7 |
| 25 | 18 | BRENTFORD | D | 1-1 | 0-1 | 1447 | Butler | | | | 9 | 5 | 6 | | 8 | 10 | 7 | 3 | | 11* | 1 | 12 | 2 | | 4 | |
| 26 | Feb 8 | Bolton Wanderers | D | 0-0 | 0-0 | 6609 | | | | 3 | 9 | 5 | 6 | | 8 | 10 | 7* | 11 | | 12 | 1 | | 2 | | 4 | |
| 27 | 11 | EXETER CITY | W | 5-2 | 3-1 | 871 | Butler (2), Rimmer, Abel (pen), Comstive | | | 3 | 9 | 5 | 6 | | 8 | 10 | 7 | 11 | | | 1 | | 2 | | 4 | |
| 28 | 15 | Shrewsbury Town | D | 2-2 | 2-1 | 2807 | Rimmer, Lightfoot | | 14 | 3 | 9 | 5" | 6 | | 8 | 10 | 7* | 11 | | 12 | 1 | | 2 | | 4 | |
| 29 | 18 | WIGAN ATHLETIC | W | 1-0 | 0-0 | 1065 | Rimmer | | 5 | 3 | 9" | | 6 | | 8 | 10 | 7* | 11 | | 12 | 1 | 14 | 2 | | 4 | |
| 30 | 22 | HARTLEPOOL UNITED | W | 2-0 | 2-0 | 1072 | Butler (2) | | 5 | 3 | 9 | | 6 | | 8 | 10 | 7 | 4 | | | 1 | 11 | 2 | | | |
| 31 | 25 | Bury | W | 2-1 | 2-1 | 2283 | Lightfoot, Bennett | | 5 | 3 | 9* | 12 | 6 | | 8 | 10 | 7 | 11 | | | 1 | | 2 | | 4 | |
| 32 | 29 | Darlington | D | 1-1 | 0-0 | 2579 | Rimmer | | 5" | 3 | 9 | 14 | 6 | | 8 | 10 | 7* | 11 | | 12 | 1 | | 2 | | 4 | |
| 33 | Mar 3 | Brentford | L | 0-2 | 0-1 | 6869 | | | 5 | 3 | 9 | 14 | 6" | | 8 | 10 | 7* | 11 | | | 1 | 12 | 2 | | 4 | |
| 34 | 7 | BURY | W | 3-1 | 1-1 | 1228 | Bennett (2), Abel | | 5* | 3 | 9" | 12 | 6 | | 8 | 10 | 7 | 11 | | | 1 | 14 | 2 | | 4 | |
| 35 | 10 | PETERBOROUGH UNITED | L | 2-4 | 1-1 | 1063 | Butler, Abel (pen) | | | 3 | 9* | 5 | 6 | | 8 | 10 | 7 | 11" | | 14 | 1 | 12 | 2 | | 4 | |
| 36 | 14 | Preston North End | W | 3-0 | 2-0 | 3909 | Rimmer, Bennett (2) | | 2 | 3 | 9 | 5 | 6 | | | 10 | 7 | 11 | | | 1 | 12 | 8* | | 4 | |
| 37 | 21 | HULL CITY | D | 1-1 | 1-0 | 1269 | Comstive | 1 | 2 | 3 | 9 | 5 | 6 | | | 10 | | 11 | | 7* | | 12 | 8 | | 4 | |
| 38 | 24 | STOCKPORT COUNTY | W | 3-2 | 1-0 | 3747 | Abel (2,1 pen), Bennett | | 2" | 3 | 9 | 5 | 6 | | | 10 | 7 | 11 | | | 1 | 14 | 8 | | 4 | |
| 39 | 28 | Reading | D | 0-0 | 0-0 | 2813 | | 1 | | 3 | 9* | 5 | 6 | | 8 | 10 | 7 | 11 | | | | 12 | 2 | | 4 | |
| 40 | 31 | BRADFORD CITY | D | 0-0 | 0-0 | 1149 | | 1 | 14 | 3 | 9* | 5 | 6 | | 8" | 10 | 7 | 11 | | | | 12 | 2 | | 4 | |
| 41 | Apr 3 | AFC Bournemouth | L | 0-2 | 0-1 | 5974 | | 1 | | 3 | 9* | 5 | 6 | | 8 | 10 | 7 | 11 | | | | 12 | 2 | | 4 | |
| 42 | 11 | BIRMINGHAM CITY | L | 0-1 | 0-0 | 4895 | | 1 | | 3 | 9* | 5 | 6 | | 8 | 10 | 7" | 11 | | 14 | | 12 | 2 | | 4 | |
| 43 | 18 | West Bromwich Albion | D | 1-1 | 1-0 | 10137 | Abel (pen) | | 2 | 3 | 9 | 5 | 6 | | | 10 | 7 | 11 | | 12 | 1 | 8* | | | 4 | |
| 44 | 20 | TORQUAY UNITED | W | 2-0 | 1-0 | 1317 | Rimmer, Lightfoot | | | 3 | 9 | 5 | 6 | | 8" | 10 | 7 | 11 | | | 1 | 14 | 2 | | 4 | |
| 45 | 25 | Stoke City | W | 1-0 | 0-0 | 18474 | Bennett | | | 3 | 9 | 5 | 6 | | 8 | 10 | 7 | 11 | | | 1 | | 2 | | 4 | |
| 46 | May 2 | LEYTON ORIENT | W | 1-0 | 0-0 | 2008 | Barrow | | | 3 | 9 | 5 | 6 | 7" | 8 | 10 | | 11 | | 12 | 1 | 14 | 2 | | 4* | |
| | | | | | | | Apps. | 9 | 30 | 44 | 36 | 40 | 44 | 21 | 40 | 44 | 40 | 33 | 3 | 18 | 37 | 12 | 26 | | 28 | 1 |
| | | | | | | | Subs. | | 2 | | 5 | 4 | | | | | 2 | 2 | 4 | 14 | | 22 | 3 | 1 | | |
| | | | | | | | Goals | | | | 6 | 10 | 4 | 4 | 2 | 13 | 11 | | | | | 2 | | | 3 | |

Own goals 1

## F.A. CUP

| Round | Date | Opposition | | FT | HT | Att. | Goalscorers | Siddall B. | Whelan S. | Albiston A. | Butler B. | Abel G. | Lightfoot C. | Bishop E. | Barrow G. | Rimmer S. | Bennett G. | Pugh D. | McGuinness P. | Croft B. | Stewart W. | Morton N. | Preece R. | Allen A. | Comstive P. | Nolan D. |
|---|---|---|---|---|---|---|---|---|---|---|---|---|---|---|---|---|---|---|---|---|---|---|---|---|---|---|
| 1R | Nov 16 | GUISELEY | W | 1-0 | 1-0 | 1851 | Barrow | 1 | 2 | 3 | 4 | 5 | 6 | 7 | 8 | 9 | 10* | | | 11 | | 12 | | | | |
| 2R | Dec 7 | Crewe Alex. | L | 0-2 | 0-0 | 5299 | | | 2 | 3 | 11 | 5 | 6 | 7 | 8 | 9* | 10 | | | | 1 | 12 | | | 4 | |

## LEAGUE (RUMBELOWS) CUP

| Round | Date | Opposition | | FT | HT | Att. | Goalscorers | Siddall B. | Whelan S. | Albiston A. | Butler B. | Abel G. | Lightfoot C. | Bishop E. | Barrow G. | Rimmer S. | Bennett G. | Pugh D. | McGuinness P. | Croft B. | Stewart W. | Morton N. | Preece R. | Allen A. | Comstive P. | Nolan D. |
|---|---|---|---|---|---|---|---|---|---|---|---|---|---|---|---|---|---|---|---|---|---|---|---|---|---|---|
| 1R1 | Aug 20 | LINCOLN CITY | W | 1-0 | 0-0 | 1018 | Barrow | 1 | 2 | 3 | 4* | 5 | 6 | 7 | 8 | 9 | 10 | 11" | 12 | 14 | | | | | | |
| 1R2 | 28 | Lincoln City * | L | 3-4 | 1-1 | 2170 | Bennett, Rimmer (2) | | 2 | 3 | 4* | 5 | 6 | 7 | 8 | 9 | 10 | 11 | 12 | | 1 | | | | | |
| 2R1 | Sep 25 | Manchester City | L | 1-3 | 0-0 | 10987 | Bennett | | | 3 | 12 | 5 | 6 | 7* | 8 | 9 | 10 | 4 | 2 | 11" | 1 | 14 | | | | |
| 2R2 | Oct 8 | MANCHESTER CITY @ | L | 0-3 | 0-1 | 4146 | | | 5 | 3 | 12 | | 6 | 7 | 8 | | 10 | 4 | 2 | 11 | 1 | 9* | | | | |

* Extra time played following score of 2-3 after 90 minutes. Chester won on away goals.

@ Played at Stockport County

## ASSOCIATE MEMBERS (AUTOGLASS) TROPHY

| Round | Date | Opposition | | FT | HT | Att. | Goalscorers | Siddall B. | Whelan S. | Albiston A. | Butler B. | Abel G. | Lightfoot C. | Bishop E. | Barrow G. | Rimmer S. | Bennett G. | Pugh D. | McGuinness P. | Croft B. | Stewart W. | Morton N. | Preece R. | Allen A. | Comstive P. | Nolan D. |
|---|---|---|---|---|---|---|---|---|---|---|---|---|---|---|---|---|---|---|---|---|---|---|---|---|---|---|
| GM | Nov 19 | Crewe Alex. | L | 1-2 | 0-1 | 1779 | Lightfoot | 1 | 2 | 3 | 4 | 5 | 6 | 7 | 8 | 9 | 12 | | | 11 | | 10* | | | | |
| GM | Jan 7 | DARLINGTON | W | 2-1 | 2-0 | 416 | Morton, Bennett | | | | 12 | 5 | 6 | | 8 | 9 | 7 | | | 11 | 1 | 10 | 2 | | 4 | 3* |
| 1R | Jan 21 | Rotherham United | L | 0-3 | 0-2 | 2543 | | | | | 9 | 5 | 6 | | 8 | 10 | 7* | 3 | | 11 | 1 | 12 | 2 | | 4 | |

## FRIENDLIES

| | Date | Opposition | | FT | HT | Att. | Goalscorers |
|---|---|---|---|---|---|---|---|
| 1 | Jul 23 | Chorley | W | 3-0 | | | Croft (2), Abel |
| 2 | 30 | Colwyn Bay | W | 1-0 | 1-0 | | Morton |
| 3 | Aug 2 | Morecambe | D | 1-1 | 0-0 | | McGuinness |
| 4 | 7 | Hereford United * | D | 1-1 | 0-1 | 1501 | Butler |
| 5 | 10 | Macclesfield Town | L | 2-3 | 1-0 | | Bennett, McGuinness |
| 6 | Apr 7 | Wrexham @ | D | 1-1 | 0-0 | 1984 | Butler |

* Herefordshire Senior Cup Final  @ Mike Williams Testimonial

**1991/92 Season:**

(Back) Pugh, Butler, Abel, Stewart, Siddall, Lightfoot, Whelan, Bennett, Hinnigan (Physio).
(Front) Albiston, McGuinness, Croft, McNally (Manager), Crofts (Chairman), Barrow (Assistant Manager), Preece, Bishop.

**1992/93 Season:**

(Back) Allan (Secretary), Bishop, Goodwin, Pugh, Comstive, Stewart, Tyrell, Abel, Lightfoot, Whelan, Butler, Hinnigan (Physio).
(Middle) Preece, Kelly, Barrow (Assistant Manager), McNally (Manager), Crofts (Chairman), Rimmer, Morton, Ryan.
(Front) Allen, Barthrop, Limbert, Miller.

# SEASON 1992-93

## FOOTBALL (BARCLAYS) LEAGUE DIVISION 2

| | Date | Opposition | | FT | HT | Att. | Goalscorers | Stewart W. | Preece R. | Comstive P. | Butler B. | Abel G. | Lightfoot C. | Kelly J. | Thompson D. | Rimmer S. | Bishop E. | Pugh D. | Ryan D. | Whelan S. | Morton N. | Keeley J. | Goodwin C. | Barrow G. | Limbert M. | Garnett S. | Albiston A. | Came M. | Wheeler P. |
|---|---|---|---|---|---|---|---|---|---|---|---|---|---|---|---|---|---|---|---|---|---|---|---|---|---|---|---|---|---|
| 1 | Aug 15 | Bradford City | L | 1-3 | 1-0 | 5780 | Bishop | 1 | 2 | 3 | 4 | 5 | 6 | 7• | 8 | 9 | 10 | 11 | 12 | | | | | | | | | | |
| 2 | 22 | Hull City | D | 1-1 | 0-0 | 4906 | Rimmer | 1 | 2 | 3 | 4 | 5 | 6 | | 8 | 9 | 10 | | 11• | 7 | 12 | | | | | | | | |
| 3 | 29 | Preston North End | L | 3-4 | 2-1 | 4471 | Bishop, Rimmer, Morton | | 2 | 3 | | | 6 | 4 | 8 | 9 | 10 | 11 | | 5 | 7 | 1 | | | | | | | |
| 4 | Sep 1 | Hartlepool United | L | 0-2 | 0-1 | 3061 | | | 2 | 3 | | | 4 | 11" | 7• | 9 | | | 12 | 5 | 10 | 1 | 6 | 8 | 14 | | | | |
| 5 | 5 | BURNLEY | W | 3-0 | 2-0 | 4981 | Morton, Lightfoot, Comstive | | 2 | 3 | | 5 | 6 | 11 | 7 | 9 | | | | 4 | 10 | 1 | | 8 | | | | | |
| 6 | 12 | Leyton Orient | L | 3-4 | 1-1 | 4158 | Barrow, Rimmer, Ryan | 1 | | 3 | | 5 | 6 | 11 | 7 | 9 | | | 12 | 2 | 10 | | 4• | 8 | | | | | |
| 7 | 15 | MANSFIELD TOWN | L | 1-2 | 1-1 | 3326 | Rimmer | 1 | | 3 | | 5 | 6 | 11 | 7 | 9 | 4 | | | 2 | 10 | | | 8 | | | | | |
| 8 | 19 | STOCKPORT COUNTY | L | 0-3 | 0-0 | 3627 | | 1 | | 3 | | 5 | | 11 | 7 | 9• | 4 | 6 | 12 | 2 | 10 | | | 8 | | | | | |
| 9 | 26 | Port Vale | L | 0-2 | 0-0 | 6392 | | 1 | 2 | 3• | | 5 | 6 | 11 | 7 | | 10 | | 12 | 4 | 9" | | | 8 | 14 | | | | |
| 10 | Oct 3 | STOKE CITY | D | 1-1 | 0-0 | 5237 | Bishop | 1 | 2 | | 4• | 5 | | 11 | 7 | 9 | 10 | | 12 | 14 | | | 3" | 8 | | 6 | | | |
| 11 | 10 | Plymouth Argyle | L | 0-2 | 0-1 | 7182 | | 1 | 2 | | 4 | 5 | | 11 | 7 | 9 | 10 | | | 3 | | | | 8 | | 6 | | | |
| 12 | 17 | BOLTON WANDERERS | D | 2-2 | 2-0 | 3394 | Ryan, Comstive (pen) | 1 | 2 | 7 | 4 | 14 | | 11 | | | 10• | 3 | 9 | 5 | 12 | | | 8" | | 6 | | | |
| 13 | 24 | Fulham | L | 0-1 | 0-0 | 3753 | | 1 | 2 | 3 | 4 | | 6 | 10" | 7 | 9 | | 11 | 8• | 14 | 12 | | | | | 5 | | | |
| 14 | 31 | BRIGHTON & HOVE A. | W | 2-1 | 2-0 | 2735 | Rimmer, Morton | 1 | 2 | 3 | 4" | | 6 | 10• | 7 | 9 | | 11 | 12 | | 8 | | | 14 | | 5 | | | |
| 15 | Nov 3 | Rotherham United | D | 3-3 | 2-2 | 4188 | Rimmer, Pugh (2) | 1 | 2 | 3 | | | 6 | | 7 | 9 | | 11 | 12 | 4" | 8• | | 14 | 10 | | 5 | | | |
| 16 | 7 | SWANSEA CITY | W | 3-2 | 2-1 | 2861 | Lightfoot, Pugh (2) | 1 | 2 | 3 | | | 6 | 4• | 7 | 9 | | 11 | 8 | | | | 12 | 10 | | 5 | | | |
| 17 | 21 | Exeter City | L | 0-2 | 0-0 | 2452 | | | 2 | 4 | 8 | | 6 | | 7 | 9 | | 11 | 12 | | | 1 | | 10• | | 5 | 3 | | |
| 18 | 28 | WIGAN ATHLETIC | L | 1-2 | 1-0 | 2395 | Rimmer (pen) | 1 | 2 | | 8 | | 6 | 4 | 7 | 9 | | 11 | 14 | | 10" | | | | | 5 | 3 | | |
| 19 | Dec 12 | READING | L | 0-3 | 0-1 | 2011 | | 1 | 2 | 10• | 8 | | 6 | 4 | 7" | | 12 | | 11 | 14 | 9 | | | | | | 3 | 5 | |
| 20 | 19 | Huddersfield Town | W | 2-0 | 1-0 | 4626 | Rimmer, Kelly | 1 | | | 8" | 14 | 6 | 4 | | 9 | 10 | 11 | | 2 | | | | 7 | | | 3 | 5 | |
| 21 | 26 | West Bromwich A. | L | 0-2 | 0-1 | 15209 | | 1 | 2" | | 8 | 14 | 6 | 4 | | 9 | 10• | 11 | 12 | | | | | 7 | | | 3 | 5 | |
| 22 | 28 | BLACKPOOL | L | 1-2 | 1-2 | 3787 | Barrow | 1 | 2 | | 8 | 14 | 6 | 4" | 12 | 9 | 10 | 11 | | | | | | 7 | | | 3 | 5• | |
| 23 | Jan 2 | LEYTON ORIENT | L | 1-3 | 1-0 | 2510 | Bishop | 1 | 2 | 14 | 8 | | 6 | 4 | 12 | 9 | 10 | 11" | | | | | | 7• | | | 3 | 5 | |
| 24 | 9 | Mansfield Town | L | 0-2 | 0-0 | 2659 | | 1 | | 3• | 8 | | 6 | 4 | 7 | 9 | 10 | 11 | 14 | 2" | | | | | | | 12 | 5 | |
| 25 | 16 | PORT VALE | L | 1-2 | 1-0 | 4367 | Pugh | 1 | | 3 | 4 | | 6 | | 7 | 9 | 10 | 11 | | 2 | | | | 8 | | | | 5 | |
| 26 | 22 | Stockport County | L | 0-2 | 0-2 | 4427 | | 1 | | 3 | 4• | 14 | 6 | 12 | 7 | 9 | 10 | 11 | | 2 | | | | 8 | | | | 5" | |
| 27 | 26 | PRESTON NORTH END | L | 2-4 | 1-1 | 2901 | Rimmer (2 1 pen) | 1 | | 3 | | 5 | 6 | 14 | 7 | 9 | 10 | 11 | | 2 | 12 | | | 4" | | | | | 8• |
| 28 | 30 | HULL CITY | W | 3-0 | 3-0 | 2232 | Rimmer (2), Bishop | 1 | | 3 | | 5 | 6 | 14 | 7 | 9 | 10 | 11 | | 2 | | | | 4" | | | | | 8 |
| 29 | Feb 6 | BRADFORD CITY | L | 2-5 | 1-3 | 2594 | Rimmer, Bishop | 1 | | 3 | | 5 | 6 | 14 | 7 | 9 | 10 | 11 | | 2 | 12 | | | 4" | | | | | 8• |
| 30 | 13 | Burnley | L | 0-5 | 0-4 | 9434 | | 1 | 2 | 3 | | 5 | 6 | 12 | 7 | 9 | 10 | 11 | | | | | | 4• | | | | | 8 |
| 31 | 20 | HARTLEPOOL UNITED | W | 1-0 | 1-0 | 1912 | Rimmer (pen) | 1 | 2 | | 10 | 5 | 6 | 7 | 12 | 9 | | 11• | | | | | | 4 | | | 3 | | 8 |
| 32 | 27 | PLYMOUTH ARGYLE | L | 1-2 | 0-0 | 2163 | Rimmer | 1 | 2" | 14 | 4 | 5 | | 6 | 7• | 9 | 10 | 11 | | | 12 | | | | | | 3 | | 8 |
| 33 | Mar 6 | Stoke City | L | 0-4 | 0-2 | 14534 | | 1 | | 4 | 10 | 5 | 6 | 7 | 12 | 9 | | 11 | | 2• | | | | | | | 3 | | 8 |
| 34 | 9 | AFC BOURNEMOUTH | W | 1-0 | 1-0 | 1614 | Abel | 1 | | | 8 | 5 | 6 | | 7 | 9 | | 11 | | 12 | 10 | | | | 2 | | 3 | 4• | |
| 35 | 13 | Swansea City | L | 2-4 | 1-2 | 4056 | Rimmer (2) | 1 | | | 10• | 5 | 6 | | 7 | 9 | | 11 | | | 8 | | | | 2 | | 3 | 4 | 12 |
| 36 | 19 | ROTHERHAM UNITED | L | 1-2 | 0-0 | 2265 | Thompson | 1 | | | 8 | 5 | 6 | | 14 | 9 | | 11 | | | 10• | | | 7" | 2 | | 3 | 4 | 12 |
| 37 | 23 | Wigan Athletic | W | 2-1 | 2-0 | 1861 | Comstive, Rimmer | 1 | | 6 | 8 | 5 | | | 14 | 9 | | 11 | | | 10 | | | 7" | 2 | | 3 | 4 | |
| 38 | 27 | EXETER CITY | L | 0-3 | 0-1 | 2047 | | 1 | | 6 | 8• | 5 | | 14 | 12 | 9 | | 11 | | | 10 | | | 7" | 2 | | 3 | 4 | |
| 39 | Apr 3 | AFC Bournemouth | D | 0-0 | 0-0 | 2829 | | 1 | | | 8 | 5 | 6 | | | 9 | | 11 | | | 10 | | | 7 | 2 | | 3 | 4 | |
| 40 | 7 | Reading | L | 0-1 | 0-0 | 3754 | | 1 | | | 8 | 5 | 6 | 14 | | 9 | 12 | 11 | | | 10• | | | 7" | 2 | | 3 | 4 | |
| 41 | 10 | WEST BROMWICH A. | L | 1-3 | 0-1 | 4812 | Morton | 1 | | | 8 | 5• | 6 | | | 9 | 12 | 11 | | | 10 | | | 7 | 2 | | 3 | 4" | 14 |
| 42 | 13 | Blackpool | L | 0-2 | 0-2 | 5078 | | 1 | | | 4 | | 6 | | | 9 | 10 | 11 | | 5 | | | | 7 | 2 | | 3 | | 8 |
| 43 | 17 | HUDDERSFIELD TOWN | L | 0-2 | 0-0 | 3019 | | 1 | | | 7 | 4• | 6 | | 12 | 9 | 10 | 11 | | 5 | | | | | 2 | | 3 | | 8 |
| 44 | 24 | Bolton Wanderers | L | 0-5 | 0-0 | 8514 | | 1 | | | 12 | 4 | 6 | | 14 | 9 | 10• | | | 5 | 11" | | | 7 | 2 | | 3 | | 8 |
| 45 | May 1 | FULHAM | L | 2-3 | 0-1 | 2016 | Rimmer, Thompson | 1 | 2 | | | 4 | 6 | | 11 | 9 | 12 | | | 5 | 14 | | | 7• | 10 | | 3 | | 8" |
| 46 | 8 | Brighton & Hove A. | L | 2-3 | 2-2 | 6247 | Thompson, Rimmer | 1 | | | | 4 | 6 | | 7 | 9 | 10 | 11 | | 2 | | | | | | | 3 | 5 | 8 |
| | | | | | | | Apps. | 42 | 23 | 26 | 30 | 28 | 39 | 24 | 30 | 43 | 25 | 35 | 5 | 24 | 20 | 4 | 3 | 32 | 12 | 9 | 23 | 17 | 12 |
| | | | | | | | Subs. | | | 2 | 1 | 5 | | 7 | 9 | | 4 | | 12 | 4 | 7 | | 2 | 1 | 2 | | 1 | | 3 |
| | | | | | | | Goals | | | 3 | | 1 | 2 | 1 | 3 | 20 | 6 | 5 | 2 | | 4 | | | 2 | | | | | |

## F.A. CUP

| | Date | Opposition | | FT | HT | Att. | Goalscorers | Stewart W. | Preece R. | Comstive P. | Butler B. | Abel G. | Lightfoot C. | Kelly J. | Thompson D. | Rimmer S. | Bishop E. | Pugh D. | Ryan D. | Whelan S. | Morton N. | Keeley J. | Goodwin C. | Barrow G. | Limbert M. | Garnett S. | Albiston A. | Came M. | Wheeler P. |
|---|---|---|---|---|---|---|---|---|---|---|---|---|---|---|---|---|---|---|---|---|---|---|---|---|---|---|---|---|---|
| 1R | Nov 14 | ALTRINCHAM | D | 1-1 | 1-0 | 4033 | Ryan | 1 | 2 | 3 | | 5 | 6 | | 7 | 9 | | 11 | 8• | 4 | | | 12 | 10 | | | | | |
| 1Rr | 25 | Altrincham | L | 0-2 | 0-0 | 3000 | | 1 | 2 | 3 | 8 | 5 | 6 | 4• | 7" | 9 | | 11 | 12 | | 14 | | | 10 | | | | | |

## LEAGUE (COCA COLA) CUP

| | Date | Opposition | | FT | HT | Att. | Goalscorers | Stewart W. | Preece R. | Comstive P. | Butler B. | Abel G. | Lightfoot C. | Kelly J. | Thompson D. | Rimmer S. | Bishop E. | Pugh D. | Ryan D. | Whelan S. | Morton N. | Keeley J. | Goodwin C. | Barrow G. | Limbert M. | Garnett S. | Albiston A. | Came M. | Wheeler P. |
|---|---|---|---|---|---|---|---|---|---|---|---|---|---|---|---|---|---|---|---|---|---|---|---|---|---|---|---|---|---|
| 1R1 | Aug 18 | Stockport County | D | 1-1 | 0-1 | 2785 | Comstive | 1 | 2 | 3 | 4 | 5" | 6 | | 7 | 9 | 10 | 11 | 8 | 14 | | | | | | | | | |
| 1R2 | 25 | STOCKPORT COUNTY | L | 1-2 | 0-1 | 4505 | Bishop | 1• | 2 | 3 | | 5 | 6 | | 8 | 9 | 10 | 4 | 11" | 7 | 12 | | 14 | | | | | | |

## ASSOCIATE MEMBERS (AUTOGLASS) TROPHY

| | Date | Opposition | | FT | HT | Att. | Goalscorers | Stewart W. | Preece R. | Comstive P. | Butler B. | Abel G. | Lightfoot C. | Kelly J. | Thompson D. | Rimmer S. | Bishop E. | Pugh D. | Ryan D. | Whelan S. | Morton N. | Keeley J. | Goodwin C. | Barrow G. | Limbert M. | Garnett S. | Albiston A. | Came M. | Wheeler P. |
|---|---|---|---|---|---|---|---|---|---|---|---|---|---|---|---|---|---|---|---|---|---|---|---|---|---|---|---|---|---|
| GM | Dec 5 | CHESTERFIELD | L | 0-1 | 0-1 | 1276 | | 1 | 2 | 11 | 4 | | 6 | 12 | 7• | | | | 8 | | 9 | | | 10 | | | 3 | 5 | |
| GM | 15 | Stockport County | L | 0-2 | 0-0 | 2064 | | 1 | | | 4" | 14 | 6 | 8 | | | 10 | 11 | 12 | 2 | 9 | | | 7• | | | 3 | 5 | |

## FRIENDLIES

| | Date | Opposition | | FT | HT | Att. | Goalscorers |
|---|---|---|---|---|---|---|---|
| 1 | July 25 | East Stirlingshire | W | 5-2 | | | Bishop (3), Rimmer, Kelly |
| 2 | 27 | Dumbarton | D | 0-0 | 0-0 | | |
| 3 | 29 | Cowdenbeath | D | 0-0 | 0-0 | | |
| 4 | Aug 1 | Altrincham | L | 0-2 | 0-1 | | |
| 5 | 4 | Ellesmere Port Town | W | 4-1 | 0-0 | | Bishop (2, 1 pen), Ryan, Morton |
| 6 | 7 | Cambridge United * | W | 1-0 | 0-0 | 1129 | Kelly |
| 7 | Oct 13 | MANCHESTER UNITED | W | 2-0 | 1-0 | 3491 | Kelly, Butler |

* Cambridgeshire Professional Cup

# SEASON 1993-94

## FOOTBALL (ENDSLEIGH) LEAGUE DIVISION 3

| | Date | Opposition | | FT | HT | Att. | Goalscorers | Stewart W. | Preece R. | Jakub J. | Bishop E. | Came M. | Greenall C. | Thompson D. | Lightfoot C. | Rimmer S. | Leonard M. | Pugh D. | Jenkins I. | Donnelly D. | Wheeler P. | Whelan S. | Barrow G. | McIlhargey S. | Felgate D. | Flitcroft D. | Lancashire G. | Bagnall J. |
|---|---|---|---|---|---|---|---|---|---|---|---|---|---|---|---|---|---|---|---|---|---|---|---|---|---|---|---|---|
| 1 | Aug 14 | DONCASTER ROVERS | L | 0-1 | 0-0 | 2752 | | 1 | 2 | 3* | 4 | 5 | 6 | 7" | 8 | 9 | 10 | 11 | 12 | 14 | | | | | | | | |
| 2 | 21 | Wycombe Wanderers | L | 0-1 | 0-1 | 5607 | | 1 | 2 | 3 | 4* | 5 | 6 | 7 | 8 | 9" | 10 | 11 | 12 | 14 | | | | | | | | |
| 3 | 28 | CHESTERFIELD | W | 3-1 | 0-1 | 2283 | Lightfoot, Rimmer, Thompson | 1 | 2 | 3 | | 5* | 6 | 7 | 8 | 9 | 10 | 11 | 4 | | 12 | | | | | | | |
| 4 | 31 | Lincoln City | W | 3-0 | 0-0 | 4038 | Pugh, Leonard, Rimmer | 1 | 2 | 3 | | | 6 | 7 | 8 | 9" | 10 | 11 | 4 | 14 | | 5 | | | | | | |
| 5 | Sep 4 | Rochdale | L | 0-2 | 0-2 | 3063 | | 1 | 2 | 3 | | | 6 | 7 | 8 | 9 | 10 | 11 | 4 | | | 5 | | | | | | |
| 6 | 11 | SCUNTHORPE | L | 0-2 | 0-1 | 2195 | | 1 | 2* | 3" | 12 | 5 | 6 | 7 | 8 | 9 | 10 | 11 | 4 | 14 | | | | | | | | |
| 7 | 18 | Scarborough | W | 1-0 | 0-0 | 1510 | Leonard | 1* | 2 | 3 | | 5 | 6 | 7 | 8 | 9 | 10 | 11 | 4 | | | | 12 | | | | | |
| 8 | 25 | CARLISLE UNITED | D | 0-0 | 0-0 | 2911 | | | 2 | 3 | | 5" | 6 | 7 | 8 | 9 | 10 | 11* | 4 | 14 | | | 12 | 1 | | | | |
| 9 | Oct 2 | Wigan Athletic | L | 3-6 | 1-3 | 1889 | Leonard (pen), Wheeler (2) | | 2 | 3" | 12 | 5 | 6 | 7 | 8 | 9 | 10* | 14 | 4 | | 11 | | | | 1 | | | |
| 10 | 9 | Darlington | W | 2-1 | 1-1 | 1787 | Rimmer, Wheeler (pen) | | 2 | 3 | | 5 | 6 | 7 | 8* | 9 | | 10 | 4 | | 11 | | 12 | | 1 | | | |
| 11 | 16 | SHREWSBURY TOWN | W | 1-0 | 1-0 | 3052 | Rimmer | | 2 | 3 | | 5 | 6 | 7 | 8 | 9 | | 10 | 4 | | 11 | | | | 1 | | | |
| 12 | 23 | Mansfield Town | W | 4-0 | 0-0 | 2545 | Wheeler (3), Rimmer | | 2 | 3 | | 5 | 6 | 7 | 8 | 9 | | | 4 | | 11 | | 10 | | 1 | | | |
| 13 | 30 | TORQUAY UNITED | D | 1-1 | 0-0 | 2563 | Bishop | | 2* | 3 | 14 | 5 | 6 | 7 | 8 | 9 | | | 4 | 12 | 11 | | 10" | | 1 | | | |
| 14 | Nov 2 | BURY | W | 3-0 | 1-0 | 2540 | Lightfoot (2), Rimmer | | 2 | 3 | | 5 | 6 | 7 | 8 | 9 | | 10 | 4 | | 11 | | | | 1 | | | |
| 15 | 6 | Hereford United | W | 5-0 | 2-0 | 2092 | Anderson (og), Wheeler, Lightfoot (2), Pugh | | 2 | 3 | 14 | | 6 | 7 | 8 | 9" | | 10 | 4 | | 11 | 5 | | | 1 | | | |
| 16 | 20 | NORTHAMPTON TOWN | W | 1-0 | 0-0 | 2650 | Pugh | | 2 | 3 | | | 6 | 7 | 8 | 9 | | 10 | 4 | | 11 | 5 | | | 1 | | | |
| 17 | 27 | Crewe Alex. | L | 1-2 | 1-0 | 4749 | Lightfoot | | 2 | 3 | 10 | 5 | 6 | 7 | 8 | | 9 | | 4 | | 11 | | | | 1 | | | |
| 18 | Dec 11 | WYCOMBE WANDERERS | W | 3-1 | 0-0 | 3195 | Rimmer, Leonard, Pugh | | 2 | 3 | 7 | 5 | 6 | | | 9 | 10 | 11 | 4 | | 8 | | | | 1 | | | |
| 19 | 17 | Doncaster Rovers | W | 4-3 | 0-1 | 1914 | Leonard (3), Pugh | | 2 | 3 | 14 | 5 | 6 | 12 | 8 | 9* | 10 | 11 | 4" | | 7 | | | | 1 | | | |
| 20 | 27 | Preston North End | D | 1-1 | 1-1 | 12790 | Nebbeling (og) | | 2 | 3 | | 5 | 6 | 7 | 8 | | 10 | 11 | 4 | | 9 | | | | 1 | | | |
| 21 | Jan 1 | Colchester United | D | 0-0 | 0-0 | 3170 | | | 2 | 3 | | 5 | 6 | 7 | 8 | 12 | 10 | 11 | 4 | | 9* | | | | 1 | | | |
| 22 | 15 | Shrewsbury Town | L | 0-3 | 0-2 | 5365 | | | 2* | 3 | 14 | 5 | 6 | 7 | 8" | 9 | 10 | | 4 | | 11 | | | | 1 | 12 | | |
| 23 | 22 | DARLINGTON | D | 0-0 | 0-0 | 2777 | | | 2" | 3 | 8 | | 6 | 7 | | 9 | 10 | | 4 | 12 | 11* | 5 | | | 1 | 14 | | |
| 24 | 29 | Torquay United | W | 3-1 | 1-1 | 2959 | Greenall, Flitcroft, Thompson | | | 3 | 10 | | 6 | 7 | | 9 | | 11" | 2 | 14 | | 5 | 8 | | 1 | 4 | | |
| 25 | Feb 1 | LINCOLN CITY | D | 1-1 | 0-1 | 2648 | Lancashire | | 2 | 3 | 8 | | 6 | 7 | | 9* | | 11 | 4 | | | 5 | | | 1 | 10 | 12 | |
| 26 | 5 | MANSFIELD TOWN | D | 1-1 | 1-0 | 2664 | Lancashire | | | 3 | 4 | | 6 | 7" | 8 | | 12 | 11 | 2* | 14 | | 5 | | | 1 | 10 | 9 | |
| 27 | 12 | Walsall | D | 1-1 | 1-0 | 4602 | Pugh (pen) | | 2 | 3" | | | 6 | 7 | 10 | | 14 | 11 | 4 | | | 5 | 8 | | 1 | | 9 | |
| 28 | 19 | Chesterfield | W | 2-1 | 1-1 | 2847 | Lancashire, Leonard | | 2 | | | | 6 | 7 | 5 | 12 | 4 | 11 | | | 10 | 3 | 8 | | 1 | | 9* | |
| 29 | 25 | ROCHDALE | W | 3-1 | 0-1 | 3472 | Pugh (2 1 pen), Rimmer | | 2 | | | 5 | 6 | 7 | 4 | 12 | | 11 | | | 10* | 3 | 8 | | 1 | | 9 | |
| 30 | Mar 1 | GILLINGHAM | W | 1-0 | 1-0 | 3128 | Pugh | | 2 | | 14 | 5 | 6 | 7 | 4 | 9 | 12 | 11 | | | 10* | 3 | | | 1 | 8" | | |
| 31 | 5 | Scunthorpe United | D | 1-1 | 1-0 | 2669 | Lightfoot | | 2 | | | 5 | 6 | 7 | 4 | 9 | 12 | 11 | | | 10 | 3 | 8* | | 1 | | | |
| 32 | 12 | SCARBOROUGH | W | 4-1 | 3-1 | 2882 | Thompson (3), Came | | 12 | | 14 | 5 | 6 | 7 | 4 | | 9 | 11 | 3 | | 10" | 2 | 8* | | 1 | | | |
| 33 | 15 | WALSALL | W | 2-1 | 1-0 | 3324 | Lightfoot, Thompson | | 4 | 14 | 10* | 5" | 6 | 7 | 8 | 12 | 9 | 11 | 3 | | | 2 | | | 1 | | | |
| 34 | 19 | Carlisle United | L | 0-1 | 0-0 | 4193 | | | 2 | | 14 | | 6 | 7 | 4 | 12 | 9 | 11 | 3 | | 10" | 5 | 8* | | 1 | | | |
| 35 | 26 | WIGAN ATHLETIC | W | 2-1 | 2-1 | 3542 | Pugh (pen), Preece | | 8 | 3 | | | 6 | 7 | 4 | | 9 | 11 | 2 | | | 5 | | | 1 | | 10 | |
| 36 | Apr 2 | PRESTON NORTH END | W | 3-2 | 1-2 | 5638 | Lancashire (2), Leonard | | 4 | 3 | | 5 | 6 | 7 | | 12 | 9 | 11 | | | | 2 | 8* | | 1 | | 10 | |
| 37 | 4 | Gillingham | D | 2-2 | 1-1 | 3165 | Pugh, Green (og) | | 8 | 3* | | 5 | 6 | 7 | 4 | 12 | 9" | 11 | | | 14 | 2 | | | 1 | | 10 | |
| 38 | 9 | COLCHESTER UNITED | W | 2-1 | 1-1 | 3394 | Lightfoot (2) | | 2 | 3 | | 5 | 6 | 7 | 8 | 12 | 9 | 11 | | | 4* | | | | 1 | | 10 | |
| 39 | 16 | Bury | D | 1-1 | 1-0 | 3142 | Lancashire | | | 3 | | 5 | 6 | 7 | 8" | 12 | 9 | 11 | 14 | | 4* | 2 | | | 1 | | 10 | |
| 40 | 23 | HEREFORD UNITED | W | 3-1 | 1-0 | 3845 | Pugh, Lancashire, Preece | | 4 | 3 | | 5 | 6 | 7 | 8 | | 9 | 11 | | | | 2 | | | 1 | | 10 | |
| 41 | 30 | Northampton Town | L | 0-1 | 0-1 | 6432 | | | 4 | 3" | | 5 | 6 | 7 | 8* | 9 | 10 | 11 | 12 | | | 2 | | | 1 | 14 | | |
| 42 | May 7 | CREWE ALEX. | L | 1-2 | 1-1 | 5550 | Lightfoot | | 4 | 3 | | 5 | 6 | 7 | 8 | 9 | 10 | 11* | 2 | | | | | | 1 | 12 | | |
| | | | | | | | Apps. | 7 | 38 | 35 | 9 | 30 | 42 | 40 | 37 | 26 | 28 | 36 | 30 | | 23 | 22 | 10 | 1 | 34 | 4 | 10 | |
| | | | | | | | Subs. | | 1 | 1 | 9 | | | 1 | | 9 | 4 | 1 | 4 | 9 | 2 | | 3 | | | 4 | 1 | |
| | | | | | | | Goals | | 2 | | 1 | 1 | 1 | 6 | 11 | 8 | 9 | 12 | | | 7 | | | | | 1 | 7 | |

Own goals 3

## F.A. CUP

| Rd | Date | Opposition | | FT | HT | Att. | Goalscorers | Stewart W. | Preece R. | Jakub J. | Bishop E. | Came M. | Greenall C. | Thompson D. | Lightfoot C. | Rimmer S. | Leonard M. | Pugh D. | Jenkins I. | Donnelly D. | Wheeler P. | Whelan S. | Barrow G. | McIlhargey S. | Felgate D. | Flitcroft D. | Lancashire G. | Bagnall J. |
|---|---|---|---|---|---|---|---|---|---|---|---|---|---|---|---|---|---|---|---|---|---|---|---|---|---|---|---|---|
| 1R | Nov 13 | Bradford City | D | 0-0 | 0-0 | 6204 | | | 2 | 3 | | | 6 | 7 | 8 | 9 | | 10 | 4 | | 11 | 5 | | | 1 | | | |
| 1Rr | 30 | BRADFORD CITY | W | 1-0 | 1-0 | 3707 | Lightfoot | | 2 | 3 | 12 | 5 | 6 | 7" | 8* | | 9 | 10 | 4 | | 11 | 14 | | | 1 | | | |
| 2R | Dec 4 | HULL CITY | W | 2-0 | 2-0 | 4333 | Preece, Leonard | | 2 | 3 | 12 | 5 | 6 | | 8 | 9 | 10 | 11* | 4 | | 7 | | | | 1 | | | |
| 3R | Jan 8 | Plymouth Argyle | L | 0-1 | 0-0 | 9170 | | | 2 | 3" | 14 | 5 | 6 | 7 | 8 | 12 | 10 | 11 | 4 | | 9* | | | | 1 | | | |

## LEAGUE (COCA COLA) CUP

| Rd | Date | Opposition | | FT | HT | Att. | Goalscorers | Stewart W. | Preece R. | Jakub J. | Bishop E. | Came M. | Greenall C. | Thompson D. | Lightfoot C. | Rimmer S. | Leonard M. | Pugh D. | Jenkins I. | Donnelly D. | Wheeler P. | Whelan S. | Barrow G. | McIlhargey S. | Felgate D. | Flitcroft D. | Lancashire G. | Bagnall J. |
|---|---|---|---|---|---|---|---|---|---|---|---|---|---|---|---|---|---|---|---|---|---|---|---|---|---|---|---|---|
| 1R1 | Aug 17 | Sunderland | L | 1-3 | 1-0 | 9484 | Rimmer | 1 | 2 | 3* | 4 | 5 | 6 | 7 | 8 | 9 | 10 | 11 | 12 | | | | | | | | | |
| 1R2 | 24 | SUNDERLAND | D | 0-0 | 0-0 | 2903 | | 1 | 2* | 3 | 4 | 5 | 6 | 7 | 8 | 9 | 10 | 11" | 12 | 14 | | | | | | | | |

## ASSOCIATE MEMBERS (AUTOGLASS) TROPHY

| Rd | Date | Opposition | | FT | HT | Att. | Goalscorers | Stewart W. | Preece R. | Jakub J. | Bishop E. | Came M. | Greenall C. | Thompson D. | Lightfoot C. | Rimmer S. | Leonard M. | Pugh D. | Jenkins I. | Donnelly D. | Wheeler P. | Whelan S. | Barrow G. | McIlhargey S. | Felgate D. | Flitcroft D. | Lancashire G. | Bagnall J. |
|---|---|---|---|---|---|---|---|---|---|---|---|---|---|---|---|---|---|---|---|---|---|---|---|---|---|---|---|---|
| GM | Sep 28 | Blackpool | W | 2-1 | 1-1 | 2633 | Rimmer, Lightfoot | | 2 | 3 | | 5 | 6 | 7 | 8 | 9 | 10 | | 4 | | 11 | | | | | | | 1 |
| GM | Oct 19 | CREWE ALEX. | D | 2-2 | 1-1 | 2370 | Greenall, Came | | 2 | 3 | | 5 | 6 | 7 | 8 | 9 | | 10 | 4 | | 11 | | | | 1 | | | |
| 1R | Dec 7 | ROTHERHAM | W | 1-0 | 1-0 | 1553 | Lightfoot | | 2 | 3 | 7 | 5 | 6 | | 8* | 9 | 10 | | 4 | | 11 | 12 | | | 1 | | | |
| NQF | Jan 11 | Lincoln City | L | 0-1 | 0-1 | 1733 | | | 2 | 3 | 14 | 5" | 6 | 7 | 8 | 12 | 10 | 11* | 4 | | 9* | | | | 1 | | | |

## FRIENDLIES

| | Date | Opposition | | FT | HT | Att. | Goalscorers |
|---|---|---|---|---|---|---|---|
| 1 | Jul 24 | Chorley | D | 1-1 | | | Leonard |
| 2 | 29 | Flint Town United | W | 2-1 | 2-0 | | Rimmer, Pugh |
| 3 | 31 | Witton Albion | D | 0-0 | 0-0 | 560 | |
| 4 | Aug 4 | NOTTS COUNTY | W | 1-0 | 1-0 | 924 | Leonard |

**1993/94 Season:**

(Back) Berry, Greenall, Pugh, Stewart, Leonard, Moss, Whelan.
Standing - Allan (Secretary), Donnelly, Thompson, Bishop, Wheeler, Jenkins, Rimmer, Limbert, Hinnigan (Physio).
Sitting - Jakub, Lightfoot, Crofts (Chairman), Barrow (Manager), Came, Preece.

**1994/95 Season:**

(Back) Page, Burnham, Alsford, Felgate, Whelan, Newland, Lightfoot, Milner, Chambers.
(Front) Shelton, Preece, Bishop, Ratcliffe, Pejic (Manager), Flitcroft, Jenkins, Rimmer.

# SEASON 1994-95

## FOOTBALL (ENDSLEIGH) LEAGUE DIV. 2

| | Date | Opposition | | FT | HT | Att. | Goalscorers | Felgate D. | Jenkins I. | Burnham J. | Ratcliffe K. | Alsford J. | Whelan S. | Flitcroft D. | Rimmer S. | Preece R. | Milner A. | Chambers L. | Page D. | Lightfoot C. | Bishop E. | Newland R. | Anthrobus S. | Hackett G. | Priest C. | Shelton G. | Jackson P. | Murphy J. | Richardson N. | Aunger G. | Tolson N. | Gardiner M. |
|---|---|---|---|---|---|---|---|---|---|---|---|---|---|---|---|---|---|---|---|---|---|---|---|---|---|---|---|---|---|---|---|---|
| 1 | Aug 13 | BRADFORD CITY | L | 1-4 | 0-1 | 4459 | Milner | 1 | 2 | 3 | 4 | 5* | 6 | 7 | 8 | 9" | 10 | 11 | 12 | 14 | | | | | | | | | | | | |
| 2 | 20 | Birmingham City | L | 0-1 | 0-1 | 12188 | | 1 | 2 | 3 | 4 | 9 | 5 | 14 | 10* | 6 | 7" | 12 | 11 | | 8 | | | | | | | | | | | |
| 3 | 27 | HUDDERSFIELD TOWN | L | 1-2 | 0-1 | 2895 | Bishop | | 2 | 3 | 4 | 5* | 11 | 7 | | 6 | 9 | 12 | 8" | | 14 | 1 | 10 | | | | | | | | | |
| 4 | 30 | Cambridge United | L | 1-2 | 0-0 | 2520 | Page | | 2 | 3 | 4" | 8 | 5 | 7 | | 6 | 9* | 12 | 11 | 14 | | 1 | 10 | | | | | | | | | |
| 5 | Sep 3 | Hull City | L | 0-2 | 0-1 | 3615 | | 1+ | 2 | 3 | | 4 | 5 | | | 6 | | 12 | 11 | 9* | 8 | 15 | 10 | 7 | | | | | | | | |
| 6 | 10 | BRIGHTON & HOVE A. | L | 1-2 | 0-1 | 2063 | Page | | 2 | 3 | | 4 | 5 | | | | | | 11 | 9 | 8 | 1 | 10 | 7 | 6 | | | | | | | |
| 7 | 13 | CARDIFF CITY | L | 0-2 | 0-0 | 1671 | | | 2 | 3 | | 4* | 5 | 8 | | | 12 | 14 | 11 | 9 | | 1 | 10 | 7" | 6 | | | | | | | |
| 8 | 17 | AFC Bournemouth | D | 1-1 | 1-0 | 3025 | Lightfoot | | 2 | 3 | | 4 | 5 | | | | | 14 | 11 | 9 | | 1 | 10" | 7 | 8 | 6 | | | | | | |
| 9 | 24 | Plymouth Argyle | L | 0-1 | 0-1 | 5329 | | | 2 | 3 | | 4 | 5" | 12 | | 14 | | 10 | 7 | 9 | | 1 | 11 | | 8* | 6 | | | | | | |
| 10 | Oct 1 | OXFORD UNITED | W | 2-0 | 1-0 | 2324 | Hackett, Priest | | 2 | | 3 | 4 | | 12 | | 7 | | | 10 | 9 | | 1 | | 11 | 8 | 6* | 5 | | | | | |
| 11 | 8 | SWANSEA CITY | D | 2-2 | 1-1 | 2186 | Page (pen), Shelton | 1 | 2 | | 3 | 4 | | 12 | | 7 | 14 | | 10 | 9" | | | | 11 | 8* | 6 | 5 | | | | | |
| 12 | 15 | Leyton Orient | L | 0-2 | 0-1 | 3309 | | | 2 | | 3 | | | 9 | | 7 | 14 | | 10 | 4 | | 1 | | 11 | 8" | 6 | 5 | | | | | |
| 13 | 22 | York City | L | 0-2 | 0-1 | 2820 | | 1 | 2 | | 3 | | | 12 | | 9 | 14 | 7" | 10 | 4 | | | | 11 | 8* | 6 | 5 | | | | | |
| 14 | 30 | WREXHAM | D | 1-1 | 1-0 | 4974 | Hackett | 1 | 2 | | 3 | 4 | | 12 | | 9* | | 7" | 10 | | | | | 11 | 8 | 6 | 5 | 14 | | | | |
| 15 | Nov 2 | STOCKPORT COUNTY | W | 1-0 | 0-0 | 2400 | Shelton | 1 | 2 | | 3 | 4 | | 12 | | 9 | | 7" | 10 | | | | | 11 | 8 | 6 | 5* | 14 | | | | |
| 16 | 5 | Peterborough United | L | 0-2 | 0-1 | 4610 | | 1 | 2 | | 3 | 4 | | 12 | | 9 | | 7" | 10* | | | | | 11 | 8 | 6 | 5 | 14 | | | | |
| 17 | 19 | BLACKPOOL | W | 2-0 | 1-0 | 3114 | Milner, Page | 1 | 2 | | 3 | 4 | | 8 | 14 | 9 | 7" | | 10 | | | | | 11 | | 6 | 5 | | | | | |
| 18 | 26 | Rotherham United | L | 0-2 | 0-0 | 2947 | | 1 | 2 | | 3 | 4 | | 8 | 12 | 9 | 7 | | 10" | | | | | 11 | | 6* | 5 | 14 | | | | |
| 19 | Dec 10 | BIRMINGHAM CITY | L | 0-4 | 0-2 | 3946 | | 1 | 2 | 3 | | 4 | | 8 | | 9 | | 14 | 10* | 7 | | | | 11" | | 6 | 5 | 12 | | | | |
| 20 | 17 | Bradford City | D | 1-1 | 0-1 | 4555 | Milner | 1 | | | 3 | 4 | | | | 2 | 7 | | 10" | 9 | | | | 11 | | 6 | 5 | | 8 | 14 | | |
| 21 | 26 | Crewe Alex. | L | 1-2 | 1-0 | 5428 | Page (pen) | 1 | | | 3 | 4 | | | | 2 | 7 | | 10" | 9 | | | | 11 | | 6 | 5 | | 8 | 14 | | |
| 22 | 27 | BRENTFORD | L | 1-4 | 1-3 | 2266 | Richardson | 1 | | | 3 | 4 | | | | 2 | 7* | | 12 | 9 | | | | 11 | | 6 | 5 | | 8 | 10 | | |
| 23 | 31 | Bristol Rovers | L | 0-3 | 0-2 | 5629 | | 1 | | | 3 | 4 | | | | 2 | 7 | | 10" | 9 | 11 | | | 12 | | 6* | 5 | | 8 | 14 | | |
| 24 | Jan 7 | YORK CITY | L | 0-4 | 0-0 | 1844 | | 1 | 2 | | 3" | 4 | | | | 7 | 11 | | | 9 | 14 | | | | | 6* | 5 | | 8 | 12 | 10 | |
| 25 | 14 | Shrewsbury Town | L | 0-1 | 0-0 | 3879 | | 1 | 3 | | | 2 | | 7 | | 4 | 9 | | 14 | 6 | 12 | | | 11* | | | 5 | | 8 | | 10" | |
| 26 | 28 | PETERBOROUGH UNITED | D | 1-1 | 0-0 | 1501 | Hackett | 1 | 3 | | | 2 | | 7 | 14 | 4 | 9 | | | 6 | 8 | | | 11" | | | 5 | | | | 10 | |
| 27 | 31 | WYCOMBE WANDERERS | L | 0-2 | 0-2 | 1524 | | 1 | 3* | | | 2 | | 7 | 10 | 4 | 9" | | | 6 | 8 | | | 11 | | 12 | 5 | | | | 14 | |
| 28 | Feb 4 | ROTHERHAM UNITED | D | 4-4 | 3-2 | 1794 | Hackett, Rimmer, Milner, Preece | 1 | 3 | | | 2 | | | 10" | 4 | 9 | | 14 | 6 | 8 | | | 11 | | 7 | 5 | | | | | |
| 29 | 11 | Stockport County | D | 2-2 | 2-0 | 4405 | Preece, Dinning (og) | 1 | 2 | | 3 | 5 | | | 10 | 4 | 9* | | 12 | 6 | 8 | | | 11" | 14 | 7 | | | | | | |
| 30 | 14 | Wrexham | D | 2-2 | 1-2 | 5698 | Bishop (pen), Milner | 1 | 3 | 14 | | 5 | | 7" | 10* | 2 | 9 | | 12 | 6 | 11 | | | | 8 | 4 | | | | | | |
| 31 | 18 | SHREWSBURY TOWN | L | 1-3 | 0-1 | 2720 | Bishop (pen) | 1 | 3 | | | 2 | | 7 | 10 | 4 | 9 | | | 6 | 11 | | | | 8 | | 5 | | | | | |
| 32 | 21 | Blackpool | L | 1-3 | 1-2 | 4649 | Milner | 1 | 2 | | 3 | 5" | | 14 | 10 | 7 | 9 | | | 4 | 8 | | | | 11 | | 6 | | | | | |
| 33 | 25 | Oxford United | L | 0-1 | 0-0 | 4930 | | 1 | 2 | 14 | 3 | | 6 | 7 | 10" | 4 | 9 | | | | | | | 11 | 8* | 12 | 5 | | | | | |
| 34 | Mar 4 | PLYMOUTH ARGYLE | W | 1-0 | 1-0 | 1823 | Rimmer | 1 | 2 | | 3 | | 5 | 14 | 10 | 4 | | | 9 | | | | | 11" | 7* | 8 | 6 | | | | | 12 |
| 35 | 11 | Huddersfield Town | L | 1-5 | 1-3 | 9606 | Booth (og) | 1 | | 3 | 6 | 2 | 5 | | 10 | 4 | 9 | | 12 | | | | | 14 | 7* | 8 | | | | | | 11" |
| 36 | 18 | CAMBRIDGE UNITED | L | 1-3 | 0-3 | 1720 | Milner | 15 | | 3 | | 2 | 6 | 14 | 10 | 4 | 9 | | | | | 1+ | | 11" | 12 | 7 | 5 | | | | | 8* |
| 37 | 22 | Brighton & Hove A. | L | 0-1 | 0-1 | 5979 | | 1 | 2 | 3 | | 14 | 6 | | 10 | 4 | 9 | | | | | | | 11" | 7 | 8 | 5 | | | | | |
| 38 | 25 | AFC BOURNEMOUTH | D | 1-1 | 0-0 | 1618 | Jackson | 1 | 2 | 3 | | | 6 | | 10 | 4 | 9 | | | | | | | 11 | 7 | 8 | 5 | | | | | |
| 39 | 28 | HULL CITY | L | 1-2 | 0-0 | 1191 | Lightfoot | 1 | 2 | 3* | | | 6 | 12 | 10 | 4 | 9 | | | 8 | | | | 11 | 7 | | 5 | | | | | |
| 40 | Apr 1 | Cardiff City | L | 1-2 | 0-1 | 4405 | Hackett | 1 | 2 | 3" | | | 6 | 8 | 10 | 4 | 9 | | 14 | 5 | | | | 11 | 7 | | | | | | | |
| 41 | 8 | BRISTOL ROVERS | D | 0-0 | 0-0 | 2241 | | 1 | 2 | 3 | | | 6 | | 10 | 4 | 9 | | | | | | | 11 | 7 | 8 | 5 | | | | | |
| 42 | 15 | Brentford | D | 1-1 | 1-0 | 8020 | Lightfoot | 1 | 2 | 3 | | 12 | 6 | 7 | 10 | 4 | 9 | | | 5* | 11 | | | | | 8 | | | | | | |
| 43 | 17 | CREWE ALEX. | L | 0-1 | 0-0 | 3054 | | 1 | 2 | 3 | | | 6 | 7 | 10 | 4 | 9 | | | | 11 | | | 14 | | 8" | 5 | | | | | |
| 44 | 22 | Wycombe Wanderers | L | 1-3 | 1-2 | 5284 | Whelan | 1 | 2* | 3 | | 12 | 6 | 7 | 10 | 4 | 9" | | | | 11 | | | 14 | | 8 | 5 | | | | | |
| 45 | 29 | LEYTON ORIENT | W | 1-0 | 0-0 | 1596 | Bishop | 1 | 2 | 3 | | | 6 | 7 | 10 | 4 | 9 | | | | 11 | | | | | 8 | 5 | | | | | |
| 46 | May 6 | Swansea City | W | 1-0 | 1-0 | 2065 | Milner | 1 | 2 | 3 | | | 6 | 7" | 10 | 4 | 9 | | | | 11 | | | 14 | | 8 | 5 | | | | | |
| | | | | | | | Apps. | 37 | 40 | 22 | 23 | 32 | 23 | 20 | 22 | 42 | 32 | 6 | 22 | 26 | 16 | 9 | 7 | 30 | 22 | 31 | 32 | | 6 | 1 | 3 | 2 |
| | | | | | | | Subs. | 1 | | 2 | | 3 | | 12 | 3 | 1 | 4 | 7 | 8 | 2 | 3 | 1 | | 5 | 2 | 2 | | 5 | | 4 | 1 | 1 |
| | | | | | | | Goals | | | | | | 1 | | 2 | 2 | 8 | | 5 | 3 | 4 | | | 5 | 1 | 2 | 1 | | 1 | | | |

Own goals 2

## F.A. CUP

| | Date | Opposition | | FT | HT | Att. | Goalscorers | Felgate D. | Jenkins I. | Burnham J. | Ratcliffe K. | Alsford J. | Whelan S. | Flitcroft D. | Rimmer S. | Preece R. | Milner A. | Chambers L. | Page D. | Lightfoot C. | Bishop E. | Newland R. | Anthrobus S. | Hackett G. | Priest C. | Shelton G. | Jackson P. | Murphy J. | Richardson N. | Aunger G. | Tolson N. | Gardiner M. |
|---|---|---|---|---|---|---|---|---|---|---|---|---|---|---|---|---|---|---|---|---|---|---|---|---|---|---|---|---|---|---|---|---|
| 1R | Nov 12 | WITTON ALBION | W | 2-0 | 2-0 | 2666 | Page, Alsford | 1 | 2 | 3 | 5 | 4 | | 8 | 14 | 9 | 7* | | 10 | | | | | 11 | | 6" | | 12 | | | | |
| 2R | Dec 4 | BURNLEY | L | 1-2 | 0-0 | 4231 | Milner | 1 | 2 | | | 4 | | 7 | | 9 | 14 | | 10 | 3 | 8" | | | 11 | | 6 | 5 | | | | | |

## LEAGUE (COCA COLA) CUP

| | Date | Opposition | | FT | HT | Att. | Goalscorers | Felgate D. | Jenkins I. | Burnham J. | Ratcliffe K. | Alsford J. | Whelan S. | Flitcroft D. | Rimmer S. | Preece R. | Milner A. | Chambers L. | Page D. | Lightfoot C. | Bishop E. | Newland R. | Anthrobus S. | Hackett G. | Priest C. | Shelton G. | Jackson P. | Murphy J. | Richardson N. | Aunger G. | Tolson N. | Gardiner M. |
|---|---|---|---|---|---|---|---|---|---|---|---|---|---|---|---|---|---|---|---|---|---|---|---|---|---|---|---|---|---|---|---|---|
| 1R1 | Aug 16 | Lincoln City | L | 0-2 | 0-1 | 2531 | | 1 | 2 | 3 | 4 | | 5 | 7 | 10 | 6 | 9 | | 11 | | 8 | | | | | | | | | | | |
| 1R2 | 23 | LINCOLN CITY | L | 2-3 | 0-3 | 1568 | Whelan, Chambers | 1 | 2 | 3 | 4 | 9 | 5 | | 10* | 6 | 12 | 7 | 11 | | 8 | | | | | | | | | | | |

## ASSOCIATE MEMBERS (AUTO WINDSCREENS) SHIELD

| | Date | Opposition | | FT | HT | Att. | Goalscorers | Felgate D. | Jenkins I. | Burnham J. | Ratcliffe K. | Alsford J. | Whelan S. | Flitcroft D. | Rimmer S. | Preece R. | Milner A. | Chambers L. | Page D. | Lightfoot C. | Bishop E. | Newland R. | Anthrobus S. | Hackett G. | Priest C. | Shelton G. | Jackson P. | Murphy J. | Richardson N. | Aunger G. | Tolson N. | Gardiner M. |
|---|---|---|---|---|---|---|---|---|---|---|---|---|---|---|---|---|---|---|---|---|---|---|---|---|---|---|---|---|---|---|---|---|
| 1R | Sep 27 | Preston North End | D | 1-1 | 1-1 | 3242 | Page | | 2 | 3" | 14 | 4 | | 11 | | 5 | | 10* | 7 | 9 | | 1 | | | 8 | 6 | | 12 | | | | |
| 1R | Oct 18 | BURY | W | 3-1 | 2-0 | 841 | Shelton (2), Page | 1 | 2 | 3 | 4 | | | | | 9 | | 7 | 10 | 5 | | | | 11 | 8 | 6 | | | | | | |
| 2R | Nov 29 | CREWE ALEX. | L | 0-6 | 0-3 | 1890 | | 1 | 2 | | 3 | 4 | | 8 | 12 | 6 | 7 | | 10 | | 14 | | | 11* | | | 5 | 9" | | | | |

## FRIENDLIES

| | Date | Opposition | | FT | HT | Att. | Goalscorers |
|---|---|---|---|---|---|---|---|
| 1 | Jul 19 | PORT VALE | L | 1-3 | 0-1 | 1173 | Bishop |
| 2 | 24 | Tranmere Rovers * | L | 0-1 | 0-0 | 1017 | |
| 3 | 25 | Isle of Man X1 * | W | 5-1 | 0-1 | | Bishop (3), Page, Rimmer |
| 4 | 29 | Carlisle United * | W | 1-0 | 1-0 | | Rimmer |
| 5 | Aug 6 | PRESTON NORTH END | L | 0-1 | 0-1 | 1010 | |
| 6 | 8 | WIMBLEDON | L | 0-2 | 0-2 | 2057 | |

* Isle of Man International Football Festival

# SEASON 1995-96

## FOOTBALL (ENDSLEIGH) LEAGUE DIV. 3

| | Date | Opposition | | FT | HT | Att. | Goalscorers | Stewart W. | Jenkins I. | Burnham J. | Preece R. | Jackson P. | Whelan S. | Fisher N. | Priest C. | Regis C. | Milner A. | Bishop E. | Flitcroft D. | Murphy J. | Shelton G. | Alsford J. | Rimmer S. | Chambers L. | Noteman K. | Richardson N. | Rogers D. | Kenworthy J. | Brown G. | Davidson R. | Ryan D. | Brien A. | Cutler N. | Brenchley S. |
|---|---|---|---|---|---|---|---|---|---|---|---|---|---|---|---|---|---|---|---|---|---|---|---|---|---|---|---|---|---|---|---|---|---|---|
| 1 | Aug 12 | HARTLEPOOL UNITED | W | 2-0 | 1-0 | 2286 | Bishop, Priest |1|2|3|4'|5|6|7|8|9"|10|11|13|14|||||||||||||||
| 2 | 19 | Bury | D | 1-1 | 1-1 | 3211 | Bishop |1||3|||6|7|8|9|10*|11|2||4|5|12||||||||||||
| 3 | 26 | PLYMOUTH ARGYLE | W | 3-1 | 1-0 | 2660 | Bishop (2), Regis |1|4|3||5||7|8|9"|10*|11|2|14||6|12||||||||||||
| 4 | 29 | Wigan Athletic | L | 1-2 | 1-1 | 2555 | Rimmer |1|4|3||5|12|7|8|9|||2*||11'|6|10|13|||||||||||
| 5 | Sep 2 | HEREFORD UNITED | W | 2-1 | 2-0 | 3385 | Regis, Noteman |1|2|3||5|6*|4|8|9|14||7"|||12|10||11||||||||||
| 6 | 9 | Colchester United | W | 2-1 | 0-0 | 3422 | Priest, Regis |1|2"|3||5|6|4|8|9*|10'||13|||14|12||11|7|||||||||
| 7 | 12 | Scunthorpe United | W | 2-0 | 2-0 | 1875 | Richardson, Priest (pen) |1|2|3||5|6|4|8|9'|10*||11|13|||12|||7|||||||||
| 8 | 16 | LINCOLN CITY | W | 5-1 | 3-1 | 3049 | Burnham,Fisher,Milner,Priest(pen),Murphy |1|2|3||5|6|4|8|9'|10*||11|13|||12|||7|||||||||
| 9 | 23 | GILLINGHAM | D | 1-1 | 0-0 | 3886 | Flitcroft |1||3||5||4|8||10"|11'|7|14||2|9|||6|13||||||||
| 10 | 30 | Preston North End | L | 0-2 | 0-0 | 8544 | |1||3||5||2|8|9||7||14||6|10||11"|4|||||||||
| 11 | Oct 7 | DONCASTER ROVERS | L | 0-3 | 0-0 | 2374 | |1||3||5|6|4||9|14|11|||8*|2|10"||12|7|||||||||
| 12 | 14 | Leyton Orient | W | 2-0 | 2-0 | 6036 | Regis, Noteman |1||3||5|6|4||9'|10*|13|||8|2|12||11|7|||||||||
| 13 | 21 | FULHAM | D | 1-1 | 1-0 | 2752 | Bishop |1||3||5|6|4||9|10*|11|||8|2|12|||7|||||||||
| 14 | 28 | Scarborough | D | 0-0 | 0-0 | 1847 | |1||3||5|2|4|13|9"|10||||8'|6||14|11|7|||||||||
| 15 | 31 | Rochdale | W | 3-1 | 1-0 | 3018 | Regis, Noteman, Shelton |1||3||5|2||4|9"|10|12|||8*|6||14|11|7|||||||||
| 16 | Nov 4 | TORQUAY UNITED | W | 4-1 | 2-0 | 2535 | Regis, Milner, Whelan, Noteman (pen) |1|13|3||5'|2||4|9"|10||||8|6|12|14|11|7*|||||||||
| 17 | 18 | Mansfield Town | W | 4-3 | 2-1 | 2415 | Rimmer (3), Noteman |1||3||5|2|8|4|9||||||6|10||11|7|||||||||
| 18 | 25 | DARLINGTON | W | 4-1 | 1-0 | 2652 | Rimmer (2), Priest (2, 1 pen) |1||3||5|2|8|4|9*||||||6|10|12|11|7|||||||||
| 19 | Dec 16 | PRESTON NORTH END | D | 1-1 | 1-1 | 5004 | Richardson |1||3||5|14|2||9|12||||4"|6|10||11|7||8*|||||||
| 20 | 23 | BARNET | L | 0-2 | 0-1 | 3081 | |1||3"||5|2|4|||9|||12||6'|10||11|8|13|7*|14||||||
| 21 | 26 | Cardiff City | D | 0-0 | 0-0 | 6046 | |1||3||5|2|8|||9||||||10||11||4|7|6||||||
| 22 | 30 | Exeter City | W | 2-1 | 2-0 | 3324 | Rimmer, Noteman |1||3||5|6|2|8||9||||||10||11||4"|7|14||||||
| 23 | Jan 6 | Cambridge United | D | 1-1 | 1-0 | 2643 | Rimmer |1||3|||2|4|7|9|8|||||6|10||11*|5|12||||||||
| 24 | 9 | Gillingham | L | 1-3 | 0-0 | 9191 | Kenworthy |1||3|||5|2|8|9*|12|||||6|10||11|7|4"|14|||||||
| 25 | 13 | BURY | D | 1-1 | 1-0 | 3283 | Regis |1||3|||6|2|8|9|13|||||5|10'||11|7*|4|12|||||||
| 26 | 20 | Hartlepool United | L | 1-2 | 1-1 | 1864 | Rimmer |1||3|||5|2|8|9|12|||||6|10||11||4|7*|||||||
| 27 | Feb 3 | Plymouth Argyle | L | 2-4 | 0-3 | 5114 | Priest, Richardson |1||3"||5|6|7|8|9*|13||||4'||10||11|12|14|||2|||||
| 28 | 17 | SCUNTHORPE UNITED | W | 3-0 | 1-0 | 2401 | Noteman, Fisher, Jackson |1||||5|6|4|8|9*|10||||||12||11|7|3|||2|||||
| 29 | 20 | Hereford United | L | 0-1 | 0-0 | 1827 | |1||||5|6|4|8|9|10||||||||11|7|3|||2|||||
| 30 | 24 | Lincoln City | D | 0-0 | 0-0 | 2533 | |1||11||5|6|4|8||10||||||9|||7|3|||2|||||
| 31 | 27 | COLCHESTER UNITED | D | 1-1 | 0-0 | 2001 | Richardson |1||11*||5|6|4|8||10|||13|||9'||12|7|3|||2|||||
| 32 | Mar 2 | CARDIFF CITY | W | 4-0 | 2-0 | 2308 | Davidson, Priest, Rogers (pen), Rimmer |1||||5|6|4*|8||10|||12|||9||11|7|3|||2|||||
| 33 | 9 | Barnet | D | 1-1 | 0-0 | 2195 | Priest |1||11||5*||4|8||10|||||6|9||12|7|3|||2|||||
| 34 | 16 | EXETER CITY | D | 2-2 | 1-1 | 2043 | Priest, Blake (og) |1||6||||4|8|9*|10|||||5|11|12||7|3|||2|||||
| 35 | 19 | WIGAN ATHLETIC | D | 0-0 | 0-0 | 2825 | |1||6|||5|4|8|9*|10||||||12|||7|3|||2|11||||
| 36 | 23 | Northampton Town | L | 0-1 | 0-1 | 4810 | |1||11|||6|4|8||10||||13||9||12|7|3*|||2'||5|||
| 37 | 26 | CAMBRIDGE UNITED | D | 1-1 | 0-1 | 1623 | Noteman |1||3|||6|4|8|9|10||||||||11|7||||2||5|||
| 38 | 30 | Doncaster Rovers | W | 2-1 | 0-1 | 1548 | Whelan, Murphy |1||3||5|6|13|8|9"|10|||14|||12||11*|7'||||2||4|||
| 39 | Apr 2 | LEYTON ORIENT | D | 1-1 | 1-1 | 2097 | Rimmer |1||3||5|12|6|8||7*|||9"|||10||11'||14|||2|13|4|||
| 40 | 6 | SCARBOROUGH | W | 5-0 | 3-0 | 2485 | Milner (2), Noteman, Priest, Rimmer |1||3||5'|13|4|8||10|||12|||9*||11|7||||2"|14|6|||
| 41 | 8 | Fulham | L | 0-2 | 0-2 | 3777 | |1||3"||5|11*|4|8||10'|||13|||9||12|7|14|||2||6|||
| 42 | 13 | ROCHDALE | L | 1-2 | 1-1 | 2158 | Ryan (pen) |1|3|11*||5||4|||10|||12|||9|||7||||2|8|6|||
| 43 | 20 | Torquay United | D | 1-1 | 0-0 | 2549 | Priest ||3|||5||4|8||10|||12|||9||11*|7||||2||6|1||
| 44 | 23 | NORTHAMPTON TOWN | W | 1-0 | 0-0 | 1674 | Murphy |1|3|||5|6|4|8||10|||12|||9||11*|7||||2|||||
| 45 | 27 | Darlington | L | 1-3 | 0-0 | 4510 | Rimmer |1|2|3*|||6|4|8||10|||12||5|9|11||7||||||||||
| 46 | May 4 | MANSFIELD TOWN | W | 2-1 | 0-0 | 2935 | Chambers, Priest |1|3|||5|6|4|8||10|||14|||9|11"|12|7*||||2|||||
| | | | | | | | Apps. |45|12|40|1|36|35|43|38|29|35|7|7|1|10|22|30|2|27|36|14|5|1|19|2|8|1||
| | | | | | | | Subs. ||1||||4|1|1||7|2|2|17|1|2|11|6|6|1|6|2|2||2||||
| | | | | | | | Goals |||1||1|2|2|13|7|4|5|1|3|1||13|1|9|4|1|1||1|1||||

Own goals 1

## F.A. CUP

| | Date | Opposition | | FT | HT | Att. | Goalscorers | Stewart W. | Jenkins I. | Burnham J. | Preece R. | Jackson P. | Whelan S. | Fisher N. | Priest C. | Regis C. | Milner A. | Bishop E. | Flitcroft D. | Murphy J. | Shelton G. | Alsford J. | Rimmer S. | Chambers L. | Noteman K. | Richardson N. | Rogers D. | Kenworthy J. | Brown G. | Davidson R. | Ryan D. | Brien A. | Cutler N. | Brenchley S. |
|---|---|---|---|---|---|---|---|---|---|---|---|---|---|---|---|---|---|---|---|---|---|---|---|---|---|---|---|---|---|---|---|---|---|---|
| 1R | Nov 11 | Blackpool | L | 1-2 | 0-0 | 5004 | Milner |1|14|3"||5|2|8|4|9|10|||||6|||11|7|||||||||

## LEAGUE (COCA COLA) CUP

| | Date | Opposition | | FT | HT | Att. | Goalscorers | Stewart W. | Jenkins I. | Burnham J. | Preece R. | Jackson P. | Whelan S. | Fisher N. | Priest C. | Regis C. | Milner A. | Bishop E. | Flitcroft D. | Murphy J. | Shelton G. | Alsford J. | Rimmer S. | Chambers L. | Noteman K. | Richardson N. | Rogers D. | Kenworthy J. | Brown G. | Davidson R. | Ryan D. | Brien A. | Cutler N. | Brenchley S. |
|---|---|---|---|---|---|---|---|---|---|---|---|---|---|---|---|---|---|---|---|---|---|---|---|---|---|---|---|---|---|---|---|---|---|---|
| 1R1 | Aug 15 | WIGAN ATHLETIC | W | 4-1 | 2-0 | 2626 | Whelan, Bishop, Milner, Murphy |1||3|||6|7|8|9"|10|11*|2|14|4'|5|12|||||||||||13|
| 1R2 | 22 | Wigan Athletic | W | 3-1 | 2-0 | 2061 | Milner (2), Bishop |1|4'|3||5||7|8|9"|10|11|2*|14||6|12||||13||||||||
| 2R1 | Sep 20 | Tottenham Hotspur | L | 0-4 | 0-3 | 17645 | |1|2"|3||5|6|4|8|||11*|7|9|12|14|10||||||||||||
| 2R2 | Oct 4 | TOTTENHAM HOTSPUR | L | 1-3 | 1-2 | 5372 | Bishop |1||3||5|6|4||9'||11"|||8|2|10|7*|||13||||||||

Other players - Quinn P. 2R2/12, Barlow B. 2R2/14

## ASSOCIATE MEMBERS (AUTO WINDSCREENS) SHIELD

| | Date | Opposition | | FT | HT | Att. | Goalscorers | Stewart W. | Jenkins I. | Burnham J. | Preece R. | Jackson P. | Whelan S. | Fisher N. | Priest C. | Regis C. | Milner A. | Bishop E. | Flitcroft D. | Murphy J. | Shelton G. | Alsford J. | Rimmer S. | Chambers L. | Noteman K. | Richardson N. | Rogers D. | Kenworthy J. | Brown G. | Davidson R. | Ryan D. | Brien A. | Cutler N. | Brenchley S. |
|---|---|---|---|---|---|---|---|---|---|---|---|---|---|---|---|---|---|---|---|---|---|---|---|---|---|---|---|---|---|---|---|---|---|---|
| PR | Sep 26 | ROTHERHAM UNITED | L | 0-1 | 0-0 | 774 | |||3||5||2|8|||11|7|9"||6|10||14|4|||||||||
| PR | Nov 7 | Burnley | D | 1-1 | 0-1 | 3225 | Richardson |1|2|3|||5||4'||10*|||||6|9"|12|11|7|8||13||||||

Other players - Newland R. PR1/1, Jones J. PR2/14

## FRIENDLIES

| | Date | Opposition | | FT | HT | Att. | Goalscorers |
|---|---|---|---|---|---|---|---|
| 1 | Jul 15 | Bangor City | W | 1-0 | 0-0 | 500 | Rutter (og) |
| 2 | 19 | Newcastle Town | W | 1-0 | 1-0 | 250 | Ratcliffe |
| 3 | 22 | Caldicot Town | W | 4-1 | 1-1 | | Priest (2), Rimmer (2) |
| 4 | 24 | Cheltenham Town | W | 2-0 | 2-0 | | Milner, Bishop |
| 5 | 26 | Merthyr Tydfil | W | 1-0 | 0-0 | | Flitcroft |
| 6 | 28 | STOKE CITY | W | 1-0 | 0-0 | 1134 | Priest |
| 7 | Aug 4 | Altrincham | L | 0-2 | 0-1 | | |

**1995/96 Season:**

(Back_Cannon, Barlow, Brenchley, Murphy, Whelan, Alsford, Rogers, Milner, Quinn, Briggs
(Standing) Walker (Physio), Burnham, Bishop, Newland, Chambers, Stewart, Rimmer, Regis, Mann (Youth Coach), Kerr (Community Officer)
(Sitting) Cattell, Flitcroft, Jenkins, Preece, Ratcliffe (Manager), Shelton (Player\Coach), Jackson, Priest, Fisher, Dobson
(Front) Hussaney, Warrington, Giles, Wood, Smith, Brown, Jones, Clinch

**1996/97 Season:**

(Back) Noteman, Milner, Knowles, Richardson, Sinclair, Preece, Rogers.
(Middle) Fogg (Youth Team Manager), Brown, Alsford, Flitcroft, Woods, Whelan, Murphy, Walker (Physio).
(Front) Jenkins, Rimmer, Jackson, Shelton (Assistant Manager), Ratcliffe (Manager), Priest, Davidson, Fisher

# *SEASON 1996-97*

## FOOTBALL (NATIONWIDE) LEAGUE DIV. 3

| | Date | Opposition | | FT | HT | Att. | Goalscorers |
|---|---|---|---|---|---|---|---|
| 1 | Aug 17 | Brighton & Hove A. | L | 1-2 | 1-0 | 5263 | Murphy |
| 2 | 24 | CAMBRIDGE UNITED | D | 1-1 | 1-1 | 1923 | Rimmer |
| 3 | 27 | SWANSEA CITY | W | 2-0 | 1-0 | 1946 | Shelton, Milner |
| 4 | 31 | Wigan Athletic | L | 2-4 | 1-1 | 3854 | Milner, Noteman |
| 5 | Sep 7 | LINCOLN CITY | W | 4-1 | 2-1 | 1802 | Rimmer (2), Davidson, Noteman (pen) |
| 6 | 10 | Rochdale | W | 1-0 | 0-0 | 1774 | Shelton |
| 7 | 14 | Torquay United | D | 0-0 | 0-0 | 2341 | |
| 8 | 21 | SCUNTHORPE UNITED | W | 1-0 | 0-0 | 1901 | Fisher |
| 9 | 28 | Hartlepool United | L | 0-2 | 0-2 | 2042 | |
| 10 | Oct 1 | NORTHAMPTON TOWN | W | 2-1 | 0-0 | 1791 | Flitcroft, Noteman |
| 11 | 12 | Scarborough | D | 0-0 | 0-0 | 2352 | |
| 12 | 15 | Leyton Orient | D | 0-0 | 0-0 | 3115 | |
| 13 | 19 | EXETER CITY | W | 2-1 | 1-0 | 1941 | Helliwell, Milner |
| 14 | 26 | HEREFORD UNITED | L | 1-3 | 1-2 | 2301 | Noteman |
| 15 | 29 | Carlisle United | L | 1-3 | 1-0 | 4187 | Noteman |
| 16 | Nov 2 | Doncaster Rovers | W | 1-0 | 0-0 | 1534 | Jackson |
| 17 | 9 | HULL CITY | D | 0-0 | 0-0 | 2085 | |
| 18 | 22 | COLCHESTER UNITED | L | 1-2 | 0-2 | 2028 | Whelan |
| 19 | 26 | CARDIFF CITY | L | 0-1 | 0-0 | 1540 | |
| 20 | 30 | Hereford United | W | 2-1 | 1-0 | 2210 | Norton (og), Flitcroft |
| 21 | Dec 3 | FULHAM | D | 1-1 | 0-0 | 1762 | Reid (pen) |
| 22 | 14 | DARLINGTON | W | 2-1 | 1-0 | 2073 | McDonald (2) |
| 23 | 21 | Barnet | W | 2-1 | 1-0 | 1581 | Noteman (pen), McDonald |
| 24 | Jan 11 | HARTLEPOOL UNITED | D | 0-0 | 0-0 | 1885 | |
| 25 | 14 | ROCHDALE | D | 0-0 | 0-0 | 1679 | |
| 26 | 18 | Northampton Town | L | 1-5 | 1-3 | 4434 | Noteman |
| 27 | 28 | Lincoln City | D | 0-0 | 0-0 | 2330 | |
| 28 | Feb 1 | Hull City | L | 0-1 | 0-0 | 2513 | |
| 29 | 4 | Mansfield Town | W | 2-0 | 1-0 | 1688 | Flitcroft, McDonald |
| 30 | 8 | DONCASTER ROVERS | W | 6-0 | 2-0 | 2347 | Milner (4), Alsford, Jones (pen) |
| 31 | 14 | Colchester United | D | 0-0 | 0-0 | 3855 | |
| 32 | 18 | Scunthorpe United | W | 2-0 | 1-0 | 1524 | Flitcroft, Priest |
| 33 | 22 | MANSFIELD TOWN | W | 1-0 | 1-0 | 2385 | Noteman |
| 34 | 25 | CARLISLE UNITED | D | 1-1 | 1-0 | 2750 | Noteman |
| 35 | Mar 1 | Fulham | D | 1-1 | 1-0 | 5780 | Priest |
| 36 | 8 | BARNET | W | 1-0 | 0-0 | 2291 | Campbell (og) |
| 37 | 11 | TORQUAY UNITED | D | 0-0 | 0-0 | 2064 | |
| 38 | 15 | Darlington | D | 1-1 | 1-1 | 2348 | Milner |
| 39 | 22 | Cambridge United | D | 2-2 | 2-2 | 3044 | Rimmer, Milner |
| 40 | 29 | BRIGHTON & HOVE A. | W | 2-1 | 0-1 | 3613 | Woods, Milner |
| 41 | 31 | Swansea City | L | 1-2 | 0-1 | 6284 | Alsford |
| 42 | Apr 5 | WIGAN ATHLETIC | D | 1-1 | 1-0 | 4005 | Flitcroft |
| 43 | 12 | Cardiff City | L | 0-1 | 0-1 | 4079 | |
| 44 | 19 | SCARBOROUGH | W | 1-0 | 1-0 | 2311 | Milner |
| 45 | 26 | Exeter City | W | 5-1 | 0-1 | 4300 | Davidson, McDonald(2), Milner, Flitcroft |
| 46 | May 3 | LEYTON ORIENT | L | 0-1 | 0-1 | 3622 | |

| | Sinclair R. | Davidson R. | Rogers D. | Fisher N. | Jackson P. | Alsford J. | Richardson N. | Priest C. | Murphy J. | Milner A. | Noteman K. | Shelton G. | Rimmer S. | Jenkins I. | Knowles C. | Cutler N. | Flitcroft D. | Woods M. | Brown G. | Helliwell I. | Whelan S. | Brown W. | Reid S. | McDonald R. | Jones J. | Aiston S. | Tallon G. | Giles M. |
|---|---|---|---|---|---|---|---|---|---|---|---|---|---|---|---|---|---|---|---|---|---|---|---|---|---|---|---|---|
| 1 | 1 | 2* | 3 | 4 | 5 | 6 | 7 | 8 | 9 | 10 | 11" | 12 | 14 | | | | | | | | | | | | | | | |
| 2 | 1 | | 3 | 4 | 5 | 6 | 7 | | 9 | 10 | | 8 | 11 | 2 | | | | | | | | | | | | | | |
| 3 | | | 3 | 4 | 5 | 6 | 7 | | 9 | 10 | 12 | 8* | 11 | 2 | 1 | | | | | | | | | | | | | |
| 4 | | | 3 | 13 | 5 | 6 | 7 | 8 | 9* | 10 | 12 | 4' | 11 | 2 | | 1 | | | | | | | | | | | | |
| 5 | | 2 | | 12 | 5 | 6 | 8 | | 14 | 10" | 11 | 4* | 9 | 3 | | 1 | 7' | 13 | | | | | | | | | | |
| 6 | | 2 | | 12 | 5 | 6 | 8 | | 13 | 10' | 11 | 4* | 9 | 3 | | 1 | 7 | | | | | | | | | | | |
| 7 | | 2 | | 12 | 5 | 6 | 8 | 14 | | 10 | 11* | 4 | 9 | 3" | | 1 | 7 | | | | | | | | | | | |
| 8 | | 2 | 14 | 3 | 5 | 6 | 4 | 8 | 13 | 10' | 11 | 12 | 9* | | 1 | | 7" | | | | | | | | | | | |
| 9 | | 2 | | 12 | 5 | 6 | 8* | | | 10 | 11 | 4 | 9 | 3 | | 1 | 7 | | | | | | | | | | | |
| 10 | 1 | 2 | | 4 | 5 | 6 | | | | 10 | 11 | 8" | 9 | 3 | | | 7 | | 14 | | | | | | | | | |
| 11 | 1 | 2 | | 4 | | 6 | | 8 | | 10* | 11 | 12 | | 3 | | | 7 | 5 | | 9 | | | | | | | | |
| 12 | 1 | 2 | | 4* | 5 | 6 | | 8 | | 10 | 11 | 7 | | 3 | | | 12 | | | 9 | | | | | | | | |
| 13 | 1 | 2 | | 4 | 5 | 6 | | 8" | | 10 | 11 | 7 | | 3 | | | 14 | | | 9 | | | | | | | | |
| 14 | 1 | 2 | | 4 | 5' | 6 | | | | 10* | 11 | 8 | 12 | 3 | | | 7 | 14 | | 9" | 13 | | | | | | | |
| 15 | 1 | 2 | | 4* | | 6 | | | | 14 | 11 | 8 | 10" | 3 | | | 7 | 12 | | 9 | 5 | | | | | | | |
| 16 | 1 | 2 | | 14 | 5 | 6 | | | | 12 | 11 | 8" | 10* | 3 | | | 7 | 4 | | 9' | 13 | | | | | | | |
| 17 | 1 | 2 | | 12 | 5 | 6 | | | | 14 | 11 | 8* | 10 | 3 | | | 7 | 4 | | 9" | | | | | | | | |
| 18 | 1 | 2 | | 3 | 5 | | | 12 | | 8 | 11 | | 10 | | | | 7 | 4* | | 9 | 6 | | | | | | | |
| 19 | | 2 | | 3 | 5 | 6 | | 8 | | 13 | 11 | | 10 | | | | 7 | | | | 12 | 1 | 4* | 9' | | | | |
| 20 | 1 | 2 | | 11 | 5 | 6 | | 8 | | 13 | | | 10' | | | | 7 | | | 14 | 3 | | 4 | 9" | | | | |
| 21 | 1 | 2 | | 11 | 5 | 6 | | 8 | | 12 | | | 10* | | | | 7 | | | | 3 | | 4 | 9 | | | | |
| 22 | 1 | 2 | | 11 | 5 | 6 | | 8 | | 13 | | | 10 | 3 | | | 7 | | | | | | 4 | 9' | | | | |
| 23 | 1 | 2 | | 8 | | 6 | | | | 12 | 11* | | 10 | 3 | | | 7 | | | | 5 | | 4 | 9 | | | | |
| 24 | 1 | | | 11* | 5 | 6 | | | | 7' | 13 | 8 | 10 | 3 | | | | 12 | | | 2 | | 4 | 9 | | | | |
| 25 | 1 | 7 | | 11 | 5 | 6' | | 8 | | 10 | 13 | | | 3 | | | | | | | 2 | | 4 | 9 | | | | |
| 26 | 1 | 2 | | 7" | 5 | | | 8 | | 10 | 11 | | | 3 | | | | 14 | | | 6 | | 4 | 9 | | | | |
| 27 | 1 | 2 | | | 5 | 6 | | 8 | | 10" | 11 | | | 3 | | | | 7 | | | | | 4 | 9 | 14 | | | |
| 28 | 1 | 2* | | 13 | 5 | 6 | | 8 | | 10 | 11' | | | 3 | | | 7 | 12 | | | | | 4 | 9 | | | | |
| 29 | 1 | | | 13 | 5 | 6 | | 8 | | 10 | 11" | | | 3 | | | 7 | | | | 2 | | 4 | 9' | 14 | | | |
| 30 | 1 | 2 | | | 5' | 6 | | 8* | | 10 | 11 | | | 3 | | | 7 | 12 | | | 13 | | 4 | 9" | 14 | | | |
| 31 | 1 | 2 | | | 5 | 6 | | 8 | | 10' | 11 | | | 3 | | | 7 | | | | 13 | | 4 | 9 | | | | |
| 32 | 1 | 2* | | | 5 | 6 | | 8 | | 10 | 11 | | | 3 | | | 7" | 12 | | | 13 | | 4 | 9' | 14 | | | |
| 33 | 1 | 2 | | | 5 | 6 | | | 14 | 10 | 11 | 8 | | | | | | 12 | | | 3 | | 4 | | 9" | 7* | | |
| 34 | 1 | 2 | | | 5 | 6 | | | | 10 | 11 | 8 | | 3 | | | | | | | 13 | | 4 | | 9' | 7 | | |
| 35 | 1 | 2 | | | | 6 | | 8 | | 10 | 11 | | | 3 | | | | | | | 5 | | 4 | 9" | 14 | 7 | | |
| 36 | 1 | 2 | | | 5 | | | 8 | | 10 | 11 | 13 | | 3 | | | | | | | 6 | | 4' | 9" | 14 | 7 | | |
| 37 | 1 | 2 | | | | 6 | | 8 | | 10 | 11* | | | 3 | | | | 12 | | | 5 | | 4 | 9" | 14 | 7 | | |
| 38 | 1 | 2 | | | | 6 | | 8 | | 10" | 11 | | 9* | 3 | | | | 12 | | | 5 | | 4 | | 14 | 7 | | |
| 39 | 1 | 2* | | | | 6 | | 8 | | 10 | 13 | | 9" | 3 | | | 7 | 12 | | | 5 | | 4 | | 14 | 11' | | |
| 40 | 1 | | | | | 6 | | 8 | | 10 | | | 9" | 3 | | | 7 | 2 | | | | | 4 | | 14 | 11 | 5 | |
| 41 | 1 | 2 | | | | 6 | | 8 | 14 | 10 | | | | 3 | | | 7 | 5 | | | | | 4 | | 9" | 11 | | |
| 42 | 1 | 2 | | | | 6 | | 8 | | 10 | | 4 | | 3 | | | 7 | | | | 5 | | | 9 | | 11 | | |
| 43 | 1 | 2 | | | | 6 | | 8 | | 10 | | | | 3 | | | 7 | | | | 5 | | 4 | 9" | 14 | 11 | | |
| 44 | 1 | 2 | | | | 6 | | 8 | 13 | 10" | | | | 3 | | | 7 | | | | 5 | | 4 | 9' | 14 | 11 | | |
| 45 | 1 | 2 | | 12 | | 6 | | 8 | 13 | 10' | | | | 3 | | | 7 | 5 | | | | | 4 | 9" | 14 | 11* | | |
| 46 | | 2 | | | | 6 | | 8 | | 10 | | | 13 | 3 | | | 7' | 5 | | | | 1 | 4 | 9" | 14 | 11 | | |
| Apps. | 37 | 40 | 4 | 19 | 32 | 43 | 9 | 30 | 4 | 38 | 30 | 18 | 22 | 39 | 2 | 5 | 30 | 9 | | 8 | 18 | 2 | 27 | 22 | 3 | 14 | 1 | |
| Subs. | | | 1 | 10 | | | | 2 | 7 | 8 | 5 | 4 | 3 | | | | 2 | 12 | 1 | 1 | 7 | | | | 14 | | | |
| Goals | | 2 | | 1 | 1 | 2 | | 2 | 1 | 12 | 9 | 2 | 4 | | | | 6 | 1 | | 1 | 1 | | 1 | 6 | 1 | | | |

Own goals 2

## PLAY OFFS

| | Date | Opposition | | FT | HT | Att. | Goalscorers |
|---|---|---|---|---|---|---|---|
| SF1 | May 11 | SWANSEA CITY | D | 0-0 | 0-0 | 5104 | |
| SF2 | 14 | Swansea City | L | 0-3 | 0-2 | 10027 | |

| | Sinclair R. | Davidson R. | Rogers D. | Fisher N. | Jackson P. | Alsford J. | Richardson N. | Priest C. | Murphy J. | Milner A. | Noteman K. | Shelton G. | Rimmer S. | Jenkins I. | Knowles C. | Cutler N. | Flitcroft D. | Woods M. | Brown G. | Helliwell I. | Whelan S. | Brown W. | Reid S. | McDonald R. | Jones J. | Aiston S. | Tallon G. | Giles M. |
|---|---|---|---|---|---|---|---|---|---|---|---|---|---|---|---|---|---|---|---|---|---|---|---|---|---|---|---|---|
| SF1 | 1 | 2 | | | | 6 | | 8 | | 10 | | | | 3 | | | 7 | 5 | | | | | 4 | 9 | | 11 | | |
| SF2 | 1 | 2* | | | | 6 | | 8 | | 10" | | | 13 | 3 | | | 7 | 12 | | | 5 | | 4 | 9' | 14 | 11 | | |

## F.A. CUP

| | Date | Opposition | | FT | HT | Att. | Goalscorers |
|---|---|---|---|---|---|---|---|
| 1R | Nov 16 | STALYBRIDGE CELTIC | W | 3-0 | 0-0 | 3151 | Rimmer (2), Milner |
| 2R | Dec 7 | BOSTON UNITED | W | 1-0 | 1-0 | 3344 | Milner |
| 3R | Jan 4 | Middlesbrough | L | 0-6 | 0-3 | 18684 | |

| | Sinclair R. | Davidson R. | Rogers D. | Fisher N. | Jackson P. | Alsford J. | Richardson N. | Priest C. | Murphy J. | Milner A. | Noteman K. | Shelton G. | Rimmer S. | Jenkins I. | Knowles C. | Cutler N. | Flitcroft D. | Woods M. | Brown G. | Helliwell I. | Whelan S. | Brown W. | Reid S. | McDonald R. | Jones J. | Aiston S. | Tallon G. | Giles M. |
|---|---|---|---|---|---|---|---|---|---|---|---|---|---|---|---|---|---|---|---|---|---|---|---|---|---|---|---|---|
| 1R | 1 | 2 | 13 | 8 | 5 | 6 | | | | 9 | 11' | | 10 | 3* | | | 7 | 4 | | | 12 | | | | | | | |
| 2R | 1 | 2 | | 11' | 5 | 6 | | 8 | | 9* | 13 | | 10 | 3 | | | 7 | 4 | | | 12 | | | | | | | |
| 3R | 1 | | | 4 | | 6 | | 8 | | 9 | 11" | 7* | 10 | 3 | | | | 2 | 12 | | 5 | | | | | | | 14 |

## LEAGUE (COCA COLA) CUP

| | Date | Opposition | | FT | HT | Att. | Goalscorers |
|---|---|---|---|---|---|---|---|
| 1R1 | Aug 20 | Carlisle United | L | 0-1 | 0-1 | 4042 | |
| 1R2 | Sep 3 | CARLISLE UNITED | L | 1-3 | 0-1 | 1947 | Noteman |

| | Sinclair R. | Davidson R. | Rogers D. | Fisher N. | Jackson P. | Alsford J. | Richardson N. | Priest C. | Murphy J. | Milner A. | Noteman K. | Shelton G. | Rimmer S. | Jenkins I. | Knowles C. | Cutler N. | Flitcroft D. | Woods M. | Brown G. | Helliwell I. | Whelan S. | Brown W. | Reid S. | McDonald R. | Jones J. | Aiston S. | Tallon G. | Giles M. |
|---|---|---|---|---|---|---|---|---|---|---|---|---|---|---|---|---|---|---|---|---|---|---|---|---|---|---|---|---|
| 1R1 | 1 | 2" | 3 | 4 | 5 | 6 | 7 | | 9 | 10 | | 8 | 11 | | | | | 14 | | | | | | | | | | |
| 1R2 | | | 3 | 4 | 5 | 6 | 7 | | 9* | 10 | 12 | 8' | 11 | 2 | 1 | | 13 | | | | | | | | | | | |

## ASSOCIATE MEMBERS (AUTO WINDSCREENS) SHIELD

| | Date | Opposition | | FT | HT | Att. | Goalscorers |
|---|---|---|---|---|---|---|---|
| 1R | Dec 10 | Hull City | L | 1-3 | 1-2 | 553 | McDonald |

| | Sinclair R. | Davidson R. | Rogers D. | Fisher N. | Jackson P. | Alsford J. | Richardson N. | Priest C. | Murphy J. | Milner A. | Noteman K. | Shelton G. | Rimmer S. | Jenkins I. | Knowles C. | Cutler N. | Flitcroft D. | Woods M. | Brown G. | Helliwell I. | Whelan S. | Brown W. | Reid S. | McDonald R. | Jones J. | Aiston S. | Tallon G. | Giles M. |
|---|---|---|---|---|---|---|---|---|---|---|---|---|---|---|---|---|---|---|---|---|---|---|---|---|---|---|---|---|
| 1R | 1 | 2 | | 11" | 5' | 6 | | 8 | | 12 | 14 | | 10 | 3 | | | 7 | 4 | | | 13 | | | 9* | | | | |

## FRIENDLIES

| | Date | Opposition | | FT | HT | Att. | Goalscorers |
|---|---|---|---|---|---|---|---|
| 1 | Jul 20 | Macclesfield Town | W | 2-0 | 1-0 | | Flitcroft, Richardson |
| 2 | 23 | Flint Town United | D | 1-1 | 1-1 | 300 | Preece |
| 3 | 29 | Weymouth | W | 2-1 | 1-0 | | Milner (2) |
| 4 | 31 | Bath City | W | 5-2 | 2-0 | | Noteman(2,1 pen),Murphy,Shelton,Rimmer |
| 5 | Aug 2 | Bangor City | W | 1-0 | 1-0 | | Milner |
| 6 | 5 | BURNLEY | W | 2-0 | 2-0 | 1057 | Murphy (2) |
| 7 | 9 | SUNDERLAND | L | 0-2 | 0-2 | 1663 | |
| 8 | Jan 25 | Halifax Town | L | 0-2 | 0-1 | 200 | |

# FINAL LEAGUE TABLES: 1996/97 - 2003/04

## Final League Table 1996/97 Division 3

| | | Pl | Home W | D | L | F | A | Away W | D | L | F | A | F | A | Pts |
|---|---|---|---|---|---|---|---|---|---|---|---|---|---|---|---|
| 1 | Wigan Athletic | 46 | 17 | 3 | 3 | 53 | 21 | 9 | 6 | 8 | 31 | 30 | 84 | 51 | 87 |
| 2 | Fulham | 46 | 13 | 5 | 5 | 41 | 20 | 12 | 7 | 4 | 31 | 18 | 72 | 38 | 87 |
| 3 | Carlisle United | 46 | 16 | 3 | 4 | 41 | 21 | 8 | 9 | 6 | 26 | 23 | 67 | 44 | 84 |
| 4 | Northampton Town | 46 | 14 | 4 | 5 | 43 | 17 | 6 | 8 | 9 | 24 | 27 | 67 | 44 | 72 |
| 5 | Swansea City | 46 | 13 | 5 | 5 | 37 | 20 | 8 | 3 | 12 | 25 | 38 | 62 | 58 | 71 |
| ***6*** | ***Chester City*** | ***46*** | ***11*** | ***8*** | ***4*** | ***30*** | ***16*** | ***7*** | ***8*** | ***8*** | ***25*** | ***27*** | ***55*** | ***43*** | ***70*** |
| 7 | Cardiff City | 46 | 11 | 4 | 8 | 30 | 23 | 9 | 5 | 9 | 26 | 31 | 56 | 54 | 69 |
| 8 | Colchester United | 46 | 11 | 9 | 3 | 36 | 23 | 6 | 8 | 9 | 26 | 28 | 62 | 51 | 68 |
| 9 | Lincoln City | 46 | 10 | 8 | 5 | 35 | 25 | 8 | 4 | 11 | 35 | 44 | 70 | 69 | 66 |
| 10 | Cambridge United | 46 | 11 | 5 | 7 | 30 | 27 | 7 | 6 | 10 | 23 | 32 | 53 | 59 | 65 |
| 11 | Mansfield Town | 46 | 9 | 8 | 6 | 21 | 17 | 7 | 8 | 8 | 26 | 28 | 47 | 45 | 64 |
| 12 | Scarborough | 46 | 9 | 9 | 5 | 36 | 31 | 7 | 6 | 10 | 29 | 37 | 65 | 68 | 63 |
| 13 | Scunthorpe United | 46 | 11 | 3 | 9 | 36 | 33 | 7 | 6 | 10 | 23 | 29 | 59 | 62 | 63 |
| 14 | Rochdale | 46 | 10 | 6 | 7 | 34 | 24 | 4 | 10 | 9 | 24 | 34 | 58 | 58 | 58 |
| 15 | Barnet | 46 | 9 | 9 | 5 | 32 | 23 | 5 | 7 | 11 | 14 | 28 | 46 | 51 | 58 |
| 16 | Leyton Orient | 46 | 11 | 6 | 6 | 28 | 20 | 4 | 6 | 13 | 22 | 38 | 50 | 58 | 57 |
| 17 | Hull City | 46 | 9 | 8 | 6 | 29 | 26 | 4 | 10 | 9 | 15 | 24 | 44 | 50 | 57 |
| 18 | Darlington | 46 | 11 | 5 | 7 | 37 | 28 | 3 | 5 | 15 | 27 | 50 | 64 | 78 | 52 |
| 19 | Doncaster Rovers | 46 | 9 | 7 | 7 | 29 | 23 | 5 | 3 | 15 | 23 | 43 | 52 | 66 | 52 |
| 20 | Hartlepool United | 46 | 8 | 6 | 9 | 33 | 32 | 6 | 3 | 14 | 20 | 34 | 53 | 66 | 51 |
| 21 | Torquay United | 46 | 9 | 4 | 10 | 24 | 24 | 4 | 7 | 12 | 22 | 38 | 46 | 62 | 50 |
| 22 | Exeter City | 46 | 6 | 9 | 8 | 25 | 30 | 6 | 3 | 14 | 23 | 43 | 48 | 73 | 48 |
| 23 | Brighton & Hove A. | 46 | 12 | 6 | 5 | 41 | 27 | 1 | 4 | 18 | 12 | 43 | 53 | 70 | 47 |
| 24 | Hereford United | 46 | 6 | 8 | 9 | 26 | 25 | 5 | 6 | 12 | 24 | 40 | 50 | 65 | 47 |

## Final League Table 1997/98 Division 3

| | | Pl | Home W | D | L | F | A | Away W | D | L | F | A | F | A | Pts |
|---|---|---|---|---|---|---|---|---|---|---|---|---|---|---|---|
| 1 | Notts County | 46 | 14 | 7 | 2 | 41 | 20 | 15 | 5 | 3 | 41 | 23 | 82 | 43 | 99 |
| 2 | Macclesfield Town | 46 | 19 | 4 | 0 | 40 | 11 | 4 | 9 | 10 | 23 | 33 | 63 | 44 | 82 |
| 3 | Lincoln City | 46 | 11 | 7 | 5 | 32 | 24 | 9 | 8 | 6 | 28 | 27 | 60 | 51 | 75 |
| 4 | Colchester United | 46 | 14 | 5 | 4 | 41 | 24 | 7 | 6 | 10 | 31 | 36 | 72 | 60 | 74 |
| 5 | Torquay United | 46 | 14 | 4 | 5 | 39 | 22 | 7 | 7 | 9 | 29 | 37 | 68 | 59 | 74 |
| 6 | Scarborough | 46 | 14 | 6 | 3 | 44 | 23 | 5 | 9 | 9 | 23 | 35 | 67 | 58 | 72 |
| 7 | Barnet | 46 | 10 | 8 | 5 | 35 | 22 | 9 | 5 | 9 | 26 | 29 | 61 | 51 | 70 |
| 8 | Scunthorpe United | 46 | 11 | 7 | 5 | 30 | 24 | 8 | 5 | 10 | 26 | 28 | 56 | 52 | 69 |
| 9 | Rotherham United | 46 | 10 | 9 | 4 | 41 | 30 | 6 | 10 | 7 | 26 | 31 | 67 | 61 | 67 |
| 10 | Peterborough Utd. | 46 | 13 | 6 | 4 | 37 | 16 | 5 | 7 | 11 | 26 | 35 | 63 | 51 | 67 |
| 11 | Leyton Orient | 46 | 14 | 5 | 4 | 40 | 20 | 5 | 7 | 11 | 22 | 27 | 62 | 47 | 66 |
| 12 | Mansfield Town | 46 | 11 | 9 | 3 | 42 | 26 | 5 | 8 | 10 | 22 | 29 | 64 | 55 | 65 |
| 13 | Shrewsbury Town | 46 | 12 | 3 | 8 | 35 | 28 | 4 | 10 | 9 | 26 | 34 | 61 | 62 | 61 |
| ***14*** | ***Chester City*** | ***46*** | ***12*** | ***7*** | ***4*** | ***34*** | ***15*** | ***5*** | ***3*** | ***15*** | ***26*** | ***46*** | ***60*** | ***61*** | ***61*** |
| 15 | Exeter City | 46 | 10 | 8 | 5 | 39 | 25 | 5 | 7 | 11 | 29 | 38 | 68 | 63 | 60 |
| 16 | Cambridge United | 46 | 11 | 8 | 4 | 39 | 27 | 3 | 10 | 10 | 24 | 30 | 63 | 57 | 60 |
| 17 | Hartlepool United | 46 | 10 | 12 | 1 | 40 | 22 | 2 | 11 | 10 | 21 | 31 | 61 | 53 | 59 |
| 18 | Rochdale | 46 | 15 | 3 | 5 | 43 | 15 | 2 | 4 | 17 | 13 | 40 | 56 | 55 | 58 |
| 19 | Darlington | 46 | 13 | 6 | 4 | 43 | 28 | 1 | 6 | 16 | 13 | 44 | 56 | 72 | 54 |
| 20 | Swansea City | 46 | 8 | 8 | 7 | 24 | 16 | 5 | 3 | 15 | 25 | 46 | 49 | 62 | 50 |
| 21 | Cardiff City | 46 | 5 | 13 | 5 | 27 | 22 | 4 | 10 | 9 | 21 | 30 | 48 | 52 | 50 |
| 22 | Hull City | 46 | 10 | 6 | 7 | 36 | 32 | 1 | 2 | 20 | 20 | 51 | 56 | 83 | 41 |
| 23 | Brighton & Hove A. | 46 | 3 | 10 | 10 | 21 | 34 | 3 | 7 | 13 | 17 | 32 | 38 | 66 | 35 |
| 24 | Doncaster Rovers | 46 | 3 | 3 | 17 | 14 | 48 | 1 | 5 | 17 | 16 | 65 | 30 | 113 | 20 |

## Final League Table 1998/99 Division 3

| | | Pl | Home W | D | L | F | A | Away W | D | L | F | A | F | A | Pts |
|---|---|---|---|---|---|---|---|---|---|---|---|---|---|---|---|
| 1 | Brentford | 46 | 16 | 5 | 2 | 45 | 18 | 10 | 2 | 11 | 34 | 38 | 79 | 56 | 85 |
| 2 | Cambridge United | 46 | 13 | 6 | 4 | 41 | 21 | 10 | 6 | 7 | 37 | 27 | 78 | 48 | 81 |
| 3 | Cardiff City | 46 | 13 | 7 | 3 | 35 | 17 | 9 | 7 | 7 | 25 | 22 | 60 | 39 | 80 |
| 4 | Scunthorpe United | 46 | 14 | 3 | 6 | 42 | 28 | 8 | 5 | 10 | 27 | 30 | 69 | 58 | 74 |
| 5 | Rotherham United | 46 | 11 | 8 | 4 | 41 | 26 | 9 | 5 | 9 | 38 | 35 | 79 | 61 | 73 |
| 6 | Leyton Orient | 46 | 12 | 6 | 5 | 40 | 30 | 7 | 9 | 7 | 28 | 29 | 68 | 59 | 72 |
| 7 | Swansea City | 46 | 11 | 9 | 3 | 33 | 19 | 8 | 5 | 10 | 23 | 29 | 56 | 48 | 71 |
| 8 | Mansfield Town | 46 | 15 | 2 | 6 | 38 | 18 | 4 | 8 | 11 | 22 | 40 | 60 | 58 | 67 |
| 9 | Peterborough Utd | 46 | 11 | 4 | 8 | 41 | 29 | 7 | 8 | 8 | 31 | 27 | 72 | 56 | 66 |
| 10 | Halifax Town | 46 | 10 | 8 | 5 | 33 | 25 | 7 | 7 | 9 | 25 | 31 | 58 | 56 | 66 |
| 11 | Darlington | 46 | 10 | 6 | 7 | 41 | 24 | 8 | 5 | 10 | 28 | 34 | 69 | 58 | 65 |
| 12 | Exeter City | 46 | 13 | 5 | 5 | 32 | 18 | 4 | 7 | 12 | 15 | 32 | 47 | 50 | 63 |
| 13 | Plymouth Argyle | 46 | 11 | 6 | 6 | 32 | 19 | 6 | 4 | 13 | 26 | 35 | 58 | 54 | 61 |
| ***14*** | ***Chester City*** | ***46*** | ***6*** | ***12*** | ***5*** | ***28*** | ***30*** | ***7*** | ***6*** | ***10*** | ***29*** | ***36*** | ***57*** | ***66*** | ***57*** |
| 15 | Shrewsbury Town | 46 | 11 | 6 | 6 | 36 | 29 | 3 | 8 | 12 | 16 | 34 | 52 | 63 | 56 |
| 16 | Barnet | 46 | 10 | 5 | 8 | 30 | 31 | 4 | 8 | 11 | 24 | 40 | 54 | 71 | 55 |
| 17 | Brighton & Hove A. | 46 | 8 | 3 | 12 | 25 | 35 | 8 | 4 | 11 | 24 | 31 | 49 | 66 | 55 |
| 18 | Southend United | 46 | 8 | 6 | 9 | 24 | 21 | 6 | 6 | 11 | 28 | 37 | 52 | 58 | 54 |
| 19 | Rochdale | 46 | 9 | 8 | 6 | 22 | 21 | 4 | 7 | 12 | 20 | 34 | 42 | 55 | 54 |
| 20 | Torquay United | 46 | 9 | 9 | 5 | 29 | 20 | 3 | 8 | 12 | 18 | 38 | 47 | 58 | 53 |
| 21 | Hull City | 46 | 8 | 5 | 10 | 25 | 28 | 6 | 6 | 11 | 19 | 34 | 44 | 62 | 53 |
| 22 | Hartlepool United | 46 | 8 | 7 | 8 | 33 | 27 | 5 | 5 | 13 | 19 | 38 | 52 | 65 | 51 |
| 23 | Carlisle United | 46 | 8 | 8 | 7 | 25 | 21 | 3 | 8 | 12 | 18 | 32 | 43 | 53 | 49 |
| 24 | Scarborough | 46 | 8 | 3 | 12 | 30 | 39 | 6 | 3 | 14 | 20 | 38 | 50 | 77 | 48 |

## Final League Table 1999/2000 Division 3

| | | Pl | Home W | D | L | F | A | Away W | D | L | F | A | F | A | Pts |
|---|---|---|---|---|---|---|---|---|---|---|---|---|---|---|---|
| 1 | Swansea City | 46 | 15 | 6 | 2 | 32 | 11 | 9 | 7 | 7 | 19 | 19 | 51 | 30 | 85 |
| 2 | Rotherham United | 46 | 13 | 5 | 5 | 43 | 17 | 11 | 7 | 5 | 29 | 19 | 72 | 36 | 84 |
| 3 | Northampton Town | 46 | 16 | 2 | 5 | 36 | 18 | 9 | 5 | 9 | 27 | 27 | 63 | 45 | 82 |
| 4 | Darlington | 46 | 13 | 9 | 1 | 43 | 15 | 8 | 7 | 8 | 23 | 21 | 66 | 36 | 79 |
| 5 | Peterborough Utd. | 46 | 14 | 4 | 5 | 39 | 30 | 8 | 8 | 7 | 24 | 24 | 63 | 54 | 78 |
| 6 | Barnet | 46 | 12 | 6 | 5 | 36 | 24 | 9 | 6 | 8 | 23 | 29 | 59 | 53 | 75 |
| 7 | Hartlepool United | 46 | 16 | 1 | 6 | 32 | 17 | 5 | 8 | 10 | 28 | 32 | 60 | 49 | 72 |
| 8 | Cheltenham Town | 46 | 13 | 4 | 6 | 28 | 17 | 7 | 6 | 10 | 22 | 25 | 50 | 42 | 70 |
| 9 | Torquay United | 46 | 12 | 6 | 5 | 35 | 20 | 7 | 6 | 10 | 27 | 32 | 62 | 52 | 69 |
| 10 | Rochdale | 46 | 8 | 7 | 8 | 21 | 25 | 10 | 7 | 6 | 36 | 29 | 57 | 54 | 68 |
| 11 | Brighton & Hove A. | 46 | 10 | 7 | 6 | 38 | 25 | 7 | 9 | 7 | 26 | 21 | 64 | 46 | 67 |
| 12 | Plymouth Argyle | 46 | 12 | 10 | 1 | 38 | 18 | 4 | 8 | 11 | 17 | 33 | 55 | 51 | 66 |
| 13 | Macclesfield Town | 46 | 9 | 7 | 7 | 36 | 30 | 9 | 4 | 10 | 30 | 31 | 66 | 61 | 65 |
| 14 | Hull City | 46 | 7 | 8 | 8 | 26 | 23 | 8 | 6 | 9 | 17 | 20 | 43 | 43 | 59 |
| 15 | Lincoln City | 46 | 11 | 6 | 6 | 38 | 23 | 4 | 8 | 11 | 29 | 46 | 67 | 69 | 59 |
| 16 | Southend United | 46 | 11 | 5 | 7 | 37 | 31 | 4 | 6 | 13 | 16 | 30 | 53 | 61 | 56 |
| 17 | Mansfield Town | 46 | 9 | 6 | 8 | 33 | 26 | 7 | 2 | 14 | 17 | 39 | 50 | 65 | 56 |
| 18 | Halifax Town | 46 | 7 | 5 | 11 | 22 | 24 | 8 | 4 | 11 | 22 | 34 | 44 | 58 | 54 |
| 19 | Leyton Orient | 46 | 7 | 7 | 9 | 22 | 22 | 6 | 6 | 11 | 25 | 30 | 47 | 52 | 52 |
| 20 | York City | 46 | 7 | 10 | 6 | 21 | 21 | 5 | 6 | 12 | 18 | 32 | 39 | 53 | 52 |
| 21 | Exeter City | 46 | 8 | 6 | 9 | 27 | 30 | 3 | 5 | 15 | 19 | 42 | 46 | 72 | 44 |
| 22 | Shrewsbury Town | 46 | 5 | 6 | 12 | 20 | 27 | 4 | 7 | 12 | 20 | 40 | 40 | 67 | 40 |
| 23 | Carlisle United | 46 | 6 | 8 | 9 | 23 | 27 | 3 | 4 | 16 | 19 | 48 | 42 | 75 | 39 |
| ***24*** | ***Chester City*** | ***46*** | ***5*** | ***5*** | ***13*** | ***20*** | ***36*** | ***5*** | ***4*** | ***14*** | ***24*** | ***43*** | ***44*** | ***79*** | ***39*** |

## Final League Table 2000/01 Football Conference

| | | Pl | Home W | D | L | F | A | Away W | D | L | F | A | F | A | Pts |
|---|---|---|---|---|---|---|---|---|---|---|---|---|---|---|---|
| 1 | Rushden & Diamonds | 42 | 14 | 6 | 1 | 41 | 13 | 11 | 5 | 5 | 37 | 23 | 78 | 36 | 86 |
| 2 | Yeovil Town | 42 | 14 | 3 | 4 | 41 | 17 | 10 | 5 | 6 | 32 | 33 | 73 | 50 | 80 |
| 3 | Dagenham & Redbdge | 42 | 13 | 4 | 4 | 39 | 19 | 10 | 4 | 7 | 32 | 35 | 71 | 54 | 77 |
| 4 | Southport | 42 | 9 | 5 | 7 | 33 | 24 | 11 | 4 | 6 | 25 | 22 | 58 | 46 | 69 |
| 5 | Leigh RMI | 42 | 11 | 5 | 5 | 38 | 24 | 8 | 6 | 7 | 25 | 33 | 63 | 57 | 68 |
| 6 | Telford United | 42 | 13 | 1 | 7 | 33 | 23 | 6 | 7 | 8 | 18 | 28 | 51 | 51 | 65 |
| 7 | Stevenage Borough | 42 | 8 | 7 | 6 | 36 | 33 | 7 | 11 | 3 | 35 | 28 | 71 | 61 | 63 |
| ***8*** | ***Chester City*** | ***42*** | ***9*** | ***8*** | ***4*** | ***29*** | ***19*** | ***7*** | ***6*** | ***8*** | ***20*** | ***24*** | ***49*** | ***43*** | ***62*** |
| 9 | Doncaster Rovers | 42 | 11 | 5 | 5 | 28 | 17 | 4 | 8 | 9 | 19 | 26 | 47 | 43 | 58 |
| 10 | Scarborough | 42 | 7 | 9 | 5 | 29 | 25 | 7 | 7 | 7 | 27 | 29 | 56 | 54 | 58 |
| 11 | Hereford United | 42 | 6 | 12 | 3 | 27 | 19 | 8 | 3 | 10 | 33 | 27 | 60 | 46 | 57 |
| 12 | Boston United | 42 | 10 | 7 | 4 | 43 | 28 | 3 | 10 | 8 | 31 | 35 | 74 | 63 | 56 |
| 13 | Nuneaton Borough | 42 | 9 | 5 | 7 | 35 | 26 | 4 | 10 | 7 | 25 | 34 | 60 | 60 | 54 |
| 14 | Woking | 42 | 5 | 10 | 6 | 30 | 30 | 8 | 5 | 8 | 22 | 27 | 52 | 57 | 54 |
| 15 | Dover Athletic | 42 | 9 | 6 | 6 | 32 | 22 | 5 | 5 | 11 | 22 | 34 | 54 | 56 | 53 |
| 16 | Forest Green Rov. | 42 | 6 | 9 | 6 | 28 | 28 | 5 | 6 | 10 | 15 | 26 | 43 | 54 | 48 |
| 17 | Northwich Victoria | 42 | 8 | 7 | 6 | 31 | 24 | 3 | 6 | 12 | 18 | 43 | 49 | 67 | 46 |
| 18 | Hayes | 42 | 5 | 6 | 10 | 22 | 31 | 7 | 4 | 10 | 22 | 40 | 44 | 71 | 46 |
| 19 | Morecambe | 42 | 8 | 5 | 8 | 35 | 29 | 3 | 7 | 11 | 29 | 37 | 64 | 66 | 45 |
| 20 | Kettering Town | 42 | 5 | 5 | 11 | 23 | 31 | 6 | 5 | 10 | 23 | 31 | 46 | 62 | 43 |
| 21 | Kingstonian | 42 | 3 | 5 | 13 | 19 | 40 | 5 | 5 | 11 | 28 | 33 | 47 | 73 | 34 |
| 22 | Hednesford Town | 42 | 2 | 6 | 13 | 24 | 38 | 3 | 7 | 11 | 22 | 48 | 46 | 86 | 28 |

## Final League Table 2001/02 Football Conference

| | | Pl | Home W | D | L | F | A | Away W | D | L | F | A | F | A | Pts |
|---|---|---|---|---|---|---|---|---|---|---|---|---|---|---|---|
| 1 | Boston United | 42 | 12 | 5 | 4 | 53 | 24 | 13 | 4 | 4 | 31 | 18 | 84 | 42 | 84 |
| 2 | Dagenham & Redbdge | 42 | 13 | 6 | 2 | 35 | 20 | 11 | 6 | 4 | 35 | 27 | 70 | 47 | 84 |
| 3 | Yeovil Town | 42 | 6 | 7 | 8 | 27 | 30 | 13 | 6 | 2 | 39 | 23 | 66 | 53 | 70 |
| 4 | Doncaster Rovers | 42 | 11 | 6 | 4 | 41 | 23 | 7 | 7 | 7 | 27 | 23 | 68 | 46 | 67 |
| 5 | Barnet | 42 | 10 | 4 | 7 | 30 | 19 | 9 | 6 | 6 | 34 | 29 | 64 | 48 | 67 |
| 6 | Morecambe | 42 | 12 | 5 | 4 | 30 | 27 | 5 | 6 | 10 | 33 | 40 | 63 | 67 | 62 |
| 7 | Farnborough Town | 42 | 11 | 3 | 7 | 38 | 23 | 7 | 4 | 10 | 28 | 31 | 66 | 54 | 61 |
| 8 | Margate | 42 | 7 | 9 | 5 | 33 | 22 | 7 | 7 | 7 | 26 | 31 | 59 | 53 | 58 |
| 9 | Telford United | 42 | 8 | 6 | 7 | 34 | 31 | 6 | 9 | 6 | 29 | 27 | 63 | 58 | 57 |
| 10 | Nuneaton Borough | 42 | 9 | 3 | 9 | 33 | 27 | 7 | 6 | 8 | 24 | 30 | 57 | 57 | 57 |
| 11 | Stevenage Borough | 42 | 10 | 4 | 7 | 36 | 30 | 5 | 6 | 10 | 21 | 30 | 57 | 60 | 55 |
| 12 | Scarborough | 42 | 9 | 6 | 6 | 27 | 22 | 5 | 8 | 8 | 28 | 41 | 55 | 63 | 55 |
| 13 | Northwich Victoria | 42 | 9 | 4 | 8 | 32 | 34 | 7 | 3 | 11 | 25 | 36 | 57 | 70 | 55 |
| ***14*** | ***Chester City*** | ***42*** | ***7*** | ***7*** | ***7*** | ***26*** | ***23*** | ***8*** | ***2*** | ***11*** | ***28*** | ***28*** | ***54*** | ***51*** | ***54*** |
| 15 | Southport | 42 | 9 | 6 | 6 | 40 | 26 | 4 | 8 | 9 | 13 | 23 | 53 | 49 | 53 |
| 16 | Leigh RMI | 42 | 6 | 4 | 11 | 29 | 29 | 9 | 4 | 8 | 27 | 29 | 56 | 58 | 53 |
| 17 | Hereford United | 42 | 9 | 6 | 6 | 28 | 15 | 5 | 4 | 12 | 22 | 38 | 50 | 53 | 52 |
| 18 | Forest Green Rov. | 42 | 7 | 7 | 7 | 28 | 32 | 5 | 8 | 8 | 26 | 44 | 54 | 76 | 51 |
| 19 | Woking | 42 | 7 | 5 | 9 | 28 | 29 | 6 | 4 | 11 | 31 | 41 | 59 | 70 | 48 |
| 20 | Hayes | 42 | 6 | 2 | 13 | 27 | 45 | 7 | 3 | 11 | 26 | 35 | 53 | 80 | 44 |
| 21 | Stalybridge Celtic | 42 | 7 | 6 | 8 | 26 | 32 | 4 | 4 | 13 | 14 | 37 | 40 | 69 | 43 |
| 22 | Dover Athletic | 42 | 6 | 5 | 10 | 20 | 25 | 5 | 1 | 15 | 21 | 40 | 41 | 65 | 39 |

## Final League Table 2002/03 Football Conference

| | | Pl | Home W | D | L | F | A | Away W | D | L | F | A | F | A | Pts |
|---|---|---|---|---|---|---|---|---|---|---|---|---|---|---|---|
| 1 | Yeovil Town | 42 | 16 | 5 | 0 | 54 | 13 | 12 | 6 | 3 | 46 | 24 | 100 | 37 | 95 |
| 2 | Morecambe | 42 | 17 | 3 | 1 | 52 | 13 | 6 | 6 | 9 | 34 | 29 | 86 | 42 | 78 |
| 3 | Doncaster Rovers | 42 | 11 | 6 | 4 | 28 | 17 | 11 | 6 | 4 | 45 | 30 | 73 | 47 | 78 |
| ***4*** | ***Chester City*** | ***42*** | ***10*** | ***6*** | ***5*** | ***36*** | ***21*** | ***11*** | ***6*** | ***4*** | ***23*** | ***10*** | ***59*** | ***31*** | ***75*** |
| 5 | Dagenham & Redbdge | 42 | 12 | 5 | 4 | 38 | 23 | 9 | 4 | 8 | 33 | 36 | 71 | 59 | 72 |
| 6 | Hereford United | 42 | 9 | 5 | 7 | 36 | 22 | 10 | 2 | 9 | 28 | 29 | 64 | 51 | 64 |
| 7 | Scarborough | 42 | 12 | 3 | 6 | 41 | 28 | 6 | 7 | 8 | 22 | 26 | 63 | 54 | 64 |
| 8 | Halifax Town | 42 | 11 | 5 | 5 | 34 | 28 | 7 | 5 | 9 | 16 | 23 | 50 | 51 | 64 |
| 9 | Forest Green Rov. | 42 | 12 | 3 | 6 | 41 | 29 | 5 | 5 | 11 | 20 | 33 | 61 | 62 | 59 |
| 10 | Margate | 42 | 8 | 9 | 4 | 32 | 24 | 7 | 2 | 12 | 28 | 42 | 60 | 66 | 56 |
| 11 | Barnet | 42 | 9 | 4 | 8 | 32 | 28 | 4 | 10 | 7 | 33 | 40 | 65 | 68 | 53 |
| 12 | Stevenage Borough | 42 | 7 | 6 | 8 | 31 | 25 | 7 | 4 | 10 | 30 | 30 | 61 | 55 | 52 |
| 13 | Farnborough Town | 42 | 8 | 6 | 7 | 37 | 29 | 5 | 6 | 10 | 20 | 27 | 57 | 56 | 51 |
| 14 | Northwich Victoria | 42 | 6 | 5 | 10 | 26 | 34 | 7 | 7 | 7 | 40 | 38 | 66 | 72 | 51 |
| 15 | Telford United | 42 | 7 | 2 | 12 | 20 | 33 | 7 | 5 | 9 | 34 | 36 | 54 | 69 | 49 |
| 16 | Burton Albion | 42 | 6 | 6 | 9 | 25 | 31 | 7 | 4 | 10 | 27 | 46 | 52 | 77 | 49 |
| 17 | Gravesend & Nthflt | 42 | 8 | 5 | 8 | 37 | 35 | 4 | 7 | 10 | 25 | 38 | 62 | 73 | 48 |
| 18 | Leigh RMI | 42 | 8 | 5 | 8 | 26 | 34 | 6 | 1 | 14 | 18 | 37 | 44 | 71 | 48 |
| 19 | Woking | 42 | 8 | 7 | 6 | 30 | 35 | 3 | 7 | 11 | 22 | 46 | 52 | 81 | 47 |
| 20 | Nuneaton Borough | 42 | 9 | 4 | 8 | 27 | 32 | 4 | 3 | 14 | 24 | 46 | 51 | 78 | 46 |
| 21 | Southport | 42 | 6 | 8 | 7 | 31 | 32 | 5 | 4 | 12 | 23 | 37 | 54 | 69 | 45 |
| 22 | Kettering Town | 42 | 4 | 3 | 14 | 23 | 39 | 4 | 4 | 13 | 14 | 34 | 37 | 73 | 31 |

## Final League Table 2003/04 Football Conference

| | | Pl | Home W | D | L | F | A | Away W | D | L | F | A | F | A | Pts |
|---|---|---|---|---|---|---|---|---|---|---|---|---|---|---|---|
| ***1*** | ***Chester City*** | ***42*** | ***16*** | ***4*** | ***1*** | ***45*** | ***18*** | ***11*** | ***7*** | ***3*** | ***40*** | ***16*** | ***85*** | ***34*** | ***92*** |
| 2 | Hereford United | 42 | 14 | 3 | 4 | 42 | 20 | 14 | 4 | 3 | 61 | 24 | 103 | 44 | 91 |
| 3 | Shrewsbury Town | 42 | 13 | 6 | 2 | 38 | 14 | 7 | 8 | 6 | 29 | 28 | 67 | 42 | 74 |
| 4 | Barnet | 42 | 11 | 6 | 4 | 30 | 17 | 8 | 8 | 5 | 30 | 29 | 60 | 46 | 71 |
| 5 | Aldershot Town | 42 | 12 | 6 | 3 | 40 | 24 | 8 | 4 | 9 | 40 | 43 | 80 | 67 | 70 |
| 6 | Exeter City | 42 | 10 | 7 | 4 | 33 | 24 | 9 | 5 | 7 | 38 | 33 | 71 | 57 | 69 |
| 7 | Morecambe | 42 | 14 | 4 | 3 | 43 | 25 | 6 | 3 | 12 | 23 | 41 | 66 | 66 | 67 |
| 8 | Stevenage Borough | 42 | 10 | 5 | 6 | 29 | 22 | 8 | 4 | 9 | 29 | 30 | 58 | 52 | 63 |
| 9 | Woking | 42 | 10 | 9 | 2 | 40 | 23 | 5 | 7 | 9 | 25 | 29 | 65 | 52 | 61 |
| 10 | Accrington Stanley | 42 | 13 | 3 | 5 | 46 | 31 | 2 | 10 | 9 | 22 | 30 | 68 | 61 | 58 |
| 11 | Gravesend & Nthflt | 42 | 7 | 6 | 8 | 34 | 35 | 7 | 9 | 5 | 35 | 31 | 69 | 66 | 57 |
| 12 | Telford United | 42 | 10 | 3 | 8 | 28 | 28 | 5 | 7 | 9 | 21 | 23 | 49 | 51 | 55 |
| 13 | Dagenham & Redbdge | 42 | 8 | 3 | 10 | 30 | 34 | 7 | 6 | 8 | 29 | 30 | 59 | 64 | 54 |
| 14 | Burton Albion * | 42 | 7 | 4 | 10 | 30 | 29 | 8 | 3 | 10 | 27 | 30 | 57 | 59 | 51 |
| 15 | Scarborough | 42 | 8 | 9 | 4 | 32 | 25 | 4 | 6 | 11 | 19 | 29 | 51 | 54 | 51 |
| 16 | Margate | 42 | 8 | 2 | 11 | 30 | 32 | 6 | 7 | 8 | 26 | 32 | 56 | 64 | 51 |
| 17 | Tamworth | 42 | 9 | 6 | 6 | 32 | 30 | 4 | 4 | 13 | 17 | 38 | 49 | 68 | 49 |
| 18 | Forest Green Rov. | 42 | 6 | 8 | 7 | 32 | 36 | 6 | 4 | 11 | 26 | 44 | 58 | 80 | 48 |
| 19 | Halifax Town | 42 | 9 | 4 | 8 | 28 | 26 | 3 | 4 | 14 | 15 | 39 | 43 | 65 | 44 |
| 20 | Farnborough Town | 42 | 7 | 6 | 8 | 31 | 34 | 3 | 3 | 15 | 22 | 40 | 53 | 74 | 39 |
| 21 | Leigh RMI | 42 | 4 | 6 | 11 | 26 | 44 | 3 | 2 | 16 | 20 | 53 | 46 | 97 | 29 |
| 22 | Northwich Victoria | 42 | 2 | 8 | 11 | 15 | 38 | 2 | 3 | 16 | 15 | 42 | 30 | 80 | 23 |

* Burton Albion 1 point deducted

# SEASON 1997-98

## FOOTBALL (NATIONWIDE) LEAGUE DIV. 3

| | Date | | Opposition | | FT | HT | Att. | Goalscorers | Sinclair R. | Davidson R. | Jenkins I. | Fisher N. | Whelan S. | Alsford J. | Bennett G. | Richardson N. | Rimmer S. | Flitcroft D. | Thomas R. | Woods M. | Murphy J. | Milner A. | McDonald R. | Priest C. | Jones J. | Shelton G. | Brown W. | Dobson R. | Giles M. | McKay M. | Wright D. | Shelton A. |
|---|---|---|---|---|---|---|---|---|---|---|---|---|---|---|---|---|---|---|---|---|---|---|---|---|---|---|---|---|---|---|---|---|
| 1 | Aug | 9 | LINCOLN CITY | W | 2-0 | 0-0 | 2478 | Flitcroft, Bennett | 1 | 2 | 3 | 4 | 5 | 6 | 7" | 8 | 9 | 10 | 11* | 12 | 14 | | | | | | | | | | | |
| 2 | | 23 | CAMBRIDGE UNITED | D | 1-1 | 0-1 | 2167 | Bennett | 1 | 2 | 3 | 4 | 5 | 6 | 7 | 8* | | 10 | 11 | 12 | | 9' | 13 | | | | | | | | | |
| 3 | | 30 | Barnet | L | 1-2 | 0-0 | 1790 | Simpson (og) | 1 | 2 | 3 | 4 | 5 | 6 | 7 | 8 | | 10 | | 12 | | | 9 | 11* | | | | | | | | |
| 4 | Sep | 2 | Scunthorpe United | L | 1-2 | 1-0 | 2633 | Bennett | 1 | 2 | 3 | 4' | 5 | 6 | 7 | 8* | | 10 | 13 | 12 | 14 | | 9" | 11 | | | | | | | | |
| 5 | | 5 | HULL CITY | W | 1-0 | 1-0 | 2271 | Bennett | 1 | 2 | 3 | 11 | 5 | 6 | 7 | 12 | | 10* | 13 | 4 | | | 9' | 8 | | | | | | | | |
| 6 | | 13 | SHREWSBURY TOWN | W | 2-0 | 1-0 | 2853 | Bennett (2) | 1 | 2 | 3 | 11 | 5 | 6 | 7 | 12 | | 10 | | 4* | 14 | | 9" | 8 | | | | | | | | |
| 7 | | 16 | Cardiff City | W | 2-0 | 2-0 | 3949 | Alsford, Davidson (pen) | 1 | 2 | 3 | 11' | 5 | 6 | 7" | 12 | | 10 | 13 | 4* | 9 | | | 8 | 14 | | | | | | | |
| 8 | | 20 | Mansfield Town | L | 1-4 | 1-3 | 2183 | Davidson (pen) | 1 | 2 | 3 | 11' | 5 | 6 | 7 | 4 | | 10 | 13 | | | | 9 | 8 | | | | | | | | |
| 9 | | 27 | Rotherham United | L | 2-4 | 0-3 | 3061 | Alsford, Priest | 1 | 2* | 3 | 11" | 5 | 6 | 7 | 4 | | 10 | 14 | | 12 | | 9 | 8 | | | | | | | | |
| 10 | Oct | 4 | HARTLEPOOL UNITED | W | 3-1 | 2-1 | 2163 | Whelan, Bennett, Murphy | 1 | 2* | 3' | 12 | 5 | 6 | 7 | 4 | 13 | 10 | 11" | | 9 | | 14 | 8 | | | | | | | | |
| 11 | | 11 | BRIGHTON & HOVE A. | W | 2-0 | 1-0 | 2402 | Bennett (2) | 1 | | | 3 | 5 | 6 | 7" | 2 | 14 | 10 | 11* | | 9 | | 12 | 8 | | 4 | | | | | | |
| 12 | | 18 | Torquay United | L | 1-3 | 0-3 | 2047 | Richardson | 1 | | 3 | 13 | 5 | 6 | 7" | 2 | 14 | 10 | 11 | | 9* | | 12 | 8' | | 4 | | | | | | |
| 13 | | 21 | Scarborough | L | 1-4 | 0-2 | 1451 | Thomas | 1 | | 3 | 4 | 5 | 6 | 7" | 2 | 14 | 10* | 11 | | 9 | | 12 | 8 | | | | | | | | |
| 14 | | 25 | MACCLESFIELD TOWN | D | 1-1 | 0-0 | 3245 | Priest | 1 | | 3 | 4 | 5 | 6 | 7 | 2 | 14 | 10 | 11" | | | | 9 | 8 | | | | | | | | |
| 15 | Nov | 1 | ROCHDALE | W | 4-0 | 1-0 | 2431 | McDonald, Bennett, Rimmer (2) | | | 5 | 3 | | 6 | 7' | 4 | 14 | 10 | 11" | | | | 9 | 8 | 13 | | 1 | 2 | | | | |
| 16 | | 4 | Notts County | W | 2-1 | 0-0 | 3104 | McDonald, Bennett | | | 5 | | | 6 | 7 | 4 | 11* | 10 | | | 12 | | 9 | 8 | | | 1 | 2 | 3 | | | |
| 17 | | 8 | Leyton Orient | L | 0-1 | 0-1 | 3894 | | | | 5 | | | 6 | 7" | 4 | 11 | 10 | 12 | | 14 | | 9 | 8 | | | 1 | 2* | 3 | | | |
| 18 | | 18 | PETERBOROUGH UNITED | D | 0-0 | 0-0 | 2612 | | | | 2 | 3 | 5 | 6 | 7 | 4 | 9 | 10 | 11" | | | | 14 | 8 | | | 1 | | | | | |
| 19 | | 26 | SWANSEA CITY | W | 2-0 | 1-0 | 1510 | Flitcroft (pen), Thomas | | | 2 | 3 | 5 | 6 | 7' | 4 | 9 | 10 | 11 | | | | 14 | 8" | 13 | | 1 | | | | | |
| 20 | | 29 | EXETER CITY | D | 1-1 | 0-1 | 2288 | Rimmer | | | 2 | 3 | 5 | 6 | 7 | 4 | 9 | 10 | 11 | | | | | 8 | | | 1 | | | | | |
| 21 | Dec | 2 | Doncaster Rovers | L | 1-2 | 1-1 | 864 | Jones | | 2 | 3 | | 5 | 6 | | 4 | | 10 | 11 | | | | 9 | 8 | 7 | | 1 | | | | | |
| 22 | | 13 | DARLINGTON | W | 2-1 | 0-0 | 1812 | McDonald, Alsford | | 2 | 3 | 8' | 5 | 6 | | 4 | 9 | 10" | 11 | | | | 13 | | 7 | | 1 | | | 14 | | |
| 23 | | 19 | Colchester United | L | 0-2 | 0-1 | 1867 | | 1 | 2 | 3 | | 5 | 6 | 7 | 4 | 9 | 10 | 11" | 14 | | | 8 | | | | | | | | | |
| 24 | | 26 | Hull City | W | 2-1 | 0-0 | 6807 | Whelan, Thomas | 1 | 2 | 3 | | 5 | 6 | 7 | 4 | 9 | 10 | 12 | 8" | | | 11* | | 14 | | | | | | | |
| 25 | | 28 | SCUNTHORPE UNITED | W | 1-0 | 0-0 | 2263 | Priest | 1 | 2 | 3 | 13 | 5 | 6 | 7 | 4 | 9 | 10 | 11' | | | | | 8 | | | | | | | | |
| 26 | Jan | 10 | Lincoln City | W | 3-1 | 2-0 | 2913 | Priest, Jenkins, Rimmer | 1 | 2* | 3 | | 5 | 6 | 7 | 4 | 9 | 10 | 12 | 11 | | | | 8 | | | | | | | | |
| 27 | | 17 | BARNET | L | 0-1 | 0-0 | 2479 | | 1 | | 3 | 2 | | 6 | 7 | 4 | 9 | 10' | 11 | 5" | | | 13 | 8 | | | | | | 14 | | |
| 28 | | 24 | Cambridge United | W | 2-1 | 0-0 | 2473 | Rimmer, McDonald | 1 | | 2 | 3 | | 6 | 7 | 4 | 9 | 10 | | 5 | | | 11 | 8 | | | | | | | | |
| 29 | | 27 | CARDIFF CITY | D | 0-0 | 0-0 | 1757 | | 1 | | 2 | | | 6 | 7' | 4 | 9 | 10 | 11 | 5 | 13 | | | 8 | | | | | 3 | | | |
| 30 | | 31 | Shrewsbury Town | D | 1-1 | 0-1 | 3002 | Woods | 1 | | 3 | | 5 | 6 | 7 | 4 | 9 | 10 | 12 | 2 | | | 11* | 8 | | | | | | | | |
| 31 | Feb | 7 | MANSFIELD TOWN | L | 0-1 | 0-0 | 2055 | | 1 | | 2 | | | 6 | 7" | 4 | 9 | 10 | 11* | 5 | 14 | | 12 | 8 | | | | | 3 | | | |
| 32 | | 14 | Hartlepool United | D | 0-0 | 0-0 | 2186 | | 1 | 2 | | | | 6 | | 4 | 9 | | | 5 | 10 | | 11 | 8 | | 7 | | | 3 | | | |
| 33 | | 21 | ROTHERHAM UNITED | W | 4-0 | 0-0 | 2432 | Murphy, Alsford, Priest (2) | 1 | 2' | | 13 | 5 | 6 | 12 | | 9* | | 7 | 4 | 10 | | 11 | 8 | | | | | 3 | | | |
| 34 | | 24 | TORQUAY UNITED | L | 1-3 | 0-2 | 2163 | Woods | 1 | 2 | | 13 | 5 | 6 | 12 | | 9* | 14 | 7 | 4 | 10 | | 11" | 8 | | | | | 3' | | | |
| 35 | | 28 | Brighton & Hove A. | L | 2-3 | 1-2 | 2510 | Flitcroft, Murphy | 1 | 2 | | 3* | 5 | 6 | 14 | 4 | 9" | 7 | 12 | 11 | 10 | | | 8 | | | | | | | | |
| 36 | Mar | 3 | LEYTON ORIENT | D | 1-1 | 0-1 | 1650 | Richardson | 1 | 2 | 3 | 14 | | 6 | 7 | 4 | | 10 | 11" | 5 | 9 | | | 8 | | | | | | | | |
| 37 | | 7 | Rochdale | D | 1-1 | 0-0 | 1955 | Murphy | 1 | | 2 | 3 | | 6 | 7 | 4 | | 10 | | 5 | 9 | | 11 | | | | | | | 8 | | |
| 38 | | 14 | NOTTS COUNTY | L | 0-1 | 0-0 | 2753 | | 1 | | 2 | 3 | | 6 | 7 | 4 | | 10 | 11 | 5 | 9 | | | | | | | | | 8 | | |
| 39 | | 21 | Peterborough United | L | 1-2 | 1-1 | 4817 | McDonald | 1 | 2 | 3 | | 5 | 6 | 7* | 4 | 14 | 10 | 12" | | 9 | | 11 | | | | | | | 8 | | |
| 40 | | 28 | Swansea City | L | 0-2 | 0-1 | 2500 | | 1 | 2 | | 8 | 5 | | 7* | 4 | 12 | 10 | | 6 | 9 | | 11" | | 14 | | | | 3 | | | |
| 41 | Apr | 4 | Exeter City | L | 0-5 | 0-3 | 2965 | | 1 | 2 | | 3 | 5 | | 7 | 4 | 11" | 10 | 12 | 6* | 9 | | | 8 | | | | | | | 14 | |
| 42 | | 11 | DONCASTER ROVERS | W | 2-1 | 2-1 | 1593 | Flitcroft (pen), Rimmer | | | | 3 | 5 | | 7* | 2 | 4 | 10 | 11 | 6 | 9 | | | 8 | | | 1 | | | | 12 | |
| 43 | | 13 | Darlington | L | 0-1 | 0-0 | 1901 | | | | | 3 | 5 | | 12 | 2 | 4 | 10 | 11" | 6 | 9 | | | 8 | | | 1 | | 14 | | 7* | |
| 44 | | 18 | COLCHESTER UNITED | W | 3-1 | 3-0 | 1780 | Whelan, Fisher, Rimmer | | | | 3 | 5 | | 7' | 4 | 11 | 10 | | 6 | | | | 8 | | | 1 | 2* | 13 | | 9 | 12 |
| 45 | | 25 | Macclesfield Town | L | 2-3 | 0-1 | 5982 | Whelan, Thomas | | | | 3 | 5 | | | 4 | 11 | 10 | 12 | 6 | 9 | | | 8 | | | 1 | 2 | | | 7* | |
| 46 | May | 2 | SCARBOROUGH | D | 1-1 | 0-0 | 2719 | Rimmer | | | | 3 | 5 | | | 4 | 10 | 7 | 11 | 6 | 9 | | | 8 | | | 1 | 2' | | | | 13 |
| | | | | | | | | Apps | 33 | 24 | 34 | 29 | 35 | 39 | 37 | 41 | 26 | 43 | 25 | 24 | 19 | 1 | 21 | 37 | 2 | 3 | 13 | 6 | 8 | 3 | 3 | |
| | | | | | | | | Subs | | | | 6 | | | 4 | 3 | 8 | 1 | 13 | 5 | 8 | | 10 | | 5 | | | | 2 | 2 | 2 | 2 |
| | | | | | | | | Goals | | 2 | 1 | 1 | 4 | 4 | 11 | 2 | 8 | 4 | 4 | 2 | 4 | | 5 | 6 | 1 | | | | | | | |

Own Goals 1

## F. A. CUP

| | | | Opposition | | FT | HT | Att. | Goalscorers | Sinclair R. | Davidson R. | Jenkins I. | Fisher N. | Whelan S. | Alsford J. | Bennett G. | Richardson N. | Rimmer S. | Flitcroft D. | Thomas R. | Woods M. | Murphy J. | Milner A. | McDonald R. | Priest C. | Jones J. | Shelton G. | Brown W. | Dobson R. | Giles M. | McKay M. | Wright D. | Shelton A. |
|---|---|---|---|---|---|---|---|---|---|---|---|---|---|---|---|---|---|---|---|---|---|---|---|---|---|---|---|---|---|---|---|---|
| 1R | Nov | 15 | WINSFORD UNITED | W | 2-1 | 0-1 | 3885 | Richardson, Priest | | | 2 | 3 | 5 | 6 | 7" | 4 | 12 | 10 | 11 | | 14 | | 9* | 8 | | | 1 | | | | | |
| 2R | Dec | 5 | WREXHAM | L | 0-2 | 0-2 | 5224 | | | 16 | 2 | 3~ | 5 | 6 | 7 | 4 | 9* | 10 | 11 | | | | | 8 | 12 | | 1 | | | | | |

## LEAGUE (COCA COLA) CUP

| | | | Opposition | | FT | HT | Att. | Goalscorers | Sinclair R. | Davidson R. | Jenkins I. | Fisher N. | Whelan S. | Alsford J. | Bennett G. | Richardson N. | Rimmer S. | Flitcroft D. | Thomas R. | Woods M. | Murphy J. | Milner A. | McDonald R. | Priest C. | Jones J. | Shelton G. | Brown W. | Dobson R. | Giles M. | McKay M. | Wright D. | Shelton A. |
|---|---|---|---|---|---|---|---|---|---|---|---|---|---|---|---|---|---|---|---|---|---|---|---|---|---|---|---|---|---|---|---|---|
| 1R1 | Aug | 12 | CARLISLE UNITED | L | 1-2 | 0-1 | 2367 | Woods | 1 | 2 | 3 | 4 | 5 | 6 | 7 | 8 | 9 | 10' | 11* | 12 | | 13 | | | | | | | | | | |
| 1R2 | Aug | 26 | Carlisle United | L | 0-3 | 0-2 | 4208 | | 1 | 2 | 3 | 4 | 5 | 6 | 7' | 8* | | 10 | 11" | 12 | 14 | 13 | 9 | | | | | | | | | |

## ASSOCIATE MEMBERS (AUTO WINDSCREENS) SHIELD

| | | | Opposition | | FT | HT | Att. | Goalscorers | Sinclair R. | Davidson R. | Jenkins I. | Fisher N. | Whelan S. | Alsford J. | Bennett G. | Richardson N. | Rimmer S. | Flitcroft D. | Thomas R. | Woods M. | Murphy J. | Milner A. | McDonald R. | Priest C. | Jones J. | Shelton G. | Brown W. | Dobson R. | Giles M. | McKay M. | Wright D. | Shelton A. |
|---|---|---|---|---|---|---|---|---|---|---|---|---|---|---|---|---|---|---|---|---|---|---|---|---|---|---|---|---|---|---|---|---|
| 1R | Dec | 9 | Scunthorpe United | L | 1-2 | 0-0 | 813 | Flitcroft (pen) | | 2 | 3 | 11 | 5 | 6 | | 4" | 9 | 10 | | | | | | 8 | 7 | | 1 | | | | 14 | |

## FRIENDLIES

| | | | Opposition | | FT | HT | Att. | Goalscorers |
|---|---|---|---|---|---|---|---|---|
| 1 | Jul | 12 | Bangor City | L | 1-2 | 0-1 | 329 | Fisher |
| 2 | | 15 | PRESTON NORTH END | W | 2-1 | 1-1 | 1315 | Priest, Fisher |
| 3 | | 19 | Newtown | L | 2-5 | 1-4 | | Jones, Ratcliffe |
| 4 | | 21 | AFC Newport | W | 2-0 | 0-0 | 382 | Rimmer, Thomas |
| 5 | | 23 | Aberystwyth Town | L | 2-3 | 1-2 | | Fisher, Bennett |
| 6 | | 25 | Caernarfon Town | W | 4-1 | 3-1 | | Thomas, Bennett (2), McDonald |
| 7 | | 29 | WEST BROMWICH ALBION | L | 0-1 | 0-0 | 1538 | |
| 8 | Aug | 2 | Leek Town | L | 0-1 | 0-0 | 417 | |

**1997/1998 Season:**

Back – Warrington, Clench, Woods, Richardson, Whelan, Milner, Jones, Bennett, Priest
Middle –Walker (Physio), Murphy, Alsford, Flitcroft, Sinclair, Saunders (Sponsor), Brown, Reid, Thomas, Fogg (Youth Manager)
Front – Dobson, McDonald, Fisher, A Shelton (Assistant Manager), Jenkins, Ratcliffe (Manager), Rimmer, Davidson, Giles.

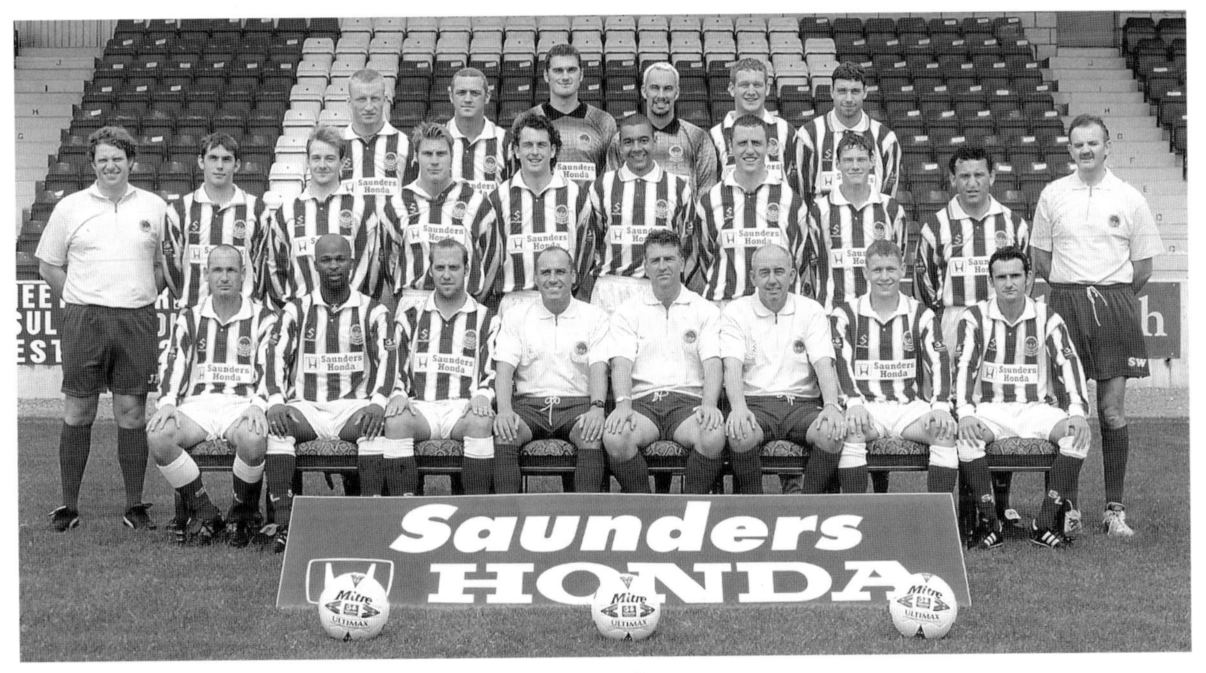


**1998/1999 Season:**

Back –Beckett, Woods, Cutler, Brown, Thompson, Murphy
Middle – Kerr (Football in Community), Jones, Priest, Flitcroft, Richardson, Whelan, Crosby, A Shelton, Bennett, Reid, Walker (Physio)
Front – Thomas, Davidson, G Shelton (Assistant Manager), Ratcliffe (Manager), Fogg (Youth Manager), Wright, Smith.

# SEASON 1998-99

## FOOTBALL (NATIONWIDE) LEAGUE DIV. 3

| | Date | | Opposition | | FT | HT | Att. | Goalscorers | Brown W. | Davidson R. | Cross J. | Richardson N. | Crosby A. | Woods M. | Flitcroft D. | Priest C. | Murphy J. | Beckett L. | Smith A. | Bennett G. | Thomas R. | Shelton A. | Wright D. | Jones J. | Reid S. | Cutler N. | Lancaster M. | Moss D. | Aiston S. | Carson D. | Conroy M. | Alsford J. | Smeets J. | Fisher N. |
|---|---|---|---|---|---|---|---|---|---|---|---|---|---|---|---|---|---|---|---|---|---|---|---|---|---|---|---|---|---|---|---|---|---|---|
| 1 | Aug | 8 | LEYTON ORIENT | L | 0-2 | 0-1 | 2541 | | 1 | 2 | 3 | 4 | 5 | 6 | 7* | 8 | 9 | 10 | 11 | 12 | | | | | | | | | | | | | | |
| 2 | | 15 | Brighton & Hove A. | D | 2-2 | 1-0 | 2703 | Smith, Flitcroft (pen) | 1 | 2 | 3 | 4 | 5 | 6 | 10 | 8 | 9 | | 11 | 7* | 12 | | | | | | | | | | | | | |
| 3 | | 23 | HULL CITY | D | 2-2 | 1-1 | 2577 | Flitcroft (pen), Crosby | 1 | 2 | 3 | 4 | 5 | 6 | 10 | 8 | 9 | | 11 | 7* | 12 | | | | | | | | | | | | | |
| 4 | | 29 | Southend United | W | 1-0 | 0-0 | 4241 | Bennett | 1 | 2 | 3 | 4 | 5 | 6 | 10' | 8 | 9 | | 11 | 7 | | 13 | | | | | | | | | | | | |
| 5 | Sep | 1 | CAMBRIDGE UNITED | L | 0-3 | 0-1 | 2199 | | 1 | 2 | 3 | 4 | 5 | 6 | 10 | 8 | 9 | | 11 | 7" | | | 14 | | | | | | | | | | | |
| 6 | | 5 | Exeter City | W | 1-0 | 0-0 | 2551 | Richardson | 1 | 2 | 3 | 4 | 5 | 6 | 7 | 8* | | | 11 | | | 13 | 10 | 9' | 12 | | | | | | | | | |
| 7 | | 8 | Peterborough United | L | 0-3 | 0-3 | 4548 | | 1 | | 3 | 2 | 5 | 6 | 7 | 8 | | | 11 | 12 | | | 10 | 9* | 4 | | | | | | | | | |
| 8 | | 12 | TORQUAY UNITED | W | 2-0 | 1-0 | 1729 | Richardson, Murphy | 1 | 2 | 3 | 4 | 5 | 6 | 7 | 8 | 13 | | 11 | 9" | 14 | | 10' | | | | | | | | | | | |
| 9 | | 19 | Carlisle United | D | 1-1 | 0-0 | 2971 | Flitcroft | 1 | 2 | 3 | | 5 | 6 | 7 | 8 | 9 | | 11 | | 10 | | | | 4 | | | | | | | | | |
| 10 | | 26 | CARDIFF CITY | D | 2-2 | 0-0 | 2842 | Priest, Thomas | 1 | 2 | 3 | 14 | 5 | 6 | 7 | 8 | | | 11 | | 10 | | 9 | | 4" | | | | | | | | | |
| 11 | Oct | 3 | Scarborough | W | 4-2 | 2-0 | 1832 | Priest, Thomas (2), Flitcroft | 1 | 2 | 3 | 4 | 5 | 6 | 7 | 8 | 9" | 14 | 11 | | 10 | | | | | | | | | | | | | |
| 12 | | 11 | Barnet | D | 0-0 | 0-0 | 2236 | | 1 | 2 | 3 | 4 | 5 | 6 | 7 | 8 | 9 | 10" | 11 | | | | | 14 | | | | | | | | | | |
| 13 | | 17 | SWANSEA CITY | D | 1-1 | 1-1 | 3926 | Murphy | 1 | 2 | 3 | 4 | 5 | 6 | 7' | | 9 | 10 | 11 | | | 13 | | | 8 | | | | | | | | | |
| 14 | | 20 | HARTLEPOOL UNITED | D | 1-1 | 1-0 | 2182 | Woods | 1 | 2 | 3 | 4 | 5 | 6 | 7 | | 9 | 10 | 11 | | | | | | 8 | | | | | | | | | |
| 15 | | 31 | SHREWSBURY TOWN | D | 1-1 | 0-0 | 3699 | Murphy | 1 | 2 | 3 | 4 | 5 | 6 | 7 | | 9 | 10 | 11 | | | | | | 8 | | | | | | | | | |
| 16 | Nov | 7 | Scunthorpe United | L | 1-2 | 0-2 | 3160 | Murphy | 1 | | 3 | 2 | 5 | 6 | 7 | 8 | 9 | 10 | 11* | | | | 12 | | 4 | | | | | | | | | |
| 17 | | 10 | Halifax Town | L | 2-3 | 0-1 | 2427 | Beckett, Murphy | | 2' | 3 | 4 | 5 | 6 | 7" | 8 | 9 | 10* | 11 | | | 13 | 12 | | 14 | 1 | | | | | | | | |
| 18 | | 21 | ROCHDALE | D | 1-1 | 1-0 | 2495 | Wright | | 2 | 3 | 4* | 5 | 6 | 7 | 8 | 9 | | 11' | | | 13 | 10" | 14 | 12 | 1 | | | | | | | | |
| 19 | | 28 | Brentford | L | 1-2 | 0-1 | 5173 | Davidson | | 2 | 3 | | 5 | | | | 9 | | 11 | | | 8 | 12 | 14 | 4' | 1 | 6 | 7" | 10* | 13 | | | | |
| 20 | Dec | 12 | DARLINGTON | W | 1-0 | 0-0 | 2011 | Shelton | | 2 | | 4 | 5 | 6 | 7 | | 9 | | 3 | | | 8* | 12 | 14 | | 1 | | | 11 | | 10" | | | |
| 21 | | 18 | Rotherham United | W | 4-2 | 1-0 | 2696 | Priest, Conroy (2), Murphy | | 2 | | 4 | 5 | 6 | 7 | 8 | 9 | | 3 | | | | 12 | | | 1 | | | 11* | | 10 | | | |
| 22 | | 26 | Hull City | W | 2-1 | 2-0 | 6695 | Flitcroft, Whitney (og) | | 5 | | 2 | | 6 | 7 | 8 | 9 | | 3 | | | 13 | 12 | | 4 | 1 | | | 11' | | 10* | | | |
| 23 | | 28 | MANSFIELD TOWN | D | 1-1 | 0-1 | 3320 | Reid | | 5 | | 2" | | 6 | | 8 | 9 | | 3 | | | 7* | 12 | | 4 | 1 | 14 | | 11 | | 10 | | | |
| 24 | Jan | 2 | SOUTHEND UNITED | D | 1-1 | 0-0 | 2574 | Murphy | | 2 | | | | 6 | | 8 | 9 | | 3 | | | | 7 | | 4 | 1 | 5 | 14 | 11 | | 10" | | | |
| 25 | | 9 | Leyton Orient | D | 2-2 | 1-1 | 4132 | Murphy, Smith (pen) | | 2" | | 14 | | 6 | 7 | 8 | 9 | | 3 | | | | | | 4 | 1 | 5 | | 11 | | 10 | | | |
| 26 | | 15 | BRIGHTON & HOVE A. | D | 1-1 | 1-0 | 3869 | Conroy | | | | 4 | 5 | 2 | 7 | 8 | 9 | | 3 | | | 13 | | | | 1 | 6 | | 11' | | 10 | | | |
| 27 | | 23 | Cambridge United | L | 1-2 | 1-1 | 3635 | Crosby (pen) | | 2 | | 4 | 5 | 3 | 7 | 8 | 9 | 14 | | | | | | | 11" | 1 | 6 | | | | 10 | | | |
| 28 | | 30 | Mansfield Town | L | 0-3 | 0-0 | 2654 | | | 2' | | 4 | | 6 | 7 | 8 | 9 | 14 | 3 | | | 13 | | | 11 | 1 | 5 | | | | 10" | | | |
| 29 | Feb | 6 | EXETER CITY | D | 0-0 | 0-0 | 2243 | | | 2 | | 4 | 5 | 3' | 7 | | 9 | 12 | 11 | | | 13 | | | 8 | 1 | | | | | 10* | 6 | | |
| 30 | | 13 | PETERBOROUGH UNITED | W | 1-0 | 1-0 | 2087 | Murphy | | 2 | | 7 | 5 | | | 8 | 9 | 10' | 3 | | | 13 | | 14 | 4 | 1 | | | 11" | | | 6 | | |
| 31 | | 20 | Torquay United | W | 3-0 | 1-0 | 2384 | Beckett, Alsford, Cross | | 2 | 14 | 4 | 5 | 12 | 7 | 8* | 9 | 10" | 3 | | | 13 | | | | 1 | | | 11' | | | 6 | | |
| 32 | | 23 | Plymouth Argyle | L | 0-2 | 0-2 | 4208 | | | 2 | 14 | 4 | 5 | 12 | 7 | 8* | 9 | 10" | 3 | | | 13 | | | | 1 | | | 11' | | | 6 | | |
| 33 | | 27 | CARLISLE UNITED | W | 2-1 | 0-0 | 2450 | Richardson, Murphy | | 2 | 3 | 4 | 5" | 8 | 7 | | 9 | 10* | | | | 11' | | 12 | | 1 | 14 | 13 | | | | 6 | | |
| 34 | Mar | 5 | Cardiff City | D | 0-0 | 0-0 | 7526 | | | 2 | 3 | 4 | 5 | 8 | 7 | | 9 | 10* | | | | | 12 | | | 1 | 11 | | | | | 6 | | |
| 35 | | 9 | SCARBOROUGH | L | 1-3 | 0-1 | 1954 | Beckett | | | 3 | 4 | 5 | 8 | 7 | | 9 | 10 | | | | 13 | | | | 1 | 11 | 2' | | | | 6 | | |
| 36 | | 13 | SCUNTHORPE UNITED | L | 0-2 | 0-1 | 2115 | | | 2 | 3 | 4 | 5 | 8 | 7 | | 9 | 10 | | | | 11* | 12 | | | 1 | 13 | | | | | 6' | | |
| 37 | | 20 | Shrewsbury Town | L | 0-2 | 0-1 | 2903 | | 1 | 2 | 3 | 4 | 5 | | 7 | | 9 | 10 | 11 | | | 14 | | | | | | | | 8" | | 6 | | |
| 38 | | 27 | PLYMOUTH ARGYLE | W | 3-2 | 0-1 | 1982 | Beckett (2), Murphy | 1 | 2 | 3 | 4 | 5 | 6 | 7 | 8' | 9 | 10 | | | | | | | | | | | | | | 13 | 11* | 12 |
| 39 | Apr | 3 | Swansea City | D | 1-1 | 0-1 | 5994 | Beckett | 1 | 2 | 3 | 4 | 5 | 6 | 7 | 8 | 9 | 10* | | | | | | | | | | | | | 12 | | | 11 |
| 40 | | 5 | BARNET | W | 3-0 | 2-0 | 2122 | Murphy, Crosby (pen), Beckett | 1 | 2 | 3 | 4 | 5 | 6 | 7 | 8 | 9* | 10 | | | | | | | | | | | | | 12 | | 14 | 11" |
| 41 | | 10 | Hartlepool United | L | 0-2 | 0-1 | 2413 | | 1 | 2 | 3 | 4 | 5 | 6 | 7* | 8 | | 10 | | | | | 12 | | | | | | | | 9 | | 14 | 11" |
| 42 | | 13 | BRENTFORD | L | 1-3 | 0-2 | 1766 | Crosby (pen) | 1 | 2 | 3 | 4 | 5 | 6 | 7 | 8 | 9 | 10 | | | | | | | | | | | | | 12 | | | 11* |
| 43 | | 17 | Rochdale | L | 1-3 | 1-0 | 1712 | Beckett | 1 | 2 | 3 | 4 | 5 | 6 | 7 | 8 | 9 | 10 | | | | | | | | | | 11* | | | 12 | | | |
| 44 | | 24 | HALIFAX TOWN | D | 2-2 | 1-1 | 2461 | Priest, Beckett | | 2* | 3 | 4 | 5 | 6 | 7 | 8 | 9 | 10 | | | | 13 | | | 12 | 1 | | | | | | | | 11' |
| 45 | May | 1 | Darlington | W | 2-1 | 1-1 | 2564 | Flitcroft, Beckett | | | 3 | 4 | 5 | 6 | 7* | 8 | 9 | 10 | | | | 13 | | | 12 | 1 | | 2 | | | | | | 11' |
| 46 | | 8 | ROTHERHAM UNITED | D | 1-1 | 1-0 | 3792 | Beckett | | | 3 | 4 | 5 | 6 | 7 | 8' | 9 | 10 | | | | 13 | 14 | | 12 | 1 | | 2* | | | | | | 11" |
| | | | | | | | | Apps | 23 | 40 | 33 | 41 | 41 | 41 | 42 | 35 | 41 | 24 | 32 | 5 | 3 | 5 | 6 | 2 | 16 | 23 | 8 | 5 | 11 | 1 | 11 | 9 | 1 | 7 |
| | | | | | | | | Subs | | | 2 | 2 | | 2 | | | 1 | 4 | | 2 | 3 | 17 | 12 | 6 | 6 | | 3 | 2 | | 1 | 4 | 1 | 2 | 1 |
| | | | | | | | | Goals | | 1 | 1 | 3 | 4 | 1 | 6 | 4 | 12 | 11 | 2 | 1 | 3 | 1 | 1 | | 1 | | | | | | 3 | 1 | | |

Own Goals 1

## F. A. CUP

| | | | | | | | | | Brown W. | Davidson R. | Cross J. | Richardson N. | Crosby A. | Woods M. | Flitcroft D. | Priest C. | Murphy J. | Beckett L. | Smith A. | Bennett G. | Thomas R. | Shelton A. | Wright D. | Jones J. | Reid S. | Cutler N. | Lancaster M. | Moss D. | Aiston S. | Carson D. | Conroy M. | Alsford J. | Smeets J. | Fisher N. |
|---|---|---|---|---|---|---|---|---|---|---|---|---|---|---|---|---|---|---|---|---|---|---|---|---|---|---|---|---|---|---|---|---|---|---|
| 1R | Nov | 14 | Cardiff City | L | 0-6 | 0-3 | 4220 | | | 2 | 3~ | 4 | 5 | 6 | 7 | 8 | 9 | | | | | | 11 | 14 | 10" | 1 | 16 | | | | | | | |

## LEAGUE (WORTHINGTON) CUP

| | | | | | | | | | Brown W. | Davidson R. | Cross J. | Richardson N. | Crosby A. | Woods M. | Flitcroft D. | Priest C. | Murphy J. | Beckett L. | Smith A. | Bennett G. | Thomas R. | Shelton A. | Wright D. | Jones J. | Reid S. | Cutler N. | Lancaster M. | Moss D. | Aiston S. | Carson D. | Conroy M. | Alsford J. | Smeets J. | Fisher N. |
|---|---|---|---|---|---|---|---|---|---|---|---|---|---|---|---|---|---|---|---|---|---|---|---|---|---|---|---|---|---|---|---|---|---|---|
| 1R1 | Aug | 11 | Port Vale | W | 2-1 | 2-0 | 3478 | Beckett (2) | 1 | 2 | 3 | 4 | 5 | 6 | 7 | 8 | 9 | 10* | 11 | 12 | | | | | | | | | | | | | | |
| 1R2 | | 18 | PORT VALE | D | 2-2 | 0-1 | 2461 | Smith, Snijders (og) | 1 | 2 | 3 | 4 | 5 | 6 | 10 | 8 | 9 | | 11 | 7* | 12 | | | | | | | | | | | | | |
| 2R1 | Sep | 15 | Sunderland | L | 0-3 | 0-2 | 20618 | | | 5 | 3 | 2 | | 6 | 7 | 8 | 9 | | 11 | | 12 | | 10* | | 4 | 1 | | | | | | | | |
| 2R2 | | 22 | SUNDERLAND | L | 0-1 | 0-1 | 2738 | | 1 | 2 | 3 | | 5 | 6 | 7 | | 9" | | 11 | | 10* | 8 | 12 | 14 | 4 | | | | | | | | | |

## ASSOCIATE MEMBERS (AUTO WINDSCREENS) SHIELD

| | | | | | | | | | Brown W. | Davidson R. | Cross J. | Richardson N. | Crosby A. | Woods M. | Flitcroft D. | Priest C. | Murphy J. | Beckett L. | Smith A. | Bennett G. | Thomas R. | Shelton A. | Wright D. | Jones J. | Reid S. | Cutler N. | Lancaster M. | Moss D. | Aiston S. | Carson D. | Conroy M. | Alsford J. | Smeets J. | Fisher N. |
|---|---|---|---|---|---|---|---|---|---|---|---|---|---|---|---|---|---|---|---|---|---|---|---|---|---|---|---|---|---|---|---|---|---|---|
| 1R | Dec | 8 | HARTLEPOOL UNITED | L | 1-2 | 1-0 | 960 | Shelton | | | 3 | 2 | 5 | 6 | 7 | | 9 | | 11 | | | 8" | | | 4 | 1 | 14 | | 10 | | | | | |

Score 1-1 after 90 minutes. Hartlepool win on Golden Goal.

## FRIENDLIES

| | | | | | | | | |
|---|---|---|---|---|---|---|---|---|
| 1 | Jul | 11 | Caernarfon Town | W | 7-1 | 2-0 | | Richardson(2, 1 pen), Beckett(3), Bennett, Shelton |
| 2 | | 14 | Connah's Quay Nomads | D | 2-2 | 0-1 | 750 | Bennett (2) |
| 3 | | 17 | TRANMERE ROVERS | L | 2-4 | 1-2 | 1624 | Bennett (2) |
| 4 | | 20 | Cwmbran Town | W | 4-0 | 4-0 | 200 | Murphy (2), Cross, Beckett |
| 5 | | 22 | Bath City | W | 2-1 | 1-0 | 362 | Bennett (2) |
| 6 | | 25 | EVERTON | D | 1-1 | 0-0 | 5324 | Beckett |
| 7 | Aug | 1 | TNS (a) | W | 3-2 | 3-0 | 200 | Murphy, Bennett, Beckett |

## SEASON 1999-2000

### FOOTBALL (NATIONWIDE) LEAGUE DIV. 3

| Date | Opposition | | FT | HT | Att. | Goalscorers | Brown W. | Davidson R. | Cross J. | Reid S. | Lancaster M. | Woods M. | Shelton A. | Richardson N. | Wright D. | Beckett L. | Fisher N. | Moss D. | Doughty M. | Jones J. | Blackburn C. | Berry P. | Blackwood M. | Agogo M. | Milosavijevic G. | Nash M. | Carver J. | Finney S. | Spooner N. | Eve A. | Laird K. | Hobson G. | Keister J. | Eyjolfsson S. | Pickering A. | Robinson J. | Hemmings T. | Porter A. | Hicks S. | Heggs C. | Carden P. | Malone S. | Carson D. |
|---|---|---|---|---|---|---|---|---|---|---|---|---|---|---|---|---|---|---|---|---|---|---|---|---|---|---|---|---|---|---|---|---|---|---|---|---|---|---|---|---|---|---|---|---|
| Aug 7 | BARNET | L | 0-2 | 0-2 | 2234 | | 1 | 2 | 3 | 4 | 5 | 6 | 7* | 8 | 9 | 10 | 11' | 12 | 13 | | | | | | | | | | | | | | | | | | | | | | | | |
| 14 | Rotherham United | L | 0-4 | 0-0 | 2966 | | 1 | | 3 | 4' | 5 | 6 | 7* | 8 | | 10 | 11 | 2 | 12 | 9" | 13 | 14 | | | | | | | | | | | | | | | | | | | | | |
| 18 | NORTHAMPTON TOWN | L | 0-2 | 0-0 | 1904 | | 1 | 2 | 3 | 4 | 5 | 6 | 7 | 8 | 12 | 10 | 11 | | | 9* | | | | | | | | | | | | | | | | | | | | | | | |
| 28 | Torquay United | D | 2-2 | 1-0 | 2345 | Beckett, Berry | 1 | 2 | 3 | | | 6 | 7 | 4 | 9 | 10 | 11 | 5 | | 8* | | 12 | | | | | | | | | | | | | | | | | | | | | |
| 30 | ROCHDALE | L | 0-2 | 0-1 | 2644 | | 1 | 2 | 3 | | | 6 | 7 | 4 | 9 | 10 | 11* | 5 | 12 | 8' | | 13 | | | | | | | | | | | | | | | | | | | | | |
| Sep 3 | Hull City | L | 1-2 | 1-1 | 6137 | Richardson | 1 | 2' | 3 | | 5 | 6 | 7 | 4 | 13 | 10 | 11* | 12 | | | | | 9 | 8 | | | | | | | | | | | | | | | | | | | |
| 11 | EXETER CITY | D | 1-1 | 0-0 | 1855 | Beckett | 1 | 2 | 12 | | 5 | 6 | 13 | 8 | 9' | 10 | 14 | 4 | 3* | | | | 7 | 11" | | | | | | | | | | | | | | | | | | | |
| 18 | Brighton & Hove A. | W | 3-2 | 0-0 | 5810 | Beckett, Watson(og), Agogo | 1 | 2 | | | 5 | 6 | 13 | 8 | 9 | 10 | 12 | | 3 | | | | 7' | 11 | 4* | | | | | | | | | | | | | | | | | | |
| 25 | LINCOLN CITY | L | 1-3 | 1-1 | 2161 | Blackwood | 1 | 2 | | | 5 | 12* | | | 9 | 10 | 11' | | 3 | 14 | | 13 | 7" | 8 | 13 | 4 | | | | | | | | | | | | | | | | | |
| Oct 2 | York City | D | 2-2 | 0-0 | 2452 | Blackwood, Agogo | 1 | | | | 5 | 6 | | 4 | 9 | 10 | | 2 | 3 | | | | 11 | 8 | 7 | | | | | | | | | | | | | | | | | | |
| 9 | Peterborough United | L | 1-2 | 1-2 | 4965 | Beckett | 1 | 2 | 13 | | 5 | 6' | | 8 | 9 | 10 | | 4 | 3" | | | | 7* | 11 | | 14 | 12 | | | | | | | | | | | | | | | | |
| 16 | MACCLESFIELD TOWN | L | 1-2 | 1-2 | 2506 | Agogo | 1 | | 3* | | 5 | | | 6 | 9 | 10 | 11 | 12 | | | | 13 | 7 | 8 | | 4 | 2' | | | | | | | | | | | | | | | | |
| 19 | CHELTENHAM TOWN | W | 2-1 | 0-0 | 1705 | Agogo (2) | 1 | | | | 5 | 6 | | 8 | 9 | 10 | | 2 | 3 | | | | 7 | 11 | 4 | | | | | | | | | | | | | | | | | | |
| 23 | Lincoln City | L | 1-4 | 1-1 | 3790 | Agogo | 1 | | | | 5 | 6 | | 8 | | 10 | 12 | 2 | 3 | | | | 9 | 11 | 4' | 7* | | 13 | | | | | | | | | | | | | | | |
| Nov 2 | Shrewsbury Town | W | 1-0 | 0-0 | 2523 | Richardson | 1 | | | | | 6' | 7" | 8 | 9 | 10 | 11 | 2 | 3* | | | 13 | | 4 | 5 | 12 | | 14 | | | | | | | | | | | | | | | |
| 6 | PLYMOUTH ARGYLE | L | 0-1 | 0-1 | 2027 | | 1 | | 13 | | | | 6 | 8 | 9* | 10 | 11 | 2 | 3 | | | | | | 4 | 12 | | 7' | 13 | | | | | | | | | | | | | | |
| 13 | Hartlepool United | L | 0-1 | 0-1 | 2266 | | 1 | | 2 | | | | 7 | 8* | 9 | 10 | 11 | | 3 | | | 12 | | | 4' | 6 | | 13 | 5 | | | | | | | | | | | | | | |
| 23 | SOUTHEND UNITED | D | 0-0 | 0-0 | 1906 | | 1 | | 9 | 4' | | 5 | | 8 | | 10 | 11 | 2 | 3 | | | 13 | | | | 7* | | 12 | 6 | | | | | | | | | | | | | | |
| 27 | SWANSEA CITY | L | 0-1 | 0-0 | 2713 | | 1 | | 9 | 4* | | 5 | | 8 | | 10 | 11 | 2 | 3 | | | | | | | 7 | | 12 | 6 | | | | | | | | | | | | | | |
| Dec 4 | Barnet | L | 0-2 | 0-1 | 2252 | | 1 | | | 4 | | 5 | | 8 | 2 | 10 | 11 | | 3 | | | | | | | 7 | | 9 | 6 | | | | | | | | | | | | | | |
| 15 | Darlington | L | 1-3 | 0-2 | 3553 | Samways (og) | 1 | | 9 | 4 | 12 | 5 | | 8' | 13 | 10 | 11 | 2 | 4 | 14 | | | | | 6* | 7" | | | | | | | | | | | | | | | | | |
| 18 | HALFAX TOWN | W | 2-1 | 2-0 | 2037 | Laird, Eve | 1 | | | | | 13 | | 8 | 12 | 10 | 11 | 2 | 3 | | | | | | 6' | 7 | | | 5 | 4 | 9* | | | | | | | | | | | | |
| 26 | Mansfield Town | L | 1-2 | 0-1 | 3234 | Doughty | 1 | | 3* | | | 6 | | 8 | 14 | 10 | 11 | 2 | 12 | | | | | | 9 | 7" | | | 5' | 4 | 13 | | | | | | | | | | | | |
| 28 | LEYTON ORIENT | L | 1-5 | 0-2 | 3160 | Wright | 1 | | | 12 | | 6 | | 8* | 13 | 10 | 11 | 2 | 3 | | | | | | | 7 | | | 5 | 4 | 9' | | | | | | | | | | | | |
| Jan 3 | Carlisle United | L | 1-4 | 0-1 | 4565 | Eve | 1 | | | 14 | | 13 | | 8 | 9' | 10 | 11 | 2 | 3 | | | | | | 6 | 7" | | 13 | 5* | 4 | | | | | | | | | | | | | |
| 8 | DARLINGTON | L | 1-2 | 1-1 | 2067 | Beckett | 1 | | 13 | 4* | | 6 | | 8' | 12 | 10 | 11 | 2 | 3 | | | | | | | | | | | | | 5 | 7 | 9 | | | | | | | | | |
| 15 | ROTHERHAM UNITED | L | 0-2 | 0-1 | 2398 | | 1 | | 3 | | 5 | 6 | | 8' | 14 | 10 | | 12 | | | | | | | | 13 | | | | 11 | | 4 | 7 | 9" | 2* | | | | | | | | |
| 22 | Northampton Town | L | 1-3 | 1-1 | 5332 | Pickering | 1 | | | 4' | 12 | 6 | | 8 | 13 | 10 | 11 | | 14 | | | | | | | | | | | | | 5 | | 9" | 2* | 3 | 7 | | | | | | |
| 29 | TORQUAY UNITED | W | 2-1 | 0-0 | 2229 | Eyjolfsson, Beckett | 1 | | | 4* | | 6 | | 12 | | 10 | 11 | | | | | | | | | | | | | 13 | | 5 | 7 | 9' | 2 | 3 | 8 | | | | | | |
| Feb 5 | Rochdale | L | 1-2 | 0-1 | 3093 | Beckett | 1 | | | | | 6 | | | | 10 | 11' | 13 | 12 | | | | | | | | | | | 14 | | 5 | 7 | 9 | 2* | 3 | 8" | 4 | | | | | |
| 12 | HULL CITY | D | 0-0 | 0-0 | 2802 | | 1 | | | | | 6 | | 13 | | 10 | | 4 | 12 | | | | | | | | | | | | | 5 | 7' | 9 | 2 | 3 | 8* | 11 | | | | | |
| 18 | Swansea City | L | 1-2 | 1-0 | 6336 | Eyjolfsson | 1 | | | | | 6 | | 12 | | 10 | 13 | 4 | | | | | | | | | | | | | | 5 | 7* | 9 | 2 | 3 | 8' | 11 | | | | | |
| 26 | BRIGHTON & HOVE A. | L | 1-7 | 0-2 | 2743 | Beckett | 1 | | | | 6 | | | | | 10 | 13 | 3 | 12 | | | | | | | | | 14 | | | | 5 | 7" | 9 | 2' | | 8* | 11 | 4 | | | | |
| Mar 4 | Exeter City | W | 2-0 | 2-0 | 2391 | Eyjolfsson, Beckett | 1 | | | | | 6 | | | | 10 | 11 | 4* | 2 | | | | | | | | | | | | | | 12 | 9 | | 3 | 8 | 7 | 5 | | | | |
| 7 | Plymouth Argyle | D | 0-0 | 0-0 | 4140 | | 1 | | | | | 6 | | 13 | | 10 | 11 | 2' | 12 | | | 14 | | | | | | 9* | | | | 4 | | | | 3 | 8" | 7 | 5 | | | | |
| 11 | SHREWSBURY TOWN | D | 0-0 | 0-0 | 4002 | | 1 | | | | | 6 | | 4* | | 10 | 11 | 2 | | | | | | | | | | | | 12 | | 5 | 7 | | | 3 | 8 | | | 9' | 13 | | |
| 18 | Southend United | L | 1-3 | 1-2 | 3483 | Beckett | 1 | | | | | 6 | | | | 10 | 11' | 2 | 12 | | | | | | | | | | | 14 | | 4 | | | | 3* | 8" | 7 | 5 | 9 | 13 | | |
| 21 | HARTLEPOOL UNITED | D | 1-1 | 1-0 | 1816 | Hemmings | 1 | | | | | 6 | | | | 10 | 12 | 2 | 13 | | | | | | | | | | | 11* | | 4 | | | | | 8 | 7 | 5 | 9' | 3 | | |
| 25 | MANSFIELD TOWN | W | 5-0 | 3-0 | 1953 | Heggs,Beckett,Hemmings,Eve(2) | 1 | | | 14 | | 6 | | | | 10* | 13 | 2 | | | | | | | | | | 12 | | 11 | | 4 | | | | | 8 | 7 | 5 | 9' | 3" | | |
| Apr 1 | Halifax Town | W | 1-0 | 1-0 | 2431 | Beckett (pen) | 1 | | | | | 6 | | | | 10 | 11 | 2 | | | | | | | | | | | | | | 4 | | | | | 8 | 7 | 5 | 9 | 3 | | |
| 8 | CARLISLE UNITED | L | 0-1 | 0-0 | 5507 | | 1 | | | | | 6 | | | | 10 | 2 | | | | | | | | | | | 12 | | 11 | | 4 | | | | | 8 | 7 | 5 | 9* | 3 | | |
| 15 | Leyton Orient | W | 2-1 | 1-1 | 4123 | Heggs, Fisher | 1 | | | | | 6 | | 11* | | 10 | 2 | | 12 | | | | | | | | | | | | | 4 | 13 | | | | 8' | 7 | 5 | 9 | 3 | | |
| 22 | Macclesfield Town | D | 1-1 | 0-1 | 3456 | Beckett | 1 | | | | | 6 | | 11 | | 10 | 2 | | | | | | | | | | | | | | | 4 | | | | | 8 | 7 | 5 | 9 | 3 | | |
| 24 | YORK CITY | W | 2-0 | 0-0 | 3503 | Dower (og), Beckett | 1 | | | | | 6 | | 13 | | 10 | 2 | | 12 | | | | | | | | | | | 11* | | 4 | | | | | 8' | 7 | 5 | 9 | 3 | | |
| 29 | Cheltenham Town | L | 0-1 | 0-0 | 5391 | | 1 | | | | | 6 | | 11* | | 10 | 2' | 12 | 14 | | | | | | | | | | | 13 | | 4 | | | | | 8" | 7 | 5 | 9 | 3 | | |
| May 6 | PETERBOROUGH UNITED | L | 0-1 | 0-0 | 4905 | | 1 | | | | 14 | 6 | | | 13 | 10 | 2' | 12 | | | | | | | | | | 11* | | | | 4 | | | | | 8" | 7 | 5 | 9 | 3 | | |
| | | | | | | Apps | 46 | 9 | 13 | 10 | 14 | 40 | 9 | 31 | 15 | 46 | 34 | 28 | 19 | 4 | | | 9 | 10 | 11 | 12 | 1 | 4 | 9 | 9 | 2 | 20 | 8 | 9 | 7 | 9 | 19 | 16 | 13 | 11 | 9 | | |
| | | | | | | Subs | | | 4 | 3 | 3 | 2 | 2 | 5 | 10 | | 7 | 7 | 14 | 2 | 1 | 9 | | | 1 | 4 | 1 | 9 | | 5 | 1 | | 2 | | | | | | | | 2 | | |
| | | | | | | Goals | | | | | | | | 2 | 1 | 14 | 1 | | 1 | | | 1 | 2 | 6 | | | | | | 4 | 1 | | | 3 | 1 | 2 | 2 | | | 2 | | | |

Own goals 3

## F. A. CUP

| Rd | Date | Opposition | | FT | HT | Att. | Goalscorers | Brown W. | Davidson R. | Cross J. | Reid S. | Lancaster M. | Woods M. | Shelton A. | Richardson N. | Wright D. | Beckett L. | Fisher N. | Moss D. | Doughty M. | Jones J. | Blackburn C. | Berry P. | Blackwood M. | Agogo M. | Milosavijevic G. | Nash M. | Carver J. | Finney S. | Spooner N. | Eve A. | Laird K. | Hobson G. | Keister J. | Eyjolfsson S. | Pickering A. | Robinson J. | Hemmings T. | Porter A. | Hicks S. | Heggs C. | Carden P. | Malone S. | Carson D. |
|---|---|---|---|---|---|---|---|---|---|---|---|---|---|---|---|---|---|---|---|---|---|---|---|---|---|---|---|---|---|---|---|---|---|---|---|---|---|---|---|---|---|---|---|---|
| 1R | Oct 30 | Whyteleafe | D | 0-0 | 0-0 | 2164 | | 1 | | | | 5 | 6 | 13 | 4 | 9 | 10 | 11' | 2 | 3 | 12 | | | | | 8 | 7* | | | | | | | | | | | | | | | | | |
| 1Rr | Nov 9 | WHYTELEAFE | W | 3-1 | 1-1 | 2183 | Cross (2), Beckett | 1 | | 9 | | 12 | | 6 | 8 | 7 | 10 | 11 | 2' | 3 | | | | | | 4 | 13 | | | | | | | | | | | | | | | | 5* | |
| 2R | 20 | Stalybridge Celtic | W | 2-1 | 1-1 | 3312 | Cross, Beckett | 1 | | 9 | 4 | | 12 | 13 | 7 | | 10 | 11 | 2 | 3 | | | | | | 5* | 8' | | | 6 | | | | | | | | | | | | | | |
| 3R | Dec 12 | MANCHESTER CITY | L | 1-4 | 1-1 | 5469 | Richardson | 1 | | 12 | 4 | | 5 | | 8 | 9* | 10 | 11 | 2 | 3 | | | 13 | | | | 7' | | | 6 | | | | | | | | | | | | | | |

## LEAGUE (WORTHINGTON) CUP

| Rd | Date | Opposition | | FT | HT | Att. | Goalscorers | Brown W. | Davidson R. | Cross J. | Reid S. | Lancaster M. | Woods M. | Shelton A. | Richardson N. | Wright D. | Beckett L. | Fisher N. | Moss D. | Doughty M. | Jones J. | Blackburn C. | Berry P. | Blackwood M. | Agogo M. | Milosavijevic G. | Nash M. | Carver J. | Finney S. | Spooner N. | Eve A. | Laird K. | Hobson G. | Keister J. | Eyjolfsson S. | Pickering A. | Robinson J. | Hemmings T. | Porter A. | Hicks S. | Heggs C. | Carden P. | Malone S. | Carson D. |
|---|---|---|---|---|---|---|---|---|---|---|---|---|---|---|---|---|---|---|---|---|---|---|---|---|---|---|---|---|---|---|---|---|---|---|---|---|---|---|---|---|---|---|---|---|
| 1R1 | Aug 10 | PORT VALE | W | 2-1 | 1-1 | 2102 | Richardson, Beckett (pen) | 1 | 2 | 3 | 4 | 5 | 6 | 7 | 8 | | 10 | 11 | 12 | | 9* | | | | | | | | | | | | | | | | | | | | | | | |
| 1R2 | 24 | Port Vale | D | 4-4 | 2-2 | 2625 | Beckett (2,(1p)), Shelton, Jones | 1 | 2 | 3 | 8* | | 6 | 4 | 7 | 9 | 10 | 11 | 5 | | 12 | | | | | | | | | | | | | | | | | | | | | | | |
| 2R1 | Sep 14 | ASTON VILLA | L | 0-1 | 0-0 | 4364 | | 1 | 2 | | | 5 | 6 | 4 | 7 | 9 | 10 | 11 | | 3 | | | 12 | | | 8 | | | | | | | | | | | | | | | | | | |
| 2R2 | 21 | Aston Villa | L | 0-5 | 0-2 | 22163 | | 1 | 2 | | | 5 | 6 | 7* | 4 | 9 | 10 | 11" | | 3 | 13 | | 12 | | | 8' | | | | | | | | | | | | | | | | | | 14 |

## ASSOCIATE MEMBERS (AUTO WINDSCREENS) SHIELD

| Rd | Date | Opposition | | FT | HT | Att. | Goalscorers | Brown W. | Davidson R. | Cross J. | Reid S. | Lancaster M. | Woods M. | Shelton A. | Richardson N. | Wright D. | Beckett L. | Fisher N. | Moss D. | Doughty M. | Jones J. | Blackburn C. | Berry P. | Blackwood M. | Agogo M. | Milosavijevic G. | Nash M. | Carver J. | Finney S. | Spooner N. | Eve A. | Laird K. | Hobson G. | Keister J. | Eyjolfsson S. | Pickering A. | Robinson J. | Hemmings T. | Porter A. | Hicks S. | Heggs C. | Carden P. | Malone S. | Carson D. |
|---|---|---|---|---|---|---|---|---|---|---|---|---|---|---|---|---|---|---|---|---|---|---|---|---|---|---|---|---|---|---|---|---|---|---|---|---|---|---|---|---|---|---|---|---|
| 2R | Jan 11 | Hull City | L | 0-2 | 0-1 | 1680 | | 1 | | 3 | 4" | 6 | | 14 | 8* | 12 | 10 | 11 | 2 | | | | | | | 5 | | | | | 13 | | | 7 | 9' | | | | | | | | | |

Chester received a bye in the 1st Round

## FRIENDLIES

| No. | Date | Opposition | | FT | HT | Att. | Goalscorers |
|---|---|---|---|---|---|---|---|
| 1 | Jul 10 | Northwich Victoria | W | 2-1 | 2-0 | 514 | Murphy, Beckett |
| 2 | 13 | Warrington Town | W | 2-1 | 2-0 | 200 | Jones, Fisher |
| 3 | 17 | TNS (a) | D | 2-2 | 1-0 | 250 | Wright (2) |
| 4 | 20 | EVERTON | L | 2-3 | 0-0 | 5800 | Beckett (pen), Wright |
| 5 | 24 | WIGAN ATHLETIC | D | 1-1 | 1-0 | 1121 | Murphy |
| 6 | 26 | Maesteg Park | D | 0-0 | 0-0 | | |
| 7 | 28 | Cwmbran Town | W | 2-0 | 0-0 | | Murphy, Reid |
| 8 | 31 | STOKE CITY | D | 0-0 | 0-0 | 1249 | |

**1999/2000 Season:**
Back – Atkins (Director of Football), Berry, Beckett, Hemmings, Robinson, Richardson, Lancaster, Carson, Wright, Shelton, Smith (Owner-Manager)
Front – Hobson, Doughty, Reid, Conkie, Saunders (Sponsor), Brown, Finney, Fisher, Woods.

**2000/2001 Season:**
Back – Fisher, Kerr, Lancaster, Greygoose, Woods, Brown, P Beesley, Carden, Fitzhenry
Middle – Hill (Youth Coach), M Beesley, Shelton, Spink, Ruscoe, Richardson, Moss, Blackburn, Gaunt, Vile (Youth Coach)
Front – Wright, Berry, Smith (Chairman), Barrow (Manager), Hinnigan (Physio), Doughty, Finney.

# SEASON 2000-01

## NATIONWIDE CONFERENCE

| | Date | Opposition | | FT | HT | Att. | Goalscorers | Greygoose D. | Lancaster M. | Doughty M. | Gaunt C. | Beesley P. | Woods M. | Carden P. | Blackburn C. | Finney S. | Wright D. | Kerr D. | Richardson N. | Ruffer C. | Beesley M. | Shelton A. | Evans A. | Brown W. | Fisher N. | Moss D. | Whitehall S. | Woodyatt L. | Porter A. | Ruscoe S. | Haarhoff J. | Priestley P. | Berry P. | Price M. | Mackin L. |
|---|---|---|---|---|---|---|---|---|---|---|---|---|---|---|---|---|---|---|---|---|---|---|---|---|---|---|---|---|---|---|---|---|---|---|---|
| 1 | Aug 19 | Rushden & Diamonds | L | 0-2 | 0-0 | 3966 | | 1 | 2" | 3 | 4 | 5 | 6 | 7 | 8' | 9 | 10 | 11* | 13 | 12 | 14 | | | | | | | | | | | | | | |
| 2 | 22 | DONCASTER ROVERS | W | 3-0 | 1-0 | 2616 | M Beesley (2), Carden | 1 | 2 | 3 | 4 | 5 | 6 | 7 | 8 | 9* | 12 | | | 11 | 10' | 13 | | | | | | | | | | | | | |
| 3 | 26 | DOVER ATHLETIC | W | 1-0 | 0-0 | 2273 | Wright (pen) | 1 | 2* | 3 | 4 | 5 | 6 | 7 | 8 | 9' | 14 | | | 11 | 10" | 12 | 13 | | | | | | | | | | | | |
| 4 | 30 | Boston United | D | 0-0 | 0-0 | 2078 | | | 2 | 3 | 4 | 5 | 6 | 7 | 8 | 12 | | 13 | | 11' | 10* | | 9 | 1 | | | | | | | | | | | |
| 5 | Sep 2 | SOUTHPORT | L | 0-1 | 0-1 | 2860 | | | 2" | 3 | 4 | 5 | 6' | 7 | 8* | 13 | | | 12 | 11 | 10 | 14 | 9 | 1 | | | | | | | | | | | |
| 6 | 5 | Morecambe | W | 2-0 | 1-0 | 1557 | Blackburn, Woods | | 14 | 3 | 4 | 5 | 6 | 7 | 8 | | 11' | 2" | 12 | | 10* | | 9 | 1 | 13 | | | | | | | | | | |
| 7 | 9 | Yeovil Town | L | 1-2 | 0-1 | 2862 | Bent (og) | | | 3 | 4 | 5 | 6 | 7 | 8 | 12 | 11" | 2' | 14 | | 10 | | 9* | 1 | 13 | | | | | | | | | | |
| 8 | 12 | NORTHWICH VICTORIA | D | 1-1 | 0-1 | 1717 | Blackburn | | | 3 | 4 | 5 | 6* | 7 | 8 | 11 | | | | 12 | 10 | | 9' | 1 | 13 | 2 | | | | | | | | | |
| 9 | 23 | Kingstonian | W | 3-1 | 1-0 | 1125 | Whitehall (2, (1 pen)), Evans | | 5 | 3 | | | 4 | 7 | 8 | 14 | | 13 | 11' | | 9* | | 12 | 1 | 6 | 2 | 10" | | | | | | | | |
| 10 | 26 | NUNEATON BOROUGH | W | 4-0 | 1-0 | 1708 | Crowley (og), M Beesley (2), Evans | | 2 | 3 | | 6 | 5 | 7 | 8 | | | | | | 9* | | 12 | 1 | 11 | 4' | 10 | 13 | | | | | | | |
| 11 | 30 | Hednesford Town | D | 0-0 | 0-0 | 1435 | | | 12 | 3 | 5* | 6 | 4 | 7 | 8 | 14 | | 13 | | | 9" | | | 1 | 11 | 2' | 10 | | | | | | | | |
| 12 | Oct 3 | Scarborough | W | 2-0 | 1-0 | 1193 | Whitehall, Blackburn | | 5 | 3 | | 6 | 4 | 7 | 8 | | | | | | 9 | | | 1 | 11 | 2 | 10 | | | | | | | | |
| 13 | 8 | KETTERING TOWN | W | 2-1 | 0-0 | 2102 | Whitehall (2) | | 5 | 3 | | 6 | 4 | 7 | 8 | | 12 | | | 13 | 9' | | | 1 | 11 | 2* | 10 | | | | | | | | |
| 14 | 14 | Forest Green Rovers | D | 1-1 | 0-0 | 943 | Fisher | | 5 | 3 | | 6 | 4 | 7 | 8 | | 12 | | | | 9 | | | 1 | 11 | 2* | 10 | | | | | | | | |
| 15 | 21 | LEIGH RMI | D | 1-1 | 0-0 | 1858 | Wright | | 5 | 3" | | 6 | 4' | 2 | 8 | | 12 | | | 13 | 9 | | | 1 | 11* | | 10 | | 7 | 14 | | | | | |
| 16 | Nov 4 | Dagenham & Redbridge | D | 1-1 | 0-0 | 1244 | Porter | | 2* | 3 | | 6 | 4 | 7 | 8" | | 13 | | | 5 | 9' | | | 1 | 12 | | 10 | | 11 | 14 | | | | | |
| 17 | 11 | STEVENAGE BOROUGH | D | 1-1 | 0-0 | 1708 | M Beesley | | | 3 | | 6 | 4 | 7 | 8 | | 10 | | | 5 | 9 | | | 1 | 2* | | | | 11 | 12 | | | | | |
| 18 | Dec 2 | WOKING | D | 3-3 | 2-3 | 1692 | Fisher, Whitehall, Porter (pen) | | 5" | 3 | 14 | | 4 | 7 | 8* | | 12 | | | 6 | 9' | | | 1 | 2 | | 10 | | 11 | 13 | | | | | |
| 19 | 16 | Doncaster Rovers | L | 0-1 | 0-1 | 2553 | | | 6 | 3" | 4' | 5 | 14 | | 11* | | 13 | | | 7 | 9 | | | 1 | 2 | | 10 | | 8 | 12 | | | | | |
| 20 | 23 | HAYES | D | 0-0 | 0-0 | 1658 | | | 6 | 3 | 4* | | | 7 | 11 | | 13 | | | 5 | 9 | | | 1 | 2 | | 10 | | 8 | 12' | | | | | |
| 21 | 26 | HEREFORD UNITED | W | 2-1 | 1-0 | 2244 | M Beesley, Whitehall | | 4 | 3 | | 6 | | 7 | 8 | | 12 | | | 5 | 9 | | | 1 | 2 | | 10 | | | 11* | | | | | |
| 22 | Jan 1 | Hereford United | L | 0-2 | 0-0 | 2321 | | | 4 | 3 | | 6 | | 7 | 8 | | 14 | | | 5 | 9* | | | 1 | 2 | 12 | 10 | | | 11' | | | | | |
| 23 | 27 | MORECAMBE | W | 1-0 | 1-0 | 1717 | Lancaster | | 5 | 3 | | 6 | 4" | 7 | 8 | | 13 | | | | 9 | | | 1 | 2 | | 10' | 14 | | 11* | 12 | | | | |
| 24 | Feb 10 | YEOVIL TOWN | W | 2-1 | 2-0 | 2265 | M Beesley, Ruscoe | | 4 | 3' | | 6 | 9 | | 8* | | 12 | | | 5 | 10 | | | 1 | 2 | | | 13 | | 11 | 7 | | | | |
| 25 | 17 | Northwich Victoria | D | 1-1 | 1-0 | 2651 | Haarhoff | | 4 | 3' | 13 | 6 | 9 | 7 | | | | | | 5* | 10 | | | 1 | 2 | 12 | | | | 11 | 8 | | | | |
| 26 | 20 | TELFORD UNITED | W | 1-0 | 1-0 | 1362 | Woods | | 4 | 3 | 5 | 6 | 9 | 7 | | | | | | | 10 | | | 1 | 2 | 12 | | | | 11 | 8* | | | | |
| 27 | 27 | BOSTON UNITED | D | 2-2 | 0-0 | 1087 | Woods, Doughty | | 5 | 12 | 4* | 3 | 9 | 7 | | | | | | | 10' | | | | 6 | 2 | 13 | | | 11 | 8 | 1 | | | |
| 28 | Mar 3 | Hayes | W | 3-1 | 1-0 | 784 | M Beesley (2 (1 pen)), Woods (pen) | | 4 | 3 | 5 | 6 | 9 | 7 | | | | | | | 10* | | | | 8" | 2 | 13 | 14 | | 11' | 12 | 1 | | | |
| 29 | 13 | Southport | L | 0-1 | 0-1 | 1279 | | | 6 | 3' | 4* | | 9 | 7 | | | | | | 5 | 8 | | | 1 | 2 | 13 | 10" | | 12 | 11 | 14 | | | | |
| 30 | 17 | HEDNESFORD TOWN | L | 0-1 | 0-0 | 1451 | | | 4 | 3 | | 6 | 13 | 7 | | | 14 | | | 5 | 9 | | | 1 | 2 | | 10' | | 8" | 11* | 12 | | | | |
| 31 | 23 | Nuneaton Borough | W | 2-1 | 2-1 | 1363 | M Beesley, Whitehall | | 4 | 3' | | 6 | 12 | 7 | | | | | | 5 | 9* | | | 1 | 8 | 2 | 10" | 13 | | 11 | 14 | | | | |
| 32 | 27 | Telford United | L | 0-3 | 0-2 | 1058 | | | 5 | | 12 | 6 | 4 | 7' | | | 9 | | | | | | | 1 | 8 | 2 | 10 | 3* | | 11 | 13 | | | | |
| 33 | Apr 3 | Dover Athletic | D | 1-1 | 0-1 | 1112 | Whitehall | | 4 | | | 6 | 5 | | 7 | | 11 | | | | | | | | | 2 | 10 | 13 | 8' | 3 | 9* | 1 | 12 | | |
| 34 | 14 | FOREST GREEN ROVERS | L | 0-1 | 0-0 | 1292 | | | 4 | 3' | | 6 | 5 | 7 | 8 | | 12 | | | | 9* | | | 1 | 13 | 2 | 10 | | | 11 | | | | | |
| 35 | 16 | Stevenage Borough | W | 2-1 | 2-1 | 1748 | Fisher, Wright | | 2 | 12 | 5 | 3 | 4 | 7 | 8 | | 9' | | | | 13 | | | 1 | 6 | | 10 | | | 11* | | | | | |
| 36 | 18 | Leigh RMI | W | 1-0 | 1-0 | 501 | Wright | | 2 | 3' | 13 | | 5 | 7 | 8 | | 9* | | | | 12 | | | 1 | 6 | | 10 | 4 | | 11 | | | | | |
| 37 | 21 | DAGENHAM & REDBRIDGE | D | 1-1 | 0-0 | 1202 | Woods | | 2 | 13 | 5 | 3 | 4 | 7 | 8* | | 9 | | | | 12 | | | 1 | 6 | | 10" | 14 | | 11' | | | | | |
| 38 | 24 | Kettering Town | L | 0-4 | 0-2 | 1216 | | | 3 | 12 | 5 | | 4* | 7' | 8 | | 9 | | | | 10 | | | 1 | 6 | 13 | | 2 | | 11 | | | | | |
| 39 | 26 | KINGSTONIAN | D | 0-0 | 0-0 | 834 | | | 4 | 3' | 5 | | | 7 | 8 | | 9 | | | | 11" | | | 1* | 6 | | 10 | 2 | | 13 | 14 | 12 | | | |
| 40 | 28 | Woking | L | 0-1 | 0-0 | 2264 | | | 4 | 3 | 5 | | | | 8* | | 7 | 13 | | | 9 | | | | 6 | 11 | 10' | 2 | | 12 | | 1 | | | |
| 41 | May 1 | SCARBOROUGH | W | 3-2 | 1-1 | 805 | Fisher, M Beesley, Piercewright og | | 4 | 13 | | | 5' | | 8 | | 7* | 14 | | | 9 | | | | 11 | 2" | 10 | 6 | 12 | 3 | | 1 | | | |
| 42 | 5 | RUSHDEN & DIAMONDS | L | 1-2 | 0-0 | 4040 | Gaunt | | 4 | 3 | 5 | | | | | | 12' | 7* | | | 9 | | | 1 | 6 | 2 | 13 | 11 | 8 | 10" | 14 | | | | |
| | | | | | | | Apps | 3 | 37 | 35 | 21 | 32 | 33 | 36 | 33 | 4 | 13 | 4 | 1 | 16 | 36 | | 5 | 34 | 31 | 16 | 26 | 7 | 9 | 20 | 5 | 5 | | | |
| | | | | | | | Subs | | 2 | 5 | 4 | | 3 | | | 5 | 16 | 5 | 4 | 4 | 4 | 3 | 3 | | 5 | 5 | 3 | 7 | 2 | 8 | 8 | 1 | 1 | | |
| | | | | | | | Goals | | 1 | 1 | 1 | | 5 | 1 | 3 | | 4 | | | | 11 | | 2 | | 4 | | 9 | | 2 | 1 | 1 | | | | |

Own goals 3

## F.A. CUP

| | Date | Opposition | | FT | HT | Att. | Goalscorers | Greygoose D. | Lancaster M. | Doughty M. | Gaunt C. | Beesley P. | Woods M. | Carden P. | Blackburn C. | Finney S. | Wright D. | Kerr D. | Richardson N. | Ruffer C. | Beesley M. | Shelton A. | Evans A. | Brown W. | Fisher N. | Moss D. | Whitehall S. | Woodyatt L. | Porter A. | Ruscoe S. | Haarhoff J. | Priestley P. | Berry P. | Price M. | Mackin L. |
|---|---|---|---|---|---|---|---|---|---|---|---|---|---|---|---|---|---|---|---|---|---|---|---|---|---|---|---|---|---|---|---|---|---|---|---|
| 4Q | Oct 28 | Easington Colliery | W | 2-0 | 1-0 | 478 | Whitehall, M Beesley | | 2 | 3 | | 6 | 4 | 7 | 8* | | | | | 5 | 9 | | | 1 | 12 | | 10 | | 11 | | | | | | |
| 1R | Nov 18 | PLYMOUTH ARGYLE | D | 1-1 | 0-0 | 3393 | Wright | | 4 | 3 | 14 | 6 | | 7 | 8 | | 12 | | | 5 | 9* | | | 1 | 2' | | 10 | | 11 | 13" | | | | | |
| 1Rr | 27 | Plymouth Argyle * | W | 2-1 | 1-0 | 3264 | Whitehall, Ruscoe | | 4 | 3 | | 6 | 12 | 7 | 8* | | 12 | | | 5 | 9 | | | 1 | 2' | | 10" | | 11 | 13 | | | | | |
| 2R | Dec 9 | OXFORD UNITED | W | 3-2 | 1-2 | 2798 | P Beesley, Whitehall (2) | | 4 | 3 | | 5 | | 7 | 11 | | 12 | | | 6 | 9' | | | 1 | 2* | | 10 | | 8 | 13 | | | | | |
| 3R | Jan 6 | Blackburn Rovers | L | 0-2 | 0-0 | 15223 | | | 4 | 3* | | 6 | 13 | 7 | 11" | | 14 | | | 5 | 9 | | | 1 | 2' | 12 | 10 | | 8 | | | | | | |

* Extra time played following score of 1-1 after 90 minutes

## F.A. TROPHY

| | Date | Opposition | | FT | HT | Att. | Goalscorers | Greygoose D. | Lancaster M. | Doughty M. | Gaunt C. | Beesley P. | Woods M. | Carden P. | Blackburn C. | Finney S. | Wright D. | Kerr D. | Richardson N. | Ruffer C. | Beesley M. | Shelton A. | Evans A. | Brown W. | Fisher N. | Moss D. | Whitehall S. | Woodyatt L. | Porter A. | Ruscoe S. | Haarhoff J. | Priestley P. | Berry P. | Price M. | Mackin L. |
|---|---|---|---|---|---|---|---|---|---|---|---|---|---|---|---|---|---|---|---|---|---|---|---|---|---|---|---|---|---|---|---|---|---|---|---|
| 3R | Jan 13 | DONCASTER ROVERS | W | 2-0 | 2-0 | 1479 | Whitehall (2) | | 4 | | | 6 | 12 | 7 | 11* | | | | | 5 | 9 | | | 1 | | 2' | 10 | 13 | 8 | 3 | | | | | |
| 4R | Feb 3 | ST ALBANS CITY | W | 3-2 | 1-1 | 1442 | Ruffer, Blackburn, Ruscoe | | 4 | 3" | | 6 | 12 | 7 | 8 | | | | | 5* | 10 | | | 1 | 2 | 13 | | 14 | | 11' | 9 | | | | |
| 5R | 24 | BLYTH SPARTANS | W | 4-2 | 2-0 | 1831 | Haarhoff, M Beesley, P Beesley, Whitehall | | 4 | 3 | 5* | 6 | 9" | 7 | | | 13 | | | | 10 | | | 1 | 2 | 12 | 14 | | | 11 | 8' | | | | |
| 6R | Mar 10 | SOUTHPORT | W | 1-0 | 0-0 | 3204 | Woods | | | 3 | 6 | | 4 | 7 | | | 14 | | | 5 | 9 | | | 1 | 8 | 2* | 10" | | 13 | 11 | 12' | | | | |
| SF1 | 31 | Canvey Island | L | 0-2 | 0-1 | 1221 | | | 4 | 3 | 12 | 6 | 9 | 7 | | | | | | 5* | 10" | | | 1 | 2 | 13 | 14 | | 8 | 11' | | | | | |
| SF2 | Apr 7 | CANVEY ISLAND | L | 0-2 | 0-1 | 2647 | | | 4 | 3 | 13 | 6' | 5 | 7 | 8 | | | | | | 9 | | | 1 | 2* | | 10 | | | 11 | 12 | | | | |

## ASSOCIATE MEMBERS (AUTO WINDSCREENS) SHIELD

| | Date | Opposition | | FT | HT | Att. | Goalscorers | Greygoose D. | Lancaster M. | Doughty M. | Gaunt C. | Beesley P. | Woods M. | Carden P. | Blackburn C. | Finney S. | Wright D. | Kerr D. | Richardson N. | Ruffer C. | Beesley M. | Shelton A. | Evans A. | Brown W. | Fisher N. | Moss D. | Whitehall S. | Woodyatt L. | Porter A. | Ruscoe S. | Haarhoff J. | Priestley P. | Berry P. | Price M. | Mackin L. |
|---|---|---|---|---|---|---|---|---|---|---|---|---|---|---|---|---|---|---|---|---|---|---|---|---|---|---|---|---|---|---|---|---|---|---|---|
| 1R | Dec 5 | HULL CITY | W | 1-0 | 0-0 | 770 | Carden | | 6 | 3 | 4 | | 12 | 7 | 11* | | 13 | | | 5 | | | | 1 | 2 | | 10 | | 8 | 9' | | | | | |
| 2R | Jan 30 | Port Vale | L | 0-2 | 0-1 | 2507 | | | 5 | 3' | | 6" | 4* | 7 | 8 | | 10 | | | 11 | 9 | | | 1 | 2 | 14 | | | | 13 | 12 | | | | |

## NATIONWIDE VARIETY CLUB TROPHY

| | Date | Opposition | | FT | HT | Att. | Goalscorers | Greygoose D. | Lancaster M. | Doughty M. | Gaunt C. | Beesley P. | Woods M. | Carden P. | Blackburn C. | Finney S. | Wright D. | Kerr D. | Richardson N. | Ruffer C. | Beesley M. | Shelton A. | Evans A. | Brown W. | Fisher N. | Moss D. | Whitehall S. | Woodyatt L. | Porter A. | Ruscoe S. | Haarhoff J. | Priestley P. | Berry P. | Price M. | Mackin L. |
|---|---|---|---|---|---|---|---|---|---|---|---|---|---|---|---|---|---|---|---|---|---|---|---|---|---|---|---|---|---|---|---|---|---|---|---|
| 2R | Oct 17 | HEDNESFORD TOWN* | D | 2-2 | 1-0 | 584 | Blackburn, M Beesley | | 5 | 3 | | | 4 | 13 | 8* | 10 | 12 | | 7' | 6 | 9 | | | 1 | 14 | 2 | | | | 11" | | | | | |
| 2Rr | Dec 18 | Hednesford Town' | W | 3-1 | 0-0 | 147 | Ruffer, Carden, Woods | | | | 4 | 6 | 12 | 7 | | | 10* | 13 | | 5 | 9 | | | | 3' | 2 | | | 8 | 11 | | | | 1" | 14 |
| 3R | Feb 6 | Southport | W | 3-0 | 2-0 | 685 | M Beesley (2), Carden | | 6 | 3 | | | 4 | 7 | 8 | | 12 | | | 5 | 10* | | | 1 | | 2" | | 14 | | 11 | 9' | | 13 | | |
| SF | May 3 | NUNEATON BOROUGH" | W | 2-1 | 1-1 | 602 | Blackburn, Wright | | 4 | 3 | 5 | | | | 8' | | 14 | 2* | | | 9 | | | 1 | 7 | 12 | 10 | 6 | 13 | 11" | | | | | |
| F | 7 | Kingstonian + | W | 0-0 | 0-0 | 495 | | | 4 | 3* | 5 | | | | 11" | | 13 | 12 | | | 9' | | | 1 | 7 | | 10 | 6 | 8 | 2 | 14 | | | | |

Chester received a bye in the 1st Round * Extra time played following score of 2-2 after 90 minutes ' Extra time played following score of 1-1 after 90 minutes " Extra time played following score of 1-1 after 90 minutes

+ Extra time played following score of 0-0 after 90 minutes. Chester won 4-2 on penalties. (Porter, Whitehall, Wright, Fisher)

## FRIENDLIES

| | Date | Opposition | | FT | HT | Att. | Goalscorers |
|---|---|---|---|---|---|---|---|
| 1 | Jul 16 | Connah's Quay Nomads | D | 1-1 | 0-1 | 676 | M Beesley |
| 2 | 25 | Runcorn | W | 2-1 | 1-0 | 469 | Wright, Ruscoe |
| 3 | 29 | Aberystwyth Town | W | 2-1 | 1-1 | 300 | Wright, Shelton |
| 4 | Aug 1 | BRISTOL CITY X1 | W | 1-0 | 1-0 | 917 | Wright |
| 5 | 4 | Bangor City | W | 3-0 | 0-0 | 250 | Gaunt (2), Finney |
| 6 | 7 | BOLTON WANDERERS | D | 0-0 | 0-0 | 1205 | |
| 7 | 12 | Stafford Rangers | W | 4-0 | 2-0 | 459 | Carden,Eccleston(og).M Beesley,Shelton |

# SEASON 2001-02

## NATIONWIDE CONFERENCE

| | Date | Opposition | | FT | HT | Att. | Goalscorers | Brown W. | Rose S. | Rose M. | Porter A. | Ruffer C. | Blackburn C. | Hill S. | Kerr D. | Wright D. | Woodyatt L. | Ruscoe S. | Haarhoff J. | Hopwood C. | Roberts P. | Lancaster M. | Malkin C. | Beesley M. | Spink D. | Kilgannon W. | Linighan D. | McNiven D. | Lopez C. | Halford S. | Baxter B. | O'Brien C. | O'Brien M. | Williams G. | Higgins A. | Carden P. | Jenkins I. | Brown D. | Collins D. | Brabin G. | Bolland P. | Whittaker S. | McGorry B. | Williams M | Carey S. | McElhatton M. | Tate C. |
|---|---|---|---|---|---|---|---|---|---|---|---|---|---|---|---|---|---|---|---|---|---|---|---|---|---|---|---|---|---|---|---|---|---|---|---|---|---|---|---|---|---|---|---|---|---|---|---|
| 1 | Aug 18 | WOKING | L | 0-2 | 0-2 | 745 | | 1 | 2" | 3 | 4 | 5 | 6 | 7 | 8 | 9' | 10* | 11 | 12 | 13 | 14 | | | | | | | | | | | | | | | | | | | | | | | | | | |
| 2 | 21 | Southport | L | 2-3 | 0-1 | 1554 | Beesley, Wright | 1 | 2 | 3 | 4 | 5 | 8' | 7" | 13 | 12 | | 11 | 14 | | | 6 | 9* | 10 | | | | | | | | | | | | | | | | | | | | | | | |
| 3 | 25 | Hayes | W | 3-1 | 2-1 | 507 | Beesley (2), Spink | 1 | 2 | 3 | 4 | 5* | | 7' | 8 | 13 | | 11 | 12 | | 14 | 6 | | 10 | 9" | | | | | | | | | | | | | | | | | | | | | | |
| 4 | 27 | NUNEATON BOROUGH | W | 1-0 | 0-0 | 770 | Hill | 1 | 2 | 3 | 4 | | 13 | 7* | 8' | 12 | | 11 | 9 | | | 6 | | 10 | 5 | | | | | | | | | | | | | | | | | | | | | | |
| 5 | Sep 1 | Barnet | L | 1-3 | 0-1 | 1197 | Beesley | 1 | 2 | 3 | 4 | | | 7" | 8 | 14 | 13 | 11 | 9* | 12 | | 6 | | 10 | 5' | | | | | | | | | | | | | | | | | | | | | | |
| 6 | 4 | TELFORD UNITED | D | 2-2 | 1-0 | 605 | Spink, Ruscoe | 1 | 2 | | 4 | 5 | | 7* | 8 | 12 | 3 | 11 | | | | 6 | | 10 | 9 | | | | | | | | | | | | | | | | | | | | | | |
| 7 | 8 | FarnboroughTown | D | 1-1 | 0-1 | 954 | Beesley | 1 | | 3 | 4 | 5 | | 7* | 8" | | 2' | 11 | 12 | | 13 | 6 | | 10 | 9 | 14 | | | | | | | | | | | | | | | | | | | | | |
| 8 | 11 | STALYBRIDGE CELTIC | D | 0-0 | 0-0 | 695 | | 1 | 2* | 3 | 4 | 5 | | 7' | | | | 11 | 12 | | 13 | 6 | | 10 | 9 | 8 | | | | | | | | | | | | | | | | | | | | | |
| 9 | 15 | BOSTON UNITED | L | 1-2 | 0-1 | 821 | Beesley | 1 | 12 | 11 | 4' | 5 | 13 | 7 | | | | | | | | 2 | | 10 | 6* | 8 | 3 | 9 | | | | | | | | | | | | | | | | | | | |
| 10 | 18 | Leigh RMI | L | 0-3 | 0-2 | 547 | | 1 | | 3 | 4 | 5 | 8* | 7 | | | | 11' | | 14 | 13 | 2 | | 10 | | 12 | 6 | 9" | | | | | | | | | | | | | | | | | | | |
| 11 | 22 | DAGENHAM & REDBRIDGE | L | 0-1 | 0-0 | 643 | | 1 | | 3 | 4 | 5 | 8 | 7' | 11 | | 14 | 12 | | | | 2 | | 10 | | 13 | 6" | 9* | | | | | | | | | | | | | | | | | | | |
| 12 | 29 | Stevenage Borough | L | 1-2 | 1-0 | 1690 | Beesley | 1 | 13 | 3 | 4 | | | 7 | 9' | | 8 | 11 | | | 2* | 5 | 12 | 10" | 6 | | | | 14 | | | | | | | | | | | | | | | | | | |
| 13 | Oct 2 | Scarborough | L | 1-2 | 0-1 | 783 | Ruscoe | 1 | | 3 | 4 | | | 7 | | 12 | 5 | 11 | | | | 2 | 9* | 10 | 6' | 8 | | | 13 | | | | | | | | | | | | | | | | | | |
| 14 | 6 | MARGATE | L | 0-3 | 0-2 | 835 | | 1 | | 3 | 13 | | | | | 9" | 2 | 7' | | 14 | | 4 | | 10 | | 12 | | | | 5 | 6* | 8 | 11 | | | | | | | | | | | | | | |
| 15 | 9 | HEREFORD UNITED | W | 2-0 | 0-0 | 1142 | Haarhoff, Ruscoe | 1 | | 3 | 4 | | 8' | | | 12 | | 13 | 9 | | | 6 | | 10 | | 2* | | | | 5 | | 7 | 11 | | | | | | | | | | | | | | |
| 16 | 13 | Morecambe | W | 3-0 | 1-0 | 1764 | M Rose, M O'Brien (2) | 1 | | 3 | 4 | | 8 | | | | | 12 | 9 | | | 6 | | 10* | | 2 | | | | 5 | 12 | 7 | 11 | | | | | | | | | | | | | | |
| 17 | 20 | DONCASTER ROVERS | D | 1-1 | 0-1 | 2148 | Ruscoe | 1 | | 3 | 4 | | 8 | | | 13 | | 12 | 9' | | | 6 | | | 10 | 2* | | | | 5 | | 7 | 11 | | | | | | | | | | | | | | |
| 18 | Nov 3 | Yeovil Town | W | 1-0 | 1-0 | 2833 | Beesley | 1 | | 3 | 4 | 6 | 8 | | | | | | 9* | | | | 12 | 10 | | 2 | | | | 5 | | 7 | 11 | | | | | | | | | | | | | | |
| 19 | 10 | FOREST GREEN ROVERS | L | 2-3 | 0-1 | 1330 | M Rose, Beesley | 1 | | 3 | 4" | 5 | 8 | | 14 | | | 13 | 9* | | | 6 | 12 | 10 | | 2 | | | | | | 7 | 11' | | | | | | | | | | | | | | |
| 20 | 24 | Dover Athletic | L | 0-1 | 0-0 | 905 | | 1 | | 3 | 4 | 6 | | | 8 | 11 | | 2 | | | | | 9 | | | | | | | 5 | | 7 | | 10* | 12 | | | | | | | | | | | | |
| 21 | Dec 1 | Woking | L | 1-2 | 0-2 | 1793 | Blackburn | 1 | 7 | 3 | 4 | | 8 | | | | | 2 | | | | 6 | 9' | 10 | | | | | | 5 | | | 13 | 12 | | 11* | | | | | | | | | | | |
| 22 | 8 | MORECAMBE | D | 1-1 | 0-1 | 1466 | Beesley | 1 | 13 | 3 | | | 8 | | | | | 11 | | | | 6' | 9* | 10 | | | | | | 5 | | 7 | | 12 | | 4 | 2 | | | | | | | | | | |
| 23 | 15 | SOUTHPORT | L | 0-2 | 0-0 | 1473 | | 1 | | 3 | 4 | 6 | 8 | | | | | | 12 | | | | | 10 | | | | | | 5 | | | 11 | | | 7 | 2 | 9* | | | | | | | | | |
| 24 | 26 | Northwich Victoria | L | 1-3 | 0-1 | 1930 | Blackburn | 1 | | | 4 | 11 | 8 | | | | | | | | | | | 12 | 6 | | | | | 5' | | 7 | 10 | | | 2 | 3 | 9* | 13 | | | | | | | | |
| 25 | 29 | HAYES | W | 3-1 | 1-0 | 1250 | Ruffer, Blackburn, Porter | 1 | | | 4 | 5 | 8 | | | | 7 | 11 | 12 | | | | | 10* | 6 | | | | | | | | | | | 2 | 3 | 9' | 13 | | | | | | | | |
| 26 | Jan 8 | NORTHWICH VICTORIA | L | 1-2 | 1-1 | 1660 | Blackburn | 1 | | | | 5* | 7" | | | | 2 | 3 | 14 | | | 6 | | 10 | 12 | | | | | | | | | | | 8 | 4 | 9' | 13 | 11 | | | | | | | |
| 27 | 19 | BARNET | W | 1-0 | 0-0 | 1421 | Porter (pen) | 1 | | | 7 | | 8 | | | | 4 | | 12 | | | 2 | | 10 | | | | | | | | | | | | 3 | | 9 | | 6 | 5 | 11* | | | | | |
| 28 | 22 | Telford United | W | 3-0 | 1-0 | 1047 | Woodyatt, Beesley (2) | 1 | | | 7 | | 13 | | | | 2* | | | | | 4 | | 10 | | | | | | | | | | | | 3 | 12 | 9 | | 6 | 5 | 11' | 8 | | | | |
| 29 | Feb 9 | Margate | D | 0-0 | 0-0 | 984 | | 1 | | 3 | 12 | | 8 | | | | | | | | | 2 | | 10 | 11 | | | | | | | | | | | 4 | | 9* | | 6 | 5 | | 7 | | | | |
| 30 | 19 | Nuneaton Borough | W | 3-1 | 2-0 | 760 | Woodyatt, M Rose (2) | 1 | | 3 | | | 13 | | | | 2 | | | | | 4 | | 10" | 9* | | | | | | | | | | | 12 | | | 14 | | 5 | | 8' | 6 | 7 | 11 | |
| 31 | Mar 2 | LEIGH RMI | D | 1-1 | 1-1 | 1572 | Brabin | 1 | | | | | 14 | | | | 2 | | 13 | | | 4 | 12 | 10* | 9' | | | | | | | | | | | 3 | | | | 6 | 5 | | 8" | | 7 | 11 | |
| 32 | 5 | SCARBOROUGH | D | 0-0 | 0-0 | 1475 | | 1 | | 3 | | | 4 | | | | 12 | | 13 | | | 2 | | 10' | | | | | | | | | | | | | | | | 6 | 5 | 11* | | | 7 | 8 | 9 |
| 33 | 9 | Stalybridge Celtic | W | 4-0 | 1-0 | 1002 | Beesley, Tate, McElhatton(2) | 1 | | 3 | | | | | | | 2 | | | | | | | 10 | | | | | | | | | | | | | | | | 6 | 5 | | 8 | 4 | 7 | 11 | 9 |
| 34 | 23 | Boston United | W | 1-0 | 0-0 | 2519 | Beesley | 1 | | 3 | | | | | | | | | | | | 4 | | 10 | | | | | | | | | | | | | | | | 6 | 5 | | 2 | 12 | 7 | 8* | 9 |
| 35 | 26 | Hereford United | L | 0-1 | 0-1 | 1295 | | 1 | | 3 | | | 13 | | | | | | 14 | | | 4 | | 10 | | | | | | | | | | | | | | 12 | | 6 | 5 | | 2 | | 7' | 8 | 9* |
| 36 | 30 | Doncaster Rovers | L | 0-2 | 0-2 | 2089 | | 1 | | 3 | | | 14 | | | | 12 | | | | | 2 | | 10 | 13 | | | | | | | | | | | | | 9" | | 6 | 5 | | 4* | | 7 | 8' | |
| 37 | Apr 1 | YEOVIL TOWN | D | 1-1 | 0-1 | 1807 | Lancaster | 1 | | 3 | | | | | | | | | 14 | | | 2 | | 10 | 9' | | | | | | | | | | | 12 | | 13 | | 6 | 5 | | 8 | 4 | 7* | | |
| 38 | 6 | Forest Green Rovers | W | 2-0 | 0-0 | 802 | Beesley (2) | 1 | | 3 | | | 13 | | | | 4' | | | | | 2 | | 10 | 9" | | | | | | | | | | | 7 | | | | 6 | 5 | | 8 | 12 | | 11 | |
| 39 | 13 | DOVER ATHLETIC | W | 3-0 | 1-0 | 1660 | D Brown, Brabin (2) | 1 | | | | | 4 | | | | | | 12 | | | 2 | | | 9' | | | | | | | | | | | 3 | | 10" | 13 | 6 | 5 | 14 | 8 | | 7 | | |
| 40 | 16 | FARNBOROUGH TOWN | W | 1-0 | 0-0 | 1386 | Whittaker | 1 | | 14 | | | 4 | | | | | | 13 | | | 2 | | | 10' | | | | | | | | | | | | | | 9 | 6 | 5 | 3" | 8 | 12 | 7 | | |
| 41 | 20 | STEVENAGE BOROUGH | W | 5-1 | 1-0 | 1866 | Whittaker (3),D. Brown,Ruffer | 1 | | 3 | | 13 | 8 | | | | | | 12 | | | 2 | | | | | | | | | | | 14 | | | | | 10 | 9* | 6 | | 11 | 4' | 5 | 7" | | |
| 42 | 27 | Dagenham & Redbridge | L | 0-3 | 0-0 | 3939 | | 1 | | 3 | | 12 | 7 | | | | 14 | | 13 | | | 2 | | | | | | | | | | | | | | 4" | | 9" | 10 | 6 | | 11' | 8 | 5 | | | |
| | | | | | | | Apps | 42 | 8 | 33 | 25 | 16 | 22 | 13 | 9 | 3 | 14 | 17 | 7 | | 1 | 35 | 5 | 34 | 19 | 8 | 3 | 3 | | 10 | 1 | 9 | 8 | 1 | | 13 | 5 | 11 | 3 | 16 | 14 | 6 | 14 | 5 | 11 | 8 | 4 |
| | | | | | | | Subs | | 3 | 1 | 2 | 2 | 8 | | 2 | 8 | 5 | 5 | 17 | 4 | 5 | | 4 | 1 | 2 | 4 | | | 2 | | 1 | | 2 | 2 | 1 | 2 | 1 | 2 | 5 | | | 1 | | 3 | | | |
| | | | | | | | Goals | | | 4 | 2 | 2 | 4 | 1 | | 1 | 2 | 4 | 1 | | | 1 | | 16 | 2 | | | | | | | | 2 | | | | | 2 | | 3 | | 4 | | | | 2 | 1 |

## F.A. CUP

| | Date | Opposition | | FT | HT | Att. | Goalscorers | Brown W. | Rose S. | Rose M. | Porter A. | Ruffer C. | Blackburn C. | Hill S. | Kerr D. | Wright D. | Woodyatt L. | Ruscoe S. | Haarhoff J. | Hopwood C. | Roberts P. | Lancaster M. | Malkin C. | Beesley M. | Spink D. | Kilgannon W. | Linighan D. | McNiven D. | Lopez C. | Halford S. | Baxter B. | O'Brien C. | O'Brien M. | Williams G. | Higgins A. | Carden P. | Jenkins I. | Brown D. | Collins D. | Brabin G. | Bolland P. | Whittaker S. | McGorry B. | Williams M | Carey S. | McElhatton M. | Tate C. |
|---|---|---|---|---|---|---|---|---|---|---|---|---|---|---|---|---|---|---|---|---|---|---|---|---|---|---|---|---|---|---|---|---|---|---|---|---|---|---|---|---|---|---|---|---|---|---|---|
| 4Q | Oct 27 | Barrow | L | 0-1 | 0-0 | 2833 | | 1 | | 3 | 4 | 7 | 8 | | 11* | 13 | | 2' | 9 | | | 6 | | 12 | 10 | | | | | 5 | | | | | | | | | | | | | | | | | |

## F.A. TROPHY

| | Date | Opposition | | FT | HT | Att. | Goalscorers | Brown W. | Rose S. | Rose M. | Porter A. | Ruffer C. | Blackburn C. | Hill S. | Kerr D. | Wright D. | Woodyatt L. | Ruscoe S. | Haarhoff J. | Hopwood C. | Roberts P. | Lancaster M. | Malkin C. | Beesley M. | Spink D. | Kilgannon W. | Linighan D. | McNiven D. | Lopez C. | Halford S. | Baxter B. | O'Brien C. | O'Brien M. | Williams G. | Higgins A. | Carden P. | Jenkins I. | Brown D. | Collins D. | Brabin G. | Bolland P. | Whittaker S. | McGorry B. | Williams M | Carey S. | McElhatton M. | Tate C. |
|---|---|---|---|---|---|---|---|---|---|---|---|---|---|---|---|---|---|---|---|---|---|---|---|---|---|---|---|---|---|---|---|---|---|---|---|---|---|---|---|---|---|---|---|---|---|---|---|
| 3R | Jan 12 | STOURPORT SWIFTS | D | 1-1 | 0-0 | 1006 | Haarhoff | 1 | | 8 | 4 | | 7' | | | 13 | 2 | | 12 | | | 5 | | 10 | 6 | | | | | | | | 11 | | | | 3 | 9* | | | | | | | | | |
| 3Rr | 15 | Stourport Swifts | W | 3-0 | 1-0 | 630 | Beesley (2), D Brown | 1 | | 3 | 12 | | 8 | | | | 2 | | | | | 4 | | 10 | 6 | | | | | | | | 11* | | | 7 | 5 | 9 | | | | | | | | | |
| 4R | Feb 2 | SOLIHULL BOROUGH | D | 0-0 | 0-0 | 1282 | | 1 | | | 7* | | 12 | | | | 2 | | 14 | | | 4 | | 10 | 13 | | | | | | | | | | | 3 | | 9" | | 6 | 5 | 11' | 8 | | | | |
| 4Rr | 12 | Solihull Borough | W | 4-2 | 1-1 | 721 | Spink (3), Bolland | 1 | | 3 | 13 | | 8 | | | | 14 | | | | | 2 | | 10* | 11 | | | | | | | | | | | 4" | | 12 | | 6 | 5 | 9' | 7 | | | | |
| 5R | 23 | HEREFORD UNITED | W | 2-1 | 1-0 | 1747 | Bolland, Haarhoff | 1 | | | | | 8 | | | | 2 | | 12 | | | 4 | | 10 | 9 | | | | | | | | | | | 3 | | | | 6 | 5 | 11* | 7 | | | | |
| 6R | Mar 16 | Burton Albion | L | 0-2 | 0-0 | 3584 | | 1 | | 3 | | | | | | | 2 | | 13 | | | 4 | | 10 | | | | | | | | | | | | 7 | | 12 | | 6 | 5 | | 8 | | | 11* | 9' |

## J C THOMPSON CHAMPIONSHIP SHIELD

| | Date | Opposition | | FT | HT | Att. | Goalscorers | Brown W. | Rose S. | Rose M. | Porter A. | Ruffer C. | Blackburn C. | Hill S. | Kerr D. | Wright D. | Woodyatt L. | Ruscoe S. | Haarhoff J. | Hopwood C. | Roberts P. | Lancaster M. | Malkin C. | Beesley M. | Spink D. | Kilgannon W. | Linighan D. | McNiven D. | Lopez C. | Halford S. | Baxter B. | O'Brien C. | O'Brien M. | Williams G. | Higgins A. | Carden P. | Jenkins I. | Brown D. | Collins D. | Brabin G. | Bolland P. | Whittaker S. | McGorry B. | Williams M | Carey S. | McElhatton M. | Tate C. |
|---|---|---|---|---|---|---|---|---|---|---|---|---|---|---|---|---|---|---|---|---|---|---|---|---|---|---|---|---|---|---|---|---|---|---|---|---|---|---|---|---|---|---|---|---|---|---|---|
| F | Nov 13 | Rushden & Diamonds | L | 2-2 | 0-1 | 937 | G. Williams, Beesley | 1 | | 3 | 4* | 6 | 8 | | 13 | | | 2' | | | | 13 | 9" | 10 | 12 | | | | | 5 | 14 | 7 | | 11* | | | | | | | | | | | | | |

* Extra time played following score of 2-2 after 90 minutes. Chester lost 3-4 on penalties (Kerr, Beesley, W. Brown)

## FRIENDLIES

| | Date | Opposition | | FT | HT | Att. | Goalscorers |
|---|---|---|---|---|---|---|---|
| 1 | Jul 19 | Connah's Quay Nomads | W | 3-0 | 1-0 | 350 | Lancaster, Ruscoe, M Beesley |
| 2 | 28 | PORT VALE | W | 1-0 | 0-0 | 254 | Whitehall |
| 3 | Aug 2 | TNS (a) | L | 0-2 | 0-1 | 150 | |
| 4 | 4 | MANCHESTER CITY X1 | L | 2-3 | 2-2 | 440 | Hill, Kilgannon (pen) |
| 5 | 9 | Caernarfon Town | D | 3-3 | 1-1 | | Hill (2, (1 pen)), Ruscoe |

**2001/2002 Season:**
Back – Blackburn, Malkin, Spink, Lancaster, Brown, Jago, M Rose, Porter, S Rose
Middle – Haarhoff, Halford, Roberts, Chamberlain, Woodyatt, Ruscoe, C O'Brien, Stevens (Physio)
Front – Wright, Berry, Ruffer, Kilgannon, Mungall (Manager), Beesley, M O'Brien, Kerr.

**2002/03 Season:**
Back - Sugden, Guyett, Hatswell, Lancaster, Ruffer, Cameron, Worsnop, Bolland, Brown, Collins, Beesley, Brown, McIntyre, Kelly, Twiss
Front - Blackburn, Haarhoff, Whittaker, Brodie, Hinnigan (Physio), Wright (Manager), Bleasdale (Assistant Manager), Alan Cottrell (Chief Scout), Carey, Davies, Woodyatt, Carden.

# SEASON 2002-03

## NATIONWIDE CONFERENCE

| | Date | | Opposition | | FT | HT | Att. | Goalscorers | Brown W. | Woodyatt L. | McIntyre K. | Ruffer C. | Guyett S. | Hatswell W. | Blackburn C. | Kelly J. | Twiss M. | Beesley M. | Davies B. | Sugden R. | Cameron D. | Harkness S. | Carey S. | Brown M. | Brodie S. | Carden P. | Bolland P. | Lancaster M. | McCaldon I. | Brady J. | Clare D. | Tate C. | Clifford M. | Collins D. | Griffin A. | Quayle M. | Joy I. | Worsnop J. | [illegible] |
|---|---|---|---|---|---|---|---|---|---|---|---|---|---|---|---|---|---|---|---|---|---|---|---|---|---|---|---|---|---|---|---|---|---|---|---|---|---|---|
| 1 | Aug | 17 | KETTERING TOWN | D | 0-0 | 0-0 | 2367 | | 1 | 2' | 3 | 4 | 5 | 6 | 7 | 8 | 9 | 10* | 11 | 12 | 13 | | | | | | | | | | | | | | | | | | |
| 2 | | 19 | Telford United | W | 1-0 | 0-0 | 1409 | Sugden | 1 | | 3 | 13 | 5 | 6 | 7 | 8 | 9 | | | 10* | 11 | 2 | 4' | 12 | | | | | | | | | | | | | | | |
| 3 | | 24 | Barnet | W | 3-0 | 0-0 | 1347 | Sugden, Twiss, Beesley | 1 | 4 | 3 | 13 | 5 | 6 | 7 | 8 | 9 | 12 | | 10' | 11* | 2 | | | | | | | | | | | | | | | | | |
| 4 | | 26 | SCARBOROUGH | D | 0-0 | 0-0 | 2292 | | 1 | 13 | 3 | 4 | 5 | 6 | 7 | 8 | 9 | 12 | | 10* | | 2 | | 11' | | | | | | | | | | | | | | | |
| 5 | | 31 | Forest Green Rovers | W | 2-0 | 2-0 | 812 | Beesley (2 (1 pen)) | 1 | | 3 | 4 | 5 | 6 | 7 | 8 | 9* | 10 | 13 | 12 | | 2 | | | 11' | | | | | | | | | | | | | | |
| 6 | Sep | 3 | MORECAMBE | W | 2-1 | 0-0 | 2039 | Sugden, Twiss | 1 | | 3 | 12 | 5 | 6 | 7 | 8 | 9 | 10' | 14 | 11" | | 2* | | 13 | | 4 | | | | | | | | | | | | | |
| 7 | | 6 | LEIGH RMI | W | 2-1 | 0-1 | 2273 | Sugden, Beesley | 1 | | 3 | 2 | 5 | 6 | 7 | 8 | 9 | 12 | | 10* | | | | 11 | | 4 | | | | | | | | | | | | | |
| 8 | | 14 | Hereford United | D | 0-0 | 0-0 | 2289 | | 1 | | 3 | 2 | 5 | 6 | 7 | 8 | 9 | 10' | | 12 | | | | 11* | 13 | 4 | | | | | | | | | | | | | |
| 9 | | 17 | Halifax Town | D | 0-0 | 0-0 | 2178 | | 1 | 7 | 3 | 6 | 4 | | | 8 | 9 | 13 | | 10' | | 2 | | 12 | 11* | | 5 | | | | | | | | | | | | |
| 10 | | 21 | DAGENHAM & REDBRIDGE | W | 5-2 | 2-2 | 2231 | Sugden(2),Kelly (p),Bolland,Guyett | 1 | | 3 | 6 | 4 | | 7 | 8 | 9 | | | 10 | | 2 | | 12 | 11* | | 5 | | | | | | | | | | | | |
| 11 | | 24 | BURTON ALBION | W | 2-1 | 0-1 | 2440 | Sugden (2) | 1 | | 3 | 6 | 4* | | 7' | 8 | 9" | | | 10 | 14 | 2 | | 13 | | 11 | 5 | 12 | | | | | | | | | | | |
| 12 | | 28 | Doncaster Rovers | D | 0-0 | 0-0 | 4867 | | 1 | 11 | 3 | 6 | 4 | | 7* | 8 | 9' | 13 | | 10 | | 2 | | 12 | | | 5 | | | | | | | | | | | | |
| 13 | Oct | 5 | Margate | W | 1-0 | 0-0 | 925 | Cameron | | | 3 | 6 | | | 12 | 8 | 9" | | | 10' | 14 | 2* | | 13 | | 11 | 5 | 4 | 1 | 7 | | | | | | | | | |
| 14 | | 8 | NUNEATON BOROUGH | L | 1-2 | 0-1 | 2564 | Sugden | 1 | | 3 | 2 | | 6 | 7 | 8 | 14 | | 12 | 10" | 9 | | | 13 | | 4* | 5 | | | 11' | | | | | | | | | |
| 15 | | 13 | GRAVESEND & NORTHFLEET | D | 1-1 | 1-1 | 2210 | Sugden | | | 3 | 2 | | 6 | | 8 | 12 | | | 10 | 9 | | 4 | 7* | | | 5 | | 1 | 11 | | | | | | | | | |
| 16 | | 19 | Woking | L | 0-1 | 0-0 | 2019 | | 1 | | 3 | | | 6 | 7 | | 13 | 14 | 12 | 10" | 9' | | 4 | 11* | | | 5 | 2 | | 8 | | | | | | | | | |
| 17 | Nov | 2 | YEOVIL TOWN | D | 2-2 | 1-0 | 3821 | Clare (2) | 1 | 3 | | 6 | 4 | | 7 | | | | 11 | 10' | | | | 12 | | 2 | 5 | | | 8* | 9 | 13 | | | | | | | |
| 18 | | 9 | Stevenage Borough | W | 1-0 | 1-0 | 1716 | Clare | 1 | | 3 | 13 | 4 | 6 | | | | | 11 | 10* | | | 8' | | | 2 | 5 | | | 7 | 9 | 12 | | | | | | | |
| 19 | | 23 | MARGATE | W | 5-0 | 4-0 | 1930 | Clare (3), Hatswell, Sugden | 1 | | 3 | | 4 | 6 | | | 14 | 13 | 11 | 10' | | | 8 | 12 | | 2 | 5 | | | 7* | 9^ | | | | | | | | |
| 20 | | 30 | Southport | W | 3-1 | 1-0 | 2447 | Carden, Carey, Ruffer | 1 | 12 | 3 | 13 | 4 | 6 | | | | | 11 | 10" | | | 8' | 14 | | 2 | 5 | | | 7* | 9 | | | | | | | | |
| 21 | Dec | 14 | Leigh RMI | W | 4-0 | 3-0 | 851 | Clare (2), Sugden, Guyett | 1 | | 3 | | 4 | 6 | | 12 | 13 | | 11 | 10' | | | 8 | | | 2 | 5 | | | 7* | 9 | | | | | | | | |
| 22 | | 20 | HEREFORD UNITED | L | 0-1 | 0-0 | 2507 | | 1 | | 3 | | 4 | 6 | | | | | 11 | 10' | 13 | | 8 | 12 | | 2 | 5 | | | 7* | 9 | | | | | | | | |
| 23 | | 26 | Northwich Victoria | D | 1-1 | 0-1 | 2305 | Twiss | 1 | | 3 | 14 | 4 | 6 | | 12 | 10" | | 11 | | | | 8* | 13 | | 2 | 5 | | | 7' | 9 | | | | | | | | |
| 24 | | 28 | TELFORD UNITED | W | 4-1 | 1-0 | 2594 | Clare (2, (1 pen)), Beesley, Davies | 1 | | 3 | 12 | 4' | 6 | | | 11 | 10 | 7 | | | | 8* | 13 | | 2 | 5 | | | | 9 | | | | | | | | |
| 25 | Jan | 1 | NORTHWICH VICTORIA | L | 2-3 | 1-0 | 3151 | Clare (2) | 1 | | 3 | 4 | | 6 | | 14 | 11" | 10* | 7 | | 12 | | | 8' | | 2 | 5 | | | 13 | 9 | | | | | | | | |
| 26 | | 4 | Kettering Town | W | 1-0 | 1-0 | 1788 | Clare | 1 | 3 | | 4 | | 6 | | 8 | 11 | | 7 | 10 | | | | | | 2 | 5 | | | | 9 | | | | | | | | |
| 27 | | 18 | BARNET | D | 1-1 | 0-1 | 1944 | Clare | 1 | | 3" | 6 | 4 | | | 7 | 13 | | 11 | 10' | | | | 12 | | 8 | | | | | 9 | | 2* | 5 | 14 | | | | |
| 28 | | 25 | Scarborough | W | 1-0 | 0-0 | 1938 | Clare | 1 | | 3 | 5 | 4 | 6 | | 7 | | | 11 | 10 | | | | 12 | | 8 | | | | | 9* | | | 2 | | | | | |
| 29 | Feb | 8 | FOREST GREEN ROVERS | L | 0-1 | 0-1 | 2245 | | 1 | | 3 | 4 | | 6 | | 7' | 13 | 12 | 11" | 10* | | | 8 | 14 | | 2 | 5 | | | | 9 | | | | | | | | |
| 30 | | 15 | Morecambe | D | 1-1 | 0-0 | 2012 | Twiss | 1 | | 3 | | 4 | 6 | | 7 | 12 | | 11 | 10* | | | | | | 8 | 5 | | | | 9 | | | 2 | | | | | |
| 31 | | 22 | Dagenham & Redbridge | L | 0-1 | 0-1 | 1870 | | 1 | | 3 | | 4 | 6 | | 7 | 13 | | 11* | 14 | | | | | | 8 | 5 | | | 12 | 9" | | | 2 | | 10' | | | |
| 32 | Mar | 1 | HALIFAX TOWN | W | 2-0 | 1-0 | 2928 | Clare, Quayle | 1 | 2 | 3 | | 4 | 12 | | | 10 | | | | | | 7 | | | 8 | 5 | | | | 9 | | | 6 | | 11* | | | |
| 33 | | 8 | Burton Albion | L | 0-2 | 0-1 | 2183 | | 1 | 2" | 3 | 4 | | | | 7 | 10' | 14 | | 12 | | | | | | 8 | 5 | | | 13 | 9 | | | 6 | | 11* | | | |
| 34 | | 17 | DONCASTER ROVERS | W | 1-0 | 0-0 | 2928 | Twiss | 1 | 2* | 3 | 5 | 4 | | | 7" | 12 | | 11 | | 13 | | 14 | | | 8 | | | | | 9 | | | 6 | | 10' | | | |
| 35 | | 22 | SOUTHPORT | W | 2-0 | 0-0 | 2292 | Carden, Lane (og) | 1 | | 3 | 5 | 4 | | | 7 | 10' | 8* | 11 | | | | 13 | | | 2 | | | | | 9 | | | 6 | | 12 | | | |
| 36 | | 29 | Farnborough Town | W | 2-1 | 1-1 | 1050 | Davies, Cameron (pen) | 1 | | 3 | 6' | 4 | | | 7 | 14 | 10" | 11 | | 12 | | 13 | | | 8 | 5 | | | | | | | 2 | | 9* | | | |
| 37 | Apr | 5 | Gravesend & Northfleet | W | 1-0 | 0-0 | 1273 | Beesley | 1 | | 3 | 6 | | 12 | | 7 | 13 | 10' | 11 | | | | 4* | | | 8 | 5 | | | | | | | 2 | | 9 | | | |
| 38 | | 12 | WOKING | D | 2-2 | 0-1 | 2165 | Ruffer, Twiss | 1 | | 3 | 2 | 4 | 6' | | 7 | 13 | 10* | 11 | | | | | | | 8" | 5 | | | 14 | 9 | | | | | 12 | | | |
| 39 | | 15 | FARNBOROUGH TOWN | L | 0-2 | 0-2 | 1869 | | 1 | 2* | 3 | | 4 | | 12 | | 13 | | 11 | 10" | | | 8 | | | | 5 | | | 7 | 9 | | | | | 14 | 6' | | |
| 40 | | 19 | Nuneaton Borough | L | 0-1 | 0-1 | 1371 | | | | 3 | | 4 | | 14 | 7 | 13 | | 11 | 12 | 10* | | | | | 2 | 5 | | | 8' | 9 | | | | | | 6" | 1 | |
| 41 | | 21 | STEVENAGE BOROUGH | W | 2-0 | 0-0 | 1745 | Brady, Clare (pen) | 1 | | 3 | | 4 | 6 | 14 | | 13 | | 11" | 10* | 12 | | 8 | | | 2 | 5 | | | 7 | 9' | | | | | | | | |
| 42 | | 26 | Yeovil Town | D | 1-1 | 0-1 | 8111 | McIntyre | 1 | 2 | 14 | | | 6 | 10 | 7 | 11" | | 13 | 12 | 9* | | | | | 4' | 5 | | | 8 | | | | | | | 3 | | |
| | | | | | | | | Apps | 39 | 11 | 39 | 24 | 32 | 27 | 15 | 29 | 21 | 10 | 24 | 26 | 7 | 10 | 15 | 6 | 3 | 31 | 30 | 2 | 2 | 15 | 23 | | 1 | 10 | | 6 | 3 | 1 | |
| | | | | | | | | Subs | | 2 | 1 | 7 | | 2 | 4 | 3 | 16 | 9 | 5 | 7 | 8 | | 3 | 17 | 1 | | | 1 | | 4 | | 2 | | | 1 | 3 | | | |
| | | | | | | | | Goals | | | 1 | 2 | 2 | 1 | | 1 | 6 | 6 | 2 | 12 | 2 | | 1 | | | 2 | 1 | | | 1 | 17 | | | | | 1 | | | |

Own goals 1

## PLAY OFFS

| | Date | | Opposition | | FT | HT | Att. | Goalscorers | Brown W. | Woodyatt L. | McIntyre K. | Ruffer C. | Guyett S. | Hatswell W. | Blackburn C. | Kelly J. | Twiss M. | Beesley M. | Davies B. | Sugden R. | Cameron D. | Harkness S. | Carey S. | Brown M. | Brodie S. | Carden P. | Bolland P. | Lancaster M. | McCaldon I. | Brady J. | Clare D. | Tate C. | Clifford M. | Collins D. | Griffin A. | Quayle M. | Joy I. | Worsnop J. | [illegible] |
|---|---|---|---|---|---|---|---|---|---|---|---|---|---|---|---|---|---|---|---|---|---|---|---|---|---|---|---|---|---|---|---|---|---|---|---|---|---|---|
| SF1 | May | 1 | Doncaster Rovers | D | 1-1 | 1-0 | 6857 | McIntyre | 1 | | 3 | | 4 | 6 | | | | | 11 | 10' | 12 | | | | | 8 | 5 | | | 7 | 9* | | | 2 | | 13 | | | |
| SF2 | | 5 | DONCASTER ROVERS * | D | 1-1 | 1-0 | 5702 | Hatswell | 1 | | 3 | | 4 | 6 | | | | | 11 | 10* | 12 | | | | | 8 | 5 | | | 7' | 9 | | | 2 | | 13 | | | |

* Extra time played following score of 1-1 after 90 minutes. Chester lost 4-3 on penalties (Quayle, Davies, McIntyre)

## F.A. CUP

| | Date | | Opposition | | FT | HT | Att. | Goalscorers | Brown W. | Woodyatt L. | McIntyre K. | Ruffer C. | Guyett S. | Hatswell W. | Blackburn C. | Kelly J. | Twiss M. | Beesley M. | Davies B. | Sugden R. | Cameron D. | Harkness S. | Carey S. | Brown M. | Brodie S. | Carden P. | Bolland P. | Lancaster M. | McCaldon I. | Brady J. | Clare D. | Tate C. | Clifford M. | Collins D. | Griffin A. | Quayle M. | Joy I. | Worsnop J. | [illegible] |
|---|---|---|---|---|---|---|---|---|---|---|---|---|---|---|---|---|---|---|---|---|---|---|---|---|---|---|---|---|---|---|---|---|---|---|---|---|---|---|
| 4Q | Oct | 26 | Radcliffe Borough | W | 4-2 | 0-0 | 1138 | Sugden (3), Cameron | 1 | | 3 | 14 | 4 | 6 | 7 | | | | 11 | 10" | 13 | | | 12 | | 2 | 5 | | | 8* | | 9' | | | | | | | |
| 1R | Nov | 16 | Colchester United | W | 1-0 | 0-0 | 2901 | Tate | 1 | | 3 | 13 | 4 | 6 | 14 | | | | 11 | | | | 8 | 12 | | 2 | 5 | | | 7* | 9" | 10' | | | | | | | |
| 2R | Dec | 7 | Morecambe | L | 2-3 | 2-2 | 4293 | Bolland, Clare | 1 | | 3 | 13 | 4 | 6 | | 12 | | | 11" | 10 | | | 8* | 14 | | 2 | 5 | | | 7' | 9 | | | | | | | | |

## F.A. TROPHY

| | Date | | Opposition | | FT | HT | Att. | Goalscorers | Brown W. | Woodyatt L. | McIntyre K. | Ruffer C. | Guyett S. | Hatswell W. | Blackburn C. | Kelly J. | Twiss M. | Beesley M. | Davies B. | Sugden R. | Cameron D. | Harkness S. | Carey S. | Brown M. | Brodie S. | Carden P. | Bolland P. | Lancaster M. | McCaldon I. | Brady J. | Clare D. | Tate C. | Clifford M. | Collins D. | Griffin A. | Quayle M. | Joy I. | Worsnop J. | [illegible] |
|---|---|---|---|---|---|---|---|---|---|---|---|---|---|---|---|---|---|---|---|---|---|---|---|---|---|---|---|---|---|---|---|---|---|---|---|---|---|---|
| 3R | Jan | 15 | WORKSOP TOWN | L | 1-2 | 0-0 | 1393 | Twiss | 1 | 2' | 3 | 6 | 4 | | | 7 | 10 | | | 9" | 12 | | 8 | 11* | | | | 5 | | 13 | | | | | | | | | 14 |

## LDV TROPHY

| | Date | | Opposition | | FT | HT | Att. | Goalscorers | Brown W. | Woodyatt L. | McIntyre K. | Ruffer C. | Guyett S. | Hatswell W. | Blackburn C. | Kelly J. | Twiss M. | Beesley M. | Davies B. | Sugden R. | Cameron D. | Harkness S. | Carey S. | Brown M. | Brodie S. | Carden P. | Bolland P. | Lancaster M. | McCaldon I. | Brady J. | Clare D. | Tate C. | Clifford M. | Collins D. | Griffin A. | Quayle M. | Joy I. | Worsnop J. | [illegible] |
|---|---|---|---|---|---|---|---|---|---|---|---|---|---|---|---|---|---|---|---|---|---|---|---|---|---|---|---|---|---|---|---|---|---|---|---|---|---|---|
| 1R | Oct | 22 | PLYMOUTH ARGYLE | L | 1-2 | 1-1 | 1126 | Guyett | | 13 | 3 | | 4 | 6 | 7" | | 9 | 10* | 11 | 12 | | | | 14 | | 2 | 5 | | 1 | 8' | | | | | | | | | |

## FRIENDLIES

| | Date | | Opposition | | FT | HT | Att. | Goalscorers |
|---|---|---|---|---|---|---|---|---|
| 1 | Jul | 22 | Buckley Town | W | 4-1 | 1-0 | 750 | Cameron (pen), Beesley (pen), Twiss, Brodie |
| 2 | | 25 | Holywell Town | W | 7-0 | 4-0 | 200 | Cameron (2), Twiss, Beesley, Sugden (2), Brodie |
| 3 | | 27 | Bangor City | D | 1-1 | 1-0 | 400 | Brodie |
| 4 | | 29 | Colwyn Bay | L | 0-1 | 0-0 | 400 | |
| 5 | | 31 | EVERTON X1 | L | 0-1 | 0-1 | 3141 | |
| 6 | Aug | 3 | MANCHESTER CITY X1 | L | 1-2 | 1-1 | 632 | Beesley (pen) |
| 7 | | 6 | MANCHESTER UNITED RES | L | 1-3 | 0-2 | 1342 | Guyett |
| 8 | | 10 | Vauxhall Motors | W | 7-0 | 3-0 | | Guyett,Twiss,Brodie,M Brown(2),Sugden,Thompson(og) |
| 9 | | 13 | LIVERPOOL X1 | W | 1-0 | 0-0 | 5172 | Blackburn |

# FINAL LEAGUE TABLES: 2004/05 - 2009/10

## Final League Table 2004/05 Division 2

| | | Pl | Home W | D | L | F | A | Away W | D | L | F | A | F | A | Pts |
|---|---|---|---|---|---|---|---|---|---|---|---|---|---|---|---|
| 1 | Yeovil Town | 46 | 16 | 4 | 3 | 57 | 28 | 9 | 4 | 10 | 33 | 37 | 90 | 65 | 83 |
| 2 | Scunthorpe United | 46 | 16 | 5 | 2 | 43 | 16 | 6 | 9 | 8 | 26 | 26 | 69 | 42 | 80 |
| 3 | Swansea City | 46 | 15 | 5 | 3 | 36 | 16 | 9 | 3 | 11 | 26 | 27 | 62 | 43 | 80 |
| 4 | Southend United | 46 | 13 | 5 | 5 | 31 | 14 | 9 | 7 | 7 | 34 | 32 | 65 | 46 | 78 |
| 5 | Macclesfield Town | 46 | 15 | 3 | 5 | 39 | 24 | 7 | 6 | 10 | 21 | 25 | 60 | 49 | 75 |
| 6 | Lincoln City | 46 | 11 | 8 | 4 | 37 | 22 | 9 | 4 | 10 | 27 | 25 | 64 | 47 | 72 |
| 7 | Northampton Town | 46 | 11 | 9 | 3 | 35 | 20 | 9 | 3 | 11 | 27 | 31 | 62 | 51 | 72 |
| 8 | Darlington | 46 | 13 | 4 | 6 | 33 | 21 | 7 | 8 | 8 | 24 | 28 | 57 | 49 | 72 |
| 9 | Rochdale | 46 | 11 | 8 | 4 | 34 | 21 | 5 | 10 | 8 | 20 | 27 | 54 | 48 | 66 |
| 10 | Wycombe Wanderers | 46 | 8 | 7 | 8 | 28 | 26 | 9 | 7 | 7 | 30 | 26 | 58 | 52 | 65 |
| 11 | Leyton Orient | 46 | 10 | 8 | 5 | 40 | 30 | 6 | 7 | 10 | 25 | 37 | 65 | 67 | 63 |
| 12 | Bristol Rovers | 46 | 10 | 12 | 1 | 39 | 22 | 3 | 9 | 11 | 21 | 35 | 60 | 57 | 60 |
| 13 | Mansfield Town | 46 | 9 | 8 | 6 | 29 | 24 | 6 | 7 | 10 | 27 | 32 | 56 | 56 | 60 |
| 14 | Cheltenham Town | 46 | 10 | 5 | 8 | 27 | 23 | 6 | 7 | 10 | 24 | 31 | 51 | 54 | 60 |
| 15 | Oxford United | 46 | 11 | 4 | 8 | 29 | 24 | 5 | 7 | 11 | 21 | 39 | 50 | 63 | 59 |
| 16 | Boston United | 46 | 11 | 8 | 4 | 39 | 24 | 3 | 8 | 12 | 23 | 34 | 62 | 58 | 58 |
| 17 | Bury | 46 | 8 | 9 | 6 | 26 | 18 | 6 | 7 | 10 | 28 | 36 | 54 | 54 | 58 |
| 18 | Grimsby Town | 46 | 8 | 10 | 5 | 28 | 19 | 6 | 6 | 11 | 23 | 33 | 51 | 52 | 58 |
| 19 | Notts County | 46 | 6 | 7 | 10 | 21 | 27 | 7 | 6 | 10 | 25 | 35 | 46 | 62 | 52 |
| **20** | **Chester City** | **46** | **7** | **8** | **8** | **25** | **33** | **5** | **8** | **10** | **18** | **36** | **43** | **69** | **52** |
| 21 | Shrewsbury Town | 46 | 9 | 7 | 7 | 34 | 18 | 2 | 9 | 12 | 14 | 35 | 48 | 53 | 49 |
| 22 | Rushden & Diamonds | 46 | 8 | 6 | 9 | 29 | 29 | 2 | 8 | 13 | 13 | 34 | 42 | 63 | 44 |
| 23 | Kidderminster Harriers | 46 | 6 | 6 | 11 | 21 | 39 | 4 | 2 | 17 | 18 | 46 | 39 | 85 | 38 |
| 24 | Cambridge United * | 46 | 7 | 6 | 10 | 22 | 27 | 1 | 10 | 12 | 17 | 35 | 39 | 62 | 30 |

Cambridge United 10 points deducted

## Final League Table 2005/06 Division 2

| | | Pl | Home W | D | L | F | A | Away W | D | L | F | A | F | A | Pts |
|---|---|---|---|---|---|---|---|---|---|---|---|---|---|---|---|
| 1 | Carlisle United | 46 | 14 | 3 | 6 | 47 | 23 | 11 | 8 | 4 | 37 | 19 | 84 | 42 | 86 |
| 2 | Northampton Town | 46 | 11 | 8 | 4 | 30 | 15 | 11 | 9 | 3 | 33 | 22 | 63 | 37 | 83 |
| 3 | Leyton Orient | 46 | 11 | 6 | 6 | 29 | 21 | 11 | 9 | 3 | 38 | 30 | 67 | 51 | 81 |
| 4 | Grimsby Town | 46 | 13 | 3 | 7 | 37 | 18 | 9 | 9 | 5 | 27 | 26 | 64 | 44 | 78 |
| 5 | Cheltenham Town | 46 | 10 | 7 | 6 | 39 | 31 | 9 | 8 | 6 | 26 | 22 | 65 | 53 | 72 |
| 6 | Wycombe Wanderers | 46 | 9 | 9 | 5 | 41 | 29 | 9 | 8 | 6 | 31 | 27 | 72 | 56 | 71 |
| 7 | Lincoln City | 46 | 9 | 11 | 3 | 37 | 21 | 6 | 10 | 7 | 28 | 32 | 65 | 53 | 66 |
| 8 | Darlington | 46 | 10 | 7 | 6 | 32 | 26 | 6 | 8 | 9 | 26 | 26 | 58 | 52 | 63 |
| 9 | Peterborough United | 46 | 9 | 7 | 7 | 28 | 21 | 8 | 4 | 11 | 29 | 28 | 57 | 49 | 62 |
| 10 | Shrewsbury Town | 46 | 10 | 9 | 4 | 33 | 20 | 6 | 4 | 13 | 22 | 35 | 55 | 55 | 61 |
| 11 | Boston United | 46 | 11 | 7 | 5 | 34 | 28 | 4 | 9 | 10 | 16 | 32 | 50 | 60 | 61 |
| 12 | Bristol Rovers | 46 | 8 | 6 | 9 | 30 | 29 | 9 | 3 | 11 | 29 | 38 | 59 | 67 | 60 |
| 13 | Wrexham | 46 | 12 | 6 | 5 | 36 | 19 | 3 | 8 | 12 | 25 | 35 | 61 | 54 | 59 |
| 14 | Rochdale | 46 | 8 | 7 | 8 | 34 | 30 | 6 | 7 | 10 | 32 | 39 | 66 | 69 | 56 |
| **15** | **Chester City** | **46** | **7** | **6** | **10** | **30** | **29** | **7** | **6** | **10** | **23** | **30** | **53** | **59** | **54** |
| 16 | Mansfield Town | 46 | 9 | 7 | 7 | 37 | 29 | 4 | 8 | 11 | 22 | 37 | 59 | 66 | 54 |
| 17 | Macclesfield Town | 46 | 10 | 9 | 4 | 35 | 27 | 2 | 9 | 12 | 25 | 44 | 60 | 71 | 54 |
| 18 | Barnet | 46 | 9 | 8 | 6 | 24 | 22 | 3 | 10 | 10 | 20 | 35 | 44 | 57 | 54 |
| 19 | Bury | 46 | 6 | 9 | 8 | 22 | 25 | 6 | 8 | 9 | 23 | 32 | 45 | 57 | 52 |
| 20 | Torquay United | 46 | 7 | 9 | 7 | 33 | 31 | 6 | 4 | 13 | 20 | 35 | 53 | 66 | 52 |
| 21 | Notts County | 46 | 7 | 11 | 5 | 30 | 26 | 5 | 5 | 13 | 18 | 37 | 48 | 63 | 52 |
| 22 | Stockport County | 46 | 7 | 11 | 5 | 34 | 29 | 4 | 8 | 11 | 23 | 49 | 57 | 78 | 52 |
| 23 | Oxford United | 46 | 7 | 7 | 9 | 25 | 30 | 4 | 9 | 10 | 18 | 27 | 43 | 57 | 49 |
| 24 | Rushden & Diamonds | 46 | 8 | 5 | 10 | 25 | 31 | 3 | 7 | 13 | 19 | 45 | 44 | 76 | 45 |

## Final League Table 2006/07 Division 2

| | | Pl | Home W | D | L | F | A | Away W | D | L | F | A | F | A | Pts |
|---|---|---|---|---|---|---|---|---|---|---|---|---|---|---|---|
| 1 | Walsall | 46 | 16 | 4 | 3 | 39 | 13 | 9 | 10 | 4 | 27 | 21 | 66 | 34 | 89 |
| 2 | Hartlepool United | 46 | 14 | 5 | 4 | 34 | 17 | 12 | 5 | 6 | 31 | 23 | 65 | 40 | 88 |
| 3 | Swindon Town | 46 | 15 | 4 | 4 | 34 | 17 | 10 | 6 | 7 | 24 | 21 | 58 | 38 | 85 |
| 4 | Milton Keynes Dons | 46 | 14 | 4 | 5 | 41 | 26 | 11 | 5 | 7 | 35 | 32 | 76 | 58 | 84 |
| 5 | Lincoln City | 46 | 12 | 4 | 7 | 36 | 28 | 9 | 7 | 7 | 34 | 31 | 70 | 59 | 74 |
| 6 | Bristol Rovers | 46 | 13 | 5 | 5 | 27 | 14 | 7 | 7 | 9 | 22 | 28 | 49 | 42 | 72 |
| 7 | Shrewsbury Town | 46 | 11 | 7 | 5 | 38 | 23 | 7 | 10 | 6 | 30 | 23 | 68 | 46 | 71 |
| 8 | Stockport County | 46 | 14 | 4 | 5 | 41 | 25 | 7 | 4 | 12 | 24 | 29 | 65 | 54 | 71 |
| 9 | Rochdale | 46 | 9 | 6 | 8 | 33 | 20 | 9 | 6 | 8 | 37 | 30 | 70 | 50 | 66 |
| 10 | Peterborough United | 46 | 10 | 6 | 7 | 48 | 36 | 8 | 5 | 10 | 22 | 25 | 70 | 61 | 65 |
| 11 | Darlington | 46 | 10 | 6 | 7 | 28 | 30 | 7 | 8 | 8 | 24 | 26 | 52 | 56 | 65 |
| 12 | Wycombe Wanderers | 46 | 8 | 11 | 4 | 23 | 14 | 8 | 3 | 12 | 29 | 33 | 52 | 47 | 62 |
| 13 | Notts County | 46 | 8 | 6 | 9 | 29 | 25 | 8 | 8 | 7 | 26 | 28 | 55 | 53 | 62 |
| 14 | Barnet | 46 | 12 | 5 | 6 | 35 | 30 | 4 | 6 | 13 | 20 | 40 | 55 | 70 | 59 |
| 15 | Grimsby Town | 46 | 11 | 4 | 8 | 33 | 32 | 6 | 4 | 13 | 24 | 41 | 57 | 73 | 59 |
| 16 | Hereford United | 46 | 9 | 7 | 7 | 23 | 17 | 5 | 6 | 12 | 22 | 36 | 45 | 53 | 55 |
| 17 | Mansfield Town | 46 | 10 | 4 | 9 | 38 | 31 | 4 | 8 | 11 | 20 | 32 | 58 | 63 | 54 |
| **18** | **Chester City** | **46** | **7** | **9** | **7** | **23** | **23** | **6** | **5** | **12** | **17** | **25** | **40** | **48** | **53** |
| 19 | Wrexham | 46 | 8 | 8 | 7 | 23 | 21 | 5 | 4 | 14 | 20 | 44 | 43 | 65 | 51 |
| 20 | Accrington Stanley | 46 | 10 | 6 | 7 | 42 | 33 | 3 | 5 | 15 | 28 | 48 | 70 | 81 | 50 |
| 21 | Bury | 46 | 4 | 7 | 12 | 22 | 35 | 9 | 4 | 10 | 24 | 26 | 46 | 61 | 50 |
| 22 | Macclesfield Town | 46 | 8 | 7 | 8 | 36 | 34 | 4 | 5 | 14 | 19 | 43 | 55 | 77 | 48 |
| 23 | Boston United | 46 | 9 | 5 | 9 | 29 | 32 | 3 | 5 | 15 | 22 | 48 | 51 | 80 | 36 |
| 24 | Torquay United | 46 | 5 | 8 | 10 | 19 | 22 | 2 | 6 | 15 | 17 | 41 | 36 | 63 | 35 |

## Final League Table 2007/08 Division 2

| | | Pl | Home W | D | L | F | A | Away W | D | L | F | A | F | A | Pts |
|---|---|---|---|---|---|---|---|---|---|---|---|---|---|---|---|
| 1 | Milton Keynes Dons | 46 | 11 | 7 | 5 | 39 | 17 | 18 | 3 | 2 | 43 | 20 | 82 | 37 | 97 |
| 2 | Peterborough United | 46 | 14 | 4 | 5 | 46 | 20 | 14 | 4 | 5 | 38 | 23 | 84 | 43 | 92 |
| 3 | Hereford United | 46 | 11 | 6 | 6 | 34 | 19 | 15 | 4 | 4 | 38 | 22 | 72 | 41 | 88 |
| 4 | Stockport County | 46 | 11 | 5 | 7 | 40 | 30 | 13 | 5 | 5 | 32 | 24 | 72 | 54 | 82 |
| 5 | Rochdale | 46 | 11 | 4 | 8 | 37 | 28 | 12 | 7 | 4 | 40 | 26 | 77 | 54 | 80 |
| 6 | Darlington | 46 | 11 | 7 | 5 | 36 | 22 | 11 | 5 | 7 | 31 | 18 | 67 | 40 | 78 |
| 7 | Wycombe Wanderers | 46 | 13 | 6 | 4 | 29 | 15 | 9 | 6 | 8 | 27 | 27 | 56 | 42 | 78 |
| 8 | Chesterfield | 46 | 9 | 8 | 6 | 42 | 29 | 10 | 4 | 9 | 34 | 27 | 76 | 56 | 69 |
| 9 | Rotherham United * | 46 | 12 | 4 | 7 | 37 | 29 | 9 | 7 | 7 | 25 | 29 | 62 | 58 | 64 |
| 10 | Bradford City | 46 | 10 | 4 | 9 | 30 | 30 | 7 | 7 | 9 | 33 | 31 | 63 | 61 | 62 |
| 11 | Morecambe | 46 | 9 | 6 | 8 | 33 | 32 | 7 | 6 | 10 | 26 | 31 | 59 | 63 | 60 |
| 12 | Barnet | 46 | 10 | 6 | 7 | 37 | 30 | 6 | 6 | 11 | 19 | 33 | 56 | 63 | 60 |
| 13 | Bury | 46 | 8 | 6 | 9 | 30 | 30 | 8 | 5 | 10 | 28 | 31 | 58 | 61 | 59 |
| 14 | Brentford | 46 | 7 | 5 | 11 | 25 | 35 | 10 | 3 | 10 | 27 | 35 | 52 | 70 | 59 |
| 15 | Lincoln City | 46 | 9 | 3 | 11 | 33 | 38 | 9 | 1 | 13 | 28 | 39 | 61 | 77 | 58 |
| 16 | Grimsby Town | 46 | 7 | 5 | 11 | 26 | 34 | 8 | 5 | 10 | 29 | 32 | 55 | 66 | 55 |
| 17 | Accrington Stanley | 46 | 7 | 1 | 15 | 20 | 39 | 9 | 2 | 12 | 29 | 44 | 49 | 83 | 51 |
| 18 | Shrewsbury Town | 46 | 9 | 6 | 8 | 31 | 22 | 3 | 8 | 12 | 25 | 43 | 56 | 65 | 50 |
| 19 | Macclesfield Town | 46 | 6 | 8 | 9 | 27 | 31 | 5 | 9 | 9 | 20 | 33 | 47 | 64 | 50 |
| 20 | Dagenham & Redbridge | 46 | 6 | 7 | 10 | 27 | 32 | 7 | 3 | 13 | 22 | 38 | 49 | 70 | 49 |
| 21 | Notts County | 46 | 8 | 5 | 10 | 19 | 23 | 2 | 13 | 8 | 18 | 30 | 37 | 53 | 48 |
| **22** | **Chester City** | **46** | **5** | **5** | **13** | **21** | **30** | **7** | **6** | **10** | **30** | **38** | **51** | **68** | **47** |
| 23 | Mansfield Town | 46 | 6 | 3 | 14 | 30 | 39 | 5 | 6 | 12 | 18 | 29 | 48 | 68 | 42 |
| 24 | Wrexham | 46 | 6 | 7 | 10 | 16 | 28 | 4 | 3 | 16 | 22 | 42 | 38 | 70 | 40 |

Rotherham United 10 Points deducted

## Final League Table 2008/09 Division 2

| | | Pl | Home W | D | L | F | A | Away W | D | L | F | A | F | A | Pts |
|---|---|---|---|---|---|---|---|---|---|---|---|---|---|---|---|
| 1 | Brentford | 46 | 13 | 8 | 2 | 39 | 15 | 10 | 8 | 5 | 26 | 21 | 65 | 36 | 85 |
| 2 | Exeter City | 46 | 13 | 5 | 5 | 36 | 25 | 9 | 8 | 6 | 29 | 25 | 65 | 50 | 79 |
| 3 | Wycombe Wanderers | 46 | 11 | 9 | 3 | 32 | 16 | 9 | 9 | 5 | 22 | 17 | 54 | 33 | 78 |
| 4 | Bury | 46 | 14 | 4 | 5 | 36 | 19 | 7 | 11 | 5 | 27 | 24 | 63 | 43 | 78 |
| 5 | Gillingham | 46 | 12 | 7 | 4 | 38 | 21 | 9 | 5 | 9 | 20 | 34 | 58 | 55 | 75 |
| 6 | Rochdale | 46 | 11 | 6 | 6 | 40 | 24 | 8 | 7 | 8 | 30 | 35 | 70 | 59 | 70 |
| 7 | Shrewsbury Town | 46 | 14 | 6 | 3 | 41 | 16 | 3 | 12 | 8 | 20 | 28 | 61 | 44 | 69 |
| 8 | Dagenham & Redbridge | 46 | 12 | 3 | 8 | 44 | 24 | 7 | 8 | 8 | 33 | 29 | 77 | 53 | 68 |
| 9 | Bradford City | 46 | 11 | 10 | 2 | 39 | 18 | 7 | 3 | 13 | 27 | 37 | 66 | 55 | 67 |
| 10 | Chesterfield | 46 | 8 | 8 | 7 | 32 | 28 | 8 | 7 | 8 | 30 | 29 | 62 | 57 | 63 |
| 11 | Morecambe | 46 | 9 | 9 | 5 | 29 | 24 | 6 | 9 | 8 | 24 | 32 | 53 | 56 | 63 |
| 12 | Darlington * | 46 | 11 | 6 | 6 | 36 | 23 | 9 | 6 | 8 | 25 | 21 | 61 | 44 | 62 |
| 13 | Lincoln City | 46 | 6 | 11 | 6 | 26 | 22 | 8 | 6 | 9 | 27 | 30 | 53 | 52 | 59 |
| 14 | Rotherham United * | 46 | 11 | 6 | 6 | 32 | 21 | 10 | 6 | 7 | 28 | 25 | 60 | 46 | 58 |
| 15 | Aldershot | 46 | 9 | 10 | 4 | 36 | 31 | 5 | 2 | 16 | 23 | 49 | 59 | 80 | 54 |
| 16 | Accrington Stanley | 46 | 9 | 5 | 9 | 25 | 24 | 4 | 6 | 13 | 17 | 35 | 42 | 59 | 50 |
| 17 | Barnet | 46 | 7 | 7 | 9 | 30 | 35 | 4 | 8 | 11 | 26 | 39 | 56 | 74 | 48 |
| 18 | Port Vale | 46 | 6 | 6 | 11 | 23 | 33 | 7 | 3 | 13 | 21 | 33 | 44 | 66 | 48 |
| 19 | Notts County | 46 | 6 | 6 | 11 | 22 | 31 | 5 | 8 | 10 | 27 | 38 | 49 | 69 | 47 |
| 20 | Macclesfield Town | 46 | 7 | 4 | 12 | 23 | 37 | 6 | 4 | 13 | 22 | 40 | 45 | 77 | 47 |
| 21 | Bournemouth * | 46 | 11 | 6 | 6 | 28 | 15 | 6 | 6 | 11 | 31 | 36 | 59 | 51 | 46 |
| 22 | Grimsby Town | 46 | 6 | 7 | 10 | 31 | 28 | 3 | 7 | 13 | 20 | 41 | 51 | 69 | 41 |
| **23** | **Chester City** | **46** | **4** | **7** | **12** | **24** | **34** | **4** | **6** | **13** | **19** | **47** | **43** | **81** | **37** |
| 24 | Luton Town * | 46 | 7 | 8 | 8 | 34 | 34 | 6 | 9 | 8 | 24 | 31 | 58 | 65 | 26 |

* Points deductions: Luton 30, Bournemouth 17, Rotherham 17, Darlington 10.

## Blue Square Premier League Table 2009/10 - as at February 6th

| | | Pl | Home W | D | L | F | A | Away W | D | L | F | A | F | A | Pts |
|---|---|---|---|---|---|---|---|---|---|---|---|---|---|---|---|
| 1 | Oxford United | 27 | 10 | 2 | 1 | 28 | 6 | 8 | 4 | 2 | 22 | 13 | 50 | 19 | 60 |
| 2 | Stevenage Borough | 29 | 10 | 5 | 0 | 32 | 9 | 7 | 4 | 3 | 17 | 11 | 49 | 20 | 60 |
| 3 | York City | 29 | 11 | 4 | 0 | 30 | 11 | 6 | 4 | 4 | 14 | 13 | 44 | 24 | 59 |
| 4 | Mansfield Town | 30 | 8 | 4 | 2 | 27 | 11 | 7 | 1 | 8 | 21 | 25 | 48 | 36 | 50 |
| 5 | AFC Wimbledon | 29 | 7 | 3 | 4 | 25 | 7 | 7 | 4 | 4 | 23 | 17 | 48 | 24 | 49 |
| 6 | Rushden&Diamonds | 28 | 8 | 2 | 4 | 24 | 18 | 6 | 5 | 3 | 26 | 11 | 50 | 29 | 49 |
| 7 | Luton Town | 27 | 6 | 3 | 4 | 21 | 14 | 8 | 4 | 2 | 16 | 11 | 37 | 25 | 49 |
| 8 | Kettering Town | 29 | 4 | 5 | 5 | 17 | 13 | 10 | 1 | 4 | 18 | 12 | 35 | 25 | 48 |
| 9 | Kidderminster Harriers | 29 | 9 | 1 | 4 | 23 | 11 | 3 | 6 | 6 | 16 | 19 | 39 | 30 | 43 |
| 10 | Crawley Town | 29 | 8 | 3 | 4 | 23 | 18 | 4 | 3 | 7 | 11 | 20 | 34 | 38 | 42 |
| 11 | Altrincham | 27 | 4 | 5 | 5 | 19 | 17 | 7 | 3 | 3 | 17 | 10 | 36 | 27 | 41 |
| 12 | Tamworth | 29 | 6 | 4 | 5 | 18 | 18 | 3 | 7 | 4 | 12 | 13 | 30 | 31 | 38 |
| 13 | Wrexham | 27 | 7 | 3 | 4 | 17 | 11 | 3 | 4 | 6 | 11 | 14 | 28 | 25 | 37 |
| 14 | Histon | 28 | 5 | 7 | 3 | 20 | 16 | 4 | 2 | 7 | 14 | 21 | 34 | 37 | 36 |
| 15 | Cambridge United | 29 | 6 | 2 | 7 | 25 | 16 | 2 | 7 | 5 | 17 | 23 | 42 | 39 | 33 |
| 16 | Hayes & Yeading | 31 | 4 | 5 | 6 | 23 | 27 | 4 | 4 | 8 | 17 | 30 | 40 | 57 | 33 |
| 17 | Salisbury City * | 29 | 5 | 4 | 5 | 15 | 12 | 7 | 0 | 8 | 17 | 29 | 32 | 41 | 30 |
| 18 | Ebbsfleet United | 32 | 4 | 4 | 8 | 17 | 23 | 4 | 2 | 10 | 15 | 33 | 32 | 56 | 30 |
| 19 | Eastbourne Borough | 29 | 4 | 5 | 5 | 16 | 17 | 2 | 6 | 7 | 11 | 26 | 27 | 43 | 29 |
| 20 | Barrow | 26 | 3 | 8 | 3 | 17 | 21 | 3 | 2 | 7 | 11 | 20 | 28 | 41 | 28 |
| 21 | Forest Green Rovers | 30 | 4 | 4 | 7 | 13 | 20 | 2 | 4 | 9 | 16 | 35 | 29 | 55 | 26 |
| 22 | Gateshead * | 29 | 4 | 3 | 7 | 13 | 16 | 3 | 2 | 10 | 19 | 30 | 32 | 46 | 25 |
| 23 | Grays Athletic | 30 | 3 | 3 | 10 | 14 | 33 | 0 | 5 | 9 | 13 | 31 | 27 | 64 | 17 |
| **24** | **Chester City *** | **28** | **3** | **1** | **9** | **13** | **19** | **2** | **6** | **7** | **10** | **23** | **23** | **42** | **-3** |

* Points deductions: Chester 25, Salisbury 10, Gateshead 1.

# SEASON 2003-04

## NATIONWIDE CONFERENCE

| No. | Date | | Opposition | | FT | HT | Att. | Goalscorers | Brown W. | Collins D. | McIntyre K. | Carden P. | Ruffer C. | Hatswell W. | Heard J. | Davies B. | Rapley K. | Gill R. | Harris A. | Beesley M. | Foster I. | Brodie S. | Carey S. | Twiss M | McCaldon I. | Bolland P. | Stamp D. | Brady J. | Clare D. | Guyett S. | Smith A. | Regan C. | Turner I. | Williams D. | Lane C. | Woods A. | Elam L. | Buckley D. | Dogun P. |
|---|---|---|---|---|---|---|---|---|---|---|---|---|---|---|---|---|---|---|---|---|---|---|---|---|---|---|---|---|---|---|---|---|---|---|---|---|---|---|---|
| 1 | Aug | 9 | Stevenage Borough | D | 0-0 | 0-0 | 2502 | | 1 | 2 | 3 | 4 | 5 | 6 | 7 | 8 | 9* | 10' | 11 | 12 | 13 | | | | | | | | | | | | | | | | | | |
| 2 | | 12 | TAMWORTH | W | 1-0 | 0-0 | 2267 | Ruffer | 1 | 2 | 3 | 4 | 5 | 6 | 7 | 8 | 9' | 10" | 11* | 13 | 12 | 14 | | | | | | | | | | | | | | | | | |
| 3 | | 16 | FOREST GREEN ROVERS | W | 1-0 | 0-0 | 1881 | Davies | 1 | 2 | 3 | 4 | 5 | 6 | 7 | 8 | 9' | 10" | | | 13 | 14 | 11* | 12 | | | | | | | | | | | | | | | |
| 4 | | 23 | Exeter City | L | 1-2 | 1-1 | 3030 | Foster (pen) | | 2 | 3 | 7 | 4* | 6 | | 8 | | | | 13 | 10' | | | 12 | 1 | 5 | 9 | 11 | | | | | | | | | | | |
| 5 | | 26 | SHREWSBURY TOWN | W | 2-1 | 1-0 | 4665 | Stamp, Bolland | 1 | 2 | 3 | 4 | | 6 | 7 | 8 | | 12 | | | 10* | | | 13 | | 5 | 9 | 11' | | | | | | | | | | | |
| 6 | | 30 | Gravesend & Northfleet | W | 4-0 | 2-0 | 939 | Stamp, Bolland, Twiss (2) | 1 | 2 | 3 | 4" | 14 | 6 | 7* | 8 | | | 13 | | 10 | | | 12 | | 5 | 9' | 11 | | | | | | | | | | | |
| 7 | Sep | 6 | Margate | W | 2-1 | 1-1 | 634 | Stamp, Brady | 1 | 2 | 3 | 4 | | 6 | | 8 | 13 | | 11* | | 10' | | | 12 | | 5 | 9 | 7 | | | | | | | | | | | |
| 8 | | 13 | HALIFAX TOWN | W | 2-0 | 1-0 | 2628 | Hatswell, Stamp | 1 | 2 | 3 | 4 | | 6 | | 8 | 12 | | 11 | | 10* | | | | | 5 | 9 | 7 | | | | | | | | | | | |
| 9 | | 20 | Farnborough Town | W | 2-1 | 1-0 | 748 | Stamp (2) | 1 | 2 | 3 | 4 | 6 | | | 8 | 12 | | 11 | | 10* | | | | | 5 | 9 | 7 | | | | | | | | | | | |
| 10 | | 23 | NORTHWICH VICTORIA | W | 4-0 | 1-0 | 2817 | Collins, Carden, Foster, Rapley | | 2 | 3 | 4 | 6 | | | 8 | 13 | | 11 | | 10* | | | 12 | 1 | 5 | 9 | 7' | | | | | | | | | | | |
| 11 | | 27 | TELFORD UNITED | D | 0-0 | 0-0 | 2688 | | 1 | 2 | 3 | 4 | 6 | | | 8 | 13 | | 11 | | 10" | | | 12 | | 5 | 9' | 7* | 14 | | | | | | | | | | |
| 12 | Oct | 4 | Dagenham & Redbridge | D | 0-0 | 0-0 | 1497 | | 1 | 2 | 3 | 4 | 6 | | | 8 | 12 | | | | 10' | | | 11* | | 5 | 9 | 7 | 13 | | | | | | | | | | |
| 13 | | 8 | Burton Albion | D | 1-1 | 0-0 | 1711 | Stamp | | 2 | 3 | 4 | 6 | | 7 | 8 | 10' | | | | 11* | | | 12 | 1 | 5 | 9 | | 13 | | | | | | | | | | |
| 14 | | 11 | WOKING | W | 2-1 | 1-0 | 2085 | Davies, Twiss | | 2 | 3 | 4 | 6* | | 7 | 8 | 13 | | | | 14 | | | 11 | 1 | 5 | 9" | | 10' | 12 | | | | | | | | | |
| 15 | | 18 | HEREFORD UNITED | D | 0-0 | 0-0 | 4481 | | | 2 | 3 | 4 | 6 | | 7 | 8 | 13 | | | | 12 | | | 11' | 1 | 5 | 9* | | 10 | | | | | | | | | | |
| 16 | Nov | 1 | Scarborough | D | 2-2 | 2-0 | 1441 | Stamp, Clare (pen) | | 2 | 3 | 4 | 6 | | | 8 | | | | | | | 11 | 13 | 1 | 5 | 9* | 7 | 10' | 12 | | | | | | | | | |
| 17 | | 11 | Morecambe | W | 1-0 | 0-0 | 1959 | Clare | 12 | 2 | 3 | 4 | 6 | | | 8 | | | | | 13 | | | | 1* | 5 | 9 | 7 | 10' | 14 | 11" | | | | | | | | |
| 18 | | 15 | BARNET | W | 1-0 | 1-0 | 2638 | Smith | 1 | 2 | 3 | | 6 | | | 8 | | | 12 | | | | 4 | 13 | | | 9 | 7 | 10' | 5 | 11* | | | | | | | | |
| 19 | | 22 | Aldershot Town | D | 1-1 | 1-1 | 3610 | Stamp | 1 | 2 | 3 | 12 | 6' | | 13 | 8 | | | | | 14 | | 4 | | | | 9 | 7" | 10 | 5 | 11* | | | | | | | | |
| 20 | | 25 | ACCRINGTON STANLEY | D | 3-3 | 3-1 | 2432 | Davies, Clare (2) | 1 | 2 | 3 | | | | | 8 | 12 | | 6 | | 13 | | 4 | | | | 9* | 7 | 10' | 5 | 11 | | | | | | | | |
| 21 | | 29 | MARGATE | W | 3-0 | 0-0 | 1971 | Davies, Clare, Stamp | 1 | 2 | 3 | | 6 | | | 8 | 9' | | | | 12 | | 4 | | | 14 | 13 | 7* | 10 | 5" | 11 | | | | | | | | |
| 22 | Dec | 6 | Halifax Town | W | 3-0 | 1-0 | 1928 | Davies, Collins, Clare | 1 | 2 | 3 | 13 | 6 | | 7* | 8 | 9 | | | | | | 4 | | | 12 | | | 10 | 5 | 11' | | | | | | | | |
| 23 | | 13 | STEVENAGE BOROUGH | L | 1-2 | 0-1 | 2145 | Twiss | 1 | 2 | 3 | | 6 | | | 8 | 9' | | | | | | 7 | 12 | | 5 | 13 | | 10 | 4* | 11 | | | | | | | | |
| 24 | | 20 | Tamworth | W | 5-1 | 2-0 | 1520 | Ruffer, Clare (3), Smith | | 2 | 3* | 4 | 6 | | | | 13 | | 14 | | | | 8 | | 1 | 12 | 9 | | 10' | 5 | 11" | 7 | | | | | | | |
| 25 | | 26 | LEIGH RMI | W | 5-0 | 3-0 | 3044 | Clare, Stamp (3), Rapley | | 2 | 3 | 4 | 6 | | | 12 | 13 | | | | | | 8 | 14 | 1 | | 9" | | 10' | 5 | 11* | 7 | | | | | | | |
| 26 | Jan | 1 | Leigh RMI | W | 6-2 | 2-0 | 2002 | Clare (3), Stamp (2), Smith | | 2 | 3' | 4 | 6 | | | | | | | | | | 8 | 13 | 1 | 12 | 9 | | 10 | 5* | 11 | 7 | | | | | | | |
| 27 | | 3 | GRAVESEND & NORTHFLEET | D | 2-2 | 2-0 | 2670 | Clare (2) | | 2 | | 4 | 6 | | | 13 | 14 | | | | | | 8' | 3 | 1 | 12 | 9" | | 10 | 5 | 11* | 7 | | | | | | | |
| 28 | | 17 | Forest Green Rovers | L | 1-2 | 1-0 | 1164 | Clare | | 2 | 3 | 4 | 6 | | 7 | | 13 | | 8 | | | | | 12 | 1 | 5 | 9' | | 10 | | 11* | | | | | | | | |
| 29 | | 24 | Northwich Victoria | W | 4-0 | 2-0 | 2141 | McIntyre, Stamp (2), Clare | | 2 | 3 | 4 | | | 7 | 14 | 13 | | | | | | 8" | 12 | 1 | 5 | 9* | | 10' | 6 | 11 | | | | | | | | |
| 30 | Feb | 7 | FARNBOROUGH TOWN | W | 3-2 | 2-0 | 2665 | Stamp, Clare (2) | | 2 | 3 | | | | 7 | 8 | | | | | | | 4 | 12 | | 5 | 9 | | 10 | 6 | 11* | | 1 | | | | | | |
| 31 | | 21 | DAGENHAM & REDBRIDGE | W | 2-1 | 1-0 | 2990 | Clare (pen), Stamp | | 2 | 3 | | | | 7 | 12 | | | | | | | 4* | 13 | | 5 | 9 | | 10 | 6 | 11' | | 1 | 8 | | | | | |
| 32 | | 28 | Woking | W | 2-1 | 0-1 | 2554 | Collins, Twiss | | 2 | 3 | 4 | | | 7 | | | | | | | | | 12 | | 5 | 9 | | 10 | 6 | 11* | | 1 | 8 | | | | | |
| 33 | Mar | 6 | BURTON ALBION | W | 3-1 | 2-1 | 3318 | Clare (2), Guyett | | 2 | 3 | 4 | | | 7 | | | | | | | | 12 | | | 5 | 9 | | 10 | 6 | 11 | | 1 | 8* | | | | | |
| 34 | | 13 | MORECAMBE | W | 2-1 | 0-0 | 3512 | Smith, Clare | | 2 | 3 | 4 | | | 7 | 12 | | | | | | | | | | 5 | 9 | | 10 | 6 | 11 | | 1 | 8* | | | | | |
| 35 | | 20 | Barnet | D | 0-0 | 0-0 | 2455 | | | 2 | 3 | 4 | | | 7* | | 14 | | | | | | | 13 | | 5 | 9 | | 10" | 6 | 11' | | 1 | 8 | 12 | | | | |
| 36 | | 30 | Telford United | W | 2-0 | 0-0 | 3503 | Clare (2, 1 pen) | | 2 | 3 | 4 | | | 7 | 13 | | | | | | | 8 | 12 | | 5 | 9' | | 10 | 6 | 11* | | | | | 1 | | | |
| 37 | Apr | 3 | Accrington Stanley | W | 2-0 | 1-0 | 2561 | Guyett, Clare (pen) | | 2 | 3 | 4 | | | 7 | | | | | | | | 8 | 11 | | 5 | 9* | | 10 | 6 | | | 1 | | 12 | | | | |
| 38 | | 6 | ALDERSHOT TOWN | W | 4-2 | 2-1 | 3432 | Bolland (2), Clare (2, 1pen) | | 2 | 3 | 4 | | | 7" | 13 | | | | | | | 8* | 11 | | 5 | 9' | | 10 | 6 | | | 1 | | 12 | | 14 | | |
| 39 | | 10 | EXETER CITY | W | 3-2 | 0-0 | 4046 | Twiss (2), Clare | | 2 | 3 | 4 | | | 7 | 14 | 13 | | | | | | 8" | 11 | | 5 | 9' | | 10* | 6 | | | 1 | | | | 12 | | |
| 40 | | 13 | Shrewsbury Town | D | 0-0 | 0-0 | 5827 | | | 2 | 3 | 4 | | | 7 | 12 | 10 | | | | | | 8* | 11 | | 5 | 9 | | | 6 | | | 1 | | | | | | |
| 41 | | 17 | SCARBOROUGH | W | 1-0 | 1-0 | 5987 | Stamp | | 2' | 3 | 4 | | | 7 | 8 | 14 | | 12 | | | | | 11* | | 5 | 9 | | 10" | 6 | | | 1 | | | | 13 | | |
| 42 | | 24 | Hereford United | L | 1-2 | 0-1 | 7240 | James (og) | | | | | | | 7 | 8 | 9" | | 10 | | 12 | | 4* | 11 | | 5 | 14 | | | 6 | | | 1' | | 2 | 13 | 3 | | |
| | | | | | | | | Apps | 16 | 41 | 40 | 33 | 23 | 8 | 24 | 26 | 9 | 3 | 10 | | 10 | | 21 | 10 | 13 | 30 | 35 | 15 | 27 | 24 | 20 | 4 | 12 | 5 | 1 | 1 | 1 | | |
| | | | | | | | | Subs | 1 | | | 2 | 1 | | 1 | 9 | 17 | 1 | 4 | 3 | 10 | 2 | 1 | 20 | | 5 | 3 | | 3 | 3 | | | | | 3 | 1 | 3 | | |
| | | | | | | | | Goals | | 3 | 1 | 1 | 2 | 1 | | 5 | 2 | | | | 2 | | | 7 | | 4 | 20 | 1 | 29 | 2 | 4 | | | | | | | | |

Own Goals 1

## F.A. CUP

| Rd | Date | | Opposition | | FT | HT | Att. | Goalscorers | Brown W. | Collins D. | McIntyre K. | Carden P. | Ruffer C. | Hatswell W. | Heard J. | Davies B. | Rapley K. | Gill R. | Harris A. | Beesley M. | Foster I. | Brodie S. | Carey S. | Twiss M | McCaldon I. | Bolland P. | Stamp D. | Brady J. | Clare D. | Guyett S. | Smith A. | Regan C. | Turner I. | Williams D. | Lane C. | Woods A. | Elam L. | Buckley D. | Dogun P. |
|---|---|---|---|---|---|---|---|---|---|---|---|---|---|---|---|---|---|---|---|---|---|---|---|---|---|---|---|---|---|---|---|---|---|---|---|---|---|---|---|
| 4Q | Oct | 25 | Blyth Spartans | W | 1-0 | 1-0 | 1105 | Clare | | 2 | | | 6' | | 7 | 8 | 14 | | | | 11* | | 4 | 3 | 1 | 5 | 9 | 12 | 10" | 13 | | | | | | | | | |
| 1R | Nov | 8 | GRAVESEND & NORTHFLEET | L | 0-1 | 0-1 | 2251 | | | 2 | 3 | 4 | 6 | | 7' | 8 | 14 | | | | 11* | | | 12 | 1 | 5 | 9 | 13 | 10" | | | | | | | | | | |

## F.A. TROPHY

| Rd | Date | | Opposition | | FT | HT | Att. | Goalscorers | Brown W. | Collins D. | McIntyre K. | Carden P. | Ruffer C. | Hatswell W. | Heard J. | Davies B. | Rapley K. | Gill R. | Harris A. | Beesley M. | Foster I. | Brodie S. | Carey S. | Twiss M | McCaldon I. | Bolland P. | Stamp D. | Brady J. | Clare D. | Guyett S. | Smith A. | Regan C. | Turner I. | Williams D. | Lane C. | Woods A. | Elam L. | Buckley D. | Dogun P. |
|---|---|---|---|---|---|---|---|---|---|---|---|---|---|---|---|---|---|---|---|---|---|---|---|---|---|---|---|---|---|---|---|---|---|---|---|---|---|---|---|
| 3R | Jan | 10 | HALIFAX TOWN | L | 1-2 | 1-1 | 1561 | Bolland | | 2 | | 4 | 6 | | | 12 | 13 | | | | 10 | | 8* | 3 | 1 | 5 | 9' | | | | 11 | 7 | | | | | | | |

## LDV TROPHY

| Rd | Date | | Opposition | | FT | HT | Att. | Goalscorers | Brown W. | Collins D. | McIntyre K. | Carden P. | Ruffer C. | Hatswell W. | Heard J. | Davies B. | Rapley K. | Gill R. | Harris A. | Beesley M. | Foster I. | Brodie S. | Carey S. | Twiss M | McCaldon I. | Bolland P. | Stamp D. | Brady J. | Clare D. | Guyett S. | Smith A. | Regan C. | Turner I. | Williams D. | Lane C. | Woods A. | Elam L. | Buckley D. | Dogun P. |
|---|---|---|---|---|---|---|---|---|---|---|---|---|---|---|---|---|---|---|---|---|---|---|---|---|---|---|---|---|---|---|---|---|---|---|---|---|---|---|---|
| 1R | Oct | 14 | DONCASTER ROVERS | L | 0-1 | 0-0 | 1141 | | 1 | 2 | 3 | | | | 7 | | 9 | | 6 | 12 | 10* | | 4" | 8' | | | | 11 | | 5 | | | | | | | | 13 | 14 |

## FRIENDLIES

| No. | Date | | Opposition | | FT | HT | Att. | Goalscorers |
|---|---|---|---|---|---|---|---|---|
| 1 | Jul | 19 | F.C. NORDSJAELLAND | L | 0-2 | 0-1 | 854 | |
| 2 | | 21 | Cammell Laird | W | 1-0 | 1-0 | 200 | Harris |
| 3 | | 23 | ADO DEN HAAG | W | 2-0 | 1-0 | 750 | Davies (2 (1 pen)) |
| 4 | | 26 | Buckley Town | W | 4-1 | 2-0 | 450 | Brodie, Carden, Heard, Byrne |
| 5 | | 29 | Connah's Quay Nomads | W | 2-1 | 1-0 | 755 | Davies (2) |
| 6 | Aug | 2 | Vauxhall Motors | D | 1-1 | 0-0 | 515 | Foster |
| 7 | May | 9 | CHESTER CITY ALL STARS * | L | 4-5 | 1-3 | 1658 | Rapley, Brodie, Durkin, Brown |

* Wayne Brown Testimonial

**2003/04 Season:**

Back - Guyett, McCaldon, Bolland, Cameron, Brown, Collins

Middle – Krol (Assistant Physio), Carey, McIntyre, Ruffer, Beesley, Rapley, Twiss, Brady, Kelly, Hinnigan (Physio)

Front – Foster, Davies, Byrne, Cottrell (Chief Scout), Wright (Manager), Liversage (Chief Exec.), Vaughan (Chairman), Burford (General Manager), Allan (Secretary), Bleasdale (Assistant Manager), Brodie, Harris, Carden.

**2004/05 Season:**

Back - Kroll (Physio), Hope, Belle, Bolland, Collins, Drummond, Ellison, Stamp, Gray (Coach)

Middle - McMillan (Players Liason), Burford (Chief Exec.), Knox (Comm. Dir.), Aizelwood (Asst. Man.), Hessey, Edmonson, Brown, McKenzie, Navarro, Rapley, Mathias (Dir. of Football), Allan (Secretary), Liversage (Vice Chair.)

Front - S Vaughan, Clare, Branch, Carden, Vaughan (Chair.), Rush (Manager), Davies, Cook, Watson, Harris.

# SEASON 2004-05

## FOOTBALL LEAGUE CHAMPIONSHIP 2

| No | Date | Opposition | Res | FT | HT | Att. | Goalscorers | Brown W. | Vaughan S. | Edmondson D. | Harris A. | Bolland P. | Collins D. | Drummond S. | Branch M. | Clare D. | Davies B. | Ellison K. | Carden P. | Rapley K. | McIntyre K. | Hessey S. | Navarro A. | Belle C. | Stamp D. | Whalley S. | Hope R. | MacKenzie C. | Booth R. | Bayliss D. | Hillier I. | Brown M. | Walsh M. | Elokobi G. | O'Neill J. | Lynch G. | Atieno T. | Foy R. | Sestanovich A. | Nicholas A. | Lowe R. | Regan C. | Anaclet E. | Doyle C. | Watson A. |
|---|---|---|---|---|---|---|---|---|---|---|---|---|---|---|---|---|---|---|---|---|---|---|---|---|---|---|---|---|---|---|---|---|---|---|---|---|---|---|---|---|---|---|---|---|---|
| 1 | Aug 7 | Notts County | D | 1-1 | 0-0 | 6423 | Rapley | 1 | 2 | 3 | 4 | 5 | 6 | 7 | 8' | 9 | 10* | 11 | 12 | 13 | | | | | | | | | | | | | | | | | | | | | | | | | |
| 2 | 10 | WYCOMBE WANDERERS | L | 0-2 | 0-1 | 2881 | | 1 | 2 | 3* | 4 | 5 | 6 | 7 | 8 | 9 | 10' | 11 | 12 | 13 | | | | | | | | | | | | | | | | | | | | | | | | | |
| 3 | 14 | MANSFIELD TOWN | L | 0-3 | 0-0 | 2648 | | 1 | 2 | | 10* | 5 | 6 | 7 | 8 | 12 | 13 | 11 | 4' | 9 | 3 | | | | | | | | | | | | | | | | | | | | | | | | |
| 4 | 21 | Bury | D | 1-1 | 1-0 | 2870 | Branch | 1 | 2 | | | 5 | 6 | 7 | 8 | | | 11 | 13 | 9* | 3 | 4 | 10' | 12 | | | | | | | | | | | | | | | | | | | | | |
| 5 | 28 | DARLINGTON | L | 0-3 | 0-2 | 2392 | | 1 | 2 | | | 5 | 6 | 7* | 8 | | 12 | 11 | 14 | 9' | 3 | 4 | 10" | 13 | | | | | | | | | | | | | | | | | | | | | |
| 6 | 30 | Boston United | L | 1-3 | 0-2 | 2698 | Branch (pen) | 1 | 2 | | | 5 | 6 | 12 | 8 | | 10 | 11* | | | 3 | 4 | 7 | 9 | | | | | | | | | | | | | | | | | | | | | |
| 7 | Sep 4 | MACCLESFIELD TOWN | W | 1-0 | 0-0 | 2913 | Collins | 1 | | 2* | 12 | 5 | 6 | 7 | 8 | | 10 | 11 | 4 | | 3 | | | 9 | | | | | | | | | | | | | | | | | | | | | |
| 8 | 11 | Scunthorpe United | W | 2-1 | 2-0 | 4203 | Bolland, Ellison | 1 | | 2 | 12 | 5 | 6 | 7 | | | 10 | 11 | 4* | 8' | | 3 | | 9 | 13 | | | | | | | | | | | | | | | | | | | | |
| 9 | 18 | CAMBRIDGE UNITED | D | 0-0 | 0-0 | 2771 | | 1 | 14 | 2 | 12 | 5 | 6 | 7" | | | 10* | 11 | 4 | 8 | | 3 | | | 9' | 13 | | | | | | | | | | | | | | | | | | | |
| 10 | 25 | Lincoln City | D | 1-1 | 1-1 | 3985 | Ellison | 1 | 13 | 2 | | 5 | 6 | 7 | | | 10 | 11 | 4 | 8' | | 3 | | | 9* | | 12 | | | | | | | | | | | | | | | | | | |
| 11 | Oct 2 | SWANSEA CITY | D | 1-1 | 1-0 | 3803 | Rapley | 1 | | 2 | 13 | 5 | 6 | 7 | 12 | | 10 | | 4' | 8 | 11 | 3 | | 9* | | | | | | | | | | | | | | | | | | | | | |
| 12 | 8 | Cheltenham Town | D | 0-0 | 0-0 | 3670 | | 1 | | 2 | | 5 | 6 | 7 | 12 | | 10 | 11 | 4 | 8* | | 3 | | 9 | | | | | | | | | | | | | | | | | | | | | |
| 13 | 16 | Rushden & Diamonds | W | 1-0 | 0-0 | 2735 | Drummond | | | 2 | | 5 | | 7 | 8* | | 10 | 11 | 4 | 12 | | 3 | | 9 | | | 6 | 1 | | | | | | | | | | | | | | | | | |
| 14 | 23 | GRIMSBY TOWN | W | 2-1 | 2-1 | 3233 | Branch (2) | | | 2 | 13 | 5 | | 7 | 8" | 14 | 10' | 11 | 4 | 12 | | 3 | | 9* | | | 6 | 1 | | | | | | | | | | | | | | | | | |
| 15 | 19 | KIDDERMINSTER HARRIERS | W | 3-0 | 1-0 | 2968 | Branch, Davies, Ellison | | 14 | 2 | | 5 | | 7* | 8 | 13 | 10 | 11 | 4 | 12 | | 3" | | 9' | | | 6 | 1 | | | | | | | | | | | | | | | | | |
| 16 | 30 | Yeovil Town | L | 1-4 | 0-1 | 5741 | Clare (pen) | | | 2" | 14 | 5 | | 7 | 8' | 13 | 10 | 11 | 4 | 12 | | 3 | | 9* | | | 6 | 1 | | | | | | | | | | | | | | | | | |
| 17 | Nov 6 | LEYTON ORIENT | D | 1-1 | 0-1 | 3125 | Belle | | 14 | 2" | 13 | 5 | | 7* | | 9 | 10' | 11 | 4 | 12 | | 3 | | 8 | | | 6 | 1 | | | | | | | | | | | | | | | | | |
| 18 | 19 | Northampton Town | D | 1-1 | 1-1 | 5625 | Ellison | | | 2 | 10' | 5 | | 7 | | | 13 | 11 | 4 | 8 | 3 | 6* | | 9 | | | 12 | 1 | | | | | | | | | | | | | | | | | |
| 19 | 27 | OXFORD UNITED | L | 1-3 | 1-1 | 2791 | Ellison | | | 2 | 4 | 5 | | 7 | | | 10 | 11 | | 9 | 3 | | | | | | 6 | 1 | 8 | | | | | | | | | | | | | | | | |
| 20 | Dec 7 | Bristol Rovers | L | 1-4 | 1-2 | 5524 | Ellison | 1 | 2 | | | 5 | | 7 | 8 | | 10* | 11 | 4 | 9 | 13 | 3 | | | | | 6' | | 12 | | | | | | | | | | | | | | | | |
| 21 | 11 | SHREWSBURY TOWN | D | 1-1 | 0-0 | 3219 | Branch (pen) | 1 | | | 2 | 5 | | 7 | 8 | | 13 | 11 | 4 | 12 | 3' | | | 9" | 14 | | 6 | | 10* | | | | | | | | | | | | | | | | |
| 22 | 17 | Southend United | L | 0-1 | 0-0 | 4837 | | 1 | 13 | | 2 | 5 | | 7 | 8* | | 10' | | 4 | 14 | | 3 | | 9 | | | | | 12" | 6 | 11 | | | | | | | | | | | | | | |
| 23 | 26 | SCUNTHORPE UNITED | D | 1-1 | 1-1 | 3216 | Ellison | 1* | | | | 5 | | 7 | 8 | | 10' | 11 | 4 | | | 3 | | 9 | | | | 12 | | 6 | 2 | 13 | | | | | | | | | | | | | |
| 24 | 28 | Rochdale | D | 2-2 | 1-0 | 3724 | Ellison, Branch | | | | 12 | 5 | | 7 | 8 | | 13 | 11 | 4 | | | 3* | | 9" | | 14 | | 1 | | 6 | 2 | 10' | | | | | | | | | | | | | |
| 25 | Jan 1 | Macclesfield Town | W | 2-1 | 0-1 | 3076 | Drummond, Ellison | | | | | 5 | | 7 | 8 | | 12 | 11 | 4 | | | 3 | | 9 | | | | 1 | | 6 | 2 | 10* | | | | | | | | | | | | | |
| 26 | 3 | LINCOLN CITY | L | 0-1 | 0-0 | 2839 | | | 12 | | 13 | 5 | | 7 | 8" | | | 11 | 4 | | | 3* | | 9 | | 14 | | 1 | | 6 | 2' | 10 | | | | | | | | | | | | | |
| 27 | 15 | Cambridge United | D | 0-0 | 0-0 | 3185 | | | 8 | | | | | 7 | 9 | | 2 | | 4 | | | 3' | | 12 | | | 5 | 1 | 11* | 6 | | 10 | 13 | | | | | | | | | | | | |
| 28 | 22 | ROCHDALE | D | 0-0 | 0-0 | 2985 | | | 8' | | | 5 | | 7 | 9 | | 2 | | 4 | 10* | | 13 | | 12 | | | 3 | 1 | | 6 | | 11 | | | | | | | | | | | | | |
| 29 | 29 | Swansea City | L | 0-3 | 0-1 | 8989 | | | 8 | | 4 | 5 | | | 9 | | 2 | | | | | 12 | | | | | | 1 | | 6 | 7' | 10* | 11" | 3 | 13 | 14 | | | | | | | | | |
| 30 | Feb 1 | CHELTENHAM TOWN | L | 0-3 | 0-1 | 1643 | | | 8* | | 4" | 5 | | 7 | 9 | | 2 | | | | | 12 | | | | | | 1 | | 6 | 11' | | 14 | 3 | 10 | | 13 | | | | | | | | |
| 31 | 5 | RUSHDEN & DIAMONDS | W | 3-1 | 2-0 | 2340 | Atieno, Hessey,O'Neill | 1 | | 2* | | 5 | | 7 | 8 | | 10 | | 4 | | | 3 | | | | | 6 | | | | 12 | | | | 11 | | 9 | | | | | | | | |
| 32 | 12 | Kidderminster Harriers | W | 1-0 | 1-0 | 2779 | Drummond | 1 | | 2 | | 5 | | 7 | 8* | | 10 | | 4 | | | 3 | | | | | 6 | | | | | 12 | | | 11 | | 9 | | | | | | | | |
| 33 | 19 | YEOVIL TOWN | L | 0-2 | 0-2 | 3072 | | 1 | | 2 | | 5* | | 7 | | | 10 | | 4 | | | 3 | | | | | 6 | | | | | 11' | | 12 | 14 | | 9" | 8 | 13 | | | | | | |
| 34 | 22 | Grimsby Town | L | 0-1 | 0-0 | 3144 | | 1 | | | | | | 7 | | | 2 | | 4 | | | 3 | | | | | 6 | | 12 | | | 11 | | 5 | 10* | | | 9 | 8 | | | | | | |
| 35 | 26 | Shrewsbury Town | L | 0-5 | 0-2 | 4859 | | 1 | | 2 | | | | 7 | | | 10 | | 4 | | | 3 | | 12 | | | 6 | | | | | 13 | | 5 | 11' | | | 9 | 8* | | | | | | |
| 36 | Mar 5 | SOUTHEND UNITED | D | 2-2 | 1-1 | 2396 | Walsh, Davies | 1 | | 2 | | 5 | | 7 | 8 | | 10 | | 4 | | | 3 | | | | | 6 | | | | | | 11 | | | | | 9 | | | | | | | |
| 37 | 12 | Wycombe Wanderers | L | 2-4 | 1-1 | 8124 | Branch (2 (1 pen)) | 1 | 4 | 2 | | 5 | | 7 | 8 | | 10 | | | | | 3 | | | | | 6 | | | | | 11* | | | | | | 9 | 12 | | | | | | |
| 38 | 19 | NOTTS COUNTY | W | 3-2 | 1-1 | 2324 | Drummond, Branch(2) | | | 2 | | 5 | | 7 | 8 | | 10 | | | | | | | | | | 6 | 1 | 13 | | | 4 | | | 12 | | | 9* | 11' | 3 | | | | | |
| 39 | 25 | Mansfield Town | D | 0-0 | 0-0 | 3437 | | | | 2* | | 5 | | 7 | 8 | | 10 | | 4 | | | | | | | | 6 | 1 | | | | | | | | | | 9 | | 3 | 11 | 12 | | | |
| 40 | 28 | BURY | W | 2-1 | 0-1 | 3107 | Lowe (2) | | | 12 | | 5 | | 7 | 8 | | 10 | | 4 | | | | | | | | 6 | 1 | | | | | | | | | | 9 | 13 | 3 | 11' | 2* | | | |
| 41 | Apr 2 | Darlington | L | 0-1 | 0-0 | 3778 | | | | 2 | | 5 | | 7 | 8 | | 10" | | 4' | | | | | | | | 6 | 1 | | | | 14 | | | 13 | | | 9 | 12 | 3 | 11* | | | | |
| 42 | 9 | BOSTON UNITED | W | 2-1 | 1-1 | 2040 | Booth, Lowe | | | 2 | | | | 7 | | | 10 | | 4 | | | 5 | | | | | 6 | 1 | 8 | | | | | | | | | 11 | | 3 | 9 | | | | |
| 43 | 16 | BRISTOL ROVERS | D | 2-2 | 0-2 | 2475 | Drummond (2) | | | 2* | | 5 | | 7 | | | 10 | | 4 | | | 3 | | | | | 6 | 1 | 8' | | | 14 | | | 13 | | | 11" | | | 9 | 12 | | | |
| 44 | 23 | Leyton Orient | L | 0-2 | 0-2 | 3192 | | | 12 | | | 5* | | 7 | 8' | | 10 | | 4 | | | 3 | | | | | 6 | 1 | | | | 14 | | | 13 | | | 11 | | | 9" | 2 | | | |
| 45 | 30 | NORTHAMPTON TOWN | L | 0-2 | 0-1 | 3455 | | | 2 | | | 5 | | 7 | | | 10 | | 4 | | | | | | | | 6 | 1 | 8* | | | 12 | | | | | | 11 | | | 9 | 3 | | | |
| 46 | May 7 | Oxford United | W | 1-0 | 0-0 | 5055 | Lowe | | 2 | | 13 | 5 | | 7 | | | 10 | | 4' | | | | | | | | 6 | 1 | 8* | | | 11 | 12 | | | | | | | | 9 | 3 | | | |
| | | | | | | | Apps | 23 | 14 | 26 | 9 | 42 | 12 | 44 | 31 | 3 | 38 | 24 | 36 | 12 | 9 | 31 | 3 | 17 | 2 | | 26 | 23 | 7 | 9 | 7 | 11 | 2 | 4 | 5 | | 3 | 13 | 3 | 5 | 8 | 4 | | | |
| | | | | | | | Subs | | 7 | 1 | 10 | | | 1 | 2 | 4 | 6 | | 4 | 9 | 1 | 3 | | 5 | 2 | 3 | 2 | 1 | 4 | | 1 | 7 | 3 | 1 | 6 | 1 | 1 | | 4 | | | 2 | | | |
| | | | | | | | Goals | | | | | 1 | 1 | 6 | 11 | 1 | 2 | 9 | | 2 | | 1 | | 1 | | | | | 1 | | | | 1 | | 1 | | 1 | | | | 4 | | | | |

## F.A. CUP

| Rd | Date | Opposition | Res | FT | HT | Att. | Goalscorers | Brown W. | Vaughan S. | Edmondson D. | Harris A. | Bolland P. | Collins D. | Drummond S. | Branch M. | Clare D. | Davies B. | Ellison K. | Carden P. | Rapley K. | McIntyre K. | Hessey S. | Navarro A. | Belle C. | Stamp D. | Whalley S. | Hope R. | MacKenzie C. | Booth R. | Bayliss D. | Hillier I. | Brown M. | Walsh M. | Elokobi G. | O'Neill J. | Lynch G. | Atieno T. | Foy R. | Sestanovich A. | Nicholas A. | Lowe R. | Regan C. | Anaclet E. | Doyle C. | Watson A. |
|---|---|---|---|---|---|---|---|---|---|---|---|---|---|---|---|---|---|---|---|---|---|---|---|---|---|---|---|---|---|---|---|---|---|---|---|---|---|---|---|---|---|---|---|---|---|
| 1R | Nov 13 | Stafford Rangers | W | 2-0 | 1-0 | 2492 | Belle, Rapley | | | 2 | 14 | 5 | | 7 | | 9' | 10" | 11 | 4 | 13 | 12 | 3* | | 8 | | | 6 | 1 | | | | | | | | | | | | | | | | | |
| 2R | Dec 4 | Halifax Town | W | 3-1 | 1-0 | 4497 | Branch(2 (1p)), Rapley | 1 | 10 | 2* | 7 | | | | 8" | | | 11 | 4 | 12 | 3 | 5 | | | | | 6 | | 9' | | | | | | | 14 | | | | | | | 13 | | |
| 3R | Jan 8 | AFC Bournemouth | L | 1-2 | 0-1 | 7653 | Ellison | | 8" | | | 5 | | 7 | | | 2 | 11 | 4 | 9* | | 3' | | 12 | | | | 1 | 14 | 6 | | 10 | 13 | | | | | | | | | | | | |

## LEAGUE (CARLING) CUP

| Rd | Date | Opposition | Res | FT | HT | Att. | Goalscorers | Brown W. | Vaughan S. | Edmondson D. | Harris A. | Bolland P. | Collins D. | Drummond S. | Branch M. | Clare D. | Davies B. | Ellison K. | Carden P. | Rapley K. | McIntyre K. | Hessey S. | Navarro A. | Belle C. | Stamp D. | Whalley S. | Hope R. | MacKenzie C. | Booth R. | Bayliss D. | Hillier I. | Brown M. | Walsh M. | Elokobi G. | O'Neill J. | Lynch G. | Atieno T. | Foy R. | Sestanovich A. | Nicholas A. | Lowe R. | Regan C. | Anaclet E. | Doyle C. | Watson A. |
|---|---|---|---|---|---|---|---|---|---|---|---|---|---|---|---|---|---|---|---|---|---|---|---|---|---|---|---|---|---|---|---|---|---|---|---|---|---|---|---|---|---|---|---|---|---|
| 1R | Aug 24 | Sunderland | L | 0-3 | 0-1 | 11450 | | 1 | 2 | | | 5 | 6 | 7 | 8* | | 12 | 11 | 13 | | 3 | 4 | 10 | 9' | | | | | | | | | | | | | | | | | | | | | |

## LDV TROPHY

| Rd | Date | Opposition | Res | FT | HT | Att. | Goalscorers | Brown W. | Vaughan S. | Edmondson D. | Harris A. | Bolland P. | Collins D. | Drummond S. | Branch M. | Clare D. | Davies B. | Ellison K. | Carden P. | Rapley K. | McIntyre K. | Hessey S. | Navarro A. | Belle C. | Stamp D. | Whalley S. | Hope R. | MacKenzie C. | Booth R. | Bayliss D. | Hillier I. | Brown M. | Walsh M. | Elokobi G. | O'Neill J. | Lynch G. | Atieno T. | Foy R. | Sestanovich A. | Nicholas A. | Lowe R. | Regan C. | Anaclet E. | Doyle C. | Watson A. |
|---|---|---|---|---|---|---|---|---|---|---|---|---|---|---|---|---|---|---|---|---|---|---|---|---|---|---|---|---|---|---|---|---|---|---|---|---|---|---|---|---|---|---|---|---|---|
| 1R | Sep 29 | Sheffield Wednesday | W | 2-1 | 0-1 | 7640 | Ellison, Hope | | 2 | | 7 | 5 | | 14 | | | 12 | 11 | 4* | 8' | 3 | | | | 9 | 13 | 6 | 1 | 10" | | | | | | | | | | | | | | | | |
| 2R | Nov 2 | ROCHDALE | W | 1-0 | 0-0 | 1419 | Hessey | | 2 | | 7 | 5' | | 14 | 12 | 9 | | | 4" | 8 | 3 | 6 | | | | | 13 | | 10 | | | | | | | | | | | | | | | 1 | 11* |
| QF | 30 | WREXHAM | L | 0-1 | 0-1 | 5028 | | 1 | 2 | | 8 | 5 | | 7" | | | 10* | 11 | 4 | 9 | 3' | 6 | | | | 14 | 13 | | 12 | | | | | | | | | | | | | | | | |

## FRIENDLIES

| No | Date | Opposition | Res | FT | HT | Att. | Goalscorers |
|---|---|---|---|---|---|---|---|
| 1 | Jul 17 | WALSALL | W | 3-0 | 3-0 | 1335 | Branch (2), Ellison |
| 2 | 20 | CARDIFF CITY | W | 2-0 | 1-0 | 1080 | Sheron, Branch |
| 3 | 22 | Colwyn Bay | W | 1-0 | 0-0 | 390 | Clare |
| 4 | 24 | QUEEN OF THE SOUTH | D | 2-2 | 1-0 | 1016 | Branch, Davies |
| 5 | 29 | Connah's Quay Nomads | W | 2-0 | 1-0 | 420 | Collins, Davies |
| 7 | Aug 2 | BLACKBURN ROVERS | D | 0-0 | 0-0 | 1472 | |

# SEASON 2005-06

## FOOTBALL LEAGUE CHAMPIONSHIP 2

| | Date | | Opposition | | FT | HT | Att. | Goalscorers | MacKenzie C. | Regan C. | McNiven S. | Curtis T. | Bolland P. | Dimech L. | Drummond S. | Branch M. | Richardson M. | Lowe R. | Davies B. | Walker J. | El Kholti A. | Artell D. | Vaughan S. | Bertos L. | Blundell G. | Hessey S. | Dove C. | Curle T. | Rutherford P. | Brookfield R. | Ruddy J. | Gillet S. | Asamoah D. | Corden W. | Horwood E. | Roberts M. | Robertson C. | Tait P. | Albrighton M. | Ellender P. | Harrison P. | Edwards J. |
|---|---|---|---|---|---|---|---|---|---|---|---|---|---|---|---|---|---|---|---|---|---|---|---|---|---|---|---|---|---|---|---|---|---|---|---|---|---|---|---|---|---|
| 1 | Aug | 6 | Peterborough United | W | 1-0 | 0-0 | 4980 | Drummond | 1 | 2 | 3 | 4 | 5 | 6 | 7 | 8 | 9 | 10* | 11 | 12 | | | | | | | | | | | | | | | | | | | | | | |
| 2 | | 9 | LINCOLN CITY | D | 2-2 | 0-2 | 2637 | Davies, Branch (pen) | 1 | 2 | 3* | 4' | 5 | 6 | 7 | 8 | 9" | 10 | 11 | 13 | 12 | 14 | | | | | | | | | | | | | | | | | | | | |
| 3 | | 20 | Rushden & Diamonds | D | 1-1 | 0-0 | 2682 | Lowe | 1 | 3 | 2 | 12 | 5 | | 7 | 8 | 9' | 10 | 11 | 4* | | 6 | 13 | | | | | | | | | | | | | | | | | | | |
| 4 | | 27 | DARLINGTON | D | 4-4 | 0-2 | 2469 | Richardson (2), Blundell (2) | 1 | 3* | 2 | 13 | 5 | 6 | 7' | 8 | 14 | | 11 | 10 | | | | 4" | 9 | 12 | | | | | | | | | | | | | | | | |
| 5 | | 29 | Torquay United | W | 1-0 | 0-0 | 2245 | Lowe | 1 | 3 | 2 | 10 | 5 | | 13 | 8 | 9* | 12 | 11 | | | 6 | 7' | 4" | 14 | | | | | | | | | | | | | | | | | |
| 6 | Sep | 2 | MANSFIELD TOWN | W | 3-1 | 1-0 | 3079 | Blundell (2), Lowe | 1 | 2 | 3 | 4 | | 6 | 7 | 8" | 13 | 10 | 11* | 12 | | 5 | | 14 | 9' | | | | | | | | | | | | | | | | | |
| 7 | | 6 | GRIMSBY TOWN | L | 1-2 | 0-0 | 3095 | Lowe | 1 | 2 | 3" | 4 | 5 | 6 | 7 | 8 | 12 | 10 | 11' | | | 14 | | 13 | 9* | | | | | | | | | | | | | | | | | |
| 8 | | 10 | Notts County | D | 1-1 | 0-0 | 5404 | Davies | 1 | | 2 | 4' | 5* | 12 | 7 | 8 | 9" | 10 | 13 | 11 | | 6 | | | 14 | 3 | | | | | | | | | | | | | | | | |
| 9 | | 17 | BRISTOL ROVERS | W | 4-0 | 3-0 | 2874 | Lowe, Artell, Richardson ,Blundell | 1 | | 2 | 4" | | 6 | 7 | | 9* | 10 | 11' | 14 | | 5 | 13 | | 8 | 3 | 12 | | | | | | | | | | | | | | | |
| 10 | | 24 | Stockport County | D | 0-0 | 0-0 | 4873 | | 1 | 3 | 2 | 4 | | 6 | 7* | 13 | 9' | 10 | 11 | | | 5 | 12 | | 8 | | | | | | | | | | | | | | | | | |
| 11 | | 27 | CARLISLE UNITED | W | 2-0 | 2-0 | 3394 | Artell, Blundell | 1 | 2 | 3 | 13 | | 6 | 7 | 8' | 14 | 10* | 11 | 4" | 12 | 5 | | | 9 | | | | | | | | | | | | | | | | | |
| 12 | Oct | 1 | Wycombe Wanderers | D | 3-3 | 2-2 | 5145 | Drummond, Branch (2) | 1 | 3 | 2 | 4 | | 6 | 7 | 8 | 9' | 10* | 11 | 13 | | 5 | | | 12 | | | | | | | | | | | | | | | | | |
| 13 | | 7 | ROCHDALE | L | 2-3 | 0-1 | 4327 | Drummond, Davies | 1 | 3 | 2 | 4 | 13 | 6 | 7 | 8 | 9" | 12 | 11 | | | 5' | | 14 | 10* | | | | | | | | | | | | | | | | | |
| 14 | | 15 | Barnet | W | 3-1 | 2-0 | 2206 | Branch, Lowe, Curtis | 1 | 3* | 2 | 4 | | 6 | 7 | 8" | 9' | 10 | 11 | 13 | | 5 | | | | 12 | | 14 | | | | | | | | | | | | | | |
| 15 | | 22 | BURY | D | 1-1 | 0-1 | 3471 | Lowe (pen) | 1 | | 2 | 4 | 14 | 6 | | 8 | 9' | 10 | 11" | 7* | 13 | 5 | 12 | | | 3 | | | | | | | | | | | | | | | | |
| 16 | | 29 | Shrewsbury Town | L | 1-3 | 1-2 | 5430 | Lowe | 1 | | 2 | 4 | | 6 | | 9 | 13 | 10 | 11 | 12 | | 5 | 8* | | | 3 | 7' | | | | | | | | | | | | | | | |
| 17 | Nov | 12 | NORTHAMPTON TOWN | D | 0-0 | 0-0 | 3295 | | 1 | 3 | 2 | 4 | | 6 | 7 | 8 | 9* | 10 | 11 | | 12 | 5 | | | | | | | | | | | | | | | | | | | | |
| 18 | | 19 | Rochdale | D | 2-2 | 1-0 | 3618 | Bolland, Davies | 1 | 3 | 2 | 4 | 5 | | 7 | 8* | 9 | 10 | 11 | | | 6 | 12 | | | | | | | | | | | | | | | | | | | |
| 19 | | 26 | PETERBOROUGH UNITED | W | 3-1 | 1-0 | 2701 | Branch (pen), Drummond, Lowe | 1 | 2 | 3 | | | 6 | 7 | 8' | 9* | 10 | 11 | 4 | 12 | 5 | | | | | | | 13 | | | | | | | | | | | | | |
| 20 | Dec | 6 | Leyton Orient | W | 1-0 | 1-0 | 3463 | Drummond | 1 | 2 | 3 | 4 | 5 | 13 | 7 | | 9' | 10" | 11 | 8* | 12 | 6 | | | | | 14 | | | | | | | | | | | | | | | |
| 21 | | 10 | Lincoln City | L | 1-3 | 0-0 | 3563 | Richardson | 1* | 2 | 3 | 4 | 5 | | 7 | | 9 | 10 | 11 | 8' | 13 | 6 | | | | | | | | 12 | | | | | | | | | | | | |
| 22 | | 17 | RUSHDEN & DIAMONDS | L | 1-2 | 1-1 | 2265 | Davies (pen) | | | | 2 | 5 | 6 | 7 | | 9 | | 11 | | 3 | | 8 | | | | 4* | 12 | 10 | | 1 | | | | | | | | | | | |
| 23 | | 26 | Cheltenham Town | L | 0-1 | 0-0 | 3819 | | | 3 | 2 | 13 | 5 | | 7 | | 9 | 10 | 11 | | 4* | 6 | 8' | | | | | | 12 | | 1 | | | | | | | | | | | |
| 24 | | 31 | Macclesfield Town | L | 0-1 | 0-0 | 2910 | | | 2 | 3^ | 4 | 13 | 6 | 7 | | 9* | 10 | 11 | 14 | 12 | 5 | | | 8' | | | | | | 1 | | | | | | | | | | | |
| 25 | Jan | 2 | OXFORD UNITED | L | 0-1 | 0-0 | 2624 | | | 3' | 2" | 4 | 14 | 6 | 7 | | 9 | | 11 | 8* | 13 | 5 | | | 10 | | 12 | | | | 1 | | | | | | | | | | | |
| 26 | | 14 | BOSTON UNITED | L | 0-1 | 0-0 | 2956 | | | 6 | 2 | 4" | | | 7 | 14 | 9* | | 13 | 8' | 3 | 5 | | | 12 | | | | | | | 1 | 10 | 11 | | | | | | | | |
| 27 | | 21 | Bristol Rovers | L | 1-2 | 0-2 | 6310 | Davies | | 3 | 2 | 4" | | 6 | 7 | 8 | 14 | 10 | 12 | | | 5 | 13 | | | | | | | | | 1 | 9' | 11* | | | | | | | | |
| 28 | | 24 | Mansfield Town | W | 2-1 | 0-0 | 3219 | McNiven, Asamoah | | 3 | 2 | 4 | | 6 | 7 | 14 | 13 | 10" | 11 | | | 5 | 12 | | 9' | | | | | | | 1 | 8* | | | | | | | | | |
| 29 | | 28 | NOTTS COUNTY | L | 0-2 | 0-0 | 2599 | | | 2 | 3 | 4 | | 6' | 7 | | 9* | 10 | 11 | | | 5 | 13 | | 12 | | | | | | | 1 | 8 | | | | | | | | | |
| 30 | Feb | 4 | Carlisle United | L | 0-5 | 0-2 | 6561 | | | 6 | 2 | | | | 7 | 8" | 13 | 10 | 11 | | | | 4 | | 14 | | | | | | | 1 | 9' | | 3 | 5* | 12 | | | | | |
| 31 | | 11 | STOCKPORT COUNTY | L | 1-2 | 0-0 | 3446 | Lowe | | 3 | 2 | | | | 7 | 13 | | 12 | 11 | 4 | | 5 | | | 10* | 6 | | | | | | 1 | 8' | | | | | 9 | | | | |
| 32 | | 18 | LEYTON ORIENT | L | 0-2 | 0-1 | 2210 | | | 3' | 2 | 4 | | 6 | 7 | 8 | 13 | | 11 | 10* | | 5 | | | 12 | | | | | | | 1 | 14 | | | | | 9" | | | | |
| 33 | | 25 | Grimsby Town | L | 0-1 | 0-1 | 4058 | | | 3 | 2 | 11 | | | 7 | 8' | 13 | 10 | | | | 12 | | | 9 | 4 | | | | | | 1 | | | | | | | 5 | 6* | | |
| 34 | Mar | 7 | TORQUAY UNITED | D | 1-1 | 0-1 | 1806 | Blundell | | 2* | 3 | 14 | | | 7 | | 13 | 10" | 11 | | | | | | 9 | 4 | | | | | | | 12 | | | | | 8' | 5 | 6 | 1 | |
| 35 | | 11 | Darlington | L | 0-1 | 0-0 | 3593 | | | 2* | 3 | 8 | | | 7 | | | 10 | 11 | | 13 | | | | 9 | 4' | | | | | | | | | | | | 12 | 5 | 6 | 1 | |
| 36 | | 18 | CHELTENHAM TOWN | L | 0-1 | 0-1 | 2281 | | | 2' | 3 | 4* | | | 7 | 8 | 14 | 10 | 11 | | 12 | | 13 | | 9" | | | | | | | | | | | | | | 5 | 6 | 1 | |
| 37 | | 26 | Wrexham | L | 1-2 | 0-2 | 7240 | Edwards | | 2* | 5 | | | | 7 | 8 | | 12 | 11 | | 3' | 6 | | | | | | | 13 | | | | | | | | | | 4 | 10 | 1 | 9 |
| 38 | | 29 | Boston United | W | 3-1 | 1-0 | 1651 | Asamoah (3) | 1 | 2* | 5 | | | 12 | 7 | | | | 11 | | 10 | 6 | | | | 3 | | | 14 | | | | 8^ | | | | | 13 | 4 | | | 9' |
| 39 | Apr | 1 | MACCLESFIELD TOWN | W | 2-1 | 0-0 | 2939 | Asamoah (2) | 1 | 2 | 5 | | | | 7 | | | | 11 | | | 6 | | | 10* | 3 | | | 12 | | | | 8 | | | | | | 4 | | | 9 |
| 40 | | 8 | Oxford United | W | 1-0 | 1-0 | 5754 | Asamoah | 1 | 2 | 5 | 12 | | | 7 | | | | 11 | | | 6 | | | 10* | 3 | | | | | | | 8 | | | | | 13 | 4 | | | 9' |
| 41 | | 12 | WREXHAM | W | 2-1 | 0-0 | 4801 | Davies (pen), Asamoah | 1 | 12 | 5 | 11 | | | 7 | | | | 2 | | 13 | 6 | | | 10* | 3' | | | | | | | 8 | | | | | 14 | 4 | | | 9" |
| 42 | | 15 | WYCOMBE WANDERERS | W | 1-0 | 0-0 | 2797 | Drummond | 1 | 12 | 5* | 11 | | 4 | 7 | | | | 2 | | 13 | 6 | | | 10 | 3 | | | | | | | 8 | | | | | | | | | 9' |
| 43 | | 17 | Bury | D | 0-0 | 0-0 | 3421 | | 1 | 2 | | 11* | | 4 | 7 | | | | 3 | | 12 | 6 | | | 10 | 5 | | | | | | | 8 | | | | | 13 | | | | 9' |
| 44 | | 22 | BARNET | D | 0-0 | 0-0 | 2367 | | 1 | 2 | | 11 | | 4 | 7* | | | | 3 | | 12 | 6' | 13 | | 10 | 5 | | | | | | | 8 | | | | | | | | | 9 |
| 45 | | 29 | Northampton Town | L | 0-1 | 0-1 | 7114 | | 1 | 2 | | 4 | | 6 | | | | | 11 | 7* | 3 | | 8 | | 10 | 5 | | | | | | | 12 | | | | | 13 | | | | 9' |
| 46 | May | 6 | SHREWSBURY TOWN | L | 0-1 | 0-1 | 3744 | | 1 | 2 | | 4 | | 6 | | | | | 11 | | 3 | | 7 | | 10 | 5 | | | | | | | 8 | | | | | | | | | 9 |
| | | | | | | | | Apps | 30 | 39 | 41 | 34 | 12 | 27 | 41 | 23 | 22 | 28 | 42 | 13 | 7 | 34 | 7 | 2 | 23 | 17 | 2 | | 1 | | 4 | 8 | 14 | 2 | 1 | 1 | | 3 | 9 | 5 | 4 | 10 |
| | | | | | | | | Subs | | 2 | | 6 | 4 | 3 | 1 | 4 | 12 | 4 | 3 | 8 | 15 | 3 | 10 | 3 | 7 | 2 | 3 | 2 | 5 | 1 | | | 3 | | | | 1 | 6 | | | | |
| | | | | | | | | Goals | | | 1 | 1 | 1 | | 6 | 5 | 4 | 10 | 7 | | | 2 | | | 7 | | | | | | | | 8 | | | | | | | | | 1 |

## F.A. CUP

| | Date | | Opposition | | FT | HT | Att. | Goalscorers | MacKenzie C. | Regan C. | McNiven S. | Curtis T. | Bolland P. | Dimech L. | Drummond S. | Branch M. | Richardson M. | Lowe R. | Davies B. | Walker J. | El Kholti A. | Artell D. | Vaughan S. | Bertos L. | Blundell G. | Hessey S. | Dove C. | Curle T. | Rutherford P. | Brookfield R. | Ruddy J. | Gillet S. | Asamoah D. | Corden W. | Horwood E. | Roberts M. | Robertson C. | Tait P. | Albrighton M. | Ellender P. | Harrison P. | Edwards J. |
|---|---|---|---|---|---|---|---|---|---|---|---|---|---|---|---|---|---|---|---|---|---|---|---|---|---|---|---|---|---|---|---|---|---|---|---|---|---|---|---|---|---|
| 1R | Nov | 5 | FOLKESTONE INVICTA | W | 2-1 | 0-1 | 2503 | Branch (pen), Lowe | 1 | 2 | 3 | 4 | | 6 | 7 | 8 | 9* | 10 | 11' | | 12 | 5 | 13 | | | | | | | | | | | | | | | | | | | |
| 2R | Dec | 3 | NOTTINGHAM FOREST | W | 3-0 | 1-0 | 4732 | Lowe (2 (1 pen)), Richardson | 1 | 2 | 3 | 4 | | 6 | 7 | | 9* | 10 | 11" | 8' | 12 | 5 | 13 | | | | 14 | | | | | | | | | | | | | | | |
| 3R | Jan | 7 | Cheltenham Town | D | 2-2 | 0-0 | 4741 | Richardson, Drummond | | 2 | 3* | 4 | 12 | 6 | 7 | | 9 | | 11' | 8 | 13 | 5 | 14 | | 10" | | | | | | | 1 | | | | | | | | | | |
| 3Rr | | 17 | CHELTENHAM TOWN | L | 0-1 | 0-0 | 5096 | | | 2 | 3' | 4 | | 6 | 7 | 8 | 12 | | 11 | 10* | 13 | 5 | | | 9 | | | | | | | 1 | | | | | | | | | | |

## LEAGUE (CARLING) CUP

| | Date | | Opposition | | FT | HT | Att. | Goalscorers | MacKenzie C. | Regan C. | McNiven S. | Curtis T. | Bolland P. | Dimech L. | Drummond S. | Branch M. | Richardson M. | Lowe R. | Davies B. | Walker J. | El Kholti A. | Artell D. | Vaughan S. | Bertos L. | Blundell G. | Hessey S. | Dove C. | Curle T. | Rutherford P. | Brookfield R. | Ruddy J. | Gillet S. | Asamoah D. | Corden W. | Horwood E. | Roberts M. | Robertson C. | Tait P. | Albrighton M. | Ellender P. | Harrison P. | Edwards J. |
|---|---|---|---|---|---|---|---|---|---|---|---|---|---|---|---|---|---|---|---|---|---|---|---|---|---|---|---|---|---|---|---|---|---|---|---|---|---|---|---|---|---|
| 1R | Aug | 23 | Wolverhampton W. | L | 1-5 | 0-1 | 9518 | Davies | 1 | 4' | 2 | 10 | 5 | 6 | 7 | 9" | | | 11 | 8* | | | 14 | 13 | 12 | 3 | | | | | | | | | | | | | | | | |

## LDV TROPHY

| | Date | | Opposition | | FT | HT | Att. | Goalscorers | MacKenzie C. | Regan C. | McNiven S. | Curtis T. | Bolland P. | Dimech L. | Drummond S. | Branch M. | Richardson M. | Lowe R. | Davies B. | Walker J. | El Kholti A. | Artell D. | Vaughan S. | Bertos L. | Blundell G. | Hessey S. | Dove C. | Curle T. | Rutherford P. | Brookfield R. | Ruddy J. | Gillet S. | Asamoah D. | Corden W. | Horwood E. | Roberts M. | Robertson C. | Tait P. | Albrighton M. | Ellender P. | Harrison P. | Edwards J. |
|---|---|---|---|---|---|---|---|---|---|---|---|---|---|---|---|---|---|---|---|---|---|---|---|---|---|---|---|---|---|---|---|---|---|---|---|---|---|---|---|---|---|
| 1R | Oct | 18 | Cambridge United | L | 0-3 | 0-0 | 1224 | | 1 | | 12 | | 5 | | | | 9 | | 13 | 7 | 3 | | 6 | 2 | | 4 | 8 | 10' | 11* | | | | | | | | | | | | | |

## FRIENDLIES

| | Date | | Opposition | | FT | HT | Att. | Goalscorers |
|---|---|---|---|---|---|---|---|---|
| 1 | Jul | 14 | Rainworth MW | W | 3-0 | 2-0 | 850 | Drummond, Branch (pen), Richardson |
| 2 | | 16 | Burton Albion | W | 1-0 | 0-0 | 1341 | Jephcott |
| 3 | | 19 | Tavistock AFC | W | 9-0 | 5-0 | 150 | Jephcott, Curtis(3), Richardson(2), Drummond, Regan, Davies |
| 4 | | 20 | St Blazey | W | 5-2 | 2-0 | 175 | Lowe (2 (1 pen)), Blundell, Walker, Bruce-Lowe |
| 5 | | 23 | Droylsden | W | 4-1 | 2-0 | 298 | Richardson (3), Davies |
| 6 | | 26 | TNS (a) | W | 3-1 | 1-0 | 307 | Lowe (2), Davies |
| 7 | | 30 | Blackpool | L | 0-6 | 0-2 | 1632 | |

**2005/06 Season:**

Back - Gannon (assistant manager), S Vaughan, T Curle, MacKenzie, Davies, Curtis, Bruce-Lowe (fitness consultant)
Middle - Bell (assistant manager), Dimech, Walker, Dove, Drummond, Bolland, Artell, Richardson, Hessey, Goodyear (physio)
Front – Regan, McNiven, Blundell, Vaughan (chairman), K Curle (manager), Branch, Lowe, El Kholti.

**2006/07 Season:**

Back – Walters, Hessey, Artell, Marsh-Evans, Palethorpe, Danby, Bolland, Linwood, Broughton, Hand
Middle Bennett, Cadwallader, Sandwith, Westwood, Blundell, Allen, Holroyd, Rutherford, Cotterell (kitman)
Front – J Vaughan, Marples, Cronin, Hinnigan (physio), Wright (manager),
Barrow (Assistant Manager), S Vaughan, Wilson, Martinez.

# SEASON 2006-07

## FOOTBALL LEAGUE CHAMPIONSHIP 2

| | Date | Opposition | | FT | HT | Att. | Goalscorers | Danby J. | Vaughan S. | Wilson L. | Linwood P. | Westwood A. | Artell D. | Bennett D. | Martinez R. | Broughton D. | Walters J. | Hand J. | Blundell G. | McSporran J. | Marples S. | Ravenhill R. | Holroyd C. | Hessey S. | Sandwith K. | Allen G. | Bolland P. | Steele L. | Semple R. | Rutherford P. | Yeo S. | Meechan A. | Kearney A. | Brownlie R. | Maylett B. | Cronin G. | Vaughan J. | Kelly S. |
|---|---|---|---|---|---|---|---|---|---|---|---|---|---|---|---|---|---|---|---|---|---|---|---|---|---|---|---|---|---|---|---|---|---|---|---|---|---|---|
| 1 | Aug 5 | ACCRINGTON STANLEY | W | 2-0 | 1-0 | 3779 | Broughton, Blundell (pen) | 1 | 2" | 3 | 4 | 5 | 6 | 7 | 8' | 9* | 10 | 11 | 12 | 13 | 14 | | | | | | | | | | | | | | | | | |
| 2 | 8 | Bury | W | 3-1 | 1-1 | 2719 | Walters (2), Woodthorpe (og) | 1 | 2' | 3 | 4 | 5 | 6 | 7 | 8* | 9 | 10 | 11 | | | 13 | 12 | | | | | | | | | | | | | | | | |
| 3 | 12 | Hereford United | L | 0-2 | 0-0 | 3834 | | 1 | 2" | 3 | 4 | 5 | 6 | 7* | 8 | 9' | 10 | 11 | 13 | | 14 | 12 | | | | | | | | | | | | | | | | |
| 4 | 20 | WREXHAM | L | 1-2 | 0-1 | 4206 | Hand | 1 | 2 | 3 | 4 | 5* | 6 | | 8 | 13 | 10' | 11 | 9" | | 12 | 7 | 14 | | | | | | | | | | | | | | | |
| 5 | 26 | Torquay United | D | 2-2 | 0-1 | 2541 | Broughton, Martinez | 1 | 2 | 3 | 4 | | 6 | 7* | 8 | 12 | 10' | 11 | 9 | | | | 13 | 5 | | | | | | | | | | | | | | |
| 6 | Sep 1 | SWINDON TOWN | L | 0-2 | 0-0 | 3382 | | 1 | 2 | 11 | 4 | | 6 | | 8 | 9* | 10 | 7 | 12 | | | | 13 | 5 | 3' | | | | | | | | | | | | | |
| 7 | 9 | Wycombe Wanderers | L | 0-1 | 0-1 | 4277 | | 1 | 2 | 11 | 4 | 5' | 6 | | 8 | 9* | 10" | 7 | 12 | | 14 | | 13 | | 3 | | | | | | | | | | | | | |
| 8 | 12 | NOTTS COUNTY | D | 0-0 | 0-0 | 1818 | | 1 | 8 | 3 | 4 | 5 | 6 | | 11 | 9 | | 7 | 10* | | 2 | | 12 | | | | | | | | | | | | | | | |
| 9 | 16 | GRIMSBY TOWN | L | 0-2 | 0-0 | 1957 | | 1 | 8 | 3 | 4 | 5 | 6 | | 11 | 9' | | 7 | 10 | | 2* | | 13 | | 12 | | | | | | | | | | | | | |
| 10 | 23 | Milton Keynes Dons | W | 2-1 | 0-1 | 5476 | Westwood, Walters | 1 | 2" | 11 | 4 | 5 | 6 | 13 | 8 | 9* | 12 | 7 | 10 | | 14 | | | | 3' | | | | | | | | | | | | | |
| 11 | 26 | Macclesfield Town | D | 1-1 | 0-1 | 2022 | Sandwith | 1 | 8 | 3 | | 5 | 6 | | 11 | 9* | 12 | 7 | 10 | | 2 | | | | 4 | | | | | | | | | | | | | |
| 12 | 30 | BRISTOL ROVERS | W | 2-0 | 2-0 | 2151 | Sandwith, Martinez | 1 | 4 | 11 | | 5* | 6 | | 8 | 13 | 10' | 7 | 9 | | 2 | | | | 3 | 12 | | | | | | | | | | | | |
| 13 | Oct 6 | WALSALL | D | 0-0 | 0-0 | 3241 | | 1 | 4* | 11 | | | 6 | 9 | 8 | 12 | 10 | 7 | | | 2 | | | | 3 | 5 | | | | | | | | | | | | |
| 14 | 14 | Rochdale | D | 0-0 | 0-0 | 3149 | | 1 | | 11" | | 5' | 6 | 4 | 8 | 12 | 10 | 7 | 9* | | 2 | | | 14 | 3 | | 13 | | | | | | | | | | | |
| 15 | 20 | HARTLEPOOL UNITED | W | 2-1 | 1-1 | 2580 | Westwood, Walters | 1 | | 11* | 12 | 5 | 6 | 4 | 8 | | 10 | 7 | 9 | | 2 | | | | 3 | | | | | | | | | | | | | |
| 16 | 28 | Barnet | L | 0-1 | 0-1 | 2301 | | 1 | 7' | 11 | 12 | 5 | 6* | 4 | 8 | | 10 | | 9 | | 2 | | 14 | | 3" | | 13 | | | | | | | | | | | |
| 17 | Nov 3 | Darlington | L | 0-1 | 0-1 | 3630 | | 1 | | 3 | | 5 | 6 | 11* | 8 | | 10' | 7 | 13 | | 2 | | | | 12 | | 4 | 9 | | | | | | | | | | |
| 18 | 17 | STOCKPORT COUNTY | D | 1-1 | 0-1 | 3624 | Walters | 1 | 4* | 11 | | | 6 | 12 | 8 | | 10 | 7 | 13 | | 2 | | | | 3 | | 5 | 9' | | | | | | | | | | |
| 19 | 25 | Shrewsbury Town | L | 1-2 | 1-0 | 4464 | Blundell | 1 | 8 | 12 | 4 | | 6 | 11 | | | 10 | 7 | 9" | | 2' | | | 13 | 3* | | 5 | | 14 | | | | | | | | | |
| 20 | Dec 5 | BOSTON UNITED | W | 3-1 | 0-0 | 1527 | Blundell (2, 1 pen), Walters | 1 | 4' | 11 | | 5 | 6 | 12 | 8 | | 10 | 7 | 9* | | 2 | | | | 3 | | | | 13 | | | | | | | | | |
| 21 | 9 | LINCOLN CITY | W | 4-1 | 1 0 | 2142 | Martinez, Walters, Blundell, Wilson | 1 | 4 | 11 | 12 | | 6 | | 8 | | 10 | 7 | 9 | | 2* | | | | 3 | | 5 | | | | | | | | | | | |
| 22 | 16 | Peterborough United | W | 2-0 | 2-0 | 4491 | Walters, Arber (og) | 1 | 11 | 3 | 4 | 5' | 13 | | 8 | | 10 | 7 | 9" | | | | | 2* | 12 | | 6 | 14 | | | | | | | | | | |
| 23 | 26 | MACCLESFIELD TOWN | L | 0-3 | 0-1 | 3365 | | 1 | 2 | 3 | 4 | 5 | | | 8 | | 10 | 7 | 9* | | | | | 11' | | | 6 | 12 | 13 | | | | | | | | | |
| 24 | 30 | MILTON KEYNES DONS | L | 0-3 | 0-0 | 2271 | | 1 | | | 4 | 5* | 6 | 11' | 8 | | 10 | 7 | 9 | | 2 | | | 3 | | | 12 | 13 | | | | | | | | | | |
| 25 | Jan 1 | Notts County | W | 2-1 | 1-1 | 4019 | Walters, Westwood | 1 | | 11 | | 5' | 6 | 13 | 8 | | 10 | 7 | 9* | | 2 | | | 3 | | | 4 | 12 | | | | | | | | | | |
| 26 | 9 | Grimsby Town | W | 2-0 | 0-0 | 3012 | Artell, Blundell | 1 | | 3 | 4 | 5 | 6 | 11 | 8 | | 10' | 7 | 9* | | 2 | | | 12 | | | | 13 | | | | | | | | | | |
| 27 | 13 | WYCOMBE WANDERERS | L | 0-1 | 0-0 | 2336 | | 1 | | 3 | 12 | 5* | 6 | 11" | 8 | | 10 | 7 | 9' | | 2 | | | | 14 | | 4 | 13 | | | | | | | | | | |
| 28 | 20 | Bristol Rovers | D | 0-0 | 0-0 | 5694 | | 1 | | 11 | 4 | | 6 | | 8 | | 10 | 7 | 9 | | | | | 2 | 3 | | 5 | | | | | | | | | | | |
| 29 | 27 | MANSFIELD TOWN | D | 1-1 | 0-1 | 2129 | Steele | 1 | | 3* | | | | 11' | 8 | | | 7 | 9 | | 2 | | 13 | 4 | 12 | 6 | 5 | 10" | | 14 | | | | | | | | |
| 30 | Feb 3 | Accrington Stanley | W | 1-0 | 1-0 | 1900 | Linwood | 1 | | | 4 | | 6 | 11 | 8 | | | 7 | | | | | 13 | 2 | 3 | | 5 | 10* | | | 9' | 12 | | | | | | |
| 31 | 18 | Wrexham | D | 0-0 | 0-0 | 6801 | | 1 | | | 4 | | 6 | 11 | 8 | | | | | | 2 | | 13 | 7" | 3 | | 5 | 10* | | | 9' | 12 | 14 | | | | | |
| 32 | 21 | BURY | W | 1-0 | 0-0 | 1642 | Yeo (pen) | 1 | | 13 | 4 | | 6 | 11' | 8 | | | | | | 2 | | | | 3 | | 5 | 10* | | | 9 | 12 | 7 | | | | | |
| 33 | 24 | Swindon Town | L | 0-1 | 0-1 | 5462 | | 1 | | 13 | 4 | | 6 | 11' | | | | 7 | | | 2* | | 14 | 12 | 3 | | 5 | | | | 9 | 10" | 8 | | | | | |
| 34 | 27 | HEREFORD UNITED | D | 1-1 | 0-0 | 1842 | Yeo | 1 | | 12 | 4 | | 6 | | | | | 7 | | | | | 13 | 2 | 3 | | 5 | 10' | | | 9 | 11* | 8 | | | | | |
| 35 | Mar 2 | TORQUAY UNITED | D | 1-1 | 0-0 | 1996 | Bennett | 1 | | 12 | 4 | | 6* | 11 | | | | 7 | | | | | | 2 | 3 | | 6 | | | | 10' | | 8 | 9 | 13 | | | |
| 36 | 6 | Mansfield Town | L | 1-2 | 1-1 | 2366 | Maylett | 1 | | 11 | 4 | | | 8 | | | | 7 | | | 2 | | | 6 | 3 | | 5 | 12 | | | | 13 | | 9* | 10' | | | |
| 37 | 10 | Walsall | L | 0-1 | 0-0 | 5282 | | 1 | | 3 | 4 | | 6 | 11* | | | | 7 | | | 2 | | 9 | | | | 5 | 10" | | | | | 12 | 14 | 8' | 13 | | |
| 38 | 16 | ROCHDALE | L | 0-1 | 0-1 | 2197 | | 1 | | 3 | 4 | | 6 | | | | | 7 | | | 2 | | 13 | 8 | | | 5 | 12 | | | 10 | | | 9* | 11' | | | |
| 39 | 24 | BARNET | W | 2-0 | 1-0 | 1591 | Bolland, Hand | 1 | | 3 | 4 | | 6 | 13 | | | | 7 | | | | | 9 | 8 | | | 5 | | | 11* | 10 | | | | 12 | | 2' | |
| 40 | 30 | Hartlepool United | L | 0-3 | 0-2 | 6059 | | 1 | | 11 | 4 | | 6 | 8 | | | | 7 | | | | | 9 | 2 | 3 | | 5 | | | 12 | 10* | | | | | | | |
| 41 | Apr 6 | DARLINGTON | D | 1-1 | 0-0 | 1942 | Yeo | 1 | | 12 | 4 | | 6 | 11 | | | | 7 | | | | | 9' | 5 | 3 | | | 13 | | 8 | 10* | | | | | | 2 | |
| 42 | 9 | Stockport County | L | 0-2 | 0-1 | 5719 | | 1 | | 11" | 4 | | 6 | 8 | | | | 7 | | | | | 12 | 2' | 3 | | 5 | 10* | | 14 | 9 | | | | | | 13 | |
| 43 | 15 | SHREWSBURY TOWN | D | 0-0 | 0-0 | 3266 | | 1 | | | 4* | | 6 | 11 | | | | 7 | | | | | 9 | 5 | 3 | | | | | 8 | 10' | 13 | | | | | 2 | 12 |
| 44 | 21 | Boston United | L | 0-1 | 0-0 | 1752 | | 1 | | 12 | 4 | | 6 | 11 | | | | 7 | | | | | 9* | 5 | 3 | | | | | 8" | 10 | | | | | 13 | 2' | 14 |
| 45 | 28 | PETERBOROUGH UNITED | D | 1-1 | 1-0 | 1905 | Yeo | 1 | | 3 | 4 | | 6 | | | | | 7 | | | | | 12 | 2 | | | 5 | 10* | | 8' | 9 | 13 | | | | 11 | | |
| 46 | May 5 | Lincoln City | L | 0-2 | 0-0 | 5267 | | 1 | | | 4 | | 5 | 11' | | | | 7 | | | | | 9* | 6 | 3 | | | 10 | | 8 | 12 | | | | | 13 | 2 | |
| | | | | | | | Apps | 46 | 20 | 34 | 33 | 21 | 42 | 27 | 31 | 9 | 24 | 43 | 21 | | 24 | 1 | 7 | 22 | 27 | 2 | 23 | 11 | | 6 | 14 | 2 | 4 | 3 | 3 | 1 | 5 | |
| | | | | | | | Subs | | | 7 | 4 | | 1 | 5 | | 5 | 2 | | 6 | 1 | 6 | 2 | 15 | 4 | 5 | 1 | 3 | 9 | 3 | 3 | 1 | 6 | 2 | 1 | 2 | 3 | 1 | 2 |
| | | | | | | | Goals | | | 1 | 1 | 3 | 1 | 1 | 3 | 2 | 9 | 2 | 6 | | | | | | 2 | | 1 | 1 | | | 4 | | | | 1 | | | |

Own Goals 2

## F.A. CUP

| | Date | Opposition | | FT | HT | Att. | Goalscorers | Danby J. | Vaughan S. | Wilson L. | Linwood P. | Westwood A. | Artell D. | Bennett D. | Martinez R. | Broughton D. | Walters J. | Hand J. | Blundell G. | McSporran J. | Marples S. | Ravenhill R. | Holroyd C. | Hessey S. | Sandwith K. | Allen G. | Bolland P. | Steele L. | Semple R. | Rutherford P. | Yeo S. | Meechan A. | Kearney A. | Brownlie R. | Maylett B. | Cronin G. | Vaughan J. | Kelly S. |
|---|---|---|---|---|---|---|---|---|---|---|---|---|---|---|---|---|---|---|---|---|---|---|---|---|---|---|---|---|---|---|---|---|---|---|---|---|---|---|
| 1R | Nov 11 | Clevedon Town | W | 4-1 | 1-0 | 2261 | Wilson, Hand, Walters, Blundell | 1 | 13 | 11' | | | 6 | 4 | 8 | | 10* | 7 | 12 | | | | 14 | 2 | 3 | | 5 | 9" | | | | | | | | | | |
| 2R | Dec 2 | Bury | D | 2-2 | 0-0 | 3428 | Steele (2) | 1 | 2 | 10 | 4 | 5 | 6 | 12 | 8 | | 9 | 7 | | | | | | | 3* | | | 13 | 11' | | | | | | | | | |
| 2Rr | 12 | BURY * | L | 1-3 | 1-1 | 2810 | Wilson | 1 | 4 | 11 | 12 | | 6 | | 8 | | 10 | 7 | 9" | | 2' | | | | 3* | | 5 | 13 | 14 | | | | | | | | | |
| 3R | Jan 6 | IPSWICH TOWN | D | 0-0 | 0-0 | 4330 | | 1 | | 3* | | 5 | 6 | 12 | 8 | | 10 | 7 | 9 | | 2 | | | 11 | | | 4 | | | | | | | | | | | |
| 3Rr | 16 | Ipswich Town | L | 0-1 | 0-0 | 11732 | | 1 | | 3 | | | 6 | 11 | 8 | | 10 | 7 | 9 | | 2 | | | 5 | | | 4 | | | | | | | | | | | |

* Chester reinstated. Bury played ineligible player

## LEAGUE (CARLING) CUP

| | Date | Opposition | | FT | HT | Att. | Goalscorers | Danby J. | Vaughan S. | Wilson L. | Linwood P. | Westwood A. | Artell D. | Bennett D. | Martinez R. | Broughton D. | Walters J. | Hand J. | Blundell G. | McSporran J. | Marples S. | Ravenhill R. | Holroyd C. | Hessey S. | Sandwith K. | Allen G. | Bolland P. | Steele L. | Semple R. | Rutherford P. | Yeo S. | Meechan A. | Kearney A. | Brownlie R. | Maylett B. | Cronin G. | Vaughan J. | Kelly S. |
|---|---|---|---|---|---|---|---|---|---|---|---|---|---|---|---|---|---|---|---|---|---|---|---|---|---|---|---|---|---|---|---|---|---|---|---|---|---|---|
| 1R | Aug 23 | Leeds United | L | 0-1 | 0-0 | 10013 | | 1 | 2 | 3 | 4 | 5 | 6 | | 8' | 9* | 11 | 7 | 10 | | | | 12 | | | | | | | 13 | | | | | | | | |

## JOHNSTONE PAINT TROPHY

| | Date | Opposition | | FT | HT | Att. | Goalscorers | Danby J. | Vaughan S. | Wilson L. | Linwood P. | Westwood A. | Artell D. | Bennett D. | Martinez R. | Broughton D. | Walters J. | Hand J. | Blundell G. | McSporran J. | Marples S. | Ravenhill R. | Holroyd C. | Hessey S. | Sandwith K. | Allen G. | Bolland P. | Steele L. | Semple R. | Rutherford P. | Yeo S. | Meechan A. | Kearney A. | Brownlie R. | Maylett B. | Cronin G. | Vaughan J. | Kelly S. |
|---|---|---|---|---|---|---|---|---|---|---|---|---|---|---|---|---|---|---|---|---|---|---|---|---|---|---|---|---|---|---|---|---|---|---|---|---|---|---|
| 2R | Oct 31 | STOCKPORT COUNTY | W | 3-0 | 1-0 | 1229 | Hand, Blundell, Wilson | 1 | | 11 | | | 6 | 8 | | | 12 | 7 | 9 | | 2 | | | 5 | 3 | | 4 | 10* | | | | | | | | | | |
| QF | Nov 29 | Chesterfield * | L | 4-4 | 2-2 | 2414 | Linwood, Wilson, Blundell, Bolland | 1 | 2^ | 11* | 4 | 5 | | 7 | 8 | | | | 9 | | | | 13 | 3 | | | 6 | | 10' | 12 | | | | | | | 14 | |

Chester received a bye in the 1st Round

* Chester lost 1-3 on penalties (Blundell)

## FRIENDLIES

| | Date | Opposition | | FT | HT | Att. | Goalscorers |
|---|---|---|---|---|---|---|---|
| 1 | Jul 11 | STOKE CITY | L | 0-2 | 0-0 | 1277 | |
| 2 | 13 | CERCLE BRUGGE | L | 0-1 | 0-0 | 269 | |
| 3 | 19 | Cammell Laird | W | 3-0 | 1-0 | 250 | Broughton, McSporran, Walters |
| 4 | 22 | CHESTERFIELD | L | 0-2 | 0-0 | 551 | |
| 5 | 24 | BLACKPOOL | L | 1-2 | 1-0 | 692 | Sandwith |
| 6 | 30 | HUDDERSFIELD TOWN | D | 0-0 | 0-0 | 1669 | |

# SEASON 2007-08

## FOOTBALL LEAGUE CHAMPIONSHIP 2

| | Date | | Opposition | | FT | HT | Att. | Goalscorers | Danby J. | Vaughan J | Wilson L. | Hughes M. | Butler P. | Linwood P. | Partridge R. | Grant A. | Murphy J. | Lowndes N. | Ellison K. | Yeo S. | Holroyd C. | Hand J. | Roberts K. | Rutherford P. | Sandwith K. | Bolland P. | Marples S. | Carroll N. | Dinning A. | McManus P. | Rule G. | Newton S. | Welsh J. | Kelly S. | Lindfield C. | Mitchell A. | Palethorpe P. | Ward G. |
|---|---|---|---|---|---|---|---|---|---|---|---|---|---|---|---|---|---|---|---|---|---|---|---|---|---|---|---|---|---|---|---|---|---|---|---|---|---|
| 1 | Aug | 11 | CHESTERFIELD | D | 0-0 | 0-0 | 3183 | | 1 | 2 | 3 | 4 | 5 | 6 | 7 | 8" | 9' | 10* | 11 | 12 | 13 | 14 | | | | | | | | | | | | | | | | |
| 2 | | 18 | Rochdale | W | 2-1 | 0-1 | 3243 | Grant, Ellison | 1 | 2 | 3 | 4* | 5 | 6 | | 8 | | 10" | 11 | 9' | 13 | | 7 | 12 | 14 | | | | | | | | | | | | | |
| 3 | | 25 | DAGENHAM & REDBRIDGE | W | 4-0 | 0-0 | 2098 | Yeo (2), Murphy (2) | 1 | 2 | 3 | 4 | 5 | 6 | 7 | 8 | 9 | | 11 | 10 | | | | | | | | | | | | | | | | | | |
| 4 | Sep | 1 | Rotherham United | D | 1-1 | 0-0 | 4036 | Roberts | 1 | 2 | 3 | 4 | 5 | 6 | 7 | 8* | 9' | | 11 | 10 | 13 | | 12 | | | | | | | | | | | | | | | |
| 5 | | 7 | MORECAMBE | L | 0-1 | 0-0 | 3199 | | 1 | 2 | 3 | 4 | 5 | 6 | 7 | 8' | 9" | 14 | 11 | 10* | | | 13 | 12 | | | | | | | | | | | | | | |
| 6 | | 15 | Bury | W | 2-0 | 1-0 | 2539 | Butler, Hughes | 1 | 2 | 3 | 4 | 5 | | 7 | 8 | 9 | 12 | 11 | 10* | | | | | | 6 | | | | | | | | | | | | |
| 7 | | 22 | BRENTFORD | L | 0-2 | 0-0 | 2453 | | 1 | | 3 | 4 | 5 | | 7* | 8" | 9 | 13 | 11 | 10' | | | 14 | 12 | | 6 | 2 | | | | | | | | | | | |
| 8 | | 29 | Macclesfield Town | W | 2-1 | 2-0 | 2647 | Murphy, Wilson | 1 | | 3 | 4 | 5 | 6 | 7' | 8 | 9 | 13 | 11 | | | | | | 12 | | 2 | 10* | | | | | | | | | | |
| 9 | Oct | 2 | Grimsby Town | W | 2-1 | 1-1 | 3479 | Murphy, Ellison | 1 | | 3 | 4 | 5 | 6 | 7 | 8' | 9 | 10* | 11 | 12 | | | | | 13 | | 2 | | | | | | | | | | | |
| 10 | | 7 | SHREWSBURY TOWN | W | 3-1 | 0-0 | 3057 | Partridge, Murphy, Yeo | 1 | | 3 | 8 | 5 | 6 | 7' | | 9 | | 10 | 12 | | | | | 11* | | 2 | | 4 | 13 | | | | | | | | |
| 11 | | 12 | HEREFORD UNITED | D | 1-1 | 0-0 | 3430 | Yeo | 1 | | 3 | 8 | 5 | 6 | 7" | | 9 | | 11 | 12' | 13 | | | 14 | | | 2 | | 4 | 10* | | | | | | | | |
| 12 | | 20 | Stockport County | W | 2-1 | 0-1 | 5566 | Partridge (2) | 1 | | 3 | 8 | 5 | 6 | 7 | | 9 | | 11 | | 10* | | | 12 | | | 2 | | 4 | | | | | | | | | |
| 13 | | 27 | WYCOMBE WANDERERS | D | 2-2 | 2-1 | 2598 | Holroyd, Murphy | 1 | | 3 | 8 | 5 | 6 | 7 | | 9 | | 11 | 12 | 10* | | 13 | | | | 2' | | 4 | | | | | | | | | |
| 14 | Nov | 2 | Lincoln City | W | 1-0 | 0-0 | 3960 | Dinning (pen) | 1 | | 3 | 8 | 5 | 6 | 7 | | 9 | | 11 | 12 | 10* | | | | | | 2 | | 4 | | | | | | | | | |
| 15 | | 6 | Bradford City | L | 1-2 | 0-1 | 13211 | Ellison | 1 | | 3 | 8 | 5 | 6 | 7* | | 9' | | 11 | 14 | 10" | | 13 | 12 | | | 2 | | 4 | | | | | | | | | |
| 16 | | 17 | MILTON KEYNES DONS | L | 0-2 | 0-1 | 3102 | | 1 | | 3 | | 5 | 6* | 7 | 12 | 9 | 10' | 11 | 13 | | | 8 | | | | 2 | | 4 | | | | | | | | | |
| 17 | | 25 | Wrexham | D | 2-2 | 2-1 | 7687 | Roberts, Linwood | 1 | | 3 | 8 | 5 | 6 | 7 | 12" | | 9' | 11 | 14 | | | 10 | | | | 2 | | 4* | 13 | | | | | | | | |
| 18 | Dec | 4 | BARNET | W | 3-0 | 2-0 | 1858 | Partridge, Ellison (2) | 1 | | 3 | 4 | 5 | 6 | 7" | | 9' | 10* | 11 | 12 | 13 | | 8 | | | | 2 | | | 14 | | | | | | | | |
| 19 | | 8 | PETERBOROUGH UNITED | L | 1-2 | 1-0 | 2291 | Hughes | 1 | | 3* | 4 | 5 | 6 | | | 9 | 10" | 11 | 14 | | | 8 | 7' | 12 | | 2 | | | 13 | | | | | | | | |
| 20 | | 22 | BURY | W | 2-1 | 1-1 | 2260 | Hughes, Ellison | 1 | 3 | | 4 | 5 | 6 | 7 | | 9' | 10* | 11 | 12 | 13 | | 8 | | | | 2 | | | | | | | | | | | |
| 21 | | 26 | Morecambe | L | 3-5 | 1-4 | 3419 | Ellison (2), Holroyd | 1 | 3 | | 4 | 5 | 6 | 7 | | 9* | | 11 | 12 | 13 | | 8 | | | | 2 | | | | 10' | | | | | | | |
| 22 | | 29 | Brentford | L | 0-3 | 0-1 | 4323 | | 1 | 2 | | 4 | 5 | 6 | 7 | | | | 11 | 10* | 9 | | 8 | 12 | | | 3 | | | | | | | | | | | |
| 23 | Jan | 1 | GRIMSBY TOWN | L | 0-2 | 0-0 | 2255 | | 1 | 2 | | 13 | 5 | 6 | 7 | | | | 11 | 12 | 9* | | 8 | | | | | | | 10' | | 3 | 4 | | | | | |
| 24 | | 5 | Accrington Stanley | D | 3-3 | 1-1 | 1311 | Holroyd (2), Wilson | 1 | 2 | 11 | 8 | 5* | 6 | 7' | | | | | | 9 | | 10 | | | | | | | 13 | | 3 | 4 | 12 | | | | |
| 25 | | 12 | MANSFIELD TOWN | L | 0-1 | 0-0 | 2092 | | 1 | 2 | 3 | 8' | | 6 | 7* | | | | 11 | | 9 | | 10 | 13 | | | | | | 12 | | | 4 | 5 | | | | |
| 26 | | 19 | Notts County | L | 0-1 | 0-0 | 3774 | | 1 | 2 | 3 | 8* | 5 | | 7 | | | | 11 | | 9 | | 6 | | 10 | | | | | | | | 4 | | 12 | | | |
| 27 | | 26 | ROTHERHAM UNITED | L | 0-1 | 0-1 | 2536 | | 1 | 2 | 3 | 13 | 5 | 6 | 7 | | 9 | | 11" | | 10* | | 8' | | 14 | | | | | | | | 4 | | 12 | | | |
| 28 | | 29 | ROCHDALE | L | 0-4 | 0-2 | 2131 | | 1 | 2 | 3 | 14 | 5 | 6* | 7' | 8^ | 9 | | 11 | | | | 12 | | 13 | | | | | | | | 4 | | 10 | | | |
| 29 | Feb | 2 | Chesterfield | D | 1-1 | 0-0 | 3701 | Murphy | 1 | 2 | | 7 | 5 | 6* | | 8 | 9 | | | | | | 11 | | 3 | | | | 4 | | | | | 12 | 10 | | | |
| 30 | | 9 | ACCRINGTON STANLEY | L | 2-3 | 2-1 | 1957 | Butler, Murphy | 1 | 2 | 11 | 7 | 5 | | 12 | 8* | 9 | | | | 13 | | 6 | | 3 | | | | 4 | | | | | | 10' | | | |
| 31 | | 12 | Dagenham & Redbridge | L | 2-6 | 0-3 | 1328 | Roberts, Murphy | 1 | 2 | 3 | 7 | 5 | 6 | 12 | 8* | 9 | | | | | | 11 | | | | | | 4 | | | | | | 10 | | | |
| 32 | | 16 | NOTTS COUNTY | L | 0-1 | 0-0 | 1798 | | 1 | 2 | 3* | 8" | 5 | 6 | 7 | | 9 | | | | 13 | | 11 | 14 | 12 | | | | 4 | | | | | | 10' | | | |
| 33 | | 23 | Mansfield Town | W | 3-1 | 0-1 | 2362 | Ellison (2), Dinning (pen) | 1 | 2 | 3 | 8 | 5* | 6 | 7 | | 9 | | 11 | | 12 | | 10 | | | | | | 4 | | | | | | | | | |
| 34 | Mar | 1 | Milton Keynes Dons | L | 0-1 | 0-0 | 8172 | | 1 | 2 | 3 | | 5 | 6 | | 8* | 9 | | 11 | | 7 | | 10 | 12 | | | | | 4 | | | | | | | | | |
| 35 | | 4 | Darlington | L | 0-1 | 0-1 | 3294 | | 1 | 2 | 3 | | | 6 | | | 9 | | 11 | | 10 | | 5 | 7* | 8 | | | | 4 | | | | | | | 12 | | |
| 36 | | 9 | WREXHAM | L | 0-2 | 0-1 | 3849 | | 1 | 2 | 3* | 7 | | 6 | | | 9 | | 11 | | 10' | | 5 | 12 | 8 | | | | 4 | 13 | | | | | | | | |
| 37 | | 12 | BRADFORD CITY | L | 0-1 | 0-0 | 1566 | | 1 | 2 | 3 | 8 | | 6 | | | 9 | | 11 | | | | 4 | 7 | | | | | 5 | 10 | | | | | | | | |
| 38 | | 15 | Barnet | L | 1-3 | 0-0 | 1663 | Hughes | 1 | 2* | 3 | 8 | | 6 | | 13 | 9 | | 11 | | | | 4 | 7' | 12 | | | | 5 | 10" | | | | | | 14 | | |
| 39 | | 22 | DARLINGTON | W | 2-1 | 2-0 | 1759 | Rutherford, Partridge | 1" | | 3 | 8 | 5 | 6 | 7' | | 9 | | | | 10* | | 2 | 11 | 13 | | | | 4 | 12 | | | | | | | 14 | |
| 40 | | 24 | Peterborough United | L | 0-1 | 0-0 | 6457 | | 1 | | 3 | 8 | | 6 | 7" | | 9 | | | | | | 2 | 11* | 13 | | | | 4 | 12 | 10' | | | 5 | | 14 | | |
| 41 | Apr | 5 | Hereford United | D | 2-2 | 0-2 | 3210 | Sandwith, Ellison (pen) | 1 | | 3 | 8 | 5' | 6 | 7* | | 9 | | 10 | | | | 2 | 11 | 4 | | | | | 12 | | | | 13 | | | | |
| 42 | | 12 | LINCOLN CITY | L | 1-2 | 1-2 | 2089 | McManus | 1 | 12 | 3 | 8 | | 6 | | | 9 | | 11 | | | | 2 | 7' | 4 | | | | | 10 | 13 | | | 5* | | | | |
| 43 | | 19 | Wycombe Wanderers | L | 0-1 | 0-0 | 5497 | | 1 | 2 | 3 | 8 | | 6 | | | 9 | | | | 12 | | 11 | 7 | 4 | | | | | 10* | | | | 5 | | | | |
| 44 | | 26 | Shrewsbury Town | D | 0-0 | 0-0 | 6417 | | 1 | 2 | 3 | 13 | | 6 | 7 | | 9 | | 11* | | | | 8 | 12 | 4 | | | | | 10' | | | | 5 | | | | |
| 45 | | 29 | STOCKPORT COUNTY | D | 0-0 | 0-0 | 3060 | | 1 | 2 | 3 | 8 | | 6 | 7* | 12 | 9 | | | | | | 11 | 13 | 4 | | | | | 10' | | | | 5 | | | | |
| 46 | May | 3 | MACCLESFIELD TOWN | D | 0-0 | 0-0 | 2396 | | 1 | 2 | | 4 | | 6* | 7" | 8 | 9 | | | | | | 12 | 11' | 3 | | | | | 10 | 14 | | | 5 | | 13 | | |
| | | | | | | | | Apps | 46 | 29 | 40 | 39 | 35 | 42 | 34 | 15 | 39 | 8 | 36 | 7 | 14 | | 30 | 10 | 12 | 2 | 16 | 1 | 20 | 9 | 2 | 2 | 6 | 7 | 5 | | | |
| | | | | | | | | Subs | | 1 | | 4 | | | 2 | 4 | | 4 | | 14 | 11 | 1 | 7 | 13 | 10 | | | | | 10 | 2 | | | 3 | 2 | 4 | 1 | |
| | | | | | | | | Goals | | | 2 | 4 | 2 | 1 | 5 | 1 | 9 | | 11 | 4 | 4 | | 3 | 1 | 1 | | | | 2 | 1 | | | | | | | | |

## F.A. CUP

| | Date | | Opposition | | FT | HT | Att. | Goalscorers | Danby J. | Vaughan J | Wilson L. | Hughes M. | Butler P. | Linwood P. | Partridge R. | Grant A. | Murphy J. | Lowndes N. | Ellison K. | Yeo S. | Holroyd C. | Hand J. | Roberts K. | Rutherford P. | Sandwith K. | Bolland P. | Marples S. | Carroll N. | Dinning A. | McManus P. | Rule G. | Newton S. | Welsh J. | Kelly S. | Lindfield C. | Mitchell A. | Palethorpe P. | Ward G. |
|---|---|---|---|---|---|---|---|---|---|---|---|---|---|---|---|---|---|---|---|---|---|---|---|---|---|---|---|---|---|---|---|---|---|---|---|---|---|
| 1R | Nov | 10 | Bradford City | L | 0-1 | 0-1 | 4069 | | 1 | | 3 | 8 | 5 | 6 | | 7' | | 9* | 11 | 10 | | | | 13 | | | 2 | | 4 | 12 | | | | | | | | |

## LEAGUE (CARLING) CUP

| | Date | | Opposition | | FT | HT | Att. | Goalscorers | Danby J. | Vaughan J | Wilson L. | Hughes M. | Butler P. | Linwood P. | Partridge R. | Grant A. | Murphy J. | Lowndes N. | Ellison K. | Yeo S. | Holroyd C. | Hand J. | Roberts K. | Rutherford P. | Sandwith K. | Bolland P. | Marples S. | Carroll N. | Dinning A. | McManus P. | Rule G. | Newton S. | Welsh J. | Kelly S. | Lindfield C. | Mitchell A. | Palethorpe P. | Ward G. |
|---|---|---|---|---|---|---|---|---|---|---|---|---|---|---|---|---|---|---|---|---|---|---|---|---|---|---|---|---|---|---|---|---|---|---|---|---|---|
| 1R | Aug | 14 | NOTTINGHAM FOREST * | L | 0-0 | 0-0 | 2720 | | 1 | 2 | 3 | 4 | 5 | 6 | | 8" | | 10* | 11' | 9 | 12 | 7 | 14 | 13 | | | | | | | | | | | | | | |

* Chester lost 2-4 on penalties (Hand, Butler)

## JOHNSTONE PAINT TROPHY

| | Date | | Opposition | | FT | HT | Att. | Goalscorers | Danby J. | Vaughan J | Wilson L. | Hughes M. | Butler P. | Linwood P. | Partridge R. | Grant A. | Murphy J. | Lowndes N. | Ellison K. | Yeo S. | Holroyd C. | Hand J. | Roberts K. | Rutherford P. | Sandwith K. | Bolland P. | Marples S. | Carroll N. | Dinning A. | McManus P. | Rule G. | Newton S. | Welsh J. | Kelly S. | Lindfield C. | Mitchell A. | Palethorpe P. | Ward G. |
|---|---|---|---|---|---|---|---|---|---|---|---|---|---|---|---|---|---|---|---|---|---|---|---|---|---|---|---|---|---|---|---|---|---|---|---|---|---|
| 1R | Sep | 4 | CREWE ALEXANDRA * | W | 1-1 | 0-1 | 2126 | Partridge | 1* | 2 | 3 | 4 | 5 | 6 | 7 | 8" | 9 | 13 | 11 | 10' | | | 14 | | | | | | | | | | | | | | | 12 |
| 2R | Oct | 9 | Carlisle United | L | 2-4 | 1-2 | 2414 | Partridge, Holroyd | 1 | | 3' | 8" | | 6 | 7* | | | | | 10 | 14 | | | 12 | 11 | 5 | 2 | | 4 | 9 | 13 | | | | | | | |

* Chester won 4-2 on penalties (Butler, Partridge, Lowndes, Murphy)

## FRIENDLIES

| | Date | | Opposition | | FT | HT | Att. | Goalscorers |
|---|---|---|---|---|---|---|---|---|
| 1 | Jul | 17 | AFC Telford | W | 5-3 | 3-1 | 1130 | Fitzpatrick (og), Yeo (3), Murphy |
| 2 | | 26 | Connah's Quay Nomads | W | 8-1 | 2-1 | 720 | Murphy, Lowndes, Yeo, Partridge Holroyd (2) , Bolland, Roberts |
| 3 | | 28 | Droylsden * | D | 1-1 | 1-0 | | Bennett |
| 4 | | 31 | Vauxhall Motors | W | 5-1 | 4-0 | 410 | Holroyd (2), Ellison, Hand, Hughes |
| 5 | Aug | 4 | BRIGHTON & HOVE ALBION | L | 0-1 | 0-4 | 725 | |

* Tony Downes Memorial Cup

**2007/08 Season:**

Back – Newton, Sandwith, Hand, Murphy, Danby, Ward, Palethorpe, Bolland, Linwood, Westwood, Roberts
Middle – Rutherford, Marples, Hughes, Yeo, Cronin, Marsh-Evans, Ellison, Bennett, Kelly, Wilson, Carroll
Front – Holt (Physio), Partridge, Holroyd, Grant, Thompson (Assistant Manager), Williamson (Manager), Butler, J Vaughan, Lowndes, Gerrard (Kitman).

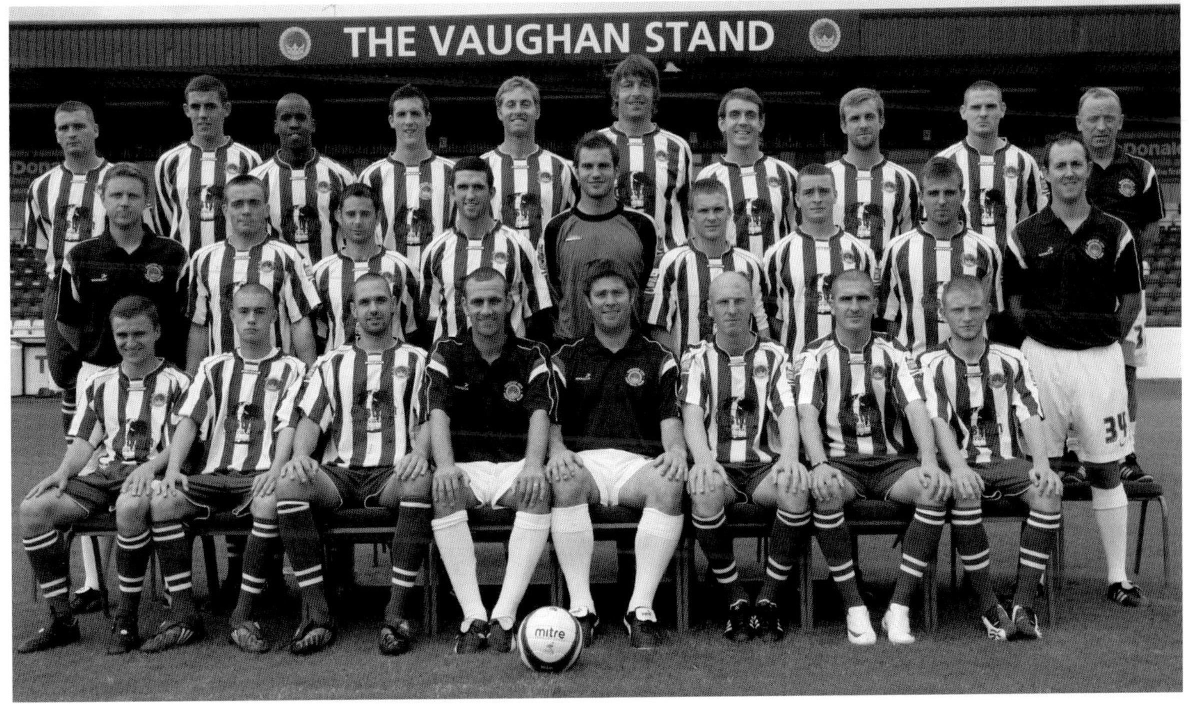


**2008/09 Season:**

Back – S Vaughan, Rule, Mozika, Kelly, Dinning, Butler, Hughes, Wilson, Barry, Gerrard (Coach)
Middle – Owen (Coach), Taylor, Partridge, Mannix, Danby, Harris, J Vaughan, Roberts, Holt (Physio)
Front - Rutherford, Mitchell, Linwood, Davies (Manager), Griffiths (Assistant Manager), Ellison, Lowe, McManus.

# SEASON 2008-09

## FOOTBALL LEAGUE CHAMPIONSHIP 2

| No | Date | Opposition | | FT | HT | Att. | Goalscorers | Danby J. | Vaughan J | Wilson L. | Mozika D. | Butler P. | Roberts K. | Partridge R. | Barry A. | Lowe R. | Harris J. | Ellison K. | Mannix D. | Taylor P. | Dinning A. | Linwood P. | Kelly S. | Hughes M. | Vaughan S. | McManus P. | Rutherford P. | Rule G. | Johnson E. | Jones B. | Owen J. | Ellams L. | Smith P. | Spencer J. | Platt K. |
|---|---|---|---|---|---|---|---|---|---|---|---|---|---|---|---|---|---|---|---|---|---|---|---|---|---|---|---|---|---|---|---|---|---|---|---|
| 1 | Aug 9 | Dagenham & Redbridge | L | 0-6 | 0-2 | 1434 | | 1 | 2 | 3 | 4 | 5 | 6 | 7' | 8 | 9 | 10* | 11 | 12 | 13 | | | | | | | | | | | | | | | |
| 2 | 16 | WYCOMBE WANDERERS | L | 0-2 | 0-1 | 1419 | | 1 | 2 | 3 | 7 | | | 12 | 8 | 9 | 10' | 11 | | 13 | 4* | 5 | 6 | | | | | | | | | | | | |
| 3 | 23 | Rotherham United | L | 1-3 | 1-3 | 3462 | Ellison | 1 | 2 | 3 | 7 | | 4' | | 8 | 9 | 10* | 11 | | 12 | | 5 | 6 | 13 | | | | | | | | | | | |
| 4 | 30 | BARNET | W | 5-1 | 1-0 | 1295 | Ellison,Lowe(2),Linwood,Roberts | 1 | 2 | 3 | 7 | | 6 | | | 10 | | 11 | | 9 | | 5 | | 8 | 4 | | | | | | | | | | |
| 5 | Sep 6 | BURY | D | 1-1 | 1-0 | 2327 | Mozika | 1 | 2 | 3* | 7 | | 6 | | | 10 | | 11 | | 9 | | 5 | 12 | 8 | 4 | | | | | | | | | | |
| 6 | 13 | Grimsby Town | W | 3-1 | 1-0 | 2950 | Ellison (3) | 1 | 2 | | 10 | | 3 | 7' | 12 | 9* | | 11 | | | | 5 | 6 | 8 | 4 | 13 | | | | | | | | | |
| 7 | 21 | SHREWSBURY TOWN | D | 1-1 | 1-1 | 2891 | McManus | 1 | 2 | 3 | 7 | | 6 | 12 | | 9' | | 11 | | 13 | | 5 | | 8 | 4 | 10* | | | | | | | | | |
| 8 | 27 | Luton Town | D | 1-1 | 0-1 | 5731 | McManus | 1 | 2 | | 7' | | 3 | | 13 | 9 | 14 | 11* | | 12 | | 5 | 6 | 8 | 4 | 10" | | | | | | | | | |
| 9 | Oct 4 | LINCOLN CITY | L | 0-2 | 0-1 | 1962 | | 1 | 2 | 3 | 7 | | | 13 | 14 | 9' | | 11 | | 12 | | 5 | 6 | 8 | 4" | 10* | | | | | | | | | |
| 10 | 11 | Chesterfield | D | 1-1 | 1-0 | 3042 | Linwood | 1 | 2 | | 7 | | 3 | | 8 | 9' | 12 | 11 | | | | 5 | 6 | 4 | | 10* | 13 | | | | | | | | |
| 11 | 19 | PORT VALE | L | 1-2 | 0-1 | 3102 | Lowe | 1 | | | 7 | | 3 | | 8' | 10 | | 11 | | 13 | | 5 | 6* | 4 | 12 | 14 | | 2 | 9" | | | | | | |
| 12 | 21 | Rochdale | L | 1-6 | 0-2 | 2162 | McArdle (og) | 1 | 2 | | 7 | | 6 | | 12 | 10 | | 11 | | | | 5 | | 8 | 4 | | | 3 | 9* | | | | | | |
| 13 | 25 | Gillingham | L | 0-2 | 0-0 | 4852 | | 1 | 2 | | 7 | | 6 | | 3 | 10 | 8 | 11 | | | | 5 | | 4 | | | | | 9 | | | | | | |
| 14 | 28 | BRENTFORD | W | 3-0 | 1-0 | 1301 | Lowe (2), Roberts | 1 | 2 | | 7 | | 6 | | 3 | 10 | 8 | 11 | | | | 5 | | 4 | | | 12 | | 9* | | | | | | |
| 15 | Nov 1 | Exeter City | L | 0-2 | 0-1 | 4448 | | 1 | 2 | | 7 | | 6 | | 3 | 10 | 8 | 11 | | | | 5* | 12 | 4 | | | | | 9 | | | | | | |
| 16 | 15 | MORECAMBE | L | 1-2 | 0-1 | 1647 | Johnson | 1 | 2 | 3 | | | 6 | 13 | 8' | 10 | 7 | 11 | | | | 5 | | 4 | | | 12 | | 9* | | | | | | |
| 17 | 22 | ALDERSHOT TOWN | L | 0-1 | 0-0 | 1653 | | 1 | 2 | 3 | | | 4 | | 7 | 10 | 12 | | | | | 5 | 6 | 8 | | 13 | 11' | | 9* | | | | | | |
| 18 | 25 | Darlington | W | 2-1 | 1-1 | 2416 | Lowe, Kelly | 1 | 2 | 3* | | | 4 | 13 | 7 | 10" | 11 | | | | | 5 | 6 | 8 | | 9' | 14 | 12 | | | | | | | |
| 19 | Dec 6 | Bournemouth | L | 0-1 | 0-0 | 4154 | | 1 | 2 | 3 | | | 4 | 12 | 7 | 10 | | | | | 13 | 5 | 6 | 8 | | 9* | | 11' | | | | | | | |
| 20 | 13 | NOTTS COUNTY | W | 2-0 | 1-0 | 1767 | Lowe, Roberts | 1 | 2 | 3 | 12 | | 4 | 13 | 7 | 9' | 10* | 11 | | | | 5 | 6 | 8 | | | | | | | | | | | |
| 21 | 20 | Bradford City | D | 0-0 | 0-0 | 12092 | | 1 | 2 | 3 | 7 | | 4 | | 10 | 9* | | 11 | | | | 5 | 6 | 8 | | | | | 12 | | | | | | |
| 22 | 26 | ACCRINGTON STANLEY | W | 2-0 | 1-0 | 2223 | Lowe (2 (1 pen)) | 1 | 2 | 3 | 8 | | 6 | 7* | 10 | 9' | | 11 | | | | 5 | 12 | 4 | | | | | 13 | | | | | | |
| 23 | 28 | Macclesfield Town | L | 1-3 | 0-1 | 2219 | Lowe | 1 | 2 | 3 | | | 4 | 13 | 7 | 9 | 10' | 11* | | | | 5 | 6 | 8 | | | | | 12 | | | | | | |
| 24 | Jan 13 | LUTON TOWN | D | 2-2 | 1-2 | 1652 | Lowe (pen), Ellison | 1 | 2 | 3 | 10 | | 4 | 7* | 12 | 9 | 13 | 11' | | | | 5 | 6 | 8 | | | | | | | | | | | |
| 25 | 17 | CHESTERFIELD | L | 1-3 | 0-1 | 1806 | Mozika | 1 | 2 | 3 | 10 | | 4 | 7* | 6 | 9 | | 11 | | | | 5 | | 8 | | | | | | 12 | | | | | |
| 26 | 24 | Lincoln City | D | 1-1 | 1-0 | 3760 | Barry | 1 | | | 10* | | 3 | 7' | 6 | 9" | 12 | 11 | | | 4 | 5 | | 8 | | | 14 | 2 | | 13 | | | | | |
| 27 | 27 | Port Vale | L | 0-3 | 0-0 | 4448 | | 1 | | 3 | | | 6 | 7' | 10 | 9 | 12 | 11 | | | 4* | 5 | | 8" | | | 13 | 2 | | | 14 | | | | |
| 28 | 31 | GILLINGHAM | L | 0-1 | 0-0 | 1541 | | 1 | 2 | | | | 3 | 7* | 10 | 9 | 4 | 11 | | | | 5 | 6 | 8 | | | 12 | | | | | | | | |
| 29 | Feb 3 | ROCHDALE | L | 0-2 | 0-0 | 1357 | | 1 | 2 | | | | 3 | 7* | 10 | 9 | 4 | 11 | | | | 5 | 6 | | | | 8' | | | | | 12 | 13 | | |
| 30 | 7 | Brentford | L | 0-3 | 0-3 | 4719 | | 1 | 2 | | | | 3 | | 10 | 9 | 4 | 11 | | | | 5 | 6* | | | | 7' | 8 | | 13 | | | 12 | | |
| 31 | 14 | Morecambe | L | 1-3 | 0-3 | 1795 | Wilson | 1 | 2* | 3 | | | 4 | | 10 | 9" | 7 | 11 | 8' | | | 5 | | | | | 13 | 6 | | 12 | | | 14 | | |
| 32 | 17 | Shrewsbury Town | L | 0-1 | 0-0 | 6133 | | 1 | 2 | 3 | | | 4 | 7' | 10 | | 8 | 11 | 14 | | | 5 | | | | | 13 | 6" | | 9* | | 12 | | | |
| 33 | 21 | EXETER CITY | D | 0-0 | 0-0 | 1649 | | 1 | 2 | 3 | | | 4 | 7* | 10 | 9 | | 11 | 8 | | | | 5 | | | | | 6 | | 12 | | | | | |
| 34 | 28 | DAGENHAM & REDBRIDGE | D | 2-2 | 0-2 | 1416 | Mannix, Roberts | 1 | 2 | 3 | | | 4 | 13 | 7 | 10 | | 11 | 8 | | | 5* | 6 | | | | | 12 | | 9' | | | | | |
| 35 | Mar 3 | Wycombe Wanderers | L | 0-2 | 0-1 | 3713 | | 1 | 2 | 3* | | | 4 | 7' | 10 | 9 | | 11 | 8" | | | 5 | | | | | 13 | 6 | | | 12 | | 14 | | |
| 36 | 7 | Barnet | L | 1-3 | 0-0 | 2085 | Ellison | 1 | 2 | 3 | 7* | | 4 | 12 | 10" | 9 | 8 | 11 | 13 | | | 5 | | | | | 14 | 6' | | | | | | | |
| 37 | 10 | ROTHERHAM UNITED | L | 1-5 | 1-3 | 1235 | Ellison | 1 | 2 | 3 | | | 4 | 12 | 10 | 9 | 7 | 11 | 8* | | | 5 | | | | | | 6 | | | | | | | |
| 38 | 14 | GRIMSBY TOWN | D | 1-1 | 0-1 | 2836 | Lowe | 1 | 2 | 3 | | | 4 | | 10* | 9 | 7 | 11 | 8 | | | 5 | | | | | 12 | 6 | | | | | | | |
| 39 | 21 | Bury | D | 1-1 | 0-1 | 3049 | Lowe | 1 | 2 | 3 | | | 4 | | 10 | 9 | 7 | 11 | 8* | | | 5 | | | | | 13 | 6' | | 12 | | | | | |
| 40 | 28 | BRADFORD CITY | D | 0-0 | 0-0 | 2735 | | 1 | 2 | 3 | | | 4 | 7 | 10 | 9 | 8 | 11* | | | | 5 | | | | | | 6 | | 12 | | | | | |
| 41 | Apr 4 | Notts County | W | 2-1 | 1-0 | 4025 | Mannix, Lowe | 1' | 2 | 3* | | | 4 | 7" | 10 | 9 | | | 8 | | | 5 | | | | | 11 | 6 | | 13 | 12 | | 14 | | |
| 42 | 11 | MACCLESFIELD TOWN | L | 0-2 | 0-2 | 2248 | | | 2 | 3 | | | 4 | 7 | 10 | 9 | 12 | | 8* | | | 5 | 14 | | | | 11" | 6' | | 13 | | | | 1 | |
| 43 | 13 | Accrington Stanley | W | 1-0 | 1-0 | 1100 | Lowe (pen) | | 2 | 3 | | | 4 | | 10 | 9 | 8 | 11* | | | | 5 | 6 | | | | | 13 | | 12 | 7' | | | 1 | |
| 44 | 18 | BOURNEMOUTH | L | 0-2 | 0-1 | 3349 | | | 2 | 3 | | | 4 | 12 | 10' | 9 | 8 | 11* | | | | 5 | 6" | | | | 13 | | | 14 | 7 | | | 1 | |
| 45 | 25 | Aldershot Town | D | 2-2 | 1-1 | 3100 | Lowe, Ellams | | 2 | 3 | | | 4 | 13 | 10' | 9 | 8 | | | | | 5* | 6 | | | | | 12 | | 14 | 7 | 11" | | 1 | |
| 46 | May 2 | DARLINGTON | L | 1-2 | 0-0 | 1945 | Miller (og) | | | 3 | | | 4 | | 10 | 9 | 8 | | 6* | | | | 5' | | | | | 2 | | 12 | 7 | 11 | | 1 | 13 |
| | | | | | | | Apps | 41 | 42 | 34 | 21 | 1 | 44 | 15 | 38 | 45 | 24 | 39 | 10 | 2 | 3 | 43 | 23 | 25 | 7 | 6 | 5 | 18 | 7 | 2 | 4 | 2 | | 5 | |
| | | | | | | | Subs | | | | 1 | | | 13 | 5 | | 7 | | 3 | 7 | 1 | | 4 | 1 | 1 | 3 | 14 | 4 | 3 | 13 | 3 | 2 | 5 | | 1 |
| | | | | | | | Goals | | | 1 | 2 | | 4 | | 1 | 16 | | 8 | 2 | | | 2 | 1 | | | 2 | | | 1 | | | 1 | | | |

Own goals 2

## F.A. CUP

| Rd | Date | Opposition | | FT | HT | Att. | Goalscorers | Danby J. | Vaughan J | Wilson L. | Mozika D. | Butler P. | Roberts K. | Partridge R. | Barry A. | Lowe R. | Harris J. | Ellison K. | Mannix D. | Taylor P. | Dinning A. | Linwood P. | Kelly S. | Hughes M. | Vaughan S. | McManus P. | Rutherford P. | Rule G. | Johnson E. | Jones B. | Owen J. | Ellams L. | Smith P. | Spencer J. | Platt K. |
|---|---|---|---|---|---|---|---|---|---|---|---|---|---|---|---|---|---|---|---|---|---|---|---|---|---|---|---|---|---|---|---|---|---|---|---|
| 1R | Nov 8 | MILLWALL | L | 0-3 | 0-0 | 1932 | | 1 | 2 | 12 | 7* | | 6' | | 3 | 10 | 8 | 11 | | | | 5 | | 4 | | | 13 | | 9 | | | | | | |

## LEAGUE (CARLING) CUP

| Rd | Date | Opposition | | FT | HT | Att. | Goalscorers | Danby J. | Vaughan J | Wilson L. | Mozika D. | Butler P. | Roberts K. | Partridge R. | Barry A. | Lowe R. | Harris J. | Ellison K. | Mannix D. | Taylor P. | Dinning A. | Linwood P. | Kelly S. | Hughes M. | Vaughan S. | McManus P. | Rutherford P. | Rule G. | Johnson E. | Jones B. | Owen J. | Ellams L. | Smith P. | Spencer J. | Platt K. |
|---|---|---|---|---|---|---|---|---|---|---|---|---|---|---|---|---|---|---|---|---|---|---|---|---|---|---|---|---|---|---|---|---|---|---|---|
| 1R | Aug 12 | LEEDS UNITED | L | 2-5 | 1-5 | 3644 | Lowe (2 (1 pen)) | 1 | 2 | 3 | 4 | 5* | | 7' | 8 | 9 | 13 | 11 | 10 | | | 6 | 12 | | | | | | | | | | | | |

## JOHNSTONE PAINT TROPHY

| Rd | Date | Opposition | | FT | HT | Att. | Goalscorers | Danby J. | Vaughan J | Wilson L. | Mozika D. | Butler P. | Roberts K. | Partridge R. | Barry A. | Lowe R. | Harris J. | Ellison K. | Mannix D. | Taylor P. | Dinning A. | Linwood P. | Kelly S. | Hughes M. | Vaughan S. | McManus P. | Rutherford P. | Rule G. | Johnson E. | Jones B. | Owen J. | Ellams L. | Smith P. | Spencer J. | Platt K. |
|---|---|---|---|---|---|---|---|---|---|---|---|---|---|---|---|---|---|---|---|---|---|---|---|---|---|---|---|---|---|---|---|---|---|---|---|
| 2R | Oct 7 | MORECAMBE * | D | 1-1 | 0-1 | 926 | Ellison | 1 | 2 | 3 | 10 | | 6 | 7' | 8 | 13 | | 11 | | 12 | | 5 | | 4 | | 9* | | | | | | | | | |

Chester received a bye in the 1st Round

* Chester lost 1-3 on penalties (Lowe)

## FRIENDLIES

| No | Date | Opposition | | FT | HT | Att. | Goalscorers |
|---|---|---|---|---|---|---|---|
| 1 | Jul 14 | Southport | D | 2-2 | 1-0 | 505 | Wilson, McManus |
| 2 | 19 | Vauxhall Motors | W | 2-1 | 2-1 | 473 | S Vaughan, Dinning |
| 3 | 22 | CARLISLE UNITED | L | 1-3 | 1-1 | 611 | Ellison |
| 4 | 31 | SWANSEA CITY | L | 2-3 | 0-2 | 889 | Harris (2) |
| 5 | Aug 2 | AFC Telford | L | 1-4 | 0-1 | 820 | Barry (pen) |

# SEASON 2009-10

## BLUE SQUARE PREMIER

| No. | Date | | Opposition | | FT | HT | Att. | Goalscorers | Danby J. | Rule G | Meynell R. | Roberts K. | Ryan T. | Barry A. | Vaughan S. | Lea M. | Ellams L. | Wilkinson B. | Ashton N. | Chadwick N. | Owen J. | Platt K. | Rawlinson C. | Lynch C. | Kay A. | Alessandra L. | Blundell G. | Vaughan J. | Kelly S. | Murphy A. | Keltie C. | Beesley M. | Flynn J. | Coulson M. | Rea J. | Freeman J. | Davidson R. | Jones B. | Coulter S. |
|---|---|---|---|---|---|---|---|---|---|---|---|---|---|---|---|---|---|---|---|---|---|---|---|---|---|---|---|---|---|---|---|---|---|---|---|---|---|---|---|
| 1 | Aug | 15 | CAMBRIDGE UNITED | L | 2-2 | 2-4 | 1757 | Wilkinson, Chadwick | 1 | 2 | 3 | 4" | 5 | 6* | 7 | 8' | 9 | 10 | 11 | 12 | 13 | 14 | | | | | | | | | | | | | | | | | |
| 2 | | 18 | Oxford United | L | 0-4 | 0-0 | 5135 | | 1 | 13 | 3' | 2 | 5 | | 7 | 8 | 10* | 6" | 11 | 9 | 12 | 4 | 14 | | | | | | | | | | | | | | | | |
| 3 | | 22 | Luton Town | D | 0-0 | 0-0 | 6563 | | 1 | | 13 | 2 | 5 | | 7 | 3 | | 6' | 11 | 9 | 12 | 14 | | 4 | 8* | 10" | | | | | | | | | | | | | |
| 4 | | 29 | MANSFIELD TOWN | L | 0-1 | 0-1 | 1734 | | 1 | | | 2 | 5 | | 7 | 3 | | 6 | 11 | 9 | | | | 4 | 8* | 10 | 12 | | | | | | | | | | | | |
| 5 | | 31 | Altrincham | D | 1-1 | 0-1 | 1737 | Wilkinson | 1 | | | 2 | 5 | | 7 | 3 | | 6 | 11 | 9 | | | | 4 | 8* | 10 | 12 | | | | | | | | | | | | |
| 6 | Sep | 5 | HISTON | W | 2-0 | 1-0 | 1171 | Roberts, Chadwick | 1 | | | 8 | 5 | 13 | 7" | 3 | | 6' | 11 | 9 | | | | 4 | | 10* | 12 | 2 | 14 | | | | | | | | | | |
| 7 | | 8 | TAMWORTH | L | 1-2 | 0-1 | 1199 | Chadwick | 1 | | | 2 | 5 | 7* | | 3 | 13 | 8' | 11 | 9 | | | | 4 | 12 | | 10 | | 6 | | | | | | | | | | |
| 8 | | 12 | Eastbourne Borough | D | 1-1 | 1-1 | 968 | Blundell (pen) | 1 | | 3* | 2 | 5 | 7 | | 8 | | 13 | 11 | 9 | | | | 4 | 6' | | 10 | | 12 | | | | | | | | | | |
| 9 | | 15 | GATESHEAD | W | 2-1 | 1-0 | 994 | Blundell (pen), Chadwick | 1 | 12 | 14 | 8 | 2 | | | 3* | 13 | 7' | 11 | 9 | | | | 4 | 6 | | 10" | | 5 | | | | | | | | | | |
| 10 | | 19 | STEVENAGE BOROUGH | L | 0-1 | 0-1 | 1089 | | 1 | 2 | 14 | 6 | 3 | | | | 12 | 7' | 11 | 9 | 13 | | | 4 | 8" | | 10* | | 5 | | | | | | | | | | |
| 11 | | 22 | Salisbury City | D | 1-1 | 0-0 | 838 | Wilkinson | 1' | 2* | | 6 | 3 | | | 12 | | 7 | 11 | 9 | | | | 4 | 8 | | 10 | | 5 | 13 | | | | | | | | | |
| 12 | | 27 | Wrexham | D | 0-0 | 0-0 | 5913 | | 1 | 13 | | 2 | 5 | | | 3 | 14 | 7 | 11 | 9 | | | | 4* | 8' | | 10" | | 12 | | 6 | | | | | | | | |
| 13 | | 29 | FOREST GREEN ROVERS | L | 1-2 | 0-2 | 1019 | Roberts | 1 | | 14 | 2 | 4 | 13 | | 3 | 10* | 7" | 11 | 9 | | | | | 8' | | 12 | | 5 | | 6 | | | | | | | | |
| 14 | Oct | 3 | Hayes & Yeading United | D | 0-0 | 0-0 | 351 | | 1 | 2 | | 4 | | 7" | | 3 | 14 | 13 | 11 | 9 | | 12 | | | 8' | | 10 | | 5* | | 6 | | | | | | | | |
| 15 | | 10 | RUSHDEN & DIAMONDS | L | 0-1 | 0-1 | 1089 | | 1 | 2 | | 13 | 4 | 8 | | 11 | | 7' | 3 | 12 | | 5 | | | | | 9* | | | | 6 | 10 | | | | | | | |
| 16 | | 17 | Gateshead | W | 1-0 | 0-0 | 631 | Beesley | 1 | | | 2 | 4 | 8 | | 11 | 14 | 12' | 3 | | | | | | 13 | | 9* | | | | 6 | 10 | 5 | 7" | | | | | |
| 17 | | 31 | AFC WIMBLEDON | W | 3-1 | 2-1 | 1666 | Chadwick,Gregory(og),Blundell | 1 | 2' | 14 | 8 | 4 | | | | | | 3 | 9^ | 13 | | | | 7* | | 12 | | | | 6 | 10 | 5 | 11 | | | | | |
| 18 | Nov | 7 | Grays Athletic | W | 3-1 | 2-1 | 480 | Coulson, Chadwick (2) | 1 | | 2' | 8 | 4 | | | | | 13 | 3 | 9* | 7 | | | | 14 | | 12 | | | | 6 | 10 | 5 | 11" | | | | | |
| 19 | | 10 | York City | L | 2-3 | 0-2 | 2164 | Barry, Kelly | 1 | | 2" | 8 | 4 | 12 | | | | 14 | 3 | 9' | 7* | | | | | | 13 | | 5 | | 6 | 10 | | 11 | | | | | |
| 20 | | 14 | Tamworth | L | 1-3 | 0-1 | 955 | Beesley | 1 | | 3 | 2 | 4 | 8 | | | | | | 9 | | | | | 7* | | 12 | | 5 | | 6 | 10 | | 11 | | | | | |
| 21 | | 21 | ALTRINCHAM | L | 1-3 | 0-2 | 1132 | Rule | 1 | 2 | 3 | 5 | 4 | 8 | | | 13 | 12 | | 9 | 7* | | | | | | 10' | | | | 6 | 11 | | | | | | | |
| 22 | | 24 | Stevenage Borough | L | 0-2 | 0-1 | 1487 | | 1 | 3 | | 2 | 4 | 8 | | | 14 | 13 | | 9" | 7' | | | | 11* | | 12 | | 5 | | 6 | 10 | | | | | | | |
| 23 | Dec | 1 | Cambridge United | L | 0-1 | 0-0 | 2239 | | 1 | 2 | 3 | 6 | 4 | 8 | | | 10 | 11* | | 9 | 7 | | | | | | | | 5 | | | | | | 12 | | | | |
| 24 | | 5 | LUTON TOWN | D | 0-0 | 0-0 | 1352 | | 1 | 3 | | 4 | | 8 | | | 10' | 11* | | 9 | 7 | | 12 | | | | | | 5 | | | | | | 6 | 2 | 13 | | |
| 25 | | 26 | Kidderminster Harriers | L | 0-2 | 0 1 | 1755 | | 1 | 2 | | 4 | 3 | | | 8 | 10 | 11 | | | 7 | | | | | | | | 5 | | | | | | 6' | | 12 | 9* | 13 |
| 26 | Jan | 19 | SALISBURY CITY | L | 0-1 | 0-0 | 425 | | 1 | 2 | 8 | 6 | 4 | | | 3 | 10 | 11 | | | | | | | | | | | 5 | | | | | | | | 7 | 9 | |
| 27 | | 23 | Mansfield Town | L | 0-4 | 0-3 | 2882 | | 1 | 2 | 6 | 4 | | | | 3 | 10 | 11 | | | | | | | | | | | 5 | | | | | | | | 7 | 9 | 8 |
| 28 | Feb | 6 | EBBSFLEET UNITED | L | 1-2 | 1-2 | 460 | Rea | 1 | 2 | 6 | 4 | | | | 3 | 10' | 11 | | | | | 13 | | | | | | 5 | | | | | | 7 | | 12 | 9* | 8 |
| | | | | | | | | Apps | 28 | 14 | 11 | 27 | 24 | 11 | 6 | 18 | 9 | 19 | 19 | 21 | 7 | 2 | | 10 | 13 | 4 | 10 | 1 | 15 | | 11 | 8 | 3 | 5 | 3 | 1 | 2 | 4 | 2 |
| | | | | | | | | Subs | | 3 | 5 | 1 | | 3 | | 1 | 8 | 7 | | 2 | 5 | 3 | 3 | | 3 | | 9 | | 3 | 1 | | | | | 1 | | 3 | | 1 |
| | | | | | | | | Goals | | 1 | | 2 | | 1 | | | | 3 | | 7 | | | | | | | 3 | | 1 | | | 2 | | 1 | 1 | | | | |

Chester expelled from Conference on February 26th. All results expunged.

Own goals - 1

## F.A. CUP

| Rd | Date | | Opposition | | FT | HT | Att. | Goalscorers | Danby J. | Rule G | Meynell R. | Roberts K. | Ryan T. | Barry A. | Vaughan S. | Lea M. | Ellams L. | Wilkinson B. | Ashton N. | Chadwick N. | Owen J. | Platt K. | Rawlinson C. | Lynch C. | Kay A. | Alessandra L. | Blundell G. | Vaughan J. | Kelly S. | Murphy A. | Keltie C. | Beesley M. | Flynn J. | Coulson M. | Rea J. | Freeman J. | Davidson R. | Jones B. | Coulter S. |
|---|---|---|---|---|---|---|---|---|---|---|---|---|---|---|---|---|---|---|---|---|---|---|---|---|---|---|---|---|---|---|---|---|---|---|---|---|---|---|---|
| 4Q | Oct | 24 | Barrow | D | 1-1 | 1-0 | 1579 | Flynn | 1 | | | 2 | 4 | 8 | | | 12 | 11* | 3 | | 13 | | | | 7' | | | | 14 | | 6 | 10" | 5 | 9 | | | | | |
| 4Qr | | 27 | BARROW | L | 0-4 | 0-0 | 1287 | | 1 | | | 2 | 4 | 8* | | 11 | 12 | | 3 | | 13 | | | | 7' | | | | | | 6 | 10 | 5 | 9 | | | | | |

## F.A. TROPHY

| Rd | Date | | Opposition | | FT | HT | Att. | Goalscorers | Danby J. | Rule G | Meynell R. | Roberts K. | Ryan T. | Barry A. | Vaughan S. | Lea M. | Ellams L. | Wilkinson B. | Ashton N. | Chadwick N. | Owen J. | Platt K. | Rawlinson C. | Lynch C. | Kay A. | Alessandra L. | Blundell G. | Vaughan J. | Kelly S. | Murphy A. | Keltie C. | Beesley M. | Flynn J. | Coulson M. | Rea J. | Freeman J. | Davidson R. | Jones B. | Coulter S. |
|---|---|---|---|---|---|---|---|---|---|---|---|---|---|---|---|---|---|---|---|---|---|---|---|---|---|---|---|---|---|---|---|---|---|---|---|---|---|---|---|
| 1R | Dec | 12 | FLEETWOOD TOWN | L | 0-1 | 0-0 | 518 | | 1 | 3 | | | 4 | 8 | | 12 | 10 | 11' | | 9 | 7 | | | | | | | | 5 | | | | | | 6* | 2 | | 13 | |

## FRIENDLIES

| No. | Date | | Opposition | | FT | HT | Att. | Goalscorers |
|---|---|---|---|---|---|---|---|---|
| 1 | Aug | 1 | Droylsden * | W | 1-0 | 1-0 | | Alessandra |

* Tony Downes Memorial Cup

**2009/10 Season:**

Back – Owen, Rawlinson, Platt, Ellams, Smith, Meynell, Blundell

Middle – Gerrard (Coach), Kelly, Hurst, Roberts, Murphy, Danby, Lea, Wilkinson, Davidson, Holt(Physio)

Front - S Vaughan, Yantorno, Ryan, Wadsworth (Manager), Davies (Assistant Manager), Ashton, Barry, Rule.

**Chester FC**

**Evo-Stik Division 1 North Champions 2010/11**